TIME TO DECLARE

DAVID OWEN

MICHAEL JOSEPH
LONDON

MICHAEL JOSEPH LTD
Published by the Penguin Group
27 Wrights Lane, London w8 5tz, England
Viking Penguin Inc., 375 Hudson Street, New York, New York 10014, USA
Penguin Books Australia Ltd, Ringwood, Victoria, Australia
Penguin Books Canada Ltd, 10 Alcorn Avenue, Suite 300, Toronto, Ontario, Canada M4V 3B2
Penguin Books (NZ) Ltd, 182–190 Wairau Road, Auckland 10, New Zealand

Penguin Books Ltd, Registered Offices: Harmondsworth, Middlesex, England

First published in Great Britain 1991

Copyright © David Owen 1991

Printed in England by Clays Ltd, St Ives plc
Filmset in Monophoto 11½/12 pt Ehrhardt

A CIP catalogue record for this book is available from the British Library
ISBN 0 7181 3514 8

The moral right of the author has been asserted

The author and publishers wish to thank the following for permission to reproduce extracts from copyright material:

Oxford Univeristy Press Ltd for ''Twas at the pictures, child, we met', from *The Works of Thomas Lovell Beddoes*; Peters Fraser & Dunlop Group Ltd for 'Henry King, who chewed bits of string, and was early cut off in dreadful agonies' and 'Jim, who ran away from nurse, and was eaten by a lion', from *Complete Verse* by Hilaire Belloc; The Hogarth Press and Chatto & Windus Ltd for 'Body Remember', from *The Complete Poems of Cavafy*; Henry Holt Inc. for 'The Road Not Taken', from *Mountain Interval* by Robert Frost; A. P. Watt Ltd for ''Twas at the pictures, child, we met', by A. P. Herbert; Laurence Pollinger Ltd and the Estate of Frieda Lawrence Ravagli for 'Green' from *The Complete Poems of D. H. Lawrence*; Macmillan Ltd for 'Sea Fever' by John Masefield, and for eight lines from *Poems* by Rabindranath Tagore; Hodder & Stoughton Ltd for 'Drake's Drum' by Sir Henry Newbolt; David Higham Associates Ltd on behalf of J. M. Dent for 'Ceremony After a Fire Raid', from *The Poems* by Dylan Thomas; Hansard (House of Commons) for the following extracts from *Parliamentary Debates*: p. 96 (16 May 1966, Col 1013, p. 103 (22 July 1966, Cols 1112–17), p. 103 (Standing Committee F, 1 February 1967, Col 144), p. 143 (28 January 1970, Col 1662 and Col 1672), p. 184 (25 October 1971, Col 1259), pp. 184–5 (25 October 1971, Cols 1251–2), p. 185 (26 October 1971, Cols 1636–8), p. 242 (22 January 1975, Col 1554), p. 255 (21 February 1977, Col 1034), pp. 330–1 (26 October 1971, Col 1634), p. 401 (20 February 1979, Cols 266–7), p. 445 (15 July 1980, Col 1237), p. 504 (26 March 1981, Col 1074), p. 545 (29 March 1982, Col 40), pp. 546–7 (3 April 1982, Cols 633–4, 641, 647, 666), p. 549 (7 April 1982, Col 967), p. 613 (26 July 1984, Col 1265), p. 638 (27 January 1986, Col 660), p. 679 (6 April 1987, Col 22), p. 771 (6 September 1990, Col 788), pp. 780–1 (13 November 1990, Col 465), p. 784 (22 November 1990, Col 451).

Every effort has been made to trace copyright material and the publishers apologize for any omissions to the above list.

CONTENTS

LIST OF ILLUSTRATIONS

Copyright holders are indicated in italics.

To Debs.
Id est semper idem, amor.

ACKNOWLEDGEMENTS

To all those who have worked in my private office in the House of Commons over the last twenty-five years I have a special debt. They have dealt with constituency cases, articles, speeches and books with dedication and skill. To those who have helped me with writing this book, I owe particular thanks to Maggie Smart, who has been with me for fourteen years, and to Ruth Smith and Ruth Willetts. The research has been done by Tony Hockley, and the House of Commons library have as usual answered questions and researched facts with patience and skill. My editor at Michael Joseph, Susan Watt, not only suggested that I should write this book, but has been the key person in bringing it to fruition. I am also immensely grateful for the work that Danny Finkelstein, Alexander Stilwell and Antonia Till have done on the text. But, in the last analysis, my biggest debt is to the voters of Plymouth, who in seven elections have chosen me to represent them in Parliament; and to Alf and Ruth Sweetland and Barbara Furzeman, who over those years have been my eyes and ears in the constituency.

PART ONE

THE PHYSICIAN

I

FAMILY

I can hear it now, the tap of a stick against the wall as he walked down to the library which was his study. I was crouched in the corner almost holding my breath, waiting. He opened the door, closed it and, wearing dark glasses, walked over to his favourite chair. On the table was a large book, the size of a big atlas of the world, although this was lighter and thicker. He leant over, picked it up, put it on his lap and began to turn the pages as if to find his place. I started to munch the boiled sweet in my mouth and the cracking noise was far louder in my ear than in the room. Then he bent down, took his slipper off and held it in his hand, his head cocked listening intently, then suddenly the slipper left his hand winging its way with unerring accuracy at my head. I ducked and it fell against the wall. Then we both began to laugh and I rushed over to his chair to give my grandfather Gear a big hug. I was then only six.

I adored 'Gear' (i). He was a most remarkable man. He had been blind ever since, as a boy of twelve, a pocket knife with which he had been playing slipped out of his hands and cut one of his eyes. He lost the sight of that eye and in spite of all the care and skill with which he was treated, the other eye became infected and total blindness followed. His father searched high and low, and eventually found the only place in the country where blind students were prepared for university – at Powyke near Worcester. There, as far as possible, he lived the life of a normal schoolboy, playing cricket with a bell inside the ball so that the boys, though blind, could hit it, and even catch it in the field. He became expert in Braille. The Bible in Braille occupied a whole wall in his library. I can almost smell it now, that big book with its thick brown pages on his knee. I would sit on the arm of the chair while he passed his delicate fingers lightly over the raised dots and read out one of his favourite passages, St Paul's letter to the Ephesians:

* Roman numerals refer to illustrations.

be strong in the Lord, and in the power of his might. Put on the whole armour of God, that ye may be able to stand against the wiles of the devil. For we wrestle not against flesh and blood, but against principalities, against powers, against the rulers of the darkness of this world, against spiritual wickedness in high places.

Gear taught me to read, often from editorials in *The Times*, listening carefully as I attempted to pronounce the difficult words and, when necessary, spelling them out. We would walk together down from his Rectory to Llandow Church where he would read morning service and I would go to the village school. Living in Llandow I started to learn Welsh, and Gear, who spoke Welsh fluently and listened to the news on the radio in Welsh, would help me. It was an enchanting period. When I was fourteen I read Siegfried Sassoon's *Memoirs of a Fox-Hunting Man*. I loved the passages describing the languid pace of country life because they evoked that time in the closing months of the Second World War in the beautiful vale of Glamorgan.

My father was away fighting in the war and Gear became my substitute father, mentor and friend. For many years he cycled on a machine made of two bicycles bolted alongside each other. But I remember riding along the lanes on the crossbar of a single bicycle with him pedalling and me steering. My mother says this is fanciful nonsense. I retort that she was not there, having gone back to Plymouth to reclaim our house and to prepare for the war's end. But it does not matter whether it is fantasy or not, for this is how I saw our relationship. I was the eyes and he was the brain and the power.

A blind person develops a compensating hypersensitivity in all his other senses. In Gear's case his hearing was so sensitive that he could locate any noise, not just me munching sweets but cars a long way off in the country lanes. He walked those lanes by himself for years, his stick tapping the road and swinging out to touch the hedges. He was never confined to the house and apart from his dark glasses and white stick you would hardly have known he was blind. What fascinated me as a child was his consideration. On getting out of his pyjamas in the morning, he would always fold them neatly on the bed and reprimand me if I did not do so as well. He insisted on maintaining the acetylene gas plant which made the gas for the lights in the rooms, all of which had to be individually lit every evening. He would always change the tyre on a car if there was a puncture while Granny Llew was driving. The blackout during the war was no problem for him since he knew where everything was in the house. He would collect the coal and firewood and light the fires. I still feel his influence on me. Rarely have I taken any important decision in my life before asking myself what he might have done in the same circumstances.

It was in early 1945 that I went to stay with Gear and Granny Llew at Llandow Rectory. My mother had been brought up there and I have a photograph (ii) of her sitting on an outside window-sill with her sister Aileen, and with Granny and Gear in deck-chairs. Up to then, we had been living in Govilon, but now my mother returned to Plymouth. So as not to disrupt her schooling, my sister Susan, two and a half years older than I, stayed with a vicar's family at Llanfoist Rectory very near the house in Govilon. The four months I spent in Llandow on my own with my grandfather and my grandmother was one of the happiest periods of my life and the most formative. The Rectory was big and had a well stocked orchard with lots of apple, plum and pear trees and a big loganberry bush by the door in the wall of the garden. I can recall the musty smell of the gas lights all over the house, even in the bathroom which I remember particularly well for the Mabel Lucie Attwell drawing and poem on the wall over the bath:

> Please remember, don't forget
> never leave the bathroom wet.
> Nor leave the towels upon the floor.
> That's a thing one never o'er.

Bath nights in the glow of the gas were also story times. There, as Granny Llew read stories, and in particular poems, my imagination had me going to sea in a sieve in the land where the Jumblies lived. Or with the Pied Piper of Hamelin demanding 'a thousand guilders! The Mayor looked blue; so did the Corporation too!'

Here I first discovered love for books and respect for learning. Gear was a wonderful teacher, feeling that knowledge was something vital to impart. After school at Powyke, he went to Jesus College, Oxford, where he took his MA degree in history with honours. Then he went to the Welsh Methodist College. He was ordained a Methodist but the need to go on the circuit and move around frequently made it very difficult for him to learn the geography of each parish. Low church and preferring simple services, he found it easy to transfer to the Anglican Church, becoming a curate at Gilfach Goch. Then he took the Jesus College living at Llandow which later became part of the Welsh disestablished Church. While at Llandow, he took further exams and became a Doctor of Law from Dublin University, where he was studying at the time of the Easter Uprising.

In church he conducted the whole service himself, reading the lessons as well as preaching, and people were amazed to find he could read with such ease and rapidity. He was also a good musician, playing the piano with some skill. He coached mature students for the universities and one of these, a local miner, went on to become the Bishop of Bath and Wells. He could find his way around his parish without assistance and apparently it was not uncommon for him to walk alone from Gilfach Goch to Ogmore Vale to visit his parents.

Gear's father, my great-grandfather, Alderman William Llewellyn (iii), was chairman of Glamorgan County Council and chairman of the Bridgend Bench of Magistrates. A staunch Liberal, he was a moving spirit in first the Mid-Glamorgan then the Ogmore Divisional Liberal and Labour Party, of which he also became chairman. To this day it is difficult for English people to understand the high levels of support for the Labour Party among the professional middle classes in Wales. This, I suspect, flows at least in part from the bonds forged early this century between the then strong Liberal Party and the newly emerging Labour Party. It has strangely evocative echoes for the present day. More than once my great-grandfather was approached with a view to representing the Division in Parliament but he always declined. He apparently disliked Asquith but liked Lloyd George. He was a leading member of the Calvinistic Methodists and a deacon of the church at Ogmore Vale. He had started life as a grocer and provision merchant in Ogmore, having moved there from Llantrisant. Over the years The Gwalia, as his shop was called, grew until it was described as 'a mecca of the valley and neighbourhood'. But the old original shop was retained. Today, that hundred-year-old building, painstakingly dismantled and transported brick by brick, has been rebuilt at the Welsh National Folk Museum at St Fagans. My great-grandfather lived a prosperous life with a chauffeur-driven Daimler, a large house and servants. When he died in 1923 at the age of seventy-three he left an estate of £44,240 gross value, which in present day values is a little less than a million pounds.

Alderman Llewellyn had seven sons and one daughter. Gear, his second son, was christened George. The eldest son, Tom, took over the family business, eventually leaving it in his will to the longest-serving employees. Mr Tom, as he was called, was described by someone who worked there as a short rotund man, with a beaming face, very blustery of speech, like a character from Dickens. I met him once as a small boy and can only remember his vast tummy, his cheerfulness and swollen legs. His brother Dill, who developed tuberculosis and was unable to follow a profession, also worked for their father. Another brother, David, became a solicitor in Bridgend; William, a mining engineer and Beve a doctor in public health. The only daughter, Elizabeth, married a clergyman.

The brother whose career most closely paralleled my own was Edgar. He was a family doctor in Splott which is an area of Cardiff dominated by the steel-works. He was a great character and adored by his patients. His unique way of sorting out their ailments was, according to my mother, to go into his surgery and announce, 'Those buggers who are ill can move to the right-hand side of the room and be seen now; those who are not can wait on the left and see me later or chance their luck tomorrow.' After the war he became infuriated by the politicians on the City Council and so decided to join his wife who was already a Ratepayer Councillor. He was elected in 1951. A photograph of him in a pony and trap, bedecked in a massive rosette, electioneering (vi) shows the first combination of doctor-politician in the family's history. His wife Jenny, who had first stood and won as a Ratepayer in 1946, was a strikingly good looking woman and a considerable character. She was the first person in eighteen years to beat the Labour candidate in her Ward. She stood again in 1949 and won and then lost her seat three years later. The wish to be an independent in local government and to stand against party politics was later mirrored by my mother and, some will say, by me too.

My mother brought me back to join her in the West Country in the early summer of 1945 to prepare for my father's return from the Army. My sister was still in Llanfoist. We lived in rented rooms in Tavistock, fifteen miles from Plymouth. I started as a day boy for the summer term at Mount House School on the outskirts of the town, and became a boarder after my seventh birthday. We celebrated VE Day on board a Royal Naval ship alongside in Devonport. There I ate the first banana in my life and also tinned pineapple.

With my father still in the Army, the family went back to Llandow for VJ Day where the village put on a concert in the hall. The party piece we children sang to the tune of Crawshaw Bailey, was:

> We have socked the Japanese
> And we did it with great ease
> Since we found the atom bomb
> Which is really very strong
> Was you ever see – Was you ever see –
> Was you ever see such a funny thing before?

The fact that we could have even put those wholly inappropriate words together shows how delayed was the impact of the Atom bomb on unsophisticated public opinion. Years later I visited Hiroshima, and the effect was so powerful that I felt ashamed of that little doggerel.

My mother, Molly (iv), is half Welsh. She was born in 1910 in Gilfach Goch. While Gear was wholly Welsh her mother, Elizabeth Phillipe, was Irish. Granny Llew's family name was Sealy from County Cork. Her mother had eloped with a wandering German-Swiss minstrel, apparently a great charmer called Phillipe. He had been at a Jesuit school, preparing for the priesthood, but had broken away in his late teens and joined a touring German band.

My father met my mother when she was seventeen at a mixed hockey match in Lysworney, a village which, with Llandow, made up my grandfather's parish. She went to Bridgend County School and trained as a dentist, first at Aberystwyth University, and then at the Royal Dental School in London. They had a long, loving but stormy relationship as students. When eventually they were married by my grandfather at Llandow church they suggested that one of the hymns for the service should be 'Fight the Good Fight'. He put his foot down on the grounds that the congregation, knowing the nature of their relationship, would burst out laughing. They argued, often and fiercely, throughout their marriage but the clashes were those of two strong personalities who loved each other. Most people who know my family think of my mother as the dominating influence, but the few of us who are really close know that this was an illusion which my father was happy to foster. When the crunch came, his was the commanding position in the family.

My father, John Owen (v), was born in 1907 in Gleneath, the eldest son of a Merchant Navy captain whose family was in shipping in Penarth, and who had tragically died in an accident on his ship during the First World War, when my father was still very young. Because of my own love of the sea I have always wanted to know more about him. He used to fascinate my father and his brother with stories from all over the world. One story was of navigating his ship through the Magellan Straits when the relevant charts had been lost, no mean feat of navigation. My father went to Brecon College and then to Cardiff University, to start his medical studies, followed by St Mary's Hospital, London.

I did not know my father's mother, always called 'Granny O', anywhere near as well as Granny Llew. I think probably because she never got on very well with my mother. Her father, my paternal great-grandfather, Dr Morris, had been a noted and fiery Welsh Congregationalist Minister. He spent some time 'hot gospeling' in Plymouth in the state of Pennsylvania in the USA. My father's brother, my uncle, the Reverend Douglas Owen, always referred to by my father as 'that saintly man, my brother' also had the Welsh *hywl* and could preach a mesmerizing sermon. Sadly there was a tension between the two of them, probably instigated by their mother, who too openly showed that Uncle Douglas was her favourite. Even so my father was his best man for his wedding in December 1934. He was for many years the Rector of St Peter upon Cornhill, a church built by Sir Christopher Wren in the City of London. He was an engaging man with many friends, and I grew very fond of him when I came to study in London. A considerable gossip, he managed to live well despite being a hard-up clergyman. In his hands a cheap bottle of wine would become an exceptional vintage through his description and the manner in which he would open and taste it. His career was extraordinary. He went to Christ's Hospital School and left to go and farm in Saskatchewan, Canada. He studied at Cambridge where he learnt more about horse racing than history, spending much of his time at Newmarket. He had friends who were bookies and he was always laying small telephone bets right up until he died in St Bartholomew's Hospital. He travelled to South Africa as a journalist, broadcasting radio commentaries on rugby matches. Only after he had sowed his wild oats did he return to Westcott House, Cambridge to study theology. He was ordained and then had a distinguished war record as an Army Chaplain. He was at Dunkirk and Tobruk with the 4th Battalion Tank Regiment, being invalided out with tuberculosis in 1942. Chaplains are seldom if ever decorated but he was mentioned twice in despatches for conspicuous bravery under fire. On one occasion he drove an ambulance, picking up wounded under direct artillery fire, through what was called 'hell fire gap'. When independent television first started he was put in charge of religious broadcasting with a programme called *About Religion*, which he rapidly built up from nothing to over a million viewers. He was made a Prebendary of St Paul's Cathedral and one of his duties was to be present when the judge at the Old Bailey passed the death sentence. He was expected to say, 'Amen and may the Lord have mercy on your soul' but as a convinced abolitionist he would never have agreed to participate. Fortunately no one was hanged during his term of office.

So chapel and church runs right through both sides of my family and perhaps accounts for my fondness for these words of Dylan Thomas:

> Into the organpipes and steeples
> Of the luminous cathedrals,
> Into the weathercocks' molten mouths
> Rippling in twelve-winded circles
> Into the dead clock burning the hour
> Over the urn of Sabbaths
> Over the whirling ditch of daybreak
> Over the sun's hovel and the slum of fire
> And the golden pavements laid in requiems
> Into the bread in a wheatfield of flames
> Into the wineburning like brandy,
> The masses of the sea.

Members of my family describe themselves as 'of the blood' and, as my family tree shows, my blood is three-quarters Welsh with a little Irish and German-Swiss to liven it up. I was born into this passionate Celtic family on 2 July 1938. Appeasement was at its height that summer and two months after my birth, the Prime Minister, Neville Chamberlain, returned from Munich claiming 'Peace in our time'. To this day Mother refers contemptuously to Chamberlain waving 'that silly bit of paper'. Father had come down to live in Plympton to start in medical practice a year before my parents married in December 1934. The family continues to live in Plymouth, which absorbed Plympton, and so I am both a West Countryman and a Welshman.

Neither of my parents before the war was in the slightest bit political. Yet perhaps because Plymouth's social life was dominated by the Royal Navy families who were their friends, neither of them was fooled by Chamberlain's fawning policies. Nor did they approve of the activities of Nancy Astor, then the MP for Plymouth Sutton and a key figure in the Cliveden set. This was named after her country house where she and her friends planned the appeasement of Adolf Hitler. My father had gone into the Territorial Army, in 1936, as much for the social life as anything else. By 1938 my parents were waiting for a war that seemed inevitable. My mother recalls an almost forced gaiety as they milked the last few months, sensing that their pleasant way of life was going to end.

My sister, Susan, and I were looked after by a nanny, whom we called Nurse Nora. She was a McElroy from Northern Ireland who spoke with a strong Irish lilt to her voice and had a kind and happy temperament. We also had a full-time live-in maid. Father was a partner in the only medical practice then in Plympton. The senior partner, 'Old Dr Stamp', still wore a black morning coat and top hat, and had only just given up driving around in a horse and carriage. His often reiterated advice to my father was, 'Conserve your energy, my boy'. His son, 'Young Dr Stamp', who was in his fifties, effectively controlled the practice and lived in Castlehayes, Plympton St Maurice, which became our family home when he retired in 1948. When I was a schoolboy, he taught me everything I ever knew about boats and fishing.

Portland House, our family home in 1938, was a comfortable, fairly large, semi-detached house. Plympton was then a small town, five miles from Plymouth's city centre. A few miles to the north lay the edge of Dartmoor and a few miles to the south, the Devon coast and the River Yealm. The old saying that 'Plympton was a borough town when Plymouth was a furry down' is literally true. Long before Plymouth existed, Plympton had a priory dating from Saxon times, and a castle which was one of the seats of the Redvers, Earls of Devon. Plympton was the main port in the area, and records of cargoes of slate exist from the year 1178. But the silting of the River Plym from the tin streaming valleys on Dartmoor meant that the Laira estuary and the creek up to Plympton became progressively more shallow. Sutton Pool and the fishing village of Sutton at the mouth of the Plym became a more attractive port. Plympton was so worried about losing its maritime trade to Plymouth that it insisted on being made a stannary town along with the other Devon towns, Tavistock, Ashburton and Chagford. The growth of the Port of Plymouth, however, could not be stopped. By 1334 Sutton was paying more to the Crown than all the Cornish ports put together. Plymouth finally won its independence and its self-government with the granting of a borough charter in 1439.

On the day war broke out, my father was called up, joining the RAMC as a Captain. He was soon posted to the 9th Lancers in Wimborne. My mother packed up the house in Plympton, after difficult negotiations with my father's partners over the future of the practice, and moved up to Wimborne with my sister and myself. There we loved driving around with my father's batman, Penny. After the phoney war period in the spring of 1940, the 9th Lancers sailed for France with their newly delivered tanks. My mother had been persuaded to take up dentistry again, as the school dental service was desperately short staffed. She felt it would be easier to do this in Wales with our relatives nearby to help her bring up my sister and myself. So she took a house in Newport, where we had our first experience of bombing, sleeping either under the stairs or in a small steel cage in the sitting room which offered some protection if the ceiling fell in.

As the Germans surrounded Dunkirk my father's regiment was evacuated by ship from Brest. When it anchored next day, he pulled aside the blackout from the porthole and found to his amazement that he was anchored in Plymouth Sound. All his personal belongings had had to be left behind in France and all he had was his khaki trousers, shoes, a shirt and jersey in which he turned up, out of the blue, outside our Newport house. He was then stationed in various parts of Britain and my mother travelled to be with him whenever she could. For me, as a small boy, his infrequent visits were not a success. 'Send that man back to the Army, Mummy', was my plaintive cry. I did not like his hold on my mother's attention; I did not accept his attempts to discipline me. Indeed I did not really understand who this strange man was, who occasionally came into our life and disrupted it.

In 1942 my father, now a Major, went with the Third Army to North Africa where he experienced the fall of Tunis. He saw a lot of action as he was commanding a small mobile field ambulance. He developed a long-running story about a character called Dick, based in the desert, and would regale us with it throughout my childhood. He succeeded in doing the same with my children. Dick was a combination of his own favourite hero, John Buchan's Richard Hannay, and whoever was the child's own hero at the time, Biggles, Dick Barton Special Agent or even Dan Dare. Dick would always triumph over the Germans, albeit with a little help from my father.

The war was a much more traumatic experience for him than he ever admitted and the memory of the shelling, the burnt-out tanks and all the horror of the desert war haunted him throughout his life. When the war ended he was a Lieutenant-Colonel commanding a convalescent hospital in Rome. Mother had not seen him for three years when he was eventually demobbed in Taunton in October 1945. Immediately afterwards they came with my sister to take me out from school for the weekend. I walked up to a strange man with a moustache, shook him by the hand and he said, 'What's your name?'

'Owen, sir.'

'In that case, I'm your father.'

At the age of seven I could not recognize my own father.

Even for my generation, the war was a formative experience. Mother and a Scottish fellow dentist, Betty Young, moved out of Newport to avoid the bombing and went to Penpergam, near Abergavenny, but even so the war could never be forgotten. As a young child in that lovely rural part of Monmouthshire I could still sense the tension every day when my mother listened to the *Six O'Clock News* on the radio. I did not realize at the time why she listened so intently, why any noise that we might make would be pounced upon with unusual severity. It must have been a great strain waiting and listening for any hint of what might be happening to my father in North Africa. The familiar airmail letters or photocards from my father were hastily read in fear that they might contain bad news. For a child it seemed that most adult conversation was dominated by war talk. Nevertheless my childhood was fun. Aunty Betty was a wizard at telling stories in the fire. She would make us put our faces near enough to the fire for the skin to feel red and for the eyes to smart. Then with a poker she would point out the detail of the story. It is like watching a red and white movie. You imagine that there are people moving around and the story comes alive. I used the same technique for my own children and they too were enthralled.

In Pempergam the peppery old farmer in whose house we were staying virtually adopted me, refusing to allow reproofs. He called me King David and fed me with cheese and pickled onions which he kept under his bed. No doubt that fed my vanity and spiced my tongue, and my mother had to keep me very firmly in my place. My cousins were evacuated to a farm close by and so we lived an extended family life. We were not short of food for when my mother and Aunty Betty took their mobile dental clinic up into the Welsh valleys they would often return with eggs, cheese and meat which parents would give them, grateful for the dental care of their children. We then moved to Govilon where we had our own house and I went to the local village school. Eventually, when 'bugger' became my every second word, my mother in desperation sent me to a private school in Abergavenny (vii). I used to travel in the dental van in the holidays and one of my tasks was to be the model patient with mouth wide open, showing that the drill did not hurt. As a demonstration it was most convincing to the watching schoolchildren, but since the drill never touched my teeth, it was all show. My mother had to have a car and though petrol was rationed we managed some outings. Sweets were also rationed and we would call out to any passing lorryload of American GIs, 'Got any gum, chum'. They would usually throw us a few packets.

Looking back on the war, my mother is amazed that she never doubted for one moment that we would win. When I began to read the history of those years, and realized the grave risk of invasion I was staggered that people like my mother were not more frightened and that their fear was not transmitted to us children. I can never remember having nightmares about the war and it is a remarkable testimony to the way the bombing and news of casualties was handled by those around me and to their fortitude that I never felt afraid.

Friends in Plymouth kept us very aware of the devastation of the city. In two intense attacks on 20 and 21 March 1941 and in five fearful attacks in April a rain of destruction fell on the city of Plymouth with thousands of high explosive bombs and tens of thousands of incendiary bombs. The devastation by blast and fire meant that Plymouth was the worst blitzed city in the country. Our house was not affected, but when we returned in 1945 not a single part of the city, industrial, business or residential, had escaped the bombing. The City Council bravely decided to plan for a new city actually during the war and they asked the town planner, Abercrombie, to draw up plans so that building could start immediately peace came.

In the General Election of 1945 Plymouth voted in three new Labour members of Parliament. The ousted Devonport MP was Leslie Hore-Belisha of Belisha Beacon fame. He held the seat first as a Liberal then as a National Liberal. In the 1935 election, as a member of the National Coalition, he had argued that, in the name of true Liberalism, Liberals should vote against Isaac Foot in the Bodmin constituency. Isaac Foot was a prominent West Country Liberal. He was a leading solicitor in the City, a Methodist lay preacher, a bibliophile and a world authority on Oliver Cromwell. He had been an MP for only a few years. No one in the West Country was neutral about Isaac Foot nor, indeed, about the entire Foot family. You loved them or you hated them. After being defeated, a furious Isaac Foot hired Devonport Guildhall and staged a full scale denunciation of Hore-Belisha's political record. He quoted Lord Alfred Douglas:

> Let him on graves of buried loyalty,
> Rise as he may to his desired goal;
> Ay and God speed him there, I grudge him not.
> And when all men shall sing his praise to me
> I'll not gainsay. But I shall know his soul
> Lies in the bosom of Iscariot.

Which just goes to show that hell hath no fury like a Foot scorned, something I too was to experience.

In 1940 Churchill, on becoming Prime Minister, removed Hore-Belisha from the wartime Cabinet. In 1945 Hore-Belisha was defending Devonport as a National Independent having become virtually a Conservative. It was nemesis that he should lose, by just over two thousand votes, to Michael Foot, Isaac's son. He had been the Member of Parliament from 1923 to 1945, the longest serving MP in Devonport's history until I surpassed his record in 1988.

Victory would have tasted sweeter for Isaac if Michael had still been a member of the Liberal Party but far better a Labour MP than a Conservative. After the war, Isaac Foot followed in the steps of Lord Astor, Nancy's husband, who had held the post of Lord Mayor throughout the wartime years. In his year of office Isaac Foot resolved that the children of the City should know more about its famous men. He sent every schoolchild a copy of the radio broadcast he had made in the war about Sir Francis Drake, and quoting Newbolt's poem 'Drake's Drum'. This became the poem I would declaim as my party piece. He also instigated annual memorial services for Captain Scott in the City schools and at the Scott Memorial at Mount Wise. Both Drake and Scott, men with strong Plymouth connections, became my boyhood heroes.

The rebuilding of Plymouth is an abiding childhood memory. Each year the ruins shrank and buildings grew. Years after the war was over, Genoni's, a restaurant we used to go to, carried on its business in a Nissen hut. Shops were in temporary buildings, and there were endless road diversions and a sense of a city being reconstructed out of the ashes. That experience gave me a fellow feeling for other cities bombed in Europe. In particular it explains why I always identified with the city of Berlin. At the time of the Berlin blockade in 1947 and the Allied airlift, the cinema newsreels were like television news today. I used to enjoy them almost as much as the main film. The Movietone News or Pathé News, rather than newspapers, were the means through which I as a child gained whatever knowledge I had about current affairs.

As a family we entertained ourselves, playing card games around the fire, acting charades, reciting poetry and above all with frequent Welsh singsongs. It was a happy childhood. One family tradition was reading books out loud and my favourite was *The Snow Goose* by Paul Gallico, a poignant story about a hunchback sailing over to Dunkirk to rescue men off the beaches and guided by a goose flying overhead. Car rides in our family were a constant singsong with Gilbert & Sullivan's *HMS Pinafore* the favourite. 'Stick close to your desk and never go to sea and you all may be rulers of the Queen's Navee' was a commentary on F.E. Smith becoming First Lord of the Admiralty. Little did I think how aptly it would apply to me when later I became Navy Minister having never been in the Royal Navy.

My sister and I would also sing the First World War marching song, 'Lloyd George knew my father, my father knew Lloyd George', to the tune of 'Onward Christian Soldiers'. But it was not until I began to research my family background that I realized that not only did my great-grandfather know Lloyd George well, but that Lloyd George had cast a long shadow over all my family's political attitudes. Far from coming from a non-political family as I used to claim, I now recognize that there was considerable family involvement in local politics. Moreover, the family has had a surprisingly large number of clerics and doctors which have probably had their influence as well.

As I walk from the Members Lobby into the House of Commons Chamber I pass the statues of our two great wartime Prime Ministers, David Lloyd George and Winston Churchill. Both were called to that office at a time when our fortunes were at a low ebb. Both men's passionate patriotism gave their leadership distinctive quality. Churchill was the greater war leader but Lloyd George left the more permanent mark on the political development of this country. It was Churchill who, in March 1945 in the House of Commons, speaking on Lloyd George's death and on the eve of his own great victory, said that when historians surveyed the first quarter of the twentieth century they would see how far the history of Britain, in peace and in war, had been moulded by the life of this one man. Undoubtedly he was the greatest single political influence on my maternal great-grandfather and also my grandfather Gear.

This political tradition did not involve only my mother's side of the family. It was also present in my father's. Two of his relatives were Lord Mayors of Cardiff – Sir Illtyd Thomas, who was his grandmother's first cousin, and Alderman Lewis, his great-great-grandfather, who held the office in the 1880s. After the war my father was approached by the local Plympton Labour Party to stand as a candidate for the Rural District Council. It must have become known that he had asked my mother to vote Labour by proxy for him in the 1945 Election while he was still serving in the RAMC in Italy. The approach from the Labour Party was written up in the local newspaper and infuriated my godfather, Dr Ball, who believed it would harm their joint practice. So, in deference to his partners, my father told the Labour Party that his politics were still 'fluid'. This did not stop the local Constitutional Club demanding that he should resign immediately from being vice-president; he had been bliss-fully unaware that this was a Conservative organization, believing it to be a drinking club. Somewhat bruised by this encounter with party politics he never took any further interest, voting for all the parties at different times. But he always joked that no member of our family 'ever votes Tory without a stiff drink before and after'. He became chairman of Plympton St Maurice Parish Council as an Independent and would walk annually around the borders of the parish 'beating the bounds', dressed up in robes with mace bearers and having all the paraphernalia of a truly 'rotten borough'. They would deliberate in Plympton St Maurice's lovely Town Hall surrounded by portraits painted by Plympton's most distinguished MP, Sir Joshua Reynolds the famous artist.

My father also took me to my first political meeting in February 1950. It was half term and my grandfather Gear was staying with us. All three of us went off to the Exmouth Hall, Devonport to hear Aneurin Bevan, the then Minister of Health, speak in support of Michael Foot. The meeting was packed. Well over a thousand people were present, some in a large overflow meeting downstairs and several hundred standing outside in the rain and wind. The meeting started with everyone singing the first verse of 'Land of my Fathers'. I was allowed to squeeze to the front. I watched spellbound as Bevan spoke for eighty-five minutes without a script, freely quoting figures to strengthen his argument and weaken his opponents. If I read his words reported in the local newspaper, I can recapture his oratory with his Welsh accent, a slight stutter and long pauses between sentences:

I addressed a meeting in this city a little over four and a half years ago. It is most unusual that politicians should behave like murderers. We are informed that murderers have a desire to return to their crimes. I have not the slightest diffidence in coming back here to speak to you, because so far from wanting to talk about what happened then, I want you to remember it.

Asked how he thought he was going to get the vote of the middle classes when he called them 'lower than vermin', Aneurin Bevan replied, 'For heaven's sake, don't continually parade around the country sentences maliciously selected from their context in public speeches'. Asked what the socialists were going to do to prevent communism spreading he said, 'Communists are weakest in Britain where socialists are the strongest', adding that 'the communists are stronger in France and Italy where the socialists are not in power'. For a young eleven-year-old this was a heady experience and my grandfather had no doubt that we had listened to the future Prime Minister. It also meant that when later locked in controversy with Michael Foot I was able to claim that I had known him man and boy. That same night Winston Churchill spoke in the Forum Cinema, Devonport in support of his son, Randolph Churchill. Plymouth politics retained their rumbustious reputation.

In 1957 my mother became a Devon County Councillor as a genuine Independent. I canvassed for her on the slogan 'Keep politics out of local government'. She was never defeated, serving for over seventeen years and becoming an Alderman. When Plymouth took over Plympton as a result of Richard Crossman's controversial local government boundary changes my mother led the 'Hands off Plympton' campaign while I, as a Plymouth MP, supported the takeover. My mother has never let me forget it! Like her grandfather, she became chairman of the Bench of Magistrates.

I used to think my going into politics was an accident, and often said so. Now I believe it was a more natural development than I realized.

All of us, my father, my sister and myself, agree that the exceptional personality in the family is my mother. She bubbles with energy and has the brightest mind of anyone I know. Now over eighty, she has miraculous recall and effervescence. I love her as dearly as any son can. She has been the major influence on my life. The Irish blood from her mother makes her, and she would say her son as well, instinctively agin the Establishment. Throughout her life she has championed the case of the minority or underdog, and almost as a principle, has argued cases that would otherwise go by default.

It is hard to describe the effect of this small, feminine, well-dressed, combative, tenacious person on any committee on which she sat. She had her admirers and her detractors, since few felt neutral about her activities. Yet the mentally handicapped in Devon and beyond benefited immensely from her being their champion, whether as vice-chairman of the Health Committee on Devon County or on the Plymouth Hospital Management

Committee. The clashes of personality were sometimes ferocious, none more so than her fight with Alderman Harry Wright, longstanding Labour chairman of the Hospital Management Committee. He was a self-educated man, a dockyard worker, and he brooked no disagreement. His dominance of that Committee was like a red rag to my mother and eventually he ensured she was thrown off. She was chairman for many years of the Plymouth Townswomen's Guild. She loved acting and the whole family once appeared in *The Farmer's Wife* by Eden Phillpotts (viii). She was very active in the Plympton Wrangler Dramatic Society and a tower of strength to a whole host of organizations to which she gave her support. When my sister and I were at home in the school holidays, a typical breakfast would start with Mother saying, 'The plan now is . . .'. She would then outline exactly what we would do and not a moment would be wasted. She would lay out our programme for the day in minute detail, whether it was to go swimming on the moor or the sea, to play badminton or perhaps to go Scottish dancing. At the same time, she would be stimulating an argument over breakfast on ways in which Devon County could introduce comprehensive education, hotly defending the ending of the eleven-plus examinations and proposing radical reforms of schools, for social services and health centres for family doctors. It was an invigorating environment in which to grow up.

My father was, by contrast, much lower key. His attitude can be summed up by the Welsh word didoreth; not idleness, nor complacency, perhaps laid-back is the closest description. Blessed with a delicious sense of humour he could delight those around him, particularly women. He was, in Devonian terms, also extremely 'ansom. When I was a medical student working at Christmas for the Post Office, I was delivering letters with a postal worker called Blanche who had helped clean in our house before the war. To my intense chagrin, she said, 'You think you're good looking. I tell you you're not a patch on your father.' He was a good athlete, having played rugby for St Mary's Hospital, and when I was a youngster, he won my devotion for hitting a massive six in a fathers' and sons' cricket match. He adored fishing for sea bass and mackerel but was clumsy in boats and did not inherit any of his father's maritime skills.

He found getting back to civilian medical practice difficult. He was used to ordering his patients around and some Plymptonians in those early years did not take kindly to being treated as if they were in the Army. There was constant friction with my godfather in the practice and the joy of the pre-war partnership was never recaptured. As with so many other couples, it was also a strain after all the absent years for my parents to pick up as if the war had not happened. They had to grow back together.

A love of my father's life was Dartmoor and in particular those of his patients who worked in the china clay pits on the edge of the moor, in Wotter and Lee Moor. I think he found there some of the charm and community spirit of the Welsh mining villages. He had first started medical practice in Ynysbyl and he really admired what he called the Moor Men. I often used to drive the four or five miles up with him. Sometimes in the afternoon when I was home on holiday, we would visit a remote farm and then go swimming naked near Cadover Bridge. The hut circles on Dartmoor are the foundations of the homes of Bronze Age men. They add to the mystery of Dartmoor with its swirling mist and granite face. It is a National Park that is always under threat by encroachment. I am a 'Not-an-incher' myself, feeling that if you once breach the existing boundary it will never stop, so I oppose anything on Dartmoor, whether a reservoir, a house or a new road.

When I was a medical student I would go on night calls with my father. We would discuss the patient and the symptoms in the car, and sometimes, if they had no objection, I would even go in and see patients with him. It was through these late-night car trips that we consolidated our relationship which because of his absence in the war had taken time to develop. Our love flowered slowly. I probably did not discover the full delight of his personality until I was over twenty-one and studying at St Thomas's Hospital. In later years his patients still loved him and long after he retired they would stop me in the street and ask about him, saying, 'He would listen to you, not like doctors do these days.' His practice extended down to Laira, including quite a large part of the Plymouth Sutton constituency which I initially represented in 1966. I still attribute my small majority of only 747 in the 1970 election to patients of my father voting for him through voting for me.

Given these strong family connections with local politics, medicine, religion and the sea my own interests are perhaps less surprising. My roots are in the Welsh radical political tradition. It was always considered perfectly natural by my family that when I did start to commit myself politically it would not be to the Conservative Party.

My days at Mount House were happy and adventurous. The headmaster, Mr Wedd, was a retired Lieutenant-Commander from the Royal Navy. He ran the school, initially with the help of another godfather, Toby Bailey. Two more different teachers would be hard to find. Uncle Toby was a gentle aesthete who agonized over every decision and eventually went to run his own preparatory school in Somerset. Mr Wedd, by contrast, was a reserved but outdoor person. A little gruff, somewhat rough and certainly hard to bluff. One of his skills, according to my father, was that almost everyone seemed to be head-boy, probably because he arranged a new one each term. Dormitories were named after sailors: Hood, Blake and Rodney, Hawkins and Drake. At this time I intended to go to the Royal Naval College, Dartmouth at the age of thirteen. Fortunately or not, I shall never know, this young entry into the Navy was stopped and I never fulfilled my childhood dream of following in Drake's footsteps.

Drake he's in his hammock till the great Armadas come,
    (Capten, art tha sleepin' there below?)
Slung atween the round shot, listenin' for the drum,
    An' dreamin' arl the time o' Plymouth Hoe.

Poetry was my love and to this day I can still recite from Henry V's speech at Agincourt, from *Hamlet* or from Shakespeare's sonnets and these words in particular from Macaulay's poem, 'Horatius' still ring in my ears:

To every man upon this earth
    Death cometh soon or late.
And how can man die better
    Than facing fearful odds,
For the ashes of his fathers,
    And the temples of his Gods.

I also became interested in collecting epitaphs and still love to browse through churchyards. My favourite at that time came from a Welsh gravestone:

Here lies the body of Mary Jones,
who died of eating cherry stones.
Her name was Smith it was not Jones,
but Jones was put to rhyme with stones.

At school, we were expected to keep everything shipshape, to sweep up, clean and make our beds. In the summer most of us slept out under canvas, swam in the River Tavy and devoted more time to playing games than studying; living as if we were in one large scout camp. On a summer evening when we were all in bed, Mr Wedd would breeze into the dormitory and lead us all down to the weir to swim naked in the river under the stars. It was a refreshing school. Yet I was always upset when I had to return after spending the weekend at home. The problem was the contrast between the warmth and comfort of home and the starkness of the physical surroundings at school. No amount of special cooking from my mother would help, perhaps it made it worse. Her steak and kidney and lemon meringue pie before I returned might have been labours of love but they were also a reminder of the awful food that awaited. Boarding schools are a mechanism for desensitizing the young and boarding school boys had the best possible training for National Service, finding it easier to adapt.

My hero of this time is still one of my heroes today. Edward Wilson died with Captain Scott in their tent on the Great Ice Barrier in a blizzard, eleven miles from food and safety. He was a medical doctor and a thinking Christian who wrote:

Religion is not a test to judge by, but an immense aid for those who use it to live by. The main thing is whether a person has the Spirit of God in him, which to my mind means simply the power to love and be kind and unselfish; and many people have this in a very perfect form without professing any religious belief at all, or using any religious practices to keep it.

I gave my sister his book, *The Faith of Edward Wilson*, on her confirmation in 1953. The service was somewhat enlivened by my father and me leaving Queen Anne School Chapel at Caversham in the middle of the service to go to Kempton Park races. One of the Welsh relatives was heard to remind us in rather too loud a whisper of the name of the horse, the time of the race and the amount of the bet. My sister and I were separated by boarding school and were not at that stage much more than friends. Our friendship became very close and warm when we were both living in London in the 1960s. With her husband away at sea, I was needed and became devoted to her. She is my dearest friend.

My last report from Mr Wedd said, 'If I had to select an expedition to go to the South Pole he would be the first person I would choose. But I would make sure that he was not on the return journey!' The reason for this barbed but perceptive comment was that he disliked my infuriating habit of retrospective analysis and carping criticism. It is an unattractive trait that I still retain.

I left Mount House to go to Bradfield College near Reading in 1952. This was a much more conventional school. I nearly went to Bryanston but both my father and my grandfather had been put off it by finding that the first eleven was playing another school with no one there on the touchline to cheer them on. Bradfield was not a wholly happy experience, mainly because I fell victim to the constant homosexual talk and was teased in a most unpleasant way. I used to fight those who called me 'Dahlia' after my initials D.A.L.O. I doubt if it did much good, most of them were bigger than I was and I got plenty of physical bruises, but perhaps it stopped me being mentally bruised. In any case, I never went through a stage of finding boys attractive and by fifteen I was starting to ogle the young Welsh maids who came up in groups from a couple of Valley towns.

My first Bradfield headmaster was John Hills. He had a twinkle in his eye and more sensitivity than one might guess given that he was a stickler for discipline. A formal man, always impeccably turned out, he said in my report, 'Can be a scruffy urchin, must be a decent citizen.' The next headmaster was Anthony Chenevix Trench, a strange small man who went on to be headmaster of Eton. I could never make him out. He said in my report, 'Rare moral courage has not made him a prig as it could have done.' He seemed to me to believe too much in the cane. I have always supported the abolition of corporal punishment. The occasional cuff delivered at the time of an offence by a parent or friend is a natural and sometimes necessary response, but formally inflicting pain is not justifiable.

The most important gift I had from Bradfield was my friendship with Clive Gimson. He was my form master in my first year. He had been a very young Major in the war, winning a Military Cross, before catching tuberculosis and losing part of his lung. This did not stop him getting a Blue in Fives at Cambridge after the war. He, with Philip Stibbe, my kindly housemaster, founded the 1952 Society, an informal debating club in which masters and boys were for a few hours equals. We would argue with no holds barred on topics like, 'Does the end justify the means?' It was a stretching experience where one learnt the art of argument and felt the excitement of ideas. In January 1955 I went skiing to St Anton in Austria in a school party with Clive and, apart from twisting my knee, which had to be put in plaster, I began to form a friendship which transcended the fact that he was a schoolmaster. That summer Clive took three of us rock climbing in Snowdonia. It was my first experience of sustained fear. Only after we had finished the climbing holiday and were sitting around the camp fire on our last night did I discover that everyone else had been just as terrified. Indeed, that mild terror is the normal accompaniment to climbing. Good climbers believe that when you lose your fear it is time to get worried. On Tryfan, in particular, we had a stupendous climb. Swimming, arguing, questioning, we became true friends, with the difference in our age of no account. The next term I found it difficult to treat Clive formally, as a master – we had crossed the Rubicon in our relationship. Fortunately he then went to Australia to teach, so he was not at Bradfield during my last two terms. Before he went he gave me the watch he had had throughout the Second World War. It was a special gesture and filled me with so much emotion that I had to gulp my thanks, turn and flee. He replaced my grandfather as the person I most admired. In 1958, when I was at Cambridge, he and his wife Fiona asked me to be the godfather of their first son, Andrew. I have a letter he sent me at that time which taught me about patience. Patience had been forced on him when he developed tuberculosis and it is a quality I wish I had. This is his letter:

One of the keys to all this which I by the grace of God have been presented with in some measure is patience but which at your age you can hardly have discovered the value of yet, and which often I lose faith about – thinking that I have achieved so little and may soon be too old to catch any of the various buses which seem worth catching. But if I had gone flat out to catch some particular bus I am sure I should have become a real shit – perhaps I am – because to achieve success it seems necessary to throw over many of the ideals of youth by trampling on the weak and putting oneself first.

You are right to find in love such power – it is the most powerful thing in existence – that's why I agree God is love. It is a consuming thing. But it must be controlled to have a practical value and that is where I have found patience so valuable – not at the time or by my own merits – patience has nearly always been forced upon me, though now that I have experienced the value of it I can begin to use it occasionally.

He sent me a poem written in Trieste at the end of the war when he was nearly twenty-five, and I quoted it years later on the BBC's *With Great Pleasure*.

We remained very close friends until he died, tragically early, of cancer of the oesophagus. Our friendship was as close as I have found it possible for two men's to be. I do not know what it was that enabled us to bridge the years between us. He was a devout but questioning Christian and when we would meet, schoolboy, student, doctor or Foreign Secretary, as likely as not we would talk for four or five hours with hardly a stop for a meal. I lying on the carpet, he in a chair. I stayed with him once when I was wrestling with a particularly difficult decision over Rhodesia, beginning to hate Ian Smith for the atrocities that the white-led Selous Scouts had done in the name of the Patriotic Front. He forced me to think through what it all looked like from the white settlers' viewpoint, desperate as they faced defeat.

Initially I thought I was going to study law and go to Oxford. Only after I was sixteen and had taken my O levels did I decide to be a doctor. Both my parents had been at great pains not to influence me towards medicine. My father, however, was delighted when I decided to be a doctor. My mother would have preferred me to be a lawyer, and since I had neglected science and concentrated most on English and history, it was going to be very difficult to get into Oxford. Then someone suggested I should try Sidney Sussex College, Cambridge. My parents and I went up to see it and were met by the Master of Sidney, Tommy Knox-Shaw, a small, bouncy, bespectacled man. His first act was to punch me in the solar plexus which was a rather odd way to start. Commenting that my stomach muscles were good, he proceeded to show us around the College. Without formal interview or meeting any other dons he told me that if I got my First MB in physics, chemistry and biology by the summer of 1956 I could come to Sidney that autumn. When one compares this with the complicated entry procedures today and the vastly higher academic threshold for medicine, I have no doubt that I would not have been able to study medicine at Cambridge. I crammed for physics in December, my mother seeking out one of her old textbooks which, in its new edition, proved to be far better than anything I had at school. I took chemistry in March and then biology in June. I forgot each subject as soon as I had passed it. With General Classics as an easier way round the compulsory Latin at O level, I just scraped into Cambridge. My school days were over. Though they are important, in my case I think the years I spent at Cambridge were the most formative.

In my early teens I read Paul Gallico's love story *The Lonely* and for the first time began to understand what love really meant. Since there was no television in our house, a visit to the 'flicks' was the main form of entertainment and the big cinemas in Plymouth were packed. For a popular programme, one would have to queue to get in. Today's television and video generation has little understanding of how important the back row of the stalls was to the course of true love, something well captured by A.P. Herbert, in his poem "'Twas at the Pictures, Child, We Met':

> For, while those clammy palms were clutched,
> By stealthy slow degrees
> We moved an inch or two and touched
> Each other with our knees.
>
> No poet makes a special point
> Of any human knee,
> But in that plain prosaic joint
> Was high romance for me.
>
> Thus hand in hand and toe to toe,
> Reel after reel we sat;
> You are not old enough to know
> The ecstasy of that.

It was in the cinema in Plymouth that the ecstasy of first love began.

2

FIRST LOVE

> Try as he will, no man breaks wholly loose
> From his first love, no matter who she be.
> Oh, was there ever sailor free to choose,
> That didn't settle somewhere near the sea?

We fell in love while we were both still at school. I was seventeen and she sixteen. For years that love generated a fire which at times nearly consumed me. I cannot describe the heights to which our love took me, nor the depths to which I sank in periods of rejection. More thinking and writing were devoted to her than to all my medical studies put together. She was fair-haired, thin-boned, and beautiful:

> She opened her eyes, and green
> They shone, clear like flowers undone
> For the first time, now for the first time seen.

Poetry was a way of expressing our love. During the time that I was close to her, I both wrote poetry and read most of the major poets in the English language. Soon after our love had finally died, I put together a complete anthology of nearly seventy romantic poems.

Two poems written in her own hand I have kept. I do not know when they were written out. I suspect from their dog-eared look and their flowery diction that it was in the early years before I went to Cambridge. If I look back through old photograph albums I can capture some of the feeling of being in love; if I visit the places where we went I can recall some of the atmosphere, but when I read the poems the tears flood into my eyes. It is as if I am there again experiencing it all. These two poems, because of the paper being hers and the writing too, are particularly precious to me. They also recapture the innocence of our early love.

> Thro' all the hours that life shall go,
> Sweet hours or sad, hours swift or slow,
> Each passing moment brings to me
> Full blooming rose-life thoughts of thee.

The other poem poses the question lovers often ask.

> How many times do I love again?
>   Tell me how many beads there are
>   In a silver chain
>   Of evening rain,
> Unravell'd from the tumbling main,
>   And threading the eye of a yellow star:-
> So many times do I love again.

Alone in a railway carriage on my way to Cornwall, reading these poems from the past, I looked up, and saw a woman's face at the window. She looked at me aghast and apprehensive as if I were ill or in pain. I could not understand why until I realized that tears were flooding down my face and on to my shirt. I smiled back reassuringly and she passed down the corridor. I was miles away, reliving my first love, indulging my memory.

The emotions that surrounded this love moulded my life. Dramatists, novelists and musicians have all been able to evoke the intensity of a young man's feeling for the woman he loves. But nothing can really recapture its consuming nature, the longing, the yearning and the tension as well as poetry.

The torture of suppressed sexuality that the Church's teaching engendered in me was immense. I do not know why in those years I chose to live up to its stern and unyielding message equating sex with sin. The people closest to me took a more relaxed attitude. My parents had the natural scientist's attitude to sex and my grandfather Gear was never a preacher of hell fire and damnation on its evils.

Our love remained for all its years spiritual and every bit as sensual, possibly more so, for not having been consummated. This was the decade before the contraceptive pill, and the fear of accidental pregnancy was ever present. For young lovers to remain chaste was probably commoner than people now realize. We travelled together with great freedom and a confidence in each other which we might not otherwise have had. It meant we had no sense of guilt in our relationship and that was very precious.

Even at eighteen we would discuss how our love could last. We could see most of our friends, even then, moving in and out of love. Our love was precious, and we believed that sexual self-control was the way to ensure that our love would last for years, perhaps for life. This was a wholly private decision, initially taken as much out of mutual respect as a fear of conception, although that fear was reinforced when close friends of ours had to get married because they were having a baby. Perhaps releasing our physical frustration might have meant less mental tension, but other strains would have emerged. And even if we had had no

Christian belief, we would probably still have felt that mutual respect dictated abstinence. So we lived near the edge of frustration. Emotions were often wrought-up without being spent. Once when I allowed that frustration to break out she was hurt and cried.

Our love flowered while I was at Cambridge, punting on the River Cam on hot days, gliding through the willow trees, visiting Grantchester. Today it is little different from what it was when I was there or when Rupert Brooke wrote that poem. There is the same apparent self confidence and yet underlying uncertainty as undergraduates grow and feel their way.

It was at Cambridge that I first discovered the poems of T.S. Eliot. 'The Hollow Men' is the one which I most often recall, not because of its most famous line about the world ending 'not with a bang but a whimper', but because for me it is a poem which expresses sexual tension.

Separation had some advantages. There was less need for me to join the endless search for women undergraduates in what was then an unnaturally male-dominated community. This was still the time when there were only three women's colleges at Cambridge; all the rest were male and no women were admitted as students. Her absence meant that I had more time to soak up what Cambridge offered. In case this sounds all too good to be true, I had the unique advantage of access to the 'Bevanry' where there was a seemingly unlimited intake of beautiful women, mainly from Scandinavia, studying English for a year. Edward Bevan, a medical student with my father at St Mary's and my doctor at Cambridge, coached the University boat crew. At the start of each winter term I went to the Bevans' first party at home. This ensured I met a number of girls whom I could ask out over the months ahead.

To an extent rare these days, with the telephone now the main method of communication, we courted each other through letters. Each morning brought the wait for the post to drop through the letter box, the hurried steps to pick it up, the excitement if a letter was there, often in a coloured envelope, and the anxiety if it was not.

> The solemn Sea of Silence lies between us;
> I know thou livest, and thou lovest me:
> And yet I wish some white ship would come sailing
> Across the ocean, bearing word from thee.

The first time we kissed was on a South Devon headland to which we repeatedly returned. The only noise was the lashing of the sea on the rocks below and the seagulls circling in the sky. There was a deserted holiday house on the cliff path, grey walled, slated and timbered. We would climb in during the winter months when there was no one around and it would become our home. Duffle coated against the cold, we would lie on the floor and warm each other, talking the hours away.

Always I sense the sea when I recall our love. We would sail together in *Agnes*, my little white sailing boat in almost any weather. I was very lucky to own *Agnes* (xi) for she was one of the most beautiful boats ever designed, one of three original X-One designs, a small day boat with a fixed keel and, unlike its modern design, clinker built with overlapping boards and gaff-rigged with a long boom that went over the counter at the stern of the boat. If I sailed into a strange harbour as often as not someone would come alongside and ask what sort of boat she was. Her lines were very striking, fast in even the lightest wind, and I hardly ever had to use the outboard motor.

The year after my motor bike accident, when my leg had mended, we went cruising together. We sailed from Newton Ferrers, where *Agnes* was moored, and went down the south-west coast to Cornwall. At Looe harbour *Agnes* had to lean against the sea wall for when the tide dropped mudflats appeared. We both slept in sleeping bags on the cockpit floor without a cover over the boom. At night we could hear people walking above us on the quay and we lay snug, looking up at the stars for company. Coming into Fowey harbour after a vigorous day's sail, we anchored and then brewed up baked beans with butter on the little Primus stove, washed down with hot chocolate. All the time we were very close to each other and to nature. All these memories came flooding back when I recently reread John Masefield's poem which I had marked '*Agnes*, Cornwall 1958'.

> I must go down to the seas again, for the call of the running
>   tide
> Is a wild call and a clear call that may not be denied;
> And all I ask is a windy day with the white clouds flying,
> And the flung spray and the blown spewm, and the seagulls
>   crying.

Coming back to the River Yealm off Rame Head, just before one can see Plymouth Breakwater and into the Sound, the seas became very steep. Water crashed into the cockpit even though the sails were tied down to the lowest reef points. There was little time for fear. She pumped and the water swilled around our feet for an hour or more. The danger we had been in only struck home when we picked up our mooring that evening in the dark, cold and wet.

The struggle with the elements is the reason why sailing has such a hold on me. The contrasts between a placid, boisterous and cruel sea make the difference between a tranquil, vigorous and dangerous sail. It is no accident of language that boats are always described as being feminine for boats have many of the characteristics of women and I cannot imagine a life without either. Nor of being unable to smell and see the sea. I have spent thirty years living on or by the Thames where the sea surges up with the tide every day and then the river floods away down to the sea,

and there is comfort in the rhythm of time and tide. I suppose I have
spent more nights of my life with the rhythm of the sea beating on the
shore or the river bed than times away from the sea. The sea is in my
blood, in part, perhaps because of my father's father, the sea captain.

> We two were lovers, the Sea and I;
> We plighted our troth 'neath a summer sky.
>
> And all through the riotous, ardent weather
> We dreamed, and loved, and rejoiced together.
>
> At times my lover would rage and storm.
> I said: 'No matter, his heart is warm.'
>
> Whatever his humour, I loved his ways,
> And so we lived through the golden days.

The chance to go on an expedition to Afghanistan in the summer before
starting at St Thomas's was too great an adventure to miss. Yet by going
I probably reinforced her suspicion that I was selfish. This was, after all,
a self-induced separation. It must have appeared to her that when it came
to the crunch I would always put my interests before hers. She never
complained but I think I lost an important part of her love in taking
those five months away.

I wrote to her as we drove through Turkey, Iran, Afghanistan,
Pakistan and India but the experience was hard to share. I quoted to her
what I think was Leavis writing about D.H. Lawrence, but it could have
been Lawrence himself, and I have not been able to trace which.

> Isolation is a kind of progressive depersonalization intellectually and
> emotionally. Our qualities are joint enterprises: my intelligence is your
> criticism, my sincerity your simplicity, my warmth your depth.

The spiritual experience of the trip wound itself into my life. I threw
myself into the mysticism of Asia. My companion as I travelled on the
road to Samarkand was Robert Byron's book *The Road to Oxiana*, the
first of the travel books to combine scholarship and rich description.
Since then I have learned to collect books connected with a country,
whether novels or history, and then read them while visiting. I find it
deepens the atmosphere as I travel and I can relive it afterwards.

Sleeping in the Afghani tents, sharing the tribe's food as they wandered,
I began to understand and respect the Islamic faith. As they grazed their
animals on the parched mountain ranges at over ten thousand feet, I was
witnessing a way of life unchanged down the centuries. They were
generous and welcoming, killing and cooking a sheep when we arrived
unexpectedly, sometimes after the sun had fallen at their camp site. We
would arrive exhausted from hours in the saddle riding on horses that
picked their way like mountain goats over the extraordinary terrain. We
slept like spokes in a wheel with our feet round the central fire. Then as

we left I would look back on the camps, refreshed by an insight into a new life. Women were unveiled and respected. The Afghanis elected their own leader, in one case a tall handsome bearded figure with a natural authority. Listening to him talk with the Koran open on his lap, even though I could not understand what he was saying, I sensed respect for religious laws that had been handed down and were still genuinely revered. One night when our interpreter had explained that two of us were young doctors we were taken to see a woman who was having difficulty delivering her baby. It was pretty clear that her pelvis was too small for the child's head. We could do nothing and knew that without a Caesarean operation, both would die. It was a harsh world up there in the mountains, but it was magical.

India was very different. I discovered there the poetry of Rabindrinath Tagore and as we joked and laughed among ourselves I would think,

> They who are near to me do not know that
> you are nearer to me than they are.
> They who speak to me do not know that my heart
>   is full with your unspoken words.
> They who crowd in my path do not know that
>   I am walking alone with you.
> They who love me do not know that their love
> brings you to my heart.

Tagore, a Bengali poet, philosopher and renowned musician, was the first Asian to receive the Nobel Prize for Literature. At that time he was an immensely popular writer in all English-speaking countries. For me, brought up within a few miles of Dartington Hall in South Devon, it was a revelation that Tagore had been a close friend of Leonard Elmhirst. After administering Tagore's model village at Srinikeran, Elmhirst, with his rich American wife, founded the Dartington Trust.

Visiting Benares I smelt the fecundity of the Hindu faith. In the Temples I saw its joyous eroticism in the explicit carvings. I watched as the bodies from the funeral pyre were slid into the bubbling surging Ganges River and far from being repelled I felt that this religion had a message about the sanctity of all forms of life.

We drove back into Iran from Pakistan via Dr Holland's missionary eye hospital in Quetta. One could not but be impressed by the dedication of Dr Holland and his fellow missionaries but I was shocked to see Muslims being converted to Christianity merely by the miracle of having their cataracts removed. They came in blind and they left seeing. Not surprisingly, in that atmosphere of prayer, some were converted. They then faced, as Christians, the penalty of becoming outcasts when they returned to their villages. I could not see any Christian virtue in this. What right did we Christians have so blatantly to interfere with a Muslim community? By now my own religious faith bore little relation to the Church of England or for that matter to the simpler, and to me preferable, Church of Wales. I felt that there was a far wider spiritual horizon than that which could be covered by the teachings of any one Church. I became and have remained a convinced ecumenicist.

Travelling through Iran on the way out to Afghanistan we had visited Meshed, the holiest Muslim place of worship after Mecca, and seen the pilgrims lashing each other's naked backs with chains. Coming back through Iran and visiting Isfahan, we saw the splendour and the beautiful mosques. It all added to the understanding of the power of Islam. The depth of Islamic culture in Iran was still immense, particularly considering that, unlike Afghanistan, Iran was fast becoming industrialized under the Shah. The Shiite faith was never likely to be destroyed by the Shah as Ataturk had done in Turkey but Western attitudes were challenging its teachings and even then the mullahs felt under attack.

I read from the Rubaiyat of Omar Khayyam while visiting his tomb in Iran. Architecturally the tomb is rather disappointing but in the surrounding flower gardens I found a peace that I have rarely experienced.

> . . . There was the Door to which I found no Key
> There was the Veil through which I might not see:
> Some little talk awhile of Me and Thee
> There was – and then no more of Thee and Me.

In many ways the travelling deepened my understanding of love. The Muslim faith accepts that man is not monogamous, that he can love more than one woman at the same time. Initially when the West discovered this facet of Islam it tended to joke about it, even to see it as a sign of an inferior faith. But as we have come to understand that the obligations for the second or third wife are no less binding than for the first; as we have seen the way mutual respect is built into such relationships, there is much less scoffing. For me at that stage in my life the realization that a wise and deep religious faith had a wider perspective on love was enriching. I began to question the narrowness behind some of the Anglican Church's teaching, particularly on chastity and the view that one can only love one woman.

When I returned from India she was already back at her university and though we still wrote to each other there was a chill of doubt in her letters. It was hard to identify what was wrong but something was missing. She explained to me later that she felt that I was destroying her love by always analysing it, probing it and not just accepting it. Her other boy-friend accepted her love and did not want to turn it upside down. She wanted the mysteries and the beauty of love but felt I treated it as if I were trying to split the atom. Eventually in a turmoil she told me she doubted whether she loved me and we stopped seeing each other and wrote less. Early the following year, after she had been in France for three months, we started seeing each other again. Yet there was a distance between us that would never completely disappear. Even so we grew back into love and in the summer of 1960 we drove to Italy together, camped on the Lido and I saw Venice for the first time travelling in across the sea. We then took a boat down to Greece, sleeping out on deck. We were very happy travelling together and on the island of Poros I read for the first time Cavafy's

> Body, remember not only how much you were loved,
> not only the beds on which you lay,
> but also those desires for you
> that glowed plainly in the eyes,
> and trembled in the voice – and some
> chance obstacle made futile.
> Now that all of them belong to the past,
> it also seems as if you had yielded
> to those desires – how they glowed,
> remember, in the eyes gazing at you;
> how they trembled in the voice, for you, remember, body.

On the beautiful island of Hydra I think of the cats. They were the animals she loved most and it is cats with which I will always associate her. They sensed her affection and used to hang around our table on the waterfront hoping to pick up some food. A little striped kitten used to lie outside the restaurant of a man who made us omelettes and gave us pickled octopus to taste. The kitten would be taken by the local boys for a swim in the sea. Instead of fighting them the kitten revelled in it and swam around with them. I have never seen that happen since.

In Delphi we slept out on the Temple steps and I remember looking down on the bay below from a restaurant where we ate tomatoes stuffed with meat, rice and bay leaves. But the doubts she had about my love were not assuaged by the magic of our Greek holiday.

We returned from Greece and she went to Ireland. I started to live on my houseboat *Amanda* on the Thames (xiii). That autumn she was due to come over for my closest friend's wedding at which I was the best man. Suddenly she cancelled. It really seemed as if our love was finally over. I felt I was no longer capable of drawing her out and that she existed behind a veil through which I could not penetrate. She then wrote to say she no longer loved me. I took it badly but never showed it. My Celtic emotions were too bottled up. Not for the first or last time an apparent aloofness stemmed from a reluctance to display my emotions. I know this can appear as arrogance. But it stems more often than not from uncertainty, even shyness.

She told me later that she decided that she did not love me enough because I did not need her enough. I probably did not show her the depths of my need. The tragedy was that we did not meet to discuss it. She was, though I did not know it at the time, terribly run down and what she later described as a complete physical wreck, worn out by examinations. London seemed far away across the water and with the wedding all mapped out for me and my friends, she thought that I did not need her. Perhaps if I had known that the combination of exams and illness had shattered her, I would have handled it all more sensitively and not taken her decision as final. I learnt only later that she had hardly slept at all for nights before she wrote the letter which, I thought, had irrevocably ended our love. I, for my part, responded hastily and foolishly, only reinforcing her suspicion that I was too conceited to care enough about her feelings.

That Christmas, three months after we had broken up, I told her about a new love. She claimed later that she sensed some uncertainty and warned me against falling in love on the rebound. Sadly I did not listen. I had often seen my new love across medical lecture theatres and the dissecting room at Cambridge; I even mentioned in my note book that I was attracted to her but we had never really talked to each other.

Early in 1961, as a medical student (xiv), I became formally engaged. We were studying medicine in London, though at different hospitals. We saw each other all the time and, as we were at exactly the same stage in our medical studies, it appeared that we had everything in common. All seemed perfect. My parents liked her; she was exceptional at everything; warm, kind, loving fully without any of the doubts and hesitations which I had grown used to in my first love. We shared a love of poetry and philosophy. I thought that I loved her and that we would be happy for life. Yet within three months I had broken off our engagement.

I alone was responsible and it was the worst hurt I have ever dealt anyone. The only explanation is that I was unable to free myself from my first love, something I sensed when I wrote to tell her about my engagement. I wept as I wrote. I refused to recognize this as a sign that I had not stopped loving her.

Sensing that something was wrong, I decided in a fit of virtuousness to get rid of the hundred and more letters which I had kept from the past five years. This distressed me so much that I barely managed to finish destroying them, and kept the two poems I have quoted from. I can see now that it was a desperate attempt to rid myself of the nagging fear that I was still in love with her.

Soon after we got engaged I had to do my statutory three months as a student of midwifery at the Lambeth Hospital, delivering babies and living inside a hospital for the first time. Sometimes I felt soaked in disinfectant and I missed going to *Amanda* on the Thames. Up at all times of the day and night, I found the beauty of birth downgraded to a production line. Women no longer seemed so beautiful; I felt restless, frustrated, and my libido went down. Feeling like this and being met by my new love's warmth irritated rather than comforted. I began to miss the very detachment and coolness of my first love.

I had also begun to convince myself that marriage would fence me in. I had just started to be interested in politics, had already joined the

Labour Party and subconsciously perhaps begun to see politics as a wholly new horizon – a horizon which would never be reached if I was involved in both marriage and medicine. Lots of little things, such as the demise of a car which I could not afford to replace, had begun to coalesce in my mind as being linked with marriage. And I worried about her encroachment on my territory. Humans need to mark out their own territory, in much the same way as animals, something Robert Ardrey has popularized in *The Territorial Imperative*. My houseboat, *Amanda*, was my territory. She would rock me to sleep before settling on the mud. She was a haven and I feared to lose her. I sensed we would not easily be able to carve out new territory and that financial pressures might force us to live a suburban life. Of course I should have thought about all of this well before getting engaged. It was indefensible that I had not anticipated these doubts and fears, but it was traumatic to realize what misery my own deficiencies were bringing to someone for whom I care deeply to this day and for others close to her whom I liked.

Only weeks into an engagement which should have been a liberation, I began to feel trapped. I started to act like a cornered animal. I snapped and snarled and even hoped that I might provoke my fiancée to break off our engagement. This indefensible behaviour only made the situation worse for she responded by being endlessly understanding and forgiving. That only made me even more desperate. Eventually I plucked up the courage to tell her of my doubts.

> Yet each man kills the thing he loves,
> By each let this be heard
> Some do it with a bitter look,
> Some with a flattering word,
> The coward does it with a kiss,
> The brave man with a sword.

She whose love I killed then wrote me the most remarkable letter I have ever received. She alluded to Oscar Wilde's poem which we had recited to each other, but she reminded me that he had written something even greater in 'De Profundis' just before he left prison, from which she took succour:

> To regret one's own experiences is to arrest one's own development. To deny one's own experiences is to put a lie into the lips of one's own life. It is no less than a denial of the soul . . .
>
> The important thing, the thing that lies before me, the thing that I have to do, if the brief remainder of my days is not to be maimed, marred, and incomplete, is to absorb into my nature all that has been done to me, to make it part of me, to accept it without complaint, fear or reluctance.

What was staggering was that, despite being surrounded by friends and family who were bandying about words like 'recrimination', 'bitterness' and 'forgiveness', she would have none of it. She wanted only to try to understand and to look to the future, and compared the uncertainty and apprehension of love to the feeling of being frightened of woods and the dark spaces between trees. As a child I had known this fear vividly, and even now if walking alone down a country lane at night I hasten, afraid to linger.

In a way it is surprising that we even contemplated getting married as impecunious students and did not wait until we were both qualified doctors. But then we would have faced immediate separation, since after qualifying we should have had to sleep in the hospital for two years, working inhuman hours. Once the engagement was broken off I felt utterly wretched. I refused to take comfort from any excuse. I alone was responsible for the hurt, had broken her trust and had smashed our love. There was no explanation to offer.

The person who gave me most comfort was the very person whose love I had destroyed. In her long letter she reminded me of the complexity of marriage and that it was understandable that no one person could meet all its demands. She ended her letter with a gift that has stayed with me for ever, the discovery of Shelley and his words from 'Prometheus Unbound':

> To suffer woes which hope thinks infinite,
> To forgive wrongs darker than death or night,
> To defy Power which seems omnipotent,
> To love and bear: to hope till hope creates,
> From its own wreck the thing it contemplates,
> Neither, to change, nor falter nor repent
> This like thy glory Titan is to be
> Good, Great, Joyous, beautiful and free
> This is alone Life, Joy, Empire and Victory!

She told me I had to stand as a person, and so had she, not bowed down by other people's disapproval. We have met a few times and she remains understanding, with no rancour. One other person understood – Mervyn Stockwood. He was then Bishop of Southwark, himself going through an agonizing time – a very public row over a consistory court case. He wrote:

> It is at times like this that we find our true bearing and find the worth of our convictions. And I have no doubt that in spite of the wind, the fire and the storm of your present unhappiness you will discover the still, small voice. I wish so much that I could help you but I know that in the affairs of the heart we have to settle our problems for ourselves. But you have my thoughts, my prayers and my love.

Eventually I emerged from my despair. With the help of friends, my sister Susan in particular, I slowly rebuilt my self-confidence. My father, a family doctor for whom there were few surprises in human behaviour, had seen and understood what had happened. Guessing that I was still tortured by sexual longing and torn by the Church's teaching on chastity, he chose to quote a saying which, he claimed, had been a favourite of my grandfather Gear, 'If God meant sex to be so sinful, he would not have made it so enjoyable.' I will never know whether my father invented the quote, but I doubt if he did. He had been very close to Gear, and knew that his was the advice I would take most notice of. Gear had a wicked sense of humour but above all a practical Christianity, always preaching the essence of the Christian message, love.

Some weeks after the engagement was broken off, I saw my first love again. She gave freely of her friendship and it was a great help. But if love there still was between us, it remained locked up, both of us too afraid of what had happened. Also my behaviour must have confirmed the wisdom of her previous doubts. We wrote, and a few months later we met again. This time we were both more relaxed and even contemplated going on holiday together. But she was wiser than I, and after reflection, wrote to say no. It had been a kind thought but it also revealed that she still felt something between us. Crazily but temporarily she had allowed sentiment to override her other commitments. That did more for my morale than any words.

By the summer of 1961 I was working hard in hospital and starting to take an even more active interest in politics. It was the Fabian Society which absorbed my energies and my membership of the Labour Party was nominal. Two women, both Catholics, who had been through their own moral questioning before rejecting their Church's teaching, taught me to love. One, Brazilian, all too quickly had to return to Rio de Janeiro, while the other, French, simply surrounded me with uncomplicated love. Whenever I tried to ask any question or analyse she would put her finger on my lips. Her English was poor and for once I talked less and lived more. She invited me to the South of France in the late summer and as I absorbed the last rays of the sun my emotional scars healed. Her father was away in Algiers and her mother, sophisticated and beautiful, conspired to let us love in peace. The family was bitterly hostile to General de Gaulle who they felt had betrayed them. They had no doubt that his famous speech, '*Je compris*' was a pledge to keep '*Algerie française*'. All over the South of France that slogan could be seen in graffiti. By the end of my stay I was not sure which one, the mother or the daughter, I was more in love with. Her mother knew that our love would now have to fade and that her daughter would marry the Frenchman already earmarked by the families. On the last evening, when I took them both out to a restaurant by the sea, she quietly made sure that I knew that too. She quoted the saying '*Aimez ce que jamais on ne verra deux fois*', or 'Love that which you will never see twice'. Then she tactfully departed, leaving us to face the morning. I have never seen either of them again.

Next morning I drove off to Zurich to stay with Jan Fisher, the medical student friend with whom I had travelled to Afghanistan. As I drove through Provence I cried – tears not of sorrow but of happiness. I was whole and alive again, the trauma of the broken engagement finally behind me.

I had been given leave of absence to study psychiatry in Zurich and it turned out to be a wonderful time to think and read. Jan was working at the Burgholzli Psychiatric Clinic, where Carl Jung had started his work and I stayed with him in his flat in the old part of the city. Enthralled by Jung's writing during the week, we climbed together in the Swiss Alps at the weekend.

As I wrestled with the analyst's approach to patients, I found comfort in Freud's description of the goal of psycho-analysis as being 'to substitute for neurotic misery ordinary human unhappiness'. I found in the writings of Karl Jasper's new insights into the spiritual world. 'Who knows the meaning of the universe, or where it is going? Perhaps it is only the purity of this not knowing which makes possible that which we call truth or reason or the service of God'. The organized Church for me became less of a focus and its overall importance declined, never again to become dominant. In its place stood the recognition of a power outside myself, but that power was no longer clothed with all the structures or dogmas of the Church. I started to draw from a well deeper than just the Christian faith, one from which Muslims, Buddhists and Hindus also draw. Asked if I was a Christian, my answer was yes, but I was very conscious that the qualificiations were now immense. I had come to believe that spiritual and physical love went naturally together and that marriage was not the exclusive entry certificate. I saw marriage as a structure devised to sustain and deepen mutual respect, to bring together not just two lovers but to provide a framework within which to forge a family. And I felt that love not founded on mutual respect was worthless. Now I shared Shelley's view:

> I never was attached to that great sect,
> Whose doctrine is that each one should select
> Out of the crowd a mistress or a friend,
> And all the rest, though fair and wise, commend
> To cold oblivion, though it is in the code
> Of modern morals . . .
> With one chained friend, perhaps a jealous foe,
> The dreariest and the longest journey go.
>
> True Love in this differs from gold and clay,
> That to divide is not to take away.
> Love is like understanding, that grows bright,
> Gazing on many truths . . .

My first love and I still wrote to each other and though we rediscovered many of our feelings for each other, our love was of a different quality.

We were still friends and spiritual lovers but there was more of the friend than lover. In early 1962 I drove over to Germany where she was teaching and we travelled to Berlin in my car. For the first time I saw this city for which I had felt an early affinity. The Movietone News film of the Berlin Airlift in 1947 was my first international political memory, and Berlin, divided, became a symbolic city for me. For her it was where her mother had been born and where relatives still lived. Later, in June 1963, when President Kennedy had gone to Berlin and made his famous speech, 'Ich bin ein Berliner', I had felt that emotional attachment deepen. Over the years, I travelled to Berlin many times as a politician, and accompanied the Queen there as part of her official visit in 1978. So when the Berlin Wall came crashing down in 1989 I relived those memories and, like many other people around the world, my heart lifted.

There was a palpable tension in the city during those early months of 1962. We drove towards the obscene Wall and waited interminably at passport control before crossing over at Checkpoint Charlie into East Berlin. It was my first visit to a communist country. Its drabness, its smell and its poverty left an indelible impression. In light snow we drove across East Germany to Prague. Arriving in the dark, we drove in a flurry of snow up the cobbled, winding streets to the Castle. Hearing the noise of the wheels echoing from the walls and seeing the snowflakes in the headlights, we felt as if we were travelling in a horse drawn carriage. Next morning we found that Prague, no longer with its snow white covering, was besmirched by the tell-tale signs of Soviet Communism. But there was an underlying beauty to the city that not even a massive statue of Stalin could blight. We knew that this city would some day be free. It took twenty-seven years.

We wrote intermittently and saw each other occasionally through the following year. But, perhaps for the first time in all our years together, her whole love belonged to someone else. That summer, when I qualified as a doctor, she wrote a beautiful letter gently, warmly explaining much of what had happened over the years. I still have it. The following year she wrote to tell me she was engaged to the man she had known at university. There was no pain. I was happy for her. Our love had lasted at varying intensity from 1956 to 1963.

We saw each other for the first time for nearly twenty-nine years, when I had finished writing about our love and she was just as enchanting and as beautiful. Afterwards she wrote, reminding me of this poem which we had shared together and which she still remembered:

We have known treasure fairer than a dream
Upon the hills of youth. And it shall stay
Jewelled in the distance, untarnished and supreme
For the dark tentacles of life's decay shall never shadow it

Nor overthrow its years like hours grown golden in the sun
Its years lived full in the gathered light
An amethyst across the sea of night
For dawn and dusk we knew and caught our breath
With the exquisite imaginings of spring,
Lived deep, talked lightly of this stranger death
And love grown wistful with remembering
A half familiar tune we used to sing, these were ours
Love's touch upon our hands, music and flowers,
Though in the faithless years they have no part
These are the endless things, the real of hearts.

3

MEDICAL STUDENT

My student days were a kaleidoscope of experiences – six years of joy with occasional despair. Looking back I have the advantage of the four notebooks which were an intermittent diary of thoughts rather than events over these years. I have also kept almost all the books that I owned at the time and some of them are revealingly marked. They show that while I had throughout one objective, to qualify as soon as possible as a doctor, I was strangely detached from my medical studies. Examinations were an obstacle to be overcome and I worked hard to pass but not much more. I wanted and found time to study and question the broader philosophical issues. The thinking was often naïve but the time spent pondering, agonizing and wondering was not wasted.

In July 1956, eighteen and no longer a schoolboy, I was doing a holiday job while waiting to go to Cambridge University. My employer was Costain's the construction firm, and the project a new sewage works near my home. Starting at 6 a.m. and often doing overtime in the evenings and on Saturdays, I earned good money. Then, suddenly, Colonel Nasser seized the Suez Canal. The Prime Minister, Sir Anthony Eden, said that Nasser could not be allowed 'to have his thumb on our windpipe'. That was mild language compared with what I was hearing as we dug trenches for the sewer pipes. Most of my fellow workers had done their National Service and some had served in the Second World War. They were adamant from the start that the Egyptians should not be allowed to get away with it. Prior to Suez the only subject of conversation was sex. Suddenly that was swept away. We were all military strategists and the question that dominated was when to go in and retake the Suez Canal.

Whenever the *Daily Mirror* or the *Daily Herald* had any reports of Labour MPs objecting to Britain using force against the Egyptians my workmates went wild. Castigating the newspaper, expressing their disagreement with Labour in abrasive terms, soon they saw even Hugh Gaitskell, Labour's leader, as a backslider. Not for them sensible warnings that while force could not be excluded if it was used it should be consistent with the Charter of the United Nations. For them it was clear cut. The 'Gippos' had hit us, so we should hit them. This was a political eye-opener for me. It was not simple jingoism. What they were expressing was their gut understanding that sometimes force has to be met by force. It left me with an understanding of some of the basic attitudes of millions of Labour voters. I disagreed with them because I did not see that nationalization of the Suez Canal Company was an invasion, it was more a confiscation. Nevertheless, Suez taught me one vital political lesson – never automatically to follow the assumptions of the small group that tends to dominate Labour and Liberal Party thinking on defence and foreign affairs. These people are afraid of exercising military power and have been for decades. Yet they do not speak for public opinion in Britain. There are more people prepared to match force with force than is often apparent. The average person does believe that for a deterrent to be of any value, one has to be prepared to use it, and they expect their politicians to be able to stand up for British interests even in the age of imperial decline. Suez brought home to me, and it was reinforced at the time of the Falklands War, that there is a robustness about the British people's character which is often underestimated by the liberal intelligentsia or what some now call the chattering classes.

Some Labour leaders have always understood this robust nature. Hugh Dalton during the 1930s stood out with Winston Churchill over appeasement. Clement Attlee and Ernest Bevin in the immediate aftermath of the Second World War, despite the yearning for peace, did not ignore the ominous build up of Stalin's power and influence. They took the decision for Britain to manufacture its own atomic bomb when our wartime nuclear co-operation with the US was suddenly shut off. Hugh Gaitskell, Harold Wilson and Jim Callaghan were all patriots in their way and capable of standing firm on the need at times to use force. The equivocation of Denis Healey over the Falklands and the outright opposition of Edward Heath and Denis Healey to our responding with force to Iraq's invasion of Kuwait serve as a warning, however, that not all politicians will even accept that invasion and occupation of another country's territory justifies military action.

Labour's ambivalence to military power has hinged on the attitudes of key trade union leaders. When Ernest Bevin told the pacifist Labour leader, George Lansbury, to stop hawking his conscience around the Conference Hall before the Second World War, he was speaking as a leader of the Transport and General Workers Union (T&GWU) who was in touch with the feelings of his members. When Frank Cousins attacked Hugh Gaitskell and campaigned to ban the bomb, he won the Conference vote, but in 1961 eventually lost because he was out of touch with people like those on the building site with me. When Jack Jones spoke as leader of the T&GWU for unilateral nuclear disarmament against Harold Wilson and James Callaghan he was unrepresentative. Both leaders were prepared to stand up to Jack Jones and as a consequence he lost too. Ron Todd, his successor was only able to win with his block vote at Party Conference from 1980–88 because Michael Foot and then Neil Kinnock were paid up members of CND. When Neil Kinnock decided to shift and endorse Trident in 1989, he had no major difficulty in changing Conference policy for the average Labour supporter had never agreed with it. The Conservatives always thrive if Labour give them the political ammunition they want to depict Labour as soft on defence. Wise Labour leaders never give them that chance.

It makes my blood boil when the Conservative Party have the brass neck to hold political meetings with the Union Jack draped over the table, as if their party had a monopoly on patriotism. It irritated me to see Prime Minister Margaret Thatcher take the salute at the march past outside the Guildhall after the Falklands War. The great wartime Prime Ministers, Lloyd George and Churchill, would never have taken the salute at such a parade. They understood that that role was the Monarch's on behalf of the whole nation. It was the correct decision for John Major to invite the Queen to take the salute at the Gulf War parade. The Conservatives have often tried to monopolize patriotism at election time, particularly in the Naval dockyard constituencies which were bastions of working-class Toryism. When canvassing for Labour votes in Plymouth, I have often put my foot in the door when it was being slammed in my face on a council estate by a dockyard worker saying, 'We're true blue here', or 'I'm for Queen and Country'. Their vote was almost certainly lost but I still felt the need to challenge face to face their belief that Labour and later the SDP was any less patriotic than the Conservatives. The Conservative argument that Labour cannot be trusted with the defence of our nation always stuck in my gullet when I was a member of the Labour Party. Sadly, from 1981–89 I too have not been able to trust Labour on defence and I was glad not to have to defend them from within during this period.

The Suez Canal in 1956 did not just run through Lady Eden's drawing room in No. 10 Downing Street, it ran also through my parents' sitting room. My sister Susan was due to marry Garth Mumford, a Lieutenant in the Royal Navy, and the invitations had already been sent out. He was serving as an engineer on the aircraft carrier HMS *Theseus* and the whole ship's company was put on full alert to sail for the Mediterranean. The wedding was cancelled and then suddenly reinstated when he was given three days' surprise leave. They were married in our local church in Plympton St Maurice and the village came out to see the bride (ix) who walked from the church the hundred yards to our home at 'Castlehayes' where we had a marquee in the garden. Then on 4 August *Theseus* set sail from Portsmouth for Cyprus with men of the 16th Parachute Brigade on board. Our family was like the family of every other serviceman with an impending war and worried about Garth's safety.

All through those summer months the Suez crisis was on everyone's lips. My parents, particularly my mother, were against Eden and for Gaitskell. The *Observer* was strongly critical of the Government and provided me with most of my facts and counter arguments on the building site. Whether sitting eating a snack, leaning on our shovels or waiting to lay concrete we argued over the rights and wrongs of using force. I backed Hugh Gaitskell though I did not know him. In particular I liked his emphasis on the need to retain the support of President Eisenhower. That just seemed common sense. Going it alone was nostalgic nonsense. I knew very little then about the political and military ins and outs of the Suez Crisis. But the Conservative Party and most of the press seemed to many of my generation to be still living in an imperial age that had passed. Nasser never struck me as even remotely like Hitler or Saddam Hussein. For Britain to act only with France and clandestinely with Israel seemed both risky and wrong. At the time Hugh Gaitskell's enemies succeeded in giving the impression that he had copped out, initially supporting Eden's policy of using force and then changing his mind under pressure from Labour MPs. Looking back now at what he said, the criticism hardly seems justified. But in the House of Commons it is so often the impression that counts. The actual words are never as important as the feel which the words leave.

Memories of the Suez debacle were to influence me strongly on two future occasions. I became convinced that Selwyn Lloyd, the Foreign Secretary, was lying to the House of Commons when challenged over the involvement of Israel. We now know that he and Eden systematically deceived Parliament. They were not the first nor will they be the last to mislead Parliament but their deception was on a massive scale. As a consequence, in January 1971 I was one of the fifty-five MPs who voted against Selwyn Lloyd becoming the Speaker of the House of Commons. I felt that no one with his record of deceit should be placed in that particular position. I have to admit that he turned out to be an excellent Speaker but that did not make me regret my vote.

I was also influenced by the anger and contempt that servicemen like my brother-in-law felt when being asked to go to war against a background of bitter party in-fighting in the House of Commons. Because of that experience I tried very hard to contribute to all-party agreement over the Argentine invasion of the Falklands and over Iraq's invasion of Kuwait. Waging war is too serious and too dangerous to be conducted against a background of a political battle in Westminster.

The Suez affair rumbled on through the summer and in September with my parents and newly married sister, I drove to Cambridge to start as a freshman at Sidney Sussex College. All freshmen had to share a set of rooms. Above the door of the rooms allocated to me was the name

B.W.C.C. Christopher. I had no idea who he was or where he came from but my sister suggested that with four initials he must be what Nancy Mitford's then fashionable book described as 'U'. When he turned up I found that Bryan Christopher was certainly 'U': a dark, tall, thin, good looking Etonian. He now practises as a family doctor in East Grinstead and remains a close friend. Each of us is godfather to the other's eldest son. We got on well together from the start, so well that we decided to share rooms in our second year. This meant living out of college in a digs in Chesterton Road run by two spinsters. We had separate bedrooms and sitting rooms but all the residents had breakfast together in the basement. One of my vivid memories is of one of the Miss Fullers leaning over with a milk jug, only to drop her false teeth into my porridge. Bryan and I went on to share the same flat in Lexham Gardens in London, as clinical students, until he married. I learnt much from him, above all the value of true friendship.

Within a few weeks of term starting the British, French and Israeli forces went into Suez at the very moment that Hungary was being raped by the Russians. Anatomy and physiology studies were set aside and like many other Cambridge undergraduates I plunged into the frenzy of political debate. I attended frequent demonstrations and protests against government foreign policy. We were furious over the sheer ineptitude of the Conservative Government, let alone the folly of their military action. I felt disgust at our inability to do anything to help Hungary as it rose up in revolt against Soviet occupation, though for a while, with the release of Cardinal Mindszenty, it looked as if they would succeed. In Cambridge we agonized long into the night about whether we should go to Hungary as our counterparts had done during the Spanish Civil War. Circumstances were very different this time but nevertheless some went even though it was pretty clear that they would have difficulty in getting into Hungary. I regretted not going, even if it had meant the frustration of waiting on the Austrian border.

Then on 5 November before dawn, while the US was putting on pressure for an Anglo-French and Israeli withdrawal from Egypt, one thousand tanks of the Red Army attacked the Hungarian forces in Budapest. The West watched, impotent. The Hungarian people overturned trams to use as barricades, the young fought with Molotov cocktails. But the Russians used heavy shells, their tanks fired at the barricades, and the deeply repressive side of Soviet Communism was there for all to see. We listened to the sound of Radio Budapest. I have never forgotten the last words when it was silenced: 'Help Hungary . . . Help . . . Help . . . Help . . .' My generation of students were as influenced by this as the generation a decade later were affected by Vietnam.

What happened in Hungary left me fiercely hostile to Soviet Communism. From that moment I never ceased to oppose its practice and ideology. My feelings were reinforced by the Soviet suppression of the

Prague uprising in the spring of 1968. Initially it all appeared hopeful with Dubcek, the Czech Prime Minister, appearing to be in control. I was Navy Minister at the moment Czechoslovakia was invaded. Again I felt the frustration that we in the West were not prepared to respond more vigorously. Logic told me it would be foolish to attempt to use force, but I believed there should have been serious sanctions. Then, over the invasion of Afghanistan in 1979, the West should have instituted tough sanctions. I supported our athletes not attending the Moscow Olympics but the collective will did not exist in Europe. Most of my big political battles inside and outside the Labour Party were destined to be about how the Western democracies could defeat through NATO, the European Community and the UN, the ideology of Soviet Communism. The seed of my defiance was sown in Cambridge as I watched Hungary go under.

Surprisingly, despite these highly political events in 1956 and the response it evoked in me, I did not become involved in party politics at Cambridge. I never joined any political party. I went along to the Cambridge Union and took a life membership for ten pounds but the one debate I attended put me off. I disliked, and still do, the mannered style of both the Oxford and Cambridge Union debates and have only rarely accepted invitations to debate, preferring to speak and answer questions. During my three years at Cambridge, if one excludes a number of comments about apartheid in South Africa, there are only two political references in my notebooks and they refer to my horror of nuclear weapons. The first was a reference to a NATO conference, asking whether we were right to use A-bombs as the ultimate deterrent, saying no one would be fool enough to start a war and how easily a small strife could work into a world cataclysm. The second was a reference to a letter which I had written to *The Times*, though it was not published, arguing that though the nuclear bomb was a deterrent it was nevertheless morally evil to believe that one could use it.

The underlying morality of nuclear deterrence has always fascinated me. I was persuaded by the speeches of Hugh Gaitskell in 1961 that the West needed nuclear weapons for military deterrence, and by Harold Wilson and Denis Healey in 1965 that Britain should continue to build Polaris. Far from finding that the closer I came to influencing nuclear policy, the more hardened I became, I found the nearer, the more I worried. After Hiroshima the nuclear genie was out of the bottle. But I was to spend a lot of my life trying to keep it in though I have never believed that once out it can be put back. To use any weapon of mass destruction, chemical, biological or nuclear, is to cross a threshold of immorality far higher than that involved in conventional war. How to ensure that nuclear weapons are never actually used, while being prepared to threaten credibly to use them is the moral dilemma. For there to be any morality to deterrence there has to be a subtle and determined strategy underpinning it which fosters public horror at any nuclear release and yet does not undermine the credibility of threatening release. Continued debate on the morality of nuclear deterrence is essential in order to buttress the politicians in their reluctance ever to authorize the military to use nuclear weapons. Despite this moral questioning, I never felt the remotest temptation to join CND or any of the student peace movements. They seemed to me even then to be escaping rather than confronting these dilemmas.

The closest I came to finding a political forum in Cambridge was Great St Mary's Church where the vicar was Mervyn Stockwood. That November he preached a whole sermon on the politics of Suez and reading it now brings back the sense of outrage. Mervyn Stockwood was a priest who saw that Christianity could thrive on controversy. For nineteen years before coming to Cambridge he had been in Bristol, first as the curate, and then as vicar of St Matthew's, Moorfields. He had also been a Bristol City Labour councillor. He was a socialist who managed to be a close friend of both Stafford Cripps and Walter Monckton when they were respectively Labour and Conservative Members of Parliament for Bristol. Coming to Great St Mary's in 1955, he had been determined to make Christianity relevant and he succeeded beyond anyone's expectations. Queues of undergraduates would form outside the church before a service. Inside, even without a famous preacher, the pews were packed with undergraduates. In part this was a tribute to Mervyn Stockwood's electric personality and his ability to generate controversy but there must have been at the same time a religious revival among undergraduates. In Church matters he was often surprisingly conservative, also very High Church; far too high for my liking. His flamboyant personality made him far fonder than I of ritual and ceremony.

In November 1958 Mervyn was asked by the Prime Minister, Harold Macmillan, to become Bishop of Southwark. Explaining to us in a sermon why he had agreed to go to Southwark, he laid stress on the virtue of the apostolic succession. Then, typically, to lighten the congregation's gloom, he told us about the Somerset farmer who, when visiting the Vatican was shown some hens which were said to be in direct succession to the cock which crew when St Peter denied our Lord. The farmer, being of a practical turn of mind, made one comment, 'Be they good layers?' So Mervyn joked that he was more interested in apostolic success than in apostolic succession. No shrinking violet, he enjoyed being the 'red' bishop. He had always refused to wear a dog collar, and made much of wearing a tie. On becoming a bishop he used to wear a deep red-purple cassock which struck my father's brother, who was then a prebendary of St Paul's Cathedral, as the height of ostentation. He used to regale me with how the then Bishop of London, seeing Mervyn at a party in this garb, sidled up and said, 'Ah, Mervyn, incognito I presume'.

Mervyn Stockwood attracted such criticism. Of course he was a showman, but he was also a devout private man and a man of prayer. He certainly had a profound influence on my life.

My first two terms were different from the rest of my time in Cambridge and more typical of a medical student. Released from the discipline of school, I tasted new freedoms with relish. One evening a group of us went 'Bulldog baiting'. The Bulldogs were college servants who accompanied the Senior Proctor patrolling the streets at night. They were chosen for being fleet of foot, and wore top hats. For sheer devilment I stole up behind one, tipped off his hat and ran with it down the streets. They gave chase but I managed to escape. Eventually I returned the hat anonymously when I heard that he would have to buy the replacement. I frequently accompanied Bryan, who was already what was then referred to as a 'Deb's Delight', to debutante balls in London. These were lavish affairs, very different from the barn dances or Scottish reel parties I was used to in the West Country. We used to come back on the 'milk train' to Cambridge, climbing over the College wall with dawn breaking and still in white tie and tails. We both did the minimum of work and the maximum of play. I played rugger, rowed in the rugger boat, watched the University rugby team, drank much beer and eventually became president of the Lunatiks, a Sidney drinking club. My heart meanwhile was miles away with my first love. Though Bryan had a constant flow of girls coming through our rooms, I felt little need to do the same. One girl-friend from that time reminded me recently that after a dance I deposited her at her college after hours and she was thrown out. I apparently redeemed the situation by returning to London with her in order to explain to her mother that it was my fault. I had totally forgotten the incident but her mother has been a firm political supporter of mine ever since.

The first girl I asked out in Cambridge was a medical student called Deborah Bliss. She later married my other close medical student friend in Cambridge, Anthony Pollock. He was a comfortable, extremely kind man who infuriated me by pretending to be more reactionary than he was. His warmth and solidity was a great help to me over the years whenever I was emotionally strained. He was someone who, puffing away on his pipe in a tweed suit, typified Cambridge as distinct from Oxford, and radiated common sense. Anthony, to the great loss of all his friends, was electrocuted using a drill outside his rambling, ramshackle stately home in Northern Ireland which he had bought for not much money from a friend while still a medical student. I am godfather to their second daughter, Lucy. After his death Deborah married the then Second Sea Lord, Admiral Sir Desmond Cassidi. My own children still remember going to dinner on his last weekend as Commander-in-Chief Home Command in Portsmouth. After a very formal meal with all the Naval silver set out on the long table, they found themselves in the dark under the same table playing Rescue, encountering a crawling Desmond as 'It'.

Those early Cambridge months were hedonistic but, like all good things, they came to an end. I was driving along the straightest stretch of road between Plymouth and Cambridge with my motor bike at full throttle and the needle of the speedometer coming up close to 100 m.p.h. Suddenly a Walls ice cream van coming towards me on the opposite side of the road turned across the road into the petrol station on my left. In a fraction of a second I had to decide whether to swing out on to the other side of the road and risk a head-on crash if anything was coming or to swing into the forecourt in the hope that the driver would see me and brake. I swung left. I was hit side on, thrown up into the air over the van's bonnet and hit the petrol sign high above the ground with my helmet. I can recall it as vividly as if it happened yesterday. As I hit the ground I heard the swoosh of a car going fast down the other side of the road and saw above me the sign swinging wildly. I realized then that if I had turned out, instead of in, I would be dead. As it was, my helmet was split open and if I had not been wearing it I would have had a severe head injury. Ever since, not surprisingly, I have been a strong advocate of the compulsory wearing of motor bike helmets.

Taken by ambulance to Taunton Hospital I was operated on by the Conservative Mayor, who was also an orthopaedic surgeon. It was a bad compound fracture of the tibia and only healed after eight painful and frustrating months in plaster. Over the next few days in Taunton, unable to sleep at night because of the pain, I read the early memoirs of Charles de Gaulle, and discovered what a complex and formidable man he was. I have remained an admirer ever since, particularly of his ruthless ability to judge every policy by its worth to France. Even then, four years before his veto of Harold Macmillan's application to join the European Community, it was clear that for him the acid test about membership of the European Community was how far it served the best interests of France. His analysis of what makes a leader, written while he was still a Colonel, his understanding of the need for a certain distance from one's followers, and his period of self-imposed political exile in Colombey les Deux Eglises had a strong influence on me. We have grown accustomed, since Harold Wilson, to political leaders who seem to have only one purpose – to cling to the conventional vehicles of power. It is hard for them to imagine a life without politics. One of the least known aspects of de Gaulle's life was the tender way in which he looked after his mentally handicapped daughter. He was 'un homme serieux' – for me one of the highest compliments.

Transferred to Mount Gould Hospital in Plymouth, I was an in-patient there for over four months. From my notebook it is clear that I was dogged by pain for nearly a year. To this day I feel bone pain in certain types of weather and have the knee joint of a seventy-year-old. As a consequence the £750 that Walls paid out in compensation has over the years appeared somewhat less generous. Feeling lucky to be alive, I found it easier to put up with the pain and disruption to my studies. It also gave me time to think. I became more serious, more introspective for the next few years. I refer to it jokingly as my Cromwellian period when the inheritance of my Calvinistic ancestors brought out the puritan in my make up.

The whole summer term was lost while I was in hospital. Fortunately I was granted a dispensation for the term, so I did not have to stay on in Cambridge for an extra year which I would have loathed. By missing my first year's examinations I was spared failing, a fate which befell Bryan Christopher. He was sent down from Cambridge and could have failed to become a doctor. But he lived a charmed life and fortunately was reinstated, one reason being that he was so popular in Sidney Sussex College. An excellent conjuror and member of the Magic Circle, he was the life and soul of any party. And so even the dons in Sidney were sensible enough to bend the rules and let him continue.

Returning to Cambridge in the winter for my second year, I still had my leg in a full length plaster and Bryan would tow me around Cambridge on my bicycle with his medical school scarf tied round the handle bars. But at Christmas the proctors responsible for discipline allowed me a motor car – cars were still banned for most undergraduates and I was only given permission because of my leg. I bought a pre-war Morris coupé with my compensation money and called it the 'Bambino' (x).

It was a chastened and altogether more serious student who settled down to catch up. Anatomy in particular is a subject you can master only by long hours of dissection and memorizing pages and pages of detail. My anatomy book, which I still have on my shelves, had been written by Solly Zuckerman when he was Professor of Anatomy at Birmingham University. Twenty years later, when I was Navy Minister, we came to know each other because of his involvement with Polaris. Then ten years after that he became my adviser over nuclear disarmament in the Foreign Office while he was working in the Cabinet Office and I greatly valued his friendship. It was an unusual appointment but his whole career had been an extraordinary one, helped by being on Admiral Mountbatten's staff as scientific adviser during the war. Few have wielded so much influence in Whitehall over so long a period, irrespective of the political complexion of the government. He always believed in nuclear deterrence but was a fervent critic of battlefield nuclear weapons and was the man behind Earl Mountbatten's often quoted speech to the Stockholm International Peace Research Institute, SIPRI, in 1979 when he said 'wars cannot be fought with nuclear weapons'. His career is an example of how the trained mind can turn to other disciplines with considerable effect. By his own engaging personality, he saved Britain billions of pounds. For without his friendship with the prickly Admiral Rickover of the US Navy we would never have had the Polaris and then the Trident Agreement which allowed us access to US missile technology at knock-down prices. In Britain we do not use academics in Government to anywhere near the same extent as in the United States and we miss the rigour of the good mind and the freshness they can bring to the stale atmosphere of Government.

I was determined to return to examining the moral and philosophical questions that I had started to explore at Bradfield. I had barely touched on these in my first year, except for worshipping at the University Church. Studying the History and Philosophy of Science as part of my tripos examination helped extend my mind beyond medicine. I also became a regular attender at F.R. Leavis's lectures on English Literature. He was a renowned lecturer – categorical, uncompromising – and fed my interest in the writings of D.H. Lawrence, in particular his novel *The Rainbow*. He also opened up for me the poems of T.S. Eliot. He could castigate Eliot for being so disparaging of Lawrence and yet in the same breath extol his merits as a poet and critic. The Humanist Society meetings were fascinating too, the most valuable part being at the end when its elderly president, E.M. Forster, would give a short but precise synopsis of what had been discussed. My exploration of humanism was undertaken deliberately to offset the predominance of Christianity hitherto. My religious views were already beginning to change. The certainties of my faith were becoming a little frayed at the edges and I found myself questioning more of the Church's teaching.

The college's main claim to fame is that Oliver Cromwell was one of its students. At Cambridge I read and greatly enjoyed C.V. Wedgwood's short life of Cromwell. It was a trick of fate that my wife became her literary agent and actively stimulated Dame Veronica's publisher to bring out a new edition of that very same volume. The Cromwellian Society, which a group of us revived, was dedicated to good food. The Society justified using Cromwell's name on the grounds that the Great Protector was a formidable trencherman. To this day I have never been able to find out whether or not this is true. The Owen family claim a link to Cromwell through the Williams family on my grandmother's side. Plymouth was a Cromwellian city and Freedom Fields marks the place where the citizens held out against the Crown. I believe this radicalism of the then Plymothians explains in part why, for twenty years, I was the only Labour or Social Democrat MP in the south-west peninsula from Bristol downwards. As if to demonstrate my Cromwellian streak, I put his portrait up in the Foreign Secretary's room but not surprisingly my successor Lord Carrington took it down.

One of my close friends in the Cromwell Society was the College organ scholar; older than I, having already graduated from the Royal College of Music, he introduced me to the art historian and collector Jim Ede. At Kettle's Yard Jim explained to me the significance of his collection of art. It was there that I became entranced by the Cornish primitive painter Alfred Wallis and I now treasure two of his paintings, both given to me by my wife.

Very little is known about Alfred Wallis. He was born in Devonport on 18 August 1855 and went to sea at the age of nine, probably never having gone to school. He was a deep sea fisherman, sailing on the windjammers, and then fished for pilchards and mackerel with the Newlyn and Mousehole fleets. He came to St Ives in 1890 as a marine rag-and-bone dealer and only began to paint at the age of seventy, claiming he did it 'for company'. He died seventeen years later, in 1942, in a workhouse near Penzance. Having been discovered by the painters Christopher Wood and Ben Nicholson, he undoubtedly influenced their work and that of the sculptress Barbara Hepworth and the potter Bernard Leach. Jim Ede had the finest collection of Wallis' work, which started when he was Assistant at the Tate Gallery. Some of Wallis' pictures are still on display today at Kettle's Yard which has now been extended into a proper art gallery, but it was then Jim's house, where he lived. The house itself also influenced me for its plain white walls and plain wood all gave a simplicity and an uncluttered feel that was new for me. I have tried to reproduce this since in my own home.

Looking through my notebooks for the two years at Cambridge after my accident, I find they reflect a constant adolescent debate between materialism and idealism, sexuality and celibacy, all overlaid by a pretty strong Christian commitment. There are frequent references to sermons preached at Great St Mary's where from time to time I read the lesson and I noted once that I had read a little too fast but felt no longer a listener but an actual spokesman of the faith. The Archbishop of Dublin said that, 'a university is the scene of the constant conflict of seeing things in relation'. In many senses that is what I, like many others, was doing. New ideas and new sensations were bubbling out all over the place and I was trying to absorb them and put them in some form of order. I could see the danger of becoming too introverted and one entry expressed a horror of becoming a religious fanatic, worthy and narrow minded. Then, Bertrand Russell's *Why I am not a Christian* found me doubting the very existence of God.

A sense of living simultaneously in two worlds was ever present. Two books, the *Journals of Kierkegaard* and *The Phenomenon of Man* by the Jesuit Teilhard de Chardin were important to me. The first explored an inner melancholy and the latter what shapes our existence. I noted that Emerson said, 'God offers to every man the choice between truth and repose, take which you please, you can never have both'. The then Archbishop of Canterbury, Michael Ramsey, preached and I questioned him afterwards about whether the celibacy of Jesus Christ reduced the impact of his sin-free life. He answered carefully and patiently and struck me as a man who spent much time on his knees in prayer. He has been the best Archbishop in my lifetime apart from William Temple, whose contribution I was too young to judge.

I returned to the debate about whether the end justifies the means which had started at Bradfield. Isaiah Berlin's classic *The Hedgehog and the Fox* absorbed me. I identified myself as a fox distrusting those who knew one big idea. I sat next to Isaiah Berlin at a dinner when I was Foreign Secretary and listened entranced. I have read and re-read his collected works: his understanding of the nature of compromise makes him for me one of the great philosophers. When one should compromise, the limits of compromise and its nature have always fascinated me.

Religion, through all this period, was a constant companion. I was starting to explore comparative religion and I became particularly interested in the struggle for racial equality in South Africa. The Reverend Michael Scott preached on South Africa. Even then I did not think that the immorality of apartheid would be of itself a sufficient lever for change and that economics would have to become a determining factor. Trevor Huddleston's book *Naught for Your Comfort* had a profound effect, giving a stark description of life in the black townships. When twenty years later I spent a lot of time negotiating for peace in Southern Africa, I saw for myself that his description was not exaggerated and came to know and respect Bishop Huddleston even more.

It was not just clergymen who came to Great St Mary's. Malcolm Muggeridge spoke witheringly and wittily. Aneurin Bevan demonstrated his oratory, again bringing back to me memories of his political speech in Devonport. He used his stutter to describe a gold plate and with his Welsh lilt I can hear him saying, 'It sh- shi- sh- shi- sh-i-i-im-im-ered', and the plate did shimmer. Stephen Spender talked on the frustration and the revolt of youth and how the young tend to blame the older generation. All this time the kaleidoscope was throwing up different experiences, new ideas. My life was a constant exploration.

One evening with Mervyn Stockwood and a fellow priest we discussed spiritualism and as a joke ended up trying to move a glass around the table. We decided to conduct more formal experiments and agreed to arrange a visit to a medium.

My visit to Mrs Twigg, who was thought to be one of the best mediums in the country at that time, was much more serious. Bryan and I had taken the precaution of booking our appointments anonymously and giving no indication of our background. I had driven up to Cambridge in my 'Bambino' which I had only recently sprayed red, and parked it some way away from our meeting.

Mrs Twigg was charming, middle-aged and middle-class and could have been one's aunt. She never assumed a different voice. She just chatted quite normally in an armchair opposite me. Very soon into our interview she described my driving up that morning in an open red sports car which was certainly a pretty good guess. I was already convinced that some mediums have a telepathic capacity and can draw from one's mind, not just present knowledge, but information that is stored away in its recesses. Mrs Twigg was certainly telepathic. What I was searching for, however, was clairvoyance, any evidence of extra-sensory perception. We were trying to find correct information that could not have come from one's own mind but only from being able to contact people who were in her words 'in spirit'. My interview gave no such information. She described pretty accurately and got into conversation with my dead grandfather Gear, and some of the words and expressions that she relayed back to me were thought later by my mother to be familiar in content and phraseology. But they could all have been taken from the back of my mind, since I had often heard him speaking.

Bryan Christopher had one fascinating tale of his visit to Mrs Twigg. In describing his family she mentioned that he had two brothers. He said he only had one brother. She thought further and turned back to him saying, 'Are you sure? I am in contact with an elder brother born in Cairo and actually gave the date of his birth. She remained adamant that his brother was 'in spirit'. Bryan noted this fact down and thought no more about it. He recalled this exchange to his parents a few days later, dismissing this particular incident as of no relevance and as an example of how quite a lot of the information was wrong. Next morning over breakfast his parents said that although they had never told him, his mother's first child had been a stillborn boy and born in Cairo. But again this was not proven clairvoyance. On the strict criteria we were applying it just might have been discussed while he was a babe in arms and stored away in a part of his brain, without his being aware that he ever knew the information.

After this experience I decided quite cold-bloodedly that I did not wish to probe this area any further – not out of fear, more out of an anxiety that one could become dependent on meeting with mediums. I felt that I had heard enough. I did not wish to know more; I was content to wonder. I have never had anything to do with spiritualism since but believe that telepathic powers exist though I remain unconvinced about extra-sensory perception.

With all these experiences shaping the future, my notebooks show that in the end hard work was dominant. Anatomy was a particularly hard taskmaster. I noted that I would never be a top grade scientist and one entry, with my finals only six weeks away, has me disciplining myself to:

7.00	Wake up
7.30	Start work
8.30–9	Breakfast
9–1	Work
2–5	Work
5.30–7.30	Work
8–11	Work = 13 hours

I also planned to get up earlier and go to bed earlier alternately and to take one topic a night. Whether I did any of this I cannot recall but I ended up with a second class degree. I deluded myself on occasions that without my motor bike accident I would have got a First but the examiners assessed me correctly. In my experience the really bright minds sail through examinations with ease, without a lot of work. They are able to retain information without difficulty and many have an almost photographic memory. I remember conversations better than written text and often where and when the conversation took place, even to the exact bend in the road. But I have never been able to recall words or numbers in their place on a piece of paper.

What little spare time was available during the last few months in Cambridge was spent preparing for what we rather grandly called on our notepaper 'The 1959 Cambridge University Afghanistan Expedition'. The four of us have kept up with each other. John Lonsdale is now a don at Trinity College, Bill Purver an industrialist, Andrew Gerry a solicitor and Jan Fischer a professor of medicine at Zurich University.

The prime purpose of our trip had emerged before I joined through discussion with experts on Afghanistan in Cambridge: it was to visit the Minaret de Jham in a remote mountain valley in the centre of Afghanistan. The minaret which marked the site of Firuzkoh, the capital of the Ghorid Empire, had only been discovered the year before by a French archaeologist and many experts wanted more photographs. It was amazing that such a beautiful minaret in such perfect condition should have remained undiscovered all those years. The Qutab Minar outside Delhi is very famous but it was built after the Minaret de Jham by the same conquering Ghorids as they extended their empire into India. After all our planning and travelling it was a thrilling experience to ride down on horseback from Afghanistan's parched high mountain range into the emerald green valley and see this slender minaret piercing the bright blue sky.

Sir Mortimer Wheeler, whose famous archaeological career had been mainly in the Indian subcontinent, then lived in Cambridge and he had, after questioning me closely, agreed to sponsor our expedition. We also needed a scientific purpose, to encourage commercial sponsorship. The physiology department agreed that Jan and I should investigate diurnal rhythm – the clock in one's own body which controls not just sleeping and waking but most bodily functions and is affected by jet lag. The uniquely wide temperature difference in Afghanistan, very cold at night and very hot during the day, was known to affect people's diurnal rhythm. We had to collect and measure the volume of all our urine in large measuring cylinders. We had to note the volume, the time and the outside temperature. This routine two or three times a day provided us with endless amusement, but I doubt if the science of diurnal rhythm was much advanced.

The expedition was an enriching experience. We drove out in a Land-Rover, which was christened the 'Bugger' (xii), through Bulgaria, Turkey and Iran. In Tehran I had my first stormy encounter with the

British Diplomatic Service. It was not to be my last. We found our
Embassy totally useless in helping us to obtain permission to drive in to
the centre of Afghanistan. No doubt they were fed up with young people
driving through without the proper entry permits. But when we went
with Jan Fischer to the Swiss Embassy we were given a first class helpful
service. Even though only one of our party was Swiss, they made us
welcome, took infinite trouble over our visas and helped us find out
about Andrew Gerry who had contracted typhoid and whom we had had
to leave behind at Erzurum in Turkey to recover. He eventually caught
up with us in Kabul.

After Afghanistan we drove into Pakistan via the Khyber Pass and
India. The expedition lasted over four months and we never once slept in
a hotel, though we relented to the extent of taking a bath in a hotel in
Delhi. We lived alongside very poor people in a way that I would never
do again. Countries which had previously been names on a map came
alive.

We drove back via Switzerland, dropping Jan off in Zurich where he
was to resume his medical studies. On my return my mother took one
look at my beard and demanded that it should be shaved off. I started at
St Thomas's Hospital in October and lived in a Lexham Gardens flat
with Bryan Christopher. I started to write in my notebook again and
noted that it was the poverty and the sickness that I had seen in Asia and
in the Indian sub-continent to which I hoped I would return when I was
qualified. I wanted to go out to these countries when young enough to
give a little of my medical knowledge to people who so badly needed
help. I always hoped that one day I would work for the World Health
Organization.

The most intriguing comment in my notebook at that time, given what
was to come, is the first real political entry commenting on the defeat of
the Labour Party in the 1969 Election, when I had voted for the first
time, and for Labour. I noted Harold Macmillan's comment, 'You've
never had it so good', and revealed my own Left-wing views.

Can any party ever have won an election on a more immoral slogan, a
positive disgrace and a sign of the moral depravity of our life? People
seem to vote solely on their bellies. Of course Labour deserved little
more but the really worrying fear is that it looks ominously as if they
are going to forsake the socialist principles to which they owe their very
foundation. I feel one can't go on criticizing for ever. There comes a
time for action and taking one particular side whilst realizing that no
one side will ever answer to one's every wish. At the moment it looks
as if I will have to join the Left wing of the Labour Party. But will I be
able to stand their class hatred? I do believe passionately that H-bombs
should be unilaterally renounced and I also believe in nationalization in
principle and in practice. Ways must be found of making it more of an
economic possibility. I cannot go on stomaching the Conservative

complacency, the 'life's better' touch, so it bloody well ought to be, but *much* better.

So at twenty-one, and starting as a clinical medical student, I was still committed to unilateralism and to nationalization. My notebook also shows how a long-lasting commitment to abortion law reform was made. A friend, clearly very troubled, eventually told me about an abortion she had had near the Elephant and Castle and the terrible time following it. She was afraid that it would scar her for life. At least her boy-friend had helped to arrange the abortion but I felt wretched for her that she had had to go through such an experience. I became committed as a medical student to the reform of the abortion laws, little realizing that I would in six years be in Parliament and on the committee dealing with the new abortion legislation.

It was also an eye-opener to start living an inner-city life for the first time. The poverty I found in Lambeth around St Thomas's Hospital shocked me, for I had lived so far a very sheltered, relatively prosperous southern life. I will never forget helping a district nurse to deliver a baby in a home with my backside outside the window sill, the bedroom being too small for it to be anywhere else. At that stage the farthest north I had ever been in Britain was Cambridge. Bad housing, far far worse than anything I had seen in Plymouth or Cambridge, was commonplace and Rachmanism, the exploitation of property, was being exposed. These bad social conditions helped me make up my mind to join the Labour Party, and to take more interest in politics.

I joined the Labour Party in Vauxhall in 1960 after some months' delay because the office was always closed whenever I went to join up. I attended meetings organized by the mainly Bevanite Victory for Socialism Group, but also joined the Fabian Society and was becoming more and more interested in Hugh Gaitskell's rethinking of the Labour Party's principles.

I remember clearly hearing Gaitskell decry the fact that there were too many 'armchair socialists' and in 1960 I heard extracts from a speech on the radio which appears to be one he made in Nottingham in February. He was justifying his belief that Clause 4 in the Labour Party Constitution, which talks of 'common ownership of the means of production, distribution and exchange . . .' should be changed. He emphasized that what was wrong with Clause IV was the vague threat that it carried to all private property and he described it as meaningless phrases and mere theology. I had not hitherto realized that he was not against public enterprise and very much in favour of co-operative ownership. From that day on he was the British politician in whom I placed the greatest trust. His arguments and intellectual authority persuaded me that my earlier attitudes to both nationalization and unilateral nuclear disarmament had not been properly thought through. By the time he gave the famous speech when he promised to 'Fight and fight again to save the Party we love' in 1960, I was a fervent admirer. But it was from afar. I never met him personally or even saw him speak, other than on television, yet he demonstrated to me that one could retain one's integrity in politics and that a politician could stick with the policies he believed in through thick and thin. I have little doubt that it was because he was the leader that I put my name forward for selection as a parliamentary candidate in 1962.

When facing some of the more difficult choices of my career, I have asked myself how would Hugh Gaitskell have handled a similar situation. That he loved the Labour Party there is no doubt and perhaps there could never have been circumstances in which he would have left it. Yet his biographer concludes that he had felt in 1960 that he should, and would have to, resign the leadership if Conference went against him again in 1961 on unilateral nuclear disarmament. Fortunately they did not and he succeeded in having the earlier decision reversed.

I relished the opportunity in 1985 to give the Gaitskell Memorial Lecture at Nottingham University on Ownership. I said then:

> This does not mean that Hugh Gaitskell, who would have been nearly seventy-five when the SDP was formed, would have left the Labour Party. I do not personally believe he would have done so, if for no other reason than, had he lived, I suspect the need for a creation of the SDP would never have existed.

For a clinical student St Thomas's was fun and exciting. Many of the incidents described in Richard Gordon's novel *Doctor in the House* were true. I have assumed the model for Richard Gordon's perpetual student was Alfie Evans, one of my father's closest friends. Alfie went to St Bartholomew's at the same time as my father started at St Mary's. He studied there all through the 1930s. Eventually his father, in desperation, sent him to a psychiatrist who reported back that young Mr Evans knew an immense amount about the theatre, music and sport, indeed everything except medicine. After a few years of war he was eventually called up and served in the Royal Army Medical Corps as a surgical orderly. There he was quite happy to nudge the surgeon, often a student friend, with advice as to where to cut, all taken in the spirit in which it was intended, for everyone liked him. He then went back to Bart's after the war, this time at His Majesty's expense, not his father's. Finally it was mutually agreed he should give up taking his medical exams in the 1950s. He then ran the British Sailors Society for many years and was a great success.

Being a clinical student is not like a normal student. One is with real patients at long last. Even so, I started expressing in my notebook a dislike of hospitals. I felt the atmosphere was as sterile as the dressings. To this day I find the smell of disinfectant and the impersonal nature of hospitals very disagreeable. St Thomas's is, however, an unusually beautiful hospital. The old building had the high ceilings and long wards that

Florence Nightingale designed. They were light and airy and, if a little noisy, at least not smelly. The horror was the new buildings. Two attempts at a new design, both half-built, are a monument to the scandalous way in which the NHS managed its capital building programme after the war. Situated on the South Bank of the Thames, St Thomas's looks out across the river to the House of Commons. Defacing this landscape is vandalism on a scale that future generations will not lightly forgive.

To have lived under the shadow of Big Ben for years before I entered the House of Commons gives me a strange feeling of continuity to my life. Working late at night in the hospital when the lights of London were out, I used to look over the river and see the House of Commons sitting late, all ablaze. Later I looked back from the terrace in front of Parliament into the wards of the hospital. In those early years I never contemplated becoming a Member of Parliament.

St Thomas's Medical School was a stimulating place. It has never been afraid of taking on older students or people with an unconventional background and has an inner sense of superiority: the saying is 'You can tell a Thomas's man anywhere but you cannot tell him anything!' Students were split up into 'firms', under a surgeon or physician, and were allocated patients for whom they had a special responsibility. The firm of about nine people with the ward sister, house physician or house surgeon and registrar, would go around all the beds under the particular consultant at least once a week. There we were taught by example. The good doctors taught us not just about the case but about how to treat patients as people; the bad doctors saw only a patient and rarely the person.

One old Londoner, in with a heart attack, put a particularly obnoxious and disdainful consultant in his place in front of all of us. The consultant having talked about this man's intimate anatomy for twenty minutes at the end of the bed without once talking directly to him, was about to leave without even acknowledging the patient. The old man asked him, 'Well me old cock, what's your name?' The consultant, most offended, started to bluster, 'You know me. I am your consultant.' In fact the old man had never met him and said, 'I don't care if you're Christ Almighty, you're my doctor, mate.' All of us, including the formidable ward sister, could barely suppress our laughter.

I was not an idle student but nor was I the most active. I remember soon after I qualified my neighbour in the doctor's dining room, who had been at Oxford and was only three months ahead of me as a medical student at St Thomas's, asking me what hospital I had trained at. He was not joking. Clearly my attendance had been neither sufficiently frequent nor sufficiently marked to make any impact on him.

My great interest was not the operating theatre but the dramatic theatre. It has been a long tradition of theatre-land to give free tickets to nurses in the London teaching hospitals. Nurses had the first call on the tickets but any that were left over were available for medical students. For three years there was hardly a show in London that I did not see. Then the Royal Court Theatre became my favourite haunt. It was the time when John Osborne and Arnold Wesker were putting on their plays and it was a lively and stimulating theatre. One evening after attending the Royal Court I wandered out into a small street at the back of the theatre and found a little bistro in Bourne Street. I peered in through the window, opened the door and was immediately asked, in a none too civil tone by a woman of indeterminate age dressed all in black, who I was and what I was doing coming to her restaurant. Somewhat taken aback, I said I was a medical student looking for a cheap supper. Whereupon, to my amazement, she suddenly embraced me and announced to everyone present that she loved medical students. She sat me down in front of a plateful of goulash which looked awful but tasted magnificent. That was my introduction to Elizabeth Furse. I have loved her ever since and eaten more of her meals than anyone's other than my wife's or mother's.

My houseboat, *Amanda*, which I bought for six hundred pounds when I moved out of Lexham Gardens was moored alongside the Chelsea Embankment. It had the fashionable address of 106 Cheyne Walk, Chelsea. She had been a ship's lifeboat, hanging in the davits. Although she was only thirty feet long there was room for a bed in the bow of the boat, where there was no head-room at all. Then a small cabin with a central ladder coming out on to the deck through a hatchway. A small bath and a chemical closet were on one side and a minute kitchen with a calor gas cooker and water heater. There was room for a desk and a spare bunk bed. In the stern was a glass walled sitting room which was the only place where I could stand upright. There was a telephone and mains electricity. The water tank on the deck was filled every day and my rent was one shilling a foot or thirty shillings a week paid to the Chelsea Yacht and Boat Company. It was an idyllic life. Next door to me there was a large converted Thames barge on which there were four girls. They were part of the Bluebell dancing team. We were like brother and sisters, never getting involved in each other's relationships but flitting in and out of our boats, going to the cinema or the theatre together if anyone was free. The contrast with hospital life could hardly have been more marked. On my boat I lived a relaxed bohemian life. Dorothy Tutin, the actress, had a boat a few hundred yards from mine which gave us some notoriety, but in those days the houseboats had not yet become fashionable and it was a cheap place to live. We had our own community, presided over by the old night watchman who guarded the gangway. He knew exactly who was seeing whom, when and where, and was a marvellous source of gossip and intrigue.

The other part of my non-medical life was politics. I was helping to draft a Young Fabian pamphlet on the pharmaceutical industry. It was because someone heard me speak at a Fabian School in 1961 on the drug industry that I was asked early in 1962 to speak on the subject in Devon to a Labour Party women's conference. Following this meeting some of the women attending from the Torrington Constituency Labour Party suggested my name for their selection of prospective parliamentary candidates. The South-West Regional Labour Party wrote to ask if I had any objection to being shortlisted for this parliamentary seat. I had just qualified as a doctor and had started work at the Royal Waterloo Hospital. I rang up the Regional Office and asked what was involved and on being told that it did not mean much more, if selected, than going down to Torrington over a weekend once a month, I agreed that my name could go forward to the selection conference. So in a small way my parliamentary career started in the same week as my becoming a newly qualified doctor.

4

DOCTOR ON THE WARDS

No threshold I have crossed in my life has been as dramatic as that between medical student and doctor. A life of relative irresponsibility suddenly had to become responsible. I was now treating patients on my own and their lives depended on what I did. Decisions had sometimes to be taken very quickly. Often there was no time for consulting anyone else, only to make the diagnosis and to start treatment. My six years of training was under the real test.

In those days, medical students were not given as much to do clinically before qualifying as they are today. There was no gradual transition. I walked into the small Royal Waterloo Hospital on Waterloo Bridge in the morning and by lunchtime the house physician I had replaced had left. I was now responsible for the male and female medical wards, two small wards with skin patients and the children's ward.

The atmosphere of a busy hospital ward has a rhythm to it which pulses through twenty-four hours a day. When a death comes it casts a pall for a few hours but the open wards encourage patients to worry about others and a camaraderie develops: off-putting to some, supportive for others. The ward sister's personality imprints itself on the nurses and through them on to the patients. The doctors are not as important as they think. The people who clean the floors and do the domestic chores contribute to the patients' lives in a way far more satisfying than just working in an office. In St Thomas's a legacy of Florence Nightingale is that the School of Nursing, named after her, insists on prayers taking place each evening when the night and day staff change over. To see the nurses and sister in their striking head gear kneeling around the central table with all the main lights off, lit only by a table lamp, evokes a sense of vocation which is still a very important part of the nursing profession's tradition.

I was eating lunch in the little doctor's dining room with a contemporary who had just started as house surgeon to the hospital when the telephone rang. It was the emergency bed service asking if I had a spare medical bed. Blind panic tempted me to say we were full but I knew that this moment had to be faced. So before accepting the patient I asked as much detail as was decent about the ambulanceman's description of his symptoms. I then rushed off to the privacy of my ground-floor bedroom where I tried to match the description I had been given with a differential diagnosis in the house physician's 'bible'. This book was literally to become a life-saver during the next few days. Slim enough to be carried in the pockets of my long white coat, it was an instant reference point.

All too soon the noise of the ambulance at the front door meant that I had to put the book away and meet as a doctor my first sick patient undiagnosed by any other doctor. He was rushed up in the lift to the ward and I was then summoned by the ward sister. I can see him now, in his middle sixties, propped up in bed, gasping for breath, quite unable to speak, with a rapid irregular pulse. I examined his heart and chest and it did not require much skill to tell that he had acute heart failure, with fluid retained in his lungs and in his legs. The difficult question was whether his heart failure was responsible for his lungs being full of water, or whether he had respiratory failure due to primary lung disease and it was this that had strained his heart. If the primary diagnosis was heart failure, the urgent treatment was an injection of morphia, but if he suffered primarily from respiratory failure then morphia would kill him because it would suppress his breathing. Fortunately my 'bible' had already given me the answer – if in doubt, give an injection of aminophylline, the house physician's friend. It would treat both the heart failure and the respiratory failure and one could sort out later which came first with the aid of chest X-rays, electro-cardiographs and all the other modern technological diagnostic aids. I decided on an injection of aminophylline and the ward sister tactfully did not ask for the definitive diagnosis. She had seen it all before and probably guessed that I had not got a clue at that stage. When I went to see the patient an hour later he was a different man, able to talk. It soon became clear that his chest was the main problem and that if I had given him morphia I would probably have killed him.

The next emergency admission was in the middle of the night. A family doctor rang me up from Lambeth wanting a bed urgently for a very sick two-year-old child as there were none available in either St Thomas's or the Lambeth Hospital. When I saw the child in his cot in a cubicle in the children's ward he was barely moving, invariably a sign that a very young child is really sick. As I examined him, beating away in the back of my mind were the words of the paediatrician, Dr Wilson, who had taught me as a medical student and was the consultant in charge of this ward, 'If in doubt don't hesitate to do a lumbar puncture.' I dreaded doing a lumbar puncture on so small a child. I tried to argue myself out of it, and to convince myself it could wait until the morning. I had only done three lumbar punctures on my own as a student and all of these were on adults. The skill is in placing a needle through the narrow gap between the vertebrae at the bottom of the spine and into the sac of fluid which protects the spinal cord. I knew that I had to face up to doing it and so I scrubbed my hands, put on gloves and picked up the special needle. It looked massive in relation to the child's tiny spine. With the sister's help, we curled the child up into a ball, with his back bent and lying on his side, and I pushed in the needle. Fortunately, the child, being nearly comatose, did not move and, more by luck than skill, after an ominous pause when no fluid came, a blob of white appeared at the hole in the needle. It was almost pure pus. One barely needed to smear the fluid on to a slide, stain it and look under the microscope to diagnose meningococcal meningitis. I then injected penicillin direct into his spinal fluid and through a drip into his veins. Within thirty-six hours he was sitting up in bed eating and laughing.

Without antibiotics that child would have died. It is the rare miraculous case like this that fuels one's optimism and enables one to instil hope in others, so important in medicine. The will to live can be very powerful. A good doctor can infuse that will in a patient. Some patients find that their religious faith gives them the will. It was for me personally a tonic to have had such a case so early in my career.

No doctor forgets his first few cases. They are indelibly imprinted on the mind because of the fear which surrounds the diagnosis and treatment. The psychological trauma of being out of one's depth is always frightening, devastatingly so in times that one has sole responsibility, however good the training. The magic of medicine is built around this very special relation-ship of doctor to patient. Nurses can assist, even other doctors, but the decision as to what to do can frequently only be taken by one person for neither medicine nor surgery is easy to practise collectively. It is individu-als who practise the art and science of medicine and that, for many doctors, is its strength and fascination. I have never ceased to love medicine and have often longed to return to it. A sign that medicine is still there in the back of my mind is that in anxiety dreams I often find I can wake in a sweat, having dreamt that I have failed my medical examinations. Sometimes the anxiety is all the worse for dreaming that I am actually practising medicine while still unqualified. Freud explained anxiety dreams as being a mechanism for reassurance, pointing out that invariably if the dream involves something like examinations, the dreamer already knows the result, and that the particular exam had been passed. The dream is a way of achieving reassurance. But the fact that it keeps recurring is also likely to be a subconscious wish to be successful. Anxiety dreams are common, as Gilbert and Sullivan recognized with their song, 'In your shirt and your socks (the black silk with gold clocks) crossing Salisbury plain on a bicycle'.

For the next six months I lived and breathed medicine. I had been the first medical student at St Thomas's to apply for the associated Royal

Waterloo job as my first choice. Normally most students placed it on their list after the twelve casualty jobs in the main hospital which were always considered to be the most desirable and were followed automatically by another six months as a house physician or a house surgeon on the wards of St Thomas's. I felt that the casualty job was nowhere near as challenging or absorbing, for once the initial diagnosis had been made, the patient either left the hospital or went up to the wards into the care of another young doctor. It was a gamble choosing the Royal Waterloo first. I had to accept, when I was chosen, that I was most unlikely to do my second job at St Thomas's.

The consultant dermatologist, Hugh Wallace, was a considerable character. He had a spinal disease when very young which had left him with a hunch-back. He reminded me of Rhaedar in Paul Gallico's *The Snow Goose*. He had a lovely, low, deep voice and a delicious sense of humour, something which was a tremendous asset when dealing with intractable skin diseases. A visit from him was like a tonic for his patients. He would leave them laughing and almost forgetting their often distressing symptoms, for only patients with really severe psoriasis or some rare skin complaint were accepted for in-patient treatment. I learnt more from Hugh Wallace about handling the emotions and moods of patients than from any other doctor. The paediatrician, Brian Wilson, was a dry, clipped, small, moustached, dapper person; at first, rather unprepossessing and not like the engaging, outward going paediatricians whom I had known through my uncle, the Professor of Paediatrics at the Welsh School of Medicine. He did not have a very high reputation among his colleagues and was an unfashionable, uncharismatic doctor. But what did matter was how well he was regarded by the parents of the children he treated. By the end of my six months I would not hear a bad word said of him. I knew I could ring him up at any time of night and if he detected the slightest note of anxiety in my voice he would be in the hospital straight away to see a child. He was a permanent example to me, for I tended then, and still do, to judge people too often on first appearances.

Only a week into working at the Royal Waterloo, I had a letter from the South-West Regional Labour Party to ask if I would be prepared to have my name put forward for the shortlist to choose a prospective Labour candidate for the Torrington constituency. I am amazed that I said yes. I was assured that if I was chosen it would not make major demands on my time and that as long as I visited one weekend a month that was all that would be needed until the election campaign when I should take three weeks off work. I had always been very troubled by the way in which my medical student friends, once becoming doctors, lost all interest in life outside the hospital. They appeared to be medical vegetables and I was loath to see this happen to me. Anyhow I did not expect to win the selection contest. Another factor was that Elizabeth

Furse had a charming thatched cottage near the village of Dolton in the heart of the Torrington constituency. In those days as a junior hospital doctor I was on duty twenty-four hours a day for twelve days at a stretch. I could plan on having two weekends off a month, leaving at midnight on Friday and returning in the early hours of Monday morning. To commit one of my two weekends was not an impossible burden, when I knew that I was going to a beautiful part of Devon, the northern edge of Dartmoor on the River Torridge. Knowing too that I would have somewhere to stay and bring friends was crucial. Although travelling down would take time, it would be a real break from hospital when I got there. The advantage would be that I would be forced to read newspapers and to keep up with current affairs. Nevertheless, my decision to accept nomination was a pretty extraordinary one since most junior doctors find little time for anything else during this hectic period in their lives.

I decided not to tell anyone in the hospital of my candidacy. I was intent on a serious medical career and I felt that if the consultants knew that I was involved in politics they would not consider I was really committed to medicine. A few weeks later, on a fine sunny Saturday morning in August, I drove down to Bideford for the selection conference in my Morris Minor convertible. I still have the long speech which I had written out for my selection conference while stopping at a couple of roadside cafés. It was my first party political speech. Hitherto, whenever I had spoken to Fabian Society meetings it had been about the drugs industry or social services. Even I could not have actually delivered to the selection committee all of the detail about what should be our negotiating position to enter the EEC, though I suspect I sent some of them to sleep. But reading the text of my speech now, it is clear that it follows in all major respects a Gaitskellite approach. It started with a short section about how I saw the aims of the Labour Party:

> to form a society where there are no social classes, where there is equal opportunity for everyone to achieve the level that their varying talents and application will allow, where there is a high degree of economic equality, full employment and a rising level of productivity, a democracy in all spheres of society due to a general spirit of co-operation between its members. Yet even as I say these words, I realize how much there is still to be done and since we believe that such changes must come through parliamentary democracy, they will of necessity come gradually, step by step, and we must persuade our fellow citizens that our ends are just and that the means we choose are right.

A few sniping attacks on the 'pitiful sight' of Harold Macmillan sacking a third of his Cabinet and at Lord Home for obstructing the UN was all that it contained of party politics. Indeed I said that I felt 'strongly that politics is more than mudslinging and popular rhetoric. The task of the Labour Party is to make people think and realize for themselves the cost of a society founded on an ill-gotten and insecure affluence'. After only a short section in the speech on social problems it went on:

yet because I believe that the issue of the Common Market is more important than anything in our history for the last fifty years, I feel I cannot and will not shirk examining the main factors that confront us ... If it were to be a liberal, outward looking institution, imbued with vigour and enterprise, I would welcome it – but should it be a tight, parochially exclusive European bloc, I would distrust it and actively do all in my power to stop our entry.

Enumerating the difficulties I nevertheless took a rather more optimistic line than Gaitskell:

I believe that with care these difficulties are surmountable. We cannot cling to the past forever – we must accept that only by putting aside some of our most treasured nationalistic traditions will any real form of International Government come about.

There were two other people on the shortlist and after the delegates had heard all three of us, they voted. Much to my surprise they chose me to fight the seat.

The sitting MP was Percy Browne who had won it back for the Conservatives in the 1959 General Election from the Liberal, Mark Bonham-Carter. Mark Bonham-Carter had won the by-election in March 1958 with a majority of only 219, polling 13,408 votes. His Conservative opponent in the by-election was Anthony Royle, who later became MP for Richmond. Though Royle was a charming person, it was not hard to depict him as a city slicker, using the constituency as a convenience en route to Parliament, and he was the wrong choice for that constituency. Yet even though Mark Bonham-Carter increased his vote to 15,018 in the 1959 General Election it was not enough for him to keep his seat. Percy Browne, who was challenging him, was a very popular local farmer and steeplechase jockey who had taken part in the Grand National, and something of a local hero. Percy Browne polled 17,283 votes and Ray Dobson who was the Labour candidate and later became MP for Bristol managed 5,633 votes in 1959.

My candidature, not surprisingly, provoked no national publicity so no one in St Thomas's realized what I was doing. Hugh Gaitskell was then the Leader of the Labour Party and a general election was expected in the autumn of 1963 at the earliest. Later that afternoon I drove down to Plymouth and told my parents what had happened. Much to my surprise it was my mother who was violently opposed to what I had done: 'You're a bloody fool!' She feared that I had ruined a promising medical career. Yet my father, whom I had expected to be opposed, was wholly in favour. Amused rather than annoyed he wisely judged that as long as I continued to work hard and the consultants did not discover for some months they would not hold it against me. He proved to be correct. Eventually the story leaked out in the hospital but by the time it did everyone could see it made not the slightest difference to my ability to work very long hours. As the election drew near it was surprising how many consultants drew me aside and told me they were going to vote Labour. There was no doubt that Labour was starting to appeal to the middle class again as it had in 1945.

A fortnight after my selection I drove down to North Devon for my first public engagement, a garden fete organized by the local Labour Party. I was asked if I would judge the baby show. This was my first major political mistake. I thought that all one did was to choose the most attractive baby's face. What an error. Judging a baby show is an accomplished skill, in which weight, length, hair and colour are as carefully assessed as by a racehorse owner at a yearling sale. When, after a cursory glance, I announced the winner, uproar followed from angry mothers who felt that they had been cheated. I must have lost at least fifty votes that afternoon and though I have a photograph of me surrounded by mothers, a careful look shows that I am the only one who is smiling.

My first political speech in public as the adopted prospective candidate was slightly more successful. It was on the European Community. The report in the local newspaper gives some clues as to why this issue was to become so central to my whole political career.

> Dr David Owen said that in the Common Market issue the country was facing one of its most important decisions. The question was fundamental to everything we had or held dear. We must all realize that entry into the Common Market would be something irrevocable – it was not something one joined and got out of, but something one entered and had to stay in. It was not just an economic Common Market but fundamentally political with its motives including some form of federation or supra-national authority. The Labour Party had been accused of sitting on the fence about the issue. He, personally, thought Mr Gaitskell's recent TV statement on the Common Market most statesman-like and would be the line upon which the Labour Party would make up its mind when they knew more. There were such questions as whether British agriculture was going to be safeguarded, whether the people of this country would be able to control their country, whether it was possible to carry out a socialist programme and for a Socialist Government to carry out any legislation they might wish. He believed that socialism was international and the EEC might well be a step towards international government. While it might be very foolish to cling to nationalistic ideals he thought it would be equally foolish to take the Liberal view that we should just go into the Common Market which he thought 'just juvenile'. Referring to nationalization, Dr Owen said they did not believe that everything should be nationalized. They believed in free enterprise but they also believed that the government should be able to control basic things.

From that day on, my political career has been dominated by the question of British membership of the European Community. I have twice resigned, with this as the most important issue: firstly in 1972 with

Roy Jenkins from being a junior defence spokesman for the Labour Party, and then in 1980 from the Shadow Cabinet when Michael Foot was elected leader. But I have never been at any stage a federalist, or a believer in a United States of Europe. On 21 September 1962, I watched Hugh Gaitskell reply on television to Prime Minister Harold Macmillan's broadcast of the night before. He asked if Macmillan wanted to enter a European federation. If so it 'means the end of Britain as an independent nation; we become no more than "Texas" or "California" in the United States of Europe. It means the end of a thousand years of history; it means the end of the Commonwealth to become just a province of Europe.' I liked Gaitskell's warning against a federalist Europe and broadly accepted his line of questioning the terms in my own speeches but I also definitely wanted us to join the European Community, though I saw no reason why it should be inevitable that it became a single European state.

I was so busy in hospital that I did not attend the Labour Party Conference on 3 October when Gaitskell made his detailed assessment of the case for entry. I did not realize how much his speech was interpreted by his friends as coming down against it. Later, Charlie Pannell, a fellow Leeds MP with Gaitskell, told me how his wife Dora had said, 'Charlie, all the wrong people are cheering.' I think if I had been there I too would have cheered. George Brown had to wind up the debate and many say he managed brilliantly in very difficult circumstances to put the case for entry, which Hugh Gaitskell's speech had brushed aside. The part of Gaitskell's speech which I childishly relished was his rubbishing of my Liberal opponent in Torrington.

Gaitskell recalled that at the Liberal Party Conference the idea of our going into a European federation was greeted with wild enthusiasm by all the delegates. 'They are a little young, I think. I am all for youth but I like it to be sensible as well. After the conference a desperate attempt was made by Mr Bonham-Carter to show that of course they were not committed to federation at all. Well, I prefer to go by what Mr Grimond says.' Gaitskell then quoted Grimond that if you are going to 'control the running of Europe democratically, you've got to move towards some form of federalism and if anyone says different to that they are really misleading the public', and then Gaitskell exclaimed, 'That is one in the eye to Mr Bonham-Carter!'

It was more than one in the eye for I frequently thereafter quoted Gaitskell's speech in the constituency against Mark Bonham-Carter. It probably did more for my morale than for my tally of votes – this sort of party political badinage is only of any real interest to party activists. It warms the immediate, not the wider, audience. Fighting this marginal seat, Bonham-Carter must have thought that the Liberal commitment to federalism was a vote loser. Jo Grimond, by contrast, then leader of the Liberal Party, was more cavalier, a quality that made him one of our most engaging politicians and won him admiration throughout his career. I have always felt that it is good for politics that the federalist cause should have a political party ready to push its case and the Liberal Party has always been broadly federalist ever since. I was never a federalist then nor am I now and it was to be one of the reasons why, twenty-five years later, I did not want to merge with the Liberal Party.

My six months at the Royal Waterloo attached to St Thomas's were enriched by having Brendan Devlin as the surgical registrar. He was then, and in some ways still is, a wild Irishman. His irreverence blew through the corridors with a freshness and vigour that some found enervating and others intensely irritating. I revelled in it. Even then he was a brilliant surgeon and he has gone on to build an impressive career in the North-East, masterminding the extremely important confidential enquiry reports into post-operative deaths from his unit in the Royal College of Surgeons. He supported Labour at the time. Now one of his sons, Tim Devlin, is an MP having won the Stockton South constituency for the Conservatives from Ian Wrigglesworth, the SDP MP, in 1987, even though Brendan was then a strong SDP supporter.

Brendan and I were always on duty at the weekends together and I would assist him in any operating that had to be done. To Brendan surgery was not just a job but sheer enjoyment. On Sundays when all was quiet he would get a little restless and itch to start cutting. So around 11 o'clock in the morning we would ring the Emergency Bed Service without telling anyone in the hospital and say that if they could offer us a couple of emergencies by lunchtime we would be ready to accept them. They could not be just any emergencies: Brendan would then indicate the type of case, largely based on whether or not he thought that I had yet assisted in enough operations on the stomach or the gall bladder or the chest. The Emergency Bed Service, only too happy to have a teaching hospital accept patients, would invariably come back with an acceptable offer, whereupon Brendan, with a twinkle in his eye, would ring up to tell the sister in charge of the operating theatre that he was under great pressure to admit two emergency cases and could she open the theatre so as to start operating after lunch. She knew exactly what Brendan was up to but since she was on duty anyhow she was usually content. We would then spend four or five happy hours operating in the afternoon and early evening, all timed so we could be off by supper. I learnt enough general surgery on these occasions to confirm that I was not made to be a surgeon. The reasons that surgeons are called Mr and not Dr is that they were originally barbers. In the olden days the man who shaved you and cut your hair would also be the person to amputate your leg. I wanted to be a doctor only from the neck up. I was becoming more and more interested in the brain and not much in what lay below. I then thought of an ingenious wheeze. I would apply to do the eye houseman's post at St

Thomas's for my compulsory six months house surgeon's job. Very wisely, the General Medical Council have now closed this loophole and insist that a young doctor's pre-registration surgical job must include general surgery. Fortunately, Hugh Wallace, the dermatologist whose ward I was looking after, was a close friend of Harold Ridley the senior eye surgeon at St Thomas's. He strongly backed my application and I was accepted.

Harold Ridley was world famous for his operation to insert a lens actually into the eye to replace the opaque lens removed in a cataract operation. He was small, dapper and a Conservative. It is to his credit that he took me on knowing I was a prospective Labour candidate. During the six months I worked for him in the main hospital we got on extraordinarily well. There was far more humour and fun to him than many people realized. He was extremely conscientious and if one did anything for any of his private patients he insisted on paying very generously. Like most people who worked for him I became very attached to him.

Gradually I was allowed to do more routine operating which I enjoyed. Unlike general surgery, there is no smell, virtually no blood and it requires considerable precision. Before I finished I was doing simple cataract operations on my own. Few patients are more grateful than those who have their eyesight restored or improved. When I was campaigning in the European Election in 1984 in a Milton Keynes shopping centre an old man came charging across to greet me, saying to the accompanying crowd, 'This is the man who saved my eyesight'. He then proceeded to tell the television cameras, journalists and well-wishers how I had done a brilliant operation on his eyes. This gratitude was heartening but in fact removing a mature cataract in most cases is relatively simple and the lens pops out, rather like shelling a pea.

One night when I was on duty in St Thomas's Hospital, an extraordinary coincidence took place. I was asked by a friend to look after one of his patients who had been admitted that day, very seriously ill. He mentioned the patient was a Conservative MP and had a nasty thrombosis in his lungs. When I went to see the patient he was asleep with his face turned away from me. I picked up his wrist to take his pulse and literally gasped when I read his name tag. The man lying in front of me was Percy Browne, the MP for Torrington. I urgently telephoned a friend and got him out of bed moaning and groaning to take over responsibility. Having this particular MP dead on my hands would have been very embarrassing. Fortunately Percy Browne survived and I used to drop in and chat to him as he recovered. Like most people I became captivated by his charm and I was very glad when he stood down on health grounds since I never had to campaign against him. He told me the story of the then Professor of Medicine, Sharpy-Schaffer, who on being shown his electro-cardiograph and being told that he was an MP said, 'This is a by-election heart.'

One day I was assisting Harold Ridley in the operating theatre when he asked whether I had thought about applying for the neurology house physician's post when my job with him ended. I expressed surprise that I might be even considered, for it was the plum job in the hospital, desired by everyone who had just finished their compulsory pre-registration year. He said that if I wanted to apply he would strongly recommend me. I was appointed and it proved to be a fascinating job. It meant that I stood in for the children's house physician on alternate weekends so I could reinforce what I had already learnt about paediatrics. But before starting, I had nearly three weeks' holiday. Having worked non-stop for a whole year and been in hospital over Christmas, I was pretty exhausted.

Before I flew to Greece in the summer of 1963 I visited Torrington and attended the Annual General Meeting of Torrington Labour Party. The Conservative candidate for the next election, in Percy Browne's place, was Peter Mills, a West Country farmer, active in the Church and prominent in a local TV programme, *Faith for Life*. It was possible that we could have had an autumn election but because of John Profumo's involvement with Christine Keeler and resignation in June, it looked more likely to be in 1964.

The Torrington Constituency Party President was Dr C.G. Jones who was a very popular general practitioner in Okehampton. With the almost feudal nature of North Devon politics he gave the party a badge of respectability and made it easier for the more timid Labour supporters to declare themselves. The chairman of the party was Fred Dennis, a stalwart of the NUR, who worked in the Meldon quarry, then under threat of closure, which produced the ballast between sleepers on railway tracks all over the country. My agent was Len Mullholland who lived in Bideford, over the water on the Barnstaple side of the River Torridge. His whole life was bound up with the Labour Party. Without his efforts over many years, the Torrington Labour Party would never have been anywhere near as strong. These and people like Nora Gee in Okehampton and George Allan, the man who delivered all the post in Chagford, made the atmosphere of the local Labour Party. They were genuine people with nothing to gain from being associated with the Labour Party and not infrequently something to lose. They took me into their homes, their wives mothered me, fed me and treated me as one of their own.

It was during the two years as their prospective candidate that I began to understand why Hugh Gaitskell had felt able to say he would fight for the party we 'love'. It is hard for those who take a cynical view of politics and the role of party to understand the emotional attachment that can easily develop. I have never believed that one should elevate party loyalty beyond reasonable limits, and obviously not beyond loyalty to the vital interests of one's country, but I too grew to love the atmosphere of the Torrington Labour Party. These people saw the Labour Party as a vehicle for helping to create a more generous, fair and just society. There was no envy or malice in their aspirations, their politics came from generous hearts. For them, fairness or a more equitable society was to evolve not out of confiscation but from persuasion. Many of them were devout Methodists and they saw their political activity as an extension of their chapel going. Many such people are still in the Labour Party and even when I now clash with Labour I try always to remember it.

I then left Torrington and St Thomas's far behind, flying off for a holiday in Greece. Before I left London I had agreed, in Elizabeth's bistro, to meet a diplomat, Martin Morland, whom I barely knew, in order to travel by car to Mount Athos. At the stroke of three, he drove up alongside the café in Athens where we had agreed to meet. After a long drive north we took a boat to Mount Athos. No female, not even a female cat, is allowed on the peninsula, which is governed by the Greek Orthodox monks in numerous monasteries. You have to have a special permit to visit but the experience is a profound one. Walking from monastery to monastery along paths softened by pine needles you catch breathtaking views of the sea. The monasteries themselves were in bad repair, their former wealth long dissipated. In my hand I had Robert Byron's book *The Station*, written when he was twenty-two, full of the spirit of Byzantium and describing 'the Holy Mountain Athos, station of a faith where all the years have stopped'. The monks offer their hospitality free to their visitor though one is expected to give a donation. It was all very frugal, sleeping on hard beds and eating very simple fare, an unforgettable experience. We then drove south to Athens and took a boat to Hydra, where I had been in 1960 with my first love. I was fancy free at the time and ripe to fall in love which I promptly did with Martin's beautiful cousin, Tessa Fraser. These friendships lasted. I am godfather to Martin's daughter and Tessa is godmother to my eldest son.

On my return, my heavy work load as the neurology house physician left little time for politics, though I continued to visit Torrington once a month. During the autumn the political conference season was particularly dramatic. Labour was doing well in the opinion polls, Harold Wilson having spelt out the main theme of modernization for the forthcoming election and striking a chord in a very receptive country. The Conservative Conference was both dramatic and bruising. Since the start of the year, with de Gaulle's veto of Britain's attempt to get into the Common Market, Macmillan's 'Supermac' image had begun to crack. Macmillan wrote in his diary at that time, 'All our policies at home and abroad are in ruins'. Despite Macmillan's declaration that he was not going to be brought down 'by a couple of tarts', the Profumo affair further tarnished the Party. There was a feeling that after twelve years of the Conservatives it was time for a change.

Macmillan told the Cabinet of his decision to stay on and fight the next election while in some pain in the morning, and that afternoon his surgeon advised him to have a prostatectomy. Harold Macmillan might never have actually resigned if Sir John Richardson had been there from the outset. The surgeon, Macmillan thought, had advised a three to four month period off work, whereas Sir John Richardson, his physician, was adamant that after six weeks he would be fit and well. Unfortunately Sir John, who had known Macmillan since the war in North Africa, was away on holiday. Such are the vagaries of life. John Richardson, who taught me as a medical student at St Thomas's, believed strongly that he could have prevented the resignation and he was not given to exaggeration. Had he done so, Harold Wilson might never have won the 1964 election against Macmillan. Becoming Prime Minister always owes more to accident than design.

On 18 October it was announced from King Edward VII's Hospital for Officers that Macmillan had seen the Queen and tendered his resignation. The Queen then sent for Lord Home who resigned his earldom to become Sir Alec Douglas-Home. He proved to be a more formidable opponent than most of us in the Labour Party were ready to accept at the time. Given Labour's then large poll lead and political memories of the Tory Party Conference, dominated by the power struggle between Lord Hailsham, Rab Butler and Reginald Maudling, it was amazing that the Conservatives came so close to winning the election in 1964, particularly since Iain Macleod, the most brilliant of the up and coming Cabinet Ministers, and Enoch Powell refused even to serve under Home.

At the time, the very welcome upshot of Macmillan's resignation for me was that an election was now unlikely until the autumn of 1964 and I could concentrate on medicine. I was still learning much about how best to handle patients. A woman who was well known in the communications world came into the hospital with a suspected brain tumour. She was much older than she looked, always beautifully dressed, charming and sophisticated. She managed the indignity of having her head shaved for the operation with great panache and wore an excellent wig afterwards. Most of her glamorous visitors had no idea how serious her operation had been – her brain tumour was unfortunately found to be far advanced and there was no case even for radiotherapy. Initially it was felt better to tell her that we thought the tumour would turn out to be benign. Gradually as the days went by she persisted in her demand to be told the true diagnosis. Her consultant, Dr Reginald Kelly, was a wise man and sensed that she did not really wish to know the whole truth. He kept delaying telling her. I talked to her a lot in the evenings and I was becoming almost too fond of her as a person, anxious that we were not being truthful with her. On a number of occasions I said that I thought we ought to reveal the diagnosis. Eventually Reggie Kelly suggested that I should tell her. I told her one evening and she was very brave, seeming to take it extremely well. Next morning in the ward I was surprised to find she was not in her bed. I asked the ward sister where she was. The sister said, 'What do you mean? She's there, in her normal bed.' We walked back and I saw the truth. She had removed her wig, abandoned her make-up, the scar on her scalp was visible and she looked thirty years older. She died a few days later. She had simply given up the will to live and I felt deeply responsible. It was an object lesson. Despite the fashionable enthusiasm for doctors always to tell every patient their diagnosis there are still some cases where it is better to let people live in hope.

Around that time the same message of caution was reinforced for me in dealing with another patient. This man was a doctor and he came in under a consultant who had been a great friend of his as a medical student. He was a very buoyant personality and was talking all the time about how he knew he had cancer and that his friend had told him that he would let him know the diagnosis as soon as the pathology reports were back. He did indeed have cancer and his consultant told me he thought in view of their friendship it would be better if he saw him alone and gave him the results. Next day I went in to see him and he made no mention at all of the tests and rather oddly talked about everything else but his own medical condition. When the consultant came round I asked him whether he had given the diagnosis since it appeared that he still did not know. He assured me he had. Soon it became obvious that this patient, though an intelligent doctor, was determined to block out the conversation he had had and the diagnosis he had been given. He proceeded to lead his life for the next few months with absolutely no regard whatever to the diagnosis. He divorced his wife, married again and never told anyone until he came into hospital to die. It was a bizarre incident but once again it showed that there are no rules of general application in medicine. Everyone is an individual and each case has to be judged on its own merit.

When my six months ended in January 1964 I went to the National Heart Hospital to do cardiology as a preparation for my higher examination for membership of the Royal College of Physicians. Sadly Dr Elkington, the senior neurologist at St Thomas's, had died. I was asked if I would help out and do a locum as neurology registrar. It was a wonderful opportunity and I jumped at it, even though it meant I did not have much time to study for my membership. After a few months, a permanent vacancy for the post of neurology and psychiatric registrar came up, and I was fortunate to be chosen.

That spring, Jim Callaghan, the Shadow Chancellor of the Exchequer, came to Exeter. It was the first time we had met and a photograph of us together appeared in the local press which was a help. He was very friendly but if anyone had said that thirteen years later he would make me his Foreign Secretary we would both have been dumbfounded.

The General Election was called for September 1964. I simply took three weeks' unpaid leave from the hospital for the campaign and drove down to Bideford and tried to rent a flat. The estate agents were clearly frightened of having any property linked with Labour and so we eventually took one in my mother's name. It was a completely amateur campaign; we had very few people who owned cars in the constituency and it was so far-flung that it was difficult to canvas. The main enjoyment was having three and sometimes four village meetings a night. A very close girl-friend and her sister came down to help and we all enjoyed ourselves and were seen to do so. We had hardly any money, barely enough to cover the cost of printing an election address, but fortunately Courage beer decided to launch a national campaign with big posters saying, VOTE FOR COURAGE. My supporters decided to take advantage of this and fly-posted all over the constituency with a large 'Owen', so that it read, VOTE OWEN FOR COURAGE. All we could hope for was to avoid losing our deposit. No Labour MP came near the constituency throughout the campaign. My only visiting speaker was a Labour peer who was a great expert in inland waterways and who came to speak in the little seaport of Appledore.

Mark Bonham-Carter made few inroads into the Conservative vote during the campaign. My election message to the constituency had at least a certain brutal frankness to it and it showed I had little time for the Liberals:

> The party of our dreams is usually far removed from the party of reality. Possibly the most unpleasant feature of politics is the inherent compromise that it demands from each of us. Yet, if we are not to end up with a party for each individual voter, we all know that we have to come to terms with this situation. Politics, with its overall concern with power, poses the question at each election, which party is to govern? Minority groups and small parties like the Liberals who, because of their gradual decline, no longer appear as a party that can possibly govern, serve merely to confuse the issue. They may provide a comfortable alternative to the dissatisfied voter who shirks compromise, but they do not represent a serious alternative.

The Liberals believed that they would win back Torrington in the 1964 General Election. It was clear to everyone that as the Labour candidate the only question for me was whether I could save my deposit. It was a seat for a one-off, light-hearted candidature or one out to earn his spurs towards being selected later for a safe seat. Mark Bonham-Carter was Asquith's grandson and the son of Lady Violet Bonham-Carter. He was almost as unsuitable a candidate for this rural constituency as Anthony Royle. In a cattle market surrounded by rubicund West Countrymen he stood out, wan and ill at ease. He had about him the cultivated effortless superiority that marks out many of those who pass through Balliol College, Oxford. 'Life', the old joke goes, 'is one Balliol man after another', and there were not many Balliol men among Liberal voters in Torrington. The more I saw of him at close quarters, the more I was put off by his political manner. His attractive wife was a considerable asset but his mother a dubious one. On polling day Lady Violet insisted on entering all the polling stations. Electoral law clearly says that this is only allowed if you are the candidate or the candidate's agent. The Torrington Labour Party, already fed up with her 'Lady Bountiful' act, complained to the Returning Officer but, despite that, and much to our fury, she continued on her way, saying she had done this at every election since her father was Prime Minister. Mark Bonham-Carter's commitment to the European Community, which he had vigorously championed in the House of Commons following his by-election success, began to wilt in the constituency as he tried to win over the Devon dairy farmers who were in those days firmly against going into the Common Market. It was the first of many reminders of how Liberal candidates try to win votes by saying different things to different people. Admittedly this candidate did it with considerably more style and elegance than normal. But he played the same game and earned more scepticism than votes from the farmers who are notoriously hard-headed.

Mark Bonham-Carter told me years afterwards at Roy Jenkins's house in East Hendred that he believed that my intervention had robbed him of the seat. This was nonsense for I increased the Labour vote by less than two hundred. Once he had lost the seat in 1959, he no longer had the advantage of incumbency. To have a chance of recovering the seat in 1964 would have required him to go and live in the constituency and nurse it day by day which was what Peter Mills was doing. Even so he would have great difficulty in winning. At the count, when my pile of votes passed the point at which the deposit was saved, a cheer went up from the Labour Party, generously supported by the Conservatives. This was not based on the old two-party conspiracy against the Liberals: both Labour and Conservative Party workers agreed that the Liberals had fought the dirtiest campaign.

The final result was:

Peter Mills	Conservative	16,899
Mark Bonham-Carter	Liberal	14,831
David Owen	Labour	5,867

I returned to London, quite happy to switch right out of politics and to concentrate on medicine. I was now living in a stylish, black floored, white walled basement flat in Chesham Street, Belgravia, having sold my houseboat, *Amanda*, for a thousand pounds. I later heard that *Amanda* had sunk in the middle of the night, holed below the waterline after settling on a milk bottle. At the hospital I was now combining what I had always wanted to do, psychiatry with neurology, and working for Dr William Sargant. He was a giant both physically, a second row rugby forward who played for St Mary's Hospital, and clinically, a dominating personality with the therapeutic courage of a lion, author of a best selling book on brain-washing called *Battle for the Mind*. That generation of psychiatrists who worked at the Maudsley Hospital transformed British psychiatry. They pioneered the unlocking of all doors and the treating of psychiatric patients in all respects like patients in medical wards of general hospitals. Before the war psychotherapy and psychoanalytical treatments had done nothing to cut the size of the large remote Victorian psychiatric hospitals. People were protected in hospital wards rather than treated. The most many psychiatrists could hope to do was to shield them against the three Ss: starvation, sleeplessness and suicide. Even after the war patients were still virtually imprisoned with wards locked and, in all too many cases, patients neglected. The transformation of their life during the 1950s was a social revolution. Psychiatric patients began to be treated with physical methods like electro-convulsive therapy (ECT) and the special anti-depressant drugs began to appear.

Dr Sargant came to St Thomas's as a consultant from the Maudsley Hospital in 1948. He found, when he arrived, no real Department of Psychiatry. He was given a dark, dank basement bed store for his outpatients. It was aptly called Scutari after the depressing hospital in the Crimean War which Florence Nightingale had done so much to transform. In 1965 we were still treating seventeen thousand new and old patients a year in Scutari and giving some of them ECT in those same appalling working conditions. Sargant had initially only been given two token beds in the hospital for psychiatric patients. When allocated Ward 5, the top floor of the Royal Waterloo Hospital, he transformed it into an open, attractive unit of twenty-two beds in single and double rooms where some two hundred patients a year were treated. He also persuaded other clinicians who were impressed with psychiatric physical methods of treatment at St Thomas's Hospital to use around twenty of their beds to treat their own patients. Sargant also acquired another ten patients in the wartime country annexe to St Thomas's at Hydestile near Godalming. Here there were also two wards for chronic neurological cases.

When I was Senior Neurology and Psychiatric Registrar, I drove down every week to this hospital. Through the hospital I met a remarkable woman, Megan Du Boisson. She was suffering from multiple sclerosis and, with another woman, had just started the Disablement Income Group (DIG). I became their unofficial medical adviser. Later, when they became established as the most powerful lobbying group for disabled people, they could call on the very best neurologists in the country. One of my most fulfilling moments was addressing, as a young MP, a mass rally which DIG organized in Trafalgar Square. A policeman, escorting us in a procession of wheelchairs to No. 10 Downing Street to present a petition, turned to Megan and said, 'This is the first time I have been on duty in Trafalgar Square that I have not resented giving up my weekend.' It was very moving but, we all felt, something that could not be repeated. I remain a patron of DIG.

William Sargant was a human dynamo. Controversial, committed, he was the sort of person of whom legends are made. He was adamant that no doors should be locked and no windows barred. He believed that patients should be trusted and treated in general wards even if suicidal. He was confident that with a combination of drugs and electric shock therapy even seriously ill psychiatric patients could be safely treated in general hospitals. What was more important, he practised what he preached.

Sargant delighted in being the *bête noire* of the psychoanalysts. The previous psychiatrist at St Thomas's was a Freudian who, with Dr Ernest Jones, led the British psychoanalytic movement. Sargant claimed that he used to tell students during the war, much to their amusement, that they did not fear Zeppelins or bombs as such, their alarm was due to the accident of these being also phallic symbols which aroused subconscious homosexual libido and other fears. While Sargant was seen as the hammer of the analysts, he actually believed that they had something to contribute to neurotic patients. But he was adamant in his belief that analysis provided absolutely nothing of clinical value for patients suffering from the psychoses.

To work for Sargant was a delight because he was so enthusiastic. He was, as his critics claimed, often infuriating and he did at times stretch the evidence and exaggerate the effects of his preferred treatment. However, the bias in some of his results came about only through his personal dominance, not any deliberate tampering. For patients under his treatment to admit that they were still depressed after being treated was an act of bravery almost amounting to foolhardiness. 'You're better, aren't you?' was his standard greeting. While I was working with him, he would comment to me that a patient was improving before coming through the door, because of the speed with which the door handle was turned. He willed his patients to get better and most of them did. The massive and all-redeeming feature of the man was his optimism. He had a passionate commitment to lifting his patient's depression. He was able to understand that those who were depressed were in many senses far more ill than people with cancer or in severe pain. In part this was because he himself had become depressed in 1934 when he had first developed tuberculosis as a young doctor and had begun to lose interest in his medical research work. He would punch home to students how dreadful it was to be depressed by reminding them how rare it was for patients suffering from intractable pain to commit suicide. By contrast the sheer horror of feeling depressed drives many to suicide. Sargant claimed that he was entitled to take some risks with the treatment of a depressed patient in the same way that a surgeon takes risks with his patients. When side-effects were discovered for such successful drugs as chlorpromazine hydrochloride, commonly called Largactil, used in the treatment of schizophrenia, or the then newly discovered monoamine oxidase inhibitors used for anxiety depression, Sargant would not only refuse to stop dispensing them but he would defend the side-effects by reference to the number of patients who were expected to die just by virtue of having an anaesthetic. He would also argue that the fact that you did not know how a drug worked should not preclude one using it if it alleviated symptoms. After all, he would say, clinicians used quinine for years in the treatment of malaria without the slightest idea how it was acting in the patient's body.

To his critics all this was dangerous bravado. To his supporters it was robust common sense. He himself would admit that he was hopeless when dealing with neurotic patients. He did his best to pass them on to other doctors including those with a knowledge of psychotherapy. But he was often impatient and brusque with them. One of his patients who had a long history of hysterical fainting fits once told me how she had collapsed on his private consulting room floor and come round to see him leaning over her with a pen and an open cheque book saying, 'Sargant with two As.' Exaggerated perhaps, but revealing of how some of his patients saw him.

In the psychiatric department a great deal of careful thought was given as to whether to refer schizophrenic patients to the neuro-surgeons for a modified leucotomy operation. The operation Sargant favoured cut the lower medial quadrants of the frontal lobe of the brain and specifically avoided the outer quadrant. Sargant found in a careful follow-up that when all other treatments had failed many of these carefully selected patients did well. Leucotomy also helped some very bad obsessional cases, people with rituals such as having to wash their hands non-stop, provided that they had a good previous, albeit obsessive, personality. For some psychiatrists the fact that Sargant was even prepared to contemplate recommending a leucotomy was a sign of derangement and his conduct aroused bitter controversy.

The widespread use of electro-convulsive therapy in St Thomas's also shocked people. Yet I saw too many patients respond dramatically to ECT to harbour many doubts about its efficacy in carefully selected patients suffering psychotic rather than neurotic symptoms. I remember a professor I treated through three episodes of depression. He came down with depression at exactly the same time of the year and had done so for a decade. The early signs were a disturbed sleep rhythm and lethargy and within a few weeks he became classically depressed, slowed up, indecisive, weeping involuntarily and quite unable to teach his students. Each year he resisted ECT until in desperation he accepted our advice and agreed to have it. After three treatments his depression would lift and he would be dramatically better. I remember too how women who had become depressed after childbirth responded to ECT with as few as one or two treatments. Such cases are a medical emergency, since these women can become so distressed that they kill their new born child as well as themselves.

I was reminded how controversial all this treatment was when some years later I was having lunch in Soho with Anthony Howard, then editor of the *New Statesman*, and a doctor friend of his. Talking as one might among doctors I used the shorthand description for ECT and said that if my wife ever got depressed after childbirth 'I wouldn't hesitate to plug her into the mains.' A few months later he used that quote in a profile and, ever since, it keeps recurring without any linkage to post-puerperal depression. So I simply became the man who would not hesitate to plug his wife into the mains!

The good diagnostician picks up the minutiae which others ignore. I once interviewed a policeman for over an hour and at the end of it pronounced him quite sane. Sargant diagnosed him as a paranoid schizophrenic within five minutes purely on the strength of an unguarded admission that he would leave Scotland Yard well after midnight and walk home and then do the return journey in the very early morning. I thought when he first said this that it was bizarre behaviour but nothing more. Sargant had the wit to look at the distance between his home address and Scotland Yard and calculate that each walk would take him over one and a half hours. When he put it to the policeman that this meant walking three hours every day in addition to his long hours at the Yard, he admitted it without blinking an eyelid. Normal people do not behave like this but even so for Sargant to certify him, much to the anger of senior officers in the Metropolitan Police who thought he was sane, was a big risk. The vindication came many months later when the policeman, by then in a psychiatric hospital, developed florid schizophrenia.

Another doctor working in St Thomas's was H.J. Shorvon, who during the war had developed with Sargant the technique of abreaction. He allowed me to treat one of his old patients who had first come with a totally paralysed arm having been strafed by German fighter planes in the water off the beaches of Dunkirk. If left untreated for more than a few weeks the arm would become completely paralysed. The treatment was to inject him with sodium amytal so that he would become drowsy and then help him to re-enact the traumatic experience of Dunkirk. When his tension was relieved, his arm would immediately start to function normally. The key to the treatment was for him to act out, as he became relaxed, his wartime experience. This meant I would have to help by generating the same atmosphere, shouting urgently, 'The bombs are dropping! There's the splash of the bomb! The boat's sinking! You've got to get off! Swim to the lifeboat! The plane's coming in to attack! The tracer bullets are coming towards you!' As I did this he would gradually react until the moment when the excitement and tension had come back he would suddenly virtually drown in front of one. His throat would gurgle. He would cough, splutter and retch and one could almost hear the water in his mouth and lungs. Then as quickly as it had come, it would all stop. He would go to sleep for an hour or more and then walk out of the hospital with his arm swinging normally.

We did not use this abreaction technique a lot but once it led to a medical emergency. A young woman was referred to Shorvon for a second opinion by a dermatologist. She was thought to be suffering from a rare peripheral vascular disease. Her nails and the tips of her fingers had been literally rotting for a couple of years and no treatment had alleviated it. The question was whether there was any underlying pyscho-pathology. Under abreaction Shorvon, without much difficulty, got her to reveal that she had been putting her fingers every day into phenol. This was her way of drawing attention to herself and to her underlying mental anxiety. He decided that this revelation was too dramatic for her to wake up and face so soon. So she was given continuous sleeping drugs for a week and then gradually brought around, by which time the skin on her fingers was beginning to heal. She was then treated with a mixture of psychotherapy and anti-depressants.

Not surprisingly in this fascinating atmosphere of positive psychiatry, I decided that I would not become a consultant neurologist but aim to be a professor of psychiatry. Before doing so I needed an academic research background and so after two years as the neurology and psychiatric registrar, I left to take up a research fellowship on the medical unit.

I had by then also embarked on a more serious attempt to become an MP in Plymouth, although I was still loath to admit it to myself. Early in 1965 I had been asked if I would allow my name to be put forward for the constituency of Plymouth Sutton by Alderman Fred Stott, who was a much respected Labour member of the Social Services Committee and a Justice of the Peace with my mother. Dr John Dunwoody, who had nearly won for Labour in 1964, had decided not to contest it again, preferring to wait for a safe constituency. His readiness to leave that seat helped to lull me into a false sense of its being impossible to win. I felt he would not be leaving it if he thought it could be won and therefore it was not likely to return me to Parliament and so disrupt my medical career.

I well remember the day on which I decided to let my name be placed on the short list for this Plymouth Sutton constituency. It was a sunny day and we were waiting for a case conference due to start in the sitting room on Ward 5 of the Royal Waterloo Hospital. Sargant burst into the room, demanding to know where the ward sister was. He was clearly enraged. It transpired that the sister in charge, finding that many of her nurses were burning their stiff white aprons on the electric fires when turning around in the patient's small rooms, had arranged for grills to be put over the electric bars. Sargant saw this as symbolic of going back to the bad old days of locked wards and treating psychiatric patients like imbeciles. Eventually the sister managed to persuade him that nothing like this was intended, nor could fairly be construed. Even so he continued to act like a spoilt child. In a flash forward I saw myself in

Sargant's position in thirty years' time, behaving in exactly the same way. Medicine then appeared to me to offer only a constricted vision and politics a much broader canvas. Over the years as I have watched eminent politicians and physicians, that superficial judgement has certainly not been borne out. Both are capable of behaving childishly, often with remarkable pettiness and Sargant's tirade on Ward 5 has been mirrored often enough, even in my presence, by Cabinet Ministers. But at the time it was an incident that overcame my hesitation and helped me to continue in politics. That night I wrote to the Constituency Labour Party accepting nomination.

A few weeks later I attended the selection conference, having been placed on the short list. The strongest challenge came from an extremely attractive candidate, Betty Boothroyd. She spoke far better than I, as many of the General Management Committee teasingly reminded me over the years, but I was the local boy, known to some of them when fighting Torrington. A few of the delegates were patients of my father's or knew my mother and no doubt they gave me the benefit of the doubt. Betty Boothroyd later became MP for West Bromwich West and a highly successful Deputy Speaker.

British politics is unusual in having so many MPs who have not been born or bred in their constituency. In America such politicians are called carpet-baggers and are only very rarely chosen. The fact that I am a Plymothian has been a considerable help in holding my seat against the tide of public opinion in 1970, 1974, and 1979. It means that visiting my constituency is going home. As I step off the train at Plymouth station I smell the sea and feel instantly different. It is as if I have gained an extra lung. I had also been shortlisted for a selection conference, on the day before the Plymouth selection, for the Falmouth and Camborne seat. This was an existing Labour seat where Frank Hayman MP was due to retire. I had driven down there a few weeks before and concluded that it was not the best constituency for me. The extra seventy miles made the journey from London too far. Also, looking around and assessing the constituency, I did not believe it was as safe in reality as it looked on paper. When I withdrew my name, Sarah Barker, the then Labour National Agent, horrified on being told that I had withdrawn in order to take my chance on being selected for Plymouth Sutton, shrieked down the phone so that everyone in the neurology clinic where I was working heard every word, that my decision was incomprehensible. Her attitude reinforced my feeling that Plymouth Sutton was not winnable and right up until the last week of the general election campaign I believed that I was still heading for a medical not a political career. I compromised with Sarah Barker to the extent that I agreed to go down to Falmouth for the selection conference and to tell them then why I was withdrawing before they voted. This ensured no adverse press speculation. As things turned out Falmouth was not as safe as people thought and while John

Dunwoody won the seat in 1966 he lost it in 1970, as did his wife Gwyneth in Exeter. I was left thereafter as the only Labour MP west of Bristol.

On the Medical Unit I carried forward the work which I had already begun with David Marsden. Our first paper, published in December 1965 in the *Lancet*, was entitled, 'The effect of Adrenergic Beta Blockade on Parkinsonian Tremor' David Marsden has since gone on to have a very successful career in neuro-pharmacology, being now the Professor of Neurology at the National Hospital for Nervous Diseases, Queen's Square, London. We tried, first on normal subjects, to measure the effect of adrenaline on the fine tremor of the outstretched fingers which all normal people have. If anxious or tense, this tremor increases its amplitude. This is because anxiety and emotional stress provoke increased catecholamine release from the adrenal glands which lie on top of the kidneys and this increases the excretion of adrenaline in the urine. It was reasonable to expect to be able to reproduce this effect by injecting adrenaline directly into the veins. The problem for us as research workers was that injecting adrenaline into the veins or arteries is a hazardous experiment. It is perfectly all right as long as the adrenaline is sufficiently diluted but if the concentration is too high then the injection is lethal. We used volunteers, medical students or fit patients. For ethical reasons we felt the first experiments ought to be done on ourselves. Never have I watched the dilution of a substance so carefully. We both checked, double checked and checked again. The injection was rather like having a glass of sherry: there was a slight increase of heart rate, a greater awareness of breathing and a general feeling of well-being. We then injected adrenaline into the artery, enabling us, by blocking the arterial supply in different parts of the limb and also using beta blockers, to show that the beta receptors concerned with tremor were located in the forearm. It was not earth-shattering research but it added some useful knowledge which we took further by repeating the experiments on patients with Parkinson's disease, thyrotoxicosis and anxiety states. We wrote together, and with others, five main papers over the next two years, some while I was an MP. David Marsden was undoubtedly the brains behind our research while I provided some of the drive. He taught me the discipline of scientific method. Politics has helped corrupt that discipline of forming judgements on facts but I have avoided making some major political errors by insisting on obtaining the facts first. I have also tried to ensure I learnt by trying to conduct a post mortem on decisions taken that have gone wrong. The sheer indiscipline of political decision-making still sometimes shocks me. Hunch, panic, prejudice are all major determinants and this will continue while we retain an adversarial parliamentary and legal system on which a peculiarly ideological media industry thrives.

Despite this, politics was destined eventually to push out medicine, though not without a struggle. I eventually won the seat in Plymouth but I turned up at St Thomas's Hospital on the Monday morning after the general election, determined to continue as a doctor while an MP. In the hospital everyone thought my being an MP was a great joke but the Professor of Medicine, Bill Cranston, and Reggie Kelly were delighted that I wished to continue to do research and both felt it would be a great waste if I gave up medicine entirely. So for the next two years I tried to be both a doctor and a politician. Foolishly I did not sit for the third part of my membership examination for the Royal College of Physicians.

In my passport I went on calling myself a medical practitioner until I became Foreign Secretary, when my passport 'to allow the bearer to pass freely without let or hindrance', was issued by myself to myself. It then seemed wiser to stop the pretence and to call myself a politician. But by then it was too late to drop the courtesy title of Doctor, even if I had wanted to. The general public are often surprised to find Ph.D.s calling themselves Doctor and they still say to me, 'You're a proper Doctor.'

In 1967 the Labour Government's prices and incomes policy dictated wage restraint for everyone and I became rather guilty about continuing to take a part-time salary from the St Thomas's Endowment Fund while also being paid as an MP. I decided to work on the medical unit, unpaid. This was an error because while I was being paid I felt an obligation to attend the hospital but once that sense of obligation was removed, the demands of the House of Commons began to take precedence. Nevertheless, until the moment I became Minister for the Navy in July 1968, when I was no longer allowed to continue as a doctor, medicine came first and politics second in my heart. This ordering of my priorities was helped by Kenneth Robinson, the then Minister of Health, appointing me as a governor of Charing Cross Hospital. This was an investment for me for I began to learn about the difficulty of administering the National Health Service which proved invaluable when I became Minister of Health in 1974. At that stage we were planning the new hospital in Fulham and the move from the Strand, opposite Charing Cross Railway Station. It would be helpful if more MPs were appointed to public bodies and gained practical experience of administering the public sector as some already do for payment in the private sector. There is now ministerial reluctance to do this and, as a result, the debates in Parliament on the NHS and other public services risk getting out of touch with the realities within these services.

In one other way medicine and politics came together. There is no doctor employed in the Palace of Westminster and the medical MPs are expected to cope with any emergencies. The police wisely call the doctors with the most knowledge first. In my early years I was near the top of their list. As the years passed they wisely dropped me to the bottom. Diagnosing and examining these medical emergencies was not easy as the facilities in the early days were pretty dreadful, just a small box of a room with a couch. This has now improved. If I was certain of the diagnosis I sent them off to St Thomas's, confident that when I met my colleagues next day in the hospital they would not be able to rib me. If I was doubtful of the diagnosis I sent them to the Westminster Hospital so as to avoid my friends in St Thomas's smiling at my expense. On one occasion an elderly Conservative MP appeared to have had an acute heart attack. But there was something odd about his case and because of this I sent him to the Westminster Hospital. I had doubts because I had felt his femoral arteries for a normal pulsation and had not been able to detect any pulse. If absent, it meant that he had a coarctation of the aorta. This is when the wall of the artery splits and blood flows in and compresses the inner wall so that virtually no blood passes through and this split can spread up to involve the coronary arteries. So I wrote in the referral letter, '? Heart attack? Coarctation of the aorta.'

I was later told by the consultant, in a generous letter of thanks, that the MP was in hospital for a few days not responding to treatment; the consultant asked the young house physician who had referred the patient and was told laughingly, an MP who was a doctor. When the consultant asked what the MP doctor had diagnosed, he was told, with even louder laughter, coarctation. The consultant then leant over and felt for a femoral pulse and finding none ordered an immediate X-ray. A few hours later the MP was operated on successfully for a coarctation. I have dined out on that story, suitably garnished, for years.

Another problem was when I was asked to see an MP who had collapsed in the Chamber. I arranged for the MP to be taken and put on the couch in the medical emergency room. After a while I left, asking the policeman to look in from time to time and promising to return in half an hour. I came back at intervals over the next few hours. By this time the young policeman was so concerned at this comatose MP being left in the room that he called the Police Superintendent. When I arrived, they were both there and asked politely if I did not think it wise to call an ambulance and arrange for the MP to be admitted to hospital. I said no and continued periodic visits for another few hours, by which time the MP was ready to leave to go home. I am not sure the young policeman ever realized the diagnosis. The MP was, quite simply, drunk.

To be a 'Doctor in the House', gives one a special vantage point to observe the psycho–pathology within the body politic. There are haunting parallels between medicine and politics. I wrote about them when aged thirty, in this letter to Debbie shortly before we were married. At that time I had less of a tendency to romanticize medicine and more up-to-date experience of combining the two professions. Now nostalgia for medicine would cloud my judgement; in 1968 I was more realistic.

Who is to judge which is the more important, politics or medicine?
As a doctor one's currency was individuals because of their disease

or pain. They felt insecure, often frightened. You as an individual were in a position for them of power – often rather frightening power. The relationship was too unequal. There is a saying, 'A lawyer sees the worst of a man, a clergyman sees the best of a man, but a doctor sees a man as he is.' It carries an essence of truth but it is also basically fraudulent – it wasn't until I met people as a politican that I realized how unequal the doctor's relationship is. It is as if people have consciously vested in the doctor an air of mystique because he affects their most precious desire – that of keeping alive. They do not allow themselves often the luxury of doubt or criticism. Of course this, like so many ingrained attitudes, is increasingly being challenged but it is still the dominant theme and the doctor for his part knows how much of his life is patching up, postponing the inevitable. Frequently uncertain that he is actively contributing. Yet preserving the aura that he is to cover for his own inadequacies. The truest doctor is the one who recognizes his own limitations. He sees his true role as an observer able to interfere only rarely, often having to give for appearance's sake, a picture of activity but in reality often deliberately choosing that hardest of all courses, 'masterly inactivity'.

A great physician, Sir Robert Hutchinson, once prayed 'from inability to leave well alone, good Lord deliver us'. Yet the consolation for the doctor is by and large one for his own self esteem. His motives are respected. His profession exudes responsibility. He is in a position where his motives are largely unchallenged. It is one of my basic beliefs that we are all self-centred and indeed selfish. All too often close examination reveals the unselfish act to be an illusion, that the only difference is in the timescale of the pay off. For some gain satisfaction from pain, even misery and vilification. One of my hardest problems in believing in Christianity is to accept the unselfish act as being within our grasp, that instead, if one probes deeply enough it is merely a reflection of enlightened self-interest. You may ask what difference in reality is there – yet it is not just a semantic problem. In essence it is the difference between the humanist and the Christian; both can lift themselves on to an outward appearance of selflessness, yet which has the true motive? Perhaps it doesn't matter. Maybe they are but different approaches to having a coherent life and that all we can or even should strive for is individual coherence, self justification and internal happiness.

Yet to return to my starting off point. One can argue that medicine is one of the greatest escape routes open to man. It allows one to luxuriate in an aroma of self satisfaction – and yet the politician, is he so different in essence? You could argue this no doubt for the lawyer, architect, painter or bus conductor, but perhaps the doctor and the politician are more comparable. One tends to involve predominantly the individual and his problems; the other the group or the mass or even the nation but these are only accumulations of individuals. They both derive power over the individual from their position. Both are observers to a certain extent. The decision making process they both use is that of a natural science. Before I became a politician I thought economics was a pure science. Now I see it and recognize it as a biological science. It has no absolute value for its fabric is made up of individuals, its variables are human variables. The good politician, like the good doctor, should be able to leave well alone and then, perhaps pushing the parallel too far, one can distinguish in both, two types – the activist and interventionist and the passive non-interventionist in political descriptions. The radical or socialist is opposed to the Conservative traditionalist. As I am by temperament an interventionist I not surprisingly believe that in both medicine and politics these are the wisest and best of men but with one major and in fact crucial qualification. The intervention must be finely judged for there is a greater onus on the interventionist to make his case to assess the indications for intervention than for the non-interventionist to justify his inactivity. Because we are, whether we like it or not, creatures of evolution not revolution there is a higher probability that inactivity in a given situation is a more appropriate response than activity.

Perhaps this is why only infrequently does the democratic process give power to a radical government. Revolution is too disruptive and painful a process. Change is nothing but an alien to *homo sapiens* who prefer to have it served in a form so slow and disguised that the rough edges have been erased.

I feel myself to be stretched by politics to an extent that medicine could never have given me. Every day produces a challenge. The very variety of the problems is fascinating and the technical complexity is matched by the consistently large human element, whether it be Parliament, MPs or constituents. One is not thanked; one's motives are suspect. There is little gratitude, and uncertainty and insecurity are ever with one. Yet for all that I would still describe politics as the supreme adventure, the ultimate test of so many qualities. As I never weary from saying and I'm sure you've heard: I really believe the Greek aphorism 'that he who is bored by politics is bored by life'. But always too in the back of my mind there is the inescapable inner voice which asks one to weigh up the relative value of one's contribution as a doctor or as a politician. In a strange way the easy way out would be to return to the certainty and self-satisfaction of medicine – maybe one day this is what I will do, but this experience I cannot ever regret. One's relationship with the individual in politics is a fantastic combination of being servant and yet master, of being venerated and despised, loved and hated. As a doctor one grew accustomed to being and even expecting to be loved – how different. To some, politics is a stage. In this sense I think I am a failure and this may be a fatal weakness. Not that I don't like the theatre part of it but I don't think I'm very good at it. I'm basically too restless and dissatisfied to be a non-interventionist but I despair as I see my whole philosophical political stance cheapened by ill thought out interventions based on prejudices and not facts.

That letter to Debbie summed up the conflict between the doctor and the politician while the two were still running in harness. I have often regretted the lack of any scientific discipline in politics – facts are far from being sacred and politicians are only just beginning to take seriously the behavioural sciences. If I had to relive my life, knowing that I was going to go into the House of Commons at the age of twenty-seven, I would still choose to have first been a doctor of medicine.

5

DOCTOR IN THE HOUSE

The early 1960s were a heady time in politics and British life. Satire was the medium, two fingers to the politicians was the message. It was exemplified by the show *Beyond the Fringe*, the magazine *Private Eye* and the television series *That Was The Week That Was*. All guyed politicians and a typical jibe was David Frost's summing up of the General Election between Sir Alec Douglas-Home and Harold Wilson as a battle between Dull Alec and Smart Alec. Michael Shank's *The Stagnant Society* hit a raw nerve. Anthony Sampson's *The Anatomy of Britain* and a series of Penguin Specials, asking what was wrong with Britain, pointed to the answer – 'the Establishment'. What the Establishment was, was harder to define. We, who were on the outside, felt those who were on the inside were the reason for our decline. Where we went wrong was to believe that it would be enough to change the players. We underestimated the extent to which the new Labour arrivals were going to be absorbed by the old Conservative players. Soon they would ape their habits and their prejudices, become obsessed about editorial opinion in top people's newspapers and fall for all the flummery surrounding 'the Palace' – even become members of the same all-male clubs.

I was part of the medical Establishment at St Thomas's Hospital. Politicians and other eminent people came in fairly frequently as patients, and this helped me to see different facets of the Establishment and to look sceptically at its values. Yet at that stage I did not look sceptically at Harold Wilson. I was staggered that as many as 103 Labour MPs had voted for George Brown to be Leader of the Labour Party in 1963. It seemed amazing to me that Harold Wilson should have won with only 144 votes. Within a few months of entering the House of Commons, I was to find out why sound, sensible MPs had voted for George despite their anxieties about his personality and his weakness for alcohol. They simply did not trust Harold Wilson. But to me, Harold Wilson's 'white heat of the technological revolution' seemed to match the needs of the country. He appeared classless, modern and, with a statistician's mind, able to reverse the 'brain drain' and understand the scientific needs of the country. To my generation Britain was still languishing in nostalgia, looking back to 1940, to the Battle of Britain when we stood alone.

I first met Harold Wilson on Plymouth North Road Railway Station, twelve days before the March 1966 general election. Traditionally Prime Ministers are welcomed by the station master. Harold Wilson stepped off the train in his famous Gannex coat, pipe puffing, accompanied by Mary, his wife. I was just part of the group, along with other West Country candidates, when suddenly his aide sought me out, no doubt because I was the candidate for the most marginal seat. I went up to Harold Wilson to shake hands but before I knew what was happening, he took me by the arm and propelled me forward to walk alongside him towards the television cameras at the end of the platform. The all-important television pictures that night were of me talking animatedly to the Prime Minister as if we were intimate friends. It was brilliant politics and the first of many incidents that demonstrated his recognition of Marshall Macluhan's gospel that 'the medium is the message'.

The press handout and the closed, ticket-only political meeting of the 1990s are killing off some of the magic of the hustings but it was still there in the 1960s. In Chatham in 1964, Wilson had rhetorically asked, 'Why do I speak about the Navy?' and a heckler had shouted back, 'Because you're in Chatham'.

He had given a rollicking speech in the 1964 Election in the Forum Cinema in Devonport which I went to as the candidate for Torrington. Ridiculing the overstaffed Navy, he reverted to being the statistician. 'We have 101 ships in commission. We have of course plenty of Admirals – eighty-five. Our Admiral warship co-efficient is 0.851.' His audience loved it, it was our Harold the 'Cheeky Chappy'.

I admired what Wilson had said in 1964 to the Scottish Labour Party at Rothesay, 'The Labour Party is a moral crusade or it is nothing. We shall not suffer this party, on which the hopes of millions depend, to become either a soulless bureaucracy or a vote-dealing Tammany Hall.' I laughed when at Bellevue in Manchester in 1963 after Lord Home had succeeded Harold Macmillan as leader of the Conservative Party, he derided the Tories as the party of privilege:

> The selection had been through the machinery of an autocratic cabal. I am worried to know how a scion of an effete establishment can understand the scientific revolution. After half a century of democratic advance the whole process has ground to a halt with a 14th Earl.

Sir Alec Douglas-Home had the good humour to reply that one could say that Harold was the 14th Mr Wilson. Wilson was a political Walter Mitty and I was to discover those fourteen Mr Wilsons in the years to come.

It is very easy in retrospect to downplay the way in which Harold Wilson dominated British politics in the 1960s. *The Economist* was correct when it entitled an editorial during the 1966 election, 'The issue is Wilson'. To someone like myself, outside the inner workings of either Parliament or the Labour Party, Wilson was something of a miracle worker and even a hero.

In Plymouth that afternoon Harold Wilson was for me, and many others, after the death of Gaitskell simply the best leader the Labour Party and the country could possibly have. Before he spoke to that enthusiastic meeting of party workers from all over the West Country in Plymouth Guildhall, I made a eulogizing introductory speech. I can still hear myself quoting President Kennedy:

> We are not here to curse the darkness, but to light a candle that can lead us from the darkness into a safe and sane future. Prime Minister you have lit that candle, may it always burn – welcome to Plymouth.

Even allowing for politician's rhetoric, I did in a way believe it.

My attitudes had been influenced by reading *The Making of the Prime Minister* by Anthony Howard and Richard West, a breathless and somewhat euphoric account of what had led up to the hair's breadth victory in 1964. Modelled on Theodore White's 1960 classic, *The Making of the President*, it suggested parallels with Kennedy. It was why I had used the Kennedy quotation in my welcoming speech and this image had been reinforced by Wilson's own attempt to mirror JFK's 'first hundred days'. Since those days, apart from his skilful handling of the Cuban missile crisis, I have become more and more disenchanted with President Kennedy's actual record both as a politician and as a person. He now seems more style than substance. In those early days too I thought the gritty Yorkshire pipe smoking Harold Wilson was like my favourite US President, peppery old Harry Truman who really did give them hell. But I was soon to realize that Wilson had none of the Truman decisiveness.

Nevertheless it was a heady day for a young candidate to have the Prime Minister coming down to help in one's campaign. It was naïve of me given that Sutton was a highly marginal seat but I did not realize, or perhaps did not want to realize, that I was likely to get into Parliament. I was still deeply ambivalent about whether I wanted to forsake medicine for politics and only Peter Shore's parting remark at the station, 'See you at Westminster', made me recognize that this might be about to happen. When I almost automatically said, 'You're joking', it became very apparent that he meant every word of it.

Peter Shore was right; the general public watching the seventeen months of the 1964-66 Government, starting with a majority of only five and a horrendous balance of payments deficit, estimated at £800 million, did feel that the problems had been handled with great skill and were ready to renew Wilson's mandate. I now know that most of the key economic decisions taken in this period were wrong. Britain was then part of the post-war Bretton Woods system of fixed exchange rates.

While devaluation was possible, it was frowned on, particularly by the Americans, since sterling was a reserve currency. If devaluation was to have been avoided then government spending should have been ruthlessly cut back. Since manifesto commitments and thirteen years of accumulated good intentions in Opposition made this virtually impossible, Labour should have devalued. Reggie Maudling, the outgoing Conservative Chancellor, would almost certainly have done so. Harold Wilson's own resistance to devaluation perhaps stemmed from his experience in 1949 when Hugh Gaitskell had championed devaluation. Moreover, his strange deference to President Johnson meant that we were left defending an unrealistic parity for far too long and we also maintained a level of defence spending greatly in excess of any other European country long after it was clear we could not afford to do so.

In my defence it was easy as a young hospital research worker to be unaware of how serious were Britain's economic problems. Reading Harold Wilson's speeches and broadcasts helped to shield one from reality and a passage from the introduction to Wilson's book *Purpose in Power* gives the flavour of the man and to some extent the time.

> Success or failure depends on the reaction to it of millions, whose co-operation can in our democratic society never be compelled, but whose productive effort, and often whose restraint, and self-discipline, must be forthcoming if our national effort is to succeed. So to purpose, planning and priorities is added a fourth: partnership. This is our socialism: the assertion of social responsibility for our economic welfare and for the welfare of the individual family.

I am afraid that looking back I can only laugh at those words. For purpose, planning, priorities and partnership were all too soon shown to be empty vessels. In reality it was the pursuit of power without purpose. Purpose became drift. Planning collapsed with the National Plan. Priorities were abandoned with deflation, and partnership went down with the trade union reform package. By 1967 my belief in this rhetoric, and my original high hopes were all dashed. The experience of watching Wilson in the House of Commons left me exasperated. My notebook, even by 1 January 1968, shows clearly the development of this disillusion from that first heady meeting in Plymouth.

> Deep down I feel this will be a critical year. I can't help doubting if HW will still be PM by 1969 and for the first time ever I wish fervently that we could get rid of him. Of course it's a long story, the disillusionment. In a way I'd prefer to think it was just the mundane process of getting to know and seeing the way he operates.
>
> Since the enthusiasm of 1966 it is as if an age has passed and I wonder to myself why I ever did it. At this moment, even allowing for flu, I feel *shabby* – no other word really describes it. One cannot be in Parliament and pass through the division lobbies too often with a sick

heart, and know that one is nominally approving of actions and decisions that one doesn't approve of without some of the dirt passing off on oneself.

The actual 1966 General Election campaign in Plymouth was surprisingly uneventful. Despite its potential for damage, defence never became a major political issue in the constituency. The cancellation of the aircraft carrier building programme did not have the expected local effect that I had feared the month before when Christopher Mayhew had resigned as Minister for the Navy. Mayhew was in favour of drastic defence cuts, but argued that there must also be cuts in commitments to match. He did not see how we could maintain a world role in the 1970s, including a presence East of Suez, with an entirely arbitrary defence cost ceiling which had forced the exclusion of new carriers. He was proven to be right. Denis Healey's resistance to cutting our world commitments only staved off the inevitable.

On election day I was carried to a surprisingly large victory on the coat tails of one person – Harold Wilson. I had a majority of 5,222 votes over Ian Fraser, overturning his 1964 majority of 410 over John Dunwoody. There was a large swing to Labour and we won Falmouth and Camborne and Exeter. We had not had three Labour MPs in the West Country since the 1945 Labour landslide. The Labour Government had an overall majority of seventy-five. The seventy-two new MPs in the 1966 intake were mainly young professionals, only fourteen were manual workers. But across the whole Parliamentary Party of 363 MPs there was still a broad cross-section. The first or formative occupation of 109 Labour MPs was a manual trade or work on the railways. Some 186 had attended university and sixty-six had been to public schools. The House of Commons contained eleven doctors, only twenty-seven women and no blacks. Today there are fewer genuine trade unionists in the sense of ever having led and negotiated for their members – there are three black MPs and women are still grossly under-represented, something which will remain until we have proportional representation.

On the Sunday after the election I drove back to London to my house in Limehouse, 78 Narrow Street, on the Thames. It was still virtually a building site. I had bought it for three thousand pounds the year before and I was slowly doing it up using odd-job men and doing a lot myself. The roof was leaking and only one room was habitable where I had to eat and sleep. My plan had been to rebuild the house around me but this would now have to change. As long as I could keep working at both St Thomas's and Parliament I felt I would have enough money to have builders in and increase my mortgage. The next day I turned up at St Thomas's Hospital determined to show that nothing had happened that would stop me continuing as a doctor. I was greeted with a mixture of amazement and humour but even the most Tory of consultants seemed genuinely pleased.

When Parliament reassembled a few days later I walked over the bridge to take the Oath of Allegiance and started to find my way around the maze that is the Palace of Westminster. I suppose I ought to have felt very proud or very humble but I am afraid my memories are more mundane. The hardest thing was to discover where the lavatories were; as if to demonstrate its clublike nature, all the doors are unmarked. I was not eligible for even a desk, let alone a room. All I had was a locker for my papers, not even as large as a golf locker in a club room. The policemen became for me, as for all MPs, guides, guardians and friends and gradually I settled in and got used to the Palace of Westminster as a place of work.

On that first day there was a note on the message board to ring Gerry Reynolds, the MP for Islington North in the Ministry of Defence. Gerry had come down to speak for me in the election and we had got on extremely well. His Private Secretary said that the Minister wanted me to come over and have a cup of tea. After being directed to where the Ministry was, such was my ignorance of Whitehall, and passing through security, I found myself admitted to a large sitting room dominated by a picture of Kitchener. It was almost like looking at the famous poster 'Your country needs you'. Gerry asked me if I would become his Parliamentary Private Secretary. A PPS, I was told, is the Minister's eyes and ears in the House of Commons, where civil servants could not go. The disadvantage was that I would not be able to speak on defence matters because I could not be seen to be critical of the Ministry. Silence seemed to me to present great problems in view of the fact that the Royal Naval Dockyard in Devonport was by far the largest employer in the city. But Gerry explained that I would be able to claim to have the Minister's ear and that becoming a PPS would be considered by the press to be an unusually rapid promotion. I accepted without really knowing what I was letting myself in for. It was, as it turned out, an excellent decision and we became good friends, our friendship ending only with Gerry's tragically early death in 1969.

Gerry Reynolds was then thirty-nine years old. He was a rising star in the Labour Government. He had previously been Local Government Officer in the Labour Party Headquarters at Transport House. What I did not know, though I should have done, was that Gerry had also been George Brown's campaign manager in the leadership election against Harold Wilson and that by becoming his PPS I was aligning myself with the right wing of the Labour Party. Staunchly in favour of Britain becoming a member of the European Community, Gerry was also a federalist, a path along which I was never even tempted to follow. Gerry had a pronounced political profile within the Labour Party with which I was thereafter inevitably identified. As events turned out I had no problem with such an identification but I had taken it on in a rather haphazard way, especially as my main interests then were in social policy

I had just edited a book called *A Unified Health Service*. That foreign and defence policy became my area of expertise was fortuitous.

Gerry was a marvellous person to work with and, though robust in his views, popular with most Labour MPs. He spoke faster than anyone else in the House of Commons, presenting a real problem for the shorthand writers. I learnt from him more about the inner workings of the Labour Party than I could ever have just picked up on my own and this proved invaluable over the years. It was Gerry who proposed my name for the 1963 Club, a dining club for people who were closely identified with Hugh Gaitskell. At my first dinner the conversation kept referring to CDS, and eventually I asked my next door neighbour Jack Diamond, who had also come down to speak for me in the general election, what the initials meant. He was amazed to discover that I had not been involved in the Campaign for Democratic Socialism which Bill Rodgers, who was also a member of the club, had brilliantly masterminded. The Campaign had been a crucial element in swinging the votes in the 1961 Conference to defeat the unilateralist nuclear defence motion which had been passed the previous year. Members of the 1963 Club included Tony Crosland, Roy Jenkins, Dick Taverne, Chris Mayhew, Woodrow Wyatt and Dick Mabon. David Marquand joined with me and though he was also a new MP he had had a long association with CDS and knew most of the other members of the club.

Thus within months of becoming a Member of Parliament, I was pitched into the inner circle of people who, at their mildest, were highly suspicious of Harold Wilson, and at their strongest, loathed his guts. I was totally ignorant of all the tensions and bitterness of the past, much of which stemmed from the Bevanite period and was reinforced in 1960 when Wilson had challenged Gaitskell for the leadership. Slowly as I read more about the Bevan-Gaitskell clash and talked to people who were involved in the controversies, I began to understand why Harold Wilson was not quite the knight in shining armour that I had allowed myself to believe in. I also became aware of the inner tensions within the 1963 Club. While Roy Jenkins, Jack Diamond and Gerry Reynolds had staunchly supported George Brown in the leadership election, Tony Crosland had supported Jim Callaghan. Even during our dinners one could sense the intense competition between Roy Jenkins and Tony Crosland. The two were longstanding friends since before the war at Oxford. Tony had become close to Roy's parents while a student. Both had been in the Army during the war. Roy had become an MP first, in 1948, and pursued his interest in biography by writing a book on Clement Attlee for whom his father, Arthur Jenkins, had been Parliamentary Private Secretary. Tony had come into the House of Commons in 1950. His main interest was economics and in 1956 when he was out of the House of Commons, he had written *The Future of Socialism*, a book which had a profound influence on me and many of my generation.

The dinners themselves and the friendships that were opened up were a revelation. For a young backbencher, listening as we went round the table, each contributing to the discussion, it was fascinating, particularly hearing Tony and Roy talk, often indiscreetly, about what was going on in Cabinet. It is impossible to exaggerate how ignorant and innocent I was about so much of the internal politics of the Labour Party.

My routine working day was to go to St Thomas's and work in the medical unit laboratory from nine in the morning through lunch until Prime Minister's Questions at 3.15 p.m. or the opening of interesting debates. If I was on a Committee sitting in the morning, I would have lunch at a big table seating seven, in the Labour end of the Members' dining room. Anyone would sit there – Charlie Pannell, the Leeds MP, and Bob Mellish from Bermondsey, were regulars full of earthy common sense; Jim Callaghan and on occasions Harold Wilson might join us. There was always a friendly atmosphere and I learnt much about politics round that table. When the SDP was formed and we were no longer welcome, I missed the camaraderie and the House became a much lonelier place.

I began quickly to learn about parliamentary procedure as Gerry Reynolds was guiding legislation on the Territorial Army through the House of Commons and I had to be on the Committee with him while the Bill was examined line by line. My actual responsibilities as PPS were, however, pretty minimal. I had to see that Gerry was paired but that presented little problem since his Tory pair never wanted to vote if there was the slightest chance of avoiding being in the House.

The first big parliamentary occasion was on 3 May when Jim Callaghan, as Chancellor of the Exchequer, introduced his first post-election budget. I described the scene in my notebook:

> Everything new, the occasion exciting, waiting for something which one felt would be unpleasant. All through the election one had muttered small caveats about the economy, it seemed certain we would have to have a few relatively tough measures. Suddenly there was Jim, confident as always at the despatch box, a far bigger man than one ever realizes, tall, long thin legs and buttocks, ugly nose but otherwise someone of presence. Confidently he produced, like a conjurer, SET, the Selective Employment Tax, to take effect in September and everyone cheered. Only Iain Macleod said it was not deflationary enough. Only he warned. I breathed a sigh of relief and forgot about everything except for regional variations in SET and brushed aside the criticism that it had all been thought up in a few weeks, arguing that all taxes had teething troubles.

It was pretty clear by then that the voluntary incomes policy was not working. It was a budget born of the creative tension between the new Department of Economic Affairs and the Treasury. George Brown had argued for growth as First Secretary of State and zealously guarded his incomes policy 'baby'. The Treasury was more pessimistic and wanted deflation immediately. They had had to make do with deflation in the autumn. That postponement turned out to be a fatal error.

On 16 May I made my maiden speech on the Second Reading of the Industrial Development Bill. I cannot recall being very nervous but I had written out large chunks of my speech. It was certainly not a great oratorical occasion. I referred to the radical spirit which had run through Plymouth for generations, how the city had welcomed the Reform Act with peals of bells, and paid tribute to a family which had added lustre to that radical tradition.

> Isaac Foot fought Sutton on many occasions. He brought up his family within the Division bell and we on this side of the House are grateful for the contribution which three members of his family have made to this party, from Michael who represented Devonport with fiery independence, to Hugh for his international contributions to this country, and to Dingle for his legalistic skill. But one brother remains in Plymouth and serves the city, and for this, too, the citizens are grateful. I hope, in the years to come, in some measure to represent a radical tradition in this House.

Michael Foot who had come in to listen to my speech sent me a generous note of congratulations which finished with 'Up Argyle!' As the years passed, support for Plymouth Argyle Football Club was one of the few issues on which we were in total agreement.

Around this time the seamen's strike started. This showdown with the National Union of Seamen caused some strain in my relations with the small Plymouth branch since I supported the Government line and the declaration of a state of emergency. Wilson's allegations that the strike committee was under Communist influence led by 'a tightly knit group of politically motivated men', heightened the drama and his words inflamed the Left outside as well as inside the Labour Party. The strike ended on 1 July, but since that was also the same day as the Steel Nationalization Bill was published, international confidence was not restored. When Frank Cousins then resigned as Minister of Technology in order to fight the imposition of an incomes policy, international bankers, or as Labour preferred to call them 'the gnomes of Zurich', began to get restless. On 13 July I was present in the House of Commons when Wilson foolishly announced that steps were about to be taken to reduce demand at home and cut back spending overseas. Far from reassuring world opinion, this was construed as meaning that a devaluation was imminent. A dramatic run on the pound developed. By now in Parliament I and other new Labour MPs were beginning to realize that the Government we had been voted in to support was facing a real crisis.

For the first time the Cabinet actually discussed devaluation. George Brown argued the case in favour and was supported by Roy Jenkins and Tony Crosland. They stressed that, with demand down, if the pound was devalued, the British economy would have the chance of breaking out of the stop-go cycle with improved export orders. George Brown also mentioned that Pompidou, the French Prime Minister, had said the devaluation was a necessary prerequisite if Britain was to enter the Common Market. Harold Wilson was still adamantly opposed to devaluation and at one time said if George wanted to resign on the issue, that was fine by him. Wilson invoked the Anglo-American Alliance, saying that devaluation would bring trouble to the dollar and threaten the whole monetary system. He was supported by Denis Healey and Michael Stewart. Jim Callaghan wobbled. My notebook has Peter Jay claiming that on 11 July Jim Callaghan told George Brown that he too wished to devalue and that he said it again on the Sunday while the Prime Minister was in Moscow, though he was then dissuaded by Wilson. The respective memoirs of the key participants, Harold, Jim and George, throw surprisingly little light on what exactly happened over those few days. The chaos inside the Government machine was, however, pretty clear to see, especially when Treasury officials initially announced that cigarettes were going up by five pence, then had to apologize, saying that was on yesterday's list. The fifty pound travel allowance was fixed by Jim Callaghan, after inspecting a sample of travel brochures. It was not too surprising that, even to its supporters, the Government looked incompetent and indecisive.

I watched all this unfold with horror and I listened in a state of shock in the House on 20 July as Harold Wilson announced a deflationary package which clearly amounted to a massive stop to the economy. We were back in the very stop-go cycle which I, along with all other Labour MPs, had attacked the Conservatives for inflicting on the country.

A six month standstill on wages and dividends was to be followed by another period of restraint and a twelve month price freeze. Iain Macleod summed it all up when he said later of those July measures:

> The truth about this Parliament is that it died three months after the last general election, when it was clear that they were elected on a false prospectus. And four years is a terrible time to wait for a burial service, while the corpse lies cold in the lobbies of Westminster.

Iain Macleod was the most attractive senior Conservative politician facing me across the Chamber. I was not put off by the quip that 'he was too clever by half'. I already respected him for what I knew of his tenure as Minister of Health and also as Secretary of State for the Colonies. Tough on the trade unions, as he showed over the London bus strike, and a believer in incentives, he was liberal in outlook and extremely principled over race. But what I discovered, watching him as Shadow Chancellor, was that he had a genuine interest and concern about unemployment and in particular shared my interest in child poverty. I worked with him on a new charity called Crisis at Christmas, addressing a candlelit vigil off the back of a lorry one evening at Hyde Park. It was strangely disconcerting to discover this degree of commitment and concern in a Conservative, who was no closet egalitarian. He would have been an effective, possibly the most outstanding, post-war Chancellor, had he not died in 1970, within a month of achieving the office. He was superbly well-equipped, both in parliamentary skill and intellectual grasp, to master the Treasury as it has never been mastered in my time in Parliament. Nigel Lawson was the Chancellor intellectually able to dominate the Treasury. Roy Jenkins was the best Chancellor in the House of Commons but conventional in policy. The only Chancellor to leave behind a strong and thriving economic legacy was strangely enough Geoffrey Howe. Perhaps history will be kinder to his record than his contemporaries, who could never forgive him for three and a half million unemployed, a million of which many felt was unnecessarily imposed.

The night after Wilson's statement in the House of Commons, every Labour MP seemed to be pacing the corridors or sitting in the tea room. Ministers who had never talked to me before suddenly stopped for a chat in the corridor. 'Has George resigned?' 'Anything on the tapes?' The whole cliff-hanging episode was a farce, with George Brown's resignation announced over the BBC and then contradicted. A year later George Brown admitted to David Marquand and me that he wished he had gone then. With hindsight he speculated that if he had, things might have been very different. I wonder whether they would. He claimed that he had been influenced to stay by the 100 backbench MPs, who had signed a round robin urging him to stay. I rather doubt this view, though obviously as an emotional man he would have been affected by this sign of broad-based support. The presence of Bert Bowden, the Chief Whip, at the late-night No. 10 Downing Street meeting was crucial, for Bert was as straight a politician as one can find, a decent, honourable man who tapped directly into George's own sense of loyalty to the Party. His appeal not to resign, which from Harold Wilson's mouth had had little effect, worked. Eventually George, helped or hindered by Harold's brandy and with Bert beside him, announced emotionally on the pavement outside No. 10 that he was staying.

The tolerance of the public to 'Brother George' throughout this period owed a lot to his being seen as a character with much the same vices and weaknesses as most of us recognize in ourselves or someone close to us. But the nonconformist voters in the Celtic fringe were not as amused and he was never very popular in my constituency. George's opposition to the July measures embarrassed the Left for they thought they had a monopoly of conscience. That night I saw for the first time the old relics of the back handed in-fighting that went on at the height of the Bevanite crisis. But it was not just the conventional Left who poured out the filth on George, other people were going around with the Whips, eroding his position. There were dark hints about 'things which we can't say but if you only knew'. If these were just a reference to George's drinking habits, there can have been no MP who was not well aware of his weakness. Even after one glass of sherry he could appear tight.

Indeed, George Brown did not even need alcohol to appear drunk, as a story told to me by one of his detectives well illustrates. His Special Branch protection team had driven him back to the Foreign Secretary's house in Carlton Gardens and George had jumped out of the car and told them not to wait since he knew his wife Sophie was in the flat. George, in high spirits, proceeded to play 'God Save the Queen' on the door bell. Sophie, thinking he had had too much to drink again, refused over the intercom to open the door. The detectives, disappearing down the street, fortunately looked back and saw George out in the road, gesticulating wildly. They backed the car up and George explained what had happened. He then asked his detective to speak to his wife on the intercom which he did, assuring Sophie Brown that he had been with George all day and that he had not had a drop of alcohol to drink. So Sophie agreed to open the door and the detectives drove off. If even his own wife could not tell whether George was drunk or not, it was far harder for us. The truth was that George's normal ebullience and manic mood swings were exacerbated but not always triggered by alcohol.

It was inevitable that George Brown would have to leave the Department of Economic Affairs after the July 1966 deflation but the decision to appoint him Foreign Secretary was highly significant for it meant that Wilson was ready to join the Common Market. George's longstanding enthusiasm for membership ensured that the balance of opinion in the Cabinet would shift decisively in favour of applying to join. Supported by Roy Jenkins, Tony Crosland and Ray Gunter, George Brown proceeded to push toward the Common Market with gusto. In doing so, he made light of the very serious reservations which the French had about Britain's membership. In May 1967 the House of Commons debated the issue and the Government had a majority of 426 for what George Brown called 'a clear, clean and uncluttered application'. In view of the equivalent vote in 1971 when sixty-nine of us Labour MPs voted with the Conservative Government it is worth noting that few Labour MPs thought it disreputable then, in 1967, to be accompanied into the division lobby by most Conservative MPs.

However, a few days later, General de Gaulle described the obstacles to British entry as 'formidable' and asserted that Britain had to undertake a 'deep economic and political transformation' before membership would be possible, even though, he said, there had 'never been any question of a veto'. Wilson described the French position as 'Yes, but'. It was clear to most of us that the French 'but' had not been overcome. Yet George Brown had chalked up a major achievement – the Labour Party, after five years of deep scepticism about the Common Market, was now

formally committed to join. Somewhat naïvely I believed that the matter
was now resolved and that the arguments in the Party over the principle
of entry would never recur. How wrong I was.

The Common Market represented a real issue within the Labour Party
because membership carried with it an explicit, not just implicit, acceptance of the market economy. I never had any hang-ups about accepting a
market economy. Competition meant in most cases more choice and from
an early stage I wanted membership of the EEC. It just seemed the
natural state of affairs for me. For those on the Left in the Labour Party
who did not accept the need for competition, profits and the dominance
of the market economy, the EEC did represent a threat to implementing
their form of socialism. This fight over accepting market economics had
to be faced up to and those like Wilson who tried to avoid or circumvent
the fight in the 1960s and again in the 1970s laid the foundation for the
far more divisive fight in the 1980s. In 1971, sixty-nine of us Labour
MPs chose the market economy as well as the European Community.
Labour rejection of the European Community in 1980 became the trigger
for the creation of the SDP and our emphasis on the social market as
our contribution to Margaret Thatcher's market orientated counter-
revolution.

Harold Wilson's character is too complex to allow simple analysis. I
have never been able to write or speak about him without checking
myself halfway through, to toughen my criticism if I have been speaking
favourably of him or to soften what I have been saying if I have been
critical. The pendulum of opinion about him from political commentators
as well as that of the public has swung wildly, both while he was actively
engaged in politics and even when in retirement. Another notebook entry
in 1968 reads:

> The more I see of HW the more I feel we are seeing the archetypal
> meritocrat.
> > Clever
> > Fabulous memory
> > Articulate
>
> Not a shit, he *feels*, mainly over things like South Africa. Yet very
> conservative on all Home Office issues . . . His weaknesses are:
> 1)–Indecision.
> 2)–Incurable optimism and conceit in his own ability to be Mr Fixit.
> 3)–To surround himself with deadbeats, sycophants etc. yet at the
> same time he shows courage and foresight in some of his Cabinet ap-
> pointments.
> 4)–To play things off the cuff.
> 5)–To be congenitally, it appears, incapable of believing that he has
> made or can make a mistake.

This sounds a formidable list of weaknesses for any PM to possess
yet it would be absurd to deny his attributes. For instance his ability to
sense issues that are important to the Party. His sense of party

management is first class . . . He can work very hard and with almost total recall of information he can keep immensely well-informed. This has to be offset against a tendency to be bogged down by detail e.g. aluminium smelters and minute day-to-day news management, foibles almost endearing until they end up in the D-notice debacle.

Historians will take some time to put Harold Wilson's contribution to British politics in the 1960s and 1970s in its proper perspective. He was, though I only attended Cabinet subcommittees under him, a good chairman of committees. His presidential period of dominance in the Cabinet lasted for less than two years. After July 1966 he was only *primus inter pares* and at times not even that. He had cronies but he did not pack his Cabinet with them, keeping them to his Kitchen Cabinet. A virtue, frequently underestimated, was his courage and at times he could show an insouciance bordering on recklessness when his policies were under attack. He went right to the cliff edge over trade union reform and only abandoned 'In Place of Strife' when he had been disowned by the entire Cabinet, with only Barbara Castle staying loyal.

He suffered badly from the politician's illness – press paranoia. But he was also paranoid about his colleagues. Admittedly sometimes this had some justification for all the senior politicians around him were manoeuvring for advantage and he never had a major figure totally loyal to him. Everyone exhibits some traits of paranoia but for Wilson this characteristic became ever more overt. It debilitated his judgement and his performance. At one time he seemed obsessed about being bugged in No. 10 and his relationship with the Secret Service was a touchy and difficult one. Some say that the suspicious side of his nature was fed by Marcia Williams, his political secretary, who later became Lady Falkender. That she fought to prevent Wilson being taken over by the civil service is in no doubt. In my few dealings with her, I always found her a highly political, kind and efficient person and in a sense she was right to be concerned about the effect of the civil service on Wilson. He had been a civil servant during the war and was an instinctive bureaucrat. She sensed that unless the Labour Party view was championed by someone very close to him, its interests would go by default.

Personally I have cause to be grateful for he promoted me three times in his governments and without this I would never have had the political good fortune to become Foreign Secretary under Jim Callaghan. Yet no other politician has driven me closer to despair about the practice of politics, perhaps because I was young and he promised so much and achieved so little.

Whereas Harold Wilson was paranoid, George Brown was deeply emotional. Yet George Brown's instincts as a politician made me forgive his vices as a Minister. I am very glad I never had to work for him. In the Foreign Office even his exceptional private secretaries, normally people who support the most controversial holder of the office, could not abide him. Stories involving George at the Foreign Office abound, most of them considerably garnished and some probably apocryphal. One such story was that at a reception abroad, when George was slightly less than sober, the band started to play some music and he approached a guest wearing a beautiful purple dress and requested the pleasure of a dance. He received a polite but firm refusal. He persisted. 'No', said his intended partner, 'for two reasons: the first is that this is the National Anthem. The second is that I am the Bishop of Montevideo!'

Iain Macleod, at the Conservative Party Conference that year, said, 'There is a national society for not being beastly to George Brown, and I pay my dues like anyone else. And now that he is Foreign Secretary, I only hope [pause] I only hope!' He was not the only one. George Brown could be a bully and a braggart. But he also had a sharp intellect with a mind that had the capacity to cut through waffle and focus on the core of a problem. He had a deep affection for Britain and the courage to speak his mind. He showed this when he said, 'May God forgive you' to Bulganin and Khruschev on their visit to London as they were talking cant while being entertained by the Labour Party in the House of Commons. His instinctively decent values owed a lot to his Christian beliefs and when the history of Britain's membership of the European Community can be properly assessed there will have to be a special place for his passionate advocacy. His eventual resignation as Foreign Secretary in humiliating circumstances was sad but by then inevitable. In fairness, Harold Wilson showed more patience over George's conduct than was probably wise for maintaining the respect of the public in his Government. But it was a measure of George's following in the Labour Party that he could not easily be sacked and had to be allowed to destroy himself politically.

George Brown remained an interesting person. He came to see me in 1978 before going to Iran in an attempt to influence the Shah and his analysis of the situation was clear and concise. He was financially helped in those later years by the textile industrialist Sir David Alliance in an act of unselfish generosity. Lunches with George Brown at the RAC towards the end of his life when he supported the SDP were always interesting. He was, in the words of Lord Ted Willis in his funeral address, 'a steam engine of a man'.

In those difficult times when economics dominated politics and financial stringency limited Parliament's initiatives, one of the things a young Labour MP like me could do was to support enthusiastically legislation for social reforms that cost little but could have a considerable beneficial effect for individuals. Two Private Member's Bills, one legislating on abortion and the other on homosexuality, were particularly worthwhile and though they were later to be glibly dismissed as contributing to a so-called 'permissive society', they were in fact long overdue.

The case for reform of the abortion law had deep roots going back to before the war when a consultant at St Mary's Hospital Paddington, Alex Bourne, invited prosecution in order to expose the restriction of the law. It also had considerable cross-party support including Dame Joan Vickers, my constituency neighbour as MP for Devonport. Her support helped me when dealing with the local Plymouth anti-abortion campaign for I could argue that it was a cross-party issue.

I also supported David Steel's 'Medical Termination of Pregnancy Bill' and on its Second Reading I tried to explain some of the complex medical aspects that underlie the legislation.

> This is an extremely difficult issue. People who relate abortion to tonsillectomy are doing their cause a great disservice. This is a very different issue. The whole reproductive cycle of a woman is intimately linked with her psyche. We know that a woman is susceptible to depression at times of pregnancy, at times of the menopause and at times of menstruation. Interfering with a natural course of pregnancy is something which a doctor does only with great care, knowing full well that he is doing something which could have adverse effects ... We should think of the doctor who is faced with the problem of a woman with seven children who tells him that she shares her bed with her husband and two children, with perhaps two other children living and sleeping in the same room. This sort of thing still occurs in this country, and we must face it.

I had seen such overcrowding in Lambeth. I had experienced in the Welfare Clinic, near the Royal Waterloo Hospital, the agonies that women felt finding themselves pregnant again while living in such appalling conditions. It was not that the child itself was unwanted, it was the predictable consequences of having that child on the other children in the family and on their marriage that made them want an abortion. I later went on to serve on the Committee of the Bill and landed myself in my first political controversy in the national newspapers when I said:

> Only a short distance away I have coached patients to say to the doctor, when asking for a termination, that they are desperate and are thinking of suicide, because I know that doctors will not terminate pregnancy on social grounds. I have seen doctors themselves encourage patients to widen their case – because they do not feel that social grounds are of themselves sufficient.

I was attacked by Mrs Jill Knight, a Conservative MP on the Committee, for directing women to lie and to cheat. I had to clarify my statement for I had never intended to imply that patients should say anything other than what they felt to be true but it served to highlight their dilemma. If they talked only about social factors this damaged their chances of having an abortion under the old legislation. They had to talk about any suicidal feelings they had and ignore the effects on their family.

The other controversial Private Member's Bill I supported was Leo

Abse's to reform the law on homosexuality. This was again legislation
that had long been asked for by a broad section of opinion following the
recommendation of the Wolfenden Report. I made a speech supporting
the Bill on Second Reading in the full knowledge that in a naval port,
where homosexual behaviour was not uncommon, it was strongly disliked.
My stance was bound to upset some of my constituents. But as a
psychiatric registrar I had been appalled by the fear of blackmail under
which many homosexuals then lived. Within the privacy of their own
homes I felt they had the right to behave as they wished provided they
were over twenty-one. Since then society has been able to move on and
systematically try to remove the undoubted discrimination which exists
against homosexuals in jobs and over housing. Generally the public mood
has become more understanding and less censorious since that legislation
was passed.

The Child Poverty Action Group was another area in which I was
involved and I had instituted a separate debate on child poverty just
before the Christmas recess in 1966. I have always believed that the
mother needs a direct payment for help in bringing up children and I
have campaigned for generous Child Benefit through all my years in the
House of Commons. It gave me great pleasure when John Major's
government in 1991 reversed Conservative policy under Margaret
Thatcher and agreed to inflation-proof Child Benefit. In this way perhaps
it will become like pensions, part of the common ground of politics in the
1990s.

All this activity on social questions which were not popular with
everyone led to a trenchant exchange in my constituency General Management Committee. An older engine driver and stalwart in ASLEF got up
after hearing my parliamentary report and said, 'David, I accept that
you're all in favour of abortion and that you support family allowances
for unmarried mothers but I do draw the line at buggery.' He was rather
upset when the entire committee burst into uncontrollable laughter.
They were decent, tolerant people in my constituency Labour Party and
they never tried to inhibit me from exercising my judgement on such
questions even if on occasions they felt the backlash in Plymouth pubs or
even the Labour club.

The widespread disillusionment that stemmed from the July 1966
deflationary measures was debilitating for the entire Labour Party. It
haunted us as candidates still in the 1970 General Election and
contributed to our defeat. It could never be, for us young idealists, 'glad
confident morning again'. The general public knew we had adopted
wholesale the very economic measures that we ourselves had helped them
to identify as Tory. Labour could not avoid paying a heavy electoral
price. Worse, a few of us young iconoclastic MPs knew the measures
were doomed to fail from the start. By the time the forced devaluation of
the pound came in November 1967 we were part of a demoralized

Parliamentary Party where Harold Wilson was derided privately by both the Left and the Right wings of the Party.

It was not easy for an MP like me, with no economic expertise, to advocate devaluation prior to its happening in 1967. When we did, we were charged with irresponsibility for selling the pound short or were accused of being out-of-touch middle-class academics. We devaluationists on the Right formed informally what we called the 'Snakes and Alligators', a very loose grouping with MPs like Eric Heffer and others on the Left. It was also the time when I began to build important friendships with three MPs: David Marquand, John Mackintosh and Jack Ashley.

My political guru was Tony Crosland who used to say that he was completely excluded from any true economic discussion, and that it was just Jim and Harold fixing things between them. Tony was Jim Callaghan's choice to succeed him as Chancellor and he was bitterly disappointed when Roy Jenkins was chosen by Wilson instead. To some extent one has to restrict discussion on as sensitive a subject as devaluation but devaluation became unmentionable. For Wilson defence of the pound was a symbol of patriotic fervour. To advocate devaluation was to him the equivalent of hauling down the flag.

All this time I was closer to Tony Crosland and saw more of him than I did of Roy Jenkins. One reason was that I found he was more interested in discussing serious policies. He, like Roy, gossiped but his gossip was funnier and mostly about the Labour Party, whereas Roy's gossip was more about personalities and life outside politics – interesting, but not as relevant. Both were very ambitious. Tony was jealous of Roy and vice versa. Their friendship had not been helped when Roy had let everyone know that he had turned down Wilson's offer to go to Education before it was taken up by Tony. Tony was a better choice for Education, not because Roy's children were going through private schooling – after all, so were Harold Wilson's – but because Tony was more interested in education. Both in practice would have followed education policies pretty similar to Edward Boyle, the former Conservative Education Minister. Tony refused to impose comprehensive schooling, adopting an evolutionary approach to its introduction. I was at the time lobbying Tony, against the advice of his civil servants, to give Plymouth a polytechnic. Fortunately he did and it has since become a great success. Tony was also starting to rethink his earlier optimism about automatic economic growth. Growth was not capable of funding the public expenditure levels he felt were essential and he recognized that we would have to develop greater public acceptance of higher taxes to achieve greater equality even in times of low growth.

In June 1967 Tony had asked David Marquand and me to his room to help him write a speech about an alternative economic strategy and I found Shirley Williams there as well. It was the first real conversation we had ever been involved in together. She had come into the House of

Commons in 1964 and our paths had never crossed. She made a lively contribution and the issue we were discussing was whether to go on preaching the hitherto accepted wisdom, namely that direct taxes were fairer than indirect taxes. For the first time I began to question whether Value Added Tax might be a more acceptable way of raising revenue and since then I have steadily moved towards wanting an Expenditure Tax which would encourage saving and not reduce the incentive to earn more.

David Marquand, John Mackintosh and I wrote a fifteen-page pamphlet which was published by *Socialist Commentary*, to coincide with that year's Party Conference. We called it *Change Gear* and, for ambitious backbenchers, the pamphlet represented a considerable risk, being a comprehensive rebuttal of most of Government policy.

By the autumn of 1967 the Government had at long last accepted that we could not continue with military bases east of Suez. General de Gaulle was delaying the whole question of opening negotiations over British membership of the Common Market. Sterling was weak and the Government was still resisting the devaluation which we had all three publicly advocated. In our pamphlet we tried to stress positive new policies and directions. We committed ourselves to Value Added Tax as part of joining the Common Market; higher social expenditure but with selectivity in social services through negative income tax and some charging; positive discrimination on race; devolution for Scotland and Wales, regional government in England; and the televising of Parliament. The pamphlet was featured in the *Observer* and generated a fair amount of press comment as it seemed to help fill a widely perceived intellectual vacuum. It was, however, comprehensively rubbished by the No. 10 Press Office and started to feed their paranoia that we were malcontents, using our charm on the *Observer* political correspondent, Nora Beloff, to promote adverse publicity and plot the downfall of the Prime Minister.

David Marquand was MP for Ashfield in Nottingham. His immense skill is with words and he writes beautifully though painstakingly. A gentle and thoughtful person, he is now strongly critical of me but somehow it never hurts because I feel he is still a friend. He left Parliament in 1967 to join Roy Jenkins in Europe. It was in effect a non-job and he soon wisely left to become a professor at Salford University. He nearly joined the Liberals in late 1979 but David Steel claims he dissuaded him. He was then a firm supporter of the creation of the SDP and soon became, or perhaps always was, a convinced believer in merging with the Liberals. Now a Liberal Democrat and a Euro-Federalist, he still writes feelingly about social democracy. His official biography of Ramsay MacDonald is unmatched and his recent book is the nearest we have to a contemporary Crosland. He has, however, even less understanding of what drives a market economy than Tony Crosland did and I find his economic writing as unrealistically warm and comfortable as his own personality.

John Mackintosh was the MP for Berwick and East Lothian. He died of a heart tumour in 1978 at the age of fifty-eight. It was a sad commentary on the practice of our modern politics that he never held even the most junior government office. Talent is not always rewarded in politics for, as Winston Churchill said, 'The House of Commons is not a race on the flat – it is a steeplechase.' Yet John was a steeplechaser. He was not just the ablest but also the best speaker by far of our 1966 intake of MPs. His book *The British Cabinet* has become a classic. His prodigious capacity for work meant that besides his constituency duties, over which he was very conscientious, he was also able to be Professor of Politics at Edinburgh as well as joint editor of the *Political Quarterly*, a columnist in the *Scotsman* and a frequent broadcaster. He taught me a great deal, particularly about political history which my medical training had virtually excluded. It was my fault that we drifted apart when I was in government because I felt, guiltily, that he should have been in government, not me. In those early years he was my closest political friend and I tried at his memorial meeting, when Foreign Secretary, to say why he meant so much to me and to others.

> What is the word that comes to mind – I keep trying both to reject it and use it – it was recklessness that sums up John. It was not just adventurousness, it was not just boldness, courage. He was reckless, deliciously reckless, lovingly reckless. He knew the risks, he calculated the risks, and he used his intellect to the full. John was a thoughtful, intellectual man who was prepared to take a risk, prepared to gamble, and I hope our political system and our country have still got a place for that sort of person. He was a whole man, he was a rounded man, he was a solid friend.

I ended by quoting from T.S. Eliot's 'The Hollow Men'.

Our pamphlet had some effect but the economic storm clouds were gathering. The dockers in London and Liverpool were out on strike over the Government's de-casualization scheme. Jack Dash, the small Communist docker from the East End, was a public figure. Vital exports were stuck in the docks. The Arab-Israeli Six Day War meant that the Suez Canal was still blocked so the balance of trade was bound to be severely distorted. On top of all that, in November there was much talk about Britain being about to be granted a new international loan. The October trade figures showed a trade gap of £107 million, the highest in our history. Speculation followed and the Bank of England lost as much as £90 million in one day defending the £1/$2.80 parity.

Robert Sheldon, a Labour MP who had long argued for devaluation, put down a Private Notice Question to ask the Prime Minister to make a statement on the rumour that a £1,000 million loan was being negotiated with foreign banks. None of us knew that the Cabinet had that morning agreed to devalue by 14.3 per cent and also accept a consequential deflationary package. Representation was made by the Government to the Speaker, Dr Horace King, to disallow the question. Not having been told about the Cabinet's devaluation decision, he refused. I was in the House when Jim Callaghan rose and declined to say much, relying on, 'It would clearly be wrong for the Government either to confirm or to deny a press rumour of this kind.' Iain Macleod made a helpful intervention but Jim Callaghan was in an impossible position and when he sat down there was immediate and massive selling of sterling. The Bank of England was the only one buying sterling and it could not stop the biggest ever run on the pound. On Saturday 18 November at 9.30 in the evening, devaluation was announced and the new sterling exchange rate against the dollar was set at $2.40 to the pound. The bank rate went to 8 per cent.

Harold Wilson then went on television and made probably the biggest political mistake of his life when trying to explain what devaluation meant. 'It does not, of course, mean that the pound here in Britain, in your pocket or purse or in your bank, has been devalued.' It was left to Lord Cromer, the former Governor of the Bank of England, who intensely disliked Wilson, to say that the Prime Minister was talking nonsense and that the pound in the pocket as well as in savings had been reduced by two shillings and ten pence. The Conservative Party never allowed Wilson to forget his words. There was a very angry debate in the House of Commons and Wilson, in his opening speech, sounded to me like a ferret in a sack. John Boyd-Carpenter, from the Tory benches, said what I privately thought, 'When he is in a corner with a thoroughly bad case he lashes out with personally offensive references, wholly irrelevant historical allusions and does everything to distract attention from the main issue.' Summing up, Jim Callaghan made a more sombre and dignified speech and few of us doubted when he sat down that it would not be long before he ceased to be Chancellor. Because of this he was not given a hard time: the House has a sense of these occasions. In fact he had sent a letter of resignation to Wilson before devaluation was announced and had agreed to stay on for only a few days.

Eleven days after devaluation Jim Callaghan swapped places with Roy Jenkins, Jim becoming Home Secretary and Roy Chancellor of the Exchequer. It was the correct decision to have a new Chancellor and probably to choose Roy rather than Tony Crosland. The Government lacked authority and credibility and only a new Chancellor could restore confidence. Wilson was himself totally discredited and the Government was still having a terrible press. By then the initial misplaced euphoria among many Labour MPs had been replaced by the realization that we were going to be very lucky, despite our massive majority, to win the next election. Dick Crossman wrote in his diary on 31 December 1967, 'This Government has failed more abysmally than any Government since 1931.' At that time Dick was going through one of his loyalist phases and rallying round Harold Wilson, so his private judgement was all the more interesting. My notebook in January 1968, reads:

The whole thing is so depressing but next time my loyalty will not carry me through. I will not again be privy to sordid, squalid manoeuvring for if one does, then our political system will be debased. The newspapers exaggerate but there is truth and substance to all too many of the charges.

My New Year message to my constituents at the start of 1968 was also pretty blunt:

I do not hide that mistakes have been made by the Government I support. I think it is humbug to pretend otherwise. But devaluation offers the prospect of sustained economic recovery.

Over the previous year I had campaigned vigorously for devaluation, had broken my self-imposed public silence in the budget debate earlier in the year and with others been afterwards accused by Jim Callaghan of losing around £35 million across the exchange rates, because of our so-called irresponsibility. David Marquand was attacked for losing rather more millions than I and this was, I used to joke, a pretty accurate reflection of the respective weight of our economic judgements. In May we had sent together a detailed ten-page memorandum to Harold Wilson, arguing the case for devaluation and had received a pretty unsatisfactory reply. The arguments had been specifically phrased to appeal to Wilson, so we conceded his earlier arguments against devaluation.

In 1969 Sir William Armstrong, who had been Permanent Under-Secretary at the Treasury in 1967, told me informally at a lobby lunch that my joint memorandum with David had been used by the Treasury officials who had to draft a reply for No. 10, as the vehicle and excuse for reopening the arguments for and against devaluation. Devaluation had been a strictly forbidden subject in any official documents for over a year. The civil service system which ensures that letters from the Prime Minister to MPs are handled by a department with the greatest care and at a high level has some real value on such occasions. The process of answering an MP's query can act as the focus for a major policy reassessment. In retrospect, it appeared that our memorandum had achieved rather more than we could have judged from the rather defensive reply.

In those days I was far too cavalier about the effect of public expenditure on inflation, though, with Jack Ashley in particular, we were on the side of those who wanted a permanent incomes policy. David Marquand and I had already, in March, helped draft a speech for Tony Crosland, which he delivered in Norwich, asking for the maintenance of higher levels of public expenditure and reacting against the constant plea from the then Chancellor, Jim Callaghan, to reduce public expenditure further so as to allow people, many of whom were disaffected Labour voters, to experience what he called the 'jingle in the pocket'.

After devaluation, public expenditure had to be further cut. The strength of Roy Jenkins's opposition as the new Chancellor to the defence commitments and foreign exchange spending in the Far East and the Persian Gulf only became apparent in the January 1968 Cabinet meetings on public expenditure. In December 1967, just before the Christmas recess, I went with David Marquand to Roy Jenkins's room at the Treasury to discuss the impending cuts in public expenditure which we had all been warned to expect as a consequence of devaluation. My own knowledge of Roy was, at that time, limited – friendly, but certainly not intimate – the result of the odd conversation in the smoking room and his presence at the monthly 1963 Club dinners. David Marquand knew Roy far better than I, going back through their involvement in the Campaign for Democratic Socialism – when I was a busy medical student. It was David who, no doubt, felt most at ease during our conversation. Roy revealed to us in that meeting that he was determined to achieve the cancellation of the F-111 aircraft which he clearly saw not only as too expensive, but also as a symbol of the world-wide defence strategy and of the East of Suez presence and commitment that he wanted to reverse.

It was also interesting that, although the EEC 1967 application had already been rejected by de Gaulle in his 27 November press conference, for Roy Europe was still our prime area of national interest. Listening to him talking, remarkably frankly, about the short-term expenditure cuts, one sensed a much deeper philosophical approach, for he started by analysing the long-term objectives and then putting together the individual expenditure savings, within the long-term framework. It was an approach which the Government hitherto had so singularly lacked. Yet he was perhaps too cautious for my liking – he did not have, like Tony Crosland, a passionate and overriding commitment to redistributing income and opportunities more widely. But looking back I have little doubt that Roy's attitude to public expenditure was correct and if Tony had been Chancellor he would have had to reduce his enthusiasm for public spending.

Roy Jenkins was obviously most worried about the political consequences of postponing the school-leaving age and reducing the overseas aid budget and though we discussed prescription charges on this his mind was made up. He categorically, and I believed rightly, rejected the only other short-term alternative within the health budget, that of slowing down the hospital building programme. One felt that, for him, prescription charges were necessary, not so much for the revenue, but for their psychological impact on the Cabinet and the Party. It would be a sign of Britain's resolve really to come to grips with the economic realities which had been progressively fudged since 1964 and he never sought to hide that the underlying economic situation was far worse than most people recognized.

The one other important issue we discussed at some length was the need to increase family allowances. I had been campaigning for this since

Christmas 1966 and had spent much of the previous year-and-a-half attempting first to have family allowances increased and then to stave off, with Peggy Herbison's active connivance, the imposition of a means-tested family allowance. This was, therefore, an issue of very great personal importance. The new factor was that Roy was open-minded and obviously interested in the concept of marrying together income tax allowances for children and family allowances. Moreover, he was familiar with the Child Poverty Action Group's suggestion of a claw-back mechanism. In marked contrast to Jim Callaghan, he did not reiterate the old Treasury incantations of how such schemes would undermine the integrity of the Inland Revenue system. At last I sensed a far more radical basic attitude.

I left the meeting, fearing the worst for prescription charges but with a resolve to defend it if reimposed, regardless of my own personal views, and very depressed about the school-leaving age. I was, however, certain that at long last we had a Chancellor in control of events. He was prepared to reduce social expenditure far more than I thought desirable but he was going to push Denis Healey hard for real and easily justifiable defence cuts and, in the process, would insist on reassessing Britain's whole role and future in the world. It was evident too that Europe was going to be a major element from now on in British foreign and defence policy. All the decisions had yet to be made but that the new Chancellor was going to assert his authority was unquestionable and, after the drift and indecision of the last few years, this alone was a welcome relief.

Before the budget, in February 1968, still punch-drunk from the expenditure measures, Labour MPs were faced with a searing emotional issue as to what to do about the Kenyan Asians who, fearing that their livelihood was threatened by a programme of 'Africanization', were coming in increasing numbers into Britain. For some time, between six thousand and seven thousand immigrants a year had come in from Kenya, mainly but not exclusively Asians. But this number had rapidly increased in the latter part of 1967. By January 1968 the number arriving was eight times that of January of the previous year, and almost all were Asians.

Under the 1963 Kenya Independence Act, holders of British passports had the right to return to the United Kingdom at any time. This loophole was designed by Duncan Sandys, the Minister responsible, to encourage white settlers to stay in Kenya. It was felt that giving them the safeguard of being able to come back to Britain would be a stabilizing factor at Independence but it could not exclude Indians without introducing flagrant discrimination. Now the Duncan Sandys promise was being taken up but by blacks, not whites. It was argued that Britain was entitled to slow the flow of immigration while not putting an absolute stop to it. This argument soon led us into the absurd situation of legislating to stem the flow of immigration that had been stimulated by fear of that very legislation. Press comment, built up by Enoch Powell, had already fanned the flames of racial prejudice.

In October 1967 in a speech at Deal, chosen to coincide with the Tory Conference at Brighton, Enoch Powell had called for the so-called 'legal loophole' which allowed the immigration of Asians from Kenya to be stopped. In Walsall on 9 February 1968 he talked about 'a problem which at the present rate will, by the end of the century, be similar in magnitude to that in the United States now'. But the speech also referred to the 'one white child in a class' of a constituent in Wolverhampton. The chairman of the Education Committee said that this had only happened temporarily for one day but the telling point had been made. Night after night television pictures of Kenyan Asians arriving at airports created an atmosphere of panic. Jim Callaghan, who had inherited the build up in the numbers from Roy Jenkins, then brought forward the Commonwealth Immigrants Bill which had already been prepared by the Home Office in case of such an emergency. It was given its second reading on 27 February and its committee stages were rushed through the House of Commons in two days with the co-operation of the Conservative Opposition.

That Duncan Sandys, the man responsible for the original legislation, should have allowed himself to join Enoch Powell in his campaign was disgraceful. It was Iain Macleod, a former Colonial Secretary, who challenged him trenchantly in a *Spectator* article: 'Your Kenya Constitution is devastatingly clear. So is *Hansard*. So are all the statutes. And so therefore is my position. I gave my word. I meant to give it. I wish to keep it.' Despite Macleod's position, the Conservative Opposition under Ted Heath decided to support the Labour Government's legislation. Later, when Enoch Powell spoke in Birmingham in April, saying, 'Like the Roman, I see the River Tiber flowing with much blood', Heath removed him from the Shadow Cabinet. This was to Heath's immense credit because public opinion was wholly with Enoch Powell and many Conservative activists saw Powell as the saviour of the nation. Heath thought the whole tone of the speech was incompatible with the Conservative Party's attitude to race relations and demonstrated to me for the first time the decisiveness and principle which I later learnt to respect.

I agonized as to how to vote. Too often we just voted like sheep. The House dividing ritually along purely party lines. On this bill I felt I would take my own decision; it was undoubtedly racial in character but perhaps it had to be racial since it was dealing with deep-seated racial prejudice in Britain. Many of my closest friends were split on the question. John Mackintosh was determined to vote against it. David Marquand in the end abstained. I vacillated hour by hour. Yet I was never tempted to abstain since I felt that was a cop-out. I forced myself to ask what would happen if the immigration continued, as it undoubtedly would, at these levels for a few more months. What would happen in the areas of highest immigration? The answer, I felt, was violence, for the tension in these areas was mounting. It would put an intolerable strain on race relations. This was a vote with a straight choice. Continuing with no controls or legislating to slow the rate of immigration. Principle dictated continuing, prudence indicated slowing. I was determined not to let those MPs in Government do my dirty work for me. If I believed that taking this emergency action was necessary, I should vote for it openly as a backbencher. I listened to every word of the debate and found myself being moved by speakers on both sides of the argument, particularly Dingle Foot, Labour MP for Ipswich, who was against the bill in principle, and Renee Short, Labour MP for Wolverhampton North-East, who was in favour and spoke of the housing, education and employment problems that her constituents currently faced. I was very upset when David Ennals, winding up the debate, tried to defend the legislation, claiming that it was not racial. I felt, by admitting what we all knew, that Britain was riddled with racial prejudice, we could get on top of prejudice and root it out. Only if we accepted the charge of institutionalized racialism would we be able to improve race relations in those urban centres where Asian immigrants were concentrated. As ten o'clock approached, I had to decide. With a heavy heart I voted for the bill.

I have fluctuated since then on whether or not I voted in the correct division lobby that night. I have felt particularly guilt-ridden because I believe that my vote helped to make me a Minister and that John Mackintosh's vote against gravely damaged his chances. It was to the credit of Iain Macleod, at the cost of some strain in his relations with the Shadow Cabinet, that he voted against, with Liberal and some Labour MPs. He was joined by a few Conservatives, among whom were three from the West Country: Dame Joan Vickers (Plymouth Devonport), Michael Heseltine (Tavistock) and John Nott (St Ives). This all added to my distress and made me question my own claim to be a radical. I left for America, still arguing with myself and pondering the deeper issues involved. I felt less proud to be an MP than at any time since I had entered Parliament. But that vote illustrates what being a Member of Parliament is about – exercising one's judgement. I could have voted either way. I chose to vote as I thought I would have acted had I been Home Secretary at the time.

PART TWO

THE POLITICIAN

6

MARRIAGE

I flew in to New York for my first visit to the United States of America on Leap Year Day 1968 and went that night to the English Speaking Union for a welcoming reception. I was tired after all the heartsearching over my vote on the Kenyan Asian legislation but buoyed up by the vibrancy of New York.

The reception seemed like any other cocktail party. As I moved about, talking to people, I met a tall, athletic, good-looking girl called Anne Curtis who explained that she was a medical student. We chatted about medicine. I liked her and as I was looking for someone to show me New York I thought she would fit the bill. Then out of the corner of my eye I saw John Pardoe, in those days the Liberal MP for North Cornwall, talking animatedly to the most beautiful girl in the room. She had long, dark, wavy hair, long legs and a splendid figure. I strolled over to join them and as we all talked I became more and more captivated. She had a flashing smile, but it was her effervescence that was so unusual. My first task was to move on John Pardoe who was showing much interest in her, so I began to inject into the conversation the odd reference to John's wife and family. It was a dirty trick but it worked. Gradually she was content for the conversation to develop into a dialogue between the two of us and John drifted off.

I knew the party would not last long and I could feel the jet lag catching up on me. So I acted far more boldly than I would normally do and I asked her whether she would show me New York. She hesitated, said she could not do the next day but what about Saturday.

I had two free days in front of me before I was due to fly down to Washington on the Sunday. I kicked around New York seeing various tourist sites, all the time looking forward to meeting this stranger of whom I knew little more than that she worked in the Time Life Building for a French publisher whose name I could barely pronounce let alone spell.

We met as agreed at her flat and went to the restaurant she suggested, sat down and began to look at the menu. It soon became clear that this was a pretty expensive place. I was travelling with only a £50 allowance which was part of the post-devaluation stringency package to keep sterling in the United Kingdom. For starters we had clams with a sharp spicy tomato dip. Inside I was writhing with embarrassment for if we went on to a full meal I would have virtually no money left for the next two weeks. Eventually, blushing to the roots of my hair, I simply had to explain the situation and said we would have to go somewhere cheaper. It was then her turn to be embarrassed but she carried it all off with great style. They were my first ever clams and I have never eaten clams since without smiling. They had provided our love with its first test and it gave our evening together something special from the start. As we walked down to Greenwich Village in search of a steak house, she was kicking herself for suggesting a place which many of her boy-friends would go to as a matter of course with no thought for the bill and wondering what this strange Brit was thinking. I was thinking how well she had handled it all and what fun she was.

As the hours passed under the magic of this vast electric city, we simply fell in love. To meet a new girl-friend is always exciting. To meet one in a different continent, yet with a common language, multiplies the excitement. Everything needs explaining, every hour is precious, hours spent sleeping are stolen hours. We filled every moment with ourselves and the city became just a backdrop. We described our different lives, families, friends. Night turned to day and still we talked. In the morning we walked through Central Park. It was my first experience of sharp clear East Coast days without a cloud in the sky. We played records, went to the Chock-full-o'-Nuts for a brunch and still we talked. It soon became apparent how lucky I was for she normally left New York at weekends to go out to her family home on Long Island. She had only gone to the English Speaking Union party as a favour to her friend Betsey Brown, who had invited some of her close friends to entertain these British Members of Parliament. At that time she barely knew what an MP was. She had also inherited from her father no great love of the British; she thought them stuck-up and cold. She had apparently said some years before that she would never marry a politician, doctor or an Englishman. My first task was to explain that the Welsh are not English and that a Celt is a very different animal to her idea of a typical Brit, much more passionate and emotional. We soon discovered a shared love of singing. Unlike any of my other girl-friends, it was music which made her fly. Poetry, books, art all mattered to her but music was an essential part of her life.

On Sunday, after less than twenty-four hours together, I had to leave to fly down with the others on the delegation to Washington. I had no idea whether I would be able to return. We were due to be in Maryland the following weekend so I vowed, without the slightest idea how I would manage it, that somehow I would get back, the question was when I could break away from the rest of the group.

Arriving in Washington the group met up again with Betsey Brown who was organizing the English Speaking Union tour and was our hostess for the trip. She was a beautiful southern belle, straight out of *Gone With The Wind*. Warm, lively and far shrewder than she would allow us to think, she ran our trip with great efficiency and charm. I decided that the best reason I could give to her and to my fellow MPs for returning to New York was that I had been invited to look around one of the hospitals there. It was Betsey's then husband Preston Brown whose eyes arched knowingly when I gave this explanation. Preston, a man of laconic humour and wit, was capable of keeping people in stitches of laughter and sensed before we even knew each other that it was a woman not medicine that was taking me back to New York. He became my eldest son Tristan's godfather and we treasure his friendship.

On Wednesday, just in case I did not get through on the telephone, I wrote our first love letter.

> Hotel Lafayette
> Washington, D.C.

Deborah,

Tonight before dinner I've walked miles around Washington. My real sorrow was that you were not here as well – I must confess to having fallen fast and hard for you and your country. There is something almost noble about the whole way in which the political institutions are constructed – of course one knows that there is a deep shabbiness not far beneath the surface as there is in all political life – but where else would you see a Jefferson and a Washington memorial enriching politics on an almost Platonic level.

You feel here something of the Greek spirit that politics is life and that to be bored with politics is to be bored with life. At night the reflections on the lake, the clear sky and the warmth make me feel almost transported away from twentieth-century living. Still, the reason for writing is to tell you that I will be at Washington Airport at 3.30 p.m. on Friday and that I'll take the nearest shuttle flight down to New York. Love is like a wildflower that grows on the edge of a precipice, if you don't dare you don't touch it – I'm glad we dared. The fragrance is still with me and I long for Friday. Till then if you've a clear sky in New York think of each one of the stars as being a kiss.

David

I arrived back in New York that Friday evening and we went to a party which she had already accepted. Next morning we hired a car and drove out to St James, Long Island, on another clear crisp day. Apparently her parents were quite used to her bringing people home at next to no notice.

It was a strange sensation being driven along the Long Island expressway, eight lanes in places and quite unlike any other road I had experienced. I had no idea of what sort of house we were going to or even what sort of people to expect but as we drove through the hideous suburbia I started to imagine the house. Nothing that I saw in those seventy miles prepared me for it. A sign at the entrance to the driveway said 'By the Harbour' and through the trees there was a long, graceful, white, wooden clapboard house with one high spruce tree on its left and surrounded by woods. Charging around the drive in front of the house were two dogs which leapt up to welcome Debbie as we opened the car door.

I was introduced to her father Kyrill Schabert and Mickey, her lively, attractive stepmother. Barely had I seen the inside of the house before, in borrowed old clothes, I was outside helping to cut down and trim back an old apple tree with a power saw. Then Debbie and I went for a long walk by the Long Island Sound. We felt the rush of air on our faces from the wild geese flying past, so near that I felt I could touch them. On my return I found the inside of the house as enchanting as the outside with roaring wood fires in both the dining room and the study which was lined with books. It was a house that had a lived-in elegance. Everywhere there was good, mostly European, taste. Kyrill's father and grandfather had been German and Mickey's family were from Hungary. The pure American blood in Debbie came from her mother, Mary Smith, who died when Debbie was seven but remains a continued presence in her life. Everyone who knew her mother says they are uncannily similar and share the same gaiety and *joie de vivre*.

All over the house were books from the Pantheon publishing house which Kyrill had helped found. One book which took my eye in the library was *Tristan and Iseult* with wood engravings by Maillot. It became a lovers' book for us, one to which we would often return and from which we took the name of our first-born.

Sunday morning came all too quickly and before I left St James I scribbled a quick note for Debbie to read after she had dropped me at John F. Kennedy Airport from where I was to fly to New Hampshire.

> By the Harbour
> St James
> Long Island

Dearest Deborah,

I'm writing this very quickly before we leave today. Maybe I'll never
say enough of what I feel, but now I cry, perhaps I'll be able to
hide this as I say goodbye – I'll certainly try. This has been
something I will never *ever* forget. I long for it to be more than just
a few days. Real love is not just a happening, it grows. Perhaps this
too will grow but the ground on which it has been sown contains
more obstacles than it is right for any two people to have to contend

with. Distance, background, everything can act as an obstacle.
Perhaps too, they could act as a bond – I hope so. I almost pray so
but who really can know. Last night I could have said lots of
extravagant, lovely things but in a way to think them was better than
to say them. *Je t'adore* and in Latin, *Id est semper idem amor*. My
dearest Deborah, this I promise I will *never* forget.

Your David who will always love and remember. I can't see to
write for my tears.

For all I knew, this might have been our last meeting. We had been
together for just two short periods, in total a little less than four days. I
promised to try and fly back but it was not going to be easy. We were
due to fly the following Friday to London from Boston and we expected
an important vote and a three-line whip in Parliament on the Monday we
were back.

When I caught up with the others in their hotel, the New Hampshire
Primary was in its final stages. It proved to be fascinating. Senator Gene
McCarthy was pushing ahead fast every day against all the other
Democratic presidential candidates. Running on a Vietnam peace ticket,
Gene McCarthy was an intellectual but had captured the imagination in
this mainly rural state. Bobby Kennedy had not yet declared that he was
a presidential candidate. Voting was due while we were there on Tuesday
12 March. By then most of my colleagues and certainly Betsey realized I
had seen a little more in New York than a hospital.

On Wednesday we and the rest of America were sent reeling. Senator
McCarthy had won the Democratic Primary by a landslide with 42.5 per
cent of the vote. President Lyndon Johnson's name was not theoretically
on the ballot but as a write-in candidate, he had received only 49.5 per
cent. It was a sharp rebuff for the President's Vietnam policy. Bobby
Kennedy, to no one's surprise, announced his candidacy four days later,
and soon afterwards President Johnson announced his intention not to
run for a further term. Whether or not he was influenced to stand down
by the New Hampshire Primary, we will never know. A complex man
behind the folksy image over Vietnam, his motivation full of self-doubt
defied analysis. For me he was never the hate figure of the Left's chant,
'Hey, hey, LBJ, how many kids did you kill today?' It was rare for a
Southerner to champion civil rights as he did, unusual to be a Roosevelt
New Dealer in Congress. He had an extraordinarily good legislative
record on trying to grapple with poverty and racial discrimination.
History should be kinder to him than the generations who still blame him
for Vietnam. I, like most people, had agonized over the conduct of the
Vietnam War and by 1968 I was finding it harder and harder to justify.
Debbie was against the Vietnam War and wanted McCarthy to do well.
She hoped that Bobby Kennedy would run and supported him when he did.

On Friday in Boston I finally decided to say to hell with the whips in
London and fly to New York. I flew down with Betsey Brown and that

Saturday in New York Debbie and I went to a party where we met Sandy Cortesi and his wife Lale who was then nearly nine months pregnant. We all agreed to have dinner the following night. Sandy was to become my closest friend and godfather to my second son, Gareth.

On Sunday there was the St Patrick's Day parade down Fifth Avenue. It was a fun affair with most people wearing green. Bobby Kennedy marched at the head of the parade as a New York Senator and as a newly announced Democratic presidential candidate. He was given a great welcome and I felt happy for him for it seemed as if he was coming out of his brother's shadow. I never knew him but at that stage in his political development he seemed both more mature and sincere and his discovery of poverty genuine. He was certainly Debbie's candidate for, unlike me, she did not have much time for Hubert Humphrey. Central Park was full of people with Irish connections and I saw for the first time how strong America's links are with Ireland. Irish-Americans' tendency to see a united Ireland as an obvious and simple right is reinforced by a strong anti-colonial streak which after their struggle for independence still runs deep in most Americans. A surge of unrest in Northern Ireland was growing in 1968 though the build up of the IRA's campaign of violence was yet to come.

I did not have to fly off to London until Monday morning so, though we still talked a lot, now as we walked we could afford the odd silence between us. On our last night, Nannas came to stay in the flat. She was a Southerner whom Debbie treasured for she had lived with the family for some years. She was not a nanny in the British sense but a family friend who had been married to a local vicar on Long Island. What she thought of me was obviously important to Debbie and luckily we clicked; she proved to be the most discreet chaperone I have ever encountered.

Those last days I read to Debbie from Cavafy's poems and left her his complete works with an introduction from W.H. Auden, inscribing it 'I will always remember, New York, March '68'. The poem 'Return' was to become our special favourite.

> Return often and take me,
> beloved sensation, return and take me –
> when the memory of the body awakens,
> and old desire again runs through the blood;
> when the lips and the skin remember,
> and the hands feel as if they touch again.
>
> Return often and take me at night,
> when the lips and the skin remember . . .

On Monday 18 March I flew back to London, too late to vote, but that could not have mattered less to me. I was head over heels in love despite the fact that we had seen each other in total for less than seven days.

George Brown had resigned on the morning I arrived back in London. Like almost all resignations it was the accumulation of events not just the event itself. He had been particularly upset ever since the decision, taken as part of the expenditure cuts, to go back on raising the school-leaving age from fifteen to sixteen. For George, who had left school without any chance of going to university, this was an emotional issue and he had found it very hard to accept. Roy Jenkins argued this was vitally necessary as part of his overall package. I had felt that the psychological effect of imposing prescription charges would be enough, but Roy was Chancellor and I felt strongly we had to back his judgement.

The trigger incident, which had taken place while I was away, had been Harold Wilson, accompanied by Roy Jenkins and Peter Shore, going to the Palace for an emergency meeting of the Privy Council without consulting George Brown. Roy Jenkins had wanted to declare a Bank Holiday so that the exchange markets could have time to absorb the decision to suspend the sale of gold while the Central Banks agreed standby credit. To Roy Jenkins and Harold Wilson this was a technical British response to an international crisis. To George this was a constitutional issue about collective responsibility.

The emotion was whether or not Wilson had tried to contact him as Wilson claimed he had. George asserted, not without justification, that he had not. In my experience a Prime Minister who really wants to contact the Foreign Secretary can do so almost anywhere in the world within minutes not hours, let alone in London. In truth, George's resignation had been inevitable for years, not just months, and it passed without much impact. Roy Jenkins's first budget speech followed on 19 March and this speech only underlined his personal authority and demonstrated that the Government was on a new course.

On 3 April I wrote, having just got back from the Anglo-German meeting of parliamentarians, journalists and academics, inspired by Lilo Milchsack, at Königswinter; meetings which have done much since the war to deepen understanding between our two countries.

House of Commons
London SW1

Dearest Debbie,

Life is rather hectic – I've just arrived back from Germany where I had a very drunken stay – too much Moselle until the most unearthly hours. Our hotel overlooked the Rhine which was fun but I find Bonn very dull and Königswinter is little more than a suburb. Your letter was waiting for me which was a particular delight. Still the rain pours in to my house and I'm fed up with it but I hope something gets done when I'm away in the Persian Gulf. Politics here is very depressing. The Johnson decision burst in like a ray of hope but it's been quickly shattered by the knowledge that bombing raids are continuing 200 miles into N. Vietnam.

I'm still really collecting all my memories. At present they are all scattered around. I need a few days of solitude just for thought. I love the desert. Perhaps I might get a few hours off and drive up to a small hill and watch the sun set over the desert and think and remember. If I do it will be of you I will think. In Persia and Afghanistan, I often used to go off alone and do this. I'll write anyhow again probably on the plane out to Kuwait if not before.

I wish very much that you were with me now. I feel very tired and a little fed up. It's sheeting outside and quite cold as if winter having gone away has now come back for a final fling. Yes, I envy you New York – I worry about you sometimes, living alone in that city – but somehow your flat is a refuge from it all. I hope everyone around you is happy and haven't allowed you to get depressed. Read *De Profundis* by Oscar Wilde. Yesterday I saw for the first time *Dr Zhivago* and loved it. Some of the scenes almost reminded me of St James in the snow. Well I must go to a meeting on a very controversial issue relating to our Prices and Incomes policy and the Union members won't allow it to pass through. We'll have to fight once again among ourselves, but when all is difficult and ugly I'll float back in time to you and past happiness and it will feel like a haven.

Your David

The Johnson decision I referred to briefly was the announcement that 'I shall not seek and I will not accept the nomination of my party as President'. But the Vietnam War showed every sign of grinding on. On 17 March there had been an angry demonstration around the American Embassy in London. Grosvenor Square was likened to a battlefield and three hundred arrests were made.

Then out of the blue she rang up on Tuesday 9 April because she thought I was off to Kuwait the next day. It was a wonderful surprise and joy to hear her voice. Now it seems surprising that we did not use the telephone more. But I was still living in a world where to ring London from Plymouth was a costly decision not to be indulged in too often. To ring New York was an expensive luxury to be done but rarely. Now we ring with barely any hesitation and what is even more expensive, so do our children.

On Thursday 11 April I wrote to her.

House of Commons
London SW1

Dearest Debbie,

Life is in such a rush. I'm writing this letter in a little Bistro in Chelsea. It's a strange place. Sometime I'll bring you here. It's run by a friend of mine, a middle European called Elizabeth who I've known for years. She fed me when I was really poor. It's very unEnglish.

Hearing your voice was absolutely marvellous and gave me a strange thrill – it was so unexpected. I'd planned that one day I would surprise you. We postponed going to Kuwait till Friday because of public holidays. I've now left the Bistro. Someone I know well came and we chatted far too late. Now I'm in bed and it's well gone midnight. I wish you could hear the barges knocking each other outside and the wash and beat of the waves on the beach as a ship goes by and an occasional hoot from a ship rounding the bend by the Isle of Dogs. It's hard to believe that one is in London.

How strange it will be to be back again in the Middle East in less than twenty-four hours. Look after yourself. It can't be easy in America now – we read and hear a lot about it, everything concentrating on the violence, perhaps to too great an extent. I miss you very much, Debbie, and I'll write soon. In the meantime,

Much love,
David

My reference to violence was to the rioting in some of the American cities that followed the murder of Martin Luther King. In New York the Mayor, John Lindsay, was stoned by a black crowd in Harlem. In Washington, a mob of black people had burned and looted a building within three hundred yards of the White House. Having just been in those places, it was all very vivid to me. It also fed the apprehensions of those who feared our own black immigration. It gave Enoch Powell the opportunity to warn about America and say ten days later that Britain must 'be mad, literally mad as a nation' to allow 50,000 dependants of immigrants into the country. He went on to say we were a nation 'busily engaged in heaping up its own funeral pyre'.

I wrote of a different world from Qatar in the Persian Gulf.

The Oasis Hotel

Dearest Debbie,

This notepaper in my bedroom finally proved irresistible. I wish I could describe what we have seen of the Gulf so far. Kuwait is so rich that it has completely turned its back on its past, full of middle-class rather horrible pseudo modern architecture. The Emir is pretty Westernized and there are some 40,000 Palestinians which tends to push it in that direction. Perhaps it's best summed up by the Sheraton Hilton.

Bahrain is very different though still fairly rich and Westernized. The ruler is much more of a Bedouin holding a Majlis every day where anyone can come and complain and speak to him and then this is followed by a banquet. We were the guests of honour and really the whole thing is out of a 1930s film scenario. You have to pinch yourself that it's happening. The big Black British Humber drives out into the desert with Union Jack flying, twinkling lights in

the desert become larger, vast palace appears, past horses, halt outside
big courtyards, clatter of arms as Laurel and Hardy assemble thirteen
or so scruffs in uniform. When they are at attention the car moves
into courtyard whereupon we find a ragged army in which at any
moment you expect a few rounds to fly off by accident. Courtyard
lit, and all around about three hundred tribesmen most in white
gowns all with white head-dresses sit around and just watch. Out
comes the ruler who speaks English then you march into vast hall
in which all the other guests, some three hundred, are sitting around
the wall. They get up and you proceed with the ruler to his couch
where you wash hands – drink coffee and tea all in the Eastern way
where they just pour sufficient for one swig – then out into a massive
dining room with about three hundred seats, a long table with about
thirty whole sheep on the table, curry nearly piled to the ceiling.
Even in Iran I've never seen such food – you pick the mutton off
the carcass with your fingers. The whole meal is very quick and has
to be followed by a long belch – my belch was one of the best I've
ever done. It curled round my big belly a couple of times before
coming out with a force that won me admiring glances from the
Sheikhs around me. The British Agent looked horrified. After the
meal you again wash hands, rub in scent and have a man burning
incense coming round. With your hand you blow it all over yourself.

The whole thing is really an unforgettable experience. All
accompanied by a very Western political talk, largely about our
decision to withdraw our military commitment in 1971.

Look after yourself my dearest Debbie and I send you a lot of
love and *much* desire. There are *no* women within even sight let alone
reach so at night I want you even more than usual and that's a lot.

Very much love,
David

My next letter, from Limehouse, reflects the 'Harold Wilson must go'
mood which was running strongly, and I felt he could be ousted by July.

Darling Debbie,

Back to dear old England and somehow this weekend I'm very
depressed. There seems so very little that one can do – I wonder
whether I should be doing what I am. I should get down seriously
to medicine but I don't seem to be able to do so. I don't feel alive,
just a little dead. Maybe this is getting older. Certainly these moods
seem a bit more frequent. Perhaps it's the contrast from travelling
around like a King with everything organized, living very well and
suddenly back in England wondering about money, future, all the
sort of tedious things that in a way for a fortnight I'd been able to
forget. If ever someone was made to live not in luxury but with the
freedom that money can buy, it's me.

By the way, Abu Dhabi *is* a place. It's part of the Trucial States
below Saudi Arabia near the mouth of the Persian Gulf. It's suddenly
got oil revenues of £100 million a year and is exploding with

buildings – a transformation from an Arab mud-built town to a
modern city in about three years. We came back via Jordan and I
crossed over the Allenby Bridge and through occupied territory to
Jerusalem. At last united, it is nevertheless depressing. On 2 May
the Israelis are holding a victory march. They've built wooden stands
all over the place and are taking over Arab land. It will be like some
Roman victory parade. It is an incredibly insensitive act to the Arabs.
It will clearly influence opinion in the Arab World and I wouldn't
be surprised if there aren't some bomb incidents.

Life is full. With a little luck we might be able to oust the Prime
Minister in about June, July. It certainly will be difficult but
something really has to be done – there are signs that he is developing
mild paranoia apart from everything else. The race picture is pretty
gloomy. There is no doubt we have all been kidding ourselves about
this problem, trying to ignore the very real feelings that exist deep
down. Powell was of course irresponsible and intemperate in his
approach but there is little doubt that it was a calculated stroke.
Still, how I wish you were here to tell you about these things.

America is in our papers so much that I don't really feel you're
very far away. Outside it's raining. The river looks very gloomy
because on the weekend there are very few boats moving about.

Travel too makes one realize how absurd distance now is but still
the gap is there and when one is sad it's got a habit of widening.
The future is too obscure and too daunting to discuss too much so I
ignore it. For the moment I'll just send lots of love and tell you 'I'm
dreaming of a half grey opal' and 'Body Remember'. I'll write in a
better mood sometime soon. Till then,

Your David

My attempt to get to America with the Select Committee on Science and
Technology fell through and it looked as if I was not going to get to the
States for a long time. I believed if our relationship was to last it was vital
that we both kept our freedom. I wrote on 10 May, 'We must just be
patient and worry not – live your own life, see everyone, do everything
but just reserve a little time each day to remember. In this way my
presence won't intrude or interfere but just exist in a good sense.'

She replied with a four-leaf clover which she had found with one other
in a field in St James. This clover I found years later in my book of
Cavafy poems under the poem 'Gray'.

I wrote from Limehouse.

I think you will love this house – in some ways it is the most
romantic house I've ever lived in with the ships flashing past. Even
on a dull overcast day there is activity and life everywhere.

Political life is difficult still. There can be no doubt now that the
Prime Minister must be removed but watching him cling on one
realizes what an immense service President Johnson did for your
country. He spared you the trauma and the indignity of removing

him – he realized that your wounds are deep enough without having
to add another bloodbath with all the conflicting loyalites and
acrimony that his pursuit of the Presidency would have involved. I
only pray that he doesn't contemplate reversing this decision for if
he did the standing of politicians the world over would be savaged.
Our Prime Minister could just conceivably stand down in the Autumn
if the pressure continues but there is little that is generous in his
political attitudes to date that could suggest that this would be his
chosen path – yet faced with ignominy, persistent denigration, I
suppose it is just possible, but not likely. Till then we will continue
to struggle in a situation which is difficult enough without this
appalling credibility gap. People simply do not believe us and since I
don't believe a word he says, why should the electorate? To be a
great leader there must be an air of indifference, or perhaps
detachment is a better word. We will see what happens in France
but again the way De Gaulle is acting in a crisis shows to my mind
his unique capacity for leadership. Maybe the rot is too deep but
even now as France grinds to a halt, I'd lay my bet that he'll come
out on top.

Your David who loves you.

My reference to the riots in Paris reflected the growing concern about
what was developing in early May with students, led by Daniel Cohn-
Bendit, fighting the police, who responded with tear gas, provoking what
was described as the worst street fighting since the Liberation in 1944.
By contrast she wrote back describing the dogwood blossom out at St
James as one of America's proudest possessions. 'It's a middle-sized
graceful tree with white or pink flowers in the shape of a rounded Greek
cross and you'll simply have to come to see for yourself.' There were
apparently a few souvenirs of our visit together – jeep tracks and the old
lopsided apple tree that I had pruned with no hope it would survive but
which was now in full blossom. All these little links with our few days
together helped to feed our memories and bridge the Atlantic.

My letters became more political as I tried to give her a flavour of my
strange life, too often staying night after night in the House of Commons,
until well past midnight. It was ludicrous, given our large majority, that
the whips refused to let our majority drop in some misguided belief that
our people in the country expected us all to be voting even when the
majority of Conservatives had long since gone home. I wrote of my
'despair at the way things are going'.

Yet I think this is one's challenge to fight back, to fight for one's
ideals. But mine are so different. I refuse to take refuge in what I
call gesture politics; to espouse causes and policies with little real
thought as to the implications or even as to their effect – so much of
our policies are synthetic. The end is willed without serious attempts
having been made to provide the means. We stop supplying arms to
South Africa as a gesture yet continue to export more goods to her

than any other nation. We choose to ignore that the French will
supply her with any arms and we argue that this is a moral stand.
True, it is, and in some ways it is admirable as I don't think anyone
loathes apartheid more than I – but is this morality in fact not
bogus? The real moral political action, if one can describe politics in
moral terms, is to apply economic sanctions but this would damage
our already feeble economy so we chose just arms. Maybe it's OK
but this sort of posturing can lead inexorably to a slippery path.

In Rhodesia we have, by adopting moral attitudes without due
regard to the practical politics, put ourselves in a difficult position –
sanctions here are largely ineffective. Slowly we are being made to
look foolish – yet to do nothing would have been equally
reprehensible. Some day one will have to cut one's losses – but this
will require an admission of failure. So many of the faults of this
Government are due to the Prime Minister but one cannot make him
the scapegoat. The Party itself seems to want this type of leadership.
It wants to fudge issues. It wants to talk morality and tough
purposive action but it shrinks from making the words a reality. Yet
another division is now being called so I must stop.

She telephoned me to say she was coming over for a summer holiday and
how shattered she felt when Robert Kennedy was shot and killed on 5
June in Los Angeles, the night of his California primary victory over
Senator McCarthy. Coming after the assassination of Martin Luther
King in April, she really feared what was happening to American society.

I wrote back in June, a rather depressed letter, but at least now I knew
she was coming over on 26 August.

Even as I turned over to answer the phone somehow I knew it was
you. Robert Kennedy dead, the world is savage and the passionate so
often fall victim to the emotions they arouse. Still, can one really
expect anything else? He was one who lived on the precipice and
that means living dangerously but also well. There are grave dangers
in trying to love each other by paper. It can easily lead to
misunderstanding and it's difficult to talk as well as we did in Central
Park that rainy afternoon, but what else can we do? You wrote about
Bernard Geis. Today in the *Sunday Times*, there is a big feature on
him. I must say, to reiterate your words, having you 'working in
London would have its tempting aspects'.

What can I tell you about me? In a strange way, since I came
back from New York I've been gradually withdrawing from a lot of
longstanding relationships and willing myself to be free though
knowing that this also involved being lonely. It's almost as if I want
to ache but it has many dangers, not least is the sheer absurdity of
being free and yet not being able to see you. I wonder whether one
can ever love enough, seeing one so infrequently. And yet too much
would perhaps breed boredom. I've never lived with anyone in my
life but I think I could with you if I came to New York or you to
London. Because one wouldn't have any roots it would really be

absurd to live apart. The whole thing is impossible. A great chunk of
me now wants ten children and when I'm still young enough to
enjoy them – another chunk of me dreads poverty, not for it itself,
but for its limitations on my own freedom to move about, to do
things, to entertain. If only I could be serious about making money I
probably could, but I'm altogether too casual about it. I don't like it
enough and while I'm single I have enough – not to live extravagantly
but to live reasonably well. I don't save anything but I don't think
much about what I spend. On top of this is this horrible hesitation
about what to do with one's life. What's going on here at present
isn't enough. I don't find it the challenge that I used to. It's sad and
I'm trying to snap out of it but it's all a maze of conflicting views. I
think I will now settle down to some psychiatry.

But one could tell how little we still knew of each other because I had to
ask when her birthday was! She had also written, 'Shocking to see how I
scan the newspaper for London dispatches. I'm supposed to be anti-
British.'

My next letter was written in the early hours of 2 July, my thirtieth
birthday. I had been dining in the House of Commons with Robert
Maclennan, then the Labour MP for Caithness and Sutherland. The
main topic we discussed was how to get rid of Harold Wilson when a
message was brought to me by one of the badge holders who circulate all
around the House of Commons asking me to go over to No. 10 Downing
Street immediately to see the Prime Minister.

Dearest Debbie,

What a fantastic day. It's midnight and soon to be 2 July, my
birthday. I've opened your kooky present and it really felt like a
birthday. All fun and rather mad and a welcome relief. But Debbie
there is something more to tell you, in a way frightening, in a way
exciting. This evening I was called to No. 10 Downing Street by the
Prime Minister and asked to be the Minister for the Royal Navy and
to join the Government. My full title, as from the Queen accepting
the appointment, will be Parliamentary Under-Secretary to the
Ministry of Defence for the Royal Navy. It means a bigger salary, an
official car and some work which I can get my teeth into.

It does, however, involve me in this Government. I thought as
deeply as I could if I should serve but everyone I spoke to was
insistent that I should, even though my view of the Prime Minister
has not changed. It's part of the political game that you operate
inside. I know all this. I know my friends would have taken the job
if offered. I know that to refuse would have been jejune and revealed
a disdain for politics. But I really did question whether I should
have done it. Of course the Prime Minister knows what I feel – he
knows that I'm potentially dangerous on the back benches so he has
in effect bought me off – all this is true and it worries me that I

have allowed myself in effect to be a pawn on his cynical chess board but for all this it offers me a real job, a position in which I can really try to influence events and to start on the ladder of political office.

Isn't it fantastic on my birthday in effect, though I knew while still twenty-nine. You're the first person to know because it won't be announced until possibly late today. I daren't even tell my parents yet. Oh, Debbie how I wish you were here. For holidays we'll have to see when I know all the commitments that I inherit from my predecessor. I might try and persuade the Navy to take me over to the States for a visit and then take time off for a holiday. Perhaps we can keep to our original plan. I very much hope so. I'm sorry to land you with all this. I'll write as soon as I can but the next week will I expect be hectic in the extreme. I'm excited but worried. The Government is still in a very shaky position.

If you buy *The Times* for July 4th and 5th you may well see two articles by me on the NHS. Normally one can't write articles in the press as a Minister but since this was written before, the Prime Minister has given me permission. Of course I'm only a very junior Minister. There is the Secretary of State for Defence, two Ministers of State for Equipment and Administration, then three Parliamentary Secretaries for the Royal Navy, Army and Air Force.

I don't think I'm going to sleep well tonight. It's certainly all very exciting. I've always adored the Navy. As a twelve-year-old this was going to be my career. I'll certainly love the work and there is far more freedom and responsibility than is given to some junior Ministers. It's anyhow a challenge but don't fear that it will stop us seeing each other. I'll have to go via the States whenever possible. The trouble is I'll now have to be the soul of discretion as the Secret Service watch Ministers carefully for security leaks. We can't have another Profumo!! How I wish you were here. Life is in a whirl. I need to feel your hands kneading my back and relaxing me with love. Happy, Happy birthday to you. I wish I was there but I'll be thinking of you.

Your David

Being offered the job by Harold Wilson was all the more incredible since I had spoken sharp words to him two months before in a lift in the House of Commons. I had asked him to stop his staff briefing the press against Brian Walden, John Mackintosh, David Marquand and myself. We were all supposed to be having affairs with Nora Beloff, the highly respected middle-aged journalist who was then the political correspondent of the *Observer*. She had not thought it funny when I laughingly said to have all four was a compliment. I was fed up with the constant innuendos and the intrigue that surrounded his Kitchen Cabinet. Meeting by chance in a lift alone seemed a good opportunity to tell him this, and I did so, but afterwards I expected that I had completely burnt my boats. What an unpredictable man Harold Wilson was.

I wrote to Debbie on 24 July.

> Happiness starts, I know, when you come through the customs
> barrier. Till then I'll just wait. There is simply masses of work to
> complete so I can't complain on that score. Today I apologized for
> the mistakes of my Ministry to the House. It went remarkably well,
> particularly when I said I accept full responsibility when the whole
> House knew it had nothing to do with me at all. It's strange how a
> fulsome apology deflates opposition.

An interesting feature about that incident was that Jim Callaghan just
happened to be sitting on the Front Bench and asked why I was making a
statement. I explained that it was because Roy Roebuck, the Labour
MP, was demanding an explanation of why a mistake over a factual
statistic in a written answer had been changed by the technique of a
pursuant written answer without his permission. 'Grovel,' said Jim. 'Lard
it on and that way the House will realize you are not really at fault and it
will rebound on him.' It was excellent advice which I followed to the
letter.

On 22 August Soviet troops invaded Czechoslovakia. Alexander
Dubcek and other liberal Communist leaders were herded into a troop
carrier, driven off and deprived of all power. The Prague Spring was
crushed by Russian tanks and the Brezhnev doctrine that the USSR had
the right and the will to use force to stop any country in Eastern Europe
from breaking out towards the West was brutally established. The most
bizarre feature of what happened as far as I was personally concerned was
the discovery of how bad was NATO intelligence. That evening, before
I left the Ministry of Defence, I was reading highly classified reports
which said there would be no invasion. I was then woken up to be told
that the Russians were invading. There was nothing NATO could do.
Indeed, nothing was what NATO had already decided to do. Nevertheless, I felt almost as bad about our inactivity as I had about Hungary in
1956. I had now learnt an inportant word, *realpolitik*, the acceptance of
reality. I was often to use it in the future. I never felt comfortable over
letting the Soviet Union go unchallenged in their so-called spheres of
influence. Gradually in the 1970s, through the human rights campaigns,
we began to develop a more principled and active foreign policy towards
the USSR. Still at this time the conventional wisdom was that the West
had no alternative but to take such repression on the chin and virtually to
turn the other cheek.

On the evening of 27 August, Debbie walked through customs in a
colourful jungle print dress. I knew now that everything was going to be
all right. Our seven days together had not been a dream. All the
anguished writing and physical frustration of the last five months just
disappeared in a wave of certainty. We drove to have supper with
Elizabeth at her bistro. This was certainly pushing Debbie in at the deep

end of my life. Elizabeth's perceptiveness, and the fact that she had deeply loved an Indian girl-friend of mine, would be a major test. She had in the past been very rude to some of my girl-friends. It was not going to be easy for a new one to win her over. I knew that all was going to be well between them when Elizabeth announced that she too was going to France and asked us to pick her up at Orly and drive her down to Gassin in the South of France. This was no request, just a *fait accompli* which I, with my usual bad grace on such occasions, only grudgingly accepted. Debbie took it all in her stride but I felt that for Elizabeth to land herself on us at this of all times was a liberty. I left the bistro that night more confident of Debbie and my love than I had dared to hope.

We had two days together in London before flying from Lydd to France with my Volkswagen Beetle. We drove to Paris and stayed on the Left Bank near Robert Laffont's publishing house. On Saturday he took us both out to lunch and, although he spoke little English and I virtually no French, all went well. He and his daughter were very fond of Debbie. They surveyed me carefully, wondering whether I was good enough for her. That made a welcome change – my friends in London had looked at her from my point of view. On Monday we drove out to Orly: not only was Elizabeth there but also her fourteen-year-old daughter Anna and two massive suitcases. Somehow we managed to cram everything into the Volkswagen. It was goodbye to privacy and a terrible squash in the back of the car. But we all laughed and set off happily for the South of France.

When we stopped to buy some food for a picnic Elizabeth and Debbie went off together and watching them return, talking vociferously in French I felt for the first time, I really am going to marry this girl. We all seemed to fit so well. The car journey was great fun and I was glad that Elizabeth had come. We arrived very late at Gassin and next day, after dropping her and Anna at a camp used by Russian émigrés, we drove on to the French-Spanish border but could only look across. I was banned as a Minister from going to Spain, not just because it was still Fascist under Franco, but because the naval confrontation over Gibraltar was hotting up and it was felt I should not risk being discovered staying in Spain. We then drove back through the Dordogne, staying near Cahors in a very expensive castle hotel. We had stuffed ourselves full of rich country pâté at lunch and, appalled by the cost of everything in the hotel, we decided we could only afford to have a little for dinner but that it should be of the very best. So we ordered champagne and a plate full of truffles. The waiter raised his eyebrows but served a memorable meal, made all the more so by a thunderstorm which put out all the lights and left us to eat by candlelight amidst flashes of lightning. By now we knew we were both deeply in love, the only unspoken question was whether we were going to marry. I was still loath to commit myself, remembering my broken engagement of six years ago. I was determined I would not let another person down. But I also knew I had to decide, for our love would not easily withstand another long separation, particularly since this time it would be the product of indecision.

We flew back to Lydd and I rang up my sister Susan to see if we could visit her in Bromley. Not only was her husband, Garth, home but my mother and father were staying with them. I wanted Debbie to meet my parents just as I had been able to meet hers, and we all had dinner together. It was clear that both my parents were enchanted with Debbie. Afterwards they told me they were surprised we did not tell them we were getting engaged that evening.

Next morning, on my first day back at work, I had to go to a Cabinet Sub-Committee on the Royal Dockyards. There was no way of absenting myself so I dropped Debbie at the air terminal at Victoria. The meeting ended surprisingly quickly and I drove fast to Victoria and found her in the coach. We left her suitcase, since it was booked through and drove out to the airport stopping at the top of Constitution Hill so we could have a quick walk and a final kiss before reaching the airport.

She wrote twice in late September, the second letter was justifiably tough in the absence of hearing from me:

> My far away love. I'm angry and herewith stage a transatlantic temper tantrum. Silent gaps are horrible, more horrible than I can bear. To be together in silence is poetry, to be apart in silence is the demon of distortion. Letters are warm hellos which I hoped could be exchanged more often than once every full moon. I care very much about your well-being and about this precipice we're on.
>
> David, you know I hate routine things but writing is about the only means of expression we have, except for strong thought waves.
>
> End of written tantrum (but my brown eyes still flash).

I wrote back – if there was any remaining hesitancy over whether to ask her to marry me it was fast disappearing.

> Dearest Debbie,
>
> Rude letter received and contents noted – deserved I admit, though in a way I'm in no fit state to write now but I will do this weekend. I'm worked off my feet as all the other Ministers seem to have flu. But that isn't the reason I've not written because of course I'd find time – the reason is a much more complex one. I felt devastated after you left. I wanted time before I wrote, time to try to sort out my feelings, time to feel the longing ache inside me and with it a certainty that time can only bring. So despite your letter, I'm not going to write more. I miss you desperately and long and ache for you.
>
> I'll write soon.
>
> Your David who loves you.

A few days after she would have had that letter I telephoned her at St

James in October and asked her to marry me. She said one word – 'Sure'. We planned to get married in America over Christmas, hopefully with my family. Her father wrote me a heartfelt welcoming letter and I knew it was going to be very difficult for him – Debbie was a constant reminder of his first wife and a tonic which would be lost when she crossed the Atlantic. He finished with words which showed how much part of him was still European, having been born and brought up in Germany but with an American mother, 'On the Continent men hug each other at times – it's a nice custom and I am sending a warm one to you.' We hugged from then on whenever we met until he died after heart surgery in 1983. He was a man who liked to be surrounded by friends; cultured, gregarious and yet insecure. After an initial wariness between us, we grew ever closer. Eventually he became a father in reality not just in law as did my mother for Debbie.

The next two months were spent in anticipation of flying to America for the wedding. Most of our letters became nuts and bolts affairs dealing with my house, the wedding arrangements and a rearguard action, which I lost, against wearing a morning coat or cutaways as the Americans call them. I even warned her in one letter that skirts were higher in Britain.

But one letter written late at night in the House of Commons in early December left these mundane matters behind. A long letter, it dealt with my attitude to medicine and politics which I quote in the chapter Doctor in the House. This part of the letter deals with my views on marriage.

December 1968

Dearest Debbie,

It's 12.30 at night and it looks as if we are all set for an all-night sitting, one of the more ludicrous facets of British Democracy and one to which I am not wedded to put it at its mildest. How lunatic to have people who make critical decisions sitting up all night and then working all day – thank goodness it doesn't happen too frequently. If it has one good side effect it might mean that I write a long letter. It also makes one ask oneself why – why is one here in politics. Looking across the river at St Thomas's Hospital and seeing lights on in my own wards I wonder deeply. So many memories rush back – often of being up in the night.

But perhaps enough of politics, medicine, life. What of us and love? What will it look like in five, ten or even twenty years time? Will we look back on successes or failures? I fear that for me the Gods have been too kind, far beyond that which any man can expect. Paradoxically, though the outward and visible aspects of my life appear successful so frequently, I myself see only failure and missed opportunities – too arrogant, too self-centred, wanting to love and yet yearning for variety, for an elusive freedom. Perhaps people like me shouldn't marry but I so want children, to watch them grow but not I hope to envelop them. To give them love and security but from a distance. Ever present but as a background.

Maybe we can do that. I hope so. So many of the things I totally
lack, you have. But you must retain these. Avoid for always becoming
a mirror image and remember your prime function is not as a mother
but as a lover. I have seen far too many wives forget that that and
that alone is the supreme relationship. Children are side effects,
important but not of primary consequence. Being a good mother is
of course a way of loving and showing your love to your husband
and likewise the position applies to me as a father but it is a
secondary role. My prime function is to love you not in an all
pervading way, not necessarily even exclusively but pre-eminently.
You must always matter more than anyone else.

Still it's time I lay down on the floor and tried to snatch some
sleep. I feel shagged out, almost too tired to sleep. I need to have
every one of my limbs massaged by your hands so that they no
longer bear any weight but float in a sensuous field of oblivion, of
warmth and softness.

Soon it will come. I yearn for it and you. Tonight I feel alone but
the distance is not far today. I feel as if you were asleep in bed at
home. I hope very soon Narrow Street will feel to you as being
home.

My parents had never before been to America, they had never met
Debbie's parents, they had never spent Christmas outside our own family
since 1945. It was nevertheless an amazingly happy and tension-free
Christmas and wedding. Any worries the two families might have had
were greatly helped by my father getting deliciously tight on the first
evening. He discovered that an American dry Martini has a lot more gin
and very little Martini. It is a large stiff drink, I would guess, four times
the usual English strength.

In America a bridal dinner is often given on the eve of the wedding for
very close friends and relatives. Ours was held in a tent alongside the
house, well warmed by blower heaters. My father-in-law was determined
that no expense be spared and the food and wine were excellent. It
seemed that every relative spoke after dinner. It was in danger of getting
a little too heavy when Lale Cortesi got to her feet. A young, elegant and
sophisticated New Yorker, she was speaking to a much older Long
Island, typical WASP (White, Anglo-Saxon, Protestant) gathering. Her
husband, she announced, would like to make a speech but she hoped
everyone would understand if he made it in Japanese as that was his
native tongue. Sandy Cortesi spoke entirely fake Japanese to an attentive
audience for what felt like nearly a minute, until they realized their leg
was being pulled. Then their laughter sounded as if it might split the tent.
What was already a happy evening became a riotous one. Malcolm
Borthwick, my next-door neighbour in London, made a wicked best
man's speech, entirely in verse and dressed up in a kilt he presented a
great theatrical performance.

We had a late-afternoon rather English wedding service next day in St

James's Church (xx). Then everything was repeated – another dinner and another dance. This time there were only a few very short speeches. Ever since, every 28 December, the band leader, Dutch Wolff, has sent a Happy Anniversary card. His marketing sense, as well as his kindness, we repaid when twenty years later to the day we returned for a dinner dance at Debbie's family home at St James. He played again and this time our three children helped us to dance the years away with all Debbie's family, except sadly her father. Some of our closest American friends were there including Anne Curtis, Debbie's bridesmaid, now a Professor of Radiology at Yale, and Sandy Cortesi with Wendy Mackenzie. Debbie's four brothers were all there: Michael and his family from Chicago, Peter from New York, Johnny from Arizona and Buzz who was at school in Massachusetts.

We left the wedding dance in an old jeep to the accompaniment of shots from a yacht-racing starter cannon. Up the driveway was Debbie's brother, Peter's, car and by now I was confident of driving on the right hand side of the road. But I forgot that American cars pack more horsepower than ours and accelerated away with a tail spin that put us in the ditch.

We managed to get ourselves out and arrived none the worse at the Plaza Hotel on Fifth Avenue. I had booked a room and actually had a receipt. I had also sent a bunch of red roses to await us. With our luggage we went to book in and our car was driven off down to the garage. The booking clerk checked off our name and then calmly announced that there was no booking and there were no spare rooms. Eventually, after much to-ing and fro-ing, we were shown to a dismal room. It had two single beds, only an internal window and it was dirty. There was no way we were going to spend the first night of our honeymoon in such a room. We went back down to the front desk and called for our car. By which time they had discovered from the first edition of the Sunday *New York Times* that I was the British Minister of the Navy. Suddenly we were offered the bridal suite. This only fuelled our anger and so we drove off to stay the night in the empty flat of 'Uncle Storer' and Margaret Lunt, two of Debbie's most cherished friends.

We had married having seen each other for only twenty-four days. We had met in one continent and were now to live in another.

7

NAVY MINISTER

To enter the Government on one's thirtieth birthday would be a thrilling enough experience in any junior ministerial post. But to have overall responsibility for the Royal Navy was the best job I could possibly have been offered. I have never doubted the need for relatively strong armed forces. I believe that laws not underwritten by force are ignored or circumvented. My father as a doctor and my uncle as a clergyman had both served in the Army during the Second World War. Moreover it is hard to be born and bred in Plymouth without having a special place in one's heart for the Navy. I would have joined the Royal Navy as a cadet at Dartmouth if the thirteen-year-old entry had been retained. So here I was, at a time when I might have been a mere lieutenant, Gilbert and Sullivan's 'ruler of the Queen's Navee' (xv). It was a daunting task, though my post was nowhere near as powerful or as grand as that of the First Lord of the Admiralty. That historic post, held twice by Winston Churchill, had been abolished in 1964, the holder having ceased to be a member of the Cabinet in 1940. Gradually the role of a Minister of State for the Navy was eroded too as the power of the Secretary of State for Defence grew, until only a mere Parliamentary Under-Secretary was responsible for the Navy. In the reorganization of 1984 all three of the single services lost even this junior Minister. The Admiralty Board, however, still existed, as did the Admiralty Board Room. Thanks to the restoration work after it was bombed in 1941, the first time I sat in the Chair of a Board meeting I was looking on a scene which differed little from that which my predecessors saw as they drew up orders to the fleet before the Battle of Trafalgar. The wind dial operated by a vane on the roof told the Admirals which way the wind was blowing in Whitehall, but as one of the Admirals said to me, 'Your job is to tell us which way the political wind is blowing and then we can bear off to take account of it.' That was as good a job description as I would or could get.

There were 100,000 officers, ratings and Royal Marines in naval service when I was appointed and 226 ships, excluding survey vessels and depot and supply ships, though only 166 of these were operational. In a Supplementary Statement on Defence, presented to Parliament in the month that I joined the Ministry, it was announced that the plan was to withdraw British forces from bases in the Persian Gulf and in South-East Asia by the end of 1971. For the next two years, therefore, I was heavily involved in the withdrawal from East of Suez. I visited the Navy and the Royal Marines in Singapore (xix) and was amazed to find that the naval dockyard buildings and equipment covered a vast area. Though we were acting against the Government of Singapore's wishes, in fact our withdrawal was the stimulus which helped create the dynamic market economy which has since transformed Singapore. In preparing to close down the Royal Naval base in Bahrain there was more heart-searching. At a minimal cost that base enabled us to offer some stability to countries which needed a few more years to settle in as independent states. But unfortunately we had moved forces from Aden to the Gulf instead of taking them home, and in doing so had given our military deployment in the Gulf a higher political profile. So it had been decided to remove all our service bases.

As a backbencher I had campaigned to concentrate our defence effort in Europe believing that our forces were grossly overstretched. I also supported reducing defence expenditure, although I knew that this would have adverse consequences in my own constituency. But at least now I would be in the driving seat and able to soften some of the impact on Plymouth; I resolved to block any attempt to close Devonport Dockyard. I knew that some inside the Ministry favoured reducing Plymouth to just a Fleet Maintenance Base, believing it better to keep open Chatham Dockyard now that the new nuclear submarine refitting base was virtually completed. Cynics within the Labour Party were predicting that my promotion was Harold Wilson's way of making one of his critics live with the consequences of glibly advocating defence cuts. The more charitable explanation of his motives, and the one to which I subscribed, was that he realized the only way my marginal seat could be held was if its own MP was seen to protect its interests. Nevertheless, it was in some sense poetic justice that a rebellious backbencher, who had argued for devaluation, defence cuts and withdrawal East of Suez, should now defend and implement that policy at home and abroad.

The British military presence in the Far East had been one of the few disputed features of what had been a largely bi-partisan defence policy since 1940. Some of us who were against such an extensive deployment in the Far East could nevertheless see the virtues of having a permanent, stabilizing military presence. But with our chronic balance of payments deficit, the high cost of these commitments in foreign exchange meant that we could no longer support them. Also our military forces were insufficiently strong to match our commitments and the continued presence of a military force outside Europe was no guarantee of effective action. We felt we should concentrate on developing the ability to deploy quickly and to sustain logistically a credible fighting force from Europe.

Staying East of Suez became an emotive issue in the Labour Party. It was the Boy Scout in Harold Wilson, the spirit of Baden-Powell, that made him come out with the ludicrous claim that 'our frontier is on the Himalayas'. That was taking the Gurkha's magnificent contribution to our armed forces more than a bridge too far. After 1964 it was as if Harold Wilson merely mimicked the old poseur Harold Macmillan in his top table posturing and bogus summiteering. Against a background of continued economic decline it lacked credibility. This was nowhere more obvious than Wilson's attempt to bring about a settlement in Vietnam in 1965. It bordered on farce to use Harold Davies MP, an old Left-winger who had had some dealings with Ho Chi Minh and who was Parliamentary Secretary to the Ministry of Pensions and National Insurance. A later attempt with Kosygin also failed because of President Johnson's lack of trust in Wilson once he, unlike Australia's Prime Minister, refused to commit British troops to help in Vietnam. So much of Wilson's gimmicky diplomacy was doomed. His response to Ian Smith's illegal declaration of Rhodesian independence in terms of activity was prodigious. But he lacked the sinews of someone who understood or exercised real power. The similarity between Macmillan and Wilson owed something to the way both men were depicted by cartoonists. Supermac's approach had greater panache than Wilson's but the two men's style was surprisingly similar. They were both illusionists who at times brilliantly manipulated their parties, Parliament and the public. Yet both failed to come to grips with Britain's real international position and both foundered on the intransigence of General de Gaulle.

What was more surprising was how slow Denis Healey was to grasp the reality of Britain's position between 1964 and 1967. He has always been more radical in Opposition, away from civil service advice, than in Government where he has a long record of following such advice and being extremely conventional. In fairness, the Ministry of Defence was heavily committed to confrontation with Indonesia when Denis Healey took office in 1964. It can be argued that this inhibited him and the incoming Labour Government in 1964 from taking a strategic decision to reduce overseas military commitments. The mistake was not to realign British foreign and defence policy immediately after the 1966 General Election victory. Then the new Indonesian Government was discussing with Malaysia the possibility of ending confrontation. The opposition to doing this came from President Johnson and his Secretary of State, Dean Rusk, who saw any British withdrawal as undermining the American position in Vietnam and leaving them vulnerably exposed as the only foreign power with overseas bases in the Far East. Harold Wilson deferred to Washington but he was also personally very susceptible in those days to Lee Kuan Yew's arguments against withdrawal.

The Americans strongly resented our withdrawal, particularly from the Persian Gulf. Dean Rusk had told George Brown, 'For God's sake act like Britain', and that our opting out of our responsibilities was the end of an era; he sensed, he said, 'the acrid aroma of a *fait accompli*'. Australia and New Zealand were also upset; Malaysia and Singapore felt let down. Service morale in Britain probably sank lower than at any time since the abortive invasion in 1956 of Suez.

In 1972 I wrote a book called *The Politics of Defence* in which I argued that, if a firm decision to withdraw had been made in the summer of 1966 at the latest, millions of pounds would have been saved, the absurdity of transferring troops from Aden to expensive new barracks in the small Gulf states would have been avoided and the re-equipment programme for the services could have been logically developed to support primary British defence interests within Western Europe. Also a major realignment of British foreign and defence policy would have been given an overall coherence and logic which would have shown it to be the historic and long overdue decision that it essentially was. In the event, the historic perspective was completely lost, the decision was seen by the world and presented inside Britain by a Conservative Opposition as an undignified scuttle, a panic reaction to financial pressures and as an example of incompetent and ill-considered government.

Denis Healey was my boss for two years and a very stimulating one to have. All Ministers must to some extent identify with and defend the interests of their departments and this is healthy, allowing for better Cabinet discussion and decisions. But Denis Healey became too powerful an advocate of the vested interests of the Ministry of Defence East of Suez. After devaluation in 1967, an early decision was needed on whether to cancel the F-111 fighter bomber aircraft. The new Chancellor of the Exchequer, Roy Jenkins, with the expertise of a former Minister of Aviation, was determined we would cut our coat according to our cloth and was adamant that the F-111 should be cancelled. Its cost had soared but, even so, Denis was prepared to offer exactly equivalent cuts in defence spending in order to save the F-111. He argued, unconvincingly, that the F-111 was needed for operations entirely within Europe but the real reason for his and the Ministry's support for the F-111 was that with its long range it provided a general military capability. George Brown was quite explicit that the F-111 was the key to being able to stay East of Suez which he wanted us to do. Denis fought like a tiger for the F-111 but Roy knew that the only way he could hope for real savings on the defence budget was to make a strategic cut and eventually he proved too formidable an adversary for Denis.

When Denis returned to the Ministry after Cabinet he may have expressed his frustration to some intimates but, within hours of this defeat, he proceeded to lecture one very senior officer on the merits of the cancellation. This was altogether too much for the man who told me he had come prepared to be sympathetic but left contemptuous. The epithet of 'the tank' has stuck to Denis – not a tank that bulldozes over all opposition, as is sometimes implied, but a tank that can turn through 180° on the pull of a lever and head off at the same speed in the opposite direction. Dick Crossman, near the end of his life, said to me of Denis, with real vehemence, 'He has a totalitarian mind.' This was a tough judgement but it is an insight from another powerful intellect. Crossman's biographer, Anthony Howard, describes him as a don at Oxford before the war, as a Right-winger at the very time a youthful Denis Healey was a member of the Communist Party. Crossman then became Left-wing as Denis moved to the Right. Though Denis can change his opinion with ease, he often does so because of another characteristic, loyalty. Of all the senior politicians I have known, Denis was by far the most loyal to decisions he did not like, to colleagues he served or who served him, to Labour Party policy he disliked and above all to his wife Edna and his family. This quality of his, more than any other, means that I have always measured Denis by a stringent but more generous yardstick than I use for any other politician. He also has great style. I can hear him, as if it were yesterday, getting up from a dinner at Admiralty House and announcing with a chuckle that he was off 'to vote for the people against privilege'. It was not just a joke. There was always a hint of 'Denis the Menace' against privilege, and justly so. For all his faults he is a big man and I have been lucky to learn from him and to know him.

When I took office the First Sea Lord was Admiral Sir Varyl Begg GCB, DSO, DSC; an Admiral with salt both in his ears and his tongue. He adored the Navy and once he saw that I loved it too we got on well. But he did not suffer fools gladly and on my first day he told me straight out that he was still recovering from the shock of having a thirty-year-old put in charge of the Navy. He was shortly to retire, having taken the Navy through the trauma of the aircraft carrier cancellation following the resignation of the then First Sea Lord, Sir Richard Luce. He had extracted one significant concession from Denis Healey, that three new cruisers should fill the gap left by the aircraft carriers. Apart from providing excellent command and control facilities, no one really knew what would be the maritime role of these large surface ships.

The new First Sea Lord, Sir Michael le Fanu, was a completely different character. He was red-headed, red-blooded and particularly incensed about the loss of the carriers. Amid much publicity he flew 8,000 miles to Singapore as a navigator in a Buccaneer within days of taking office. Then irreverently called 'Lee Fan Yew', or the 'Chinese Admiral', he called on Lee Kuan Yew the Prime Minister of Singapore. Totally devoid of pomposity and the friendliest of men, he had a fund of funny rather schoolboyish stories, usually at his own expense. He was loved by almost everyone who knew him in the Navy. Stories about him abounded. Once, when he was Commander-in-Chief of the Middle East, charged with withdrawing from Aden, he was on an airfield dressed in plain khaki uniform and unselfconsciously started to help an airman unload an aircraft. The airman, not seeing the four stars on his shirt and sensing after a while that he was slowing down, said, 'Come on, Ginge, get a bloody move on!' When Mike le Fanu was asked what he did then, he replied, 'Exactly what I was told to, I got a move on.'

When the Second Sea Lord, Admiral Sir Frank Twiss, persuaded all of us on the Admiralty Board to get rid of the naval tot Mike le Fanu realized its political sensitivity and did everything to show that this was a naval decision, earning another nickname, 'Dry Ginger' – later the title of a breezy book about him by Richard Baker. The rum ration was the equivalent of four-and-a-half pub measures. After the bosun at the wheel had had his midday tot he would have failed a breathalyser test. The Admiralty Board feared a backlash and at one meeting we solemnly talked about the risk of mutiny. A doggerel going around the lower deck at the time went like this:

> Jack's always done his duty
> To country and to throne,
> And all he asks in fairness
> Is: leave his tot alone.

We softened the blow by allowing spirits in the Petty Officers' mess for the first time and extra beer for the ratings was also given at my suggestion. I had to defend the decision to abolish the tot in a debate in the House of Commons in January 1970. Jim Wellbeloved, Labour MP for Erith and Crayford, had instigated the debate as 'a matter of the utmost gravity' but it began with much hilarity. Soon Mr Speaker was intervening to say, 'This is a serious debate. If there is too much interruption, I may have to hang an Honorable Member from the yardarm.' The debate was wound up for the Conservatives by Rear-Admiral Morgan-Giles (Winchester). 'This is a terrible day', he began to cries from Roy Roebuck (Harrow, East), 'Hoist the main brace!' and Mr William Hamling (Woolwich, West) 'Shiver me timbers!' Rear-Admiral Morgan-Giles went on, 'Rum has been issued to the Royal Navy for two hundred years.' In fact he supported the decision. I announced £2.7 million for a Sailors' Fund so that all the rum savings went back in improved leisure facilities. In those days the annual Navy Estimates debate was quite an occasion and it mattered to the Navy what was said. Sadly, over the years, its importance has declined as have the number of MPs who have served in the Navy, though the Royal Marines are rather better represented.

With Mike le Fanu I embarked on one of the more delicate Whitehall operations that I have been involved in. He was determined to retain naval air power in one form or another despite not being able to build new aircraft carriers. He had already, largely to boost morale, taken and passed a helicopter pilot's course. Indeed on one occasion I put my life and that of my wife and father-in-law in his hands when he flew us to Holbrook, a school for the sons of seafarers for the annual prize-giving where the year before the Queen Mother had given the prizes (xviii). Mike le Fanu knew that the Royal Air Force, having won the inter-service battle over the carriers, was watching the Navy very carefully. He was determined to move with stealth. His surprising first decision was to take me into his confidence. This must have been difficult since he could not be sure which way I would go on the issue and whether or not I would tell Denis Healey. I was flattered to be trusted but also I had never been party to the earlier decision to cancel the carriers and privately had considerable reservations about its wisdom. If we could retain air power at minimal cost, this would be very attractive and I felt at liberty to authorize the Navy to explore this new option entirely on a single service basis. Denis Healey would have to agree any eventual decision but meanwhile there was no point in putting a naval cat among the light blue pigeons.

The first step, at the existing design stage of the new cruiser, was to move the command and control centre from midships to the side. Our justification was that we needed the space for the large Sea King helicopters necessary for the agreed anti-submarine warfare capability. Then the number of helicopters necessary for twenty-four-hour a day cover was increased and so the size of the deck increased. Mike Le Fanu was adamant that it should not be re-christened a mini-carrier and that we should stick to calling it a cruiser, albeit a through-deck cruiser. He also knew, because he had very close links with the US Navy, that the US marines were very interested in our Harrier jump jet. After a suitable interval I was asked to authorize the flying of a Harrier on and off the helicopter deck of the existing cruiser, HMS *Blake*. I feared that this would trigger off press comment about the return of the aircraft carriers, so I briefed the Head of the Royal Naval Press Office to angle all the publicity towards export sales of the Harrier to the Americans and to keep clear of any implications for the Royal Navy. Gradually, as it became clear that the US Navy was likely to buy Harriers, it was possible to discuss having special Sea Harriers designed to be embarked on naval vessels, and to make provision for a few as part of the mix with helicopters on the through-deck cruisers. The problem then was who should fly the Harrier.

I suggested to Mike le Fanu that the Navy should propose that these Harriers be flown by RAF pilots. He saw the virtue of this immediately and, despite some criticism from the Fleet Air Arm that we were selling out, we got it agreed within the Ministry that the Harriers should not be permanently based at sea and that the Navy should stick to flying helicopters. Soon Mike le Fanu's readiness to play along was justified: as he had predicted, RAF pilots lost any initial enthusiasm for going to sea.

Some found themselves sick in rough weather and others disliked living aboard ship. After a while it became generally accepted, along with the fact that the through-deck cruiser was really a mini-carrier, that the Fleet Air Arm should fly Naval Harriers.

One of the last decisions that Denis Healey took before we left office in 1970 was to approve HMS *Invincible* as the first of that particular class of ship. It was a fateful decision. When Argentina invaded the Falklands in 1982, the then First Sea Lord, Admiral Leach, who had been Captain of Naval Plans in my time, knew very well that he had indigenous air power available both on the old carrier HMS *Hermes* and the new mini-carrier HMS *Invincible*. It is widely acknowledged that Leach personally made the crucial difference, with his strong recommendation to Margaret Thatcher when they met in the House of Commons on the night of the invasion, that a Task Force should be sent to repossess the Islands. I have no doubt that without the Harrier jets the Task Force would have had far greater difficulty in defeating the Argentines. Indeed without them it might well have been impossible. To me one surprising feature of the Falklands engagement was how vulnerable our ships were to incoming missiles. This weakness had been well known in the Ministry of Defence when I was there and I thought we had instigated provision for new anti-missile defences years before. I only discovered during the Falklands War that these had been cancelled in the 1970s because of financial constraints. We were very lucky not to lose even more ships.

A fascinating part of my job was dealing with the Polaris nuclear deterrent programme. The four submarines were not yet complete and we were still building up the operational base in Faslane. The whole programme was on a very tight schedule so that the transfer of the deterrent role would coincide with the phasing out of the aging V-bomber force.

The biggest problem we had with the Polaris Agreement was Admiral Rickover's hostility to the whole concept of collaboration over nuclear matters with anyone, the British included. The head of the US Navy programme, he guarded US nuclear submarine secrets with a ferocity that bordered on paranoia. Yet when he authorized the two navies to exchange information it could and often did save the Royal Navy millions of pounds. Rickover was the 'father' of nuclear-powered submarines, a prickly customer by any standards, but nevertheless a remarkable man who, with the help of Congressional leaders, had built his own empire. He was in an inviolable position, with even successive Presidents of the United States unable to force his retirement. Fortunately, as I have already mentioned, he got on well with Solly Zuckerman, who had been Scientific Adviser in the Ministry of Defence, and thereafter was based in the Cabinet Office. In order to improve relations with Rickover's team on the naval network, a fellow naval engineer, Rear Admiral (Lou) Le Bailly, was sent to Washington as Naval Attaché. Years before he had worked with Rickover in connection with HMS *Dreadnought*. It was an inspired choice, for Lou's charming and gregarious nature was ideally suited to overcome suspicions from American naval officers influenced by Rickover. Gradually the atmosphere between Rickover and the Royal Navy thawed. When I visited Washington, to everyone's surprise, I had a long and fascinating talk with Rickover, having beefed-up my own scientific expertise. This was helped by my having studied our civil nuclear power programme when on the Science and Technology Select Committee. In Lou's book, *The Man Around the Engine*, he tells how Rickover was asked by a West European naval attaché, 'When are you going to tell us about your nuclear submarines, Admiral?', to which Rickover replied, 'I take my orders from God, but I'm not communicating with him at the moment. When I do I'll send you a telegram.'

The Polaris programme was criticized by some of the Left-wing Labour MPs in the Tribune Group and there were a few demonstrations in Scotland. But the domestic controversy was nowhere near as great as that which was to develop later. Most Labour MPs forgot that they had fought the 1964 Election on getting rid of Polaris, and in the 1966 Election its continuation was assumed. I have pondered long and hard the case for Britain keeping a nuclear deterrent which we can threaten to use independently. With an American wife and all three of my children with dual citizenship, I have profound respect for the United States. But I believe Clem Attlee and Ernest Bevin were right in 1946 that Britain should make her own atom bomb. I will never forget that the US only had troops on the ground in the 1914–18 War by its closing stages; that, even with the most powerful President in their history, Franklin Roosevelt, they did not come into the Second World War until America had been attacked by the Japanese at Pearl Harbor; that, despite making available all our nuclear know-how and scientists for the A-bomb programme, the US Congress turned around immediately after the war and tried to freeze the UK out of any further nuclear co-operation and that President Harry Truman went along with their decision. I do not wish my country to be wholly dependent on the reaction of a US President if we are ever threatened by nuclear blackmail. Our possession of nuclear weapons, as for the French, also ensures that no US President can ignore our views on major security questions, nor those of Western Europe. These facts are sufficient to convince me that it is a crucial national interest to maintain an independent nuclear deterrent.

I travelled to Florida for a test firing of a Polaris missile by HMS *Renown*. I boarded the ship in the early morning and we sailed for the missile firing range, returning the same night. The actual firing was remarkable: only a slight judder in the ship confirmed that the missile had been launched. Later the result was radioed back to us showing, over hundreds of miles, pinpoint accuracy. The whole Polaris programme and now that of Trident is a remarkable testimony to the relationship, not just between the United States and the United Kingdom, but also to the warm friendship that exists between the two navies. Britain has had a fantastic bargain, being able to purchase sophisticated hardware without paying anything near the full research and development costs.

I developed a keen interest in submarine warfare and, after studying the analysis of the relative vulnerabilities, I became convinced that in an age of satellite photography old fashioned naval terms like 'over the horizon deployment' were out of date. It seemed that the shrouding quality of the sea meant that we should put the balance of the Navy underwater. I argued for submarines at the expense of the surface fleet. I could put these iconoclastic views forward best at the 'brood-ins' for the Admiralty Board that Mike le Fanu arranged. Wherever I looked in the Navy Department, I found stimulating intellectual challenges and naval officers well able to think through the issues involved.

I well remember travelling to a naval establishment with Sir Frank Twiss, a small bird-like figure who had been a Japanese prisoner of war. I was being rather casual about the possibility of arriving a few minutes late. Quietly but icily, he told me what it was like as a young rating to be out on a parade ground waiting in the rain for the guard of honour to be inspected. I vowed there and then to try hard always to be on time. In this service atmosphere I also began to study leadership, reading about Lord Nelson. It surprised me to find that the man who understood Nelson's greatest quality was General de Gaulle who would often quote Admiral Fisher's comments on Admiral Jellicoe after the Battle of Jutland: 'He has all Nelson's qualities but one: he doesn't know how to disobey.'

General de Gaulle had fascinated me since I was eighteen. I had watched in May 1968, the 'month of the barricades', when France was shaken and brought to a virtual standstill with rioting students and two million workers out on strike, how President de Gaulle had waited and, when he had secretly sought and been assured of the support of the armed forces, clamped down. François Mitterrand, the leader of the Left, attacked him for provoking a civil war and said, after de Gaulle's broadcast, 'the voice we have just heard is the voice of dictatorship'. At the end of June, de Gaulle won a resounding victory in a general election, in the process ensuring that the Communists were blamed, as Le Monde put it, for 'barricades they did not put up and for strike pickets they did not command'. Yet by April 1969, at the age of seventy-eight, having only achieved a 47 per cent 'yes' vote on a constitutional referendum to reorganize regional government, he resigned. It was hubris that led him to make the referendum in effect a vote of confidence which brought about his own dramatic fall from power. By threatening to resign if he did not win the referendum, he invited his own downfall. Yet that he would use such a tactic could have been predicted from reading his own views on leadership, published when he was only a young Colonel. In

The Edge of the Sword, originally published in France in 1932, he reveals views which he followed throughout his life:

> This passion for self-reliance is obviously accompanied by some rough-
> ness of method. The man of character incorporates in his own person
> the severity inherent in his effort. This is felt by his subordinates and
> at times they groan under it. In any event, a leader of this quality is
> inevitably aloof, for there can be no authority without prestige, nor
> prestige unless he keeps his distance.

Appropriately this formidable leader was toppled by the people speaking directly to him in a referendum, for it had been successive referenda which had given him the authority he needed to defeat the Colonels in Algeria, to replace the constitution of the Fifth Republic, and to revive the fortunes of France.

His successor as President, Georges Pompidou, lifted the veto on British entry. Yet de Gaulle's legacy remains: he knew that the much needed renovation of Europe would only be accomplished by retaining the vitality and drive that stems from the nation state. That is an insight which Margaret Thatcher had as well. A Europe that denigrates or downplays nationhood will never achieve its full potential. De Gaulle's vision of a 'Europe des patries' goes with the grain of European history. The vision of another eminent Frenchman, Jean Monnet, of a United States of Europe goes not only against the grain of our history but is a bureaucrat's dream. I have always believed that politicians in France or Britain, preferably both, while supporting European unity, will also feel strongly about the need to maintain the sinews of nationhood. And that they will use the power of veto within the European Community treaties to halt any development which crosses the threshold to a federal Europe. It is a hard distinction to make but instinct, on which all political leadership in the last analysis rests, must guide these decisions.

The Labour Government decided to open negotiations for entry to the European Community just before the calling of the general election. There was little party political difference on the issue. Each party had its small but vocal group of anti-marketeers but it was reasonable to expect a successful outcome to the negotiations and when Edward Heath, in a speech in Paris, talked of the wholehearted consent of the British people, most people assumed that this was already present.

An issue close to my heart, which ran on right up to the 1970 Election, was what to do with the Royal Naval Dockyards. In 1968 we had four fully operating, in Rosyth, Chatham, Portsmouth and Plymouth. Rosyth Dockyard was inviolable as we were building it up in order to refit Polaris submarines. Chatham Dockyard had just had millions of pounds spent on it to refit the new hunter-killer nuclear-powered submarines. Portsmouth and Plymouth had as yet no nuclear refitting facilities and were confined to refitting surface ships and diesel submarines. It was obvious to me that if Devonport Dockyard was going to survive it had to move into nuclear submarine refitting. Fortunately Devonport had far more berthage space than Chatham for surface ships and far better and quicker access to the Atlantic. Yet even so, the best short-term financial choice for the Navy was to close Devonport Dockyard. This appalling prospect dawned on me in my first few weeks in office and I realized I was facing an acute political challenge. I did not see how I could be the Minister who closed down by far the largest industrial employer in the city of Plymouth, for at that stage the general manager's department of Devonport Dockyard employed 18,000 people. So within a few months of taking office I was looking down the barrel of a political gun, loaded and aimed at my head. If we had to close Devonport, resignation might have helped me in Plymouth but it would have been an admission to my Parliamentary colleagues that I was not prepared to let the national good override my fear of losing my marginal seat. I decided that I would tough it out. I would fight my corner for Plymouth but only on its intrinsic merits. I felt that if it once looked as if I put my constituency interests before the best interest of the Navy, my influence within the Ministry of Defence would be immediately marginalized.

Fortunately for me the Chief of Fleet Support, Vice Admiral Turner, showed remarkable understanding of the political difficulties I faced. He was also very worried about the difficulty of retaining skilled workers at Chatham when there was so much competition for labour from local industry. In Devonport, where unemployment levels were high, retention of skilled people was much easier. Soon it was the Naval Staff who wanted Plymouth developed as a nuclear refitting base. But they also wanted all four dockyards to be retained with the largest cutback in the labour force being concentrated in Devonport. They preferred no cutbacks in Portsmouth because there were so many other naval installa-tions nearby and because so many of them had their own houses there. I, however, wanted Portsmouth to take its share of the cutback in dockyard numbers, in part to reduce the number of jobs lost in Plymouth. Gerry Reynolds, as Minister of Defence for Administration, knew that financial savings only come from strategic cuts and he was adamant in wanting one dockyard to close completely. If we closed Chatham, the political problem was that we would have to spend a lot more capital on building alternative nuclear refitting facilities in Plymouth as well as explaining away Christopher Mayhew's earlier decision to build up Chatham.

After a lot of in-fighting, it was time for a decision which could only come from Denis Healey. I was visiting the Royal Naval Air Station in Yeovilton and in the morning I flew, for the first time supersonic, in a Phantom jet. I had previously flown in the propeller-driven Gannet, on and off an aircraft carrier. To land on a carrier is one of the more terrifying things I have done in my life. Each time I would arrive at the air station and be introduced to a pilot. After take off, there would be the carrier, like a speck in the ocean. Then as the plane lined up for the descent all I could see was the hair on the back of the pilot's neck. Descending I would find myself reading into that neck more than one would believe possible, for the person in front literally had my life in his hands. The actual landing on an aircraft carrier is a sophisticated crash. Suddenly the deck of the carrier emerges and then simultaneously the hook on one's plane catches on the arrester gear. The deceleration is massive. It is far more powerful than the kick in the kidneys I experienced when accelerating off a steam-launch catapult.

That morning in Yeovilton I was passed fit by the doctor to fly and kitted out with all the sophisticated equipment. I climbed into the Phantom behind the pilot, was strapped in and we took off. Flying straight out into the Irish Sea, it seemed only a few minutes before he said that we would go supersonic though I was quite unaware of the exact moment that we did. When the plane turned to come back I began to feel very odd and the pilot, who was chatting most of the time, asked me if I was OK. I did not like to complain so said nothing, but when he started to turn the plane more tightly, what had been a minor feeling of discomfort became acute. I felt flattened against the back of the seat and my face began to pull as if the flesh was peeling off. I described this feeling to the pilot and he asked whether I had a pressure suit on. I said that I assumed so but I did not know for I had just climbed into whatever had been put out for me. He immediately slowed the plane down flying as straight as possible and we landed, with me feeling somewhat drained. We then discovered that in all the fuss surrounding my visit I had not been given a pressure suit and so had been subjected to considerable gravity pressure, far more than was healthy.

On landing I was told that Denis Healey had called a meeting on the dockyards for late afternoon and if I was to be present I had to fly back to Northolt immediately. At the dockyard meeting I was distinctly below par, feeling as if I had been dragged through a hedge backwards. Fortunately Denis Healey accepted the package which we had hammered out. Chatham was to close completely, Devonport was to be extensively modernized with a new nuclear refitting base and three new covered slips for refitting Leander frigates. Portsmouth was to lose some of its labour force. Devonport was eventually to lose 5,000 jobs over a period of years. My task was to convince everyone that the £75 million modernization of the dockyard guaranteed its future and that the job losses were a necessary and unavoidable evil. Fortunately the dockyard unions were very understanding. They knew that at one stage Devonport had been very near to being closed and were well aware of all the fighting I had done on their behalf. Nevertheless, the announcement, coming at the start of 1970, ensured that the future job losses risked becoming a major issue at the general election even though we hoped to achieve it all by natural wastage. It was unusual for any Minister to face an issue of such magnitude, intimately involving his own constituency. I had had to balance any number of different interests: the Treasury need for savings, the Navy's need for greater dockyard efficiency and the needs of my own constituents for jobs and spending power within the city. Fortunately the outcome was far better than I could ever have hoped when I first started to grapple with it eighteen months earlier.

Quite apart from strategic decisions about the dockyards, I was also heavily involved in the struggle to make them more efficient, something which has eluded everyone who has tried since Samuel Pepys. I was directly responsible for 45,800 industrial civil servants with very different needs from the much larger number of non-industrial civil servants. I chaired the Whitley Council and was closely involved with trade union leaders. It was very educative and meant that far from being solely involved in naval matters I was dealing with domestic industrial issues. It also brought me into quite close contact with the Treasury and Barbara Castle's new Department of Employment and Productivity. We tried to bring in new efficiency techniques, getting rid of the Admiral Superintendents and bringing in general managers. We also introduced a new Chief Executive, the first being Leslie Norfolk, who had been in the private sector, mainly with ICI. I also tried but failed to get the Treasury to accept the case for a separate Dockyard Fund, which would not be constrained by existing civil service rules. These are designed for administrative departments and wholly inappropriate for an industrial enterprise. I remember on one occasion, the Deputy Under-Secretary, the Chief of Fleet Support, the Chief Executive of the Dockyards and myself sitting around a table and deciding in which naval dockyard a particularly ineffective general manager would do the least damage. For months we had tried to persuade the Treasury to allow us to retire him early with a 'golden bowler', but they were adamant in refusing. Yet the Treasury were content to accept the continuation of a manager, who, through inefficiency, would cost them far more in a few months than any generous redundancy scheme. It was during these years that I started to be convinced that it was impossible for Government departments, under Treasury rules, to run any industry, either directly themselves or even indirectly through nationalized boards. Treasury control was too strong and too restrictive; parliamentary control was too pettifogging and unrealistic. The only way these industries might ever have been run efficiently would be if the Treasury had given up its year by year control of their revenue, capital accounts and manpower numbers. Successive Labour Governments in the 1960s and 1970s, with an ideological wish to see the public sector flourish, were not prepared to free up the management of these industries sufficiently. In many respects the privatization programme of the 1980s was the logical outcome of the failure of Labour Governments to free the public sector from unacceptable Treasury accounting procedures.

When Barbara Castle embarked on preparing her White Paper, 'In Place of Strife', I was involved, not because of attending Cabinet Sub-Committees, for that was normally done by the more senior Ministers in the Department, but because the Navy Department was the largest industrial employer within Government. In its own right the Department was part of the consultation process within and outside Government. My trade union contacts through the Whitley machinery also ensured that I was hearing the views of the trade unions directly. Until this time I had given very little thought to the place of the trade union movement in British society, or the underlying philosophical issues surrounding industrial relations. As a backbencher I had merely noted the Donovan Report, published in March 1968 when I was falling in love in America. Creating a Royal Commission was one of Harold Wilson's characteristic ways of resolving pressing problems. This one, appointed in April 1965, when the Government barely had a majority, was a committee de-liberately chosen to produce a consensus, not provoke a crisis. I did not feel strongly either way about the Commission's recommendations and the 145,000-word report, lengthy like most Royal Commission reports and covering all aspects of the trade unions' and employers' associations, seemed destined to gather dust.

It was A.P. Herbert, speaking in the House of Commons with the candour and independence of a man elected by Oxford graduates under the old system of university seats, who wisely said, 'A Royal Commission is generally appointed not so much for digging up the truth, as for digging it in: and a Government department appointing a Royal Commis-sion is like a dog burying a bone, except that a dog does eventually return to the bone.' As Peter Jenkins wrote in *The Battle of Downing Street*, after more than three years the dog returned to the bone, and the dog was called Barbara Castle.

The Donovan Report went down like a lead balloon with the press and the general public. This was not surprising given the recent spate of industrial action. Strikes had become commonplace and they were widely felt to be damaging our export performance and giving Britain a reputa-tion as an unreliable supplier. George Woodcock, the TUC General Secretary, bizarrely having been made one of the Commissioners, was rightly judged to have pulled the wool over the eyes of the chairman, Lord Donovan, himself a former Labour Member of Parliament. Harold Wilson had no doubt, like many other people, that it was still necessary to 'do something about the unions'. Barbara Castle was never a legislative laggard and responded to the challenge. Not for her some minor legislative adjustment! What she wanted was far more ambitious, a wholly new philosophy of industrial relations. She succeeded, for the White Paper, 'In Place of Strife – A Policy for Industrial Relations', published on 18 January 1969, was a major document of State, whatever one thought of its contents.

I doubt if I had exchanged more than a few words with Barbara Castle throughout that Parliament. I could see even then though that she was a lady of quality. She moved in a circle of contacts on the Left, I on the Right, and we had no reason to talk. She believed she was offering a bargain. The unions were to be strengthened and allowed to retain the legal right to organize and negotiate, while in return they had to accept additional obligations to act constitutionally, particularly over unofficial strikes. The problem was that she was not offering much of a bargain for most trade union leaders. They found it impossible to imagine that their Labour Government was not going to keep their immunities, so to them this was no concession; they would have been truly shattered if Labour had not continued the status quo. Their fear was the old trade union negotiator's nightmare of 'the thin end of the wedge'. The concessions they were being asked to make to Labour might not be onerous now but what would an incoming Conservative Government be able to do with them?

The really controversial proposals were the twenty-eight-day 'conciliation pause', which was Barbara Castle's brainchild, and the compulsory strike ballots, which were Harold Wilson's own favourite. They had sought and won the full support of Roy Jenkins for their proposals. They did not go to the Industrial Relations Committee of the Cabinet on which Jim Callaghan, a predictable critic, sat. Instead they used a small committee of experts, then went, with George Woodcock's support, to the General Council of the TUC before the proposals were even discussed by the Cabinet. Not surprisingly, the Cabinet deeply resented being bounced. But pique was only a small factor; the actual proposals were objected to in principle. Jim Callaghan was by then Home Secretary but he had also, in 1967, been elected Treasurer of the Labour Party. He believed that neither the conciliation pause nor the strike ballot would work. Moreover, his whole political philosophy was based on the importance of the link between the unions and the Labour Party. He was convinced that this, for him, precious link, was going to be strained to breaking point and, though he denied it, he must have feared that it would mean a less generous response to his pre-election appeal for funds. The Cabinet Ministers on the right who felt most strongly were Dick Marsh, then Minister of Transport, and Roy Mason, a former coal miner. On the left, Dick Crossman and Judith Hart were adamantly against.

Despite Ministerial opposition, the White Paper was pushed through Cabinet by Wilson. From then on, members of the Government were bound to support it at least in public. I believed that the proposals were broadly correct and initially it seemed as if the generally favourable press would carry a somewhat reluctant group of trade union MPs along with the reforms. Yet it became clear to me, even in Plymouth with no history of militant trade unionism, that there was trouble ahead. On 26 March, the NEC of the Labour Party rejected 'In Place of Strife', with Jim Callaghan once again voting against Barbara Castle. Jennie Lee, Aneurin Bevan's widow, and the Minister responsible for the Open University, voted with Jim Callaghan as did Tom Bradley, Roy Jenkins's Parliamentary Private Secretary, who was, like me, a member of the 1963 Club. For all his protestations of innocence, Jim Callaghan was daring Wilson to sack him. He had now become, in Peter Jenkins's words, 'The Keeper of the Cloth Cap.'

I did not know Jim Callaghan well. I was not, however, as instinctively hostile to him personally as many of the other young professional Labour MPs. Some close to Roy Jenkins had privately and semi-publicly pilloried Jim over the Kenyan Asians. But I felt that Roy had been lucky to escape from the Home Office in time and that it was bad luck on Jim that he had inherited this particular poisoned chalice on taking office. My occasional meetings with Peter Jay gave me insight into Jim's thinking on some issues and I disliked patronizing talk about his populism. It seemed instinctive and not false to me. Populism is a strange political characteristic, it can be as much a vice as a virtue. Tony Crosland nurturing his own image as friend of the Grimsby fishermen and sup- porter of Grimsby Town Football Club had its amusing side but I understood his feelings for they were genuine. The fishermen around the Barbican in Plymouth, although in those days much fewer in number than the Grimsby fishermen, were also full of character, adding something to my constituency as well. Having watched Plymouth Argyle from the terraces ever since I was a small boy, I could also identify with his enthusiasm for football. What I disliked intensely was people pretending to be what they were not. As a medical student, working on building sites, well before becoming a politician, I sensed that no people were quicker at detecting a phoney than the British working class. They far prefer people to be what they are. To relate to popular feeling is a political strength. What is self-defeating is to be seen to be at the beck and call of public opinion.

Now Jim Callaghan had an issue on which to campaign. At the end of 1967 Jim's political career had looked as if it were destined to decline. Devaluation had been a severe blow to his self-esteem. Yet now with his self-confidence recovered he skilfully began to use his power base as Home Secretary to considerable effect. He had a natural public persona rather like Dixon of Dock Green, the policeman everyone could trust. He was helped in this by the knowledge he had gained when, for years in Opposition, he had been spokesman for the Police Federation. He instinctively targeted trade unionist opinion with which he felt comfort- able and had known well since he started as Assistant Secretary of the Inland Revenue Staff Federation. Jim Callaghan's political weakness at that time was not just his record as Chancellor but that he appeared to have too many chips on his shoulder. He could be very edgy, but disguised this with a breezy bonhomie. He resented the bitter criticism that had come his way over the Kenyan Asians and, as someone who loved and knew Africa from the time he had shadowed the Colonial Office, he could never understand why President Kenyatta virtually escaped criticism for first depriving Kenyan-born Asians of their livelihoods and then expelling them. Fortunately, towards the end of 1968 the Kenyan Government did slow and then essentially end the withdrawal of Asians' work permits. This meant that the UK voucher system did not have the dire effects that were once feared. But the politician in Jim knew that he had to defuse the slur of racialism and in June 1968 he introduced legislation to create the Race Relations Board. He peremptorily threw out Barbara Wootton's well-argued report arguing that legislation on the drug cannabis should be relaxed. But as if to balance that tough action he identified with the Home Office's role of responsibility for children. It was he who set up, on Leo Abse's prompting, the committee to look into reform of the law of adoption, which I was a few years later to take up for my Private Member's legislation. Soon he had established a distinctive image: hard on immigration but soft on race relations, hard on drugs but soft on children, hard on gaming but soft on bingo.

Jim Callaghan had made a formidable political recovery and it even meant that his name began to be tentatively floated as a candidate to oust Harold Wilson. In the House of Commons tea room, where some Labour MPs virtually live, Jim always retained a following. It was these people who saw, early on, that Barbara's trade union reform package was going to end in tears. At one stage, John Mackintosh went to see Jim to ask if he was willing to stand for the leadership to replace Harold. George Lawson, an older, centrist figure and Scottish Whip, then went with the same request. Callaghan told them both that he did not think there was a solid body of opinion in the Party in favour of a change of leadership. On a later occasion Denis Healey sent Alan Lee Williams, his Parliamentary Private Secretary, to see if Jim would support Denis Healey making a move for the leadership. Jim told Alan bluntly, 'No' and added that he did not believe that Denis would ever make a move. When he was asked why he came to that conclusion he said, not without justification, that if Denis had been serious he would have come himself, rather than sending a boy to do a man's job. These refusals did not stem from any love of Harold Wilson or lack of ambition. He simply calculated correctly that after devaluation, despite his wise handling of the situation in Northern Ireland, he was never in a sufficiently strong position to challenge Wilson himself. He judged too that all the emissaries wanted him to do was to open up a contest and then they would vote for someone else, most frequently Roy Jenkins. He could not have been unaware that Roy rarely missed an opportunity in private to put him down, nor that at one stage, with Barbara Castle, Roy had wanted Harold Wilson to sack him. Woodrow Wyatt, a good friend of Roy's and indeed of mine, not a man to shrink from either controversy or publicity, called for Jim to be sacked and so he deserved to be. For he was now in open rebellion against the Cabinet majority on trade union reforms. Attlee would have demanded loyalty or promptly had his resignation. But Wilson was no Attlee. He always disliked sacking people and was chronically indecisive. At that time in particular he lacked the self-confidence to act and so used the Wilsonian device of briefing the press that he had reprimanded Callaghan in Cabinet when in fact he had done nothing of the sort.

Jim's and Roy's rivalry was fed by mutual dislike. It was well concealed, but the combustible contempt lay not far below the surface. Roy thought Jim was unintelligent and philistine. Jim thought Roy arrogant and effete.

The Cabinet was now beginning to turn in on itself and we junior Ministers began to hedge our bets on 'In Place of Strife', by leaving it for Barbara Castle to champion. Wilson looked weak, the Government divided. It was in this debilitated state that the Cabinet drifted towards a commitment to legislate. On 15 April 1969, making his second budget statement, Roy Jenkins first won cheers on the Labour side by announcing that there would be no renewal of the powers under the 1968 Prices and Incomes Act but then stimulated the Conservative benches to cheer when he announced that there would be immediate legislation on 'In Place of Strife'. In his years as Chancellor it was one of Roy's few political mistakes to ally himself to a sinking ship and then abandon it. He, like most of his friends, wanted legislation. But he had enough battles as Chancellor and these reforms were never essential for short term economic recovery. Roy was in a commanding position at this time and his personal authority at its height. He was the most credible figure in the Cabinet and though I was closer to Tony Crosland, Roy was the figure I most admired.

By early May the mood in the Parliamentary Party was sulphurous. Those of us with marginal seats could see Harold Wilson was a liability not just in public opinion terms but with opinion formers; for example, Methodist ministers, who had previously believed in his idealism for War on Want, were now openly sceptical. But no one really knew how he could be removed. Some wanted a meeting of the Parliamentary Party to debate the leadership. But the Callaghanites wanted the Jenkinsites to move first and vice versa. Roy Jenkins was still committed to supporting Barbara Castle and Harold Wilson over the legislation. Then Jim Callaghan overplayed his hand by again criticizing and voting against the trade union reforms at a meeting between the Cabinet and the National Executive Committee of the Labour Party. In the midst of this intrigue, Harold Wilson went public; 'May I say for the benefit of those who have been carried away by the gossip of the last few days, that I know what's going on – I am going on.' Meanwhile, Tom Bradley, who, as well as being very close to Roy Jenkins, was President of a white collar railway union, the Transport and Salaried Staff Association, was desperately trying to persuade Roy to dump his commitment to the bill. Roy's friends were divided. Many of them wanted legislation to control the trade unions but they also wanted Roy to become Prime Minister. In the 1963 Club, conversation was dominated by the leadership question. But there was ambivalence and some embarrassment over pushing Roy's claim when Tony Crosland was sitting at the same table. Roy's view was, 'It's too early to strike.' Some began to wonder whether he had it in him to strike. But he knew that a false move could lead to the pound plummeting on the exchange market. He used to liken his position to someone balancing on a cliff face. It was a highly exposed position.

Legislation on the trade unions was then set back by the opposition of two important people in the Parliamentary Party. Douglas Houghton was the Parliamentary Party Chairman, and Bob Mellish had only recently taken on the job of Chief Whip because John Silkin was thought to be too weak. At the fateful Cabinet meeting on 17 June it was Bob's unscheduled intervention right at the start which smashed any hope of carrying the legislation. 'Prime Minister, before you consult your colleagues of the Cabinet, I feel you and they should hear what your Chief Whip has to say.' He told them bluntly that there was not a hope of the measure being carried in the House of Commons, that the Party would not stand for it and that the penal clauses had to go. As Peter Jenkins describes it in his book, 'The scene now resembled the interruption of the preacher in the dockyard church when, in the words of the old seaman's song, "up jumped Jack, in the third row back" and mouthed some dreadful obscenity.' Then, as one colleague put it later, 'Roy slid elegantly on to the fence.' Once that happened Harold Wilson knew that the desertion was complete. He was being told to settle with the General Council on the best terms available. Now Wilson showed the one quality that no one can deny him – guts. He refused to be browbeaten by the Cabinet and was adamant that he would not be instructed as to what to say when he met the General Council next morning. That evening the buzz I was picking up in the tea room of the House of Commons was that Harold and Barbara were totally isolated. Even so the defiant message from No. 10 was 'The little man's not going to go.' Barbara Castle went to bed thinking that this might be her last day as a Cabinet Minister and that tomorrow there might be another tenant in No. 10.

Next morning a cocky Harold Wilson weaved and ducked with the General Council but they knew they had him on the ropes. Over lunch, Barbara Castle and he decided that they had to deal. They would grasp the lifebelt that had been thrown to them by Victor Feather, the TUC General Secretary. The Bridlington Declaration of 1939 had always been much loved by the trade union movement. It is the voluntary code preventing unions from poaching members. So Harold Wilson announced, after the lunch interval, that he was ready to enter into negotiations over 'a solemn and binding undertaking' which the TUC must accept as having the same standing as the Bridlington Declaration. This provoked the wisecrack from a civil servant in the Department of Employment about Solomon Binding being a character out of George Eliot. It was agreed the TUC would place an obligation on trade unions 'to take energetic steps to obtain an immediate resumption of work', where they, the TUC, thought strike action unreasonable.

Harold Wilson went on television that night to explain the Government's climb-down. He was followed the next evening by Edward Heath, who said of Wilson, 'He knows, you know, the world knows after last Wednesday, that although they may still wear the trappings of office, the power resides elsewhere.' Who could have guessed that within five years Edward Heath would suffer an even greater humiliation at the hands of the trade unions in No. 10 Downing Street. For those of us watching this miserable spectacle from within the Government there were many lessons, not least of which was that reform of the trade union movement once started by the Government had to be followed through, for no vested interest could be seen to defeat a democratic Government without damaging that Government and the country.

What I, and I suspect many others, did not realize then was that it was not Harold Wilson's nerve that had cracked but the Cabinet's. Wilson had gone to the limit. Indeed, in fairness, he had gone well beyond most Prime Minister's limits. He was like a man hanging over a cliff edge who had had to be pulled back up to safety. I took the view that Harold and Barbara should never have got us into this mess in the first place. But that was too easy a conclusion. The truth was more unpalatable for moderates like me. It was we, the supposedly hard men on the Right, who had lost our nerve. First and foremost of those who had backed off was Roy Jenkins. It is impossible to know what would have happened if he had stuck with Harold and Barbara and defied the Cabinet. In retrospect, that is what he should have done, for if that Labour Government had stood up to the trade unions and been seen to win, Labour would have won in 1970. Roy Jenkins would within a year or so have succeeded Harold Wilson as Prime Minister. Wilson, to his credit, knew this. In a bitter exchange with Hugh Scanlon, then President of the AEU, at Chequers in June he showed that he understood the penalty of backing down. Scanlon said, 'Prime Minister, we don't want you to become another Ramsay MacDonald.' To which Wilson replied, 'I have no intention of becoming another Ramsay MacDonald. Nor do I intend to be another Dubcek. Get your tanks off my lawn Hughie!' The tanks stayed on the lawn until Arthur Scargill's defeat by Margaret Thatcher in 1985.

At that time I had no inkling that the Cabinet was likely to fold. I was defending the forthcoming legislation in my own constituency and slowly winning the argument. It was not until after the general election, that I became fully aware of the true story. In the interval I had done what many other MPs on the Right tended perhaps too often to do – blamed Harold Wilson. I had made him the scapegoat and had depicted him as the softie on the trade unions, when in truth he was the hard man. The whole incident only demonstrates yet again the complex personality of Harold Wilson, both the man and the politician.

During these critical months of TUC-Government confrontation, I have to admit that my main preoccupation was saving Lundy Island, a three and a quarter mile stretch of granite off the coast of North Devon. The press was full of stories that the scientologists were ready with £300,000 to buy the island. Jeremy Thorpe, Leader of the Liberal Party and MP for North Devon, asked me to come to a meeting with him and Peter Mills, the Conservative MP for Torrington, in an attempt to launch an all-party national appeal to raise the money for the island and give it to the National Trust. On our first meeting in Jeremy's room, the telephone rang and Jeremy was told that a Mr Jack Hayward was calling from the Bahamas. He told Jeremy that he had read about the three of us getting together in the *Sunday Express* and he wanted to know if he could help. Jeremy, always the showman, at one point broke off to consult us about what size contribution we were looking for. I remember suggesting £10,000 but Jeremy ignored my puny proposition and calmly announced that £150,000 would fit the bill. I was staggered when Jack Hayward promised that sum and Jeremy graciously said it would not matter if it did not come for a few days. This meant that we were now able to buy the island. But the National Trust had made it clear that they had no funds to maintain it so I then spoke to John Smith, the Conservative MP for Westminster who funded and ran the Landmark Trust and he agreed to maintain Lundy. In less than two hours we now knew that the island would be saved.

Later, Jeremy Thorpe arranged for a thank you lunch in the House of Commons for 'Union Jack' Hayward. I sat next to him and talked about a project that Richard Gould-Adams had asked me to help with: the s.s. *Great Britain*, the first British sailing ship with a metal hull, lay rusting in shallow water on the Falklands. Money was desperately needed to tow her back to Britain. Hayward offered to help so I put him in touch with Gould-Adams. Within a few days he had agreed to finance the ship's being towed back to Bristol, where she had been built. After a lot of persuading, Bristol City Council co-operated and today the s.s. *Great Britain* can be seen in all its restored splendour in its original dock. It was a wonderful act of generosity from Sir Jack Hayward to save, so spontaneously and imaginatively, both Lundy Island and the s.s. *Great Britain* for the nation. There is a fine old print of the s.s. *Great Britain* sailing past Lundy Island which can be seen as anticipating this extraordinary sequence of events.

The morale of both the Government and the Parliamentary Labour

Party improved after the summer recess of 1969. With Roy Jenkins in control of public expenditure and a balance of payments surplus assured, there was increased confidence abroad and we started to look like, and more important, behave like a coherent Government.

Over these years I gradually began to see more of Roy. On two occasions I had lunch alone with him in No. 11, and we chatted over many difficult aspects of policy. He showed a definite interest in achieving further sensible defence cuts and, somewhat to my surprise, was very sceptical about the value of a nuclear hardening programme for Polaris. In the main, we discussed internal politics. I remember vividly, at one lunch early in 1970, Roy saying that it had been only a few months ago, towards the end of 1969, that he had really felt able to sleep soundly for fear of another deterioration in the balance of payments. I then realized that, following devaluation, we had remained on the knife edge for far longer than I or most people had thought. It was undoubtedly this experience of – to use his own analogy – bruising his arm against the cliff-face of a mountain path for fear of the precipice on the other side, that had built in the caution in his economic policies, in such striking contrast to his period in the Home Office. The interesting question was whether caution or boldness was his dominating characteristic.

Inside the Ministry of Defence I was increasingly interested in ensuring that we had indigenous air power in the Fleet. In March 1970 I sent a personal memo to Denis Healey about the future shape of the Royal Navy, saying I was happy for it to be seen by the First Sea Lord. It argued for the Royal Marine Commandos to stop operating as a permanently embarked marine force, but rather that they should be a highly trained mobile force, capable of amphibious operations, but also specialists in cold-weather warfare. I argued for a refit of HMS *Hermes*, operating her flexibly with Sea King helicopters and between three and five uprated Harrier jet aircraft, so that she would become in effect the lead ship for the new cruisers. HMS *Ark Royal* and HMS *Hermes* would be phased out in the early 1980s when the cruisers with helicopters and Harriers became operational.

I also argued for increasing the build rate for the hunter-killer submarines nearer to the target of one every twelve months. I showed, under the ten-year long-term costing, how we could pay for these changes by altering the shape of the Fleet and by phasing out as early as possible some of the larger surface ships, *Albion*, *Lion*, *Blake* and *Tiger*. The surface ship lobby was 'fighting hard' and, as so often, putting submarines and the Fleet Air Arm under threat. Yet all the operational research, in the US Navy as well as our own, showed how vulnerable big ships were to attack by hunter-killer submarines. Some of the thinking behind this memo, particularly that relating to HMS *Hermes*, became accepted later in the MOD, but the potential for undersea warfare continues to be underplayed by a Navy that is happier operating upon rather than under the waves.

Given the political traumas of the four years of government, it is amazing that, when Harold Wilson announced on 18 May that a general election was going to be held on 18 June 1970, it was possible for me to believe that Labour would win the election. On 12 May a Gallup Poll had actually shown Labour $7\frac{1}{2}$ per cent ahead of the Conservatives. Even as late as December 1969, the Conservatives looked comfortably ahead. But the local election results in May and the opinion polls all indicated that the Conservative lead had melted like the spring snow.

The reason for the polls changing was Roy Jenkins's budget, delivered on 14 April. It was variously described as honest, dull, not a bribing budget, and, by the *Financial Times*, as a political non-event. Nevertheless, Labour found itself ahead in the opinion polls for the first time since 1967. After the general election conventional wisdom held that Roy's third budget was too responsible and had lost us the election. The budget justly concentrated on taking two million people out of paying any tax at all and the judgement of most people, even on the Left, in May or early June, was that Roy's integrity was an electoral asset. The mistake was to go for an early election and that was Harold Wilson's decision. The press was carefully massaged so as to make a June election acceptable and by the time it was announced most Labour MPs, including myself, were in favour of going. In retrospect it was a foolish decision and people remembered the bad years. I do not believe that the electorate switched around during the campaign because England lost to Germany in the World Cup in Mexico or because the trade figures showed a freak deficit because of the purchase of two jumbo jets.

An incident which gave an indication of Roy's deep-seated commitment on Europe occurred during the campaign. On the Thursday before polling day he travelled down from Birmingham to speak to a crowded meeting at the Plymouth Polytechnic. After the meeting Roy, John Harris and Peter Jenkins came back to my parents' house for a meal which Debbie had prepared. It was a relaxed evening and the only topic of conversation was who was going where to do what when we had won the election. Roy, somewhat incautiously, in view of Peter Jenkins's presence, made it clear that he had very recently been offered the Foreign Secretaryship. Peter, no doubt thinking of his *Guardian* column, began to question Roy in some detail and, to my amusement and surprise, much of it later appeared in the *Guardian*. The interesting comment was when Roy described his strategy. He would immediately break the Government's 'absurd, almost craven silence' over Vietnam; he would openly criticize the US and, at the same time, move fast towards Europe.

Roy disapproved of the whole of the US's Vietnam policy and was strongly influenced by his Democrat friends in the US. Debbie's brother, Peter, was awaiting a possible draft to Vietnam and I too wanted to see a rapid ceasefire. Roy also recognized the need to nurse the Left and Right wings of the Labour Party through the European transition. He saw it as part of the Foreign Secretary's duty to involve himself in all major aspects of the EEC negotiations and I could not help feeling that he would need a rather more junior Minister than George Thomson to conduct the negotiations. Much later in 1971, Roy mentioned that, when Harold Wilson had asked him whether he was prepared to go to the Foreign Office, he had replied by saying that before he could accept he would have to know whether Wilson was really committed to Britain's entering the EEC. 'Not just committed, dedicated', was the reply and apparently he was very dismissive about even the possibility, raised by Roy, of any difficulty emerging in the negotiations over the terms.

Harold Wilson came to Plymouth for a quick visit on 11 June (xvi). He was in cracking form. He had had flour thrown at him in Exeter and said, 'I've had eggs elsewhere, flour now. I just need a bit of milk to make pancakes.' He was generous about me and when someone outside Beaumont Hall thrust his head through the windows, he warned, 'Don't cut your throat on that window. There's someone else who might want to do it.' His cocky manner was that of a man coasting to victory. He believed he was winning and I did too.

I did not realize until very late the extent to which the electorate had not been taken in by the Government's recent successes with the economy. I began to be uneasy towards polling day but put that down to nerves. It was not until I was driving in to my count in Plymouth Guildhall and heard on the car radio that Gwyneth Dunwoody had lost her seat in Exeter that I realized I was in trouble. The pundits were predicting that, on the national swing, I would lose in Plymouth Sutton. The Conservatives very nearly made a clean sweep of all the constituencies in Devon and Cornwall. I held on in Plymouth Sutton by 747 votes, but John Dunwoody lost Falmouth and Camborne, showing that I had made the correct choice in 1965 and that Sutton was a safer seat than Falmouth. Jeremy Thorpe kept his leadership of a decimated Liberal Party by a mere 369 votes in North Devon and John Pardoe held North Cornwall by 630 votes. Edward Heath had vanquished his critics to become Prime Minister with a deceptively effective campaign that appeared to peak at exactly the right moment. Only one poll had predicted a Conservative victory and that only at the last moment in the London *Evening Standard*. On the Sunday before the election the weighted average of five national opinion polls showed Labour having a 6.4 per cent lead.

Why did Labour lose? On the doorstep I found the overwhelming reason was that people did not trust us over the economy. They remembered the traumas of the past and doubted our ability to protect their standard of living. A success over the balance of payments was not enough. Try as I might to convince people that Roy Jenkins had turned the economy round, I found too many clearly sceptical. It was often women who were unconvinced and, though they did not say how they intended to vote, the firm, polite way in which the doorstep conversation was ended and the door was shut left me certain they were going to vote independently of their husbands. They wanted new faces and were readier to listen to Edward Heath than to Harold Wilson. In many ways the result was a vindication of democratic judgement. It showed that just heading opportunistically for a patch of clear sky in the opinion polls was insufficient. As the campaign developed, people remembered the past abysmal record. Of that record, devaluation and the abandonment of the trade union reforms were what people remembered most. But their unhappiness with Labour stemmed from their loss of spending power. There was not the jingle in the pocket for which they yearned. But there was also something indefinable about that Labour Cabinet that people did not like. The tensions, the rivalries and the ambitions of its leading figures had made an unhappy spectacle. At no time did the public sense that these significant figures, individually people of considerable substance, had worked together as a team. Edward Heath's own foreword to the Conservative Election Manifesto, captured the mood:

> During the last six years, we have suffered not only from bad policies, but from a cheap and trivial style of government. Decisions have been dictated simply by the desire to catch tomorrow's headlines. The short-term gain has counted for everything: the long-term objective has gone out of the window. Every device has been used to gain immediate publicity and government by gimmick has become the order of the day.

Harold Wilson had failed to weld a team together but the personalities did not lend themselves to working as a team. With a large parliamentary majority, a Left-Right split was inevitable but that was not the reason for the failure of this Government. With people of the calibre of George Brown, Jim Callaghan, Roy Jenkins, Dick Crossman, Tony Crosland, Denis Healey and Barbara Castle there was as much talent as in the 1945–50 Labour Government. But they never worked together or were held together in a way which would have maximized their strengths. The post-war Labour Cabinet had had its tensions too. Herbert Morrison never stopped manoeuvring and Hugh Dalton, Stafford Cripps, Aneurin Bevan, and later Hugh Gaitskell and Harold Wilson were none of them shrinking violets. The difference was the exceptional quality of Clement Attlee and of Ernest Bevin, loyally supporting the Prime Minister. A few loyal Cabinet Ministers supported Wilson, like Michael Stewart, the Foreign Secretary, but he had neither Bevin's strength nor his broad based support in the Party. Right up to the general election, senior members of the Government were manoeuvring against each other and it showed. A revealing JAK cartoon is published in Harold Wilson's own account of 1964–70. It is presumably how he sees his premiership too, a ringmaster surrounded by undisciplined fighting lions.

As I waited anxiously for my result during the count in Plymouth

Guildhall, I felt convinced that I had lost and a strange calm came over me as I thought through my next step. As I went round talking to friends and supporters, scrutinizing the count, I felt no sadness to be leaving Parliament. It had been an amazing experience and I had no regrets. But there was no sense of shock that it was over. I decided that I would ring the Maudsley Hospital, which specialized in psychiatry, next morning and see if I could be accepted as a Registrar. I recognized that I would have to catch up by taking the final part of my membership and working for a diploma in psychological medicine but I felt a keen sense of anticipation and even joy at the prospect of returning to medicine.

My agent, Alf Sweetland, was with the Returning Officer counting all the bundles and it was impossible to tell who was ahead. He was not allowed to tell me the result but suddenly he looked at me. He then deliberately turned around and put his thumb up behind his back. I had won. I experienced no elation. If anything, I was rather disappointed. I was still an MP but it was pretty clear by then, from the results already in, that Labour was going out of government. As Debbie and I mounted the platform to hear the official result I galvanized myself into believing that we had won a great victory in Plymouth. We had and yet it all felt very hollow. My idealistic beliefs in what a Labour Government could do had made my victory four years ago a thrilling one. Now those ideals lay shattered.

8

SHADOW SPOKESMAN

On the Friday morning of 19 June 1970, Harold Wilson conceded defeat. Apart from waiting for the Queen to return to Buckingham Palace from the Ascot races, our system allows no time even to catch one's breath before a new Prime Minister has kissed hands and assumes control. On television that night and in the newspapers next day there were humiliating photographs of Harold Wilson leaving by the back door of No. 10 Downing Street while Ted Heath was coming in at the front.

The new Conservative Government had a working majority with 330 MPs to Labour's 287 and the Liberals' six. They could expect to run for the full five years if they needed to. That morning I spoke to my Private Office for the last time as Minister. It was my first experience of the sudden transfer of power.

Leaving the Ministry of Defence was a massive wrench for, in a small way, I had exercised real power. Losing the accoutrements of power did not bother me, although I was devoted to my cockney driver, Mr Taylor. But it was no problem to give up an official car; I far preferred to drive myself. Nor was there a problem with money for there was only a small pay differential in those days between a junior Minister and a backbencher.

My anxiety was what I would do to keep myself busy. I knew the House of Commons by itself would not fill my working day. Two years earlier when I had been a backbencher I had worked in medicine part time and I wondered whether I should try to become a clinical assistant in the Department of Psychiatry at St Thomas's.

Then, that weekend, Sandy Cortesi rang from America, first to commiserate over our losing the election but also to ask if I would be interested in becoming chairman of Decision Technology International as there was likely to be a vacancy very shortly. Sandy had talked a lot about Decision Technology on his visits from the US. It was a fast growing computer based consultancy, with its head office in Boston and another office in New York. The presiding genius was Arnold Amstutz

from the Massachusetts Institute of Technology. He had designed a
computer model of the New York stock market. He had also designed a
model of the US pharmaceutical industry as a marketing tool. In Europe
the company had a contract with Rolls-Royce to build a computer model
to mirror the production line of the RB-211 Rolls-Royce aero-engine. I
was interested in this contract as I had been involved in the Navy
Department with the future of Rolls-Royce and with the programme to
uprate the Pegasus Mark II engine for Harriers operating off ships. Even
then it was clear that Rolls-Royce was going to need special financial
support for high technology developments. One of our last acts in
government had been to lend Rolls-Royce £20 million to add to the £47
million of government support which had already been put
predominantly into developing the RB-211.

Decision Technology had also developed a sophisticated method of
measuring political views through studies of attitude and awareness.
They had worked with Robert Kennedy and a number of other politicians.
I saw in Sandy's offer a unique opportunity to learn about business. I
also felt it would be easier to combine politics with business than with
medicine. While medical research would be fairly easy to combine with
politics, once I was involved with patients there would be problems. It
would be difficult to change clinics at the behest of the parliamentary
timetable and, with legislative committees, I could not even rely on being
free in the mornings.

As Navy Minister, I had found the industrial management questions
relating to the dockyards fascinating. Yet I was very conscious that I had
not had experience of private industry or of the workings of the
marketplace, a weakness I shared with most Labour MPs. The chairmanship of Decision Technology offered me an opportunity to learn about
management and the ethos of the private sector. It would also make a
very useful addition to our family income. So I accepted and for two
years it gave me a valuable insight into a different world.

Returning to the House of Commons in Opposition meant sitting on
the other side of the Chamber for the first time and, far more importantly,
changing my whole approach. Now the task was to exploit weaknesses in
the government machine, not to paper over the cracks. Being in government transforms people: Edward Heath, never very impressive in Opposition, suddenly had new-found authority as Prime Minister. With Iain
Macleod as his Chancellor, it looked a competent team and in their
inevitable honeymoon there was little for us to do as an Opposition. To
those who can only remember Edward Heath in the 1980s in constant
opposition to Margaret Thatcher, it is worth recalling how similar his
own Prime Ministerial action and style was. He polarized politics from
the start. His creed was announced from the Selsdon Park Hotel before
the election: higher incentives, lower taxes, reduced public expenditure
and higher profits. All industrial intervention was to be halted, the

Industrial Reconstruction Corporation was to be wound up and the Prices and Incomes Board abolished. Apart from Europe, there was virtually no continuity or attempt to continue with consensus politics. Welfare milk went and, despite the protest in Cabinet by the Secretary of State for Education, Margaret Thatcher, free milk for school children from seven to eleven was eventually dropped.

However, the first political issue was an internal one – the deputy leadership of the Labour Party. Despite a vigorous campaign, criss-crossing the country as Deputy Leader, making many excellent speeches on the stump and receiving a great deal of favourable TV coverage, George Brown had lost his seat which had been adversely affected by boundary changes.

The deputy leadership of the Labour Party has never been considered an important position. It was created for Herbert Morrison and only Michael Foot succeeded in using it as a stepping stone to the leadership of the Party. Nevertheless, the holder is automatically a member of the National Executive of the Labour Party and the NEC, in Opposition, becomes a powerful body.

Somewhat to my surprise I was asked to a meeting in Dick Taverne's London flat to decide whether or not Roy Jenkins should stand. Prior to this, though I knew they went on, I had not been involved in any of the meetings which were attended only by committed Jenkins supporters. In retrospect I suppose it was from this moment that I became classified as a Jenkinsite. Yet my political heart remained with Tony Crosland. I did not make a wholehearted commitment to Roy as the future leader of the Labour Party until the summer of 1971, when it became clear to me that Tony Crosland was not prepared to recognize that Britain's entry into the European Community was a major issue. Susan Crosland has since revealed that Tony was discovered to have high blood pressure soon after the election and that may have contributed to a political lassitude not easy to distinguish from Tony's natural and rather attractive laid-back manner. He still worked very hard in the 1970 Parliament, particularly on local government questions, but some of his vivacity had gone.

At the Taverne meeting the general conviction was that at some point Roy should run for the leadership. George Thomson and Bill Rodgers were the most militant, arguing strongly that Roy should stand for the deputy leadership, even if Jim Callaghan stood. In fact it was pretty clear by then that he preferred to remain Treasurer of the Party, which carried an automatic seat on the NEC and had the virtue of being the only office elected by all sections of the annual conference. At the other end of the spectrum, David Marquand, and I to a lesser extent, questioned whether it was wise to be bound to Harold Wilson by becoming his Deputy. Eventually Roy agreed to stand but not without clearly warning us all that for him the European Community was a central political issue and if the Party was to oppose entry it would be no good any of us invoking

Party loyalty or the fact that he was Deputy Leader. We should know
that now, he said, rather than finding it out later.

On 8 July the Parliamentary Party gave Roy an overall majority
with 133 votes. Michael Foot got sixty-seven votes and Fred Peart
forty-eight. It was clear that Roy's period as Chancellor had earned him
the respect of many Labour MPs whose political opinions tended to
move with the centre of gravity of the Party. These MPs are sometimes
referred to as the 'tea-room vote' and they are an essential element for
anyone wishing to lead the Labour Party from the Centre-Right. But the
vote also sent a warning, which pro-marketeers underestimated at the
time, in the form of the large number of anti-EEC moderates, also part
of the tea room, voting for Fred Peart. Michael Foot had yet to widen his
support beyond the traditional Left but Peart's vote meant there was now
a body of MPs whose hostility to the European Community would be
likely to determine who in the parliamentary leadership had their
support.

George Thomson was made Shadow Defence Minister and intriguingly
Harold Lever was Party Spokesman on Common Market matters with
Denis Healey Shadow Foreign Minister. This line-up gave Harold Wilson
tactical control of a pro-European policy. I was at the UN in New York
and was told by a diplomat in our delegation that *The Times* had listed
me as a junior Defence Spokesman. This was done without any consultation but, in fairness, Harold was usually scrupulous in observing the
courtesies and, anyway, I was perfectly content; busy enough as the part-
time chairman of Decision Technology International not to want to
devote time to learning about an entirely new area of policy. When
Parliament went down for the summer recess, the Heath honeymoon was
still under way and it looked as if we were in for a long and frustrating
period of opposition. Since the junior posts in the Shadow Cabinet are
not full-time jobs, it was a good time to learn about business and to
widen my horizons.

Before the election, Debbie had been working as a literary agent with
Nicholas Thompson, but now she planned to leave as she was expecting
our first child in September. We decided that we needed a house well
down on the road from London to Plymouth where I could leave Debbie
and any children for the weekend before driving on to the constituency.
We did not have the money for a deposit on a house but fortunately
Debbie's father loaned us some.

We had been tipped off about a run-down old rectory by a close friend
who had seen a For Sale sign peeking out of the trees as she drove up to
an out-of-the-way hamlet called Buttermere. When we visited it in early
August we were enchanted by its position. The hamlet sits on top of the
southern ridge of the Kennet and Avon valley, three miles up above the
Domesday book village of Ham, and it also looks over Inkpen which
nestles under the fold of the ridge. There are spectacular views, and

because there is no mains water the surrounding countryside is totally unspoilt and devoid of any houses.

The Old Rectory was built in 1887 of red brick and flint on the site of an older, smaller parsonage. It had been lived in by a woman who had become a recluse. Since her husband's death she had not gone upstairs at all and every single ceiling had collapsed. As a point of principle she had never killed a living thing so no plant or tree had been cut and the house was invaded by vines, plants and trees that had gone completely wild. It was in an appalling condition and we later discovered that two friends of ours, far wealthier than we, had both wanted to buy it but had been dissuaded from bidding because of the estimated cost of putting it right.

In the middle of August, Debbie's blood pressure rose and she had to go into hospital. So she was not with me when one Thursday, late in that month, I drove down to Hungerford Town Hall for the public auction. It was a cold, wet, dank day and Elizabeth Furse drove down with me lecturing me most of the way against a socialist having two houses. So I was not in the best of moods when we dropped in on the Rectory so she could see it before the auction. Normally she had great imagination about what could be done with houses but on this occasion even she was daunted and her lack of enthusiasm was evident. In the Town Hall, just before the auction started, a man got up at the back to ask the auctioneer if, in view of a recent Council by-law, they could guarantee that any purchaser would be allowed to live in a house which relied only on rain water. The auctioneer consulted someone on the platform and then replied in a manner which I was all too used to, waffling like a Minister at Question Time, without a clue as to the correct answer. This was the final straw for me and I decided not to bid.

The bidding got under way and had reached £5,000 when Elizabeth suddenly jabbed me in the side and pointed to the very man who had queried the water supply. He was quietly bidding by surreptitiously raising his finger. This infuriated me so much that I entered the bidding. After £6,000 this man, who later turned out to be a local builder, pulled out. Eventually the house and the very small school, all set in 4½ acres, was knocked down to me for £7,200. It later transpired that Mr Waters, our closest neighbour in Manor Farm, had only been bidding because he had heard that some hippies were after the house. I returned to the Lambeth Hospital, triumphant, and we celebrated the purchase with champagne.

On 8 September 1970, Debbie gave birth to a son in the Lambeth Hospital, where I had done my midwifery training. I always intended to be present for the birth but I nearly missed it. The midwife said I would be safe to travel with Sandy Cortesi to Rolls-Royce at Derby but Debbie's face showed so much disappointment when she heard this that I decided to stay. I was very glad I did, for she started labour while I would have been travelling back. It is fascinating how different it is to watch your own child being delivered compared with delivering other people's children. In that same suite of delivery rooms I had delivered over thirty babies and yet on this occasion it was as if it was a completely new experience. I had none of the clinical detachment of the doctor, only the anxiety of the father. The relief that our child was born without any deformity was a far stronger parental feeling than the medical textbooks reveal. We decided to call him Tristan, after our favourite story of *Tristan und Iseult*.

For the next year we would drive down to Buttermere at weekends with a plastic container of fresh water and with Tristan in a carry cot, we would camp in one room while we did up the house ourselves, clearing the garden whenever the weather was fine. It was all very good therapy for the frustration of politics. Eventually, for a fraction of the price that we would have had to pay to a contractor, we made the house habitable. It became a haven for us and later a place where I could relax when I became Foreign Secretary. I was not in the slightest bit interested in taking over Dorneywood, the stately home then available to the Foreign Secretary, far preferring Buttermere. One slight complication is that if, late at night in London, we say we are driving to Buttermere, people tend to look at us askance, thinking we are heading off to the Lake District's well known beauty spot.

In Parliament it rapidly became clear that Europe would dominate. The incoming Conservative Government took up the negotiating stance that we had already been preparing over the last six months and the speech which Anthony Barber eventually gave at the opening of the EEC negotiations in Brussels was very little different from the draft approved during the Election campaign by George Thomson. He was to have been the Labour Government's negotiator, had we won. The negotiations began but public opinion was still against entry, with only 22 per cent positively in favour. So keeping bipartisan agreement, which was not the natural state of affairs in Parliament, was in the Government's interest.

Yet for a time it did seem as though, on Europe, the consensus would hold. At the Labour Party Conference, Harold Wilson's speech made a reference to Europe which was fairly unexceptional, though, as usual, it was capable of being interpreted in a number of different ways. Apart from a narrow vote at Conference in favour of the NEC's cautious resolution on the EEC – a majority of only 95,000 – there was little real evidence to justify the sceptics who predicted that Wilson would eventually reject the EEC.

The next few months passed pretty quietly on the European side. Denis Healey was convinced with his usual certitude that the French would once again reject British entry. Parliament listened restlessly to the rather drab reports from Geoffrey Rippon who had replaced Anthony Barber as chief negotiator. Only Peter Shore had staked his career on the issue, refusing the offer of a relatively minor Front Bench appointment and going to the back benches where he was rapidly taking over from Douglas Jay as the official anti-Market spokesman.

It seemed to me, and I expect to many others, that there was nothing much to be worried about: superficially, it appeared that, to Harold Wilson and most of the influential members of the Shadow Cabinet, the commitment to entry was irrevocable and that everything, as before, would depend on France.

Soon things began to change. In the early months of 1971, it became increasingly obvious that the high unemployment figures, the Government's total inability to restrain prices and their determined commitment not to intervene in industry, were making them very unpopular. It also affected the whole issue of entering the EEC. A new factor too, was Jim Callaghan's attitude. Ever sensitive to any change of feeling in the Party, he was starting to tell his friends that he was less and less convinced of the case for British entry into the EEC. The manner in which by nudge and wink Jim began to indicate his impending change, was reminiscent of the way he handled his disapproval in 1969 of the proposed legislation, envisaged in 'In Place of Strife'. The shift was initially almost imperceptible, never anything one could actually seize upon to criticize, always leaving enough room to swing back to support entry if the climate changed. But unlike in 1969 there was no prime ministerial patronage to check his movement and others like him away from the official line.

It is hardly surprising that the agreement over Europe felt the strain of polarized politics as economic growth slowed, output fell and unemployment rose. It can be argued with some justice that the only difference between Thatcher's and Heath's early years in No. 10 is that when confronted with high unemployment her nerve held and his did not. The Heath U-turn came with the one-clause bill to rescue Rolls-Royce, followed by an interventionist Industry Act in 1972. Then came the statutory income policy of 1972 and 1973 which marked the big U-turn distorting the market economy and raising the question about whether it was compatible with Conservative philosophy. However, for the first few years, Heath out-Thatchered Thatcher. His style came from his days as a Colonel in the war: peremptory, prickly, authoritarian; but it was also accompanied by a basic decency, a rigid incorruptibility, yet you had to look for it buried under an off-putting veneer of executive efficiency. So from the Labour side in those days there was very little respect, indeed there was considerable animosity towards Heath.

Perhaps the most divisive issue was the whole Industrial Relations Act, a serious though misguided attempt to grapple with the trade unions. Barbara Castle was foolishly retained by Harold to shadow the Department of Employment. Embarrassed by the failure of her own policy, she was soon opposing every measure in the Conservative package, irrespective of its merits, even when they were virtually identical or had much in common with her own legislation. The Heath approach to trade union reform was to impose a highly legalistic structure. The Government soon had egg all over its face and any reputation for competence was shattered. Once again, an attempt to reform the trade unions had failed, with potentially profound consequences. This was all the more surprising since, in the early months after the election, Edward Heath's Government looked omnicompetent. Perhaps the rot set in with the early death of Iain Macleod, the Chancellor of the Exchequer; a grave blow that deprived Heath of advice which, even if unwelcome, he could not ignore.

As the Government's reputation fell, Labour leaders found it increasingly difficult to agree with them on anything and the European Community became another issue for instant opposition. Yet it was the Labour Party which was to damage itself on this issue from 1971 to 1987. The true story of the formation of the SDP begins here in early 1971.

On the night of 19 January 1971, when a running three-line whip kept a large number of MPs in the House of Commons, a straight anti-EEC motion was touted around and received 119 signatures from Labour MPs. This eventually rose to 132. It was a formidable achievement. From that moment on, there could be justified doubt as to whether there was a genuine majority for British entry to the EEC among the Parliamentary Labour Party. The key sponsors of this motion were John Silkin and Brian O'Malley – respectively former Chief Whip and Deputy Chief Whip. Ironically, during the May 1967 application debate, these two had whipped vigorously for the Labour Government to achieve a substantial majority, convincing 260 out of 361 Labour MPs to support entry in principle. Since the 1970 Election defeat, they felt free to reveal their hostility to the EEC and had joined the Tribune Group of Left-wing MPs. They were seasoned Parliamentary tacticians, capable of dressing up initiatives which might otherwise have been dismissed as pure 'Tribune' moves so as to have a much wider appeal. If Harold Wilson had been seriously contemplating sticking to the EEC, this motion must have been very influential in pushing him towards opposing entry.

For the pro-marketeers, the situation was now very worrying. We could no longer count on a majority in the Parliamentary Labour Party and voting in the NEC was increasingly going against the advice of the Party leadership. A resolution, stating that a future Labour Government should not pay compensation to shareholders owning stock in companies that had been hived off from nationalized industries under the Conservative Government was passed by the NEC on 24 February by 13–7, despite strong objections from Harold Wilson, Roy Jenkins and Jim Callaghan. It was yet another indication that Harold Wilson could not now control the NEC. We began to realize that even if he held to the need for entry to the EEC, we faced a debilitating fight. By the spring of 1971, it was obvious that the Party Conference in October would be strongly against entry. The NEC might remain narrowly in favour of entry but it would be difficult to hold, and the PLP would need to be given vigorous leadership if the slow erosion in the commitment of many centre MPs to entry was to withstand the inevitable pressures building up from trade unions and constituency parties.

In this climate, in March, John Roper, David Marquand, Bob Maclennan and I left the House of Commons for a quick dinner in an Italian restaurant before voting at 10 p.m. I proposed a suggestion for a counter-attack. A parliamentary motion was out of the question for we could not match John Silkin's numbers for his anti-Common Market motion. We needed, in contrast, to demonstrate both the quality of the support for entry in the PLP and the extent of support that still existed in the Shadow Cabinet. My suggestion for a European Declaration, signed by prominent socialists in the ten countries which would, hopefully, make up the new Europe, was accepted as a way of obtaining a commitment from some of the people whose open support was now vital. None of us had any illusions about the logistical difficulty of producing such a statement in such a short time. We first had to sound out Roy Jenkins, who was cautiously enthusiastic. Then we began to talk to others. The most encouraging response by far was from Douglas Houghton who pledged total and complete support and said he could see no reason, as Chairman of the PLP, why he should not sign. Shirley Williams, George Thomson and Harold Lever, all welcomed the proposal and agreed to sign. Shirley promised to approach Ted Short: David Marquand and I went to see Tony Crosland. Tony, who had said very little about Europe for the last few months, was happy to sign but he felt that it must attract more than just the known, committed pro-marketeers. He astutely attached great importance to Ted Short, and even went so far as to say that he would need to reconsider his position about signing if Ted Short decided not to sign.

Denis Healey was a much more difficult problem. He had reached the same conclusion as Hugh Gaitskell in 1962, coming down marginally against Britain's entry on the terms likely to be available. He admired Scandinavian socialism, and later admitted that he overestimated the Commonwealth's potential to influence world affairs. Denis had supported Douglas Jay in the Cabinet in opposing a second application for membership in 1966 but had, without too much unhappiness, gone along with the majority decision. It was decided that Roy Hattersley and I should approach him, for we had worked with him in the Ministry of Defence and had considerable respect for him. However, only a few days before, Denis had made a speech which left some wondering whether he too was not starting to change. We were ready to have a stand-up row. Dealing with Denis Healey is quite different from dealing with most politicians: he respects straight talk. In the event, we did not need to say anything – Denis seemed to know that this was different from most meetings. As often, when nervous, he hid it by talking in a joke Yorkshire dialect. 'Well, lads, what can I do for you?' was his opening gambit. We showed him the declaration and, to our surprise, he signed immediately and promised to discuss it with Willy Brandt, the former German Chancellor, whom he was due to see at Königswinter. This was important since it was obvious from the start that Willy Brandt's signature would be crucial in obtaining the support of other Europeans. In fact, Roy Jenkins had already written to him and told him that David Marquand and Bob Maclennan would discuss the wording of the declaration with him in Bonn, since they too were going to Köningswinter.

With most of the key European figures either having agreed to sign or already being approached, we met on Thursday 6 May, in Roy Hattersley's house in Gayfere Street. The negotiations were due to come to a major decision point in Brussels on the Wednesday of the next week. There was no doubt that the time for our declaration was now; we had eight Shadow Cabinet members – could we obtain our maximum support by Monday? The decision to go immediately was strongly argued by David Marquand and myself and all agreed. Though we decided to confirm it with Roy, he would have had to have strong objections to change our minds. We felt we should be able to obtain slightly more than seventy signatures. Not for the last time, we totally underestimated our support. All through the weekend people were contacted, telegrams sent to European capitals. The end response was remarkable. On Monday morning it was apparent that we might even reach 100, although I was adamant that we should not take topping-up signatures from the Lords. We decided to put the advertisement only in the *Guardian* and ten minutes before the 2 p.m. deadline on Monday 10 May, we had the 100 signatures.

The statement in the *Guardian*, after various redrafts and problems with the translated meaning, said:

> We, the undersigned Parliamentarians, are convinced that the causes of social democracy, world peace and economic advance in both developed and developing countries would be strengthened by the addition of the United Kingdom, Norway, Denmark and Ireland to the European Economic Community.

Since the wording was fairly bland, it was vital that no one of substance should sign and then later announce their opposition to entry on the basis that it was not incompatible with signing the declaration.

The greatest danger of this, we thought, could come from either Tony Benn, who was at that stage nominally a supporter of entry, or from Jim Callaghan. Roy felt that both should have the opportunity of signing the declaration. It would be hard, he felt, to justify their exclusion before the other members of the Shadow Cabinet, since they were supposed to be in favour of entry. Harold Wilson had been informed of the proposed declaration some time before by Roy and had also been told that Willy Brandt would be asked to sign. We quite deliberately did not ask Harold

Wilson to sign, though it was always understood that if he had wished to we would have been delighted. In public Harold's position was that he thought it inappropriate to sign but he raised no objections to the declaration.

So I spoke to Tony Benn with the express hope of not obtaining his signature. It proved an easy task. He clearly had no intention of signing, making it plain that his opposition was not to entry but to the manner in which the decision was being made. He seemed genuinely shocked that I could believe that we could go in without calling an election or a referendum.

Jim Callaghan was a much more formidable proposition and I was uneasy in having to tackle him. Over the years I had developed a wary regard for him. Unlike so many of the other people close to Roy, I could not help but like him and it was perhaps because of this that I was delegated to approach him. I waited until late on the Sunday. I wanted to make him a totally genuine offer to sign but to resist any argument for delay. I had difficulty in contacting Jim and eventually had to ring Peter Jay, who first rang his father-in-law to see if I could be given his number on the farm. When I got through we both fenced hard: Jim was trying to find out who else had signed in the Shadow Cabinet, which I was quite happy to reveal, but he was also arguing for a delay, presumably so that it could be discussed at the Wednesday Shadow Cabinet. He told me he would not be in London on the Monday but I pleaded newspaper deadlines and international co-ordination problems and this eventually led Jim to say that if the machinery was already in motion and could not be stopped, he would have to accept that the declaration must go ahead. We then agreed a formula: he would say that he had been approached but refused to sign on the grounds that it was better for the Shadow Cabinet members to stay outside such an initiative. He had not, in consequence, been given the wording of the declaration which meant that he had no view on it.

I had no complaints. It meant Jim could not brief the press to say the statement was innocuous and the sort of statement he would be usually quite happy to sign. To have him downplaying the whole initiative would have been very damaging. It was now also too late for him to brief the press for the Monday editions.

The *Guardian* declaration had a major impact, steeling the ranks of the pro-marketeers inside the PLP and raising the morale of our supporters outside Parliament. For all this, the harsh fact was now becoming clear: the Party outside was moving relentlessly against entry and Harold Wilson's position on the fence was looking very lopsided. In conversation with middle-of-the-road Labour MPs one could sense that many were preparing for a retreat from any previous commitment to entry, claiming that the EEC was not that important and that we should really be concentrating on housing, education and health.

The shift was also becoming apparent to the press, not least to David Watt, political editor of the *Financial Times*, and who, with his wife Susan who works in publishing, had become close friends of ours. David knew the Labour Party inside out from his time as Common Market Correspondent on the old *Daily Herald*. He was getting more and more concerned that the Labour Party was about to switch away from its support for entry. On 7 May he wrote in the *Financial Times* that

> If the leader of the Labour Party starts at this late stage to discover a sudden burning indignation on behalf of the Caribbean sugar produc-ers, Scottish fishermen and New Zealand farmers, many of us will be quietly sick, but quite a lot of the Parliamentary Labour Party may find it convincing.

Many of us were soon to be sick. The Heath-Pompidou breakthrough meeting took place on 20–21 May 1971 and it was now clear that France was going to accept Britain as a member of the Community. Just four days later, the pro-marketeers were dealt a major blow. Jim Callaghan made his devastating 'Language of Chaucer' speech at a by-election meeting for Bob Mitchell in Southampton. Bob later became an SDP MP but he was a rarity, being against the European Community but firmly on the Right of the Party. While paying lip service to the on-going negotiations, Jim did not even attempt to disguise his belief that the Labour Party should reject entry. He defined terms of entry that were not remotely negotiable and he knew it. Picking up on a *Panorama* interview when President Pompidou had referred to French as the language of Europe, Jim played shamelessly to the gallery. 'Millions of people in Britain', he declared, 'have been surprised to hear that the language of Chaucer, Shakespeare and Milton must in future be regarded as an American import from which we must protect ourselves if we are to build a new Europe.'

However, the speech cannot simply be dismissed as the small change of an internal party battle. In a perceptive passage Jim anticipated the controversy of the 1990s over whether a single currency meant a federalist Europe.

> I understand there is to be a confederation of member states whose Ministers will retain full powers of decision. That is to say, they can disagree with decisions taken by other countries and so can prevent action by the EEC countries. This is a contradictory position for, if there is to be a successful economic and monetary union, then member states will have to subordinate their own fiscal, taxation and monetary policies to a central governing body.

This was a direct reply to Edward Heath who had said decisions would have to be taken unanimously with a veto retained. By exposing that a unified economic and monetary policy meant a big step towards a United

States of Europe, Jim also drew attention to the way Heath, throughout this period, sold entry to the British public as joining a Community of nation states. I never realized that Edward Heath was hiding his own federalist opinions at every stage of the negotiations as well as during the passage of the legislation. He was not the only one. I only later discovered that Roy Jenkins was a closet federalist. The dubious tactic of the federalists throughout was to deny they wanted a single Executive European President, a European Cabinet or an authoritative European Parliament but to quietly push in this direction over a whole series of small decisions. In this sense the anti-Europeans were right – there was a secret agenda. Yet many of the pro-Europeans were, like me, deeply suspicious of a federalist Europe. An uneasy truce was reached in British politics to postpone serious discussions on this question until Britain was firmly embedded within the European Community. It is revealing that the federalist debate in Britain only surfaced from 1988 onwards, the moment when it was clear that Labour's internal battle against membership was perhaps finally over.

It is quite extraordinary that Jim Callaghan's autobiography, *Time and Chance*, has no account of his '*Non merci beaucoup*' speech in Southampton. The impact of the speech on Harold Wilson and its effect within the Labour Party was tremendous. I have no doubt that if Jim Callaghan had supported entry in 1971, as he had as Chancellor when it was debated in 1967 and as Home Secretary when Labour formally applied in 1970, then Harold Wilson would not have come out against the terms of the negotiations. For Harold did not need to understand French to know what Jim was up to. He had already had reported to him Jim's reputed comment to a journalist not willing to go to Southampton, 'Well, if you want to hear the next Leader of the Labour Party, you'd better arrange to be there.' As he had done with 'In Place of Strife', Jim was putting himself at the vanguard of mainstream Labour Party opinion. If Harold Wilson wanted to stay true to the application for membership which he had launched, he was going to have to fight Jim Callaghan once again and with no certainty as to the outcome. And if Wilson had any doubts as to which way the wind was blowing the conduct of two other members of the Shadow Cabinet, Denis Healey and Tony Crosland, would have convinced him.

Denis Healey had reinforced his signature on the *Guardian* advertisement with a positive pro-European article in the *Daily Mirror* on 26 May.

> I've changed my mind too . . . I know it's unfashionable. Some of my friends say it is politically inconvenient too. But the world has changed a lot in the last nine years and so has the Common Market . . . failure in Brussels will be a great chance lost for everyone concerned. It would mean another quarter of a century in which what happens to all of us in Europe is decided mainly by the Americans and Russians.

No sooner had we celebrated Denis's support than a few weeks later he began stressing entry terms that were not negotiable. The Healey tank had turned, only to bulldoze off in the opposite direction. It was as cynical a piece of politics as I have ever seen. The turn was so sharp that on 13 July a BBC TV debate had to be rearranged because he had been invited to speak as a pro-European in the mistaken impression that was his view. In his autobiography, *The Time of My Life*, he glosses over it all, describing the *Guardian* advertisement as 'intended for our socialist colleagues abroad'. If so it was rather odd that we chose to place it in a British newspaper. He also describes his article in the *Daily Mirror*, as one 'which put the arguments on each side'. He certainly managed to confuse the BBC! A man I had deeply respected, one of the better Defence Secretaries since the war, had shown an unscrupulous side to his character that I had not seen before. Sadly, I was to see it displayed all too often during the next twenty years over Europe, the nuclear deterrent and the Falklands. It culminated in 1991 with a deplorable attack on President Bush when Saddam Hussein refused to withdraw from Kuwait and Denis was arguing against using force to expel Iraq.

Tony Crosland's 'apostasy', as it was woundingly described by the *Sunday Times*, leaked out from the General Management Committee in his Grimsby constituency on the same day as Denis Healey's *volte-face* was complete. For Tony, we were told, membership of the European Community was not that important, perhaps seventh in his list of priorities. There was no way in which Tony could make this argument sound convincing. He had been a longstanding supporter of entry into the European Community, and he had been upset by Hugh Gaitskell's anti-Community stance in 1962. How could he behave like this? Undoubtedly he was influenced by jealousy of Roy Jenkins who was ahead of him in the leadership stakes and by the fact that many who supported Roy had acted with monumental insensitivity towards Tony. None of us had done nearly enough to keep Roy and Tony working together. We had lined ourselves up in separate camps as if preparing for war. I kick myself for not having learnt the lesson of nursing bruised egos in my dealings with the three other members of the Gang of Four after our 1983 election defeat. Too often it is lack of communication as well as ambitions and animosities which determine people's political positions.

Not surprisingly, as David Watt had foreseen, Harold Wilson discovered New Zealand farmers at the Labour Party's Special Party Conference in the Central Hall, Westminster. Eleven days later the National Executive of the Labour Party voted by sixteen votes to six to invite the Parliamentary Labour Party to unite wholeheartedly in voting against the Government's policy over the European Community. Roy Jenkins, Shirley Williams, Jack Diamond, Fred Mulley, Tom Bradley and Walter Padley voted against. The stage was set for a monumental clash inside the Parliamentary Party.

At this stage, though I was still working with the group around Roy Jenkins, I was nevertheless on good terms with Tony Crosland. Dick Leonard, who was very close to Tony, was every bit as strong as I was on the issue of Europe and determined to act as a bridge between friends of Tony and Roy. Roy Hattersley, who at this time was gung ho for Europe, was saying that it was typical of Tony that his nerve was giving out. It all became very nasty. People became beleaguered, backs were turned, military metaphors were the order of the day. It was said that Tony Crosland's weakness was that he would 'never put his head over the parapet'. He was only ready to 'fight the enemy over the next hill'. I found this military language somewhat inappropriate for Tony had volunteered for the Parachute Brigade during the war. Nevertheless, I was infuriated by Tony's attitude, and incensed by Denis Healey's. I respected both men's intellect and liked their general manner and outlook but gradually I found myself looking to Roy Jenkins for consistency. It was noticeable how personal animosities usually reflected past Labour Party political battles in which I had not been involved. Perhaps because I had no legacy to bring to this new battle, I felt less vitriolic.

The clash of personality can never be divorced from politics. It of course occurs in all walks of life but is peculiarly heightened by the cockpit of politics that is the House of Commons. Wilson was naturally determined to hold on to the leadership. Callaghan, Jenkins, Crosland and Healey were all fighting in their various ways to become Leader. The clash of personality had debilitated the Wilson Government of 1964–70 and was now haunting Labour in Opposition. Superficially the discord between Roy Jenkins and Tony Crosland was the least defensible. Longtime personal friends, they were supposed to agree on most political issues. Although Tony was a far more ideological politician than Roy, both were fiercely ambitious and deeply emotional, though they desperately tried to hide these characteristics both from themselves as well as from their friends. Roy gave the impression to some of not giving a damn about the Labour Party, seeing the issue only in terms of editorials in *The Times*, and of being also unduly obsessed about his own personal position; whereas Tony appeared to elevate the Labour Party, particularly in Grimsby, to a position where its interests came well before those of the country. He was also never as uninterested as he pretended to be in jockeying for position as a potential Leader of the Labour Party. Tony's problem was that Roy was thought to have a far better chance of winning the leadership. It was becoming very hard to be a friend of both men.

The Special Labour Party Conference in the summer of 1971 was a qualified success for the pro-marketeers. It was at least a genuine democratic debate. Harold Wilson's wind-up speech was firmly against entry. John Mackintosh spoke extremely well and turned on Peter Shore, who had also made a good demagogic speech reminding everyone of the last Labour Government. 'I wonder if he has been living in the same world as I have. Does he remember the cuts and the deflation which we had to explain all round the country?' I had been attempting to speak but could not have come near to John's speech. Conference delegates knew little about the radical Right's record of dissent and that was our fault. We had played within the conventions and decencies of Parliament. We had not taken our criticism of the Labour Government into the constituencies. Our views on civil liberty issues – race, homosexuality, abortion, divorce law reforms – had become known but not our dissent on the more central political issues. To some extent it was known over East of Suez but not sufficiently over devaluation or over Vietnam. It was a lesson for the future; I vowed I would never again tie myself into the conservative attitudes of the dead-centre.

On Monday evening, 19 July, the PLP met for a final series of discussions on the EEC. It had been agreed that Roy Jenkins and Barbara Castle would represent the differing views in the Shadow Cabinet. But the most significant speech came from the floor of the meeting. Bert Oram MP, a strong member of the Co-op wing of the Party with a firm longstanding commitment to overseas development, was an unusual voice to be heard in favour of entry. In a quiet, controlled contribution, he spoke with great dignity and in a reference to Harold Wilson's critical speech on the previous Saturday made it clear that he did not like hearing George Thomson, in effect, called a liar. The meeting exploded. The thumping on the desks conveyed the pent-up fury of many moderate people and interestingly it was not only coming from the well-known pro-marketeers. It was a response from the centre of the Party. However gratifying it was, I sensed it was also dangerous and I stopped applauding for the atmosphere was getting nasty. Barbara Castle made, for her part, a quite dreadful speech. She was a bad choice – Willie Ross or even Fred Peart would have been much better. Coming after Barbara, Roy's speech seemed, in contrast, far better than it actually was. After all the years of shuffle, smudge and slither, the PLP saw, at long last, what can happen when a leader leads from the front. They responded that evening, not just to the man, not just to the words, nor even to the obvious emotion of the occasion, but to leadership – even those who did not agree on the issue were moved to applaud.

As if to reinforce the feelings of the PLP, at the next meeting Harold launched into an all too familiar indirect and snide attack, without mentioning any names. He talked about those who 'can find it in their hearts to sully their purity by continuing to sit on the Front Bench on invitation'.

This deliberate attack could not go unchallenged. Next day, Bill Rodgers, Dick Taverne, Denis Howell, Dick Mabon and I asked for an urgent meeting with Harold to demand a withdrawal. The one useful commitment to come out of the meeting was the public statement that open espousal of the case of British entry was not incompatible with membership of the Front Bench.

Over the weekend of 19–20 June I saw a lot of Willie Whitelaw, then Leader of the House, since we were both at Ditchley, at an Anglo-American Parliamentarians' Conference. He made it clear that he was arguing in the Cabinet for a free vote and he insisted the door was not shut on a free vote, though he conceded it was unlikely. The wording used by Heath in the House had been deliberately chosen to leave open the possibility of having a free vote in the autumn. Whitelaw was adamant that, after the vote in principle, the Government would have to be responsible for the subsequent legislation but he attached great importance to the achievement of a substantial pro-entry vote in principle in October and clearly felt that if there was a free vote many more Labour MPs would feel it possible to vote for entry than if they had to flout a three-line whip. In retrospect, there can be no doubt that, if Whitelaw had been able to convince the Cabinet in July to support a free vote, it would have been very difficult for the Labour Party to have insisted on a three-line whip. Unfortunately he failed and the Cabinet made the major tactical blunder of holding out until forced to concede a free vote in October.

The widely used argument was that it was necessary to hold the prospect of a three-line whip over Conservative MPs during the summer so that Conservative Associations could pressurize their anti-Market MPs. But the numbers who would have been so pressured were very small, probably ten MPs at most. The real reason was that Edward Heath believed he could carry the vote relying only on Conservative votes and attached great importance to doing so. Over the summer, the momentum therefore built up for a Labour three-line whip against entry. Our resolve to support entry was undiminished. About fifty of the Labour pro-marketeers met under Bill Rodgers's chairmanship just before the summer recess. At that meeting, it was made clear that there were sixty-plus who were committed to vote for entry, even against the expected Conference decision, and against a three-line whip. This did a lot to strengthen people's morale and I went away for the summer feeling I had made a commitment before close colleagues and that there could now be no turning back. Nor did I want to. Not for the first or last time in my political career I was rejecting Disraeli's dictum 'damn your principles and stick to your party'.

It was remarkable how firm our group's resolve proved to be. Instead of the summer months showing a steady slipping in support, the group's strength actually increased. By Conference we were certain of at least sixty-five pro-votes and throughout October Bill Rodgers's figures were far more accurate, as events proved, than the underestimates made by the official Opposition Whips. Although it was not widely discussed, Roy Jenkins's intention to vote for entry, finally confirmed in October in answer to pleas from the Left to abstain, was never in doubt.

Throughout August I replied to a fairly large mail bag from my constituency asking about my voting intentions with the comment that individual MPs were unlikely to make their final voting decision until October and I said that it was still possible that the Government would decide on a free vote which I believed would be the right way for Parliament to decide an issue of principle. I went on to say that politicians could not simply chop and change sincerely held views and, however bitterly opposed I was to many of the divisive policies of the Conservative Government, in my view the nation could not lose this historic opportunity.

The constituency pressure on a few MPs like Dick Taverne in Lincoln was becoming massive and some of us were becoming very worried that he might be deselected. It was to his great credit that he never wavered and was determined at all times to vote in Parliament as he felt his best judgement dictated.

Before the Brighton Conference I had to face a selection conference for the new Devonport constituency. I was determined that there should be no misunderstanding and so I told the GMC that within weeks I had every intention of voting for the principle of entry contained in the Government White Paper. I was the single candidate under the then rules since I was the sitting MP for parts of the new constituency and I only had to get 50 per cent of the votes. I did this easily, but there was some dissent so the chairman asked if the meeting would agree, for press purposes, to take another vote in order to make it unanimous. To her credit, one of the delegates who was passionately anti-Common Market objected to this procedure.

When Parliament reassembled, it became ever clearer that Bob Mellish's earlier promise that a three-line whip would be imposed only over his dead body was not going to be honoured. It was argued by some MPs that the pro-marketeers were so eager for a showdown and so insensitive to Labour Party unity that they never looked seriously at the alternatives. This was not the case. I have a scientist's respect for the patience of paper when weighing problems and, determined that we should seriously consider other options, had circulated a memorandum back in May among our group putting the case for a reasoned amendment rather than a straight vote backing Heath. It meant claiming that only a Labour Government could handle the transition period so there had to be a general election before entry. But it committed Labour to entry. I was not convinced even by my own arguments and they were rightly exposed in discussion as being merely a device which would not convince a majority of the PLP. Even Jim Wellbeloved MP, who managed that summer to raise a round robin supporting abstention, could point to very few MPs whose vote depended on whether we were or were not abstaining. Roy Jenkins held firmly to the view that this was one of those rare occasions when an MP had to reach a definite conclusion. He likened it to the Great Reform Bill, the Repeal of the Corn Laws and, crucially for me, who had little historical knowledge of either of these, to the May 1940 vote in the House of Commons, when the Conservative rebels changed the direction of the war, bringing about Chamberlain's resignation and Churchill's coalition Government.

The case for an abstention anyhow faded further after Heath's belated announcement that all Conservative MPs would have a free vote. Yet in my own constituency the pressure was mounting against my voting for entry, with many activists urging me to abstain. On 25 October I wrote to Alf Sweetland, my agent, a close friend but very unhappy about my stance, enclosing a letter which I had sent to every member of the Sutton GMC. I told Alf that I did not believe that I could abstain and that for an MP not to have a view on this issue was impossible to justify, however uncomfortable I would feel voting in a Tory lobby.

In other letters to members of the Party I reminded them that I had never abstained or voted against the Party in the six years that I had been in Parliament. I pointed out that in 1967, when Labour applied to join, we were bitterly unpopular and that the Tories did not choose to play party politics with the issue but voted in support of the application to the EEC on the basis that this was an issue that transcended party politics.

> Party unity means a very great deal to me. I have never been prepared, however, to become a slave to party unity or just a delegate. Who can doubt now that in 1938 those Tory and Labour MPs who voted against the official view of their party and against appeasement were not right to do so? They rightly resisted the call of party unity and put the future of Britain first. History alone will judge whether my decision to support entry into the Common Market is right; but I would be denying everything I have said in the past if I change my mind now purely because the Labour Party, in my mind, has changed its mind ... To those of you who may say that by taking this stand I will harm my future political career I would say that politics is not just about the pursuit of personal power. It is also, and perhaps more fundamentally, about the pursuit of a political philosophy. Every now and then in political life an MP will have to choose not just the course of ambition or the course of simply staying in power but the course he believes is right.

Telegrams started to flow in and resolutions were passed at one ward party meeting after another. Alf Sweetland wrote on 27 October:

> I know the agony of mind you are having to contend with. I still cannot accept your reasoning. You are placing your decision against that of the Party, freely arrived at and voted on. You are taking this step with your eyes wide open, and you must take the backlash afterwards. I have been your eyes and ears since 1965 and on no issue such as this have I found the rank and file so much against you. For your political future, THINK!

The Plymouth Central Labour Party Executive met on the Tuesday
before Thursday's vote and passed a resolution:

> The Executive Committee strongly criticize any Member of Parliament
> who supports the Tory motion in the House on 28 October and calls
> on the MP Dr David Owen to support the Labour Party's call to
> oppose the motion before the House and to give loyalty to the Party
> which has given him the honour of being an MP.

The resolution was carried by ten votes to one. The delegate who voted
against was the same woman who had refused to make my selection for
Devonport unanimous. Despite her own passionate opposition to the
European Community she told the Executive that it was humbug to
censure me now when I had honestly told them of my voting intention
before selection. Her action was a demonstration of the basic decency of
most people in the Labour Party. In the end there was no savage
backlash, in part because I had never hidden my views. But its absence
owed much to Alf Sweetland. Deeply respected within the Party, he
loyally threw his weight behind me and defused party activists' anger.
Significantly, there was no backlash from the general public in Plymouth
who seemed to like their MPs to have the courage of their convictions.

The six-day debate to approve the Government's decision of principle
to join the European Community on the basis of the arrangements which
had been negotiated was the most important debate in my time in the
House of Commons. Over two hundred MPs were trying to catch the
Speaker's eye and it was called 'The Great Debate'. John Mackintosh
spoke at 6.30 a.m. and even at that unearthly hour it was a lucid
demolition of the nineteenth-century concept of sovereignty. I had earlier
challenged Michael Foot on this point, intervening in his speech to say:

> Before my Honourable Friend gets carried away by his own rhetoric,
> on the important point of principle which he rightly raised on the issue
> of sovereignty, how does he square the fact that membership of the
> United Nations also carries with it some secession of sovereignty, and
> membership of any treaty or any organization involves sharing,
> compromise and, if he likes, haggling?

Earlier that day Geoffrey Rippon quoted President Pompidou's explanation about sovereignty and the Treaty in a press conference held on 21
January 1978 and it remains the best description I have heard of the
realities of Community membership.

> How will the Council of Ministers be able to take its decision? I ask
> everybody and in particular our partners to consider how coalition
> governments work. When everybody is of the same opinion all goes
> well. If that is not the case, there is a majority and a minority. At that
> point either the minority considers the question is not vital and yields,
> or thinks the contrary and breaks the coalition. It is plain that, in our

construction of Europe, one cannot break without everything collapsing. I therefore conclude that important decisions can only be taken on the basis of unanimous agreement and that what is at issue here is political reality rather than juridical rule. If one ignores that reality everything would be destroyed.

There is no possible interpretation of President Pompidou's words or the fact that it was quoted by our chief negotiator in that debate which gives any evidence for the argument that we were joining up for a United States of Europe and that Britain would have no right to veto such a development.

I spoke in the debate at 11.13 p.m. on 26 October with my father-in-law and Debbie in the gallery. It was not a brilliant speech but it was the first I had made in the House of Commons without reading extensive notes and it reads a little unevenly in Hansard. I ended by saying:

I support entry now, just as I supported it in 1962 when it was unpopular in this Party, and just as I resisted the temptation, in fighting an agricultural seat in Devon in 1964, to change my mind for cheap votes which were then easily obtainable. I stayed constant to Europe then.

I saw my Party change its mind because it saw the economic realities facing it when it took office in 1964. It was no accident that we changed our minds. We lived through the experience of July, 1966. I have never voted against my Party, nor abstained, but the one decision I regret is that I did not vote against my Government in July 1966, because the deflationary policies which we followed then were wrong, but I knew then I should be voting against a party when it was in Government.

Today I feel a free man. In 1967 we decided to enter the European Economic Community. We on this side should remind ourselves that we were very unpopular as a Government in 1967. It was not all that easy for the then Tory Opposition to vote with us. They did so because some of them genuinely wanted the issue of European unity not to become a party political issue. It should not be a party political issue.

I shall vote on Thursday to support British entry, but I shall do so in a mood of sadness that I have to make a decision to go against the will of my Party. I believe in party unity. I believe that we exercise power here because we have been sent here as representatives of our Party, not as individuals. But, equally, I believe that the electorate expect us to make our decisions on this of all issues on the way ahead that we think will be good for the country for decades to come. They will expect us to exercise judgement, and my judgement is that Britain should enter the European Economic Community.

The debate grew tense towards the end. When the division was called I, along with sixty-eight other Labour MPs, voted to support entry into the Common Market and twenty, including Tony Crosland, abstained. There was a majority of 112 for the principle of entry into the European

Community. Had every Labour MP and all the Conservative rebels voted against, Britain would not have become a member of the European Community. It was the best parliamentary vote that I have ever cast and I have no regrets whatever for voting as I did.

What I do regret, and bitterly, was thereafter voting against the legislation necessary to ensure that entry was enshrined in our law. Now that the White Paper on the principle was passed, we faced months of votes on the mechanics, each bit of which was essential to entry. The truth is that we allowed ourselves to drift into a messy compromise over how to vote during the next few months. It is easy to see how it happened. There was a strong case to be made for those of the sixty-nine who were in the Shadow Cabinet not resigning and putting themselves up instead in the Shadow Cabinet elections due to follow in only a few weeks' time. Roy was correct to argue that to resign, only to stand a few weeks later, was just a gimmick. There was no group decision before the White Paper vote to vote against the subsequent legislation, instead it emerged over a period of time. It would not have been very comfortable for us, given the unpopularity of the Conservative Government, to let them off the hook by providing them with a majority for their legislation. Their Whips feared too that if we took the pressure off their rebels by virtually guaranteeing the legislation, the number of Conservative MPs rebelling would only increase, weakening the authority of the Government. A rather bogus logic was also developed to justify our behaviour, namely that it was not the job of an Opposition to carry Government legislation. I never really accepted this and believed that voting against would be very embarrassing. This was one reason why I had shown interest in abstaining on the White Paper for I felt we could hold to that and abstain throughout the legislation.

When Bruce Millan, ostensibly in all innocence, asked at a Parliamentary Party meeting how Roy intended to vote in subsequent divisions he was put on the spot. It was ruled from the chair that all the candidates for the deputy leadership should answer the question at the next week's meeting. As happened too often, Roy Jenkins's personal position then became paramount. It was thought, in retrospect quite wrongly, that it would damage him if he got fewer votes for the deputy leadership than in the previous year. To hold support from some MPs, Roy devised a totally unsatisfactory form of words. In effect, he said that he would vote against the legislation in all divisions unless he judged that he was being asked to deny the principle of entry. Whether it was successful in ensuring the votes of Millan and a few others we will never be sure but it meant we were caving in quite unnecessarily to the vicious propaganda line that it was a great sin to ever vote 'with the Tories'. That criticism was taken so far that many Labour activists outside Parliament believed that the sixty-nine of us were responsible for keeping the Tory Government in power. In fact, very few of those Tory rebels were ready to vote in a way which meant that their Government would have had to call a general election.

I have no doubt that, immediately after the White Paper vote, we should have said that we would abstain on the subsequent legislation and that we could have held that line. As it was we humiliated ourselves night after night voting against what we believed in. For what? To ensure that Roy got 140 votes on the first ballot for the deputy leadership, seven up on the previous year. It did not stem the tide. Michael Foot got ninety-six votes and Tony Benn forty-six. On the second ballot, Roy polled 140 again but Michael Foot this time polled 126. The Labour cleavage was no longer a Left/Right political divide, it was for or against the European Community, something that Tony Crosland in fairness had always held would be the most dangerous, as well as the most likely, outcome of making entry into the European Community an issue of high principle. While there is no doubt that the margin of Roy's victory might have been reduced if he had refused to concede the principle of voting against the legislation, he had enough votes to win. What is more important, to win in such circumstances would have meant it was quite unneccessary to resign a few months later. He then would have been in a position to challenge Wilson for the leadership in the autumn. In such a leadership battle, Roy would have lost against Wilson, but it was at least openly knocking at the door. It is a terrible indictment of the so-called Labour moderates that we never challenged Harold Wilson openly for the leadership. When one considers that both Edward Heath and Margaret Thatcher were defeated it is to our discredit that from 1963 to 1976, Harold Wilson was never democratically opposed as Leader in the PLP.

The pro-marketeers entered the new year fearful, in many cases, of being undermined in their constituencies. On 19 January 1972 Harold Wilson unceremoniously sacked Bill Rodgers from his position as a second-tier spokesman on the Opposition Front Bench. This was a direct challenge to Roy Jenkins for Bill had acted as chief of staff of the pro-market campaign and was known to be very close to Roy. But, cleverly, Wilson did reappoint Dick Taverne. It was a neatly judged knifing of Roy Jenkins, diminishing him without provoking him. Other people who had voted for the European Community, including Cledwyn Hughes, a former Cabinet Minister, and four other junior spokesmen, one of them David Marquand, were not reappointed. I survived, although I was neither asked for nor gave an assurance that I would abide by the so-called 'Houghton formula' to vote against the forthcoming legislation. Wilson's action showed how impotent Roy had become as Deputy Leader. People tempted to support him began to wonder who he could shelter if he had not got the authority to protect even Bill Rodgers. This must have been Wilson's intention.

On the night of 17 February, on the Second Reading of the European

Communities Bill, I cast the worst vote I have ever cast in Parliament and the one of which I am most ashamed. It was the first of the votes to put in place the necessary mechanisms for entry. I felt physically sick, passing through what I knew to be the wrong division lobby and voting against the bill. That night I was closer to leaving Parliament than at any other time. I had had dinner in the House with Roy and we had all drunk rather too much, trying to hide our feelings. It was a very emotional occasion. All the indications were that the Government would have a fairly comfortable majority of a little under twenty. As 10 p.m. came nearer it became obvious that it might be close. I talked to Austen Albu, who was uncertain what he would do, and also to the veteran Labour MP George Strauss, who was upset that most of us intended to vote against the Second Reading and felt strongly that we should abstain. Roy decided not to wait for the result and went up to his room. Voting against the bill had been a desperately difficult decision for him personally: he really felt it might be better to resign. Like us all, however, he buoyed himself up with the false belief that this would be the last hurdle.

The division result was announced to a tense House and the majority of only eight was shattering news. We had boosted our Party but nearly broken the bill. There was a snarling, vicious scene as the Labour benches erupted, with Jimmy Hamilton and others rounding on the Liberals who had quite reasonably voted for entry. I left and walked up with Roy Hattersley to Roy Jenkins's room. On the way, Roy Hattersley talked about how we must dissuade Roy from resigning. In the room were Harold Lever, Shirley Williams and a few others, all dejected. It seemed that Harold and Shirley both wanted to resign immediately and this was the general mood. We agreed, however, that this was not the time to make such a decision and that we should think about it over the weekend.

I left for Paris the next day and rang Bill from Paris on Saturday, quite expecting that Roy might have decided to resign. Instead I found that no decision had been made and generally the situation seemed calmer. The ugly scenes with the Liberals had taken most of the publicity.

The next few weeks were, in many respects, one of our worst periods. The pro-market forces were in disarray, guilt was the dominant emotion – most people felt deeply distressed at how near we had come to seeing our entry to the Community rejected. Once again, the anguish had to be faced over what was more important – Britain going into the Common Market or splitting the Labour Party. The anti-market forces – both Tory and Labour – had scented blood. The successful alliance between Enoch Powell and Michael Foot, which had forced the shelving of the House of Lords Reform Bill, might succeed once again. The legislation on the European Bill was now clearly threatened and there would be tremendous pressure for frequent three-line whips.

Bill Rodgers, on this occasion emotionally fraught, was strongly in favour of resigning. Roy Hattersley was firmly against resignation but in a highly tendentious fashion started to brief the press that he and Tom Bradley were the doves, advising Roy Jenkins to sit tight, but that there were some wild hawks, such as Bill Rodgers, in favour of resignation. I was not named, although if I had been it would have been as a dove, largely on the grounds that resigning after the event was the worst possible time. Roy Jenkins himself talked to many people, perhaps too many, and the resulting speculation was damaging. He was opening himself up to the charge of 'hawking his conscience around'.

Of the original sixty-nine Labour pro-marketeers who had abstained on the White Paper, five were the true Labour Party heroes of Britain's entry into the European Community. They were Freda Corbet, Austen Albu, Carol Johnson, George Lawson and Christopher Mayhew who bravely went on abstaining. We hid behind their bravery and were demeaned. It was the memory of this shabbiness that sustained my resolve when it came to the agony of leaving the Labour Party and creating the SDP in 1981.

Partly to break out of this frustrating downward spiral, Roy Jenkins had agreed some months before to embark on a course of speeches. Debbie helped Roy with the publishing arrangements for *What Matters Now* and he generously gave her a Persian rug as thanks. We still have it in our sitting room and it serves to remind us both of a happy time when Roy and Jennifer Jenkins were our friends. A number of us put a great deal of time and effort into these speeches. David Marquand contributed most to the writing, often while staying in Buttermere for the weekend, and he included a reference to 'breaking the mould', a concept later taken up by the SDP. The ideas came from a large number of people whom we consulted. Roy, of course, provided his own distinctive gloss but at times I wondered whether he was focusing sufficiently on the radical nature of many of the suggestions. They were put to him and were easily accepted but when he had the opportunity to put some of them into action in government, particularly on poverty and the inner cities, Roy singularly failed to champion them. As chairman of the Home Affairs Cabinet Sub-Committee between 1974 and 1976 Roy could have instigated a radical programme, even though we were then in a very difficult financial situation but he showed precious little interest in pushing forward the ideas established in his own programme. More than any other single thing, this eroded my commitment to him as a future leader.

The intention behind the speeches was straightforward and political. It was to be the 'Unauthorized Programme'. Just as Joseph Chamberlain, another Birmingham MP, had used this vehicle in 1885 to stamp his own distinctive mark on British politics, we hoped it would provide a rallying point for people who wanted to see Roy Jenkins succeed Harold Wilson as Leader of the Labour Party.

So when the first speech on poverty was delivered to the Worsley

Labour Party on Saturday 11 March, not surprisingly, it was marked by Sunday newspaper headlines: 'JENKINS OPENS HIS BID TO OUST WILSON'; 'JENKINS OPENS HIS BID FOR LABOUR LEADERSHIP'; 'JENKINS'S BID FOR THE TOP'. The next day I was sitting out in the spring sun in Buttermere, extremely pleased by what had been achieved, and listening to *The World This Weekend*. I heard Gordon Clough ask Roy, 'A bid to oust Mr Wilson? How do you react to those headlines?' Roy replied, 'Well, I react by regarding them as a totally distorting picture ... I rather resent it when the whole press reacts to this as though it is a personal issue, which it is not, and tries to create a great leadership crisis which does not exist.' It was the first time that Roy Jenkins, the politician, totally exasperated me. If he was going to take this line, I believed he should not have gone on the programme. It was certainly not necessary to deny he was challenging for the leadership in terms which came close to those we now laugh at in *Yes Minister*.

I had thought that Roy accepted that we were embarking on an outright challenge to Wilson and all that his style of leadership implied. Yet here he was, having demonstrated his readiness to strike, showing his disinclination to wound. It reflected many things, not least Roy's ambivalence towards Wilson. I understood this because it was something I had shared but by then I had no doubts whatever about Wilson's leadership. I wanted him out and would have preferred any of the likely alternatives – Roy, Jim or Denis. Roy of course had only one preference – to replace Wilson himself. Roy was always unsure as to whether he could use Wilson as the ladder to No. 10 or whether he had to destroy Wilson to achieve it. Whereas he would be scathing about Jim Callaghan, he was then not as vicious about Wilson. He despised Denis Healey's twists and turns and was uneasy dealing with Tony Crosland but to Wilson there was a sense of indebtedness. However, this was not the time to be paralysed by ambivalence and for the first time I developed a deep anxiety about whether Roy, despite his ambition, had the stomach for an open fight to achieve it, or whether he would always prefer the indirect, less overt feline approach.

Whatever he said on the radio, one of the effects of Roy's speech was that Harold Wilson believed that he was now after his job. Although this was not a new feeling, the intensity with which Wilson felt it was. Not even in 1969 had Wilson looked so vulnerable, for now in Opposition he had very little patronage. He must have been only too well aware of how damaging his somersault over the European Community a few months earlier had been to what was left of his reputation. Yet he saw the situation very differently from us. He felt resentful that he had been left to wade around in the shit, as he put it, while Roy and others like me could ignore the responsibility for Party unity and bask in the glow of a favourable press which called us men of integrity. From then on Wilson seemed determined to face down the Jenkins challenge.

On 15 March the Shadow Cabinet met for the first discussion on the referendum. Tony Benn had been campaigning for some time in favour of a referendum but the issue now was specific – whether or not to support a Tory backbencher's amendment to the European Communities Bill that supported a referendum. In the Shadow Cabinet there were only four votes in favour of the amendment and on this first occasion Harold Wilson spoke against. Then fate intervened. The very next day President Pompidou announced that there would be a referendum in France on the question of enlarging the Community. It was purely a constitutional ratification procedure in France, though having the advantage of splitting the socialists from the communists, but in Britain its effect on the Labour Party was dramatic for it gave Wilson the opportunity to use the issue to isolate Jenkins. The referendum issue was brought by Tony Benn to Labour's NEC on 22 March and they voted in favour by thirteen votes to eleven, with Wilson, Jenkins and Callaghan not attending. This was even though at the previous Brighton Conference the NEC had called successfully for the defeat of a similar referendum motion. Then on 24 March, Edward Heath announced a plan for occasional referenda in Northern Ireland on the issue of union with the South and the momentum for a European referendum was now building up. So much so that when the Shadow Cabinet met on 29 March the pending referendum amendment vote in the House of Commons was on the agenda yet again. This time Harold Wilson spoke early, advocating support for the referendum amendment. Neither Willie Ross nor Denis Healey, who had previously been against, attended and, in the case of Ross at least, Wilson's influence was felt to be at work. Usually loyal to Wilson, Ross was passionately anti-referenda, believing that the Scottish Nationalists would use it to force through separatism or even the devolution which he opposed. So, by eight votes to six, the Shadow Cabinet reversed its position and recommended the Labour Party to vote with Enoch Powell in favour of a consultative referendum.

After the decision had been taken Tony Crosland said that he hoped nobody would take the issue as one of principle. Roy deliberately made no comment. He was determined not to start yet another period of press speculation about his voting intentions and about a possible resignation. He had learned his lesson from the too-wide and extensive consultation that took place over the Second Reading.

Next morning, when I met Roy in his room with David Marquand, John Roper and Bob Maclennan to discuss a speech he was due to deliver, he took a telephone call from Harold Lever. It was clear from listening to Roy's half of the conversation that Harold now believed that resignation was inevitable and essential. Roy had previously talked to George Thomson and George had apparently made it clear that he felt he personally had no other option than to resign; that in speeches up and down the country he had deeply committed himself against a referendum.

Roy remained enigmatic, giving no real indication of his feelings, except that it was a serious situation and he wanted a week to think things over. He then asked me to drive down to the country with him, so I arranged for Debbie to drive down with Tristan and for me to go in Roy's Rover and be dropped off at Buttermere.

9

RESIGNATION

As Roy Jenkins drove out of the House of Commons he said slowly but with determination, 'I think I will have to resign.' Just before leaving the House, I had photostated transcripts of Harold Wilson's two election interviews – on *Panorama* and on ITV – where he had categorically stated his rejection of a referendum on the EEC, and also Attlee's sharp denunciation of the Churchill proposal for a referendum on continuing the coalition after 1945, and read parts of these statements to Roy. We discussed these and stopped for lunch at a pub in Chiswick.

Why had Harold Wilson and Bob Mellish switched over the referendum? The more we looked at it, the more we were led to the conclusion that Wilson had switched, not as on previous occasions to cover his flank from Benn and the Left who could have been easily held, but deliberately to engineer an open breach with the pro-marketeers in the Shadow Cabinet. Unlike the principal issue of entry, there was no evidence that, on the referendum issue, Jim Callaghan was pushing Harold Wilson.

We also wondered if more could have been done to win on the issue in the Shadow Cabinet. Ted Short, who had somewhat surprisingly supported Wilson in the vote, had been attending an education meeting at County Hall before the Shadow Cabinet meeting and had only come to the Shadow Cabinet with the greatest reluctance. Maybe it would have been different if Roy had spoken to Ted Short but on this issue there had seemed little reason to doubt his position. On the EEC generally, following his abstention in October, Ted had voted consistently with the pro-market section of the Shadow Cabinet on all critical issues and was, in many ways, thought to be more reliable than Tony Crosland who had voted against a referendum. Roy, however, was fed up with the constant lobbying: every Shadow Cabinet was a battle, as was every meeting of the NEC. He had just lost the battle to ensure that Gwyn Morgan, the Assistant General Secretary, would take over the General Secretaryship of the Labour Party from Sir Harry Nicholas. John Cartwright, who was on the NEC and voted albeit without much enthusiasm for Gwyn, believed that the last-minute switching of votes was influenced by the controversy building up over the European Community. The whole European issue had been one long emotional struggle. In addition the scars of our vote on the Second Reading had gone pretty deep and the press reaction and speculation over Roy's critical speech in Lancashire had stifled support for Harold. That controversy too had been more than he had reckoned with, so his guard was down while Wilson's was up.

It is easy to forget the exhaustion and emotional strain of politics. One thing I had learnt over the previous few months was that Roy Jenkins was as emotional as every Celt and to vote against the Second Reading was for him as for me one of the hardest things we had ever done in politics.

Discussing the situation, I was certain of one thing, that in the end Roy would make his own decision and would not be easily persuaded to stay his hand. I remembered how, some months back in the Reform Club at lunch, he had said that the decisions he most regretted taking in his life were those where he had been most cautious. Looking ahead, we were already worried about the forthcoming vote on Clause 2, which was the core of the bill, for to lose that clause would be to lose the legislation. If Wilson and the Shadow Cabinet could reverse their decision on the referendum with such apparent disregard for everything that had been said before, it was only a matter of time before they could engineer another crisis to embarrass us.

The Times editorial on Harold Wilson – 'What can one say of such a man, save that he should never be Prime Minister again'[1] – must have hurt for he always took press criticism, from whatever source, far more seriously than it merited. Sensitive, embittered and lonely, his paranoid feelings about the press only intensified by criticism, to Wilson the story was very different. He was the martyr, the man who had put Party unity before his own personal position. Roy had allowed his personal commitment to come before Party unity; only he, Harold, had withstood, as he described it, the 'mud, filthy mud' that was being thrown.

It is hard, even now, not to feel real sympathy for Wilson in his European predicament now also facing his Deputy Leader's challenge on the very basis of the Party's social philosophy. Roy's Lancashire speech on the new challenge of injustice was, we all knew, a fervent attack on Wilson's values, leadership and standing. Previously Wilson had never seen Roy Jenkins as a rival because he lacked a base in the Party. Callaghan was always the real danger. Perhaps after the Lancashire speech Wilson had now decided to ignore the short-term cost to his own credibility and would force his Deputy Leader to severe humiliation and compromise so that his image would be tarnished. This was typical of the restless insouciance which often characterized Wilson's approach. Wilson must have recognized that this could mean Roy's resignation but he might have thought that Roy would swallow even this.

One further aspect of our conversation, which I had recorded in my notebook, in the light of subsequent events had particular significance. When I, for the first time, raised the whole question of us perhaps being forced into a new political party, Roy said that, if one was a Chartist, one would take the view that this was highly possible but it was clear that it had no attraction whatever for him – his roots were then still too deep in the Labour Party

Roy was under no illusion at all that resignation would damage his chances of becoming Leader. I only wanted one promise – that he would fight back for a number of years. I got my assurance with the wry comment that this was not a commitment for a decade. It was clear that Roy intended to fight – he would not go off and write, to the exclusion of politics, or take some financially lucrative appointment in the City. Unlike Jim Callaghan, he remarked, he was not intending to become a director of an Italian bank.

Having put my point vigorously about the need for him to still attend Prime Minister's questions and Party meetings, I told Roy that whatever decision he made on resignation, whether I agreed with it or not, I too would resign. I felt that he needed to have the certain knowledge that some of us would come with him. In these situations we had to retain a basic cohesion and loyalty and, though I still felt unsure which was the right course and indeed went on putting the case against resignation, over the last year I had developed enough confidence in his judgement to make his decision my decision. Over that Easter weekend Tony and Susan Crosland came to stay at Buttermere for the night. It was a delightful visit. The preliminaries, however, amused us. Before they finally accepted, Debbie was telephoned to find out whether we had more than one bath, to which we had to say no; it took all Debbie's self-control not to add that we did have two lavatories.

We only had a short talk about politics. It was clear that Tony could see no reason why the referendum vote should pose any substantial difficulty. He had voted against but there it was, they had lost in the Shadow Cabinet. The situation was awful, yes, but there was nothing anyone could, or should, do. The only time I think I shook Tony's argument at all was when I reminded him of his own attitude to unilateralism in 1961. There must, I asked, be some issues on which one has to fight. The referendum might not be the issue, but the compromises were increasing. He was off to Japan in a few days so I warned him that the referendum could turn out to be a major turning point, although I felt I could not tell him that I thought Roy was about to resign. We left the issue thereafter for it was pointless to argue further, our basic positions were so different. Tony had convinced himself that the EEC was a minor issue; starting from such a premise, any discussion of resignation, conscience or principle was bound to be meaningless.

His was a breathtaking position – intellectually impudent as well as suspect. It flew in the face of all the conventional wisdoms. There was scarcely any significant figure, Left, Right or Centre in the EEC controversy, who thought entry a minor issue. However, the attraction of the position for anyone not wanting a fight within the Labour Party, yet wanting to remain consistent, was immense. I never dismissed Tony's views without thought, for since 1966 he had been proven right more often than anyone else on the main issues. Tony's one-page memo to Cabinet on why Barbara Castle's 'In Place of Strife' proposals were misconceived was a brilliant demolition job, written when he was President of the Board of Trade. Typically, he had bothered to read the Donovan Report, called together a few outside experts to discuss the issue and proceeded to expose both the impracticality and the lack of realism that lay behind some of the proposals. On public expenditure, Tony had at least been consistent and courageous even if he was wrong. He believed that Roy was going for overkill in his 1968 and 1969 budgets and argued persuasively for a different strategy, in particular for the retention of the planned date for raising the school-leaving age. He had underestimated the uncertainty of foreign investors, as he would again in 1976. But, for all his intellectual rigour, Tony's political judgement was somehow suspect. The criticism that he always wanted to decide tomorrow, to fight another day, had substance. It was an intellectual wish to postpone decisions until he had every last fact, which probably prevented him from ever making the political impact to be expected of someone with his intellect, ability and personality.

After this weekend, having had time to reflect, I drove back with Debbie and Tristan to London very worried that we were in danger of making the decision to resign without looking at the options. I had had a telephone conversation with Roy on the Sunday, when he was clearly very disturbed by the massive majority in favour of a referendum revealed by a newspaper poll. Even allowing for the loaded way in which the question was put, it was clear that the poll would put greater pressure on pro-market Labour MPs and lukewarm Tory anti-market MPs. As we had always recognized, the cry to 'let the people decide' was a heady one and hard to counter. On top of this, there were the 'elitist' jibes. Finally, the escape hatch of the referendum was a tempting one for anyone under pressure in their constituency.

It was against this background that I decided, once again, to try another option. It might not be viable but it needed to be discussed. As in May 1971 on the White Paper vote, I was determined that we should not be open to the charge of failing to look at all the options rationally and objectively. My memo was typed by Debbie on Thursday morning and I showed it to Bob Maclennan as we drove down in the car to East Hendred for lunch and a discussion on Roy's forthcoming regional speech.

The memo started from three basic assumptions: that the PLP would support a consultative referendum before ratification, despite any opposition we might put up at the Party meeting; that less than half of the eighty-nine pro-European voters or abstainers would consider abstention even if Roy and the other members of the Shadow Cabinet resigned; and finally that the Labour Party Conference in October would support the commitment for any incoming Labour Government to have a referendum on whether or not Britain should stay within the EEC. If these assumptions were correct, by far the most important was that relating to the likely position of the Party at the next election. To vote now against a referendum, quite apart from any short-term problems, would make for immense difficulties over the general election manifesto. It would, in my opinion, make it impossible for Roy to become Leader this side of the general election, and the continued existence of the commitment would make it difficult for Roy to challenge to be leader in the early years following an election defeat. Given that the pressures for a commitment to come out of the EEC were now pretty strong, the only way of holding off such a commitment would be to compromise on the referendum. Therefore to vote against a referendum could well start a process whereby a group of us would have no option other than to reverse our earlier position or not to stand at the next election.

In accepting under these unique circumstances the need for Britain to enter the EEC united, and thus the desirability of a referendum, I stressed that to have any meaning it must be genuinely democratic and not used as a vehicle for removing the Government of the day from office. My own acceptance of a referendum was wholly conditional on certain safeguards being agreed to and being maintained. Firstly, all political parties would accept that this referendum would not establish a precedent and its introduction would not be used as an argument for the extension of referenda into the British system of parliamentary government. Secondly, the political parties would agree to conduct a referendum, not on the basis of party political confrontation, but allowing MPs and other politicians the normal party facilities to put forward their views even if they conflicted with the general position of the political party to which under normal circumstances they owed their allegiance. Thirdly, there would be a responsibility on the BBC and ITV to reflect a fair balance in the factual arguments and the Press Council should be asked to ensure that this was done as far as possible in the national and regional newspapers. Fourthly, there would be no advertising or free or subsidized propaganda published relating to the referendum. The referendum would have to take place on the basis of a straight 'yes' or 'no' as to whether Parliament should ratify the Treaty four weeks after the necessary consequential legislation had passed through the normal parliamentary procedures. Most of these conditions were in fact those adopted for the 1975 referendum on membership of the EEC. The memorandum also spelt out a possible speech for Roy to explain our position.

By the time we arrived at Roy Jenkins's home for lunch, Bob Maclennan was an enthusiastic supporter of my memorandum. He did not feel anyhow very hostile to referenda in terms of the constitution and, for local constituency reasons, was not happy to commit himself against referenda. He did, in the event, vote for the EEC referendum amendment, though he had previously after a difficult two days of indecision resigned on the wider issue of the Party attitude to the EEC.

I gave a copy of my memo to David Marquand who read it very briefly and was unenthusiastic. Having been ignominiously sacked by Wilson in a savage piece of discrimination the previous November, David was very hawkish. He had also arrived for lunch earlier than most of us and already knew that Roy believed that there was no viable compromise and that resignation was becoming inevitable. Roy's argument was now clear: he was convinced that to have a referendum would destroy the Party. He kept reiterating that the central activity of constituency parties was to get Labour supporters to the polls to put their crosses on a ballot paper on polling day. Whatever might be said at the start, as the campaign progressed, a referendum would become identified with a general election in Party workers' minds. He said, with immense passion, that he was convinced that, whatever people's intentions at the start of the campaign, before the end he and others would inevitably run a very substantial risk of being expelled from the Party. To the argument that we would have to have a written undertaking that pro-marketeers would be free to campaign, he forcefully reminded us of other similar pledges on Europe. What about what the Party had already said over the referendum? Though he was well controlled, I could detect very considerable emotion – he was stretched like taut elastic. He did not believe a word that Wilson now said. Certainly the catalogue of lies, half-truths and twists and turns was a depressing background against which to travel down a new referendum road, particularly one dependent on assurances from Harold Wilson.

I left Roy's late that Thursday afternoon, totally convinced that he was going to resign. My memo and views on referenda notwithstanding, I was determined not to leave him alone and isolated: not only did he need a few people to resign with him but I had also felt throughout a sufficient doubt about the referendum to be content to accept his judgement. On the drive back, however, Bob Maclennan was still adamantly against resignation and he asked if I minded him showing my memo to George Thomson. Bob had been George's Parliamentary Private Secretary when we were in Government and was very close to him. I had no fear that it would go any further. George, it turned out, was unconvinced and did a great deal to persuade Bob to resign.

The day after the East Hendred lunch, Roy Hattersley rang and spoke to Debbie: it appeared to her that he had spoken to Jennifer Jenkins on the telephone and was aware of everything, including my memo. He asked me to drop by for a chat, which I did, on Friday evening on my way down to Wiltshire. Debbie was waiting in the car with Tristan, so I was in a hurry. Mistakenly, I gave a copy of my memo to Roy Hattersley. He was extremely enthusiastic, so much so that I even found myself forced to argue against it, stressing the problems of being able to actually support entry in any referendum. I think he really wanted Roy Jenkins to vote for a referendum but for the rest of us to ensure that the referendum was lost by sufficient abstentions. Yet it was not clear whether he was prepared to abstain himself and I told him of Bill Rodgers's view that, without some form of leadership, it was hard to see that we would get enough abstentions. He knew George Thomson and Harold Lever wanted to resign and that it was impossible for Roy Jenkins to stay while they went. In sum, I was not certain what Roy Hattersley wanted or that he was either. But he did say as I left that he was an animal who hunted in a pack and that we would both have to resign if Roy Jenkins did. The one thing he felt very strongly about was that, since we were both reluctant to see Roy Jenkins resign, we should not let him know our intention to resign in advance. I said I could not threaten Roy Jenkins like this. He had always known that I would go if he did and anyhow I had already told him that I would resign. I could not, I said, use this as an indirect bargaining chip. It was, anyhow, a pretty worthless one: Roy Jenkins was going to make this decision on his own.

Roy Hattersley asked if he could keep my memorandum, with the intention of showing it to John Harris on his arrival from America. Some sixth sense made me reluctant to part with it but I did. I felt slightly that in giving it to him I was moving behind Roy Jenkins's back for I knew in my heart that Roy Jenkins was now going to resign. Roy Hattersley claimed to know of the existence of a first draft of his resignation letter, though I was not sure whether he had seen it.

I left Roy Hattersley's house tired and rather depressed. I told Debbie that we would both be resigning together with very much the same doubts, anxieties and beliefs. She flatly refused to believe that Roy Hattersley would resign. I shared Roy Hattersley's dislike of resignation as a tactic in most circumstances in politics; the arguments for holding one's ground and fighting from within are usually overwhelming. However, this situation was quite different. Apart from other considerations, the referendum vote in the House of Commons promised to be the closest yet. There was a real possibility of a far larger number of Tory rebel votes or abstentions than hitherto and the morale of the pro-marketeers was being progressively undermined. The pressure being put on pro-market members in the constituencies was also mounting – not only was Dick Taverne in deep trouble but Edward Lyons was being seriously threatened in his new Leeds constituency and others like Pat Duffy were feeling pressure too. The climate could not have been worse to attempt to rally a mass abstention and Bill Rodgers felt this would be

particularly difficult if all the Shadow Cabinet pro-marketeers voted for
the referendum. I greatly valued Bill Rodgers's judgement, but decided
to conduct a straw poll of my own and its conclusion was very similar.
The will to fight was disappearing. Normally tough people like Maurice
Foley were quite prepared to go along with the referendum and they
would only fight it if given a lead.

That evening at Buttermere, Roy Jenkins rang to ask Debbie and me
over for lunch the next day. Bob McNamara and some others were
coming and he wanted, I suspected, to tell me his decision. It was a
lovely spring day. I talked to McNamara about the Cuban Missile Crisis
and it was clear that he still considered control of nuclear weapons to be
one of the central world problems and, with population control, the
most urgent issue facing mankind. He was fascinating about the Nassau
meeting in 1962, confirming that it was Macmillan's powers of persuasion
with Kennedy over Polaris which were the key factor. He was also
brutally frank about the Gulf of Tonkin, an incident which I had written
about in my book on defence, saying that he felt that it was quite possible
that no torpedoes were ever fired. Throughout lunch, the conversation
never touched on the Common Market or the referendum and it was as
though we were unconscious of the slow-burning fuse that was relentlessly
moving towards detonation. Then, once we had eaten, Roy and I went
into his study for a private chat and he showed me a handwritten draft of
his resignation letter to Wilson. It came as no surprise, although after
Roy Hattersley's remark I had been expecting it to be a typed letter.
When he had claimed to have seen the letter he implied that Roy's
secretary had typed it out. This might not have been the case if he had
made the whole thing up to sound me out and to see if I knew of the
existence of a resignation letter. I made a few detailed suggestions but the
letter was very clear and the only point over which I was very strong was
the need to say that Roy did not wish his other friends to resign as well.
This seemed to me to be important in terms of Party unity and to
prevent ill-feeling between those who wanted to resign and those who
wished to remain.

As we left, Roy and Bob McNamara were going for a walk on the
Downs and I knew nothing would change his mind. Technically he was
leaving his options open until he discussed it with Tom Bradley and
George Thomson over lunch on Sunday but he knew their views before
they came – George wanted him to resign and Tom was strongly
opposed. John Harris would be flying in on the Sunday but Roy felt that
he would not be in a position to form a considered judgement having
been in the United States for the last few months, following McGovern's
Primary campaign.

When one looks back at the possibilities of a compromise solution at
any stage between Wilson and Jenkins, the element of sheer distrust
dominates everything. Neither Roy nor Jennifer really believed a single

word Wilson said and, whether this was a fair assessment or not, it was a central feature of their attitudes on how to handle all the issues in relation to entry into the EEC.

I now knew I was spending my last few days as a front bench spokesman. On Sunday, both David Watt and David Marquand rang. I felt I could not reveal Roy's decision but I prepared the ground and David Watt wrote a very useful and sympathetic piece in the *Financial Times* on the Monday morning. On Sunday, I worked on my speech for the Navy Estimates debate certain that this would be my last speech from the front bench. I was determined to speak out even more strongly than before on the inability of the Admiralty Board to shift expenditure in favour of submarines and underwater warfare.

On Monday after lunch I was sitting in the House of Commons library when Roy Hattersley came in. He said that Roy Jenkins had put his resignation letter in and that it would be public later in the afternoon. Though he still regretted the resignation and talked wistfully of my alternative proposal, he did nothing to indicate he was not intending, personally, to resign. He was clearly overwrought but seemed to be facing the inevitable. Suddenly, our conversation was interrupted by one of the staff of the Whips' office coming in to say that Harold Wilson wished to see him immediately. He got up straightaway, almost as if he had been expecting the call. It seemed to me rather odd that he should be summoned so soon but I assumed that Harold Wilson would try and persuade him not to resign.

In the course of winding up my speech in the debate, I hinted at my intention to resign. It seemed that there might be some advantage in indicating this to my friends and it might also serve to prevent any blandishments aimed at persuading me to stay on. It had to be a veiled reference because I wanted to tell Harold Wilson personally first but if, as had been agreed, we were not resigning until Wednesday there seemed to be no harm in stiffening the resolve of others.

After my speech at about 6.30 that evening, a quick word with Roy Hattersley in the House made it clear that he was very unhappy about resigning. He tried to persuade me to stay on but I said I was definitely going, though adding that I could see no reason why he should go. I felt that nothing could be worse than Roy Hattersley resigning but briefing the press constantly over the succeeding months that he had only acted out of loyalty and that the resignations were against his advice. This seemed a certain recipe for discontent. Roy Jenkins had made it clear to the lobby in a press briefing – not, as I suggested, in the resignation letter – that he did not wish all his friends to resign office as well. So I understood Roy Hattersley's position. It would undoubtedly have strengthened the position of the three in the Shadow Cabinet if they had been accompanied by more influential ex-Ministers than me, like Shirley Williams and Roy Hattersley, but anyone who resigned was taking an immense risk with their career. Since I knew Shirley was not going to resign, it seemed not unreasonable for Roy Hattersley to stay and far better to keep his goodwill. He was very dejected and clearly upset by his internal conflict and I felt rather sorry for him. I had a quick chat with Dick Taverne who had no doubts about resigning and we confirmed that we would resign together but agreed to wait until Wednesday. However, my speech had triggered off speculation and Peter Kirk, the Navy Minister, was quick to see the connection between Roy Jenkins's resignation on the tapes and my closing remark that it might be some time before I spoke again from the front bench. He paid a very gracious tribute when winding up the Navy Estimates debate and I left the House that evening having answered none of the press calls, resolved to sit tight.

On Tuesday it became apparent that Harold Wilson was trying to pass off the whole episode as 'a little local difficulty' like Harold Macmillan at the time of Peter Thorneycroft's resignation. He was very keen to limit the number who joined Roy Jenkins and thus prevent a full-scale revolt. Shirley Williams made a statement explaining why she was not going to resign, always the worst of statements to make. Although some people read her words as meaning that her resignation later, possibly over Clause 2, was inevitable, I doubted she would resign even then. Shirley had been almost hysterical in her advocacy of resignation on almost all the previous occasions so it was for me a source of amusement rather than anger. Now, like many others, she had decided that the referendum proposal, with which she had some sympathy, was not a major breaking point. Douglas Houghton had left for America over the weekend and had told Roy Jenkins that he would leave his position open until his return but he was clearly not convinced that resignation was the best course. He had held his post as chairman of the PLP with amazing tenacity and skill for a man of his age, and there were advantages to us in him staying.

Now Roy Hattersley became the prime target for Harold Wilson's wooing. He was, apart from John Harris, supposedly Roy Jenkins's closest confidant and principal adviser. On the same Monday afternoon that he had talked to Hattersley, Harold Wilson saw Selwyn Lloyd, the Speaker of the House, on other business and confided that he was not unduly worried. Roy Jenkins would go off and write biographies, he said, and he had, in effect, bought off the most ambitious of his lieutenants in Roy Hattersley which would stop a large number of consequential resignations. I presumed that Roy Hattersley had been offered the Defence post earlier that Monday afternoon.

On Tuesday evening I had a message that Wilson wished to see me. On my way I talked to Bob Maclennan who, having seen Wilson himself, told me that Frank Judd was already pencilled in to replace me as Shadow Navy Minister. Frank Judd was Harold's Parliamentary Private Secretary and I bumped into him as I was going into the Leader of the Opposition's room. I could not resist congratulating him, which caused him slight embarrassment. As I walked in, I also told Harold how pleased I was that Frank Judd was taking my job. He mumbled that if I wanted to stay on this of course would not apply but he had obviously been well briefed on my attitude – presumably by Roy Hattersley. It was a civilized and friendly conversation. I thanked him genuinely for his kindness in the past and for giving me the opportunity to serve in his Government. I told him that what most concerned me was that, irrespective of his own wishes, there was beginning to be a real risk that, with the shift against entry to the EEC gathering momentum in the PLP, even if we won an election he might not be able to keep Britain in the EEC and that a referendum commitment would take the decision out of his hands.

What embarrassed me was Harold Wilson's obvious knowledge of the memorandum I had sent to Roy Jenkins arguing the case against resigning. He realized that I had advised Roy against resigning and went so far as to talk about the contents of what he described as a detailed letter. I left, furious at what I thought could only have been the divulging of my memorandum by either Bob Maclennan or Roy Hattersley. I was quickly able to eliminate Bob from suspicion as I spoke to him immediately afterwards. He was rather upset; he had decided not to resign and was embarrassed and uncertain about his position, having had a drink in the Harcourt Room with George Thomson. He confirmed that Harold had already had the memo and had specifically mentioned its existence. Bob had told him, quite reasonably, once he knew that Wilson was aware of its existence, that he had strongly supported my arguments.

Leaving Bob, I then issued a short statement to the Press Association saying that I had resigned but would be issuing no further statement or resignation letter. This was Denis Healey's advice to say no more than that my reasons were the same as those of Roy Jenkins and that I had no wish to exacerbate the situation. Roy Hattersley, it was announced, would now take over from George Thomson as Shadow Minister of Defence, though since he was not elected he could not formally be a member of the Shadow Cabinet. Had he not resigned and not accepted preferment, he would have been only doing the same as Shirley Williams, Tom Bradley, Alex Lyon, Denis Howell, Ivor Richard and, at that stage, Bob Maclennan. However, actually filling dead men's shoes when you were as closely involved with them as Roy Hattersley had been caused considerable offence and looked disreputable. He then published a pompous and self-seeking letter which reaffirmed his support for the European Community in a blatant attempt to mollify his friends. Since he later boasted that Harold Wilson had encouraged him to write it and virtually helped draft it, it was a transparently synthetic gesture.

On Wednesday, the Party meeting was told to endorse the recommendation of the Shadow Cabinet to support Neil Marten's pro-referendum amendment when it came before the House. The pro-marketeers lost on the vote, as expected, but we polled surprisingly well. It was amazing to see some people talking tough who, only a few days before, had indicated that they were in favour of accepting the referendum proposal. Roy Jenkins spoke in a restrained way but well, the most striking moment being when he said, simply and rather emotionally, that he had never expected to hold such high office in the Party and thanked everyone for their support. It was as if he knew that this was the end of the road for him in the Labour Party.

After the meeting, I tackled Roy Hattersley about my memorandum and he denied having told Harold Wilson about it. I demanded his copy back, which he did return but it caused deep offence, and the incident soured our relationship for some time. Roy Hattersley's behaviour throughout had been that of tortured ambition. I could not help feeling how much stronger he would have been if, while deciding not to resign, he had refused Harold's offer, letting it be known that he had refused George Thomson's post. If he had done this he would certainly have been elected to the Shadow Cabinet next time round in his own right. As it was he had put himself at Harold Wilson's mercy and Harold excluded him from his real Cabinet in 1974; Roy only came into the Cabinet in 1976 at the invitation of Jim Callaghan.

There rarely is an objectively right time to resign. The politically right time is usually seen as a tactical resignation which is damaging because it reeks of opportunism. A delayed resignation damages because it attracts the stigma of weakness and indecision. History itself can be a poor judge of political resignation, for each has its unique character, risks, opportunities, pressures and frustrations. They all coalesce at the time, so that the whole can only be seen as the expression of a multitude of factors. In the end, most individuals do what they feel they have to do and damn the consequences.

Our resignation did not end the battle over EEC entry. It is Edward Heath to whom most of the credit must go for first negotiating entry and then having the nerve to take the legislation through Parliament. He had to contend with a serious, open and long-running revolt among his own members; and listen to endless jibes from Enoch Powell and others that he had failed to get the full-hearted consent of the British people. Yet he never wavered and his position in history will be assured by this singular act of statesmanship.

The commitment to introduce a referendum became, as I had predicted in my memorandum, a settled commitment for the Labour Party at the next election. Personally, never having had much problem with the concept, I was quite content to fight an election promising a referendum but it remained a difficulty for Roy Jenkins as he had wound himself up into a rather pedantic posture over the referendum as an undesirable constitutional innovation. It is true that they had often been used by Fascist governments and tended to be a mechanism for preserving the status quo but they also have the potential to let public opinion express itself outside the straitjacket of party allegiance and I have argued since 1982 that they should be the mechanism for introducing proportional representation.

There were many casualties within the Labour Party from the European Community debacle. In personal terms the one I most regretted was my alienation from Tony Crosland. After Roy had resigned I argued within our group that we should vote for Tony as Deputy Leader. This was viewed with the utmost horror. I had voted for Tony in the Shadow Cabinet elections after the White Paper vote as had Bill Rodgers but even then others had withheld their vote on the basis that Tony had behaved badly and ought to be punished. This time, however, Bill was adamantly against voting for Tony, not wanting him to profit at Roy's expense. I was in a minority of one so when Tony Crosland rang me and asked if I would vote for him I was very embarrassed. I told him there was a debate going on but like a fool I promised that I would let him know when I had decided. Even more foolishly I kept that promise and wrote to him, trying to justify my supporting his opponent, Ted Short. Instead of just saying that I felt bound by group solidarity I tried to produce some specious arguments which I did not believe as to why Ted Short would be a better Deputy Leader. The letter had a stench about it and deserved to be treated with contempt. Our relationship only came close to recovering a few months before Tony's death in February 1977.

Roy Jenkins continued to give his series of speeches but for me the spice and excitement had gone out of the whole exercise, particularly since he had given a crazy commitment to Harold Wilson not to stand against him in the autumn for election as Party Leader. The year after would be the eve of an election and it would be virtually impossible to stand. So his pledge meant he had given up any attempt to oust Wilson before the election. It was the action of a man too cautious to risk all or too proud to be defeated. In politics you must be ready to suffer the humiliation of running for an office you do not expect to win. Roy was always rather disdainful about putting down markers.

In a mood of anti-climax, a group of us, around Roy Jenkins, continued to meet from time to time usually at Harry Walston's flat in Albany. Inasmuch as there was any strategy within the group it seemed to be based on the assumption that Labour was bound to lose the next election and Roy's best chance of winning the leadership was after an election which we had lost. This was all right if, like Roy Jenkins, you were sitting on a safe seat in Birmingham. For me, in a marginal seat in Plymouth, a Labour defeat would mean that I would almost certainly lose. I not unnaturally bridled at such a depressing scenario and felt a slight alienation from the group. I tried to make a more positive contribution to the Labour Party and since my main interest was in health policy I was fortunately co-opted on to an NEC working party. Then I started for the first time to work with Barbara Castle. Hitherto I had barely known her and it was during this time that, in order to block a move to abolish all private medicine, I helped devise the concept of phasing pay beds out of the NHS.

On 9 January 1972, for the first time since 1926, the National Union of Miners called an official strike nationwide. It was clear that miners' wages had fallen quite dramatically against their counterparts in skilled manual work. I had great sympathy at that time for the miners. Though I believed an MP should always advocate negotiation and very rarely, if ever, endorse strike action, on this occasion I did feel that they had been sorely provoked. Politically, it was a remarkable period. On 22 January 1973, Edward Heath signed the Treaty to make the UK a member of the European Community. As he went in to the Egmont Palace to sign, he was splattered with ink by a woman demonstrating not against Europe but, of all things, against the redevelopment of Covent Garden. Unemployment was rising over the million mark and in the middle of February came some nine-hour electricity blackouts and industry was placed on a three-day week.

One of the new developments was the spontaneous emergence of the flying picket, with miners taking to the road instead of staying in their isolated villages. This had a personal impact. One morning, coming out of my house in Limehouse, I saw that a picket had been established outside the Stepney coal-fired power station, only a hundred yards from my house. They looked pretty cold, with only a Dormobile van for protection, and I asked them if they would like a hot drink. I went back in to tell Debbie, and she brewed them a cup of tea. I asked them if they would like to use our lavatory and telephone while they were picketing, and they were grateful. When I returned that evening, I found most of the miners in our house and that Debbie, in her open American way and fearing that their van would be too cold for them, had invited them not only to use our kitchen but to sleep the night. They were delightful company. Having driven down from Nottinghamshire, and finding nothing to do, they had chosen to go to this power station, which was not even generating electricity. By pure chance their picket proved to be very effective, because inside was stored the fuel which lit up the furnaces for many other power stations in the south of England. During all this time we had twelve miners staying in our house in Narrow Street. Four men used to sleep in shifts on the floor in our spare bedroom and they all shared our kitchen and bathroom. They were incredibly neat and tidy, immensely considerate and, given the smallness of our house, for we had not yet expanded next door, remarkably unobtrusive. That is, apart from the smell of fry-ups drifting up from the kitchen into our bedroom in the middle of the night when the night shift came back from picket duty. After a fortnight the Nottingham miners were replaced by miners from Kent who were different in character, but equally engaging. When the Nottingham miners left they called Debbie down to the garage and their spokesman proceeded to make a short speech, finally bringing a bunch of flowers out from behind his back and presenting a Dinky toy to Tristan. For her it was a very moving occasion which she has never forgotten. Eventually the miners' case went to an independent tribunal chaired by Lord Wilberforce and their stance was vindicated with a 17 per cent pay award.

Twelve years later, in 1984, at Buxton in Derbyshire a miner appeared outside the SDP Conference claiming to have been one of those who stayed with us, and got some mileage out of this with the press. But the miners' strike in 1984–85 had none of the validity or the dignity of the 1972 dispute. Large intimidating pickets were by then developing into a grave threat to the nation. The NUM leaders of 1972, Joe Gormley and Lawrence Daly, were very different from Arthur Scargill and Peter Heathfield both in ideology and behaviour. I felt my support for the Conservative Government in 1984 was as justified as my refusal to support them in 1972.

On 23 August 1972 Debbie and I had another son, delivered in the Lambeth Hospital and christened Gareth. She had worked in her literary agency right up to the birth and started again soon afterwards. She was now having to juggle job, husband, two children, a house in London, another in Wiltshire and the demands on the wife of an MP with a constituency 252 miles on the motorway from London. We started to entertain less, rarely at home in London and only for very close friends in Buttermere at weekends. That pattern has stayed ever since. Large dinner parties, late-night drinking and even dancing with the carpets rolled up at home, ended as we found that the only way to see enough of our family, while both my political life and her literary activity grew, was to cut down ruthlessly on our own entertaining and social life. We always take our holiday together as a family. The children learnt to sleep in sleeping bags stretched out in the back of the car so we could painlessly cover many miles and stay sailing all Sunday in Plymouth or leave Buttermere late on Sunday arriving back in London after the traffic had died down. Our main celebration is a family one in July on the last Saturday of Wimbledon, between my birthday and Debbie's, to mark America's Independence Day. Over eighty family friends with children come and play baseball in our field at Buttermere and we grill hamburgers outside and fly the American flag.

By the summer of 1972 it had become more sensible to operate Decision Technology International from Paris in association with a small French consultancy with whom we were doing a lot of work. This change suited me for I felt that it was time, at the halfway mark in the Parliament, to give more attention to politics. I had learnt much about the market place and enjoyed commercial life and the experience was to have an important influence on me politically. Without the knowledge I gained during those years I would never have started to challenge the

Tony Crosland revisionist economic stance which had paid scant attention to making markets work efficiently. It led also to my championing of the social market in 1981 and, as Leader of the SDP, to try to bring competitiveness and compassion into a new synthesis around the social market. Business, like politics, cannot be a part-time activity. If one wants to go to the top one has to choose. It was time now for me to choose and after a lot of thought and despite all the disillusionment surrounding Labour's attitude to the European Community, I chose politics. The die was cast; only if I lost my seat could I now envisage returning to medicine. A factor in my decision to choose politics and not go back to medicine was that I had already been asked to become director of the World Security Trust. The Trust had existed for over ten years and was aimed at promoting new conceptual approaches to the problems of international security. My book *The Politics of Defence* had recently been published and I was eager to develop further my ideas on nuclear disarmament and strengthening the United Nations. In particular I was fascinated by the ideas put forward by Leonard Beaton in his book *The Reform of Power* about how the superpowers might be harnessed to creating a world security system more effective than the existing UN. It meant too that I could afford to travel further afield than Europe and have some additional income to cushion the lost salary from Decision Technology.

When she was Secretary of State for Education, I had my first meeting with Margaret Thatcher. A medical friend had come to dinner with her and when she bumped into me in the division lobby she asked if I would go down to the Harcourt Room and have a drink. Debbie was waiting for me in the Family Room, so she came as well. It was a revealing occasion, for as the conversation developed Margaret Thatcher's best and worst qualities were on display: consideration for a constituent and the wish to get to the bottom of a problem coupled with a total inability to comprehend that depression affects adolescents. To her it appeared more a matter of what used to be called 'lack of moral fibre'. She turned to Debbie to say that she had never been able to understand how any seventeen-year-old could be depressed. Debbie listened aghast. Eventually, as we were walking away from the table, Margaret Thatcher turned to me and said, with Debbie two feet away, 'Is your wife always so quiet?' Anyone who knows Debbie will realize how unusual was her silence. She was simply amazed at her sheer insensitivity. But Margaret Thatcher has never been able to understand the non-achievers or how society, whose existence she denies, has a public responsibility to help shoulder some of their burdens.

In early 1973 I made extensive visits to both Israel and Egypt. After Israel had allowed former Vice-President Nixon to visit without any official notice being taken of him, only to find him becoming President, it developed a sophisticated system for spotting visitors who might have influence in the future. Though I was only a backbench MP, every door was opened for me and I met all the significant leaders, tramped over the Golan Heights, visited Gaza and got a real feel for the security problems on the ground. In Egypt too I had no difficulty in seeing all the key people, in particular General Shazli, the Commander of the Egyptian forces. I came away convinced there was going to be another war with Israel. I also developed detailed ideas for the demilitarization of Sinai and spoke about them in a foreign affairs debate in the House of Commons in June 1973. Predictably, war did follow. On 6 October, as Israel celebrated Yom Kippur, the Day of Atonement, Egyptian forces stormed across the Suez Canal. I was appalled when the Foreign Secretary, Lord Home, and Prime Minister, Edward Heath, refused to supply, during the actual fighting, shells for the Centurion tanks that Israel had bought from us. I considered it then, and still do, the most cynical act of British foreign policy since Suez. It showed not just the Arab influence within the Foreign Office but a total lack of principle in standing by one's commitments from two politicians whom I had hitherto respected. For the first time I began to wonder whether Alec Douglas-Home had shaken off attitudes towards appeasement that he had held as Parliamentary Private Secretary to Neville Chamberlain. British influence with Israel never recovered, for perfectly understandable reasons. Israeli politicians on the Left as well as the Right were confirmed in the distrust which had developed when we were in control of Palestine. It was a craven act which had everything to do with the threat of being cut off from Arab oil and for which I had nothing but contempt.

One other consequence of my involvement with the World Security Trust was that I got to know not only David Astor who was still editor of the *Observer* but also two interesting Conservative politicians who were trustees. Duncan Sandys was, I soon discovered, far from being the simple Tory Right-winger I had labelled him after his 1968 stance over the Kenyan Asians. He had an invigorating mind, he understood the use of power and military might, yet he was always looking for new approaches to international security. Lord Harlech had been a Conservative MP as David Ormsby Gore and in 1961 was appointed Ambassador to Washington by Macmillan to capitalize on his friendship with President Kennedy. He had held an insider's position of some influence during the Cuban Missile Crisis and I found him intuitive and deceptively shrewd once his mind was engaged.

It was not just the Trust work that enabled me to give up Decision Technology without much of a financial setback. Debbie's literary agency was becoming very successful. I had helped finance her agency in early 1971 but now it was profitable. Her office started in our garage, which we had specially converted, though the surroundings were never ideal. Watching other married women with young children working, I was convinced that if she operated from home she would find it far easier to cope and the children would see more of her. Debbie was initially opposed to this. She felt that, after seven years in New York publishing, she was too accustomed to office life. Working from home seemed too dilettantish. However, she agreed to give it a go and after a short time realized that working from home had considerable advantages. We are all now total converts to Alvin Toffler's concept of the cottage office. In the twenty-first century we will be amazed at the way we all stubbornly continued to travel to work when, with modern technology, much of that work could so easily come to us.

Soon we managed to buy the ground floor and basement of the house next door and knock the intervening wall down to make a large office. So, as her business expanded, Debbie worked from one of the loveliest offices in London, with two large picture windows overlooking the Thames from which she is able to feed ducks and swans from the catwalk. The family also now swim off the catwalk when the tide is slack at high water. The Thames has become progressively cleaner; as pollution has been reduced fish have returned to the river. When I was a medical student if someone fell into the Thames it meant an automatic stomach washout, so foul was the water. Along with the ending of the smog and the clean up of buildings, the London of the 1990s is transformed from the London I first knew in the 1950s.

Initially Debbie had started off with only one author, a young cook called Delia Smith whom she had met while working in Nicholas Thompson's agency. She was soon to become Debbie's bestselling author in Britain with the cookbooks based on her well known BBC series. They also became very close friends. Then came one of those fortuitous happenings that so often transform businesses. While my mother was staying in Cardiff she mentioned to her friend Eve Godfrey that Debbie had started her own agency. Eve said she knew a literary agent called Joyce Weiner who had just told her that she was retiring on doctor's advice. Debbie contacted Joyce and discovered that she had known her father, Kyrill Schabert, when he was at Pantheon, the New York publishing house, and that Joyce had been quietly monitoring Debbie's career since her arrival in London. Soon they came to a mutual arrangement whereby Debbie took over most of Joyce's authors and this gave her business a tremendous boost.

The most successful of Joyce's authors was Georgette Heyer. Before agreeing to be represented by Debbie, she insisted on a meeting with Debbie and me. She felt she would have a clearer picture of Debbie once she had met her husband. Georgette Heyer was, to put it mildly, no socialist and at first meeting a rather intimidating person. Much to my surprise, and no doubt hers, we got on extremely well. Debbie found working for her a delight and grew very fond of her husband, Ronald Rougier, a judge. One of the reasons for Georgette Heyer's extraordinary success as a historical novelist was that her grasp of history was so complete. She was a very private person and only much later did she take Debbie into her confidence and let her see her notebooks. They were enthralling, full of hand-drawn pictures of costumes, coats of arms and maps of Bath as well as detailed information about the Regency and mediaeval periods.

The historian Dame Veronica Wedgwood also came from Joyce Weiner. It was her book on Cromwell which had so enthralled me when I was an undergraduate at Cromwell's old college and I was pleased when Debbie managed to have it republished. Another author, who in more recent years has become a very popular novelist, was Edith Pargeter, whose mediaeval novels about Brother Cadfael are written under the name of Ellis Peters. Two younger authors who came to Debbie were Penelope Farmer, an adult and children's book writer, and Amos Oz, the Israeli novelist. Both are now close friends. We have visited Amos and his family regularly, first at Kibbutz Hulda and more recently in Arad. In 1977, when Foreign Secretary, I raised a few diplomatic eyebrows by visiting his kibbutz. One day I hope he will be awarded the Nobel Prize for Literature, for his writing has true quality. Amos is not a politician but he, like most Israelis, is absorbed by politics. He is one of Israel's most interesting doves. No one who fought his way up the Golan Heights in 1967 has any illusions about the horror of war. What singles him out is that he also understands the necessity at times to fight. It is Amos's rare gift to be confident that peace has to be fought for morally, intellectually, politically and sadly, at times, physically.

Debbie was also my agent, even managing to persuade Praeger to bring out *The Politics of Defence* in America. I understood that the advance that she had so skilfully negotiated was in pounds and so on the strength of that I went off and ordered a tennis court for Buttermere. Only when the bulldozers had carved up our field did I discover that it was only in dollars. Nevertheless, it was an improvidence we have never regretted. At this time we were seeing a lot of Bill and Sylvia Rodgers and their two daughters at Buttermere. Both their girls were much older than Tristan and Gareth but they were wonderful fun with our boys who, in return, adored them. The Rodgers lived in a rented cottage on the north side of the Kennet and Avon Valley. I remember particularly celebrating one New Year's Eve at Buttermere, when Roy and Jennifer Jenkins came over as well. We were playing charades and Roy was given *The Decline and Fall of the Roman Empire*, which he depicted with a hilarious impression of a drunkard. Like many basically shy people, when relaxed he was very funny and not in the least pompous.

Meanwhile, my political life in Westminster was not very happy. Dick Taverne's position in his Lincoln constituency was particularly distressing for us all, even more so for Roy and Bill since Dick was a close friend of theirs. I did not know Dick well but felt, as they did, that we ought to do more to help and yet it was impossible to do so unless we were ready to be expelled from the Labour Party. It was nonsense to say, as some Labour MPs did, that Dick Taverne deserved to be in trouble in Lincoln. A myth was propagated that he was a bad constituency Member whereas in fact an ORC poll in October 1972 showed that 82 per cent of his constituents thought he was a good Member of Parliament and only 2 per cent a bad one. The truth was that he was the victim of a particularly dedicated group of Left-wing activists, ably led by Leo Beckett, now the husband of Margaret Beckett, the MP for Derby South.

The deselection of Dick Taverne in Lincoln was a foretaste of things to come and he quite rightly decided not to take it lying down. He resigned in October after the 1972 Party Conference, having held off the announcement for a few months to reduce the pressure on Roy and other friends. It was not in the interests of the Labour Party to have the by-election quickly when they knew Dick was determined to fight. So they delayed moving the writ until February which, under a parliamentary convention, it is their right to do. The by-election was not therefore held until 1 March 1973. This highly dubious delaying tactic was one of the reasons why, when the SDP was formed, Labour MPs who joined the SDP were not keen to force by-elections in their constituencies. Delay can give a massive advantage to the party defending the seat, for allowing the party whose MP had resigned to fix the by-election date keeps the former MP in limbo for five or six months without pay or influence. It was to Dick Taverne's credit that he pressed on, standing as Democratic Labour and campaigning to win. If any of us had gone to campaign for him we would have been instantly thrown out under the rules of the Labour Party. So the opening meeting of his campaign was addressed not by fellow MPs but by my old friend Mervyn Stockwood, still Bishop of Southwark, and by Bernard Levin, the columnist on *The Times*. In the event Dick Taverne had a spectacular victory with a majority of 13,000, gaining 58 per cent of the vote to Labour's 23 per cent and the Conservatives 18 per cent. Although he managed to hold on to the seat again in the February 1974 Election, he lost it the following October.

Should the pro-Europe, moderate Labour MPs have split from the Labour Party and fought with Dick Taverne then? Should we have created the SDP when we rebelled over Europe in 1971 rather than in 1981? I have no doubt that it would not have been possible to do so. We all of us had to go through the traumas that lay ahead and also feel within ourselves that we had fought our corner before most of us would have dreamt of leaving the Labour Party. Even so, leaving Labour in 1981 was hard enough. Without that ten-year struggle behind us very few, if any, would have come to the SDP. A fairer criticism was that we did not fight vigorously enough within the Labour Party during that ten-year interval. In our defence, it is hard to fight the Left if the Party Leader is not interested in doing so. This was the decade of what I called in 1980 'fudge and mudge'. Neither Harold Wilson nor Jim Callaghan felt it prudent openly to confront the Left in the 1970s. Each in his different way formed a partnership with Michael Foot to head off the Left rather than face them down. All the while the balance of power was shifting. The full extent of the shift in the Labour Party was masked while we were in government from 1974–1979 and it only became obvious to those outside in 1980 when the Left forced changes to the Party's constitution. Then we really saw how the Left had come to dominate the constituencies and could use deselection to intimidate Labour MPs. We on the inside knew it was happening and never really mobilized the centre ground when we were in government, in part because many of us were too busy as Ministers, in part because we had grown used to the protection of the trade union block vote, fixed up mainly by the Leader and helped by the use of patronage.

To have split off in 1971 would also have been to break on a single, albeit major, issue of policy, the European Community. By 1981 there were several major issues of policy: the European Community, nuclear deterrence, nationalization, as well as a major constitutional issue with the trade union-dominated electoral college. Indeed, by 1981, the Labour position on Europe had become even less defensible than in 1971. For by then the European Community had been given a massive endorsement in the 1975 referendum. In 1980 Labour indefensibly committed itself to come out of the Community without even another referendum. It was on that policy that they fought the 1983 General Election. It was inconceivable, after all we had gone through in 1971–72 to get Britain in, that we could have stood as Labour MPs in 1983.

Uncomfortable though it was, I think Dick Taverne had to fight Lincoln without the help of his friends in the Labour Party. It would have been quixotic for Roy Jenkins to have spoken on his platform in Lincoln and, though it deeply upset Roy to have to stand on the sidelines, I do not believe he should feel guilty about this decision. At this time in 1973, unfortunately, Lincoln appeared to depress Roy rather than to energize him. He became even more convinced that Labour would lose the next election and indeed began to make his wish that this would happen all too obvious. Such a position was an untenable indulgence for a senior politician: he could not operate effectively within a political party while, even temporarily, wanting its defeat.

In 1973 and in 1974, on the eve of the election, we had a number of group discussions about what would happen if Labour won. Almost everyone present believed that Roy should insist on being Chancellor of the Exchequer if he was to serve in the Government. Some even believed that he should bargain for this with Wilson before finally deciding whether to stand for the Shadow Cabinet in the autumn. What I think frustrated a number of us was Roy's reluctance even to contemplate negotiating for the Chancellorship. His reasoning was that he needed Wilson's full support if he was to have authority within the Party to do the job properly.

A few of us returned to this argument in Bob Maclennan's house on the eve of the February 1974 Election but Roy was still very reluctant to bid for the Chancellorship. He argued that the effect of the oil shock was such that he would have to be as draconian a Chancellor as he had been in 1967 and that, while then he had had the full support of Wilson, he would not be able to operate successfully if he imposed himself on Wilson. There was more than a grain of truth in his arguments but the real anxiety was his defeatist mood.

By this time a far more significant and long-lasting anxiety than anything in politics had entered my life. The family all spent the summer of 1973 in America, staying with Debbie's parents at St James, Long Island. Gareth was still a baby, nearing his first birthday, and Tristan was approaching his third birthday. His personality was developing and he was as bright and thoughtful a child as we could have asked for. We were lucky parents. Then in America Tristan had a mysterious, though minor, illness involving a slight temperature and swollen glands which was thought to be a virus called locally Cat's Fever. He recovered quickly and we thought no more about it. When we came back to Britain we went down to the constituency and stayed in Noss Mayo in a house which my parents had bought to retire to. I noticed that a small cut which Tristan had was taking a long time to heal. He then developed a temperature and large glands in the neck. He was initially diagnosed by a local GP as having mumps. This diagnosis never seemed right to me and after a few days, rather worried about some ominous bruising on his body, I took him to see a consultant paediatrician in Plymouth.

In the children's ward at Freedom Fields Hospital I could tell that something was wrong the moment the consultant asked me to leave Debbie with Tristan and go into the Sister's private room off the ward for a chat about the tests. I suppose, as a doctor, I sensed that he was making sure that I was sitting comfortably before he raised a serious problem. The news was that Tristan's blood showed some evidence of acute lymphatic leukaemia – though it would be necessary to do more tests before he could really confirm it. He told me that if I rang him at home in the early evening he would have all the results. I had been away from paediatric medicine for nine years but I remembered only too clearly having to do exactly what I thought he was doing, giving a parent a sense of hope when in one's heart one knew that their child was going to die. Suddenly I experienced the sense of depersonalization that is described in medical text books. It was as if there were two of me, the one looking in on the other. One was sitting in the chair listening as a doctor and trying to assess what I was being told, the other, the father, divorced from what was happening, in a state of shock, detached and feeling as if I were floating in the air. I can almost hear the words of the paediatrician now – soft, gentle, considerate: 'You will be amazed at the changes that are taking place. Leukaemia is no longer an automatic death sentence for

i. My grandfather, Revd George Llewellyn – Gear.

ii. *Top:* The Llandow Rectory – mother on the window sill, Gear and Granny 'Llew' sitting.

iii. *Above:* My great-grandfather, Alderman W. Llewellyn, in his Daimler.

iv. *Left:* My mother, Molly Owen. v. *Right:* My father, John Owen.

vi. Dr Edgar Llewellyn r. (Gear's brother) campaigning for the Cardiff
City election.

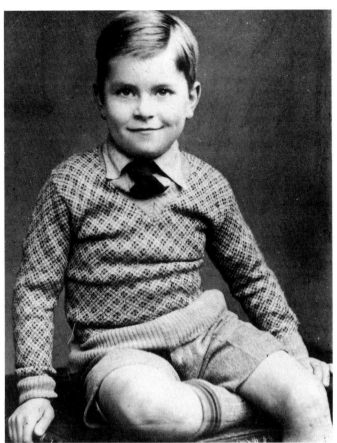

vii. *Left:* When I was five years old.

viii. *Below:* 'The Farmer's Wife'. Mother, the maid, myself, Susan and my father in a bowler.

xii. *Above:* The 'Bugger' in Afghanistan, 1959.

xiii. *Right: Amanda* – 106 Cheyne Walk, Chelsea, 1960.

OPPOSITE

ix. *Top left:* My sister, Susan, and Garth Mumford, 1956.

x. *Top right:* The 'Bambino' – my first car at Cambridge – with Bryan Christopher and Hugh Guinness standing, 1958.

xi. *Bottom: Agnes* at her mooring in front of our cottage on the River Yealm, 1957.

xiv. Medical student, St Thomas's Hospital, 1961.

children. We are at the breakthrough point, probably we have passed the breakthrough. There is a real chance your son could survive.' He explained that a big breakthrough had just been confirmed from a clinic in Tennessee in America. Radiotherapy treatment had successfully prevented a relapse in the nervous system, killing off any abnormal blood cells which had crossed over the blood–brain barrier. Normally that barrier is very effective in preventing the nervous system from being infected. But some abnormal leukaemia cells did cross through nature's filter. Having crossed, they multiplied and many children died, not from a relapse in their blood, but from leukaemic cells in their brain and nervous system. When I pressed the paediatrician he had to admit that the odds were still stacked against Tristan but my problem was that I did not really believe what he was saying. He was a good man and I knew I should trust him but I knew how often I had given an optimistic picture myself in order to instil hope. It was as if the dispassionate doctor and the passionate father had collided and compromised with each other by not letting any feeling come out at all. I could not even cry. I delayed telling Debbie the bad news, saying the test results would be available that night.

Becoming a parent had been an experience beyond my imagining and I had been wrong in 1968 to write to Debbie that children were not of primary consequence. I had never anticipated until Tristan was born how much love could be directed towards any one person and it followed in exactly the same way for our other children, Gareth and Lucy. It is quite different from any other love I have ever felt, totally different from my love for any woman, even the love for my wife. I suppose it is because they are our creation. People had spoken to me before of how the love of a parent for a child was different but I was nevertheless quite unprepared for its all-pervasive nature. Part of this unique feeling stems from the whole process of conception which is a miracle of science and however many times I watch it and despite knowing the embryology, I feel awed by the wonder of it all. A child, born in wonder, that most compelling emotion, goes on to provide for its parents wonder at every stage of development. For wonder is not just a feature of the early, wholly dependent months and it does not lessen with maturity. I understand why Bismarck, when asked in the latter part of his life what had given him the greatest satisfaction during it, did not choose his formidable political achievements but simply said, 'That God did not take away any of my children.'

To believe that your child is going to die is devastating. If Tristan had already died I think I might have found it easier to cope. It was the knowledge that I was going to have to watch him die and, worse, to be powerless to prevent it that added to my grief. I had never experienced any other death that might act as a yardstick, such as my mother, father, sister, brother or wife unexpectedly dying. Debbie's mother did die when she was eight and she told me once when we were talking about our feelings that the news about Tristan was far worse for her to handle than the sudden shock of knowing that her mother was dead.

The consultant confirmed the diagnosis and I walked back the few hundred yards to the house to tell Debbie. I was determined to be the doctor and to give her some glimmer of hope, even though I was convinced that there was none. With the greatest difficulty I tried to put myself into the same frame of mind as often in the past when talking to the mother of an ill child. Although part of me had been outside the conversation, as if I was overhearing it, I could and did repeat the doctor's words of hope to Debbie. As she quietly began to cry I was still able to tell her clinically and dispassionately what chances the doctor had given of Tristan's survival. It was only when I had finished telling her all the information that had been fed into me that I let the mask slip. I was like a pilot who having landed, then switches off the automatic pilot. Debbie looked at me and on her face I could see clearly that she knew that I knew that he was going to die. Suddenly my attempt to be a doctor had to be completely abandoned. We were just two parents, desolate, as we clung to each other, crying. Never have I felt so empty and I doubt if I could ever feel so empty again. There was nothing but a void, a blackness. There were no shapes, nothing to hold on to, to fix one's sights to, or sounds to attune one's ear to. Only slowly did we begin to talk, to weigh the options and consider all the possibilities.

For years afterwards we both had an unconsolable ache that sometimes we would discuss and sometimes we would leave alone, both knowing what we were thinking. It only left us thirteen years later, when for the first time we allowed ourselves to answer the numerous queries about Tristan's health with the simple words, 'He is cured now.' Up until that moment neither of us ever said, 'I think he's cured', as the prospects improved. We deliberately tried to avoid making any judgement lest we tempted fate. We would either just shrug our shoulders or say, 'Keep your fingers crossed', or if we knew the inquirer had prayed for him, say 'He still needs your prayers.'

We agreed with the consultant in Plymouth that we would travel back to London straightaway and that Tristan would be admitted to the Hospital for Sick Children at Great Ormond Street which had already offered a bed. From the moment we met the Registrar on duty at Great Ormond Street and accepted his advice that Tristan should come into hospital immediately, we never took any other medical opinion and never used any other drugs than those which they prescribed. Every night he was in hospital one of us slept by his bed. We were given a constant infusion of strength from everyone we met in the hospital over all those years. From the porters at the door and the admission clerks to the nurses, sisters, registrars and consultants, we received innumerable kind-nesses. We never paid a single penny for his treatment which at times was very expensive. New, costly drugs were used and on one occasion when he developed chickenpox he was given a new anti-viral agent which had barely been used before in the UK and almost certainly saved his life.

It is hardly surprising, therefore, that as a family we believe that the National Health Service is the finest public good that this country has. Our American relatives are lost in admiration for the NHS as they have seen it during Tristan's illness. I am not starry-eyed about the problems and deficiencies of the NHS but I fervently believe that its ethical foundations are sound and should not be fundamentally changed. No politicians would ever have my vote if I thought they would damage the NHS. When Margaret Thatcher announced her NHS reforms in January 1989 she confirmed all my worst fears. Only when John Major succeeded her did I breathe again and believe that we were in the same principled position as when Iain Macleod became Minister of Health in 1951 and ensured that the NHS would be safe in Conservative hands.

Debbie and I resolved that since Tristan was going to have to fight for his life we were going to have to fight with him. We both felt then that if he was going to live it would not be just because of the medicines or the skills of the doctors, it would be because of his inner fight. If the doctors' claims for the treatment were right, the drugs would kill the abnormal cells. But if he was to survive it would be because the poisons were not also killing the healthy blood cells. The therapy had to work with his body and not carry his body down to ill health. We knew he had to mobilize an inner strength to fight the disease. Our job was to will him to live; to give him the love and strength which would help him to fight. At various times people suggested faith healers whom they had used. Often we were given names of different medical doctors who had treated children successfully in different parts of the world. Despite the obvious temptations, we held firm to our initial course. We would rely on Tristan, Great Ormond Street and ourselves.

It was impossible for us to prevent my constituents knowing that Tristan was ill. Rather than have rumours and constant questions we decided to be quite open about it. Within days both the *Western Morning News* and the *Evening Herald* carried short statements about his illness. We called it leukaemia, explained why I had to cancel some constituency engagements and said that we wanted him to be treated in every way as a normal child. From that day to this those two newspapers treated his illness with the utmost delicacy and tact; they never once used photographs which could have been embarrassing to him or to us and we are indebted to them. Nor was his story picked up by the national newspapers for many years. When I became Minister of Health, for example, my attending hospital with him and waiting my turn like other people in outpatients could easily have become a news story. By the time I became Foreign Secretary all the main newspapers knew of Tristan's illness and they never exploited their knowledge, for which he and we will always be grateful. Eventually one popular newspaper broke the story when Tristan was fifteen. By then we were becoming more confident that he was cured. The story talked of his courage and it did no harm. Only when it became clear that he was fully cured did I feel able to talk about it in public. Tristan understands that his example has been used by doctors to inspire a number of other families facing the same news as we were given. It can help them to relate to a family they know about and, for that reason, Tristan is content for it to be referred to publicly.

It was a formidable treatment for him to undergo over all those years and he coped wonderfully well, attending his primary and comprehensive schools all the time. I was fortunate to be a backbench MP in the early months because I had the freedom to attend hospital with him, as did Debbie running her own business. Later, when I went into Government, she had to devote the most time to taking him to hospital. Through all these years the doctors were testing different drugs and doses, trying for a mix strong enough to kill the immature abnormal blood cells but not so strong as to kill the normal body cells. The side effects of the drugs were nasty if the dose was too strong. These trials were supervised by the Medical Research Council. Information was being shared by doctors around the world and I read every medical paper I could find, even in the most specialized of journals. The frontiers of medical science were expanding and, knowing the scientific risks and opportunities, with one's own son's life depending on the rapidity of medical advance, was a nail-biting experience.

Almost as if fate had intervened deliberately to take my mind off worrying about Tristan, in November 1973 I won a high position in the Private Members' Ballot. This brought me back into political activity. I had to present my Private Member's Bill to the House of Commons in the New Year and, if I could assemble a majority for its Second Reading debate, it would have a good chance of becoming the law of the land. A Departmental Committee on the Adoption of Children had been set up by Jim Callaghan, when Home Secretary, in 1969 under the chairmanship, first of Sir William Houghton, and then on his death just before publication, of Judge Stockdale. It had reported in 1972 and its recommendations provided a sound foundation for the nationwide organization of a professional adoption service in which central and local government and voluntary agencies formed a partnership; it also suggested a new procedure to enable parents to give early final consent to adoption, put forward a new custodianship order midway between that of adopter and a foster parent and extended the powers of local authorities for the greater protection of children. It had been hoped that the Government would announce legislation in the Queen's Speech to deal with all its many complex but integrated recommendations but it had not done so. A lobbying group had been formed to try and ensure that legislation was brought forward and they were very keen to support me. Influenced I am sure in a strange way by Tristan's illness, I decided to choose adoption for my Private Member's Bill and to widen the coverage to include protection against child abuse and call it the Children's Bill. I went to Sir Keith Joseph, then Secretary of State for Health and Social Security, to see if he was prepared to support my legislation since the Government had claimed that it was only a shortage of legislative time that had led it to postpone the bill.

Sir Keith Joseph was a very interesting politician, far removed from his stereotype as a harsh Right-winger. A highly strung, deeply sensitive intellectual with the social awareness and concern that is often found in leaders of the Jewish community, he had just developed a research programme to discover the facts behind his concept of the 'cycle of deprivation'. It was a concept that drew attention to the interaction of poor educational attainment, poverty, emotional impoverishment, depression and despair. Sir Keith obviously thought that all any ambitious backbencher would be interested in was quick, headline-catching legislation. So he offered me Government support for a short bill to implement the findings of the report into the tragic case of child abuse involving Maria Colwell. This was tempting in that it would ensure that my bill passed into law but it was also dangerous in that if the Government could take the heat off reforming the law of adoption in this way, the Houghton Report could well be pigeonholed indefinitely. Its recommendations were meant to be taken as a whole and I had become convinced that legislation should not be piecemeal. Sir Keith was puzzled when I refused his offer and asked how I could possibly draft legislation for such a major report on my own. I replied that I had a team of lawyers who, on a voluntary basis, were already far advanced and that we would challenge the Government to reject comprehensive legislation which would also cover the Maria Colwell recommendations. He smiled, probably amused more by my audacity than anything else, and I left believing I could negotiate a deal with him if I managed to obtain a Second Reading.

My anxiety was whether the necessary 100 MPs would be in the House at 2.30 p.m. on the Friday afternoon in February which had been allocated for the bill's Second Reading. With that number we could ensure the closure of the debate and thereby stop the Government Whips from making sure that someone was still talking when the vote was due. This was the tactic for killing a bill like this, for I doubted whether the Government would have dared to formally vote against it. On the *Jimmy Young Show* I appealed for people who wanted the legislation to write to their MP and ask them to be present. This produced an astounding response and MPs were deluged with letters demanding they reserve time to be present. The press was very sympathetic and when the bill was published the experts were amazed that so complex a piece of legislation could be drawn up without the backing of the Government's

Parliamentary draftsmen. The team of volunteers, many of whom were specialists in the law affecting children, had done a remarkable job. It looked as if the Government was going to be gravely embarrassed, but sadly the Dissolution of Parliament for the February 1974 Election took place on the very day that the bill was due for its Second Reading. It was now inevitable that whoever won the election would have to bring forward immediate legislation. Nevertheless, my disappointment was intense and the team of drafters shared this. Little did I or they know that fate was to ensure that within months I would bring forward, as the Minister responsible, virtually the same legislation and be in the key position to guide it on to the statute book as the 1975 Children's Act. Also, despite Barbara Castle's scepticism, I maintained all the research work that Sir Keith Joseph had instigated on the 'cycle of deprivation', believing that it was a concept that needed serious scientific assessment.

The cause of the February 1974 General Election was the struggle that Edward Heath's Government was having with the second miners' strike. On this occasion I was not as sympathetic to the miners' case. Having rolled the Government over in 1972, they were coming back for more and if they won again with the strike weapon it would augur ill for parliamentary democracy. I had spoken out strongly in my constituency on 16 December, saying, 'The miners should return to normal working; the train drivers should stop their industrial action immediately and allow people to return to their families for Christmas; the power technicians should work normally.' I felt strongly that we had to check the abuses of trade union power and anyway the last thing I wanted was a snap election with the Conservative Party decked out in the Union Jack supporting the people versus the trade unions.

When Heath called the election I thought the Conservatives would win and I was facing the fight of my life in the Devonport constituency. We now had three constituencies in Plymouth. The new Devonport had been carved out of my own Sutton seat and Dame Joan Vickers's old Devonport and there was a new Drake constituency. We were fighting each other as sitting MPs. Dame Joan was a formidable adversary. Statuesque, looking far younger than her age, with blue hair and a long and devoted record as the Member for Devonport, she presented a very strong challenge.

I tried to divert attention from the miners' strike and instead emphasized local questions, particularly Plymothians' resentment at the Conservative Government's local government reforms. These had smashed the City of Plymouth's independence, leaving us to be virtually governed from Exeter as part of Devon County Council. The emphasis in all my election literature was also on my youth and time as Minister for the Navy. It was not very subtle – an example being a picture of me with the Devonport Gun Crew. For the first time I felt an election actually swinging during the campaign. A change of public mood came very early on, when they were angered by the cynicism of the Government's decision to restore television in the evening, since that had been stopped up to then to save electricity. It was seen as typical of politicians to deprive them of many of their favourite evening TV programmes until the moment when it suited them to put out their own election propaganda. As the campaign built up I sensed that people were voting against Heath's Government even if they were not voting positively for a Labour Government. Jeremy Thorpe conducted a very effective campaign on the basis that neither Heath nor Wilson could unite the country and the Liberal vote soared to 6,059,519 which was 19.3 per cent of votes in the UK. The result of all these factors was that Labour squeezed home but without a real working majority. Our Plymouth campaign was summed up in a letter from my hard-working constituency secretary, Barbara Furzeman, 'It was worth every foot-weary, rain-sodden inch of the way.' Three minutes before the polling stations closed, I met my sister, Susan, whom I had not seen all day as she had been dragging people out to vote in appalling weather conditions and she bent down and literally wrung the water out of her skirt. Despite the traditional Labour Party fear that their voters would stay away in the rain, we won but the margin was a mere 437 votes. Still, I had won the seat back for Labour for it was Dame Joan Vickers who had defeated Michael Foot, the sitting MP in 1955, and then beaten him again in 1959 after which he had gone to Ebbw Vale to take over Aneurin Bevan's seat. I was thrilled for many reasons but first because I could go on representing Plymouth in Parliament.

Next day it was clear that Edward Heath, who only had 297 MPs against Labour's 301, would try and stay on, with the help of the fourteen Liberal MPs. He asked Jeremy Thorpe to come to No. 10 and in his eagerness Jeremy made, I thought, a tactical mistake. He would have been well advised to say that, though he was ready to come and talk to the Prime Minister, he could only do so on the basis that the Liberal Party was ready to contribute to a government of national unity. He then should have consulted a few prominent centrist figures before going in to see Edward Heath, strengthening his negotiating hand in the process. Instead he got ensnared in problems with his activists who disliked Heath and had no experience of the problems of government. The Liberal Party had not been involved in government since the wartime coalition, and before that, not since Lloyd George resigned in 1922. After the Conservative election victory in 1951, Winston Churchill had asked the Liberal Leader, Clement Davies, to serve in his Cabinet on a personal basis but he had refused. Most of Jeremy Thorpe's colleagues appeared to be basically against any arrangement with the Conservatives, let alone Heath. Heath offered Thorpe a Cabinet position and a Speaker's Conference on electoral reform. Even with Liberal support, the Conservatives would have been short of an overall majority but the potential for a bargain of mutual advantage existed as Heath was ready to offer the Nationalists

Scottish and Welsh Assemblies. The Liberal Party failed to seize their opportunity, but on the spin of the electoral roulette wheel, it will no doubt return.

Harold Wilson meanwhile had decided to sit tight and wait. The Sunday following the election, Roy and Jennifer Jenkins came over to Buttermere for lunch. We first gossiped about the election and Heath's tactics in trying to stay on and then went for a long walk on the ridge overlooking the Kennet Valley. Tristan was on my shoulders and Gareth in a backpack, and we looked like ramblers. The conversation, however, was very much to the point. I discovered that Roy was not just contemplating the prospect of becoming Chancellor but was even working up some enthusiasm for the task. He had actually drafted an outline of the economic policy which he thought he would have to pursue. I was thrilled that he was at last showing his old fight. There had been some Sunday press speculation about him going to the Treasury but it was far more than speculation. Roy told me that he had spoken to Harold Wilson and had gained the impression that Wilson might want him to be Chancellor. Roy's earlier desire to be Wilson's positive choice and not forced on him looked as if it might be fulfilled. As we walked he mentioned in passing a health problem he had developed. My advice was that he should put himself into the hands of a good doctor and I suggested a few names. We parted in a mood of optimism such as I had not felt since dining together in Plymouth just before the 1970 General Election. Sadly, it proved as then to be a false dawn.

The Shadow Cabinet met on Monday while the whole nation was watching the comings and goings at No 10. It began to look more and more likely that Harold Wilson would be called to form a new government. That evening, after Edward Heath had resigned, a group of us met with Roy for dinner at Harry Walston's in Albany. Everyone was tired and there was a great sense of let down when Roy said he had been told by Wilson that he would not be Chancellor but Home Secretary. I felt particularly dismayed since only thirty-six hours earlier he had told me it looked pretty likely that he would be Chancellor.

I do not recall Roy mentioning that evening that Wilson had also offered him the task, as Home Secretary, of co-ordinating policy towards Northern Ireland. My notebook says he told me when we talked in the Home Office two days later. Anyhow, it transpired that he could have made his own choice for a Northern Ireland Minister and he could have insisted on whoever it was being in the Cabinet, working to him as Home Secretary, rather as the Chief Secretary to the Treasury works to the Chancellor and, as Roy had insisted in 1968, should be in the Cabinet. If Roy had accepted, his obvious choice to go to Northern Ireland would have been Bill Rodgers. Bill would have been extremely good in that testing post, particularly since he would have had to face the backlash against the Sunningdale Agreement from the Protestant Ulster Defence

Force. More importantly, Roy himself would have had the authority and the nerve to insist that when these self-styled Protestant loyalists went on strike they were faced down. Merlyn Rees, who became the Secretary of State for Northern Ireland, estimable man though he is, was asked to confront too big a challenge too early in his Cabinet career. Merlyn was persuaded that the Loyalists were able to hold the Province to ransom. Perhaps they could, though I believe that was an error of judgement, at least it was something which should not have been conceded before it was proven and they should have been resisted all the way. We should have attempted to openly draft in volunteer power station workers from the mainland and tried to persuade them to teach servicemen and to break what was a political not an industrial strike.

If Roy had taken the additional responsibility for Northern Ireland, I am convinced that the Sunningdale Agreement and its breakthrough power-sharing Executive would not have been overthrown. Bill Rodgers would have had his position in the Party greatly strengthened and Roy would have been in the centre of British politics as Home Secretary, not on the fringe during the crucial years before Wilson's resignation. It was not to be. During that depressing dinner, without exactly knowing why, I felt that Roy, and by association all of us in that room, had been outmanoeuvred yet again by Harold Wilson. It was a dismal start to a Labour Government and as yet I did not know whether I would even be part of that Government.

10

MINISTER OF HEALTH

On Monday 4 March Edward Heath resigned and Harold Wilson was summoned to the Palace. It was the shabbiest victory I have ever taken part in: we were back in government by courtesy of the National Union of Mineworkers. We gave the face workers their full claim and strike action ceased. Edward Heath's folly was in calling an election on the issue of 'who governs the country'. It seemed pathetic for a Prime Minister to be calling into question his own authority. Heath should have told the country that there was no alternative to paying the miners, but that before a general election in the summer he would put before them specific proposals to ensure that the trade unions would not again hold the country to ransom. He would then have trounced Labour.

For Harold Wilson the victory was neither shabby nor depressing. For him, it was one of those rare occasions when the humiliation of previous defeat is avenged and victory is especially sweet. He would have been less than human if he had not felt some satisfaction seeing the press photographs of Edward Heath's famous piano leaving No. 10.

The Cabinet met on Tuesday at 5 p.m. and it was clear that the junior Ministerial appointments would not be announced that night. I waited with no great anticipation of office. I was so disillusioned with Harold Wilson that I did not even care very much. My victory in Devonport was behind me, I still had the World Security Trust job, my son Tristan was having to attend hospital frequently and I had more than enough to keep me busy. Ministerial office was not the be-all and end-all so I did not hang around at the end of a telephone waiting for a call from No. 10.

Barbara Castle had been told on the first night that she would be going to the Elephant and Castle as Secretary of State for Health and Social Services and that she would have Brian O'Malley as Minister for Pensions. Barbara decided that she did not want Shirley Summerskill in her team because she felt that she did not carry enough weight and, talking to Harold that evening, discovered that David Ennals was already earmarked for another job. It was Elizabeth Shore, Peter Shore's wife, a medical doctor in the Department, who suggested my name to Barbara for the Health side. Barbara then proposed to Harold on the telephone that I should be appointed. Harold's reply was, 'I like the idea. Let me think about it.'

On Wednesday morning I went to No. 10 and Harold offered me the job of Parliamentary Under-Secretary of Health. In retrospect I am amazed that I quibbled and said I did not believe the job could be done effectively without the more senior status of Minister of State, if I or anyone else was to deal effectively with the doctors in the dispute over pay beds that undoubtedly lay ahead. Harold was somewhat taken aback and obviously anxious to get on with compiling his list of junior Ministers, rather than wrangle with a young pup who ought to have been grateful for the bone thrown to him. He suggested that I should mull it over and talk to Barbara Castle but just as I was walking out he promised that if I accepted I would have responsibility as Under-Secretary for introducing the same children's legislation that I had put forward as a Private Member. He knew well that this would more than tempt me.

On leaving No. 10 I went over to the Home Office to see Roy Jenkins. We talked in a desultory way about all the events since Sunday at Buttermere. He seemed surprised that I had not accepted Harold's offer but wisely he did not seek to influence me either way. Barbara had gathered from Harold that my acceptance was a little dicey so she rang me up and suggested that I come round to the Elephant and Castle. Although I did not know it at the time, she had already had to persuade Brian O'Malley that he could not be made a full Minister for Pensions. The last thing she wanted to hear me say was that I did not think it was worth my while to come merely as a Parliamentary Secretary. I explained that unless I had greater authority over the pay beds controversy the doctors would be appealing over my head to her all the time. Also, it meant I had not advanced in seniority since I was last in Government. She totally agreed about my needing more authority to deal with the doctors and she promised to try to persuade Harold to make me a Minister of State. She cleverly bypassed my doubts, however, by suggesting that I should sit in on a meeting to discuss the implementation of the former Secretary of State, Keith Joseph's, NHS reorganization.

As Sir Philip Rogers, the Permanent Secretary to the Department, explained the situation I became more and more absorbed in the immense problems the NHS was facing. I had edited a book on the organization of the NHS in 1966, *A Unified Health Service*, and I had studied its structure in depth when I had been a Governor of Charing Cross Hospital. Sir Keith Joseph had published his White Paper in 1972 and I had opposed the structure which he had then outlined to the House. It was widely felt to be developing into a bureaucratic nightmare, owing too much to the management consultants McKinsey and too little to NHS needs. The National Health Service Reorganization Act had, however, been given Royal Assent on 5 July 1973. It was the law of the land and implementation of the new structure was set for 1 April 1974. For us to reverse the reorganization, Sir Philip argued, would require immediate legislation and the ensuing delay would be chaotic. Everything was geared up for its introduction over the next few weeks. Barbara explained to him that she opposed important aspects of the legislation. I said nothing, having no official status at the meeting. Personally I was opposed to the whole concept of reintroducing an executive regional health authority; I thought the NHS needed the ninety area health authorities for England as a single tier and that it was madness to have third-tier districts as well. Suddenly Barbara turned to me and asked what I would do. I reluctantly told her that she would have to keep the proposed structure. Tempting though it was to stop the reorganization in its tracks, the arguments against doing so were massive. I hoped we could make some evolutionary changes but regrettably the reorganization would have to stay on its planned timetable. Hardly were the words out of my mouth than I realized she had hooked me in. How could I give her this unpalatable message and then walk away from implementing it?

Although I continued to affect caution, she knew then that I would say yes. When I rang her that night she had spoken to Harold who had assured her that the only reason he could not make me a Minister of State was that he was over the statutory number allowed and that he hoped to legislate to raise the limit in the summer. She promised to do her best to ensure that I was given the next vacancy. My main anxiety then was to confirm that I was actually in charge of the Department of Health and that I would not have to deal with her through Brian O'Malley. In this way, although officially a Parliamentary Secretary, I would in effect be the Minister of Health. She gave me a categoric assurance on this and so I promised to come. My appointment was duly announced the next day and Harold kept his promise. I became a Minister of State in the summer.

The then combined Department of Health and Social Security used to be affectionately called by its staff the Department of Stealth and Total Obscurity. It was one of the super-ministries which Harold Wilson had created in 1968 for Dick Crossman to be Secretary of State. No Secretary of State could master every aspect of it and there had to be considerable delegation to the two Ministers of State. Though there had been some limited interchange, the Department was still stratified between the old Ministry of Health and the Ministry of Social Security, further strengthening my independence. One of the most attractive features of the Ministry of Health is the way that its civil servants traditionally identify with the values and aspirations of the NHS. If a Minister supports the principles of the NHS he is assured of as loyal and as dedicated a service as you can get anywhere in Whitehall. I cannot think of any instance where the Department tried to frustrate my decisions. As Minister of Health, I spent two and a half of the happiest and most constructive years I have had in Government. If I had never held any other office it alone would have justified my decision to go into politics.

In the main being a doctor was an advantage rather than a hindrance. At that time only one other medical doctor, Lord Addison, had been Minister of Health. Many of the issues faced by the Minister have a large scientific content and to be trained in that discipline means that the complexities are easier to unravel. On the other hand, there is the temptation as a doctor to ride hobby horses and follow prejudices. Also, the social workers might have been more suspicious of a doctor if I had not already shown my interest in reforming the law affecting children; they were eagerly awaiting new legislation on adoption which I hoped to bring forward into law by 1975. Generally speaking, the practice that Ministers exercise judgement in areas in which they are not experts is worth maintaining. However, in the climate of early 1974, it was a bonus to have as the Minister responsible for the NHS someone who knew its inner workings. Inflation was heading towards 27 per cent, the NHS was facing a fundamental administrative upheaval and the medical profession was militant and determined to overthrow the Government's manifesto commitment over pay beds.

There were any number of specific instances where it helped to be a doctor. Twice, the Chief Medical Officer of Health, Dr Yellowlees, asked for assistance to keep the World Health Organization's smallpox eradication campaign on course. The WHO campaign had started in 1969 when there were ten million smallpox cases worldwide. On one occasion we were asked for an extra £1 million and on another for £$\frac{1}{2}$ million. The need was desperate but Dr Yellowlees had been quite unable to find these sums within his own budget. As a doctor I needed no convincing that tracking down those last few cases of smallpox, mainly in the Horn of Africa, was a critical health priority. I rode roughshod over the Departmental objections and just told them to find the money. With this push they easily found the cash and, with contributions from a few other major countries, the programme continued and was brought to a successful conclusion. The last naturally occurring case was in Somalia in 1977. Now even the need for a smallpox vaccination has vanished. It is almost incredible to think that that vital WHO programme could ever have been in danger because of financial trouble. Yet WHO could, if it had the money, mobilize resources totally to eradicate malaria and some other world killers like bilharzia, a worm found in rivers and reservoirs. If only a fraction of the money invested in modern drugs were put into such preventive health programmes the health of the world would be transformed. If only a UN Secretary-General had the standing and the authority to mobilize all the special agencies for a few targeted programmes, the sum of human happiness could be greatly enhanced. Meanwhile, the UN and the special agencies often pull against each other and there is no firm ordering of priorities.

It also helped that I had studied the pharmaceutical industry when writing an unpublished pamphlet for the Young Fabians and had worked with pharmaceutical companies when I was chairman of Decision Technology. This gave me the background knowledge to counter some of the industry's special pleading. This was buttressed by Dr Fred Wrigley. Within a few days of my taking office, Sir Philip Rogers came to say that he assumed that I would not want to use the services of Wrigley, Sir Keith Joseph's part-time adviser, who had previously been managing director of Burroughs and Wellcome. I said he should make no such assumption, that knowledge from private industry could be invaluable and that I would like to see him. When I met him I was enthused by his Yorkshire realism and he became a valued adviser. I like to believe that, despite my tough demands to restrict lavish promotion budgets, the part of the industry which is research based realized they had a friend in court. I did all I could to encourage inward investment and had some success with Merck, Sharpe and Dohme's decision to invest in a major research laboratory in Britain. I knew from my own experience with ICI when on the Medical Unit at St Thomas's Hospital that the best of the British pharmaceutical industry are world beaters and that this was an area of excellence which Britain could develop. Thankfully it has evolved since then. The voluntary system of profit and quality controls that has been developed in the UK is an amazing example of Government and private industry co-operation. It is a totally managed market with profits being fixed by a civil servant in the Department. Everything depends on the integrity of a very few civil servants who have to have access to a whole range of highly confidential commercial information and are in a position of immense trust. In theory it should be a more open market, but, in its defence, it does work and no one has yet found a better way of squaring so many conflicting objectives. It stimulated my interest in developing internal markets and, in the mid 1980s, I advocated internal market reforms for the NHS itself.

My medical background also helped in dealing with two controversial issues: cigarette smoking and abortion. Both were subjects that Barbara Castle wanted to have little to do with. Since she smoked like a chimney she knew that it would be humbug for her to lead an anti-smoking campaign and yet she could see that this was the biggest health hazard that we faced. She supported me to the hilt in my determination to control the tobacco industry. The voluntary agreements we made became progressively tougher but I felt that tobacco products should come under the 1968 Medicines Act, a very sophisticated piece of legislation capable of protecting the legitimate needs of industry while balancing independent scientific advice on the danger of certain products to an individual's health. After a bitter interdepartmental battle, I won acceptance in Government for legislation to designate tobacco as a product to be controlled under the act. Unfortunately, when I went off to the Foreign

Office, the tobacco industry mobilized their supporters among the MPs and they used their considerable influence over the legislation programme to ensure that it was postponed indefinitely.

On abortion Barbara Castle was untypically extremely nervous of public opinion. She apparently felt that a controversy over abortion had lost her in the past a number of votes with Catholics in her Blackburn constituency. Anyhow, whatever the reason, in the main she preferred me to handle it. She did, however, throw her whole political weight in the Parliamentary Labour Party against the setting up of another Select Committee to examine the Abortion Act. We had been forced to concede a Select Committee in 1974 but we were confident we had the votes to resist its re-establishment. Abortion was an issue on which I found it a help openly to use my medical knowledge when handling public and parliamentary debate and to defuse controversy.

The headlines in the London *Evening Standard* when we took office were all about London becoming the abortion capital of the world. The growth and abuse taking place in private clinics was shocking, threatening the more liberal abortion law that I had supported as a backbencher in 1967. At the committee stage of this bill tougher powers to regulate private clinics were urged on David Steel, the sponsor of the 1967 bill, but he had resisted, probably on Government advice. Now I was told by the Departmental lawyers that we needed fresh primary legislation in order to clamp down. I was anxious about introducing any new legislation for the mood of the House of Commons in the middle of 1974 was very different from the reformist mood in 1966 when Labour had a large majority. I judged that any new legislation risked the imposition of restrictive amendments to the actual grounds on which an abortion could be authorized. I decided therefore to try to use existing legislation, though I might be taken to court for going beyond the powers those laws gave me. We presented regulations to the House of Commons to enable us to clamp down on this private abortion racket. I told our lawyers that, if challenged, I would be ready to go to court and defend my decision since it was so clearly in the public interest for us to act. Even legislation to fix the number of weeks beyond which no abortion could take place could have had a restrictive amendment attached to it. So I deliberately delayed this legislation as well. The time limit was eventually settled and passed in Government legislation during a free vote on embryo research fifteen years later.

Of all my ministerial jobs, Minister of Health was the one for which Debbie felt least resentment at the long hours I had to work. It was constructive work and she could see I was engrossed. She too was expanding her literary agency. In early 1975, on a Friday evening at Buttermere, sitting by the fire and wanting something light to read, I picked up one of her manuscripts. It had just been sent to Debbie by Jeffrey Archer, who had been the Conservative MP for Louth from

1969–74. He had rung her up at the end of 1974 having heard of her agency through an American friend of hers, Elise Smith. Jeffrey had mentioned at a party that he was writing a book and Elise had warned him against doing what the author of *The Graduate* had done, signing away all rights to his book and losing a fortune in the process. She had told him that he needed a literary agent and suggested he should contact Debbie. As I read the manuscript I found myself chuckling and turning the pages avidly. When I finished that same evening I told Debbie that I did not think she would want to return the manuscript and that it was amazingly good for a first novel. She read it, liked it too and they started on fifteen years of a close, fruitful and enjoyable working relationship. She sent the manuscript to seventeen different publishing houses until it was reconsidered by Jonathan Cape, who had earlier rejected it. It was published as *Not a Penny More, Not a Penny Less* and I have always felt that it is one of Jeffrey's best books.

In those days Jeffrey was out of politics. Having resigned his seat because of a threat of bankruptcy, he wanted to build up his finances and his independence. His path to being a successful novelist is an amazing saga in itself. Watching his progress left me full of admiration for his energy. It is not easy to become a bestselling author, but to do it without using sex or violence, just good story telling, is even more difficult.

Jeffrey Archer is the subject of endless jealousies and controversy. When he became Deputy Chairman of the Conservative Party and I was Leader of the SDP, Debbie's position as his agent could have become very difficult. We all kept, with a few exceptions, to a self-denying ordinance about commenting on each other's activities. Jeffrey, at Conservative Party functions, raised many a laugh by claiming that he was financing the SDP and he joined David Steel as the only person on whom I could vouchsafe no comment for fear of it being passed on to journalists. I knew my weakness for a colourful phrase too well – silence was the safest course. When his libel action against the *Daily Star* was taking place, Jeffrey asked us to his annual summer party at his family home at The Old Rectory, Grantchester. We both decided that we would attend, whether he won or lost, and fortunately, following the judgement, it turned into a celebration not a wake. Debbie enjoyed his pizazz and chutzpah, both New York terms which do not easily translate – the best equivalents I can think of are animation and cheek. They are qualities not found in great measure in the English and she, as a New Yorker, especially enjoyed the fun and zest he brought to her agency.

In 1990 Jeffrey felt he no longer needed an agent to negotiate his contracts for new books in the US and UK. Debbie always works for her authors worldwide, very rarely using sub-agents in other countries, and has never accepted numerous offers to be a sub-agent herself. In particular she always enjoyed negotiating in the United States, for many of the publishers were personal friends. It was a decision for Jeffrey to make and she was determined that they would part without involving lawyers and with only good memories of what had been. She gave an 'Archer Departure' lunch for him and for the key people they had worked with. The gossip writers were deprived of any chance to write about bitter clashes or to involve me in any way.

The success of Debbie's agency has doubly enriched our life together. It has given the family a far greater degree of financial freedom and meant that I could remain a full-time politician throughout the 1980s when I would have found it very hard to have worked part-time in either medicine or business. It has also ensured that Debbie had her own fulfilling life and that I could switch off from politics at home and take an interest, as a director of her company, in the world of publishing.

In the Department of Health the task which took up much of my time was supervising the legislation to reform the adoption laws. It was a most unusual situation, with me bringing all the volunteers who had helped me as a backbencher together with the Departmental officials. Instead of being prickly, the officials welcomed this outside involvement and as a result we built on and improved my Private Member's Bill. Our problem was the innate conservatism of the Home Office but Alex Lyon, who was a junior Minister there, was a great help and did his best to swing opinion round, particularly over the new concept of guardianship. I found the Lord Chancellor's Department surprisingly progressive in comparison to the Home Office. I could also always rely on Leo Abse, an influential Labour MP who had been the most important single influence behind the adoption reform movement, to put a little pressure on in the correct places. He was generous with his advice, having steered through more controversial legislation than any other MP.

My main concern was to ensure that we had the balance right between the natural parents and the child. The British Association of Social Workers helped to ensure this by going out on a limb for the rights of the natural parent and this concentrated people's attention on a substantive issue. The Directors of Social Services were a wiser group and they did much to reorientate the social work profession to ensure that it took greater account of the child's interest than hitherto. I was always vexed over giving an eighteen-year-old the right to see their adoption certificate, thus making it easier to trace their natural parents. The right already existed in Scotland. It was not technically the retrospective legislation that its critics alleged it to be but it came too close to being retrospective for my comfort, besides raising deep ethical questions. I agonized for those parents who would live in fear of unpleasant emotional encounters. In practice the counselling safeguard we introduced worked well and there have been very few distressing cases. There have, however, been many happy reunions and many more adoptees, satisfied just to know the names of their natural parents, have taken the matter no further. The legislation has adapted to changing attitudes and it did provide the framework for a living law, with the reporting-back and research procedures that I had always wanted. It represents the most constructive legislative contribution I have made to British politics but it could never have been done without the help of many hundreds of people.

At the same time as we were making satisfying progress here, we became entangled in a controversy that was to have a much less desirable outcome. In the summer of 1974 Sir Philip Rogers came to see Barbara Castle and myself to discuss privately our controversial manifesto commitment to phase pay beds out of NHS hospitals. Sir Philip deployed a strong case against our taking any action. He warned us that the mood of the medical profession was very brittle and said that the considered judgement of himself, the Chief Medical Officer and all the top officials was that, in the best interests of the NHS, we should avoid a confrontation with the doctors on this issue. Rather movingly, he insisted that if the Secretary of State, having heard him out, came to a different conclusion then that was the last that she would hear of it and everyone in the Department would carry out her policy faithfully and to the best of their abilities. Barbara handled him very well, thanked him for his courtesy and his memo and then concisely and clearly put the counter arguments for phasing out. For my part, I made it clear that I agreed completely with her judgement. I had been one of the architects of the policy in the National Executive Sub-Committee before the election. It was a painfully achieved internal Party compromise and at the time it was the only way we could avoid being committed by manifesto to abolish private medicine in its entirety. I have always thought that abolition was wrong in principle. It is a fundamental human right to use one's after-tax income to pay for private education or private health. The private option provides a safety valve, a source of experimentation and variety in what is otherwise monopoly state provision. There is in my judgement, however, no case for public subsidy for private health provision or tax relief to encourage private health insurance.

Sir Philip kept his promise and from then on defended our decisions and refused to let the British Medical Association get away with the attempt to present officials as not being fully behind our policy. It was a fine example of the best of the civil service tradition of serving governments irrespective of party. The civil service must, however, be able to warn Ministers of the pitfalls and perhaps we would have been wiser to drop our policy. But it would have been very hard, almost impossible to do. The predictions about the reaction of the medical profession were totally accurate. Eventually, after a protracted struggle, we forced pay-bed legislation on to the statute book, only for it to be removed by the incoming Conservative Government. The fight left a damaging legacy, for many consultants never again gave the NHS the long hours of extra unpaid effort which they had willingly given before.

In justification of our stand, it is very easy to forget how sensitive this issue had become with the Health Service unions. It was the queue-jumping within the same hospital which had pay beds that caused so much offence. Most people did not object to private patients using a separate private hospital. It was not primarily the co-location of private and public medicine in NHS hospitals that aroused resentment but the difference in waiting time when the same operating theatres were being used, with private cases gaining preference sometimes on the same operating list. We tried unsuccessfully to work out schemes for common waiting lists and I was glad to see in 1990 this concept coming back on to the agenda. A particular grievance with the staff was to see a consultant operating on varicose veins or a hernia for a private patient when they would leave such operations for a junior doctor to do on the same list if they were NHS patients.

The pay-bed dispute today is just a vignette of history, a symbol of how very different attitudes were in the 1970s from the 1990s. But then we were in the last throes of the corporatist state. Leaders of the trade unions and the BMA expected to bargain directly with Ministers. It was the era of beer and sandwiches at No. 10 which ended with the Winter of Discontent in 1979 and with the defeat of the Labour Government. The union pressures were strong. In any case, to Barbara Castle, phasing out pay beds for the NHS was a sacred mission. It was the means whereby she would redress the historic error of her hero, Aneurin Bevan. In her mythology he had been simply led astray when he agreed to keep pay beds, whereas in truth it was part of his historic compromise with the consultants and had smoothed the path for the original legislation. He recognized it was the consultants' price and it allowed him to say, with contempt, 'I stuffed their mouths with gold.' The deal had been brokered by Sir Charles Wilson, the Dean of St Mary's – 'Corkscrew Charlie' to his students, who included my father. As Winston Churchill's doctor he later became Lord Moran.

To Barbara Castle personally the manifesto commitment itself was compromise enough. Left to her own devices, I always felt she would have legislated without a qualm for a total ban on private practice. The doctors also sensed this and, however much she said that she was only committed to phasing out pay beds and was not proposing the abolition of private medicine, they detected an ulterior motive. The BMA strategy was to present pay beds as merely the thin end of the wedge: that we were abolishing private medicine through the back door by phasing out pay beds so fast and they could not build private facilities outside the NHS. Just when I was beginning to convince the profession that she was not opposed to private medicine outside the NHS, she insisted on legislating for licensing arrangements to control the building of new private health facilities. Logically, there was a good case for such controls but politically it was madness to propose them at that time for it fed BMA propaganda and it was the touch paper that the BMA leaders used to ignite the profession. The BMA always wanted to fight on the fundamental principle of their right to practise privately. If the BMA were allowed to get away with fighting on this ground, I knew they would be able to rely on the support of the many thousands of doctors who, like myself, had never charged a patient in their life and never had any intention of doing so. So most of my battles with Barbara over licensing were to try to win back those doctors who believed in working full-time for the NHS but who nevertheless prized the independence of the profession. No politician who has ever had to deal with the BMA has escaped unscathed. It was David Lloyd George who said on 11 June 1911 in Birmingham:

> I had two hours' discussion with the medical men themselves the other day. I do not think there has been anything like it since the days when Daniel went into the lions' den . . . but I can assure you they treated me with the same civility as the lions treated my illustrious predecessor . . . except these lions knew their anatomy.

In July 1974 the pay-beds issue, which was festering beneath the surface, was suddenly splashed across the headlines of every popular newspaper. It provided an incident which starkly illustrated the state of corporatist Britain. 'Granny', 'Ma' or 'Mrs' Brookestone, depending on which paper you read, was leading a strike action against pay beds on the private fifteenth floor of Charing Cross Hospital. She was demanding that the privileges of the private patients should be shared with NHS patients so as to shorten waiting lists. Until this was conceded she and her colleagues were prepared to withhold basic domestic services to private patients. At one stage it looked as if a compromise between the local consultants and the local hospital administrators would solve the strike but then the BMA intervened to stiffen the consultants' line, refusing to let their members moderate the right to fill the predetermined number of private beds. Before we knew where we were, Barbara Castle and I were negotiating directly with the BMA and the General Secretaries of NUPE and COHSE on this one local dispute.

The negotiations had their funny moments. One was late at night when we needed to locate Albert Spanswick, the Leader of COHSE. He was traced to a caravan site and came on the telephone to speak to Barbara Castle. She was explaining in her usual animated way the intricacies of the agreement, whereby the private floor was to become a mixed ward, and found Albert, to her disappointment, uninterested in the detail and only too happy to agree. What she did not realize was that he had been hauled out of bed and had walked in his pyjamas in the pouring rain across the camp site to take her call in a public telephone box.

After we had won round the union bosses someone had to undertake the task of convincing Mrs Brookestone and her colleagues who had brought on the whole action. In those days it seemed quite natural for

Barbara and I to talk to the local strike leaders together with the local consultants to explain the complicated arrangements agreed with their national leader. When private patients were treated in special units elsewhere in the hospital the equivalent number of beds on the private floor would be occupied by NHS patients. In her diary, Barbara Castle captures Mrs Brookestone's reaction very well, 'All we have got is one for one,' she complained. 'Yes, Brooky,' explained one of the consultants – now free from the shadow of the BMA to renew his normal friendly relations with Ma B. and her staff – 'but you know that the private floor is always under-occupied. In future these beds will not be kept empty. When we move a private patient to a specialized unit, as we do frequently, we will move an NHS patient immediately into the empty bed.' The issue was resolved, but what a farce. We should never have been involved in this local dispute. But there was very little alternative, given the militant mood of NUPE and their wish to force the pace, fearing that Labour would lose the election which everyone knew could not be postponed for much longer.

Another consequence of the agreement was that the so-called Owen Working Party on a new consultants' contract was speeded up with the aim of reaching an agreement by November. Meanwhile, we agreed not to undertake any arbitrary reductions in pay beds. Despite the fact that the contract negotiations were meant to be separate from pay beds, the two issues had become intertwined. This linkage suited the BMA and their more vigorous challenger for members, the Hospital Consultants and Specialists Association, the HCSA. They agreed to call off their threatened work-to-rule; they were only biding their time but so were we.

On 11 October Labour won the general election but with an overall majority of only three. Labour had 319 MPs and the Conservatives 276. The Liberal vote slumped but they had only one less MP. I again fought Dame Joan Vickers in Devonport but this time I had a majority of over 2,000 and I felt fairly confident of victory throughout my campaign. I was greatly helped by the extensive favourable publicity for the Children's Bill.

Just before Christmas, with the election safely out of the way, Barbara and I met the leaders of the BMA and the HCSA in addition to the members of the Working Party. We also made available to them, half an hour before the meeting, copies of our contract proposals. It was very clear that their leaders were intent on a showdown and ready to call industrial action. Immediately Barbara was asked in hectoring tones whether our proposals were on a take it or leave it basis. No, said Barbara sweetly, they were a statement of the Government's decisions. Were they negotiable? Obviously, she replied, but the principles were not negotiable. What, asked their main negotiator, was the borderline between principle and detail? Well, said Barbara, it could not be rigidly defined but it would be misleading for her to pretend that there was any hope of the

Government accepting an 'item of service' contract. That was the signal for some of the consultants to explode and the meeting deteriorated sharply. It finished with our telling them that we would put our proposals directly to the medical profession and that we were quite happy to arrange to send out copies of the BMA's views on our proposals at Government expense. That rather bowled them over. It all reminded me of Hilaire Belloc's lines:

> Physicians of the Utmost Fame
> Were called at once; but when they came
> They answered, as they took their Fees,
> 'There is no Cure for this Disease.'

Interestingly my main support on the Working Party came from Professor Ian McColl, then as now Professor of Surgery at Guy's Hospital. Totally dedicated to the NHS, he had no time for the BMA's position and served as an independent member. He continues to be independent. He agreed with my advocacy of the internal market in the middle 1980s, became involved with the Conservative NHS reforms and was made a Life Peer. He now strongly supports the Guy's Hospital Health Trust. His position is perfectly logical: as a good Christian he likes the ethics of the NHS but also wants it to be efficient.

We were now on a collision course. At this critical juncture the *Daily Telegraph* ran a story, fed to them by the BMA, that I was at odds with Barbara Castle. I strongly denied this and she agreed that we should go on television to explain our proposals and make clear that there was no major difference between us on the substance. We did differ in the style of our negotiating. At one stage, I had, perhaps ill-advisedly, flirted with having a face-saving study of 'item of service' payments. But Barbara had, probably correctly, overruled me, citing the slippery slope argument. From time to time, her diaries reveal tensions in our relationship but no more than those which would occur between any two passionate individuals working under immense pressure. Generally speaking, considering we were at opposite poles of the Party, our working partnership was remarkably harmonious.

One of Barbara's diary entries captures our relationship pretty well. The Chief Medical Officer of Health, Dr Yellowlees, though a pleasant person, was not tough enough either with us Ministers or with the BMA. His predecessor Sir George Godber, had been a commanding figure of quite exceptional calibre and had stood up even to Dick Crossman. I told Barbara that the officials in the Department did not really understand our rows, 'They don't realize that we can argue like that but that basically we agree.' Barbara replied that if we had had someone like George Godber, who would have argued ferociously with us, we should not have had to conduct so much of the argument between ourselves. I took her point, saying, 'Yes, I shouldn't then have felt I had to put so much of the medical point of view.'

On many occasions, as is clear from her *Diaries*, I believed that a greater readiness to compromise would have meant less confrontation. But Barbara revelled in confrontation. When it came, her adrenalin pumped round and she saw everything in terms of a battle that had to be won. On one occasion, after being up all night negotiating with the doctors, with the sun rising over the Elephant and Castle and all sane people in bed, Barbara was still at it, seizing on the wording of a particular sentence, juggling it around and sending it back to the BMA. They, poor blighters, then agreed, more I suspected out of exhaustion than conviction.

Eventually she went too far. We already had the consultants working to rule and the junior hospital doctors in the north-west stepping up their unofficial industrial action, with newspaper headlines like 'BLAME CASTLE IF PATIENTS DIE'. To cap it all the GPs were getting restless. Barbara seemed to me to be interested only in keeping the Left in the Party happy by getting a tough commitment on pay beds in the Queen's Speech. I was getting more and more apprehensive about the developing risks to patients' lives.

Harold Wilson must also have been worried for he then intervened, ringing her up and casually suggesting that she might have a private word with Arnold Goodman, who had been retained by the Independent Hospitals Group to fight the pay-beds legislation. Barbara knew then that if she did not compromise soon Harold Wilson would settle the issue over her head. Simultaneously the profession met with the Prime Minister in No. 10 Downing Street to try and persuade him to refer the whole pay-beds issue to the Royal Commission which it had been agreed would be set up to look at the NHS as a whole. This would have been a very bad move since the Royal Commission was not an appropriate vehicle and would have got bogged down in this relatively unimportant issue. It was designed to examine the NHS in all its aspects and I had juggled the membership to ensure that it was at least composed of sympathizers, not antagonists to its principles. Barbara just managed to persuade Harold to let her keep the negotiations in her own hands but she was now being watched carefully from No. 10.

She initially met with Arnold in secret without letting me know. I then joined Barbara, her political adviser, Jack Straw, her Private Secretary, Norman Warner, and Sir Patrick Nairne, her new Permanent Under-Secretary, in clandestine meetings with Arnold Goodman and the BMA. We met in Arnold's flat in Portland Place so as not to alert the press and in ten days of almost continuous negotiation, by telephone, paper and meetings, we bridged the gap. It soon became apparent that we made more progress when Barbara was not in direct contact with the BMA. At some points I would meet Arnold in the hall of his flat to compare notes. I would then return to Barbara, he to the BMA. Arnold's relationship with the BMA was rather an odd one. He had declined to take any fee and he used to adopt a bullying tone with them when we were present, I suspect as much to impress Barbara with his impartiality as anything else. She, however, remained suspicious of Arnold, describing him as being slippery as an eel. She suspected, almost certainly correctly, that he was reporting her every move to Harold Wilson behind her back. Eventually these rather odd negotiations bore fruit – agreement was reached to phase out pay beds with an independent board charged with arbitrating on the speed of the phasing so as to allow sufficient time for alternative private facilities to be built up. I genuinely hoped that the agreement would carry support across party lines.

Harold Wilson's resignation took place at a special Cabinet meeting on the morning of 16 March 1976. It came as no surprise to me because Roy Jenkins had told me when walking after lunch at Buttermere in early January that Wilson was going to resign. Roy did not tell me then who had tipped him off but it later emerged that it was Arnold Goodman, acting on Harold Wilson's instructions. As I discussed with Roy in January what we should do to organize over the next few months, I felt he was listless and not even enthused about the prospect of standing. He felt that he could not tell any of his friends and I was surprised that he had told me. Jim Callaghan has revealed that he was told at about the same time by Harold Lever and it was confirmed to him directly by Harold Wilson after his sixtieth birthday party on 11 March.

There are many murky rumours surrounding Wilson's surprising resignation in 1976. Some of them were perhaps fed by the same people involved in the misinformation and denigration that did undoubtedly stem from MI5 in the early 1970s in relation to Northern Ireland. I was also named in this campaign, as was Merlyn Rees. Whether my label as a subversive was due to my support, back in 1966, for the human rights movement in Northern Ireland I do not know. I had come across sloppy MI5 labelling once before, when I was Navy Minister. Jim Callaghan was then Home Secretary and he told me over lunch in the Members' dining room how an ashen faced civil servant had arrived in his room to say that a traitor had been unmasked and that it was a Labour MP, David Owen. Jim's reaction was one of disbelief. When they checked back with MI5 they found it was the Labour MP Will Owen, not me, who was under suspicion. Will Owen was in fact acquitted at the Central Criminal Court in May 1970 of passing state secrets to Czechoslovakia.

The explanation I favour for Harold Wilson's resignation is that he had some health problem in the early 1970s and that he had promised his wife, Mary, when it was discovered, that he would not stay long if he won the election. Whether or not this was true, Wilson knew that a round of public cuts was inevitable and he understandably after the success of the referendum on the EEC could not face having to preside over yet another dismal period of IMF-induced expenditure constraint and internal Party strife.

Three weeks later, at the age of sixty-four, Jim Callaghan became Prime Minister. I never for one moment believed that Roy would beat Jim and I suspect nor did Roy. I tried, as did others, to whip up some enthusiasm for him among Labour MPs but he just did not have the basic support. Most of his potential voters had sensed some years before that his moment was past and they had switched allegiance. In the main their votes had gone to Jim Callaghan, with a few going to Denis Healey. Once the result of the first ballot was known, Roy was determined to withdraw. Tony Crosland, who was bottom of the poll, automatically dropped out. There was no need for Roy to do so but he had lost any stomach he might once have had for the contest. I felt disinclined even to try to persuade him to keep his name on the ballot. I was then rung up by Denis asking for my vote and I promised that I would vote for him on the second ballot, though I could see he had no chance of beating Jim. Barbara Castle reports in her *Diaries* that she tried to persuade me to vote for Michael Foot in the final ballot. She did so but, if I gave her the impression that there was any hope of my voting for Michael, that was purely tactical. But I cannot say I was a great enthusiast for Jim Callaghan.

Roy Jenkins was not surprised to lose but he was hurt when Jim Callaghan kept him at the Home Office, making it plain he was not prepared to risk the uneasy truce in the Party over the European Community by appointing Roy Foreign Secretary. Jim judged that Tony Crosland would arouse less suspicion. It was also a matter of personality; Jim liked Tony and disapproved of Roy. I suspect too that, knowing from his own time as Foreign Secretary that they would be thrust into constant contact, he thought that it would be more enjoyable travelling with Tony Crosland. Roy, who had already been sounded out by Harold Wilson over whether he would like to be President of the European Commission, later went to see Jim Callaghan and he agreed to nominate him as President. Since both Giscard d'Estaing and Helmut Schmidt had indicated they would like Roy to take the job there was little doubt it would be his.

I had told Roy after a meal at East Hendred that I thought he should accept the Presidency. It was not, as some people later alleged during our leadership contest in 1982, done brutally or in an unkindly way. We discussed the options in a warm and affectionate mood. There was no sense of pushing him out of British politics and my advice was in line with a decision he had already virtually made in his own mind. I felt that if he stayed his frustration level would rise and I feared conflict with Jim and resignation in a fit of pique. Roy made it clear he would stay active and not rule out coming back to the House of Commons, though I was very sceptical of that ever happening.

One of Jim's first acts as Prime Minister was to sack Barbara Castle, with whom he had never got on. It was a sad end to a distinguished career. Politics is a brutal business and it would have been kinder for Jim to have let her carry the pay-beds legislation and relieve her of office in the summer. But he must have felt a need to put his own stamp on the Government and Barbara was very much a part of Harold's era. David Ennals succeeded her. Barbara then insisted on going on the Committee of the Pay Beds Bill and we had to put up with her brooding presence, like Banquo's ghost, zealously guarding every line of her sacred agreement. When Labour lost the election, the Conservatives repealed our legislation and the whole exercise proved to be fruitless. I, who had supported the phasing out of pay beds, learnt a valuable lesson, namely that reforms have to have a reasonable chance of taking root for it to be worth embarking on legislation in the first place. It is a lesson that I doubt Barbara ever accepted.

I admired Barbara Castle. She is a lady of quality and one of our great women politicians. She had the ability to be the first woman Prime Minister had the Labour Party not then been so deeply chauvinistic. Harold Wilson had wanted to give her serious economic responsibilities in 1968 but this was blocked by Roy Jenkins as Chancellor of the Exchequer who did not want a repeat of the divided responsibility for economic questions which had haunted Labour from 1964–66 with Jim Callaghan at the Treasury and George Brown at the Department of Economic Affairs. She was an excellent Minister for Overseas Development and an innovative Minister of Transport. The main thrust of her proposals as Secretary of State for Employment, 'In Place of Strife', were correctly judged and her courage in standing by them was exemplary. Even six years later, though past her prime, as Secretary of State for Health and Social Security she had the ability to grasp the core of any problem. She had a formidable intellect and instinctive judgement which, in government, usually triumphed over ideology. Only in Opposition did she revert to being a rather typical Left-wing member of the National Executive Committee, where ideology governed intellect. She could also abandon her prejudices. I remember, for example, persuading her to go to the Play Group Movement's annual meeting. Begrudgingly she agreed but was dismissive of my claim that they were a splendidly irreverent and radical force in society. She came back enthused and started to lecture me about their merits and how we should help. Typical Barbara!

Above all she had tremendous fighting spirit which permeated everything. One of her favourite and true sayings was that politics is all about guts. From the outside she appeared as tough as nails but there was a softer streak which one saw when she talked about or involved her husband, Ted. I increasingly felt that this streak should have been more visible but if it had been she might not have survived in the still depressingly male-dominated world of politics. She survived on her sheer toughness. One night she fell and hurt her leg quite badly but insisted on staying and voting into the early hours of the morning. After I had helped her home and into her flat, the last thing she said was that she had to write her diary before going to bed. Most of us would have gone to bed and written it when we woke up. But then the great value of her *Diaries* is that they were despatches written from the battlefield. They lack objectivity but they convey immediacy.

Barbara was feminine and proud of it. Sometimes in our all-night negotiating sessions, when I was exhausted and longing for sleep, I would look across at her, immaculate, not a hair out of place, her stockings smooth, her skirt uncrumpled and would be amazed that I was looking at a woman of sixty-five. She seemed more like someone in her late forties. Of course she could be impossible at times. She simply had to toughen up any negotiating position she was presented with: so much so in fact that sometimes I used deliberately to propose something slightly weaker than I wanted in the full knowledge that she would strengthen it. We would then achieve a position which was at least negotiable. However, she was always open to argument and I knew that if my case was strong I could usually convince her. Most of her criticisms of me in her *Diaries* have some substance and are perceptive.

Barbara Castle had many of the characteristics which later came to be associated with Margaret Thatcher. Interestingly, she respected Margaret Thatcher from the moment she was chosen as Leader of the Conservative Party in February 1975. Her diary entries make this clear and they tally with my recollection of what she was saying at the time. While Margaret Thatcher was only a candidate fighting Heath, Barbara wrote:

> The papers are full of Margaret Thatcher. She has lent herself with grace and charm to every piece of photographer's gimmickry, but don't we all when the prize is big enough? What interests me now is how blooming she looks – she has never been prettier. I am interested because I understand this phenomenon. She may have been up late on the Finance Bill Committee; she is beset by enemies and has to watch every gesture and word. But she sails through it all looking her best. I understand why. She is in love: in love with power, success – and with herself. She looks as I looked when Harold made me Minister of Transport. If we have to have Tories, good luck to her!

That is a description one would not hear from a male MP – the open admission of being in love with power and success is not something men find easy to acknowledge and it also shows the solidarity of a woman across the political divide in the man's world of politics. I wonder whether Margaret Thatcher ever had reciprocal views about Barbara. It was as so often on the floor of the House of Commons, where leaders are made or unmade, that Margaret Thatcher made her own victory possible. In January 1975 the *Daily Telegraph* had already referred to her as having 'dimples of iron' and Denis Healey was not getting it all his own way in the economic debate. He had referred to her as 'La Pasionaria of privilege'. To be compared with Dolores Ibarruri, the Spanish communist whose fiery speeches instilled confidence into those fighting in the Civil War, was a tribute not an insult. But Margaret Thatcher decided to hit back hard: 'Some Chancellors are micro-economic, some Chancellors are fiscal. This one is just plain cheap.' Conservative doubts about her fighting capacity as a woman were laid to rest. From that moment on Heath was in trouble. On the first ballot she had 130 votes and Heath only 119. Heath resigned and on a second ballot she trounced the Establishment's candidate, Willie Whitelaw, with 146 votes to Whitelaw's seventy-nine; Howe and Prior had only eleven apiece. The Conservative Party had chosen a new Leader who was to become its most atypical and radical Prime Minister since Disraeli.

Not many people believed in 1975 that Margaret Thatcher would be a threat to Labour. Barbara sensed it immediately and I remember being surprised at that assessment. It showed that her political antennae were well tuned to the voters of middle England, even if her own political stance was anathema to them. She understood people, even when she disagreed with them.

Then, in September, the Prime Minister rang to ask if I would go to the Foreign and Commonwealth Office as Tony Crosland's deputy in place of Roy Hattersley who was going into the Cabinet. I was delighted, though I should have liked to go into the Cabinet myself. I managed to mention this in passing to Jim and he said that after I had widened my experience he would certainly not rule it out. He emphasized that my task was to prepare for and carry through our six-month Presidency of the Community and he implied he would consider another move up for me after July 1977. Meanwhile, since for much of the time I would be putting the British case in the Council of Foreign Ministers, I would have a responsible position.

I left the Elephant and Castle at the best time. Health expenditure had increased every year. Barbara had fought the Department's corner with the Chief Secretary of the Treasury, Joel Barnett, very effectively – probably too effectively for the good of the economy. Health spending was now 6 per cent of GDP having increased by a full 1 per cent over the last two years – the biggest step-like increase in the history of the NHS. Sadly, the weakness of our economy meant that it was not capable of being sustained and in relative terms health spending slipped back over the remaining years of the Labour Government. But I enjoyed myself and it had been perhaps the most fulfilling two-and-a-half years of my life.

PART THREE

FOREIGN SECRETARY

II

THE FOREIGN OFFICE

The Secretary of State for India's Oval Office is a small but beautifully proportioned room with a striking curved window looking out over St James's Park. On the south-west side of the room are two doorways, designed to allow visiting Indian princes of equal rank to enter the room simultaneously so that neither lost face. There is also an exquisite domed ceiling. It was in the midst of this splendour that, as Minister of State in the Foreign Office, I now found myself authorizing or querying expenditure often of only a few thousand pounds. In the Ministry of Health, from my ugly glass box overlooking the railway line at the Elephant and Castle, I rarely saw any spending proposal that was not expressed in millions. The Diplomatic Service employed six thousand people; the Department of Health was responsible for over a million. The contrast was immense. Now every day I was dropped off at the Foreign Office entrance by the statue of Clive of India and I almost felt as if the Empire were still with us. Nor for my generation, who can still remember school maps with the British Empire coloured pink and covering a quarter of the globe, is the Empire a totally remote concept. Our childhood reading – whether old copies of *Chums*, *Boys Own* or books and poems – was often rooted in Empire. Perhaps that gave me too nostalgic a view of our imperial past without an appreciation of the offsetting realities of having lived through the harshness and the problems of exercising power across such vast and diverse cultures.

My main task was to brief myself thoroughly on the European Community. As I did, it dawned on me that the UK really did have a lousy deal. The Agricultural Policy, which we had always known worked against our interests, was out of control – big surpluses were building up in milk products, olive oil and wine and costs were soaring. It was also clear that in a few years' time the UK budgetary contribution would rise so much that we were quite likely to find ourselves the nation making the largest contribution. We also had to cope with a Fishing Policy which had been cobbled up by the original Six members on the eve of the

Community's expansion and which could hardly have been more unhelpful to UK fishing interests. On top of this we had Iceland drastically limiting our fishing rights. In those early weeks I was almost driven to conclude that Harold Wilson had been right after all in 1971 and that the terms had been unacceptable. Certainly they were far more adverse than I had ever realized and it was clear that we would face a grinding, acrimonious debate to recoup lost ground. Yet talking to Foreign Office officials, with some notable exceptions, I found the senior diplomats so dismissive, even light-hearted, about these realities that I soon despaired of being able to develop a tough negotiating stance which we would stick to.

The Head of the Diplomatic Service, Michael Palliser, had had a brilliant career, having been Private Secretary to Harold Wilson in No. 10 and a key figure in the negotiations over entry to the European Community. He was married to Marie-Louise, the charming, kind and sensitive daughter of the former Belgian Prime Minister, Paul Henri Spaak, one of the founding fathers of the European Community. Michael was an Old Etonian and had served as an officer in the Brigade of Guards but he was neither stuffy nor class conscious. I liked and respected him. The problem I had with the Foreign Office was never over Africa, Israel or any of the world's flashpoints, it was overwhelmingly over the European Community. The problem was, however, deep-seated. Too many of the Euro-diplomats were reluctant to embark on any course which put us at serious loggerheads with the majority of Community members. They were intelligent people but they never had the tenacity to fight for British interests in the same way as the French diplomats fight at every level for France. The French Foreign Office at the Quai d'Orsay infiltrate the Commission systematically with high-flying officials who know they have a direct route back to top posts in Paris. They talk European and think France. The Germans have no such equivalent. Probably the Dutch are nearest the French in defending and championing their interests. Until we build up a core of élite European officials drawn from the Treasury and the Foreign Office and inculcate in them a pride in British interests and the determination to uphold those interests we will never challenge the domination of France within the Community. In France their Euro-officials give the impression when working in the Commission that they are dedicated to a wider vision of a United States of Europe, but they channel this impression in ways which safeguard French interests. It is a very sophisticated operation.

Many of the British diplomats by contrast are Euro-federalists, believe in an eventual United States of Europe and do think this is a higher calling than the more mundane task of fighting the British corner. Few of the very best would dream of serving in the Commission, believing rightly that it would not help their promotion prospects in the Foreign Office or the Treasury. The nearest they will go to the Commission is to serve in cabinets of British Commissioners.

It is a feature of life that sects within a faith often have greater difficulty in working together harmoniously than they have in their relationship with non-believers. So it was over Europe. They and I clashed, sometimes fairly violently, because we all believed in Europe. It was not a matter of indifference to them or to me, Europe was high on both of our lists of priorities. Trouble arose because we differed over what sort of European Community the UK had joined in 1973 and what its future shape should be. I believed the Community should be a union of independent nations, they believed it had to develop into a single state. The Foreign Office generally keeps coming back to the intentions of the founding fathers. No one can deny that these wanted an eventual European state, but that ignores what people and countries have wished since General de Gaulle won his battle for the recognition of a veto with the Luxembourg compromise. Moreover, Edward Heath specifically disavowed a federalist intention at the time of British entry. To argue later that a United States of Europe is what Britain signed up for is retrospectively to change the interpretation of the kind of Community we entered.

Yet I was only Minister of State; policy questions were determined ultimately by Tony Crosland. When I took over from him I was immensely grateful, however, for the detailed knowledge I had acquired earlier. I vowed then to shift the whole emphasis of the Foreign Office to a more self-confident, assertive stance towards the Community. I suspect the Labour Government's problems with Euro-federalists over those years would have been more difficult if our Permanent Representative in Brussels had been anyone other than Sir Donald Maitland. A diminutive, determined Scot, he had all their best qualities. His speciality was as an Arabist. He had been Edward Heath's impartial and fair-minded Press Secretary in No. 10 and went on to be our representative at the UN just before the 1974 Election. He was then rather abruptly shunted aside for Ivor Richard, giving the impression that Labour did not trust him. In fact he was a fine public servant. Anyone who has survived being bullied by George Brown, as Private Secretary, and then served Edward Heath as Press Secretary, has staying power. His career ended as Permanent Under-Secretary for the Department of Energy, an excellent example of the interchange between the Home and Diplomatic Service which must be made even more extensive if we are to develop our membership of the Community as an integral part of the governance of the UK.

He handled me superbly and he and his wife made my frequent visits to Brussels a far more enjoyable experience than they would otherwise have been. Dealing with all the complex issues with calm precision, he was ready to fight the UK corner with tenacity and skill, even if he did not agree the ministerial line. It was easier to be convinced by him that a particular course was wrong because I felt that he too could be converted by discussion.

The biggest source of friction I had to contend with at the Foreign Office was a relatively small number of senior diplomats who had got used to having a campaigning role over the European Community and had built up strong links with journalists sympathetic to Europe. Over the years they had been given more political licence by Conservative and Labour politicians than is normal for officials. In the process some of them had become zealots for the European Community and all its works and were none too keen to accept political control. In particular, they found it hard to understand that my determination to spill a little blood on the diplomatic carpets of Europe from time to time was not playing to anti-European sentiment but stemmed from the belief that having a sticking point and being prepared to stand one's ground on occasions was necessary to protect British interests. They also did not comprehend that my distaste and disdain for moves designed to pave the way for the Euro-federalists' dream, the United States of Europe, was all of a piece with my long-standing and strong commitment to Britain's playing a full part in the European Community. The principal pro-European politicians with whom they were in contact, like Edward Heath, Roy Jenkins and Jo Grimond, were federalists and when I joined the Foreign Office they too easily assumed, due to my resignation with Roy, that I would be too.

The Foreign Office had also developed a passionate commitment to the Arab cause as well as to the European Community. Why there is this marked Arab identification among British diplomats is the subject of much speculation. Some see it as a phenomenon similar to the fascination that Arabia held for T.E. Lawrence, others to a basic British anti-Semitism. The Foreign Office explanation is that there is only one Israel and many Arab countries and therefore many more diplomats serve in Arab countries and learn to empathize with the Arabs and their support for the Palestinian cause. The other factor is that over the years oil has been a vital British interest, first because we had none of our own and then because we needed to co-operate as we became through the North Sea a significant oil producer.

By contrast, many British politicians have always admired Israel's democracy and the courage of its people. They have developed strong links with Israeli politicians. It was Israel that was the issue on which Ernest Bevin, when Foreign Secretary, had the most trouble with the Labour Party. Though Bevin was a great Foreign Secretary, it was widely felt that his attitude to the Palestinian problem was far too pro-Arab and quite unduly influenced by the Foreign Office. Sir Alec Douglas-Home and Edward Heath have been the Prime Ministers most critical of Israel; Winston Churchill, Harold Wilson and Margaret Thatcher her most deeply committed friends.

The Foreign and Commonwealth Office has other legacies, some inherited from the separate ministries which it has absorbed and which brought their own traditions and attitudes. In 1920 the staffs of the

Foreign Office at home and the Diplomatic Service abroad were amalgamated. In 1943 Consuls and Commercial Officers were joined to the Foreign Office. In 1947 the India Office and the Dominions Office became the Commonwealth Relations Office. The Colonial Office remained separate until 1966 when it was merged with the Commonwealth Relations Office. Then in 1968 a single Foreign and Commonwealth Office was formed. Those who were not from the Foreign Office tended to be rough diamonds, less polished than the diplomats. There were still, in my time, old Africa hands who had been District Officers and I found them good allies and very keen to stand firm against Mr Smith in Rhodesia.

The Foreign Office has been likened to a Rolls-Royce, so efficiently does it serve its politicians. It is, however, far from being a machine – personalities play a very big part. It is, primarily, a reactive organization, with sensitive tentacles everywhere in the world, though not so well developed within Whitehall. It is alert for and reports on every nuance of international affairs. The main anxiety people have about the Foreign Office stems from its reputation as being the home of appeasers. This began with its pre-war involvement in, and support for, Chamberlain's appeasement policy which culminated in Munich. Post-war, the Foreign Office had a shadowy role – shared with most of our leading politicians – over whether or when to join the European Community. Britain's failure in 1956 to attend the Messina Conference which negotiated the terms of the Rome Treaty was a refusal to help shape the European Community. It was the major error of our post-war foreign policy. The Foreign Office, however, was not alone in being slow to anticipate the development of European unity. Politicians of the calibre of Attlee and Bevin, Churchill and Eden, saw European unity as a purely continental matter, desirable for those countries but not a matter to trouble ourselves with. The Foreign Office was vigorous in its internal opposition to Eden's ill-fated Suez venture, taking the lead from its Arabists, and on this occasion was proved right. Foreign Office diplomats also had a good record in support-ing the free spirits in Eastern Europe and were always in favour of the eventual reunification of Germany. So the Foreign Office's record of being proved correct on foreign policy questions is a mixed one. As to their tendency to split the difference, that is part of the art of diplomacy. Any lack of backbone in the operation of foreign policy is a reflection on the personalities involved, the Foreign Secretary in particular, rather than the Foreign Office itself. If the Foreign Secretary is weak, the official view predominates and that too reflects personality, especially that of the Permanent Under-Secretary. With the new generation of senior diplomats in the 1990s the tendency towards appeasement is fading. But it was there in the Foreign Office from the 1920s to the 1980s and at times became the predominant mood. I hope it never returns.

In September 1976 Tony Crosland's mind was on the looming domestic financial crisis and, apart from the fishing interests of his constituency, he had no great enthusiasm for the detail of the European Community. It is easy to see why the domestic crisis preoccupied Tony at this time. The great weakness of all Labour Governments has been their inability to restrain public spending in their early years. Instead the discipline has had to come from external pressures. This depressing pattern started with Ramsay MacDonald's Labour Government which split in 1931 over the need for economies in order to raise short-term credit. Stafford Cripps's period as Chancellor came after the free-spending Hugh Dalton had resigned in 1947 and was haunted by the need to limit spending up to and beyond devaluation, a problem later exacerbated by the costs of rearmament for the Korean War. It was surprising that Wilson had not learnt the public expenditure lesson from his first period in office but Jim Callaghan had and in 1976 he was determined to change the Government's spending pattern. Even Harold Wilson must have been aware of the risks he was running in keeping expenditure levels up in 1975. But by then he wanted the European referendum to be won and he knew that the referendum was far more likely to endorse staying in the Community if the economy was buoyant. Harold Wilson had hoped to resign soon after the referendum in 1975 but the economic deterioration led him to postpone his resignation.

When Jim Callaghan became Prime Minister in April 1976 he knew that before many months had passed he would have to persuade his colleagues to submit to financial constraints dictated by the International Monetary Fund. In his autobiography Jim recalls that the day after taking office on 15 April he met with the Governor of the Bank of England, Gordon Richardson, and writes that it was uncannily like stepping back twelve years and listening, as the new Chancellor of the Exchequer, to the then Governor, Lord Cromer. The message was about the weakness of sterling, the fact that the United States was gloomy about its future and that the borrowing requirement was too high, threatening to crowd out much needed private investment.

My attitude to Jim Callaghan became much more positive at the Labour Party Conference at Blackpool while listening to his speech on 28 September. I felt that, for the first time since Roy Jenkins opened his Budget in 1968, someone in the Labour Party leadership was really grappling honestly with the economic situation facing the country. That speech is renowned for the words widely attributed to Peter Jay:

> We used to think that you could spend your way out of recession and increase employment by cutting taxes and boosting Government spending. I tell you in all candour that that option no longer exists, and that insofar as it ever did exist, it only worked on each occasion since the war by injecting a bigger dose of inflation into the economy, followed by a higher level of unemployment as the next step. Higher inflation followed by higher unemployment. We have just escaped from the

highest rate of inflation this country has known; we have not yet escaped from the consequences: high unemployment. That is the history of the last twenty years.

It was a brave speech. The Conference audience recognized it as such and, in the main, responded warmly to its frankness. The next day, from the Imperial Hotel in Blackpool, Jim Callaghan rang President Ford to warn him that we would need a stand-by loan from the International Monetary Fund and a safety net for sterling.

From then on, the more I saw of him as Prime Minister the more I admired Jim Callaghan. He was an example of someone who grew in office. Having achieved his ambition he relaxed more and lost his personal chippiness and wholly unwarranted sense of inferiority. Though he never went to university, he had a good mind and considerable experience and his leadership qualities now came to the fore. The Cabinet began to trust each other and the Downing Street press office stopped denigrating Cabinet colleagues. The one exception was Tony Benn whom Jim could never understand, though he tried hard. Ministers were supported even when they had made mistakes. An atmosphere of genuine trust started to emanate from No. 10. It was a wonderful change from Wilson's paranoia and was a formidable transformation. So it was that 'Honest Jim' became the public image and fortunately it had real substance to back it up.

On 18 November the Prime Minister told the Cabinet that the Government was at a critical phase in its life and that the negotiations with the IMF team which were needed to secure its support would prove crucial. I became indirectly involved in these Cabinet discussions because Tony Crosland was deeply unhappy with Denis Healey's demands as Chancellor for planned levels of public spending to be reduced. Tony felt that, with over one and a quarter million people unemployed, there was enough spare capacity to allow exports to rise and that further public expenditure cutbacks would destroy trade union co-operation to keep wages down and lower industrial costs. He could see a value in cosmetic expenditure cuts for IMF purposes and was ready to sell the Government shares in Burmah Oil but he was not prepared to jeopardize the so-called Social Contract between Government and unions. Tony, for a period, led the opposition to Denis Healey in the Cabinet, talking frequently to Shirley Williams, Roy Hattersley, Bill Rodgers, David Ennals and Harold Lever. Nine Cabinet meetings were held during a period of three weeks and Tony Crosland ensured that I saw all the relevant papers while he agonized over what he should do. Neither of us liked the idea of further cutbacks in social spending but I could sense that Tony was becoming more and more anxious about Jim's personal position and recognized that he could not be disowned without the whole Government collapsing. What changed Tony's initially relaxed response to all the international pressures was Helmut Schmidt's stance when Tony and Jim discussed the matter with the German Chancellor at the European Council meeting in The Hague at the end of November. On his return Tony told me that if even Schmidt would not help in restraining the IMF's demands there was no escaping its draconian discipline, however economically illiterate it was. The Cabinet finally agreed the IMF package with Tony Crosland siding with the Prime Minister, more out of loyalty than conviction. In retrospect I believe Tony was wrong on the substance. If your economy is weak it is impossible in an increasingly global economic market to ignore the perceptions, even if mistaken, of the international financial community.

Watching the IMF discussions from the sidelines convinced me that modern Cabinet Government becomes almost impossible unless the four most senior Cabinet Ministers resolve any differences before they come to full Cabinet. It becomes very difficult to handle Cabinet discussion, let alone Cabinet cohesion, if the Chancellor of the Exchequer, the Foreign Secretary or the Home Secretary disagree openly in Cabinet with the Prime Minister. It is incumbent on them to discuss issues thoroughly, to try very hard to agree, and to only go to Cabinet to fight their corner as a last resort. In the end Tony Crosland put his loyalty to Jim first. He was experienced enough to know that the Cabinet could not reject Jim Callaghan's advice once he had declared his support for the Chancellor of the Exchequer.

That experience also convinced me that the relaxed attitude to public expenditure favoured by those of us close to Tony Crosland needed to be considerably revised. 'Sound money' could be scoffed at but without it inflation eroded the social purposes of public expenditure. Ever since 1976 I have been far more cautious about expanding public spending and far more resistant to accepting inflation as the price of growth. Denis Healey had learnt that lesson and started monetary targets and monetary discipline in his last few years as Chancellor of the Exchequer, with my full support. It is a myth fostered by the Labour Party in Opposition that monetarism started with Margaret Thatcher.

On Sunday 13 February, Tony Crosland had a stroke at his country home in Adderbury, Oxford. My family and I were staying with Prue and Malcolm Borthwick in Essex. Malcolm had been best man at my wedding and Prue was Tristan's godmother. I was called up by Ewen Fergusson, Tony Crosland's Private Secretary, and told that Tony was ill, and from his tone and brief description I could sense that it was serious, for Tony was partly paralysed. I was shocked, even though I had guessed for some time, travelling with him in Europe, that Tony was not well. In 1971 he had been diagnosed as having high blood pressure and that is one of the commonest causes of strokes. His lifestyle, the long hours, good food, little exercise, alcohol and cigars could not have helped.

It was hard to accept that a life so full should now be ebbing away.

Only a few weeks before he, Susan, Debbie and I had had lunch together in the kitchen of their house in Lansdowne Road. Susan had cooked an excellent meal. Tony and I had drunk too much and Tony had gossiped deliciously and flippantly about the diplomats we knew, all in a haze of cigar smoke. We had driven back together for a meeting at the Foreign Office and I had gone to my room to pick up my papers. By the time I arrived Tony had started the meeting and he had looked up ferociously and berated me for being late. The officials seemed rather stunned. Only Ewen Fergusson was grinning broadly, knowing that we had had lunch together.

Tony loved to tease. He particularly enjoyed teasing the European press. On one of the last occasions I was with him we had been up most of the night negotiating once again in Brussels over fish. Tony had been in the chair as President of the Council of Foreign Ministers and I had argued the British case. The Council started at 10 a.m. on Tuesday and finished at 5 a.m. on Wednesday. After the Council – as dawn broke – Tony had to brief the press. He was in hilarious form and we all laughed our way through the complex fish quotas we had been discussing and which he, as the MP for Grimsby, was the only one fully to understand. We then flew back to Northolt military airport so that we could all be back in the Foreign Office for a normal working day on the Wednesday. The strain of such a lifestyle was bound to tell.

When I returned to London on that Sunday evening, I had a telephone call from Jim Callaghan. He asked about Tony's condition and I told him that from what little I knew it sounded as if he had had a stroke, with a blood clot on the brain, rather than just an arterial spasm. He questioned me about how much work Tony had been doing and if I had noticed whether or not he had been ill. He then asked me to look after the Department and not to hesitate to let him know if there were any problems. So, on Monday morning, I went to my own room in the Foreign Office and prepared to look at areas of policy in which I had not been previously involved. I was quickly thrown in at the deep end. Ewen Fergusson came in to tell me that there was an important meeting on Rhodesia that afternoon and he felt that I should chair it. After some thought about exactly what was appropriate, we decided to hold it in Tony's room since we could not fit everyone into mine. We agreed that I would continue to work from my own room for the rest of the time.

I had not been involved in policy over Rhodesia at any time before for it was handled mainly by Tony Crosland as Secretary of State. The ill-fated Geneva Conference had been Tony's initiative to build on Henry Kissinger's proposals for a Council of State, half-white and half-black. The objective of the Conference was to thrash out arrangements for an interim Government which would eventually lead to black majority rule in Rhodesia. In September 1976 Ian Smith had for the first time publicly conceded 'majority rule' in two years but, far from being a change of heart, this just served as a platform for his own delaying tactics. Smith attended the conference in Geneva merely to agree the nuts and bolts of Kissinger's Council of State. The black Rhodesian leaders, however, were in the main totally opposed to a Council of State. The ill-fated Geneva Conference was adjourned in December 1976 after seven weeks of unsuccessful and largely acrimonious negotiation. During the Geneva Conference I had read most of the main telegrams from Ivor Richard, who was acting as the Chairman though his real job was as our Permanent Representative at the United Nations in New York. Ivor was a former Labour MP who had lost his Barons Court seat in February 1974. After the collapse of the Conference he had visited Southern Africa but since most people there regarded the Geneva Conference as a dead duck he had had a rather difficult reception. The more I read of the background papers, the more complex it all seemed.

My attitude was also influenced by a more personal encounter. A few weeks before, I had had dinner with my cousin, who had been critical of Tony over Rhodesia. 'He keeps telling us on television that Rhodesia is the most serious problem facing the world and Britain,' he said, 'and yet all I see is him in London or Brussels, not even going to Geneva or Southern Africa, while the situation deteriorates.' That made me think very hard. I knew that Tony was working long hours on Rhodesia, indeed it was the dominant issue on his agenda, yet here was my cousin, intelligent if apolitical, totally unaware of the extent of Tony's involvement. Tony might have made eleven foreign trips in three months but by not identifying himself publicly with Rhodesia he was in danger of being judged as doing too little.

With the meeting due that afternoon, Ivor Richard asked to see me. He came into my room, sat down on the sofa and proceeded to tell me what to do about Rhodesia. Whether it was his manner or whether it was because he seemed to show few signs of wanting to rethink policy after the collapse of the Geneva Conference I decided to keep an open mind.

I then spoke to Ted Rowlands, who had been junior Minister in the Department since 1975 and had been focusing on Africa. I had not had many dealings with him before but I had always felt that he had a good feel for politics; presumably this was why Jim Callaghan had liked having him as a young colleague. He warned me against seeing any merit in an internal settlement which involved only Mr Smith's regime and the black nationalist leaders inside Rhodesia. An internal settlement was deliberately designed to exclude Mugabe and Nkomo. He was very worried about an internal settlement and put down a strong marker against accepting any advice in that direction. He clearly felt that the Geneva approach had failed. The more I heard, the more I felt it necessary to stand back and try to analyse what had been the main stumbling blocks to the success of the Geneva Conference.

I chaired the meeting that afternoon, feeling uneasy. Sir Anthony

Duff, the Deputy Permanent Under-Secretary, was present. He was a former High Commissioner to Kenya and an experienced Africa hand. Ivor Richard and Ted Rowlands were also there. So were a whole range of other people, none of whom I knew. I suppose everyone was haunted by thoughts of Tony Crosland and I began to regret that I had agreed to hold the meeting in Tony's room. We made no decisions of any substance.

It was a difficult week for everyone. Tony was dying and the Department was on hold. I took only those decisions that could not be postponed. On Wednesday 16 February I received a message to say that I was to attend the Cabinet on Thursday morning and that, rather surprisingly, the Prime Minister wanted me to feel free to speak on subjects other than foreign affairs. Before the meeting started, Jim asked me what I was going to speak on in Cabinet under the foreign affairs item. I had thought it had been arranged between our two Private Secretaries that there was nothing to report but Jim Callaghan mentioned subjects which he thought I should raise. In retrospect it is clear that he wanted me to speak at the Cabinet meeting because he had already decided to make me Foreign Secretary.

On Saturday 19 February, having been unconscious for some days, Tony Crosland died, with Susan and his two step-daughters at his bedside. Like so many people in the country I was deeply saddened. We had been friends, never very close, but in recent months getting closer. I admired his razor-sharp mind and his debonair style. I was enchanted by his gaiety, when he allowed it to break through, for it danced like rays of sunlight banishing the other impression of cynicism and world weariness.

On Monday 21 February Prince Saud (the Saudi Foreign Minister who still retains that position), the Prime Minister and I had lunch in the small dining room which links the big dining room and the reception rooms on the first floor of No. 10. Jim made no mention of who was to succeed Tony, though his mind must have been on this as well as his forthcoming tribute to Tony in the House. But he did keep joking about how young Prince Saud was, at only thirty-six. Later, down at the House, Jim gave a moving tribute to Tony Crosland, wistfully saying that he was 'gifted beyond the reach of many of us'.[2] The House was full and there was an overwhelming mood of sorrow for someone who had been such an attractive Member of the House – good looking, arrogant, rude and yet intellectually honest and fundamentally decent. The manner of his dying and the daily medical bulletins had moved the House more than Tony had ever done in his lifetime for he was never a great speaker. Yet everyone felt that something had gone from the Chamber of the Commons. There was a massive intellectual gap, and also, of course, an immediate political gap. Tony had undoubtedly seen himself succeeding Jim Callaghan as leader in a few years' time and so his death was also that of a lost leader.

I walked back to the Foreign Office wondering what Jim Callaghan would do and how it would affect me. There had been much speculation in the newspapers but it was all rather diffuse. A *Times* editorial had hinted at an interim arrangement where I might be asked to continue to run the Foreign Office until the Budget, which was not far off, and then Jim would move Denis across to be Foreign Secretary and appoint someone else as Chancellor of the Exchequer, bringing me into the Cabinet in a junior post. This was certainly the summit of my hopes. Denis Healey was definitely the favourite to succeed, with Edmund Dell taking over from him. Some suggested Shirley Williams for the Foreign Office and a few Roy Hattersley. No one suggested me.

When I arrived back in the Foreign Office my Private Secretary told me that No. 10 Downing Street had been on the telephone. Would I go and see the Prime Minister in his room in the House? I found Jim Callaghan sitting alone. He asked me to sit down and said simply, 'David, I am going to make you Foreign Secretary.' I was stunned. Jim says in his autobiography that I went as white as a sheet. It took me a few seconds to reply and then he said that this was not going to be a temporary appointment. He had discussed the situation with Denis Healey and Denis really did not quite know what he wanted to do. So, as Jim put it, he had decided the issue for him – he would stay at the Treasury. He would be telling the press that I was not a stop-gap appointment and that I should look on it as if I were going to remain Foreign Secretary for a reasonable period of time. The one warning he gave me was that if the good of the Government made a change necessary, by which I took him to mean if Denis Healey ran into serious political unpopularity as Chancellor of the Exchequer, then I could be moved to make room for him. But otherwise I could expect to stay until the election. The one thing over which he went out of his way to reassure me was that he was not promoting me to this seniority in Cabinet only to demote me in a few months' time. I left promising not to tell anyone until it was announced at 6 o'clock.

I felt it was impossible not to tell Debbie. So I went quietly back to the Foreign Office and mentioned casually that I was going home. When I got home, I took Debbie upstairs and sat her down on the bed. When I told her the news she was even more surprised than I. Hardly had I finished telling her when the telephone rang – the Prime Minister wanted to see me again. I drove up in my own car to the Commons. Jim was in his room, pacing up and down, anxious to get on with making the changes. He was clearly somewhat surprised that I had gone home. He suggested that my deputy should be Judith Hart. I had to react very quickly for I thought it would be a bad appointment. As a Left-winger Judith Hart had a long record of opposition to the European Community. To have her dealing with Europe would not be easy. I also did not want as deputy somebody who was older than I and had such a well known position in the Party. It was uncomfortable to have to reject Jim's first proposition in our new relationship but it had to be done. I suggested that I should have Frank Judd and that Judith Hart should in turn replace him by going back to Overseas Development. Though she would still come under me in the Foreign Office, it would be far easier to manage her if she had independence as Minister of Overseas Development, an issue where we were anyhow in broad sympathy. I knew Frank Judd would be very disappointed to be moved, having only just recently taken over from Reg Prentice, but I liked him and felt I could work well with him. Jim seemed sympathetic and promised to look at this, making it clear he had not as yet approached anyone.

I drove home again by myself. It would be the last time for two-and-a-quarter years that I would be alone in a car: tomorrow Detective-Superintendent Alan Dickinson would come. He was the most senior member of Tony's Scotland Yard protection team and a cultured, modest and delightful person. It would be hard to find anyone more considerate, discreet and pleasant. He managed an excellent team and at all times they were friends of the family. My two boys, in particular, enjoyed having them around and found them willing companions in football. But it is difficult to exaggerate the effect on one's personal freedom of being constantly accompanied, always having to think of the impact on the detectives of any change of plan. I enjoy my own company, finding strength in solitary reflection and peace in being alone. To have that curtailed was the single most unattractive feature of my new job.

Debbie and I decided we would not say anything to the press that night. There was more than enough news. We both needed time to think about my appointment without making any statements. We settled down to have supper alone and to talk. We quickly decided not to move to the Foreign Secretary's flat at the top of Carlton Gardens and instead to go on living in our own home. We also decided that Debbie would continue with her agency. The telephone rang pretty incessantly as we watched reaction on the television news bulletins. I spoke only to a few people from Plymouth and to close relatives. Debbie put off all newspaper commentators. Our telephone number was in the directory and, despite some very unpleasant anonymous calls, of which 'nigger lover' was the most printable, we have never gone ex-directory. The hardest task that night was to persuade the journalists and photographers assembled outside the door in Narrow Street to go home. At one time I even had to restrain Debbie from putting the dustbins out for that would have provided them with an unusual photocall. Eventually at about 11 o'clock they cleared away, bribed by our agreeing to a photocall next morning with the boys.

12

FOREIGN SECRETARY – THE FIRST THIRTY-TWO DAYS

Arriving for the first time as Foreign Secretary at the Ambassador's Entrance of the Foreign Office which overlooks Horse Guards Parade on that Tuesday morning, 22 February 1977, I felt a tinge of awe. I had already worked there for nearly six months. But today I was accompanied by a Special Branch detective and was now referred to by diplomats as Secretary of State. Every telegram that went out from the Foreign Office would have Owen at the bottom and a selection from the large number of those telegrams would come to me every day wherever I was in the world to provide a briefing system of immense value. Even something as simple as getting in the lift to my Private Office was a reminder of the history that lay behind my new post. It still travelled at the slow pace demanded by Ernie Bevin's doctors when he developed his heart condition.

My office too was full of history. The Secretary of State's room is the loveliest office in the whole of Whitehall with its big windows looking out west to St James's Park and north across Horse Guards Parade (xxii). It is huge; difficult to envisage as a working office. I used to imagine it with three double decker buses parked in a row. That is a slight exaggeration, but gives some indication of its size. Yet, particularly at night, it had a warmth and intimacy that evoked Sir Edward Grey in 1914 watching the lamps going out all over Europe. My desk faced the mantelpiece above which hung a portrait of Palmerston brought in by George Brown to replace one of George III. In those early days, with the Government about to lose its majority in the House of Commons, I thought I might stay in office for an even shorter time than Patrick Gordon-Walker. Only when I had been there for a decent interval did I feel confident enough to remove Palmerston and replace him with a painting of General Jung Bahdour Koowar Ranajee who was Prime Minister and Commander-in-Chief of Nepal at the age of thirty-two. Tony Benn was very sniffy about this picture, saying that at least Lord Palmerston was a British Foreign Secretary. The Ranajee picture, in its size and colour, matches the room's green and gold ceiling and walls, brown curtains and chairs but I took Tony's point and I later balanced this image of Empire by introducing a portrait of Oliver Cromwell. Lord Carrington perhaps not surprisingly removed that. But interestingly Ranajee still looks down on the Foreign Secretary's desk, a reminder of distant shores and broader responsibilities.

When the Israeli Prime Minister Begin came over to London he asked me if he could see my room because it was where the Balfour Declaration was signed in 1917. This Declaration was the first authoritative pledge to create a homeland for the Jews. As Begin walked in a hush fell and I sensed it was like a shrine for him. He was deeply moved and was obviously praying. Feeling I should mark the occasion, I took from the shelves a leather-bound volume of Hansard. I chose it carefully to include the speech I had made in 1973 on the demilitarization of Sinai, hoping it might concentrate his mind. He appeared thrilled by the gift and I gathered later from his son that he treasured the book thereafter. Others were not so pleased as they were never able to replace it. The particular skilled bookbinder had died and, when I returned after I had ceased to be Foreign Secretary, I would notice the gap in the bookcase with a smile.

The outer office was where four Private Secretaries worked. The Principal Private Secretary, Ewen Fergusson, had served Jim Callaghan as well as Tony Crosland. His physique was that of a big, burly, Scottish rugby international forward, but it disguised a delicate mover within the Whitehall machine. He got on extremely well with everyone but that too was deceptive – he was shrewd, holding firm opinions which he carefully hid in order to generate a climate of bonhomie. He was a wise counsellor and always fun to be with but he worked within the system. George Walden succeeded him in 1978. George was robust with the Department believing that his prime duty was to serve the Foreign Secretary and he did that loyally, flowering under Peter Carrington.

Ewen was helped by two younger diplomats, who acted as Assistant Private Secretaries. For most of my time they were Kieran Prendergast, independent and tough-minded, and now High Commissioner in Zimbabwe, who dealt with Europe; and Stephen Wall, imaginative, immensely thorough and hard-working, who dealt with Africa and is now Private Secretary to the Prime Minister, John Major. At the desk as people came in through the door of the Private Office sat Maggie Turner, disciplined and an extremely competent keeper of the Foreign Secretary's diary. One of the first things I had to do was to persuade her to stay. She was an attractive Home civil servant of twenty-five who had been Tony Crosland's Diary Secretary in the Department of the Environment. He had created a huge kerfuffle in the Diplomatic Service by demanding that she should come with him to the Foreign Office. Now she agreed to remain and since she had by then earned the respect and affection of everyone who worked with her, it was not difficult to arrange. She proved vital, since a Foreign Secretary, more than most, depends on someone who can juggle the diary to fit in the demands of the Foreign Office at home and abroad, the Cabinet Office, Parliament, and, in my case, Plymouth, family and friends. Foreign statesmen were flying in and out of London with increasing frequency, often giving no notice or cancelling without warning. It was impossible to fit in all the requests. She was able to say no firmly but without ruffling too many feathers, soothe bruised feelings and settle the debris I too often left in my wake. After losing the General Election, I managed to persuade her to come out of the civil service and run my office in the House of Commons which, as Maggie Smart since her marriage, she has done with consummate skill.

We also incorporated into the Private Office Ham Whyte, the Head of the News Department. Ham was a diplomat with a difference. Pink socks flashing as he rode his bicycle around Whitehall, he breezed in and out of the office like a Peter Pan. We all loved him and he was no slouch at public relations. He was both affable and ruthless, loyal to me on everything. Ham loved all things American. With Cy Vance's then Press Secretary, Hodding Carter, he would put on a hilarious double act, jointly briefing the press around the world, and was very popular with journalists which helped me put across our policy. On my first anniversary in office he put out, without the slightest consultation with me, a press statement saying I had travelled 'x' thousand miles and personally signed 'y' number of photographs. Even Ham's friends in the press seized on this press release and gave me the full treatment for vanity. I summoned Ham next morning, having read the appalling press, to demand an explanation. 'Well, Secretary of State, it seemed a good wheeze at the time.' What could one do with such a character but laugh?

Throughout my period as Secretary of State, these people in my Private Office were a delight and a tonic. Everyone worked with dedication and immense skill. It became a power house, full of zest, from which I was determined to get to grips with the Foreign Office. We were an irreverent guerrilla force. At times I was too tough on the Foreign Office but the pace had to be fast and my reactions were at times too furious. Late at night I would sometimes write irreverent comments on carefully crafted diplomatic papers like 'balls', 'guff', 'ugh', 'creep'. Such comments were obviously not meant for circulation but to guide my Private Office in their sanitized memos back. Unfortunately a few of the raw comments got back, I hope only through inadvertence.

The Carter Administration in 1977 was quickly establishing its own radical foreign policy agenda and this, particularly when it was ill-thought-out, added to the pressures. But the ferment in Washington helped us to think afresh, whether on human rights, conventional arms limitation or nuclear non-proliferation. It was an exciting time to be involved in international affairs.

The Private Secretary in the Foreign Office has an internal authority I have not found anywhere else in Whitehall. He – there has never yet been a woman – acts as the hinge for two crucial relationships: that between the Foreign Secretary and the Prime Minister, and that between the Foreign Secretary and the Head of the Diplomatic Service. Of the two, the link across the road to No. 10 is by far the most important and sometimes preserving it means that the Foreign Secretary is wise to differ from the collective wisdom of the Diplomatic Service. An example of this came some months later when Jim Callaghan sent a note over from his Private Secretary to mine asking what the Foreign Secretary thought of inviting the new Israeli Prime Minister Menachem Begin for an official visit. The Prime Minister, I later discovered, remarked at the time, 'Now we will discover who is in charge of the Foreign Office.' He knew the bias towards the Arab viewpoint. As he had guessed, the reaction was to advise me to say no and to explain as my justification that public opinion in Britain would not welcome a visit from the former leader of Irgun, the organization thought to be responsible for the blowing up of the King David Hotel in 1946. I overruled their advice and wrote back to say I thought he should be invited.

Soon after my appointment, Jim mentioned informally that Harold Wilson had said when he retired that he would loyally support Jim's Government even if he thought it was wrong, with one exception. The exception was Israel. I knew, therefore, that I had to watch this issue carefully. Fortunately, once President Sadat flew to Jerusalem in November 1977, we were into a highly positive round of diplomacy leading up to the Camp David Agreement and the Egyptian-Israeli Treaty. Prime Minister Begin had to cancel his visit to Britain because of Sadat's visit but he was so keen to come that he reinstated it for early December, even announcing the date before we had agreed it. This almost accidentally put us in a more influential role than any other European country and both Begin and Sadat tended to call in on us in London en route to or from the United States. Prior to this, despite George Brown's sponsorship of the famous Resolution 242 in the UN Security Council in 1967, Britain had not had much involvement in the peace process, mainly because we had progressively lost influence where it counted, in Jerusalem.

Relations between Jim Callaghan and I, and between No. 10 and the Foreign Office, were exceptionally good for two-and-a-quarter years. Indeed we barely had a hiccup. When I was appointed I hardly knew Jim at all and the good initial relationship owed much to Ewen Fergusson who had worked for Jim. It helped to know how his mind worked and to be able to anticipate his reactions. It was also helped by Jim's ability to drop hints about his inner thinking. He did this particularly on plane or car trips when there were no officials present for, apart from those officials who worked close to him, he was suspicious of Whitehall. I was amazed how Jim consciously chose not to interfere, once actually going to the lengths of ringing me up to apologize for fixing up a meeting with President Kaunda without consulting me first. The advantage to me, within the Foreign Office, of being seen to have the ear of the Prime Minister was immense and some of the senior officials would have been wiser to have adapted rather quicker to the change of pace and priorities instead of resisting and having them imposed.

For years I had chafed at Britain's relative economic decline and I never accepted that we had to resign ourselves to its continuance, nor that it meant that we had to give in continuously when we negotiated in Europe. In my first Commons speech as Foreign Secretary I deliberately struck an expansive note, saying that it was time to stop selling ourselves short, that we needed more self-confidence, more national buoyancy, that we were in danger of exaggerating our weaknesses and under-playing our potential. The battle over Europe within the Foreign Office began very soon after I took office since it was high time that we developed a strategy to cut farm prices and challenge the growing percentage of the Community Budget taken by the Common Agricultural Policy. In the spring of 1977, John Silkin and I agreed to aim for a zero farm price rise by the spring of 1979. Inflation generally was so high that farm prices could only be taken down in three steps. The Commission, under Roy Jenkins, supported this strategy. They were surprised and even annoyed when the Conservative Government abandoned this sensible stance in the early summer of 1979 and left the Commission in the lurch supporting a zero farm price settlement.

In 1977 the Euro-diplomats were still in the first flush of post-referendum euphoria and were very reluctant to sound warnings about the manifest unfairness of the British budgetary contribution. It was all too easy for them to dismiss even serious criticism as being anti-European because too many in the Labour Cabinet were still at heart against the Community. But these diplomats had become far too protective of their own handiwork. Criticism of the terms of their negotiations was, for some, a personal slight. It would have been much wiser if we had had a new team of diplomats to deal with the European Community after entry, people with no hang-ups from the past, people who understood that the compromises which were legitimate for getting into the European Community might have to be disowned and renegotiated once in. Some of the Euro-diplomats found it easy to explain my stance as deriving from a wish to curry favour with the Left in order to win more votes and get elected to the Labour Party NEC. A quite prominent diplomat told me much later that it was only when he saw me, out of office, in 1980, fight within the Labour Party for the European Community that he understood what I had been working for inside the Foreign Office. When Margaret Thatcher became Prime Minister, those same diplomats began to realize that standing up for one's interests in the European Community was not just part of an internal Labour Party battle. The climate in the press changed too and the budgetary consequences of entry were more clearly seen as unfair to the UK, so that it became more widely accepted that we had to fight for the terms to be changed.

I tried to build on the Foreign Office's Planning Staff by creating my own Policy Section within the Private Office. It was made up of a variety of experts. One was Michael Stewart, working part-time while still teaching Economics at University College. Michael Stewart had originally had the much more challenging task of advising Tony Crosland, who really knew about economics. He agreed to stay on in the less satisfying role of educating me in economics. As a result I felt more confident participating in domestic Cabinet economic discussions and in the mysteries of international economics. His expertise was also very helpful when the Prime Minister invited me to the seminars he chaired on monetary and exchange rate policy. This was not a formal Cabinet Sub-Committee. Attended by Gordon Richardson, the Governor of the Bank of England, it was a vehicle for the Prime Minister to involve himself in what had hitherto been the sole preserve of the Chancellor of the Exchequer. It was generous of Jim Callaghan to invite me along, and I suspect it was to educate me as much as anything.

Paul Lever, a bright, iconoclastic diplomat, dealt with security questions, particularly the nuclear deterrent and arms control and later succeeded Kieran Prendergast in my Private Office. What was important was that Paul appeared to have a good relationship with the Head of the Defence Department, David Gillmore, an astute, determined person, now the Permanent Under-Secretary in charge of the Diplomatic Service. David Stephen was my political adviser. These advisers are paid as civil servants but given a special dispensation to be involved in party politics. He was involved in all aspects of my activity. He had worked for the International Department of the Labour Party and as Secretary of the Runnymede Trust. A Spanish speaker, he had strong links with the human rights movements in Latin America, and the Latin American Department to their credit used his knowledge to the full. He visited Ovamboland in Namibia, to report on the SWAPO guerrilla campaign, and Maputo, with Robin Renwick whom we had brought into the African Department. They reported very fully on Mugabe and Robin Renwick used his knowledge of the mentality of a liberation leader to excellent effect in the Lancaster House conference and later in South Africa; he is now our Ambassador in Washington.

To control all the activities of the Foreign Office is a superhuman task. As a strong pillar of the British Establishment, it is all too adept at appearing to change its shape and direction to accommodate the passing concerns of a particular Foreign Secretary. Its capacity to revert as soon as the Secretary of State's attention is diverted is considerable. Like an octopus it can squirt up diversionary clouds in order to escape scrutiny. Its ministerially unauthorized rubbishing of both the individuals concerned and the recommendations of the Central Policy Review Staff examination of the Diplomatic Service will long be admired by connoisseurs of *Yes Minister*. I am afraid the chief culprit in this was Ham Whyte. Peter Jenkins, an old friend of Ham's, had a story in the *Guardian* in April: 'Think Tank suggests an end to the FO' saying the Cabinet Office would be responsible for foreign policy. This was calculated to raise the alarm and the 'chief villains' were the women members of the team, Kate Mortimer and Tessa Blackstone who was labelled 'The dark-eyed evil genius'. When I tackled Ham about all this he looked sheepish while disclaiming all knowledge. When I had my first sight of the report in June I was perplexed at its strange mixture of perceptiveness and trendy criticism. Its folly was to pitch such a despairing image of Britain in the opening chapter. Our decline was too obvious to need pointing up so vividly and depressingly. It would have been far better if Sir Kenneth Berrill had reported directly to the Prime Minister and me with oral briefings and suggested action points rather than attempt a wide-ranging published review.

The CPRS recommendation that we should amalgamate the Diplomatic Service with the Home Civil Service was a product of the centralizing mind that had given us the large Ministries in Whitehall, with very mixed results. The flexible career structure which I believed essential and the responsiveness to world events which were so needed seemed to me to be far easier to develop in a small, separate Diplomatic Service. My conclusion was that it was easier to kill off the Report and then try to extract its wisdoms, implementing them in-house without the prejudice or publicity that had been engendered. Most of the Report's detailed recommendations were brought into effect and it triggered off some important changes of attitude in the Diplomatic Service but it was not the sort of investigation that the CPRS had been designed to undertake and the adverse reaction sadly contributed to its eventual demise.

The Foreign Office is a hierarchical organization. That hierarchy is not to be taken on lightly and it is rare for a Foreign Secretary even to attempt it. I am glad I did. Dissatisfaction with foreign policy advice had quite frequently been expressd by previous Prime Ministers. Margaret Thatcher was its most virulent critic but many of her frustrations were shared by Churchill, Macmillan and Wilson. The Foreign Office had grown complacent and, apart from my differences over Europe with Sir Michael Palliser, I felt he too wanted to build afresh. Our problem was that the Central Policy Review Staff Report on our overseas representation provided, when it came out, a disappointing base on which to build.

The Foreign Office is staffed by dedicated and often brilliant people and I am dubious about whether it has an appeasing identity. As far as there is one it stems from the fact that the culture of diplomacy elevates, splitting the difference to an art form. Also 'going native', which means empathizing with the country within which one is living, is inevitable. Much can be learnt about the conduct of foreign policy by watching the relationship between the Treasury and the Foreign Office as they battle for dominance in the co-ordination of Britain's European Community negotiating stance. The Foreign Office's skills ought to make it pre-eminent, but if its key officials are thought to lack backbone then the Treasury becomes more powerful with Ministers. The Treasury is less hierarchical, more irreverent and readier to fight Britain's corner but it does not always know when it is better to bend, wiser to settle. Tension between these two great Ministries need not be a disadvantage so long as it is creative and overseen by an independent-minded Foreign Secretary.

I sense that Foreign Office officials are more robust in protecting British interests in the 1990s than they ever were in the 1970s. The new generation of diplomats are less effete and more realistic. An example of an important development is that our Permanent Representative in Brussels, John Kerr, has served in the Treasury. A young and brilliant diplomat, he was Michael Palliser's Private Secretary in my time. He went on to the Treasury and was, exceptionally, chosen by the Chancellor to be his Private Secretary. That sort of interchange is vital for the future. Today's key diplomats were young men when I was Foreign Secretary and I singled out a number of them for preferment. They have become determined negotiators in the Community. I like to believe that some of that has its origins in the counter-culture of defiance that I tried to generate and which later Margaret Thatcher also encouraged.

My own style as Foreign Secretary was not above reproach and at times I left myself open to justified criticism for I was too brash and abrasive. It is easy to make excuses – the pace I set myself was taxing, even given my relative youth. But my impatience was too often on display and a little more time should have been spent on mollifying bruised egos. It was a pity that Peter Jenkins, then columnist on the *Guardian* and since on *The Independent*, did not come as my political adviser for that first year. He thought very seriously about the job and would have been given leave of absence from the *Guardian* for a year. Foolishly I thought it would be a serious disadvantage to have someone advising for only a year and Peter felt it would put at risk his professional independence. However, Peter would have been tough enough to stand up to me where it was needed, particularly within the Private Office, and I would have been a better Foreign Secretary for having him near at hand, giving me a broader base with his experience.

Wiser, older, I would now handle myself differently. Set against this as the years have passed, so has the exuberance and the irrepressibility of youth. Issues I tackled then I would probably shirk now. Age softens and whether the advantages of that outweigh the disadvantages is not easy to determine. Suffice to say, I was not a paragon of virtue and the critics of my style had some fair points. Some, though, like the allegations that I got rid of numerous chauffeurs, were a total myth. Despite having to put up with some of my less attractive qualities, the Foreign Office, particularly the younger diplomats who seemed to like my iconoclasm and activity, served me well.

The Diplomatic Service covers everyone who works for the Foreign Office at home and overseas. It generates an *esprit de corps*, without which it could not maintain its high standards in so many trying and difficult posts. It is a great mistake to imagine that all Embassies or Commonwealth High Commissions are luxuriously appointed or in pleasant places to live. For many, service overseas is uncomfortable, trying and beset by constant health problems for their families and themselves. Yet that very spirit, so essential for life in the Diplomatic Service, can envelop like a cocoon. It is that which breeds what appears, at times, to be superciliousness. This problem is reinforced by the fact that the Diplomatic Service offers the same guaranteed career structure to the age of sixty that is a feature of the much larger Home Civil Service. While both high-fliers and burnt-out cases can be accommodated in a large organization, it is harder to do so in a small organization like an Embassy.

For the separate Diplomatic Service to survive, as I believe it should, it must maximize the advantages of being small and independent. It has started to introduce the 'up or out' system which I tried to develop on lines similar to that for officers in the armed services. Just as no ship can be captained by anyone who is second-rate without affecting the performance and morale of everyone on board, so no Embassy can afford a fading diplomat as an Ambassador. The Diplomatic Service's career structure is still too much like a rectangle rather than, as it should be, a pyramid. To work, the 'up and out' system must have the lubrication of generous redundancies and I fear this is still being resisted. Too many older people, of no great merit, are accommodated with Ambassadorships or made High Commissioners in Commonwealth countries. This only holds back the brightest and the best.

I was and remain a blue-water diplomatist. I want our reach to go out from Europe across the oceans of the world. I believe we should have some presence in virtually every country represented in the UN, however small. We should not be ashamed of having one-person Missions operating with a telephone, a fax and a small safe, with none of the paraphernalia of a full-blown Embassy. Wide coverage is a responsibility that comes with being a permanent member of the Security Council, a status that is a fortuitous consequence of our history but one which we should retain and defend with vigour. There is a reluctance among some to shoulder this worldwide responsibility. It is seen as an embarrassing relic of Empire to be abandoned rather than as an opportunity to be exploited. It would be folly for Britain to acquiesce and allow its own and France's seats on the Security Council to become European Community seats rotating with whoever has the Presidency.

In my first few days in office I was fortunate in being familiar with most of the issues I had to deal with. I also knew most of the people with whom I would be working. My first priority was to talk individually to all the Ministers who were in London. I wanted to build the sense of a Ministerial team for no one person could handle that massive workload. We had not hitherto had much contact and I suggested we should all meet for a sandwich lunch every Wednesday, something which had worked well with Barbara Castle in the DHSS. These meetings were particularly valuable when we dealt with political questions outside foreign affairs, since one of the hardest things for a Foreign Secretary is to keep in touch with domestic politics.

As a team of Ministers they had differing qualities. Most of what they decided, day to day, I never even saw. If I felt at times that they tended to succumb too easily to Departmental advice, that was mainly because I was only involved on relatively few issues. Either because of their importance or their political sensitivity, these were the ones on which I was most likely to want to put my personal stamp. Ted Rowlands has since been woundingly critical of those years, which saddens me. However, this criticism only surfaced after I had left Labour for the SDP and after he had invited me to be his guest of honour at his constituency annual dinner in the autumn of 1979 in Merthyr Tydfil. In my experience a fellow MP is not invited to such a function if strongly disliked. I have therefore tended, perhaps wrongly, to discount some of Ted's retrospection. For my part I valued working with him.

Ted was abroad on my first day, but each of the other Ministers was available to see me. Lord Goronwy Roberts came in first. He had a wise Welsh head on which I was to rely a great deal. Much older than I, he was almost embarrassingly deferential. Sometimes I had to force him to be blunter in his advice. His years as an MP meant that he was a safe pair of hands in the House of Lords and I was fortunate to be able to delegate whole parts of the world, particularly Hong Kong, Brunei and Australasia, to him and to know that he would refer back anything that I should know about. On one occasion I let him down badly by criticizing him in his absence in front of one of his officials. He had taken a decision to try to improve the compensation terms for the Banabans which I had agreed with the Australian Foreign Minister, Andrew Peacock. What he did not know was that I had promised Andrew that I would under no circumstances come back and reopen our financial settlement. Even so, it was disloyal of me to grumble and he was promptly told by the official what I had said, no doubt garnished in the telling. Goronwy Roberts came to see me, deeply distressed, and offering to resign. I apologized profusely to him and also wrote him a letter. He then returned, doubly upset, with tears in his eyes, saying that I should not have written such a letter. It was all very Welsh. He was a good man, and politics is enriched by people like him.

Then Frank Judd bounced in, as enthusiastic as ever. I was glad, though, that he did not pretend to hide his disappointment at losing Overseas Development. We agreed that he would take over my previous role in dealing with the European Community. I explained to him how I intended to chair the Cabinet Committee on European questions. While he would put the office view, agreed between us before the meeting, I would be free in the chair to sum up, on occasions against the Foreign Office. I felt it was vital that in the all-important co-ordination of our negotiating position in Brussels I should not feel bound in the chair. Of course I could not be wholly impartial, but I should at least be free to move with the argument and discussion.

That European Cabinet Committee (EQ) was all-important, but it was difficult to chair. The Cabinet anti-Europeans, Peter Shore, John Silkin, Stan Orme, Tony Benn and Albert Booth, regularly attended in person while the main pro-EEC Cabinet members, Shirley Williams, Roy Hattersley, Bill Rodgers and Edmund Dell, kept sending their junior Ministers who were often less enthusiastic. The pros remained in the majority, but only just, and Peter Shore's arguments were substantive and persuasively put. For some Cabinet Ministers it was already as if the 1975 referendum had never taken place. Their hostility to the principle of entry had not abated. I told Frank he should feel free to comment on any aspect of the Department, and over the years he did so fairly frequently. He was a loyal and conscientious deputy. I used to say he was my conscience for he had a moral, idealistic view of politics which he maintained at all times, never succumbing to cynicism. When he lost his seat in Portsmouth, he took that idealism into his work as a highly committed Director of VSO and then Oxfam. In the fast moving world of realpolitik in which I was operating, Frank's worries and doubts were a necessary, if not always welcome, reminder. We laughed about his memos in Private Office and, though I could not always accommodate them, I certainly never resented them. Ewen Fergusson christened these memos 'Judders', which, in a way, is what they were.

Evan Luard was a junior Minister when I took office. An academic, with considerable experience of international affairs, he had done extremely well to win his Oxford seat. He dealt mainly with the UN, with quiet competence and skill. I asked him early on to report on whether we could increase our influence in Afghanistan, for this was a country to which I was still attracted. Sadly and rightly, he concluded that the USSR was too firmly entrenched for us to be able to carry much influence. It reminded me of how we were prevented from driving north to Mazar-i-Sharif in 1959 because of Soviet military manoeuvres. Evan later became an active member of the SDP and died of cancer in 1991.

The other junior Minister was John Tomlinson, a robust and committed European, full of common sense. Sadly he was moved on to another department once the heavy work load associated with the British

Presidency of the European Community ended in the summer. He lost his seat in 1979 and became a European MP.

Peter Hardy, who had been Tony's Parliamentary Private Secretary, agreed to stay on and help me. He was a former teacher and MP for Rother Valley, a safe mining seat. His position in the Party was in the centre. Liked and respected, he helped keep me in touch with MPs whose views matter but are rarely recorded in the newspapers or on radio. He was a good friend over those years but perhaps too kind to be sufficiently critical. He was one of the people whose friendship in the House of Commons I most regretted losing following the creation of the SDP. There was never any doubt that he would stay with the Labour Party and I respected his position. In the ghastly climate of that time at least we remained civil to each other but to remain friends was virtually an impossibility.

Judith Hart and I also had a pleasant chat. I did not get the impression that Jim had told her about my objection to her as my deputy and so said nothing. We agreed demarcation lines for her Overseas Development responsibilities and we kept to those without any ruffled feathers. I argued vigorously in Cabinet on her behalf for higher public expenditure on overseas aid, with some success, so that by the end of our period in office overseas aid was the fastest growing area of public expenditure on the expenditure forecasts. Her position on the Left stemmed from the days of her youth and she was too intelligent to let old prejudices interfere with her Ministerial responsibilities. Yet she would go off and support nonsense upon nonsense on the NEC. That dichotomy between party activist and parliamentary realist is peculiar to the Labour Party.

That afternoon I also had my first introduction to the diplomatic press when I gave an on the record press briefing. There were a number of questions about the work load in the light of Tony's death. I reminded them that I had arguably worked harder in the distant days when I had been a junior hospital doctor. I also told them that I had had a letter from an old age pensioner, saying that now I had become a statesman did I not think it was about time I had a hair cut! Looking back on the photographs throughout that period I am amazed at how long my hair and sideburns were. When asked to explain the significance of the fact that four of my five Ministers, including myself, were Welsh, I replied 'It's all in the blood.'

By and large this good humoured occasion set the tone for our relationship. The diplomatic press were pretty good to me over the years ahead, even when their editors were baying for my blood. Certainly the rollercoaster, on which all politicians ride, was then surging upwards. But John Junor and the *Sunday Express* were a reminder of how swiftly it can swoop down. Over Rhodesia the *Sunday Express* led a vicious campaign. It was not unusual for me to be the subject of abuse in the editorial, main feature article, Crossbencher and John Junor's own column. One day

John Junor took my wife out to lunch to talk about serializing a Jeffrey
Archer book and made it abundantly clear that he loathed me. Debbie
expressed her surprise that he could dislike someone so much without
ever having met them. He did not rush to put this right, indeed we only
met after a rather bizarre incident. He had written in his column after the
General Election:

> Isn't it in some ways a mercy that Dr David Owen has been re-
> elected and so will not be forced to resume his medical career? And if
> you disagree, then just imagine yourself with acute appendicitis in a
> hamlet cut off by snow and finding Dr Owen as the one and only
> general practitioner advancing upon you with a scalpel. Wouldn't you,
> in these circumstances, be wishing to God he had stayed in Parlia-
> ment?

I wrote to the proprietor, Lord Matthews, saying that while my political
views were fair game I objected to my medical prowess being attacked. I
did not want to sue but felt an apology was called for. He wrote a
conciliatory reply and suggested that John Junor and I should meet. So at
lunch, as much to his surprise as mine, we found we liked each other and
thereafter I used to write for the *Sunday Express* from time to time.

My first day ended in a meeting with John Davies, the Conservative
Shadow Foreign Secretary. He was honourable and decent in our dealings
and I would regularly give him confidential information, sure that he
would never exploit it. Francis Pym, who followed him, was far more
political. Neither approached Lord Carrington's grasp and understanding
of foreign affairs. It has been a happy tradition that as far as possible
foreign policy is conducted on a bi-partisan basis. The Foreign Secretary is
never refused a pair for voting and this eases the burden of travel
considerably. Apart from the European Community, Suez and Rhodesia
were the post-war issues which had put cross-party co-operation under
most strain. I was going to come under severe attack from the Conservative
Right wing on Rhodesia, particularly since Margaret Thatcher sympathized
with their views. She knew very little then about Africa and her main
adviser seemed to be Laurens van der Post who, when I met him at her
request, was concerned about the Shona/Matabele tribal divide in Rhodesia.
She unwisely committed herself to Bishop Muzorewa and gave a pre-
election commitment to support the internal settlement which undoubtedly
hindered our diplomacy. When she won the election she found it was the
first promise she was unable to fulfil. I always found John Davies and Peter
Carrington, by contrast, far more sceptical of Muzorewa and more realistic
about the strength of the guerrilla movements fighting for independence.

Many of these people I would meet most days to work, to argue and to
compromise with. While Iran, the Falklands, the Middle East and
nuclear weapons would all later play their part, the immediate issues
seemed clear – Rhodesia and Europe.

On European questions I was already well briefed. But on Rhodesia I needed to think out the fundamentals. Over the previous week, while Tony was ill, I had started to come to grips with the problem but now it was truly my responsibility. In those first few days I formulated the main outlines of a new policy, described in the next chapter, which culminated in the Anglo-American proposals which were published in a White Paper on 1 September. I also had to decide whether I should be seen to be personally involved. Sitting back and using a surrogate like Ivor Richard was not temperamentally acceptable to me. Politics at home also dictated that I should accept full responsibility for the deterioration in internal security while the mounting loss of life from the fighting was becoming headline news. In Parliament, with Labour's majority under constant threat, I had to hold the support of the Liberal Party and this would be easier if I was seen to be active. The public, I felt, wanted the new Foreign Secretary to adopt a much higher profile than hitherto. Yet Rhodesia had already proved to be a political graveyard for British Ministers and diplomats. I was not carried away by any thought of instant glory. I knew that a policy of involvement in Rhodesia had high risks both domestically and internationally. I had no intention of contributing to Mr Smith's already formidable number of political scalps.

Henry Kissinger's belated involvement in Southern Africa taught me that US power was crucial. But if the US was to be involved there had to be close partnership and a working relationship with British diplomats. American diplomats had not had the experience in Africa that we had built up over the years and there was room for a lot of misunderstanding if we acted separately. In any case, the new Carter Administration was already far more actively engaged over South Africa and apartheid than the Ford Administration, so Washington needed to be sounded out by our officials quickly to see if we could work more closely together on Rhodesia.

The critical question was how to persuade and pressurize South Africa. We needed the classic combination of stick and carrot. There was no doubt that South Africa was able to deliver a settlement at any time but they had to be convinced it was in their interests. For them, a dependent white-dominated buffer state of Rhodesia had its advantages. We had to persuade them of the disadvantages, raise the price of their support and increase the incentive to co-operate. The previous strategy of playing both ends, South Africa and black Africa, against the middle, Rhodesia and Namibia, had diminished British influence in Africa and in the world. White minority governments in Mozambique and Angola had collapsed with the fall of the Portuguese Empire. Britain looked, and indeed was, a paper tiger over Rhodesia. It was obvious that sanctions against South Africa had to be progressively invoked, something which Britain had shrunk from doing under Labour as well as Conservative Governments. That did not mean comprehensive all-out economic sanctions but it did mean a readiness to squeeze their economy.

Over Namibia and Rhodesia, and South Africa itself, there was a choice to make and I was determined we would make it. Majority rule, and soon, was where both principle and interest now lay. The white minority groups were not viable and they were playing for time at a heavy price in lives and in human misery. Eventually, even in South Africa, blacks would gain the vote. I believed Britain's trading interests, as well as our political interests, lay in ensuring that we were not identified with sustaining racial discrimination or minority rule. This meant abandoning neutrality and being partisan in our determination to have fair elections. It meant that we would no longer because of our history, our culture or racial prejudice, act as apologists for the minority governments in Rhodesia, Namibia and South Africa which held power by exploitation and violence. I was not advocating a starry-eyed policy divorced from self interest. On the contrary, I believed that Britain had to curb and put its large financial interests in South Africa at risk in the medium term in order to be able to secure them in the long term.

Politically we would now have to hold back from promoting settlements involving a qualified franchise and we would have to refuse to identify ourselves with any internal solutions. We had to understand that the black leaders and their supporters who came from Rhodesia and Namibia were fighting outside the countries because there was no hope of gaining their freedom by staying and living under white domination. Many were principled people, active Christians, forced to become liberation fighters. For others, their Marxism was secondary to their nationalism. We could not supply them with arms, for this would disqualify us from any diplomatic influence in South Africa but we would champion negotiations and fair elections in order to minimize the influence of the communist countries who were supplying the freedom fighters with arms. A hard core of the guerrilla fighters were not committed to the ballot box at all. We had a role here too. We had to restore faith in democracy and support those black politicians who were democrats. Some, like Denis Healey, argued that all we could realistically do was to wait until the freedom fighters won. That was far too fatalistic. It would also have been a politically impossible position to adopt in the House of Commons or in the UN. It would have encouraged those who wanted to impose their rule by force of arms and we would have been seen as ignoring the ballot box.

Britain, whether we liked it or not, was held responsible internationally for Smith's UDI. We had to have an active diplomatic role. Some in the Cabinet disliked any active Rhodesian policy for the domestic political risks due to family links, and militarily due to the danger of being sucked in. Jim Callaghan had warned me in our first conversation after my appointment that a majority in the Cabinet was opposed to any commitment of British military forces in Rhodesia. Even then my mind was turning on how to involve the United Nations.

There were two immediate decisions. Instead of focusing on Rhodesia, Ivor Richard would now go back to New York. This was interestingly what Michael Palliser wanted too. There was a lot of Departmental discontent, some of it unfair, about Ivor's handling of the Geneva Conference. I also had to agree a policy framework for Rhodesia with Jim Callaghan which we could both put to President Carter when I accompanied the Prime Minister to Washington in early March.

I wanted to turn the earlier strategy upside down. Instead of attempting to establish an all-party interim government and then taking eighteen months to produce a constitution we with the US would produce a draft constitution by the summer and hold an all-party constitutional conference to discuss it. Since the collapse of the Sunningdale Arrangement in Northern Ireland, I was deeply suspicious of trying anything which smacked of power sharing. Power sharing was based upon an idealistic interpretation of how political men and women behave. Like it or not, the whole basis of democratic politics is the clash of different views and different ideologies. Compromise, not consensus, is the dynamic of politics. Trying to put everyone together in government was political engineering on a grand scale. Essentially unstable anywhere, in Rhodesia it was totally unworkable. The weakness of Geneva was that we had tried to put together the newly developed Patriotic Front of Nkomo and Mugabe, itself divided, with Bishop Muzorewa, the Reverend Sithole and the Smith regime, and hoped to weld them together into a team of Ministers under the benign chairmanship of a Resident Commissioner. It was asking too much to expect them to work together in government while producing not only a constitution but also plans for holding elections which they would all then contest. Even if we had been able to reach nominal agreement, it would have broken down within a few months. The four main factions would have been jockeying for power, attempting both to rig the elections and the constitution in their favour. Even without the experience of Geneva, it seemed too optimistic to believe that such a combination could work. Subsequent events at the Lancaster House Conference in 1980 only confirmed that judgement. The Patriotic Front immediately split and Mugabe and Nkomo fought each other for power. Lancaster House also confirmed that dealing with the constitution first was the right strategy since, when that conference started in 1979, they had been discussing virtually the same Constitution for two years. Our Anglo-American plans proved a good investment and the old saying about the need to 'palaver' in Africa meant that our two-year diplomatic effort was not in vain.

Whatever my own priorities, world events had a habit of blowing us off course. When I was working on Rhodesia, problems would blow up in Tehran or in Buenos Aires; when I was grappling with budget problems in Brussels I would have to fly to the other end of the world to fulfil a long-standing engagement. Being Foreign Secretary is not a job that allows for neat and ordered tackling of problems. If I ever doubted this, my first Cabinet meeting showed why. I was keen to inform my colleagues of progress on Rhodesia, where talks between the US and ourselves had begun. In the end, however, the discussion turned to Idi Amin.

Cabinet always has on its agenda a separate and early item on foreign affairs, and the Foreign Secretary normally makes an oral report. This is a useful convention allowing Cabinet to be kept informed without the formality of detailed papers. It was the time to encourage early discussion in areas of foreign policy which were likely to become controversial. I reported that our soundings in the Commonwealth had shown that we were a long way from being able to mobilize a majority to oppose Uganda's General Amin attending the London Conference of Commonwealth Heads of Government. This issue was to plague us over the next few months. The black Commonwealth, led by Nigeria, was suspicious of our motives for wanting Amin excluded, blithely ignoring the monstrous nature of the human rights abuses he was perpetrating in Uganda. Days before the Commonwealth Conference, I was told by Merlyn Rees in the middle of the Lord Mayor of London's lunch that he had just been informed that Amin had flown into Dublin. We had agreed we would have to mobilize the police to hold his plane while it was refuelled and then insist that it fly off. If he just flew into Heathrow we had already decided that we would not let him off his plane. Fortunately it all turned out to be a false alarm; Amin never came. But the Amin issue did not go away. Later he was ousted by Tanzanian armed intervention, and we aided Julius Nyerere in the attempt. I will never be sure whether it was wise to do so. The price we extracted from Nyerere for our material support was the promise that a mild, decent former children's doctor should be President rather than Milton Obote. Unfortunately the doctor did not have the necessary authority. The end result was that Obote returned to the Presidency, Uganda was riven again and human rights were trampled. Although not quite as bad as Amin's, Obote's rule was still a disaster.

After Cabinet, Bill Rodgers and I had a sandwich lunch in my office. We were good friends then and I was anxious that he would not feel I was too busy to seek his advice and talk domestic politics, particularly about the Campaign for Labour Victory which he had just launched to try and combat the influence of the hard Left and Militant Tendency. The most immediate political problem was how to handle the British Presidency of the European Community and the related issue of direct elections for the European Assembly. This was the first time since we had entered the Community that the UK had held the chair and it was an opportunity to try and nudge the development of the Community in directions which we favoured. In the 1990s, directly electing members to the European Parliament seems logical but in 1977 it was a controversial issue within the Labour Party. It was seen by Michael Foot as a challenge to the authority of the House of Commons and was threatening to split the Party. Before the special Cabinet on the European Elections the next day, I had arranged to see Merlyn Rees, the Home Secretary, and Ron Hayward, the General Secretary of the Labour Party, to sound them out over the different methods of voting. I was attracted by the Finnish system of regional lists and proportional voting. I found Merlyn Rees totally open-minded on which system we should adopt. Even more surprisingly, Ron Hayward, though he had the natural caution of a Labour Party agent about abandoning the old, well-tried system, did not commit himself to opposing proportional representation for Europe. If we went for a regional list system of proportional representation, confined strictly to Europe, the Labour Party might be better represented. We were expecting that Labour would suffer badly under the first-past-the-post system since Europe was likely to be unpopular in 1979 and the large European constituencies would make it hard to raise enthusiasm.

We had an enjoyable and good-natured special Cabinet meeting on the Friday to discuss direct elections. It was not so much a decision-making meeting as an attempt to harmonize the diverse opinions. Hitherto our representation at the European Parliament had come from existing MPs and peers and, purely in terms of British interests, this was working rather well. It provided a valuable link between the two Parliaments and was educating MPs about continental politics. Some on the Left, like John Prescott, were developing as European socialists and becoming adept at handling the politics of the European Parliament. Most Ministers, including me, would have preferred this indirect representation to continue, but eventually I and others managed to convince the majority of the Cabinet that this was not an achievable option, that the other eight member states were determined to have the Europe-wide elections provided for in the Treaty and there was no way that we could block this. I had not realized until then quite how vehemently Michael Foot was opposed to the whole concept of a European Parliament. He believed that it would gradually challenge the Westminster Parliament since all parliaments fight to expand their power base. Michael had a romantic attachment to the Westminster Parliament. He saw its power as stemming only from debate on the floor of the Commons. He opposed Select Committees and reform of the Lords. All he wanted was the cut and thrust of debate. His Cornish blood made him ready to take up the mantle of Trelawney, except that it was the English Channel rather than the River Tamar which was to be his frontier. He was deaf to the argument that the Treaty of Rome made legislation imperative. Tony Benn too was opposed to any direct election, on the not unreasonable grounds of its potential for stimulating a move towards Euro-federalism. The Cabinet was clearly heading for major trouble. Merlyn Rees feared problems in the House too, worrying that any legislation might suffer the same fate on the floor of the House as Dick Crossman's attempt to reform the House of Lords.

I was more sanguine and thought that the Conservative pro-marketeers would see the legislation on to the Statute Book in the end.

Without great enthusiasm, the Cabinet turned to the voting mechanism for the elections. I proposed the regional list system of proportional representation and was surprised that it was given a good hearing. A clear majority preferred it for Europe to first-past-the-post voting. It was an important moment. Already, proportional representation had been introduced into the UK for the Northern Ireland Assembly by Edward Heath and for their three seats in the European Parliament it was the only way to ensure minority representation. This discussion was the first time that a Cabinet had been minded to introduce a proper system of proportional voting for an election in all parts of the UK. Even Tony Benn seemed to be concerned about the dangers a Conservative landslide in European elections would present to a Labour government at Westminster. As practical politicians, the Cabinet majority sensed, in view of the specific commitment in the Treaty of Rome, that early legislation and a proportional voting system was the best of all the unappealing courses open to us. Roy Hattersley alone thought our obligation would end by trying and failing. The rest of us thought this was a ploy which would rebound on us if we tried it.

I soon experienced the politics of Europe first-hand, for, on the same day as the special Cabinet I flew with Debbie to Paris. For many personal and political reasons I wanted France to be the first country I visited as Foreign Secretary. Debbie had worked in Paris, Gareth's godmother is a Parisian and I love travelling in France. I share the ambivalence of many British people towards France and the French, but affection easily outweighs suspicion. In my bones politically I know that on the big issues, when the chips are really down, the French, of all the European Community countries, are the most likely to react like the British and be there with us in times of crisis. We are destined to be linked together and yet separate. The incipient tension in our relationship has more constructive than destructive aspects. I wanted then, and do to this day, improved Anglo-French relations.

To stay in the grandeur of the British Embassy in Paris is a delightful experience at any time but in the first flush of my promotion to Foreign Secretary it was something very special. The French Foreign Minister, Louis de Guiringaud, had laid on at no notice a sumptuous, large dinner party at the Quai d'Orsay. I was not expecting to speak but when he rose to propose a toast it became clear that his speech was going to need more than a cursory response. Our Ambassador Sir Nicholas Henderson's fertile mind came to the rescue, frequently passing menu cards along to me with excellent suggestions as to what I should say. The end result was a far better speech than it would have been if I had carefully prepared it.

In handling the tensions that lay ahead between myself and the Euro-federalists I was adamant that I would not be party to any gossip about how awful the Callaghan Government was, and with Roy Jenkins coming on Saturday I had to be also wary of any attempt to develop between the President of the Commission and the Foreign Secretary anything that could even remotely be seen as a hostile axis to Jim Callaghan. Admittedly I had not been a great proponent of Jim Callaghan. However, I genuinely thought that in his initial period as Prime Minister he had shown himself to be a far better leader and more trustworthy politician than ever he had been before. I certainly owed him my loyalty and unless that loyalty proved to be misplaced he would have it in full measure. Also, I believed strongly that Roy Jenkins could not be a good President unless he managed to distance himself from Britain and removed any suspicion in Brussels of bias. We had different roles to play and by the very nature of these different roles we would inevitably clash from time to time, for British interests and the wider good of the European Community could not invariably coincide.

Sir Nicholas Henderson's views on the European Community were of course familiar to me but were more formally conveyed in his original typed valedictory despatch in early April 1979. We were on the eve of the May General Election. Moreover, I instantly thought that it had the flavour of having been written for publication. I asked my Private Secretary, George Walden, to arrange for the few other copies in the Department to be returned to our office immediately. I then instructed that it should be sent to be formally printed which, given the normal printing delay, meant it would only circulate after the election.

This supposedly confidential report from Paris was then published as I had predicted in full by *The Economist* on 2 June 1979. His approach to the Community is revealing for it indicates what I had to cope with and on occasions to counter from the Foreign Office hierarchy. In one passage, while admitting that there was an acute budgetary problem, he said there was only one way to go about it if we were to get our way: 'That is to have a heart-to-heart talk with the leaders of the other eight countries on the basis that we are unreserved and constant members interested in the fortunes of the Community as a whole.' In fact this approach had been tried by Jim Callaghan with Helmut Schmidt in 1978 to little effect. It can work on minor matters but on the big questions involving money each country's Treasury interests override heart-to-heart arrangements between friendly leaders. Sir Nicholas Henderson also commented on British economic problems and I supported the analysis, if not all the history, of Britain's continued decline. Sir Nicholas Henderson was appointed by Lord Carrington, an old friend, to be Ambassador to Washington to replace Peter Jay in 1979. It was essentially a political appointment, though it was treated as an extension of his diplomatic service. He proved, particularly over the Falklands crisis, an attractive expositor of the British case.

During their first few months, the new Conservative Government in

1979 did indeed adopt the Henderson approach, developing a heady pro-European stance under Lord Carrington. Most unwisely they agreed to lift our carefully organized zero farm price settlement and accepted the exact farm price increase which I had rejected out of hand only a few weeks before. No doubt the same Foreign Office official persuaded Lord Carrington using the same arguments I had refused. But I wonder whether they ever revealed to him that this was the lever by which we hoped to prise open a budgetary agreement at the European Council meeting in Dublin. A few months later Margaret Thatcher, still in her 'be nice to the Community' mode, found herself bargaining at Dublin with no leverage at all and was totally rebuffed. Thereafter the 'be nasty' view prevailed as she realized that one has to have some bargaining counters to exert leverage in any negotiations. How to negotiate to protect British interests is again an issue in the 1990s and siren voices want to revert to the Henderson approach.

European Community membership is a continuous negotiation. If you have an interest to protect, particularly as majority voting becomes more frequent, you need allies and you have to find them among those who also have an interest to uphold; not always the same interests as one's own. We, like every other Community country, have to assemble coalitions, sometimes quite brazenly scratching their backs if they will scratch ours. Also, since we, like every other Community nation, have a veto power under de Gaulle's Luxembourg compromise, it must be seen that, selectively and very occasionally, we are prepared to use it if vital interests are involved. In one sense the veto is a deterrent, more powerful for never being used. The Labour Party throughout the 1980s could not make up its mind whether to support or to criticize Mrs Thatcher for being tough towards the Community. What was important was that many Foreign Office Euro-diplomats slowly adapted to the Thatcher style. Where Margaret Thatcher came unstuck was in pushing too hard on all issues and in not varying her tone. She became too strident and demanding for the strength of her own European negotiating stance. But, nevertheless, her hard line from No. 10 was often essential. The welcome change of tone towards the Community which came with John Major in No. 10 means that it will be easier to mobilize other countries to challenge the loose and wishful thinking which lies behind Commission thinking on a single currency and particularly the timing of a single currency. But Britain will also need Margaret Thatcher's nerve and resolve if Euro-federalism is to be repulsed. In one sense it helps to have Margaret Thatcher in the wings. The other European Ministers know that on this issue she is a volcano about to erupt and they show some sign of being sensitive to Britain's political problem and ready to give us some leeway. But, as I argue in the final chapter, we do face now a choice between developing a European state or a Europe of nation states.

When Roy Jenkins arrived at the Paris Embassy we had a friendly chat. We were both having to adjust to a potentially fraught relationship. He had been my mentor and now, as President of the Council of Foreign Ministers for the next few months, though not actually his master, I was the mouthpiece of European Community Ministers. It was bound to be difficult for him as a new President of the Commission and vastly more experienced than I to have me holding the very office which only some months back Callaghan had denied him. I have no major complaints about how Roy handled our relationship throughout the next two-and-a-quarter years. Various bits of gossip would come back to me about what he was saying but, apart from minor irritation, I cannot say I objected to his odd put downs, most of which are faithfully recorded in his book *European Diary*. My work load was so great that I did not have the time or inclination to get excited about petty jealousies. Slowly, however, our friendship ebbed away. It was not long before he was being referred to by the nickname which first surfaced in Brussels, '*Le Roi Jean Quinze*', both at home and in my Private Office. For the most part it was good natured ribbing. Over the so-called battle of 'Jenkins's seat' at the London Economic Summit I was far more supportive of Roy than I think he ever realized. It really does matter where the President is placed in the hierarchy of the Community and whether he is treated as a Head of Government or as a mere Foreign Secretary. Fighting for position is an occupational hazard of becoming President of the Commission. Yet Jacques Delors has threatened to turn the office of President into a real power position. That has meant the ultimate accolade, a *Sun* headline 'UP YOURS DELORS'. Previously the President of the Community was ignored by the *Sun*, and even *The Times* never presented this position and that of the Commission as being a seat of power. Sadly for Roy he was unable to turn the Presidency into the influential position that he had hoped for and this manifested itself in periodic frustration.

An added difficulty was the seething contempt in which Roy held Jim Callaghan and the deep suspicion that underlay Jim's reaction to Roy. Gradually this improved, particularly as Jim became ever more European. As they grew older and less competitive they started, in the middle 1980s, even in private, to speak more warmly about each other. Now it is the warmth of old punch-drunk pugilists working out in the verbal gymnasium provided by the House of Lords for politicians no longer in the House of Commons.

President Giscard d'Estaing, himself fond of position, had spotted the Jenkins weakness for pomp and recognition and began to play Roy like a fish on a line. A photo call confined initially to Heads of Government, would, at Giscard's rather imperious invitation, be widened to include the President of the Commission. Roy, lurking in the background, would then join the group, but Giscard would only put him on the end of the row or in the back. It was all absurd but while some people would have

taken it as a source of amusement, for Roy it was torture. Leaving Roy
fretting on the sidelines or pleasing him by meeting him at the front door
or providing a guard of honour, became a sort of game for the Elysée
Palace. European Community protocol is pretty tedious and the French
President was forever standing on his own dignity, even with as good a
friend as Helmut Schmidt. On one occasion when Germany was the host
for a European Council, Helmut decided he had had enough of Giscard
always arriving last because he was a Head of State. So they both circled
the driveway in their cars until Giscard cracked.

Helmut Schmidt was the European politician I most admired. He
seemed to me the archetypal Social Democrat – market-orientated on
economic questions, resolute on defence, socially aware and with an
understanding and sympathy for trade unionism. When he talked of
social partnership it had real meaning. He was never sucked in by any of
the interest groups that play in the foothills of politics. He represented
the strength and solidity of that great seaport, his home town, Hamburg.
He also knew how to make a deal. Once in Buckingham Palace he and I
settled a three-year formula for ending the Anglo-German financial offset
arrangement which covered the cost of our forces in BAOR. Hans-
Dietrich Genscher, as Foreign Minister, would not commit himself,
whereas Helmut with no hauteur healed what was a running sore literally
on the back of an envelope, which I kept for years but unfortunately now
seem to have lost.

In fairness to Roy, the fight to ensure that he was represented at the
Economic Summit in London was a matter of some substance. As host,
Jim was bound to want to conduct his own show without having Roy in
his shadow. Why Giscard, who had previously pressed Roy to become
President in the first place, was now so anxious to keep the Commission
outside and in its place was beyond rational explanation. The Benelux
countries were determined that the President of the Commission should
come to the Summit to represent them. Eventually it was agreed that the
President should attend for those parts of the discussion that dealt with
trade. The Americans thought we Europeans were crazy with these petty
arguments. Giscard even refused to attend the opening dinner at No. 10
because Roy was going to be present. Thankfully, now the President of
the Commission attends throughout Economic Summits and the whole
absurdity has been put to rest.

My private advice to Jim had been to let Giscard argue the case and
take the political flak. I suspect Roy was being told by Crispin Tickell,
the Foreign Office diplomat on attachment to him as Chef de Cabinet,
that I was refusing to sign the letter to the Prime Minister supporting
Roy's presence at the London Summit which the Department was
pressing me to send. What he did not know was that I had already
discussed the issue frequently with Jim Callaghan and was jollying him
along to accept the inevitable. The last thing needed was a formal letter

from me. This was a typical example of the constant flow of gossip among private secretaries which sometimes inflames relations instead of smoothing them. One such piece of Foreign Office gossip arose from an incident that took place on my appointment. Roy's office had sent a routine formal telegram of congratulations. On receiving it, and not realizing that Roy had had nothing to do with its wording, I cursed loudly about its pomposity. Doubtless my expletives were not deleted in transmission from my Private Secretary to his Chef de Cabinet. For me, it was only a transient irritation of no consequence whatever. But passed on in this way it obviously nagged at Roy and he mentioned it to me years later. Of such small molehills are mountains made. I suspect our friendship, founded as it was on inequality of position, could never have been sustained on the basis of any equality of position which only pointed up the differences in our personalities. No doubt I should have tried harder and for a short period at the turn of the year in 1980 we did grow closer and almost became friends again. But that ended only a few months later in the autumn of 1981.

A major speech which I had inherited from Tony Crosland and on which he had already done invaluable work was to be delivered in early March to the Diplomatic Writers Association Dinner. Andrew Shonfield came along with some other people from Chatham House to discuss it on my fourth day as Foreign Secretary. It was a stimulating occasion and showed the Foreign Office diplomats at their best, in particular Reg Hibbert and Iain Sutherland. Both had the intellect for extremely successful academic life but they had also built up a practical knowledge of the Russian mind.

Reg Hibbert had been Ambassador in Outer Mongolia and was the person I most enjoyed arguing with in the Foreign Office. He gave no quarter and expected none in return. People were surprised at the ferocity with which we two would engage. I found his robustness all too rare and insisted on appointing him Ambassador to France. Near the end of my period in office, it was clear that a row over our budgetary contribution was inevitable and I felt we would need an Ambassador in Paris who was his own man. So unusual was Hibbert's style that Margaret Thatcher, in one of her periodic clashes over the European Community Budget, surprised to have a telegram from Paris telling her to stand firm and to keep the heat up on the French, asked how he had ever been appointed.

Iain Sutherland was a perceptive adviser on the Soviet Union and later became a friend as we often used to meet him and his wife over dinner at Elizabeth Furse's house. After being Ambassador to Greece, he went to Moscow where he built a considerable reputation. I was particularly glad that David Lipsey came to that meeting. He had been Tony's devoted political adviser and was utterly demoralized by his death. I had asked him to stay as a form of therapy, in the full knowledge that for his own development he needed to move on, which he did, going to work at No. 10. But in those early days he needed time to absorb the shock and to help Susan Crosland in sorting out the aftermath of Tony's death. Tony's Thanksgiving Service was held in Westminster Abbey on 7 March 1977 and my lasting memory of the service was the belated discovery of the splendid second verse to the National Anthem which I wish could be sung more often.

> Not on this land alone –
> But be God's mercies known
>   From shore to shore.
> Lord make the nations see
> That men should brothers be,
> And form one family
>   The wide world o'er.

My attention switched quickly back to Rhodesia and to my first official visit to the US. On the early evening of 9 March the Prime Minister and I flew out on Concorde to Washington to meet President Carter. Audrey Callaghan was on the plane, as was Debbie. Concorde had been taken as part of a promotion campaign since we were still locked in the battle to achieve landing rights in New York. Jim was the first European Head of Government to visit President Carter. In part this was because he was the President of the European Council but it was also because, as a dyed-in-the-wool Atlanticist, he wanted to establish his own special relationship with the new President. It was a thrill to fly Concorde and for Debbie it was going home. She had voted for Jimmy Carter and to visit her capital city in such style was exciting.

Before leaving, Jim Callaghan had agreed that I should put to President Carter the idea of a constitutional conference for Rhodesia. The conference would be based on discussing a specific constitution which our countries would present jointly after consultation with all the parties vying for power in an independent Zimbabwe. On the trip we talked about some of the details and I got a fascinating first glimpse of the small political mafia that surrounded Jim. Bernard Donoughue, the Head of the Policy Unit, was a sensitive operator who paced round the Whitehall jungle like a political leopard. He coupled highly manipulative skills with a good academic mind. Tom McCaffrey, the Press Secretary, was solid and sensible, older than the others and had Jim's total trust. Unassuming and friendly he had considerable newspaper management skills. When he had come over from the Home Office with Jim to run the Foreign Office News Department, a post zealously guarded by the diplomats, he was viewed with the utmost suspicion but his sheer professionalism won through. Then there was Tom McNally, Jim's political adviser, who had been International Secretary to the Labour Party and also with him in the Foreign Office. He had a gritty guile, became a Labour MP and then joined the SDP and became for a time close to me. Finally, there was Roger Stott, Jim's Parliamentary Private Secretary, a young mainstream MP with his ear close to the ground. I sensed that Jim would not be diverted too far from domestic politics with them around, and since that is where the votes were, this was reassuring. Whenever I travelled with the Prime Minister I was always struck by the way he surrounded himself with these four and never allowed the pomp and circumstance of foreign travel to supplant the nitty-gritty of party politics at home. Jim was a domestic Prime Minister and this was one of the reasons why he chose to interfere so little in foreign policy. The home front, he knew, was where the next general election would be won or lost.

We drove from the airport to the lovely Blair House, across the street from the White House, where the Callaghans were staying. Jim's decision to stay there, rather than at the Embassy, was deliberate. He had little time for our Ambassador, Sir Peter Ramsbotham. From that moment I knew that Sir Peter would have to be moved on, regardless of his considerable merits. It is simply unacceptable, in the principal capital of the world, to have an Ambassador who does not have the fullest confidence of the Prime Minister. However, Debbie and I did stay at the Ambassador's residence and were made very welcome. It is a large impressive Lutyens house. Some argue that this Embassy is too grand and costly but I believe it to be an excellent investment for Britain. The US relationship, however one describes it, is the most crucial one for the prosperity and security of our country. A lovely house and garden, which over the years Presidents, Vice-Presidents, Senators and Congressmen have all enjoyed being invited to visit, cannot be bad for Britain.

We went into the first session with President Carter next morning after brief welcoming speeches but without the traditional speeches on the White House lawn since this was one of the trappings banished by Carter at the outset of his Administration. The nineteen-gun salute for the Prime Minister had also been cancelled for fear of provoking a besieged gunman in the City Hall two blocks away.

The President and Prime Minister went off to the Oval Office and I was left in the Cabinet Room with Secretary of State Cyrus Vance, whom I had never met before. We soon developed as close a working partnership and friendship as I suspect has ever existed between a US Secretary of State and British Foreign Secretary. Our first discussion was on Rhodesia. In less than fifteen minutes, helped by a prior meeting between officials, we had agreed the outline of a joint approach. When the President and Prime Minister came back I summarized what had been discussed and it was quickly endorsed by President Carter. In this brisk fashion, the Anglo-American initiative on Rhodesia began.

The only difference during the trip between Jim and me arose when he talked to the British press about this initiative. He tried to downplay US involvement over Rhodesia and talk up the extent of British control.

However, I did not want it thought that Britain was in the driving seat, with a little American help. I wanted it seen that we were sharing the driving and that the initiative would carry all the clout of American diplomacy. In this way I hoped it would be impossible for Ian Smith or for the South Africans to divide and rule. Picking Britain off and isolating us was a tactic that had been used to considerable effect in the past. I eventually managed to counteract his presentation. Also Johnny Apple, a good friend, arrived in London as the *New York Times* correspondent.

Another reason for my anxiety to bind in the Americans was the way Mr Smith had been able, over the years, to exploit domestic divisions in Britain. I calculated that some Conservative critics would now hesitate before backing Smith by, for instance, opposing the renewal of sanctions, since they would not want to put themselves against the US. For some on the Right support for Rhodesian UDI had become the vehicle for expressing racial prejudice. The Tory Right also enjoyed the Salisbury connection and they would not hesitate to block, if they could, the tougher line I intended to take with Smith. Given the small Labour majority, the Cabinet's proven reluctance to risk any military involvement and our weakened economic position, we could not take even these people on alone. For me to attempt to settle Rhodesia on our own would be to risk another abject failure. With American strength and power I had a renewed opportunity. I kept saying publicly that I had no *amour propre*, that Africa needed American strength and American commitment. The British attempt to keep responsibility for Rhodesia to ourselves had always been a mistake and the outcome of Wilson's posturing on HMS *Fearless* and HMS *Tiger* only revealed our weakness.

On that first day Cy Vance understood completely why I wanted his support and he never wavered throughout the whole exercise. Once, while walking up the stairs of State House in Dar es Salaam to see President Nyerere, he told me he did not agree with me over retaining the Rhodesian police force in the transition but that he would back me none the less which he proceeded to do with the utmost conviction. With friends like that one can do business. Another advantage of our joint initiative was that it had a new momentum. Andrew Young, a young black politician, had been appointed as the US Ambassador to the United Nations. He was a civil rights activist, had been a close associate of Martin Luther King and was a long-time political associate of Jimmy Carter in Atlanta, Georgia, the State of which Carter had been Governor. Andy Young was able to enthuse Third World countries in a way I never could. The price of his participation was more than a little unevenness in negotiations and some unconventional diplomacy but it was a price worth paying, even if he did shoot from the 'lip'.

Another significant policy development stemmed from a discussion I had with Jim one evening in Blair House before Carter's ceremonial dinner in the White House. Jim could see that the proliferation of nuclear weapons was of massive concern to Carter and that we would have to develop our policies quickly to match his. Jim himself had been involved in forming the London Nuclear Suppliers Group and had taken a special interest in this area with a particularly thoughtful diplomat, John Thomson, who had become our High Commissioner in Delhi. It was decided, with Sir John Hunt, Secretary to the Cabinet, to form a special Cabinet Sub-Committee on nuclear non-proliferation which I would chair. Jim was obviously pleased to discover that this was an area in which I was not only interested but reasonably well-informed thanks to my periodic lunches with Solly Zuckerman.

The White House dinner was an enjoyable occasion. When Jim spoke he said that he was shy about talking about the special relationship but since the President had mentioned it earlier he felt it did describe with accuracy the ease and common feelings we had for each other. He quoted Shakespeare on friendship, 'Grapple them to thy heart with hoops of steel', and gave the President some worsted fabric with the almost imperceptible repeat of the letters JC, forming a silver silk pinstripe, which he had already had made up for himself into a suit. We ate roast beef and an American tenor sang the Welsh hymn 'All Through the Night'. As farmers and fellow Baptists the two got on very well together.

In my more detailed conversations with Cy Vance in the State Department the vexed question of sanctions against South Africa kept recurring. Both of us were in no doubt that any initiative on Rhodesia and Namibia was doomed unless we were able to bring pressure on South Africa. I had sensed before that one of the levers which the Americans had used during Henry Kissinger's time was the Shah of Iran, who was the main supplier of oil to South Africa. That was now confirmed. We agreed to do all we could discreetly to mobilize this pressure again in support of our Anglo-American initiative.

In the UN Andy Young was much seized by the prospect of bringing, under the UN Charter, mandatory sanctions against South Africa. This meant declaring that, because of apartheid, a threat to peace existed, in or around South Africa. In the early months of the new Administration there was a great deal of unreality about what was said on this subject. Andy Young was playing to the Third World gallery in the UN and Walter Mondale, the Vice-President, had had an abrasive and fruitless meeting with the South Africans in which the threat of sanctions had been raised. Cy Vance was encountering powerful resistance over sanctions in Congress and from some sections of American business interests and this countered the support they were getting in the UN.

I had a similar problem over South Africa for I had to cope with a Labour Cabinet which included a powerful group of Ministers who were against any trade or economic sanctions because they would reduce exports, as well as a Whitehall machine which was adamantly opposed. I had first to overcome the traditional bureaucratic argument about the slippery slope and it took me some time before I made any headway. My first task was to make Cabinet colleagues and Whitehall officials aware that the Americans were already definitely heading towards some sanctions and, if we were not to slip down towards total sanctions, we had at the very least to keep the US State Department alongside. To say that Britain would use our veto against economic sanctions on our own was unrealistic. Even in the unlikely event that a Cabinet majority agreed to a lone veto, they would never agree to continue it once they had felt the worldwide hostility that would break around us. However, it would be a completely different and far more acceptable proposition to use our veto at the same time as the US. So the key Cabinet Sub-Committee had to be persuaded to bend at least to the extent of having some sanctions considered as an option. The Foreign Office had to be persuaded too. Within Whitehall it was virtually a forbidden subject and to outwit the Whitehall consensus I had to first win the battle within the Foreign Office. I was not to find it easy and I needed Cy Vance. He was in tune with the Congressional realities and ready to curb Andy Young's exuberance, so we slowly began to develop a coherent joint policy over sanctions.

On 17 March the Cabinet met and Jim Callaghan reported on our trip to Washington and to Ottawa. I felt on top of the world. My office was a hive of activity and everywhere I looked there were important, challenging things to be done. My anxiety was whether or not Labour would be in office long enough to achieve any of them. That night in the debate on public expenditure, the Government faced almost certain defeat. To avoid a vote the Whips used the tactical device of moving the Adjournment of the House and abstention when a division was forced by the Scottish Nationalists. It was a pretty disreputable exercise and Margaret Thatcher, as Leader of the Opposition, was within her rights to demand an early debate on a motion of no confidence. It was by no means certain we would win it. There were then 311 Labour MPs, 280 Conservative MPs, 13 Liberal MPs, 8 Ulster Unionists, 11 Scottish Nationalists, 3 Welsh Nationalists, 1 SDLP MP, 2 Scottish Labour Party, 1 Independent Ulster Unionist, 1 Independent Irish Republican and 1 Vanguard Unionist Progressive Party. The Labour Government, if ever faced by a combination of all the other parties, would lose the vote by ten.

The debate was arranged for Wednesday 23 March and that weekend the press was full of speculation about discussions between the Leader of the Liberal Party, David Steel, and Michael Foot, on behalf of the Government. Yet while this was winning all the attention a vital hard-nosed deal was being stitched up between Michael Foot and Enoch Powell, now an Ulster Unionist. They were old friends, a friendship rooted in their mutual love of Parliament and their unrealistic interpretation of parliamentary sovereignty. They had combined frequently in the past to fight European Community legislation and reform of the House of

Lords. They trusted each other and understood how parliamentary deals are made. In addition, the Ulster Unionist MPs had long felt aggrieved by their under-representation in the Commons. Since this was a fair complaint, a decision to bring their constituency numbers in line with the average constituency in Britain was a fairly simple concession. After the weekend, the Prime Minister saw Jim Molyneaux, the Leader of the Ulster Unionists, with Enoch Powell and Michael Foot, and promised an all-party conference under the chairmanship of Mr Speaker to examine the case for an increase in the number of Northern Ireland seats. There was no formal agreement but the understandings reached were sufficient for three Ulster Unionists to abstain. Thus was born the informal Labour-Unionist pact, which lasted until 1979. It was commented on much less than the formal Lib-Lab pact, both at the time and subsequently. Yet I believe that it was a more stable relationship and was at least as important in the survival of the Labour Government.

All eyes were on the probability of the Liberals doing a deal with Labour. Pacts between political parties can take many forms. To retain power you can swap political influence for MPs' votes, to gain power you need the most MPs and that is best done by standing down candidates in key seats. With rare exceptions since 1918 both the Liberal and Labour Parties have fought shy of standing candidates down. The Conservatives, far more ruthless about winning and retaining power, have never shown the same restraint over either type of pact. Lord Salisbury was prepared to make a pre-election pact by standing down for Liberal Unionists under Joseph Chamberlain and Stanley Baldwin was ready to participate in a National Government under Ramsay MacDonald. Winston Churchill was always ready to work with his former Liberal colleagues. After the Second World War, Conservatives readily absorbed Liberals into the Conservative Party. But they also had an electoral pact with the Liberals in 1951 and 1955 involving four seats in Bolton and Huddersfield. Until Edward Heath, they were more than willing, despite occasional differences of policy, to link up with Ulster politicians. The SDP was ready to work in the Alliance with the Liberals but most people would have been ready to consider a pact with the Conservatives or Labour if policy were agreed.

It may eventually be seen to be in both Labour's and the Liberal Democrats' interests to strike a formal pre-electoral seat pact but there is still a lot of suspicion. Much of the suspicion relates to past events in which, by a quirk of history, my great-grandfather was deeply involved because of a by-election in the constituency of Mid Glamorgan in which he lived. The first Lib-Lab pact had mainly operated in South Wales at the start of this century. There were twenty-four Lib-Lab MPs after the 1906 Election. They were trade unionists and could only be distinguished from Labour MPs by their taking of the Liberal Whip. When the Executive of the South Wales Miners recommended that Vernon Hartshorn, the miners' agent for the Maesteg area, should fight the parliamentary by-election in Mid-Glamorgan in 1910 for Labour, they were choosing an able and articulate critic of the then Lib-Lab pact. The Liberal Chief Whip who had been involved in negotiating the Memorandum with Labour had already promised the seat to Vernon Hartshorn. But the local Liberal Association felt betrayed and in the teeth of strong opposition from the Parliamentary Liberal Party they fought and beat Labour. My great-grandfather, Alderman Llewellyn, was the Honorary Treasurer of the Association. The Conservatives failed to contest as their candidate was away on a yacht cruise. No Liberal MP, however, came down to help in the local Liberal campaign and great damage was done to the concept of Lib-Labism not just in Wales but in the country at large. The Conservatives began to profit from battles between Liberal and Labour candidates and virtually all Lib-Lab co-operation had ceased by the time of the Coupon election in 1918.

On Monday 21 March, David Steel came to see the Prime Minister for a preliminary meeting. It went well and on Tuesday Michael Foot, David Steel and his Liberal colleague, John Pardoe, were in almost constant touch. Jim Callaghan also twice met with David Steel and eventually very late that night an agreement was reached between the two of them.

The Cabinet was called for noon. It was a momentous meeting. We all knew that, unless Jim had been successful in his discussions, we were going to lose the vote of confidence that night. The agreement was circulated and I read the document carefully; it seemed to me that apart from what I saw as the window dressing of joint consultation, the key section of the agreement related to proportional representation. But I later realized that this perspective was wrong. For David Steel, it was the joint consultation which was the essence of the agreement and that was Jim Callaghan's understanding too. I suppose David Steel thought consultation would develop into more than the fig leaf that it became. But by emphasizing this side of the agreement he let slip a golden opportunity to make progress on proportional representation.

The section of the agreement relating to proportional representation was incredibly weak. It read simply:

> We agree that legislation for direct elections to the European Assembly in 1978 will be presented to Parliament in this session. The Liberal Party reaffirm their strong conviction that a proportional system should be used as the method of election. The Government is publishing next week a White Paper on direct elections to the European Assembly, which sets out the choices among different electoral systems but which makes no recommendation. There will now be consultation between us on the method to be adopted, and the Government's final recommendation will take full account of the Liberal Party's commitment. The recommendation will be subject to a free vote of both Houses. We agree that progress must be made on legislation for devolution, and to this end consultations will begin on the detailed memorandum submit-

ted by the Liberal Party today. In any future debate on proportional representation for the devolved assemblies there will be a free vote.

When Jim explained exactly what he had agreed, I was astonished that the Liberals had not been able to extract a firm Government commitment to proportional representation for the European Parliament. The Liberals knew that a majority of the Cabinet had already accepted that proportional representation should be in the legislation since I had personally told Jeremy Thorpe that this was the case. If they had dug their toes in and refused a pact without Labour officially supporting proportional representation for the European elections, Jim would have had to persuade the Cabinet. In my judgement the majority of the Cabinet would have accepted this as a necessary price. I doubt if even Tony Benn would have resigned: he had stomached many more indigestible items than this over his years in Cabinet. The MPs from Northern Ireland, where there was already proportional representation, could not have objected, nor would the Scottish Nationalists.

I was doubly amazed at the agreement that David Steel had signed because I knew well that Liberals still resented the way that Labour had exploited an earlier Lib-Lab pact. People like John Pardoe were determined that the Liberals should not be taken for a ride again. They wanted something concrete and a Government commitment to support proportional representation for Europe fitted the bill. So what happened? John Pardoe was clearly under the impression that he and David Steel had agreed on their sticking point – 'No proportional representation, no pact.' Yet, whatever David Steel's intention, when he met Jim late that night his resolve weakened. He allowed himself to be persuaded that Jim could not deliver a firm commitment to proportional representation and he signed up for the watered-down version that was presented to us in Cabinet. The Liberal MPs were then trapped, unable to disown the pact without disowning their Leader and leaving the Party in disarray.

David Steel points out that he had been given Jim Callaghan's private assurance that, as Prime Minister, he would vote for proportional representation on a free vote when the time came. This is, of course, true but was never going to be enough to swing the issue. For proportional representation to win the day there would have had to be a whip on all Labour MPs and only a few voting against it. The Liberals had lost a chance to change the voting system. Proportional representation may well come first for the European Parliament and, only after experience with this, for the Westminster Parliament.

The Liberals had had a better opportunity during the 1916–17 Speaker's Conference presided over by Sir James Lowther and set up with the support of Asquith. That Conference recommended proportional representation in rural areas unanimously and the Alternative Vote in the Boroughs by eleven votes to eight. The House of Commons then rejected proportional representation and by a majority of one supported the Alternative Vote whereby voters go 1,2,3,4 and so on down the ballot paper showing a preference for the candidates in a single constituency. The Lords then reinstated proportional representation and rejected the Alternative Vote. Lloyd George, by then Prime Minister, disliked the idea of proportional representation because he saw it as a challenge to the two-party system, then made up of Conservatives and Liberals. As the historian Lord Blake said of the Liberals who had voted against proportional representation:

> The Party has been kicking its collective self ever since. And Britain has bumbled along to this day with what is virtually a unicameral sovereign legislature elected on the first-past-the-post system – the least fair, most arbitrary and least democratic of all methods of election in the democratic world.

It was a dramatic moment as we went round the Cabinet table each saying whether he supported the Lib-Lab Pact. I could see no point in making a long contribution so I just said 'I support the agreement'. My main surprise was the opposition of Bruce Millan on the grounds that it would gravely damage the Party. In my eyes he had always been a staunch Callaghanite and indeed Jim looked amazed. It showed the depth of scepticism towards any form of pact-making. The opposition of Peter Shore was predictable for he was implacably opposed to direct elections. Stan Orme's and Tony Benn's opposition were along the traditional Left-wing exclusive view that any association with any other party was always wrong. But then I was even more surprised when Albert Booth and John Silkin supported the agreement. So the Cabinet, by twenty votes to four, were in favour of the Lib-Lab Pact. The Prime Minister made it clear that he would expect all members of the Cabinet to be in the Division Lobby to vote in effect for the agreement that night.

In a packed House, Mrs Thatcher's motion of no confidence was rejected by 322 votes to 298. If the Liberals had voted against us we might just have been able to persuade more Ulster Unionists to abstain. If we had not, the Government would have lost by two votes. A general election would then have been held which we would have lost. I would have been in my post for thirty-two days, the shortest time of any British Foreign Secretary. I would have accomplished nothing, for all I had done so far was lay the foundations, and I would have been very lucky to hold Devonport.

13

AFRICA

The time of pussyfooting around over Rhodesia's independence was past. I was determined to bring UDI to an end and ensure majority rule for Zimbabwe. With the Government's future now assured well into 1978, I had the necessary political authority for a trip to Africa. It would have been impossible to push Mr Smith into serious negotiations if he had thought an election was imminent and the Conservatives likely to win. But before flying off, the question of sanctions had to be confronted. It was now clear that I was sitting on top of one of the biggest scandals in British post-war history. It looked as if, with the full connivance of the British Government, British oil companies had been breaking oil sanctions against Rhodesia. Revelations from Tiny Rowland, the Chief Executive of Lonrho, backed by letters and memoranda which he had already shown to President Kaunda of Zambia, contained what appeared to be *prima facie* evidence of sanction-breaking by BP and Shell. I immediately talked to Sam Silkin, the Attorney-General, and he asked me to send the correspondence directly to him. In this way we were able to circumvent any departmental discussion. Sam's view was that, although there was insufficient evidence to refer the case immediately to the Director of Public Prosecutions, it did warrant urgent investigation. Armed with that legal opinion, the inter-departmental discussion which then took place was loaded in my favour, although some still attempted to block an enquiry. These officials now had to cope with my open suspicion of past complicity and impropriety over Rhodesian sanctions. It was a tense time in the Department. To abandon minority white rule, Mr Smith now had to be pressurized either directly or, more credibly, indirectly by the South African Government. That meant the threat of economic sanctions had to encompass South Africa too.

The Cabinet Office was commissioned to make a factual assessment of the balance of economic advantage between Black Africa and South Africa in terms of trade and other aspects. However, officials came up with a paper which gratuitously introduced the familiar arguments of principle against sanctions and issued grave warnings about their dangers. How the Foreign Office representatives could have signed it I could not understand. In addition the Foreign Office sent out an incredibly slanted telegram asking for the views of our overseas posts.

This was a central test of political control. I worked on the simple principle that the Foreign Office should speak in Departmental Committees with the same voice that I spoke in Cabinet. The Foreign Office officials concerned with Africa were totally supportive, the problem came from those who were dealing with economic and trading questions and the Foreign Office representatives on the Whitehall committees. I had no hang-ups over internal dissent, in fact I enjoyed the clash of opinion, and sanctions was a vexed enough question for many different views within the Foreign Office to be wholly legitimate. What was not acceptable was that, after officials had had the opportunity to put their viewpoint, they should go to inter-departmental committees and try to undermine my decision. I was facing a difficult enough battle as it was with implacable opposition in Cabinet to any form of economic sanctions against South Africa coming from Edmund Dell, Denis Healey and Harold Lever. From then on I tried to ensure that nothing of substance on sanctions that had not first been vetted by my Private Office went out within Whitehall from the Foreign Office.

The history of sanctions-busting was that, in 1965, the Labour Government, having forsworn the use of force, imposed oil sanctions one month after Rhodesia had become a colony in rebellion against the Crown. Under Ian Smith, Rhodesia had simply issued a unilateral declaration of independence on 11 November 1965, in effect putting two fingers to the world and Britain. To have landed troops would have necessitated first destroying the Rhodesian Air Force and this was ruled out as it meant extensive bombing of airfields close to civilian housing and would inevitably have led to a loss of life. Britain acted under a non-mandatory resolution of the Security Council. The principal route for the supply of oil to Rhodesia was the Umtali pipeline from Beira in Mozambique. From 19 December 1965, no oil ever reached Beira and from 31 December no oil from the pipeline reached Rhodesia's only refinery. Oil did, however, reach Rhodesia overland through South Africa. Once the Beira Patrol was established, ships went to Lourenço Marques to offload and this continued until 1975, when it ceased following the Portuguese revolution and Mozambique's independence. Oil then came to Rhodesia through South African ports.

The Labour Government in 1965 felt there was no practicable way of monitoring or controlling the flow of oil through Lourenço Marques without a major confrontation with South Africa, since it was to South African law that the South African subsidiaries of the oil companies were subject. So British oil companies continued shipping oil to the Transvaal Province, Botswana and Swaziland through Lourenço Marques even when, after the failure of Harold Wilson's talks on HMS *Tiger* at the end of 1966, mandatory sanctions were applied to Rhodesia's major exports and to key imports, particularly oil. It was believed in Africa and in Britain that the British oil companies, BP and Shell, were not using that oil to supply Rhodesia. So President Kaunda was deeply shocked when he read the documents that cast serious doubt on that belief.

President Kaunda, by raising the profile of the Lonrho allegations and making it crystal clear that he would not see me personally when I was due to visit Lusaka on my African tour unless sanction-breaking was investigated by the British Government, ensured serious action. Jim Callaghan, to his credit, saw at once that my visit could be completely ruined by a black leader's boycott and that this could develop into a far worse snub than had been delivered to Ivor Richard on his tour. So the Prime Minister joined me in insisting on an investigation, which meant that the arguments of those in Whitehall who did not want an investigation on Africa were overruled.

Before I left, I saw the heads of Shell and BP and received their confirmation that they would henceforth stop all supplies of oil to Rhodesia; I was also able to tell Kenneth Kaunda that there would be a full investigation. Even so, there was persistent prevarication in Whitehall and it was only in May that I was able to announce that Thomas Bingham QC would conduct the investigation. His remit was to establish the facts concerning the operations whereby supplies of petroleum and petroleum products had reached Rhodesia since 17 December 1965.

The Department was instructed that no documents were to be withheld from the Bingham Inquiry and Bingham saw the Cabinet papers for 1967 and 1968, which were still on the departmental files. Much later, in the winter of 1978, such was the ludicrous furore over this in Whitehall that I actually had to apologize to the Cabinet for this breach of security. The Foreign Office should, under Whitehall rules, have returned these papers to the Cabinet Office. Personally I was delighted Bingham had seen the papers. It meant that my officials were not part of what would otherwise have been seen as a Whitehall cover up. Already the press were calling it Oilgate, comparing the scandal with President Nixon's Watergate. It would have been indefensible for Bingham not to have examined the role of Labour Ministers in 1967–68 under the guise of Cabinet secrecy. It never occured to me that Bingham, on whose positive vetting officials had insisted, could be refused access to Cabinet papers. Even so, when it was discovered that he had seen the relevant Cabinet papers, he was not allowed under the Official Secrets Act to admit to having done so in his report or describe what exactly had been decided by Ministers in Cabinet or in Cabinet subcommittees.

The real issue was political, namely the refusal of Britain in the middle 1960s to take the issue to the Security Council to apply mandatory oil sanctions on South Africa. To be effective this would have meant a UN-backed maritime blockade against South Africa, not just Mozambique. The Soviets would not have vetoed such a resolution and it is an open question whether the French and the US would have vetoed. The French had abstained on an early resolution but they would have been wary of alienating French Africa. Iran and Oman would not have sought to evade a mandatory UN Resolution. The truth is that Britain never tried in 1965. With no majority, that was excusable. After 1966, when Labour had a large majority, I and many other MPs felt it was inexcusable. Had we tried, Mr Smith's UDI might have been ended long before 1980 and many lives would have been saved. The Beira Patrol by the Royal Navy showed that it was feasible to stop tankers and turn them round but, in the light of what we now know about the swap arrangement, the Patrol was just a cynical exercise. Stopping oil going to Beira while ignoring the oil going to South Africa either through South African ports or Lourenço Marques was always dubious. To waste money on doing this from 1968 to 1977 while British companies were either supplying direct or simply swapping oil in order for others to supply Rhodesia was a major scandal.

One spin off from learning about potential oil sanction-breaking was that I could no longer recommend to Jim Callaghan that George Thomson be made Ambassador to Washington, as had been my intention. George had just finished as a European Commissioner and would in normal circumstances have been the obvious choice. He had supported Jim Callaghan for the leadership of the Party as far back as 1963 and had maintained friendly relations. Officials legitimately have access to past Cabinet papers which I could not see, and I was warned that George Thomson might be implicated in the Bingham investigation. Given the sensitive mood about sanctions in Carter's Administration, an incoming British Ambassador linked in any way to possible sanction-busting would be an embarrassment. It was also awkward for Michael Palliser who was then Harold Wilson's Private Secretary and who would have been expected to have read minutes of George Thomson's meetings sent over to No. 10.

The Bingham Report came out in September 1978.[1] It was always going to be published, for I would have resigned rather than let it be pigeon-holed. The controversial swap arrangement which BP and Shell agreed with Total in 1967 was described in detail. In order that no British owned company could be said to be supplying oil direct to Rhodesia, Total supplied the oil and were compensated by Shell and BP. This arrangement operated until 1971. The Report made clear that the swap arrangements had been revealed in full by the oil companies to the British Government in 1968 and that the British Government had taken no steps at the time to consider prosecution for the breaches in the law which the oil companies admitted had already taken place. The swap itself was within the letter of the law. When this swap arrangement lapsed in 1971, Bingham found no evidence that the British Government knew thereafter that these British oil companies supplied oil direct to Rhodesia in clear breach of the law. The oil companies, in their defence, would have been entitled to claim that the law had already been breached in spirit for three years from 1968–71 with the compliance of a Labour Government.

The main scandal within the Report, which was never focused on sufficiently, was the revelation that there had been no reference to the Director of Public Prosecutions in 1967 when the evidence of breaches of the sanctions law was first known in Whitehall. It is simply not open to Ministers or officials to ignore illegality because it is politically convenient. In that limited sense what was revealed really was the equivalent of Nixon's Watergate. Why did officials in the various departments not insist that the Attorney-General was consulted? Why did Ministers not so insist? We never had these questions answered satisfactorily; Bingham was prevented from publishing what he had seen in the Cabinet papers and, in my view, did not point this issue up with sufficient shock and outrage. It was an excellent factual report but strangely devoid of the moral indignation that some of the great investigations of the past have brought to bear.

When the Bingham Report was referred to the DPP it became obvious that the illegality prior to the swap in 1968 and after the swap in 1971 could form the basis of a prosecution. But, since the defence would have had every right to refer back to the Cabinet decisions concerning sanctions policy, a court would either have had to have access to those papers or be unable to form a judgement on all the material facts. To hear members of a Labour Cabinet preaching the absolute sanctity of Cabinet documents was alarming. The doctrine they and others outside the Cabinet sought to defend was that Cabinet documents should never be revealed in any circumstance, even when a breach of the law was at issue, until thirty years had expired. It was soon obvious that, in order to investigate the role of Ministers under both Labour and Conservative Governments, Parliament would have to lift the cross-party agreement on not revealing Cabinet papers. After much Cabinet soul searching, a Commission of Inquiry into the whole affair, whose terms of reference were announced in December 1978, was put forward for Parliament's approval. The Commission was to be chaired by a High Court judge and would have had the opportunity to look at all the Cabinet papers for the period, Labour and Conservative. Its creation was met with the utmost scepticism and then voted down in the House of Lords.

So, with a good deal of cross-party complicity, the cover up continued. Thereafter, it was almost inevitable that the Attorney-General in the incoming Conservative Government would decide against the DPP proceeding with any prosecution. To have made officials in BP or Shell a scapegoat once Parliament had refused to investigate the role of the politicians would have been an even shabbier end to what was an already sordid affair. The ingrained attitudes of secrecy that the response to Bingham revealed in politicians' and civil servants' minds horrified me. It also made me very concerned that any future reform of the Official Secrets Act would tighten their grip. Their refusal to accept a public interest defence in the new legislation leaves me very concerned that it might still be impossible to expose a similar scandal.

When the Bingham Report came out, George Thomson and Michael Stewart admitted in dignified speeches in the House of Lords that they knew about the swap arrangements but, although they put what had happened in the context of the time, they never explained why the Law Officers were not called in. Harold Wilson denied that he knew about the swap and said he had not read the minutes of the meetings that George Thomson had had with the oil companies, in fairness he would only read such minutes if put before him by his Private Office.

The political decision had been made in 1967 when George Brown, as Foreign Secretary, put a paper to Cabinet which told them that they had a straight choice: to apply sanctions against South Africa or to turn a blind eye to Rhodesian sanctions being evaded with the help of South Africa. Characteristically, George Brown wanted to confront the South Africans. Equally characteristically, Harold Wilson wanted to duck out of the real choice. The Cabinet deliberately continued with the rhetoric of sanctions while avoiding the reality and this is all too apparent in Harold Wilson's account of what happened in his speech to the House of Commons on 7 November 1978.

It was claimed by Edward Heath and others that in June 1970 top Foreign Office officials did not tell the incoming Conservative Government about the swap arrangement. If so, that was a disgraceful omission. Bingham reported that officials did not monitor what happened after 1970 and so did not pick up the change in the swap arrangement in 1971. That too was negligent, compounding the error of not telling Ministers about its existence. The civil service have no excuse while incoming Governments are not told of a predecessors' domestic decisions; new governments are meant to be told about on-going policy in international affairs. It has, however, become very necessary to clarify this obligation since officials did not tell Lord Carrington until March 1982 about the Labour Government's deployment of naval vessels to the Southern Atlantic in 1977, which was also negligent.

The depressing overall result of the Bingham enquiry was that neither the politicians nor the civil servants involved in sanction-breaking were ever held to account. It exposed the total inadequacy of the powers of Parliament to scrutinize the Executive. Parliament should not have had to wait for the Cabinet to come forward with an ad hoc new type of commission. In those days, there was no Select Committee on Foreign Affairs, though I had supported its creation while Foreign Secretary. One problem was Michael Foot, who disliked Select Committees and had a romantic view of the value of questioning Ministers at the despatch box. Now the House of Commons has Departmental Select Committees, introduced when Norman St John Stevas was Leader of the House. But even so, civil servants would not answer what advice was given to Ministers and, just as the Select Committees that looked at the Westland affair were never able to question Bernard Ingham, the Prime Minister's Press Secretary, they would not have been able to question Michael Palliser about whether Harold Wilson did see the papers about George Thomson's meeting with the oil companies when the swap arrangements were discussed. Also, all Cabinet papers and decisions would be closed to the Select Committee. At the very least, we need to reform and agree new procedures for the equivalent of the old Tribunals of Enquiry and get away from the one-off enquiries which are fraught with problems.

While the outcome of Bingham was deeply unsatisfactory, the issue helped me break Whitehall's resistance to contemplating sanctions against South Africa. Officials preparing evidence for Bingham were well aware that there was truth in Lonrho's revelations about oil. Tiny Rowland's allegations were to be vindicated and, even though at one stage he threatened to sue me, our shared love of Africa meant that later he and his wife, Josie, became friends. When in the autumn of 1977 Steve Biko, the charismatic young black-consciousness leader, was brutally beaten to death in a prison cell in South Africa, the climate of opinion inside Cabinet changed further, helped by world anger at the clumsy restrictions on black newspapers. I now had little difficulty in obtaining authorization to apply UN mandatory sanctions against South Africa in relation to all arms supplies.

That decision had a sobering effect on South Africa for, although a voluntary arms embargo had been in place for some years, they now knew the world community had broken the psychological barrier over mandatory action and was more likely to agree further sanctions. It took a long time for sanctions to bite. It was not until the US congress overturned President Reagan's veto on the Comprehensive Anti-Apartheid Act that South Africa was really pressurized to change policy in 1986 and the harshest economic sanction was in 1985 when foreign bank loans dried up following the refusal of the Chase Manhattan Bank to roll over short-term loans. A myth was propagated by Margaret Thatcher that sanctions never had any effect on the changes that came in 1990 with President de Klerk. That was never the view of the South African business community.

In 1986–87, Reagan's seemingly failed policy of constructive engagement in Southern Africa produced real movement. The regional negotiations achieved a breakthrough over the US-imposed linkage of Namibian independence and Cuban troop withdrawals from Angola. A combination of US-Soviet co-operation and South African loss of air supremacy in Angola, following Cuba's strengthening of their forces, also changed the dynamics. In 1988 the South African *Weekly Mail* wrote that this 'was the year financial sanctions struck home.' Indeed, the 1989 National Party Manifesto recognized that 'Boycotts, sanctions and disinvestment have strained the economy of the country and of every business and household.' It is very difficult to calculate whether the ban on new investment hurt the South African economy but a reasonable assessment is that it depressed attainable GDP growth by 1–1.5 per cent per annum by 1988–89.

By 1989 the world was facing a very different situation. The Soviet Union was no longer a superpower. Its economic weakness, known privately to the leadership for at least a decade, was now publicly exposed. The winding down of the Soviet Empire was inexorably underway. Cuban troops were due to withdraw from Angola in 1991 and in Eastern Europe the communist satellite countries began to collapse. Some of these countries, like East Germany, had hitherto had strong links in Southern Africa with the liberation movements. More importantly many of the slogans of the liberation movements were having to be revised. Support for the one-party state in Africa was incomprehensible judged against what was happening in Czechoslovakia, Hungary, East Germany, Poland and even in the Soviet Union itself. Ritual denunciation of capitalism sounded bizarre in view of the proven failure of Soviet Communism and the command economies. But equally the South African Government could no longer claim to be a bastion against communism and the strategic significance of the Cape sea routes, always exaggerated, was now exposed to be of little relevance.

But the realism of 1990 was totally absent in 1977. In the run up to my visit to Africa I tried to consult as wide a range of opinion as I could. Over lunch at No. 10 with Jim Callaghan and the President of Senegal, I tried to enlist the President's help as he was influential in French-speaking Africa. That same evening I took the issue to the Parliamentary Labour Party and found them in good heart. They clearly liked the activist stance that I was taking over Rhodesia. Yet it was interesting how warmly a number of influential MPs spoke of Bishop Muzorewa: the important role he had played in mobilizing opinion inside Rhodesia to convince the Pearce Commission that Lord Home's initiative in the early 1970s did not carry majority support had made him many friends. I also managed to use an EEC Council of Ministers meeting in Luxembourg to lobby support for our policy among foreign ministers. One of the most interesting meetings I had was one I requested with Lord Goodman. He had had many meetings with Smith and gave me excellent advice on how to handle him. He had no doubt that Smith was a frequent stranger to the truth but the more he had his back against the wall, the more he twisted and turned. He suggested that I should propose starting off with a completely new sheet at a meeting with only the two of us present.

Given the Lib-Lab Pact, a meeting with Jeremy Thorpe was an obligation but also a pleasure for he was knowledgeable about Africa.

Over the years, he had developed strong links with Kenneth Kaunda and on Rhodesia he warned me that the Tory Right wing were just waiting for an opportunity to put a motion of censure down on me personally. Like some of my Labour colleagues he stressed the importance of Muzorewa, whom I was due to see next day. When I did, try as I might, I found it hard to believe that Muzorewa was likely to emerge as a key figure. He was doing a lot of lecturing on the Methodist circuit in the United States and seemed pretty out of touch with the younger, radical nationalists who were becoming more and more influential inside as well as outside Rhodesia. Jeremy and I also took the opportunity to talk about the Lib-Lab Pact. I had known Jeremy from West Country politics since 1962 and I knew that when one could stop him acting the showman he was an astute politician. I was worried about the survival of the pact. Labour Ministers had been pretty shattered to find out after the Budget that the Liberals had decided that they would have to vote against the £10 rise in Vehicle Excise Duty and the 5p a gallon increase on petrol. This could have lost the Exchequer a cool £670 million in revenue besides dealing a devastating political blow to the pact's credibility. Fortunately, the Liberals eventually backed down but only after an expensive compromise had been arranged. I well understood the antagonism to such measures in rural areas where a car is essential and I wanted to know if Denis Healey had been aware of their feelings. Jeremy explained that John Pardoe and Denis Healey were an explosive combination, that there was no trust and he felt that Denis had set out deliberately to rub Liberal feelings up the wrong way in his budget. They were bound to protect the rural voter. Nevertheless, he was confident that the pact would last for two years.

Perhaps the most important meeting before my trip was with Cy Vance, who came through London and met with the Prime Minister and myself. Next day we had extensive discussions on a range of issues and co-ordinated what I would say on my African trip. We agreed that in Cape Town I should raise our deep anxieties about an internal settlement for Namibia which excluded nationalist leaders fighting for independence outside the country. We also decided we would both try to persuade the Shah to support our Namibian and Rhodesian initiatives. We hoped for a private threat from the Shah that he would stop supplying oil to South Africa if the UN viewpoint on Namibia were ignored.

I also recorded a long interview for *Weekend World* with Peter Jay at Buttermere. Peter stayed for supper and we had a good yarn about politics and how he saw the economic situation. He had a mind like a machine-gun and even though he saw only the warts of the European Community, he had come to terms with the reality of our membership. He was ready to be constructive about how to improve things in Brussels and it was apparent that he was still seeing a lot of Jim Callaghan and that Jim was listening to what he had to say. He also liked and admired

Denis Healey as Chancellor, while disagreeing with him from time to time. Since this was my attitude too, I became more and more convinced that he was the right person to be our Ambassador in Washington.

We spent Easter weekend as a family in Plymouth. The logistic problems of juggling our private and public life were immense. We left London on the Thursday and drove down in our own car. The detectives on this occasion travelled in the car behind us. Although sometimes they felt obliged, for form's sake, to travel with me in the car, even when I was with the family, they were very understanding of our needs as parents with two young children. I was speeding too fast down the motorway and was flagged down but the detective on duty, with great presence of mind, got out of the car, thanked the Devon police for flagging us down and asked what message they had for the Foreign Secretary. This approach rather took the local police aback; pleasantries were exchanged and no further mention was made of our speeding. Debbie and I returned to London on the Sunday evening, leaving Tristan and Gareth to be looked after by my sister while we were away. Before flying out I had a meeting with Joshua Nkomo. He was the oldest of the nationalist leaders, a vast man with a laugh that rumbled around his large belly; friendly, earthy but shrewd. There was little doubt that he would come to a constitutional conference but he held his negotiating hand close to his chest, as one would have expected from such a veteran negotiator. Like an elephant, he had a long memory but despite his bulk moved with care and precision.

It was the first time I had flown in the RAF VC-10. They are the quietest and most comfortable of planes and the advertisements to try a little VC tenderness were accurate. It was fitted out with a few bunk beds and there was a table for working and eating on. The press corps which accompanied me and helped cover the cost of the plane, were eager to have a press conference, which I conducted in the aisle. The question on the lips of every reporter was 'Are you going to Rhodesia?'. All I would say at that time was that, if I thought it would help I would consider it. My intention was to see Mr Smith in South Africa first and only then decide whether to go into Rhodesia, although in my own mind I was certain that I would go. No Labour Cabinet Minister had visited Rhodesia since UDI, though Alec Douglas-Home, when Foreign Secretary, had gone there in 1971. When Jim Callaghan was Foreign Secretary, he had visited six African countries, including South Africa, but he had not felt it right to go to Rhodesia. He had been uneasy about me going but had agreed to the strategy. As Debbie and I slipped into bed that night, we laughed about the time, in 1969, when we had flown in the US Secretary for the Navy's plane overnight from Virginia to San Francisco and I had leant across and said, 'Its downhill all the way from now.'

My purpose in Africa was to win acceptance to opening discussions about a constitution for an independent Zimbabwe – to get the South Africans to put pressure on Smith and persuade the Front Line Presidents to put pressure on the Patriotic Front of Nkomo and Mugabe. The first port of call was Tanzania and we arrived at Dar es Salaam, having slept well. I met Robert Mugabe there for the first time. He was like a coiled spring, tense and very prickly and also somewhat withdrawn. He was quite convinced that the conflict could only be settled by 'a bitter and bloody war', which could be 'resolved only on the battlefield'. I countered his line by telling the press that our American backed proposals could bring majority rule to Rhodesia through 'the ballot rather than the gun', but it was painfully apparent that, after Geneva, Mugabe had lost any faith he might ever have had in diplomacy. 'The struggle might be protracted, bitter and bloody, but this is the price Zimbabweans should be prepared to pay,' he told reporters. 'Dr Owen has failed to convince us that Britain is in a position to effect the transfer of power to the people of Zimbabwe.' At that stage, it was impossible to convince him that he should talk to Mr Smith. When I raised the question of an amnesty for crimes committed since UDI he was not just adamantly opposed but outraged that the idea should even be contemplated. He and I were to return to this issue time and time again but he was implacable about the need for retribution, which made his speech of reconciliation after his ballot victory in 1980 even more remarkable. Despite the unpromising nature of the discussion and my sense that he was talking to a collective brief, as befitted a good Marxist, I nevertheless felt that I was dealing with an honest man. That feeling never left me. We had numerous, often extremely heated, arguments. Ferocious words were sometimes exchanged between us which have left their scars, but Robert Mugabe never once lied to me. That truthfulness was precious and I can confidently say it of only one other person with whom I negotiated for over two years in Southern Africa and that was Samora Machel, the young President of Mozambique.

During my visit to Rhodesia Debbie made an interesting trip to a Mission School and met a priest called Father Dove who had Robert Mugabe's sister teaching in the school. He said he had a message for me, 'Tell your husband that Robert is still a Christian.' I recalled that advice many times in the years ahead and asked our intelligence service to find out if he was a practising Christian. I suspect that Mugabe was then, and still remains, a Jesuitical Marxist. This goes some way to explain his obduracy when powerless and his readiness to reconcile when he had power.

Mugabe was the panther, Nkomo the elephant, both true beasts of the forest and exceptional people. We were all pacing around each other, knowing we needed each other but each wanting it to be on his own terms.

I then went to State House in Dar es Salaam to talk to President Nyerere.

Nyerere was the most influential figure among the leaders of the so-called Front Line States. Tanzania was miles from the Rhodesian border but Julius Nyerere had established his position as the moral voice of Africa. People in the Foreign Office tend to have passionate views one way or the other about him. Peter Carrington distrusted him while I liked him. Highly intelligent, flagrantly manipulative, he was suspicious at times to the point of paranoia about British motives. He believed, on good past evidence, that when the crunch came we would never put economic pressure on South Africa. Our talks went reasonably well and I left him with more good will than I had hoped. A face-to-face meeting was not my only way of communicating with Nyerere. I knew he listened to the BBC World Service as he shaved each morning. Sometimes, in a broadcast, I would angle what I was saying at a delicate moment as if I were talking back to him from his shaving mirror.

I also met with the Reverend Sithole. Since my father always inadvertently called him 'Shit holy', I lived in mortal dread that I might make the same mistake in pronouncing his name!

Next day we flew to Mozambique, having stayed overnight in Dar es Salaam. The Foreign Secretary, now President, Joaquim Chissano, intelligent and sensitive, came out to meet me at the airport. Driving into Maputo one could see the depressing effect of the sudden withdrawal of the Portuguese in 1975. There was a desolate feeling to most of the white suburbs and a marked deterioration in the city. But my meeting with President Machel was a delight. He bounced into the room and, though speaking only Portuguese, radiated a warmth and openness in marked contrast to the suspicion of almost everyone else I had met. Allegedly a Marxist, he seemed to be more a genuine nationalist leader and I liked him. The Mozambicans were desperate for a solution to the Rhodesian problem, but not at any price. Machel felt honour-bound to support the Zimbabwean nationalist leaders who were fighting for their independence, as he had done. But there was a streak of realism in his nature, which came from being a genuine bush fighter, and made me believe he could become a supporter of the ideas that we were developing in the Anglo-American initiative.

And so we flew on to Cape Town where we stayed with the Ambassador, Sir David Scott, a seasoned sage adviser and one on whom I relied a great deal over the years ahead. The Government and Parliament spend part of the year in Cape Town by the sea and part in Pretoria on the veldt at 5,000 feet. Prime Minister Vorster, whom I met next morning and later had lunch with, was a dour ponderous Afrikaner. He thought carefully before he reacted but I found that, as long as I did not offend his pride in South Africa, he could take criticism of his policies. His reaction, however, to even a hint of a threat was to become intransigent. He was the hippopotamus. I spent some time explaining the thinking behind the new initiative over Namibia which was sponsored by five nations on the Security Council – the US, UK, France, Germany and Canada. I told him straightforwardly we could not accept the Turnhalle internal agreement. Vance and I had both agreed that we simply had to turn the South African Government round on this issue. Unless we could do so the UN would obstruct any chance of establishing a constructive dialogue with South Africa over Rhodesia and the pressure for sanctions in relation to apartheid would grow. The Namibian Contact Group, or the Western Five as it was variously described, was purely an ad hoc grouping. It allowed Britain, the US and France, as permanent members of the Security Council, to work with Canada, who had genuine interest in, and generous aid programmes for Africa, and Germany which had been the colonial power in Namibia. It was just our good fortune that these two countries happened to be members of the Security Council at that time. Andrew Young and a very effective black State Department official, Don McHenry, were the driving force behind the Namibian initiative. Namibia was part of a three-pronged approach to Southern Africa alongside the Anglo-American initiative on Rhodesia and the pressure on South Africa to abandon apartheid. Vorster and I got on well and he made this clear when briefing the press afterwards. Also, once he realized that I had every intention of going to Rhodesia, he became more enthusiastic for my proposal to take the constitutional questions first.

That afternoon, at our Ambassador's house in Cape Town, I met Mr Smith for the first time. Because he was the head of an illegal government I never referred to him as Prime Minister and relations were always formal and stiff, in keeping with his own manner. As I had planned, we went for a walk in the garden before we all sat down for the formal meeting. I suggested that he and I should open a new page and try to develop trust by talking frankly together. I would far prefer that he was rude to me directly than that he misled me behind my back. He professed to be quite unaware that I was actually intending to visit Rhodesia. Only when he realized that I really was planning to come did his mood change and we quickly agreed certain safeguards and who he would release from prison so I could see them. His problem now, he explained, was that his people were expecting him to be angry with me and to persuade me to come to Rhodesia. I said I had no objection if he wanted to make that case when the meeting started and I would listen and then concede gracefully. This is exactly what we did. So realistically did he perform that even my Private Secretary thought that Smith had been pretty bloody to me and was amazed when I told him that we had pre-arranged the whole thing. Smith was the jackal among the key people around whom I had to build a policy. Nkomo the elephant, Mugabe the panther, and Vorster the hippopotamus. Circling overhead was the American eagle but I could not yet be sure whether on the ground the British lion was ready to roar.

What was surprising was that Smith welcomed American participation in a constitutional conference, perhaps because he was obsessed about the growth of Communist influence in Southern Africa and felt that they too would be disturbed by this development; perhaps because he thought that, as with Henry Kissinger's initiative, he could play off the US officials against the British. So it was announced that evening that we were changing our plans and I would fly to Rhodesia after having visited Lusaka.

Next day I flew to Gabarone, the capital of Botswana, to meet President Seretse Khama. Botswana was then the only true democracy in Africa. I thought back to how my young cousin, Faith, as a small girl, had been fascinated by Seretse Khama when he was always in the news, having been banished from his country by Britain. He had been treated appallingly by Britain because of his marriage to Ruth, a white English woman of quite exceptional charm and quality. Now I could understand his appeal, for Seretse Khama was considerate, thoughtful and carried himself with an impressive quiet dignity. He liked the proposals and he was a staunch friend thereafter, in part because he had known Jim Callaghan over many years and trusted him. That afternoon I flew on to Lusaka.

Next day I met President Kenneth Kaunda and there was none of the animosity which I had previously feared. Kenneth was emotional, friendly and very pleased by the promise to investigate oil sanction busting. Yet if one had to sum up the atmosphere of our meeting in one word, it would be sceptical. He had been let down too often by Britain in his own struggle for independence during the colonial days to be totally trusting. Since UDI, he had had to watch Zambia, a newly independent country, bleed because of Britain's inability to suppress a revolt against the Crown. Unspoken was the thought that if a black government had declared UDI in Rhodesia, British military might would have crushed the revolt within days. Sadly, he was quite right: Britain's failure to act had had everything to do with its being a white revolt and the reluctance to put our armed forces in was because it meant confronting our 'kith and kin'. In 1965, with only a narrow majority and an election pending, Labour did not have the self-confidence to act. He wondered whether we now had the self-confidence to uphold the principles underpinning the Anglo-American initiative. President Kaunda's courtesy and affection for Britain always remained; his attitude was more of sorrow than of anger. He wanted to believe that I would succeed but he doubted I would. One question on which he privately wanted reassurance was whether the Prime Minister was backing me because he had picked up some scurrilous press speculation that Jim was distancing himself from the Rhodesian problem. I was able to reassure him that Jim Callaghan was fully supportive.

I flew next morning into Salisbury in an RAF plane to a colony in rebellion against the Crown. Determined to distance ourselves from the illegal regime, we did not even use their official car. I stepped instead into a Rolls-Royce that had been driven up from South Africa. We stayed only thirty-seven hours, during which I met dozens of different delegations, called again on Mr Smith, went on television for a half-hour interview, managed to visit a tribal trust land and even to drink the local beer. Surprisingly the visit turned out to be a considerable success. I always spoke about the inevitability of a transfer of power. Mr Smith replied with demands for entrenched clauses in the constitution, a qualified franchise, an impartial judiciary and safeguards for white pensions, investment, land rights and the maintenance of the forces of law and order. At this stage we were still talking about the widest possible franchise, and I made it clear to him that I saw great difficulties in limiting the franchise, favouring one person, one vote.

We thought it would be worthwhile to fly back through Angola but we left Salisbury without having clearance to land in Luanda. We still had no clearance as we circled the almost deserted airport. Eventually our RAF pilot just radioed that he was coming in to land. We were then taken to the airport terminal's VIP lounge where the carpet and furniture were covered in a thick layer of dust; it looked as if no one had been there since the Portuguese left. Eventually President Neto came out to the airport and, when we had cleaned off the seats, we had a useful conversation. This was the first visit at Ministerial level of any Western democracy to Angola under its new Marxist regime. The internal war with Jonas Savimbi was already under way and I formed the impression that Angola would be too weak to play an important diplomatic role over Rhodesia and that Namibia was going to be their prime concern. Despite this, I was glad to have come – symbolically it was important to have visited all five of the Front Line Presidents.

There was one more visit to make before I returned home – Lagos. Our High Commissioner, Sam Falle, had only managed after some difficulty to fix a meeting with Commissioner Garba, the Foreign Minister. I was amazed to discover how bad bilateral relations had become. The declared reason was our refusal to return the Benin mask from the British Museum but, as is so often the case, there was an undeclared reason; it was our refusal to allow General Gowan, their former leader, to be extradited. It took time to convince Joe Garba that I was serious about a transfer of Rhodesian power to the majority but thereafter we worked together quite closely, particularly over Nkomo's meeting with Mr Smith in Lusaka in August 1978. Without Nigerian involvement we would not have been keen on the meeting. Even so, Joe Garba's presence was not sufficient to dispel either Robert Mugabe's or Julius Nyerere's suspicions. I always regret that, having sent my Assistant Private Secretary, Stephen Wall, as a special envoy to Tanzania to explain our motives to Julius Nyerere, I did not send him in after Joe Garba had been to see President Nyerere at State House. The only reason I did not do so was Joe Garba's specific request to leave Julius alone because their meeting had gone so well. In fact, Garba had completely misread Nyerere and Julius promptly set out to scupper that initiative.

On a subsequent visit to Nigeria I began a friendship with General Obasanjo, the then Head of Government, which blossomed when, throughout the 1980s, we were both members of the Independent Commission on Defence and Security Issues, initially chaired by Olaf Palme. Obasanjo believed someone had to bash heads together to stop the Patriotic Front fighting each other and was very helpful to the Anglo-American initiative throughout, particularly when he became convinced by the sincerity of President Carter. Nevertheless, relations were still so strained after my visit that Nigeria only sent Obasanjo's deputy to the Commonwealth Heads of Government Conference in London in July and they created constant problems for us when we wanted to isolate Idi Amin in Uganda.

I arrived back in London to find a mood of optimism. Debbie and I had travelled 5,000 miles in eight days and fallen in love with the African continent, its people and its beauty. The press reports of my tour had been extensive and almost universally favourable. Jim Callaghan in particular was very pleased. He wrote to say it had been one of the best weeks for his Government and said much the same in Cabinet. I had no specific agreement to show but the atmosphere was transformed, Geneva was now behind us and the Anglo-American initiative firmly launched. A momentum for dialogue and negotiation had been created which, though it would slow down very considerably, just about carried through to the Lancaster House Conference convened by Lord Carrington in the winter of 1979. The concept of a constitutional conference with all the parties represented but with no one holding a veto became firmly rooted. The strategy of close US involvement was starting to be accepted too, though it was still viewed with scepticism by the Patriotic Front, with Nkomo keener than Mugabe. In fact I felt confident that once they met the key Americans, particularly Jimmy Carter, Cy Vance and Andrew Young, it would not be long before they would be preferring to deal with America than with Britain and that was what happened. By December 1979 the Patriotic Front were looking to President Carter to stop the British from getting away with any manipulation and the US only agreed to lift sanctions when Lord Soames as Governor established an election commission.

Not everyone was enthusiastic about our two trips to France and Africa. Debbie received the following letter:

It really is the most appalling impertinence for a toothy and very plain American woman to be gallivanting around the whole of Southern Africa, shopping in Paris etc. and all at the expense of the poor clobbered British taxpayer. Furthermore, if I were you I would

cease displaying newspaper photographs of those two quite
extraordinarily unattractive little boys. The poor creatures look
mentally deficient and they are to be pitied.

The hardest task now was to maintain the momentum. Mugabe and
Nkomo started making even more critical noises, dismissing American
involvement and making the ludicrous claim that they alone should
negotiate with Britain, the colonial power. Vance and I agreed that two of
our senior officials should form an Anglo-American Consultative Group
and so John Graham, for us, and Stephen Low, who was the US
Ambassador in Lusaka, began to tour around filling in the details of the
constitution. I was also keeping up the pressure for a proper democracy
and increasingly in Parliamentary Questions and in press interviews,
spoke of one person-one vote and less and less of a qualified franchise.
What were supposed to be private discussions started in Salisbury to
spell out the concept of a resident British Commissioner to take control
of an interim administration for a period of not more than six months
and to supervise the elections. We also talked about how to ensure a
ceasefire and create viable security arrangements.

As these initiatives took place and the momentum of my trip was
maintained, Mr Smith realized in the early summer that we meant
business and that his old tactics of splitting the forces against him were not
working. The British and Americans were working in very close harmony
and one member-one vote was looking increasingly likely. Smith suddenly
reverted to his old style and briefed the press against John Graham
personally and the proposals in general, breaking confidence and destroying
the good will that had stemmed from our meetings. By July I knew we
were in for a confrontation. He had always deeply regretted his commitment
to Henry Kissinger to transfer power within two years and was trying hard
to renege on this pledge. Meanwhile a backlash was developing inside
Rhodesia in the face of the deteriorating economic and security situation.
The Rhodesian Action Party was launched on the heady premise of victory
at war, victory against the terrorists and may the best man rule. Mr Smith
used the launch as an excuse for a typical ploy, calling an election for 31
August. Everyone knew he would defeat the new party easily but it allowed
him to play for time and to stall our negotiations. In another manoeuvre,
Smith persuaded Sithole to return from exile. In terms of public opinion
this proved to be a non-event and he was of only limited significance from
then on. I realized that we had to assume that the Anglo-American
proposals would not win Smith's support and that we would have to appeal
over his head to public opinion within Rhodesia and in the wider world.
He was just looking for an opportunity to launch an internal settlement
with Sithole and Muzorewa excluding Nkomo and Mugabe. I had always
been adamant that there would be no vetoes from any side, and Mr Smith
now had to be forced to understand that this applied to him as well.

The situation in Rhodesia was deteriorating in almost every regard. The level of violence in the war between the guerrilla fighters and the Rhodesian armed forces increased. The Patriotic Front, in particular Mugabe's ZANU, were infiltrating from Mozambique and the Rhodesians were retaliating. Nkomo's forces, ZIPRA, were Russian-trained and based in Zambia. Schools were being forced to close and often burnt down. Mission hospitals and clinics were harassed and government hospitals and clinics destroyed. Farmers in remote areas lived in fear of their lives. While in the first half of the year over a thousand guerrillas had been killed, the number of guerrilla fighters in the country increased. The cost of the war soared and the economy was seriously weakened. In the first half of the year an average of 1,500 whites a month left the country. What was even more depressing was the type of violence on both sides. Vicious murders were taking place, reminiscent of Mau Mau in Kenya, carried out not only by Mugabe's people in ZANU and Nkomo's in ZIPRA but also increasingly by the Selous Scouts, part of Mr Smith's army. The Selous Scouts tried to incriminate the Patriotic Front by leaving behind ZANU or ZIPRA papers and cap badges which would then be duly shown to the press. It was a murky, messy business. On all sides Britain was being held responsible for these horrors and we had no power on the ground to reinforce our rhetoric. With each incident I was dragged down to the House of Commons to make statements of sympathy. What it demonstrated was the vital necessity of having, as part of our plan, concrete measures to keep all the different forces from fighting each other while any elections took place. In Africa it was thought that he who controlled the army and the police controlled the election. Mugabe, Nkomo and Smith were all determined to retain control of their own armies. So we had to think of an independent force capable of holding the ring.

I had already been rebuffed by the Cabinet, as Jim Callaghan had warned me I might, over my wish to have a Commonwealth force to go into Rhodesia to supervise a ceasefire and monitor the elections. My preference for a Commonwealth force rather than one provided by the United Nations stemmed from my desire to maximize British influence and minimize the risk of a Soviet veto which would be ever-present if we brought in the UN. Denis Healey, having been involved in the decisions not to use force at the beginning of the crisis in 1965, was adamant that we should not be sucked in now. His opposition to a Commonwealth peace-keeping force was decisive in a Cabinet already reluctant to commit British forces and only too keen to be swayed towards the UN. Denis's argument played on the fear that, with a Commonwealth force, we could not avoid making a sizeable British military contribution which would have to expand if the security situation worsened and other Com- monwealth contributions were shown to be inadequate. In Cabinet, my main supporter for a Commonwealth force was Michael Foot but the unlikely combination of Denis Healey, Roy Mason and Tony Benn sunk such a force in favour of the second-best option of a UN force.

That the Labour Cabinet feared the responsibilities inherent in a Commonwealth force was yet another sign of the Party's chronic incapacity to understand the exercise of power. It is to Lord Carrington's credit that he convinced Margaret Thatcher and the Conservative Government, as part of the Lancaster House settlement, to restore a fully fledged British Governor and to support him with a Commonwealth force containing a strong British element.

The Anglo–American plan was then agreed by our two Governments. First, there would have to be a ceasefire, only then and by agreement would Britain assume responsibility for governing Rhodesia. During a period of no longer than six months there would be free and fair elections on the basis of one person-one vote. All executive and legislative powers would be vested in the Resident Commissioner who would also be Commander in Chief of both the Rhodesian armed forces and the forces of the Patriotic Front. A United Nations force, under its own command, would supervise the ceasefire and assist in maintaining security.

I knew that the presence of a UN force would not, of itself, be enough to persuade many people that it would be possible to hold fair and free elections in Rhodesia. The Resident Commissioner had to be a credible figure. The only person I could imagine holding the job was Field Marshal Lord Carver. Denis Healey admired Mike Carver and he knew that Carver had also opposed the British Army's involvement in Rhodesia. I judged that if Carver was to be the Commissioner my plan would get a far easier ride in Cabinet. I saw him on 3 August for an informal chat about Rhodesia, mainly to listen to his professional judgement as to whether it was possible to integrate guerrillas with regular forces. He replied that it was difficult but not impossible: it had been done in Kenya, where he had served, in Malaya and more recently in Oman. But when at the end I asked my Private Secretary to leave and boldly asked him whether he would consider being involved, he replied that he would be 'very, very reluctant'. I was not deterred. When I mulled over our conversation I was strengthened in my conviction that Carver was the man for the job. In the middle of August I decided that I should try and persuade him before I left for Africa for a second time. The problem, however, was that no one knew where he was.

The Field Marshal was eventually traced by the local police, cruising along the Llangollen Canal in North Wales. Showing an understandable reluctance to break his holiday, he agreed to go to the nearest airfield provided he could be taken there and back to his canal boat. I flew up to meet him at an RAF base in Shropshire where he turned up in old boating clothes with a blue polo neck jersey and baggy blue trousers looking very unlike a Field Marshal. I explained to him for the first time the details of the Anglo–American plan. He looked carefully at assessments of the security situation which I had brought with me. They were pretty grim, the fighting was now even more widespread throughout Rhodesia. I then asked if he would take the job, saying that Jim Callaghan was very keen that he should, as were President Carter and Cy Vance. I sensed that he had anticipated this meeting and had thought it through but I had no doubt that he accepted only out of a sense of duty and certainly with no relish. He quoted a remark by the first Duke of Wellington who was a relative, 'I'm a *nimmuk wallah*, that is one who has tasted of the King's salt, and therefore bound to do his service.'

At this point, just before I left for Africa again, President Carter came very close to destroying the whole initiative. Following a meeting with Julius Nyerere in Washington, he wrote to Nyerere saying that under the Anglo–American proposals the future army of Zimbabwe would be 'based primarily on the liberation forces'. This was dynamite and would never be acceptable to the South African Government, particularly Vorster, who was now the crucial player, for I had given up on Smith. I managed to get the Americans to agree that the word 'primarily' should be dropped from the Anglo–American proposals but with some foreboding I felt I had to explain this significant change to Carver and give him the opportunity to back out. Fortunately, he decided he could live with this wording and I promised that the paper on law and order, on which I was now going to consult in Africa, would not be issued until he had seen it and had had an opportunity to comment. Eventually I was able to cable him a new form of words about enrolment in the future Zimbabwe National Army which I had hammered out on my second tour. 'Enrolment in this army will be open to all citizens, but it will be based on the liberation forces: it will also include acceptable elements of the Rhodesian Defence Forces.'

On 1 September, immediately after Andy Young and I had met Mr Smith in Salisbury, we issued a White Paper detailing the Constitution as well as a separate law and order paper. I also announced that Field Marshal Lord Carver would be the Resident Commissioner. Mr Smith had been obsessed about our decision to replace the head of the Rhodesian police. That decision was immutable for without it I would never have succeeded in shifting Julius Nyerere from supporting the Patriotic Front's position that the police force should be based on a mythical Patriotic Front police force. Strengthened by his victory in the election the day before, Smith used his usual intemperate language to the press, saying that integrating his forces with the 'terrorists' was 'crazy, disastrous and ill-conceived'. He also made much capital out of our use of the word 'surrender'. In the text it was clear that we were using the word in its legal, not military, sense but I was foolish not to have spotted this and he had a field day with it. Fortunately Carver, in London, gave a splendid press conference and defused a lot of Smith's propaganda. He charmed the press with a rather far-fetched reminder that the formation of the British regular army in 1660 was an amalgamation of elements of Charles II's Royalist forces and Cromwell's New Model Army. I knew that we had a defensible principled position but it was far from being an agreed position on the ground and we were also far from delivering a ceasefire. Patience would now be the order of the day.

The next task was to get the approval of the United Nations Security Council for UN involvement and authorization for the Secretary-General, Kurt Waldheim, to appoint the Indian Lieutenant-General Prem Chand, whom he had chosen as his representative in discussions with Lord Carver and all the parties on the military and associated arrangements to effect a transition to majority rule. This was only done after extensive haggling in New York where I spoke directly to Gromyko to avoid a Soviet veto. In the end they and the Chinese settled for an abstention.

With the White Paper, agreement to the UN force and Lord Carver and Prem Chand all in place, we and the Americans had a firm, principled and credible plan which was able to withstand a constant battering, from all sides, over the next two years. It was inevitable that Smith would, as always, play for time and embark on an internal settlement with Bishop Muzorewa. Not so inevitable, but understandable, was the determination of Robert Mugabe to build up his strength on the ground by continuing with his guerrilla campaign and distance himself from Joshua Nkomo who, ever the pragmatist, was far readier to seek a negotiated solution. Nkomo's miscalculation was to believe that by not splitting the Patriotic Front he would be its eventual leader. It became very obvious to me when meeting with Mugabe and Nkomo in Malta and Dar es Salaam that they were too different in temperament ever to work together as equals. Mugabe had no intention of accepting the leadership or the values of Nkomo. We met over the years separately or together in London (xxviii), Africa or in New York, but I always felt a tension between the two as they warily watched each other.

There was much secret diplomacy on all sides for the next eighteen months and I learnt a great deal about the seamier side of African politics. South Africa was using its control of the railway network and its access to ports to put a squeeze on the Front Line States and also to expose their vulnerability. It forced these countries to take South African products and to clandestinely break sanctions and then held over them the threat of public exposure. The military support South Africa was giving the Rhodesians was essential to their survival and, though they used this as a bargaining lever, it was not to settle with us and adopt the Anglo-American proposals but to avoid provoking world opinion. The South Africans were content for the Rhodesians to keep white minority rule but wanted cosmetic concessions to calm the pressures on them in the UN. Diplomacy was not very productive. The real battle was going on in the rural areas of Rhodesia with border raids into and from Mozambique

and Zambia. All the parties manoeuvred to fix the blame for the fighting
on the others. Mr Smith appealed as usual to Right-wing Conservative
sentiment in Britain and used Bishop Muzorewa's good name to help
him. The Patriotic Front had the sympathy of the UN.

The war intensified, more lives were lost, more schools were destroyed,
more agricultural land was left to deteriorate. Logic and reason had long
since been abandoned. I faced a situation where I knew that time and
time alone would resolve the power struggle. If the Rhodesian forces
could hold Mugabe's guerrilla fighters, then when the internal settlement
failed because people eventually saw that it did not involve a genuine
transfer of power to the majority, there might be a short period where
there was deadlock in the midst of devastation. This was the likely
outcome which might give one last chance for a conference and a
negotiated ceasefire. Otherwise it would be settled on the battlefield and
Mugabe's forces would win. I had always said that there could only be
one other conference after Geneva. To hold a premature conference and
fail would be a certain recipe for Rhodesia to go the way of Mozambique,
with the whites withdrawing and the guerrilla forces taking power
without an election.

To wait patiently is one of the hardest things to do in politics but it is
much easier if you have a position of principle on which to stand. The
Anglo-American proposals gave us such a position and we simply waited,
keeping up the appearance of activity. Thus began a reactive phase of
diplomacy, fascinating for a participant and student of diplomacy, full of
twists and turns, each turn subsequently overtaken by events. It is such
fruitless activity, more than the productive moments, which take up the
time of a Foreign Secretary. As if to emphasize this point, when Lord
Carver went to Salisbury in November with General Prem Chand, the
main controversy was that the Rhodesians claimed he had raised hackles
by not signing the Visitors' Book in the police officers' mess. Then Smith
kept Carver waiting while he watched a cricket match. It was petty point-
scoring and further revealed that Smith was not seriously interested in a
transfer of power. Nevertheless, Carver and Prem Chand left with more
knowledge of the way the war was going. The Graham-Low travelling
dialogue continued, laying down formulations that were eventually very
useful at Lancaster House but at this stage were just part of our active
diplomacy.

At the end of January 1978, Andy Young and I met with the Patriotic
Front in Malta. Carver came as well, having useful talks with the
guerrilla leaders, including Mugabe's military chief, Tongogara. To see
Carver and Tongogara together in animated discussion was an extraordinary sight and it gave me hope that an eventual ceasefire was
achievable and that people like Tongogara would accept a return of
British rule during an election period. But we made no obvious progress
for the Patriotic Front wanted to tilt the settlement in their favour and

control the interim administration and I was not going to concede an unbalanced settlement. Andy Young was far too relaxed about the details of all this and I was forever nudging him in the negotiations so as not to concede ground. Meanwhile, Smith was making no compromises. On the plane coming back I said to Carver that the strange atmosphere of friendship that had developed had been like that between kidnappers and hostages. Carver replied, 'Who is the kidnapper and who is the hostage?' He was rightly anxious by then that the Americans were pushing me too close to the Patriotic Front's position which was not remotely negotiable. It was a well-judged warning not to concede any more ground. We also both knew in our hearts that we were not going to get an agreement before an internal settlement had failed and that he was unlikely ever to be the Resident Commissioner. Yet he stayed on very generously, purely to help our diplomacy and to keep the Anglo-American proposals alive, for there was no better option available. I will always see his contribution as going far beyond what I had any right to expect and as a fine example of the serviceman's tradition of duty to Queen and country.

The internal agreement between Smith, Muzorewa, Sithole and Chirau was signed on 3 March 1978 and a Rhodesian Executive Council formed. Elections were promised for the end of the year, but Smith was still very much in control while pretending not to be. In the House of Commons I welcomed those parts of the internal agreement which were compatible with the Anglo-American plan but also pointed out it was seriously defective. I deliberately left it to others to identify the omissions and discrepancies. By doing this, and refusing to reject it out of hand, I was also putting pressure on the Patriotic Front to be more reasonable, for they too could not be allowed a veto. I was never in any doubt that, though this internal settlement might have been acceptable under the famous 1972 Fifth Principle of acceptability to the majority, in 1978 it was not acceptable to the people of Rhodesia. Time had moved on and attitudes with it. The fall of the Portuguese Empire and the emergence of the independent states of Mozambique and Angola meant that new, younger nationalist leaders were ready to fight, if necessary for years, to obtain true independence.

In April, Cy Vance, Andy Young, Lord Carver and I went to Dar es Salaam, Pretoria and Salisbury, mainly at the prompting of President Carter whose visit to Nigeria had made him want to force the pace. It was all too obvious that the internal settlement would go ahead and those leaders involved in the sham settlement were evasive about attending any conference. We needed to demonstrate that the Anglo-American proposals were still on the table and had our full support. It was the first time that Cy Vance had visited Rhodesia and to have his support on the ground was essential, for the whites needed to know that they were not dealing with just Andy Young. As I was about to drive away from the meeting, a white woman ran forward and threw thirty pieces of silver in my path, to

314 TIME TO DECLARE

signify my betrayal of their cause. But I could be no Judas since I never believed in their cause. Cy Vance had rotten eggs thrown at his car by Sithole supporters.

The sacking of a black Minister, Byron Hove, from the Executive Council for calling for more blacks in the police force revealed to any doubters in the British public the essentially fraudulent nature of the internal settlement. Mr Smith had total control of the transitional Government and Bishop Muzorewa was now a cipher but I judged it was far better for this to be demonstrated by events than for people to listen sceptically to me denigrating the deal. A ceasefire appeal by Muzorewa was predictably ignored which also showed, not only that he had no influence with the guerrillas, but also that his claims to have his own army were patently false. Nevertheless, as guerrilla atrocities grew, accompanied by similar savagery from the Rhodesian armed forces, the Right-wing in Britain and in the US started to mobilize support for the internal agreement.

Endless attempts were made to persuade Nkomo to be more forthcoming and to help us to pressurize Mugabe to negotiate. But Nkomo feared going too far ahead of Mugabe in negotiating when he could not be sure that Smith was moving in any substantive way. It became important for Nkomo to judge for himself whether Smith would move. Nkomo and Smith eventually met on 14 August for a secret meeting in Lusaka with Kenneth Kaunda and Joe Garba from Nigeria present. The fact that the meeting took place was leaked and various sources were suspected; Muzorewa in Salisbury, or Nyerere in Dar es Salaam. The meeting was presented by Julius Nyerere as an attempt to divide Nkomo from Mugabe. This was despite his having been told about the meeting by Joe Garba and of the firm intention to involve Mugabe at the next meeting. Joe Garba was adamant that he had squared Nyerere. The mistake was not to have President Machel present with President Kaunda, since Kaunda was adamantly against involving Nyerere. Machel's inability to speak English was the reason given for not involving him which I was keen to do. The Nigerians told an angry Mugabe why he had been excluded. I had been deeply involved in all the secret diplomacy and had kept Cy Vance personally informed, but the Americans were deliberately not involved in any direct way since they were sceptical of its chances.

On 4 September a Rhodesian Viscount airliner was shot down by a SAM 7 missile and Nkomo's Russian equipped ZIPRA forces claimed responsibility. Thirty-four passengers were killed. Then Joshua Nkomo, who was a decent man, and upset by the killing, was heard on a BBC radio interview to make a sound which some people interpreted as a chuckle. The effect was disastrous. Smith called him a 'monster' and suddenly Nkomo was no longer seen as a moderate. In this deteriorating situation wild hopes were focused on an immediate conference of all the parties, even though it had no prospect of success.

The best decision I made in my entire time as Foreign Secretary was not to convene a Lancaster House conference in November 1978. Everything was ready. The actual conference arrangements had all been thought through. The draft Constitution was even printed. For the first time for years, Smith wanted to come to a conference, in itself grounds for suspicion. Both Jim Callaghan and President Carter were under growing domestic pressure to endorse a conference. I was too, I admit, sorely tempted, for the Conservative Opposition strategy, revealed in a two-day debate on Rhodesia, was to paint me as the obstacle to a conference and to urge Jim Callaghan to chair it. So I knew that if I agreed to call a conference I would simultaneously outflank the Conservatives and put myself centre stage. The world's attention would be on London, and the gambler in me was eager to act.

At that most vulnerable moment Sir Anthony Duff, whom I had brought back to oversee African policy in the Foreign Office, asked to see me with Lord Carver. It was early evening and, with Stephen Wall, there were just the four of us. I had come to have profound respect for the judgement of both Duff and Carver. They had one simple message: 'You, Secretary of State, have always said that you would not convene a conference until you were reasonably sure that it would succeed. You know, and we know, that a conference now will fail.' Sadly, I knew in my heart that what they were saying was true. They also went as close as was decent in saying that before a conference could be successful not only would the internal settlement have to be seen to fail, as they were both certain it would, but also a general election in Britain would have to take place in order that a new British Government, whether Labour or Conservative, would have the authority to convene it and over-ride Smith. They were correct over this too and I did not try to argue otherwise. Rarely for me, I just listened and offered very few comments, except to say I would think about it. When they had gone I looked out through the windows into the November evening over St James's Park. I knew what I had to do, I had to kill off an early conference.

Once I had accepted this hard fact, it did not prove too hard to achieve. With Duff's support, I could carry Whitehall, and the way out with the public and the politicians lay in Jim Callaghan's wish to appoint a politician to report back to him about the feasiblity of a conference. I thought it would be possible to defuse the issue by convincing that person and others that there was no choice but to be patient. The key was the person Jim chose: a wise one could only report one way. I went over to No. 10 to discuss possible candidates with Jim Callaghan. He was sitting in his chair in the Cabinet room and, much to my amazement, suggested sending Willie Ross, the former Secretary of State for Scotland, to Africa. Willie Ross had many good qualities, he was tough minded and independent, but he had no experience of Africa, and I was not convinced that he had the sensitivity to pick up all the danger signs against an early conference. Instead, I urged Jim to appoint Cledwyn Hughes, who had that political sensitivity in abundance, and also the experience of being Commonwealth Secretary. Fortunately, Jim agreed. From that day on, I never doubted that Cledwyn would find against an early conference. What is more important, he did so in a way that carried conviction across party lines in the House of Commons. On 30 November Carver ceased to be the Resident Commissioner designate. I went with him to No. 10 and Jim thanked him for all he had done. All of us were aware that a settlement in Rhodesia would have to wait until the General Election, even though I never admitted that this was what we were doing. Essentially, even from September 1977 to May 1979, I was waiting for the power struggle within Rhodesia to reach deadlock.

Only a deadlock could produce the ceasefire without which there could be no fair and free election. While we had been at pains to ensure that no party had a veto on our Anglo-American proposals, we could never escape the fact that as long as either the Patriotic Front or the Rhodesian armed forces, or both, were prepared to continue the war there could be no peaceful transition. We always believed that the Commonwealth Conference due in Lusaka in 1979 would be a good opportunity for diplomacy and that was one of the key reasons why Jim Callaghan had helped Kenneth Kaunda financially and militarily at a meeting in Kano in the summer of 1978. We also both resisted attempts early in 1979 to cancel the Commonwealth Conference because of alleged danger to the Queen's life. The Queen herself wisely insisted on going to the Conference when Margaret Thatcher's new Conservative Government was wavering soon after taking office.

Towards the end of 1978 and in early 1979, there was a very real risk that the Rhodesian military led by General Walls, always a far more realistic man than Smith, might suddenly take control and end illegal independence, demanding that Britain should assume responsibility for administering Southern Rhodesia. Of course, we had detailed contingency plans for such an eventuality, but we were not prepared to return and assume authority unless the Rhodesian armed forces accepted the original Anglo-American proposals. Also, the Security Council would have had to give its authority to a UN peace-keeping force to supplement the armed forces of the Crown. We never shifted from the position that Britain would only return as a colonial power, even for the briefest transitional period, with the authority of international opinion. In practice that would have meant the Front Line States helping to enforce the ceasefire. I was also determined that in this case we would go back to our original proposal for a Resident Commissioner holding all power unencumbered by a Governing Council, which I had conceded for the transitional period only with the utmost reluctance.

Fortunately, General Walls did not preempt the situation with a military coup. He came very close to doing so after the Lancaster House settlement, actually during the election period in 1980 – sensing that Mugabe was winning – but was prevented by the firmness of Margaret Thatcher. Also, it turned out that it was President Machel's personal intervention with Robert Mugabe that was a crucial factor in persuading Mugabe to accept the Lancaster House settlement.

I had always hoped that Peter Carrington would succeed me if the Conservatives won the election, for he understood Africa better than any of their senior politicians. He had used his non-executive directorship of RTZ to keep himself well informed about Africa and whenever I had briefed him confidentially I had found him totally realistic. Flying back together on the plane from Jomo Kenyatta's funeral, we had talked very frankly. At one stage when we were looking for a Secretary-General for NATO to replace Joseph Luns, who was outstaying his welcome, I approached him, with the agreement of Cy Vance, to see if he would accept the job. He asked for time to go away and, as he put it, 'consult his mistress'. He came back and politely refused; and when I said, 'That means you have been offered my job,' his eyes had a tell-tale twinkle. So when the election was lost and I heard that he was going to take my place, I was delighted but not surprised.

Lord Carrington deserved all his success, first at the Commonwealth Conference in Lusaka, and then at the Lancaster House Conference which followed. Field Marshal Lord Carver wrote in his autobiography, *Out of Step*, that one of the principal differences between Carrington's Lancaster House settlement and my Anglo-American proposals was that he made no attempt to disband or disarm any of the military forces on either side until after the elections, when a new Government came to power. It was a gamble that paid off, helped by an overwhelming victory for Mugabe and much wise handling of the pre- and post-election period by Lord Soames, the interim Governor.

By one of those tricks of fate, because Peter Shore who was by then Shadow Foreign Minister, was out in Rhodesia in early 1980 watching the elections, I was asked by Jim Callaghan, though Shadow Energy Spokesman, to respond to the announcement in the House of Commons giving the details of Mugabe's election victory. For the Conservative Right wing it was a shattering result: even the Government had been confident that Robert Mugabe's ZANU would not win outright and a Nkomo-led coalition would be the outcome. As I rose to speak in reply there was a strange stillness in the House. Those Conservative MPs who had lambasted me month after month for insisting that the Patriotic Front, and in particular Robert Mugabe, whom they loathed, had to be a party to any settlement, were strangely silent. I decided not to utter a word of self-justification and instead to lavish praise upon the Government. Robert Mugabe's outright victory was a vindication of much that I had done as Foreign Secretary and I did not need to spell it out, for everyone in the House of Commons that day knew the score.

Only in Africa could there have been such a reconciliation. Robert Mugabe asked General Walls to stay on, citing the fact that he had tried to kill him as justification for now asking him to protect his life. The head of Rhodesian Intelligence also stayed on to serve Mugabe. When the tenth anniversary of independence was celebrated, Ian Smith walked down the still well-kept streets of Harare, without any security, unmolested and even recognized with a grin by many blacks as well as whites. One of the reasons I am still hopeful for Africa is that there is no deep seated animosity between black and white in Southern Africa. Namibian independence under President Sam Nujoma is a true democracy and it makes worthwhile all our efforts to achieve a UN solution which took twelve years to bear fruit.

Nevertheless, the Lancaster House settlement was rightly seen as the first triumph of Mrs Thatcher's Conservative Government and the euphoric partisan mood and press reporting allowed for little recognition that the Anglo-American agreement had had any role to play in the successful outcome. But those who had watched events closely knew that the achievement had been built on the foundations we laid down.

It was wise of President Carter and Cy Vance to step back and support the British Government working with the Commonwealth after the successful Heads of Government conference in Lusaka in August 1979. But the fact that the United States would not have gone along with a sell-out to Smith and Muzorewa was an important constraint on Mrs Thatcher. A generous assessment was made by Cy Vance in his book *Hard Choices*:

> The credit for the final negotiation of Zimbabwe's independence properly belongs to the British, principally to the skilful diplomacy of Peter Carrington . . . However, it is only proper to point out that the final settlement was fully consistent with the Anglo-American proposal. Further, in my judgement the successful resolution of the Rhodesia issue in the Lancaster House Conference would not have been possible, without the substantial progress that had already been made with the Patriotic Front and the front line states prior to the British elections. For this, credit must go to David Owen and Jim Callaghan.

I will always treasure Elizabeth Longford's report of the Queen's views:

> On Zimbabwe Independence Day a high official said to her, 'What a superb job Lord Carrington has done.'
> 'Yes, indeed. But we mustn't forget that it was David Owen who put it all in train.'
> The official knew this was true and admired her all the more for recognizing it.

14

FOREIGN SECRETARY – 1977

President Jimmy Carter flew in for the London Economic Summit in May, unconventionally via the North East, starting his visit in Durham at Jim Callaghan's suggestion. Carter showed his populist touch by prefacing his speech in front of Newcastle Town Hall with the Geordie cry, 'Hawaay the lads!' and so arrived in London to a good press. The Downing Street Economic Summit took place on the weekend of 7–8 May and was then followed by a NATO meeting of Heads of Government on 10 and 11 May.

Jimmy Carter was an intriguing figure and the more I saw of him at international meetings and in the White House the more complex I found his personality to be. He combines a fundamental decency and good Baptist values with a mean, competitive streak. His 'born again' religious views gave him a moral certainty which could be unattractive, but his interest in facts and his scientific approach to problems counter the fundamentalism, so that there is a greater strength to his decisions than is often at first apparent. He was too obsessed by minutiae to be able to stand back enough from the complexities of international affairs and this was probably his undoing as a President. Yet there was a romantic streak also, and he loved Dylan Thomas's writing. Sitting next to him in the NATO meeting in Lancaster House, I gave him the funniest of Dylan's short stories, *The Outing*, in a small booklet. Carter had not read it before and was enchanted. Though small in stature, there was an ease in the way he held himself and moved which gave him a quiet dignity. A Southerner and proud of Georgia, where he had been Governor, he had a tinge of contempt for the tall, confident East Coasters who still held power in the Democratic Party, despite the Texan Presidency of Lyndon Johnson.

It was Carter's misfortune to coincide in office with Brezhnev's declining years and so there was not the transformation in East-West relations for which Carter yearned. But he did not fall into the trap of pretending that the Soviet position was moving. He was attacked for not giving strong leadership but I felt he was the first US President to understand that in future America would lead more through persuasion than domination. The hostage crisis and the invasion of Afghanistan gave the impression of weakness which Reagan exploited, but Carter was brittle not weak and the uneasiness that he aroused stemmed more from concern that he would snap rather than bend.

The Summit meeting was held in the dining room at No. 10; Denis Healey and I sitting beside Jim Callaghan with Giulio Andreotti, the Italian Prime Minister, and Helmut Schmidt, the German Chancellor, opposite; the French speakers, Pierre Trudeau, Prime Minister of Canada and Giscard d'Estaing, President of France, on our left; and Takeo Fukuda, Prime Minister of Japan and Jimmy Carter on our right. Roy Jenkins came in for only part of the Summit. With the interpreters walled off behind us, the atmosphere was very intimate, if occasionally acrimonious over non-proliferation.

The most important issue was the growing controversy over Jimmy Carter's attitude towards Helmut Schmidt and Giscard d'Estaing on the implications for the spread of nuclear weapons derived from civil nuclear power programmes. We had formed a new Cabinet Committee, GEN 74, which I chaired and it was fascinating because it included some scientists. The issue which confronted us before the Economic Summit was the level of world uranium supplies. Carter held that supply exceeded demand so that expensive fast-breeder reactors which relied on plutonium were unnecessary in terms of energy supply, and very dangerous in that countries like Brazil and Pakistan might achieve the capacity for nuclear weapons. It was clear that Whitehall departments could not agree even on the facts and I had to call for further internal studies. Over the next few months, I found considerable common ground on this issue of non-proliferation with Tony Benn, for like me he took it very seriously and was prepared to challenge conventional departmental views.

President Carter, in the opening session, defused much of the tension by proposing that the Seven should set up a technical study to see if we could agree on the extent of world uranium reserves, and whether if supplying countries would expand their uranium enrichment facilities, consumer countries would accept constraints on nuclear material. He was not insisting on a ban on fast-breeder reactors. Given the strains and stresses of the previous months, probably only a meeting like this could have resolved the problems. But Helmut Schmidt was bruised by Jimmy Carter's insensitivity in implying that Germany could not be trusted over nuclear matters and relations between Carter and Schmidt never really recovered. Carter's officials should have briefed him that Helmut Schmidt had made his reputation with a speech in the German Bundestag in March 1958 for which he was labelled, 'Schmidt Schnauze', or Schmidt the lip: he had argued passionately against those CDU-CSU politicians who wanted atom bombs for the Bundeswehr. 'Give up your German megalomania once and for all; your German national megalomania', he said to a standing ovation. This made him the hero of the SPD until, typically, he deeply offended those very people a few months later by voluntarily going off to do four weeks' military service in the Bundeswehr reserve. Carter and Schmidt, two serious figures sharing much the same values, should have got on well together, but they antagonized each other to the embarrassment of all who were present.

The other important issue was Carter's determination that NATO should increase its defence spending. Over these days the seeds were sown for the decision, ratified in the Washington NATO Summit a year later, for a 3 per cent increase in defence spending. It is often forgotten that it was Carter, not Reagan, who started to strengthen NATO's defences in the light of the Soviet military build-up. That build-up, whether in terms of new aircraft carriers, large nuclear submarines, sophisticated tanks and fighter aircraft or the new SS-20 missiles in Europe, was too ominous to ignore. It presented Jim Callaghan with possibly the toughest task of his Premiership. Having less than a year earlier persuaded the Party to accept the IMF's public expenditure constraints, he was pledging himself to increased defence spending. I watched with admiration over the next few months as Jim manoeuvred to win acceptance of that 3 per cent increase. So deftly did he take it through Cabinet Committees and Cabinet itself that one felt that some members were not even aware of what was happening. One of Jim Callaghan's strengths was that in Cabinet he concentrated his efforts on a few specific issues and did not waste political capital by using his weight on others, being content to act as an impartial chairman. That did not stop him from working behind the scenes and arranging for other Cabinet Ministers to achieve his own objectives.

During Jimmy Carter's visit, Jim Callaghan sounded him out about appointing Peter Jay as Ambassador to Washington. Some weeks before I had sent Jim a handwritten letter proposing Peter's name. I warned him in that letter that charges of nepotism would be made because Peter's wife, Margaret, was Jim's daughter. I wanted Jim to be free to refuse and knew that he was pondering the matter because at one Cabinet meeting I saw my folded letter in his wallet. Eventually we discussed it and he admitted that he was worried, but could see no justification, given Peter's personal qualities, for saying no. The Foreign Office, while ready to comply with my wishes, naturally wanted to protect Sir Peter Ramsbotham, the current Ambassador. It was believed that Sir Peter's reputation depended on my announcing his move to be Governor of Bermuda simultaneously with Peter Jay's appointment to Washington. In this way it was felt that people would understand and a distinguished diplomatic career would not be blighted. It would have made for far better public relations to have made the Bermuda appointment, then later leaked that Jim Callaghan was resisting my suggestion of Peter for

Washington: a few weeks later Peter could have been appointed after journalistic pleas that nobody should be discriminated against because he happened to be married to the Prime Minister's daughter.

On the afternoon of 11 May, before flying overnight to Jeddah with Debbie, I announced Peter's appointment to the diplomatic correspondents. A number of people in the Parliamentary Labour Party jumped on the nepotism bandwagon, only too happy to settle old grievances with me and Jim, as well as expressing present jealousies. This would just have been an irritant had it not been for an off-the-record press briefing given by No. 10. A few badly chosen sentences had dismantled all the presentational wrapping that I had constructed. The *Evening Standard* headline screamed 'SNOB ENVOY HAD TO GO'. By then I was flying up from Jeddah to Riyadh with Prince Saud, the Saudi Arabian Foreign Minister, and meeting Crown Prince Fahd before calling on King Khalid. Telegrams were flashing between the Foreign Office and the Embassy and my mind was in London as much as Saudi Arabia. I issued a statement supporting Sir Peter Ramsbotham, but the damage was done.

It was a great comfort to have Debbie on the plane to talk it all over with and it was a much chastened man who stepped off the VC-10 at Tehran airport. I was pleased to be staying with Anthony Parsons, and his first comment was what an excellent appointment Peter Jay's was, which cheered me up.

It seemed astonishing that the scruffy student, virtually refused admission at the gates of the British Embassy in Tehran, should, less than twenty years later return as Secretary of State. Cy Vance, the US Secretary of State, was also attending the CENTO meeting in Tehran, so we co-ordinated our approach before he saw the Shah. The Shah gave the CENTO Foreign Ministers a lavish lunch in the Niavaran Palace. Even in the Elysée Palace I have never seen such expensive, exquisite French tableware. The food looked and tasted as if it had been flown in from Paris, and for all I knew it was, so extravagant were the Shah's habits by then. Empress Farah welcomed us, dressed in the height of Paris couture. One did not have to be very perceptive to sense a monarchy far removed from the people.

His Imperial Majesty the Shahanshah held himself like a preened peacock, but he had acquired knowledge with his years of experience. In a profitable talk we ranged over many regional and global issues. I was particularly keen to persuade him to use his oil power on South Africa with the aim of achieving both an independent Namibia and black majority rule in Zimbabwe. There had been some earlier discussion about whether I should voice our uneasiness over the internal situation in Iran. I was concerned about the human rights abuse taking place and wanted to endorse my anxiety personally. So I told the Shah that, while I did not wish to impose British views on Iran and though his moves towards liberalization had been well received in Britain, what criticism there still was would decrease if the living conditions of prisoners were improved and trials opened regularly to the public. While not belabouring the point unduly, there could be no doubt about the strength of my feeling, and there was no adverse reaction from the Shah, either at the time or later. The meeting reinforced the image of a powerful leader; not remotely akin to the dithering, indecisive Shah of 1953. I confess that it was this self-confident, assertive image which stayed with me in 1978 while we debated what we should do to bolster the Shah's Government. But it was false. People very rarely change and he was still indecisive and weak. Our big mistake was to fall for the Shah's carefully constructed self-image. This is covered in the chapter on Iran.

We flew back from Tehran late on Sunday 15 May and next day I was in the House of Commons to hear Jim Callaghan's statement on Peter Jay's appointment. Jim loyally defended his staff in No. 10 against attacks that they were responsible for denigrating Sir Peter Ramsbotham. Once again I kicked myself for getting Jim into this mess. Next day I attended the Economic Cabinet Committee while Debbie took Tristan to Great Ormond Street. During the meeting a messenger came in and left a note with Jim Callaghan who flicked it across the Cabinet table to me. It simply said, 'Would the Foreign Secretary go to Great Ormond Street urgently.' I left immediately and arrived at the hospital to find Debbie looking shattered. Tristan had relapsed again and his blood was full of the abnormal lymphocytes we thought had been poisoned by the drugs. Once again I felt I was listening to a death sentence. The doctors were talking optimistically; they had no doubt that they could, with drugs, trigger another remission and that he had a very good chance still of being cured. I did not share their confidence. I knew from the medical literature that a second relapse was bad news and that his chances were now greatly reduced. There was also a big question mark about whether it was safe to have a second dose of radiotherapy. I cancelled lunch with the Iranian Ambassador at his Embassy and tried to sound confident to Debbie and Tristan, but I was feeling far from it myself. After various tests and a snack lunch at the hospital, Debbie left to take Tristan home and I went back to the House of Commons. I knew that Jim Callaghan, at Prime Minister's Questions, was to be asked about the CPRS Review of the FCO and I felt I should be there. As I sat down on the front bench next to Jim, I felt drained. He said nothing but put his hand firmly on my thigh and kept it there for a while. It was more than a gesture of comfort: I felt a transfusion of strength. He must have been told or guessed what had happened, and his response did more for me than any words could possibly have done.

The touchiness of the Iranians caused them to interpret major political developments from my cancellation of the Ambassador's lunch, so we hurriedly arranged a sandwich lunch in my room. It was somewhat frugal fare for a man used to gourmet food, but I had an interesting discussion. A relatively young man, he owed his position to his friendship with the Shah's sister, but he was thoughtful and spoke more frankly than I had expected about the Shah's vulnerable position and the problems facing him.

My life had a completely new dimension: Debbie had coped wonderfully with my hectic life as Foreign Secretary but, now, with Tristan's illness starting all over again, she would not be able to join me on foreign visits for some time ahead, and I feared for the future. We even discussed whether I should continue as Foreign Secretary. One decision we did make was that I would try and cut down the number of days I was out of the country and do my best to fly there and back overnight and not be away at the weekends. I think this was the source of my reputation as the 'flying doctor'. Otherwise, we decided I should keep to my schedule and that we would carry on as normal, with only the minimum number of people knowing Tristan was ill.

Peter Jay's appointment had been far more controversial than it need have been. Nevertheless, he did an excellent job in Washington, every bit as good as I had hoped. He established a personal relationship with the President but, more important, he crossed the ring fence which Carter's Georgian mafia had put up around themselves. He got to know Hamilton Jordan, Carter's Chief of Staff, and Jody Powell, his Press Secretary, and intellectually was more than a match for Zbigniew Brzezinski, on and off the tennis court. My only sadness was that Washington put additional strains on Peter and Margaret's marriage which ended in divorce.

The Foreign Secretary has a powerful weapon: by making a political appointment to one of the top ambassadorships he can break the closed circuit of Foreign Office internal communications. A problem I had had with Sir Peter Ramsbotham was the hostility which the Defence and Foreign Affairs Select Committee felt towards the Washington Embassy. During a parliamentary visit to Washington the year before, a middle ranking diplomat had cabled to the Foreign Office highly critical comments about the business activities of one of the MPs. This had leaked to the press and, in a parliamentary answer and on the advice of the Department, I denied that there had been any criticism. Some time later I discovered that there had been a telegram, that the press reports were substantially correct and that the Embassy had been part of the cover-up. The Select Committee were increasingly angry about the whole business and it was beginning to look as if I would be hauled down to the House of Commons to apologize for misleading the House. Since I had previously been a member of the Committee I asked to see the Chairman, Sir Harwood Harrison, privately, and made a clean breast of it, admitting they had been misled and apologizing for what had happened. Fortunately, he agreed to persuade the Committee to drop the whole incident without taking evidence from Sir Peter Ramsbotham. During that episode I discovered the existence of many such telegrams which were completely outside the normal distribution network. Initially the Foreign Office tried to justify the denial of the telegram's existence on the basis that they were essentially private letters, of no concern to Parliament, but when I pointed out that the tax payer paid for them they dropped that line of defence.

If the Foreign Secretary has a personal friend or political ally in Washington it greatly strengthens his grip on the Foreign Office machine. Most issues have to go through Washington and an alert Ambassador can pick up what is going on underneath the surface. I found Peter Jay invaluable in keeping me abreast of such developments. One example was the Ministry of Defence's systematic attempt to undermine the British Government's position in the Comprehensive Test Ban negotiations. Indeed, things got so bad at one stage that Harold Brown, the Defence Secretary, complained to Peter Jay. The scientists in both countries were trying to sabotage a treaty by suddenly discovering that nuclear weapons were deteriorating. This 'shelf life' argument had never surfaced before, but they were using it to justify continuing tests. Worse, they were getting some support from influential opinion on Capitol Hill. Solly Zuckerman, who was my adviser on nuclear matters, was incensed. He thought the 'shelf life' issue was artificial and produced excellent scientific facts which helped me to demolish it. The whole thing was a classic example of vested interest, with the scientists collaborating across the Atlantic to protect their jobs. I wrote to Peter the sort of frank letter that it would have been impossible to have sent to a career diplomat, however good your personal relations.

Was my appointment of Peter Jay a political mistake? I have often asked myself this question. The answer depends on whether or not the incident did any permanent harm to Jim Callaghan. Up until then he had a reputation as 'Honest Jim'. The appointment did temporarily tarnish that image, but I do not think it did lasting damage. Although Jim Callaghan was wise enough to have stopped it if he had wanted to, I should have realized it was very difficult for him to do so. I had not known that, when Jim became Chancellor and Peter was already doing well in the Treasury, it had been impossible for Peter to move as planned to one of the best jobs. I should, however, have known that Jim's judgement was bound to be clouded by his own affection for Peter. One of my tasks as Foreign Secretary was to protect the Prime Minister from political flak and here I had put him into the firing line. Certainly I had mismanaged the presentation of the appointment. It was my first real setback as Foreign Secretary.

In Cabinet Jim announced that with extreme reluctance he would agree to the Cabinet having a free vote on the bill on direct elections for the European Parliament which he wanted to present to Parliament after Whitsun. Normally the rule of collective responsibility means that all members of the Government vote as one body. I, having written privately to Jim saying that he had no option but to concede to Michael Foot on this issue, supported his decision; though it would be difficult in Europe I thought I could persuade my colleagues on the Council of Foreign Ministers that the legislation would pass and that we were not backsliding. Michael Foot, ever one for an historical parallel, reminded the Cabinet that Lloyd George and Asquith had voted in different lobbies on the Conciliation Bill. No doubt Michael, with his Ebbw Vale constituency, related to Lloyd George, but a less Asquithian figure than Jim Callaghan, an abstemious Baptist, it would be hard to find. Jim then made it clear to those who were against the bill that he hoped they would abstain.

A free vote had, of course, already been conceded in the context of the Lib-Lab Pact on the method of electing MEPs. To his credit, Michael did not personally make use of this concession, even though it was available to him. When the legislation on direct elections came up he, like other Cabinet dissenters, abstained on the vote of overall principle in Second Reading on 24 November, but voted with Jim Callaghan in favour of proportional representation on 13 December. I am sure that this was more through personal loyalty to Jim than any belief in proportional representation. He would have known that 'first past the post' was going to be chosen by the House so he could feel safe in solidarity with Jim. Perhaps, having been party to the negotiations with the Liberals, he also felt it would ease future relations with them if he voted for proportional representation. It is hard to estimate how many more of the Cabinet would have voted against the Lib-Lab Pact itself if they had thought they would have to vote for proportional representation as part of the bargain. Only fourteen of the Cabinet voted for proportional representation to elect the MEPs. Tony Benn voted against and the rest abstained.

On the weekend of 21–22 May it was the British turn to arrange for a private, informal meeting of Foreign Ministers at the stunningly beautiful Leeds Castle in Kent. These are called Schloss Gymnich meetings, after the first one which was held in Germany. They are a good way of achieving informal discussion without officials and with no fixed agenda. The importance of the meeting was that for the first time we all accepted the strong political case for enlargement of the Common Market to buttress the new democracies – Spain after Franco's fascist rule, Portugal after Salazar's dictatorship and Greece following the fall of the Colonels' junta. Roy Jenkins attended and apparently did not enjoy himself: he wrote in his *European Diary* that David Owen 'is not a naturally gracious host; he is not keen enough on surroundings or food or drink to enjoy providing them for others'. That was, I suppose, fair comment; I have never been part of the country house set nor have I any knowledge of wine, but my Private Secretary, Ewen Fergusson, a connoisseur, had been involved in choosing the wine and the menu both of which seemed pretty good to me.

At the end of May we had the CIEC North-South Ministerial Meeting in Paris at the Palais Kleber. I represented the European Community in one of the three negotiations with the Third World countries which dealt with the Common Fund and also the symbolic issue for a new world economic order. With Andrew Peacock, the Australian Foreign Minister, we spoke for the developed world and, somewhat surprisingly, we forged an agreement with the under-developed nations. They attached great importance to this, though Cy Vance had less room for manoeuvre on the group dealing with economic questions. He was, rather oddly, accompanied by Senators and Congressmen present, it appears, to check that he did not give the store away. They insisted he hold out for a commitment to keep prices down from the oil-producing nations, classified as under-developed for the purpose of these talks, and disagreement became inevitable. Much to French disappointment, the whole conference failed. It was a pity, for we were far closer to agreement than any of us expected and ours had been the only serious negotiations at Ministerial level during the whole period of so-called North-South dialogue.

The Queen's Silver Jubilee Thanksgiving Service was held in St Paul's on Tuesday 7 June, followed by the Lord Mayor's Lunch in the Guildhall. Next day the Commonwealth Heads of Government Conference opened in Lancaster House. Rhodesia was a major item on the agenda and soundings showed there was no great readiness among the key Commonwealth countries to commit themselves to a Commonwealth peacekeeping force. What response I did manage to obtain was lukewarm. The most interesting part of the meeting was sitting next to Malcolm Fraser, the Australian Prime Minister, and witnessing the start of his love affair with the Commonwealth. He came to the Conference with the reputation of being a hard-line, Right-wing sheep farmer. But as he listened to one African leader after another express disenchantment with British policy in Africa, I sensed that he saw an opening which Australia could exploit. He moved in on the side of Black Africa with considerable effect and virtually made a bid to take the leadership of the old White Commonwealth over from Britain. It was not a totally cynical move either, for he stayed involved on African issues long after he ceased to be Prime Minister. It was very important that the Commonwealth did not split on African questions purely down the black-white divide. Canada had long been sympathetic to African concerns and, with Australia joining them, Britain would have to be careful to avoid being isolated. Sadly British isolation along the black-white cleavage was to be the hallmark of Commonwealth relations throughout Margaret Thatcher's period. As is usual in splits of this kind, there were faults on both sides. There was too much glib talk of comprehensive mandatory economic sanctions, but she for her part was incapable of recognizing that some sanctions were necessary and that, instead of exposing their limitations and inconsistencies in Southern Africa, she should have made a few more cosmetic concessions, not just to retain good will but to build up sanctions as a credible arm of policy in international affairs. She had wanted sanctions to work effectively against the Soviets, following their invasion of Afghanistan, and she had tried sanctions against Iraq. It is no gain for the peaceful settlement of disputes that sanctions have to date a poor record of achieving their objectives.

At the weekend the Heads of Government went to Scotland where they cobbled together the 'Gleneagles Agreement', covering sporting contacts with South Africa. For many years this assumed the sanctity of a Biblical text. Whereas it was easy for some governments to tell their people exactly which countries they could visit, there was no way that we could or should have persuaded Parliament to legislate against people playing cricket or rugby wherever they wished. I was more committed than most to having no sporting links while apartheid continued, but I was adamantly opposed to dictating how people should run their own lives. The British Government undertook to withdraw financial support from organizations that breached the guidelines and to seek actively to dissuade sporting organizations from planning fixtures with South African teams. While the Gleneagles text was being negotiated, I was able to keep in touch easily because the Trooping of the Colour was taking place on Horse Guards Parade and we had a family party, with lots of children running around my office, eating ice cream and playing games, while occasionally watching the parade ground through the window. Tristan looked so frail that day and I felt a wave of fear for the months ahead.

On Sunday 26 June an all-day unofficial Cabinet meeting at Chequers was held with no civil servants present. We had a useful political discussion, much of it about the Lib-Lab Pact. The discussion on whether we should renew it in July was somewhat artificial since everybody knew that if there was a summer or even an autumn election we would certainly lose. I maintained that we should go on into 1979 before holding an election, believing that, while some of the atmosphere of good will surrounding the Jubilee had rubbed off on the Government, it was very early days and we would need all the time available. The economic traumas of 1975–76 had scarred the public mind so deeply that I did not believe they would really trust us until they experienced a sustained period of sound and successful government. The Lib-Lab Pact had helped us by creating a more united national mood and given political stability. Of course my judgement was not purely objective: I enjoyed being Foreign Secretary and wanted it to go on for as long as possible. In effect Jim and Michael Foot were given *carte blanche* to negotiate what they could with David Steel. By the end of July, without having conceded anything of substance, they had an agreement and we were fairly sure that there would be no election before autumn 1978.

Tony Benn opposed the Lib-Lab Pact ritually rather than passionately, making his denunciation for the record and suggesting nothing in its place. He scribbled away through every Cabinet meeting; at one stage Denis Healey turned to him and, full of sarcasm, said, 'Would you like me to talk more slowly, Tony, so you can get everything down?' Tony's diary writing caused much anger to the older Cabinet members who thought it would inhibit discussion, but most of the younger members felt much less anxious. After Dick Crossman's diaries, which were so obviously tendentious and self-seeking in places, few believed that the public would take every word that Tony recorded as gospel truth.

Our Presidency of the European Community ended with the European Council in London on 29–30 June 1977. Nothing much happened. Giscard d'Estaing, aided and abetted by Helmut Schmidt, expressed his antagonism once more to Jimmy Carter on civil nuclear power and Jim defended the US President stoutly. I cannot say that our Presidency was a great success, but nor was it the disaster it sometimes looked as if it might have been. Given the continuing divisions on Europe within the Cabinet, most Ministers had co-operated fairly well and many had enjoyed chairing their specialized councils. While some of the animosity against the Community in the Labour Party was abating, we were far from having a committed, coherent line. I strongly welcomed Jim Callaghan's decision to have a special Cabinet meeting on our European position at the end of July. He asked me to ensure that the papers were written by me and not the Foreign Office. I decided to involve his staff, particularly Tom McNally, in the preparation of the papers for I knew the Department's draft contribution would be bland and likely to go down badly with those colleagues who wanted to feel that there were some political objectives underpinning our strategy.

On Thursday 28 July I went to a lunch which Harry Walston had fixed up in his Albany flat. It was the first time the Jenkinsites had met since I had become Foreign Secretary and I thought I would look a bit of a prima donna if I did not turn up. It was a good thing that I did for Bill Rodgers had clearly briefed Roy Jenkins about the Cabinet papers. Roy launched into characteristically oblique and coded criticism of people who were backsliding on Europe, without mentioning whom he was attacking. Essentially he objected to favouring enlargement because it would lead to a loosening and slowing of the momentum towards union. I had no objection to being criticized, but he was in danger of forgetting that, as President of the Commission, he represented a different interest. So I pointed out that Roy's interests were not from now on necessarily always going to be identical with British interests. I also argued the anti-federalist case and it did no harm to have the issues aired. The group was not wholly on Roy's side and there was a new petulance in his attitude which not everyone liked. Roy knew perfectly well that the pure milk of Euro-federalism could not possibly be imbibed, either by the Labour Party or by the British electorate. Yet he was already showing that being away in Brussels somewhat dulls one's political reflexes at home, and in any case he no longer had to worry about inner Labour Party arguments.

I thought little more of the meeting until I was telephoned by David Watt; he told me that he wanted to write in his *Financial Times* column next day about the forthcoming Cabinet meeting. He gave me the impression that he knew exactly what was in my Cabinet papers and he put it to me that it was being said by my supposed friends that I was chickening out of my commitment to the European Community. This was such a travesty of what I had written that I over-reacted and rebutted my critics point by point, in the process revealing practically everything in the Cabinet papers. Though a great friend, David was also a skilled journalist and beguiled me into blowing the gaffe. I had just experienced Denis Healey's leaking to Peter Jenkins of the *Guardian* that I had been overturned by the Cabinet over a Commonwealth peace-keeping force for Rhodesia, so I was a bit touchy. Next morning I arrived in the Foreign Office to find my Private Secretary, Ewen Fergusson, ominously formal. 'The Prime Minister, Secretary of State, is very annoyed.' 'Why the hell is he annoyed?' I said. Ewen produced the *Financial Times* with David Watt's article; a quick reading showed that he had given a very good precis of the papers I had put to Cabinet and the criticisms of some of my pro-market Cabinet colleagues. I went over to see Jim at No. 10, trying to appear relaxed but inwardly feeling like an errant school boy. He was in his 'honest copper' role, adopting a 'What's all this 'ere?' tone. I thought the best thing to do was to be totally honest. I apologized for the article, said it was all my fault and explained how frustration had led me to say too much. Jim was rather nonplussed to find a Cabinet Minister actually admitting responsibility for a press story. He was sympathetic to the position that I had been put in but he was also angry and talked about cancelling the Cabinet meeting. Tony Benn, in his *Diaries 1977–80* (pages 201–6), describes what then happened as one of the most remarkable Cabinets he had ever attended and, give or take a little, his is an excellent account.

The passion aroused over the years by Britain's membership of the European Community stemmed from an incipient tension over federalism. The question of federalism had been raised in 1962 by Gaitskell. It had been there in the background through the 1970–71 negotiations, but since Edward Heath had denied any federalist intention at every stage it was hard to arouse public concern about a United States of Europe.

It is not surprising that Community membership is a divisive issue for many people in the UK, and particularly politicians who in my view correctly want to retain the essentials of our nationhood and will fight to do so. Sovereignty is not an absolute yet, as I had said in my own speech to Parliament at the time of entry on 26 October 1971, it is 'foolish to try to sell the concept of the EEC and not admit that this means giving up some sovereignty. Of course it does, and I believe it rightly does. I believe this is one of the central appeals of it.' The skill is to voluntarily surrender and pool such sovereignty as is necessary to maintain the coherence of the Community, but to still retain the sinews of nationhood. As the European Community rightly strives for greater unity, the wise politicians will know what are the essentials of nationhood that must not be eroded. It was de Gaulle who in the Luxembourg Compromise developed the ultimate safeguard of a nation's vital interests once invoked acting in effect as a veto. It cannot be invoked lightly or often, but the knowledge that it is there concentrates minds and helps negotiations.

The outcome of our all-day Cabinet meeting was that, despite the passions aroused, we now had an official Government policy which was firmly pro-European, anti-federalist and committed to enlargement of the Community to include Greece, Portugal and Spain. It was Jim's and my task to sell that package first to the Labour Party at the autumn Conference and then to the country.

The emotional key to unlock the Left's suspicion and hostility to the Community was Spain. To Jack Jones, then the powerful leader of the T&GWU, Spain was the symbol of international socialism. As a young man, he had fought in the Civil War against Franco. If I could use Spanish entry to swing his heart and that of Michael Foot, the Labour Conference could be won. On 5 September I flew with Debbie to Madrid as part of my strategy for demonstrating the Labour Government's commitment to early Spanish entry. The three key people who ensured that Spain moved from fascism under Franco to democracy within the European Community were the Prime Minister, Adolfo Suárez, the Leader of the Opposition and later socialist Prime Minister, Felipe González, and the King, Juan Carlos. Each in his own way was impressive. They all represented a younger generation, but the person who played the crucial role was Suárez. Of all the Heads of Government I met during my time as Foreign Secretary, he was the one personality without whom one felt the Government would collapse. In this case that meant the transition to democracy would not succeed. For those early years of transition he exercised iron will and determination. Without his inside knowledge of the old Franco regime he would not have been able to bridge the massive gap between those whose instincts and attitudes had been shaped by decades of fascism and the new generation of young, idealistic, democratic Europeans. He had established a friendship with Felipe González and he spoke openly to me about how they both realized that the Socialist Party's time was coming but that it must not come too early. When Suárez resigned as Prime Minister in circumstances which have never been fully explained, exhausted and frustrated, it fell to the King to bridge the gap. He alone held the loyalty of the armed forces and stopped a military takeover. Only when that military threat was averted could Felipe González speak and act for the new generation of Spaniards, irrespective of their political inclinations. But this was for the future. In

1977 the issue was simple. Should we help Spain to enter the EEC and brush aside the pessimistic prophets of economic gloom who saw Spain as a millstone round the neck of the Community? The answer was 'yes', and we were a crucial help.

There were dire predictions from many quarters about the weakness of the Spanish economy, its protectionist nature and the domination of the state-owned industries. Very few people anticipated the remarkable speed with which the Spanish economy adjusted within the European Community. The British Labour Government and the German Social Democratic-Liberal coalition Government strongly supported entry for political reasons. We accepted that there would be economic problems but felt that without the buttressing of Community membership the ever present risk of a military coup would almost certainly be realized. Unlike NATO which, in my view wrongly, never made membership or its continuation dependent on being a democracy, the Treaty of Rome is quite clear: no country can remain a member of the European Community if it has abandoned democracy. I urged Felipe González to use Socialist International to mobilize opinion in favour of Spain's entry and arranged for him to come to London, as Leader of the Opposition in Spain, on an official visit.

At a Foreign Affairs Council meeting in Brussels on 20 September we firmed up on Spanish entry. The French feared the effect of Spanish agriculture on their southern voters, but in 1977 Giscard d'Estaing was very keen that Greece should join, and eventually that was the deal; all three – Greece, Portugal and Spain – or none. There are powerful echoes of this debate as the Community faces up to the need for Poland, Hungary and Czechoslovakia to enter soon after the 1992 internal market is achieved. The federalists routinely oppose enlargement. Those who fear federalism embrace enlargement. The European Community has no option other than to be a home for all European nations that espouse a true democracy and a market economy. The limit is how strict is the definition of Europe. In my judgement, it does not include Turkey or the Russian Federation.

At that time, my attention was constantly switching from Europe to Africa. I left that Council meeting in Brussels early to fly back for a memorial service for Steve Biko, the young South African leader of the Black Consciousness Movement. I had admired what he had been saying and writing in South Africa and wanted to demonstrate that his death was not going to be ignored by the Western democracies. My gesture was appreciated, and talking to people afterwards, most of those in St Paul's Crypt were amazed at my presence. It was the world-wide sense of outrage at the way Biko had been battered to death in a prison cell that led to the UN Security Council passing a mandatory arms embargo against South Africa in November 1977 on the basis that apartheid represented a threat to peace.

Each September the United Nations starts a new session and it is the traditional time for the Foreign Secretaries from all the member countries to come to New York and make a speech to the General Assembly. Because of Tristan's illness, Debbie had not been able to go in the spring for her annual visit to New York publishers so she was going to be there with me for part of the time. Before I flew to New York, I went to Plymouth to open the new laboratory for Marine Environmental Reseach and the huge covered frigate complex in the dockyard which I had planned as Navy Minister. It was a moving occasion; more important than launching a ship. For years I had visited the dockyard and watched in amazement as men worked at repairing frigates out in the open, lashed by the prevailing westerly wind and rain coming in over the Hamoaze. It seemed absurd to demand improved productivity while they worked in such appalling conditions. The old covered-in slip, where wooden boats had been made for the Royal Navy, was a constant reminder of what used to be done in Devonport and I had always vowed that if I ever had the chance I would do something to improve the disgraceful working conditions in the dockyard.

I gave a lot of thought to my speech to the UN General Assembly and developed the theme of strengthening UN peace-keeping forces. Though normally I am rather blasé about public speaking engagements, this was a vivid occasion with the vast hall full of diplomats from all over the world. My main activity was to lobby the Security Council to pass a resolution over Rhodesia which would set in motion the preliminary steps towards establishing a UN peace-keeping force. Debbie flew with me to Chicago. I had a lunchtime speaking engagement on human rights and détente. She stayed with her stepbrother before flying home. I had to go back that same afternoon for another meeting of the Security Council. Then it was on to Washington, returning at the weekend for the Labour Party Conference which started on Monday 3 October in Brighton.

For the first time, I was standing for a place on the Constituency Section of the National Executive of the Labour Party. The result was announced as usual on the Tuesday morning. I polled 176,000 votes which was more than I had expected. Jack Ashley just managed to get on as the seventh member with 287,000 votes and I was very pleased for him. Dennis Skinner was the runner-up, followed by Neil Kinnock, Peter Shore and then me. Jim Callaghan, in the speech that followed, spoke bluntly to the Conference about the need to cut inflation which was still running at 16 per cent. 'Please don't support us with general expressions of good will and kind words, and then undermine us through unjustified wage increases or price increases – either back us or sack us.' We had to a considerable extent defused the debate on the Common Market by issuing a letter from Jim Callaghan to the National Executive on the eve of the Conference. I had sweated blood with Tom McNally and others in helping Jim to draft this letter, which followed up the all-day Cabinet meeting. The letter was firm in rejecting any possibility of British withdrawal from the Community. It also warned the Party about the damage that was being done to Britain's position by constant speculation as to our basic commitment. Roy Jenkins, predictably, did not like the emphasis on a loose Community coming with enlargement and the limiting of the powers of the European Parliament. But he was far less critical than when I had first embarked on trying to defuse the issue of our membership within the Party.

It was left to Michael Foot to sum up the debate and divert attention from the hostile NEC document on the merits of which Tony Benn had regaled the Cabinet. Michael, a veteran of the Bevanite clash with Gaitskell, nevertheless evoked memories of Hugh Gaitskell's speech to the Conference in 1962 against a federalist Community. He also helpfully laid particular stress on the Community as a vehicle for continuing negotiations on the matters which Jim Callaghan's letter had placed on the agenda. The strategy of emphasizing enlargement worked, for, he said, 'I do not see how I, as an international socialist, or this movement, as an international movement, could say that we were going to slam the door in the faces of our comrades from Greece and Portugal and Spain.' This was the most forthcoming statement about British membership that I have ever known Michael Foot to make. The main interest on foreign affairs surrounded Rhodesia; I spoke in the debate on Southern Africa and Conference was broadly content with the policy I was pursuing.

On the Saturday morning I flew to the Belgian 'Schloss Gymnich' weekend at Villiers-le-Temple where I was asked to report on the Labour Party Conference. Because of my relief at having emerged unscathed from my internal battle, I was probably too complacent about the effect of the Callaghan letter on other Foreign Ministers. What sounded all right in Brighton was less attractive in Belgium for, deliberately, it contained little of the Euro-speak which they all used about union and unity. Although Hans-Dietrich Genscher was a little critical in our meeting, he gave a far more hostile briefing to the press before leaving us early that Saturday evening. On Sunday morning I had to sort out the controversy he had left behind with the British press and also answer questions about Reg Prentice who had decided to join the Conservative Party.

I talked about Reg to Roy Jenkins, who was at the meeting, for he knew him better than I and had actually spoken for Reg with Shirley Williams at a riotous meeting in Newham Town Hall in September 1975. Prentice had had a miserable life with his Left-wing dominated local party and one could well understand why he had decided to leave. It was, however, one of the first signs of the importance Margaret Thatcher would give to attracting converts to the Conservative Party. The Labour Party never understood that this was a clever strategy, diminishing Labour in the eyes of the electorate. They only compounded the effect by

accusing people like Reg Prentice of being traitors. Margaret Thatcher's
wooing in Opposition of Labour supporters like Paul Johnson, a former
editor of the *New Statesman*, and Hugh Thomas, the young historian
who had written a brilliant book on the Spanish Civil War, began to set
an intellectual climate in which the exciting ideas were felt to be coming
from the Right. She also persuaded Woodrow Wyatt, the former Labour
MP, of her worth, which had a considerable dividend in his journalism
for the *News of the World* and *The Times* and his contacts on the Left. It
was subtle politics, while being fiercely party political, to appear open
intellectually to ideas from a broader base.

That Sunday afternoon, 9 October, I left Bierset in Belgium and flew
direct to Moscow. I arrived not really knowing what sort of reception to
expect. Anglo-Russian relations had not been warm for some time. The
freeze had started when Sir Alec Douglas-Home had expelled ninety
Soviet diplomats and officials in September 1971. I had had a good
meeting with Gromyko in New York a fortnight earlier and his decision
not to veto in the Security Council our resolution over Rhodesia was
perhaps a sign that they wanted to thaw our relationship. Gromyko was
at the foot of the steps to greet me and from that moment it became clear
that the Russians were laying down the red carpet. Driving into Moscow,
he pointed out the tank memorial marking the point that the German
Panzer divisions had reached, a timely reminder of why Soviet military
chiefs over-insured. When Gromyko and I signed the Anglo-Soviet
Agreement on the Prevention of an Accidental Outbreak of Nuclear War,
not only did President Brezhnev turn up but all the senior military
figures and a number of other Politburo members. This was their way of
indicating that they wanted improved relations. The Treaty itself was of
no great significance, the US and France already having signed something
similar. What the Russians wanted was to convince us that their anxieties
about Jimmy Carter's attitude to the Strategic Arms Limitation Talks
(SALT) were genuine. They had carefully noted Jim Callaghan's developing friendship with Jimmy Carter and now they wanted us to use our
influence.

Soviet-US relations were bad that autumn not just because of SALT
but also because of the start of a Soviet sponsored Cuban military build
up in Ethiopia. Affairs in the Horn of Africa were immensely complicated,
for the Ethiopians had turned from the West to Moscow, and the Somalis
from Moscow to Washington. To add to the complexity, the Somalis had
invaded Ethiopian territory in the Ogaden. The territorial dividing line
had long been disputed but we had no illusion that this was an aggressive
act. In Washington Zbig Brzezinski, Carter's National Security Adviser,
saw the Horn only as an East-West power struggle, whereas Cy Vance
and I, with the German, French and Italian Foreign Ministers, wanted to
treat the invasion as a regional question, holding Somalia to the rules of
the Organization of African Unity which upheld the sanctity of the

existing map of Africa. I was determined that we should not acquiesce in Somalia's action, for to do so would lose any moral authority when the Ethiopians eventually, as I felt confident they would, reasserted their military dominance. When they won back the Ogaden we would have to demand from the Soviets that they would veto any Ethiopian adventurism into Somalia. This was exactly what happened in 1978, but not before a massive Cuban build up of armed forces in Ethiopia. We were then able to persuade the Soviet Union to hold the Ethiopians back, but even so an unrepentant Brzezinski said that 'Détente died in the desert of the Ogaden.'

The main source of tension between the two superpowers was, however, SALT. In the spring of 1977 Cy Vance had gone to Moscow to put a new approach to Gromyko for the SALT II negotiations which were the follow up to the SALT I signed by Nixon and Brezhnev in 1972. Jimmy Carter wanted 'deep cuts' in the number of strategic weapons. It was a proposal somewhat similar to that which Gorbachev tried on President Reagan at Reykjavik in October 1986. But in 1977 the Old Guard, who then dominated the Politburo in Moscow, were appalled. They thought that Carter was out to trick them and was going back on the Vladivostok Agreement made with President Ford. Cy Vance had sensed that the Russian bureaucracy would not like this proposition and had won from Jimmy Carter the right, if it was turned down, to put forward an alternative approach. Unfortunately, by the time Cy put forward this alternative, Gromyko had just switched off and refused to do anything for the next few months other than rubbish the deep cuts proposal as a 'cheap and shady manoeuvre'.

I found Gromyko readier than hitherto to accept that Jimmy Carter's intentions towards arms control were at least genuine but he was still perplexed about the emphasis that was being given to human rights. I was in a cleft stick. All my instincts sympathized with Carter's wish to elevate human rights and I was not afraid of embarrassing the Soviet Union. But I also wanted, as did Vance, substantive progress on arms control. Up to a point, we could aspire to both. But even though there was no explicit linkage, implicitly we did face choices. If forced to choose, I was more concerned then about the troubling build up of nuclear weapons. We in Britain also, for the first time, were represented directly in the negotiations for a Comprehensive Test Ban Treaty and we wanted progress in this area as well. Our main fear was nuclear proliferation, particularly in Pakistan and South Africa. Much of my visit was spent in trying to assess the tolerances on these issues and trying to weigh up how hard we could push in one area without adversely affecting others. My personal problem was that I was much more hostile to Soviet Communism than Jim Callaghan and the mainstream of Labour Party thinking. The Soviet military's attempt to starve Berlin in 1947, to suppress the Hungarians' bid for freedom in 1956 and to snuff out the

Dubcek reforms in Czechoslovakia in 1968 were ever present memories for me. The Union of Soviet Socialist Republics, once described as 'a lie in every word', was an empire put together by violence and held together by terror. Reagan was not wrong when he called it an 'evil empire'. It might have been imprudent, but it was accurate. I can see no redeeming features in Leninism or Stalinism. The world has rightly never forgotten Nazi crimes and the evil of the Holocaust, but I had for a long time been amazed at the way the world ignored Soviet Communism's record of mass murder and bloody suppression of ethnic minorities. Now under Brezhnev, the Soviet economy was stagnant and its totalitarian Party corrupt. I had to deal with these people within the diplomatic niceties but I despised and distrusted them. I never doubted that both Brezhnev and Gromyko would not hesitate to suppress or invade another country in their sphere of influence, so when the invasion of Afghanistan came in 1979, it was no surprise. Why Carter was so shocked, I could never understand. The Russians were afraid of Islamic fundamentalism with so many Muslims within their empire; their influence in Afghanistan was longstanding and they were not prepared to stand by while it was overturned, as had happened to the West with the toppling of the Shah.

On human rights Gromyko was as dour as usual, resenting our intervention in what he considered to be internal Soviet affairs. He listened to my representations on Sakharov and others and promised to look at the list of people we wanted them to release so they could travel to the West, but he left me under no doubt that any concessions would be made from pure cynicism, merely as a device for improving British press comment and public attitudes to the USSR. To entertain our delegations, Gromyko and his wife gave an informal supper party followed by Russian folk singing. It turned out to be a lively and enjoyable evening, with Gromyko totally relaxed and joining in the songs. The inscrutable mask was allowed to drop and I saw a different facet to his personality. But that he was ready to acquiesce in brutal suppression I never doubted.

The word 'détente' had been strongly criticized by the Right wing in America in the latter days of President Ford's period in office and the hawks were beginning to criticize President Carter for identifying with détente. All the evidence was that the détente process had, over twenty-five years, contributed to a more stable and safer East-West relationship. What President Carter was trying to do in championing human rights was immensely important. We had to rescue the Seventh Principle of the Helsinki Final Act which pledged the thirty-five signatory states to uphold human rights and fundamental freedoms and which the Russians were trying to bury. Our task over the next few decades was to move that commitment from an aspiration in some countries to a reality. In the case of the Soviet Union, since it had never even been an aspiration but a cynical commitment undertaken with no intention of fulfilment, we had to devise a political strategy which would provide incentives for the Soviets to implement reforms and disincentives if they continued abusing human rights. In the first speech I made as Foreign Secretary, I said that Britain would take its stand on human rights in every corner of the globe but we would not discriminate and we would apply the same standards and judgements to communist countries as we did to Chile, Uganda and South Africa. I warned that in many areas we were dealing with entrenched attitudes which, in the nature of things, would not change overnight, but that the Final Act was already seen as an inspiration and a point of reference, and I drew attention to the signatories of Charter 77 in Czechoslovakia.

In retrospect, the push on human rights from the Western democracies which started in 1977 was a critical influence on Vaclav Havel's ability to mobilize the peaceful protest in Czechoslovakia which won them their freedom in the end. In Eastern Europe, 1989 became, like 1848, the Springtime of Nations. It could not have occurred so quickly had there not been a past history of patriotism, pluralism and market economies. But nor could it have occurred if the Western democracies had accepted the Soviet interpretation of the Helsinki Final Act. A series of review conferences and a whole range of protests and sanctions had forced the Soviet Union to realize that they did not have *carte blanche* to ignore human rights.

Nothing in my period as Foreign Secretary gave me as much intellectual satisfaction as trying to develop this strategy for achieving greater individual freedom. Of course there were numerous inconsistencies in the British and Western approaches, and the closet supporters of Soviet Communism would always seize upon them. They would use our support for the Shah, our readiness to talk to the Argentines or our trade with South Africa as a way of devaluing our criticism of Brezhnev. After the invasion of Afghanistan, when the Third World turned against the Soviet Union, even members of the Politburo began to recognize that they could not ignore criticism.

The KGB had realized this a few years before and we were picking up straws in the wind that Yuri Andropov, head of the KGB, was aware that Soviet propaganda was becoming less effective as more countries began to see that the Soviet Empire was in decline. Perestroika and glasnost did not arrive with Gorbachev – they were first introduced when Andropov became General Secretary – and they had a firm base in the *Realpolitik* of the KGB. This should never be forgotten in interpreting the history of the 1980s. The decision to retrench to the boundaries of the USSR, to pull out of Afghanistan and pull back from Eastern Europe was KGB-led and owed nothing to respect for democracy.

The insistent demands of the Western democracies on individual cases were in the 1970s starting to have an impact. Gromyko might look at the ceiling every time I mentioned Sakharov and try to pretend he was not listening, but, provided we gauged the tolerances correctly, we could push them a little further at each stage. In 1978 I published a book called *Human Rights*, an unusual event for a Foreign Secretary given that every word had to be cleared by the various Government departments. It stimulated some debate. At times the language used and the attitudes struck by ourselves and the United States differed, and the French and the Germans too had their own style and understandably made different estimates of what was and was not tolerable. This was quite helpful in that the Soviet Union had to respond in different ways and could not portray it simply as Western propaganda. Inevitably, when arms control negotiations were at crucial stages, human rights pressures were reduced. But by encouraging the development of human rights pressures from non-governmental organizations and individuals, I hoped that the pressure from public opinion would be maintained on the Soviet Union even when Governments might be relaxing theirs. It began to be accepted that governments could not always act at the same tempo and intensity as individuals or pressure groups. But if they co-operated each could reinforce the other. It became fashionable during Reagan's Presidency to denigrate President Carter, but for raising the profile of human rights and for being ready to risk the ire of the Soviet Union in their defence, the world owes Carter an immeasurable debt.

On arriving back from Moscow, I asked, on 17 October, for a report about the threat which was building up in the Falkland Islands. It was an eye-opening background account of militancy. Why it had not come to me unprompted was beyond belief. Some of the facts I knew already, but having them brought together in this way was dramatic. The account told how, in January 1976, the dying days of Elizabelita Perón's regime, Argentina demanded the recall of our Ambassador to Buenos Aires; how in February 1976 RRS *Shackleton* was fired upon; and how in March 1976, when the military regime took office, Admiral Massera of the ruling junta said that the intention had been to hit RRS *Shackleton*, not merely fire warning shots across her bows. In 1976 the Argentines established a base on Southern Thule and planned to capture the British Antarctic survey personnel in Southern Georgia if we attempted to remove their base in Southern Thule. They had also developed their fisheries programme without consultation and showed no interest in co-operation. The document also explained how the Argentine Government had licensed two US companies to carry out geo-physical surveys in disputed waters without prior reference and had rejected our protest that this infringed our rights. The Argentines then put forward a joint administration scheme leading to a full transfer of sovereignty within eight years, with Argentine acquisition of the Falkland Islands Company and the establishment of a bank on the Falkland Islands. As if all this were not enough, the Department then went on to describe how the Argentines had arrested five Soviet trawlers in late September 1977 and arrested two

more Soviet and two Bulgarian trawlers on 1 October. They had actually
fired on one of the Bulgarian ships, wounding a Bulgarian sailor and
Admiral Massera had ordered his ships to 'sink the vessel if necessary'.
An Argentine spokesman had said there would be a similar riposte to
intrusions 'by any other flag carrier and at any other place'. This remark
was explicitly drawn to our attention by the Argentine naval attaché. The
Beagle Channel judgement, involving international arbitration, had just
come out in favour of Chile, a disappointment for the Argentines, and
there had been no progress in their negotiations with the Brazilians over
the River Plate dispute. It was felt, not unreasonably, that the Argentine
navy, from which the Foreign Minister had been appointed, was showing
signs of wanting to demonstrate its virility. There was judged to be a
definite threat with the impending presence in disputed waters of HMS
Endurance and British Antarctic survey ships, *Bransfield* and *John Biscoe*.
'We cannot be sure that they will not attempt to arrest or attack any of
these if the next round does not go well.' Against such a background I
was in no doubt that we would have to deploy at least a nuclear-powered
hunter-killer submarine in the Southern Atlantic in case the Argentines
decided to spring a surprise invasion. That is what we did and it is fully
described in the next chapter.

November dramatically changed the Middle East. I had visited Cairo
and Damascus in April, and had sensed then the frustration which Sadat
was feeling over the need to keep in step with every Arab nation. He also
emphatically did not want the Soviet Union in the driving seat. The
Egyptian economy was in a very difficult state even then and he no doubt
felt the need to reduce spending on the military and obtain US financial
help. Peace between Israel and Egypt had the potential for being a
popular issue in Cairo.

My visit to Syria in April was the first time a British Foreign Secretary
had been in Damascus since the country's independence in 1946. After our
meeting, which I had found intellectually stimulating, President Assad was
asked if he felt Britain bore a large share of responsibility for Middle East
crises. He paused for a few seconds, smiled, which was rare for him, then
said in a clear reference to my age that men should not always be held to
account for what their fathers or grandfathers had done. I wish Assad had
shown the same readiness to forget the misdeeds of the past in relation to
Israel, but he was implacable, unwilling to make any territorial compromise,
not only on the Golan Heights, which is Syrian, but in the West Bank too.
I left convinced that his hard-line sentiments would not shift, and so it
proved; but also with an impression confirmed by subsequent events that
he was one of the most interesting leaders in the Middle East and could
eventually hold the key to a comprehensive settlement. When in 1990 the
Syrians deployed forces as part of the anti-Iraq coalition to free Kuwait,
I began to hope that that an Israeli–Syrian agreement could be forged
to return Golan – demilitarized – to Syria in perpetuity.

The joint US–Soviet, Vance–Gromyko statement on the Middle East issued on 1 October 1977, and which it was hoped would provide the basis for reconvening the Geneva Conference, provoked Israel into vituperative attacks against the statement, reinforced by the Jewish community in the United States. Under considerable domestic pressure, President Carter appeared to be shifting his ground. President Sadat, who had initially welcomed the statement as a masterstroke, began to be concerned. He had private doubts about involving the Soviet Union, particularly as only a few years before he had deliberately broken away from their sphere of influence. It was Carter's handwritten note towards the end of October, appealing for a bold and statesmanlike move to help overcome the hurdles on the path to Geneva, that led Sadat on 3 November to propose a world summit in East Jerusalem to be attended by the US, the USSR, China, France and the UK as well as Israel, Syria, Jordan, Egypt and the PLO. There was some private diplomacy between Israel and Egypt and on 13 November Begin invited Sadat to come to Israel. The world was amazed when Sadat flew into Israel on 18 November. Here were the leaders of the two countries that had fought each other only four years before meeting and agreeing to the slogan, 'No more war, no more bloodshed.'

The emotion of the occasion was captured by television and flashed around the world, and Sadat returned to a hero's welcome in Cairo. Suddenly UN resolutions and the Geneva Conference were all sidelined. I and many others sensed that it could only be the personal chemistry between the Right-wing leader of the Likud Party, Prime Minister Menachem Begin, and President Anwar Sadat, the former air force officer and member of Nasser's military committee that overthrew King Farouk, which would provide a breakthrough. Sadat had put Begin in his debt. Begin was going to have to move. It transpired in 1978 that their personal relationship also needed a catalyst, which emerged in the person of Jimmy Carter. All three men had deep religious beliefs and, having spent some time with them all, I do not believe that the Camp David Accords, reached on 19 September 1978, would have been possible without their respective commitments to Judaism, Islam and Christianity. Carter's skill as a mediator was to use every psychological pressure and debating point to play on the eternal verities, to build friendship between them all and to make each feel a moral responsibility to the other. The man who risked most was Sadat and his assassination in 1981, while taking the salute at a ceremonial military parade, was by troops loyal to the extremist Islamic group, the Moslem Brotherhood.

Prime Minister Begin flew into London on Friday 2 December for a visit which had been postponed because of Sadat's decision to go to Israel. It was painfully apparent that he knew he had to respond to Sadat and yet had no idea how he could do so within the confines of his own rigid view that Judaea, Galilee and Samaria were holy places which had to lie within the boundaries of Israel. We all talked of an all-embracing agreement but, in the privacy of our own minds, knew that a comprehensive peace settlement was not going to be possible and that all we could reasonably plan for was to place the first building block of an eventual comprehensive settlement.

It had been an action-packed year and it was perhaps typical of the stubborn nature of so many of the foreign policy questions that I had to confront that I had started the year with Rhodesia, unresolved for decades, and ended it with Israel. UDI in 1965 was rooted in history and in the form in which the Colony of Southern Rhodesia came into being in 1923. The problems of Palestine were of even longer standing. While Zimbabwe was to become independent in just over two years, a homeland for the Palestinians has still to be achieved. With Syria fighting alongside the Allied forces against Iraq in 1991 and Jordan's authority reduced, having supported Saddam Hussein, we will see in the early 1990s direct talks between Israel and Syria and Israel and Jordan. With the Soviet Union acting constructively alongside the United States in the region after Iraq's defeat, it is possible that even the Arab–Israeli dispute may be solvable. Those who search for instant solutions to international disputes will not relish the long and often protracted nature of diplomacy. But the politicians who come to diplomacy, usually for short periods, should not allow their enthusiasm for action to be blunted by the world weariness of the diplomats. It is a necessary mix for success that political optimism and diplomatic caution work together.

xv. First day, Minister of the Navy, 1968.

xvi. *Top:* The 1970 General Election – Debbie, Mary Wilson, the
Candidate, the Prime Minister.

xvii. *Above:* MP for Plymouth.

xviii. *Top:* Minister of the Navy with the Queen Mother at the Royal
Hospital School, Holbrook – a school for the sons of seamen.

xix. *Above:* Minister of the Navy on HMS *Intrepid* at Singapore.

xx. Our wedding, 28 December 1968.

xxi. Gareth and the new Foreign Secretary on his first morning, 1977.

xxii. The office of the Secretary of State for Foreign and Common-
wealth Affairs.

xxiii. The Callaghan Cabinet.
Front l. to r.: Peter Shore, Tony Benn, myself, Denis Healey, Michael Foot, the Prime Minister, Lord Elwyn Jones, Merlyn Rees, Shirley Williams, Eric Varley and Roy Mason.
Back l. to r.: Sir John Hunt (Secretary to the Cabinet), John Smith, Bill Rodgers, John Silkin, Lord Peart, Albert Booth, John Morris, Bruce Millan, Fred Mulley, David Ennals, Joel Barnett, Roy Hattersley, Stan Orme and Harold Lever.

xxiv. The family call this after the advertisement, 'I'm David, fly me!'

15

MI6, GCHQ AND
THE FALKLANDS

It could only happen in Britain that the Foreign Intelligence Service, MI6, responsible to the Foreign Secretary, officially does not exist. Its wartime predecessor, SIS, is admitted to have existed and the counter-espionage service, MI5, responsible to the Home Secretary since 1952, is acknowledged officially. Yet newspapers refer constantly to MI6. The BBC refers to MI6 in broadcasts at home and abroad, and in August 1981 even produced a detailed programme, *The Profession of Intelligence*. The Heads of MI6 and MI5 are never publicly named for the good reason of protecting their lives. For most of my time the Head of MI6 was Sir Maurice Oldfield, thought by me, though he has denied it, to be John Le Carré's model for George Smiley, who is described in *The Russia House* as 'a tubby, bespectacled gentleman of a certain seniority'; and carries the flavour of the Maurice Oldfield I knew.

Intelligence can play a crucial role in defence decision making, which is literally a life or death affair. But Ministers need to understand how to use intelligence, whether military, diplomatic or obtained by covert means, through MI6 or GCHQ. In both 1977 and 1982 the factual evidence of a potential invasion of the Falklands was available to Ministers. The 1977 record shows that intelligence served as a tool for Ministerial decisions. The 1982 records show how intelligence was ignored. It is insufficient simply to garner secret information; it has to be assimilated and correctly used. The intelligence services are vital but they are rightly shrouded in secrecy and it is difficult to write about them. Yet the Falklands War has meant that there is now much more information in the public domain than would ever normally be the case and I am freer, therefore, to write about these issues.

Initially, I was sceptical about the system for referring intelligence cases with a political content to the Foreign Secretary. But after a review of six months' referrals, I was completely satisfied. I grew to respect the work of MI6, particularly in Southern Africa, where they provided me with a lot of intelligence.

As Foreign Secretary I never publicly mentioned MI6 until years later in Opposition, after Jim Callaghan had decided not to comply any longer with the pretence that it does not exist. As Prime Minister, Jim Callaghan did attempt to change this convention, and sent a memo suggesting that we should break with precedent and formally avow the existence of MI6. I consulted Maurice Oldfield and he produced, I felt, compelling arguments for continuing the convention. Admittedly it was absurd, even risible, but the protection afforded by not admitting it existed was absolute; whereas once it was acknowledged there would be a constant attempt to make Ministers answerable and a progressive erosion. While one could imagine Ministers initially holding the line on a blank refusal to discuss any detail, there was a reasonable fear that gradually, as had happened in the US Congress with the CIA, more information would be divulged under parliamentary pressure. An opponent can piece together valuable information from a series of disclosures which, though trivial of themselves, can in combination become very revealing.

The crucial question is how a democracy can have confidence in the operation of the Secret Services without risking intelligence being compromised. This must mean, first and foremost, vigilant and interested politicians holding the key offices of Foreign Secretary, Home Secretary and Prime Minister. The Prime Minister should not be given overall executive control. Harold Wilson's paranoia, justified or not, over spies and spying illustrates the danger of centralized control in No. 10. This central control occurred under Margaret Thatcher, but without any specific authorization. The other basic ingredient is for Parliament to have sufficient confidence in the intelligence services to accept that this is the one area which has to fall outside their normal procedures for holding government accountable. The only satisfactory way to ensure overview is if there is independent parliamentary scrutiny from a Committee of Privy Councillors, with Parliament accepting that there should be no probing on the floor of the House of Commons.

After a lot of discussion about whether to admit the existence of MI6, I was convinced that it cost us nothing to continue the charade and that it might cost us something to discontinue it. Interestingly, Margaret Thatcher, who was consulted as Leader of the Opposition, took a similar line and Jim Callaghan wisely concluded that the necesary level of cross-party agreement was not present, so he would continue with the policy of non-avowal. The Government in my time also did not acknowledge the full activity of the Government Communications Headquarters, GCHQ, in Cheltenham, either. This was revealed in 1983, when Geoffrey Prime was discovered passing some of the most precious secrets to the KGB. He had been doing this for years and throughout my time as Foreign Secretary. But it appeared to me that the greatest revelations about what happens in GCHQ came during the controversy over the banning of trade unionism in the establishment in the 1980s. I winced as day after day what I had thought was sensitive information was divulged, and it seemed far more damaging than any strike action.

So important did I feel it was to protect GCHQ, that I supported the Attorney-General, Sam Silkin, in his decision to go ahead with a prosecution under Section 1 and Section 2 of the Official Secrets Act in what became known as the ABC trial, after the three men who were arrested – Aubrey, Berry and Campbell. My instincts had been not to prosecute for fear of revealing information in court, but we were assured that court procedures would mean that there were no revelations. In fact it turned out to be an unwise decision and the Attorney-General instructed that important charges should be dropped.

In the early part of 1979, GCHQ was threatened with disruption by the civil service strike. I was very anxious about the effect of any serious disruption of activity. Fortunately, most of our staff agreed to keep all essential work going both in London and in Cheltenham on the day of the mass action. It never crossed my mind not to turn up that day at the Foreign Office, particularly since I was expecting the staff to come in despite the pickets. As I walked past the picket at the Ambassadors' Entrance I was sworn at and called a scab. I returned a full barrel-load for I was not going to be called a scab by anyone – and found that it was all being recorded on a TV camera which, unbeknown to me, was inside the doorway. My rather robust turn of phrase was captured on the television news bulletins. In the demonology of the Labour Party, crossing a picket looms large. Some of the Ministers who had stayed at home to avoid crossing a picket were furious at my remarks, but I was unrepentant. The strike itself was taking place weeks before the settlement date and the negotiating procedures had still not been exhausted. If civil servants had not taken industrial action either then in 1979 or in the early 1980s there would never have been a ban on trade unionism at Cheltenham. I have always opposed the ban and the justification for it was virtually removed when all but one of the civil service unions eventually agreed to a no-strike agreement for everyone working at Cheltenham. Any Government has some areas of activity which need to be protected from strike action and sensitive intelligence establishments are just such an area. But the people who staff these establishments are patriotic citizens and it was a great mistake to equate being a member of a trade union with putting the nation's security at risk. That was and remains a slur on the good name of trade unionism which should not remain, provided that all the unions can be persuaded that a no-strike pledge is acceptable as a condition of appointment.

In the debate in late 1979 on the treason of Sir Anthony Blunt, which had been concealed by successive Home Secretaries, Margaret Thatcher did not reveal the existence of either MI5, which Blunt had been in, or MI6. Yet Jim Callaghan and many other MPs referred freely to both MI6 and MI5. During the week that followed, the Table Office in the

House of Commons actually allowed questions to be put down about the Security Services provided there was a specific reference to Anthony Blunt in them. Thereafter, the Home Office announced it was not going to answer any more questions and the absolute ban was reasserted.

There has never been any reference to MI6 in a Government publication. Even on 23 April 1987, when the Prime Minister was asked about the media's allegations about Sir Maurice Oldfield's homosexuality, Margaret Thatcher, in a Written Answer, only referred to him as Security Co-ordinator in Northern Ireland. She never revealed that he had been the Head of MI6, despite the fact that every newspaper reported it. It could be argued that democratic debate was not harmed since Members of Parliament knew the former Head of MI6 had admitted, in March 1980, that he had from time to time engaged in homosexual activities. That Maurice Oldfield had repeatedly lied about this when being positively vetted was shattering news to all those who, like me, had known and trusted him completely.

Margaret Thatcher said that there was no evidence or reason whatsoever to suggest that security had ever been compromised by Oldfield and that he had contributed notably to a number of security and intelligence successes. That judgement is probably correct. Yet this was no minor matter. After the various Soviet penetrations of both MI5 and MI6 the suspicions about who one could trust were once again raised. Was there a Fifth Man spying for the Russians? That suspicion still existed while I was Foreign Secretary, for another person, never mentioned in press speculation, was investigated, though nothing incriminating was found.

I was impressed by Maurice Oldfield as were most of the few politicians who dealt directly with him. Parliament was, however, now being told that we had been wrong to trust his word as Head of MI6 and that the positive vetting procedures had been totally ineffective. I enjoyed talking privately with him about world problems, often without even my Private Secretary present, and I asked myself, should I have spotted something?

He had implemented the policy that led to many people's lives being blighted, either by being dismissed from their job or having their promotion prospects blocked, because of the security doubt about homosexuals. I had, in the Ministry of Defence in 1969, challenged that policy, feeling that mere homosexuality should not be an automatic bar to holding some jobs. I had then been visited by someone from MI6 to demonstrate how the Soviet Union and East European Communist countries had subverted people through their homosexuality. Again in the Foreign Office I had challenged the need to apply the policy so rigidly and had even spoken to Maurice Oldfield about it. Margaret Thatcher's announcement made me wonder not only whom I could trust but also whether I should have guessed. I had known Maurice Oldfield was a bachelor. He seemed well adjusted, though I noticed that after a chat in the evening he was reluctant to go, leaving an impression of loneliness. I had no idea, however, that he knew Tom Driberg and had I done so I might have been alerted, for Tom Driberg was a florid homosexual. While still a Labour MP, he had turned up uninvited and with a friend at a party in my house in the late 1960s. Hearing a noise in the bedroom I put on the light to find them engaged in a homosexual act. Tom Driberg was a friend of Guy Burgess, a homosexual, as was Anthony Blunt. A culture of homosexuality was pervasive among a whole generation of Oxford and Cambridge undergraduates before the Second World War. Many of them rose to influential and sometimes prominent positions, so we should have been on the alert. Yet Oldfield had hoodwinked us all, politicians and his fellow spies. He did not appear to be remotely like those alienated public school boys of whom Noël Annan writes in his book *Our Age*. They were still around in the Foreign Office and in the ruling establishment of the 1970s. Modernism, collectivism, pacifism and homosexuality were their gods. Maurice Bowra called the Cambridge spies of the 1930s the Hominterm. They did great harm to this country. But their soulmates who were loyal and fought for their country in the Second World War had a more lasting influence. They were the generation that lacked backbone, that had no obvious sticking points, people for whom patriotism was a bore. They were influenced by Keynes and Beveridge, they were not angry young men but cynical and essentially defeatist. Oldfield, I suspect, in part despised them while in part identifying with them. A complex man in a complex trade he hoodwinked us all.

The Oldfield affair convinced me that parliamentary scrutiny over MI6 and MI5 or, as they are referred to in the House of Commons by Ministers, the Security and Intelligence Services, had now become essential. It could only be beneficial for the Foreign Secretary and Home Secretary to be questioned on their responsibilities by a Committee of Privy Councillors, drawn from the House of Commons and Lords, and for the Heads of MI6 and MI5 to be questioned as well. A Scrutiny Committee would not be able to reveal their detailed findings nor probe individual operations. Indeed the Foreign Secretary, unless there is a need to know, steers clear of involvement in operations. A Committee would, however, be an independent check, and carry far more conviction with MPs than the existing Security Commission. I do not shift from my belief that the activities of MI6 should not be subject to questioning on the floor of the House of Commons. Yet such an absolute ban will be easier to sustain if MPs know that they have delegated their responsibility for scrutiny to a few trusted colleagues. Involving the House of Lords would allow for the Chairman to be a Law Lord and for the potential to involve crossbenchers so there need be no fear of partisan politics.

One of Britain's clandestine activities is counter-propaganda. On 4 January 1948 a Top Secret paper was put to Cabinet by Ernest Bevin, the Secretary of State for Foreign Affairs. Christopher Mayhew was one of his junior Ministers most closely involved. It is an eloquent statement about Social Democracy and the counter-propaganda it authorized deserves to be given an important place in any history of the Cold War. Even today we need to be vigilant to ensure the eventual defeat of Communism. The paper recommended:

1. We should adopt a new line in our foreign publicity designed to oppose the inroads of Communism by taking the offensive against it, basing ourselves on the standpoint of the position and vital ideas of British Social Democracy and Western civilization, and to give a lead to our friends abroad and help them in the anti-Communist struggle.

2. The only new machinery required would be a small Section in the Foreign Office to collect information concerning Communist policy, tactics and propaganda and to provide material for our anti-Communist publicity through our Missions and Information Services abroad. The fullest co-operation of the BBC Overseas Services would be desirable; but this and the provision of the necessary material by the Central Office of Information would be arranged through the usual channels.

Our anti-Communist publicity material should also be available to Ministers for use, when convenient, in their public speeches; and also to British delegations to conferences and – on an informal basis – to Labour Party and Trades Union delegations.

3. We should develop visits by important Trade Unionists from abroad and other influential, non-Communist foreigners, and set up a 'Wilton Park' in which we could offer them courses on British life and institutions, and make available to them material and ideas useful for the struggle in their own countries against Communism. In short, we should seek to make London the Mecca for Social Democrats in Europe.

The small section in the Foreign Office, which the paper refers to, became the IRD, the Information and Research Department in the Foreign Office. It occupied for many years a grey area between MI6 and the News Department. It did essential service and there is no need for anyone associated with it to feel shame: without a counter-propaganda offensive through those difficult years the Soviets' propaganda would never have been adequately countered. Gradually, however, its style of operation got out of step with our more open democracy and reform was inevitable. In 1976 Sir Colin Crowe undertook an investigation of the three information departments in the Foreign Office: the Information and Administration Department, IAD; the Guidance and Information Policy Department, GIPD; and IRD. In May 1977 I agreed that there should be a comprehensive reorganization and IRD was closed, despite the protests of its Head, Ray Whitney, who later became a Conservative MP, and a new department of information was formed out of the remainder. The aim was to achieve greater clarity and end the grey area, which for too long escaped proper scrutiny, falling neither in the open area of diplomacy nor in the closed area of spying.

It was the publication of the Report of a Committee of Privy Council-lors on the Falklands, under the Chairmanship of Lord Franks, in January 1983 that convinced me that I had been wrong and Jim Callaghan right about avowing MI6 and that we should no longer go on refusing to acknowledge its existence. In the Franks Report there is no reference to MI6, presumably because of the ban on admitting its existence. This was despite the information presented to the Committee by a former Prime Minister, Jim Callaghan, alleging that he had asked the Head of MI6 to inform the Argentines of the naval deployment in 1977 and claiming that it had therefore deterred an invasion and was not a clandestine deploy-ment. This was a deeply significant claim for the former Prime Minister to make. He also made a more serious charge, which coming from a man of notable patriotism deserved more respect than it appeared to receive, namely that Margaret Thatcher and her Government were guilty of not acting with foresight and despatch to prevent the Argentines from invading the Falklands. That charge, which I too believe to be valid, was based above all on his experience and mine of what happened in 1977. Yet the Franks Report never published any of the detailed information on the background and the decision making that led up to the 1977 deployment of naval ships to the Southern Atlantic. Why? This omission was in spite of the fact that I and others gave evidence to the Franks Committee covering this aspect in full. We are entitled to this information and I propose to give it.

The naval deployment in the Southern Atlantic in the autumn of 1977 was first revealed to the House by Jim Callaghan on 30 March 1982, just before the invasion on 2 April. He was giving the Government the chance to claim that naval vessels were in the area even if they were not. Later he developed his argument that the deployment had been declared to the Argentines. This necessitated open and careful examination. It was amazing that the Franks Report never rebuffed or corroborated his statement that he had told the Head of MI6, Maurice Oldfield, to let his contacts in the Argentine Government know that our submarines were in the vicinity of the Falklands and therefore able to act.

In his autobiography, published in 1987, Jim Callaghan toned down what he had said in 1982, saying only:

> We made no formal communication to Argentina of these precautionary moves, but I informed the Head of MI6 of our plans before the ships sailed and it is possible that, as I hoped, some information reached the Argentinian armed forces.

In fact the head of MI6 would have read all the Cabinet Committee papers on this question. He would also have been aware from the Foreign Office that I had refused an MOD request to inform the US Navy about our deployments, for the very reason that I knew they had close links with the Argentine Navy and I did not want the Argentines to know. I do not believe that Maurice Oldfield, who was primarily answerable to me as Foreign Secretary as well as to the Prime Minister, would have disclosed the naval deployment as a result of a discussion with the Prime Minister, at least not without talking to me first. Although in some delicate areas he would be entitled to respond only to the Prime Minister I do not believe this was one of them. No evidence was ever found that he had been either instructed by the Prime Minister or acted on such instructions.

The Governor of the Falkland Islands was advised at the time:

> If the talks go well the task force will quietly withdraw. But if things go wrong we will be in a position to counter any Argentine threat to the Falklands or to our shipping in the area ... What we are doing is taking a number of precautions since we believe it will be prudent not to leave ourselves unprotected or unprepared ...

Our naval deployment was an insurance policy, it did not of itself deter.

I am left with the suspicion that a tacit understanding was reached within the Franks Committee to set to one side what happened in 1977 despite its importance for assessing the actions of the Conservative Government in 1982. It is not hard to see how all the interests represented on the Committee could have acquiesced with such a course. They had first of all a ready-made excuse for doing so since they could claim that they were excluded from making any direct reference to MI6 or to Sir Maurice Oldfield. The two Labour Privy Councillors, Harold Lever and Merlyn Rees, would have naturally been keen to protect Jim Callaghan's reputation and would not have wanted to conclude that his memory was at fault and that Maurice Oldfield had not been asked to warn the Argentines. The Committee might have been told formally or informally that Maurice Oldfield's routine notes of his meeting with the Prime Minister had been examined, as were the files in MI6, for any corroboration following meetings with Jim Callaghan when Prime Minister, and that nothing had been found to substantiate his claim. The two Conservative Privy Councillors, Anthony Barber and Harold Watkinson, given the 1977 precedent, would have been quite relieved not to have to compare Jim Callaghan's robust reaction with the failure of Margaret Thatcher and Peter Carrington to send a maritime force much earlier. The other two members of the Committee, Patrick Nairne and the Chairman, Oliver Franks, had no political interests to protect but would not have wanted to focus attention on the failure of diplomats and civil servants to tell Conservative Ministers much earlier about the 1977 incident – compromises like this can develop unconsciously. It was also convenient in that the Franks Committee had no need, therefore, to confront the question of whether to break with precedent and mention MI6.

The Franks Committee was made up of senior Establishment figures, but also streetwise politicians and civil servants. As David Watt wrote in

The Times of 21 January, they knew that the bloke in the pub was not really interested in raking over the ashes. The mood of the country was 'The war's over. We won, didn't we?' This is the best explanation for the total disjunction in the report. Its bland uncritical conclusions are tacked on to a critical narrative and the conclusions do not marry with the main text. Yet even so the Report is the closest the British public will get for some many years to learning about the internal workings of the intelligence community.

Admiral of the Fleet, Sir Terence Lewin, was interviewed by the BBC on 30 January 1983. A brilliantly successful Chief of the Defence Staff during the Falklands War, he was first known to me as a Naval Captain and then junior Admiral when I was Navy Minister, then as First Sea Lord and Chief of the Naval Staff when I was Foreign Secretary. It was clear, as he criticized a speech that I had made in the House of Commons about our readiness to open fire in 1977, that even he had forgotten the terms of the Rules of Engagement which had been agreed by Ministers with the full involvement of the Ministry of Defence. He said:

> I cannot believe that any British Government in peacetime would authorize a nuclear submarine, or indeed our ships, to take hostile action, the first hostile action, against another power. No Rule of Engagement would ever be approved that would allow you to do this and it certainly wasn't approved in 1977.

What Admiral Lewin had forgotten was that Ministers had carefully defined what would constitute a hostile action or hostile intent and that Ministers did authorize Royal Naval commanders to open fire on Argentine units which displayed hostile intent. Evidence of hostile intent was to include preparing to land military forces on the Falkland Islands or manoeuvring into a position to attack British territory. It is also clear that Ministers in 1977 were ready, in the event of a sufficiently serious deterioration in relations between us and the Argentine Government, to extend the territorial limit round the Islands from three to twelve miles and to inform the Argentine Government that any of their warships and military aircraft approaching to within fifty miles would be asked to identify themselves and state their intentions. The Argentines would have been ordered to withdraw within twenty-five miles of the Falkland Islands, and if they had failed to do so, under the doctrine of minimum force they would have been subject to ascending degrees of force, from warning to the discharge of conventional weapons.

Though it was hoped that the commander of the nuclear-powered hunter-killer submarine HMS *Dreadnought* would have been under the control at all stages of the Commander-in-Chief Fleet, answerable through the Chiefs of Staff to Ministers, it was thought highly desirable that in a deteriorating military situation or where there might be difficulty in communicating with the commanders of the two frigates or of the

submarine, they should have very carefully designed political authorization to act on their own initiative.

The Rules of Engagement, agreed in November 1977, could have been
printed in the Franks Report, and they certainly should have been
commented on. It is also very clear from what Admiral Lewin said in his
broadcast that, besides his doubts about initiating hostile action in 1982,
he had another concern relating to the size of the force needed. He said:

> With the degree of Argentine frustration five years further on from
> 1977, I very much doubt whether the Chiefs of Staff would have
> recommended that a force of that small size would have been enough.
> We would have had to send a much larger force and the situation never
> really warranted it in those first early days of March 1982.

My reaction to this comment is that if the Argentines' frustration was
greater five years on, why had there not been a much earlier and far
firmer military response.

It is not every day that Britain is plunged into a war. The Falklands
War, once it began, was handled with great skill by Margaret Thatcher
and by all our military commanders. I made this very clear in the speech
on which Admiral Lewin was commenting. Malcolm Rutherford
described that speech in the *Financial Times* on 28 January 1983.

> The most devastating speech came from Dr Owen who savaged Mrs
> Thatcher in a manner to which she is plainly unaccustomed. Moreover,
> he did it from a rational basis of knowledge and experience. In brief,
> he said that it was right to respond to Argentine aggression, though
> there were some qualifications about how the invasion was allowed to
> take place. It was right in the circumstances even to sink the *Belgrano* –
> a notably brave statement. But it was wrong to fall back on Fortress
> Falklands and the 'paramountcy' of the wishes of 1,800 islanders about
> their future. 'We fought against aggression, not for a flag,' he said.
> Sometime it would again become necessary to discuss the long term
> future of the islands, not only with Argentina but with Latin America.

I always supported the sinking of the *Belgrano*, but I was opposed to the
cover-up that followed. The sinking demonstrated what I had been
arguing for for years, that the nuclear-powered hunter-killer submarines
are to modern naval engagements what the Dreadnoughts were to the
First World War. The success of the nuclear submarine HMS *Conqueror*
in 1982 showed up the scepticism of the Naval Staff in 1977 when I
requested that a nuclear submarine should be sent. The advocates of the
surface navy still dominate and the potential of the submarine navy is
constantly underrated. Even in the 1990s we are allowing the nuclear-
powered submarine fleet to be cut to a mere twelve submarines, easily the
worst single decision stemming from the 1990 'Options for Change'
exercise.

When I read the Franks Report I could not help but feel, 'there but for the Grace of God go I.' For Peter Carrington in 1982 we could have easily been reading David Owen in 1977. The Franks Report never made clear exactly what Margaret Thatcher, Peter Carrington and John Nott had been told about the detail of our naval deployment and intelligence in the autumn of 1977. For example, when the Prime Minister saw the telegram despatched from the British Ambassador in Buenos Aires on 3 March 1982 and on which she perceptively wrote, 'We must make contingency plans', was she told that contingency plans had been made four-and-a-half years earlier? She also asked John Nott on 8 March how quickly Royal Navy ships could be deployed to the Falkland Islands and no action was taken. Did they both know then that we had in 1977 diverted a submarine at sea and that two frigates had come into port for one day, stored and sailed? Also that it had been done in secret? Despite the men on the frigates and the submarine, and later no doubt their families, knowing where the force had gone, it was never disclosed until Jim Callaghan mentioned it in the House of Commons. What this past history could have shown Margaret Thatcher was that a naval deployment could be made in secret without provoking an even earlier invasion. The full seriousness of the situation was grasped in the Foreign Office on 5 March and we know that Lord Carrington was told about the 1977 incident then. Why not until then? Did this knowledge then go wider than the Foreign Office? Lord Carrington has since admitted, with characteristic honesty, that with the benefit of hindsight he wished he had sought to deploy a nuclear-powered submarine earlier.

The Franks Report draws attention to the 9 July 1981 assessment of the Joint Intelligence Committee:

> that if Argentina concluded that there was no hope of a peaceful transfer of sovereignty, there would be a high risk of their resorting to more forcible measures against British interests, and that it might act swiftly and without warning. In such circumstances military action against British shipping or a full-scale invasion of the Falkland Islands could not be discounted.

They concluded that there was no case for despatching ships before the New York talks at the end of February, but after the Argentines had disowned their negotiator, insurance was needed against Argentine action. It is bizarre, however, that the Report did not analyse in more depth why on 8 March no ships were sent as a contingency measure, particularly because of their own conclusion that there should have been a naval deployment in the light of the reports received on 24 and 25 March.

Even more extraordinary is that the Franks Committee, who were all experienced in Cabinet Government, failed to highlight their finding that the Defence Committee of the Cabinet never met to consider the July JIC assessment. Even more bizarrely they never met between February 1981 and April 1982. The country should have been alerted by the conclusions of the Franks Report to the absence of Cabinet Government and proper collective responsibility, phrases used by Sir Geoffrey Howe in his resignation speech in 1990. On the minutes passed between the Foreign Secretary and the Prime Minister, the Report is strangely silent about the Prime Ministerial replies.

I felt with sadness that it was necessary for Lord Carrington to resign, but I only hinted at that in the emergency debate when speaking on the Saturday after the invasion. I believed that he would know the honourable and correct course and that proved to be the case. The advantage of his resignation was that it cleared the air and protected the damaged authority of the Prime Minister, Margaret Thatcher, and the Secretary of State for Defence, John Nott. Without it I doubt they would have been able to successfully conduct the military operation to recover the Falkland Islands. The disadvantage was that it left the impression that the errors made in the run-up to the invasion all stemmed from the Foreign Office, whereas in fact that was not the case. Errors were in addition made in the Ministry of Defence and in No. 10. The British Ambassador in Buenos Aires and his staff in fact performed very well. The Foreign Office for many years had warned successive Labour and Conservative Governments about the danger of Argentina taking action over the Falkland Islands. It was the politicians of all parties, including me, who had failed to condition the British public to the realities. In our defence it can be fairly claimed that that was difficult to do when the popular press would blow up the sovereignty issue at the merest hint of any accommodation with the Argentines. As Foreign Secretary, I never treated the Falkland Islands as a remote problem and did not delegate it completely to Ted Rowlands, because I knew how sensitive the House of Commons was on the issue. As with Gibraltar, passions are easily aroused in defence of these small populations who, MPs of all parties sense, are only too easily betrayed.

The moment Tony Crosland, just before his death, announced to the House the re-opening of negotiations with Argentina we knew that this was going to be a very sensitive issue requiring delicate handling. The authority to negotiate had come as a result of a Defence and Overseas Policy Committee meeting in December 1976 which had specifically rejected the only other alternative of building up the defences of the Islands and providing an expensive runway so as to be able to reinforce at a few days' notice. Yet the Fortress Falklands option was ruled out, not just on grounds of expense, but also because to be seen to be abandoning a negotiated solution would exacerbate ill feeling in an already fractious region and alienate the United States as well as the countries of Latin America. Both sides of the House were rightly very angry about the military regime in Buenos Aires; people were just disappearing off the streets of Argentine cities. They were certainly no respecters of human rights at home and no one trusted them, even with joint administration, to be involved in any way with the Falkland Islands.

We were walking on glass in even negotiating with the Argentines, and what is more we knew it.

In February 1977, we had seriously considered whether to divert a Royal Naval task group to the Southern Atlantic if developments, during Ted Rowlands's visit to Argentina and the Falkland Islands, suggested that this might be prudent. So even then we were thinking of Royal Naval deployment at times of tension and it was taken as a serious option. Ted Rowlands, in his 1983 article in *The Times*, quoted a Foreign Office assessment concluding that the Southern Thule action, 'was not the compulsive act of policy in the dying days of the Peronista regime', but a continuing and increasingly aggressive policy spearheaded by the Navy. 'The Argentines are clearly pursuing their interest at two levels – on the surface a dialogue and negotiation; beneath the surface they are planning action against the Falklands . . .' Also, there was a special assessment by the Joint Intelligence Commission (JIC) concluding that action by the Argentines before his visit was unlikely. But he had sought authority: 'if during my discussion with the Argentines they were to threaten the use of force to further their claims it might be useful for me to let them know that a British task group, including a nuclear submarine, is in Atlantic waters.' While understandably expressing caution about 'playing that card', the Defence Secretary, Fred Mulley, reaffirmed 'that we could consider the possibility of moving the task force if developments make it prudent to do so . . .' Ted Rowlands's discussions went well and tension eased by 11 March when a Joint Intelligence Commission report concluded that, so long as the Argentines calculated that we were prepared to negotiate seriously, they were not likely to resort to force.

On 1 March 1977, following the Foreign Affairs debate, I minuted that the debate had shown that, though there was some pressure on us to repeat that there would be no change without the Islanders' consent, no real parliamentary opposition to our strategy had emerged.

Then on 24 March, I received a memo from Ted Rowlands with an enclosure from the Department on the negotiating strategy for the forthcoming meeting. An official had rather revealingly written on the file that the Secretary of State 'will not need to plough through the detailed arguments' and that he had asked the Department to prepare a draft minute summarizing their conclusions and recommendations. That prompted me to write on the memo:

> I agree subject to minor changes in the Private Secretary letter. I have ploughed through the papers. This is an important issue. The Department need not be afraid of asking me to do this or of being defensive about it. One needs detail on an issue like this.

It was clear to the Department that I was to be personally involved.

In view of the Franks Report criticisms about the Conservative Government's decision to withdraw HMS *Endurance* from the Southern Atlantic and the signal this gave to the Argentines, it is worth recalling how large this issue featured in my time. On 25 April 1977 I wrote to Fred Mulley, the Secretary of State for Defence, agreeing with Tony Crosland's earlier letter and saying that HMS *Endurance* should be retained and that any withdrawal would risk putting the Islanders' new-found confidence seriously at risk. I went on to say:

> news that *Endurance* was to be withdrawn would be an indication that the Government's withdrawal from the Falkland Islands and the South-West Atlantic was already under way. This is not a view which at the outset of negotiations we want the Argentines to take.

I concluded by asking that a firm decision now be taken to deploy *Endurance* again next season.

In May Fred Mulley replied that he planned to pay off HMS *Endurance* in 1978, but deployment for 1977 would go ahead. When I asked that no action should be taken without further consultation, he answered that he was not planning any deployment after the 1977/78 season and any final decision could not be delayed beyond October 1977.

In June 1977, prior to our officials' meeting with Argentine officials in Rome, I held a meeting on the Falklands and asked for the paper which was going to the Defence and Overseas Policy Commitee (DOP) to be recast. The summary of that meeting recorded that we should go ahead with the negotiations in spite of the Argentine record on human rights and that time was not on our side. Afterwards, my Assistant Private Secretary, Stephen Wall, put a note out to the Department saying that the revised paper should come back for my weekend box and later minuted that I had agreed the DOP Cabinet Committee paper with the addition of the word 'illegal' in reference to the Argentine occupation of Southern Thule. He went on to say that I had also commented that I would prefer the ministerial meeting with the Argentines to be as late in the year as possible since 'he wants to play this issue as long as he can'. The DOP Committee met and agreed the outline of our position. Officials were not authorized to table any specific proposals but just to get a feel for Argentine attitudes. That caution was followed by a number of Argentine decisions which heightened the tension.

Over the next few months, the Falkland Islands came frequently to my attention through telegrams whose traffic was considerable. On 12 September 1978, I held an office meeting attended by, among others, the Governor of the Falkland Islands, Mr Parker. The minutes recorded me as saying that, on the substance of the dispute:

> I saw little prospect of real progress until public opinion had been prepared – there was a difficult but essential educational job to do both here and in the Islands. This should have been tackled before we involved ourselves in the present negotiations. It was not only the

public and Parliament; other Government Departments still cling to the belief that resources on the other side of the world were still ours to exploit.

This was a reference, in part, to Tony Benn, who was very nationalistic on the energy side.

In early October I had read a telegram from Port Stanley reporting the Islanders' fears that we were talking behind their backs. I then asked the Deputy Permanent Under-Secretary, Sir Anthony Duff, to issue a general instruction for officials to engage in regular briefing, before and after discussions at Foreign Minister level, on the Falklands and other such situations like Belize. I said:

> I want regular arrangements for prior briefing and post briefing and press line agreed. In this way we will keep their confidence. I am not, on any of these issues, prepared to move behind their backs. We will, at all times, operate straightforwardly. This is my style and I cannot and will not change it. It may reduce flexibility a little at times. But confidence is the key to progress and keeping their confidence is essential to success. I would like this taken as a general injunction.

The day after this, Ted Rowlands sent me a draft DOP paper on our negotiating position which also asked that the Secretary of State for Defence should keep HMS *Endurance* in commission and that the Chancellor of the Exchequer should be consulted about finding funds for this. I was unhappy with the suggested negotiating position, which seemed to me to give too much ground on sovereignty, so Stephen Wall minuted the Department with my comment that DOP would not accept what was proposed and that I was not convinced either. He went on to say that he had, in explaining the softer line suggested by the Department, mentioned to me that there was some evidence that the Argentines were taking an increasingly militant attitude, that failure to make progress at the next round could lead to a hardening of militancy on their part, that I had asked what the evidence was and that he would be grateful for chapter and verse. This was an excellent example of how a politician can be the grit in the system, questioning and probing. It also shows how vital it is that the Private Office is alert, constantly looking for possible difficulties. I often wonder what would have happened had I not queried Stephen Wall and if he had not used the word militant to me. An exceptionally gifted diplomat, he had picked up the evidence of militancy from telegrams. He later served Geoffrey Howe, John Major and Douglas Hurd as Principal Private Secretary, before being appointed to act as John Major's Private Secretary for Foreign Affairs at No. 10.

The minute, entitled 'Falkland Islands: The Threat', arrived on 17 October and its clear threat assessment made it even harder to understand the Department's strange reluctance to explain the reasons why they wanted to make concessions in negotiations and why they detected an urgency for progress among the Argentines. I refer to it in detail in the preceding chapter. On 14 October I had dissented from the Foreign Office's interpretation of my talk with the Argentine Foreign Minister, Admiral Montes, at the United Nations in New York for they had implied that the Argentines had not been prepared to accept delay. I had minuted, 'Not at all, I found them encouraging in relation to a delay.' It was now clear to me that while Admiral Montes was the soft, acceptable front man for the regime, Admiral Massera was a prototype Galtieri, aggressive, ambitious and in the populist Peronist tradition.

I immediately raised questions about the readiness of the Argentines to continue negotiations and the real possibility of some militant action. Three days before receiving this memo, on 14 October, I had asked what action and decisions were going to be required in the light of the JIC assessment of the South Sandwich Islands. On 24 October the Prime Minister's Private Secretary also queried the JIC assessment on the South Sandwich Islands. My Private Secretary wrote back on 31 October, saying that the Foreign Office had decided – in fact the decision was taken by Ted Rowlands – not to go ahead with a surface-borne reconnaissance of the South Sandwich Islands which was intended to consider whether or not Southern Thule was still occupied.

We also heard, on 26 October, that the Argentines had informed our Embassy in Buenos Aires that

> in order to complete the installation erected during the 1976/77 Antarctic campaign and as part of the annual programme of scientific research carried out by Argentina, work is being carried out on Southern Thule. This work, which is purely scientific, is being done in support of Argentina's Antarctic programme during 1977/78.

What was odd was that, while the Department were considering this question in September and the JIC had made an assessment of a possible interference with any surface-borne reconnaissance, it was not reflected in the paper that came to me on 4 October. The report of 17 October was the first serious warning of possible Argentine militancy. I had had to ask for even the JIC assessment that arose out of that report.

The situation was becoming alarming and on 27 October I wrote to Fred Mulley:

> For us to announce next month the paying off of *Endurance* would be seen by the Argentines on the eve of the next round of negotiations (now set for 13–15 December) as a clear admission of weakness on our part and a lack of determination to defend our interests. Such an announcement would also have a serious effect on the morale of the Falkland Islanders themselves. I also believe we could be faced with a parliamentary and public outcry; ... we should be attacked for withdrawing defence support from the Islands at a crucial juncture and

accused of paving the way for a sell-out to Argentina. . . . There is a clear defence requirement . . .

On 28 October an official in the Foreign Office wrote to an official in the Ministry of Defence saying that, since the JIC were currently engaged in producing a paper about possible inimical action that might be taken by the Argentine Government against British interests in the event of a breakdown in the negotiations in December, it would be helpful if the Ministry of Defence could produce its own analysis of the efficacy or otherwise of our response to a possible Argentine action.

In early November I indicated that I did not think that the present draft DOP paper would be acceptable to my colleagues and that I was not myself convinced by the arguments put forward by the Department and Ted Rowlands for conceding so much on sovereignty. I was then sent a memo from the Ministry of Defence, dated 3 November, on measures to resist the Argentine threat in the Falklands area, which included an enquiry on how quickly a nuclear-powered submarine could be sent to the area. On 10 November I changed the draft DOP paper so that it concluded, 'We should work towards the solution of a lease-back of the inhabited islands for a period of 70 years and certainly not less than 50 years.' In the original it was 'for a period not less than 50 years.'

The Cabinet Overseas and Defence Committee met three times in November. It was important that we should not be obliged to negotiate from a position of total vulnerability and equally important that if the Argentines were to attack our shipping or invade the islands we should not be seen by public opinion to be unprepared. I recommended that the Secretary of State for Defence be asked to prepare urgently

> contingency plans for the defence of British shipping in the area of the Falkland Islands and for the eventuality of an Argentine invasion of the Islands and their Dependencies. Preliminary deployment of an SSN to be considered if there is any expectation of an Argentine use of force.

I felt that if we were to go into the Ministerial talks without Cabinet authority to table any ideas which had a bearing on the sovereignty issue we could, as the JIC assessment indicated, be faced with various possible military scenarios. Any of these, for example occupation of the Dependencies or interference with our own shipping, could result in public humiliation and criticism which would be every bit as difficult to handle as the public reaction we would face if we ever let it be known we were negotiating over sovereignty. Tony Benn, Secretary of State for Energy, was present at the meeting and there were some arguments as to the rights to the oil in the seabed and of the impact on negotiations with the Irish with whom we had another territorial oil dispute.

I argued that to be seen to introduce a surface warship to the

Falklands area during the negotiations would be very provocative and could provoke a serious incident. I therefore recommended that no surface task force should be despatched at present but that a single SSN (nuclear-powered submarine) should be deployed in the area with HMS *Endurance*. In subsequent discussion it was argued by the Chiefs of Staff that two frigates were necessary but that if

> it was preferable not to deploy the two frigates in the immediate vicinity. It would be adequate to have them 1,000 miles out in the Atlantic. There would be no problem to their being at sea for a month or so and they could use the time for the purpose of exercises. The fleet submarine could on the other hand be deployed close to the islands on a covert basis . . . This small task force would therefore be able to respond flexibly to limited attacks of aggression . . .

This deployment pattern was agreed as it would not be visible, and therefore not provocative to the negotiations. Also, I do remember Jim Callaghan saying that, if the Argentines saw naval ships in the Southern Atlantic from a tanker or aircraft, that might act as a sobering influence. But the clear decision was taken to deploy in secret and not to interfere with the negotiations. That was obviously Ted Rowlands's understanding too, even though he was not at that meeting, for he has since written 'it was not intended that the Argentines should know of its existence unless or until the negotiations broke down'.

As Prime Minister, Jim Callaghan summed up the DOP meeting by saying that our objectives should be to buttress our negotiating position by deploying a force of sufficient strength to convince the Argentines that military action by them would meet resistance. But that this did not necessarily mean a force of sufficient size to ensure the defeat of a determined attack with reinforcements, nor did it imply the decision to fight.

In December, at the Ministerial talks we were able to get away without disclosing any of our bottom-line positions over sovereignty. We did not concede even the principle of leasehold, just a working paper on sovereignty issues, and a joint report to the UN. Our naval force was withdrawn in late December; a hardship for the crews to be still at sea over Christmas, but an admirable example of the effective covert deployment of naval force. Yet these lessons were sadly never absorbed, even by the most senior naval commanders. Ministers of the incoming Conservative Government were not aware of the deployment or maybe even the extent of the threat from May 1979 to 5 March 1982. I, like Jim Callaghan, was quite unaware of their ignorance prior to the invasions.

I assumed, rightly as it turned out, that they did know the whole story when, in late March 1982, the situation over the Falkland Islands began to look threatening. I had hoped, even then, when events started to unfold in the House of Commons, that the Government might announce the presence of a hunter-killer submarine off the Falklands even if it had not yet arrived. The Government could, for example, have told President Reagan that one was there and was ready to sink any Argentine vessels that attempted an invasion before Reagan's last-minute telephone call to General Galtieri. That was done to warn him off invading. But if he had been able to say he knew that the British not only meant business but had the wherewithal to threaten his ships it just might have been sufficient. President Reagan is a good poker player, and even if we had told him the truth that we had no ships he might have been able to carry the bluff by saying that US intelligence had spotted Royal Naval ships near to the Islands. Yet none of this was done and it looks as if it was not even seriously contemplated.

The inescapable conclusion is that the Falklands War was an avoidable war and that the events of 1977 should have given us the knowledge and experience to have prevented the 1982 invasion. If the history of 1977 had been properly absorbed it would have been impossible for the Chief of Defence Staff, Admiral Lewin, to have been able to say on BBC radio in 1982, 'I just couldn't believe that one apparently civilized country would try and settle its dispute with another civilized country by going to war at this part of the twentieth century.' The events of 1977 showed that Argentina clearly might have invaded. There is some evidence that this refusal to think ill of military dictators was still dominant in the British and American intelligence communities in the summer of 1990 when Iraq invaded Kuwait. When will we ever learn that evil remains and that there is such a thing as original sin?

16

FOREIGN SECRETARY – 1978

We celebrated the New Year in a holiday beach house near Mombasa lent to us by the Smith family, friends of Ken and Edith Matiba, who I had got to know a few years before. The whole Owen family needed a holiday and this was the boys' first visit to Africa. We swam, sailed and fished on white coral sand under coconut trees for the first few days and my only official visit was to President Kenyatta who was down on the coast. We then went on safari into Masai Mara game reserve in our High Commissioner's Land-Rover which he had made available to us. We could not have been in better hands, and Jack Barrah, the head of the game reserves, took us under his wing. We flew in his small plane and slept out in a tented camp. At night the lions roared outside the tents and I slept with one of the boys and Debbie with the other. She was a more popular companion than I for every time the lion roared I would recite:

> He hadn't gone a yard when – Bang!
> With open Jaws, a Lion sprang,
> And hungrily began to eat
> The Boy: beginning at his feet.
> Now just imagine how it feels
> When first your toes and then your heels,
> And then by gradual degrees,
> Your shins and ankles, calves and knees,
> Are slowly eaten bit by bit.
> No wonder Jim detested it!

The boys would snuggle up to me but would also want me to go on to James' miserable end.

We saw every form of wild animal and, very excitingly, tracked a leopard from its first sighting to the eventual kill of an impala. It was an unforgettable holiday for us all and we returned refreshed. Now the whole family shared a love of Africa and we have returned whenever we can.

When I next visited Kenya it was over the New Year of 1985 and we took my mother to stay with Ken and Edith Matiba and the Smith family at their hotel on the Diani Beach south of Mombasa. It was Lucy's first visit to Africa and my mother, always called Bangy by the rest of the family, had only ever been to North Africa. Ken typically insisted on being at the airport to pick us up. He was then a Minister in President Moi's Government, having become an MP and given up being Chairman of East African Breweries. As we drove, taking the ferry at Mombasa, I could sense my mother's excitement grow at the bustle, colour and gaiety of Africa. She had just had her seventy-fifth birthday and my father's long illness had drained even her prodigious energy. As the days passed she fell in love with Africa, the Africans and above all the Kikuyu.

Ken and I flew up to have breakfast with President Moi early in January 1985 at his farm in Kabarak and I had a useful talk with him about Uganda and the Horn of Africa, still problem areas seven years on. I had met Moi a number of times before and since he had become President. I remembered how at Kenyatta's funeral the big question was whether he would be able to keep Kenya united. By common consent he had handled the transition with considerable skill. Ken and Edith had known Moi for many years since Ken had been his senior civil servant when Moi was Minister for Education and later his Permanent Secretary at the Home Office. Edith is a devout Christian and her father was one of the first Kenyan-born clergymen in the Church of Scotland. I little realized that day that in five years' time Moi would place Ken in detention.

After some days on the coast we flew up to Nairobi and then drove down past Mount Kilimanjaro to Arusha in Tanzania to stay the night, then in a Jeep across pot-holed, red-earthed roads we arrived at the Ngorongaro Crater. Salim Salim was the Tanzanian representative on the UN when I was Foreign Secretary. In 1985 he was Defence Minister and we were working together on the Palme Commission. He had helped arrange for me to visit Ngorongoro, telling me it was one of the great wonders of the world. He is now the Secretary-General of the OAU. Staying in a hotel on the rim we looked down a telescope at the wild animals below. It was a breathtaking sight, unmatched by anything I have seen anywhere else. It was as if one was looking back centuries in time. We spent all next day in the crater from the early morning. We drove through a herd of rhinoceros on the move and they kept making mock charges at our Jeep which was both exciting and rather frightening. We saw lions and almost every kind of wild beast and many rare birds. Back in Nairobi we went out to the Matibas' farm, where Edith had just started to grow orchids for export, and then flew home after a memorable holiday which had given my mother immense enjoyment and made another Owen an enthusiast for the African continent.

In January 1990 we went again to Kenya for a family holiday and stayed with the Matibas on the coast. This time the political atmosphere

was tense. Ken had resigned from the Government, having been very
critical of the undemocratic practice of 'queueing' in order to vote.
Previously Kenya had had secret balloting; now people were first counted
in a queue for a specific candidate and often did not have to go into the
polling booth. The practice had started a few years earlier. As a
consequence of his criticism Ken had been thrown out of KANU, the
only political party, and was then automatically no longer an MP. As we
talked about his concern for what was happening we never discussed
forming another political party, for Ken at that stage still believed that
the priority was to restore proper democratic procedures within KANU
and the existing political system. That February he came to London and
visited us in Buttermere on the very day that Nelson Mandela was
released from prison. Ken was glued to the television set and with his
daughter, Ivy, and my family we celebrated what we all thought was a
great day for Africa. When Ken returned he began to speak out more
about the need for Kenya to move towards multi-party democracy and
there were some troubling and untrue stories in the newspapers that he
was about to form a new party. His name was linked with me because of
the creation of the SDP. I began to be worried about Ken, as were many
of his friends inside and outside Kenya. On 13 June, late at night there
was an attack on his farm by a gang of armed men. From what they said
it was clear they believed that Ken was at home, but in fact he was on the
coast. They were not robbers after money and when they realized he was
not there they attacked his wife, Edith, with a panga knife. Her head
injuries were so bad she required brain surgery. The gang made off
before the neighbours and the police could arrive. Fortunately Edith
recovered, but on 4 July 1990, as we were celebrating American Independence Day at Buttermere, we heard that Ken had been arrested and
detained.

I had often dealt with representations about political prisoners when I
was Foreign Secretary and now it was my turn to make representations to
Douglas Hurd and to the Prime Minister. I tried to see President Moi,
but at all times I was handicapped by the need to do nothing which
would hurt Ken or delay his release. It was a deeply frustrating period.
Kenya is the country I know best and love most in Africa. The Kenyan
people must determine their own system of justice and democratic
procedures. But the frustration was intense of not being able to help one
of my best friends, until his release in June 1990, having been seriously
ill. Kenya and Africa were diminished by his detention, for free spirits
like Ken Matiba cannot have their principles imprisoned. Queueing is
now to be stopped but still KANU insists it should be the only party.

This debate about multi-party democracy started with renewed vigour
in Africa after the democratic upsurge in 1989 in Eastern Europe. All
over Africa the grass root pressures often encouraged by the churches are
building up for real democracy. Namibia in 1990 joined Botswana as a

genuine multi-party democracy. Kenya which pioneered under President Kenyatta a multi-racial, market-orientated free society and began moving towards a fully democratic independent nation, is destined to become a multi-party democracy and to eradicate the corruption which can destroy their market economy. The only question is when this happens and how long, before it does, will people like Ken Matiba have to languish in jail.

The most interesting development in the European Community during 1978 was the emergence of what became known as the European Monetary System. Roy Jenkins can fairly claim to have triggered the process with a speech in Florence on 27 October 1977, delivering the Monnet Lecture at the European University Institute. He spoke again about economic and monetary union to the European Parliament in January 1978, and it was still very much on his mind when Debbie and I went over to East Hendred for lunch on the first Sunday in February.

President Sadat came through London on Thursday 9 February 1978 and Jim Callaghan and I talked to him at London Airport. His trust in President Carter was rather touching but he was also adamant about Israel giving back territory which they currently occupied. It was evident that Sinai was crucial for him and, though he talked about the West Bank territory, he did so with none of the same zeal as President Assad of Syria.

I felt that this was a good time to visit Jordan and Israel. So on Friday 24 February I went by train to Plymouth with Debbie, talked to a sixth-form conference, held an Advice Bureau, gave a lecture on the 'Morality of Compromise' at St Andrew's Church in the evening and then went late to the General Management Committee of the Devonport Labour Party. We then left by car for RAF St Mawgan in Cornwall and flew overnight to Jordan. Next day I had a breathtakingly beautiful flight in a helicopter over the Jordan Valley. It was very depressing to see the green, irrigated fields on the Jordan side, glinting like emeralds, and the parched brown of the occupied territories where there had been so little agricultural investment. On the Sunday we flew to Israel. To my amazement I was the first British Foreign Secretary ever to have visited the State of Israel.

I had been to the Holocaust memorial at Yad Veshem on a number of occasions before, but the official visit somehow ensured that the impact on me was even more sombre. We then drove out from Jerusalem and had lunch with Amos Oz and his wife at Kibbutz Hulda. The rest of the afternoon and evening was spent with Moshe Dayan, the Israeli Foreign Minister. After the formal dinner we went to Dayan's house and saw all his archaeological treasures, most of which he had appropriated for his private collection, totally against the rules. He had a captivating quality in conversation and the Deputy Prime Minister, Yadin, who was a professional archaeologist, joined us. We were drinking outside in the warm evening air and could have been on a university campus in

California. Dayan's second wife, attractive, sophisticated and sensuous, seemed to soften him that evening and it was hard to remember that this man, with his black eye-patch, had fought and nearly lost his life in 1948, was the hero and Commander-in-Chief during the 1967 Six Day War and the scapegoat, as Minister of Defence, for the 1973 Yom Kippur War. Previously Labour, now representing only a small party, he was a strangely isolated figure, yet someone to be reckoned with.

We stayed at the King David Hotel and I met Begin in the morning. The issues were becoming clearer after his meeting with Sadat. He knew that his December proposals for the West Bank had not made much headway. The US was becoming restless at the lack of progress and critical of Israeli settlement policy which continued to be provocative to Arab opinion. Begin was due to see Carter in March in Washington. There was no flexibility in his position and, depressingly, he saw nothing wrong with continuing to create new settlements on the West Bank. When I tried to elicit his criteria for self-rule he was very defensive. He was not at that stage even prepared to give up settlements in Sinai or to put these settlements under the UN. I left the meeting very depressed, for Begin seemed totally rigid.

Next I saw Ezer Weizman, who had previously been the Head of the Israeli Air Force and was now Minister of Defence. He was far ahead of Begin in talking the language of peace with Egypt but beginning to despair. Later he was to play a critical role in challenging the Israeli chiefs of staff who were resisting giving up the large new Israeli airfield in Sinai which they thought gave them the defence in depth essential for their security. Later, over dinner at the British Embassy in Tel Aviv, I found all the senior Labour figures under Shimon Peres adamantly opposed to giving up this airfield and still talking about retaining a strip of Sinai.

I left Israel next morning against the background of a rather unpleasant newspaper story which alleged that I had criticized Begin in a hotel lift. Though the story was somewhat garnished, it was possible that I had been overhead expressing my frustration in rather too ripe a turn of phrase. Flying back and writing a speech which I had to make next day to the Labour Friends of Israel, I did not anticipate that in just over six months there would be the amazing breakthrough at Camp David. The essential element in the Israeli-Egpytian peace treaty was Begin's readiness to give back every square millimetre of Sinai. Begin must have feared that this would mean using troops to oust Israelis from their settlements in Sinai. This was very painful for him but whereas it was possible for him to do it in Sinai, it would have been impossible for him in Judaea or Samaria. Paradoxically it was easier for Likud and Begin to withdraw from Sinai than for Labour. In the 1990s it may again be easier for Likud to withdraw from Golan if there is to be another building block towards a peace treaty between Syria and Israel.

Concerned about the Bonn Economic Summit in the summer and the Americans' lack of any policy to stabilize the dollar, Jim Callaghan wanted an economic summit that actually produced co-ordinated action. Peter Jay, having been briefed in London, went back to Washington in mid-January to tell President Carter about a potential package in which each of the seven countries would be expected to make at least some contribution in five main areas – a commitment to growth, efforts to maintain currency stability, measures to promote world trade, the use of capital surpluses and energy conservation. As a result of this initiative, Jim visited Washington in March to take the planning for the Bonn Summit further. He did not wish to leave it to the Cabinet Secretary who in Britain acts with a group called the 'sherpas', consisting of influential people appointed by their respective heads of government.

It did not come as a total surprise when, over dinner with the other Heads of Government at the European Council meeting in Copenhagen on 7 April, Helmut Schmidt developed his ideas for a new monetary system for Europe. But what did surprise Jim Callaghan and the Treasury official who had come to Denmark specifically for this issue, was the boldness of the actual proposals. We in Britain had been tending to explain what was happening in terms of window-dressing to the existing currency 'Snake' arrangement so as to make it easier for France to join. It soon became clear that Schmidt's scheme was capable of developing into more than just a Deutschmark zone. While Jim Callaghan wanted currency stability, he was more worried about the dollar and felt that concentrating on the European currencies was too narrow a focus. Also he claimed that in Schmidt's system a strong Deutschmark would pull sterling up and do political damage to the British economy in the run-up to an election. When, next morning, Helmut Schmidt, Giscard d'Estaing and Jim Callaghan met for breakfast it was clear that France was going to join and Jim reserved the British position. This was not my area of expertise, but talking to him over that weekend, I inferred that he was not prepared to risk the row in the Labour Party that would undoubtedly come if we were to join the European Monetary System before the election. The irony was that in these early days, Margaret Thatcher, in Opposition, was giving the impression of being in favour of what became the European Monetary System. But that was in her rather short 'be nice to Europe' phase, which abruptly ended after the Dublin European Summit in 1979.

In April I was interviewed by Paul Callan for the *Daily Mirror* for a two-day centre-page spread headlined, 'Doctor in the House, and he has that bedside manner', and next day, in somewhat contradictory terms, 'Action Man or Mr Arrogant?' He tempted me into what he described as an undiplomatic statement about Margaret Thatcher, though I could see nothing wrong with it:

> I saw her the other evening at the House of Commons and for the first
> time she looked really rather attractive. She'd had a couple of whiskies
> and was quite glowing, in the nicest possible way. She came over,
> smiling that special smile of hers, and wafted a combination of expensive
> scent and alcohol over me.

This was described by an angry Conservative Party as the first dirty trick
of the forthcoming election campaign. It was mild compared to President
Mitterrand's remark later that 'she has the lips of Marilyn Monroe and
the smile of Caligula.' But John Junor, who had lunch with her, found
her relaxed, even flattered. It was at about this time that I had realized
that we faced in her a far more formidable opponent than it was
fashionable for most Labour politicians to admit. I remembered what
Barbara Castle had said about her and I began to wonder if she might not
attract a different type of Conservative voter.

It was also noticeable that the *Sun* newspaper was promoting Margaret
Thatcher and I felt that we could no longer rely on the automatic
support of those we had hitherto regarded as Labour voters. She had
earlier given an interview on Granada Television arguing for a clear end
to immigration and used emotive language which had been deliberately
chosen and calculated to send a signal to those many people who were
concerned about immigration. Coming in the wake of some recent rioting
in Wolverhampton when young blacks, provoked by whites, had smashed
shop windows and hurled bricks at the police, her claim that 'people are
really rather afraid that this country might be swamped by people of a
different culture' was bound to evoke a sympathetic response from
voters and denunciation from politicians. Merlyn Rees, as Home Secretary, said she was 'making racial hatred respectable', but she refused to
withdraw, using the language with which we were to become all too
familiar. The charge of racism was 'absolute nonsense' and it would have
been 'absolutely absurd not to discuss the issue'. There was none of
Enoch Powell's Messianic passion attached to her stance and she did not
obsessively repeat it, but she had flagged up her position. In the 1979
Election, a Labour canvasser encountered a district nurse who said that
she was very worried about Labour's policy on immigration. The
canvasser, with all the statistics at his finger tips, demonstrated pretty
convincingly that there was in fact very little difference between Labour
and Conservative immigration policy. But the nurse put her finger on the
electoral significance when she said, 'Ah, but Mrs Thatcher would try
harder.' She did much the same thing with the death penalty. Sending
the public a signal by voting for the return of hanging but being careful
to protect her flank with Conservative abolitionists by holding firm to the
view that this was a matter for a free vote. Nevertheless, by ensuring that
it was fairly frequently voted on she reinforced her identification with the
strong populist wish to bring back the death penalty. I was opposed to
both her stances.

Britain's reputation for racial prejudice was widespread enough in the world for it to be a problem for me as Foreign Secretary. When it was reinforced by the Leader of the Opposition supporting an internal settlement in Rhodesia and talking about swamping whites with blacks in Britain the problems were compounded, but I was not so blind that I could not see that what was bad international politics won votes at home. Although Margaret Thatcher was still not very effective in the House of Commons, she seemed to be building up authority in the country. I began to pay more attention to her speeches, particularly on the economy, and was surprised to find in relation to the market a Tory philosophy reminiscent of Edward Heath's Selsdon Park policies which stressed market forces and competition. They were not fully worked out but nevertheless different, and more interesting to me than the later stages of Edward Heath's corporatism.

On 11 May 4,000 troops invaded Zaire from Angola and occupied the town of Kolwezi. It was essentially another ethnic problem stemming from the colonial partitions of Africa, though this time it was the Belgians who were involved as the former colonial power. Henri Simonet, the Belgian Foreign Minister, was furious with Giscard d'Estaing who wanted to muscle in and display French power in Africa. There were rapes, looting and it looked as if the trouble might spread. The Angolans had not got the capacity to curb the insurgents and Zaire wanted help. A quick intervention on humanitarian grounds was called for and eventually an effective international rescue operation was put together. Belgian and French troops were flown down in the big American C-5 transport planes to Zaire and the RAF flew down to Zambia to be ready to ferry in supplies if they were needed.

In the midst of this crisis we had the Danish 'Schloss Gymnich' in Hesselo. It was incredibly inconvenient for me, but I was very fond of the Danish Foreign Minister, K.B. Andersen, who had been very supportive over Africa. I had to go up to Scotland to speak in the Hamilton by-election campaign on Thursday 18 May, address the NUM Conference in Blackpool next morning and attend the Plymouth Lord Mayor's Banquet on the Friday evening, since the new Lord Mayor was Councillor Bill Evans, one of my good friends. I caught the Plymouth sleeper up to London on the Saturday and then flew out to Denmark. It meant yet another weekend without being with the children, for I was only able to return on the Sunday evening from Denmark and on Monday had to leave with Debbie, as members of the Royal Household accompanying the Queen on a state visit to Germany.

I expected Henri Simonet to be present in Denmark in the hope of sorting out the Belgian differences over Kolwezi with the French. Despite promising to come, Simonet never turned up, which made me furious. This was by far the most important foreign policy issue that Belgium was involved in throughout my time as Foreign Secretary. Yet their Foreign

Minister could not come to the key Community forum for solving intra-Community differences. It seemed a very strange ordering of his priorities. I enjoyed Henri; he was good company, bright and with a wry humour. His absence, I soon discovered, reflected considerable differences of approach within the Belgian Cabinet which he did not wish to expose to open scrutiny, especially with the French present. Yet the attendance of Louis de Guiringaud, the French Foreign Minister, who had served as a diplomat in Africa and was both knowledgeable and committed, ensured that the French view of events dominated at the expense of the Belgians'. I felt the Community had missed an important opportunity. It was bizarre conduct given that the Belgians were federalists, constantly advocating a Community foreign policy.

What is a Community foreign policy? Initially political co-operation covering foreign affairs was seen as a mechanism to reach an agreed consensus, but I sensed even in 1978 that the federalists wanted it to be brought into the same qualified majority voting pattern as covered the Common Market. People who despised or distrusted national decision making wanted Community decisions to be binding on all member states, and almost seemed to want to have an excuse to be bound by the majority votes. They were well aware that if a nation ceases to make its own mind up on defence and foreign policy it will cease by any known definition to be an independent nation. But that is exactly what they wanted. They want a Community as a single federal state, making unitary binding decisions covering European defence and foreign policy.

On Monday 22 May I left for Germany on the Queen's Flight. It was the Queen's second state visit to Germany and just before she left an opinion poll had shown that, of all the nations in the world, Germany was the most popular with the British public. We flew to Bonn where the Queen and Prince Philip had lunch with the Federal President. I had a meeting with Hans-Dietrich Genscher and then he and his wife gave lunch for Debbie and me. One of the many advantages of this visit, as with other Royal visits, was that they give the Foreign Secretary the opportunity to meet political counterparts in the sort of relaxed and convivial circumstances which cement friendship. That evening there was a banquet at Schloss Augustusberg given by the Federal President, Dr Scheel. Debbie and I stayed with the British Ambassador. On the Tuesday morning I attended a meeting which the Queen had with Genscher at the original Schloss Gymnich where she was staying. Helmut Schmidt hosted a luncheon at the Palais Schaumberg and then we left by train for Mainz where the Queen visited the Gutenberg Museum and a dinner was given in her honour. The programme emphasized the federal nature of the German constitution. Next morning the Queen and the Royal party, which included Debbie and me, flew from Mainz to Berlin where the Queen reviewed British troops. Lunch was given at Schloss Charlottenberg by the Governing Mayor of Berlin, Dieter Stobbe, a young, friendly, perceptive Social Democrat. We then flew to Kiel, where we drove out into the country and the Queen saw a parade of Schleswig-Holstein horses. That evening we boarded the Royal Yacht *Britannia* in Kiel harbour. As we slept, the Yacht went through the Kiel Canal and Debbie and I slept in the cabin I had used when I had last been on the Royal Yacht as Minister for the Navy, when the Queen reviewed the Fleet at Torquay. Next morning, in dense fog we went out into the North Sea for a review of the Federal Navy. Since we could barely see the bows of *Britannia* we concentrated on lunch, at which the Queen entertained members of the Federal Armed Forces, underlining the extraordinary way in which our two countries had shed the bitterness of the past. That night in Bremerhaven, the Queen gave dinner in honour of the Federal President on board the Royal Yacht. The visit was a resounding success and late that night Debbie and I flew home. We had thoroughly enjoyed ourselves and had been made to feel totally at ease by other members of the Household. I had talked to the Queen privately on a number of occasions.

The value for us in Britain of these state visits is hard to exaggerate. Every detail is scrupulously planned by Palace officials in close consultation with the Queen, and as a consequence everything runs like clockwork. But the success is not automatic; it is earned by hard work and above all by the quality of the Queen's contribution.

The NATO Heads of Government meeting was due to start in Washington on Tuesday 30 May. On Saturday 3 June I flew to America with Debbie and the two boys, accompanied just by a detective, all of us travelling tourist class since the family were going on holiday and we were paying. I managed a break for a day-and-a-half out at Long Island with Debbie's parents. They then looked after the boys when she came with me to Washington. Since the Prime Minister's party was staying at the Embassy, we stayed at the Hay Adams Hotel which overlooks the White House and is the hotel I like best in Washington.

I arrived to find that Washington was in some turmoil as a consequence of Giscard d'Estaing's visit on the previous Friday, when it was pretty clear he had persuaded Carter to get far more involved in Shaba Province in Zaire than I thought wise. This meant supporting the French idea, which had been given a great deal of publicity, for a Pan-African force and an active Western role which would inevitably be pitched as part of an East-West confrontation in Africa. At a meeting on Monday evening in the State Department, Louis de Guiringaud developed the French line and, to my amazement, was supported by Cy Vance. Though he said extremely little, I had the feeling that Cy was very uncomfortable with the line, even though it was also vigorously supported by Hans-Dietrich Genscher. I bided my time and did not speak for almost an hour. Finally I took the French analysis of what was happening in Shaba Province head on. I said that we had supported the humanitarian action, though we had been involved only in a minor role, and we had no quarrel with that action. But what was now being suggested was, in our view, extremely ill-advised. I sketched out my extreme scepticism about British involvement in any Pan-African force, and particularly about the idea of physical Western support for the resolution of African problems.

I went to the Embassy early next morning to have a word with Jim Callaghan before we went into the full NATO meeting and had an interesting chat with Tom McNally. I briefly sketched my view that we were facing a serious problem, with the Americans having swung in favour of the French line on Africa, and he told me that he had had a great row with the Prime Minister the night before, which in McNally terms meant a boisterous set-to. He described the Prime Minister's mood as 'half way between Biggles and John Biggs Davidson' (a Right-wing Tory MP). This splendid definition of Jim's attitude nevertheless caused me a certain amount of anxiety, so on the way to the NATO meeting I briefed him a little on what had happened at my meeting with the three other Foreign Ministers. I found him not as hard-line as Tom had suggested, but more inclined to go down the American line than I had suspected he would be. Yet I could see that the points I was making were having some effect, and I thought that in view of the cautious line that Tom McNally had urged on him the night before and with his basic attitudes to Africa, he would probably come right. He said he would like to have some time to think about it and we discussed it a little further in the margins of the meetings.

It also became apparent from the Washington press that Zbig Brzezinski was riding high, having come back from China and given some very ill-advised interviews about his visit. The Washington press was full of him as the great policy maker. Zbig was the hard-liner on Africa and wanted the President to take a tough line, and it was this attitude that was triumphing.

At the afternoon session of the Washington meeting I was not exactly sure which way Jim was going to go but I hoped that he would counsel caution. The crucial intervention was a contribution by the Belgian Prime Minister, Tindemans, which was very vague about Belgian policy. Tindemans personally wanted to go down the French line of Pan-African-ism and Western involvement. But he was held back from saying too much by the fact that Simonet, a socialist who opposed it, was sitting beside him; a symbol of the split in his Cabinet. Tindemans' reference to the problem of the Lumba tribe in Shaba reminded Jim of the history: when he spoke he made one of the most impressive contributions I have ever heard in any international conference – low key, friendly, rather self-deprecating, saying 'of course the problem of the Lumba tribe has been around since time immemorial, rather like myself'. It was a throwaway phrase which got everybody smiling. And yet I could see that Helmut Schmidt was listening and observed that Jimmy Carter was rapt in attention. Then Jim began to expand in a way that only he could, on his involvement in Africa. He let slip that he had known Kenneth Kaunda since KK had been a student, and how he had been discussing these problems with Julius Nyerere for many years. Suddenly the conference realized that here was a man talking against a background of years of experience of African politics, visiting Africa in the late 1940s, being Shadow Colonial Secretary in the 1950s. What he said in effect was 'steady on now, let's be careful about this, let's not go absolutely slap down the line of thinking this is an East-West issue. Yes of course the Soviet Union are causing problems for us, they will exploit every difficulty, they will cause problems wherever they can; but let us recognize that Africa has to solve these problems.' Jim's contribution completely changed the debate. He was followed by the Prime Minister of Norway, by the Prime Minister of the Netherlands and by the Danes, who all made similar contributions. The whole atmosphere switched. This was crucially important, for Jimmy Carter saw that the Giscard d'Estaing-Zbig Brzezinski line that he was being manoeuvred into was not going to carry universal support in NATO.

That evening in a delightful dinner in the Rose Garden of the White House, a good deal of manoeuvring went on. In co-operation with K.B. Andersen, the Danish Foreign Minister, I encouraged the smaller countries, since I thought it would be better not coming from Britain, to sponsor an amendment to the Final Communiqué which was aimed at very considerably softening the tough passage about Cuban involvement and East-West confrontation. It was also obvious that Jim Callaghan was very pleased by the reaction to his intervention. Numerous people came up to him to say how much they had enjoyed it, what good sense he had shown and how well he had spoken. And so next morning, on the Wednesday, he was confident that he had done well the day before. He suggested he might give a press conference, and asked, 'What do you think of this phrase, "Latter-day Christopher Columbuses"?' I laughed and said I thought it was very good. This illustrated the interesting way in which Jim worked. He had a tendency to go for a phrase and then mull it over – very few things came out spontaneously. He knew that it was a risky remark and that it would make the headlines.

Jim then talked to Cy Vance, and got the feeling that Cy Vance would not mind a few broadsides flashed across Brzezinski's bows; I had no doubt that, from our point of view on Africa, Vance needed to be the crucial influence on the President. We were a little worried about the President's reaction, so it was arranged that a transcript of the press conference would be given to Jimmy Carter. During the meeting, at about 4 o'clock, Jimmy Carter leant across to Jim Callaghan and asked him if he would like to come to the White House at about 6 o'clock for a drink. Jim was delighted, and turning to me said, 'You know that shows the wisdom of not touting for a meeting; let it come naturally.' As it turned out it developed into a very long evening, eventually ending up with him and Audrey having southern fries with Jimmy Carter and his wife. Peter and Margaret Jay with their children joined them to watch a film, so the two Leaders were able to have a private chat about politics and deepen their relationship, which was becoming pretty strong. One interesting aspect was that Zbig Brzezinski came in waving the UPI tapes of Jim Callaghan's press conference, clearly very upset about it. Jimmy Carter read the tapes and said, 'I don't see what you are getting fussed about, there is nothing to worry about here'; and virtually told Brzezinski to go off and not worry about it. We all took this as a good sign.

When Jim Callaghan came back that night I saw one of his great strengths. We were wondering whether he should moderate our line, which was clearly becoming very controversial and risked being seen as an intervention in the American debate. But quite rightly he took the view that he had deliberately said what he wanted to, and thought he was right, so we should stick with it. I did a down-the-line interview for the BBC *Today* programme late that night, maintaining the line though softening it in some respects by saying that we were not gunning for Zbig Brzezinski. But of course we were and everybody knew it. However, it was necessary to go through at least that degree of subterfuge.

It was a crucial few days in Washington. If Brzezinski's line had triumphed, the West would have been poised to make a major mistake and to repeat all the errors of the Kissinger period in 1975 over Angola. In the space of a week, it would have undone most of the good achieved on Namibia, Rhodesia and Southern Africa the year before. I also think that the effect of our intervention made a decisive difference in the struggle for the ear of the President over foreign policy. It was in British and Western interests that Cy Vance should predominate in advising the President on foreign policy, not Zbig Brzezinski. Cy Vance, over breakfast on the Thursday morning in the State Department, disclosed that he had just sent a memo to the President making it quite clear that the present situation could not go on, for that day there had been an article in the *Washington Post*, briefed by Zbig, that the SALT negotiations were likely to be held up because of Soviet adventurism in Africa. I think that, while Cy was unhappy about France's new African policy and Brzezinski's statements on China, he was adamant that his view of SALT would not be challenged. He told me that he had never before intervened with the President on a personal issue but I was left in little doubt that he had sent a very tough memo to the President. Jimmy Carter rang Cy while I was still there and invited him to write down his views on détente which he would use as the basis of the speech on Soviet policy that he planned to make within a few days. It was later claimed that that speech was one which did not come down decisively between Vance and Brzezinski, but in my judgement and that of most people close to the scene, the outcome of that speech was a position closest to Vance. Vance, always very averse to personality clashes and prepared to go a long way to avoid them, knew that, though he wanted a good relationship with Zbig Brzezinski, there were limits which had here been reached. There is an inevitable tension between the White House and the State Department. It is a more difficult relationship than that between No. 10 and the Foreign Office, for once the President has decided, there is no further appeal and no requirement for collective discussion before his decision.

When we left for the UN on the Thursday morning, we were given a noticeably warm welcome by the Third World delegates; Jim Callaghan's press conference had gone down extremely well with many African states. The final irony was that Gromyko claimed to me that 'latter-day Christopher Columbuses' was a reference to the Soviet Union's involvement in Africa. I had a good meeting with Gromyko on Africa and other issues, and another with the Chinese Foreign Minister. It was an extraordinary day. I had seen Cy Vance for breakfast, Gromyko for lunch, and the Chinese Foreign Minister in the afternoon. Such is modern diplomacy.

Once back from America, we had to concentrate on European monetary matters. At the Bremen European Summit on 6 July EMS was moved further forward and I began to feel that Jim Callaghan was becoming much more ambivalent about the consequences of not joining the scheme. He still felt that the internal Labour Party politics made joining inadvisable, but I sensed that, with the Bonn Summit imminent, he knew he would not be in a strong position to argue for worldwide currency stability while dragging his feet on the European proposals. Moreover, the Americans seemed increasingly favourable towards the EMS. In fact, at the Bonn Summit Carter sounded less enthusiastic than we had anticipated. Eventually agreement on a co-ordinated package was reached by the seven, with Helmut Schmidt conceding a higher target for German growth than at one time looked likely. We will never know whether this economic programme could have achieved its objectives because it was dealt a massive blow by the oil price rise in early 1979. I suspected that Jim's emphasis at the summit on global economic management tended to exaggerate the capacity of governments to deliver, and that what was needed was much more month-to-month co-operation between finance ministers and their national banks. As in London the year before, the Bonn Summit was mainly important for the opportunity to ease some of the tensions between Helmut Schmidt and Jimmy Carter, which had been exacerbated by the fiasco over the neutron bomb.

All this time British officials were involved in discussions about the development of the EMS, even though Jim had made it clear to Helmut and Giscard that he was not going to join. It was assumed initially that we would have nothing to do with the system but a paper was put up to me suggesting that Britain should join the EMS but not the Exchange Rate Mechanism. In effect that meant standing aside from the fundamental element, a commitment to keep one's currency from fluctuating beyond certain bands. I was mulling over this possibility when Jim Callaghan passed a note across the Cabinet table during our meeting on Thursday 21 September to ask if I would have lunch with him at the Athenaeum. Prime Ministers are automatically given membership of this club, though Jim hardly ever used it. We were due to fly out to Kano in Nigeria next day to meet President Kaunda and we used the lunch, accompanied by Ken Stowe, Jim's Principal Private Secretary, to think through our strategy for what promised to be an emotional and rather difficult meeting. We feared Kenneth Kaunda was about to purchase Soviet air defences to stop the Rhodesian Air Force violating Zambian air space and putting their troops in to hit targets in Lusaka. This humiliation had already been inflicted and the President was determined to prevent its happening again.

After lunch, Jim decided to walk back through St James's Park and he motioned to Ken to hang back so that we could talk privately. He then brought up the issue of EMS. He was concerned about a speech which Denis Healey had made the day before in Canada which appeared to argue that we should join the Exchange Rate Mechanism of the EMS. Denis was soon due to speak to the IMF in Washington. Jim reiterated his view that the Party would not wear entry to the Exchange Rate Mechanism and that it would have to wait until after the election. I suggested the possibility of joining the EMS but not the ERM. Jim pondered this for a moment and then asked me what I thought Denis's attitude would be. I thought Denis, in view of what he had said in Canada, could be persuaded, and Jim suggested that I get my Foreign Office officials to square the Treasury officials. We felt that we could perhaps then sell this somewhat ingenious approach to the Party. Later Denis agreed and Jim managed to push the distinction between joining the EMS, but standing aside from the ERM through the Cabinet in early November. He cleverly did this by first getting everyone to accept that we wanted a zone of monetary stability, then that we should commit ourselves to helping to achieve this, but that we should not accept any obligations restricting our own freedom to manage the sterling exchange rate as we thought fit. I was doubtful whether all the Cabinet members really understood what we were actually going to do, and suspected that Jim had squared Peter Shore earlier. It was the ERM which was the element in the EMS which Peter was most adamantly opposed to and he certainly knew exactly what was happening for he was always vigilant and well-informed on any aspect of policy involving the Community. I do not believe, given the political climate at the end of 1978, that we could have gone any closer to being a full member of the EMS, and that it was an achievement to come as far as we did.

The Parliamentary Labour Party was very uneasy about the EMS issue. Well over a hundred backbench Labour MPs signed an Early Day Motion against it and at a meeting of the PLP there was an attempt to restrict Jim's freedom to sign up for any arrangement; he had to insist vigorously on the Government's right to settle during the give-and-take of a Community negotiation. The Irish Government, meanwhile, had cleverly winkled extra financial support out of Germany and France as their price for signing up for full EMS membership at the EEC summit in early December. Prior to the Paris summit, a Green Paper was published on EMS which the Labour Party NEC predictably attacked. We signed the EMS agreement in Paris and Giscard d'Estaing presented all the signatories with the first minted Ecus. Eventually Parliament agreed that we would be associated with the development of the European Currency Unit and we made up our national share of gold deposits and committed dollar reserves. This ensured that the Ecu had sufficient backing from all nine countries. The great advantage of this compromise was that the necessary procedural hurdles were passed by the Labour Government for full membership at a later date. When, under a Conservative Government, Britain belatedly joined the ERM in October 1990, no new authority was required and entry was fixed up quickly and conveniently over the weekend.

In the middle of October I had a meeting in Pretoria with Don Jamieson (the Canadian Foreign Minister who accompanied me in my plane), Cy Vance, Hans-Dietrich Genscher and the French Deputy Foreign Minister. It was felt that the five of us should, in a quite unprecedented meeting, confront the new South African Prime Minister, P.W. Botha and the Foreign Minister, Pik Botha, about Namibia and their intention to ignore the UN Resolution 435 and hold internal elections in December. It was a very difficult moment for our whole Southern African diplomacy.

Previously on 20 September Prime Minister Vorster had resigned in the midst of a political scandal. Pik Botha had flown back from New York to stand as Leader in the caucus election within the National Party. In order to boost Pik's candidacy, Vorster had, in his last act as Prime Minister, authorized the rejection of the UN plan and announced internal elections. But this ploy had not succeeded and the National Party had chosen P.W. Botha instead. As politicians, all five of us knew it was inconceivable that the new Prime Minister could, even if he wanted to, which was highly unlikely, reverse the decision of his predecessor. The accompanying US officials were, by contrast, wanting us to apply immediate sanctions if he refused to stop the internal elections. I insisted that we act as politicians. We therefore negotiated, with no officials present, directly with Pik Botha and Magnus Malan, then the General in charge of the South African forces. At times the new Prime Minister, P.W. Botha, also attended. He was as tough as nails, and a bully to boot. We had as stormy a dinner as I have ever attended. At one stage Hans-Dietrich, not normally a man to lose his cool, started banging his hand down on the table repeatedly and the glasses danced to each thud, 'I –

am – the Deputy – Federal – Chancellor – of Germany – and I will – not
be – spoken to – in this way.' Even P.W. Botha realized that he had gone
too far and started to back off.

After hours of negotiations we had made no progress and so we asked
our officials to tell our pilots to prepare to fly home. Sometimes this is
done as a negotiating weapon, but this was far from our minds. We were
fed up and determined to go, feeling the whole mission had been a waste
of valuable time. We went in to see P.W. Botha to say goodbye and Cy
spoke for us all: we were leaving because we could not accept their
refusal to go ahead with the UN supervised election *after* their own
internal election had been held. Suddenly P.W. Botha intervened to say
that if this was our position he had no objection. Vance, ever alert for an
opening, reaffirmed that it was our position and did not rub salt into the
wound as I might have been tempted to do by adding it had been our
constant position over the last two days.

I watched Pik Botha's face while P.W. Botha was speaking. His jaw
dropped and he looked incredulous as his own Government's negotiating
position collapsed around him. When, twelve-and-a-half years later, I
visited him in Pretoria after having seen the new Prime Minister, F.W.
De Klerk, Pik was in an expansive mood and we reminisced about old
times. He confirmed that he had been literally thunderstruck, for the
Prime Minister had totally changed his negotiating position. We stayed
long enough to confirm P.W. Botha's new position, which was not quite
as good as we hoped in that he would only say publicly that he would try
and convince the politicians inside Namibia to accept UN elections after
their own internal elections. But since we knew he virtually controlled
them, we returned to the negotiating table confident we would make a
breakthrough and told our pilots that we would not be flying out that
night.

The eventual agreement that we forged paved the way for Namibia to
become independent, although it was postponed by South African delaying tactics until 1990. The twelve-year delay meant the war continued,
but at least Reagan's insistence that Cuban forces should leave Angola
helped ensure as well a settlement in 1991 between the MPLA and
UNITA in Angola. Had we not committed P.W. Botha to accepting the
concept of UN-supervised elections in 1978 and the implementation of
Resolution 435 we might never have had Namibia move to independence
in such a well-ordered way. I have rarely felt such great pleasure as when
I returned to Windhoek in 1990 on the eve of independence and saw Sam
Nujoma just before his inauguration as President. The new constitution
for Namibia is a model for the rest of Africa. No President can remain in
office for more than two terms. It has a Bill of Rights and elections take
place under proportional representation. There has been a marvellous
spirit of reconciliation and co-operation between South Africa and the
new Namibian Government. There are excellent prospects that Walvis

Bay will be returned to Namibia. The RTZ mine at Rossing which I visited in 1990 is making an invaluable contribution to the economy of Namibia and I felt completely vindicated in defending that investment when many people wanted me, as Foreign Secretary, to intervene against it. But it shows how long the timescale can be before one sees a return in international politics.

In 1978 nuclear strategic issues began to haunt European politics and cause tense relations with the United States, which remained until the IMF Treaty was negotiated in 1986. In 1977 Helmut Schmidt, in a speech to the International Institute for Strategic Studies in London, drew attention to the build up of the Soviet SS-20s and argued for the need to maintain a Euro-strategic nuclear balance. Hitherto the conventional wisdom, which I supported, had been that the strategic balance was maintained globally and we had no need to reach a balance only within the European region. In March 1978, the French Foreign Minister expressed my own sentiments about Schmidt's speech when he said that to endorse the concept of a Euro-strategic nuclear balance was the 'equivalent to recognizing that the central, strategic forces of the US do not protect Western Europe'. Even so, we in Britain, France and the US realized that the very fact that Germany, and particularly Schmidt, a former Defence Minister, felt so anxious about the Soviet build up of SS-20s meant that it would be necessary to look at the whole question of modernizing existing nuclear weapons in Europe. But for me the strength of the case for modernizing was not primarily to match Soviet SS-20s but to join the US global deterrent firmly to Europe. It was in this mood that most of the European countries in NATO had supported the idea of the enhanced radiation weapon or neutron bomb. Some unfortunate publicity had portrayed in very simplistic terms the neutron bomb as killing people but not damaging buildings. This not surprisingly provoked an emotive public debate. While CND took it up in the UK, their protests were containable. But in Germany Helmut Schmidt began to come under considerable pressure from some Social Democrat MPs in his Party who pressed him to refuse to deploy the neutron bomb on German territory. Schmidt, assured by the US Defence Secretary that it was essential, fought and won a battle with his own Party in support of the neutron bomb. Only then did he discover that Jimmy Carter had serious reservations. Carter, in early 1978, which had been declared UN Disarmament Year, finding that the Soviet Union was seizing on the neutron bomb as a tool for their propaganda, sensed that the Soviets were likely to win that propaganda battle. Once he was briefed that NATO was itself divided he began to backtrack. The British Ministry of Defence was all in favour of the neutron bomb, though I was not. Cy Vance, like me, had gone along with the military. In my case it was because I had more important battles ahead of me over British nuclear strategy. With Jim Callaghan supporting Fred Mulley, I judged it wiser to acquiesce since my doubts stemmed from a more fundamental and longstanding questioning about the wisdom of deploying any tactical nuclear weapons, particularly nuclear artillery. I had long believed that short-range weapons were both dangerous and unnecessary and should be the first weapon system to be negotiated away. They are dangerous on many grounds but particularly because they can be overrun in a border dispute and commanders are then faced by the 'lose or use' dilemma. They are unnecessary because, with the pinpoint accuracy of the modern strategic nuclear missile, and with the new technology for cruise, one can plan to fire into the European theatre from submarines, aircraft or land bases without having nuclear weapons stationed near the East-West frontier. Cy Vance had told me that he wanted the neutron bomb like 'a hole in the head'. But the sudden manner of Carter's cancellation upset Vance as well as Schmidt and the Europeans. It raised very large questions about the reliability of an American President. Helmut Schmidt was still angry and exasperated by Carter's cancellation at the time of the Bonn Summit. The two men were utterly incompatible and unfortunately were to remain so until Carter's four-year Presidency came to an end.

In order to try and avoid any further confusion, Zbig Brzezinski was sent round Europe in the late summer to sound out Jim Callaghan, Helmut Schmidt and Giscard d'Estaing on whether they would meet with Jimmy Carter early in 1979. This was agreed and a meeting was held that January in Guadeloupe, mainly for the four to talk privately about nuclear questions. This meeting brought to a head our own discussion on the continuation of the British independent nuclear deterrent.

The political problem that we faced over nuclear deterrence lay at the heart of the Callaghan Government. The Deputy Prime Minister, Michael Foot, did not believe in nuclear deterrence and, as an original Aldermaston marcher and CND activist, was not prepared to be involved. He sat on the Defence and Overseas Policy Committee of the Cabinet but it never handled specific nuclear questions. These had been handled ever since 1974, first under Wilson and then under Callaghan, by a small and special grouping of Ministers. In my time it was a group of four – the Prime Minister, Foreign Secretary, Chancellor of the Exchequer and Defence Minister.

The Labour Cabinet had agreed after the second General Election in 1974 to update Polaris. But like all nuclear matters it was slipped through the Labour Party, avoiding discussion because to do so would risk a row. The hardening and modernizing programme for the Polaris warhead under the secret codename Antelope was first examined when I was Navy Minister in 1969. Expenditure was authorized under the codename Chevaline by Edward Heath near the end of his Government. In 1977 I became involved again after the scandalous escalation in the cost of the Chevaline project. This had quadrupled and the four of us met to consider cancelling. We decided not to cancel but for very mixed reasons.

Jim Callaghan believed it was militarily necessary to improve the warhead. Fred Mulley believed he had to keep the Chiefs of Staff happy and, since they believed it was necessary despite the ABM Treaty, he went along with it in spite of his doubts. Denis Healey wanted to be Foreign Secretary and to align himself with Jim, so, even though he disliked the cost and thought it militarily unnecessary, he acquiesced. I believed it was not militarily necessary after the ABM Treaty but, since we had spent three-quarters of the total cost, I feared cancellation would raise military questions capable of destroying the political effectiveness of Polaris as a deterrent without an improved warhead. Since nuclear deterrence is as much psychological and political as military, I therefore favoured continuing with Chevaline.

But I also believed that it was a warning to us that we had not got the financial weight to continue with a highly sophisticated nuclear deterrent, since in any new missile system that we bought from the United States, we would still have to rely on Aldermaston to manufacture and develop its nuclear warhead. They could do this for a simple system, but increasing sophistication of the new generation of Trident warheads would present us with similar problems to those we had encountered over Chevaline. I began to feel we were playing out of our league and that we needed to look at a cut-price deterrent.

The four of us examined in considerable depth the difficult question of what to do about replacing Polaris. I fought to explore the option of the cruise missile as a cheaper minimum deterrent. The Ministry of Defence were strongly against this, wanting the best available, irrespective of cost, which was undoubtedly Trident. I had to develop the arguments initially inside my own Private Office Policy Unit. When the paper the four of us had commissioned from officials eventually arrived I was, however, ready and tabled instantly a long detailed and very different paper stressing the value of cruise as a less sophisticated option. Typically, we were called to the meeting in the latter part of 1978 to discuss the officials' long delayed paper at only a few days' notice. But to everyone's surprise my detailed alternative options paper was presented simultaneously. As a result the four of us explored the Tomahawk cruise missile, a very new concept, with information which Peter Jay had sent from Washington. Given its amazing success and accuracy in the Gulf War, I hope that those who denigrated its potential for nearly a decade in Whitehall will remember and recant. Every effort was made to dismiss cruise missiles even as an option and to boost the case for Trident and for continuing with an intercontinental ballistic missile system. I never had any doubt that Trident was a highly effective super-sophisticated system and that it was necessary for the US to go ahead with it. The unanswered question for me was whether a cheaper more flexible missile system existed, a weapons system which needed an unsophisticated and therefore cheaper nuclear warhead.

The four of us never doubted that we wanted Polaris replaced and that Britain should retain its independent nuclear deterrent. Yet none of us ever felt able to go out and argue the case positively to the Parliamentary Party, let alone the Party in the country. All we did to justify nuclear deterrence was done in the context of maintaining Polaris and the need for NATO to have modern US nuclear weapons. If Jim Callaghan had won the next election he would have argued for Trident. In my judgement, Michael Foot's self-imposed exclusion from even discussing these issues during our whole period in Government made him unfit ever to be Prime Minister. I could understand his attitude while it looked as if he acknowledged that, because of his unilateralist ideas, he could never seek to be Prime Minister. Only when he decided to put himself forward as Leader of the Labour Party did I make my decision not to serve under him. During the 1983 General Election in a speech in Bristol, I declared that, for this reason, he was totally unfit to hold the office of Prime Minister.

It was at a meeting on nuclear questions on 12 December that, almost by accident, we had to decide whether to make the vote at the end of that day's debate an issue of confidence. I recall the incident in some detail because it is a vignette of how that Labour Government, without sufficient votes, constantly had to cobble together a majority. It was a daily part of the Government's life which I rarely saw at close quarters. With the benefit of hindsight, I have no doubt that this was the moment that the Labour Party lost the 1979 General Election. Many people believe that it was lost when Jim Callaghan announced to the Cabinet on Thursday 7 September that he was not calling a general election. I told Jim before this decision that, though I thought the election would be close, I did not think we would win. With my marginal Devonport constituency, I was far from confident of victory that September. I detected considerable reservations about the performance of the Labour Government in the minds of my electors. Of course, if we had had an election in the autumn of 1978, Labour would not have lost by anywhere near as large a margin as in May 1979, but Prime Ministers hold elections to win and I do not believe we would have won that October.

There were undoubted risks in facing the winter without the Lib-Lab Pact which had ended in the summer. Yet the Liberals, by bailing out at that stage, felt few of the benefits of their pact with us. They thought with one bound they would be free, but they did not escape responsibility for the Winter of Discontent in the public mind, however unjustifiably. We knew that the Ulster Unionists would stay with us at least until the legislation for the extra MPs in Northern Ireland had taken effect, and that the Scottish Nationalists would want the devolution referendum planned for early 1979 to go ahead.

By December the political situation was becoming dominated by pay policy questions. The Ford Motor Company, which had been profitable in 1978, had been ready at least to take account of the Government's pay guideline, ill-advisedly set by Jim, in a very personal decision, at the unrealistically low level of 5 per cent. However, having resisted a nine-week strike, they decided to settle with a massive pay increase of 17 per cent. Our pay policy, though predominantly voluntary, had been underpinned by some mild sanctions, one of which was that private firms who ignored the Government's pay guidelines were told that they could not expect to have any Government orders for their products. The Cabinet decided that Ford could not be an exception. A debate on the Ford sanctions was then forced by the Conservatives, and thirty members of the Tribune Group of Left-wing Labour MPs tabled an amendment expressing their opposition to any form of incomes policy. Though this amendment was not called, the Conservative Opposition's amendment was; it demanded the abandonment of any sanctions against companies which broke the pay guidelines. It was obvious that the Government could well lose if there were any Labour abstentions, since the Liberals and Scottish Nationalists were going to vote with the Conservatives. Jim Callaghan along with Michael Foot had already urged the Tribune Group not to abstain on the Conservative motion. Michael Foot, as Leader of the House, and Michael Cocks, the Chief Whip, asked to see Jim urgently that morning, having just met with the Tribune Group again. Jim decided to call them into our meeting and to open the discussion up as to our next move.

Denis Healey argued that some of the Tribune MPs threatening to abstain would think more than twice if we declared the vote to be one of confidence. In effect threatening them with a general election. Michael Foot was strongly against such a gamble, fearing that it would lead to a general election if we lost the vote. He preferred to lose that night without declaring it a matter of confidence and then have a no-confidence debate next day when the Scottish Nationalists would support us. Michael Cocks explained that eighteen of our Members were away in Luxembourg, Cledwyn Hughes was in Lagos and Arthur Irvine was ill. We realized that if we lost, having made it a vote of confidence, we would have to hold a general election in January on the old register and have a break in canvassing over the Christmas period. This did not worry me and to be standing firm against inflation seemed an ideal battleground. It would be Conservatives and Liberals who had voted for inflation and letting Ford off the hook. Clearly fed up and moving towards making it a motion of confidence, Jim decided to adjourn and meet again at 12.45 p.m. to hear a further report from the whips. In the meantime, I would try to contact Cledwyn in Lagos to see if he could fly back in time to vote.

At 12.45 p.m. Michael Cocks reported that there was a marginal chance of winning if we made it a vote of confidence. There appeared to be some uncertainty as to the exact whereabouts of the delegation to the

European Parliament, which raised a fundamental doubt about the whips' assessment that we could win. I had not been able to get hold of Cledwyn. Michael Foot had sounded out Enoch and though there was no chance of the Irish voting with us, some might conveniently be away. Denis and Jim still seemed keen to make it a vote of confidence. They felt if we won that we could hold the sanctions policy afterwards. I doubted this but said very little and Fred Mulley was also quiet.

My main anxiety was to keep Jim in a mood which would not, as we used to joke, 'send him off to the farm'. If we had an early election, it was vital for him to be in a confident mood, happy that he had decided to provoke the Left and not feeling that he had been pushed into an election against his will. We agreed to meet at 3 o'clock in Jim's room in the House as he and Fred Mulley had a lunch fixed with the Chiefs of Staff. I had lunch with Harry Walston and to my surprise found that he was against Ford's being penalized by sanctions. This shook me a little and he was also wholly relaxed about the consequences of our losing the vote that night but restoring the position next day. I felt perhaps we were exaggerating the significance of the Ford decision and that fewer people would care if Ford got away without penalty than I had hitherto thought. So when Denis argued strongly after lunch that sanctions would crumble and our anti-inflation policy would be in ruins if we did not win the vote, I was too complacent. Fred Mulley had told me that he had advised Jim to 'stick with Michael'. I wanted a decision which was Jim's, and that he could live with when he shaved next morning. I was convinced it was no use foisting anything on him. We were then told that the delegation of MPs were in Brussels, but five minutes later we heard they were in Luxembourg. This was the last straw as far as I was concerned for I felt that if we made it a vote of confidence we were likely to have our people anywhere rather than in the Division Lobby. Roy Hattersley, who was opening for us in the debate, and Joel Barnett called in. Roy strongly backed Denis while Joel also agreed to a vote of confidence, but only if we could guarantee that we could win it. Then Jim moved decisively to support Michael's argument not to make it an issue of confidence. I guessed, however, he was hoping in this way to put strong psychological pressure on Michael to deliver the Tribunites.

So the die was cast. We would not make it a vote of confidence. We would probably lose and we would call a vote of confidence next day. We did lose, by two votes, 285 to 283. Enough Tribunites had abstained, as we predicted, to lose us the vote. That night the Government tabled a motion of confidence which was debated next day. We had a majority of ten, with the Scottish Nationalists voting for us. Yet we had lost the ability to threaten anyone with sanctions. As it turned out, Denis Healey and Roy Hattersley were shown to have been correct. Sanctions were like a finger in a dyke; once removed the whole edifice of restraint collapsed.

Before we knew where we were the Winter of Discontent descended on us, dooming us to lose the general election.

I believe if we had made the Ford sanctions debate a vote of confidence we would have won, for enough Tribunites would have folded under such pressure and not abstained. Even if we had lost, I believe we would have won a general election in January. Even more important, if we had not lost the Ford vote Jim Callaghan's morale would have been much higher. He would have confronted any trouble that winter with more confidence and we might even have won a September 1979 General Election. But politics is full of 'ifs'.

The Government was beginning to look tired and was running out of steam. We were facing an increasingly confident Margaret Thatcher and a Conservative Party which had rediscovered the will to win. I had by chance witnessed this one particular incident but Jim, Michael and Denis had been facing similar issues since 1974. The whole process of maintaining a majority in the House of Commons and beating back inflation was beginning to wear them out.

17

IRAN

The toppling of the Shah by Ayatollah Khomeini at the head of the Iranian Revolution in early 1979 was, predictably, a geopolitical disaster. The power of Iran in the region was within months dissipated and destroyed. If the revolution had not occurred, there would have been no invasion of Afghanistan by the USSR in late 1979, no Iran-Iraq War from 1980–87, and in 1990 no Iraqi invasion of Kuwait. Death would not have claimed a million or more Muslims on the battlefield. The wave of Islamic fundamentalism would not have gathered such destructive force or led to such severe abuses of human rights; abuses which in retrospect make the Shah's rule look less unattractive and even the loathsome SAVAK not as odious.

I have often pondered the events surrounding the Shah's fall. Immediately after the revolution in 1979, I arranged for the Foreign Office to conduct a detailed post mortem on where mistakes might have been made. In fact that report came to my successor Lord Carrington. It is always hard to admit error, but it is my considered belief that in 1978 the Western democracies had it in their power to influence events inside Iran so that the revolution could have been averted. It would almost certainly have meant the Shah retiring on health grounds, with a Regency instituted until he could be succeeded as Shah by his son Reza, though without imperial powers. In this way I believe that Iran could have been guided towards becoming a democratic state. I take part of the blame myself for not, as Foreign Secretary, acting with sufficient foresight or being successful enough in mobilizing the Western countries to provide a firmer policy towards Iran in the late summer of 1978.

The most frequent criticism of the West during this time is that we failed to anticipate the revolution. I am not convinced that this is fair. We agonized constantly about whether or not the Shah's regime could survive. 'Is the Emperor Fully Clothed?' was the title of a despatch sent from our Embassy in Tehran in August 1977. The real criticism is not of our anticipation skills but of our handling of the Shah. We failed to remember how weak he was before he took on the airs of an autocrat. We were far too deferential before his charade of leadership while he vacillated month by month. We failed to infuse him with the decisiveness and ruthlessness which were necessary not just for his survival but for his country's rejection of an Islamic revolution.

There are no scapegoats and I attach no blame to our Ambassador during that period, Sir Anthony Parsons. I had first met him in the late 1960s when he was Political Agent in Bahrain and liked him and his wife immensely. Though unquestionably liberal-minded, he was not soft, and understood the exercise of power. He was not a Persian scholar, but as an Arabist he knew the region well and had made himself very knowledgeable on Iran. His advice was always thoughtful and, though he was unduly influenced by the panoply of power surrounding the Shahanshah, so would any Ambassador have been. It did lead him to exaggerate the Shah's capacity to influence events, but he does not deserve criticism for this. Most of us were similarly misled. My task and that of the other political leaders in the Western democracies with ranks of specialist advisers, was to stand back and assess the real Shah rather than the illusion. We failed to do this.

The Iran with which I had to deal as Foreign Secretary was a very different country from the one through which I had travelled extensively in 1959 on the way to and from Afghanistan. It had changed a lot too since my next visit in 1966 with an all-party delegation of MPs. By 1977 it was almost unrecognizable, with hugely increased wealth, power and sophistication. Iran was by then producing nearly 12 per cent of the world's oil and some 16 per cent of Britain's. British Petroleum obtained between 40–45 per cent of its total oil supplies from Iran. With its vast oil revenues Iran was a major purchaser. Britain sold Iran about £200 million worth of industrial goods, motor cars and military equipment a year. We had recently sold them 750 Chieftain tanks and some 250 Scorpions. The UK was Iran's fourth largest supplier after the USA, Japan and West Germany. France also had extensive interests and the European Community took about 13 per cent of its oil supply from Iran. After the rapid financial and political collapse of Iran following the revolution, the rule of Khomeini and the Iran-Iraq War, it is easy to forget how economically important Iran was under the Shah. Politically too; by the 1970s Iran totally dominated the Gulf region.

The overthrow of Mossadeq by an uprising of the people in 1953, engineered by the CIA and MI6, is the key event in any retrospective analysis of the events of 1978. The British proposed that Kim Roosevelt, the head of the CIA's Middle East operations, should be put in charge. Sir Anthony Eden, as Foreign Secretary, was not as convinced as Winston Churchill, the Prime Minister, that Mossadeq should be ousted, but he suddenly became ill and Churchill temporarily took charge of the Foreign Office. The crucial fact which we should never have allowed to slip our memories was the extent to which at that time the young Shah demonstrated his indecisiveness. The Shah was not only extremely nervous, he wavered and, at a critical moment, thinking the plan had failed, took flight in a small plane to Iraq with Queen Soraya. He had no idea where to go next, eventually flying to Rome. While in Baghdad he had talked to the American Ambassador and, although the British Ambassador did not see him, he sent back a revealing despatch to London describing what the Shah had said to the Americans: we were given a clear intimation of the Shah's attitude for the future. 'He had then decided that as a constitutional ruler he should not resort to force as that would lead to bloodshed, chaos and Soviet infiltration.' The Shah continued to rationalize his behaviour at that time. Even in exile, sick and dying, he still insisted on making a distinction between a dictator and a hereditary monarch in his memoirs:

> A sovereign may not save his throne by shedding his compatriots' blood. A dictator can, because he acts in the name of an ideology which he believes must triumph whatever the price. But a sovereign is not a dictator. There is an alliance between him and his people which he cannot break. A dictator has nothing to hand over. Power lies in him, and in him alone. A sovereign receives a crown and it is his duty to pass it on.

In Rome in 1953, the Shah was living in a hotel without money or much influence and it was widely felt by British diplomats that he had shown himself to be a coward. The Americans managed to stiffen him to assert his constitutional rights and denounce Mossadeq's actions as illegal. Initially the streets of Tehran were full of Mossadeq's supporters and communists from the Tudeh Party. Then the CIA paid for and mobilized counter-demonstrations. These pro-Shah crowds encouraged the Army to come out in favour of the Shah and overthrow Mossadeq. When Mossadeq was put on trial he blamed the British for his overthrow, so we gained the undeserved reputation of being the master planners while the Americans were never given sufficient credit. The Shah, however, thought his return owed everything to his people, asserting 'I knew they loved me'; another myth with which he reassured himself. Thereafter the Shah was haunted by his exile and decided to build up a fortune outside the country in order to safeguard his future. It was also, he felt, necessary to inaugurate his own National Intelligence and Security Organization, SAVAK, from its Iranian name, *Sazeman-e Ettela't va Amniyat-e-Keshvar*. He chose the CIA and Mossad, not the British MI6, as his principal advisers on this.

I blame myself for not calling in 1978 for a detailed analysis of what happened in 1953. We did not focus sufficiently on analysing the Shah's personality – if we had we would surely have concluded that he could not be trusted to assert leadership and authority in the crisis. I was trained as a natural scientist and it always shocked me how in the British system of government there is no automatic analysis of relevant past decisions, no systematic collection of historical precedents. As Foreign Secretary I tried all the time to widen my knowledge, I read extensively and insisted on talking to outside experts, but I was too dependent on my own limited knowledge of Iran and the sort of analysis made inside the Foreign Office was too superficial.

In 1959, as a student travelling with little money and meeting people far removed from the diplomatic circuit, I saw for myself how poor and feudal rural Iran was. There was, however, no mistaking the enthusiasm for the land reforms and the start of the Shah's 'White Revolution'. By 1966 the reforms still seemed to offer great hope. The Shah appeared to envisage a Literacy Corps, rights for women and electoral reform as well as land reform and nationalization of the forests. The land reform programme was seen by the poor as their opportunity to share out the vast land holdings of the rich merchants, while the mullahs were strongly resented.

The peasants wanted their own small farms and the Shah's apparent readiness to force landowners to give up their estates was widely welcomed. At that stage even the Shah's Coronation ceremony was reasonably popular. It was lavish but not gross and could be interpreted as a symbol of Iran's increased stature and confidence. He had his critics of course, but there was evidence that he was respected too and there were good grounds for cautious optimism. It was in the early 1970s that the Shah began to be assertive, challenging the dominance of the international oil companies. In 1971 he was largely responsible for the Tehran Agreement which substantially increased Iran's oil revenues. It was in the aftermath of this that the flamboyance and extravagance of the Shah's court began to develop. A grotesquely extravagant party was held at Persepolis in October 1971 to celebrate the 2,500th anniversary of the Persian monarchy. This seems to have been the moment when the Shah lost touch with reality and his people. A tented city was put up for the visiting Royals and VIPs. Maxim's prepared the food, Lanvin the uniforms, Porthault the linen. *Son et lumière* celebrated Cyrus the Great, while the prophet Mohammed and Islam were apparently ignored. The peacock and his throne were matched.

In 1969, as Navy Minister visiting Bahrain, I was involved in the reassessment of our interests in the Gulf. The Royal Naval base was due to close and all British forces were to withdraw from the Gulf. Edward Heath was challenging this and, unwisely, we continued Naval withdrawal from the Gulf along with the sensible decision to withdraw from Singapore. It was then the Shah began to fill the gap. In 1941 Iran's armed forces numbered 90,000. By 1978 they amounted to 350,000. In December 1971 Iranian troops landed at Abu Musa and the Tunbs Islands in the lower Gulf, asserting a dubious claim to the Islands, but there were very few objections. The Shah's military might inside Iran was built up to underwrite his projection of power in the region. London was pleased by this assertion of regional dominance because the Shah had agreed to purchase our Chieftain tanks. By 1973 the Shah was talking in grandiose terms of the era of the Great Civilization, and boasting that Iran had joined the ranks of the industrialized nations. He sent Iranian troops to help the Sultan of Oman. Henry Kissinger, then US Secretary of State, accepted and, what is more, encouraged him in his self-appointed imperial role as guardian of the Gulf. The Shah forced the pace in OPEC, first at the October and then the December 1973 meetings. As the Western democracies watched, the illusion of a decisive, determined monarch grew.

At the start of 1974 the Shah was the single most important influence in the Middle East. Ever more vain and imperious, he was nevertheless shrewd. Broadly, his instincts were compatible with the interests of the Western democracies, so we encouraged him. Iran was a member of the defence organization CENTO along with, initially, Iraq, Pakistan, Turkey, the UK and the USA. The Shah was also a strong supporter of the free flow of trade within the Gulf. Yet he was very conscious of having a 1,000 mile border with the USSR and always maintained a private channel to Moscow. For us in Britain, Iran's historic significance was that it lay between Russia and the warm water ports, between the USSR and India. Even in the 1970s we felt we had interests in the Indian sub-continent though, apart from sentiment, they were not easy to define. Good relations with the Shah were correctly judged to be an essential part of British foreign policy and much retrospective nonsense has been written about whether Britain should ever have supported the Shah. Economically, by the middle 1970s the Shah's favour was important to us, for we desperately needed to be able to offset the oil price shock by selling an increased proportion of our industrial output to Iran.

There was, however, an ambivalence about Anglo-Iranian relations. Britain, after 150 years of influence and, some would say, gross interference in Iran's internal affairs, was the subject of much suspicion within Iran. Almost every person one met there was ready to ascribe almost magical powers to the British Secret Service. The CIA, despite their much greater involvement in the overthrow of Mossadeq, and the Israeli intelligence service, Mossad, both powerfully represented in Iran, were treated by Persians as being of far inferior quality. The Shah also became obsessive about the hidden hand of Britain, attributing to us a role and an influence which we ourselves were never able to live up to. The Iranians were in part flattered, in part suspicious of the number of British diplomats over the years who had a profound knowledge of and love for Persian history, literature and culture.

Yet even before the late 1970s, our Ambassadors had always been watching for signs of instability. Back in the 1960s our Embassy in

Tehran was reporting that the collapse of the regime might or might not be imminent; they worried about an old-fashioned society being invaded by new ideas and how the superimposition of industrialization was destroying the traditional way of life. One of the most astute Ambassadors who ever served in Tehran, Sir Denis Wright, drew attention to the genuine dilemma that faced the Shah. If he was to carry his reforms through he needed to tighten his political grip on the country. The trouble with this, as history has so often shown, is that genuine reformist leaders who take undemocratic powers turn into reactionary dictators. Lord Acton's dictum, 'All power corrupts, absolute power corrupts absolutely', has proved true time and time again. The Shah was never an enlightened democrat but he was a genuine modernizer, though his autocratic style hid a neurotic and indecisive personality.

In retrospect, one of the Foreign Office's minor mistakes over a decade or more was to take short-term advantage of the skills of our Persian linguists to improve our commercial performance at the expense of in-depth political reporting. This mattered chiefly because it coincided with a period when we were gradually ceasing to have much diplomatic contact with Iranian opposition leaders and the leading mullahs, a decision taken because of the hypersensitivity of the Shah who saw intrigue behind any meeting, however innocent. As he grew more autocratic and intolerant, it became apparent that we could easily endanger our relationship with him if he felt that we were continuing with the long British history of intrigue. We therefore chose in the late 1960s not to deploy any of our own intelligence service in Iran, feeling that we had little option other than to rely on SAVAK. I am now certain we should have built up a separate Iranian intelligence analysis unit within MI6 in London. It would have been a valuable asset at any time and quite crucial in 1978. Better links with Mossad would have helped, but we were still suffering from our 1973 decision to withhold tank ammunition from Israel during their war. With our electronic sources, coupled with the knowledge of those people who did retain close cultural and political links with Iranian opposition figures, we could have analysed more and possibly anticipated events. It is a great mistake to think that one should only deploy MI6 or diplomats to probe on the ground.

In consequence, from the 1960s onwards, our Embassy began slowly to lose some of its intelligence about the religious, cultural and intellectual life of Iran since so many of the people who could have kept us informed were judged by SAVAK to be either hostile to the Shah or unsound. As the older diplomats with wider contacts from their youth retired, a broad understanding of Iran was increasingly lost to us. In my time as Foreign Secretary there was only one official, other than the Ambassador, in the Embassy on political duties, and these had to compete with other responsibilities.

The lesson of history for us in early 1978 was that in the nineteenth and early twentieth century a combination of intellectuals, bazaaris and mullahs had more than once combined to force Qajar Shahs into surrendering their powers or abdicating. The Shah should have bought off at least one of those elements. He underestimated the influence of the mullahs as we, the Americans and the French consistently underestimated the reach and rapport that Khomeini was building up while in exile. Yet neither we nor the Shah had any illusions about the Ayatollah. I remember reading a report spelling out how hysterically xenophobic he was, fanatically anti-Western, anti-Communist and anti-Zionist. We knew Khomeini would withdraw from CENTO, push for higher oil prices and possibly cut oil supplies to Israel and South Africa. On the other hand, since we knew he wanted the unity of all Islamic countries, we hoped he might over time abate his adverse comments on Saudi Arabia, Kuwait and the other Gulf States. We knew he would protect Iran's borders, but no one guessed that the revolution would so weaken Iran that Iraq would dare attack. But then we had no idea of how chaotic the revolution in its early years would be and how demoralized the armed forces would become under daily harassment from the Revolutionary Guard.

It is easy to be wise after the event. All of this time Foreign Office budgets were under considerable constraint and the emphasis was on helping our export drive. Also, there was exasperation with the Shah's manner which I too felt. Politicians had grown fed up with being pushed around by him and, particularly in the middle 1970s, his political criticism of Britain was resented. Few politicians in Britain had much time for him personally, disliking his ostentatious flaunting of wealth and power. The Iranian Embassy in London, in which champagne flowed and caviar abounded, was widely felt to have been too lavish for years in its representation of what was still, in the rural areas, a Third World country.

The frenetic activity which the Shah stimulated in Iran following the oil price hike meant that inflation gathered momentum. By early 1975 the Iranian economy was in serious difficulties. Soaring rents in Tehran were cutting living standards. The Shah was aware of the problem but chose not to deal with the underlying inflation, and instead embarked on an anti-profiteering initiative. This angered the bazaar merchants who guessed correctly that it was an attack on them. Ominously, it started to push them towards the mullahs. By 1976, when as Minister of State I started to examine Iran, inflation was running at over 20 per cent and corruption was rampant. A palpable malaise was creeping into Iranian society. Everyone was on the make and the Pahlevi Foundation was becoming a vehicle for the Shah's close family to amass vast sums in financial kick-backs and build up fortunes overseas. It has been argued that we in the UK were too importunate in offering arms to the Shah, as were the US and France, and it is true that successive Heads of Defence Sales were authorized to expand aggressively on the Iranian market. The contract for the Shir Iran tank gave the Shah far too big a stake in British tank production. Some highly classified military information was also released to Iran in this contract which, after the revolution, we regretted. But the alternative of unilaterally adopting a purist position, selling arms only if a regional balance in arms sales were maintained, would simply have opened the door to our competitors. We were certain to get no reciprocal response from France or even from the United States under President Carter. The Americans talked of limiting conventional arms sales but their various schemes never looked like being accepted internationally. The State Department took the high moral ground while the Pentagon pushed arms sales. Also, we knew that countries which criticized the Shah were dealt with capriciously. Holland had its imports banned, and trade was halted at various times with Sweden, Norway, Italy and Belgium. Individual companies too felt his vindictiveness.

By March 1976, the fiftieth anniversary of the Pahlevi dynasty was certainly not something for the poor people to celebrate. The Shah's credibility was weakened and he had had to cancel a number of prestige projects and even admit to having made some mistakes. More importantly, his influence in the region also began to wane. At the December OPEC meeting in Doha, the Saudi Arabians refused to agree to an Iranian demand for an oil price increase and this dented the Shah's prestige. As Minister of State I became rather apprehensive about the optimistic note struck in the annual report from the Embassy in January 1977 and wrote on it, 'I am very wary of believing that Iran is wholly atypical and that factors of instability which would be cause for alarm in other countries can be thought to have markedly less influence in Iran.' There was a tendency to believe that somehow Iran was unique, its instability different from other countries, exempt from the pressures for democratization and human rights building up worldwide.

The Shah's liberalization policy virtually coincided with my period as Secretary of State. It was initiated in 1977, a reaction to the global interest in human rights then. While it certainly suited my mood and that of the incoming Carter Administration, it was not dictated by us. The apologists for the Shah never cease to blame Carter for his downfall. But in fairness, just as Carter's stress on human rights was a reaction to trends of opinion already apparent in the world, so the Shah too was reacting. Iran's prisons were opened up for inspection by the International Red Cross. The public were admitted, for the first time since 1972, to the trials of political prisoners and some political prisoners were released. There is no evidence that the Shah made these decisions because of US pressure. It was more as if he recognized that the guided democracy, which he had tried, had largely failed. And if his son were to succeed him in a mood of peace and harmony then the popularity of the monarchy had to be safeguarded. The Shah's problem was that by then he had dismantled a viable structure within which to govern.

The Shah was aware of the organized opposition and he did try to identify ways of curbing their influence. The entrenched opposition were those who took as their symbol Ayatollah Khomeini, then exiled in Iraq, but it could also be seen round the old National Front politicians like Shahpour Bakhtiar and Mehdi Bazergan. All these people were difficult to square. The bazaar merchants were more fickle in opposition and could have been bought. But things became serious when they started to finance the mosques. The largest element of opposition and the least organized was the city dwellers, who grew restless as inflation rose. Everyone knew that the Great Civilization was coming apart at the seams, and this was emphasized by a series of power cuts demonstrating how dismally the planners had failed in making provision for power. Nevertheless, given the Shah's apparent readiness to address some of their concerns, there was no reason why urban dissatisfaction could not have been contained with more anticipation and flexibility.

In August 1977 the Shah made a critical mistake and dismissed his longstanding Prime Minister, Amir Abbas Hoveyda, whom I had met a few months earlier. If the Shah was doing this to divert criticism from himself, he should have known it would not work. But the dismissal did something else. It showed those who had been loyal to the Shah that they could not count on his loyalty in return. There is in the Persian character a marked tendency to hedge bets and thereafter there were many more important people hedging their bets against the Shah being toppled. By October public dissatisfaction was palpable, and in the Goethe Institute in Tehran readings of literature critical of the regime attracted amazingly large numbers. This was followed in November by students openly demonstrating in Tehran against the Shah before his visit to President Carter. In Washington an Iranian student demonstration outside the White House grew so violent that CS gas had to be used, whose acrid smell drifted across the White House lawn as the ceremonial welcome took place, bringing tears to the eyes of the participants.

In January 1978 I felt that the Shah must have authorized the placing of an article in the press lambasting Khomeini. To accuse him of being an adventurer and a non-believer was crass stupidity and there were predictable riots in Qom where some demonstrators were killed. This was probably the touch-paper that fired the revolution; the moment when the forces against the Shah gathered momentum, with Islamic fundamental-ism in the vanguard. It was followed by demonstrations in Qom at forty-day intervals, a Shi'a practice in commemoration of the dead. In Tabriz in mid-February there were riots where tanks were used. Anglo-Iranian relations then soured over the case of a former British Army officer, involving illegal financial inducements. He was arrested in April 1977, and found guilty in January 1978. At one stage the Iranian Prime Minister threatened a trade boycott and there were constant complaints about BBC broadcasts. Our Ambassador was told that British firms hoping for Government contracts need not bother to apply. So it was arranged that Fred Mulley, our Secretary of State for Defence, should visit in March. He took flattery to levels exceeded only by Jimmy Carter, but the Embassy view was that constant flattery of the Shah was a small price to pay. We reviewed our policy yet again and concluded that the best policy was 'support for the Shah, warts and all, while occasionally offering treatment for the warts'. Meanwhile, in May the rioting continued in Tehran. In June, the Shah dismissed General Nissiri, the Head of SAVAK. In late July there was unrest in Mashad.

It was against this background that I had to consider the Iranian request to supply CS gas to the Shah. It transpired that the Americans had either refused to supply CS gas or were sitting on the request, we could not be sure which. Whether out of embarrassment or waiting for a Presidential decision, the Americans were untypically tight-lipped. I thought long and hard that summer about what was the best course for Britain, for Iran and the region. In many ways it was a threshold for our policy towards Iran. If we refused the request we would be sidelining ourselves. Our influence would cease. It seemed to me impossible to justify protesting about the use of tanks to control rioters and then to fail to provide the Shah with the means for a more acceptable form of crowd control. I minuted Jim Callaghan to say that it was my intention to supply CS gas unless I heard to the contrary. This meant that he and other senior Ministers need not expose themselves by replying and if there was, as I fully expected, a press leak, I could take the criticism. It was a delicate time domestically. We were on the eve of a possible autumn election and I did not want to put Jim Callaghan in the firing-line on an issue which I knew would arouse a lot of adverse comment. In the event, as so often when one is expecting adverse publicity, the information about our supplying CS gas did not become public.

It was that summer that the Western democracies had the opportunity to rethink a strategy to bind Iran to the West. It was obvious by then that the Shah was vulnerable, perched on an unstable edifice. Too many people had direct access to him. There was no Cabinet to sift information and determine priorities. One young Foreign Office analyst likened the structure to a series of parallel columns with each pillar representing an independent interest, be it SAVAK, the Prime Minister, the Supreme Commanding Officer or the Central Bank. All reported direct to the Shah. It was just about manageable in normal times but an impossible structure to operate in a crisis, particularly if there was indecision at the head.

I wish, above all, that I had known that the Shah was suffering from chronic lymphocytic leukaemia. This had been diagnosed in April 1974 by the leading French haematologist, Professor Jean Bernard. He told the Shah that he had a blood complaint called Waldenstrom disease and deliberately did not mention cancer or leukaemia. At that stage he was told that he did not need treatment. Thereafter, the Shah was treated by a young French doctor, Georges Flandrin. Dr Flandrin is reported in William Shawcross' book, *The Shah's Last Ride*, as being convinced that the French Secret Service did not know. Nor, it is claimed, did the CIA, Mossad, SAVAK or MI6 ever know. Yet at one stage, the French Government did come to know. The French Foreign Minister, Louis de Guiringaud, who left office in 1978, was in London in late 1979, when I was no longer Foreign Secretary. Over dinner, he said that he had told me of the Shah's illness the year before. He was mistaken over this: no doctor would forget information like that. It would have triggered many things in my brain and I would have started to look at the Shah as a patient. But he was confirming that the French Government did know at least by the summer of 1978. If I had known of his illness, I would have been much keener to push my belief that the Shah should be persuaded to leave Tehran and a Regency appointed. If we had known he was ill, not only would that have provided the excuse for his departure but we might have realized sooner that we risked a repeat of 1953, with the Shah temperamentally unable to cope with a crisis.

Martial law was declared in Isfahan in August and the Shah promised further liberalization, saying that elections for a new Parliament due in June 1979 would be totally free and that bills would be presented to the National Assembly providing for free expression and assembly. The trouble was that no one believed it would be done. Then there was a very upsetting arson incident in the south-west city of Abadan which had an effect far beyond its local area.

If I had recognised, as I should have done that summer, that the Shah himself could not be the vehicle for the restoration of law and order, I would have urged Cy Vance to join me in pressurizing him to leave immediately. Also, I would have tried to persuade the US, France and Germany that the government which remained should have full technical help to keep the oil wells open and political support in terms of riot-control equipment in order to sustain themselves against strikes and street demonstrations. In retrospect, it was a mistake for Anthony Parsons to have taken an extended summer leave, for by the time he returned to Tehran in the middle of September bearing a message from the Prime Minister to the Shah, we had nearly lost any chance of influencing events. Holding the country off from revolution would have been difficult but possible that autumn if there had been an authoritative lead given either by the Shah or a Regent with his authority.

One of our major problems was in developing a united Western front. Even as late as October, the US Administration was split on such basic questions as whether or not to give the Iranian Government crowd-control devices. William Sullivan, their Ambassador in Tehran, and the State Department apparently opposed supply while Zbig Brzezinski wisely supported it. Brzezinski even alleges in his autobiography that the head of the Iran desk in the State Department was motivated by a doctrinal dislike of the Shah and simply wanted him out of power altogether. It is clear in retrospect that the estrangement between the White House and the State Department was even worse than I sensed it to be at the time.

Much debate has centred on whether the American stress on human rights had made the Shah act in ways that he would otherwise not have done. I doubt this, but anyhow believe that the question misses the more fundamental point that the Shah was by then an empty vessel. Was there any way that he could have been stiffened even if all our advice had tended towards his taking much tougher action? Knowing what I do now about the American Ambassador's views, I regret they were often asseverated in meetings with Anthony Parsons. I believe that the two men reinforced each other's reluctance to see any military clamp down. The British message was itself far from clear. We wanted decisive liberalization from a man who could not be decisive and was not liberal. Jean François-Poncet, Security Adviser to President Giscard d'Estaing and later, in 1978, Foreign Minister, thought by the end of October that the Shah was suffering from a crisis of will. He was right. Our problem was the Shah and yet we continued to see him as the person to restore authority. Instead, we should have vested his power in a Regent while he himself was persuaded to step aside. The Western democracies never really worked out how to bolster and demonstrate the determination and authority which should have stemmed from the Shah. For example, we ought to have discovered long before whether the Iranian Army would be able to keep the oil flowing if there was a strike on the oilfields. If we had concluded that they would be unable to preserve the flow of oil, we should have made a contingency plan to put outside experts into Iran. In the event, the virtual shutdown of the oilfields and the loss of revenue had a wildly disproportionate effect, because it came as a shock and deepened a growing sense of impotence. By the end of October 1978, oil production had fallen from 6 million to little more than 1 million barrels per day.

The Western democracies' stress on forming a coalition Government would only have worked if it had carried the full support of the military. It had to have a younger charismatic figure to head it up and they were in short supply: witness the succession of out-of-touch old people the Shah gathered around him. We needed to keep the Shah's authority, as represented by his office, intact in relation to the military. But that did not necessarily mean a military figure, as either Prime Minister or Regent. We needed someone with charisma who would only be in post for a few years, brave enough to make enemies, and ready later to step aside for the Shah's son as a constitutional monarch.

Sir Anthony Parsons was the subject of some UK press criticism when on his return to Tehran he said publicly that Britain was heartened by the Shah's determination to maintain stability and progress. It was fair comment but I told him to keep a low profile in future and let Ministers 'take the flak'. He saw the Shah on 29 September and specifically advised him to promise that free and fair elections would take place. The Embassy also contacted Ayatollah Shariatmadari, less radical than Khomeini, in Qom, informing him that the British Government still supported the Shah. Shariatmadari was in contact with the Shah during most of 1978 through his private financial adviser. We also arranged for a British expert in riot control to visit Tehran, but decided against having contact with Sadeq Qotbzadeh, one of Khomeini's entourage in Paris, and later Foreign Minister. On 10 October Jim Callaghan wrote a letter, which was deliberately publicized, saying that he could not see how countries which, like Britain, had urged the Shah to modernize the political process in Iran, could align themselves with those who now opposed modernization.

On 22 October a television interview, recorded with Brian Walden a week before, was transmitted. It was an object lesson about allowing an interview to be put in the can for later transmission. During that week the Shah's position had deteriorated and I would probably have toned down my comments. Brian, a friend who had been a fellow Labour MP, had come to Buttermere to do a general interview and it was only after this, relaxing over coffee in the kitchen, that I expressed my surprise that the new great cause of the far Left was the support of Khomeini and all he stood for in terms of turning the clock back. Brian asked me if I would put this on tape and I foolishly agreed. I argued in the interview that this was a situation where Britain could not hedge its bets, that one did not back off when one's friends were under attack and that, against the regional background, it would not be in our interests for the Shah to be deposed. I added that human rights in Iran would not be increased if Britain supported the fanatical Muslim element. It was a bravura perform-ance and the deterioration in human rights after the revolution showed its predictions to be correct in almost every particular but, to say the least, it was imprudent. It exacerbated feeling in the Labour Party and made Jim Callaghan even more hesitant about supporting the Shah.

The NEC sent a deputation to see me on 9 November. It was the first and only time I have encountered Neil Kinnock in a formal meeting. It also had a record of what was said. Otherwise we have exchanged pleasantries or the odd substantive sentence on aeroplanes to State funerals or at all-party functions. I regret this. But I suspect that only since 1989 has there been sufficient common grounds for us both to have been able to talk seriously and sadly history and circumstance combine to hold us apart. Neil Kinnock was reasonable, realistic and flattering. I was well known and admired, he said, as a proponent of human rights so they wanted to know why I had adopted my present position on Iran. In reply I emphasized that I remained unhappy about the human rights record but urged them to accept that if I were to make public what we were saying in private our influence would plummet to zero. Neil Kinnock thought that the Shah as an absolute monarch could concede more, that we should toughen up on arms sales and cancel the Queen's visit. He acknowledged Iran's strategic importance and saw the alternatives now available as either a hawkish reactionary Muslim government or an essentially unstable military regime, both of which would alarm the Soviet Union and be bad for relations with the West. The NEC delegation did not deny that our vital interests were engaged, with visible exports totalling £654 million, invisibles of the same order, export orders for four years and 100,000 jobs at stake. I felt they at least had their feet on the ground. It was obvious that there was more potential to Neil Kinnock than I had hithero recognized and I saw for the first time why Ted Rowlands was always referring to him as the rising figure in the Labour Party.

Cancelling the Queen's forthcoming visit to Iran was delicate. The trade union of monarchs has its rules, one of which is to stand by each other in times of difficulty. Deferral of her visit could only damage the Shah, and I was keen to hang on for longer than was politically convenient at home. I was strongly against making a premature decision, and so, even though No. 10 were keen to close down the option of her visit, I managed to keep it open until it was obvious to everyone, even in Tehran, that it could not go ahead.

In early November, Zbig Brzezinski telephoned the Shah saying that he did not know of a military government that had failed; it is often gleefully quoted against Brzezinski because General Azhari's government which followed was hopeless. But in fairness to Brzezinski, he never got the 'military government with the wraps off' which he had wanted, and by then anyhow it was probably too late. The mistake in Washington was to believe that a military clamp down had to come from a military government. The military, given a decisive lead, would have taken orders from any civilian who had been put in control by the Shah.

In late November the Americans made a very strange decision, bringing George Ball in as an outside adviser. He was a distinguished older man with a long liberal record and had formerly been a political appointment in the State Department. He had made his reputation as a dove over Vietnam. I thought at the time that Cy Vance was responsible for this appointment but Zbig Brzezinski admits that it was his mistake and that Ball's participation sharpened their internal disagreements and delayed basic choices. For us it certainly made the formulation of a coherent strategy with the United States virtually impossible. For the first time in my relationship with Cy Vance I found it difficult to get him to commit himself, and for crucial weeks in December American policy was on hold.

We did not lack local information at this time. I read eyewitness accounts of street demonstrations in Tasua which described a controlled situation, with slogans like 'We are Muslims not Marxists', and a readiness to halt abuse of the Shah so as not to overstep the limits of tolerance. By the next day I was reading accounts of far greater militancy in Ashara where the slogans were 'Yankee go home', 'Death to the Butcher Shah' and 'Power to Khomeini'. It was clearly turning into a true revolution and the revolutionary mood intensified daily.

By late December the situation was hopeless. I held an office meeting on 20 December and said that

> the Shah has not yet tried conducting a severe crack down and that might well be the last and only option. It would be very unpleasant politically for Britain if he did crack down but it might work in Iran where, given the absence of an alternative and the threat of chaos, there could be a greater acceptance of the ruthless exercise of power that we in the West could not easily imagine, let alone support.

I reaffirmed that I did not feel that I had been misled about Iran. We had been grossly over-committed economically but this had been a deliberate attempt to offset the oil price rise. I thought that we would get the worst of all possible worlds if we shifted policies now, but added that henceforward, 'we are not to advocate or be thought to be advocating solutions, nor should we become involved in advising the Shah or others about what they should do.' As for the BBC Persian Service, it was a liability in some ways but also a form of insurance with the internal opposition. I had taken a firm decision months earlier not to interfere with the BBC and was happy with this and felt we had this problem in its proper perspective.

Despite my decision not to advocate solutions on 29 December, I was cabled while in Algiers with a draft telegram suggesting some advice to Cy Vance. I had been attending President Boumedienne's funeral, which was an extraordinary experience. On the way to the funeral the roads were packed with people, mainly women, in black and wailing as is the tradition. Then, walking with a motley crew of Heads of State to the burial ground we heard a noise approaching in the distance. During the service the noise grew louder and louder until it became clear that a massive crowd had broken through the police cordon. The funeral service finished, perhaps was even shortened, and the VIPs scrambled, dignity abandoned, into their cars. On arriving at my aeroplane I read the cable. The Foreign Office wanted me to argue with Cy Vance against a military clamp down. I refused to send the telegram. I had decided that the causes and the cures for the present crisis lay in Iran. It was no longer for us in the West to intervene either way. As I had said with emphasis, at the earlier office meeting, in a confusing situation we should follow the old naval maxim, 'In a fog, slow right down but don't change course.'

Sir Anthony Parsons' departure on 15 January provided us in Britain with a threshold. We would not again have the same access or influence with the Shah. But nor did we want it. On 16 January the Shah left Tehran, flying first to see President Sadat in Egypt and then on to Morocco. The US gave backing to Prime Minister Bakhtiar while we in Britain steered clear. The CIA tried to establish a deal with Khomeini while also bringing in General Heyser, the Deputy Supreme Allied Commander in Europe. The street battles from 9 to 11 February scuppered any CIA hopes of a deal with Khomeini who returned to Tehran on 11 February. The streets filled with masses of people and the once proud Iranian Army simply collapsed. I recognized the new regime from the Royal Yacht in the Gulf, while the Queen was visiting Saudi Arabia.

Revolutionary committees were established all over the country. Anyone associated with the Shah's regime was dragged off to prison. The new Prime Minister, Mehdi Bazargan, was powerless to intervene. Summary trials were held and people publicly executed. The former Prime Minister, Hoveyda, was tried, sentenced to death and, in a matter of minutes, shot in the prison cell. *Paris Match* published a picture of his body with three revolutionaries, one of whom, full of smiles, was carrying a machine gun; alongside it was a photograph of one of the Shah's family swimming in the Bahamas.

The Shah had flown into the Bahamas in King Hassan's own Boeing 747 from Morocco because the United States and Britain had in effect refused him entry. In the middle of March, Cy Vance made what he called, 'One of the most distasteful recommendations I have ever had to make to the President', namely that the Shah should not come to the United States. With a similar sense of shame I had sent a note to Jim Callaghan that the Shah – who never formally applied to come – should be politely turned away. There was no honour in my decision, just the cold calculation of national interest. I had stuck to the Shah far longer than was good for my own position in domestic politics, but even so I felt it to be a despicable act. Given Britain's long history of offering political asylum, it was depressing that all but a few MPs now turned completely against the Shah. It was as if they were blind, on both Labour and Conservative benches, to what was bound to happen in Iran under the Ayatollah. On 20 February I made a statement recognizing the new Government. Unwisely, given the mood of the House, I said that I was prepared for our record of support for the Shah 'to be justified by history'. That was met with mirth and the cutting jibe from the Conservative MP, Sir Peter Tapsell, that 'history may have other things on its mind'. Yet the old adage 'He who laughs last, laughs loudest', was borne out. The passage of only a few years amply justified my stance and by then the criticism was not for defending the Shah but for letting him fall.

Margaret Thatcher, as Leader of the Opposition, got herself into a considerable mess with her off-the-record press briefing that the Government should be ashamed of itself for refusing the Shah admission, and her private promises to reverse our decision. As with her promise to recognize Bishop Muzorewa, she had to backtrack in Government. Instead of choosing to do so openly, thereby retaining some vestige of honour, she did it clandestinely. She sent Sir Denis Wright, the former Ambassador to Iran, to the Bahamas, travelling under a different name and passport. So, according to William Shawcross, it was as Edward Wilson that Sir Denis arrived at the Ocean Club in the Bahamas. It was a Mr Wilson who was called in by the Shah on 20 May for tea in his house on the beach. The Shah must have been full of contempt. The shabbiness was further compounded because the British Government wanted to be able to say, if asked, that the Shah accepted and understood the decision not to grant him asylum. It was an added humiliation to heap on the Shah, but he apparently accepted the British decision on the condition that we would acknowledge that he had never formally applied to come to Britain. He wrote in his autobiography, 'I have a longstanding suspicion of British intent and British policy which I have never found reason to alter.' In the circumstances, it was not too harsh a judgement.

In March 1980 the Shah flew to Egypt at the brave and generous invitation of President Sadat. He died in Cairo on 27 July 1980. At the state funeral were Richard Nixon and the American and French Ambassadors. Britain sent its Chargé d'Affaires.

18

FOREIGN SECRETARY – 1979

With Iran on the threshold of revolution and with the Soviet Union building up their strategic missile force and deploying more and more intermediate SS-20 missiles targeted on Western Europe, it was urgent for the West to be seen to be responding with firmness and retaining its unity. The dismay and confusion over the neutron bomb had to be put behind us and a new cohesion established.

In early January Jim Callaghan, President Carter, Helmut Schmidt and President Giscard d'Estaing held a meeting in Guadeloupe. For the first time Jim formally raised with Carter the question of replacing Polaris with Trident. He was assured that Carter could see no objection to transferring this technology to the United Kingdom. There are many people in the Labour Party who have accused Jim Callaghan of defying the Labour Party's manifesto commitment which was not to replace Polaris. There is no truth in this allegation. He never committed a future Labour Government but he also prudently never allowed the delay in calling the election to interfere with the timetable for necessary decisions about Polaris's replacement. Encouraged by the Secretary to the Cabinet, Sir John Hunt, Jim used his friendship with Jimmy Carter over Trident in much the same way that Harold Macmillan had used his personal relationship with President Kennedy over Polaris. This meant that when Margaret Thatcher came into office she found awaiting her a minute written that very day by Jim Callaghan authorizing her to see all his correspondence with President Carter on the future of the nuclear deterrent. He also made available to her the comprehensive report by officials, received in December, on the various options we had commissioned and discussed for continuing Britain's independent nuclear deterrent. That was honourable conduct.

President Carter had made it clear at Guadeloupe that he would only agree to fund the Pershing 1 missile replacement and ground-launched cruise missiles if he could be sure that the European nations would agree to them being deployed on their territory later. Then Helmut Schmidt developed the argument that Germany could not take cruise missiles alone and that at least one other European nation would have to accept cruise missiles on its territory. Carter replied to the three European Heads of Government that he would discuss with Brezhnev the build up of the Soviet SS-20s and that he would open negotiations about these, as well as American nuclear forces already in Europe, but that the negotiations would have to be predicated on the fact that some of the US systems were going to be modernized and that he was not going to accept a ban on modernization during the negotiations.

A study had been initiated in NATO much earlier, and made public at the time, to look at five options: modernizing Pershing 1; building a new intermediate ground-launched missile; deploying cruise missiles at sea, or in the air, or on the land. The eventual decision to go for land-based missiles was emerging as part of NATO's collective decision-making during the spring of 1979. No final decision was taken during the period of the Labour Government but the planning assumption at official level seemed to be moving towards land-based missiles, mainly because it was felt that sea-basing did not have as much potential for binding the US global deterrent into Europe. I favoured sea-basing because it was far less provocative in terms of public opinion and also avoided the 'use or lose' risk of forward deployment.

After Guadeloupe Jim Callaghan flew into London Airport and tried to defuse the atmosphere of crisis that had built up over the various public sector strikes. The words, 'Crisis, what crisis?', which he never actually used, were pinned on him and, fairly or unfairly, his avuncular image was transformed into complacency. Meanwhile, Debbie was in St Thomas's Hospital awaiting the birth of our third child. I was due to have lunch with Felipe González and called into the labour ward around noon. The midwife said the delivery would not be until the afternoon and that it was fine for me to go to lunch. Fortunately, I felt and timed Debbie's contractions and, although by then my knowledge of obstetrics was pretty thin, it seemed to me she could be delivered quite quickly. I stayed and, soon after 1 o'clock, on 18 January 1979 she had a girl, whom the boys later decided should be called Lucy. I could not have had better lunch partners than the Spaniards who love children, and we drank many toasts. I suspect it was a long time since Carlton Gardens had had such a riotous party.

Debbie was thrilled to have a girl for she had been convinced that this is what I had wanted. Months before, we had announced in Plymouth that she was expecting another child and much to our surprise the national press had failed to pick it up. A few weeks later, she was talking to Simon Jenkins, then editor of the *Evening Standard* and a good friend, and happened to mention that she was pregnant. Simon, ever alert for a story, asked whether it had appeared in the press and when Debbie said no, he asked if she would mind if he ran it in the *Evening Standard*. A few hours later I emerged from No. 10 to see an *Evening Standard* news stand, for in those days the public had access to Downing Street, and the big headline, 'OWEN WANTS A GIRL', which prompted Harold Lever to dig me in the ribs and say, 'What's new about that?'

Neither China nor Hong Kong were dominant issues during my period in office, but I was determined to do all I could to continue the improvement in relations with China. For some time they had been interested in establishing closer links between our armed forces, and at the end of April 1978 Air Chief Marshal Sir Neil Cameron, the Chief of the Defence Staff, visited Beijing. He made a speech which was widely quoted in the British press saying that he looked forward to closer co-operation with the Chinese armed forces against their common enemy, Moscow. The Left in the Labour Party were outraged and I had to speak at a May Day rally in Birmingham in the midst of the controversy. I also gave interviews in which I gently indicated that we did not see our good relations with China as being at the expense of the Soviet Union. Tony Benn raised the issue in Cabinet the following Thursday, taking exception to defining the Soviet Union as the common enemy. There was no general mood of antagonism to what Cameron had said in the Cabinet room, though many thought it could have been better phrased.

The more controversial decision we made was to agree in principle to selling Harrier jump jets to China. The Left on the NEC of the Labour Party repeatedly objected to this but Eric Varley, who saw the trade advantages, was helpful in getting it through Cabinet. All along I doubted whether China would actually purchase any Harriers, for with space for airfields no problem, their motive seemed to be political rather than military. What the Chinese wanted to establish was that we were ready to sell sophisticated arms to them which we would not sell to the Soviet Union. They wanted a demonstrably and qualitatively different relationship to that which we had with the Soviet Union. I could see much merit in agreeing to this, particularly since I hoped it would make them more receptive to some of the ideas we were developing over Hong Kong. The Chinese were showing signs of moving towards a market economy, in contrast to the Soviet Union, and though neither gave any evidence of endorsing moves towards democracy I felt generally more hopeful about China.

In early 1979 the Chinese came to an agreement with the Portuguese over Macao that sovereignty would pass to China, though Macao would continue under Portuguese administration. I felt that it was a good time to open a tentative dialogue with the Chinese over Hong Kong. I therefore arranged to visit Beijing on 12 April as part of a longer trip to the Far East. As a preliminary to my visit, it was agreed that the Governor of Hong Kong should visit Beijing and on 30 March he met the Vice-Premier, Deng Xiaoping.

The Governor of Hong Kong was then Sir Murray MacLehose, whom

I had urged to stay on beyond retirement because he generated much trust in Hong Kong and respect in Beijing. I had come to value his judgement after dealing with him over cases involving alleged corruption in the Hong Kong Police. After a big trial, in which a number of policemen were found guilty, there were still further charges outstanding on an even larger number of policemen. The Governor felt that it would be destructive of morale and damaging to his task of maintaining law and order if these trials went ahead and he wanted me to use my powers under an old colonial statute to amnesty them. The Foreign Office lawyers were adamant that, in order to avoid being challenged in the courts, I had personally to review each case. So for a few weeks a desk in my room was piled high with thick files relating to individual policemen in Hong Kong and I had to flick through them, observing the ritual, reviewing each case personally. Eventually, with some trepidation, the amnesty was announced and it caused not a cheep of protest in the House of Commons and not much more in Hong Kong. Thereafter, I treated the Governor's advice with even more respect.

The problem looming over Hong Kong was that the bulk of the territory had been leased from China in 1898 under an agreement which expired in 1997. The business community in Hong Kong were extremely anxious about what was to happen to these New Territories. The Chinese Government recognized none of what they called the Unequal Treaties and, in theory at least, made no distinction between those parts of the colony which we considered to be ceded to us in perpetuity – Hong Kong Island and the small area of Kowloon. As relations with China improved, we hoped that they might be ready to come to some understanding which would allow the status quo in Hong Kong to continue.

At Sir Murray MacLehose's meeting with Deng Xiaoping, Deng said that he regarded Hong Kong as part of China and that one day China would wish to make political changes. He could not say whether this would be before 1997 or even as late as the next century but, whatever happened, special arrangements would be made to maintain living standards and guarantee investments. In a famous phrase, he invited the Governor when dealing with investors in Hong Kong 'to put their hearts at ease'. The Governor explained that, although assurances like this were very welcome and helpful, they were of too general application to ease the short-term anxieties that existed about land leases. The problem which the Hong Kong Government faced was that all individual leases for land in the New Territories ended in 1997 and we could not grant leases beyond that point without special legal authority. He told Deng Xiaoping that, with leases getting steadily shorter and shorter, investors were becoming increasingly concerned about the legal limitations set on their period of ownership. The British Government felt that it would be helpful to remove this legal limit and that the best way was to remove the date from all existing leases and to issue new leases without a fixed date.

We wanted to act in a way that would maintain confidence in investment without undermining China's long-standing position on Hong Kong. It was not clear if Deng Xiaoping had actually grasped what the Governor had said. He did not specifically endorse the ideas put to him over the leases but neither did he reject them. A general election was called two days before the Governor's meeting in Beijing so my trip had to be cancelled and I never decided on what follow-up action to take. Had I gone to Beijing as planned, I had intended to reinforce what had already been said on the leases and leave behind a speaking note.

I had a clear view in my mind how I hoped to deal with the Chinese but I knew we could only move as fast as they were ready to travel. A favourite adage of mine is 'Jump your fences one by one.' The Chinese later in 1979 rejected, at official level, doing anything about the leases. But they might have shown more willingness to tackle the issue if I had been able to engage Deng Xiaoping's mind over the problem that April. If so, I would have been ready to move with him into uncharted waters. The lawyers had also wanted the Governor to raise the question of his powers, for they felt that there was a potential legal problem if the Chinese were ever to agree to let the Governor administer the New Territories beyond 1997. They argued that they needed an Order in Council on a purely permissive basis to allow continued administration under British law if the Chinese Government wished. I was very wary about this particular option. It seemed very legalistic and, if we ever reached that stage, I could not see who would challenge any continued administration by the Governor or any other body. I therefore decided that the Governor should not raise the need for an Order in Council in Beijing or even hint at any potential legal problem.

There were many options open if Deng Xiaoping was to contemplate the status quo going beyond 1997. I have always been convinced that it is in China's fundamental interests to maintain a stable, prosperous Hong Kong far into the next century. Only a perceived threat of Hong Kong's acting as a subversive element would change that self-interest assessment in Beijing. It would help if the problem over the leases could be resolved, but it was not vital. In theory we would be able to glide from 1997 to 1998 without any formalities. But the confidence factor, indefinable and yet so crucial, would be better sustained if we could ensure a formula whereby the present administration of Hong Kong was guaranteed for a specified period, which could be rolled forward each year.

In my mind, a viable option would have been to consider letting China have formal sovereignty over all the territory in Hong Kong well before 1997. On world maps Hong Kong would be part of China, but in return they would guarantee in international law that the existing administration would continue at least until 1997. Then that agreement would be subject to annual renewal from the date of signing so it could roll forward from 1997 to 1998 to 1999 and into the next century. As far as I know, these ideas were never tried out on the Chinese Government by the incoming Conservative Government and our Ambassador in Beijing, Sir Percy Craddock, only raised the proposal on the leases that summer; and this, I gather, was politely but firmly rejected by the Chinese. There was, however, no upset in our relations, and the issue of what was going to happen after 1997 then lay dormant for three years. This is the sensible answer to the argument that the Governor's visit to Beijing in March 1979 was a dramatic threshold in Anglo-Chinese relations over Hong Kong. All the evidence is to the contrary and that threshold was crossed only when Margaret Thatcher visited Beijing after the Falklands War in the summer of 1982. It was then that the sovereignty question, in the charged circumstances surrounding her visit, began to sour. It was then that Deng Xiaoping made it quite clear that China was determined to assume full sovereignty and administer Hong Kong after 1997. The subsequent negotiations, conducted by Sir Geoffrey Howe, were probably the best that Britain could by then hope to achieve. But I will always wonder what would have happened if I had been able to keep to my schedule and visit Beijing in April. Given the precedent of February 1979, when the Chinese agreed to Macao remaining under Portuguese administration, and the extremely good relations which we had established by 1979 in the wake of the Harrier decision, it just might have been possible to have nudged Deng Xiaoping to embark together on a conceptually different settlement involving a transfer of sovereignty, but accompanied by a renewable administrative tenure agreement.

I was only a bystander in the Cabinet during the Winter of Discontent, for I was not a member of the Civil Contingency Unit which was meeting constantly at Ministerial level as well as at official level. My only input was that I could not accept the arguments against declaring a state of emergency. Clearly this was what Jim wanted, and indeed at Cabinet on 18 January I thought that it had been agreed. I did intervene to say that it was psychologically necessary, for the public expected it and simply did not understand the technical arguments that all the powers necessary to use troops and commandeer ambulances already existed. Jim's authority inside the Government was by this time greatly reduced, and it was people like John Silkin with his T&GWU links who seemed able to block the declaration of a state of emergency.

On Thursday 1 February the health service unions and the local authority unions were on strike, and Jim was well aware that indiscipline and what I described as thuggery were threatening the Government. He sadly felt unable to do what I think he knew he should, namely go on television and demonstrate that he had had enough. At this stage we were not even able to bury the dead and ambulances were failing to pick up patients. If Jim had expressed his disgust on television it could have been very powerful. Most people in the country knew of his gut sympathy with the trade union movement, so if ever he placed the whole authority of his office on the line and denounced the strikers I had little doubt that their action could be made ineffective. Jim admitted, rather poignantly at one stage, that there was not a single night when he did not consider going on television but then asked himself if anything would be different next day. I felt he underestimated his own personal authority and the strength of the office he held. It was a very distressing time for me in Cabinet. Because I was slightly distanced from the day-to-day handling of events, I saw perhaps more clearly that we were witnessing the terminal stages of the Government. In a strange way, Jim knew it too. I felt that he had resigned himself to electoral defeat and only had one objective, the perfectly honourable one of keeping the Labour Party together. He, like so many of his generation, was haunted by the mythology that surrounded the figure of Ramsay MacDonald, and dreaded the thought of breaking the Labour Party. Like the captain of a ship that had lost its mast and whose crew were injured, he just wanted to get his ship to port without sinking. It was difficult to isolate our domestic position from our standing in international affairs. In Rhodesia the situation was still not ripe for a negotiated settlement, but if we had held a Lancaster House conference that winter the perception of a government losing its authority at home would have had an impact in the conference as it would only have confirmed Smith's wish to hang on in the hope of being able to manipulate a new Conservative Government. Foreign policy, to be effective, needs the clout of a government that is looking assured and confident at home.

On 1 March, St David's Day, the referenda on devolution were held in Scotland and Wales. It was the moment when the fate of the Government was sealed, and in many respects deservedly so. Devolution had not been adopted by Labour out of conviction but out of expediency. Regrettably, many people within the Party did not truly believe in it. Devolution was a political reaction to the appeal of the Nationalists. The refusal even to consider proportional representation seriously for the Scottish Parliament, which could have kept the Lib-Lab Pact going at no great price, left many convinced devolutionists fearing that, in some future political circumstances, the Scottish Nationalists might hold an overall majority. In Wales, devolution was rejected by four to one. In Scotland, though there was a small majority in favour, it did not jump the 40 per cent hurdle under the Devolution Act. The Government now had to table Repeal Orders and it was clear that we could not ask loyal MPs in the North-East who had disliked devolution all along to vote down the Order for Scotland.

On 28 March the Scottish National Party tabled a Motion of Censure and the Conservative Party gave it their support. We could have squeezed through by promising a gas pipeline to Northern Ireland, but Jim Callaghan drew the line at this. He did, however, accept the speeding-up of the promised legislation to give compensation to state quarrymen suffering from lung disease and this ensured the votes of the Welsh Nationalists. Gerry Fitt, from the SDLP, who objected to the increased number of MPs in Northern Ireland, voted against. He had been wooed assiduously by Airey Neave, the Conservative spokesman on Northern Ireland, tragically to be blown up by the IRA a few days later. We went down by 311 votes to 310, the first time since 1924 that a Motion of No Confidence in the Government of the day had been lost. As I passed Jim's room behind the Speaker's Chair after the vote, he called me in, leaving Roger Stott outside. 'Will you be all right in Devonport?' he asked anxiously. Considerate to the last, Jim was nevertheless not speaking like a man confident of victory at the polls. If he was worried about Devonport, he felt we were heading for defeat. At Cabinet next morning we all felt it was sensible to coincide the general election with voting for the council elections on 3 May. Then Jim went to the Palace to ask the Queen to dissolve Parliament.

On Tuesday 3 April, with Debbie, I went to Windsor Castle for dinner and to spend the night. It was a delightful evening. Jim and Audrey Callaghan, unexpectedly, were also present, which made it very special for both of us and it was a time to thank him for all his support during my time as Foreign Secretary. The Queen ensured that elections were the last thing any of us thought about, and after dinner the Queen's Librarian showed each of us an item of special historic interest to us personally. Next morning Debbie and I walked through Windsor Park before returning to London when Parliament was formally dissolved.

On the Friday we had an eight-hour joint meeting of the Cabinet with the NEC for the final drafting of the manifesto. I successfully opposed the anti-marketeers, making a commitment to repeal Section 2(1) of the 1972 European Communities Act by which Community Instruments take effect directly as law in the member states. They knew, and they were right, that a change in the direct applicability would put us in breach of our treaty obligations and on a collision course with our European partners. By contrast, making Ministers accountable to the House of Commons prior to forming any commitment in the Council of Ministers is a perfectly reasonable element of democratic accountability, though it is wise to preserve some degree of flexibility for Ministers in negotiating. I was also very worried about the wording over a replacement for Polaris. I was sent a note before the meeting to say that Fred Mulley wanted the nuclear section to read:

> Since 1974 we have renounced any intention of moving towards the production of a new generation of nuclear weapons or to a successor to the Polaris nuclear force *which will remain effective into the 1990s; we still believe this may be the best course for Britain.* But many great issues affecting our allies and the world are involved, and we believe there must be a full and informed debate about them, and a balanced appraisal of all the relevant considerations, including cost and arms

control factors as well as our security interest and our contributions to
NATO, before Parliament makes a final decision in a few years' time.

I supported Fred Mulley, but the all-important italicized words disappeared in the various drafting sessions, to be replaced, after 'the Polaris
nuclear force', by 'We reiterate our belief that this is the best course for
Britain.' That flatly contradicted the view that we did need to replace
Polaris, expressed by the four of us involved in nuclear decisions. To this
day I have never understood why Jim acquiesced. I think he was just too
weary to have another row. Instead he wasted valuable ammunition
shooting down the proposed abolition of the Lords, a trivial issue by
comparison.

During the election campaign in Plymouth I realized for the first time
how unpopular the Left wing of the Labour Party, and particularly Tony
Benn, had become. Though I had been scrupulous in keeping my advice
bureaux, my hectic schedule and particularly foreign travel meant that I
was more out of touch with the grass roots opinion in the consituency
than I would have liked. Whereas the Left had always been tolerated in
the Labour Party, I found that many traditional Labour voters,
particularly those working in the dockyard, now saw and described the
Left as communists. They did not mince their words about them either.
The Winter of Discontent had brought out a new mood of personal
bitterness in politics.

A distinctive feature was the racial backlash which I felt for the first
time in Plymouth. People from Rhodesia canvassing for the Conservatives
heightened press interest. A nasty, vicious card which had a letter from
another Dr Owen claiming I was responsible for a terrorist attack in
Rhodesia with a picture of a woman dead, and probably having been
raped, with her dead child by her side, was pushed through the door of
every council house in my constituency. It was despicable and I felt its
effect on the doorstep. The *Sun* ran a centre-page spread on 'Dr Smug'
and on that day of all days copies of the *Daily Mirror* missed the train to
Plymouth. Distributing my own leaflets at 6 a.m. at the dockyard gate, I
felt as if every single person took a copy of the *Sun*. Debbie was more
relaxed, saying no one would read its highly personalized attacks, but
they would like the photographs. Sure enough, in telephone calls to the
office, if the article was mentioned, it was only to say, 'lovely picture of
David in the *Sun* today'. Newspapers are not as powerful in swinging
votes as politicians think.

In Plymouth, and when I travelled to speak elsewhere in the country, I
never, throughout the campaign, believed that a Labour Government
would be returned. We started 13 per cent behind in the opinion polls
and, though slowly improving, the gap never went below 2 per cent and
realistically never looked as though it was below 4 per cent. The Winter
of Discontent hung over us like a dark cloud and justly. Unlike 1970,

when I had completely misjudged the public mood, this time I felt it was against us from the beginning to the end and at times I was certain of losing in Devonport. But despite the very adverse swing against Labour in the South-West, I managed to hold on to my seat by 1,001 votes.

When I woke up late on Friday morning, though the election was lost, results were still coming in and I was still Her Majesty's Principal Secretary of State for Foreign and Commonwealth Affairs. Then I saw on television the outgoing Prime Minister, Jim Callaghan, driving to Buckingham Palace to see the Queen. I rang the Foreign Office and sent a farewell message to every Embassy in the world to thank them for all their past service. It was to be the last of hundreds of thousands of telegrams to end with the name 'Owen'. I was no longer a Minister of the Crown. No further telegrams would come from around the world for decision at all times of the day and night. No more despatch boxes, no Cabinet papers, no intelligence reports. The scrambler telephone could be taken away and personal protection was needed no longer. I suggested to the detectives that they should go back to London and thanked them for all their kindness, patience and courtesy. They had, after all, been ready to risk their lives for mine.

I climbed into my car and for the first time for nearly two-and-a-half years, drove alone through the streets of Devonport, without either a detective beside me or a police car following. I sang at the top of my voice; strangely, my predominant feeling was one of freedom – freedom to be alone, freedom to decide what to do with the rest of the day, freedom to be with my family. I planned a bicycle ride with my boys, just us three. Gradually, as the hours passed, other emotions crowded in, including regret at so much unfinished business. As I listened to the news on the radio, there was a feeling of detachment now that the events unfolding were outside one's influence or control. I felt sadness at leaving people who had become friends – private secretaries, detectives, drivers, diplomats. The telephone rang as I watched the *Nine O'Clock News* showing Mrs Thatcher entering No. 10 for the first time. It was Cy Vance, the US Secretary of State – the first of many Foreign Ministers ringing or writing as old friends. As I put the receiver down I felt tears come to my eyes for he had been a true friend. The world of modern diplomacy is tough and exacting; there is a tremendous amount of travelling, but it is not impersonal. I had forged close friendships, built up through hours of working closely together, whether in New York, Africa or Brussels.

One thing remained constant; I was still the MP for Devonport, and this was the post I valued most of all. The telephone rang as if to reinforce this. It was a constituency problem, a young mother separated from her husband and wanting to find a flat so that she could bring her children out of temporary care. The day that had started in the early hours with the count going on in the Guildhall, ended with my parents, wife and children, sitting around the fire at the family home in Plymouth. A whole new life of Opposition now opened up. Despite the disappointment of losing a Labour Government, I comforted myself with thinking how different it would have been if I had lost Devonport. That would have left an unfillable gap. I would have felt empty, bruised and battered.

Defeat had come as no surprise to Jim Callaghan, for the defeatist mood which I had detected the night that we lost the censure vote was there throughout the campaign. His senior policy adviser, Bernard Donoughue, recalls near to polling day encouraging Jim with poll figures showing that Labour might just squeak through. Jim turned to him and said quietly:

> I should not be too sure. You know there are times, perhaps once every thirty years, when there is a sea-change in politics. It then does not matter what you say or what you do. There is a shift in what the public wants and what it approves of. I suspect there is now such a sea-change – and it is for Mrs Thatcher.

PART FOUR

LEAVING LABOUR

19

THE SHADOW CABINET

'Where there is discord may we bring harmony ... Where there is despair may we bring hope.' With these words of St Francis of Assisi, Margaret Thatcher stepped across the threshold of No. 10 Downing Street on Friday 4 May 1979. Despite having been personally well behind Jim Callaghan in all the polls, she had just won a stunning victory. A 7 per cent swing to the Conservatives had given them 339 MPs, Labour only 269, the Liberals 11, the Ulster parties 12 and the Nationalists 4. With an overall majority of forty-three, she had that most precious asset, a secure parliamentary majority, something which Jim Callaghan never achieved. It was soon apparent that she intended to use it to start a decade of radicalism that would shake the innate conservatism of this country to its foundations.

That weekend I talked to Peter Jay on the telephone. As he was about to speak to Jim, I said I hoped Jim would resign immediately. I could see no advantage in his hanging on as Leader of the Party in Opposition, he had done his best but he would be blamed for defeat. If he went now, he could go with dignity and hand over to Denis Healey. Peter promised to pass on my views and I did not attempt to intrude any further. Yet, by Wednesday 10 May, when the old Cabinet met in the suite of rooms allocated to the Leader of the Opposition, it was clear that Jim intended to stay on as Leader. Michael Foot proposed, later that morning, that Jim should be re-elected Leader by the Parliamentary Labour Party, PLP, and he hoped that it would be unanimous. No one dissented.

The next day, Tony Benn announced that he was not going to stand for the Shadow Cabinet. I thought his decision wise. Throughout my time in the Cabinet, he had been totally out of sympathy with his colleagues and his relationship with Jim was tetchy. He was correct to choose the freedom of the back benches. Rather selfishly, I also thought that it would make it easier for me to get elected to the Shadow Cabinet. However, Tony's decision also had a significant drawback. The Left would now have a redoutable activist as its leader. Tony, unfettered and in Opposition, would be far more formidable than he had ever been in government and his position on the NEC and his appeal in the constituencies gave him a growing power base. Tony's critics were mistaken about him. He was not mad, nor was he a simple militant purist ideologue. He was a deeply ambitious politician whose ambition was harnessed to a superficial intellect and a total lack of proportion.

The following Wednesday the PLP met and we started a messy post mortem on Labour's defeat. It was tense at times but it was not bitter and Jim, winding up the debate, tried to rally the PLP, urging it to look forward and give leadership to the Party in the country, quoting an old Chinese proverb, 'A fish rots from the head.' This was far too simplistic an analysis. The Labour Party was suffering from two interlocking problems. The first was at the top of the Party and it was intellectual. The Keynesian Revolution had run out of steam – instead of maintaining full employment, it had produced high unemployment and inflation at the same time. It also offered no response to increasingly flexible patterns of production, to demands for lower taxation and individual's aspiration for higher material standards as well as greater freedom, let alone to the crisis of confidence in British industry. The Labour Left moved into this intellectual gap by accepting the analysis of decline, aggressively argued by the Conservative Right as well, but putting the blame on insufficiently strong government intervention in the economy and proposing this time to take control of the commanding heights of the economy. Their recipe was more not less state socialism. There was no adequate response to the Labour Left from the Centre or Right of the Labour Party. Exhausted after years in government and intellectually demoralized, they were content to fight a defensive battle. The second and associated problem was an organizational one affecting the body of the Party. As the trade unions continued the revolt against the Party leadership that had started with the winter of strikes, the Centre retreated and started to compromise itself out of existence. Organizations like the Militant Tendency had spread their tentacles and built up their strength in the constituencies. There was little resistance as first the key office-holding positions in the constituencies changed hands and then the very nature of the constituency General Management Committees was altered to reflect activist priorities; the politics of minority interests began to flourish.

Any counter-attack would depend on the capacity to develop new ideas as well as provide organizational support. The Campaign for Labour Victory (CLV) had been formed in February 1977 as a grass roots organization to complement the Manifesto Group inside the Parliamentary Party. Of the Cabinet Ministers, Bill Rodgers had been the main force behind it. I had supported CLV, but now I started to give it more time and energy. It had many problems associated with lack of money but it was also insufficiently geared to winning the battle of ideas.

No sooner was the General Election over than it was time to fight the first direct elections for the European Parliament. This provided the Labour Left with an opportunity, which they seized, to shift the policy of the Party, with the NEC controlling the Euro-manifesto. There was little enthusiasm within Labour for the elections and the Conservatives, with their morale high, grabbed their opportunity to score a second victory. Polling took place on Thursday 7 June and counting, Europe-wide, took place on the Sunday. I spoke in different parts of the country, but it was an apathetic campaign. On Monday 4 June in Bradford and in Halifax I claimed that the Labour Party was the most 'unequivocally non-federalist of all the parties fighting in the election.' That was not without justification since the Conservatives had yet to discover their identity on Europe under Margaret Thatcher and were still Heathite. I added, however, that 'in arguing against the supranational federal Europe it is not necessary to pour scorn on the noble idea which it incorporates.' Then, speaking in Beeston, Derbyshire, on Tuesday 5 June, I argued that 'the sensible development of the European Monetary System has been bedevilled by a large dose of Euro-rhetoric and Euro-vision'. The visionaries had wanted monetary union and a common currency but their aspirations had been wholly unrealistic and it had soon become clear that the most that Germany was prepared to support was a widening of the existing membership of the 'Snake', accompanied by minor but useful changes. Instead of accepting this, I argued, the zealots had then ensured that this modest package was grandly named the European Monetary System and invested in it all the aura and significance of monetary union. So the debate had become unnecessarily polarized, with the EMS depicted by the anti-federalists as an inevitable step towards inevitable monetary union rather that what it was, a necessary step towards the sensible objective of greater currency stability.

Driving between the two speaking engagements on that fine June afternoon, I spent a few hours alone in the Peak District walking along a railway line transformed into one of the most sensational walks in England. I have often returned but have never quite recaptured the beauty of that day or the peace it gave me for reflection. It was there that I decided that, be my political life long or short, henceforth I was going to be true to myself and not repeat the miserable experience of our last time in Opposition, from 1970–74, when I had compromised so much that I had begun to loathe politics and despise myself.

It is hard to understand if you do not come from the West Country, with its strong non-conformist tradition and respect for the Liberal Party, the traumatic effect of Jeremy Thorpe's trial at the Old Bailey in the middle of May. Saturation coverage of the committal proceedings in Minehead during the previous December and now the whole saga coming out again ensured that it was a long drawn out embarrassment for the Liberal Party. The revelations about unsavoury financial dealings within the Party over many years were particularly unpleasant. And it was not just Jeremy Thorpe – also involved as a key witness was Peter Bessell, who had been a Liberal MP in the West Country, representing Bodmin from 1964–70. The effect on West Country Liberalism was considerable. The protracted trial made a dreadful background to the Liberal Party campaign for the European Elections and, not surprisingly, they did very badly.

The European campaign moved my thinking a little further on electoral reform and I was openly campaigning for proportional representation for the European Assembly. However, I was still not ready to concede the case for proportional representation for Westminster, even though my experience in Europe as Foreign Secretary meant that I had no fear of coalition government. In answering letters, I said that the difference between the two elections was that we faced immense distortion in the European elections because of the small number of very big constituencies, while in the general election there were eight times as many constituencies, allowing a much better chance of getting a more accurate spread of opinion. I did not have a closed mind on the need for electoral reform at Westminster, but at that time I did not believe that the disadvantages of the current system were sufficient to justify a change. Broadly speaking, I believed our system, with coalitions within the existing parties rather than coalition between them, had served us reasonably well. In the European elections, where there was no legislative or executive authority at stake, the need for a decisive voice was not so marked. I also believed that the case for proportional representation was particularly strong for Scottish and Welsh Assemblies, if and when they were established, and that once the European Parliamentary elections had been conducted under PR it would be possible to make a judgement about whether there was any need for a change at Westminster.

Two days after the Euro-election result, Sir Geoffrey Howe presented his first budget. Despite his having said on 21 April in a general election press release, 'We have absolutely no intention of doubling VAT', and Margaret Thatcher's saying on 23 April at a Conservative press conference 'We have no intention of doubling VAT', VAT was raised from 8 per cent to 15 per cent. No wonder people despair of finding honesty in politics, but it was, apart from misleading the electorate, a wise choice. It brought in substantial revenues and gave the Government the necessary cushioning to make progressive cuts in income tax thereafter. The standard rate of income tax was only cut by 3p in the pound, but the upper rate of tax was very sensibly reduced from 83 per cent to 60 per cent. At such a high confiscatory level, few were paying and the effect on those who did was stultifying. Yet the disadvantage was that on the Government's own estimate they were adding nearly 4 per cent to the cost of living and they forecast that inflation would now reach a maximum of 17 per cent from the 10.3 per cent level when the Labour Government left office.

In mid June the results of the Shadow Cabinet elections were announced. Denis Healey topped the poll, but with John Silkin and Peter Shore, committed anti-marketeers, coming second and third respectively, it was not hard to see trouble looming on that front. Peter Shore had not been on the slate of either the Tribune group or the Centre-Right and, as the only candidate elected without being on a slate, he had done particularly well. I was elected, coming tenth with Roy Mason and John Smith below me, and Eric Heffer the runner-up. Ian Aitken, political editor of the *Guardian*, commented that it surprised many of my colleagues that I was still on the ladder, but undoubtedly Roy Hattersley, who had come fourth, was the best placed of all of us in the Manifesto Group. Bill Rodgers, who had come eighth, was given Defence, which pleased both him and me. I interpreted it as a welcome sign that Jim did not intend any backtracking. When I saw Jim Callaghan after the result it came as no surprise that I was not going to shadow Foreign Affairs. I was quite happy that he offered me Energy since it would involve me in economic questions while keeping a foothold in international affairs. In addition, with Jim's help, I was appointed to the TUC-Labour Party Liaison Committee, a good way to meet members of the TUC General Council. It was a body which Jim hoped, in Opposition, would become as important as the NEC, if not more so.

Revealingly, when Jim spoke to me about the Foreign Affairs portfolio, he made it clear that the reason he wanted to appoint Peter Shore to shadow Foreign Affairs was because he wanted the Parliamentary Party to have a choice in the leadership election and Peter needed international experience if the Party was going to see him as a credible challenger. In this way, although he was at pains to point out that he had no preference, he showed his own doubts about Denis as Leader. He said that he thought that Michael Foot would not want to be Leader and he seemed to be building up Peter to take Michael's place as leader of the Centre-Left. His doubts about Denis were not new to me; I had picked them up on a number of occasions in the past. I also knew Jim liked Peter and recognized in him his own robust patriotism. It had been noticeable in the Cabinet how much Jim bothered to ensure that he carried Peter's support and now he was giving him a chance to shine.

In fact, as it turned out, it was another promotion that in the long run determined the leadership of the Party. Neil Kinnock, who had failed to get on the Shadow Cabinet, was made Shadow Education Spokesman. Previously Jim had offered him a junior Ministerial post which he had refused, but now it was sensible to give his career a boost and to try and detach him from the Left, particularly since he had been elected to the NEC for the first time in 1978. It was also a way for Jim to keep Michael Foot happy, for he had always been a strong supporter of Neil Kinnock.

The scene was set for a battle for control of the Labour Party. On

Wednesday 11 July the Parliamentary Party met to discuss changes to the Labour Party Constitution, which had already been published and were known as the Benn-Heffer proposals. Tony Benn introduced them, and as so often with him, they ranged from the deadly serious to the trivial, with no real connecting strand other than to rub Jim's nose in the dirt. The most serious was the proposal to change Clause 5 so as to give the NEC the final say on the election manifesto, ending the veto of the Cabinet or Shadow Cabinet. Benn and Heffer also wanted all staff, including personal aides and research assistants, to be employed by the Party organization, an indirect attack on the Leader of the Parliamentary Party and members of the Shadow Cabinet. The Left's resentment, not widely shared, was over the way in which the PLP was developing independently of the Party in the country, and controlling parliamentary assistants was one way of reining back this independence. It was also proposed that the Shadow Cabinet and principal spokespersons should be elected by the PLP, this time a direct attack on the patronage of the Leader of the Party. Jim should probably have scoffed at it and treated much of it with derision. Instead, he seemed defensive and a little rattled. Tony Benn had drawn blood and while some of the detail was eventually shelved by a decision to establish a Commission of Enquiry, there was no doubt that at the annual Conference he was going to be able to mount a pretty strong offensive.

At a joint meeting of the Shadow Cabinet and the NEC on 26 July, I concentrated on opposing any changes in the way the manifesto was drawn up. This was, I believed, the central issue. I accepted only that there was a strong case to re-establish greater trust in the Party since in the past we had suffered from a vicious circle whereby Conference resolutions that were passed had been ignored, thus provoking Conference to pass even more unrealistic resolutions which were then further ignored, and so a pattern of irresponsibility had become built into Conference resolution making. The Benn changes would only deepen the existing mistrust.

In early September Debbie and I visited South Africa at the invitation of the students of the University of Wittwatersrand, Johannesburg. My visit was thought likely to be very controversial and Pik Botha, the Foreign Minister, saw me at the airport on my arrival, thus neatly avoiding his being associated with anything controversial I might say later. I did not ask or want to see the Prime Minister, P.W. Botha, for I was convinced that as long as he remained in control, there would be no significant change in the underlying apartheid system. He was astute enough to make cosmetic changes, but I had watched him closely over hours of negotiation in October 1978 on Namibia, and even more revealingly over dinner, when he had lost his temper with Genscher, and I was convinced that he was a deeply authoritarian figure, incapable of any genuine transfer of power from white to black. I gave the fourteenth

Freedom Lecture to 2,500 students, packed into the sports hall on Wednesday 12 September. It was the second anniversary of Steve Biko's death and I reminded them of the shame of the circumstances of his dying, handcuffed and in leg irons, travelling naked for over seven hundred miles in the back of a Land-Rover. I made no bones about being a gradualist on applying economic pressure on South Africa and I argued that successful transitions in Namibia and Zimbabwe would pave the way for internal negotiations in South Africa.

Unlike all my previous visits, on this occasion, I was able to see more of the country. The stark simplicity of the Veldt and the beauty of Natal and Lesotho made a deep impression on us both, and it was fun to be travelling with students away from officialdom, either British or South African. My face was familiar to the Afrikaners and I did not escape their wrath. 'What does it feel like to be the most hated man in South Africa?' was one of the comments. Another, as we came down in the lift with our tennis racquets, was, 'Will anyone play with you?' The mood among most of the whites was very bitter. The Lancaster House Conference for Zimbabwe's independence had only just developed and no one knew what would happen. I also found among black students the almost universal belief that history was on the side of those who advocate violence and revolution. I tried to convince them that violence could only be the refuge of last resort and that peaceful, evolutionary change would come. But I left wondering whether it would, and vowing that I would not return until P.W. Botha had gone. That took nearly ten years and, despite many invitations, I refused to return until January 1990 when I visited President F.W. De Klerk and became convinced that here was a man who understood that there had to be real negotiations over a constitution, and who was ready to transform South Africa and end apartheid.

On our return from South Africa in the middle of September, it had become obvious that the Left wing had effectively mobilized the constituency parties behind the changes and Jim was left pleading for Party unity, making a speech in Swansea appealing for the withdrawal of the proposals for constitutional reform from the October Labour Conference. He wanted the proposals to be considered as part of the Commission's work on all aspects of the Party and warned that the impending conflict could be long, bitter and potentially disastrous for the Party. Tony Benn immediately rejected this plea, saying that the suggested reforms would not split the Party and adding that it would be quite wrong to see all this as part of a leadership contest: 'There is no vacancy. Jim Callaghan will go on until he retires. Then there will be candidates. I might be one of them.' The Campaign for Labour Victory also issued a statement billed by the press as being in the name of Roy Hattersley, Roy Mason, Bill Rodgers, David Owen and Shirley Williams, all of us CLV supporters. It declared that Jim Callaghan had the backing of 'the mainstream of

Labour supporters in the firm stand he is taking against constitutional
changes that would turn the Labour Party into a narrow, sectarian and
intolerant organization.'

On Friday 28 September, on the eve of the Labour Party Conference,
I spoke to my own Devonport General Management Committee. Again,
I singled out the importance of the manifesto and pointed out that if the
wording of successive Conference resolutions had been included in our
manifesto it would have been electorally disastrous in Devonport. I drew
attention to the damaging experience of the NEC having drawn up the
manifesto for the European elections and reminded everyone that, while
the founding fathers of the Labour Party could easily have established
Labour as a trade union party, the creature of a vested interest, they had
had a wider vision and insisted on a constitution that reflected the need
to establish a national base.

When the Conference met, these objections were swept away.
Fortunately, the motion for the election of the Party Leader by an
electoral college was lost and I hoped this would be the last we heard of
it. Mandatory reselection of members, once in every Parliament, was,
however, carried. Ultimate control of the manifesto, it was decided,
should now lie with the NEC. The delicate balance of power between
the Parliamentary Party, elected by the country as a whole, and the Party
activists in the NEC and the Labour Party Conference was under serious
threat. Even though all these issues would be covered by the Commission
of Inquiry and would therefore come back to the next annual Conference,
few of us had any doubt that Tony Benn was masterminding a
fundamental change in the balance of the Party, an historic shift from
elected representatives to non-elected party caucuses. In elections in the
constituency section for the NEC there was also a substantial swing to
the Left. Peter Shore, whom I had beaten the previous year, moved
ahead of me, as did Roy Hattersley; but, despite their success in the
Shadow Cabinet elections, none of us had anywhere near the votes of the
successful candidates who were elected almost exclusively from the
straight Left.

Immediately after the Party Conference, I spoke to a Hornsey Constituency Labour Party meeting. I tried to confront the constitutional arguments of the Left and, for the first time, argued that individual members
of the Party should be given the right to a postal ballot in the selection or
reselection of their candidate or MP, in the choice of the constituency
representatives to the NEC and in the annual choice of Party Chairman.
I also argued for state funding of internal party democracy on the same
basis on which the Conservative Government was making funds available
for elections in trade unions. I might as well have saved my breath. Few
in that meeting were interested in a genuine extension of democracy
within the Party; for them it was simply a power struggle against the
'Right', in which democracy was little more than rhetoric. It was one of

the most unpleasant political meetings I have ever attended; the air was full of Trotskyist sentiment and Marxist catch phrases. Afterwards, I went back to the house of a member of CLV and heard how helpless and angry the moderates felt. Someone even said that the 'yobs' were taking over the Party. But I feared it was more sinister than that. The whole experience made me even more determined to fight.

On Wednesday 24 October the NEC agreed the membership of the Commission of Enquiry. The balance was appalling. Of the five NEC members, four were hardline Left. Of the five trade union members, three were associated with the Left. David Basnett, of the GMWU was wobbly and only Terry Duffy of the AEW was on the Right of the Party. With the vice-chairman and treasurer on the Left, Jim Callaghan could only rely on the automatic vote of Terry Duffy and on the general support of Michael Foot and David Basnett. Eventually, after endless representations, the Chief Whip, Michael Cocks, was put on the Commission with observer status as a sop to the Parliamentary Party. A new leader would have been forced to fight, but I believe Jim Callaghan saw his task as one of damage limitation. If he had resigned someone like Denis Healey would at least have had self-preservation as a spur to make him mobilize the Parliamentary Party and refuse to have anything to do with such a grotesquely unrepresentative Commission.

The general backbiting against Jim Callaghan personally among Labour activists on the Left was becoming very nasty, and on 9 November, speaking at Ted Rowlands's Merthyr Tydfil Constituency Labour Party Annual Dinner, I declared that I was proud to have been a member of Jim Callaghan's Cabinet and was not prepared to see him used as a scapegoat for our defeat. Not only was he our greatest electoral asset, I did not believe that the 1979 manifesto had lost us any votes in this constituency or in my own.

On 18 November, Hugo Young, writing in the *Sunday Times*, previewed the BBC Dimbleby Lecture which Roy Jenkins was due to give the following Thursday. It started rather unkindly, saying that most people would have forgotten who Roy Jenkins was, since for three years he had been in Europe 'jetting from capital to capital as the pseudo-equal, or more often the impotent servant, of a Prime Ministers' club he never managed to join.' Predicting that within a year the Labour Party would be in the hands of the two least trusted groups in the whole of public life, the Bennite Left or the trade union leadership, he asked whether Roy Jenkins on his return from Europe would simply join the natural beneficiaries of political extremism, the Liberal Party. 'It would surely be a quixotic and futile thing for an ambitious man to do. He is not about to become the Christopher Mayhew of the 1980s.' He concluded that, since Mr Jenkins himself was scarcely a popular figure to compare with Mrs Shirley Williams, if he 'is to make any headway he is going to have to find the moment, to put it simply, when Mr Rodgers can be

persuaded that the future of Britain is more important than the sensibilities of a few party worthies in Stockton on Tees.' By emphasizing the
role of Bill, Hugo Young was stressing the need to win over the
traditional Labour Party in the North-East, a haven of moderation.

Some have tried to pretend that the Dimbleby Lecture was the first
and critical move that led inevitably to the founding of the SDP. Roy's
Dimbleby Lecture was undoubtedly for some an important milestone;
but in my view it was neither the first nor the most critical milestone. It
was of nowhere near the same political significance as, for example, the
28 October 1971 vote of the sixty-nine Labour MPs who defied a three-
line whip to support entry to the European Community, or the decision
of the Parliamentary Labour Party to elect Michael Foot as its Leader in
November 1980. The main thrust of the lecture was an elegant and
convincing case for proportional representation and coalition government.
Never before had it been championed by such a senior political figure or
taken to such a mass audience on prime time television; and Roy got a
large number of letters, overwhelmingly supportive, which increased his
enthusiasm for realignment.

For someone in my position trying, with others, to mobilize the
Manifesto Group of MPs in Parliament and the Campaign for Labour
Victory in the country to fight a desperate battle inside the Labour Party,
Roy's speech was a diversion from the task in hand. Roy was out of
British politics and was bound to see things differently. I made my view
clear the next day, speaking at the South-West Staffordshire Constituency
Labour Party dinner on Friday 23 November. 'The centre of the Labour
Party must now stand firm. We will not be tempted by siren voices from
outside, from those who have given up the fight from within.' I stressed
that I was not prepared to admit defeat, to accept that within two years
we could not turn our Party once more into a strong electoral force
capable of ousting Mrs Thatcher and regaining power as a broad-based
Party with appeal across the classes and the divisions of British society.
The Labour Party, I argued, had had that base before, idealistic and
radical, but we had to win back support. I admitted that the room for
compromise was dangerously narrow and that it might be that the battle
would be lost. I also said that new parties did not carry instant solutions
and that proportional representation of itself did not guarantee political
stability. I felt that we should be wary before giving up our system of
coalitions within parties and replacing it with the continental system of
coalitions across parties. But equally the Labour Party must recognize
that if we were to continue to resist proportional representation then this
was only credible and tolerable if the Labour Party itself represented a
coalition which mirrored the broad spread of views of Labour voters. I
stressed that if we narrowed our coalition within the Party then we would
forfeit the support of many millions of people who currently voted
Labour, and proportional representation would become irresistible.

The things that Roy was saying were not, however, lost on me or on others like Bill Rodgers. When on 27 November at a joint meeting of the NEC and the Shadow Cabinet, I once more spoke passionately against giving the NEC ultimate control of the manifesto, I warned that there was a political vacuum which could easily be filled by the Liberals if the Labour Party tore itself apart over constitutional changes. That Saturday, Bill spoke in Abertillery in even more outspoken terms, in effect giving the Labour Party one year to put its house in order and predicting that if it did not it would split.

Over the next year, the views of those of us who were to form the SDP repeatedly diverged, came together, or crossed on this crucial question of fighting inside the Party or leaving it. At this stage, I was more firmly fighting from within the Labour Party than Bill or Shirley Williams. According to Roy's European diary, while Bill was listening to the Dimbleby Lecture he claimed he had had a vision of himself sitting in the headquarters of the new party with his sleeves rolled up, actually organizing things. Even so, Roy records that when he had lunch with both of them on the day of Bill's Abertillery speech, they were anxious – Shirley perhaps a little more than Bill – to tell him that it was always possible, though not likely, that things would go sufficiently well in the Labour Party to make them want to stay. Roy thought then that Bill had reached the watershed, whereas Shirley had not. For my part, I was nowhere near the watershed and there was a lot of fight still in me. The irony was that it would be Shirley and Bill, in the latter part of 1980, who would be the ones who looked closest to backtracking and staying with Labour.

At the end of November the European Council in Dublin Castle had the British budgetary question on the agenda and Margaret Thatcher demanded 'her money' back. After the initial honeymoon with all things European, and having in the summer foolishly lifted the British veto on a zero farm price settlement, she found that she had no bargaining power and instead behaved, as one of the participants patronizingly observed, like 'the grocer's daughter'. From a nation of shopkeepers, what did one expect? Britain and the European Community were on a collision course and Margaret Thatcher was riding a populist issue with the reckless abandon that was to become all too familiar. The politics of Europe were once again set to divide Britain and not just the Labour Party. My position remained as it always had been, strongly pro-Europe but strongly against federalism. Bernard Levin had interpreted a speech of mine wrongly as paving the way for yet another Labour somersault over the EEC, referring to 'the unappetizing ersatz ectoplasm issuing from Dr Owen's mouth' and saying that my credibility stood 'somewhere between Benedict Arnold and Harold Wilson'. It was all good rumbustious stuff, even if it did misinterpret my conviction that the Right should stay and fight. I have always enjoyed Bernard Levin, whether or not I have been on the receiving end. His attacks on the North Thames Gas Board or his description of how, when listening to opera under the Wicklow Mountain, his mind would turn to Anthony Wedgwood-Benn are memorable pieces of journalism. That same evening at a party thrown by the publishers Jonathan Cape, who should be there but Bernard Levin? Connie Harman, an old friend, came up to me and urged me to hit him. I thought it better for events to prove him wrong, and by and large I think they have.

My mood at this time is best expressed in a handwritten letter which I sent to a close friend in America on 11 December.

> Politics here is difficult to assess. I broke with Roy Jenkins, which was painful but had to be done – it's meant adding Bernard Levin to my campaign honours, a price I can live with, but it's not been pleasant. From Roy's own point of view the decision is fair enough, he will be out of a job in January 1981 and needs to pave the way – yet for me, intent on fighting from within right up to the election of 1983–84 if need be, any impression that Roy was being encouraged by us would be fatal inside the Party – I disagree even with Bill Rodgers in putting down a one-year deadline. It could easily be worse next year but still we will have to fight on – the nearer the election the more the Centre will find its influence increasing. Even if in desperation we were forced to split, it is important that the split should be seen to come after we have traversed every mile – and tactically it needs to come fairly close to an election. If a new party was formed with two to three years to go, both the Tory and Labour Parties, whether under Thatcher and Benn, would have to gravitate to the Centre to squeeze out what they would both see as a threat – I am not attracted to a third party anyhow – I think it would be rootless, brought together out of frustration. It would soon split apart when faced with the real choices and could easily reflect the attitudes of a London-based liberalism that had neither a base in the provinces nor a bedrock of principles.
>
> It's very hard to see a third party having any success other than for an initial election and possibly a second unless it also went into local government and this presents a major problem. For the present, and I may change, my inclination is to go down with the ship – not search for a new boat – this one has given me a lot and I can't face the idea of sinking it by my own actions – my problem is of course Devonport. If we have a crazy manifesto and one seen to be the living embodiment of the '1984' Orwellian forecast, then I cannot win Devonport. To lose on a manifesto one can fight for is one thing, and an acceptable risk but I doubt I'd be prepared to go down on a manifesto that I didn't believe in. The options would be to dissociate even to the extent of fighting as a Parliamentary Labour Party candidate and try to take as many of my local party as possible with me, so that only a rump Labour Party supported the official candidate, or to just miss out that election and go back to medicine. If one had a safe seat one could resign the front bench and yet still

fight as the Labour candidate and know one would be returned to
fight on after a severe electoral defeat.

   The real horror is of the EEC becoming caught up in all this. I
desperately want Mrs Thatcher to succeed on the British contribution
to the Community budget and believe she is right to kick hard and
forgo the diplomatic niceties – the FCO is as usual shivering in
their boots. I believe and hope she will win in around three years
time and radically alter the budget formula, but we will have to
become very unpopular in the EEC first – 'Heath with balls' is the
best description I've heard of her tactics – but she is looking and
sounding very tense and slightly manic, on a high, with few people
to sustain her if she falls.

The situation steadily got worse. On 13 December Francis Pym announced to the House of Commons that the Government was accepting
the deployment of 160 cruise missiles in Britain, initially at Greenham
Common and then at Molesworth. Bill Rodgers replied from the front
bench for the Labour Party and managed to avoid outright opposition to
the deployment decision, concentrating more on the absence of
parliamentary debate. But the Labour Left now had a defence issue to get
their teeth into and the policy debate was about to become as divisive as
the constitutional debate.

   The Parliamentary Party discussed the cruise missile decision on 16
January and, even though the decision was overshadowed by the Soviet
invasion of Afghanistan, we knew there was enough dissent within the
Party to indicate that trouble lay ahead. Sure enough, it surfaced again at
the joint meeting of the Shadow Cabinet with the NEC on 30 January.
Tony Benn's intervention, sloganizing future policy to 'No cruise, no
Pershing and no successor to Polaris', showed that he was determined to
widen the attack from constitutional questions to the most divisive issue
within the Party, defence. The policy reversals and constitutional changes
were undoubtedly depressing. But far worse was the way that decent,
moderate people seemed to have gone into hiding. It was as if the Party
were in a collective funk and everyone was looking for the nearest hole in
which they could bury themselves for a few years in the hope that the
nightmare of the Left in control of the Party would somehow pass
without their having to do anything to prevent it. There seemed to be so
little fight left, let alone the energy to embark on the rethink of
fundamentals so desperately needed.

   The Left were also winning the crucial fight to capture trade union
support. The first national steel strike since 1926 started on 2 January
1980 and was to last until 1 April. Much steel-making capacity was lost
in the strike which unfortunately confused a much needed rationalization
with a niggardly pay offer, which had eventually to be substantially
increased. It was the first occasion since 1977 that any government had
taken on a powerful union and won, and it did a lot for Conservative

morale. But one effect of this dispute was to make the normally moderate steelworkers more militant. It had its effect on other unions too. Just as polarization under Heath had pushed labour away from the EEC, now the threatened union laws and tough economic policies pushed the trade unions into the arms of the Left and their hostility to the EEC.

I plugged away, speaking out for what I saw as common sense. On 10 January in Newcastle-upon-Tyne, at a Campaign for Labour Victory meeting, I argued that the Labour Party's most serious challenge was to re-establish its historic identification with social responsibility, social co-operation and social morality. I reminded my audience that almost every opinion poll demonstrated the fundamental gap between NEC decisions and the majority views of Labour Party members and Labour voters, and that the reason that their voice was not heard was the system of delegated democracy. We had to openly challenge authoritarianism, dogma and the elitism of the activists. The rights and views of the passive Party members could not be subordinate to those of the active members. Nor could the views of the wider electorate be ignored. As if in answer to this, *The Times* commissioned a poll showing that on the issue of a new Centre party, the public was as split as its potential leaders. A clear majority of people favoured the formation of a new party in the Centre, but rather ominously there was no consensus on its component parts. There was a strong desire to avoid a split in the Labour Party but a deep unease about the working of the political system, significantly greater among Labour and Liberal voters. At the time the poll was taken Labour was still ahead with 42 per cent, the Conservatives had 39 per cent, the Liberals 16 per cent and the Nationalists 2 per cent. What emerged was that a Centre party which consisted only of a breakaway group of moderate and Right-wing Labour candidates would succeed only in splitting the Labour vote without having any real chance of winning power. It was thought that the effect would be to give Britain two Liberal-sized parties in the Centre. If a Centre party was formed, David Steel emerged as the clear favourite to be its leader, with Edward Heath second, Shirley Williams third and Roy Jenkins fourth, with less than half the support of David Steel. Bill Rodgers, the only other candidate mentioned, had barely any support.

In early February, the Parliamentary Party witnessed a small vignette of the future when Neil Kinnock, speaking as Shadow Education Minister, gave the first sign that he might split off from his hitherto firm identification with the far Left. In a fit of righteousness he refused to commit the Party to repealing the Education Bill, and while he was prepared to say we would end the assisted places scheme, he was not prepared to pledge the reinstitution of school meals and free milk. This caused outrage on the Left and Neil tried to speak again, forgetting the old adage, 'When in a hole, stop digging.' It was, nevertheless, a sign that he was coming to grips with the realities of public expenditure, and starting to speak as though he might one day be in government. I was pleased by his speech and did not enjoy seeing him attacked, though many on the Left and the Right were bitter at what he said and delighted to embarrass him. However, eight years and two election defeats were needed before Neil Kinnock was prepared to abandon the Left-wing policies that he had espoused since his youth. At the end of February, I spoke in Birmingham to the Northfield Constituency Labour Party, again urging that the country invest in democracy and that since one member-one vote ballots were expensive it would be wise for the Government to support financially not just balloting in trade unions but balloting in political parties as well.

On 4 March 1980 Robert Mugabe won the election in Zimbabwe with an overall majority and Margaret Thatcher's Government had its first major success – albeit achieved as a result of their first U-turn. I have described in the chapter on Africa what happened in the House of Commons. The continued rise in unemployment was adding to the bitterness within the Labour Party and on 21 April unemployment topped $1\frac{1}{2}$ million. The moderates were retreating into their shell rather than defend sensible economic and industrial policies, fearing that if they attacked the Left they would be seen to be doing Margaret Thatcher's work for her. On 15 March, at a South-West Regional Labour Party Conference, we had a CLV fringe meeting which was addressed by Betty Boothroyd and Bill Rodgers. I remember it mainly, however, for the difficulty in getting people, whose moderate views I knew, to declare themselves. It was given an added piquancy by Tony Benn coming to sit in the audience.

At this time I was trying to raise money for CLV. It was not very successful, but some people helped and I had a particularly charming response from one industrialist. I had written to him in April saying that I would continue to fight from within the Labour Party and that the 'so-called moderates in the Party must never forget that the "Church Militant" is a respectable precedent for fighting hard and standing firm for one's beliefs. We need a little of that resolve if we are to overcome our own so-called militants.' He replied, saying that what I had written was just how he felt.

I have been an avowed Labour supporter all my life, since the time I first addressed envelopes, at the tender age of 13, for the late Sir Charles Edwards, then the Member for Bedwellty. My socialism was born out of my reading of the works of Charles Dickens and Emile Zola (when we had no radio or television) and the fact that in the early thirties more than 80 per cent of the insurable population of Merthyr was unemployed. I have remained loyal to those early convictions ever since. I recite that merely to emphasize my great disappointment in contemplating the prospect of the Labour Party, as I have known it, being destroyed from within.

But we did not succeed in igniting any sustained flame of resistance. We had no large financial resources, only limited union backing, and had to contend with apathy and the increasing fear of deselection. It might have been a reflection on our own personalities or the way we were campaigning, but it is significant that the Solidarity campaign which under Roy Hattersley took over from CLV in the early 1980s seemed to fare no better. It was only when the trade union leaders stirred themselves, or were stirred by Neil Kinnock, to fight Militant that any real fight-back began. Trade unionists found it easier to defeat the Militant Tendency as a separate organization if they were not encumbered by fighting Militant on policy issues as well. So the trade union leaders who backed the expulsion of militants had a justification of sorts in not shifting the policy of the Party until this arguably more damaging long-term threat to the Labour Party was removed. Moderates make bad militants and the CLV did not stop the dismal tide of organizational and political extremism as it lapped at the feet of the Callaghan leadership and threatened to engulf the Party. In fairness to CLV, it needed Jim Callaghan's overt support, not merely covert sympathy.

People who ought to have known better, not only on the Parliamentary Left, but even in the Centre, were refusing to face up to the clear evidence of the infiltration of local parties by the Trotskyist Militant Tendency. Lord Underhill, the former National Agent of the Labour Party, had at long last been given permission by the NEC to publish his report. They had repeatedly refused to publish it themselves and he had to do it at his own expense. It was a damning document. He had assembled some four hundred pages of background material demonstrating that, while the Militant Tendency had no more than two thousand fully accepted members, they were energetic, active workers who operated in secret. While he said he did not want to see a nationwide witch hunt, he had shown conclusively that the Militant Tendency had a national political organization with its own policy, its own media for propaganda and its own headquarters and printing shop with full-time staff, which included nine political workers at the Centre, four technical workers, eight regional field workers and a sales force for the *Militant* newspaper. He had struck a warning note, but the NEC, the one body with the power to act, simply ignored him.

On 26 March the NEC agreed to a suggestion from Moss Evans of the T&GWU that we needed a recall Conference to discuss industrial policy. In the event Tony Benn managed to ensure that the policy document presented at the Special Conference on 31 May, entitled 'Peace, Jobs and Freedom', became the vehicle for a massive shift towards the Left's entire policy agenda. The promise to amend the 1972 European Communities Act, for example, talked of 'restoring to the House of Commons the full control of all law-making and tax-gathering powers, now ceded to the European Community'. Defence was just as bad – we were now being told that 'the Labour Party opposes the manufacture and deployment of cruise missiles and the neutron bomb and refuses to permit their deployment in Britain by the United States or any other country.' When the document was discussed in the Shadow Cabinet, Jim Callaghan got rather exasperated when some of us suggested that these commitments were not just difficult to live with, they were impossible to live with and the Left's challenge could not simply be ignored. At one stage the NEC even looked as if they might refuse to allow Jim Callaghan, still Leader of the Party after all, to introduce the document to the Conference. The usual moderate blandishments were invoked against not reacting vigorously – the document was not binding on the Party, it did not have the status of a manifesto, and if we were low-key now we would be able to retrieve some of the commitments at a later date. I never believed any of this. The situation was deteriorating day by day.

In early April, Debbie and I went to Venice, as I was talking to a conference on Africa and we had a few days' holiday staying in the Danielli. I have always loved Venice but this visit was very special because Debbie's first cousin Trixie was married to a Venetian, Giangi Marangoni. Sadly he has since died, but seeing Venice with him and visiting his relatives in their house brought a completely different and magical dimension. Looking back at Britain from Italy, it seemed sheer madness to divorce ourselves from the European Community. I remembered how William Harvey, the famous anatomist, had frequently visited and lectured in Italy centuries earlier. Britain was inescapably European and I returned resolved to keep Labour supporting the European Community.

In mid-April 1980 our son Tristan had another relapse in his childhood leukaemia. This time it was even more serious, for it happened while still on treatment, and he had to have a second course of radiotherapy. He pluckily continued at school despite the after-effects of the treatment. Lucy was not yet two years old and it was difficult for Debbie to find all the extra time to wait long hours in hospital, since one of us had to go every day. I cancelled some of my speaking engagements. All we could do was wait, hope and pray. I suppose it was a distraction to have the Party battle raging during this time but it was also an added strain. If anything, Tristan's poor health tended to make me a little more detached from the Party fray and gave me greater perspective. On this level it all seemed so irrelevant; my family certainly came before fighting people like Tony Benn. However, Tony was but the acceptable face. There was a much more unattractive element lurking below the surface and they had to be fought. So with some reluctance, and not feeling as fully engaged as before, I began writing a book in order to confront the ideology of the centralized Left and the mistaken path of state socialism.

During the run-up to the Special Conference in May, the political atmosphere worsened. Though the Government got a certain amount of reflected glory from the successful storming of the Iranian Embassy by the SAS, it did not last. By the middle of May 1980, inflation had risen to 21.8 per cent. Though the Day of Action called by the TUC had not been a great success, it had, nevertheless, mobilized many in the trade union movement who would not normally have protested. The view that the Conservative Government was the most reactionary, divisive government in our history was widespread inside the Labour movement. This meant that the climate for the Special Conference was developing into one of deep hostility to the Conservatives. There was growing intolerance for anyone who could be depicted as in any way supporting policies which could be equated with those of the Conservative Government. The constant publicity about the excessive British budgetary contribution to the European Community with headlines like 'Mrs T asks for more' was also arousing all the old, latent hostility to everything stemming from the European Community.

Meanwhile, Tony Benn and the Campaign for Labour Party Democracy had come together with a bizarre grouping of broad Left pressure groups – Clause IV, Independent Labour Publications, Institute for Workers Control, Labour Co-ordinating Committee, National Organization of Labour Students, Socialist Campaign for a Labour Victory – all combining to form the Rank and File Mobilizing Committee.

Each of these groups, to a greater or lesser degree, lived in its own world of purist extremism. One only needs to read a magazine like *London Labour Briefing*, to see how remote they are from reality. Headlines like 'The progress of the class struggle in Bromley Ravensbourne' or 'Yes, the international banking crisis is *sexist*', would have been funny if the people who wrote it were not engaged on a serious project to wreck the Labour Party.

The Rank and File Committee launched a new publication in June which contained excerpts from a speech by Tony Benn:

> In the heart of parliamentarianism lies the continuation of the Burkeian myth. We've got to deal with that by getting every Labour candidate to sign that he supports the Manifesto. Now, that's not an innovation, we did it for the European Election. We wouldn't endorse any candidate for the European Election until they had signed that they supported the Manifesto.'

Edmund Burke was a Whig who represented Bristol in Parliament for six years from 1774 to 1780. By now, Tony Benn, as a fellow Bristolian MP, had developed a fetish about challenging everything Edmund Burke had ever said. But Burke's definition of representative government is as true today as when he first articulated it. It was not as if Burke did not understand the need for party. Long before parties had reached their present dominance, he argued that party government was the best government, for he recognized that MPs needed to unite to promote, by their joint endeavours, the national interest. But Burke also said that an MP as 'your representative owes you not his industry only, but his judgement; and he betrays, instead of serving you, if he sacrifices it to your opinion.' He was quite right. It was becoming ever more obvious that the fight we were embarked on inside the Labour Party was a fight over some of the essential tenets of parliamentary democracy.

On the day of the Special Conference, Debbie and the three children were due to drive down to Buttermere and I felt so fed up that I wanted to go with them. Fortunately Debbie persuaded me that it was ridiculous not even to attend and that I would be letting down other people in CLV if I were not there. But it was symptomatic of my mood. She dropped me off at Wembley and I arrived late. Jim Callaghan was already on his feet speaking. He had just started to deal with international issues and, watching from the back of the hall, I felt a deep foreboding. Jim's speech was lacklustre and his words on the European Community and cruise missiles were too carefully crafted to carry conviction or force. He talked about that section of the document 'that seems to point to unilateral action' and went on: 'Whilst I respect those who call for unilateral disarmament, I cannot agree that we should take an insular view of our responsibilities.' This was hardly fighting stuff and I felt the Conference was barely listening. I passed Peter Shore and asked him if he was going to speak. To my amazement he said no. I then bumped into Bill Rodgers and found that he too was not intending to speak. He was feeling guilty about it, but Jim had apparently persuaded him that it would be wiser not to. So the Shadow Foreign and Defence Ministers were not even going to challenge the Conference to stick to the policies we had pursued while in government. I went forward into the hall and sat down next to Denis Healey. I discovered that he intended to speak only on the economy and was not going to touch on foreign affairs. I had already listened to two rabidly unilateralist speeches, both of which were applauded from the platform with exaggerated enthusiasm by Neil Kinnock, so I decided that I would have to speak.

I had not prepared a speech and had no idea when I would be called. I rose at the moment that Lena Jeger, the Chairman, called Clive Jenkins and since he spoke in part on energy she must have thought that it would be a good idea to call me as Shadow Energy Spokesman. So to my surprise I was called after only one other constituency speaker.

I concentrated initially on energy questions and then switched to defence: 'It is no use expecting us to have a place at SALT III if we are going to take decisions on cruise missiles before we have even entered into the negotiations.' This provoked the expected uproar and I went on, 'Oh no, it has to be faced in this country. It is no use expecting your friends and allies to expect you to have a place in those negotiations if you are pre-empting it.' To further cries I added, 'I am telling you as someone who has dealt with those negotiations.' This provoked even louder cries of protest from the floor. 'I will say it to you again. If you think you can enter into arms control negotiations with your hands tied behind your back, with no form of leverage, you are deluding yourself.' Lena Jeger then intervened to call for order: 'The speaker has a right to be heard, comrades. Please be quiet.' I went on:

> If we want to take arms control and disarmament seriously, it cannot be on the basis of already pre-empting decisions on a unilateral national basis. We want the removal of the SS-20 and the removal of cruise missiles in Europe. Don't pre-empt that choice before you have even entered into negotiations. This Party had this argument some years ago. We do not want that again. The emphasis in this document is on negotiations and – rightly so – on peace. But peace is not won by one nation pursuing its own policy in total isolation from others. It is in pooling, in making a bargain, in making a deal, in negotiating with the Soviet Union from a position of strength, not a position of weakness.

As I returned to my seat I could sense the animosity in some parts of the hall. I wondered whether I should have stayed quiet but my old regional organizer in the South-West patted me on the shoulder and said, 'In fifteen years you'll be very proud of that speech.' The booing did not upset me. It is like boxing when you barely feel the blows; when speaking you barely hear the boos. I had been heckled enough in the past not to be put off by that – in fact I rather enjoyed it – but it undoubtedly made me more aggressive in response. A few days later Jim Callaghan, who would probably have preferred me to shut up, went out of his way to commend my speech. He did, however, add that I should not have reminded them that I had been involved in the negotiations. Of course, in a way he was right, but I was speaking spontaneously and responding to the atmosphere of the Conference. Most people in CLV, who believed we had avoided a bare-knuckle fight for far too long, were delighted by my hitting back.

The *Guardian*, on Monday 2 June, had a perceptive editorial entitled 'The World Outside Wembley'. It analysed what a Left-oriented Labour Party was trying to achieve. It said its parliamentary leadership 'would have no place for Mr Callaghan, for his presumed successor Mr Healey, for Mrs Williams, Dr Owen, Mr Rodgers or Mr Varley; even Mr Foot would only qualify for old times' sake.' It went on to put its finger on the two parts of their strategy which were inextricably interlinked. First they had to get a Left programme adopted – and by the time Tony Benn had finished building on to the document he was commending to the Conference, they were well on the way to getting it. But then, to ensure that the policies were carried out, they had to have a Left parliamentary leadership and a Parliamentary Party which would bend to the Party's will, ignoring any constraints to the contrary. Eric Heffer had told the Conference that he wanted 'a Labour Government as dedicated to carrying out our policies as Mrs Thatcher is to carrying out her policies.' It was a sign of the times that Margaret Thatcher was often invoked by the Left as legitimising their shift of policy. On the Right she was criticized as a recruiting sergeant for the Left. Partisan politics was back in Britain with a vengeance.

It had been a depressing first year out of government. Stripped of the trappings of office, too many of the former Labour Cabinet Ministers lacked authority and most were trimming on every issue to accommodate the virulence of the Left in Parliament and in their constituencies. I was looking forward to the meeting which I had fixed up with Shirley Williams and Bill Rodgers and little realized that the European Community, which had bitterly divided us three from the Labour Party in 1971–72, was now about to be brought back by the Left to actually split the Party.

20

THE GANG OF THREE

Since Shirley Williams had lost Stevenage and was no longer in the House of Commons, my opportunities of talking to her were few. We were not social friends; neither of us had ever been to the other's homes in London or in the country. In fact I had to ask Bill Rodgers for her phone number in order to fix a meeting for the three of us to meet on 6 June 1980 at her flat. He had known Shirley well since Oxford and, because his and my families saw each other frequently, had assumed I knew her; so he was surprised that we did not know each other better.

The day before we were due to meet, I was stopped by Malcolm Rutherford of the *Financial Times* as I was walking through the underpass to the House of Commons. He told me that the anti-EEC Common Market Safeguards Committee had just issued a statement saying that Labour Party policies and the demands of European Community membership were irreconcilable. The statement, signed by John Silkin, said that they were going to attempt, at the autumn Conference, to get the Party committed to withdrawing from the European Community with no renegotiation and not even a referendum. It was one more step away from sanity; one that was to precipitate a response that I was almost certain a normally cautious man like John Silkin had not expected.

I left Malcolm Rutherford, went to my office and put out an immediate press release. It argued that millions of Labour Party voters and thousands of Labour Party activists had voted to stay in the EEC and that no more certain recipe for splitting the Labour Party could be imagined than to ask members to choose between their commitment to the Labour Party and their belief that it was in the national interest to remain a member of the European Community. I said 'My party or my country' is not a happy choice, but there could be only one answer.

Next morning, I met Shirley Williams and Bill Rodgers in Shirley's flat where we had our first substantial political discussion since the election. The morning papers had been full of the impending row within the Labour Party over the European Community. We decided to issue a joint statement to catch the Sunday newspapers. Shirley's was the main draft, but we all contributed words and sentences. We declared that for the Labour Party to make a manifesto commitment to leave the European Community in 1983 or 1984 would be 'irresponsible, opportunistic and short sighted', and added that we could have no part in it. We asked, 'Is this decision to be endlessly reopened? Are the old divisions to be stirred up again and again weakening our national self-confidence and our ability to contribute constructively to economic, energy and social problems?' We ended by saying 'there are some of us who will not accept a choice between socialism and Europe. We will choose them both.' That was the first indication I had ever given that I could contemplate leaving the Labour Party for a new social democratic party. We resolved to meet over the next few weeks with a view to drafting a much more comprehensive statement covering economic and social questions for we knew that Europe was too narrow a platform. The Gang of Three was born.

The next day our defiance was headline news in the *Sunday Times*. It was an important milestone in the birth of the SDP for it brought together the critical mass needed to attract other Labour MPs. It was also a positive partnership with good humour and give-and-take. We stayed close and pretty cohesive right up until the 1983 General Election when both Bill and Shirley lost their seats.

Our decision to fight together did not imply that any of us was ready to accept Roy Jenkins's dream of a Centre party. On Monday 9 June Roy spoke to the Parliamentary Press Gallery saying that there was no question of his flickering back to British politics, like a moth to a candle, before he finished his Presidency of the European Commission on 6 January 1981. However, he talked of an experimental plane, his way of describing the Centre party with which the press associated him. Roy's experimental plane was of little interest to me at this time, except that I could see that if he ever took off it would have profound consequences for our fight within the Labour Party. I believe that Bill and Shirley shared this view. While neither of them told me much about their meetings with Roy Jenkins at this time, in Roy's *European Diary* the impression is given that they were interested in a new party. I recall, however, that in discussions at this time they were still resisting any split and were extremely reluctant to contemplate ever being part of a Centre party.

Not surprisingly, the anti-marketeers hit back at our Gang of Three statement and Peter Shore and John Silkin got involved in the controversy. Jim Callaghan stepped in and called all those in the Shadow Cabinet who were arguing in public to a meeting in his room in the House of Commons. He asked us to try and defuse the controversy. Bill and I replied that we could not stay silent, the danger to the European Community was now a very real one, for a resolution demanding withdrawal from the Community had been circulated to constituency parties by the Safeguards Campaign. If we did nothing it would become official Labour Party policy within months. All we could promise, in deference to Jim, was that we would try our best to keep personalities out of the conflict.

Then nemesis struck. The Labour Party Commission of Enquiry was having a meeting to finalize its report on reforming the Party's constitution on the weekend of 14–15 June at the ASTMS training college at Bishop's Stortford. On the Saturday the Commission had a major division over the question of mandatory reselection whereby, irrespective of whether a constituency was happy with their MP, they would have to hold a selection procedure. Even Clive Jenkins had realized that this was a deeply sensitive issue for MPs and had proposed a compromise, stipulating that two-thirds of a constituency party could reject automatic reselection. But Moss Evans voted with the Left to defeat this and the full reselection proposal was carried. Jim reacted angrily saying, 'I can't go back to the PLP with this,' but when he suggested opening MPs' selection to the wider constituency membership, it was pointed out that the PLP had itself rejected this option. The Leader of the Party was humiliatingly rebuffed.

On the Sunday the conference turned to the question of leadership. Michael Foot proposed continuing the present arrangement with the MPs alone electing the Leader. He was only supported by Jim Callaghan and Terry Duffy. It was then that Jim Callaghan was told for the first time by the unions about their concept of an electoral college made up of 50 per cent MPs and 25 per cent trade union representation: 20 per cent for constituency parties and 5 per cent for others with power to elect the Party Leader and to control the Party Manifesto. By the early evening Jim had endorsed it.

I was outraged. It was incomprehensible that Jim Callaghan put his name to such an indefensible proposition. That the Leader of the Labour Party and, worse still, when in government the Prime Minister of the country, should be elected by such a body would, I thought, have stuck in his gullet. Why had he not taken the battle to the Shadow Cabinet and from there to the Parliamentary Party? The brutal truth was that fighting would have meant defying the unions and the Conference, and this Jim was obviously no longer prepared to attempt. He would have been wiser to have resigned then and there and put all his weight behind Denis Healey to succeed him. No one could blame him for wanting to retire to his farm in Sussex, but many would blame him for putting his authority behind the electoral college.

That Sunday evening, Jim had spoken with Bill Rodgers and tried to square him before the meeting of the Shadow Cabinet on the Monday. I was glad he had not attempted to telephone me, for I think we would have had angry words. At the Shadow Cabinet, Jim Callaghan and I had our first and only row. I attacked both the concept of the electoral college and the fact that he and Michael had come to us already totally compromised. Jim, who clearly had a guilty conscience over what he had done and was behaving in an unusually furtive way, hit back. He called me a 'political infant' which stimulated Bill to jump to my defence. Suddenly the Shadow Cabinet was riven. All of us had served in Cabinet together with good will, often friendship and certainly fundamental respect for Jim Callaghan; that was now jeopardized.

For the first time I really began to wonder whether the Labour Party was now salvageable. I was still not thinking of a Centre party but I was questioning my continued membership of Labour. I had tended to agree with Jim Callaghan that 'any party in this country has to rest on organized interests', and that no party could get very far in challenging the two big dominant parties unless it could develop some equivalent organized support. The Liberals lacked such a base and constantly showed their lack of moorings in their indiscipline. The consumer provided a countervailing interest to the producer but so far that had only been mobilized in an apolitical way. But my lack of faith in a new venture no longer shielded me from the reality of what had happened to the old one. I had hitherto argued for continuing the fight within the Labour Party for two to three years more, right up to the general election if necessary. I now despaired. Waiting it out, hoping to turn things round, seemed pointless, for we had suffered a mortal blow at Bishop's Stortford. With this albatross of an electoral college, MPs had lost the last democratic safeguard of being able to mobilize the Parliamentary Party against the NEC and if need be the Labour Party Conference. It was that safeguard which Hugh Gaitskell had used in 1960–61 as the base from which to reverse the unilateralist decision. I wondered whether I would even want to stay in the Party beyond the October conference if the electoral college went through. My thoughts were turning once again towards medicine and leaving politics.

I was far from alone in my opposition to the electoral college in the Shadow Cabinet, though perhaps mine was expressed with the most vehemence. My opposition was total, and I was so angry with Jim that I felt that if he did not stand down, Denis Healey should challenge him for the leadership. Denis himself was clearly angry but did not know exactly how to get out of the mess we were in without offending Jim. He was loath to do that for he knew Jim could still influence his chances in any leadership election. Roy Hattersley appeared to be strongly opposed, but again seemed to fear offending Jim. Bill Rodgers was appalled, Roy Mason did not like it and nor did Merlyn Rees. Bill, Roy Hattersley and I attended a Manifesto Group meeting of Labour MPs later that day which passed a motion highly critical of the Commission's compromise, referring to 'dangerous proposals conjured out of thin air'. The Group called upon the Commission to go back and produce totally different proposals, fairly pointing out that an electoral college had already been overwhelmingly rejected by the Parliamentary Party. It said that a college would be 'unworkable and constitutionally unacceptable to those who believe in parliamentary democracy'. In a statement, the Campaign for Labour Victory called the proposals a complete sell-out.

Press comment was universally hostile – 'a shambles', 'a dog's dinner', 'a mess of pottage'. Bernard Levin was in sparkling form, saying that to expect Callaghan to fight the takeover of the Party was, 'akin to expecting a blancmange, left overnight on the dining room table, to rise from its plate and set about knocking down the burglars who had broken in and are busy stealing the spoons'. He continued to equate me with the backtrackers: 'Nor is it any use looking to any possible successor to Mr Callaghan, for it is not just the Owens and Hattersleys that will rat, but the very Healeys as well.' The best account came from Peter Jenkins, writing in the *Guardian* on 18 June 1980, and using his old links as an industrial correspondent to winkle out what had really happened in Bishop's Stortford:

> Mr Callaghan will not go down in the history books as another Ramsay MacDonald but he could find a place in them as the Labour Party's Neville Chamberlain. Bishop's Stortford may have been his Munich. With Mr Michael Foot as his aide, his faithful Lord Halifax, the Leader of the Labour Party returned to Westminster with the promise of unity in our time. In return for his piece of paper he conceded in effect the integrity and independence of the Parliamentary Labour Party: he did so as an act of appeasement of the superior forces of the Left and the power and wealth of the trade unions . . . The relevant question in British politics at this moment is not what prospect there is for a new Party but rather what is the chance of the old Party splitting. Dr David Owen, Mr William Rodgers and Mrs Shirley Williams will have serious decisions to make . . . Mr Jenkins might find himself joining their Party instead of trying to recruit them to his.

In fairness to Jim Callaghan, he did make one fairly desperate attempt to put things right. In a speech on 5 July 1980 in Brecon, he struggled vainly to restore his authority as Leader by setting out in full his position on the constitutional changes. On reselection of MPs, since the last two conferences had decided this issue both ways, he declared the Party should go back to the 1978 Conference decision. On electing the Leader, he urged the Party to stick with MPs choosing, but with a requirement for consultation with their constituencies. On the manifesto he stated the case, in which he fervently believed, for staying with Clause 5 where the NEC and the MPs were jointly responsible. It was as if Jim hoped his support for an electoral college could be forgotten. Sadly, it was soon clear that his Brecon speech would have no effect within the Party. I just hoped he would resign in the next few weeks, with as much of his dignity intact as was possible, and let us elect a new Leader before the summer recess and the Party Conference. Though I thought it would be a tight election, I believed Denis Healey would win against any contender, particularly if Jim backed him solidly and did not flirt with Peter Shore.

The shaky position of the Labour moderates, backed into a corner, was being constantly demonstrated. Not only could I see our position deteriorating at home, but I was also, at this time, able to compare our problems with the strong position of social democrats abroad. For the last few months I had been working very closely with Olof Palme, the Leader of the Swedish Social Democratic Party, who had been Prime Minister and was to be Prime Minister again. Together we had set about establishing an Independent Commission on Disarmament and Security Issues, modelled on Willy Brandt's Commission on Development. Bruno Kreisky, then Prime Minister of Austria and Leader of their Social Democratic Party, who had been extremely helpful, agreed to provide office facilities for the secretariat in Vienna. I was then charged with raising over two million dollars. It was also agreed that I would fly to America to talk to Cy Vance, still Secretary of State, to ensure high-level US representation, and that Olaf would go to Moscow to talk to Gromyko. Unlike the Brandt Commission, which had no Soviet representation, this Commission could not function without their participation.

Although we were very keen to ensure that we had commissioners from a wide spread of countries and with different political backgrounds, the Commission did look slightly like an offshoot of the Socialist International. Egon Bahr, the German Social Democratic politician who had been very closely involved with Willy Brandt and the development of Ostpolitik, agreed to serve as did Joop den Uyl, Leader of the Dutch Labour Party, a former Prime Minister who was to serve as Prime Minister again during the work of the Commission. Gro Harlem Brundtland, Leader of the Norwegian Labour Party, also became Prime Minister during the life of the Commission. All these prominent leaders of the Socialist International over the next nine years treated me as a colleague and friend. It was very different from the enmity between Labour and the SDP in Britain.

My trip to the United States to persuade Cy Vance to join the Commission was successful, but not before I became caught up in one of the more important resignations in recent US history. On 25 April President Carter's ill-fated attempt to rescue the fifty-three US diplomats held hostage in the US Embassy in Tehran ended in disaster. Mechanical failure had already aborted the mission when one of the helicopters collided with a tanker aircraft in the Iranian desert two hundred miles from Tehran, leaving eight Americans dead in the flaming wreckage. I was due to fly to Washington on Sunday 27 April, so contacted the State Department, expecting my visit to be cancelled. I knew that Cy would have his hands full with the crisis, and I was surprised to be told that he

was very keen for me to come. When I arrived in Washington the crisis
had deepened and there were rumours that he was going to resign. Again
I rang the State Department and again I was told that Cy still wanted to
see me. So when, next morning, Cy Vance saw President Carter and
formally resigned, I became Cy's last official visitor late that afternoon in
the State Department. It was one of the most poignant meetings I have
ever attended. Cy only wanted to reminisce and use me as a sounding
board as to whether he had made the correct decision. He told me that he
had opposed the rescue attempt from the moment it had been conceived
and had continued to oppose it in the National Security Council even
after the President had made the decision. Quite apart from his military
reservations, Cy believed that the politics were all wrong. Even if the
rescue mission had succeeded, the Iranians would simply have taken
more hostages from among the American journalists and others still in
Tehran. American lives would still have been at risk and the whole region
would have been even more inflamed. He decided that he could not
honourably remain as Secretary of State if the mission went forward. He
had actually resigned a week earlier but had agreed to stay in place until
after the mission was completed, though whatever the outcome his
decision was irrevocable. As he went over all those traumatic decisions,
Cy was visibly anguished and all I could do was listen sympathetically
and support his judgement. Cy Vance is the finest public servant I have
ever worked with in any country. That day, despite being very distressed
and physically not well, there was deep, underlying dignity about
everything he said and did, refusing to blame President Carter and
showing no hint of self-satisfaction at having been proved right. Resignations are rare in the United States but I believe this one, though it
deprived President Carter of a man of rare judgement, gave an example
of principled conduct that will enrich the public life of the United
States.

The Commission's main report, *Common Security*, was published in
book form in June 1982. After the tragic death of Olof Palme in 1986, it
became the Palme Commission and continued in a lower key producing a
final report, *A World at Peace*, in April 1989. There were many arguments
and differences among the Commission members but there was never any
question of the Commission advocating unilateral abandonment of nuclear
weapons despite the involvement of so many members of the Socialist
International. The Commission sat during the whole period in which the
British Labour Party was committed to unilateral nuclear disarmament
and was widely respected as a sane voice for disarmament. It was an odd
experience to be seen abroad as a committed disarmer while in Britain,
because I was opposing the nonsense of Labour's defence policy, I was
depicted by the Left as an unreconstructed, hard-line military hawk.
That was certainly not how the Ministry of Defence saw me when
Foreign Secretary. But later it suited Roy Jenkins and, sadly, Shirley too

to portray me as a man with a nuclear missile in each button hole. Yet in fact there is no politician in the 1970s and 1980s who has devoted more time and effort to serious disarmament.

On 15 July 1980 Francis Pym, the Secretary of State for Defence, made an important statement about Britain's strategic nuclear deterrent. He announced that, as the best and most cost-effective way of replacing Polaris, the Government had chosen the US Trident submarine-launched ballistic missile system. Bill Rodgers, who replied for the Labour Party, said, 'We believe that the case for buying Trident has not yet been made, and we cannot approve it.' Given the manifesto, he could hardly have said anything else; we were landed with the commitment to oppose Trident. What remained vital was to retain a commitment to a British contribution to NATO's nuclear deterrent – whether that was achieved through cruise missiles deployed on submarines or through air-launched nuclear missiles was nowhere near as important as keeping support for the principle.

At the time Bill Rodgers put a paper to the Shadow Cabinet with a formula for dealing with Trident. Arguing Labour could make clear

> our belief that NATO must be armed with nuclear weapons until such time as there is all-round unilateral nuclear disarmament. Second, we could oppose the decision to buy Trident, principally on the grounds of cost. Third, we could add that in matters of this kind, involving security and international relations, the Opposition was not in a position to take a wholly informed view and that a final decision on the attitude of an incoming Labour Government would have to be reached at that time.

The paper was never really discussed. By then the Shadow Cabinet had in effect accepted that we would oppose Trident with no ifs or buts. But in any case the third proposition was a wholly unsupportable policy. I thought that Bill was buying time and did not believe this could be a serious policy on which to fight an election in 1983. But incredibly, even after that election had been won by the Conservatives with a straightforward commitment to purchase Trident, Bill put forward a somewhat similar formula when he sat on the 1986 SDP-Liberal Defence Commission which I felt bound to reject.

As my depression about Labour's attitudes deepened, I increasingly turned to the possibilities and problems of a new party – its origins, its base, its relationship with other parties. These thoughts were uppermost when David Watt and his family came to stay for the weekend at the end of July. We all went to Michael Sissons, the literary agent's, annual party just over the hill from Buttermere. There, Susan Watt and Debbie were among many publishing friends and we enjoyed football matches for fathers and sons, a barbecue and dancing. Afterwards, David and I went over the new party conundrum in depth. I could speak far more frankly to him than to most others because I completely trusted his discretion. He had talked to Roy in Brussels a few months earlier and, while he was pessimistic about the chances of any new party, he had told Roy that he was convinced it could only work if it was based on a Labour Party split. In particular David felt that if Roy were merely intent on joining the Liberals, no breakthrough could ever be achieved. I thus knew Roy's thinking about the Liberals; I also knew that his Liberal friends, like Mark Bonham-Carter, would influence him towards the Liberal Party and that in many of his policy attitudes he was already close to the Liberals. Perhaps this should have worried me more but at this stage, at least, Roy was not the politican who interested me. Both David and I agreed that Denis Healey was a far more critical figure than Roy. If only Denis could be persuaded really to fight from within and split only if that failed we would be in serious business. Reluctantly, however, we both feared that Denis was now so compromised in his attempt to win votes when Jim went, which we were all expecting to be soon, that the chances of persuading him of the necessity to fight now were very slim. The result of this discussion, therefore, was that we were both pessimistic about the chances of any Liberal Centre party but felt that we could not rule out a new party of the Centre-Left and its moment could arrive when some of us might have to split from Labour, regardless of its chances.

Why did I oppose then and continue to oppose Roy's idea of a Centre party based on the Liberals? The answer had little to do with feeling myself more 'Left-wing' than Roy or even with being 'socialist'. Although this word was much bandied about, it shed more heat than light. The truth can only be understood by remembering what Britain was like in 1980. We had suffered decades of economic decline, a series of massive financial crises, a prolonged period of vicious industrial disputes and a collapse of the consensus that underpinned the Welfare State. The response of the ruling Establishment during these times had been miserable. There had been a collective failure of will and now, faced with the need to rethink fundamentals, the inclination of the Centre was to snipe from the sidelines. This was not confined to politicians – it applied, for example, just as much to the leadership of the civil service. In other words the failure of will was a failure of the entire Centre.

So I felt that joining a Centre party based on the Liberals would be jumping out of the frying pan into the cotton wool. I was determined to remain a redistributionist. I believed that the extremes of Left and Right could only be defeated by an explicitly radical alternative. Those beliefs I felt could be best expressed by remaining a part of the social democratic, Socialist International world and using continental social democracy as the starting point for a fresh political party in Britain.

For the Gang of Three the main preoccupation now was to draft a more comprehensive policy statement. My diary shows that I had at least five meetings with Bill, Shirley or both prior to the publication of an open letter in the *Guardian* on 1 August. Our long letter went through many different drafts with each of us adding and subtracting phrases or words. By the end it was genuinely the property of all three of us. Throughout, the major issue with which we had to grapple was how far we went in implying that we were ready to leave the Labour Party and help create a new party. On 3 July, with a redraft of Bill's initial draft, I wrote to Shirley:

> The hardest question I find to resolve is whether we should explicitly raise again the question of another socialist party. Again on balance I conclude we should, but fairly indirectly, and I think we need to guard against being thought to be 'opting out' rather than 'fighting on'.

On 1 August our letter duly appeared, prominently positioned in the *Guardian*. The opening sentence read, 'The Labour Party is facing the gravest crisis in its history – graver even than the crisis of 1931'. This was followed by three sections – on the commitment to the mixed economy, the commitment to international socialism and the commitment to representative democracy. However, the sting was in the tail and it was over these words that we had wrestled.

> If the NEC remains committed to pursuing its present course and if, consequently, fears multiply among the people, then support for a Centre party will strengthen as disaffected voters move away from Labour. We have already said that we will not support a Centre party for it would lack roots and a coherent philosophy. But if the Labour Party abandons its democratic and internationalist principles, the argument may grow for a new democratic socialist party to establish itself as a party of conscience and reform committed to those principles. We are not prepared to abandon Britain to divisive and often cruel Tory policies because electors do not have an opportunity to vote for an acceptable socialist alternative to a Conservative Government.
>
> There are those who say that the Labour Party cannot survive its present battles but must now tear itself to pieces. Others believe that soft words and a little skilful evasion of the issues can paper over the cracks again. We do not share either of these views. If there is one lesson it is that there can be no compromise with those who share neither the values nor the philosophy of democratic socialism. A Labour Party committed to these values and this philosophy can defeat Tory reaction. We shall fight for such a Labour Party. We ask all those who share that conviction to fight for it too. It is Britain's best hope.

What the hard Left called the capitalist press gave us, I suppose predictably, a lot of coverage and a good hearing across the spectrum. In the *Guardian* it was 'The Three Musketeers Take up Arms'; in the *Sunday Times*, 'Why the Gang of Three are Right'. *Tribune* by contrast

ran a feature for several weeks vilifying the Gang of Three, amusingly
entitled, 'The Little Blue Book: Sayings of the Gang of Three'. They had
a quotation a week, with Shirley Williams praising Reg Prentice in
1975 and me saying that the toppling of the Shah would not be in the
West's interests in 1978. Neither were sentiments we had any reason to
be embarrassed about, but in the lexicon of the Left they were great
crimes.

David Steel then wrote a letter to the three of us via the *Guardian*,
signed, 'Yours fraternally'. It only confirmed to me his superficial
approach. Its aim was publicity. He had written to Bill and sent copies to
Shirley and me. I am not sure that Bill even replied and inasmuch as we
had any view it was one of irritation. For the three of us, rightly or
wrongly, the Liberal Party was low on our agenda. There were other
priorities. Had we known it was so high on Roy Jenkins's agenda, I am
sure that prudence alone would have led us to give the issue more
thought at this stage. As it was, all three of us saw the Liberal Party as an
issue to be faced after any party was formed and, we hoped, from a
position of strength rather than weakness. Our focus was on whether we
could create a party which Labour voters could support, replacing the
Labour Party by a similar party, though not a replica, or marginalizing
the Labour Party to its hard unrepresentative Left and taking over a
substantial part of their voters.

I spent most of August on holiday in the United States with my family
at Fort Union Ranch in New Mexico. Situated on the Santa Fe trail, it
belonged to a friend's family and had been kept as a working ranch. The
ranch covers 180,000 acres and was originally given to a military member
of the family by a grateful US Government. It is an idyllic place with a
cool spring feeding a pond in which we swam after returning from long
rides. We rode with Western saddles which hold you firmly, being built
up front and back and, apart from rattlesnakes which frighten them, the
horses pick their way on the trail with barely a stumble, allowing one to
relax and enjoy scenery that makes a Hollywood Western appear rather
dull. In the evening when I could escape from Scrabble, I would finish
writing the manuscript of *Face the Future* which was due to be published
in the new year. As I chronicled Britain's decline, my resolve to try and
reverse it with radical changes in our political system increased. Here I
was able to talk to American friends about their experience of helping
John Anderson. He had campaigned as a third-party candidate for the
Presidency and their two-party system and first-past-the-post voting had
squeezed him dry. I also had time to reflect on the British historical
precedents. They were not likely to encourage anyone to split: Ramsay
MacDonald's National Government and Oswald Mosley's New Party,
the disaffiliation of the Independent Labour Party in 1932, Sir Richard
Acland's Common Wealth Party in 1942. All had failed. I returned from
America still keen to do battle from within the Labour Party.

With the difficult Blackpool Conference almost upon us, it proved easier to resolve to stay with Labour than to do it. Unemployment had just topped two million for the first time since 1935. Margaret Thatcher was determined not to be panicked into making the same U-turn on economic policies which she believed had led the Conservative Party away from the paths of righteousness under Edward Heath. There was justice in her allegation that the economy had been mismanaged, that inflation had to be controlled and that over the previous years we had paid ourselves 22 per cent more for producing 4 per cent less. But the rigidity of her stance made it correspondingly harder to argue within the Labour Party for a market economy. The Benn advocacy of seizing the commanding heights of the economy for another round of nationalization had more appeal than would normally be the case. The ideological purity which was gripping the Conservatives as well as the Labour Party was mutually reinforcing. Both Tony Benn and Margaret Thatcher were good communicators because both had simple messages. Both thrived on controversy. The difference was that the true radical was Margaret Thatcher; her ideology had never been tried in Britain. Tony Benn was merely recycling earlier, failed centralized socialism. Nonetheless, it was Benn who looked set for success in Blackpool.

Wherever I went I found an extraordinary contrast between people's public and private positions. In private there were any number of Labour MPs and Labour Party members horrified by what was happening and yet in public there were almost none who would fight back. Abroad, fellow socialists were watching with amazement what was happening to the Labour Party which for many of them had been the model for their social democracy in the immediate post-war period. Surely, I told myself, we could have continental social democracy in Britain. I became more conscious than ever of the contradictions on which British Labourism had been founded; more convinced than ever that Hugh Gaitskell had been right to single out the significance of Clause IV in the Constitution after electoral defeat in 1959.

In September, irony of ironies, a few months before I was ready to contemplate leaving the Labour Party, my Devonport constituency became a safe Labour seat. I had been in highly marginal seats for the fourteen years I had been MP, but the Boundary Commissioners now came forward with a proposal to create three constituencies, North, East and West. The northern constituency, later called Devonport, bore only passing resemblance to the original Devonport constituency. But it contained all of the post-war council estates between Dartmoor and the city. It was solid Labour territory and would probably never be won by the Conservatives.

The Gang of Three at least had the consolation of some public support. On Monday 22 September a group of twelve Labour MPs led by Mike Thomas, the MP for Newcastle-upon-Tyne East, published an article in *The Times* explaining why the Labour Party's structure must change. One of its most interesting features was that they clearly expected that the Blackpool Conference might paper over the cracks for a little longer.

> Soothing voices are to be heard telling us all is at last to be well with This Great Movement of Ours. Tony Benn and his constitutional changes will be staved off; the leadership will rest secure with the Parliamentary Labour Party, the NEC will come under control again, policy differences can be swept under the carpet; the unions will bail us out from bankruptcy; and unemployment and the Thatcher/Joseph/ Howe brand of economic masochism will ensure us victory at the next election.

But this was not to be. The Blackpool Conference was to prove to be far more disastrous than any of us expected. On Monday 29 September CLV had a meeting in the Baronial Hall of the Winter Gardens. The Gang of Three all spoke and it was a rousing affair. I said it was time for the compromising to end and the fight back to start, and Shirley warned that there was such a thing as a fascism of the Left. That evening in Shirley's room in the Imperial Hotel we heard that Clive Jenkins was confident of swinging the trade union votes to win on an electoral college and on withdrawal from the Community. On the very first day Tony Benn, replying to the economic debate on behalf of the NEC, called for three major pieces of legislation within the first month of a Labour Government. This was cloud cuckoo land. First, an Industry Bill with the power to extend common ownership, control capital movements and provide for industrial democracy to be on the statute book within a matter of days (rapturous applause). The second bill must transfer all the powers back from the Common Market Commission to the House of Commons within a matter of weeks. The third bill was to get rid of the House of Lords by creating a thousand peers and then abolishing the peerage (fervent applause). I could not believe that such flagrant nonsense could actually be taken seriously by a Party which, for all its faults, had demonstrated over the years that it had deep moorings in the British way of life. That night, at a meeting in Shirley's bedroom, I heard fellow MPs talk for the first time about leaving the Labour Party without qualifying what they were saying. Ironically many of those who spoke most fervently that night eventually stayed with the Party. But that night we all felt doom-laden.

Next morning, Tuesday 30 September, the results of the constituency section for the NEC showed that my vote had slipped. I had 106,000, votes, Jack Ashley was runner-up and Peter Shore and Roy Hattersley well ahead of me. I was paying the price for the Gang of Three letter. When Jim Callaghan spoke the next day he once again made a plea for Party unity but there was precious little of it about.

For pity's sake, stop arguing. The public is crying out for unity in order to get rid of the Thatcher Government [applause]. Mr Attlee is coming back into favour. He is being quoted by all and sundry. Every time I read an article or hear a speech I hear a quotation from Clem. I must say it only goes to show what happens to us after we are dead.

Towards the end of his speech he said, 'Nobody here, I think, talks any nonsense about Centre parties or the rest of it. It's as dead as a dodo, mere fluff.' It was sad to listen to someone, who over the years had been able to dominate the Conference, speak with so little of his former influence or power.

On the Wednesday morning it was my turn. I spoke from the floor against a Clive Jenkins motion urging the Labour Party to include the withdrawal from the European Community as a priority in our next manifesto. I said:

The TUC voted for a referendum only a few weeks ago. Why have we not had the opportunity to vote again to consult the British people? I say to Conference that it is a constitutional outrage, first to go to the British people and let them decide in 1975 and now not even to give the British people a chance to determine their own destiny.

Conference Report says there was applause then but it was mixed with cries of dissent. I went on:

This issue has divided the Party. I do not want it to continue to divide the Party. A commitment to a referendum united us in 1974. I urge that we unite again on another commitment that, if a Labour Government wants to withdraw, it will put the issue to the British people.

I left the rostrum to applause, but again there were many loud shouts of disagreement. I was followed by Bill Sirs of the steelworkers union who made a strongly pro-market speech, but it too made no difference. Peter Shore then spoke very emotionally:

At last the wraps have dropped from people's eyes and they have seen the full reality of the sell-out of what occurred when Mr Heath took us in against our will, without any Parliamentary or constitutional process, no commitment in any manifesto by Mr Heath [applause], no General Election, no referendum. What happened was a rape of the British people, and of the British Parliament and the rights of our constitution [applause].

He went on to say, 'I do not believe that if we state fairly and clearly in our next manifesto what our policy is, that we have any necessity at all to resort to yet another referendum'. The withdrawal motion was carried on a card vote by 5,042,000 to 2,097,000. The requisite two-thirds

majority was not there to ensure it was in the manifesto but nobody
listening to that debate could have had any doubt that Labour would
fight the next election on an outright commitment to withdraw and what
is more if it won it would take Britain out.

This was only the beginning of an awful day. In the afternoon the
Conference voted to widen the franchise for the election of the Party
Leader beyond Labour Members of Parliament and opted for compulsory
reselection. The only ray of light was a narrow defeat for the proposition
that the NEC should control the election manifesto. And then, that
night, I had an ugly encounter in the lounge bar of the Imperial Hotel. A
new trade union organizer had come to Plymouth and, slightly drunk, he
started to threaten me with deselection if I continued to fight against the
Left. I grabbed him by the lapels, 'I know more of your members by
their Christian names than you know by their surnames; don't come into
my constituency and tell me what Plymothians will do. They and I will
not be bullied by the likes of you.'

By the Thursday morning the Conference seemed determined to
convince the country that it was totally in the grip of the far Left by
proceeding to vote for unilateral nuclear disarmament. This was despite
Bill Rodgers's warning that, if they were to go down a road of the
single-handed renunciation of nuclear weapons, Labour would be
rejected overwhelmingly by the people whose support they needed for
victory.

These blows, coming one upon the other, were shattering and for some
of us, decisive. Indeed some of us might have preferred to make our
move that day. I certainly think Bill would have been in favour of taking
a very significant step away from Labour then. But by the time Bill had
spoken to the press after his speech, Shirley was already in full cry at a
CLV fringe meeting. We had agreed we would meet before the meeting
started to discuss what we would say, but it had not proved possible. It
was clear that the electoral college question was going to be referred to a
Special Conference and Shirley said, without consultation, that we would
take our battle there. Bill turned to me and said, 'Well it's nice to know.'
It was not Shirley's fault, she had to react, but it showed how these
deeply important issues were having to be dealt with rapidly, almost
instinctively. Events were moving so fast that we could hardly anticipate
them. My mood was very tough indeed when I got up to speak, and the
Guardian report was correct in saying that I took the whole argument a
step further by implying that Jim Callaghan should only stay as Leader if
he was prepared to join in the fight against the Left.

· We are fed up with this fudging and mudging, with mush and slush.
We need courage, conviction and hard work ... We cannot turn this
party round unless there is much clearer and more decisive leadership
... We must ask our leaders that they stand up for their beliefs with

the same conviction and passion and the same skill used by others who have won out on countless issues at this Conference.

Some thought the word 'mudging' was there only for euphony, but Eric Partridge's *Dictionary of Slang and Unconventional English* says that it is an old dialect word for 'moving very quietly'.

On Friday morning, 3 October, I worked on a speech which I intended to make on Saturday afternoon at a Labour Party meeting at Blaenau Festiniog in North Wales; not exactly a media centre. Mike Thomas came to help me and we decided there and then that we could not defeat the Left's call for a wider franchise to elect the Leader by advocating that it should be left to MPs. Our best course, and the most principled, would be to exploit the opportunity that Conference vote had left us. The Party had not been able to agree a specific mechanism for the Leader's election. It had only made the commitment to widen the franchise. We had to ensure that one member-one vote became the preferred way of widening the franchise and not the electoral college.

I also discussed my speech with Shirley before driving off to stay at the home of Barry Jones and address his East Flint Constituency Labour Party that night. Given that Barry was Denis Healey's PPS and that it was obvious that Jim Callaghan was about to resign, I did not think it was fair to involve him in what I intended to be a very tough speech. But I did try to convince Barry that Denis Healey had to put himself at the head of a group of MPs who would disown the Party Conference decisions. I think that Barry and Denis believed their best hope for winning was to conduct a low-key campaign with Denis as the unity candidate. I wanted to let them know that I thought this was a recipe for certain defeat and that there were already some Labour MPs who were so disillusioned that, even though they were on the same side as Denis, they would not vote for him if he ran as an ameliorator. I cannot say I made much headway, delightful hosts though Barry and his wife were. I drove that morning up into the mountains of Snowdonia, believing that Denis Healey would lose to either of the two likely other runners, Peter Shore or Michael Foot.

My speech that afternoon was aimed directly at the Bishop's Stortford compromise over an electoral college. I argued that it conceded a principle, and in place of a legitimate, proven, parliamentary procedure offered a mess of pottage. Only on Thursday the voters had seen on their television screens the total shambles surrounding the trade union block vote in Blackpool. If the trade unions were to participate in choosing a Prime Minister or Leader of the Opposition they must accept that their votes had to be cast as a result of balloting within their unions and then only by members who voluntarily paid the political levy to the Labour Party. I argued that, day by day, we had seen in Blackpool why an electoral college, in any of the forms proposed, was not acceptable.

We cannot have a Prime Minister chosen by block votes that do not accurately reflect the number of their members paying the political levy. We cannot have a Prime Minister chosen by block votes, cast in line with the overall policy of a union whose policy may be determined by a body which includes conservatives, communists and people who do not pay the political levy. We cannot have a Prime Minister chosen by the switching of a block vote where a Communist can influence that decision. We cannot have a Prime Minister chosen by the switching of block votes merely because the General Secretary of a trade union happens to be absent. We cannot allow the choice of the country's Prime Minister to pass from Parliament to the caucus; to unrepresentative block votes and to unrepresentative delegates.

Driving back to Buttermere late that afternoon over the twisting roads of Snowdonia, I began, really for the first time, to think in detail about what would be necessary to create a new party.

On my return others were rapidly moving in the same direction. I was greatly encouraged to receive a letter from Harold Luscombe, a young Labour councillor from my constituency. He worked on the railways and had fought West Devon as a Labour parliamentary candidate. In effect he told me that if I broke with the Labour Party, he would too. I wrote back, 'One thing I can promise you – I will not become a Liberal or join a rootless Centre party that means abandoning my socialist conviction.' True to his word, when I left in 1981 so did he, becoming the lone SDP councillor on Plymouth City Council. He lost his seat in the city council elections in 1982, won a county council seat in 1984, became Deputy Leader of the SDP/Liberal Alliance Group at County Hall and then won back his city council seat. He lost it in 1991, though remaining a Social Democrat Devon county councillor. In 1987, travelling down to David Penhaligon's funeral with a number of SDP and Liberal MPs, I was being ribbed by journalists about the SDP's middle-class claret-drinking image, something guaranteed to make me see red, when who should walk down the carriage in his railway uniform but Harold Luscombe. It gave me great pleasure to introduce him all round as the leader of the SDP in Plymouth.

Then on 15 October the inevitable happened. Jim Callaghan formally announced his resignation as Labour Party Leader. I immediately wrote to him by hand:

Dear Jim,

I have never shifted and will never shift from my judgement that your period as Prime Minister was one of which you can be proud and all those of us who served under you can feel privileged to have been part of it. For two-and-a-half years I saw the burdens you carried as close as almost anyone, other than Denis, in the Cabinet – I often marvelled at your strength and judgement – you taught me a great deal – you supported me through good times and bad –

sustained me and guided me. I am, and will remain ever in your debt. We disagreed this summer openly and sadly on a very important issue, I wish it need not have happened but I know each of us took the course they felt to be right.

I think you felt I was responsible for Peter Jenkins' wounding article after Bishop's Stortford – not so – I never leaked from Cabinet or Shadow Cabinet except on that occasion which I told you about, over the all-day Cabinet on Europe when I was indiscreet rather than leaking to David Watt. But as it turned out that helped us both get through the Cabinet and the Party a sensible policy for Europe which we held to for two years. History will credit you with handling Jimmy Carter for two-and-a-half years in a way which made his Presidency a great deal better than it might otherwise have been; of staying resolute over a genuine settlement for Zimbabwe and of helping the Party and the country to adjust to membership of the Community, quite apart from many domestic achievements.

I wish I knew which way the Party is heading. I fear for its future and its future is bound up closely with that of our country. I wish you and Audrey every happiness and for you personally I only feel warmth and respect. Thank you for all your kindness which sometime I hope I can repay.

Yours ever,
David

Jim Callaghan sent a handwritten reply on 24 October thanking me very much and wishing that he deserved half of what I had said. It was a gentle, generous letter, given our recent differences, saying that he had great hopes for me in the future and hoped that did not sound patronizing and in a kind reference to my time as Foreign Secretary, said how much he had admired my pertinacity and inventiveness on Zimbabwe and Namibia and that if the Tories had not encouraged Smith to wait in the hope of getting a better deal, I might have pulled off a settlement much earlier. In wishing me the best for the future he urged me to remember that our Party could not be led from the Right – I must be in the Centre.

We were now confronted with a battle on two fronts; we had simultaneously to elect a Leader under the old system while trying to get the PLP to reject an electoral college of any kind and support one member-one vote. And the Left were fighting these battles under new rules of their own.

A letter had been sent from the organizing secretary of the Labour Co-ordinating Committee to all Constituency Labour parties. It said:

Nominations close on 29 October and the first ballot of MPs will close on 4 November. We therefore recommend Constituency Labour Party and sitting MPs to hold emergency General Management Committees (GMCs) within this five-day period and insist that the MP brings his/her ballot paper to the GMC to be filled in after a vote has been taken there. CLP activists will, of course, be fully aware that the Conference endorsement of reselection will herald a new era of competition from MPs.

There in all its nakedness was exactly what was wrong with mandatory reselection. On 20 October, in a speech to an EETPU meeting, I warned that

> this letter is more than just to 'lean on a bloke or two', it is to fulfil all our worst fears about the tenuous nature of some people's commitment in the Labour Party to representative democracy. We are on the threshold of becoming a different party, a party where MPs are simply sent to Westminster to do what they are told by a majority of their GMC, perhaps twenty-five or thirty people, maybe less, who are able to attend emergency GMCs. Maybe now some people in the Labour Party who had thought that the Gang of Three were crying wolf will realize how dire the situation now is.

I called on all the candidates for the Party leadership election to say whether they were prepared to commit themselves to one member-one vote in every constituency; to either select an MP or to sack an MP. Sadly, there was very little chance that Denis would come out of his shell and champion one member-one vote. His strategy, such as it was, was to lie low and hope people could be frightened by the sheer implausibility of Michael Foot as Prime Minister.

It was essential to build up the number of constituency parties who would support one member-one vote and a lot of my time and effort over the next few months went into this. I argued strongly against those who were saying that it was not feasible for the Labour Party to introduce one member-one vote. Surely since this was exactly what the Liberal Party had done, we could not argue that it was beyond us. The key was to head off the argument that the great test was whether the Parliamentary Labour Party in an electoral college had 50 per cent, 40 per cent or 33 per cent of the electoral college vote. The issue of principle was that either Members of Parliament voted to choose or individual members of the Party voted to choose but that the electoral college was a fix and any percentages totally arbitrary.

I was in close touch with Shirley Williams who was an enthusiast for one member-one vote. Things were more complex with Bill Rodgers. He could see the tactical advantages of one member-one vote but he genuinely believed that it was better for MPs to choose the Leader and preferred to stick to this option, while agreeing not to do anything to damage the cause for one member-one vote. I genuinely believed that a widening of the franchise to all members of the Party was a good thing, although I could see the strength of the argument that sometimes only the MPs knew the weaknesses of the potential leadership candidates. For example, I do believe that it was because Labour MPs were aware of George Brown's weakness for alcohol that he was beaten, and that information like this is sometimes not widely known by Party members.

All the time that this battle was raging we were grappling with the problem of a new party. On Saturday 19 October Roy and Jennifer Jenkins came over to Buttermere for lunch. Their last visit had been early in 1976, when Roy had told me that Harold Wilson was going to resign, which showed how much we had drifted apart. It was more relaxed than Debbie and I had anticipated but I still could not be sure what sort of party Roy really wanted. During a walk after lunch he told me about his proposed new policy institute, to be an offshoot of the Radical Centre, a small organization he had already established. The Centre was run for him by Clive Lindley, a pleasant businessman who owned a catering company serving motorways and sports stadia and also by Jim Daly, a councillor. Both were disillusioned members of the Labour Party and active in CLV, but this did not give me a real picture of what Roy was after. I am afraid I concluded that Roy was trying to find a vehicle to make himself Prime Minister and that made me wary. I had just finished reading a book by Dingle Foot which quoted a speech by Lord Randolph Churchill delivered in June 1886 to the electors of South Paddington. He had asked why Mr Gladstone had reserved the Home Rule Bill for his closing days and had concluded it was for one reason only: 'To gratify the imagination of an old man in a hurry.' Though Gladstone was then seventy-seven and Roy was only fifty-nine, it was very obvious that Roy too was an old man in a hurry.

I was more encouraged when David Marquand came to see me. David appeared to want a new socialist party, which heartened me since he was close to Roy. He sent me some analysis by Ivor Crewe, the Essex University psephologist, whose findings in David's view pointed

to a basic contradiction between the Labour Party's policies under any conceivable leadership and the working-class Labour electorate, to a quite genuine revolt against the two-party system and (less obviously perhaps) to a possible sociological basis for a breakaway Labour Party.

Meanwhile the Campaign for Labour Victory was stepping up its activity, with Alec McGivan trying to encourage more and more constituencies to support one member-one vote. On Saturday 25 October we held a special meeting at our headquarters at Highbury Place in London, which had been made available to us by the EETPU. Though the members were split, a good number of them totally despaired of our chances of turning Labour around in anything much under a decade. What was encouraging was that Clive Lindley wrote to me before the Conference in favour of calling any new party the Social Democrats, so it began to appear that those close to Roy were coming around to our thinking on the type of new party we should be forming. I fear, however, in the light of what happened later that they were just manoeuvring; that it was a tactical change of heart rather than a sincere decision.

In the Shadow Cabinet we decided to go ahead with MPs electing our new leader and the PLP supported us. On 4 November the first ballot results from the leadership election were announced. Denis Healey had 112 votes, Michael Foot 83, John Silkin 38 and Peter Shore 32. It was obvious that Michael could win on the next ballot. On Monday 10 November he duly did so, beating Denis Healey by 139 to 129 votes.

There were press reports that some of the Right had deliberately abstained or even voted for Michael Foot in the belief that it was better to bring all the Party's problems to a head by electing Michael Foot, even though they totally disapproved of him. Bill Rodgers and I had taken the precaution of having our voting slips witnessed. Despite the deep doubts we had about Denis Healey by then, we had both voted for him. I do know of two or possibly three Right-wing MPs who might have tried that trick, but they did not change the result. Denis Healey deludes himself when he says that their few votes were sufficient to explain his defeat. When the Gang of Three had met with him in September before the Conference to try to persuade him to risk all by battling on, we had warned him that he was heading for defeat. Although an aggressive campaign would have made defeat by Michael even more likely, it would have left him free to challenge Michael Foot openly a year later and win. As it was, immediately the result was announced, he agreed to serve as Michael's Deputy and thereby locked himself into certain defeat at the General Election, with Michael still Leader.

I have said since that I would not have left the Labour Party if Denis Healey had become the Leader. The truth is that I would even have stayed and fought alongside him if he had lost the leadership provided he had shown at least the will to fight. Once Denis Healey accepted the electoral college, as he did during that leadership election, I could see no possibility whatever of shifting the Labour Party back towards sane policies before the next election. The election of Michael Foot was the final straw. I had, after all, watched Michael Foot closely in Plymouth ever since the age of eleven; there were people in the Devonport constituency whom I knew well and who also knew him, and we had many family friends in common. I never disliked him as a person but I deplored his political positions. It was beyond my worst imaginings that he would become Leader of the Labour Party. Even in the early 1970s when he started to poll well in the Parliamentary Party, it seemed something only for nightmares. Now it was reality. I knew better than most how deep-seated was his antagonism to nuclear deterrence, to serious defence spending and many of the principles on which NATO was founded. His criticism of the economic market basis of the European Community was venomous; his romantic attachment to parliamentary sovereignty and his hostility to any legislation which stemmed from the

European Communities Act were passionate. There was no prospect of reversing the shift in Labour Party policy while he was Leader or of defeating an electoral college at the Special Conference in January, and so it proved to be.

I knew that under his leadership I could not remain a member of the Shadow Cabinet. The question now was not 'if' I should leave the Shadow Cabinet but 'when'. Since I was elected by the PLP and there was the all-important special meeting of the Parliamentary Party on 13 November in which I hoped to speak, I decided to stay for my elected period but not to put myself up for re-election.

The Shadow Cabinet did not take long to distinguish itself under its new leadership by backing a Roy Hattersley motion that accepted an electoral college. It only stipulated that the unions must make sure they consulted their Labour Party supporters who paid the political levy before they cast their vote in the college. Roy Hattersley, who in early November had attacked the block vote, was bent on finding a formula that would ditch us and save his face, even though he knew his motion was unworkable and would be rejected by the NEC and Conference, which it duly was.

At the PLP on 13 November, I was allowed to put the case for one member–one vote which had been spelled out in the Shadow Cabinet paper in my name and that of Bill Rodgers. Roy Hattersley advanced his argument on which the Shadow Cabinet had devised their ingenious but disreputable hybrid. He claimed it to be a compromise between the administrative practicality of an electoral college and the genuine democracy of one man–one vote. He suggested that the PLP should be allocated 55 per cent of the votes of an electoral college, the remaining 45 per cent being distributed between the various constituent bodies on a basis that could be amicably negotiated, with the constituencies receiving the largest share. Individual constituencies would vote by a ballot of their members on a specified night and the constituency vote would then be aggregated and cast as a qualified block vote.

I spoke off-the-cuff but Mike Thomas made a note of what I said for the press:

> Any system of widening the franchise has to be legitimate and democratic, acceptable not just to the Party but to the nation as a whole. The system will be subjected to the closest scrutiny of the whole nation, as we choose not just the Leader of our Party but also their Prime Minister.
>
> If we once accept the principle of an electoral college then we can be sure that on 24 January we will end up with a scheme very similar to the NEC model resolution. The Parliamentary Committee's resolution today asks us to mortgage our future and to vacate the ground of principle. If we concede the principle today without knowing any of the details we will be doing so without being able to judge whether

what is proposed is democratic or legitimate. It is a menu not only without percentages, but a menu without the main courses.

Roy Hattersley's paper says his scheme is a compromise between an electoral college and one man-one vote. But, Roy, you cannot compromise with one member-one vote – that is a principle. The motion from the majority of the Parliamentary Committee is a proposal for an electoral college and it should fly under its true colours.

In our consideration of one member-one vote, we tried to find a way to involve the political levy payers in the trade unions. But all the trade unions we consulted said they either could not distinguish readily who their levy payers were, or if they could, could not see how to rule out Communists, Liberals or Conservatives from voting in any consultation of those levy payers. It is simply impractical to separate them.

That is why we believe one member-one vote is the only legitimate and democratic alternative to the present arrangements for electing the Leader.

The Parliamentary Party voted for Roy Hattersley and the Shadow Cabinet's electoral college by a very small majority. Of the 268 Labour MPs, barely half attended and the motion was carried by only sixty-eight votes to fifty-nine. The Hattersley compromise had, however, served its purpose. It had divided those in the Shadow Cabinet who had originally voted against the electoral college. I warned Roy in the Shadow Cabinet that it was really the Kinnock amendment and would one day be used by Neil Kinnock to become Leader. Roy Hattersley discovered in 1983 that I was right, and he was deprived of the leadership he coveted.

That same night there was a demonstration on the floor of the House of Commons which reflected very badly on the Parliamentary Labour Party. Michael Foot had failed his first real test as Leader. Bill Rodgers felt deeply affronted by what had happened and when he wrote to Michael the next day, I agreed to sign his letter. We objected to what Michael and Roy Hattersley had said on the floor of the House, asserting that most people would see it either as connivance of the front bench in the demonstration or at the very least tacit support for it. Bill let the press know what he had done and I felt that, like me, he was paving the way to stand down from the Shadow Cabinet.

I had misread Bill, not for the last time I fear. In the middle of the next week he and I went over to Shirley's flat to discuss the general situation. I came armed with a letter which I hoped to send to my constituency party the next day explaining why I had decided not to seek election to the Shadow Cabinet. In Plymouth on the Saturday before, while opening a divisional Labour Party bazaar, I had already given some indication of my disquiet. I referred in my letter to what I had said then and emphasized that the issue was not one of personalities but of profound differences over a range of policies. I had made clear in Plymouth that Michael Foot had been fairly and clearly elected by the Parliamentary Party and that he was entitled to be given every chance to see if he could unify the Party and settle our policy differences. One of my difficulties was that my agent, Ron Lemin, was a very close friend of Michael Foot, having worked for him in the constituency when Michael was the MP, and though many on the constituency GMC did not agree with Michael on policies, particularly defence, they nevertheless liked him as a person. So I stressed in my letter that I was fond of Michael and that the problem I faced was somewhat similar to that which Michael had faced when he was in opposition to Clement Attlee, and had chosen the freedom of the back benches. I also spelled out in some detail the policy differences and put them in a Plymouth context. At that time I was due to meet the President of Toshiba to persuade the Japanese company to save jobs at the Rank-Toshiba factory which was due to close. I said that Toshiba would not dream of staying in Plymouth if they seriously thought that Britain would leave the European Community and that it would put off other foreign investors whom Plymouth needed to attract. On defence I highlighted the effect of a Labour Government, if elected in 1984, unilaterally abandoning the Polaris patrols which would still then have at least ten years' potential active service ahead of them. I said that I could not stay silent on these issues, as I would have to do if elected to the Parliamentary Committee, and that I felt it necessary now to speak out from the back benches in Parliament and in the country in order, I hoped, to reverse the decisions taken by the Party. But already my closest friends in Plymouth could see that I was distancing myself from the Labour Party.

Shirley and Bill seemed stunned that I intended to leave the Shadow Cabinet and they both tried to persuade me to stay. Shirley said that if I were to stand down she would not be able to go ahead with her nomination as a prospective Parliamentary candidate in Stevenage, due to be agreed shortly at a constituency meeting. I argued, though I was not fully convinced, that it was perfectly possible for her to go ahead if she wished and also for Bill to be a member of the Shadow Cabinet. We did not have to act in an identical fashion. It was a good-natured argument, but I was not to be shifted. I had always regretted not resigning after the European vote in October 1971 and I was not going to make that mistake again. There was a deeper reason too. I wanted now to be able to talk openly to people about the pros and cons of forming a new party. I did not think it was right to do this while still a member of the Shadow Cabinet, nor could I profess loyalty to a leader whose political views were diametrically opposed to my own. Eventually it was agreed that Bill and I would go our separate ways but without any rancour. Shirley said that she would not now agree to be nominated for Stevenage. She warned me, quite rightly as it turned out, that the press would interpret my decision as being a major step towards leaving the Labour Party, however much I tried to explain that I was fighting from within. Bill misread Shirley, also not for the last time, saying to me as we left her flat that he had known her a lot longer than I and she would be persuaded to go ahead and become the prospective Labour candidate for Stevenage. In retrospect it was a critical meeting. Had Shirley not withdrawn her candidature, maybe the Limehouse Declaration would never have occurred.

I sent my letter off on the Thursday and arranged to see Michael Foot on Friday morning. It was a brief business-like meeting, for he could see my mind was made up, but it was also a sad occasion. That evening I left for a five-day visit to Brazil. I settled down in my seat, looking forward to seeing Rio de Janeiro again and leaving Labour Party problems behind me; I turned and across the aisle was surprised to see Clive Jenkins, the General Secretary of my own union, the ASTMS. He grinned. In truth, he had much to grin about.

21

THE GANG OF FOUR

When I returned from Brazil I arranged to meet Roy Jenkins at the end of November. Firstly, I was growing apprehensive about whether, in the last analysis, Bill Rodgers would be prepared to move decisively, even if we were to be saddled with the electoral college at the Special Conference in January, and I thought Roy could steady him. Secondly, since Roy Jenkins was going to take some action when he returned from Brussels in early January, there was a real risk of a foul-up with everybody getting in each other's way.

Bill had become ever more evasive when the question of creating a new party had come up in discussion. Now, with his decision to stand for the Shadow Cabinet, I could not see how he could resign immediately after the Special Conference, since this was only a few weeks away on 24 January. On 28 November, the day before I was due to see Roy, Shirley had, as she promised, told her constituency party in Stevenage that she could not accept nomination and I knew that this had cost her dear. Her main reason was that she could not, as a parliamentary candidate, honestly expound and defend Labour Party policies. She went on quite specifically to say that there was no other party in Britain that she could contemplate joining and that 'the Liberals aren't a serious alternative'. So I had no sense that she was backing away from the possibility of forming a social democratic party. My fear was that she was sufficiently sceptical about the chances of any new party to walk away from politics altogether, if she felt it was likely to be the rootless Centre party she had particularly castigated. Out of Parliament and having always disliked the hours and the male atmosphere of the House of Commons, and now without a constituency, her ties were understandably looser. She was starting to enjoy the freedom of the quasi-academic life she was now involved in, particularly in the United States, and I suspected that she could be seduced away by Yale or Harvard. She was adamantly opposed to a Centre party and, like me, wanted any new party to be part of the Socialist International. At that stage she was also rather suspicious of

Roy: she was aware of his ambition and in the past had insisted on taking her own independent line, not resigning in 1972 and being identified with no one wing of the Party. She was an important factor in our prospective success, for she was undoubtedly a vote-winner, with a natural gift for empathizing with anyone with whom she was in contact. Her attitude strengthened my resolve to make it quite clear to Roy Jenkins that we were not interested in, and would not join, a Centre party with the Liberals, based on his friendship with David Steel.

On Saturday 29 November Debbie, the children and I drove to East Hendred for a late lunch with Roy and Jennifer Jenkins. I knew this meeting would be critical. Roy had had his sixtieth birthday a few days earlier; he seemed fit but was getting impatient with what he saw as our prevarication. The rational case for making it a Gang of Four rather than continuing with the Gang of Three was overwhelming. Since I was probably the biggest obstacle to making this transformation, with my scepticism about Roy becoming our leader, it was all the more important that I should take the initiative.

However, I did not feel as though I was acting alone. In a real sense I was speaking as the representative of a number of the other younger MPs who had been talking to me very frankly about the nature of any new party. We were all adamant that it could not be a party created in Roy Jenkins's image. Most of us saw Shirley Williams as the leader and feared that, if Roy joined us, the older MPs likely to split off with us would naturally muster behind him again and vote for him as leader. Moreover, we were in the thick of the battle for one member-one vote to choose the Leader of the Labour Party, and there was some anxiety that Roy would want the old system of MPs choosing the leader for any new party.

My first task, therefore, was to get a pledge from Roy that he would accept one member-one vote in a new party. He readily conceded this – all too readily I now realize. I knew he was serious when he specifically asked if I accepted that he might run for the leadership against Shirley Williams, who, I had already told him, I thought would make the best leader. I said, of course he could stand, anyone could, that was the advantage; the members of the party would be free to choose whoever they wished. Debbie was with me at the time and later, when we discussed his reaction in the car, she felt that he had registered that this pledge was crucial to me and other MPs. Since one member-one vote for electing the Leader of the Labour Party was at the heart of the then public controversy Roy must have realized it was very important. Just before Christmas he rang me up at Buttermere, somewhat agitated, having heard from various friends of his that I was asserting that I did not think he should ever be the leader. I presumed that he had seen a memo I had sent to Bill and Shirley in early December which was highly critical of his being perceived as the leader right from the start. I then drove over to East Hendred, this being so important, and we settled it, as I thought, once and for all. If a new party were formed, the leader would be elected by one member-one vote, and if Roy won that was perfectly acceptable to me; I joked that I might even vote for him.

For Roy to pretend now that this was a matter of minimal importance is a subterfuge to cover his tracks and to pretend that we did not even focus on it in the four hours of discussion that November, defies belief. It took a mere nine months for Roy Jenkins to renege on that agreement and campaign for the leader to be chosen by the SDP MPs. When he switched, as I describe on pages 530–32, the probability was that Shirley would defeat him in a members' ballot. I was not then considered by anyone to be his likely challenger.

All this time we were moving closer and closer to the break with Labour, with many hesitations and fluctuations in mood. On 2 December, for example, Bill urged that the Gang of Three write a letter to members of CLV to say we were continuing to work together for the interests we all shared and that the fight would continue up to and beyond the Special Conference on 24 January 1981. I had to write back to him and say that I favoured deleting the words 'and beyond' for by then I was convinced that the Special Conference must be a threshold. This he accepted. But, despite differences still existing between us, Peter Jenkins rightly based a *Guardian* article in December on the premise that a breakaway from the Labour Party was no longer a mere possibility but had become a distinct probability. He flagged up the Special Labour Party Conference on 24 January as providing a convenient point of decision if not exactly a deadline. He had obviously spoken to Roy Jenkins, who was declaring that he would act on his own if nothing had been done by Easter. It also observed that Roy now accepted that any breakaway should be a social democratic party, that he did not expect to return as the leader of any such new party, and that personal ambition was no longer, if it ever had been, his chief motivation. That proved to be sheer disinformation, yet Peter's conclusion, with which I fully concurred, was very sobering:

> The Labour Party is probably in decline and in the course of time there will probably be some kind of realignment in the Centre-Left. But it could take a long while, perhaps extend over two or three elections; meanwhile, promising careers will be wasted in the wilderness, the Conservatives will probably be kept in power (although not necessarily Mrs Thatcher), and many failures will precede eventual success. Those who set out had better be prepared for a long haul into the unknown.

Despite these warnings, by early December I was ready to cast the die. A year earlier I had written to a friend in America saying that I would stay with Labour and fight right up to the election. Now I sat down to write and explain why I had changed my mind:

As to the present awful situation in the Labour Party I am well content with what Hugo Young wrote in last Sunday's *Sunday Times*, also Peter Jenkins in the *Guardian* this Wednesday; they reflect my thinking. Getting out of the Shadow Cabinet was crucial. It means I can with honour think and plan for a social democratic party. I am not yet across the Rubicon but I am rationally calculating the changes necessary and the chances of success. Whatever I decide, I know it will be a gamble. I realize full well in three years I could be without a seat in Parliament – with a busted career – to be truthful I don't mind. I contemplate starting a new life in 1984 with calm and some pleasure. I am attracted by the challenge of a new fight but I loathe the prospect of hanging on to a broken vessel, which is the Labour Party for at least eight years. We could of course win in 1984 but it will be a bad government and Britain in 1988 will be worse off as it will be if Mrs T. wins again. I see a spiral downwards of economic decline and I ask is this really inevitable?

My analysis in the book due to be published in February is that our decline is part of a resistance to change, an inertia, and yet I envisage a new party. Why could this succeed? I am not sure it can but what else can? What other way is there and if we do not try how will we ever know? I cannot urge others to be more adventurous, the country to be more adventurous, if I cling to the system, to the old politics, to the politics of nudge, fudge and mudge. In a strange way, on the Friday after the 1979 election I felt free and devoid of ambition. Fate has given me too much, too early but this means I can at least give back one thing. I can risk all to win all.

The essential is that a new party is not cast in Roy Jenkins's image – he is valuable to us provided he does not lead it. Now, ambition would say let Roy lead it, for that gives me a chance, but that would be to flaw the party before it starts. I have doubts about Shirley on many counts, but she is classless, she is soft, she does have a sense of new politics; so I will use my position to insist on her being given a lead role even within a collective leadership for the launch period. What happens after that depends on the members, for any new party must be one member-one vote.

Can we finance it? Who knows, I don't. I doubt you can ever know until you try. If there were 20,000 who would join and pay £10 a year, that would, with other contributions, probably be sufficient. I write as if I have decided to launch a social democratic party; not quite, but I am very near to trying it. It may be the benefit will never come our way. It may force the Labour Party to have its equivalent of the SPD Bad Godesberg Conference. I am as certain of anything as I can be, that we will never have such a reappraisal of the Labour Party without an external stimulus, for if the electoral college goes through we will never have the type of leader who will fight the trend, fight for the unpopular cause or rally the Parliamentary Party. I can't see a Labour Prime Minister holding a wage policy as in 1977, or holding firm on the firemen's pay, for example.

I will now take three weeks to think. I know I am thought to be impatient, but you know that I rarely act without a lot of thought. I have come to my present position slowly, reluctantly and steadily. It is this inexorableness which makes me feel that the Rubicon will be crossed. They say now is not the time, but when will it be? If we wait, 1981 will be grim in terms of unemployment. Labour will do well in the May election. Party Conference will ignore its 1980 decisions and be merely an assault on the Tory Party, the launching pad for a general election. The political atmosphere will hot up. It will be the wrong time in June, the wrong time in October and so we will wait until the election and the manifesto. Perhaps five or ten MPs will stand as independent PLP candidates. Five might win. But all the time the good MPs will be picked off one by one or they will be bent. In order to beat off reselection, commitments will be made by good people that they will not leave the Party, then, having rallied one's troops, the feeling of letting them down will be too strong. So we will rationalize; let's fight in 1985 after the election, but then perhaps we may be elected and become the Government.

In government we won't be that bad, that extreme; compromises will be made. But what a mess. Half-hearted over Europe, hesitant over NATO, even more corporatist, in hock to the trade unionists, not really redistributionist, the libertarian nerve dulled by corporatist pressures. Out of government Michael goes. Peter Shore succeeds. After all, he will be only sixty Perhaps Hattersley! Maybe Benn, though not likely. Dark horse John Smith, with Scottish votes. Kinnock probably not because never a Minister, but growing more powerful. What a prospect. Meanwhile I and others become bitter, Messianic or depressed, believing in nothing passionately, holding on and learning to compromise. Abolish private education, even Shirley is starting down that route. Well, we will say, better than other countries. Perhaps, but why not enjoy life and return to medicine, and that's what I will do.

But all my life I will know there was a time in 1981 when perhaps had we had the courage, the vision; had we been prepared to break out, cut loose, risk all and accept being called traitors, things just might have been different. Britain just might have pulled itself up by its own collective will and common sense if it had just been given the chance. Who knows?

All the bulk of the advice is against me and yet I keep knowing that they are wrong. You said trust one's instincts – I believe that is what eventually I will have to do. Jimmy Carter did it in 1976. 'Ah,' the wise, prudent men will say, 'and look what happened to him.' True, but he nearly made it, and even so his legacy for the world and the US for four years is not going to be that awful. The all-powerful US will never be the same again. Carter was a necessary adjustment factor; flawed perhaps, but not fatally.

On Friday 5 December I drove up to Leeds with Debbie to be the guest of honour at Denis Healey's constituency Labour Party dinner and dance. Denis and Edna went out of their way to be welcoming and Denis made a very generous speech about me and my period as Foreign Secretary. He had in happier times talked to journalists about my leading the Labour Party eventually. He must have known that anything said that evening could be played back against him by the Left if I left the Party, as he by now must have guessed was probable. It was typical that he ignored this danger. The evening represented all that was good in the Labour Party, full of Yorkshire common sense and decent, generous people. Denis was totally at ease in his constituency, which was really one massive council estate. It was this which made him a far more formidable Labour politician than Roy Jenkins or Tony Crosland. In my speech I steered clear of any internal Labour Party politics and that night I wondered again if Labour could be saved from within. Might Denis be persuaded to fight? Really the two of us ought to have had a blazing row that night instead of fencing around each other. The reason I could never stop liking Denis, even while disagreeing with him, was that you could have a row and clear the air with him. I remembered the row we had over his refusal to back me when the Vice-Chief of the Naval Staff had wanted authority to strike-break over a weekend at Faslane without prior reference to Ministers. I remembered the row we had after he had leaked to Peter Jenkins about him rebuffing my attempt to win Cabinet approval for a Commonwealth peacekeeping force in Rhodesia. These had not been a mild exchange of views but vigorous stand-up rows. But our friendship had been strengthened not weakened because of them. Why, given the impending crisis, did we not lock horns that night? I suspect it was the old bull and the young bull story. He knew he had one fight left in him. I knew I had many. We were bound to fight from now on against each other. Hopefully it would be done with respect.

All through December I had frequent meetings with Mike Thomas, John Horam, Ian Wrigglesworth, Edward Lyons, Tom Bradley, Tom Ellis, Bob Maclennan, John Roper and others who must remain nameless. All of them were agonizing personally about what they might do. Sometimes there were only three or four MPs, sometimes more. Time and time again we analysed the prospects for any new fourth party. One point of agreement was that it would have to be distinctive and in particular different from the Liberal Party if it were to succeed. The more we analysed the polling evidence, the more we realized we had to undercut the Labour vote, not only to survive in our own seats, many of which were Labour strongholds, but also to be a new and powerful force in British politics. At a seminar given by Professor Ivor Crewe and Professor Anthony King of Essex University in Shirley's flat, the message was that a social democratic party would have a significant impact. It was a misfortune that Roy Jenkins was in Brussels and not involved in these discussions because it became ever clearer what sort of party we needed, and a strong consensus emerged. It is true that Bill did not attend many of these early meetings either, but he was having his own meetings with MPs. He was also, unlike Roy, struggling with his own personal decision. In the first few days of January 1981 he was still not ready to commit himself to leaving the Labour Party. The advantage of my meetings was that there were always one or two people ready to talk in detail about the shape of a future party when others were going through patches of doubt and caution. Some of the younger MPs were not keen to talk openly in front of Neville Sandelson, thinking him too headstrong, a reservation which I had to respect. Neville resented it at the time when I talked to him, though the intensity of this understandable resentment only became apparent later. In fairness to Neville, he was one of the firmest and clearest of us all, having believed that a break was inevitable some time before I or others came round to his way of thinking.

In the first week of December I sent the ten-page memo to Shirley and Bill to which I have already referred. It set out the predictable decision points for the month ahead. A copy was later stolen from my office in the House of Commons and found its way into the public domain. The memo started by saying that it was essential to try and maintain the unity and strength of the Gang of Three. This was now more necessary than ever because of the debate over standing for the Shadow Cabinet, which had revealed our own understandable indecision to the public and led the press to question the existence of an underlying strategy. So as each of the difficult decisions had to be made, we had to act together.

The first of these decisions would be in early December when the NEC decided on its view of the electoral college. I argued that Tom Bradley and Shirley Williams should not resign from the NEC. The second decision would come at the PLP meeting on 11 December. We were putting down an amendment urging the PLP to decline to accept the electoral college as legitimate and democratic since the NEC and Shadow Cabinet had, as we expected, failed to reach an agreed solution. The third decision that would face us related to Roy Jenkins who would cease to be President of the European Commission on 6 January. Handling this

is immensely difficult in personal and political terms for some of our closest allies see Roy still as their political leader, others count him as a friend but do not see him as the political leader in the 1980s, but as contributing powerfully to the campaign for social democracy. Others see him as a liability, linked to the Liberal-Centre party concept and not a social democrat. The maximum unity can only be achieved if it is accepted that any social democratic organization will be based on one member-one vote and that therefore the membership will determine the roles of individuals, but that before such decisions there should be a collective leadership. The problem with leaving this leadership issue blurred is threefold. Firstly, Roy has in the past been accepted as our leader and for four-and-a-half years was actually voted for as our leader; a natural tendency if the issue is not resolved will be for him to emerge as our leader. Secondly, Roy is older, therefore letting him emerge as the leader now satisfies the ambitions of those younger by leaving the issue open. Thirdly, the media will want a leader – particularly if we widen it out from the Gang of Three which has been accepted as a collective leadership. Some will push Roy Jenkins's leadership with the media and those in the media who wish us ill will be only too happy to portray him as the leader, sensing that this will do harm to the identity of social democracy. This issue must be resolved between the Four; it is too dangerous to leave it open. There are two options: the Gang of Three launch all initiatives and Roy Jenkins supports them, clearly taking for the present a secondary role; or, if there is a collective leadership of Four, Shirley Williams becomes the openly acknowledged leader of the group until any initiative is underpinned by democratic elections. It would be undesirable for the same reasons for any initiative to start with the launching of Roy Jenkins's policy unit endorsed by the Gang of Three in advance of any other simultaneous announcement. It would also seriously undermine the whole concept of a social democrat if David Steel was involved. The policy unit is a good idea but as presently envisaged its membership is deeply embedded in old-style politics; even though the figures suggested come from outside 'politics', they are all people of Roy Jenkins's generation, and sadly were, late in November, all male names. The whole key to success for any initiative is that it is new, different, young and fresh looking.

The memo then addressed an even more important question. If we had an electoral college forced on us in January, what should we do? We would face the choice of soldiering on, breaking away close to an election, or making a clean break in February. Whatever our answer we had to decide what to do about the Campaign for Labour Victory before 24 January. This was partly for political reasons – some in the Campaign would not leave the Labour Party under any circumstances, while others wanted to go now. But it was also organizational – we had to consider whether to hand back the premises made available to us by the Electricians Union and how to find a salary for Alec McGivan. I argued that we did not have much time. For every week we waited, we lost momentum, lost the feeling that we knew where we were going and eventually we might lose the justification of the Special Conference as our breaking point. So, at the very least, we needed to turn CLV into an explicit social democrat group which could be the nucleus for a new party. To support such a new entity, no longer linked, as CLV was, to the Labour Party, we would need premises, telephones and computers with space for volunteers. Such an organization would, we knew, be running very close to the wind and be in danger of being proscribed, and all of us expelled from the Labour Party. This would be even more likely if we tried to hold on until after the October 1981 Conference. The other danger of an

xxv. The Eisteddfod – a Welshman returns.

xxvi. *Top:* With Cy Vance, US Secretary of State, and Jim Callaghan,
Prime Minister, at the Bonn Economic Summit in 1978.

xxvii. *Above:* Moscow, 1977, with Brezhnev and Gromyko.

xxviii. At the Foreign Office with Joshua Nkomo and Robert Mugabe.

xxix. Sailing with Gareth.

xxx. At home in Limehouse.

xxxi. *Above:* The Gang of Four. The Limehouse Declaration, 25 January 1981.

xxxii. *Left:* Shirley puts her bet on Crosby, 1981.

xxxiii. SDP and Liberal MPs awaiting the State Opening of Parliament
in November 1981.
Back l. to r.: David Steel, Alan Beith, David Penhaligon, Bill Pitt,
Richard Wainwright, Christopher Brocklebank-Fowler, Eric Ogden,
David Alton and Dick Crawshaw.
Front l. to r.: David Owen, Bill Rodgers, Bob Maclennan, Edward
Lyons, Dick Mabon, David Ginsberg, John Horam, Jim Wellbeloved,
John Cartwright, Ian Wrigglesworth, Tom McNally, John Roper, Mike
Thomas.

xxxiv. *Left:* With Social Democrat students at the SDP Conference at Torquay, 1985.

xxxv. *Below:* The Two Davids campaign.

organization launch, rather than a party launch, was that it looked hesitant. On the other hand, launching straight into a party was probably going too fast for MPs like Mike Thomas and Ian Wrigglesworth; possibly even John Horam. I concluded that my own instinct was for the clean break and a party launch, but I was prepared to consider seriously a gradual break and an organization launch. I even suggested a structure to solve the leadership problem of such an organization, with Shirley as Chairman of the Social Democratic organization in the country, Roy Jenkins Chairman of its policy studies unit and Bill Rodgers and I joint Chairmen of the Social Democratic Parliamentary Group.

Putting all this down on paper concentrated minds even if it did make obvious my reluctance to have the party too closely identified with Roy. It also achieved most of its objectives. We did establish a collective leadership. We did call ourselves Social Democrats and we did break quickly after the Special Conference.

While all this was going on Bill was re-elected to the Shadow Cabinet. It proved a poisoned chalice. Michael Foot did not keep him as Defence Spokesman and Bill, who was by then in low spirits and suffering from a very painful back, considered this signified that he had been dismissed. Michael Foot then offered him Health or Pensions and subsequently the Northern Ireland portfolio. This last post was a clever offer and difficult for Bill to refuse without putting himself in the wrong. But soon Michael appointed MPs outside the Shadow Cabinet to all three of the positions which he had offered Bill, demonstrating how little he really valued him. Eventually Bill decided to remain as a member of the Shadow Cabinet without any portfolio. Despite this bruising experience, however, he was still keeping his own counsel, reluctant to talk to other MPs about a break and, insofar as he was taking a position at all, seeming to want to wait until the end of 1981 before breaking. A year earlier he had been the one who was keenest to break, now our roles were reversed.

Meanwhile the PLP reaffirmed their wish to have a minimum of 50 per cent of the votes in any electoral college, voting down the CLV amendment which Mike Thomas had put before them. However, the NEC and the Shadow Cabinet did not back the parliamentarians and they remained unable to reach agreement on the exact shape of an electoral college. It was beginning to look certain that the form of electoral college introduced at the Conference would be contrary to the wishes of the PLP. But that since the PLP were so demoralized they would accept anything.

The lines of battle became ever clearer. The Social Democratic Alliance, led by Stephen Haseler and Douglas Eden, was on the point of being proscribed by the NEC and they were pressing Roy Jenkins to ally himself with them, but most of the MPs felt we needed to start any new party with a clean sheet and not on the base of old grudges or old battles. On the CLV front, Roy Hattersley told Councillor Clive Wilkinson, the

Chairman of the CLV and leader of the Labour Group on Birmingham City Council, that he no longer wanted to be associated with CLV. Two camps were emerging – the stayers and the leavers.

We spent Christmas at Buttermere. Debbie's parents came over from America and my parents came up from Plymouth. It was a traditional family Christmas with log fires in all the rooms downstairs and it started off as usual with the crib service in our little Buttermere church. Kyrill Schabert, who had given us the beautifully carved figures from Oberammergau, had special pleasure in seeing them all around the crib at the centre of the whole service. Families with children were now regularly making the trip from other parishes up to Buttermere for this Christmas Eve service, which we had started some years before, and now our boys were old enough to help with the readings. With no electricity it had to be by candlelight, even though it started at 3 o'clock in the afternoon, and afterwards all of Buttermere came for tea. The Old Rectory came alive again as in Victorian times and with Lucy not quite two years old we had great pleasure listening to Dylan Thomas's record of a 'A Child's Christmas in Wales'.

At the turn of the year Bob Maclennan rang me at Buttermere to discuss the situation. He said he was almost sure that he would break if the Conference went badly, as it was almost certain to do, but he left the door on the Labour Party just slightly ajar. I told him that I was sure of Neville Sandelson, Tom Ellis and John Horam. I believed that Tom Bradley would come too, if only out of loyalty and affection for Roy Jenkins, but I could guarantee no one else. If Bob did not come we might well be only five. David and Susan Watt and their four boys were staying with us and, after my conversation with Bob, David and I talked long into the night about the pros and cons of breaking with only five MPs. We both concluded that it was too risky and that I would have to wait. Next morning over breakfast we simultaneously both admitted to having second thoughts and felt I should make the break and damn the consequences. In a way I was turning Disrael's famous dictum 'Damn your principles, stick to your party,' on its head.

It was in this determined frame of mind that on 5 January I attended an all-day meeting of the group of Labour MPs who were most likely to break with Labour. Although my mind had been made up some weeks before, some of the all-important younger MPs with constituencies in the North were just at the point of decision: Mike Thomas, aged thirty-six, MP for Newcastle North-East with a majority of 6,170; Ian Wrigglesworth, forty-two, MP for Middlesbrough, with a majority of 4,648; John Roper, forty-five, MP for Farnworth, with a majority of 8,107. All three had every reason to expect a career in politics until their sixties with little prospect of losing their seats, however awful the Labour Party's situation nationally.

Two other MPs, John Horam and Tom Ellis, were by then certain to go. John was forty-one, with a 8,312 majority in his constituency of Gateshead West. He had talked to David Steel over several months and might at one stage have joined the Liberals. He was to join the Conservatives before the 1987 Election. In economic terms he was, even at that stage, the most market-orientated of us all. Tom Ellis was fifty-six and had a majority of 12,149 in his Wrexham constituency. He too had been close to joining the Liberals and had talked to David Steel. He had been a colliery manager, was a romantic about politics, passionate over proportional representation and a Euro-federalist.

These and others, some of whom joined us eventually and some who contemplated joining us but eventually did not, had deep, long-standing friendships with people who would stay in the Labour Party come hell or high water. They knew that they would be putting those friendships under strains so great that, in some cases, not only would the friendship end but enmity would replace it. Being a member of a political party is not like being a member of a golf or tennis club. Membership carries with it tremendous emotional overtones, particularly in the Labour Party. This is partly because at the beginning of the century the fight was against entrenched privilege, and 'unity is strength' was more than just a slogan. There is no other organization, not even the armed services, where if one leaves voluntarily one is called a traitor. In some cases, MPs had to deal with differences within their own family. John Roper's wife remained throughout a member of the Labour Party, something they handled with great tolerance, but it must have been an added strain. I was fortunate that Debbie enthusiastically supported me. Although she liked the party activists in Plymouth very much and had enjoyed Labour Party Conferences, she had never joined the Labour Party. She saw Britain as class-ridden and felt that Labour perpetuated class divisions rather than healed them.

Most of the MPs at our meeting had no problems with their constituency parties and their GMCs supported them. There was no fear that they were going to be deselected. It was the same in my own constituency. I knew I would lose many good friends, that people who had worked hard to get me elected would be hurt, puzzled and sometimes angry. The majority of my GMC had no time whatever for unilateral nuclear disarmament nor for coming out of the European Community without a referendum. But the Labour Party was a way of life for them and to leave would be like amputating a limb. Some did not seem to understand that parting with such people was deeply painful, that for all of us it was a harrowing time.

Nor was the pain and struggle confined to Labour MPs. The Conservative MP, Christopher Brocklebank-Fowler, was facing much the same dilemma. He had spoken mainly to Bob Maclennan who was an old friend, and I knew Christopher from our trip to America in 1968. We had not always agreed over Rhodesia as he was a Muzorewa supporter, but he understood and loved Africa and was one of the Conservative MPs most determined to maintain sanctions against the Smith regime. He had told me before Christmas that, if the Budget was bad and unemployment was still rising while the Government remained indifferent, he would join us. This he did, literally crossing the floor, after speaking in the Budget debate; the first Conservative MP to do so since Austin Taylor went over to the Liberals in 1906. It was a decision that cost him not only his very safe seat in Norfolk but also his livelihood. He was ostracized for many years, found numerous opportunities in business suddenly closed off to him and suffered the gravest financial loss of all the MPs who joined the SDP.

When a Manifesto Group meeting was held later that week I made what could only have been described as a farewell speech, saying that we should part as friends for we might well need each other later. But it was already clear that we would be very lucky if any friendship lasted. Roy Hattersley was determined to demonstrate that we were now beyond the pale. In fairness to him, that was inevitable. Those MPs who were close to us on the policy issues under dispute or who had campaigned with us were viewed with intense suspicion inside the Labour Party. They felt that from now on they had to be more 'catholic than the Pope'. In attacking our decision to go they were reinforcing their position of influence in the Labour Party. We were called defeatists and everyone who joined us was described as a defector, as if we were deviants from the path of truth. I have no animosity against those who decided to stay in the Labour Party. As a matter of principle I did not become an evangelist, trying to persuade people to see the light and leave. My door was open to anyone who was wavering but I made it clear that we talked in confidence and I would never reveal that they had talked to me and would never put any pressure on them to come. Later there were Conservative MPs who talked to me on exactly the same basis.

By the end of that full day's meeting I was quite convinced that more than five MPs would be prepared to help set up a Council for Social Democracy if the Special Conference went for an electoral college. The Council, we all knew, was not intended to have a life of its own. It was a way of easing people out of the Labour Party and the means for creating the shell of a party organization on which we could build in the few months we would need before we could formally launch a national party. At that time we believed this launch should wait until after May to avoid getting sucked into fighting local council seats before the party had got itself organized.

In the middle of January the Gang of Four met for the first time and it was clear that Bill Rodgers was now firmly on board and that we needed to work on a statement that we might release after the Labour Conference if, as we expected, the electoral college went through.

On Friday 16 January I recorded a *Weekend World* interview with

Brian Walden. It went out that Sunday under the title, 'The Labour Right. Moment of Truth'. Some of my emotional turmoil overflowed as I said, 'The thing that haunts me, and I think it haunts all socialists, is, if we were to split, would it mean that the Centre Left could never be able to form a government in this country?' But the real drama came in the last question. Brian Walden, as a former Labour MP and sympathetic to what we were doing, knew only too well the fury we would encounter were we to leave the Labour Party, so he asked his question in a gentle way – but, typically, inside the velvet glove was an iron fist.

BRIAN WALDEN:
I wonder if I could ask you finally what you'd say to the sort of person who says, I understand all that, and there's much that you say Dr Owen that I agree with, but, leave the Labour Party, how can you even discuss it, how can you sit there talking about such an emotional wrench, such an act of treachery, such a destruction of what endless people for many years have fought to build up. How would you reply to what I would call an old-fashioned Labour loyalist who put that point to you?

DAVID OWEN MP:
Well I would just ask them, quietly and slowly, to say what, if they used the word treachery, what is the biggest treachery; to put the Labour Party before your country or your country before the Labour Party?

Up in Grimsby, watching the programme, was the Labour MP Austin Mitchell's agent, a dentist, Paul Genny. He described his reaction on hearing my words. He jumped up in the air, said 'He is going to do it, he is going to leave,' and dashed out to a friend's house to discuss their next moves, before the programme had even ended. For him and other Labour activists, the charge of treachery was one of the greatest problems. Hearing how it could be turned back on the accuser convinced him that I and others were now heading out of the Labour Party.

He was right. The Gang of Three was becoming the Gang of Four; what was to be known as the Limehouse Declaration was starting to take shape and the new party was being openly discussed. But whatever the impression may have been, it was not a smooth ride. It had already been agreed that the Gang of Three would meet with Roy Jenkins at his house in East Hendred on Sunday 18 January. Unfortunately either Roy or his friends had talked to the *Observer* and on the morning of the meeting I woke to a front-page picture of Roy with a story revealing that we were meeting at East Hendred that Sunday. To me it was just an irritation, another example of an old man in a hurry, but Shirley Williams was outraged. She was at a conference in Ditchley Park and she announced to Roy on the telephone that she was not now prepared to come. She had a fair point: the story was slanted to give the impression that we were all being summoned by the king over the water soon to return from Brussels, and that he was in charge of the whole operation. It was a cynical way of handling publicity, and similar press stories were to become frequent over the next eighteen months. All too often the purpose was clear – to boost Roy at the expense of Shirley.

The *Observer* story nearly scuppered the meeting and it was only saved by endless telephone calls, with Roy contrite and at his most conciliatory and, of course, disowning all knowledge of the story. I thought it pretty pointless to start worrying about whether it had been leaked by John Harris, Matthew Oakshott or by Roy himself, I just wanted to get on with things. So I was pleased when eventually it was agreed that we would all meet at Bill Rodgers's house in London. But still things did not go smoothly. Shirley came late and had to face a barrage of photographers at the door. Whether or not they had been tipped off or just guessed, I do not know, but I could see steely anger on Shirley's face as she entered the room. It was an expression I recognized well: it is the same as the one my sister adopts on the rare occasions when she is furious. I often think that one of the reasons I like Shirley so much, even though she sometimes infuriated me and I her, is that she has some of the characteristics I love most in my sister. The capacity to make you feel that you are the one person who matters, a characteristic which unfortunately I all too rarely display.

The *Sunday Times* magazine on 27 September 1981 had a perceptive article by Andrew Stephen, 'How Shirley and Co made their Party', with on the front cover *Alice in Wonderland* model caricatures by Luck and Flaw of *Spitting Image* fame. We were surprisingly well cast. Shirley was Alice, Roy was the Dormouse, Bill the Mad Hatter and I the White Rabbit. The article recaptured very well what happened that day at Bill's house:

> 'I am not prepared to proceed with these discussions unless we go round the room and each person says which jounalist he has spoken to in the past two days,' Shirley said. There was an embarrassed silence for a few seconds, which Jenkins finally broke. 'I am sorry,' he murmured, 'that this great enterprise of ours is starting up in the same spirit as the worst of the Wilson Cabinets.' Mrs Williams was still enraged: 'Look, I am not prepared to be pushed out of the Labour Party by anyone.'

It was not, to put it mildly, a propitious start to the serious drafting of what later became known as the Limehouse Declaration.

Eventually, helped by some alcohol, the mood lightened and we got down to the various drafts. The best and most elegant words came as usual from Roy Jenkins, the substance of policy came largely from me, the quotable pieces for the press from Shirley and practical sense from Bill. The main argument was whether or not to talk about a realignment in British politics. For Shirley 'realignment' was too specific and meant that we were committing ourselves to leaving Labour. She fiercely resisted that at this stage. The other three had brought with them their closest political advisers so as to be able to help with the drafting and co-ordination. Roy's was Matthew Oakshott, who had been with him in the Home Office; Shirley's, John Lyttle, who had been with her in the Department of Education, and Bill's was Roger Liddle, who had been with him in the Department of Transport. My own political adviser was David Stephen, but he was still in the Labour Party, and I was not putting any pressure on him to leave. So the fourth adviser in the room was not mine. Alec McGivan came as the Secretary of CLV and the person we hoped to employ to run the Council for Social Democracy. Roy Jenkins then flew off to Washington for the presidential inauguration of Ronald Reagan and was due back by the Saturday when the three of us who were still in the Labour Party were going to stage one last political battle from within.

On Tuesday 20 January Michael Foot asked to see the Gang of Three and we had an unsatisfactory meeting. He was friendly and civil, assuring us that if we stayed in the Labour Party we would have the freedom to dissent and to argue our case, but when I challenged him by saying that surely we could not be free to disown a manifesto, he became vague and discursive. He knew, as well as we did, that dissent inside the Labour Party was only tolerated up to a point which certainly did not extend to the election campaign. In the past the Left would campaign vigorously and often bitterly for their viewpoint up to the election and then, during the campaign behave like lambs on a manifesto with which they had fiercely disagreed, sometimes on major areas of policy. They would then resume normal hostilities once the election was over. This was all justified on the grounds of loyalty to the Labour Party. I could never really understand such party games and I could not envisage behaving in the same way on the fundamental policy issues which were in dispute. But I knew that was what was required.

To some extent Michael's posture at our meeting was for public consumption. So he could say that he had gone every last mile to keep us in the Party. I do not, however, think it was his only motivation. He genuinely did want us to stay, if only because his journalistic instinct, if not his political one, told him that if we left, it would be considerably harder to convince the country to elect a Labour Government. Why could we not behave as he had done in the past, was his unspoken rebuke. We allowed you to govern when the Right was in control of the Party, you are not letting us govern now that we, the Left, are in control. He found it impossible to understand that we believed that it was against the best interests of the country that he should take us out of the European Community and call into question our continued membership in NATO. The problem with Michael was that he really believed in these, to me, dangerous and damaging policies, as did Neil Kinnock from 1983 to 1988 as Leader of the Labour Party. The cynical advantage of having Harold Wilson as Leader in 1964 was that we could all merrily campaign on a manifesto to abolish Polaris which everyone, Left and Right, knew he had no intention of ever carrying out. Wilson's skill was to convince the Left that he was really on their side, when they knew he would not follow their policies. Michael, from the old-fashioned Left, had no such flexibility; he genuinely supported unilateralism and pulling up the drawbridge to the European Community.

On Wednesday the Gang of Three, with Roy still in Washington, met at Bill Rodgers's house and revised the Limehouse Declaration. Again there was a discussion about using the word 'realignment' and we agreed to make a final decision when all four of us would meet on the Sunday morning after the Special Conference at my house. Debbie would be quite happy to type the final version and we could take account of the mood of the Conference and its final decision then. Even at this stage, if a miracle had happened and the electoral college had been thrown out, we would not have gone ahead with forming the Council for Social Democracy that weekend.

On Saturday I drove to the Wembley Conference Hall, once again ready to do battle. Debbie came with me and Bob Bishop, the Chairman of Devonport Labour Party, with his wife, Carol, who had stayed overnight with us. I knew that some form of electoral college was virtually certain. Once again I went to the floor of the Conference to argue a case which I knew, even before I began to speak, was going to be rejected since the trade union block votes had already been pledged. I called for one member-one vote.

> I have stood by this principle all through this argument. I am amazed you have to come to the Labour Party and defend the issue of one member-one vote [applause]. This Party is known throughout the world for championing the widening of the franchise to one person-one vote. In 1977 when a Labour Government told Mr Ian Smith that he would never get independence without one person-one vote you all applauded it and held firm to that principle. In South Africa we argued for one person-one vote.

I went on to say that no socialist party in Western Europe had a block vote. Trade unions had said they could not ballot their members since they could not separate out communists or conservatives, and they would not be able to organize a system involving individual trade unionists. If that was so, I argued, then trade unionists and others should have the right to vote in the Party as members of their constituencies. That was the easy and the democratic way. Of course, I said, an electoral college would be introduced – the votes had all been cobbled up, the arrangements made.

> But I say to the Party this; the day this system is used to elect a Prime Minister the whole of the country will be watching the procedures, and

then these procedures will be shown to be totally undemocratic. They will be shown to be a totally illegitimate way of electing the Prime Minister of the country.

I finished by saying that 'to allow the block vote to choose the future Prime Minister of this country is an outrage. It is a disgrace and this Conference ought not to accept it.' I had put some heart into our troops but it was like Custer's last stand, we were going down to another defeat. When voting began the only question was what percentages would determine the make-up of the electoral college. The NEC of the Labour Party backed a percentage formula of 33:33:33 in which the Parliamentary Party, the constituency parties and the trade unions all had equal votes. David Basnett of the GMBWU was the main backer of a formula in which the largest share, 50 per cent, went to the MPs. USDAW, the shopworkers union, which had also been supported by NUPE, advocated a 30:30:40 formula, in which the trade unions had the largest percentage. What had been largely forgotten by the press, but not I suspect by Clive Jenkins, was that two unions came already committed. The T&GWU executive had actually announced on 4 December that they would support the 33:33:33 formula but not support anything that would give more than 40 per cent to any constituent body. Therefore, when the NEC 33:33:33 option failed, Moss Evans of the T&GWU was likely to put his weight behind the USDAW 30:30:40 formula in preference to the Basnett 50:25:25 option. But while Moss Evans had said to David Basnett that in the last analysis he would support David's formula – deliberately or accidentally – he had not made it clear that that would only happen if the USDAW 30:30:40 formula had already fallen. What he and the T&GWU wanted was an electoral college even if it meant 50 per cent for the MPs.

Terry Duffy, the engineers leader, had less freedom for manoeuvre over his 928,000 AEW votes. He had been mandated to vote against every proposal which did not give MPs a majority. This meant that when the NEC 33:33:33 option fell the Left were able to mobilize behind the USDAW formula with David Basnett watching horrified because he thought that he had been promised Moss Evans's union vote. Most of us in the hall were unaware of all this manoeuvring and some people, including me, believed when the result was first announced that the 40 per cent referred to the Parliamentary Party. It took a few minutes before we realized that it was the trade unions who had been given the largest share. The critics of the principle of the electoral college could not have been handed a better propaganda weapon or a more obvious example of why the whole system was a democratic disgrace, open to the most flagrant political manipulation.

There were many descriptions of what did or did not happen over lunch in Clive Jenkins's suite of the Crest Hotel that Saturday. Some even recounted what had happened in the Medallion Restaurant the evening before when Clive Jenkins dined with Moss Evans. Complaints to the Press Council by Clive Jenkins about various newspaper reports never succeeded in clarifying the issues despite an adjudication by the Press Council. Which trade union leader misled who, or whether there was a misunderstanding is not a matter of great moment. What mattered was the impression, as Shirley said, that it had all been engineered by 'four trade union barons in a smoke-filled room'. Clive Jenkins rebuffed this by saying that since he detested smoking, Tom Jackson of the Post Office Workers leaned out of the window to smoke his cigar!

It was the nature of the electoral college which was displayed for all to see that Saturday which will haunt the Labour Party as long as it remains part of their constitution. It is quite possible that, until the Labour Party breaks this institutional link with the trade union movement voters will continue to withhold their support for fear that the vested interest of the trade unions will once again dominate Labour in government. Even the policy reversals of 1988–91 will be insufficient to reassure them. The horrible atmosphere surrounding that vote meant that we left the Conference Hall that day utterly disenchanted. I now knew for certain I would have to leave the Labour Party.

22

THE LIMEHOUSE DECLARATION

On the morning of Sunday 25 January the Gang of Four met at my house in Narrow Street, Limehouse. Opposite us were the Brightlingsea buildings where Clem Attlee lived when he was doing social work in the East End of London. The small group of houses was built for ships' captains in the early part of the eighteenth century when the road to Limehouse from the City of London ran through green fields. Here we settled down to the final redrafting of the document which was to become the Limehouse Declaration. Shirley was still resisting the word 'realignment' because that was barely even code for leaving the Labour Party. If she had thought that meant joint membership with the Liberal Party there could not have been the remotest chance of her signing the Declaration. Apart from this, we quickly agreed the text and settled down for lunch. Shirley mentioned that she was on the BBC radio programme *The World this Weekend*, so we listened as we ate at a long pine table overlooking the Thames. In the course of the interview Shirley made it crystal clear that she was ready to leave the Labour Party, and she had the grace to smile when we pointed out to her that the word 'realignment' was negligible compared with what she had already committed herself to. So Debbie went off to type the Declaration with its final paragraph:

> We recognize that for those people who have given much of their lives
> to the Labour Party, the choice that lies ahead will be deeply painful.
> But we believe that the need for a realignment of British politics must
> now be faced.

Looking back on the Declaration we signed that day, it is hard not to be struck by how orientated it was to the Labour Party. Nevertheless one of the changes from Roy's early draft had been the deletion of 'the party of Attlee or Gaitskell' which shows that, far from him trying to stop our being associated with the Labour Party, Roy wanted to clarify the sort of Labour Party we were ready to identify with. The Declaration was not a rallying-cry for the new Centre party with which Roy had been associated

since the Dimbleby Lecture. Indeed we specifically said that we did not
believe 'in the politics of an inert Centre merely representing the lowest
common denominator between two extremes'. Instead we addressed
those who had been 'actively and continuously engaged in Labour
politics', and some who had been engaged in the past but had given up
recently. Although we deliberately made a pitch for people active outside
the party political sphere, this was in the main an appeal to those who
wanted to resist the drift towards extremism in the Labour Party. There
was comment on the absence of a commitment to proportional representation. Interestingly, Roy had never pushed for it to be included. For me
the omission was welcome: it did not pre-empt further debate, and it
avoided the accusation that this was a statement which could have been
issued by the Liberal Party. There would be ample time to make that
commitment and none of us doubted that it would come when we wanted
to forge an electoral pact with the Liberal Party. The sentence which was
taken into the Constitution of the SDP and is most often quoted was,
'We want to create an open, classless and more equal society, one which
rejects ugly prejudices based upon sex, race or religion.' A significant
example of how much the SDP influenced the political debate in the
1980s was John Major's campaign to become Prime Minister in November
1990 on a commitment to a classless society.

Some of the MPs who had been most closely involved joined us in the
course of the afternoon. John Lyttle phoned the Press Association to say
that we would issue a statement at 4 p.m. and that there would be a
photocall but no interviews. This induced panic because all except Roy
had arrived casually dressed. Eventually Shirley wore one of Debbie's
blouses and I put on a suit, though Bill kept his casual clothes. The boys
meanwhile were talking out of the open kitchen window on the first floor
to the press assembling outside in the street and having a lot of fun. So
many photographers turned up that we could not be photographed inside
my house or even on the terrace overlooking the river, so we wandered
out into Narrow Street and posed on the little bridge marking one of the
old entrances into Regent's Canal Dock.

Though the formal launch of the SDP did not take place until 26
March, as far as the Gang of Three was concerned the rubicon had been
crossed – a Social Democratic Party was going to be formed. However, it
is now clear to me that, whatever the declaration said, as far as Roy
Jenkins was concerned a Centre party was going to be formed which
would merge with the Liberals. Within five weeks, before the SDP was
even formally launched, Roy and his foremost supporters were arguing in
the discussion over the interim constitution that people should be allowed
to be members of both the SDP and the Liberal Party; even at this stage,
it seemed that the SDP was merely to be a transit vehicle. It was as if
they wanted a cross between the Salvation Army and the Fabian Society;
a movement so broad and diffuse that it would become putty in the

hands of the Liberal activists, let alone able to withstand the pressures that were bound to be put on us by the old class-based parties. How on earth he thought such a grouping could hold together and prise workable seats and workable policies out of the Liberal Party was a mystery. Until it became all too clear that he did not envisage any pressure or leverage being put on the Liberal Party. The whole concept was flatly rejected. But those who were involved in that short debate could never again entertain any illusions as to Roy's real intentions. Nor did the concept of joint membership ever totally disappear. It would resurface from time to time with somebody proudly claiming joint membership and the National Committee having to issue an instruction for this to be stopped. As the evidence mounted that Roy was so committed to merging with the Liberals, it became ever clearer to me that in honour he should never have signed the Limehouse Declaration to create the Council for Social Democracy in the first place. He had not abandoned his concept of a Centre party linked to the Liberals; if we wanted to call ourselves Social Democrats, talk about socialism and even join Socialist International he would go along with that, biding his time until we were out of the Labour Party and had burnt our boats and then push the Liberal link.

That evening I had time to read the Sunday newspapers which commented on the Conference; a fairly common theme was that since we felt we had to leave the Labour Party, this was the time to go. The *Sunday Times* carried an extract from my book *Face the Future* which Jonathan Cape was due to publish on 29 January and we were going to have a publication party at home the night before. It had been a huge effort to write, given all the other pressures of 1980. Naturally, it is a far fuller statement of my views at that time than the Limehouse Declaration. It is also notably less concerned with the battle against extremism in the Labour Party and far more with the failures which contributed to the extremists' success within the Labour Party.

Although my political thinking developed substantially over the next ten years, as it had in the previous ten years, I am happy to stand by the basic ideas outlined in *Face the Future*. Although I did not use the phrase, 'social market economy', it was here that I began to outline the analysis underpinning this concept and develop the case for multi-party politics.

The most important theme of the book was the need to break the grip of bureaucratic corporatism. Early in its history, the Labour Party had chosen the path of Fabian paternalism personified by Beatrice and Sidney Webb; pursuing nationalization and Clause Four state socialism. I argued that this had been a historical error bedevilling every Labour Government. There was now a need to revive the 'radical democratic libertarian tradition of decentralized socialism' identified with Robert Owen, William Morris and G.D.H Cole, and developing policies for individuals, families and small communities rather than producing an uneasy consensus between the big battalions of trade unions and industry. European social democracy provided a model for Labour, although even the social democratic parties had been too corporatist and not favourable enough to diversity and decentralized decision making.

From this starting point I argued for a more market-oriented economic policy.

> It is fundamental that interventionism is not allowed to become the dominant thrust of an industrial strategy or its marginal benefits exaggerated. Far greater importance must be given to creating changes of attitude in industry rather than embarking again on a state nationalization programme on the scale of 1945–51. The centralized corporatist incomes policies of the past must now be rejected in favour of a more modest, and one hopes, more sustainable decentralized approach, where commercial realities in the market sector of industry are not obscured by overall national norms and centrally imposed pay rigidities.

This call for a new economic philosophy for non-Conservatives was accompanied by an appeal for new attitudes – aiming to foster a climate of altruism and to change our political system. The argument was put for a Scottish Parliament, regional assemblies with greater freedom for local government and a more decentralized NHS.

In many respects *Face the Future*, written while still in the Labour Party, encapsulated my hopes for the SDP – that we would be politically bold, unconstrained by the past and prepared to tackle the failures that had led to Margaret Thatcher's victory in 1979. Generally speaking, the reviewers were kind to it and it soon went into a second edition, but its reception was blurred by the unintended synchronicity with the formation of the SDP.

The day after the Limehouse Declaration, nine other Labour Members of Parliament joined Bill and me in declaring their support for the Council for Social Democracy. We announced that we would campaign individually and collectively inside and outside Parliament for the cause of social democracy. We had also agreed that everybody would make their own decision about when and how they would leave the Labour Party and that this would inevitably depend on the timings of General Management Committee meetings and other factors. No one was signed up formally for the new party but the understanding was that all of us would leave the Labour Party.

On 3 February David Steel wrote a letter, supposedly to the two hundred already adopted Liberal Parliamentary candidates, but released to the press and meant to be his reaction to the Limehouse Declaration. Its style was pre-emptive, its tone patronizing. Referring to supporters of the Council for Social Democracy, he said, 'these dissidents now accept the need for electoral reform'. Our social democracy was then redefined in his terms as a public demand for 'an effective non-socialist alternative to Thatcherism'. Socialism was as much a dirty word to the Liberal Party as to the Conservative Party and we were to come under constant pressure to abandon it. Of course we could not thrust the term at our potential friends or allies who did not come from the Left, but for a social democrat to be told they were not socialist was a liberty coming from the Leader of the Liberal Party. After all, it would have been felt to be aggressively assertive if we had said of the Liberals, 'these dissidents are now prepared to accept nuclear deterrence and to join an effective non-liberal alternative to Thatcherism'. David Steel in that same speech confessed 'to being irritated by the apparent stand-offishness towards, and ignorance of, the Liberal Party by some of the Social Democrats'; which the press were then quietly told was a reference to me. I gritted my teeth as I had to many times over subsequent years. My stand-offishness was quite deliberate; it stemmed not from ignorance but came from all too great a knowledge of what the Liberal Party was actually like.

Instinct, which was later backed by hard market-research evidence, indicated that it could only harm our new party if we were too identified with the Liberals. But we studiously avoided facing that market research. I had fought the Liberals in the West Country, where they are stronger than in most other parts of the country, for twenty years. I had a pretty good idea of their strengths as well as their weaknesses, whether from fighting Mark Bonham-Carter in Torrington or fighting in Devonport, Captain Michael Banks RM Retired. While Michael Banks was distributing leaflets outside Devonport Dockyard gate promising an increase in defence expenditure in the neighbouring constituency of Tavistock, Aza Pinney was stomping the fields in his gumboots promising to reduce defence expenditure. I had lived, only recently, for months with the story of Jeremy Thorpe, Liberal MP for North Devon, splashed across our West Country newspapers, with endless details about the involvement of the former Bodmin Liberal MP Peter Bessell, and of the Liberal Party's financial dealings, which were sleazy to say the least. The 1979 Election result in the West Country had been its worst for years. Jeremy Thorpe had lost his seat and sadly, because he was an excellent MP, so had John Pardoe. I had experienced too the Lib-Lab Pact and the problems of keeping the Liberal Party to an agreed line. I knew we had to try and work for some form of electoral deal but there was no rush. We had first to build the SDP. Meanwhile Cyril Smith was telling people that we ought to be strangled at birth, and that was not a maverick sentiment. David Steel had his problems in containing Liberals who wanted nothing whatever to do with us, but for these and other reasons for the SDP to give the impression that we could not wait to get into bed with the Liberals was the height of political madness. Nevertheless that is what some of the SDP tried to do.

Then Bill Rodgers resigned from the Shadow Cabinet, turning down a final offer from Michael Foot, made the week before, to act as a one-man

Royal Commission on regional policy. On the same day I applied to the Rowntree Trust for a grant to enable us to employ a research and administrative officer for the parliamentary section of the Council for Social Democracy. After a clarifying meeting in February, the Trust granted us £10,000 a year for three years on 6 March. We advertised and were lucky enough to appoint Dick Newby, an able young civil servant who resigned to come and work for us.

A sad and painful moment came at the end of that exhilarating week. That Friday, I flew down to Plymouth for the Devonport Constituency annual GMC. I told them that I would not be able to stand as a Labour Party candidate at the next election and would not be putting myself forward for reselection. 'I have not,' I told them, 'changed my support for the manifesto on which you and I fought the 1979 election and I will conduct myself in Parliament over the years ahead until the next election within the spirit of that manifesto.' I went on BBC TV in the South-West for a late-night interview and found it all very emotional. I was leaving behind friends of fifteen years' standing, people whose help had been invaluable in five close-fought general elections. The pangs of conflicting loyalties were acute and even my few opponents on the Left in the constituency were, I think, genuinely upset.

The strains were also showing in Parliament. The Callaghan Cabinet were planning a dinner for Jim and Audrey and, without any warning, Michael Foot wrote to Bill and me returning our cheques and saying we would not be welcome. My hand-written note to Michael reveals my mood about the impending split.

> We are all going to have to exercise the maximum of personal
> restraint over the next few difficult years if in the long term British
> socialism as a philosophy is to recover. Your action today does not
> augur very well for such restraint, and perhaps you might like to
> reflect overnight on your action for I fear it will set the tone for
> much of what is to come. By all means, attack our views, let us be
> political foes if that is what you wish. I expect you to be vigorous in
> your onslaught on our ideas and principles. But the idea that Bill,
> Shirley and I can no longer sit at the same table as yourself to
> honour Jim as former colleagues is patently absurd.

In the end Edmund Dell joined the three of us in sending the Callaghans an Ackermann print, and it says a lot for Jim and Audrey that they never used the creation of the SDP as a reason to abandon past friendship.

In the House of Commons Michael had set the tone. From then on we passed each other with an occasional nod but never exchanging even pleasantries. There are some MPs who have never spoken to me since the Limehouse Declaration. There are a few who have never allowed it to make any difference, but with the majority relations are formal. The attacks were not long in coming and for my part, I hit back; but initially more in sorrow than in anger.

The structure of the SDP developed quickly after the Limehouse Declaration. We had envisaged launching near the end of May. In response to an overwhelming demand by letters and telephone calls it was clear we had to proceed far faster and we moved the launch date to 26 March. An advertisement, placed in the *Guardian*, made possible by a cheque for £5,000 from George Apter who later became a trustee, brought an avalanche of applications. It asked for support for the Council for Social Democracy and, to help people identify with the Council, a hundred names of initial supporters were given. Again there was a heavy Labour bias but it was compiled in a hurry and largely reflected people the Gang of Four knew. The flavour of the list can be seen in a few names: Sir Geraint Evans, the opera singer; Frank Chapple, General Secretary of the EETPU; Lord George Brown; Julia Neuberger, the young rabbi; Lord Flowers, the scientist; Steve Race, the broadcaster; Lord Bullock, the biographer of Ernest Bevin; and Michael Young, the founder of the Consumers Association. That same day the Gang of Four agreed the most effective division of responsibility between us. I was to chair our activities in Parliament, Bill was to be in charge of organization, Roy, the development of policy and Shirley, publicity and the media. Within policy, Roy would deal with Treasury matters, Shirley with home affairs and social services, Bill with industry and I with foreign and Third World issues. The Parliamentary Committee, which I chaired, met for the first time and it was agreed that it would meet every Thursday. A Steering Committee was established to meet once a week with Alec McGivan as its secretary and to be chaired in rotation for a month at a time by a member of the Gang of Four. The Steering Committee membership was composed of seven MPs from the Parliamentary Group: Tom Bradley, John Cartwright, John Horam, Robert Maclennan, John Roper (who became the Chief Whip), Mike Thomas and Ian Wrigglesworth. Lord Aylestone, who as Bert Bowden had been my first Chief Whip in the Labour Party and was a former Commonwealth Secretary and Chairman of the IBA, agreed to serve, and Roy was clever enough to ensure that he had three of his supporters, Jim Daly, David Marquand and Dick Taverne, on the Committee. In June the Steering Committee was widened to include David Sainsbury, who had been chairing the Finance Advisory Committee, Christopher Brocklebank-Fowler, Polly Toynbee, then a *Guardian* columnist, Lady Stedman, a former Labour Minister with experience in local government, and two more Jenkins supporters, Clive Lindley and Matthew Oakshott, as well as Roger Liddle. There was no escaping the fact that this Steering Committee had to be self-appointed and it did undoubtedly have a crucial influence on the development of the SDP. As it turned out – though I had no detailed knowledge of it at the time – of the original fifteen members, at least seven had already engaged in discussions which involved David Steel in the formation of a Centre party. In the enlarged Steering Committee, there were nine. In many ways the surprise, with that balance in the key decision-making body, whose membership inevitably carried over in large part to the elected National Committee in 1982, was that we managed to keep the SDP from merging with the Liberals for over six years.

On 12 February the Parliamentary Committee discussed relations with the Liberals, agreeing that there was a need for a common strategy but emphasizing that there was a strong and clear social democratic point of view which had to be firmly established. The Steering Committee reported that the *Guardian* advertisement had produced nearly eight thousand replies, that two out of three letters contained money and that we possessed £25,000. Bob Maclennan was charged with consulting on the constitution. By Monday 1 March the Steering Committee was able to meet in the offices we had rented in Queen Anne's Gate, by which time we had numerous volunteers dealing with the mass of correspondence. We were hopeful of having up to 25,000 supporters on computer even before we launched the party. Mike Thomas was put in charge of the launch. Ian Wrigglesworth was dealing with finance and John Horam with the membership computer. We started to choose local convenors to help establish provisional local parties. We also settled on the party name, though it had been crystallizing for some time. At various stages we had considered Radical, Democratic Labour or the New Labour Party, but by choosing Social Democratic Party we hoped we were identifying with a proven tradition and one with deep roots in continental socialist practice and thinking.

Handling friends in the Labour Party in Plymouth was perhaps the hardest task. I wrote to one of them in early February, and this gives the flavour of how a harrowing situation was handled with mutual respect.

> Many thanks for your letter which you wrote with such sympathy and understanding. It has been a horrible period for me. I hope you will understand why I have been reluctant to involve you all in this decision. I simply do not want to put any of you in a difficult position or in any way try to persuade you to leave the Labour Party. It is different for you in Plymouth as a Labour councillor and for me in my position. There is no hurry to make decisions for you. Unfortunately events are pressing me all the time for rapid decisions. As you probably know I wanted to postpone a decision until after May to avoid damaging the Labour Party in the council elections but this looks less and less possible. There is no question of running official Social Democratic candidates in the council elections and I personally will make sure I support good Labour councillors. The main task and the main anxiety is that whatever happens good friendships remain intact. It will be difficult. Also I do not want to pressurize anyone. These are very individual and deeply agonizing decisions. You both have been among my oldest friends in Plymouth. I expect you both to stay in the Labour Party and it will not make one jot of difference to my regard for you. But for myself I am

afraid I do not want you to be under any illusion that I think I will
have to leave since I do not believe the changes in attitude that are
necessary are now possible within the national Labour Party in any
reasonable timescale.

Later in the month I wrote formally to the Chairman of the Devonport
Labour Party, Bob Bishop. He had been at pains not to put me under
any pressure for a final decision. I told him I would cease to use Labour
Party premises for my advice bureaux but that I was ready at all times to
help each and every one of them as individual constituents. I recalled
how Plymouth politics had always been remarkable for allowing disagreements on policies between parties and yet having many good friends
crossing party lines. I said that many whom I deeply respected would
decide to stay within the Labour Party and that I would not dream of
trying to change such a decision. I ended by thanking them all for their
kindness and particularly for showing tolerance and forbearance over the
last month.

The Secretary of the Constituency Party, Barbara Furzeman, and the
previous Chairman, Will Fitzgerald, did join the SDP at once, as did a
number of active Labour Party members. What was sad, as is so often the
case when ruptures like this occur, was the number of people who drifted
away from politics, ceasing to be active in the Labour Party but not
joining the SDP either.

My mailbag was vast and in particular I got a number of letters from
Liberals, either urging us to join them or suggesting ways in which we
could work together. I often found their grass roots workers more relaxed
than their leaders about the concept of keeping a partnership based on
two parties. The pressure to merge came from the top. Their President,
Richard Holme, sent me a copy of their manifesto as if I did not know
anything about the Liberal Party and had not fought them in six
successive elections. My replies were fairly standard, like this letter
written on 17 March, a few days before the launch of the Party.

I believe that it makes electoral and political sense for the Liberal Party
and the Social Democrats to go into the next election as separate parties
with a separate identity. I say this for a number of reasons. If we are to
realign British politics, it is vital that the Social Democrats cut into the
Labour vote, and particularly cut into the Labour vote in the northern
part of the country so that, in combination with disillusioned Tories
and Liberals in seats that have hitherto been considered 'safe Labour',
a Social Democrat can be returned. It is my view at present, though I
concede that the whole political scene is changing, that this can best be
achieved by having a Social Democratic identity along the lines that I
argue for in the early chapters of my recent book, *Face the Future*. I
totally accept that an electoral arrangement of itself is insufficient. The
electorate has the right to know what would happen under any of the
conceivable electoral results. For example, if the Social Democrat MPs

were to be the largest grouping, that they would see as their first and primary coalition partners the Liberal MPs and vice-versa. It would also be necessary to convince the country that a coalition of Social Democrats and Liberals would give a coherent government, and in two major areas of constitutional reform and industrial policy I believe it is vital that we are seen to have developed, before the next election, well thought out, radical and sustainable policies.

I believe an arrangement between the Liberal Party and the Social Democrats must be open with no covert deals. I believe we can preserve our separate identities without trying to highlight differences of views and approach and that jointly we act now in Opposition as we will act in government after 1984. You have roots and traditions in liberalism; we must develop the traditions and roots of social democracy that are very strong in Europe and the philosophy and decentralized socialism which was very strong in Britain in the early part of this century.

On 6 February *Now!* magazine published the results of a constituency poll in Bill Rodgers's and my seat. If there were a General Election next day in Plymouth Devonport and if I were standing for the Social Democratic Party, I would gain 55 per cent of the vote; the Conservatives came next with 25 per cent, Labour with 16 per cent and the Liberals 4 per cent. In Stockton, if Bill were standing, 41 per cent would vote Social Democrat; Labour came next with 28 per cent, then the Conservatives with 22 per cent and the Liberals with 9 per cent. In my own constituency the *Evening Herald* had very early on run a test of opinion which showed that I would win easily. There were two powerful conclusions from these polls. Firstly, if we were to call by-elections there was an extremely good chance that both of us would win and some pollsters thought all twelve MPs would win. Secondly, the Liberal vote was not essential to us, though if we stood as a Social Democrat-Liberal Alliance the margin of our victory, not surprisingly, would slightly increase.

Bill Rodgers, however, was adamantly opposed to fighting by-elections. Whether or not he feared losing his own seat I do not know, but on the basis of the *Now!* poll he should have been safe, and had he won in 1981 he would have been much less likely to have lost in 1983. His argument was that it would be harder for us to attract some of the MPs less well known in their constituencies if they thought they were going to have to fight a by-election. Also, like me, he was loath to concede any ground to Tony Benn, who was arguing that MPs are not primarily answerable to their constituents, but to a party caucus.

These were strong arguments, but there were countervailing ones. The endorsement of the electorate would have given us a more powerful position in the House of Commons and in the country. It would have also sharpened our Social Democratic image immediately and greatly enhanced our authority in dealing with the Liberal Party. Michael Foot constantly asserted that we should all fight by-elections, and I tried to persuade Bill that at least as Chairman of the Parliamentary Committee I should fight one symbolic by-election on behalf of all SDP MPs. In conversation, Bill managed to persuade me that this would be an indulgence and that it would only heighten the constituency pressure on the other eleven to fight as well. Yet I believe we made the wrong decision; we should have fought. It would have demonstrated electoral clout to the Liberals and greatly enhanced the concept of the SDP as a free-standing fourth political party. I am sure too that it would have helped MPs when they came to fight their own seats in the 1983 General Election.

The reason I did not go ahead and fight a by-election, ignoring Bill's reservation, rather as I had done when choosing to resign from the Shadow Cabinet, was that now we were involved in collective decision-making. At this stage our whole enterprise was so problematical that I was reluctant to put any strain on relations between Bill and me, or indeed between any of the other MPs who were not keen to fight and who would provide the bedrock on whom we would build the Party outside Parliament. We had above all else to stick together. Strong views were expressed among the other ten. One such was Dick Crawshaw, Deputy Speaker, who was very much in favour of standing in his constituency and indeed at one stage had told me privately that he would not join us unless he could fight his seat. Dick was highly principled, someone who would lose financially by joining the SDP: since the Deputy Speakership is an office which has an extra payment, as is the case for Ministers, the Leader of the Opposition and three Opposition Whips, Dick knew that he would have to give up his office, which he did. Eventually, with extreme reluctance, he too agreed to abide by the majority decision not to fight a by-election. The SDP repaid his loyalty in a most shameful way, acquiescing in the Liberals standing against him in the general election in Liverpool, but he never complained. That his should have been one of only two seats in the country where this happened was indefensible, and all because Roy Jenkins would never threaten David Steel with retaliatory action. Dick lost in 1983 and I was pleased, when I became Leader, to recommend him as our first SDP life peer, a small compensation for a real sacrifice.

The Labour Party stimulated many activists to write to me about fighting a by-election and I had a fairly standard reply:

MPs can and do give up the whip, while still remaining a member of their party. More frequently they vote against their whip. They can, as they have done in the past, give up the whip and change their party – all of this within the context of remaining an MP. I believe this freedom between elections is vital for parliamentary democracy. The House of Commons must be a free Parliament able to respond to events not fixed in totally rigid compartments. If thirty-five Conservative MPs did what Christopher Brocklebank-Fowler did, then we would now have a general election. That is part of our democracy and one reason why governments can lose votes of confidence. The Labour Party would accept a general election gladly if it was forced in this way.

A poll in my Devonport constituency conducted between 5 and 8 April for Westward Television showed, like the poll in *Now!* magazine, that I would get 55 per cent of the vote and put Labour second with 21 per cent, the Conservatives on 20 per cent and the Liberals only getting 2 per cent. Also 79 per cent wanted me to stay on as MP until the general election and only 21 per cent wanted me to resign immediately and hold a by-election.

I had to admit, however, that I was in a very different situation from most people; it was widely felt that I could easily win an early by-election in Devonport. But not everyone else was in that situation. I could have gone on my own ego trip, and very tempting it was for it would have boosted my position in the Gang of Four, but it was not to be, though it continued to worry me. The extent to which it did can be judged by a rather defensive speech I made around that time:

> It is not for Michael Foot, who was a Liberal and became a socialist, who did represent Devonport and then went to Ebbw Vale, to lecture me on honour – he fought the election on the same 1979 manifesto as I did, and who can doubt who has changed more? I will not use my vote in Parliament between now and the next election to run totally counter to the 1979 manifesto on which I went before the Devonport electorate.

A consequence of this stance – that we were the true protectors of the Labour Party Manifesto – was that we were a little too ready to defend some of its elements which we really needed to drop. It pushed us further towards being identified with the status quo.

I broke from a united front on by-elections only once. Michael Foot had taunted me in the House of Commons saying that he would be happy to conduct a debate in Devonport if I would fight. We exchanged public letters on that same day, 4 November 1981. I, saying I would gladly resign my seat if he would come and fight me in Devonport. He rejected it, repeating his charge that I sat in the House on false pretences. He would not even have had to resign his Ebbw Vale seat: for a quirk of Parliamentary practice would have allowed him to contest Devonport as a Labour candidate while remaining MP for Ebbw Vale and Leader of the Opposition – though naturally if he were to win it would be Devonport he would then have to represent, not Ebbw Vale. It would have been a perfect opportunity for the voters to demonstrate what sort of Labour Party they wanted, for we were both Plymouth-born and both had been Labour MPs for Devonport. Of course I did not expect him to take the bait: if I beat him, as I am confident I would have done, it would then have been impossible for him to remain as Leader, even though he would still have been the MP for Ebbw Vale.

While the Labour Party was tearing itself apart and the SDP was being formed, the Government made one of the most significant strategic decisions of its first Parliament, one which we can now see helped them to victory both in 1983 and 1987. On 18 February Margaret Thatcher made her second major U-turn, the first being over Bishop Muzorewa. In the face of a strike threat from Joe Gormley, the popular miners' President, the Government offered more money to keep the coalmines working. I had begun to realize that a remarkable feature of Margaret Thatcher's style was her refusal to admit that she ever changed her mind even when it was obvious that she had. She seemed keen to appear more ideological, less pragmatic than the record actually demonstrated. Observing successive Labour Prime Minsters from the Opposition benches had clearly made her decide that it was better to be seen as consistently resolute; never to complain, never to explain and never to admit to a U-turn. So much was this her style that whenever I heard her deny that she was turning, I immediately suspected that she was. When she made her famous Conference speech in October 1980, 'You turn if you want, the Lady's not for turning', for instance, I wondered if she had already begun to change her economic stance; but in fact she was not changing and Geoffrey Howe's budget in 1981, in defiance of 364 economists, squeezed demand and paved the way for sustained expansion from 1983–89.

Mrs Thatcher would probably much rather be remembered for her public battles than for her strategic retreats. However, her recognition that coal reserves were insufficient in 1981 and that if a strike were called the Government might be beaten, was astute and brave. It was probably the wisest political decision of her first period in office, particularly since it was linked to a decision to build up big coal reserves in the power stations and to plan for a predictable confrontation with the incoming President of the NUM, Arthur Scargill, after Joe Gormley retired. Given her temperament it could not have been easy to back off; no doubt she feared cries of chicken and a bad press. But cutting one's losses is a great political skill. Margaret Thatcher was a far more cautious political leader than is often recognized.

Meanwhile I was experiencing union troubles of a different kind. The Parliamentary Committee of the Social Democratic Party was born on Monday 2 March when twelve Labour Members of Parliament resigned the whip and became Social Democrats. I withdrew from all Labour Party organizations, though a little devil meant that I kept my membership of the Socialist Medical Association. They seemed to accept my banker's order and I did not stop it for many years. I was amazed to discover, however, that, though a member of the ASTMS, I was no longer allowed to attend meetings of its Parliamentary Committee. This was indefensible since union officials were allowed to attend without being paid-up members of the Labour Party. But Labour policy was to prevent Social Democrats from building relations with the trade union movement. From Labour's point of view, it was logical to try and show that we were not true social democrats. So Clive Jenkins made not the slightest attempt at maintaining links with the SDP, irrespective of whether it was in the best interests of his members. This was particularly evident when, as over the Toshiba industrial plant in my constituency, my endeavours to keep it open specifically affected ASTMS members. The EETPU by contrast, through their trade union officer Roy Sandelson, worked with me as the MP irrespective of whether I was Labour or SDP. But their leader, Frank Chapple, who signed the Limehouse Declaration, did not join the SDP. His problem was that he needed Labour Party moderates to ensure that the Left did not win back control of his union. His prime responsibility was to the EEPTU and if that could best be helped by staying a member of the Labour Party that was a price worth paying. It meant that we did not attract any major trade union figure into the SDP.

We were witnessing the start of an aggressive Labour counter-attack. Politics is a bruising business and we had no reason to expect any quarter from the Labour Party. Their tactic was to conflate the SDP with the Liberals. They set out to challenge our socialist, social democratic or Left credentials. So links with trade unions were to be denied, links with European socialists were to be undermined and in the House of Commons we were presented at all times as linked to the Liberals. The Fabian Society now took a ballot on whether members of the SDP should be excluded. It went narrowly against our being eligible to remain.

The fact that most of our MPs were in very safe Labour seats was bound to be an important influence on what sort of SDP they wished to establish. Most knew that in order to survive they had to win traditional Labour votes. Of all these MPs Mike Thomas was the one who became my closest friend, though I had not known him well before this time. His Newcastle-upon-Tyne East constituency was a solid safe seat with an 18.7 per cent majority. Sponsored by the Co-operative Movement, he had been very active in the National Union of Students. When he came into the House of Commons in 1974 he was identified most closely with Shirley Williams and had been Roy Hattersley's Parliamentary Private Secretary when Roy was Minister of State in the Foreign Office. He represented the younger generation, those who persuaded the Gang of Four that joining the SDP by credit card was perfectly sensible and efficient, and that we should ignore the jibes of Labour and set a new style. He saw the launch as a marketing opportunity and automatically sought the best professional advice insisting that we leave behind in the Labour Party all those hang-ups about using the skills of advertising and public relations. But behind all his veneer of modernity and thrusting

aggression lay a thoughtful, kind and gentle person, more deeply committed to the values that under pinned the Limehouse Declaration than any
of the other people most closely associated with it. Because he fought for
the SDP, it was easy to portray him as a hard, ruthless, ambitious
politician. That is a false portrait, but one which is hard to shake off. The
easiest way to lose such a reputation is of course to back away from
confrontation and concede ground to those who denigrate you. That
Mike did not choose that course is a tribute to his courage. I can truly
say that no one I know gave more of himself to the SDP and, without his
readiness to fight for the Party, it would have been absorbed into the
Liberals and have lost even more independence by 1982.

One person who, I thought, Roy would find particularly difficult to
ignore in the need to get at Labour voters and whose views I respected,
was Tom Bradley. He had served as Roy's Parliamentary Private Secretary
from 1964 to 1970 and had been Chairman of the Labour Party in 1976.
Now fifty-five, he had spent forty years in the Labour Party, having
joined in 1942 shortly before his sixteenth birthday. After a year as a
railway clerk he was called up as a 'Bevin Boy' and spent two-and-a-half
years in the pits in a Derbyshire coalmine. He won Leicester in a by-
election in 1962 as a sponsored Transport Salaried Staff Association
Trade Union MP. There was a substantial Asian vote in Leicester and
hitherto it had voted homogeneously on a high turn out for Labour. It
was going to be a very difficult seat to hold unless the SDP could attract
that Asian vote. Sadly, Tom never seemed to be ready to confront Roy
about our identification with the Liberals. He was always moaning about
them, but never seemed to reach a conclusion about our position. Edward
Lyons, in his seat in Bradford, also had to win Asian support in the 1983
election to retain the seat. He had been Roy's Parliamentary Private
Secretary from 1974–76. Edward, by contrast, fought hard to keep the
original identity of the SDP. I suspect Tom's equivocation came from
his awareness that the next election was Roy's last chance to become
Prime Minister, and his generous nature favoured a close relationship
with the Liberals to make this possible. Yet part of him, I suspect, also
knew that the Liberal link spelled electoral doom for him in Leicester.
His political head led him the way I wished the Party to go but his heart
kept him with Roy. Edward Lyon's head and heart was with the SDP.

On 9 March the Steering Committee agreed that the colours of the
Party should be red, white and blue, but that we would not want to use
the Union Jack for that belonged to everybody, irrespective of party. We
chose as the symbol of the Party, the letters SDP. This had proved itself
for other parties in Europe. The emphasis would be on 'Social
Democrats', rather than on the Party since market research showed that
people disliked the word 'party'. There was to be no minimum subscrip-
tion for members, but a general guidance figure was £9. It was agreed
that a Chief Executive should be appointed as soon as possible. It was

also decided that we would not run official candidates in the May local
elections because we were wary of cranks jumping on the bandwagon. On
16 March the Steering Committee agreed that a policy statement called,
'Twelve points for Social Democrats' should be produced for the launch
and that all MPs and members of the Steering Committee should be
invited to the launch of the Party on 26 March in the Connaught Rooms.

Did the SDP take the task of attracting Conservatives to our ranks
seriously enough? Indeed was it wise to attract Conservatives towards a
Social Democratic Party? This was a major dilemma for me. To widen
our appeal I naturally wanted Conservative support, but I knew that in
the process we could make it harder for the SDP to build a left of centre
identity. As a result I was initially rather lukewarm about welcoming
Christopher Brocklebank-Fowler and he used to rib me about this in the
early months. Helpfully, when he crossed over to us, Christopher's
speech stressed the appalling record of the Government over unemployment, and on race his stance was well-established and principled; so he
personally presented no problems. My main priority at that time, however, was to persuade sufficient Labour MPs to join. Only when we had
the eleven on board did I look seriously at the Conservatives.

At the time there were a number of young Conservative MPs who
looked as if they might join us. We spoke to each other under the same
terms of confidence as I had obtained with the Labour MPs and I do not
intend to embarrass them by breaking that confidence. A 1984 survey of
past political affiliations among those who joined the SDP showed that
most of the members – 65 per cent – had never previously been members
of any party and they became known as the political virgins. Of the 35
per cent who had once been members of other parties, the largest
proportion, 61 per cent of those previously affiliated or 22 per cent of all
members, were ex-Labour, 8 per cent were ex-Conservatives and 8 per
cent were ex-Liberal. On that basis we should have had much more than
one Conservative MP with us and it may have been a mistake not to
proselytize more actively. We also lost some Conservatives because of our
links with the Liberals and Christopher Brocklebank-Fowler was always
warning us against the Liberals' image as losers.

Another reason we did not attract more Conservative MPs concerned
the nature of the so-called Tory wets. In commenting on my book in
early March 1981, Samuel Brittan wrote in the *Financial Times*, 'There is
only one plea I would make to the Social Democrats: think several times
before seeking soul mates among the Tory "wets".' He argued
perceptively that the decentralizers among the Social Democrats should
find the Thatcherite distrust of big government less uncongenial than the
attitude of the upper-class Tory paternalists and continued, 'a social
market economy is much more radical – and in the right sense egalitarian
– than anything that has occurred to the Whitelaws, Priors and
Carringtons of our political world.' The social market concept never

attracted Roy Jenkins and since he was dominant over economics his views, rooted in the 1960s, carried the day. Even though his outlook was very similar to the Conservative paternalists, they all preferred to 'keep a hold on nurse for fear of getting something worse.'

The Conservative Party, moreover, like Labour, were counter-attacking to keep their MPs. The Gang of Four were savaged by Margaret Thatcher, of all people, on the grounds that we should have stayed and fought within the Labour Party. How she had the effrontery to argue that case, knowing we would have had to vote for Labour defence policy, shows how desperate the old parties were, and still are, to preserve their duopoly. Peter Walker, the high priest of the wets, was given the job of holding the wobblers' hands, an astute choice. I also believe that the socially aware Conservatives did gain more influence on policy between the Warrington by-election and the end of the Falklands War. But, since Margaret Thatcher denied any U-turn, only the historians will be able to judge. After the Falklands War the Conservatives did not have to take the SDP challenge very seriously again until 1984 when we won the Portsmouth by-election, and then we did become a target until 1987.

A crucial early move in identifying the SDP with the Left of Centre was taken on 2 March. With Roy Jenkins never making the slightest protest, all four of us sent a telegram to the vice-presidents of Socialist International saying:

> We wanted you to hear personally from us that we have today ceased to be members of the Labour Party and twelve Members of Parliament have become Social Democrats. We will launch a new Social Democratic Party before Easter. Eventually we hope the new party will become a member of Socialist International and we will be writing to you later in more detail.

In response, at the start of the week in which the SDP was formally launched in March, Ron Hayward, then General Secretary of the Labour Party, wrote in pretty intemperate terms to Socialist International about our desire for affiliation:

> I want to make it crystal clear that this would be strongly opposed by the Labour Party which for the reasons I have given would of course be unwilling to belong to an organization to which such a breakaway group were admitted.

This letter caused a good deal of ill feeling among Socialist International members because of the threat to withdraw. Nevertheless Joop den Uyl, as President of the Confederation of Socialist Parties of the European Community, came under a lot of pressure from the Labour Party to issue a statement saying that we would not be allowed to join the Confederation. This he did in early April, repeating the main Labour Party propaganda theme that our aim was to form a coalition with the Liberal Party and thus to occupy the centre position on the English political spectrum. Labour's counter-attack focused on this issue. They felt they could cope with a Centre party linked to the Liberals but a new social democratic party scared them. The Socialist International itself meanwhile said nothing. In Germany Helmut Schmidt, still Chancellor, was personally very sympathetic. But Willy Brandt, President of the SPD, was wary, knowing the dangers to the Left of encouraging any splitting and wanting to keep Socialist International in harmony. He was informed by Shirley that we would not make any move to apply to Socialist International until at least we had shown our strength in by-elections. I told Joop den Uyl that he was wrong about our wanting an immediate coalition with the Liberals, though we did want an electoral arrangement with them and a coalition might emerge after a general election. Since he had publicly committed himself to form the next Dutch Government in coalition with D66, a very similar grouping to the SDP, I pulled his leg about his disparagement of any link we might form with the Liberals. He took the point and personal relations remained good, but he was in a difficult position politically. The Dutch Labour Party, with its Left-wing militants, was facing some of the same problems as the British Labour Party. The Dutch Peace Movement was strong and the Dutch Labour Party deeply torn over the deployment of cruise missiles. Eventually the SDP Steering Committee recommended that we should stick to the formula set out in our telegram, concentrating on keeping good relations rather that provoking a major row over the issue and embarrassing our friends; and that we should review the situation following our first by-election victory. After Warrington, Roy's distaste for involvement in Socialist International became very clear and their rebuff made it hard to take it further. Later we were to face pressure for us to be linked with Liberals internationally, which Shirley always staunchly resisted and I supported her since they are more reactionary than the Christian Democrats.

When I was pressed about Socialist International on Granada's *World in Action* programme on 24 March, on which I appeared with David Steel, I emphasized that Social Democrats were no less keen to ally themselves with Social Democrats abroad than the Liberal Party was eager to associate itself with like-minded Liberals in other countries. In that programme I was more forthcoming than I had been earlier when the two of us had appeared together soon after Limehouse on BBC's *Question Time* with Sir Robin Day. Even so, the *Guardian*, under a headline 'OWEN REACHES OUT FOR PACT WITH LIBERALS', said that neither I nor David Steel had talked in terms of an agreement which would sink the identities of the Liberal Party and the Social Democrats into a single electoral organization. It was felt that we had both been accommodating about the way in which a deal could be reached and were agreed that a simple electoral alliance would be a second-best arrangement. When I was pressed on the programme about the repeated use of the word 'socialist' by members of the Council for Social Democracy, I insisted that that had been no barrier to a coalition in Germany between the SPD and the Liberals. If Willy Brandt, a social democrat and member of the SPD as well as being prominent in Socialist International, could coalesce with the FDP, the West German Liberals, who were also members of Liberal International, why could not we do the same in Britain? The *Guardian* on 22 April had a story under the headline, 'EUROPEAN SOCIALIST GROUP SNUBS SDP', in which their reporter from Brussels admitted that members of continental socialist parties had mixed feelings about the SDP, some of their party leaders feeling they had more in common with pro-marketeers such as Shirley Williams and Roy Jenkins.

This question of the Socialist International was important to me and to some of our activists, but I must admit it soon became irrelevant to many members and most certainly to the public and, inasmuch as it raised the word 'socialist', was damaging. Shirley and I were too slow to acknowledge that in Britain the word 'socialist' had become indistinguishable from 'Labour' and that few members of the public understood that bureaucratic Fabianism was not all the socialist tradition had to offer, whereas on the Continent the terms 'socialist' and 'social democrat' are virtually interchangeable. There was a certain cussedness about my refusal to reject identification with socialism. I could not and still cannot repudiate the great body of socialist thinking and writing about egalitarianism and its linkage to an individual's freedom. The non-Marxist socialist tradition of Christian charity and care is not one that can or should be lost in a crude equation with communism or vulgarizing of the socialist viewpoint. British socialists like Robert Owen, William Morris, Professors Tawney and Titmus and G.D.H. Cole have made a profound contribution to political thought and I will not denigrate their memory by decrying socialism. In retrospect it would have been better simply to have said, 'I am a social democrat full stop', and adamantly refused to get into any arguments about what socialism was or was not. In my book *Face the Future*, published while I was still nominally a member of the Labour Party, the words 'socialist' and 'social democrat' were interchangeable. When, in the paperback edition, I changed some but by no means all of the references to 'socialist' or 'socialism' to 'social democrat' and 'social democracy' I was taunted by Labour and teased by journalists. I rejoined that we could not expect former Conservatives who were in the SDP to use the word 'socialist'. By November, Roy Jenkins, conveniently forgetting that he was a signatory to the telegram to Socialist International only in March, was saying, 'I don't use the word. I haven't used the word socialist, or socialism, for some years past, a substantial number of years past, because I regard it as more obfuscating than clarifying.' He had by then no difficulty in convincing everyone that that was true.

Even in the Richmond by-election in 1989 I got myself into a tangle over the word 'socialist' in an interview with Jean Rook of the *Daily Express*. I had made all the right qualifications when I talked to her, but they disappeared in her text; perhaps not unreasonably since I had used the dreaded word. Some exaggerated the effect; no doubt it lost our excellent candidate, Mike Potter, a few votes, but that was probably counterbalanced by the few votes the article gained. Eventually the term 'social democrat' will I expect replace 'democratic socialist' within whatever form the Labour Party is eventually packaged. The Union of Soviet Socialist Republics in 1991 decided they would from now on be called the Union of Soviet Sovereign Republics. It is a sign of the times – though how sovereign the republics will prove to be is open to doubt. The fact that Leningrad is to revert to St Petersburg is also revealing. Maybe by the next century we will see the abandonment of the title 'Labour', and certainly 'socialist' is beginning to be used less and less by Labour politicians.

In March 1981 I was approaching the launch of the SDP with excitement and anticipation. To be a social democrat was a new release, a link with my Labour past but also a springboard for the future. I wanted to take the ethic of redistribution into our new Party, but to lose all the trappings of state socialism; to break the institutional links with but not the respect for the trade unions. I wished our SDP would spearhead a counter-revolution to reverse our relative decline, but I had not yet fully realized the extent to which a counter-revolution was already underway with Margaret Thatcher.

PART FIVE

CREATING THE SDP

23

THE LAUNCH OF THE SDP

The launch of the Party on 26 March 1981 was a brilliant success, and the credit goes to Mike Thomas. By giving sole authority to one person we evaded the problems of launching by committee. That morning everything went with a zing: we were out to show that we were a bright, modern, professional party and proud of it. There were 500 journalists when we started at 9.00 a.m. in the Connaught Rooms, and since journalists are not dedicated to early rising, this was itself an achievement. Television camera crews from all over the world were swarming everywhere and there was an infectious mood of excitement and bustle. The news coverage of the launch was vast. ITN's mid-day bulletin gave twenty-three of its twenty-five minutes to the SDP.

We had bought expertise but expert help was given freely too. For example Dick Negus, one of Britain's foremost designers, contributed the distinctive SDP logo, though it was Sylvia Rodgers who suggested thickening the line underneath the letters for additional strength. Many other professional people bestowed their time and exertions, in particular David Kingsley and John Habden; also David Abbot on advertising. This gave us the equivalent of millions of pounds' worth of free publicity – over £20 million perhaps. The London launch was followed by other launches as the Gang of Four dispersed to the provinces of Britain. Debbie and I went to Southampton by train, and then flew on to Plymouth. All round the country, volunteers came to man the phone banks so that members could be signed up on the spot. The idea of credit card membership proved a great success; and this method brought in many people who were joining a political party for the first time. I lost my prejudice against plastic money, and got my own credit card for the first time.

In the House of Commons Hansard noted our presence with an intervention during Prime Minister's Questions:

MIKE THOMAS
Far be it from me to intrude on this private quarrel, but will the
right honourable Lady ponder on the fact that the emergence of the
Social Democratic Party has less to do with her theories of
monetarism or the right honourable Gentleman's theories of socialism
than with the future of the country?

PRIME MINISTER
I recall hearing a comment on the radio this morning about the
Social Democratic Party being a new Centre party. I heard someone
say that such a Centre party would be a party with no roots, no
principles, no philosophy and no values. That sounded about right,
and it was Shirley Williams who said it.

This abrasive exchange demonstrated that launching a party was one
thing but sustaining it and building it up to withstand the buffeting of
party political warfare was, formidably, quite another. And the Government manifested its power to manipulate public opinion: that day the
Prime Minister elected to make a statement on the Security Services.
Normally this is a subject guaranteed to make headlines and divert
attention. In a statement occupying a page and a half of Hansard she
revealed the findings of the former Secretary of the Cabinet, Lord
Trend. It concerned that hardy perennial about whether or not there was
a Fifth Man in addition to Burgess, Maclean, Philby and Blunt. Although
it was impossible to prove to the contrary, Lord Trend had concluded
that Sir Roger Hollis, the Director General of MI5 from 1956 to 1965,
had not been an agent of the Russian Intelligence Service. Rather lamely
Margaret Thatcher concluded by saying that she had asked the Security
Commission to review current procedures. The Labour Party co-operated
fully in making the most of this affair. The two entrenched class-based
parties were by no means averse to combining to steal our thunder
whenever it was in their mutual interests. But although it captured
headlines, the press did not completely fall for this flagrant ploy and gave
us substantial coverage.

The three press conferences I attended were inevitably rather sterile
affairs, few members of the public being present, but I had a public
speaking engagement that evening in Taunton. It had been fixed before
the launch date and I decided to keep to it, since another launch press
conference was planned for Bristol the following morning. Driving up
from Plymouth to the school on the outskirts of Taunton, I envisaged a
normal public meeting of around 100 people. As we drew near to the
school we noticed a lot of cars. We thought this was a little odd but
conjectured that another meeting was being held there. But when we
walked into the hall I realized that the launch of the party had triggered
off a dramatic political response. It was packed, with well over 800
people present, supposedly the largest political meeting in Taunton since
Winston Churchill had spoken there in the 1945 Election. The immense

enthusiasm was captured by television and supplemented the launch publicity with new, fresh pictures for the evening news bulletins. At that moment, for the first time, I felt that the SDP just might be able to break through the two-party stranglehold that had gripped British politics since the emergence of the Whigs and the Tories.

It is worth recalling what our launch research (five discussion groups with respondents who would consider voting for an alliance of SDP and Liberals at the next general election) said about the SDP versus the Liberals:

The SDP is also seen as being qualitatively different from the Liberal Party. Policies, once again, are totally irrelevant here. The really salient dimensions on which the SDP and the Liberals are compared are ones on which the SDP is seen as having enormous advantages. The SDP is:

'New' – as against the rump of a dead party.

'Risk taking' – as against armchair 'do-gooders' ('They have won their spurs').

'Experienced' (the SDP members have practical experience of 'real' government).

These are the true criteria and on these counts the SDP is seen as radically different from the Liberals. The Liberal Party vote is at heart regarded as being a middle-class 'cop out', 'pious', a non-urgent protest vote. More to the point, the Liberals are associated with a particular set of middle-class minority values and lifestyles that are widely disliked and 'discredited'.

In this sense it is highly important that the SDP recognizes the basis of its relationship with the Liberal Party – one of considerable bargaining strength – and with 'liberalism', and in a stylistic sense continues to emphasize its basic differences. To suggest too great an identity with the Liberals is likely to limit the appeals of the SDP to an unnecessary degree. By contrast the greatest appeal of the SDP is that it appears to have a real chance of effecting change. The SDP is seen as being a party with some momentum.

The opportunities and the warnings were all encapsulated in that research. The launch was the time in the SDP's history when we were ready to seek out and accept professional advice; when it was considered natural and correct to make decisions against a background of knowledge not just hunch or instinct.

These were heady days. It was above all immense fun. We were free and unfettered. In any account of the SDP the focus is inevitably on what went wrong, on inner tensions, arguments and personality clashes, but for those of us who lived through the first ten years, it was a fascinating experience and an extremely worthwhile enterprise. I cannot say I have no regrets; I made errors, took decisions which proved to be wrong and made judgements on people and events which turned out to be false. But that is so of every ten-year segment of my life. To the question, do I regret helping create the SDP, the answer is a resounding 'no'.

By next day it was clear that everything about the launch including the opening London press conference had gone extraordinarily well. But I was very worried about one, I think spontaneous, reply by Bill Rodgers to a question on the Liberals which appeared as a new policy statement on the front page of *The Times*. The SDP intended, he said, putting up candidates in about half the 635 seats apart from Northern Ireland where they would set up no party organization. Such plans he added would have to be drawn up in consultation with the Liberals. That commitment had never been discussed among the four of us and had far-reaching implications. It implied, right from the start, parity with the Liberals; a massively important decision. What if the SDP was a great success – were we committed to fighting only half the seats? What did parity mean? Any fool could see that to have 317 seats meant nothing. It was which seats you had that mattered. It might be a more realistic and advisable bargain to fight 435 to the Liberals' 200 or vice versa. It was an odd statment to make without any consultation. It was particularly unfortunate since Mike Thomas had presciently prepared extensive briefing notes which we had all studied and agreed before the press conference, in order to cope with just such questions. We had even had a dress rehearsal. The form of words for answering the inevitable questions about our relations with the Liberal Party was deliberately bland:

Q. What kind of arrangement with the Liberals do you envisage?
A. There is no alliance at present between the SDP and the Liberals. We are determined to be a **separate** party with our own programme of policies. But there are obvious advantages in an **electoral arrange-ment** between us, because not to have one would split the vote among those who want a real alternative to the sterility of the old Labour or Conservative politics. We will seek to negotiate such an arrangement with the Liberals – this is what we believe the majority of the electorate expects us to do.

The nature of the electoral arrangement with the Liberals was one of the key questions facing the SDP and, with one comment, Bill Rodgers had pre-empted it. David Steel had been putting constant pressure on us all over this issue, both before and after the Limehouse Declaration. It was perfectly reasonable for him to do so. He was, after all, the Leader of the Liberal Party and apart from his own highly developed but perfectly legitimate ambition, his over-riding responsibility was to protect the interests of the Liberal Party. He never ceased to champion both and I have no criticism of him. Politics is not an occupation for those who are upset by anything more than the odd jostle at a vicarage tea party. Ambition drives politics as making money drives commerce. The public knows this and views politicians with healthy scepticism and disdain. David Steel never made any secret of his wish to build up the Liberal Party so that it could govern the country again. Any Social Democrat who expected him to act differently was gravely underestimating the survival instinct of the Liberal Party and, as we were to see in 1988, their capacity to come back from the most appalling self-inflicted wounds. I never underestimated David Steel's manipulative skills; if they had been matched by an interest in the policies best suited to our country, he would have been a formidable politician.

But what made Bill's statement even more infuriating was that I had written to the other three on 23 March to say we must try and make time for strategic thinking. I had enclosed a memo which suggested a Constitutional and an Industrial Commission and informed them that I had discussed this concept in very broad outline with David Steel:

> he seemed reasonably keen, though he still persists in talking about a policy document in July and keeps referring to an Alliance, both of which are to my mind premature. It should be quite sufficient to have by September a working relationship in Parliament through the Joint Committee, an arrangement for dealing with by-elections and two Commissions, one established and working, the other in prospect.
>
> I cannot see how we can proceed to talk about constituency arrangements until we have democratically elected Area Parties by September at the earliest, and hopefully a Council for Social Democracy by November, established with full national and regional representation. Obviously we should aim to have a constituency agreement before the Metropolitan and London Borough elections in May 1982.
>
> David Steel is pushing us all the time, for obvious reasons, on his timetable. We must take the initiative ourselves after the launch and lay out a timetable for co-operation which suits our timing, allowing us to establish the Social Democrat identity first. Nothing could be more damaging for us than to be forced into an Alliance before we are ready in May$June in the wake of Liberal gains in the Council elections. In late April they will want to be seen to be working with us in order to help them do well in the May elections. That is the moment when they will be most receptive to an offer and yet most likely also to accept our terms. June will be a time when we could be most vulnerable, having not fought in May, perhaps having had a few difficult by-elections to fight. I believe if we are quite firm that we will not make any commitment to an Alliance until we are a democratic party that will be understood by the general public and be an honourable not just a defensible position.

On 1 April 1981, a week after the launch, Roy Jenkins, speaking at a Gladstone Club dinner, offered the Liberals a 'partnership of principle'. That meant little in itself but then I read in the newspapers that, at the Königswinter Conference that coming weekend, ways towards a formal inter-party agreement were to be pursued between David Steel and Shirley Williams. It was nice to know: again there had been no collective discussion. At Königswinter substantive talks were held without any prior agreement by the Steering Committee or discussion at the Gang of Four lunches at L'Amico's restaurant, which used to precede the Steering

Committee. The proposals which emerged were reported in considerable detail in the *Guardian*. All hell broke loose among the SDP MPs.

Following these unauthorized talks, a special meeting was urgently called on 7 April between the Parliamentary Committee and the Steering Committee. I, like most of the MPs, was furious. Roy Jenkins was chairing all committees that month, in the Gang of Four's agreed rotation, but even he could not defuse the mood of anger. According to the very full minutes of the meeting, Ian Wrigglesworth said he felt very strongly that Social Democrats were being constantly bounced by David Steel on all aspects of the relationship, and argued that it could not be in the best interests of the Party, or of striking the best deal for the Social Democrats, to be entering into any form of negotiations, less than fourteen days after the establishment of the new Party. It was a nonsense to enter into a deal when we were weaker but had the potential to be stronger and when we had not negotiated policy within the party itself. He pointed to the indications in recent polls that there was considerably more support for Social Democrats than for Liberals. The public perceived the Liberals, loaded down with all their historical baggage, as representing failure. Our Party should not be entering into a merger before we had a national organization. Edward Lyons said the Party should maximize its membership in the current flood of good will and pointed out that there was great resistance to voting Liberal from supporters of other parties in the past. He felt we were in bed with the Liberals far too early and that this could damage recruitment. The new party should be democratic in its approach, its policy formulated by its members. Only then should we negotiate. The Liberals would choose candidates anyway and there would have to be hard bargaining in any case. It was important not to rush. The public perceived a major difference between Liberals and Social Democrats and we must acknowledge that. Robert Maclennan said we did not have to accept David Steel's interpretation of what he needed to take to his conference. It was possible to take too catastrophic a view of the urgency to achieve an agreement. Mike Thomas said that the public had a general perception of the Liberals as negative; associated with failure. The Social Democrats were new and positive. David Steel was playing a bad hand very astutely. There should be no statement for some months and electoral arrangements should not be discussed for twelve to eighteen months. I reminded the meeting that we were in a bargaining situation, and sought some form of arbitration procedure for the settling of by-election disputes since they could be highly damaging. Others, mainly those closely associated with Roy Jenkins, supported David Steel's position with varying degrees of enthusiasm, but Roy Jenkins, summing up, reflected the agreement that both parties should retain their separate identities – there was no idea of a merger: that there must be an arrangement before the next general election; that the Liberals were a loose body and varied in their support in different areas throughout the country; and that there was too much negotiation being conducted in public by the Liberals. Bill Rodgers said that he and Shirley Williams would report the widely-expressed anxiety to David Steel.

It had been a clear and firm rebuff to all the Gang of Four, and I could not escape responsibility for not having prevented these moves towards the Liberals. For a few weeks this shot across Roy Jenkins's bows meant that we could proceed with the mammoth task of building our own Party. But a trend had been set in motion which was to prove impossible to reverse. The press learnt that there had been a row and reported the dissent, but the ferocity of the encounter was toned down; it was not in our interests to repeat the fights we had experienced within the Labour Party. This became the pattern: in our wish to avoid in-fighting and bickering we presented an outward image of unity. Of course, this is attempted by all political parties, but it served us ill. Issues which should have been thrashed out were hidden under the carpet. This is very much Roy Jenkins's style. Unfortunately it became the house style of the SDP too. Many of our members never realized how strongly and for how long a merger had been pressed within the Party and resisted, until in 1987 it all erupted with pent-up ferocity on an unsuspecting public and, in some cases, unsuspecting Party members.

I had written to the Speaker, George Thomas, to ask formally that rooms should be allocated as a Whip's Office for Social Democrat MPs. Eventually the Services Committee felt obliged to accede to our request and we took the Ulster Unionists' room close to the Members' Smoking Room. In the Chamber we chose the bench below the gangway which was traditionally where those on the left of the Labour Party sat. Michael Foot had sat there throughout his years of opposition to his own front bench. Now that he was leading the Party from the front bench we deemed it an appropriate place for us. This provoked the 'battle of the prayer cards'. MPs who wish to reserve a position for Prayers, which take place for five minutes at the start of business at 2.30 p.m. every Monday to Thursday and at 9.30 a.m. on Fridays, are entitled to place a card with their name on the seat they wish to occupy. If, and only if, they attend Prayers, they are then entitled to put it in the slot on the back of their seat which reserves their place for the rest of the day. Suddenly a number of atheists on the Left discovered an interest in God in order to prevent SDP MPs from claiming their seats. But since you could claim the seat as early as 8 o'clock in the morning, it was not long before our MPs' keenness to establish themselves triumphed. Eventually, despite the occasional shoving and pushing, we managed to establish this bench as our territory, a small but significant victory. I took the view it was no good expecting our troops to challenge the other parties in the country if we were not prepared to take up the battle in Parliament. As the number of SDP MPs increased, so we occupied the whole of that bench below the gangway and, with the exception of very few Labour MPs, it became our own. On big occasions some of our MPs had to sit in the empty spaces left on the Liberal bench immediately behind us.

The 'battle of the prayer cards' was not the end of our run-ins with the Left. In the struggle to establish the SDP in Parliament we had to cope with people like Dennis Skinner, the Labour MP for Bolsover. He once called me a 'pompous sod' and, in an exchange with the Chair, the question was whether he would withdraw the word 'pompous', 'sod' or both. I was unmoved. Dennis Skinner's bark is notoriously worse than his bite. He is like a court jester, the licensed dissenter, and has lost his edge. In those days the self-appointed scourge of the Social Democrats, he was a pain to begin with, but over the years our relations improved; first when after the 1983 Election he came back to share the bench below the gangway and then after the 1987 Election when he no doubt judged we could no longer do much harm to the Labour Party.

A successful all-day policy meeting was held in the Charing Cross Hotel in London in May and we managed to involve a broad cross-section of people. The foundations were laid for some interesting and thoughtful new policies in many important areas. We also came under legal challenge for calling ourselves a social democratic party as there was another, rather Left-wing group who claimed the title. Eventually there was a court ruling that any group of people could say they were the Labour, Conservative or Social Democratic Party, and that no one had a monopoly on a name. It was a useful ruling for us in 1988. The first conference could not be more than a sounding board, since it was too early for it to be democratically elected, so we decided that we should hold three two-day conferences in early October concentrating, though not exclusively, on foreign policy in Perth, unemployment in Bradford and constitutional reform in Central Hall, London.

On 19 May, Debbie and I flew up to Glasgow where I lectured on the social market economy. In many senses it was the most important policy speech I have made in politics because it flagged up my wish for the SDP to break out of the consensual approach to the mixed economy and take up, as Margaret Thatcher was doing, the theme of market economics. Helpfully Samuel Brittan in the Lombard column in the *Financial Times* on 26 May 1981 wrote:

> The absurdity of the Left-Right view of life was demonstrated by the Fourth Hoover lecture, 'The Social Market' given at Strathclyde University last week. The cliché-monger might assume from the title that it was given by Sir Keith Joseph, who first popularized the term in Britain. But he would be completely wrong. For it was given by Dr David Owen, who is normally placed in the Centre, or just left of Centre in the spectrum.
>
> Dr Owen's starting point is the need for greater emphasis on markets and 'the commercial and competitive imperatives on which our

prosperity depends.' He also let the cat out of the bag about decentralization. It cannot mean only geographical autonomy. It must by its very
nature endorse the market mechanism because the market is a continuous referendum. But it must also challenge the concentration of
industrial and economic power.

It was a theme I was only able to develop as Leader in 1983. At that time
the key SDP voice on economics was Roy Jenkins and a big selling point
was his period as Chancellor of the Exchequer from 1967–70. It was not
the best time for arguing that the failed economic policies of the past had
to be dumped in favour of greater emphasis on the market. The SDP at
that time was, probably inevitably, given its personalities, the party of
unreconstructed Keynesian economics, and Roy's criticism of Margaret
Thatcher and Geoffrey Howe focused on macro-economics and demand
management.

We stayed the night in Glasgow with Mary Rankin, my mother's
cousin, who is married to Robert, a Professor of mathematics at Glasgow
University; and once again I experienced the sense of how different
Scotland is from England and how different is its university culture and
its institutions. It served to reinforce my belief in a Scottish Parliament .

The most important inter-party skirmishing involved the Speaker,
George Thomas. In June he sent me a personal letter. I replied that its
implications were of such constitutional importance that they would have
to be discussed by SDP MPs and I could not guarantee that they would
not become public. It arose from a debate on unemployment, when the
Chair had called Bill Rodgers and Cyril Smith close together. Afterwards
the Speaker had received strong representations that the Social
Democratic Party and the Liberal Party were, to use the words of his
letter, 'for electoral purposes, one party'. There was a real risk that on
this basis the Speaker would decide in effect to merge our parties in
Parliament. If so, on major occasions only one of our parties might be
called and most MPs considered that this would be very damaging: both
SDP and Liberal MPs could lose speaking rights. I repudiated the other
parties' view that we should count as one party, challenging it first on
the grounds that we had as yet made no electoral arrangements over
constituencies for the next election and secondly, that when we did so, it
would be on the clearly stated basis that 'our parties stem from different
traditions and have their own identities'. This phrase came from the
statement called 'A Fresh Start for Britain' which had been put out
jointly by our two parties in mid-June. It had a picture of David Steel
and Shirley sitting on the grass together and, in my circle of friends, was
christened the 'honeymoon couple' statement – all mood music and little
substance.

I reminded the Speaker that an average of recent opinion polls showed
that, in answer to the question, 'If an election were to take place
tomorrow and a candidate from the new Social Democratic Party stood,

how would you vote?' the proportion answering SDP averaged a steady 26 per cent in January and February, rose to 34.5 per cent in the fortnight of the launch of the Party, dropped to 23 per cent by late April, and until June averaged a steady 24 per cent. Moreover, MORI, using a slightly different question, gave the SDP 30 per cent in February, 29 per cent in April and 29 per cent in May, and all the pointers showed a level of support for the SDP, with or without Liberal co-operation, for which there was no precedent in the last half century. I submitted that as Speaker he had a duty to represent this national feeling in the House of Commons and if he could not do so then the House of Commons would be seen as being unable to represent political opinion in the country. What had made Parliament, and the House of Commons in particular, such a great institution, I wrote, was its ability to adapt to changed political circumstances as the forum of the nation. To allow Parliament to become a rigid box in which the balance of political views and their expression had to reflect the number of MPs would be to ensure that Parliament became a stagnant political force in the country. If the public sensed that Parliament was stifling and suppressing a public mood purely because of pressure from the two largest parties, then Parliament's standing would show a further drop.

My letter deliberately appealed to George Thomas's reverence and love for Parliament. I had frequent discussions with him about all the problems we posed for him. He was amazingly understanding and indeed courageous in the way he withstood pressure, not just from the Labour and Conservative Parties, but the Liberals as well. The Liberals frequently spoke with two voices, ready to come to an understanding over speaking arrangements at the weekly meeting David Steel and I had, together with our whips, but then using another language to Murdo Maclean from the Government Whip's Office and to the Speaker and his Secretary, demanding they be treated as the Third Party despite our having more MPs. I had no complaints about this. They were defending the interests of the Parliamentary Liberal Party, which could not always coincide with those of the Social Democrats.

In June the Liberal Party had eleven MPs and the SDP fourteen. We grew to fifteen in July when Jim Wellbeloved, the Labour MP for Bexley, Erith and Crayford, joined us. By November, when Shirley joined us after her victory at Crosby, we were twenty-five, and at the end of the year twenty-seven. Eventually in June 1982, when George Cunningham, Labour MP for Islington South, joined us, we peaked at thirty SDP MPs.

The fight to preserve our independence in Parliament, with the Labour MPs and some Conservative MPs trying to have us treated as one party, came to a head when, on 18 November, I wrote formally to the Speaker at the request of the Parliamentary Committee to reiterate what I had said on many occasions, most recently at a joint meeting with

David Steel. We were now, I wrote, the largest third party in the House of Commons since 1935 and we ought to be treated in at least a similar manner to the Liberal Party. I stressed that we did not seek to be given priority over the Liberals merely because we had more MPs:

> We value our relationship with the Liberal Party and we would not wish you to give automatic precedence to us on all occasions but equally we find it unacceptable that the Liberal Party should be given precedence to us on all occasions. David Steel is well aware of my views on this issue. We are quite separate parties. It is perfectly understandable that the Liberal Party will wish to retain their rights but the Parliamentary Committee felt that it was now necessary to put our case rather more formally to you.

George Thomas was wise enough to accept that he had to reflect the change in the political situation. He himself came from the moderate, Methodist wing of the Labour Party. There is much truth in the old crack that Labour owed more to Methodism than to Marxism, and privately he was appalled at what was happening to the Labour Party. He was a lay-preacher and a wonderful orator, much in demand in the West Country chapels, and I can remember to this day when I first heard him preach. It was far more compelling than listening to him in the House of Commons in the days when he was a Minister or backbencher. George always took a very special interest in MPs' children and often invited our boys to tea, which they greatly enjoyed, each coming away with a pound note in his pocket. I find it hard to be objective about his Speakership, because without him the SDP could have been very badly squeezed. Some felt he was too favourable to Margaret Thatcher and he certainly had little time for Michael Foot. I found him scrupulously fair.

I consider George Thomas was easily the best Speaker in my years in the House of Commons. He was a true champion of parliamentary democracy. Every time the Labour Party abused Parliament to undermine the SDP, they strengthened his resolve to uphold our rights. He understood the theatrical nature of the House of Commons, and would try to 'hold a house', following the front bench speeches with arresting ones from the back benches. Or, if people returned to the House to hear a particular speaker, as they used to do for Enoch Powell, he would choose someone to follow Enoch who would continue to hold their attention. He knew the House thrived on controversy and was not a bureaucratic Speaker, locked into a percentage allocation of speaking opportunities. Rather than daunting him, the heightened drama the SDP brought to that Parliament was welcomed and he was determined to harness it to enhance Parliament's standing in the country. Though he hoped that David Steel and I would, as far as possible, resolve between ourselves who would speak first, I found that on all major debates I could be sure that a spokesman for the SDP would be called in addition to the Liberals, and, on occasions, before the Liberal speaker. The Chair gave scant attention to the Labour allegation that the Liberals and SDP were just one party, but their propaganda continued.

It always amazed me that those in both our parties wishing for merger failed to realize that, without proportional representation there will always be grotesquely few MPs representing the smaller parties, so it is in the small parties' interests to claim speaking rights as separate parties. Provided there are three MPs – the minimum number for recognition by the House of Commons – more is gained in parliamentary terms by operating independently. The SDP demonstrated this when our numbers fell to three in spring 1988, when Bob Maclennan and Charles Kennedy joined the Social and Liberal Democrats. In parliamentary terms we were perfectly entitled to continue as the SDP, to be treated by the House authorities as a political party, to issue our own whip and receive a negotiated share of the financial help available for Opposition parties. Important constitutional safeguards built up over centuries underpinned our determination and our right to be an independent SDP.

When Roy Jenkins won Hillhead in the spring of 1982, he plumped himself down on the Liberal benches. It was a foolish decision, further identifying him as a Liberal, but also undermining the SDP's position. To those of us who had fought for months to establish the SDP place below the gangway this action was an absurd slight, but by then it was all too clear that his main interest was to win the support of Liberal MPs to ensure that he became the Leader of the Alliance. It had, however, a more serious consequence for him, which I would not have predicted. Roy had previously been a brilliant parliamentary performer but on his return he was extremely ill at ease. His oratorical skills, for no apparent reason, suddenly seemed very dated and he clearly missed the natural authority conferred by speaking from the Despatch Box. Once it became apparent to Dennis Skinner and other Labour MPs that Roy could easily be put off his stride by barracking, they would find an empty space on the bench in front of him, to interject or keep up a distracting stream of commentary. We had to muster SDP MPs to sit in front of Roy on our bench but, while we could do this for Questions, they were too busy to hang around for guard duty before Roy spoke in debates.

I stopped being Chairman of the Parliamentary Committee when Roy became our leader in the summer of 1982 after the Falklands debates. The MPs clubbed together to give me a silver tankard which I treasure. No one at that stage doubted that the SDP had been successfully launched in Parliament and was one of our four national parties, clearly distinguishable from the Liberals.

24

THE ALLIANCE

I, and many other SDP MPs, had always thought a trial of strength with the Liberals was inevitable. Any electoral pact would entail hard bargaining. The SDP was founded on the understanding that one had to bargain from strength in the international fields of defence and security. I never doubted that we must also bargain from strength in the field of domestic politics. The Liberal Party was bound to fight for its position as the third party and we would have to prove our vote-getting ability first.

My priority from the launch of the Party, for the next year at least, was to build up the SDP, its membership, its finances and a core of activists. We already envisaged our first nationwide electoral test as only coming in the May 1982 local government elections. If the SDP could make sensible deals with local Liberals at those elections over a year away, so much the better. But in order to achieve those deals the SDP had to be prepared to put up candidates where Liberals were standing in council elections up and down the country. I envisaged negotiating over parliamentary seats, with one party standing down for the other after the council elections had taken place and we had established the SDP on the ground. By that time we would have developed SDP policy independently and democratically, while of course keeping a weather eye on Liberal Party policy to ensure a sensible measure of compatibility. We would also have established our own one member-one vote democracy and have either chosen or be about to choose our own leader. Meanwhile, I thought, the right strategy was to try to agree an arbitration procedure as to which party would fight which by-elections. Unless we could agree some such procedure with the Liberals, the SDP should fight all by-elections. A by-election agreement would have the advantage of making it easier to win. Victories in by-elections make it worth losing the national profile gained from fighting every by-election. Also a by-election agreement would keep open not only the possibility of working together more extensively at the next election, but the hope of achieving agreement to step down in some parliamentary seats nearer the time. Of course the

Liberals would go ahead and choose parliamentary candidates in their best seats as they had already done, but this I felt was not disastrous, provided we would be doing the same and demonstrating our capacity to match them. If at our first general election we only reached a limited electoral pact with the Liberals and did not fight each other in the most winnable seats, say 80–100, that would not be a bad agreement. It was the way electoral pacts had worked between Labour and the Liberals at the start of the century and later between the Liberals and Conservatives.

On 6 April Mike Thomas produced a paper for discussion crystallizing many of these issues. It said why Social Democrats and Liberals ought to come to some agreement, that we shared some important aims in common and should work together to achieve them. We were likely to govern in coalition and must agree on basic matters to be able to do this. Also under our 'first past the post' system, for Liberals and Social Democrats to fight each other would or could be electorally self-defeating. To meet our objective of not fighting each other was admitted to be complicated and a number of variants were possible and discussed. In spelling out the disadvantage for the SDP of a deal with the Liberals, the paper reiterated our launch research about the SDP being seen as real and 'nitty-gritty'. We were associated with a broad, classless approach to politics and they were associated with an unpopular set of middle-class minority values and lifestyles, which the press were trying very hard to stick on us too. Above all we were seen as having a real chance of effecting change; they were seen as losers with no chance. This produced for us a problem on proportional representation, for while we could be seen as wanting it on merit, they were seen as wanting it on the basis that it was their only chance of winning anything. The SDP, therefore, had little to gain in 'image' terms from close association with the Liberals and a great deal to lose.

The next twelve months were critical. We had to quickly establish our identity and build our Party on the ground. Too close an association with the Liberals would gravely damage this. If our potential support had wanted to join the Liberals it would have done so a long time ago. It actively did not want to do so but would join us. It would not see any point in joining us if we were perceived as moving towards too close an association with the Liberals. In terms of local organization what would be the point of organizing and working for the SDP locally if you already knew or guessed that the Liberals would be fighting your constituency and there would be no SDP candidate? This was a powerful argument for delay – a practical arrangement necessitated by the election system arrived at close to the election would be wholly saleable to our potential members. Gratuitous early embrace was not.

There was very little national core consistency in the Liberal vote which is why it went up and down, even over the period of six months between the two 1974 elections, so precipitately. Only in special circumstances, mostly of peripheral geography and Conservative scandal, the paper argued, did the Liberals turn support into seats. They rarely showed any sign of turning their second places into first places. Indeed the voters almost seemed instinctively to turn back from the brink when asked to do this.

The advantages of early agreement for the Liberals were the mirror image of the disadvantages for us in the SDP. It would, enhance their image and give them the credibility they currently did not have. It would protect them from attrition of their membership, many of whom were ready to join the SDP, and attract electoral support, much of which would switch to us, over half, on examination of the current polls, could switch without a second thought. It could also push them over the top in the eighty-one seats in which they ran second, which would give them a majority of the seats won by SDP and Liberal candidates in 1983 or 1984. This would give them the dominant role in Parliament subsequently, gravely undermining our credibility even though we commanded three to five times their electoral support at that time.

The overwhelming logic of the present position, the paper argued, was for any early moves for agreement to focus solely on the minimum amount of general policy agreement to sustain friendly relationships and show good will. Even this should be played down publicly and delayed some months. A firm and public rebuff for the David Steel tactics of constantly setting us deadlines was called for and some public distancing of ourselves from the idea we were being bullied or swept along by this pressure. Also a clear and public statement was needed that our first priority for twelve months at least was to establish our own party. Meanwhile it would be helpful to have an indication from David Steel that he would call a moratorium on the adoption of further Liberal candidates. Also that he would accept that the question of candidacies must be considered *ab initio* on the basis of the considerations of who was most likely to do best in which seats, plus a nationwide spread of candidates for both parties.

It was argued that the appropriate time for moves towards both a closer policy agreement and decisions on the nature of our posture, whether to keep at arms' length, to hold hands or to cuddle-up tight in the general election campaign, should be made at least twelve to eighteen months hence. In the meantime, a practical calculation, who would do best, would determine our joint approach to by-elections. We needed an SDP candidate to win an early by-election in his or her own right. So this meant that any joint nomenclature would need careful consideration for we could not afford at any by-election for the Liberals to claim more credit than that they did not stand and had endorsed our candidate. There is no doubt, therefore, that the options were put plainly before the self-appointed SDP decision-makers in April. After the row following Bill and Shirley's unauthorized action at Königswinter, that paper represented mainstream thinking. The fact that we proceeded in the next few months to pre-empt virtually every one of those decisions which should have been taken by the members was a democratic disgrace.

To establish the SDP in the country as the third largest party within a year, with the Liberals very clearly the fourth party, was not over-ambitious. By October 1981 we did achieve this third party position in terms of numbers and political weight in the House of Commons and, on the opinion poll evidence, in the country as well. The SDP was ahead of the Liberal Party in public esteem in every poll. In Gallup from March to October if people were reminded of the existence of the SDP as a separate party we normally had double, sometimes triple, the Liberal Party support.

Our membership was over 50,000 by April and up to 78,000 by the end of 1981 which, given the exaggerated membership claims of the Liberal Party, meant we were probably larger. It could have been more – our membership drive never achieved its full potential partly because of our confused identity. Our financial position was also always considerably stronger than that of the Liberal Party.

Why was such a strategy for building up the SDP not followed that April? Why by October 1981 had we queered our own pitch by forming an Alliance and other links with the Liberal Party, and why did we disadvantage ourselves further in terms of seat negotiations? Why had we systematically blurred, diffused and damaged our separate identity as a new party by the autumn of 1982?

The answer was not the Liberal Party. We could have resisted them. Nor was it David Steel, although he was harder to resist when he was acting in cahoots with Roy Jenkins. It was the divisions within our own ranks as to whether the SDP was to be a separate party from the Liberal Party that destroyed us. I find it impossible to escape the conclusion that Roy Jenkins misled me and some of the other MPs who left the Labour Party in 1981, as well as the members of the SDP in the leadership election in 1982, about his real intentions.

When Roy and I were persuading Shirley Williams to use the term realignment in the Limehouse Declaration it was because that would be a firm indication of our intention to form a new party. We were not using realignment then, however much he now tries to pretend we were, in the way Jo Grimond had sometimes used it, bringing part of the Labour Party together with the Liberals into one party. Nor can Roy pretend that his notion of a Centre Party from the Dimbleby Lecture had been agreed. It was superseded in later Gang of Four discussions. That was reflected by the rejection of the centrist names for the Party he suggested, the Radicals or the Democrats. The choice of SDP meant that, when we four sent a telegram on 2 March saying we hoped the new party would become a member of Socialist International, we were signalling the launch of a Social Democratic Party within the socialist family. When we launched the SDP on 26 March it was an independent national fourth political party. If we were to be a catalyst, then it was by continuing with the SDP, for a catalyst by definition is something which does not change itself but brings about changes in others.

It is interesting to learn from Roy Jenkins's *European Diary* that on 7 January 1980 David Steel,

> perfectly understands that there is no question of me or anybody else joining the Liberal Party. He equally is anxious to work very closely, and possibly, if things went well, to consider an amalgamation after a general election. He would like the closeness at the time of the election itself to take the form of a non-aggression pact, but of working together on policy and indeed sharing broadcasts, etc.

Whether Roy Jenkins agreed with David Steel then about amalgamating after the general election, his *Diaries* do not reveal. What was shattering was when it first became apparent to us in the SDP Steering Committee that Roy Jenkins did want to amalgamate, and he supported joint membership for SDP and Liberal Party members. While he abandoned open advocacy of a merger until 1987, he subtly and systematically undermined the SDP's independence from 1981–87. Roy used the SDP. It would have been more honourable to have joined the Liberals in 1981.

I am confident by contrast that Shirley and Bill helped to create the SDP with the intention that it should be and remain a fourth party in British politics. Of course they never ruled out, as the relationship with the Liberal Party developed, an eventual merger but neither Shirley nor Bill saw this in those early months or even years as the desired outcome of their work. As the years passed both of them, in different ways, came to the conclusion that a merger was the correct course for the SDP and announced it publicly immediately after the 1987 General Election. I believe they were wrong but they had formed that judgement honourably in the light of events. Over the years I sensed them slowly arriving at that judgement. So did many others, and though I disagreed, it never meant I did not respect their decision. When both were adopted as candidates by joint selection for Cambridge and Milton Keynes, previously Liberal seats, the process understandably accelerated. Having been chosen by Liberal members as well as Social Democrats they began to develop a dual loyalty, and were starting to fight Alliance campaigns rather than SDP ones. I do not believe there was any deceit on their part at any stage in that process.

The event which gave Roy the opportunity to cast the SDP into an Alliance mould aimed at forging a single party was, quite simply, Warrington, and it came only two months after the launching of the SDP.

At the end of May Sir Thomas Williams, the Labour MP for Warrington, resigned his seat in order to become a judge. We had had some warning of this and I raised the likelihood of the by-election at the SDP Steering Committee on 27 May, having previously discussed it at a Gang of Four lunch at L'Amico's. There, much to my horror, Shirley expressed extreme reluctance to stand and it was all I could do to stop her closing the option completely there and then. We all agreed that she would be the obvious candidate but as her reluctance became more apparent so Roy's enthusiasm to take on the challenge increased. He was like an old stallion, sniffing the smell of the race course, hoping that if the favourite withdrew he might take her place at the starting line. Shirley agreed to think about it. The Steering Committee was firmly of the view that the SDP should field a candidate and that we should commission a poll to provide information on how we should fight the seat to the SDP's best advantage. Specific candidates, Shirley Williams, Roy Jenkins and Sir Thomas Williams's son, David, who was a member of the Party, were to be brought into the poll. It was also recognized that some discussions would be necessary with the Liberals to persuade them to stand down and it was agreed that Bill Rodgers would talk to David Steel.

On 29 May John Lyttle, the employee of the party dealing with communications, issued a press statement in the name of Bill Rodgers, saying that, subject to the wishes of our local members, in consultation with the Liberals, we intended to fight the by-election. Shirley then, largely on the advice of Tony King, the Professor of Politics at Essex University and a close friend, began to back further and further away from fighting Warrington. The word was that she could not afford to be a two-time loser, a reference to her having lost in Stevenage at the last election and implying that she could not win Warrington. Then in the early evening of 3 June we learned of a poll in the *Sun* next day which showed that, if Shirley were the SDP/Liberal candidate in Warrington, 55 per cent in Warrington would vote SDP, 36 per cent Labour and 9 per cent Conservative. Under the headline, 'You can do it Shirl', the *Sun* had a whacking 19 per cent lead for Shirley, with Labour knocked out and the Tories nowhere. Instead of rethinking her position, Shirley pre-empted pressure by rushing out a press release saying that she would not stand.

It was the worst decision Shirley has ever made in politics, and certainly the most damaging single decision for the future of the new SDP. It effectively put paid to Shirley's chances of becoming Leader of the SDP and ensured that Roy would be its first Leader. I have no doubt that Shirley could have won Warrington, with dramatic consequences for the SDP and for the country. She would have fought a predominantly SDP campaign and we would in consequence have been able to negotiate a far better seat deal with the Liberals than the miserable one we ended up with. Shirley would have been the Leader of the SDP and Bill and I would have buttressed her position. There would have been no question but that it was a Social Democratic Party, standing in its own right as one of four parties in British politics. But it was sadly not to be.

The *Sun* poll showed that if Roy Jenkins were the SDP candidate we should lose: Labour would get 46 per cent, just winning the seat from the SDP on 42 per cent, with the Conservatives at 12 per cent. That was very close to the actual outcome, when Roy polled 42.4 per cent of the vote, dramatically reducing the Labour majority from over 10,000 to 1,759. This result nevertheless gave the SDP an immense boost and it was to Roy's credit that he took up the challenge. People were getting used to the unfair press image of him as a bloated bureaucrat from Brussels. In fact he turned out to be, as he always had been, a very effective campaigner and he deservedly won accolades from the press and increased public esteem. Interestingly the *Sun* poll also showed that if David Williams had stood he would have done extremely well, achieving 40 per cent to Labour's 47 per cent; whereas David Marquand, the former Labour MP and unknown in the constituency, would have won only 36 per cent with Labour at 52 per cent.

The young SDP threw its heart and soul into the Warrington by-election. Alec McGivan became the agent and did extraordinarily well. John Lyttle was the press officer, liked and trusted by journalists. People came in from all over the country. The three other members of the Gang of Four campaigned hard for Roy, as did David Steel. But the final result was Roy's personal triumph. He had always been a strong contender for the leadership of the SDP, now he was the firm favourite. At times I felt the campaign was geared to coming a good second, but perhaps that was wise – by not raising people's hopes of winning we were able to emerge as the victors. It did not sound an exaggeration when Roy described the result at the end as 'my first defeat in thirty years in politics. And it is by far the greatest victory that I have ever participated in.' I admired his campaigning spirit immensely and was deeply disappointed with Shirley for having ducked the fight, so much so that for the next few months I became quite reconciled to the fact that Roy would be our first Leader.

Roy had stood in Warrington as a Social Democrat with Liberal support and he went out of his way to emphasize the extent of the Liberal support during the campaign, exaggerating this, I felt, to make his political point. Whatever the truth, the reality was that he had inevitably been able to run and present the campaign as he wanted to and thereafter, like any politician, he used it to reinforce his favoured approach of an Alliance, with a capital 'A', with the Liberal Party. One other consequence of Warrington was that John Lyttle's long-standing and close friendship with Shirley was ruptured – he switched allegiance and became increasingly identified both with Roy Jenkins personally and with his view of how the Party should develop. I never understood what happened. But whatever the reason, it was another factor altering the balance of power. Shirley no longer had John's wise head and organizing ability to rely on and she suffered. A subtle campaign developed to diminish Shirley's influence, which she did not help by living up to her reputation for always being late.

My main anxiety became our relationship with the Liberals. In the middle of June I wrote to David Stephen, my old political adviser in the Foreign Office and by then a member of the SDP: 'I am growing increasingly worried about the way we are merging into an amorphous amalgam with the Liberal Party. I cannot put my finger on how to stop it.' The most serious threat was joint membership with the Liberal Party. I thought we had scotched it before the launch but it kept recurring in different ways. Ian Wrigglesworth even felt it necessary to write a tough letter to *The Times* stating clearly that we were not able to accept the concept of dual membership, reflecting a decision taken earlier in the Steering Committee and recently re-endorsed. This was just one instance of the pressure to fall in with the Jenkins/Steel view of an Alliance from very early on. Another was that David Steel began to raise questions about our collective leadership. Whether he was anticipating Roy winning Warrington and then mooting a leadership election was not clear. But at this stage our will to resist was strong and we were all agreed that we would not have a leadership election until the Party's democratic procedures had been put in place, which could not be before the middle of 1982. Anyhow, to have had a leadership election with either Roy or Shirley still out of the House of Commons and therefore disqualified did not make much sense.

In the midst of the Warrington by-election another by-election presented itself in Croydon, showing once again that, in politics, the unpredictable is normality. At its meeting on 6 July, the Steering Committee was informed that our area party had agreed to a joint meeting with the Liberals to be held on 24 July with the aim of selecting a joint candidate, and a statement to this effect had been issued to the press. No one wanted a public row during the Warrington campaign but joint selection was the most dangerous device the Liberals had yet designed. I believed that if we conceded joint selection for a single by-election it would establish a precedent which would open up joint selection for all parliamentary seats and gravely undermine our integrity as an independent party. Almost by definition a party which allows members of another party to select its candidate surrenders its independence. It was decided that Bill Rodgers and John Cartwright should meet representatives of the area party as soon as possible to warn them about the issues of principle involved, and we aimed to postpone a decision until after Warrington. We were fortunate in having Tyrrell Burgess as part of the Croydon SDP. I knew him from Labour Party days as a radical educationalist and a convinced decentralist and was sure he would be open to reason. He duly reported to the Steering Committee on 20

July that the meeting with the Liberals had been cancelled and that local SDP members would find it difficult to support William Pitt, the Liberal candidate in the previous election.

The joint selection danger passed but the Croydon problem remained. We all believed that Shirley Williams should fight the seat but it was clear the local Liberals were likely to dig their heels in. We had conceded as part of the agreement over Roy fighting Warrington that the Liberals should have first refusal over the next by-election unless there were special circumstances. By any political standard, with Shirley ready to fight, this was an exceptional circumstance. We agreed to say publicly that after Warrington we needed to maintain the momentum and that our alliance with the Liberals would be best served by the nomination of a candidate of national standing.

Over the next week there was frantic activity. David Steel did try hard to persuade the local Liberals to accept Shirley Williams, even at one moment threatening to come down to Croydon to speak against Bill Pitt. It was the first clear demonstration to the general SDP membership of the nature of the Liberal Party and the very considerable autonomy of their local constituency associations. It was not even as if we were dealing with a large, active Liberal Party in Croydon, their numbers were so small that they could all meet in Bill Pitt's front room. He turned out to be a bearded Liberal activist, extremely affable, but a libertarian militant. He had not been christened William Pitt for nothing and the prospect of parliamentary greatness weighed heavily with him. Since he controlled the local party and was able to generate pressure more widely from the Liberal grass roots, the Croydon Liberals were only too happy to refuse to accept Shirley Williams while the local SDP wanted to say no to Bill Pitt. We had a choice – to fight or not to fight – but in truth we barely considered fighting the Liberals.

Had Warrington not brought about a change in the Party's perception of Shirley and Roy, the Steering Committee might well have voted to put Shirley up in Croydon regardless of local Liberal protests. As it was, on 27 July we lamely expressed the hope that a local SDP meeting would take place and endorse the local candidate, William Pitt. It was a massive error, and I blame myself for not putting up a real fight for Shirley. It would, however, have meant breaking the consensus within the Gang of Four which we were trying so hard to maintain. Even so the SDP Steering Committee should have shown more self-confidence and faced the Croydon Liberals down. My problem was that, on the Steering Committee, I knew the votes were not there for putting Shirley up in opposition to the Liberals. There was almost a feeling that she should not profit from backing off the fight at Warrington. She would have had to be prepared to insist on standing, and she was not. She was admittedly in an invidious position and, although she never said so, she must have been regretting her decision not to fight Warrington. By not pushing herself harder for Croydon, she virtually committed herself to fighting the next by-election, wherever it was and however unpromising.

At the end of July Bill Rodgers presented a paper for a full discussion on our strategy for dealing with the Liberals. It postulated negotiating an agreed and equal split of all the parliamentary seats. There was, I fear, little realization of how weak our position was likely to be within such a framework. The balance of real power within the Steering Committee now emerged. Roy's view of the future now had a majority on the self-selected Steering Committee. We were about to embark on the self-destructive seat settlement which eventually emerged by the autumn of 1982. In September we were confronted by a Liberal demand for the negotiations to be held locally, which Bill rightly insisted we resist. Our local area parties were only just being formed and they were in no position to hold their own against well-established Liberal Associations. What this showed, was how premature were any negotiations. We should have taken far more time.

Once again joint selection reared its head, both for by-elections and parliamentary elections. David Steel's view mirrored that of Roy Jenkins – since we were going to merge anyhow, there was no reason for anyone to get agitated about which party fought what seat, how many seats each party fought or whether both parties' members chose the candidate. David Steel described all this in his memoirs in 1989.

> I have no doubt at all that the SDP should have been much more relaxed about seats and numbers. This was where our strength lay. Theirs lay in their top leadership. No Liberal in either House had been even a junior minister – except the current Lord Mayhew – and in any potential Government they had not only the Gang of Four but a group of experienced parliamentarians. But a Party which relied on a mainly postal membership had no chance whatever on its own of making an electoral breakthrough. We made an alliance so long as we capitalized on and combined our different assets.

This was a logical view only if the SDP was never intended to have an independent political life of its own. Since David as a Liberal never intended that it should, who could blame him? Our problem was that Roy shared his view while being a member of the SDP. They both wrapped up their intentions in ringing declarations about the Alliance being a partnership of principle. But since they were both impatient of any fights or arguments about seats, it was inevitable that the Gang of Four would be divided over seat allocations. Before any argument began, David had an automatic ally in Roy for whom rows over seats were a costly diversion. At that stage for me, and, it must be said, for Bill and Shirley, obtaining winnable seats was the vital element for building up the SDP. But the only way to do this was to be ready to fight. But for Roy to contemplate fighting the Liberals was already considered to be a mortal sin and they soon sensed we were a pushover.

I suppose Roy would now argue there was no alternative. Whether or not he was duplicitous in helping to found the SDP, why did he become convinced that there was no alternative to amalgamating with the Liberals? He would no doubt argue that spurning the co-operative relationship offered by the Liberal Party would have meant so many scars from early by-elections battles over seats that we could never have built up the SDP. But if the Liberals had fought Roy Jenkins at Warrington, they would have lost their deposit and they would have lost it in Croydon too if they had fought Shirley. The very anarchic elements within the Liberal Party which David Steel struggled to contain would of course have relished fighting us at every stage and would not have listened to reason even if we had beaten them convincingly in the early by-elections. But by the Llandudno Conference, the Liberal Party would have been in more realistic mood. If we had to wait another year, so what.

Instead, by the time the Liberal Assembly was held in Llandudno, commentators were starting to equate our two parties whereas in the spring, we had looked and sounded very different. When Shirley had been invited to speak to the Liberal Conference, she wisely referred it to the Steering Committee. It was all for keeping our distance and only after some initial reluctance did it eventually agree she could go, and then only if she spoke on the fringe and not in the main conference hall. After Warrington Roy felt under no such constraint.

I was not very surprised therefore to read on my return from a Palme Commission meeting in Mexico that the fringe meeting at Llandudno had been turned into a meeting larger than the conference itself or that it had been addressed by Roy Jenkins as well as Shirley Williams, with Jo Grimond and David Steel on the same platform. Why did I go to Mexico for what was not after all a vital drafting meeting of the Commission? I think it was because subconsciously I wanted to keep my distance, and already saw I was being sucked into an Alliance with a big 'A' rather than a small 'a' over which I had the profoundest doubts. In retribution, perhaps, I slipped a lumbar disc, and had to submit, in fear and trepidation, to a Mexican chiropractor, who in fact put it back with considerable skill. But already by Llandudno I was in an intermittent minority of one in the Gang of Four, and that was to remain the pattern from then on when dealing with questions affecting the Liberals.

The Liberal Party was apparently in a good mood at the Llandudno Assembly. They had performed well in the local council elections; success which owed much to the launch of the SDP. No one had any doubts that the Assembly would give the necessary authority to form an Alliance, but it was a surprise that it did so by such an overwhelming vote. Yet the very day after voting for the Alliance, they proceeded to vote for a campaign against the deployment of cruise missiles. This was the result of an impassioned speech by the prospective candidate for Yeovil, Paddy Ashdown who, in 1983, went on to address a CND rally with Neil Kinnock. That was before they both trod the road to Damascus and accepted Trident in 1989. With the Assembly's existing commitment against an independent deterrent, this meant that the Liberals were in effect opposed to all nuclear weapons other than the obsolete free-fall nuclear bomb on aircraft committed to NATO! That little political adventure at Llandudno did considerable damage electorally to the Alliance until the INF Treaty was negotiated in 1987. But the SDP by then had to pretend to brush it aside as of no consequence. David Steel was so elated that in his final speech at the conference he said, 'I have the good fortune to be the first Liberal leader for half a century who is able to say to you at the end of our annual assembly: go back to your constituencies and prepare for government.' The Llandudno air was so intoxicating that not even the hardened pressmen at the conference laughed.

The Liberal Assembly decision endorsing the Alliance behind him, David Steel was able to go ahead appointing the two joint Commissions with us, which many Liberals were surprised to find that I had suggested. To establish policy Commissions between our parties was, in my judgement, perfectly compatible with the concept of a coalition between them. We had to anticipate the coalition we intended to present to the country in the election and with which we hoped to govern after the election. To be taken seriously we had to have a basic agreement on constitutional reform and economic prosperity. The commission on the British Constitution, chaired by Sir Henry Fisher, an ex-judge and President of Wolfson College, Oxford, had Vernon Bognador as its highly skilled Secretary. Roy Jenkins, David Steel, Ralf Dahrendorf and I sat on this Commission with other politicians and constitutional experts. Our main political task was to choose a system of proportional representation on which both our parties would agree. Perhaps inevitably we came down in favour of the Single Transferable Vote, long championed by the Liberal Party. The main innovation was that in grouping constituencies we did not apply too rigid a formula. Where it made sense to have a group of three constituencies, as in Plymouth, or five, as in Bristol, we went with the natural geography and sense of community even at the expense of perfect proportionality.

We were keen to avoid the absolutism and zealotry of past electoral reformers and we made it clear that our priority was reform, not one particular system. We were prepared to negotiate with other parties even if they would not agree to our preferred system, so we deliberately did not rule out the Additional Member System, practised most effectively in the Federal Republic of Germany. Personally I could even stomach the French two-ballot system if there were nothing else on offer. The first priority was breaking the log jam and initiating a change from our present first-past-the-post system. The Commission also dealt with House of Lords reform, suggesting a mixed chamber, partly elected from the regions, partly nominated. On the important issue of a Scottish Parliament we had concurred in suggesting a proper devolved system for a legislative Parliament. Wales was different. Here we toned down some of the Liberal Party's unrealistic nationalism, making a sharp distinction from Scotland by devolving less power and making no provision for primary legislation. The Welsh have yet to show that they want legislative devolution and we wisely avoided stuffing it down their throats just because a few Welsh activists demanded it.

The second Commission on employment and industrial recovery was chaired by Sir Leslie Murphy. Sir Leslie had agreed to be a trustee of the Party from the outset and remained one until 1991. A tower of strength to the SDP, he had had an interesting career. As a civil servant he had been Private Secretary to Hugh Gaitskell, when Minister of Fuel and Power; he became a merchant banker at Schroder Wragg and was Chairman of the National Enterprise Board. In addition he was a leading figure in the Church Army and a delightful person, generous with his time and always a wise counsellor to me personally. He never had any doubt in 1987 that it was not a merger but a wholesale takeover that was being proposed by the Liberal Party. Characteristically, he immediately asked me if I could turn the tables on the Liberals and take them over, and was never really convinced that I could not have done so. The other SDP trustee was Lord Diamond, a former Labour Chief Secretary to the Treasury, who later stood down in order to concentrate on being leader of the SDP peers, and David Sainsbury took his place. Jack Diamond was a good friend of Hugh Gaitskell and had been Chief Secretary to the Treasury from 1964–70 and in the Cabinet from 1968–70. He was a longstanding friend of Roy Jenkins and indeed of all of us, and acted as the co-ordinator of the Gang of Four during the 1983 General Election. He made a massive contribution to the SDP in many different ways and I was delighted when he decided not to support the merger and continued as a Social Democrat in the House of Lords.

The politicians on the Employment Commission were Shirley and Bill, Richard Wainwright MP and John Pardoe for the Liberals, along with a mixed group of other politicians and specialist economists. Inevitably the Employment Commission was more of a commentary on current political issues and it ought to have had Roy as a member but he preferred to go on the Constitution Commission. The Commission was split over the merits of the Inflation Tax which Roy was keen on and which became the policy of the Alliance. The inflation tax was an attempt to use the tax system as a constraining influence on wage inflation but even our industrial supporters like John Harvey Jones were against it, as was Leslie Murphy. The Commission was also divided on the emphasis to be given to the market economy and the extent to which we should agree at least with part of Margaret Thatcher's agenda. The Commission was not a success, and the fault lay with the politicians not with the Chairman or the specialist members.

The Commissions were a sophisticated way of developing a body of ideas and policies in key areas to provide the basis for a coalition government, but we lacked the resources of people or time to do the same in all areas of policy. Nor had I the inclination to do so. For, like Royal Commissions, these were consensual devices. A political party needs to innovate, and to strike out on its own with ideas which give it an identity and its followers something to fight for. More than an old party, a new party needs the cutting edge of sharp, even controversial, ideas and the strength of commitment to develop its identity. We needed to feel, like Cromwell's russet-coated captains, 'that we knew what we were fighting for and loved what we knew'. Too much joint activity would lead to an amorphous amalgam, the very 'inert Centre' which we had supposedly disavowed in the Limehouse Declaration. The Liberals, with their community politics, had developed an identity which made sense for them. I never decried their pavement politics for, as I used to remind people, tripping up on uneven pavements is one of the commoner reasons for attending casualty departments at local hospitals. But the SDP needed an identity of its own as a serious force for national government and leadership and we could not afford either the time or the energy for too much joint policy activity.

It was always hard to express these views publicly without seeming to want to break up the Alliance. The further the move to amalgamate went, the more difficult it was to oppose joint projects without being seen as a 'splitter'. Nevertheless, in September 1981, I risked controversy and made a speech in Andover endorsing competition between our parties. Coalition politics, I said, did not mean that the partners in the coalition had to agree on every political issue. There should be an open acceptance of competition between the parties while working together, either in Opposition or in government. We had to demonstrate a core of agreement on the central issues we would face in government and a readiness to work together for the national good but that did not mean merging or fusing our parties or our policies. It meant respecting our different political identities and distinctive traditions. I argued we would make a great mistake if we interpreted the need to avoid fighting each other in parliamentary and council elections as an injunction to blur our identities. The electorate wanted to see a civilized, friendly, co-operative dialogue between our two parties. It was, I felt, those who were wedded to the old politics who assessed the Alliance against the yardstick of a unified party, or who yearned for authoritarian, hierarchical leadership. They did not understand that coalition politics meant that government decision-making, of necessity, becomes more open because the negotiations are held between not within the parties. The compromises become overt unlike those currently made within Cabinet under the mantle of secrecy and the discipline of a single-party whip.

The problem with those in favour of merger was that they could never understand what made a good coalition partner. If people like me suggested or agreed to some joint policy-making, the next thing was that they wanted all policy-making to be joint. If, in the interests of the Alliance, we tried to downplay differences, the mergerites then pretended that there were no differences. As I wrote to a friend, 'To say anything critical of the Liberals is a sin against the Holy Ghost whereas they appear to be at liberty to brief quite hard against us.'

I conclude that the Alliance model that we developed destroyed the SDP even though it took ten years to do it. By 1991 most of the Labour policies and many of the Conservative policies which the SDP had been formed to prevent had been abandoned. The policies which the SDP had been formed to fulfil were often adopted too, but the loss of the SDP was a hard price for many of our members to pay for these changes in the other parties.

25

ONE MEMBER-ONE VOTE

By the summer of 1981 the future shape of the SDP Parliamentary Committee was becoming clearer. It was pretty certain that if both succeeded in returning to the House of Commons, the MPs would overwhelmingly elect Roy as their Leader, rather than Shirley. At that stage I was not even in contention. It was far from clear, however, whether Roy would win a one member-one vote leadership election in the Party. And it was this system which Roy had promised me he would back when we had lunch at his house in East Hendred at the end of November 1980.

We were scheduled to complete discussion of the constitution in our meetings at the end of July. But, with Bill Rodgers in the chair, it was noticeable that the detail about electing the leader was not going to be discussed. It was left to be settled in early September when everyone came back from holiday. I was concerned about what this might mean and raised my anxieties with Bob Maclennan who was handling all the constitutional negotiations. I wanted to know if behind the delay was the fact that Roy was changing his mind. I was assured that Roy had not raised any questions about one member-one vote with him nor with anyone else. But when the Steering Committee resumed its discussions in early September, with Roy in the chair it quickly became obvious that a massive volte-face was imminent. Bill Rodgers tabled a paper which he called 'a compromise' but which essentially advocated the MPs choosing the Leader and abandoning one member-one vote. The so-called compromise element was that the MP's choice had to be endorsed by the Council for Social Democracy. It did not require much political savvy to recognize that the CSD's power was purely nominal. A failure to endorse would provoke a terrible crisis of confidence between the Party in the country and in Parliament. Listening to the discussion and analysing the tactics of what was quite simply a coup, I was transported back to my time in the Shadow Cabinet. I could almost hear Roy Hattersley, the year before, preparing to ditch our one member-one vote proposal with his so-called compromise. It was an unpleasant reminder that the old politics had not died in the SDP.

I was aware, unlike many of the others, that for Bill Rodgers at least, this was not a total change of view. He had always believed that MPs should choose the Leader and his support within the Shadow Cabinet and for the campaign on one member-one vote in the Labour Party was tactical; he had recognized that there was no other viable alternative to the electoral college. Nevertheless Bill, like Roy, seemed to have kept Bob Maclennan completely in the dark about his wish to challenge one member-one vote, and for months we had all proceeded as if the issue had been decided.

As the Steering Committee discussion developed it became obvious that a great many people had known of the so-called compromise before the meeting, and that there would be a majority for it. Shirley expressed surprise and anger that there should be any question of challenging the commitment to one member-one vote we had all made from the launch of the Party. The rejoinder was there was no challenge, that one member-one vote would be retained for everything except for choosing the Leader. I backed Shirley and vigorously opposed abandoning one member-one vote to choose the Leader. Then, seeing that there was a danger of Roy summing up the meeting as being in favour of Bill's proposition without revealing his own position, I asked if it were right for him not to let us know how he felt. After humming and harring he eventually admitted, with a guilty expression, that he was in favour of Bill's position.

I said nothing. What would a row have achieved? I had been totally out-manoeuvred and to cry foul would have sounded like a spoilt child. But I vowed then that I would ensure that Roy was challenged for the leadership of the party. If need be I would fight him myself. I was no simpleton in politics and had seen some pretty shabby things in my time but this was the shabbiest act that I have ever witnessed.

Roy knew very well that he had assured me when I saw him at the end of the previous November, and again in late December, that he accepted one member-one vote for the election of the Leader of our Party. To turn around now and abjure that promise without even telling me of his change of mind meant only one thing: he was in so much of a hurry that he could not give a damn for the Party that he had helped found. The SDP was just a disposable vehicle for his ambition to be Prime Minister.

The vote was taken and, as I expected, Roy had his majority in favour of the MPs choosing the Leader. The next point was whether, provided this proposition survived consultation with the Party and the constitutional conference, a full membership ballot should be held on whether to endorse the proposition or to replace it with a proposal for one member-one vote. This was so obviously the only way of healing a deep division in the Gang of Four, let alone the Party, that it was conceded. We also agreed that Mike Thomas, who favoured one member-one vote and David Marquand who favoured election by the MPs, should each speak for five minutes at the Perth, Bradford and London conferences, putting their respective cases, to be followed by a debate from the floor. As I left the Steering Committee I wondered how much damage this issue would do to confidence within the Party and particularly within the Gang of Four. Shirley rang me that evening at home, more distressed than I can ever remember her. She knew that she had been stitched up and she, like me, was very unhappy about it.

On 12 September I left for the Palme Commission meeting in Mexico before the Liberals' Llandudno Conference, which I have already described in the previous chapter. Mexico gave me time to ponder fundamental questions about what I hoped the SDP would contribute to the 1980s. It was beginning to look as if we would continue to practise the mixed economy of the 1960s and 1970s, and to pursue very similar policies. The radicalism which I had hoped for was slipping away as Roy Jenkins's influence grew. Establishing the SDP as a force as radical as Margaret Thatcher's Government was revealing itself as quite a task. We were in danger of steering a middle course between Labour nationalization and the Conservative Government's privatization as if we were not ready to challenge the dominance of the state. There was much in the Conservative analysis of what had gone wrong in the 1960s and 1970s which our new Party should have accepted and adopted.

The Labour Party Conference at Brighton started with a meeting of the electoral college on Sunday 28 September. Since 1 April, the apt date for Tony Benn's announcement that he was going to fight Denis Healey for the deputy leadership, there had been an extensive and divisive campaign going on both in the unions and the constituencies. The Left had deliberately taken the decision not to use the electoral college mechanism to challenge Michael Foot; everything was concentrated on the Benn-Healey tussle. Significantly, Neil Kinnock announced that he would not support Tony Benn and abstained, apparently feeling unable to support Denis Healey. Nevertheless, it was a rupture with his past which paved the way for his leadership election two years later.

On the first ballot Healey won 45.3 per cent of the college vote, Benn 36.3 per cent and John Silkin, who was sponsored and supported by the T&GWU, 18 per cent. It was believed that the T&GWU would abstain on the second ballot, but instead, in full view of the TV cameras, their delegation made the decision to vote for Tony Benn. The next ballot was a cliff-hanger and I watched it on television with rapt attention. Healey had 50.426 per cent and Benn had 49.574 per cent. If that vote had gone the other way there would have been a substantial number of Labour MPs ready to come over to the SDP and we should have been able to regain some of the ground we had lost in establishing our independence vis-à-vis the Liberals. I doubt whether Denis Healey himself would have joined, but people close to him who had spoken to him during the year gave me the impression that it was not impossible that at some stage he might have been ready to join.

We had, however, reduced that possibility considerably when Roy had become involved and the Gang of Three became the Gang of Four. I think Denis might have taken up the Secretary-Generalship of NATO, a post he claims he rejected in April. He would have done it immensely well and, since he had not yet made the major concessions that he was later to do over nuclear deterrence, he should have been acceptable to the Conservative Government. The job of replacing Joseph Luns eventually went to Lord Carrington. What is certain is that, if defeated, Denis Healey would not have remained an effective force in politics as he did until 1987.

Hugo Young in the *Guardian* on 5 June 1991 revealed what Denis Healey once thought:

Mr Healey does have one claim to rightness. He once thought about joining the SDP, and decided against. He did so not out of loyalty or socialist principle, but on the basis of a hard-headed assessment that the project would fail.

I remember well the conversation in which he told me this. I was impressed as one never ceases to be by the brutally self-interested calculation – far in excess of what political journalists customarily ascribe to them – which professional politicians bring to the important moments of their life. Mr Healey thought the SDP would not make it into government, and he was right.

Predictably the electoral college was shown to be a corrupt way of electing a leader, and the Labour Party dropped further in the polls. The only ray of light was that some of the extreme Left were knocked off the NEC and, with Kinnock's shift, the foundations were being laid for the 1985 offensive against the Militant Tendency. But as yet there was no stomach for a fightback. That had to wait until Labour lost the 1983 election and the SDP was bound to play a significant and necessary role in that richly deserved defeat.

Our own first SDP Conference was surprisingly successful. We rolled with British Rail to halls in Perth, Bradford and finally London, winning coverage not just from the London-based newspapers but also the Scottish and Northern newspapers and Scottish and regional TV. In *The Times*, Frank Johnson, author of delightfully cynical parliamentary sketches, turned his attention to the train. 'Well powered by one of the gleaming Debbie Owen class of locomotive, the Social Democratic Conference Special "Spirit of Croydon North West" reached Bradford from Perth, defying all those faint hearts who said the journey was impossible.' In Bradford he wrote that it was time to catch the 'Train of Shame' for London. On those journeys we developed an *esprit de corps*, a mood of adventure and fun which carried through into by-elections and to the next year's rolling Conference between Cardiff, Derby and Great Yarmouth. Despite our internal machinations I was enjoying the SDP in ways I had never known in the Labour Party. This enjoyment continued despite the merger controversy for the whole ten years, for whenever I went out to speak to the Party in the country, in good times or in bad, I returned with all the original inspiration, determined to fight on.

'Rolling' gave an original flavour to the conference season and, in terms of newsworthiness, made up for the fact that there were no voting dramas. But even without votes this was the first time we saw our Party membership face to face and could assess its make-up. It was not a conventional Party. There were, for instance, many more women attending than at the other party conferences. The members were in good heart and the 'political virgins' manifested a freshness and open mindedness which was very attractive, despite attempts by the cynical journalists to highlight their naïvety and inexperience. We got additional publicity when several Labour MPs announced their decision to join us, although this was a double-edged sword: we were starting to look like the Mark II Labour Party Cyril Smith had predicted from the start. Many of these new SDP MPs were unreconstructed Labourites in policy terms, resistant to some of the new Social Democratic ideas, as we were to discover to our cost over trade union reform in Parliament in February 1982. Roy Jenkins astutely picked up the rumblings of resentment among Party members who had never been involved in politics before, declaring firmly in his speech in Central Hall that we were not a Mark II Labour Party. In my speech I emphasized that we were neither a Mark II Labour Party nor a Mark II Liberal Party; the broad attitude of most members. I was keen to attract disillusioned Labour voters but never believed that would be achieved by just serving 'warmed up Callaghanism' to the electorate. We had to appeal to the C2 voters, the semi-skilled working class which Margaret Thatcher had attracted so cleverly with the aid of the *Sun* newspaper in 1979 and was showing signs of losing in 1981. Her promise to sell off council houses had proved a great success with these voters. I had known it would because Plymouth City Council had been following that policy for many years. Most of these C2 voters were also repelled by Labour's defence policy. The SDP had to lose the Liberals' soft image on defence if we, not Margaret Thatcher, were to be the beneficiaries of Labour's travails with C2 voters.

The most gratifying development was that it soon became apparent that most of those who came to the Conference rejected the idea of MPs electing the Leader. They were not going to allow the Steering Committee to ditch one member-one vote. On arguably the most important early question facing the Party, they were going to stand firm. The question was what the wider membership who had not heard the debate at conferences would choose

Just before the Perth Conference, as the Croydon by-election was under way with Bill Pitt standing as the Liberal and SDP Alliance candidate, the Conservative MP for Crosby died. The Gang of Four discussed that by-election with David Steel in Perth over a meal, the first we had all had together. We all agreed that Shirley should stand. But, as the SDP travelled to Bradford, it began to be clear that the local Liberals were none too happy and we feared a repeat of Croydon with a 'grass roots' revolt. Over breakfast, before Shirley was due to speak at the start of the Bradford conference, Bill and I discussed the situation with her. It was our unanimous view that Shirley should give a firm indication of her intention to stand. Unjustly she was subsequently attacked in unattributable Liberal and SDP press briefings for having made this pre-emptive decision individually and impulsively in defiance of what had been agreed with David Steel. I was at both meetings and I have no doubt that she was correct to act. If she had teased the Conference and the public about her intentions she would have been accused of dithering.

Behind the scenes both by-elections generated difficulties. But there is no denying their fabulous public success. The Croydon by-election was won on 22 October by Bill Pitt with a majority of 3,300 over the Conservative candidate, and a swing of 29 per cent. We all helped, and the local SDP suppressed their doubts about his suitability. It was a formidable achievement given that, even in Croydon, Bill Pitt was nowhere near as well known as Shirley. In Crosby, Shirley campaigned brilliantly, attracting Labour voters on the council estates at the Bootle end of the constituency in a very impressive way. She achieved a swing of 34 per cent. Unfortunately it was a seat which would be immensely hard to win at a general election, particularly with the planned boundary changes, but for the time being it meant that the Gang of Three were united again in Parliament, and her win gave her a tremendous personal boost. I was delighted to see her self-confidence return and she was now in a far better position to challenge Roy for the leadership. She knew that, as had always been the case, she would have my full support if she wished to stand as Leader.

All this time the Party was establishing itself while finding it desperately difficult to keep up with events. We moved out of Queen Anne's Gate, having negotiated a lease on a self-contained building at 4 Cowley Street very near the House of Commons. Bernard Doyle, our new Chief Executive, started on 1 September. Aged forty, he had an MBA from Harvard Business School and had had a very good business career, being chairman of Booker McConnell Engineering and a main board director of Booker McConnell. I was amazed that he had even replied to the advertisement. Both he and we were taking a risk, for the transition from business to politics is immensely difficult. He worked very hard to overcome his political inexperience and I had few problems in my dealings with him, but it cannot have been easy to serve a collective leadership, let alone one which was deeply split on the best way forward for the SDP. After the 1983 election he left to become Chief Executive of the Welsh Water Board. It might have been wiser to have followed Shirley's inclination and appointed the other very strong contender for the post, Anne Ballard, who was running the Women's Institutes. She would have found it easier to mobilize the volunteers who were an essential part of our organization. In addition to John Lyttle and Alec McGivan, we appointed Tony Martin to oversee promotion and membership. Christopher Smallwood, who had been with the corporate planning department at BP, became a highly effective policy co-ordinator setting a very high standard for policy development. This was fully maintained by his assistant Wendy Buckley who succeeded him. Despite this, our economic policy was neither new nor exciting and when Ralf Dahrendorf, the former German Liberal Federal Minister and Director of LSE, said at the 1983 election that the SDP promised 'a better yesterday' he touched a sensitive nerve. Our policy development in those early years can best be described as worthy. Apart from constitutional reform, too much of the radicalism was coming from Margaret Thatcher.

The seat negotiations presented the trickiest problem, well exemplified by what happened in the West Country. The Liberals were strong here so again, to their surprise, I was conciliatory, proposing that the SDP should settle for fighting only five of the fifteen seats – the three Plymouth seats, Exeter, and Falmouth and Camborne. Liberals were happy to accept this regional bias in their favour but refused to agree that the SDP should be given priority elsewhere, in New Town seats, for example, where there was polling evidence that the SDP were doing better than the Liberals. They refused also in other regions of the country where the Liberals were traditionally weak and we were strong, either because of having a large number of SDP MPs or because there was a tradition of support for the moderate wing of the Labour Party which was now finding itself challenged by Left-wing militants. In these cases all logic pointed to the SDP having the largest number and the most winnable seats. The Liberals wanted to negotiate narrowly and locally because that suited them; we wanted to negotiate broadly and centrally because that suited us.

In terms of realignment it made sense for the SDP and Liberals to widen their joint appeal by appealing to different parts of the electorate. This was the so-called 'Heineken effect', which we knew from polling evidence had the potential to swing votes. But we progressively abandoned that strategy by, in effect, 'watering the workers' beer' and not enjoining the SDP to go for the Labour vote. As the Liberals showed their inability to trade off a gain in one place for a concession elsewhere, so did the SDP abandon any wish to concentrate on Labour seats. Gradually as the Liberals and SDP began to converge, the SDP tried to get its fair share of the most winnable or 'Golden' seats, whatever the local position.

Even when the Liberals were running a good second in a seat and we encouraged them to continue building support, with us recouping on the next group of 'Silver' seats, we found they fought ruthlessly against our then having a preferential allocation. It was becoming ever more hopeless and only a matter of time before the SDP put its foot down.

Plymouth was a case in point. When we agreed eventually that the Liberals should not be denied all representation and could have one seat, they got very upset when we staked a claim for St Ives and Teignbridge in compensation. Two seats as compensation for one, since the Plymouth seat was in theory highly winnable, seemed fair to us. But in the end we had to settle for the hopeless seat of Honiton rather than Teignbridge.

It was the decentralist, locally orientated Liberals who were demonstrating inflexibility up and down the country. They were political street fighters and despised this claret-swigging SDP that was intent on pinching 'their' seats. Our local people in many cases did have mettle and were prepared to fight, but the Steering Committee's advice was always to play the negotiations long and coolly. What we needed in the SDP leadership was the ability to say after a certain point, 'Well, since there is no agreement, we shall, reluctantly, have to fight.' If we were always going to back off just as things came to the crunch then the SDP negotiating position would never have any backbone.

At least Bill Rodgers did seem to understand this, which, as he was leading the negotiations, was reassuring. Although he kept his cards close to his chest I began to feel towards the end of the year that he realized that we would have to have a showdown. Sure enough, it came. In the *Observer* on Sunday 3 January 1982 the front-page headline was 'LIB-SDP TALKS ON SEATS BREAK DOWN'. Bill Rodgers had suspended talks following a collapse in the negotiations over Greenock and Derbyshire. When asked whether there was a crisis threatening the Alliance, Bill replied, 'Yes, regrettably there is.' David Steel reiterated Macmillan's notorious phrase about 'little local difficulty'. David, who had been hotting-up the atmosphere the week before by encouraging local Liberals to stand out against 'arrogance and bluster', was quoted as commenting that 'the Liberal Party is not an authoritarian party and the SDP perhaps is.' The word 'perhaps' was a nice touch; rather like a Mafioso greasing a stiletto.

Whether Bill should have gone public in this way I was not sure, but we had to trust each other in our different areas of responsibility and when the press telephoned me I made it clear that I was not prepared to criticize what he had done in any way. However, I sensed from their questions that they had been briefed by Roy Jenkins and his friends in a direction that was highly critical of Bill. On the Monday this started to appear in newspaper comment. That day there was a Gang of Four lunch at Bill's house, though Shirley was unable to come because of a tobogganing accident. I arrived early and reassured Bill that he had my total support. When Roy arrived I saw him, for the first time, express real anger with Bill. It was soon apparent why. Tam Galbraith, the Conservative MP for Hillhead and my pair, had died and Bob Maclennan was urging Roy to stand; but the Liberals already had a prospective candidate. Roy was extremely agitated that he might forfeit the chance to fight Hillhead. This could be his last chance to get into Parliament before the leadership election, and here was Bill, his closest colleague in the Gang of Four, gratuitously damaging relations with the Liberals.

Bill had allowed a *Times* photographer in and our lunch was written up under the headline, 'Some wine, no women – and Marmite', in which Roy Jenkins was depicted as subsisting cheerfully on war rations and reduced from his favourite clarets to Sainsbury's red Bergerac. Mince pies, again a Sainsbury's variety, had been laid on by Sylvia deliberately to counter David Steel's crack that Bill had eaten too many mince pies over Christmas, and for some reason a jar of Marmite was on display. It was all very trivial and, not for the first time, I cursed our claret image and obsession with food, identifying myself with the old couplet:

> There goes the toper whose untutored sense
> Finds peace in ale and can with wine dispense.
> Whose mind pale fortune never thought to stir
> Beyond the muddy ecstasies of beer.

At times the mood of our meeting was rather ugly and Bill, I felt, allowed himself to be too defensive; at the end even appearing chastened. It was not easy for him; David Steel was in close contact with Roy and had already cleverly upstaged and patronized Bill. Once again a pending by-election was throwing the SDP into the arms of the Liberals. For Roy the only issue was that he should win Hillhead. As far as he was concerned the seat negotiations in the rest of Britain were trivial, even though one of the seats in contention at Greenock was that of Dick Mabon, a Labour MP who had joined the SDP only a few months before. I left the lunch extremely depressed, wondering which party Roy was a member of and fearing that Bill would feel that he had to patch up the row and resume negotiations. If he did, his action in suspending them would look petulant and we would find our negotiating strength even further diminished. My apprehensions were well founded. Within days, over yet another publicized meal in a restaurant, Bill had climbed down and David Steel emerged looking ever more like a choirboy. Sadly, over twenty-five years, I can think of no major issue on which, in the last analysis, Bill was prepared to set his often better political judgement against that of Roy Jenkins.

I decided to write an article for the *Guardian*, spelling out the case for two separate parties. I was shattered to find, so early in the Party's life, that there was increasing evidence that the members were confused and divided. Alec McGivan, our National Organizer, had told Maggie Smart, my assistant, that he believed it was inevitable that in time the two parties would merge.

After a *pas de deux* with the local Liberals and the odd pirouette Roy Jenkins was chosen for Hillhead. Opinion polls made us optimistic about the outcome. Bob Maclennan sent me a December poll published in the *Scotsman* which showed that the Alliance was appealing to Scottish voters with our proposals for constitutional reform. In particular a majority were attracted by our intention to have another try at a workable devolution scheme, this time a more balanced one in which there would be elected assemblies for the English provinces as well as for Scotland and Wales. Given that Hillhead was a Conservative constituency, a reasoned campaign on devolution could, we all felt, easily ignite interest as well as gain wavering votes. Roy would give constitutional reform the stature it needed, particularly for Scottish Conservative voters who had never been enthused by past attempts and were worried about separatism.

However, by early February, commentators were saying our support was slipping. The evidence was mixed but a myth was created that it was all Bill's fault. His suspension of the negotiations with the Liberals had not caused immense damage. It must be remembered that polling is often completed well before the polls are published. A Marplan poll commissioned by the BBC on 26 January did indeed show the Conservatives ahead of us at 34 per cent, Labour at 32 per cent and the Alliance at 29 per cent. This was described as a slump in Alliance fortunes. But MORI, doing fieldwork on 3 and 4 February gave the lead back to the Alliance with 34 per cent, the Conservatives 33 per cent and Labour 31 per cent. Gallup, who polled from 10–15 February, confirmed the Alliance in the lead with 36 per cent, Labour at 34 per cent and the Conservatives down at $27\frac{1}{2}$ per cent. On any of these readings Hillhead still looked favourable for Roy Jenkins.

At about this time the SDP faced a crucial test of its radicalism. Trade union reform had been the single most important task facing Margaret Thatcher when she took office in 1979, and the reforms she instituted will prove to be her most enduring legacy. It was always clear that this issue would be the one on which the SDP's claim not to be a Mark II Labour Party would be tested. Once Margaret Thatcher had sent Jim Prior off to Northern Ireland and made Norman Tebbit her Secretary of State for Employment, it was inevitable that controversy would follow. Tebbit's speech at the Party Conference the previous October set the tone: 'My father did not riot. He got on his bike and looked for work.' He is a far more interesting and subtle politician than Michael Foot's crack about 'a semi house-trained pole cat' implies. He knows that elections are fought and lost among the semi-skilled workers, the C2 voters, and he never had the slightest intention of alienating these people in his approach to trade union reform. What he sensed in his own constituency in Chingford, Essex and had the self-confidence to capitalize on, was the burning resentment of many trade unionists at the conduct of the leaders of their own trade unions and, particularly, the operation of the closed shop. The characteristic, somewhat condescending, view of the liberal intelligentsia – to be found in all parties including the Conservatives – was that reforming the trade unions meant alienating trade unionists. Tebbit knew it was the other way round and that the 1980 Prior reforms, aimed at increasing the responsibility and accountability of the trade unions, did not go far enough.

Tebbit's 1982 legislation was seen to deal with the closed shop. To oppose it would line up the SDP with all the vested interests of the trade unions, but if we voted for the legislation on Second Reading we would be depicted by the Labour Party as anti-trade unionist. In the middle of January I had given a lecture at Leicester University in memory of the former General Secretary of the TUC, George Woodcock, where I had emphasized that the SDP valued trade unionism and would never be antagonistic to the concept of workers combining to safeguard their interests. But I was determined that the SDP would not duck Tebbit's challenge. When we discussed how to vote in the Parliamentary Committee, almost every MP believed that abstaining on the Second Reading was not a practical course. The overwhelming majority of the Committee felt that it was modest legislation, usefully restricting the application of the closed shop, and that, though the scope of the legislation should have been much wider, covering industrial democracy, inner trade union democracy and the political levy, we could not credibly join Labour in voting against it. Bill, Shirley and I agreed that, despite the fact that we were likely to have a split in our vote, with newcomers to the Committee, like John Grant and Tom McNally, unable to go along with the majority decision, we should not seek refuge in abstention. Of the twenty-seven SDP MPs in the House of Commons, five voted against the legislation, one abstained but the rest of us voted with the Liberals in favour. The headline in *The Times*, 'Alliance holds together in first crucial voting test', was not too bad, but other newspapers focused more damagingly on the split in our Party. In truth we were still finding our way over trade union reform. Soon we did begin to hit the right notes, emphasizing the need 'to bring the trade unions back to their members' with one member-one vote democracy. The result was that the Conservatives pinched all our ideas, even that very phrase, and put them on the statute book in the 1984 legislation, and by 1988 their legislation concentrated on giving trade union members rights; by then a well established SDP theme. We supported therefore the 1982, 1984 and 1988 reforms. I was pleased that, as a consequence, the Conservative trade union reforms were seen to be more broadly based and have substantial cross-party support. This was one of the reasons why, when Labour campaigned to 'Kill the Bill' in the hope of placating their militants, they got such a poor response even from trade unionists.

The crucial aspect about the four trade union acts was that they progressed one step at a time in an evolutionary process. Margaret Thatcher had learnt important lessons from Edward Heath's Industrial Relations Act and the TUC's response to it. She also realized that it was not enough to rely on legislation alone. Just as important was to make the trade unions understand that when the Government took a stance, it would stick to it. Thus it withstood the steel strike in 1980, the civil servants' strike in 1981, health workers in 1982, water workers in 1983, miners in 1984–85, teachers in 1985–86 and ambulance workers in 1989–90. During all these strikes Ministers deliberately distanced themselves from the negotiations surrounding these disputes. Whereas in the past Conservative Ministers had been as ready to intervene as Labour Ministers, casting themselves in the role of honest brokers, now Ministers were not visibly involved in the negotiations. They were not, however, removed from the battle. They were partisan and political in their comments and stood ready to put the boot into the trade unions whenever they could see a good opportunity. Yet even where the Government was the employer, they managed to distance themselves from the actual bargaining process. This approach meant that it was much harder to generate an atmosphere of national crisis around strike action and the average trade unionist came to be far more concerned about maintaining his job than following the call to action by trade union leaders. The SDP was sympathetic to this approach and, insofar as we were able to influence the climate, we unashamedly reinforced the Conservative trade union reform programme. I believe that this was in the national interest and helped to demonstrate that the TUC and Labour Party response was largely ritualistic and contrived.

On the weekend of 13–14 February the SDP held its Constitutional Conference in Kensington Town Hall. It was the first voting conference we had held and, given the complexity of the issues, we did well to get through it all. There was not a single amendment to prepare our constitution for a merger with the Liberals or build in any institutional links. The merger pressures within the Steering Committee were shown up as the product of a self-selected few with no widespread reflection in the Party. Exactly the same pattern followed in the review of the constitution after three years in 1985. It was obvious from conversations with the members that the conference would vote overwhelmingly for one member-one vote to elect the leader and there was a general feeling that the pressure would build up for a leadership election once the membership had authorized the full constitution. During the debate Mike Thomas stole a march on the rest of the Steering Committee. The others had all accepted they would not have speaking rights but Mike ensured his own by becoming the delegate from Newcastle-upon-Tyne. In his speech, he said that if he had not been a member of the Steering Committee himself he would have been inclined to sue it 'for breach of the Trade Descriptions Act' in supporting MPs electing the Leader when everyone had joined the Party in the belief that it would be the members' decision. It did not exactly improve internal relations but I agreed with every word he said. The Conference vote went overwhelmingly against Bill Rodgers's so-called compromise. Later when the members voted they too chose a one member-one vote election for the Leader; but Roy's volte-face had damaged personal relations, and ensured his challenge as Leader.

The rest of the conference was much less controversial. There was some controversy about measures for positive discrimination in favour of women but it did not cause bitterness. Eventually, after a tied vote, it was decided to ballot all members on the proposition that there should be equal numbers of men and women on the Council for Social Democracy. Bob Maclennan had put a tremendous effort into developing the constitution which also introduced a novel negotiated policy process to balance the interest of activists and the parliamentary leadership. We only had to use it once, over the Council's vote to ban plastic bullets used in Northern Ireland, for the Policy Committee refused to accept this as Party policy, believing it necessary as a reserve power to control crowds with potential IRA snipers in their midst.

Immediately after this conference we plunged into the Hillhead campaign. Everything depended on being able to erode the Labour vote and check the Scottish Nationalists. It turned out to be a dogged and difficult fight. Roy campaigned well but it took time to break down the Glaswegians' suspicions. The journalist, Simon Hoggart, reported one exchange on the streets during the campaign: a voter who had been undecided the week before had now made up her mind to support Roy Jenkins. 'Why?' asked the canvasser from the Labour Party. 'Because I have always been against the Common Market,' she said. The astonished party worker then emphasized that Roy Jenkins was a devotee of the EEC – Mr Europe himself. He had even been President of the European Commission. 'Aye,' she replied, 'but he packed it in.' It shows how bizarre the reasons frequently given for supporting a particular candidate are and the reasons for opposing them can be equally bizarre. One SDP candidate, having been called a 'Young Turk' on the radio, found that a voter would not support him because she preferred 'an English candidate'.

We started house meetings during the campaign for it soon became clear that the more people saw and heard Roy the better the chance of persuading them to vote for him. He dealt very effectively at a public meeting organized by the Campaign for a Scottish Assembly with the charge that he was not Scottish by meeting it head on:

I am not a Scotsman ... [loud ribaldry from the crowd] I am a Welshman, but not a Welsh-speaking Welshman [great roars of outrage, mirth, shouts of 'phoney']. I come in fact from Gwent, where only a small number of people speak Welsh as their first language ... [more shouts]. I have to confess that I don't speak Welsh, but then, how many in this hall speak Gaelic? [shocked, embarrassed, prolonged silence].

The opinion polls showed it was going to be a close-run thing but we thought by the last few days that Roy was easing ahead. So it proved. He won by over 2,000 votes and returned to the House of Commons with a very considerable personal triumph. It would not be more than a few months before the Party members would now choose which of the Gang of Four they wished to be their first Leader.

26

THE LEADERSHIP ELECTION

During the Hillhead by-election it had been agreed that the leadership election would be brought forward from the autumn to the summer. It was a proposition that was hard to resist. Roy had clearly judged that if he won Hillhead it would be better to have an election quickly while the aura of victory was still around him and he had made it pretty clear that if he lost he had no intention of fighting another by-election. He and his supporters were intent on avoiding a fight with Shirley now that they knew they had lost over the MPs electing the Leader and there would be a one member-one vote election. First Bill talked on ITN about keeping the present collective leadership. Then they began to woo Shirley with the idea of a dual leadership – Roy as Party Leader, her as President. This two-leader scenario was assiduously run for the next few months and Shirley became progressively more attracted by it. Meanwhile I was fortifying my intention to ensure a challenge to Roy. I was telling friends that if Shirley did not run, I definitely would; but if she decided to stand I might well not. The one thing I was determined to ensure was that the Party would be able to choose.

There remained a major problem with having an election – would the leadership of the SDP mean anything if there were also a Leader of the Alliance? After a weekend SDP-Liberal meeting in Oxfordshire in early February the impression was given to the press that we would announce a single Leader for our two parties before the election but it was always discussed in such roundabout terms that no one was ever sure what had been agreed. One reason was that in all the opinion polls David Steel was a far more popular choice as Leader than Roy Jenkins, yet we all knew that David Steel had privately indicated to Roy at some stage that he would accept Roy as Leader. Exactly how and when this was to be achieved was always left very vague, but part of Roy's leadership campaign strategy was to be the man whom David Steel trusted and would accept as overall Leader, in contrast to Shirley Williams or David Owen who were not acceptable as Leader of the Alliance. What worried Shirley and me was who would look after the SDP interest if Roy became Leader of the Alliance.

On 29 March there was a prime example of how important it was to watch over SDP interests. There was to be a major debate on Trident in the House of Commons. Five days before the debate I wrote to David Steel suggesting a draft motion which we could table and both agree. I said that I found it very hard to vote against Trident without registering my continued support for Polaris and did not wish to give anyone grounds for believing that the Social Democrats were ready to concede that Polaris might not continue to the end of its useful life – in the year 2000 in my judgement. The SDP could live with not mentioning Polaris in the motion so long as we could agree words for the debate which would not cause embarrassment or which the Liberal spokesman in the debate would not contradict later on. We agreed both an anodyne motion and the following form of words which I used in the House:

> Both the parties I speak for – I carefully consulted the Leader of the Liberal Party – recognize that while the Soviet Union has nuclear weapons NATO must have them, too. Pending all-round nuclear disarmament, both parties acknowledge the need for the NATO strategic deterrent, of which Polaris submarines form part. Both parties agree that, for as long as the Polaris fleet provides a useful part of a NATO deterrent, it should continue to fulfil that role. Moreover, both parties agree that the decision on whether to replace it need not be taken now.

Fortunately for us nobody noticed that despite our agreement David Penhaligon made a speech as a Liberal and flatly contradicted what I had said by disowning Polaris. Whether that was deliberate or not I do not know but the Liberal MPs also rapped David Steel's knuckles for agreeing any form of words with me. The trouble we had taken to get agreement was wasted. I would have done better to table an SDP motion, for we were not even papering over the cracks successfully. But the incident did convince me that before the next election we would need to persuade the Liberal Party to accept that Polaris should continue at least for its full operational life or there would be an open divide. In truth on the most fundamental issue of defence policy the SDP and the Liberal Party were deeply riven and yet I was under growing pressure to agree to have Alliance spokesmen, including one on defence, and to pretend there was such a thing as Alliance policy covering defence. Sometimes I had to pinch myself to realize that I had left the Labour Party; the arguments over defence were becoming so similar.

The day after this debate on 30 March Roy Jenkins took his seat in the House of Commons. It had been agreed that I would continue as Chairman of the Parliamentary Committee pending the leadership election which we began to prepare for. But that day was notable for much more than Roy's arrival. The Falklands crisis was looming. That afternoon there was a statement about South Georgia in which the Government admitted that the situation was potentially dangerous and that the question of security in the Falklands area was being reviewed, though they could say nothing in public about their precautionary measures. Three days later, on Friday 2 April, I was due to leave early for Plymouth but, listening to the morning news programmes I heard that the Argentines were claiming that they were in occupation of the Falkland Islands and that the garrison had surrendered. I cancelled travelling to Plymouth and stayed in the House of Commons, going in at 11.00 a.m. for a statement on the Falkland Islands by the Lord Privy Seal, a senior Minister in the Foreign Office. He revealed that there was now a real expectation that an Argentine attack against the Falkland Islands would take place very soon. In my interjection I said I hoped that contingency measures had been taken some weeks earlier to ensure that naval forces were in the area and were capable of intervening if necessary, adding that there should be no question of the House adjourning if there was any possibility of an invasion. At 2.30 p.m. the Leader of the House, Francis Pym, rose to make another holding statement, promising that there would be an emergency session of Parliament next day, a Saturday, if the situation in the Falklands deteriorated. By this time, MPs on all sides, hearing radio reports of Argentines dancing on the streets of Buenos Aires, were extremely concerned that we had been misled by the earlier statement, and that the Government knew that the Falkland Islands had already been invaded. At least the fact that the Government was prepared to contemplate coming back on a Saturday demonstrated they understood the seriousness of the situation. Later that night, when the fact of the invasion could no longer be held back, I went on television and strongly supported the immediate despatch of a naval task force, something which we did not know had been under active discussion in the Government since Wednesday.

On the Saturday the House assembled at 11.00 a.m. for the most dramatic debate I have ever participated in. I had had a meeting with Bill Rodgers and a few other MPs who had come in early in the room of John Roper, the SDP Chief Whip. There was never any question that I would speak in the debate for the SDP. It was a helpful discussion and Bill, though sharing my anxiety about the difficulty of an opposed landing, advised me strongly and wisely against saying anything which would make it hard to repossess the Islands. At Prayers the House was packed and the mood sombre. Immediately afterwards the Lord Privy Seal rose to apologize for misleading me and other Members in the House the day before. We then had a rather irritating vote on whether the debate should take place for longer than three hours, a fairly typical House of Commons diversion.

But soon the main debate started and the Prime Minister rose to speak: 'The House meets this Saturday to respond to a situation of great gravity. We are here because, for the first time for many years, British sovereign territory has been invaded by a foreign power.' She was clearly shaken. There was none of the self-confident hectoring that we were used to. The speech was nevertheless determined and she said with feeling, 'It is the Government's objective to see that the Islands are freed from occupation and returned to British administration at the earliest possible moment.' I believed, as I said later in my own speech, that she had misjudged the atmosphere of the House quite seriously when she said, 'It would have been absurd to despatch the Fleet every time there was bellicose talk in Buenos Aires. There was no good reason on 3 March to think that an invasion was being planned.' This was, I felt, no time for self-justification and I said directly to her in my speech, that she now had to 'examine ways of restoring the Government's authority and ask herself why Britain has been placed in such a humiliating position during the past few days.' For the first time since he had become Leader of the Opposition, Michael Foot spoke, not as a partisan politician but for the country as a whole:

> Even though the position and the circumstances of the people who live in the Falklands are uppermost in our minds – it would be outrageous if that were not the case – there is the longer-term interest to ensure that foul and brutal aggression does not succeed in our world. If it does, there will be a danger not merely to the Falkland Islands, but to people all over this dangerous planet.

In my speech I outlined the case for a naval blockade: 'There is much to be said for declaring our right to a 200-mile limit round the Falkland Islands. It would be perfectly compatible with international law to declare that no Argentine vessel should appear within that limit and that, if it did, the British Navy would take action.' Winding up the debate, John Nott, the Secretary of State for Defence, made a disastrous, defensive speech, and while dismissing the key question from his own side about why he had not put a hunter-killer submarine on station two weeks earlier, insisted on trying to score a petty point at the expense of Jim Callaghan, as if he were still in the Cambridge Union, saying that Jim and I had contradicted each other. Jim had said that Argentina had known about the naval force in 1977 and that a diplomatic solution had followed, whereas I had said it had been done in total secrecy. This provoked both Michael Foot and me to intervene and when I said: 'If the Rt. Hon. Gentleman, the Secretary of State for Defence, has not understood the value to a Foreign Secretary of being able to negotiate in a position of some military influence and strength, he should not be Secretary of State for Defence' – a sentiment which most people in the House that day shared. When John Nott sat down at the end of the debate there were few people in the House who believed that both he and Lord Carrington could stay on. At least one of them, perhaps both, would have to resign.

The House of Commons spoke for the nation that day, reflecting the humiliation that millions felt and a resolve to put this humiliation behind us, to restore our reputation and to retake the Islands. Of course there were MPs on all sides who hoped, some none too secretly, that this episode would prove to be the undoing of Margaret Thatcher, while outside the House of Commons commentators representing the liberal intelligentsia affected to yawn at the irrelevance of it all. Over the next few weeks at their London dinner parties the conversation would be full of speculation on how the Government would fall if the Task Force returned with its tail between its legs and General Galtieri's forces still ensconced on the Falkland Islands. But the great majority of MPs and of the British people wanted the Government to succeed. In this moment of grave crisis they rightly saw the fortunes of the Government and the nation as one.

I never had any doubt that what was at stake was far more than the survival of Margaret Thatcher or of the Conservative Party. It seemed to me that, if Britain were defeated, the peace movement would start to find the public receptive to its demand for swingeing cuts in our defence forces. They were already making considerable progress campaigning against cruise missiles and NATO's strategy of nuclear deterrence. What was the point, they would argue, in having all these sophisticated weapons if we could not even stand up to General Galtieri? The SDP MPs gave their full-hearted support to the Government throughout the Falklands campaign. Of course, they knew that if the Government's popularity recovered as a result of retaking the Falkland Islands, there might be adverse political consequences for our young party, but I think, like me, they felt that this was no time for the usual 'hedge your bets' type of opposition which makes it possible to point to trivial qualifications if things go wrong. We stiffened the Liberal Party and held firm in supporting our armed forces, something that was a good deal easier to do once Margaret Thatcher conceded that after the war there would need to be an inquiry into how we had lost the islands in the first place. But her tone on sovereignty became even more entrenched and unrealistic. As I constantly argued, we could *not* use the UN Charter to justify our act of self-defence and then ignore the UN Charter's demands that we negotiate. I did, however, accept that Argentina had to face the fact that there are penalties for going to war. I do not believe we can do more than share sovereignty or transfer it to the UN at some future date – as a result of Argentine aggression a straight transfer of sovereignty to Argentina is now impossible to foresee.

As the war developed I spoke frequently both in debates and on statements. The Government agreed to brief Opposition leaders on Privy Council terms but foolishly Michael Foot refused. Slowly, largely under Denis Healey's influence, Michael Foot's resolve to support the task force began to weaken. The reservations increased and the reluctance actually to use the force that had been deployed deepened. There was nothing one could really put one's finger on but the mood of Labour in the House began to change. Conservative MPs who had been welcoming the interventions from Michael Foot and the Labour front bench, started to view them with suspicion. There was no overt antagonism, the divisions never approached those which had developed at the time of Suez, but the House was nowhere near as united as it was to be over the Gulf War in 1991. The credit for that goes largely to John Major, but also to Neil Kinnock who ignored the views of Denis Healey. Denis Healey's contributions in the Falklands debates began to get wilder, his predictions increasingly dire and his language more emotive. That is not simply the view of a partisan politician. Professor Calvert of Southampton University describes in his book how Healey in the 7 April Commons debate 'badly misjudged the mood of the occasion, alternately challenging Mrs Thatcher to resign and lecturing her on the "appallingly difficult and dangerous situation to which the Government has exposed the nation"'. Calvert went on to observe, 'it almost seemed that he was more interested in defeating the Government than defeating the Argentines.' Later in the same speech Denis Healey, as Shadow Foreign Secretary, actually declared that, 'an opposed landing would inflict intolerable casualties on the Falkland Islanders, whom it is our duty to protect. They are not asking for the peace of the cemetery.' It was sad to see him losing his judgement. As Labour retreated from its initial Falklands stance, the political scene predictably began to change. In the May council elections which took place during the war a Conservative revival took place. It is true that this revival had started earlier but the war certainly gave it momentum.

The Government's conduct of the war was exemplary; even the sinking of the *Belgrano* was a necessary military operation which effectively trapped the Argentine Navy in their ports for the rest of the war. It is unfortunate that this essential military act was to give the Government so much grief in the months to come as small inconsistencies in describing what had happened became large discrepancies. For reasons which I can only assume stemmed from a desire to prevent the Argentines from gaining compensation for the *Belgrano* in international law, a cover up began. The key mistake was not to reveal everything in the published review some months after the war was over. After this the affair became more and more tangled. The misrepresentation continued to dog the Government and, during the general election, a television encounter about the *Belgrano* between Margaret Thatcher and a woman in Gloucestershire was the only occasion on which she looked rattled and vulnerable.

The British people began to see the formidable benefits of our voluntary but highly professional armed services. For me, as Devonport's MP, the actual war was an emotional experience. Thousands of my constituents were in the Southern Atlantic. I visited the wives and families of a number of servicemen who were killed or injured and it was a harrowing experience. For the people of Plymouth, who felt that a significant part of our city with Royal Marines as well as the Royal Navy participating, this was no remote war. The mood was not, however, jingoistic. People sensed the danger and the risks involved. The *Sun* with its headlines 'Gotcha!' and 'Up Yours Galtieri' may have upset the intelligentsia in London, but in the provinces it was taken in good heart; more as an amusing morale booster than a sign that jingoism was running rife in the UK.

Nor, in private, was Margaret Thatcher's mood bellicose or belligerent. On the occasions I saw her I was struck by her caution and there was no trace of rejoicing. When I mentioned privately that I hoped we would only bomb Argentine airfields *in extremis* it was I who was made to appear the hawk as she remonstrated that there were no circumstances under which we would do so. I then had to say that if one of our carriers were torpedoed and limping to safety but still in range of aircraft flying from Argentine bases, it would be our duty to try and incapacitate their airfields. No one seeing her immediately after the bombing of HMS *Sheffield* could have any doubts about her concern for the lives of our servicemen. She did not lose her nerve, although on occasions she certainly showed her nervousness. I have explained why in the chapter on the Falklands I believe Margaret Thatcher cannot escape a considerable measure of responsibility for the invasion, but she also deserves a considerable measure of the credit for our victory. The voters recognized this and were going to reward her with victory whenever she called the general election. No sensible politician could have expected the voters to react in any other way, despite Churchill's defeat in 1945.

In the council elections in May, the Conservative revival got underway; the SDP and Liberals began to suffer. Although the two parties only made an overall gain of ninety-seven seats, in most parts of the country our share of the vote doubled and between us we managed to win a quarter of the vote. Inevitably the SDP lost a large number of councillors who had previously been Labour and were in rock-solid Labour wards. The SDP reversal was most marked in Islington with Labour taking fifty-one of the fifty-two seats. Previously there had been twenty-six SDP councillors who had moved over from Labour but this was far more of a commentary on the old politics than the new. Yet our bandwagon had clearly slowed down. This was confirmed in the Beaconsfield by-election which the Liberals fought on 27 May and in the Mitcham and Morden by-election on 3 June, where Bruce Douglas-Mann lost his seat. Bruce had just joined the SDP from Labour and insisted on a by-election against the wishes of all his new colleagues. It gave the Conservatives a by-election gain, the first time the Government of the day had gained a seat in a by-election for over twenty years. Then, on 14 June, the Argentines surrendered, and from the moment the union jack was run up the flag pole at Port Stanley once more I never doubted that the Conservatives would be re-elected. At a by-election on 17 June at Coatbridge and Airdrie the fortunes of the Alliance had fallen so far since Hillhead that the unfortunate candidate's deposit was lost. Margaret Thatcher was cock-a-hoop, deservedly enjoying the aura of a successful war leader. It was now for her only a question of waiting for the earliest decent moment at which to call an election without being thought to be exploiting the issue. That did not of course stop her exploiting it.

At this inauspicious electoral moment the SDP leadership contest was finally upon us. Nominations had to be in no later than 12 noon on Friday 11 June and the ballot would be counted on 2 July, my birthday. So, in theory, the leadership election started while the war was on, but in practice it was in abeyance. My nomination was held back because of my hope that Shirley would still decide to stand against Roy. She was abroad and did not finally announce that she would not be a candidate until 18 May. I did not want to confirm my candidacy until I had spoken to her. I offered to stand down if she would prefer a two-horse race, but by then she had made up her mind that she did not want to fight. She guessed that she would lose against Roy and that she would easily win the Presidency against Bill. In February I had been worried that I would not reach the requisite threshold of MPs to nominate me. By June I had the support of half the twenty-nine SDP MPs, with John Roper, as Chief Whip, staying neutral. Shirley Williams had agreed to nominate me and I was also supported by Christopher Brocklebank-Fowler, John Cartwright, Dick Crawshaw, Edward Lyons, Mike Thomas, Michael O'Halloran, Ron Brown, James Dunn, Tom McNally, Bob Mitchell, Eric Ogden and John Grant. It is interesting to note that of those who nominated me only Tom McNally and Shirley Williams supported merging with the Liberals in 1987.

Despite, or perhaps because of this support, I had been placed under very heavy pressure not to stand. It started with a letter from Bob Maclennan on 10 May, and was followed by a letter from Bill on 11 May and another from John Horam on 14 May. All three fervently supported Roy Jenkins but also professed genuine worry about the dangers of an election, preferring no contest. I remained adamant that I would stand. I did not believe I would win, but I wanted to mobilize a counterweight to Roy's attitude to the Liberals, and I believed under his leadership the SDP would be lucky to survive being merged by the back door.

Before Hillhead, when the outcome was far from certain, Shirley had put a proposal to Roy with my full support: if we were able to form a government he should become the choice of both Liberals and Social Democrats as Prime Minister, irrespective of how many MPs each party had. The leadership and presidency of the SDP would be held by Bill, Shirley or me, whoever was elected by the membership. The Gang of

Four had discussed this briefly and Roy had said he would consider it, but made it pretty clear it had little appeal. During the by-election Roy looked at times as if he would lose, and Shirley and I then agreed that, under our plan, Roy would remain our choice for Prime Minister even though he would not yet be an MP. Our concern was that the Leader of the SDP had a massive task in building up the Party. We repeated our plan after Roy's Hillhead victory, but it was too late. It was brushed aside perhaps understandably because he wanted the power base of being SDP Leader, not just Alliance Leader. It would have undermined his leadership campaign if people felt they could have the sugar and the bun – Shirley as SDP Leader and Roy as Prime Minister. It was initially, however, put forward as a serious and genuine attempt to maintain a more collective leadership, to match the right people to the right jobs and to widen the appeal of the SDP and the Liberals. I still believed it had merit and stated publicly during the campaign that I would not rule it out if I became Leader of the SDP. It would obviously have depended on Roy's standing in the opinion polls nearer the election and the relative standing of David Steel and myself. But I emphasized that my main interest was in becoming Leader of the SDP, not the Alliance's prospective candidate for Prime Minister, already looking a remote possibility.

I started my campaign believing that I would be lucky to avoid a humiliating defeat and it was only on the day the votes were counted, when I realized how my handling of the Falklands War had been appreciated by Party members, that I allowed myself to even contemplate victory. In the Steering Committee there had been strenuous demands from the Roy Jenkins supporters that there should be no campaigning; they even got me to agree that we should not go on television to campaign, merely confining ourselves to the 750-word statements by each candidate which were circulated with the ballot paper. It was Roy who broke his own ban and went on TV, no doubt feeling disadvantaged by my Falklands-related TV appearances. As soon as I read Roy's statement to the members, I realized that whether or not we went on television, there would be no real contest on the one issue which truly divided us, namely the Liberals. Roy had simply forestalled a bare-knuckle campaign by stating:

> This is a vital Alliance which has mostly worked well on the ground. At its best it is a real partnership of principle. Our separate SDP identity is, however, essential to the whole enterprise. It is our creation which has lit a flame in the country. We can be firmly for the Alliance, while proud of our distinct SDP philosophy and membership which many have worked so hard to create.

I knew that his actions belied his words, but I could not call Roy a liar without destroying the Party nor could I reveal that in my view all his actions since the Limehouse Declaration pointed in one direction –

merger. But the fact that he had felt obliged to be so clear about the SDP's identity was a gain and enabled me and other Party members to hold him at least to the semblance of such a position while he was the Leader of the Party.

The words in my statement were not too dissimilar to his for we were both trying to edge into each other's constituencies, as happens in any election.

> The fact that many of you have never belonged to any other political party is a precious asset. It means that we have identified and mobilized a new political force. Our principled partnership with the Liberal Party is indispensable electorally and on major policy questions we are in close agreement. But we should not appear to merge into a single 'Alliance Party'. We gain strength and respect, as Liberals and Social Democrats, from being seen as two parties, working together while retaining an appeal to a broader spectrum of the electorate. In doing so, we show as part of achieving proportional representation that Social Democrats and Liberals will be natural coalition partners in government.

The newspapers did try to bring out and sharpen the coded disagreements between Roy and me, but I suspect many people had voted before they read the press comment. Should I have acquiesced in the shadow-boxing and in effect allowed myself to be in part an accomplice to Roy's strategy? Should I have challenged the Party members outright by telling them we were being merged by stealth? Though the headlines concentrated on personalities – 'Abrasive David or rounded Roy', 'Can the Doctor win without a bedside manner?', 'The good doctor versus one of nature's bankers', 'Is Dr Owen's cutting edge a shade too sharp?' – most of the comment explored the nature of our different approach to the Liberals, but not so obviously as to alert members to the true pressure to merge. The Roy Jenkins sympathizers assiduously sold the line that my election would rupture the Alliance and raised privately or by inference a question mark over whether Roy would continue in politics if he lost. This was a point taken up in the *Scotsman* by James Naughtie, 'An Owen win would certainly threaten to bring Mr Jenkins's political career to a premature close.' An editorial in *The Times*, 'The whisper of the hustings', stressed the SDP's dependence on the Liberals when it argued that I would be a better bet as leader but only of a radical new party and that Roy would be the more comfortable leader.

I do not blame David Steel for masterminding an Alliance between the SDP as far as possible on Liberal terms and later, the takeover of the SDP, for he thought that was in the best interests of the Liberal Party. I believe, however, it was only in their narrow, short-term interest. The broader interest of Liberals was and still is to do everything possible to achieve proportional representation. Apart from the safety and prosperity of the country, proportional representation should be any Liberal leader's central objective. For the diversity and disaggregation that their creed of individualism favours will flourish within the coalition politics that accompanies proportional representation. To achieve this there is one task – to enlarge the vote of those who do not wish to support the Labour or Conservative Party and force a change in the voting system to proportional representation. The best way to ensure this is by electoral pacts with other parties involving standing down candidates in seats so as to beat the distortion within the present system. It was very clear that David Steel never saw the SDP-Liberal Alliance as lasting until proportional representation was achieved. I always understood why, given his position, David Steel backed Roy Jenkins to be the Leader of the SDP and that he conducted an extremely effective campaign on Roy's behalf. They had a tacit understanding that Roy would take the lead role in the forthcoming General Election, with David Steel's support and that Roy would support David Steel to be the Leader of the by then merged party. After Roy had beaten me in our SDP leadership election, I said in an interview in the *Daily Express* in October 1982, 'if I was Leader of the Liberal Party and I was 44 and my name was David Steel I think I would be in favour of Roy Jenkins rather than David Owen winning.'

My disagreement with David Steel was that, in pursuing the course of nudging the SDP into a merged party at every opportunity, he pursued the narrow not the broader interests of the Liberal Party. It was obvious what he was up to and it had an understandable short-term benefit for him. I could understand too why Roy Jenkins's short-term interests impelled him towards this course. For those of us in the SDP who did not agree with their judgement or their tactics, it was not easy to resist without damaging public rows which we felt we had to avoid.

The *Guardian*, in its editorial, wrote 'especially because of the overwhelming importance in a first-past-the-post system of sustaining the Alliance, the best outcome would be a Jenkins victory but with a sturdy enough Owen vote to produce a continuing creative tension in the Party.' *The Economist* in its editorial 'Send for the doctor', urged the SDP to take its courage in both hands since a realignment of the Left in British politics was the real issue. It argued that I had never made any bones about my view that a strategy which rendered the SDP merely a Liberal Party front organization was a denial of the motivation which led to its formation. I suspected the hand of Nick Harman in that editorial for over many conversations in Buttermere he had consistently warned against association with the Liberals and felt if we could not replace or reform the Labour Party the whole exercise was a waste of time.

The *New Statesman* carried an article by Peter Kellner, 'Beware of the medicine man', which began 'As I wish the SDP to fail, I hope that Roy Jenkins becomes the party's leader this weekend.' Its main argument was that if I were leading the SDP with its own distinct semi-radical image it would then be a real challenge to Labour. To reinforce his message he quoted a shrewd member of the Labour Shadow Cabinet, 'I adopt the straightforward Marxist view; given the choice between two bastards, root for the older one.'

On the last Sunday of the election campaign my hopes soared when I read the front page of the *Observer*. It showed me leading Roy Jenkins easily, but when I studied the detail of the NOP poll it became apparent that the poll was not among SDP members, who were the relevant electorate, but a sample poll of the whole country. I led Roy by 47 per cent to 29 per cent on the question of who would make a better leader, and when they asked only potential SDP or Liberal Party voters the gap widened with me having 57 per cent support and Roy only 33 per cent. Yet this evidence of Roy's relative unpopularity was not new and David Steel also had a sizeable lead over Roy; the much smaller SDP membership were influenced, and in many ways rightly, by the Dimbleby Lecture, Warrington and Hillhead.

In my heart I knew that Roy was going to win but I still dared to hope. The result was announced on my forty-fourth birthday. Out of 68,000 potential voters Roy Jenkins got 26,300 votes and I got 20,900 votes. We had not spilt much political blood but perhaps that was the tragedy of that election. The real issue had been kept in the depths and not allowed to surface. Perhaps my greatest service to the SDP would have been to have exposed Roy Jenkins's pretensions, but in doing so not only would I have lost Party votes, I suspect our candidates in the 1983 General Election would have lost votes as well. Unity after the Falklands was vital for the survival of the SDP, and survival was now the name of the game.

27

DEPUTY LEADER

As soon as the school holidays allowed, I left for a long holiday in America where Debbie's younger brother was getting married. I knew there was little I could do now to stop David Steel and Roy Jenkins bringing our two parties ever closer. Shirley was bound to win the election for the presidency and a period of silence was called for from me. At the end of August I spent a week in Australia. It was my first visit and I had a number of speeches and political appointments in Sydney, Canberra and Melbourne. I will always remember one beautiful sunny day in Sydney. It started with an *al fresco* breakfast given by Malcolm Fraser, the Prime Minister, at his official residence overlooking Sydney harbour. Then I went sailing in the harbour with a good wind and it provided a spectacular vantage point from which to admire the Opera House. We ate plenty of oysters and had a lot of champagne. Then I gave a lecture in the evening to students who came back with a lot of irreverent, iconoclastic questions. It made me realize how much Australian society unleashes people's energy, how vibrant, cocky and classless it had become and how depressed and defeatist Britain was by comparison. The mother country had a lot to learn from its offspring in 1982. In the space of a month I had seen, in the United States, Canada and Australia, the advantages of a classless, market-orientated culture, with democratic structures which were more responsive and more liberal than ours. It intensified my desire for the SDP to become more aggressively radical. I stopped off to speak in Hong Kong and arrived home on 3 September convinced that there was a modern technologically-orientated world that was passing Britain by.

I had almost no enthusiasm for British politics when I returned but I had to go down to Gower and help in the by-election which was to be held on 16 September. It was not as good a result as the SDP might have hoped for and Labour retained the seat. My cousins lived in the constituency so I knew it well and I could sense that we were not clicking with the electorate. We came second with 25 per cent, despite our candidate being reasonably well known, having previously been the Labour MP for the neighbouring constituency. We were no longer exciting the electorate. I wrote afterwards to the candidate, Gwynoro Jones, to congratulate him on his effort and commiserate, but also to wonder if it had been wise to stress the Alliance name in the campaign as much as we had done. I mentioned that when I looked at his news sheet, I was hard pressed to find the terms 'SDP' or 'Social Democrat'. We needed to know, I felt, how the word 'Alliance goes down with people on the ground'. Was it thought of as a building society or did people relate to it as a political force? Having spent a lot of my time getting across the phrase 'Social Democrat', reinforced by news items from Germany and Sweden referring to social democrats, I was concerned that we were now trying to force another name on to the public, ignoring not only 'SDP' but also to some extent 'Liberal' which had positive associations in some parts of the country. I wondered how we could present ourselves in such a way that Labour supporters who were fed up with their Party felt they could vote SDP with a clear conscience, not feeling that they were betraying their class.

Perhaps my concerns over identity were heightened by the discovery that in my own borough of Tower Hamlets both seats had been handed to the Liberals by the negotiators. I tried to discourage the local party from taking unilateral action against this seat plan but I could sense how dispiriting the experience had been for them. Debbie, who was very active locally, was extremely angry that all our SDP effort in the borough over the last eighteen months had, in effect, been snuffed out. I could better understand why the Liberal Party had fought to have one of our three Plymouth seats to keep their own flame alight and it was a good lesson for the future.

The truly disastrous finding, which confirmed my fears, was in the MORI poll of 5 October. MORI asked their standard, unprompted vote intention question with an 'incliner' follow-up for those intially undecided or not intending to vote. The results, Don't Knows aside, were:

Conservative		42%
Labour		30%
SDP	4%	
Liberal	13%	27%
Alliance	10%	

We now had the ultimate indignity of the SDP in October 1982 only polling 4 per cent to the Liberals' 13 per cent. This had to be compared with a year before when the SDP was polling 40 per cent.

Dividing and reallocating the 10 per cent who said Alliance in the ratio (56/29) which the poll also suggested would be the breakdown, the SDP had the support of about 6 per cent of the electorate while the Liber were currently supported by 16 per cent. The field work was done just after the Liberal Assembly when awareness of the Liberals was high. But even so these figures, which seemed to be consistent with other current evidence, indicated the urgent need to revive support for the SDP in the interests of everyone in the Alliance, not just the SDP. But even though these findings were circulated to Roy Jenkins, I could not be sure that he was prepared to recognize the full implications. He had been ignoring the warning signs for so long, I wondered whether he cared about the make-up and was comforting himself with the fact that we were only a little way behind Labour. Yet, if we were to expand our appeal, it could only be by increasing the SDP element: only recently it was this which had been the factor giving us opinion poll ratings in the upper thirties, and until we could recapture those levels of support we would only have a negligible number of Liberal and SDP MPs after the next election.

Early that month Debbie and I had dinner with John Pardoe and his wife. It was a merry evening and we gossiped, with just a tinge of malice, about David Steel. John spent his whole time convincing me that life outside politics was much better than inside; not, at that stage, that I needed much convincing. Not only was he doing well in his business but also, as they both explained, the real delight was to have more evenings at home and time for all the things which politics had excluded. This upbeat view of non-political life was reinforced by a rather downbeat lunch with Lord Zuckerman a few days later at London Zoo. Solly, despite being a good friend of Roy Jenkins, was gloomy about the political situation. I was due to have lunch with Roy to talk about the deputy leadership and was by now in no mood for it. I needed cheering up. So I arranged to have lunch with Lord George Brown – if anyone knew anything about the perils of being deputy leader it was George. He gave a good analysis of the boundaries within which I could work in my relations with Roy, and we also discussed what it would be legitimate for me to say when I met Roy next day. We both agreed that the prospects for the SDP looked pretty grim but that all I could do was to lie low. If I spoke out publicly the Party's chances would be further damaged.

This dilemma over whether to go public was one over which all of us agonized at the time. Mike Thomas had written Roy Jenkins another letter expressing his unhappiness over the seat distribution, but by then he was viewed with so much suspicion that I doubt if any notice was taken. He had been my campaign manager, and though he understood why I had fought such a low-key campaign, concealing the extent of our disillusionment, privately, I know, he wondered whether I had played fair by the members in not revealing the truth that we were no longer acting as if the SDP was an independent party.

As I walked into the Athenaeum for lunch with Roy, I mused as to why he had asked me to this bastion of the British Establishment. He knew perfectly well that these all-male London clubs got up my nose.

Even his own club, Brooks's, had a slightly less fusty image. My last visit had been with Jim Callaghan in 1978 and we had both laughed then at the incongruity of two Labour men lunching there. In fairness, Roy did his best to make the lunch a success and it was only when we went upstairs for coffee that we got down to real business. He asked me if I would agree to chair the Finance Committee, on which David Sainsbury had sounded me out the week before. Roy had already telephoned me in the middle of July after the election to ask if I would take the job of fund-raiser and I had asked for time to think about it. I explained that I was not at all keen and felt that fundraising would be far more effective if it was done by him or somebody very close to him. In my experience donors wanted to meet the Leader and hear his views directly, and this was not a burden which could be easily parcelled out. I also explained that there was a difference in principle between us on fundraising. I did not favour joint financial appeals with the Liberals at this stage. These should, I suggested, be kept until much closer to the election. All they would do now would be to detract from the task of obtaining more money for the SDP and this was very necessary – we were already facing the probability of having to cut headquarters staffing. Nevertheless, Roy was due to speak in Plymouth Guildhall on Friday 1 October and it was obvious that he was doing his best to heal our rifts, so I said I would consider his proposition.

I did, however, assure him that I had no intention of continuing to fight the leadership election campaign: he had won and was entitled to lead in the direction he wanted. But the views of the 20,000 members who had voted for me could not be dismissed. I would not stand in the way of any amount of 'jointery' that he or David Steel could agree between them provided they did not make irrevocable steps towards a merger.

Roy also wanted me to accept a comprehensive speaking responsibility as Deputy Leader. I expressed extreme reluctance, saying it was a non-job and that I would prefer to go on dealing with foreign affairs and defence.

On 20 September the Liberals started their Conference in Bournemouth, and to improve relations, Roy and David Steel took some final decisions over the seat negotiations. These were particularly adverse for the SDP. Once again we gave ground to avoid a row. The end result gave a superficial impression of a fair distribution of seats, but in truth it was anything but fair. My reaction was to dictate my darkest thoughts to my diary on 24 September:

> When eventually the history of the Social Democratic Party is written historians may have to decide at what point it became inevitable that it merged into the Liberal Party and of all the thresholds and of all the turning points it may be that they will conclude that it was this week that the final determination was made. I hope that this will not be the outcome or the verdict of history, I hope it may still be possible to

maintain the independence of the Social Democratic Party, but realism forces me to admit that that is not now the most likely outcome. It is hard to reach such a conclusion so soon after the birth of a Party that promised so much and appeared to fulfil so much of my own personal aspirations and even dreams, but remorselessly over the last few months I have been driven back and now face a future in which I may have to accept with as good a grace as I can that I cannot reverse the momentum towards a merged Alliance party. I am, of course, against that result on two grounds. Firstly, I am temperamentally and philosophically a believer in the tradition of social democracy. I believe that it exists as a separate strand of political thought capable of being mobilized into a political party. But I am also against the merged identity of Social Democrats and Liberals as a result of a hard, analytical analysis of the electoral consequences of such a merger. It is my profound belief that if the Social Democrats and the Liberals come so close together that they are either perceived by the electorate as being one or actually merge into one entity then there will be insufficient votes to challenge the two–party monopoly of Conservatives and Labour. . . .

The reason for coming to this rather depressing assessment is that in this week Roy Jenkins has finally tipped the seat negotiations across a threshold which could be fatal for the independence of the Party. It is not fair to blame him for the entire seat negotiations for the eventual outcome is the product of much confusion, doubt and lack of commitment . . . Nothing will shift him from the course on which he is pointing. All I could do at lunch was to take my stand on a few central issues and hope that I have enough weight and authority to hold to these sticking points. Certainly Roy Jenkins knows that I will not accept in the run-up to the next election any permanent irreversible changes in the direction of a merged party. Furthermore, he knows that I will not serve in any Alliance Shadow Cabinet; that I will not accept a voting procedure involving Social Democrats and Liberals for the post of Prime Minister designate and that I will not accept that whoever is made Prime Minister designate during the run-up to the next election has the right to claim to be the Leader of the Alliance in Opposition after the next election if we have been unable to form a government.

Now those are three, in my view, permanent changes that if I acquiesced in them would make it impossible, after the next election, to retain the independence of the Social Democratic Party. In my judgement, on at least two of them – and possibly all three – David Steel will push Roy Jenkins very hard indeed. I am the victim of the politics of edging at which both Roy Jenkins and David Steel are very great exponents.

Issues are never confronted directly. There is often very little discussion about what should be done but steps are taken unilaterally and often publicly which remorselessly carve out a position. Each incident is of itself insufficient to create a row or provoke a confrontation and demand that the position be held. But each incident cumulatively has a powerful determining effect on the future.

Yet despite that mood of pessimism I still threw myself into SDP activity. My diary was full of SDP speaking engagements night after night in different parts of the country. I was not skulking away but taking a very heavy load in keeping up Party morale.

On Sunday 26 September there were numerous press rumours about my being axed as foreign affairs spokesman. They all obviously came from the same briefing and each pushed the same line – this was a 'slap down for Owen'. Roy telephoned me that morning to say that he could not understand how these stories had occurred. In fact, I did not think he had been responsible. The stories were so crude they were more likely to have come from the Liberals who wanted me out of the foreign affairs post so that David Steel could be the Alliance spokesman in the joint Shadow Cabinet they kept talking about.

The views I held over the seat distribution and loss of identity were not mine alone. A couple of months earlier a *Times* headline summed up many people's feelings: 'Will the Liberals gently walk off with the swag?' Of the fourteen MPs who had nominated me as Leader as many as ten were deeply worried about keeping their seats at the next election. On 30 September Mike Thomas sent me a copy of a note he had sent to Bill Rodgers. His frustration was intense.

As you know I strongly agree with you that the SDP should remain a distinct and separate party; but I start to wonder then, why, apart from your loyalty to Roy, you are allowing us to proceed down the slippery slope to merger with the Liberals without a word of protest. Indeed that you are allowing yourself to be made the principal apologist for it to me and others.

I am increasingly coming to the conclusion that some in our Party never wanted an SDP except as a transition camp for those of us in Parliament and in the country who could not be immediately persuaded to join the Liberal Party. As a vehicle to encourage us to make the initial break in the sure knowledge that we would eventually be put in the position where we had no option but to be part of a souped up Liberal Party – letters to *The Times* from prominent Liberals already refer, I note, to the 'Alliance Party'.

If you were a party to that thinking, Bill, then you have systematically deceived me in a way that I find hard to contemplate. I don't believe it. I think you were conned too.

Well, we have ourselves to blame for that, but conned though I may have been, I will not knowingly be party to conning others – and nor should you be. We left the Labour Party because we would not ask the electors to vote for a party that wanted us to be the figleaf in persuading the electors it was what it wasn't. Roy Hattersley can do that if he likes, we wouldn't; and we shouldn't be prepared to vote for an 'Alliance Party' either.

I write so straightforwardly not to be offensive but because I believe time is terribly short now. To put it at its bluntest, you and

I know what a year of failing to promote the SDP has done to our membership and finances. Another six months of systematic neglect and perhaps another set of bad local elections (and, given the seats deal, even quite a good general election) could finish us as an independent force.

If we continue on this road I know one thing for sure. You are not going to be able to look me in the eye when you come to the National Committee and tell them, as chairman of the Finance and General Purposes Committee, that 'in the circumstances, in view of the political, membership and financial position, there is no alternative but for us to merge with the Liberals' or some such. Every step we are now asked to agree to in the Steering Committee (when we are asked at all) is one step nearer that meeting.

The electoral consequences are already plain to see. Because we behave as though there's no difference between us and the Liberal Party (indeed we keep on saying so) the electors are starting to treat us how they treat the Liberal Party – good for a mid-term by-election protest, but not taken seriously come a general election. Every step down the 'Alliance' route strikes that chord in the public mind, drives away the millions of voters who thought we were something new and different (most of whom would never have considered voting Liberal in a million years) and demoralizes some of our most active members.

The irony is that, so cleverly has David Steel manoeuvred to make sure that the Liberal Party wasn't damaged by the start of the SDP, that he's now well on the way to killing the goose that would have laid the golden egg for Liberal candidates in large numbers before it did so for more than a handful of Social Democrats.

I can't go along with it much longer Bill – nor can you if I sense what you feel in your heart.

That letter anticipated in every respect what later happened: the determined though unsuccessful attempt to merge the SDP with the Liberal Party after the 1983 Election and the actual merger after the 1987 Election. From 1982 onwards we were embarked on a very different struggle from that which many of us had begun in Limehouse in January 1981. Our struggle now was to survive and avoid being absorbed into the Liberal Party. In 1982, I said, 'Our epitaph might be that we had saved the Labour Party' and added that 'there were worse fates than that'. After the tenth anniversary of the founding of the SDP a *Times* editorial on 27 March 1991, 'To the Four's credit', disinterred that quotation and concluded it was indeed our epitaph. Yet that editorial could not have been written after the 1987 Election. Then, it looked as if all the SDP might be remembered for was giving the Liberal Party a boost. For the Labour Party was still unreformed. By 1991 the continuing SDP could claim that Labour was reformed. This is, however, too negative an interpretation of the SDP's contribution to British politics.

After the 1983 General Election and again in 1987 we kept the SDP an independent force so as to create the climate for coalition politics and reform of the voting system as well as to contribute to the battle of ideas in British politics. It will only be historians in the twenty-first century who will be able to determine how successfully the SDP contributed to a change in political attitudes. But if coalition politics does ensue, that could prove to be a more lasting legacy than our considerable impact on reforming the Labour Party. As to our impact on ideas we now have John Major compaigning for a classless society and the Conservative Party talking about the social market; the shift has not therefore just taken place within the Labour Party.

However, in 1982, the realists among us knew that in order to be in a position to contribute our ideas we had to ensure there would be enough MPs for us to continue as a Parliamentary Party after the general election. That meant that, despite disillusionment, neither Mike Thomas nor I, nor others who thought like us, slackened our efforts to fight for the SDP – in many ways we redoubled our efforts.

For the previous six months the SDP had been discussing two different strategies – the breakthrough or the bridgehead. In April 1982 David Marquand put a strategy paper to the Steering Committee which presented only two options on our relationship with the Liberals, either a very loose association or a tight association involving a joint candidate for the Prime Ministership, Shadow Ministers, a joint programme for Government and a joint election manifesto. I replied with a paper called 'A four party structure – before and after the next election'. Broadly speaking, those like David who favoured the breakthrough believed that everything should be sacrificed for maximizing our vote for the 1983 Election. Those like me who wanted to stress the identity of the SDP believed that in the short run we should help to maximize the Alliance vote and therefore contribute to the breakthrough but, just as importantly, that it would also ensure that we were able to hold a bridgehead in Parliament if the electoral fortunes of the Conservative and Labour parties improved. That was before the Falklands war was won. Now, after the war, a breakthrough strategy was even less credible. Stressing the Alliance and downplaying the SDP had helped reduce the appeal of the Alliance and left us in the SDP with no chance of survival if the breakthrough did not materialize. The breakthrough strategy was fine for Roy Jenkins who saw this as his only opportunity to be Prime Minister, but that it required ratings of 40 per cent to be credible. With us below 30 per cent in the polls, we were facing a long haul. We needed to ensure the bridgehead and worry less about the breakthrough.

The extent to which Britain's electoral system militates against political parties whose support is evenly distributed has never been widely understood. In February 1974 the Liberals got 19.4 per cent of the vote but only 2 per cent of the seats. Despite the fact that this was a potent argument for reform, it was never in our interests to point it out, for if

people saw our opinion poll support at between 33 per cent and 34 per
cent they thought we were level-pegging with the Conservative and
Labour parties. To disabuse them would damage our credibility and
might leave people thinking we were a wasted vote. But in fact if the
SDP/Liberal Alliance got one third of the vote it would win fewer than a
hundred seats and, because of the 1982 seat agreement, the overwhelming
proportion of those seats would go to the Liberal Party. Only if we went
over the 40 per cent level would the electoral system have started to work
in our favour as, evenly spread, we would have then been over-rewarded
with seats. In the post-Falklands situation we would be extremely lucky
to get 30 per cent of the national vote and even that would only give us
around forty-two seats. Twenty-four per cent of the vote might give us as
little as twenty-two seats. To continue with a strategy geared to the
breakthrough was absurd. For a bridgehead we had to retain SDP MPs'
seats in Labour constituencies. That meant capturing C2 voters,
something which the Liberal Party had never done in sufficient numbers
in any post-war general election. It meant the SDP asking the same
questions as Margaret Thatcher did and not being too appalled if we
came up with some answers which were not very different from hers. All
the market research showed that C2 voters wanted a strong determined
defence policy of the sort that would upset many Liberals. That same
research also showed that selling council houses was immensely popular,
and yet the Liberals were very reluctant, even hostile, towards the basic
concept of selling council houses.

I decided to let Roy Jenkins go on propounding the breakthrough
while quietly trying to ensure that we were in a position to consolidate
around a dozen SDP MPs after the election. I knew from then on how
difficult it would be and that my influence was not going to be particularly
strong. When Bill Rodgers wrote to Bernard Doyle, our Chief Executive,
at the end of September 1982 saying that during the election he had
thought of doing some nationwide campaigning but had now dropped
any such thought, it was a clear sign that he too realized we were in
electoral difficulty. He said he would not accept any nationwide engagements after Easter 1983, that he did not intend to sleep away from
Stockton during the general election campaign and that in the final ten
days he would not leave Stockton at all. He intended to win and felt that
now was the time to be single-minded. His reaction was perfectly
understandable, but it was a clear sign, and read as such by other MPs,
that he knew that we were now fighting for survival.

I remained convinced that the SDP's identity held the key to this
survival and made this point again in early October, just before the
Conference, in a letter to the trustees, copied to Roy, finally agreeing to
chair the Finance Committee. I did so because I found it impossible to
refuse repeated requests from the elected Leader and the two trustees. I
pulled no punches, telling them that I was convinced that the failure to

retain and attract members was entirely related to our failure to promote the SDP, and drew attention to the recent MORI poll showing the SDP with only 6 per cent out of a total level of 27 per cent for the Alliance. We had ourselves done a recent poll which showed the SDP having 5 per cent out of total Alliance support of 22 per cent. I told them I could not see how we could increase our membership unless we had a sustained period of at least six months in which, with David Steel's agreement, we were freer than we had been in the past to promote the SDP. This would be in his interest, since restoring the fortunes of the SDP held the key to restoring the fortunes of the Alliance. I argued that if Roy or I appeared on ITN or the BBC *Nine o'Clock News* for one minute we got the equivalent of £50,000 worth of press advertising. If during that one minute we talked about the Alliance and not the SDP, then the SDP lost out. Similarly if we spoke only on Alliance platforms and neglected to build an organization and a fighting election machine it would be at the expense of our infant Party. We were too new to be able to survive without constant reinforcement of the very fact that the SDP existed.

Our newly appointed Director of Communications, Roger Carroll, who had been with Jim Callaghan in No. 10 and on the *Sun*, was urging that the Alliance partners should project themselves as two strong brands in marketing terms with the Alliance as an extra benefit, albeit a crucial one. Christopher Brocklebank-Fowler, who also had marketing expertise, strongly shared this view. The SDP had been a runaway success when we projected ourselves as a new, fresh and exciting force in British politics. We needed to rediscover ourselves if we were to put our full potential strength at the disposal of the Alliance.

On Monday 11 October the SDP's second annual Conference opened in Cardiff. It was a new, modern conference hall but too big for us and we rattled around. The question all the journalists were asking was well put by John Cole in the *Listener*. 'Can the SDP get back into the big league?', he asked, arguing that the SDP badly needed a fresh spurt of energy.

But while this was the big underlying question, it did not prove to be the issue that set the Conference on fire. *The Times*'s political editor, Julian Haviland, was the only person correctly to predict what would prove truly controversial at the Conference – the decision to go for a statutory incomes policy. This had been taken three weeks earlier on the insistence of Roy Jenkins, who thought the SDP/Liberal Joint Commission document 'Back to Work' was far too weak. Julian followed this up two days later with an article entitled 'The doctor remains a pay policy agnostic', saying that I was sceptical about its efficacy.

After Cardiff we rolled by train to Derby and then to Great Yarmouth. On the train Ruth Levitt, my research assistant, asked if I would object if she tabled a motion for the debate on a statutory incomes policy calling for a flexible policy and avoiding the Policy Committee's commitment to campaign for 'a statutory incomes policy of a conventional kind'. Ruth was the prospective SDP candidate for Nuneaton and worked for me virtually unpaid, so I felt that I could not prevent her. She argued anyhow it was by no means certain the amendment would be selected. But I should have realized this would be open to misinterpretation, that people would assume that I had put her up to it. I then compounded the mistake by listening to her speech from the platform. She spoke extremely well and I was genuinely pleased for her. The television cameras showed me applauding vigorously. When her amendment was voted on and passed, the TV commentators understandably put two and two together and made five. Suddenly the SDP was facing 'a challenge to Roy Jenkins's leadership' led by me. I had been very foolish and the papers made much of it next day.

Walking to the Conference after reading that morning's press comment, Shirley gave me a stiff but civilized reprimand. Roy Jenkins, by contrast, was incandescent with fury. I was summoned to his hotel as if he were a headmaster hauling in an errant schoolboy and I had to listen to a tirade about a 'petty ploy over an insubstantive issue' and how ruthlessly, calculatingly, personally ambitious I was. He was so incoherent with rage that there was little point in arguing and I just made notes, which I still have, while he was talking, putting down what he was saying like a doctor with a patient and only making the odd interjection. He said I seemed to interpret every olive branch or concession as weakness and only under-stood a kick in the groin. Despite my repeated apologies he was incapable of listening. Whether his purpose was to sever all personal relations between us I do not know but that was certainly the result. He accused Mike Thomas, Christopher Brocklebank-Fowler and me of constant plots and manoeuvres against him, and was smarting about a conversation I had had with Anthony Sampson which had been relayed to him so as to make me seem consumed by rivalry. In fact it was Anthony who had likened the tension in our relationship to that between Asquith and Lloyd-George and I had disagreed, saying that we had more friendship. Now even their relationship looked over-optimistic.

While I had nothing to do with suggesting Ruth's amendment, I did sympathize with her on the issue, and it was true, as Roy alleged, that I had left the meeting which had discussed the Conference document before his summing up which gave the ridiculous drafting instructions to Christopher Smallwood. Not only I but also Sir Leslie Murphy, David Sainsbury and John Horam shuddered at the thought of the new SDP actually campaigning to reintroduce an incomes policy of the conventional kind. It was an utter folly and fortunately the Party realized it, supporting the amendment by 4:1 which showed that it was not my influence alone. I had not planned to publicly embarrass him and as to his allegations that the incident had destroyed the whole effect of our Conference and gravely damaged the Party, that was utter nonsense. It had actually provided us with a little publicity to which we had become a stranger. The *Financial Times*, in an editorial, 'More than a third force', said:

> Britain's Social Democratic Party is now an established political entity. It is established in the literal sense that the meeting in Great Yarmouth at the end of last week was the first time that the Party was operating fully under its constitution ... it is established in the more cynical sense that it has begun to behave like the other parties. In Great Yarmouth there was evidence of internal dissent. A section of Mr Roy Jenkins's proposals for an incomes policy was voted down by a majority of the elected representatives to the Council for Social Democracy.

I now had to watch what I said in public very carefully and Roy held me at arm's length. I had no option but to accept Roy and Shirley drafting me in as a reluctant Deputy Leader and then to run for the National Committee in an election among the MPs. We only just won the vote to keep to an STV election in the Parliamentary Committee and even Bob Maclennan, who had drafted the constitution favouring proportional representation in internal party elections, voted for a list system. I feared a slate under first-past-the-post elections could have kept off most of my parliamentary supporters. As it turned out we were able to organize our first preference voting and I risked not voting for myself and gave my first preference to Mike Thomas. The newly elected National Committee did not assert itself sufficiently and we spent the next few months simply waiting for the Liberals to let Roy become the so-called Leader of the Alliance. At the start of 1983 the SDP/Liberal Alliance was still stuck in the opinion polls. What rather unfortunately became known as the 'Alliance re-launch' was held in January. Originally envisaged as being in the Albert Hall, it took place more modestly in Central Hall Westminster. Despite the splendid singing of the Aberystwyth male voice choir we made little impression on the television news bulletins. The press gave us little coverage either for the London or the regional meetings. One opinion poll even put us down below 20 per cent, at 19 per cent.

Then fate served us a good turn. Bob Mellish, who had offered to make way for Shirley earlier, resigned creating the Bermondsey by-election. Bermondsey had been Labour for over sixty years but now the Labour vote was split since a friend of Bob Mellish's ran independently from the official Labour candidate. Simon Hughes fought an excellent traditional Liberal community politics by-election campaign, but it was a campaign which was Labour's to lose and they lost it. Peter Tatchell, a Labour Left-winger was a totally unsuitable candidate, never likely to win the sympathy of Bermondsey council tenants. Simon Hughes won in February 1983 with a 44 per cent swing from Labour to the Liberal/SDP Alliance. It looked as if we might be back on the road to recovery when another by-election got under way at Darlington. Here the SDP was fighting the seat and had chosen Tony Cook, a regional TV interviewer, who was extremely well known. This time, however, Labour put up a tailor-made candidate for that constituency, Ossie O'Brien. The SDP campaign was a disaster from beginning to end. We had started with an opinion poll showing a 2 per cent lead. Bill Rodgers and Ian Wrigglesworth as northern MPs took responsibility for the campaign, but somehow Tony Cook, who was after all a professional, managed to blow even his television appearances. We came third and Labour held the seat. In some ways this was not, however, really a Labour gain. It was widely felt that if Labour had lost, Michael Foot would have resigned by the end of March and been replaced by Denis Healey which would have meant a huge improvement in their popularity at the general election. So perhaps Darlington should properly be recorded as a Conservative victory, keeping Michael Foot in place and stopping any possible SDP/Liberal Alliance bandwagon.

On Thursday 7 April Debbie was attending the London Book Fair and staying up in London alone. Her father had just had a heart by-pass operation and all seemed to go well. Tragically, he died the day after the operation and Debbie was rung up by her brother in the early hours. She rang me next morning at Buttermere where I was looking after the three children over the Easter holiday and by that afternoon all five of us were flying over the Atlantic to comfort the other members of the family and prepare for the funeral. It is enriching to have a family with dual nationality and I was always determined that the children should never lose the feeling of being Americans. Their Grandpa was an important figure in their lives. It was very strange to be back on Long Island without him around the house. Not to have him with us any more on trips in the old Second World War Jeep with the kids down to the harbour, or when sailing in his boat, or on fishing trips which seemed to end up with everyone catching a large blue fish. It was his energy that was so striking; playing tennis with his wife, Mickey, they were still able to beat Debbie and me. It was, nevertheless, typical of him to decide that it was worth risking the operation going wrong rather than to go on living but declining into inactivity. His passing left an unfillable hole in our family life. We had said our goodbyes much earlier for he had came over for Christmas at Buttermere and we had discussed the risks of the operation then. He had not wanted Debbie to come over for it. Burying him next to Debbie's mother was hard for her and I was glad we were all with her.

On our return it was all too obvious that with Michael Foot strengthened in office it was only the Alliance which still had a leadership question to answer. We had to decide when to announce that Roy was going to lead us or, as it was rather portentously and very revealingly expressed, become the Prime Minister designate. For months David Steel had delayed making the inevitable announcement and it was clear why. David Penhaligon, who understood polls, was incensed that there should be any question of endorsing Roy when there was such an obvious discrepancy in their respective appeal. A MORI poll in February had shown that 52 per cent of Alliance supporters wanted David Steel to lead and only 30 per cent Roy Jenkins. Among the whole electorate David had 46 per cent satisfied with his leadership whereas Roy had only 26 per cent. The most sensitive finding of all was that even SDP supporters had a higher regard for David Steel than Roy Jenkins in every respect other than that of experience. In March a MORI poll in the *Sunday Times* showed 52 per cent of voters preferring David Steel as Alliance Leader while only 14 per cent preferred Roy. These findings sat very uncomfortably with David Steel's private agreement with Roy. Shirley Williams was thought to have jumped the gun when she told the SDP Scottish Conference at the end of February that Roy Jenkins would be Prime Minister if the Alliance won and that David Steel had accepted this; but she was only revealing what we all knew had already been agreed between the two of them.

The Liberals were not happy. David Penhaligon stated on television that he thought David Steel should be chosen to lead the Alliance. At the end of March a joint meeting of MPs agreed that an announcement about a single leader would not be made until the eve of a general election and in the meantime the joint leadership should be promoted. In the middle of April Brian Walden, writing in the *Standard*, 'Two heads are better than one', anticipated that David Steel would wait until the Prime Minister named the date of the general election and then, with all the insouciance he could muster, mention that Roy Jenkins was getting the job. With no time to debate the choice in the heat of battle, the Liberals would hopefully be too preoccupied to make much fuss.

Apart from David Penhaligon, who actually went to see Roy to persuade him to stand down, there was also concern in the SDP. The Trustees of the Party, David Sainsbury and Sir Leslie Murphy, came to see me near the end of April to discuss how Roy could be moved aside. Both were convinced he was a disaster. I had to tell them that I was the last person who could do anything. David Sainsbury had voted for Roy but now regretted it. Leslie Murphy had voted for me.

As the election approached, the inevitable happened and Roy became the Prime Minister designate with David Steel called 'Leader of the campaign'. For parties which were by then facing a very difficult election, it was a dismal solution, but short of Roy Jenkins magnanimously standing down there was nothing any of us could do. Those who believed a single leader was essential had had their way, the breakthrough strategy was still being followed and we had handicapped ourselves before we started.

There was one bridgehead I would not ignore. Devonport had previously been marginal, but this election promised to be the toughest I had ever fought, for it had now become, as a result of boundary changes, on paper, a safe Labour seat. I was determined to win and to demonstrate that the Labour voters who had supported me in past elections would stay with me as a Social Democrat. Up and down the country for the last two years Michael Foot had regularly promised his audience, to shouts of joy, that one thing he could assure them, I would lose in Devonport. Not only was I intent on proving him wrong, but I was determined not to be thrown on the defensive. I would campaign as a national leader and not hole up in my constituency. But I knew I would also cut myself loose from the attitudes of the Alliance and attack Labour's policies.

28

ELECTION 1983

Thirty MPs had bravely put their careers on the line to create the SDP. In May 1983 they learned that in a month's time they would face the electorate for the ultimate test. Each of us knew that the omens were not good and that we might lose seats that, in many cases, we had held for more than a decade. Strangely, this did not make me reconsider my decision to campaign outside Plymouth. Unless the SDP/Liberal Alliance polled more than 25 per cent overall I knew I would be very vulnerable in Devonport, so campaigning nationally would also help in my constituency. I was assisted by the fact that in Plymouth the *Evening Herald* and *Western Morning News* had a long tradition of scrupulously giving all candidates the same space. I could obtain this coverage with press releases whether or not I was in Plymouth and by flitting in and out I could give the appearance that I was present more than I actually was. What I needed was a plane. Fortunately Richard Ford, an SDP member, had his own small four-seater Piper Aztec and he generously put it at my disposal for the entire campaign. Sometimes Richard flew it himself, and since he had only just learnt to fly, there were a few bumpy rides. But fortunately for my stomach – since I find being tossed around in a small plane worse than being at sea in a storm – more often than not the plane was skilfully piloted by Vicky Buxton. So mine was to be a guerrilla campaign while I would also be available to do anything that Roy Jenkins asked me to do. Despite being available, I did not expect to be asked to play a big part in the national campaign. This proved to be the case.

The Friday after Margaret Thatcher announced the election I went to Plymouth and started to plan my local campaign. This was quite unlike any other election I had ever fought. In the past I had been able to rely on the Labour Party, but in the last two years I had had to create my own party machine. My agent was Mick Quick, owner of a small boat-building business in Kingsbridge, who had virtually abandoned it for the last few months to help me. He was an archetypal SDP member, having never been involved in politics before. He was enthusiastic and everyone liked him. Will Fitzgerald and Barbara Furzeman, who had respectively been Chairman and Secretary of the Devonport Labour Party provided the experience. Will had been adopted as the SDP candidate for Drake and had taken time off from his job so he virtually worked full-time, living with his parents in Plymouth. He was totally unselfish and, seeing the council election results which projected an easy Labour win in Devonport, and a local opinion poll which had me running third, he proposed that we should virtually ignore Drake and concentrate all our effort on Devonport. It was the obvious thing to do but the obvious is by no means always performed. I shall always be grateful for this gesture of friendship. Ruth Sweetland, the wife of my former professional Labour Party agent, Alf Sweetland, was also a tower of strength. Alf was now retired and wisely stayed out of the campaign, but Ruth who had been a secretary in the Regional Labour Party offices, had plenty of experience of her own, and organized the council house estates in the north of the constituency where she had previously lived. Another key helper was Tim Brampton who walked in to our headquarters off the streets one day, offered to help and virtually took over the responsibility for my election address. He was still serving as a nurse in the Navy and he and his wife had a young baby, but together they put in formidable hours. We took as our headquarters a big old sail loft in the Barbican with stunning views of Sutton Harbour. It was in Drake constituency and not Devonport, but since we were running the campaigns in tandem it made sense to concentrate our volunteers in one place and to organize canvassing and deliveries on a ward basis. Fortunately in every ward there were people who had been active in politics, not all by any means in the Labour Party, who came almost out of nowhere to volunteer their time and experience. We were grateful for every volunteer, however inexperienced. But the campaign was not a slick, sophisticated effort.

Even before the campaign started, it suffered a bad blow. I had two assistants at the time in the House of Commons office and one of them, Sandra Brenner, moved down for the whole campaign and became the lynchpin of the Plymouth end. This was a tremendous responsibility for her as it had always been envisaged that Maggie Smart, the head of the office, would be in Plymouth too. Unfortunately that Friday she had gone into Westminster hospital for an operation for early breast cancer and it looked as if she would be out of the campaign completely.

On that first Sunday I returned to London for a campaign meeting in the National Liberal Club. The theme of the campaign was still that we should be the next government of the country, Roy the Prime Minister, and that we were equally critical of the Conservatives and Labour. I knew by now that there was no point in wasting my breath in trying to persuade them that this was a nonsensical stance. I had tried for months to stand on one issue – Labour was unfit not only to govern but to be the official Opposition; we were now the only credible Opposition and

Labour should be sidelined. I could see that I was not going to persuade Roy or David Steel to take this tack and I resigned myself to being left out of the decision loop. I would, I thought, find it very difficult to establish even a small place on a campaign with whose strategy I disagreed so profoundly. Then surprisingly, things changed.

Maggie Smart, now out of hospital, came in to tell me that she would be having radiotherapy treatment every day for six weeks. I was very upset for she had become a trusted friend. Then she told me she had talked it over with her husband and had decided that she wanted to be involved in the campaign. It would take her mind off the treatment she thought. So, suddenly, what had appeared to be a disaster became an opportunity. She had worked with me ever since I had first become Foreign Secretary, and could make decisions on my behalf even when I could not be contacted. Without her constant presence in Cowley Street we should never have been able to achieve half of what we did. She worked very closely with Roger Carroll, the SDP's Head of Communications, during the entire campaign. She just walked the hundred yards from Cowley Street to the Westminster hospital every day for thirty minutes' radiotherapy and luckily had no side-effects. She always claimed that it was the best thing possible for her because it never gave her time to think of herself. She made a complete recovery, later had her first child, and still works for me.

I travelled back to Plymouth by sleeper for the opening constituency press conference. The press were like a pack of wolves. They had scented the end of 'Dr Death'. I decided that false confidence would be a mistake. The best strategy was to be perfectly frank, admit that I was lying third in the local poll and put the issue straight to the electorate in Plymouth; they had my political life in their hands. Instead of trying to dismiss that poll as being of no significance, I promoted it, wanting people to know that I was facing the political battle of my life.

My national campaign began late that afternoon. I flew to Heathrow, where Debbie met me, and we drove to the Oxford Union where I spoke in support of Evan Luard, who had been a junior Minister with me in the Foreign Office. Evan urged me to follow my instincts and attack the Labour Party. He was a mild man with no natural aggression so I knew his advice represented a calculated political judgement. As we drove to London where I was appearing on *Newsnight*, Debbie and I decided that we risked nothing by fighting a distinctive campaign to raise the profile of the SDP within the Alliance. Otherwise we were all going to sink without trace.

In my campaign, I resolved I would present the electorate with the truth about Michael Foot's Labour Party and not make a foolish attempt to argue that Margaret Thatcher's party was just as bad. Fortunately, the Conservatives soon presented us with a theme enabling us to persuade fleeing Labour voters not to run into the arms of the Conservatives.

It happened early in the campaign when I went on *Question Time* with Francis Pym and Roy Hattersley.

Pym, Foreign Secretary at the time, quietly interjected what was to prove, for him, a fatal phrase. 'Landslides', he said, 'on the whole, do not produce successful governments.' Margaret Thatcher was furious at what she regarded as his impertinence. The next morning she said witheringly at her press conference, 'I think I can handle a landslide all right.' She had always disliked Francis Pym and that was mutual. She had only made him Foreign Secretary at the emotion-charged moment when Peter Carrington finally rejected all her entreaties to stay on after the invasion of the Falkland Islands. To him she was below the salt; to her he was a snob. His explanation for the Conservative troubles was 'we've got a corporal at the top, not a cavalry officer'. On the day after the election she summoned him to No. 10, saying 'Francis, I want a new Foreign Secretary', and peremptorily sacked him.

Often those present entirely miss the significance of political turning-points. The prospect of a landslide provided the only serious anti-Conservative campaign issue. The advantage of a general election is that it often peels off the veneer. Seeing Margaret Thatcher chair the Conservative press conferences, journalists could feel that her Cabinet must be almost a session of the Spanish Inquisition. The way she humiliated, patronized and even bullied grown men at these conferences was all too revealing. I seemed almost the only politician who did not mind admitting that there was a danger of a Conservative landslide, so when I spoke I obtained a very receptive audience in the press.

The morning after Pym's mistake, as Margaret Thatcher was responding in London, I left by train for Doncaster where I picked up the SDP bus. It was a very uncomfortable vehicle: nothing seemed to work on it and what was particularly frustrating was that the mobile telephone was useless. This meant I had to keep stopping the bus at a public telephone, ring Maggie in Cowley Street to hear the latest news and dictate any instant reaction or press release. Fighting for my political life as I was, I felt a little as Hubert Humphrey must have felt in 1960 as he bumped along to defeat in his little bus and watched his Democratic Primary rival, Jack Kennedy, soar by in his luxury airplane. Things were not helped by the fact that I felt dreadful, with an acute gastric upset. I dealt with it by frequent swigs from a bottle of kaolin and morphine.

Roger Carroll was desperate for news to give hungry reporters and when we arrived in Grimsby Town Hall by way of Hull I unleashed a pretty savage attack on the Labour Party. I had grown increasingly angry at the way the SDP/Liberal Alliance campaign had been pussy-footing around over the defence issue, pulling our punches for fear of upsetting Liberal CND activists instead of continually attacking Labour's defence policy. I was increasingly campaigning nationwide as a guerrilla, paying scant regard to the absurd emphasis on forming a government when

everyone knew that we would be hard pressed even to form a
parliamentary party. I compared the Labour Party manifesto with that of
the Communist Party:

> The similarities between the Labour Party and Communist Manifesto
> are uncanny. In many crucial sections it is not just the policy, but the
> wording, which is the same. No incomes policy; withdraw from the
> European Community; no to cruise; cancel Trident; close US bases;
> cut arms spending; extend nationalization; compulsory planning agree-
> ments; repeal anti-trade union laws. No wonder the *Morning Star*
> acclaimed Labour's manifesto. No wonder the Communist manifesto
> urges people to vote Labour where Communists are not standing . . .
> Michael Foot visits Moscow but he has not visited Washington for
> thirty years. The General Secretary of the Labour Party, during an
> election period, writes to Mr Andropov to explain Labour Party
> defence policy. He need not have bothered. Moscow is only too well
> aware of what Labour Party policy is.

Meanwhile, of course, the Plymouth fight continued. On Monday, after a
weekend tour of Cornwall, I was out in David Astor's Land-Rover with
loudspeaker and posters saying 'David Owen Again' to show as many
people as possible that I was not taking them or their vote for granted.
David is Nancy Astor's nephew and had been an active member of the
SDP from the start. He canvassed day after day on the council estates.
He was a prosperous farmer and venture capitalist in the City, but he had
not only inherited the Astor name – he had Nancy's political genes in
him. Nancy Astor had been a legendary campaigner speaking to the
fishermen down in the market off the back of a lorry and liking nothing
better than the heckling which allowed her to respond like a fishwife. In
West Country parlance David 'went down a treat' on the doorsteps. He
made many good friends among my old Labour Party workers, showing
he had no side or stuffiness, and when Drake came to choose a new
parliamentary candidate to fight the 1987 Election he was a natural
choice. It was good to have an Astor with us in the SDP to add style and
substance to the Plymouth campaign which was now picking up
momentum, and I began to think I would be able to hold on.

After speaking on the Monday in Southampton and Portsmouth, I
returned to London and slept at Narrow Street so that the next morning
I was ready to give a joint press conference with Liberal MP Richard
Wainwright. Given the resonance of the landslide issue, I felt it was time
to concentrate my attack on Margaret Thatcher and what I called
'rampant Thatcherism'. I likened her to a 'Queen Bee', unstoppable
unless there was a strong Opposition to curb her. I warned that the
'drones' were on the way out, 'Lord Carrington has been sacrificed, Mr
Prior banished, Mr Walker by-passed, Mr Whitelaw put down and Mr
Pym admonished.'

But the true issue was Labour. Next morning I flew in my small plane from Birmingham/Coventry airport to Plymouth, ready to take part in a down-the-line interview on the *Jimmy Young Show* with Michael Heseltine and John Silkin. The internal Labour Party wrangle over nuclear defence was now in full spate. On the previous day the headlines had been 'LABOUR TO DISPEL POLARIS CONFUSION' (*Guardian*), and 'FOOT FAILS TO HEAL RIFT WITH HEALEY OVER NUCLEAR POLICY' (*The Times*). Now the headlines were 'LABOUR TOTTERS ON THE BRINK OVER NUCLEAR POLICY' (*Guardian*) and 'FOOT AND HEALEY IN BIG SPLIT OVER NUKES' (*Sun*). *The Times* had a particularly damaging story alleging that Denis Healey had vetoed any possibility of Michael Foot's making a firm, unqualified pledge that Britain's Polaris nuclear deterrent would be phased out by a Labour Government. John Silkin did his best to try and pretend that there was no difference between Denis Healey and Michael Foot. Everybody knew, however, that while Denis was trying to give the impression that Labour would negotiate, Michael would simply ban all nuclear weapons immediately. In some newspapers there was also a hint of even bigger trouble to come with the revelation that Jim Callaghan was due to speak on nuclear matters in Penarth that night. Neil Kinnock had also entered the controversy with an unequivocal statement supporting Michael Foot's line that Polaris would be scrapped.

I said that 'Labour's weasel words on the defence of Britain must stop.' I suppose that this was permissible humbug because of course I did not want the Labour row to stop at all. Nothing would do us more good than emphasis on this issue. It would help the Conservatives too, but the most important thing for us was that it was the best differentiating issue between Labour and the SDP. Michael Foot had trifled with Britain's national security, I claimed, and it was about time he levelled with the British people. 'Labour's defence policy began as an organized hypocrisy, now it has become a disorganized deception.' My boot was going in and starting to leave its mark.

That night in Penarth Jim Callaghan fully demonstrated why I had been right to leave the Labour Party in 1981. You can have private reservations about a manifesto but it is devastating if a prominent figure in a political party publicly disowns a major manifesto commitment during an election. It can be argued that if Jim Callaghan felt he had to act as he did then he really should not have stood as a Labour candidate at that election. As Ian Aitken described it in the *Guardian* 'the former Labour Prime Minister took the unprecedented step of repudiating the defence policy of his own party in the middle of a general election campaign. He made it clear that he will have nothing to do with unilateral nuclear disarmament.' If I had fought as a Labour candidate in Plymouth in that election, as many people both before and since have argued that I should have done, I would have had to make the same speech as Jim Callaghan and, although it would not have had the same public impact, it too would have done considerable damage to Labour nationally. In Jim's case I believe he really had tried to be loyal but just could not keep quiet. I doubt he ever intended to speak out as he did when he decided to fight another election and be the Father of the House of Commons. But, quite apart from his own deep-seated patriotism, with his overseas friendships I suspect he could not face Gerald Ford, Helmut Schmidt and Giscard d'Estaing if he had said nothing. What is the honourable course? Shut up, put up, or get out! Certainly, the most prudent course when you disagree so fundamentally with central planks of policy that you cannot be silent is to leave. But Jim Callaghan had to stay, there could be no question of him leaving Labour and, given his circumstances, the honourable course was to speak out when Michael Foot, who had been given every opportunity, still refused to give up his unilateralism.

Margaret Thatcher used to argue that the Gang of Four should have stayed supporting Labour and struggled from within. Nothing could have suited the Conservatives better than to have our voices destroying the credibility of the Labour Party while not challenging the Conservatives by being able to take their voters. In my circumstances I will always believe that the honourable course was to leave. I personally felt far better and cleaner fighting Labour's defence and foreign policy in 1983 and 1987 from outside the party. I avoided having to nominally fight to elect Labour as the Government while at the same time desperately hoping it did not obtain the power to fulfil its election pledges.

The press had a field day with Jim Callaghan's speech. 'CALLAGHAN IN ARMS REVOLT' was the headline in the *Daily Mirror*. 'CALLAGHAN WRECKS POLARIS REPAIRS' (*Guardian*); 'CALLAGHAN'S BOMBSHELL' (*Daily Mail*) and 'CALLAGHAN'S BOMB SHOCK FOR LABOUR' (*Daily Star*). If the Labour Party had ever had a chance – which it did not – this was a blow from which it could not recover. Michael Foot was bitter with Jim, but I reflected that in January 1981, Michael had tried to persuade me to stay in the Labour Party and told me I would be free to speak out. He had not answered when I had asked whether that included speaking out in a general election period.

I now became increasingly convinced that I could hold Plymouth Devonport by taking thousands of votes that had previously gone to Labour. I decided that I would help this along by choosing my moment and exposing Michael Foot's abdication from any involvement on nuclear matters when he and I were both Labour Cabinet ministers.

I met David Steel for a chat and a photocall outside the BBC studios in Plymouth that Wednesday. The pictures of him, Debbie and me smiling together made good television, but they were only a front for a deeply serious conversation. David told me that he had told Roy at the London press conference that morning that he thought there should be a change in the leadership of the Alliance. He had asked Roy to bow out, leaving David the Prime Minister designate. The opinion poll evidence supporting such a move had been building up. An Audience Selection poll for TV-am the day before, giving the Conservatives 45 per cent, Labour 32 per cent and the Alliance at 20 per cent, had shown that if David Steel were Prime Minister designate the Conservatives would have had 42 per cent, the Alliance would have moved to second place at 29 per cent and Labour third at 28 per cent. Our current level of support was alarming. If this evidence of the fillip we could get from making a change was even half-right, then the leadership issue had to concern SDP as well as Liberal candidates. Apparently Roy had said he would think about the suggestion but had told David that I would object to any change on the grounds that it would damage the SDP. My response to David was what it had been for months. The question of a single leader was a matter between him and Roy and I would agree to whatever they settled between them. I told him that if, and I stressed that it was a very big if, Roy was prepared to step down then that was fine by me and I would do nothing to stop it. But I also warned against believing that it would, of itself, produce a dramatic turnaround in the opinion polls. I did not think we would in reality achieve anything as dramatic as a jump from 20 per cent to 29 per cent. Nevertheless the addition of even one or two per cent was a bonus and might save some of the vulnerable SDP seats. There would, however, be no point in doing any switch if Roy was not prepared to sell it positively to the press. I agreed to let Jack Diamond know of our conversation since he was acting as the link between the Gang of Four and we would discuss it further in Bristol.

When I phoned Jack Diamond his immediate reaction was strongly against it: he thought it would backfire and the press would present it adversely, but he promised to let me know Roy's considered view before I met David Steel again. I thought hard about the problem over the next twenty-four hours. It was obvious that it had been a massive error to put Roy into this leadership role, but it was not as if we had not known. One of the issues the SDP always avoided discussing was that, in opinion poll after opinion poll, even before the Limehouse Declaration, Roy had not emerged as a popular figure. However, to make a switch in the middle of an election campaign was dicey. I felt the press would present it as a 'Steel knife-job' or as 'Roy leaving the sinking ship'. That said, what else could rescue our campaign?

On the day that David Steel had first spoken to me about his view of Roy's campaign I had been accompanied by Terry Coleman who was doing a profile for the *Guardian*. This came out a few days later headlined 'Mr Clean in a crumpled suit'. In the circumstances, its opening lines were ironic with me cheerfully asking before the meeting with David Steel 'Do you want to come and see the great political love-in?' Little did he know what had been discussed. He described Debbie canvassing as 'very American, a Long Island Yankee, who never gave up all day and is obviously worth six ordinary men. Very chic, too, in a yellow suit and black sweater.' It is true that she is a tireless and very effective canvasser who, when I am travelling during elections, has taken control of the Plymouth campaign but, without anyone realizing it, a skill which I regret she has not yet been able to pass on to her husband. He then described the second and last meeting of the day in a secondary school with an audience of seventy-seven.

> There was a bit of heckling. The chairman tried, in the modern manner, to suppress it, but Owen said no, let him answer, and he did. He answered all questions with an evident weight of knowledge, and did not once raise his voice or stray from the point put to him. He made the odd jibe at Labour. It wouldn't be human nature if he hadn't. But it was the most persuasive exposition of social democracy that I have heard, and an intellectually scrupulous statement of the election issues. A reporter next to me, who has covered many elections round the world, and who I think would not agree with much of what Owen was saying, said at the end that it was difficult not to break into spontaneous applause.

I value this tribute. I do believe that my constituency are entitled to respect and to be given the opportunity for serious debate. If they choose not to attend that is up to them, but they have the right to question their future MP and it is rare for journalists to attend or describe the personal encounter of a politician with their own constituency electors.

I followed this speech with a more controversial performance the next day. David Steel and I addressed an 'Ask the Alliance' rally in the Central Hall, Bristol. Although I was speaking off-the-cuff all the television cameras were there and so I decided to attack Michael Foot. What I said was reported prominently in the main TV News bulletins and summed up the next day in the press as 'FOOT NOT FIT TO BE PM SAYS OWEN'. I revealed how, when in Government, Michael Foot never once sat with the four senior Ministers who made the decisions on nuclear policy. It reflected my very strong view that a man who had deliberately avoided sharing responsibility before was not fit to take the sole responsibility now. Under Michael Foot, Labour would not have been fit to govern.

Just before I had spoken to the meeting, I had talked once more to Jack Diamond on the telephone. He told me that Roy, as I thought he would, had decided to stay on as Leader. Travelling back to London in David Steel's battlebus we discussed this response. David accepted that nothing could be done. Ousting Roy against his will was out of the question. He did, however, want to shift the focus away from Roy and build up his own role as campaign leader, so he was very keen that I should come up to Ettrick Bridge with Shirley to make his ordinary planned meeting with Roy look like an Alliance Summit with him in the chair. Although this was tricky to arrange, given my schedule, he offered to fly me from Norwich on a jet which he had been loaned.

The following day was one long reminder of what we were up against. Its highlight was a walkabout in Woolwich with John Cartwright in the late afternoon. This had been one of Labour's safest seats and yet John thought that he might just be able to hold on. Later, when I spoke in Lewisham for Polly Toynbee and in Islington for SDP MPs John Grant and George Cunningham, the position was not so good. George had come to us late but he was a man of granite-like integrity and a parliamentarian to his fingertips, the sort we would need in the struggle ahead. His election material made no bones about the Islington Labour Party – 'You'd have to be mad to vote Labour in Islington now.' Unfortunately it looked as if too many were. John Grant had to contend not only with a safe Labour seat but also with Michael O'Halloran who had become an SDP MP for a short time and was now standing as 'the Labour candidate', simply missing out 'party' on the ballot paper. John's election address had a rare tribute for an SDP candidate. It was from Frank Chapple, leader of the EETPU and TUC President, saying that John was 'the most courageous and outspoken fighter of extremism in the trade unions'. But despite the red flag over the Town Hall, a motion banning fox hunting in Islington of all places, nuclear free zoning, twinning with Grenada and licensed squatting, the signs were that both these excellent MPs would lose.

That afternoon Debbie had rung me to say that she was getting the feeling on the doorstep that I had been away from Plymouth too long. She urged me to come down. I did not hesitate for she was my eyes and ears. I took the sleeper and spent all Saturday morning touring shopping centres and the council estates before flying up to Cambridge for a public meeting in the early evening. Then I drove with Christopher Brocklebank-Fowler to Kings Lynn where we had a packed public meeting in the lovely old Town Hall. I spent that night at Christopher's home. He was very anxious about his seat. The consistent Conservative opinion poll lead was making it hard for him to pull over enough Conservatives, even though some of them were deeply disillusioned. We were, he felt, just not credible to them; they did not like our close link with the Liberals. As we discussed the campaign we both concluded that Roy had to go immediately after the election. It would be brutal but we dare not wait more than a few days or he would use the inevitable anti-climatic mood to push for a merger. We both knew it would be hard to rally a demoralized SDP if he and David Steel acted to make it a virtual *fait accompli*. Christopher offered, whether he won or lost, to make a speech on the day after the election, saying it was time for Roy to step down.

Early on the Sunday morning, Christopher drove me to Norwich airport and I flew off to the so-called Ettrick Bridge summit in a plane belonging to Anthony Jacobs, the Head of the British School of Motoring. On the plane I read the Sunday newspapers. The *Sunday Times* headline was 'ALLIANCE STORM OVER JENKINS'S LEADERSHIP'. What had been private was now public. 'Roy Jenkins was at the centre of a web of intrigue inside the SDP/Liberal Alliance last night over his future as Prime Minister designate in an Alliance Government.' It said that Roy dismissed the report as 'absolute nonsense', with David Steel saying 'the subject is not on the agenda' but, the report continued,

> in spite of the denials there is no doubt about the dissatisfaction of Liberals and the intention of key figures to have Jenkins's position placed at the top of today's Summit agenda at Steel's home. They argue privately that this is essential if the Alliance is to take off from its present opinion poll groove of around 20 per cent and overtake Labour.

It also quoted Alliance sources claiming that both Bill Rodgers and I had signalled our assent to a 'new look' leadership with David Steel at the top.

On the way John Pardoe told me that he was determined to raise the question of Roy's leadership but I warned him off, saying that this had already been ruled out. I also warned him that I knew Roy well enough to predict his reaction. When his personal position is concerned he fights dirty. To corner him is the worst possible tactic. Far better to leave it to private pressure. We flew across to Speke Airport in Liverpool to collect Shirley Williams and then, when we arrived at Edinburgh airport ready to transfer to a helicopter, we found dense fog. So we hired a car and John Pardoe drove Shirley, Jack Diamond and me to Ettrick Bridge. I felt pretty car-sick on the twisty winding roads and we arrived far later than if we had taken a helicopter. Coming late to David's house we had to start the meeting around his dining room table straight away. Roy and David were due to brief the press, and the TV news people were anxious to get their film back for the early evening bulletins. At the meeting John Pardoe weighed in on the leadership question and, to my surprise, was supported robustly by David, despite what he had said to me coming back from Bristol. I tried to change the subject, saying that this issue could only be resolved by the two leaders together privately and we had enough to discuss in terms of electoral strategy. David persisted, with extreme toughness, saying he owed it to Liberal Party candidates to raise the issue again. Roy said he had thought it through carefully and felt it was not in the interests of the Alliance for him to step down. Shirley strongly defended him, as did Bill, but all the Liberals wanted a change.

It was an unpleasant meeting and I felt some sympathy for Roy who was obviously deeply embarrassed. We should have discussed this issue frankly months before but it had always seemed too sensitive to raise. And, after our leadership contest, I was the one person who was in no position to raise it. Public opinion on this crucial issue was well known but we had just ignored it. Stepping aside might have cost Roy the

Hillhead seat. Nevertheless if he had been prepared to sacrifice his personal position and enthusiastically endorse David I have no doubt that there would have been some electoral return – perhaps as much as ten to fifteen extra seats.

The meeting broke up with very little else of substance discussed and Shirley, Bill and I drove to Berwick-on-Tweed to pick up a train to London. The fog had cleared, it was a lovely drive and, although we were all tired, we were relaxed. Bill, I think, knew he was going to lose, Shirley was very worried and I was far from certain that I was going to win. But there were no recriminations as we re-lived the last three years from the moment in June 1980 when we had first got together as the Gang of Three. I look back on this now as the last truly happy time that we all had together. We were all three committed Social Democrats. We had had our arguments and differences but we were friends. Our next meeting would be on the Monday after the election. Both of them would have lost their seats and we were never again to recapture the comradeship of those years as 'The Gang of Three'. Looking back I blame myself. Losing their seats was a personal blow and, since neither wanted to get a job which would mean giving up standing at the next election, I should have done far more to keep open communication.

I opened the newspapers on Monday morning full of apprehension but, to my relief, no one had really picked up the row that had taken place around David Steel's dining room table. The general impression the press had of Ettrick Bridge was that David Steel had been given greater prominence. It was not written up as an attempted assassination. The television coverage on Sunday night had even looked pretty good – a relaxed group; friendly politicians being nice to each other!

Shirley came down to Plymouth and then I went up to Crosby. The next morning an opinion poll in the *Sun* showed us only 4 per cent behind Labour, with the Conservatives at 44 per cent, Labour 29 per cent and the Alliance 25 per cent. But there was better to come. The story of the day was Denis Healey's extraordinary outburst the previous evening that Margaret Thatcher after the Falklands was 'glorying in slaughter'. As Shirley and I were driving to the BBC studios for a *Today* interview, she used the word 'abattoir' about Denis's speech. I asked if she minded if I purloined it for my interview. She agreed, so I was able to produce probably the most quoted of all my remarks in the election: 'Mr Healey has moved from the politics of the gutter to the politics of the abattoir.' Everywhere I went that day I continued to twist the knife and every time I rang our HQ I was amazed to discover Denis had still not apologized. The story was running hard as I campaigned in Liverpool that morning and was still running when I arrived by plane in Newcastle in the afternoon to be met by Mike Thomas and John Horam. In Wallsend shopping centre and then on a walkabout in Newcastle the reaction of the average Geordie was unequivocal. 'Give 'im 'ell David', they called out, and the ''im' was Denis. For a few hours I thought Labour's vote would collapse. Denis was still holding out according to the journalists who were following me around when I spoke in Newcastle and again in Blyth Valley. Only when I got back to the BBC studios in Newcastle to record a *Newsnight* interview did I hear that Denis had finally made half a climbdown, saying he regretted using the word 'slaughter'. The whole episode did much harm to the Labour Party.

The Gallup poll on Friday 3 June showed the Alliance had gained 5 per cent. The Conservatives now had 47.5 per cent, Labour 28 per cent, and the Alliance 23 per cent. Our leadership problem remained. And it was clear from this poll that David Steel was a far more popular leader than Roy, with approval ratings of 71 per cent to 29 per cent. Even more worrying for us was that people were asked if they had seen each party leader on television and if so whether they felt it had increased support for their respective party or not. Again David did very much better.

At the Alliance London press conference I played once more on the threat of a landslide, saying that the Orwellian horror of Big Brother was being replaced by a fear of Big Sister. It would be a disaster for this country to give totally unconstrained power to Margaret Thatcher. But faced with Michael Foot most people preferred the devil they knew. I flew to Plymouth, campaigned all day there and David Steel arrived for an 'Ask the Alliance' West Country rally, wittily chaired by Steve Race. David had a filthy cold and the strain of the campaign was showing. He asked what I could prescribe and I said a large brandy. I feared that the big hall would not be full but it turned out to be one of our best meetings and I was grateful to him for coming. His schedule was more horrendous than mine.

I needed to concentrate on Plymouth now. I stepped up my efforts to convince reluctant Tories to switch to the Alliance, since the polls showed that a staggering 40 per cent of those planning to vote Conservative were doing so just out of fear of Labour. We needed to show that it was inconceivable that there could be a Labour Government, and capitalize on their secondary fear – that of a Tory landslide. The problem was that this undermined the Steel-Jenkins strategy for it tacitly acknowledged that the Tories were going to win. The Alliance stance, forlornly pretending we could win, was pathetic. But despite these concerns, my confidence began to rise that we would win in Plymouth. That evening, at our traditional Question and Answer session organized by Devonport Methodists for all the candidates, I could sense the tide turning my way. My two opponents were both able people but they sounded as if they knew they were losing. Nationally, too, the *Sunday Mirror* had had a sensational poll showing that we had nosed ahead of Labour, with the Conservatives on 44 per cent, the Alliance on 27.5 per cent and Labour on 27 per cent.

I campaigned all day Monday and most of Tuesday in Plymouth. The dockyard 'mateys' would say spontaneously outside the main gate in the early morning 'You're doing well, boy' or 'Good on you, David' and I knew I was home and dry when the bookies' odds moved heavily in my favour, though I suspected David Astor was doing some insider dealing!

The atmosphere surrounding my national campaign is best caught by Edward Steen of the *Sunday Telegraph* who hitched a lift with us when we flew to Leeds on the Tuesday evening:

> 'Four of us?' demanded the blonde pilot, the Hon. and charming Vicky Buxton (sister, it turned out of Cindy, the South Georgia castaway). 'I was only expecting David. I've got a full fuel load. Oh well . . .' she said tolerantly. The flight would be turbulent: a question of electric storms.
>
> We rolled out on to the runway. The Piper four-seater sounded like a Portuguese taxi, anno 1936. Vicky mentioned something about cracks and oil. 'It'll be a rough run, till it burns itself out.' Dr Owen was unperturbed, as befits a man of destiny. Then, suddenly, the engine roared more vigorously, and we vanished into the clouds. Owen's sister and temporary minder Sue Mumford – usefully, a psychiatric social worker – knitted furiously to calm her nerves.
>
> Storms raged, as promised. I wanted a cigarette: knitting makes me jumpy. Mrs Mumford offered Polo mints. Dr Owen relaxed. He slumbered over the Bristol Channel, then studied a short, powerful, and disconcertingly truthful speech on the NHS that he had run up in the last twenty minutes at his Plymouth constituency HQ.
>
> It is the third floor of an Elizabethan warehouse under conversion, decorated with images of Owen's saturnine good looks, requests not to smoke and a malicious cartoon about Roy Jenkins.
>
> Over Wales we tried to shout a conversation. (The engine was going fine.) Owen yelled a few good-humoured remarks about putting the boot into the BBC over alleged suppression of a poll showing the SDP at second place – 'all part of the political badinage'.

After this flight, I felt distinctly queasy when I arrived at Yorkshire TV studios late on Tuesday evening. Edna and Denis Healey were both there and were incredibly kind. Given what I had said about Denis and the abbatoir they would have been entitled to ostracize me but Edna was worrying about whether I could win. I took a healthy swig of medicinal brandy to settle my stomach and went in for the programme which started at 10.40 p.m. We were well into the programme and as Geoffrey Howe answered a question I fell asleep. I woke up to see Jonathan Dimbleby looking straight at me, having clearly just asked me something. I mumbled vaguely that it was all very difficult and I was not sure I had any specific view on the matter! I felt a complete idiot for the rest of the programme but afterwards, when we were relaxing over drinks, no one remarked on it. When I asked my sister and a few other people whether one of my answers had seemed slightly off the point, they said they had not noticed anything amiss. As my daughter Lucy always tells me, politics is b-o-o-ring and most people do not listen to every word on a TV programme, just absorb a general impression.

I flew down next morning to Plymouth and concentrated on collecting the last few votes. My campaign team had done wonders in my absence and Debbie had as usual proved herself a formidable campaigner. It had been a difficult campaign at the start, with jeers and shouts of traitor. But by the end even the most ardent Labour activist no longer had the gall to call me a traitor, not least because my response was so savage and full of contempt.

I wish I could say that nationally we did ourselves justice. The BBC captured the essence of the campaign by asking the three party leaders: 'Would you push the nuclear button?' Roy Jenkins prevaricated: 'I find it difficult to believe the situation would arise.' Michael Foot was obdurate: 'It would be utter criminal insanity for anyone to say they would press the button.' Margaret Thatcher considered the alternative: 'If we don't say we will press the button the Russians would sweep over Europe and us with conventional forces.' In all the hours of debate, those words on this crucial defence issue clarified the attitudes of the parties more than anything else. I vowed that never again would I go through an election campaign with a defence policy so lacking in conviction. Nuclear defence had been the dominant issue in the view of most commentators.

The *Daily Mail* summed up the campaign as the measure of one woman's ascendancy and of one party's collapse. They were sympathetic to our attempt to fill the democratic vacuum between a Tory Prime Minister in her prime and socialism in decline. They said the voters wanted to believe in the Alliance but sensed 'that it is not enough in a rough world for those entrusted with government to be pleasant and accommodating. You need bottle.' They said, quite rightly, that we had fudged the Jenkins/Steel leadership, fudged the independent deterrent, fudged on private education, fudged on council house sales and on the central issue of the economy proposed a return to incomes policy and reflation. Ruefully I had to smile. I had left the Labour Party to finish with fudging and mudging.

Until we could sharpen our policies and develop a more populist appeal, the SDP/Liberal Alliance would neither bust nor deserve to bust the system let alone break the mould. The more the SDP looked like Liberals the better for both Labour and the Conservatives. The late surge in the opinion polls did much for our morale but not much for our eventual score. In the dying days of the campaign we were also helped by Neil Kinnock who managed to put his foot in it. A member of a TV audience had shouted: 'At least Mrs Thatcher has got guts,' and Kinnock had replied, 'It is a pity that people had to leave theirs on the ground in Goose Green to prove it.' Once again the Falklands was back in the headlines, which could only help the Conservatives and hinder Labour. This also raised questions about Neil Kinnock's judgement under pressure.

The general election was won overwhelmingly by the Conservative

Party with 397 seats. Labour had 209, the Liberals 17 and the SDP 6 MPs. For the Alliance as a whole the result was disappointing, though it represented a 6 per cent improvement for the Liberals on Jeremy Thorpe's February 1974 result. Because of the way the seats had been allocated, the SDP result was a predictable disaster. We had certainly not achieved the breakthrough, had not even, perhaps, established a bridgehead. Worse still, it was hard to imagine that we would ever again fight a Labour Party in quite such a dreadful state. Michael Foot had proved to be a worse leader even than the pacifist George Lansbury. Even the *Daily Mirror* and the *Guardian* were critical. He looked old, harassed and not up to the job of being Leader of the Opposition, let alone Prime Minister. Gerald Kaufman called their manifesto the 'longest suicide note in history'. Yet even so the SDP's parliamentary force had been decimated. For its 27.6 per cent of the vote Labour got 32 per cent of the seats. The Alliance having 25.4 per cent of the vote got only 3.5 per cent of the seats, twenty-three out of the 650 in the House of Commons. Of the SDP six, Ian Wrigglesworth had only just scraped home. If his Conservative rival had not been discovered to be a member of the National Front, so that Keith Joseph refused to speak in his support, we could well have been only five. Our only new MP was Charles Kennedy who won Ross, Cromarty and Skye – a natural Liberal seat which Bob Maclennan had managed to squeeze out of the Liberals late in the Scottish seat negotiations. Charles came into the House of Commons at the age of twenty-three and now as a Liberal Democrat has a very good chance of holding the seat for as long as he wishes. He may even become their Leader.

Labour lost 120 deposits, showing how badly they had done in many parts of the country and how concentrated was their support in their safe seats. The SDP lost seven deposits. After many years of losing deposits in large numbers, the Liberals only lost five, the same number as the Conservative Party. On average in our 312 seats, the SDP added 12.4 per cent to the 1979 Liberal vote, while in their 322 seats the Liberals put on 10.4 per cent. Part of the reason for the SDP's slightly better performance was that twenty-two of our former MPs, who were fighting seats containing a substantial part of their old constituency and did not face Liberal opposition, added 20.1 per cent on average to the Liberal base, polling 31.8 per cent of the vote. But even so twenty-four former SDP MPs lost their seats and I felt both anguished and in part responsible. Also in truth by the time of the election the public saw little difference between the SDP and Liberal candidates, a fate which we had willed on ourselves.

Some people believed that if the Alliance had managed to squeeze ahead of Labour in the popular vote it would have transformed the political situation. We would, these people argue, then have had greater legitimacy when we challenged the distorted representation of the first-past-the-post voting system. I disagree. Of course it would have been better to have beaten Labour in the popular vote but, after a few months, with Labour the Official Opposition in the House of Commons, we would have seen that nothing much had changed. With all the official Opposition's Front Bench speaking rights and their right to have their amendments called by the Speaker in preference to the other parties, I believe the old familiar pattern of British politics would have been re-established. In any case, the Conservatives, who under Baldwin had done so much to establish two-party politics in the 1920s and 1930s, would certainly have helped Labour reassert their position. Time and time again, that conspiracy of interest between the two old class-based parties came together to squeeze the Alliance as they had always squeezed the Liberals. But we had helped them do so by looking like the Liberals.

What the 1983 Election should have achieved was an SDP Parliamentary Party as big as if not bigger than the Liberal Party. It was our own fault that we did not ensure it. This had been the moment for the SDP to establish a bridgehead by smashing into the Labour Party and it was the SDP which should have won some of the most vulnerable Labour seats, not the Conservatives. It was a loss to politics that so many MPs of courage and calibre had gone and what was even more tragic was that most even the younger ones would never return to the House of Commons.

All of us in the Gang of Four had a heavy responsibility for the personal trauma that underlay those losses and none of us should pretend otherwise. What promised so much that day two-and-a-half years before in Limehouse was unrecognizable now in the shadow of defeat. I knew in Plymouth on the day after the election following what *The Times* called a 'strong national campaign and outstanding personal victory', that the torch would fall to me and I feared that I might not be able to even keep it alight.

PART SIX

LEADING THE SDP

29

SDP LEADER – 1983

After every election I have driven through Plymouth to thank the electors over the loudspeaker. This time my thanks were more heartfelt than ever before. I had a majority of 4,936, the Conservatives had come second and Labour, despite having been the favourite after the boundary changes, had been pushed into an ignominious third place.

That Friday morning in addition to thanking the Plymouth electors for my personal result, I released a statement commenting on the national result. There was no point in whingeing; the present electoral system involved winning seats and we had not won enough of them. Though busting the system was our aim we had to be successful within it in order to beat it. I went on to stress that the SDP/Liberal Alliance was enriched by the diversity of the two parties, strengthened not weakened by retaining a partnership, so we should nurture their distinct identities. To champion proportional representation effectively we had to get people accustomed to the concept of coalition politics as they witnessed two parties working together. And, for the next four years, that was what I tried to do.

We drove to Buttermere late in the afternoon and it was here that *The Times* rang me up. They were on the scent of an 'oust Jenkins' story which I had to handle with care. On Saturday they carried the headline, 'JENKINS MAY FACE OWEN CHALLENGE', predicting an early contest for the leadership of what remained of the Social Democratic Party in Parliament. It quoted me as saying that the leadership was in the first instance a matter for Roy to decide. 'He has been elected Leader, it is up to him whether he wants to continue. I would want to talk to other SDP MPs even though there are not many of us.' Asked specifically if I would stand if Roy did not stand aside I replied, 'It depends what the feelings of the Party and the MPs are.' I had completely forgotton that Christopher Brocklebank-Fowler was going to call for Roy to resign, until I read a report of his speech in the newspapers. But others in the SDP were also feeding comments to the press calling for a change and these neither surprised nor dismayed me. There were a lot of telephone calls to and from Buttermere over the weekend. Bob Maclennan was the first to ring, adamant that Roy should go, and wanted him to lead a campaign on proportional representation. John Cartwright also felt Roy should go soon. I thought it was better for one of them to sound out Ian Wrigglesworth since his close links with Roy might inhibit him from talking frankly on this issue with me. Later Bob told me that Ian too thought Roy should resign and said that Charles Kennedy would almost certainly take the same view. This meant that by the time Roy and I talked I already knew that the MPs wanted a change of leader and wanted it immediately. Roy said that he favoured deferring his resignation until after the Party Conference. This would be too late, I told him, because it would cause uncertainty in the run up to what would be a very important Conference, and I suggested that he consult the other MPs. I left him with the clear message that if he did not step down quickly an election was certain. Although under our rules – since he had not yet been Leader for a period of twelve months – there could not be an election for a few more weeks I doubted whether he would want to tough it out. After Ettrick Bridge he could hardly feel obliged to stay Leader just to fight for David Steel to become overall Leader of the Alliance. That position anyhow did not now technically exist for some of us had fought against its being institutionalized.

By Sunday Michael Foot had announced he was giving up the leadership of the Labour Party. Inevitably the press then turned their attention to us and not just to the leadership issue either. The *Observer* ran a story with the title 'Liberals in favour of merger with the SDP', quoting David Penhaligon and others as urging the parties to unite. There was also mounting criticism of the national campaign – a routine event in the case of the Liberal Party – and Richard Wainwright said that he had never fought an election with such poor national support. Fortunately, because my own guerrilla campaign was perceived as having been different from the national campaign and had been widely praised, I was not sucked into that particular row.

Roy called a meeting with Shirley, Bill and me at his East Hendred home on Monday 13 June. Surprisingly, no other MPs were invited, but he had asked John Roper, the former Chief Whip, and Jack Diamond who had co-ordinated the campaign. The ostensible purpose of the meeting was to thank Jack for his tremendous effort in Cowley Street, keeping Liberals and Social Democrats on speaking terms. But at the start of the meeting Roy announced his intention to resign immediately and that he had prepared a press statement. Shirley and Bill were very upset and apparently surprised. They urged him strongly against resignation. My objective was to make the decision seem to have come spontaneously from Roy. Sensing that I was not going to change my mind, Roy went ahead and issued a statement that he thought it was desirable that the SDP should immediately have a new leader for the next election and that fortunately, with my victory at Devonport, such a leader was available. He hoped I would be elected without a contest. He said he was not withdrawing from full political activity and that he would be 'particularly active in safeguarding the unity of the Alliance'. I tried to say nothing which would detract from his statement and the *Daily Telegraph* praised him for his dignity and generosity. Fortunately his resignation occurred without public bitterness. However, it is impossible to do things like this painlessly and the incident did leave its scars.

David Steel and I arranged to meet at Buttermere the following Saturday. Just before our meeting, Russell Johnston, Liberal MP for Inverness, called for a merger before the next election. Perhaps this was fortunate for it meant that David and I could discuss the pressure for a merger quite frankly and I could make it clear that I would oppose it tooth and nail. I did, however, agree to limit what I said in public. I would say that merger was extremely unlikely but would not close the door to the possibility. In effect we ruled out merger before the next general election. I thought, wrongly as it turned out, that, in addition to accepting the formal position, he had accepted the rationale applying to our political situation. The SDP had to enhance its appeal to former Labour voters or at the very least retain that significant part of the Labour vote we had attracted at the election at the same time as aiming for more Conservative votes. We both knew that any new Labour leader would be better than Michael Foot. He could hardly be worse. We also knew the Conservatives would go through a period of mid-term unpopularity but that we should not rely on this carrying through to the next election. Tory disillusionment had been shown to be pretty ephemeral, with voters returning very rapidly to the fold even without the Falklands factor. So we must appeal to those voters who since 1945 had become increasingly disillusioned with Labour. Some of these had even joined the Conservatives, attracted by the new conviction politics of Margaret Thatcher and her challenge to the corporatist consensus. But I was convinced, indeed I remain convinced, that their natural home was with a distinct, tough, vital Social Democratic Party. The Alliance could only gain by the SDP's wooing these people who would otherwise, disenchanted with the 'Centre' image, stick to Labour in despair or vote Conservative by default.

Realignment, to which we were both committed, had to be achieved steadily, never allowing the Labour Party to return to a position where it was seen by press and public as the sole challenger. We managed to prevent this for the next four years. I told David that we had to go back to the original concept of the Alliance, with each party complementing the other's appeal, and counter-balancing strengths and weaknesses. In Scotland, for instance, and in some other parts of the country he and the Liberal Party would always be more popular than me or the SDP.

We also confronted the problem of two ambitious politicians of a similar age working so closely. Given the 'yo-yo' nature of politics there would be times when one of us was up or one of our parties was down and we would have to discipline ourselves not to exploit what would probably be only temporary changes in fortune. I considered myself bound by that conversation thereafter and never once tried to oust David Steel from our joint leadership. Much has been said and written about our relationship and most of it is false. For my part, I have no serious complaint about our partnership. Most of the tensions were predictable, arising from the necessity to safeguard the interests of our respective parties and reflect their concerns and their democratic decisions. Through all these moments of tension, our original agreement held. For instance, I resisted frequent incitements to push David aside when the SDP was in the ascendant. Shirley Williams, in particular, kept reiterating the argument for a single leader and her view that it should be me, but I always dismissed it as being impossible to achieve through agreement, which was the only option. I know that he had many similar representations made to him and that he too usually resisted them. I believed we had effectively bound ourselves to work an equal partnership until the next election and that we were two leaders of two parties, not two leaders of one. Moreover, if either of us challenged the other seriously the resultant trauma would have been very damaging. Perhaps that was the real limiting factor, rather than personal obligation, but I suspect it was a mixture of both.

Of course we differed on the merger issue, but we were conscious of this from the outset. I am often described as being surprised and angry when David called for a merger on the Sunday after the 1987 Election campaign. In fact I was neither surprised nor particularly angry. The timing and manner of his decision were more questionable, but whether or not we should merge was a legitimate question. David Steel says now that he should have pressed the case for a merger more thoroughly in 1983 and should not have allowed my objections to act as a veto. No doubt when he had dinner with Roy Jenkins after our meeting they discussed these issues and he could have reopened them if he had wished. However, he probably knew that I spoke for my Party at that stage and that Roy could no longer deliver. So whatever his thoughts now, in practice pressing the issue would have been difficult then. In any case, he did not seek to re-open the matter, apart from one letter prior to the Portsmouth by-election in 1984. What he did for the next four years was what he had been doing for the last three, namely working for a merger while denying he was doing so. My attitude to this was 'That's politics'. I never for one moment considered that David Steel was anything other than a believer in three parties not four. From his own point of view that made good sense. There was never any danger after the seat allocation in September 1982 that the Liberal Party would lose its identity in a merger. Whereas there had been a ratio of twenty-nine SDP MPs to fourteen Liberal MPs in May, in June there were seventeen Liberal MPs to six SDP MPs. Since the Alliance was formed they had gained far more councillors than we had. With a merger they were on course for a takeover. The danger for the SDP was much greater – we would be snuffed out. In politics as in business mergers are rare; takeovers, even if not always described as such, common.

In 1989 David Steel wrote of this period: 'thus within days of the general election and thanks to our joint acquiescence, David Owen secured both the leadership of the SDP and a veto over merger of the two parties into one. It was a remarkably bloodless coup.'

On Tuesday 21 June the MPs unanimously elected me as Leader of the Party and since there were no other nominations it did not go out to a ballot of the members. I cannot remember feeling particularly elated. I knew I had to weld four of them into a team while letting Roy involve himself whenever he wished. He was too valuable to lose but from now on he would be semi-detached. I thought privately that if we were able to survive as an independent party until the next election it would be little short of a miracle, but I was resolved at least to have a go. I had no illusions and very limited aspirations beyond survival. Much would depend, as it always does in modern politics, on how I stood in the opinion polls in relation to David Steel and how the SDP stood in relation to the Liberal Party. If I and/or the SDP slipped badly then David and Roy would combine to force a merger.

I was soon presented with a priceless opportunity to establish the credibility of the tiny SDP force. On 2 July, my birthday, we had our annual American independence baseball and hamburger party at Buttermere. As we put politics aside and enjoyed ourselves, unbeknown to me, David Steel was writing a formal letter of resignation as Leader of the Liberal Party. He even sent it. His resignation was only stopped, and the letter suppressed, when his wife Judy managed to organize what David called kitchen-cabinet pressure on him to stay. He ended up by taking a three-month sabbatical instead. It was an incredible situation: the official Opposition were leaderless, waiting for the electoral college to choose their Leader at their annual Conference in October, and the Liberal Party Leader was resting. Even more important was that for a few precious months Margaret Thatcher ran out of steam. After a stupendous victory with a 144 seat majority she had sacked Francis Pym, given Willie Whitelaw a Viscountcy, thus creating a by-election in Penrith, and was looking all set for another storming performance. Then, surprisingly, she seemed to lose her bearings. Perhaps this was due to the detached retina for which she needed an operation. People who are rarely ill often have more difficulty in coping when illness does strike. Perhaps what was happening in Cecil Parkinson's private life also distressed her. He was her heir apparent and she must have felt it as a personal blow. Whatever the cause, there was now a strange vacuum in British politics.

This was a wonderful chance for the SDP to make its mark. Debbie agreed to cancel our holiday in America and stay in England, sailing and fishing from our cottage in Wembury. I would be better placed from there to exploit any political news openings and to launch and to develop the policy ideas which I had long wanted the SDP to champion.

The first challenge was the Penrith by-election on 28 July. The Liberals had an excellent candidate, a young businessman and former Conservative whom I went to support, and at one stage it looked as if he might win. The Conservatives held on by 552 votes, Labour losing their deposit in a seat where on 9 June Willie Whitelaw had had a majority of 15,421. The Liberals had achieved this splendid result while technically without a leader, though David Steel did break his sabbatical and travel the few miles from his home to the constituency. Inactivity can have advantages. I remember Michel Rocard with his leg in plaster after a skiing accident showing me polls in Paris where his personal popularity soared during the months he was out of action.

Over the summer there were, as I had expected, plenty of opportunities to exploit the leadership vacuum. I had the first of many run-ins with Bernard Ingham, the Prime Minister's Press Secretary, when he said that Peter Shore was talking 'bunkum and balderdash'. This would have been acceptable from a spokesman for the Conservative Party but it was totally inappropriate language for a civil servant paid by the taxpayer. On another occasion I urged the Prime Minister to persuade President Reagan to halt the rise in US interest rates. I was also widely quoted on the Soviet shooting down of the South Korean airliner in Soviet airspace north of Japan. This all served to provide modest headlines as did the SDP policy documents released before the Conference. People were again aware of the SDP. I did not use the word 'Alliance' if I could avoid it and tried hard to not even refer to the Liberal Party. It was all SDP.

Against this background the pattern of my leadership over the next four years emerged. First, I had to face the debate over merger which continued among the two parties' activists. A new term began to surface, 'organic merger'. It arose from a Liberal Councillors' Conference, soon after the election, which had envisaged local mergers taking place in piecemeal fashion. The challenge was that no leader could oppose the democratic will of the local people. The enthusiasts for merger felt they could prove, at the grass roots, that the two parties' political interests were as one and that they could work better as an integrated operation. I realized that this organic merger was going to be helped along at our Salford Conference in September by a concerted attempt to make the decision on whether the candidates should be chosen jointly a purely local one. What we were being offered was merger by stealth.

We could only counter this by convincing people that the fact that you could work together did not mean you had to merge together. This involved familiarizing people with the mechanics of the inter-party coalitions which operated in Europe. I initiated this with a long article in the *Guardian* on 4 July. It was accompanied by a photograph of David and me in the garden at Buttermere, somewhat ambiguously captioned, 'Divided we stand for coalition'. I conceded the necessity to evolve our relationship further, deepening it while avoiding pointless overlapping and suggested that both parties should group constituencies for organizational purposes. A sensible way might be to bring together those constituencies we envisaged as being grouped under legislation for proportional representation. This would not only accustom the public to grouped constituencies but also ensure that party members would not be left without a local constituency fought by their own party. If it was not their own, it would be one next door, in the same group. Unfortunately influential Liberals were never attracted by this and clung to the autonomy of their local constituency association. The Association of Liberal Councillors, never keen on the SDP, were canny enough to see that if my suggestion were adopted it would reduce a lot of the pressure to merge or, as they saw it, take over the SDP. There were a few decentralist Liberals who understood the value of getting the public to understand the new political attitudes which must underpin proportional representation, but they could not win this point against the other activists.

As well as this party battle, so frequently frustrating and pointless, I was lucky enough to be involved in international work over the next few years. In early July I attended the first meeting of the Independent Commission on Humanitarian Issues in Geneva. This had been set up by Prince Sadruddin Aga Khan and Crown Prince Hassan of Jordan following a Jordan-sponsored resolution on humanitarianism adopted by the UN. The Commission was to follow in the steps of Brandt and Palme and examine humanitarian principles from a broader background than the purely Judaeo-Christian tradition which had hitherto predominated. A substantial number of the Commission's members came from Third World countries and Islam was well represented. There were several working-groups and I spent most of my time in the early stages working on famine, particularly as world concern built up over the situation in Sudan. We produced a Pan paperback special entitled *Famine* and I became an advocate of the view that we must restore a local market in food production and distribution if communities were to avoid the dependent culture which resulted from simple reliance on food aid.

The real task was to re-examine all policies and see whether we could start the serious work of producing social democratic ideas for the 1990s. Much would depend on the quality of these ideas. By August it was pretty clear that Neil Kinnock was going to become Leader of the Labour Party as he was accumulating a substantial majority of votes over Roy Hattersley in the electoral college. The so-called dream ticket then emerged. One bizarre incident illustrated the absurdity of the electoral college. The SDP staff were members of the APEX trade union and, as a result, the branch at Cowley Street was given a vote on the Labour Leadership and thus a say in the electoral college. They used it to vote for the 'nightmare ticket' of Eric Heffer and Michael Meacher, designed to saddle Labour with the worst leadership on offer.

All new leaders have a honeymoon when their pronouncements are given much more attention than they deserve so I had to move quickly for public impact. Most people knew where I stood on foreign policy, so I needed to carve out a distinctive position on economic policy before Neil Kinnock was given the opportunity. I decided to return to the idea of the social market economy which I had tried to project in 1981. The SDP had to break the stranglehold of the 1960s. An understanding of the market economy was the first essential step towards the radical libertarian force I wanted to create. Now that Roy had asked to have general speaking responsibilities and Ian Wrigglesworth was speaking for us on the economy it was going to be easier to make the social market the leitmotif of the SDP. We needed, however, to make a splash, otherwise no one would notice the change in our economic outlook. My speech at the Party Conference would not be enough. I could flag the change there but then I would have to reinforce it with more detail. The Institute of Economic Affairs asked me to write an article for their journal, *Economic Affairs*, and this seemed the perfect forum. It would be a clear signal, for the IEA had established itself as the progenitor of Margaret Thatcher's emphasis on the market. The series of articles to which I would be contributing had been launched by Geoffrey Howe surveying his four years as Chancellor. My article would, like his, be assessed in print by four independent economists of the IEA's choice and I would then have a chance to reply in the same issue.

I was fortunate to have a market economist as my research assistant. Alex de Mont had been an Oxford don and had come to work for Bill Rodgers in the early days of the Party. Though I did not realize it when I took him on, he had been all along privately critical of the economic policy pursued by the SDP. He was a sceptic on incomes policy and believed in only very selective state intervention. For four years he never once provided me with an inaccurate statistic and always ensured that any market solutions were properly considered even if they were rejected. His intellectual toughness was belied by his slender physique and courteous manner and it was a stimulating relationship. During August and September we worked on developing the concept of the social market economy and in the process came to the conclusion that the SDP's advocacy of incomes policy must end, to be replaced by an emphasis on the micro-economy, with far greater stress on training, trade union reform and decentralized, market orientated wage bargaining. I knew that some in the Party would resist this shift, although on this issue some in the Liberal Party would be allies.

xxxvii. *Above:* With Debbie chatting to miners pickets during the 1984 SDP Conference at Buxton.

xxxviii. *Left:* General Election, 1987, on the River Thames.

OPPOSITE
xxxix. *Above:* Election 1987 – shaving in a helicopter with assistant, Sandra Jantuah.

xl. *Below:* Debbie with two of her authors.

xli A stroll with Debbie on Plymouth Hoe after the 1987 Election.

xlii. Eyeing the daffs. With Mike Potter and stallholder during the
Richmond by-election campaign in February 1989.

xliii. The Leader of the SDP with world leaders: *Top left:* Chancellor Kohl; *top right:* Pope John Paul II; *above:* President George Bush.

OPPOSITE
xliv. *Above:* Six Foreign Secretaries – Lord Pym, Lord Carrington, myself, Douglas Hurd, Lord Callaghan and John Major.

xlv. *Below:* After the bomb scare at the Scarborough Conference in 1989, The Speech on the Beach, with John and Rosie.

xlvi. The Owen family, 1990 – David, Debbie, Lucy, Tristan and Gareth.

Incomes policy and government intervention in industry had permeated my political life up until then. I had grown used to thinking of them as an integral part of political activity and had been a supporter of many of the earlier failed initiatives. My personal revisionism had only started in 1978 when giving a Fabian lecture as Foreign Secretary, and progressed much further while writing *Face the Future*. When I was adopted as a candidate in 1962 the Conservative Government, with Selwyn Lloyd as Chancellor, had created the National Incomes Commission. Labour had then replaced it in 1964 with the Prices and Incomes Board. The Heath Government had abolished the PIB in 1970 but then set up a Price Commission in 1973 which was expanded by Labour in 1974 and abolished by Margaret Thatcher in 1979. The Labour Government had set up the Industrial Reorganization Corporation in 1966 and later the Commission for Industrial Relations. Both were abolished by the new Conservative Government in 1970, though they had created two new bodies, the Pay Board in 1970 and the National Industrial Relations Court in 1971. Both had been abolished by Labour in 1974 which then created the National Enterprise Board. This had been restructured in 1979 and then abolished. It was a record of failure.

To align myself with Margaret Thatcher in condemning all these initiatives had its political advantages, and the label of 'sub-Thatcherite' or, as Denis Healey so delicately put it, 'Mrs Thatcher in trousers' did not worry me. The public's impression was what mattered, not the pundits or politicians. It was a small price to pay to rid the SDP of the image of being stuck in the 1970s, promising a better yesterday. I was determined to rediscover some of the élan with which we had launched ourselves and this could only come from new policy development, not another re-launch. Fortunately there was tremendous scope for developing our social policies in a more egalitarian and redistributive direction. If we could simultaneously break right on the market and left on social policy I believed we would find an electorally attractive political mix. If the social market were not to be a synonym for the mixed economy, our market policies and our social policies had to be hard edged, intellectually convincing and politically engaging. The SDP would attempt, late in the day admittedly, to throw off the centrist 'splitting the difference' image with which we had been landed. We would fulfil our promise for a rebellion against the Centre as well as the extremes. For the first time we would provide the British people with a party at once sensible, compassionate and unencumbered with the mistaken corporatism of the post-war era. It was worth a gamble. In addition, if I led with my chin on policy it would divert public attention from the internal debate about merger. Few things are more unattractive than political parties washing their dirty linen in public. We had to look outward to the electorate.

A considerable ally in this strategy was Michael Young and it was all the more significant that we had come to similar conclusions without consultation. Michael was Chairman of the SDP's independent think tank, the Tawney Society, but was better known as the founder of the Consumers' Association. He saw the SDP as heir to the libertarian socialist tradition and feared that if we rushed into a new Alliance party we could never become that radical force. He knew the Labour Party well and he thought it possible then that the Labour Party could contract still further to the size of the old Independent Labour Party, with Neil Kinnock as the latter-day Jimmy Maxton. He stayed with the SDP after 1987, returning to Labour in 1989 when they made their big policy switch on the EEC, market economics and Trident. For people like Michael an emphasis on the market had to be linked to consumerism, while demonstrating that competitiveness need not be incompatible with compassion. I felt sure I could convince people that we were still a radical, redistributive party while embracing the market. There was a temptation to play down our market orientation until after the merger debate. But I was convinced that there was a window of opportunity at Salford, and if I put my whole authority as new Leader on the line I could get away with blocking the merger and turning to the market.

In early September the strategy of those promoting a merger became clear. They were not going to go for direct confrontation over immediate national merger; instead local initiatives promoting organic growth or union were to produce the same result. These people were similar to, indeed they often were, federalists in the EEC, denying their intentions but edging in with seemingly innocuous phrases and initiatives. Dick Taverne, David Marquand and Matthew Oakshott, all fervent supporters of Roy Jenkins, signed a joint declaration with a group of twenty-four Social Democrat parliamentary candidates in which joint selection was their chosen stalking horse. This was supported in an article by Bill Rodgers in the autumn edition of *Political Quarterly*; he argued that if people wished to turn a loose alliance into a close day-to-day relationship, speaking as one and jointly selecting candidates, it would be foolish to resist such pressure on the grounds that premature merger might result. Postal balloting of the Cambridgeshire SDP led to the claim that 90 per cent of their members were in favour of joint selection of Alliance candidates for parliamentary and European elections and we were being faced by a wave of jointery. This was all brought together in an article by Adam Raphael in the *Observer* entitled, 'Thin end of a merger is dilemma for Owen'. I was fortunate to have a strong opponent of merger in John Cartwright, our Chief Whip, and he made a speech on what a party's identity stands for: 'Any political party which gives up its right to choose its own candidates in accordance with its own constitution inevitably surrenders its right to a continued independent existence.' Christopher Brocklebank-Fowler had a motion before the Council which urged the Party to stick to the present constitution. Since we were never sure that we could keep a simple majority in the ruling Council for Social

Democracy, our strategy was to force those who wanted joint selection to come clean and change the constitution. This would require a much greater proportion of the party to back the move. A simple majority would not be enough.

On Thursday 8 September David Steel and I discussed the form of words on joint selection which we were trying to hammer out with the Liberals on the Joint Leaders Advisory Committee next day. He himself would not be present, leaving it to Alan Beith who was deputizing for him, but he was helpful. We did on Friday morning manage to agree a document on how to handle the next year's European election, which went to both our parties' conferences. Those of us who supported our parties' independence could not object to the Liberal Party inviting SDP members to vote in selection meetings in seats which were allocated to the Liberals. It was a clever move on their part.

The next day the SDP National Committee met in Salford as a prelude to the Party Conference. It soon became clear that our adviser on the constitution, William Goodhart QC, did not accept that joint selection was against the constitution in all circumstances, though this interpretation was challenged by Edward Lyons, an equally distinguished QC. Yet all agreed that anything resembling universal joint selection was outside the constitution. An acrimonious meeting concluded with the carrying of a motion rejecting joint selection by seventeen votes to ten, a far more convincing vote than I had expected. The press described it as a rout for the Jenkinsites, but that was not quite accurate. A crucial chink in our armour against a merger had, however, been opened up. We insisted that the SDP would ballot only its own members in the seats allocated to us unless there were 'exceptional circumstances'. The National Committee was bound by the constitution every bit as much as the area party members and had to bear this in mind when making seat deals. The arrangement that day with the Liberals was as far as we could go constitutionally and further than I wished to go.

Salford was a rather strange choice for a conference. We wanted to emphasize that, while the old parties went to the seaside, we were going to the depressed industrial heartland whose decay created social problems that were being ignored. It was where L.S. Lowry painted and the setting for the pre-war depression novel, *Love on the Dole*. Fine political gesture though it was, it turned out to be a mistake. The hall of Salford University, in which we met, had no character and, with no hotels nearby, we were unable to build up the Conference spirit that is so important. Most of us felt by the end that the seaside or a spa town would be better in future.

We had chosen Sunday for our internal debate in the Council for Social Democracy because there would be less television coverage and we had no wish to project our differences beyond the hall. Christopher Brocklebank-Fowler moved the main motion on behalf of the National

Committee, making it abundantly clear that it meant no merger before
the next general election at least and no joint selection except in
exceptional circumstances. The word 'exceptional', product of the
lawyers' interpretation of the constitution, was to bedevil us over the next
few years. Having put my leadership on the line on this issue of joint
selection, it might have been wiser to commission an independent legal
opinion on whether the SDP constitution allowed any joint selection.
But to have to amend the constitution would have been fraught with
difficulty; we should have found it awkward to mobilize a two-thirds
majority to carry a constitutional amendment.

On the Tuesday I gave my main speech to the Conference. It was
much too wordy. Debbie made me promise that I would never again read
a speech and with few exceptions I have followed her advice. It takes
considerable skill to read a speech without putting a barrier between the
speaker and the audience. The 'sincerity machines', introduced from
America, where a speech is reflected up on to glass panels in front of you
but which the audience and television cameras can look through, allow
the speakers to keep their heads up and, if well done (President Reagan
being a past master at it), can give the impression of spontaneity. I had
tried them, but the real skill is not so much in the reading as in the
writing. A written speech tends to be too dense to absorb. In a spontaneous one the arguments are looser and, although one does repeat
oneself, it goes at a pace which people can digest. Additionally there is an
ease of expression and a genuine spontaneity which can be compelling to
listen to. I know of no one who can hold the attention of the House of
Commons while reading a speech, and most people find that having to
keep to a text restricts their freedom to deal with interjections or to
respond to their listeners. Nevertheless in its content my speech was
probably one of the more important that I have given. Because I used a
conversational tone, few in the hall, I think, fully realized quite how
extensive a re-think of SDP policy I was envisaging. Though 'toughness
and tenderness' was the theme of the speech it was also a synthesis of
new policies.

It was the American philosopher, William James, who first formulated
the concept: 'The tough think of the tender as sentimentalists and
softheads. The tender feel the tough to be unrefined, callous or brutal.'
Yet the two characters are not incompatible and many people have
elements of both. Why should not a political party be tough in pursuit of
the market economy and sound defence and tender in supporting the
NHS and fixing social security benefit levels. Combining virtues seemed
good social democratic practice.

Next week was the Liberal Party Conference where I was to speak on
the Saturday. One party conference was enough for me, two excessive, so
I was very glad that Debbie agreed to drive up with me to Harrogate on
the Friday. Having unguardedly accepted David Steel's invitation to the

Liberal Assembly's glee night that evening, we felt that we could best break the ice by doing a party piece. Debbie comes from the American generation which swooned to Elvis Presley and 'Love me tender' was her suggestion. As we drove along we thought up lyrics and she tried to teach me the tune. The Liberal activists were so amazed that we were prepared to make fools of ourselves that they all joined in the chorus, rolling about with laughter:

> Love us tender, love us true,
> All our dreams fulfill;
> Truly, Liberals, we love you
> And we always will.

Next morning when I rose to speak the atmosphere in the Conference hall was far warmer than I could ever have expected. Instead of walking out, the Liberal CND-ers listened to a speech which dealt with defence, cheering whenever I used the work 'arguable'. Demonstrating that the NHS was not safe in Mrs Thatcher's hands was not hard and that meant we were all on the same wavelength.

In the first week of October the Labour Party Conference elected Neil Kinnock as Leader, at the age of forty-one. He was Michael Foot's political heir and for many years Michael had supported and sponsored Neil, so on paper it was a victory for the Left. But few of those close to Tony Benn rejoiced. They knew Neil Kinnock would eventually follow past heroes of the Left along the well-trodden path towards the Centre, impelled by electoral logic and the need to come nearer to the centre of gravity of the nation as a whole. For the moment, however, Neil Kinnock embodied every Left-wing prejudice and passion. A longstanding CND supporter, he had also made speech after speech attacking our membership of the European Community, even being a member of the council of the 'Get Britain out' campaign. It was unlikely that there would be any policy U-turns for a while, but a fresh face and a young image would, I knew, automatically boost Labour. It was bad luck for him that he slipped while walking along the beach with his wife on his first photocall and got his trousers wet in the surf. When he quipped 'Bet it wouldn't happen to Maggie', rather too many people agreed.

Labour might have ended its leadership crisis but there still remained a general political leadership vacuum. The Conservative Party Conference a week later was a miserable affair dominated by Cecil Parkinson's resignation. So the SDP came out of the conference season with a higher political profile than we had had since 1981. It was therefore apt timing that my *Economic Affairs* article, entitled 'Agenda for Competitiveness with Compassion' was published at the end of October. The *Financial Times* called it 'Thatcherism with a human face' and it was their correspondent, Peter Riddell, who really understood the true significance of my shift. I was not arguing, as we had done so far in classic centrist fashion, that we should freeze the frontier between the public and private sectors. I was welcoming change. Hitherto the SDP had been very cautious in talking about privatization, never really supporting it and over-stressing the value of stability on the frontier between public and private provision. I was now shifting our attack from opposition to all privatization towards an objection in principle to all monopoly power, whether in private or public hands. Even a *Guardian* editorial, 'Embrace with proper caution', affirmed that there was much that was correct in my message, even if it was one which the present Prime Minister had seemed to make her own for the past five years. It pointed out, to the evident chagrin of some of the IEA's *laissez-faire* commentators, that my article was studded with useful reminders of how intervention in the market can help both in correcting problems of inequality which arise from its mechanisms and help the market itself to work better by reducing uncertainty. The article provoked considerable discussion and serious criticism which in its turn helped me clarify my thinking and laid the basis for my next book, published in 1984 by Viking/Penguin, *A Future That Will Work*.

While at Salford I met John Ashworth, their Vice-Chancellor. He had previously been the Chief Scientist to the Central Policy Review Staff from 1976–81. A biologist by training, he represented the vibrancy and challenge to higher education that I hoped the SDP could bring to politics. He was turning Salford University around at the time and I liked his open-mindedness and enthusiasm. He later offered in effect to set up a think-tank for me and gathered some of the people who had been with him on the CPRS. We would meet at approximately two-monthly intervals to discuss medium- to long-term problems. It was an important discipline for me because I was having to react hour by hour to events and promote new initiatives on a day by day basis, but unless these could be set in a deeper and more fundamental framework they would look superficial. The people who came, unlike John, were not all SDP supporters but they were at least sympathetic. Because they had recently been in Whitehall but were now outside, they had that most precious characteristic, relevance, already on their agenda. From that informal think-tank came many ideas and insights. Harold Carter acted as the convenor and I added people like David Sainsbury, Christopher Smallwood and my own staff. It was a time when John's wife was very ill so we saw less of him than I should have liked, but insofar as the SDP did contribute new political ideas from 1984 to 1987, this group played a significant role. We explored the regeneration of Liverpool in depth and inner cities in general and I became convinced that restoring or even retaining the population was not crucial. The population could be built back up again and if it meant a lot of green space for a decade or more that did not matter as long as dereliction was removed. There was nothing which indicated that a declining population had to mean a declining city. We also examined direct taxation and the increase of VAT. On the vexed question of earmarking tax I became convinced of the case for a specific health tax which would fund all NHS expenditure. The case against the National Insurance contribution and the need for integration of tax and benefits featured, as did many other structural changes which would take decades to fully implement.

Establishing the SDP as a national party meant fighting hard for recognition at every level. It was never easy to judge when to make a stand but few issues were more delicate to handle than the question of an SDP wreath at the Cenotaph. The Armistice Day Remembrance Service is one occasion when the whole nation is as one and the two minutes' silence mark a precious moment which I had no wish to besmirch with partisan politics. Roy Jenkins had asked for us to be represented in 1982 but it had been turned down by the then Home Secretary. So in July 1983 I thought it best to put our case for representation privately to the Prime Minister. A convenient opportunity had arisen because the Government Whips' Office had been in touch with me over the question of political honours. I had always disliked Harold Wilson's decision to separate political honours from the honours system as a whole, with the implicit assumption that politics was different from other forms of service to the country. The practice had arisen of allocating Opposition party leaders a certain number of knighthoods, CBEs, OBEs and MBEs each year for their own personal patronage. This was undesirable for it extended and legitimized the Government's political patronage system which had been abused for decades. The SDP Parliamentary Committee had decided that, like the Labour Party, we would have nothing to do with this system until it was changed by all-party agreement.

My meeting with the Prime Minister in No. 10, our first formal one-on-one meeting, started in a friendly atmosphere. I told her about our decision and urged her to return to a system where political honours were treated like all other honours. That would mean that while Opposition party leaders could make representations there would be no formal allocation to them and the final decision would be made, on merit, with overall responsibility lying with No. 10. Margaret Thatcher seemed to be unaware of the Labour Party's reasons for not participating, but in any case she showed little inclination to reach any accommodation. I could almost see her thinking that if we were foolish enough to spurn patronage that was our affair, she knew how to use it to buttress her authority and gain support. We then discussed life peerages and I said that I hoped the SDP would be considered for them in the normal way because that was the only mechanism for ensuring that new SDP voices could be heard in the Second Chamber. On this she was studiously non-committal. Finally I raised the question of representation at the Cenotaph. I was barely halfway through my case than she intervened to reject it, declaring that she was adamantly opposed to widening representation. Suddenly the atmosphere was heated. I told her bluntly that I could see absolutely no reason why a party that had attracted $3\frac{1}{2}$ million voters should not be entitled to lay a wreath at the Cenotaph. Eventually I rose to go and said that I hoped that, since the decision was formally the Home Secretary's, she would give the matter renewed thought, otherwise I would have to take my case before the bar of public opinion. She became incandescent, alternating between a prim 'How could you?' to a furious 'How dare you?' Clearly she had not been spoken to like this for years and I left, uncertain if I should be forced to take issue with her in public. In October I had my answer. A formal letter came from Leon Brittan, rejecting our participation but promising an urgent review and admitting that the present arrangements had developed in a piecemeal way.

I decided to go public, in the uncertain hope of winning press support. My letter to the Prime Minister was outspoken: 'Many Conservative, Labour, Liberal and Social Democrat voters will see this as petty and partisan – the act of the Leader of the Conservative Party and not the act of the Prime Minister of the whole nation.' The SDP had demonstrated its support for the armed services of the Crown 'not just in words but in action during the Falklands War, when we were steadfast in our backing of British interests'. Nevertheless we were totally opposed to making a demonstration as some had suggested for this would only detract from a sombre and moving ceremony of national unity. The *Daily Telegraph* reported that the issue had already sharply divided Ministers, that many senior members of the Government were unhappy and that one of the service chiefs had actually objected to our exclusion. In its editorial column the *Daily Telegraph* said that we should be permitted to lay a wreath next year, as did the *Evening Standard*, and many other newspapers up and down the country took our side. It was a good example of the basic fairness and decency of the British people asserting itself. The British Legion demonstrated their feelings by inviting Debbie and me to the Albert Hall and then to the dinner afterwards where Margaret Thatcher was the chief speaker. Symbolically we had to get up and leave in the middle of her speech, having ensured that everyone knew beforehand that we were doing so only in order to catch the midnight sleeper to Plymouth to lay a wreath on the War Memorial on the Hoe next morning. The *coup de grâce* was when the television news bulletins that Sunday evening, after reporting the Cenotaph, had a shot of me laying a wreath in Plymouth. Over the next few months much time was spent in Whitehall producing a formula to save the Prime Minister's face, it being agreed eventually that the leader of parties with six or more MPs could lay a wreath and those with fewer would be invited to attend. In some ways it was a trivial issue, in others an important one. What the whole episode showed was that the Prime Minister, though still totally dominant, did not have an absolute hold on public opinion or newspaper editors. Even Rupert Murdoch, proprietor of the ever loyal *Sun, News of the World* and *Times* was saying 'She has run out of puff.'

30

SDP LEADER – 1984

At the start of 1984 Anthony Howard wrote an *Observer* article entitled, 'The Doctor's dilemma'. I had known Tony on and off since 1963 when he had come to the children's ward at St Thomas's to see a friend who was a nurse. At that time he was a columnist on the *New Statesman* and I, as a mere prospective candidate, saw him as a guru of the Labour Party. We had had our clashes over the years but I have respect for his political judgement so I read his article with interest and pondered his analysis with care. He wrote:

> ... his closest colleagues speak of him, quite openly, as being 'obsessed with the Liberals' – but it is scarcely a neurotic obsession. The Liberals, in fact, provide the roadblock against everything he still would like to achieve for the future. With seventeen MPs against the SDP's bare half dozen (and for what it is worth, 600,000 more aggregate national votes as well), the Liberal Party is simply not going to allow Dr Owen even the nominal supremacy it briefly accorded to Mr Jenkins. As for any talks of 'merger' Dr Owen knows full well that it is not so much that which is on the table as the threat of a 'takeover bid'. Hence his obduracy even over such matters as joint candidate selection for this summer's European Assembly elections (though here he recently suffered the indignity of being overruled by his own SDP National Committee). It is not perhaps something that Dr Owen would like to proclaim from the house tops, but his feeling seems to be that, if his party is not more careful in the future, it could easily find itself in the position of the unfortunate young lady of Riga who went for a ride on the back of a tiger.

He was correct on all counts. On the National Committee there was no automatic majority to oppose joint selection and each time a particular local deal was put forward for National Committee approval it was a toss up whether or not those of us opposed to joint selection would manage to vote it down. I certainly feared that the limerick would end:

Liberals returned from the ride,
With the SDP inside,
And the smile on the face of the tiger.

We had a Council for Social Democracy meeting in Aston in January
1984 which affirmed our policy of minimum nuclear deterrence and
support for using the deployment of cruise missiles as a bargaining
counter with the Soviets. Some commentators attacked this as being
deliberately divisive in our relations with the Liberals. This was an
absurd criticism. Cruise deployment was by then a key political issue,
protest marches and rallies were challenging NATO governments all
over Europe, Soviet propaganda was in full swing and some analysts
questioned whether NATO would be able to stick to its decisions. I now
recognized that our decision in Parliament, soon after the 1983 Election,
to find a way of voting with the Liberals on cruise missiles was the single
biggest mistake I had yet made as Leader. We had urged delay for a few
weeks while the negotiations in Geneva were still continuing. This was
distorted by the Conservatives into a claim that we had joined Labour
opposition to the deployment of cruise missiles. The fact that when the
Soviets broke off the negotiations a few weeks later in December the
SDP immediately came out firmly in favour of deployment was ignored.
Our constant support for deployment thereafter as a negotiating counter
was obscured by the Conservatives' constant invocation of the earlier
vote, and when the Liberals continued to oppose deployment inside and
outside Parliament our SDP protestations looked very thin. My mistake
was already rebounding on us in Tory speeches and propaganda and I
did not mean to repeat that same error.

The SDP was not prepared to disown cruise missile deployment, as
Labour and the Liberals wanted. We supported Britain having a dual
key, allowing us to ensure the missiles were not fired without British
involvement, but I was not prepared to support splitting the difference
by encouraging the freeze movement which, in effect, opposed deployment even if from a less anti-NATO position. I knew we were going to
have to negotiate a coalition defence policy with the Liberals and I felt it
was time we put some bargaining chips in place, otherwise we would be
pushed into actually opposing deployment. There was every reason, with
Neil Kinnock at Labour's helm, to expect defence and nuclear questions
to be as salient at the next general election as they had been at the last
one. If our stand was divisive with the Liberals it was naturally divisive
rather than deliberately so.

At the end of January I visited Japan with Zbig Brzezinski, President
Carter's National Security Adviser, in preparation for a Trilateral Commis-
sion report of which I was the principal author along with the former
Japanese Foreign Minister Saburo Okita. It was published in April as
Democracy Must Work and was an attempt to set an agenda for the

decade ahead on which Japan, the US and Europe could usefully co-operate. My particular brief was the world economy and solutions for unemployment. Michael Stewart, who had been with me in the Foreign Office and was then Reader in Political Economy at University College, was travelling with me as one of our experts and we were both able to learn something about the future impact on employment of Japan's high technology.

I had deliberately flown out via Hong Kong so as to talk to the Governor about the negotiations with the Chinese and the situation after 1997 when the New Territories were due to return to China. After our meeting in Japan I flew to Beijing to make my first ever visit to China. There I had a long meeting with Mr Wu Xueqian, the Chinese Foreign Minister, whom I already knew, and left confident that there would be an agreement which would give Hong Kong a very special status after 1997. My worry was whether the Chinese leaders fully understood the importance and the intangible nature of international financial confidence; both its fickleness and its fragility. There was not much time for tourism, but walking on the Chinese Wall, truly one of the Wonders of the World, I looked down on my coat lapel to see a pearl and realized that it was a frozen tear, so cold was the wind coming over the Northern Steppes.

In February, only fifteen months after taking over from Leonid Brezhnev, Yuri Andropov died. It had been a period of important change with the emergence of the KGB realism which had first been drawn to my attention in the late 1970s. Younger leaders had been brought to the fore by Andropov, particularly Mikhail Gorbachev, and there was a sense that the Soviet economy was going to be opened up. Margaret Thatcher flew to Moscow for the funeral and I went on her plane with David Steel and Denis Healey. The ceremony in Red Square was strangely moving with the sombre music and impressive military parade. It was freezing cold and we had to stamp our feet to keep warm. I got an interesting insight into Margaret Thatcher's attitudes to the Soviet Union over lunch in the British Embassy. They were still very Iron Maiden-ish and, unusually for her, showed a surprising degree of ignorance about both the country and its history. At the reception, as the new leader Konstantin Chernenko was wheezing away, I mentioned to some of the press that I thought he had emphysema. That little aside was flashed round the world and I spent days extricating myself from a diagnosis for which I had no proof, though it later turned out to be accurate.

A series of by-elections came up and both Alliance parties co-operated well. At Chesterfield in March Tony Benn was returned to the House of Commons, having lost at Bristol in the general election, and the Liberal candidate came second, moving up from third place in the general election. The SDP fought Stafford in May retaining our second position and increasing our vote. I was canvassing in the main street when a news flash came through that a Libyan gunman had shot and killed a police-woman on the pavement outside their Embassy as she was controlling a crowd of demonstrators. Within minutes I was asked on the radio whether we could go in and arrest them and I said that we could not, being prevented by the Vienna Convention, but that we should expel the Libyans. It looked for a few days as if I would be proved wrong, and there were a number of snide comments about my instant punditry. Leon Brittan huffed and puffed, giving the impression, egged on by the Labour Party, that he could flout the Convention. At last the Libyans were expelled and my initial reaction was vindicated, but it showed the dangers as well as the advantages of instant reactions. It meant living near the edge and relying on my memory of facts mainly learnt in government. I knew that one day I would slip and everyone would enjoy my splashdown.

In further by-elections in Surrey South-West the Liberals came very close to defeating the Conservatives, substantially increasing their vote, and in Cynon Valley the SDP remained in second place, defeating Plaid Cymru and the Conservatives. If a pattern was establishing itself, how-ever, it was that the Liberals were collecting more votes than the SDP and I guessed that if this continued the merger issue would come back with a vengeance with the Liberals insisting on David Steel as the overall leader. This meant that we must take all by-elections very seriously, even though they are totally disruptive and, in the long run, not very significant. They matter, however, for the small parties for they provide our main chance of publicity. The Leader's programme is contorted to fit in by-election meetings, extra money has to be found and the result is always exaggerated in terms of its long-term implications. Yet a slip up can be deeply damaging as Darlington had proved for the SDP and the Alliance. The SDP, I realized, would have to mobilize volunteers and learn Liberal by-election techniques while eschewing Liberal manners. Their flagrant manipulation of polling statistics and policies to fit a particular by-election had confirmed an image of irresponsibility and instability. We were going to be judged more harshly and I neither had nor sought the same freedom.

Our biggest challenge now was the European elections. An equal allocation of seats for the European election had been agreed. The most winnable seat, the Highlands and Islands, was to be fought by the Liberal MP Russell Johnston, but the SDP was to fight Plymouth and Cornwall with Jonathan Marks as our candidate. An interesting feature of our work on the joint manifesto was how little pressure came from the Liberal Party to endorse federalism, not just then but in the 1987 General Election as well. In part this was because David Steel did not seem to share Jo Grimond's federalist feelings, in part it was because Margaret Thatcher's tough stance within the Community ensured that federalism had little electoral appeal. The main focus of contention between us was the SDP's reluctance to have union in the European context written with a capital 'U'.

My relationship with David Steel by this stage was edgy but civil. A child's letter addressed to me and asking what I would do if I knew the world was going to end was erroneously delivered to David's office. He passed it on with a barbed note, which found its way into the press, suggesting that the end of the world was more my department. I replied to the press enquiry by saying that if I knew the world was going to end I would join the Liberal Party. About this time David wrote me a letter whose implications were all too clear: he would make a move to dominate the Alliance if we failed to win the Portsmouth by-election, something he clearly expected to happen. It was like a black cone warning of a storm ahead.

The by-election in Portsmouth South had been called by the Conservatives deliberately to coincide with voting in the European election on 14 June and stretch our resources. The SDP candidate was Mike Hancock, a young local councillor for the Fratton ward in the constituency whom I had known in the Labour Party. He was an AEW shop steward and a character, with great charm, though with a common touch and streetwise. He had fought the seat in the General Election for us and had been chosen to fight the by-election, amid some controversy, in preference to Bob Mitchell, our former MP for Southampton. With its naval dockyard Portsmouth was seen to be perfect SDP territory and though it would be a surprise if we won, there could be no excuses if we had a bad result. I decided virtually to ignore the European election in terms of our headquarters staff and volunteer effort and concentrate all our staff and resources on Portsmouth. Mike Hancock proved to be a far better candidate than the Conservative import and his conscientious and sensitive handling of local council problems undoubtedly helped to take Labour votes.

I went to Portsmouth frequently while campaigning nationwide for the European elections. The week before polling day I was in the West Country on the Wednesday and due to fly up to Portsmouth for the next day's press conference. Our experts in the campaign team wanted me to announce that we were ahead and were going to win. Cassius Clay politics, as I call it, with endless boasting of victory, is not my style and I was reluctant to do it. I was staying the Wednesday night with Harold Carter, my travelling companion in the Euro-campaign, at his old Rectory in Lansallos. It is a spectacular part of the south Cornish coast near Looe. On Thursday morning soon after dawn broke, wandering through the churchyard, I saw on a gravestone:

> In memory of John Perry, Mariner, who was unfortunately
> killed by a Cannon ball by a person unknown In ye year
> 1779 Aged 24yrs June ye 5

In prime of life most suddenly sad tidings to relate
Here view my utter destiny and pity my sad fate
I by a Shot which rapid flew
Was instantly struck dead
Lord pardon the offender who
My Precious Blood did shed

I was still trying to memorize this as I walked down to the sea. There was not a soul about and it was a bright clear morning. As I walked over the brow of the hill, I saw a Leander Class frigate heading west a mile or so offshore and looking spick and span yet with a hint of menace. I felt for no good reason that the Navy was sending me an upbeat message for Portsmouth. Buoyed up I flew to Southampton and when I confidently predicted victory at the by-election press conference I really believed it.

The Sunday before polling day the *Mail on Sunday* predicted a shock for the Tories and Willy Wolff, an old friend from *Daily Mirror* days, predicted in the *Scottish Sunday Mail* that we would win. Just as our confidence grew, on Monday afternoon we heard that the *Daily Mail*'s NOP poll, to be published on Tuesday, showed us lying third with 25 per cent of the vote. It was hard to keep our nerve but constituency polls are notoriously inaccurate and we had had these false alarms before. I went to the eve of poll meeting which was packed, anxious and apprehensive, but feeling certain by the end that we would win. Sure enough, we had a stunning victory. I knew then that the SDP would survive any attempt to rob us of our independence this side of the election. Mike Hancock polled 15,358 votes, the Conservatives 14,017 and Labour 10,846. We had vast publicity on the Friday and Saturday and this ensured that, when the European election results were announced on the Sunday, the relatively disappointing performance of the Alliance went largely unnoticed. The *Daily Mail* hailed our result as 'The Alliance victory that cannot be ignored'. The *Express* called it a 'Famous victory' and the *Daily Mirror*, under the headline 'SUNK' said the Tories were left 'beached, battered and bewildered'. The *Guardian* called it 'A sharp kick on the lady's ankle'.

In March 1984, a national miners' strike began, led by Arthur Scargill and called without a ballot. Here was a litmus-test issue for the Social Democrats. There was no dilemma for me – Arthur Scargill must be defeated. If he won, it would do irreparable damage to the market economy, to democracy and to the elected government's ability to govern. Once more the SDP had to show that it would not split the difference, would not call for compromise, would not show the loss of confidence that had characterized the Centre too often. We had to back the Government, and we did.

Until July there was no public difference between the Liberals and ourselves over the miners' strike, but in our inter-party discussions in Parliament we were aware that there were growing tensions within their ranks, a wish to hedge their bets and not give the appearance of being hostile to the miners. Early in July I went to a Liberal summer school and warned that if the Government were defeated by the miners it could cause an avalanche of similar disputes with a general loss of confidence in government; this was one of the few industrial disputes which were 'clearly political and should be beaten in the name of economic and political sense'. Soon after this our unity broke. David Steel, who was coming under increasing criticism from within his own ranks for allowing me to dominate the Alliance, attacked me in thinly veiled terms, saying that it was foolish of the Prime Minister to talk in terms of victory and defeat. The press were briefed that it was not just the Prime Minister he had in mind and the headlines shouted 'Steel attacks Owen line' and 'Steel's Thatcher rebuke rebounds on Owen'. For David to have asserted himself on this issue seemed to me to be very bad politics. By then there were very few among the general public who wanted Arthur Scargill to win. They rightly saw this strike as a direct challenge to the rule of law and parliamentary democracy.

On the same day as these reports, I attacked Neil Kinnock in the *Sunday Express* for not speaking up for the moderate miners at the recent Durham miners' gala. Given that his father was a miner and that the Welsh miners were far from enthusiastic about Arthur Scargill's leadership, it amazed me that he had not stuck to his initial position and held fast to the need for a pit-head ballot. It would have given him a position of principle wholly in keeping with the miners' tradition.

By then I was getting worried about the mood for compromise that was developing. I genuinely did believe that Scargill had to be beaten and was horrified at any possibility of the Government cobbling-up some face-saving formula. The SDP MPs urged me to continue to make it quite clear publicly that we were not going to be diverted by Liberal criticism. With their backing I spoke in the Adjournment Debate, before the House of Commons went down for the summer recess, demanding action on secondary picketing by miners, declaring that it was unacceptable that the law on the statute book had not been used after twenty weeks of the strike. Of course we wanted the dispute ended, but not at any price. The NUM should not be able to say which pits should or should not be closed. I ended by saying that 'Scargill's tactics of intimidation, violence, bullying and distortion are intolerable in this country.'

During the strike I established close contacts with the UDM which had been set up by moderate miners, mainly in Nottinghamshire, seeing their leaders privately. They had no money at that time and I arranged with a friend for some financial support, although I chose not to have any publicity. Their cause was too important to be mixed with the party political debate. They needed to attract Labour moderates and being portrayed as an offshoot of the SDP would not help them. During the strike I deliberately went down a pit in Nottingham, ignoring the pickets. I was given a friendly welcome at the coal face. As I emerged from the shaft I was met by television cameras asking for a comment on the death of a taxi driver in South Wales as a result of a block of concrete being dropped on his car. It was a harsh reminder of the passions underlying the dispute and of the dangers.

Unfortunately it is all too typical of the Liberal Party that when the going gets rough on a political issue they back off. We had also been having trouble with them over renewing the Prevention of Terrorism legislation for Northern Ireland. Though David was being pressurized within his own Party, our tougher stance was not damaging the Alliance and we were doing well in the opinion polls. We had also reached an agreement that our two policy committees would aim to have a draft general election manifesto ready by the summer of 1986. Yet Labour was in the lead in the polls, not so much because of positive support but because the Alliance was taking Conservative votes.

In August Ian Wrigglesworth publicly clashed with David Steel over the Government's handling of the miners' strike. David was suggesting that Peter Walker, the Energy Secretary, should meet with the TUC leaders to try and resolve the strike. Ian flatly contradicted that view and said quite rightly that the one thing the Government should not do was to be seen to intervene directly in the dispute. In effect the SDP backed Margaret Thatcher's stance throughout, rather as we had done during the Falklands War. We did, however, want more action on creating jobs in mining villages and argued that the Coal Board should set up a company, as British Steel had done, to help revive communities likely to be severely hit by heavy redundancies.

When the pit deputies union, NACODS, threatened strike action at the end of October there had to be some flexibility in the Coal Board's position and it was Ministers who leant on the NCB to give a little on the procedure for closing uneconomic pits. But it was a hostage to fortune and I was extremely worried that this could be used by Scargill as a face-saver. Fortunately his Marxism came to the rescue and because he was not prepared to compromise at any stage he did not pick up the NACODS settlement and run with it as he well could have done. At the unveiling of a plaque for WPC Fletcher on the spot where she had been shot down outside the Libyan Embassy, I took the opportunity of being in the same room as Margaret Thatcher to have a private talk with her. She seemed genuinely pleased to find that my worries about letting Arthur Scargill off the hook were exactly the same as hers. She made no attempt to conceal the fact that some of her colleagues wanted to settle but that she was adamantly against it. She was clear-sighted about the danger of Scargill being able to claim a spurious victory.

In assessing Margaret Thatcher's leadership I believe the miners' dispute showed her at her best. She had cut her losses and settled when challenged by Joe Gormley in 1981 and had then planned ahead for the inevitable confrontation with Arthur Scargill. Some critics attacked her for having chosen Ian Macgregor as head of the NCB with allegations that he was personally provocative. Admittedly his public relations sense left much to be desired, but his management skills and rhinoceros hide were considerable assets. When I talked to him I found him cool and calculating. Few of our other leading industrialists would have had the nerve to hold as firm as he did. His experience in North America had taught him that managers have to be ready to withstand strikes. He did not hold with the fashionable assumption that a shift in the management's final offer is always inevitable. We were lucky to have him in that position and there has been far too much retrospective dumping on him.

The key to victory over the miners was keeping the Government out of the firing line, at least in public, and letting Macgregor bear the brunt of the criticism. I advocated using the new picketing legislation, though I could see that there was some merit in demonstrating that Scargill could be defeated under the old legislation. The nature of the mass picketing at Orgreave damaged the reputation of the police. When the end came in March 1985, fifty-one weeks after the strike had started, it was the miners who disowned their leaders by streaming back to work with their funds running low and their self-respect in tatters. It was galling for Edward Heath to see 'that woman' defeat the very NUM which had so humiliated him and lost the Conservatives the 1974 Election. But for the country as a whole it was essential for our self-confidence that intimidation and violence could be resisted without tear gas or mobilizing the armed services. The police, with a few exceptions, did extremely well and showed that with good co-ordination between constabularies a national effort could be mobilized without the centralized danger of having to adopt a national police force. We had Devon policemen on the picket lines and talking to them about their experience I was reminded how restricted country life still is; many of them had never even been to London let alone further north.

The miners' strike also involved the SDP in a battle with the BBC. On Tuesday 19 June I had a Private Notice Question in the Commons to the Home Secretary, Leon Brittan. I put it to him that the public mood was one of increasing frustration at seeing the police force subjected night after night to violence and battering. When the TUC code of conduct provided for only six people on a picket I wanted to know why no action had been taken under the civil law to prevent mass picketing by thousands of people. I alleged that the Government had dissuaded the British Steel Corporation from using the civil law. In reply Leon Brittan said, somewhat unconvincingly, that the Government did not seek to stand in BSC's way if they wished to take action. I was incredulous that no representatives from either the SDP or Liberal Party were included in the television discussions that followed these exchanges in the House of

Commons. Nor was there any news report on what I had said. With the heartening Portsmouth result I now felt that we were strong enough to start procedures to take the BBC to court. The Liberals were extremely reluctant, preferring to continue protesting privately over occasional meals with BBC executives. However, when I explained that there would be no legal costs billable to them they then acquiesced. With the help of Anthony Lester QC, an SDP member, we set out to build our case by writing to the Chairman of the Broadcasting Complaints Commission. I claimed that in comparison with Labour the Alliance was being given grossly unfair treatment. We had resisted innundating the BBC with large numbers of small complaints, since I accepted that political balance has to be assessed in the round and over a period of time. But we had organized a monitoring exercise of BBC Television's main *Nine o'Clock News* and ITN's *News at Ten* over ten weeks between February and April. This showed the coverage of the parties' political activities in minutes and seconds:

	Conservative	Labour	Alliance
BBC	85'14"	28'26"	7'60"
ITN	88'58"	36'57"	5'31"

The Broadcasting Complaints Commission Chairman replied that they had no power to examine our complaint over whether the authorities were failing in their duty to act fairly and impartially and not to discriminate. That admission meant the way was now clear to apply for judicial review on the grounds of natural justice and this we did, hoping our case would come up before the end of the year.

It was the SDP annual Conference at Buxton which started to consolidate our new policy image and, in particular, robustly backed the social market economy. I was worried too that we were not building an electoral machine and so I emphasized, rather crudely, in my leader's speech that, 'I am only interested in one thing, that we win votes, that we win influence and that we win power.' Nevertheless the Party was now showing a good deal more self-confidence. It was noticeable that the quality of the speeches had greatly improved and that fringe meetings were well attended, particularly one with the moderate Nottinghamshire miners, which offset the flying pickets we encountered outside the Conference Hall (xxxvii). We were also building up party spirit. We had the first of what became annual conference revues in the lovely little Buxton Opera House. Roy Jenkins was a great hit when he joined the policemen's chorus singing 'A policeman's lot is not a happy one'. Debbie and I did a replay of 'Love me tender, love me tough; All our dreams fulfil'. It was a disaster! By the time I got to 'Truly Liberals we love you' I had gone flat, as if I knew I was striking a false note. The audience howled with laughter and we never got back in tune. There was also a football match, the old beating the young, but I was so exhausted that I vowed it would be the last time I took out my football boots. The young later claimed that they only lost because we had fifteen players on our side. Everyone enjoyed Buxton, and with the merger issue temporarily buried and those in favour of merger merely burrowing away beneath the surface, it was possible to hope that the SDP could establish itself as a permanent fourth political party.

The Liberal Party Conference in Bournemouth seemed a scratchier affair. The mood was not helped by the Liberal MP Stephen Ross saying he would be perfectly prepared to accept me as the 'natural Alliance leader' and describing his own Leader as a 'first class deputy'. This led David to assert, rather usefully from my point of view, that there should not be a single Alliance leader, we were a duet and that he was not playing second fiddle to anyone. Overall our partnership was working tolerably well. The worst moment came when the Liberal Assembly voted for the removal of cruise missiles 'forthwith', a policy advocated with zest by Paddy Ashdown, now an MP, who became the conference hero. This vote was despite a speech by David Steel, from the rostrum, arguing against removal. David had not even been arguing for full deployment but for the fudged solution – the freeze – which Tom McNally was always urging me to accept. Yet even that had not won sufficient Liberal support. We were all too relaxed in the SDP about Liberal defence attitudes, in retrospect foolishly so, given what was to come in Eastbourne in 1986. It should have served to stiffen some of the National Committee not just on joint selection, but on preserving our own identity. In Wales in particular we were conceding far too much ground on joint selection and the SDP's identity. The threat of a CND Liberal candidate representing the Alliance was real enough but that Liberal votes should swing a selection conference to an SDP CND candidate was my nightmare. In the National Committee I had just managed to win the vote to exclude CND supporters from our panel of candidates. But before every attempt to hold the line on defence I had to organize to ensure I had the votes and carefully lobby within the National Committee beforehand. Those who criticize me for not being interested in party management have no idea of how many hours I spent keeping a majority for sensible policies within the SDP's own democratic forums. In doing this I relied on a few people who were ready to risk unpopularity with the Liberals. Too many who ought to have known better were cuddling up to the Liberals in the hope of getting a constituency with a chance of victory, and if joint selection procedures were the price they were only too ready to pay it.

In the early hours of 12 October I was telephoned at my Sheffield hotel for a comment on the IRA bomb explosion which had gutted part of the Grand Hotel at Brighton and could well have destroyed the whole Cabinet. Margaret Thatcher had been very fortunate to escape and the IRA taunt, 'Today we were unlucky, but remember we have only to be lucky once', was revolting. But it was also a reminder of the constant

threat with which she had to live. It was a numbing moment and I was
very distressed for John Wakeham, who suffered appalling injuries himself
and lost his wife and for Anthony Berry's widow. Later I visited Norman
Tebbit and his wife in Stoke Mandeville. He was very brave but his
bounce had temporarily gone and she was showing the stoicism of a
former nurse. Driving away from the hospital I felt all my medical cool,
which had been on display, disappear and replaced by political anger.
Debbie and I attended a special performance of Andrew Lloyd-Webber's
Requiem in Westminster Abbey and felt the grieving of the whole
Conservative Party. It was a terrible incident. When, much later, there
was snide criticism of the security gates being put up at the Whitehall
end of Downing Street, I was amazed at how short people's memories
were. Can anyone believe that they would have been put up on any other
grounds than that of security? Perhaps those critics felt some embarrassment when a mortar bomb nearly killed John Major and his colleagues in
the Cabinet Room. There is very little anyone can do to stop a terrorist
or fanatic who wants to kill a politician. I had long since resigned myself
to that. Once in the Cambridge Union while Foreign Secretary, with six
detectives present, someone stole in and dumped a bag of flour on my
head while I was actually speaking.

At the end of October Indira Gandhi was assassinated by her Sikh
bodyguards. I flew off to attend the funeral with Margaret Thatcher.
Princess Anne represented the Queen and Jim Callaghan attended since
he was already in India on a lecture tour. During my time as Foreign
Secretary, Indira Gandhi had only been Leader of the Opposition. Yet
Callaghan had seen her, when she came to London, despite the protests
of the Janata Government. Watching as Rajiv Gandhi, her son and
successor, lit the sandalwood funeral pyre, I noticed the visual effect of
the family figured against the heat haze walking anti-clockwise around
the fire with their slightly distorted figures and faces. It took me back to
my childhood having stories told to me in the fire and feeling the burning
heat on my face. In Hinduism everything goes backward at the time of
death. Yet in the midst of the crowd was the uniformed figure of General
Zia, the military ruler of Muslim Pakistan, sitting on his shooting-stick,
as Jim Callaghan said, as if he was at a point-to-point. Bizarrely acting as a
reminder for all the world that he was perched on enemy territory. That
Pakistan and Indian armies faced each other across a disputed border in
Kashmir with periodic fighting. I was later to get to know Rajiv, to visit
him in his office in Delhi and hitch a lift with him on his plane from
London to Mexico when we attended a conference on the Non-Proliferation Treaty. Six-and-a-half years after his mother's assassination, he was
to suffer the same fate and the world once again watched as India, the
largest democracy in the world with over 800 million people, mourned.
For me that funeral in 1991 had a special poignancy for my son, Gareth,
aged eighteen had just returned from visiting India with a young friend

from Atlantic College. He had fallen for India just like I had when I was aged twenty-one. For a parent there is a special delight as we watch our children grow and when my children have experiences similar to my own I find myself reliving my past with them.

In December I was elected Parliamentarian of the Year by the *Spectator*, sponsored by Highland Park whisky. It was the first year of their awards which have now become a part of the parliamentary scene. The judges said that, though my aggressiveness was not to everyone's taste, I had employed it to great effect in the past year and had succeeded in putting down the hecklers on the bench on which we sat and in challenging the Government, particularly the Prime Minister, with clear, simple, well-informed interventions. This was gratifying because I had gone out of my way to use the House of Commons as a forum for political argument. In effect as a bully pulpit for the SDP. My speech of acceptance, however, was so long that the judges must have regretted their choice. It was bad judgement: journalists are not the people to harangue on proportional representation; they are not receptive to concepts – they want hard news or witty asides.

I wrote to Jim Callaghan who had been taken ill but was fortunately making a good recovery. In reply, while congratulating me on the parliamentarian award, he gently warned me not to acquire a Right-wing image – and to remember my socialist origins which went back a long way to when I first fought to enter Parliament and contained values worth advancing in today's society. He was correct, for the values of the best practitioners of the socialist vision do have an enduring relevance. It was like being back on a VC-10 flying to an international conference when a quiet word from Jim would flash a warning message. I took far more notice of his injunction than any jibe from my fellow Gang of Four members about being sub-Thatcherite.

At the end of the year I gave a party message which was once again about winning the balance of power. This irritated those in the Liberal Party and a few in the SDP who believed that we should at all times pretend that we were going to form the Government of the country. Those who actually believed this was possible could make that claim. The only claim I could make with conviction was that we could carry increased influence after the next election. The Alliance was picking up in the polls, we were emerging as the main rival of the Conservatives in the south of England and we were eroding some of the votes the Conservatives had gained from Labour. But outright victory was still far from our grasp, and I was worried about our inability to carry the fight to Labour in the Midlands and in the north.

We now had firm polling evidence that if people believed we would hold the balance they would vote for us in only slightly smaller numbers than if they believed we would win. We repeatedly confirmed this finding, but I could not get my colleagues to focus on it. Since holding the balance of power was possible and outright victory incredible it was not political prejudice but psephological evidence which dictated an electoral strategy putting the balance of power issue at the top of our agenda. Our 1983 experience demonstrated the dangers of pursuing the Prime Minister designate strategy. I found the freedom and flexibility the balance of power idea gave us very attractive, quite apart from its credibility. But prejudice triumphed and I never convinced a sufficient number of serious people in both parties that this should be our strategy. They might agree in the Alliance Strategy Committee but would abandon the policy no sooner than they were out of the door and no longer had to confront facts. The reason was that balance of power posed the problem of choice – which coalition did you prefer.

Meanwhile Roy Jenkins had started telling the press that I reminded him of Joe Chamberlain, the nineteenth-century Birmingham radical, who started on the Left wing of the Liberal Party and ended as an imperialist in alliance with the Conservatives. I began to have some sympathy with Margaret Thatcher in having to deal with Edward Heath's constant sniping. But like her I knew the best tactic was to totally ignore it. But I did become something of an expert on this part of our political history, talking with Julian Amery, Chamberlain's biographer.

When Gorbachev came over in December 1984 David Steel and I were both allocated a set time to talk to him, and we decided to amalgamate our meetings so as to have long enough to get to know his views. Even then it was clear he was likely to be the next Soviet Leader. He was certainly a new phenomenon among Soviet politicians for he talked far more freely and was more combative. I had a short verbal punch up with him over human rights in Northern Ireland and I saw why a few months later, when recommending he should become General Secretary, Gromyko had said, 'He may have a nice smile, but he has teeth of steel.' Over the years he has transformed his language and what he says now about a market economy and democracy is far more realistic. But even then he had an openness and a readiness to use a different vocabulary to that of the programmed Marxists; also to think conceptually. I sensed, however, a deep seated authoritarianism, which was not surprising in someone who had struggled up the communist ladder to the Politburo, and which even then I feared would restrict his apparent flexibility. As he has evolved as a leader he does seem to have been far readier than I then anticipated to bend with circumstances and to adapt pragmatically, even in sensitive areas like the possible secession of the Baltic States from the USSR. But he has been a leader who has never been ready to put his own authority to the democratic test. Elections have been introduced, and were often manipulated in the early days, but his own power base has been sacrosanct, never allowed to be put at risk in the ballot box. The feeling I had then that he was a Czar-like figure, a relatively benign dictator, has never left me.

Alan Clark, a junior Minister and my Conservative neighbour in Plymouth, was starting a campaign for me to join the Conservatives, with which he persisted over the years. Though anonymous, those who know him would not have found it hard to detect Alan's voice in this cavalier contribution reported in the press: 'The trouble is that he has landed himself with a real shower. The Liberals are useless and the SDP are a rabble. He is surrounded by pygmies and he is very uncomfortable company for them. They have become used to flabby chieftains.' Alan, the son of Kenneth Clark who wrote the TV series *Civilization*, is himself an accomplished military historian and an original character. He relishes being thought Right-wing but in many areas is refreshingly radical. Few revel in or generate more political gossip. I enjoy his company, both the indiscretions and the insights. We lunch together from time to time and he has a novel way of introducing me to his friends: 'Have you met my doctor?' Our friendship started over the Falklands, when we were both desperately worried about the safety of our Plymouth constituents. He was close to Margaret Thatcher, but I was not sure how influential. I have given up trying to stop him placing stories in the press about becoming a Conservative because he does it out of a mixture of affection and devilment. He knows perfectly well that I am never going to become a Conservative but gains raffish delight in perpetuating the myth.

I have never been able to decide whether these stories about me going to join the Conservatives did me and the SDP harm or not. But I had for some years refused to play the party game. David Steel used to make the odd jibe at it which never upset me much; like saying the Alliance would not succeed, 'by presenting ourselves as Crypto-Tories'. The reason this did not perturb me was that I wanted the Alliance to be seen as a potential coalition partner for whichever party – Conservative or Labour – that seemed at the time to be most likely to govern in sympathy with SDP policies. In the public mind I was inevitably associated with Labour because I had been Labour so to counter-balance this with talk of a Conservative future, as long as it did not get out of hand, might be beneficial. But I knew it was an issue to watch and I resolved to ponder the question over Christmas and in the New Year when we were in Kenya on holiday.

31

SDP LEADER – 1985

When I returned from Kenya in January 1985 I openly said on Channel 4 on 14 January 1985 that, 'I would never join the Conservative Party.' If there was any danger of me becoming too identified with the Conservatives, I now made it crystal clear that I was not going to become a Tory. Some people say that politicians should never say never. But I knew in my heart that it was true and saying so in such a public way gave me the freedom to support some Conservative policies while remaining firmly a Social Democrat. On that same programme I was adamant that, 'nothing that anyone says is going to change my fundamental position that when I think somebody is saying something right and in the country's interest I will support it, irrespective of which party they come from'.

Since 1982 I had been ready to negotiate a role in a coalition led by a Conservative Prime Minister if the circumstances were right for the SDP. Even if Labour had ever been ready to negotiate, it was not until 1989 that Labour's policies had sufficiently changed to be able to envisage the SDP being in a coalition led by a Labour Prime Minister. Coalition partners have no right to say who leads the larger party, which is why I have always resisted saying that I would never serve under Margaret Thatcher or Neil Kinnock. Coalition politics needs to transcend personalities and focus on policies. For the SDP to be open to negotiation with either of the larger national parties is not to be a political harlot. It simply means being ready to practise the coalition politics which comes with proportional representation. I have often tried, but singularly failed, to convince both David Steel and Roy Jenkins that this outlook has merit. Sadly the deep-seated nature of the party political battle in Britain has made it very hard for some sensible people involved in the SDP and Liberal parties to think in these terms.

In the middle of January our action on the BBC finally came to the High Court. We attempted to persuade them to declare that the Broadcasting Complaints Commission under the 1981 Broadcasting Act did have jurisdiction to deal with our complaint. Anthony Lester argued that our case raised the question of whether there was any effective remedy for a substantial complaint of imbalance in the way British politics were reported and discussed on the broadcasting media. He contended that television had become vital to modern politics because of its importance in influencing public opinion and that imbalance had major consequences on the competition between political parties for public support. The Alliance had obtained 25.4 per cent of the vote in the 1983 General Election – only 2 per cent less than the Labour Party. In six subsequent by-elections the Alliance share had been 36 per cent with the Conservatives polling 32 per cent and Labour 29 per cent. This change in voting patterns had not been matched by a change in the way television covered politics. Our ten-week survey had shown that Conservative spokesmen had a 70 per cent share of television time, Labour 25 per cent and the Alliance only 5 per cent. If the Commission could abdicate its responsibility on the grounds that its power was confined only to programme content it would mean the Alliance parties had no remedy. Leonard Hoffmann, QC for the Commission, said we should not have gone to the Commission but to the BBC Governors and the IBA. The Court, however, upheld our complaint that the matter fell within the jurisdiction of the Commission, but ruled that the Commission was within its rights in using its wide discretionary power to refuse to consider our complaints. We had no redress.

The then Chairman of the BBC, the late George Howard, in what David Watt described in *The Times* as a wonderfully insolent letter, laid out to David Steel and me the BBC's case: 'Parliamentary convention nominates the Opposition party with most seats as Her Majesty's Opposition. As far as I know that continues to be the convention. It is one which we shall continue to observe in our coverage when seeking official comment on announcements of public policy.' Fortunately subsequent chairmen have been readier to acknowledge the small matter of fairness, and the Howard doctrine has been consigned to the wastepaper basket. When those words were read out in court, even the BBC representative appeared embarrassed. Whereas the IBA is enjoined by the law to be 'fair', the BBC's Royal Charter has no such imperative and when the Charter is revised over the next few years it should be given the same directive as the IBA. In preparing submissions for the hearing, the BBC had to reveal more than ever before about their inner workings, and despite their denials it became clear that they did monitor on a statistical basis for balance. The BBC then behaved in a quite extraordinary manner, seeking a legally binding pledge preventing us from disclosing any of the detailed information which they had made available to us for the Court case. For an organization that prides itself on producing programmes championing open government, it was an extremely depressing action. I wanted to expose it for the humbug it was, but I was advised to concede and so I am still bound by a pledge to the Court not to make public the information which I have. Fortunately the Court was not prepared to accede to the BBC demands that we should pay anyone else's costs and ruled that everyone should be responsible for their own costs. Since that Court hearing, there has been a marked change for the better in the way that the SDP/Liberal Alliance and now the Liberal Democrats are treated on the main BBC and ITN news bulletins. Politics is no longer presented simply as a two-horse race. It was well worth taking the matter to court and we were fortunate to have the help of such an able team of lawyers.

By February the *Mail on Sunday* was carrying a headline, 'GET OWEN ORDER BY TORY BIG GUNS', predicting that alarmed Ministers had been ordered to swing their political guns on to me in an attempt to sink the Alliance. They saw our 25 per cent Gallup poll rating as a very good launching pad and opened hostilities by barracking me in an economic debate in the House of Commons. A few days later David Steel was warning me again about the danger of sounding too Thatcherite, particularly on the miners' strike. Given that the miners' strike was just about to collapse, this seemed rather odd timing. Even so I did warn the Prime Minister that she should remember Lord Nelson's words on the eve of the Battle of Trafalgar: 'May humanity after victory be the predominant feature.' The question over my leadership was whether the Alliance, which before 1983 had been a herbivorous grouping, could be led by a carnivore. It was in February too that Roy Jenkins started likening me to the Javanese upas tree, poisoning all other life nearby. This was a charge soon to be repeated by that well-established carnivore Denis Healey. It was actually too delicate a barb for Denis to handle. He is a specialist in hyperbolic abuse. To be savaged by Denis Healey is a compliment to savour, spit out and return in kind. His best crack about me was that, 'The good fairies gave the young doctor almost everything: thick dark locks, matinée idol features, a lightning intelligence – unfortunately the bad fairy also made him a shit.'

On 11 February a jury found Clive Ponting, a civil servant in the Ministry of Defence, not guilty of revealing classified information about the Falklands War. This was a snub to the Judge whose summing-up had virtually instructed them to find him guilty under the Official Secrets Act. Ponting's defence had been that he had acted from a duty to uphold the 'interests of the state' in giving information to an MP on the cover-up surrounding the sinking of the *Belgrano*. He was a member of the SDP, and I had seen him a couple of times and very carefully considered going to Court in his defence. Eventually Shirley Williams agreed to go to Court as did Merlyn Rees. I had been in favour of sinking the *Belgrano* but nevertheless appalled by the cover-up. To this day it is not clear to me why Ministers continued to refuse to tell the truth after the war was over, failing to take the opportunity to correct the record in the White Paper published months afterwards. Perhaps it will be the most favourable explanation, that they did not want to reveal information which the Argentines could use for claiming compensation under International Law, for there was some cloudiness about the legality of actions outside the exclusion zone. The worst explanation is the civil service, particularly in the Ministry of Defence, were involved in an effort to save Ministers from having to admit an error. But in the heat of war, no one in Parliament would have been greatly outraged if they had inadvertently or even deliberately misled us. But the Ponting case raised deeper questions about where civil servants owed their loyalty. To me it cannot be right that it is at all times to the government of the day irrespective of circumstance and that there can be no public interest defence. I used this case and that of the Ministry of Defence officials who briefed Churchill in the late 1930s on the German rearmament figures to urge a public interest defence on Douglas Hurd when he was Home Secretary and the law was being reformed. It was obvious to the House of Commons that he was unhappy about rejecting it. Now that Margaret Thatcher's veto no longer applies, we should have a public interest defence reinserted in our law, perhaps as part of the legislation for a Citizens Charter which is promised by every political party.

By early March 1985 the rumblings over joint selection were becoming audible. We had no hope of renegotiating the basic 1982 deal with all its inbuilt unfairness to the SDP. The most we could hope for was to hold our own. Our aim was to ensure that the SDP fought no less than 300 of the 650 seats. But to achieve this, the Liberal Party argued (with support from within the SDP), we had to concede joint open selection where members of both parties vote for candidates of either party. Eleven of these joint selections had already been agreed by the SDP National Committee, as being exceptional cases under the formula I had reluctantly conceded at Salford in 1983. I had opposed most of these in the National Committee, so the claim that the Committee did everything I wanted was quite wrong. They had also agreed twelve closed selections, which is when the combined membership choose from candidates of only one party. I had opposed most of these too. Cambridgeshire were now threatening to make a unilateral declaration of independence. This was high politics because it was an open secret that Shirley was thinking of becoming the candidate for Cambridge. The Liberals were crafty over joint selection; knowing that both Shirley Williams and Bill Rodgers wanted to get back into the House of Commons, they made it clear that Shirley could not have Cambridge or Bill Milton Keynes unless the SDP was prepared to agree to these seats being chosen by joint selection. Eventually we conceded, seriously compromising a principled opposition to joint selection within the SDP. It also provided a subtle pressure, impelling both Shirley and Bill to become Alliance-minded and increasingly favourable to merger. Despite all this merging by stealth I was not averse to trying to widen the areas of policy agreement between our two parties and had supported the establishment of two further commissions, one on defence and one on Northern Ireland. I suggested that Bill should be on the Defence Commission and Shirley on the Northern Ireland one.

On 10 March Chernenko died and Mikhail Gorbachev, at fifty-four the youngest member of the Politburo, became their Leader. Once again I flew to Moscow for the funeral with Margaret Thatcher, Neil Kinnock and David Steel. It was freezing cold and David Steel came with a hip flask of Scotch whisky which we swigged down to keep our spirits up, if not the cold out. This time it was incredible how well briefed Margaret Thatcher was on the Soviet Union and her attitudes had dramatically changed. There was no question that her meeting with Gorbachev had produced a transformation in her stance. In the receiving line Gorbachev was personally welcoming to all of us and his earlier visit to Britain had been extremely well timed. For the first time since Nixon and Brezhnev I began to feel some optimism about making progress on nuclear disarmament.

Towards the end of April the Labour Party completely lost their cool in the House of Commons and did themselves a great deal of harm when their Left wing attempted to prevent me opening a debate on trade union democracy. This was the first debate allocated to the SDP. The antics began with Labour MPs occupying the bench below the gangway when a division was called and we in the SDP had to vote. Labour MPs ran a shift system so that our bench was occupied throughout the vote and neither Ian Wrigglesworth nor I could get back on to our bench. Denis Skinner then demanded of the Deputy Speaker that we should speak from the Conservative benches, given our views on trade union ballots. By this time I was sitting in the gangway between the Opposition front bench and the bench below the gangway which SDP and Labour MPs normally shared. I then moved to exercise my traditional right as a Privy Councillor, which the Labour Party had forgotten about, to speak from the Despatch Box opposite the Government. At this point I was elbowed away by John Prescott, the Shadow Employment Spokesman. I approached the Despatch Box again only to encounter legs stretched out and feet firmly planted on the table. Amid uproar the Deputy Speaker was being continually asked whether I was entitled to speak from the Despatch Box. This continued for about forty-five minutes until finally a fifteen-minute suspension of the House of Commons was called, during which talks were held between us and the Conservative and Labour front bench. Labour finally agreed to vacate the bench below the gangway and I agreed to make my speech from there. It only served to make the Labour Party look loutish and draw attention to the SDP's popular policies on giving power to the individual trade unionist through postal ballots, a cause which had already been given a boost by the T&GWU ballot-rigging rumpus then in the news – to which Ron Todd had responded by promising to hold another ballot.

A few days later came quite a different escapade. My twelve-year-old son, Gareth, and I were out sailing in Wembury bay late on a cold windy afternoon when he saw some people waving at us from the cliff face. We took my twenty-foot gaff-rigged boat in close and saw five young men stranded on the cliff, one of them lying on the ground halfway between the sea and the clifftop. We sailed back to our cottage as fast as we could, rang the coastguards, gathered all our warm sailing clothes and ropes and, with Debbie, Tristan and Lucy, ran up to the cliff. We lowered and hurled down as much warm clothing as we could to the shivering teenagers below and, when the coastguard's Land-Rover arrived, helped haul the five young men 150 feet up the cliff to safety. A police helicopter had arrived by this time. Luckily no one was seriously hurt, though the men, from the naval training establishment HMS *Cambridge*, were all taken to hospital, frozen and shaken. An auxiliary coastguard told the press that if they had stayed out all night they would have died of the cold. Certainly the wind was gusting strongly, one of the reasons why no one had heard their cries for help. There were some dramatic photographs in Monday's newspapers, taken by an enterprising local resident, showing me hauling them up, along with headlines like 'OWEN SAVES FIVE IN CLIFFTOP DRAMA', 'OWEN IN CLIFF RESCUE' and 'SDP LEADER HELPS SAILORS IN SEA TRAP'.

The local elections took place three days later and in the Devon County elections in Plymouth the SDP did spectacularly well. We increased the SDP's strength from none to thirteen on Devon County Council – nine SDP councillors coming from Plymouth. As a result Devon County fell to the Alliance, an unbelievable result. I had assumed it would always be Tory controlled. In the country generally the county elections were a great success for the Alliance. Twenty-five of the shire authorities moved into a position of no overall control, in six councils the SDP/Liberal Alliance groups were running minority administrations, and in another three we were sharing power. The Plymouth result had been greatly helped by Michael Heseltine introducing agency management for the dockyard, seen as privatization by the back door and the cause of a tremendous furore locally. That the SDP had helped defeat the Tories so convincingly in my home patch greatly strengthened me in dealing with my SDP critics who said I was moving to the Right.

In a Tawney Society lecture two weeks later Bill Rodgers issued what was described as a warning to me against going too far towards a market economy or in appealing to Conservative supporters. In this almost completely unreconstructed speech he made public what I had known for many months – that Bill, Shirley and Roy were going to challenge the policy direction in which I was leading the Party more openly than hitherto. My reaction was to increase the pace of new thinking, propounding the theories of Professor Martin Weitzman on wider share ownership in a Gaitskell memorial lecture at Nottingham, and promoting the egalitarian concepts of Professor John Rawls, the Harvard University philosopher. I wanted privatization of the big public monopolies like gas to be accompanied by a free distribution of shares to all gas consumers, an idea originally put forward by Samuel Brittan. But I was never able to carry the Party with me on this because of the footling argument that some would cash in their shares. This did not worry me, they had the right to do what they liked with the distribution of their own asset; most would not do so and at least it would, like council house sales, spread wealth. It was better than just selling off assets to reduce the PSBR. Later that year Harold Macmillan, now the Earl of Stockton, made a witty but wrong-handed swipe at the whole concept of privatization, 'First of all the Georgian silver goes and then all the nice furniture that used to be in the saloon. Then the Canalettos go.' It was the paternalist voice of another era. Those who had shares for the first time in British Telecom, particularly the employees, were enjoying the increase in their value and were not at all keen for Labour to renationalize the Company. There was a populist appeal in spreading shareholding, the making of mini-capitalists, that the Macmillan of the 1930s writing the *Middle Way* might have well understood. The real criticism of the Government's privatization programme was that it sold shares at too favourable a price insufficiently widely. Yet on the substance the SDP supported almost all the sales, whether British Airways, Enterprise Oil, Sealink, Jaguar or Rolls-Royce. Our main criticism was over the sale of the Regional Water Authorities, but as debate raged over pollution control of the rivers, the Government conceded a National River Authority and some potentially significant statutory minimum standards. As a result, by the end the framework looked environmentally more sound than at the outset. The consumer interest, however, depends on how far the regulator is prepared to go in making new water authorities cost-effective.

The polls were now showing Labour only marginally ahead of us with the Tories third. Neil Kinnock was getting rattled and provocatively described me as 'fat on arrogance and drunk on ambition'. My best tactic was of course not to reply in kind, saying rather prissily that I would avoid putting any emphasis on personalities. This was humbug, provoking the Labour Party to such an extent that Jack Straw wrote an article to prove, not without difficulty, that I had been just as tough on Neil Kinnock, quoting me as saying 'spineless Kinnock' or 'the most vacuous leader in Labour's history' or that Kinnock was 'in Arthur Scargill's pocket'. Throughout history politicians have abused each other when they thought it was in their interests. It can go too far from time to time and then it backfires. But it does not usually cause a lot of ill-feeling. Neil Kinnock and I found ourselves a few days later outside the House of Commons helping launch a campaign to mark the UN International Youth Year, and there were smiles on our faces, though we were not revealing what was in our hearts.

In the Brecon and Radnor by-election, despite a last minute MORI poll in the *Daily Mirror* giving Labour the lead with 46 per cent, the Alliance second with 28 per cent, the actual electors voted very differently. The Liberals won with 35.8 per cent of the vote, Labour came second with 34.4 per cent and the Tories third. It was a tremendous result for everyone, especially Richard Livesey who went on to hold the seat at the general election. I was glad for David Steel. He had had a rough year and this result gave him great heart and balanced the SDP success in Portsmouth. If the partnership were to thrive, the more we could keep it in balance the better. We ended July with a joint conference of SDP/Liberal Alliance candidates in London where we both emphasized the dual leadership approach; a strategy meeting of Liberal MPs decided not to opt for one leader. It tends to be forgotten by those who wanted merger that we had had one leader during the 1983 Election. It had not been such a great success that people could argue with conviction that a single leader was a crucial ingredient. What was crucial was to be seen as a credible governing force. If only the Alliance had spent more time achieving credibility and less on mechanistic mergers we would have been seen as a more cohesive political force.

A BBC *Panorama* team were following me around then, supposedly making a serious documentary, and came with me and the family to Clement Freud's constituency summer fête. It was a good chance to see him operate in his constituency and I soon realized that behind all the joking was a dedicated constituency MP. His own jokes are hard to recapture, but explaining how he won his seat in the by-election he recalled visiting the local branch of the National Union of Railwaymen. He decided to enlist the aid of his distinguished grandfather, Sigmund Freud. 'I am not a railwayman,' he said, 'but my grandfather, Signalman Freud, was a great enthusiast.'

Also at the fête was an old friend of his, Yuri Geller, who proceeded to bend a spoon which I had chosen from the family cutlery and held in my hand throughout. All he did was concentrate and lightly pass his finger above and below the spoon as I held it out. *Panorama*, given the quality of their final offering, would have been better advised to have recaptured the whole thing on television. Try as I can, the only explanation I can come up with is that he does have the power to change the molecular structure of the metal in the spoon so that, instead of being so arranged as to give an interlocking strength, a gap occurs in the inner structure which creates a weakness. Holding the spoon I had no doubt it was not a product of pressure from his finger bending the spoon.

A gregarious and imaginative person, Clement Freud was a far more serious politician than he allowed people to believe. His defeat in the election meant more than the disappearance of an eccentric, as some saw him, but of a personality that enriched politics.

The SDP Conference started on 7 September in Torquay. It was to be the most successful in the Party's history, helped by non-stop sunshine and having the conference hall and hotel on the same site, surrounded by a semi-tropical garden. In the run-up to the Conference there had been a lot of tension in the air. Roy Jenkins had written an article about how, after Thatcher, the country would not want a 'sub-Thatcherite alternative', overt code for 'David Owen'. That was par for the course, but a more serious statement was his assertion that under no electoral system would there be room in the hearts of the British people for more than three mainstream political groups. Never before had he quite so clearly repudiated the four-party model on which the SDP had been launched.

Just before the Conference, David Steel publicly argued for a freeze on the deployment of cruise missiles, presumably in an attempt to influence our debate where the platform faced a challenge. Tom McNally had by then become obsessed with the belief that the freeze option was the way to defuse differences on defence between the two parties and was due to move an amendment to our SDP defence White Paper. Roy Jenkins was involved in the freeze movement and they were soon to recruit Shirley Williams. In the light of this we were probably lucky that most of the flak was drawn by a memorandum about the state of the Alliance which had leaked unhelpfully on the eve of our Conference. It had been written by one William Wallace, a Liberal few had heard of, who was an adviser to David Steel. Its message was reasonable enough, a warning that if the Liberals were serious about 'preparing for government' they should 'be scared stiff of arriving unprepared' and that 'ministerial experience from the SDP was a rapidly wasting asset'. Fortunately, as with so many conference crises which seem dreadful at the time, it was a one-day wonder. The more serious challenge came in a motion from Stevenage which endorsed the SDP's maintaining of many of the traditional values of the Labour Party. The wording looked fairly innocuous but it was being pushed as a proxy vote of opposition to purportedly sub-Thatcherite views.

Lucy had broken her leg and it was in plaster. She had also just lost one of her front teeth. A photo with her toothy grin looking up at me in Torquay was on the front of many Sunday papers, and it somehow summed up the mood of our young party where there seemed as many children as parents, with people taking a holiday to coincide with the meeting. As the Conference gathered momentum it became clear that this was now a confident Party, perfectly ready to sort out the wheat from the chaff, which was what it proceeded to do. Most unwisely Bill and Shirley had lined themselves up with the Stevenage motion, though it was noticeable that Roy had been a little more reluctant to do so, sensing that it was out of step with the mood of the Party. The National Committee, against Bill and Shirley's passionate argument, decided to oppose the Stevenage motion and some excellent speeches were made. Polly Toynbee, a member of the National Committee, urged the Party not to fall prey to middle-class guilt: 'Half of the Labour Party are Trotskyist Etonians, professional politicos and academic researchers assuming mock regional accents and calling each other "mate".' Sue Slipman, a former Communist, who replied on behalf of the National Committee to the debate, said that emotionally and politically she was left of Centre, a term which would not be rejected by most people in the SDP when used in the sense of supporting the have-nots rather than the haves.

> I am in this Party not because I reneged on my loyalty to my class but because I maintain it and I want them to have the same privileges and opportunities I managed to get. I know this is the Party that stands for that, not the Labour Party.

A new young star appeared in the Party's firmament. Danny Finkelstein, the chairman of the Young Social Democrats, argued that the strategy of the SDP should be based not on the old Labour Party but on the new politics of coalition. He borrowed the words of Monty Python: 'The old politics are dead. They have expired. They have ceased to be.' Danny as a youngster delivering leaflets for the Labour Party, by which he had been taught to 'lift' other parties' leaflets sticking out of letter boxes, duly pinched a number of SDP leaflets. He could not find a bin in which to dump them so when he got home he glanced at them, read them through, and converted to Social Democracy forthwith. His sister, Tamara, who tells this story, says there is a moral there somewhere!

The Stevenage motion which had been comprehensively hammered was withdrawn in favour of an amendment which talked only about the radical dimension of SDP policies. The social market was again resoundingly endorsed by the Conference. Non-nuclear defence was once again rejected, with a replacement for Polaris specifically accepted. Most people wanted a series of hard-edged, coherent policies which were distinctive and uniquely SDP. When I rose to speak at the end of the Conference I knew that we were getting close to being the sort of party I had hoped we would create back in 1981. I spoke directly without any written text and in a conversational style to the people watching on television as well as to my Conference listeners:

> Be proud of our party. Be proud of our Alliance. Respect other political opinions even if you disagree with them. Create a climate in this country which starts to end the divisions, the bitterness and the disillusion.

The rejection of the 'better yesterday' policies did, sadly, leave some tensions and hurt feelings within the National Committee; but most of those who attended the Conference left in tremendous heart, having thoroughly enjoyed the conference revue and our first cricket match which, like the revue, became an annual fixture. In the words of Peter Riddell of the *Financial Times*:

The Social Democratic Party has found itself at Torquay. After four years of introspection about whether it is a Labour Party Mark II or a Centre group aiming at disillusioned Tories, the Party's own activists have ended the debate. They have made it plain they dislike references to previous party labels and to the Left-Right spectrum. Instead, much to Dr David Owen's delight, the activists claim the Party has its own social democratic values, combining in the market economy, and radical social priorities which cannot easily be labelled Left or Right.

The opinion polls were showing the Alliance in the lead, and one had us 9.5 per cent ahead of Labour, with the Conservatives third.

The following week the Liberals held their Conference in Dundee. I had to go and speak, which I dreaded. To Liberal activists, according to the *Daily Telegraph*, I was 'a cross between a serpent in the garden of Eden and a walking threat to the eco-system, a sort of nuclear reactor on legs.' I escaped unscathed because their quarry was now Paddy Ashdown, who having as they saw it sold the pass on Liberal unilateralism during our Conference, was now referred to as 'Paddy Backdown', and had to suffer the ultimate indignity of lapel badges saying 'Ashdown has been doctored'.

After Dundee Roy sent me a card in which he was generous about my speech, saying he had watched it all on television, something he had not often done before, and commenting that though my method of speaking was obviously, and in his view rightly, very different from his own, he thought it was now more effective, particularly with the wider television audience. He went on to say that the impression of thinking as I went along came over very well and allowed me to relate general points to immediate events. He congratulated me on both Torquay and Dundee, which in general he felt went better than he had feared. This was a considerable gesture, particularly since he added, 'Incidentally, I don't think there are significant differences of policy between us now. I was slightly worried in 1983–84 but not now.'

I genuinely hoped this marked the end of our policy differences; obviously we would not agree on the merger issue but if Roy was happy with policy after Torquay I thought it meant he could now live with the social market economy and the replacement of Polaris, which made me very pleased. He even suggested that it was right to force the 'hung Parliament' issue on to the agenda, but had a point which he wanted to talk about. I am afraid this card lulled me into a false sense of security. I read it wrongly as the end of the sniping, that Roy, Bill and Shirley would now accept the new policies. Little did I realize that, through the Defence Commission, the three of them were within months going to launch the most direct policy challenge of my leadership.

The poll euphoria with which both our two parties ended the conference season was also premature. Neil Kinnock was preparing to take on Militant. At the Labour Party Conference, in a most courageous speech with moments of great theatre, Neil Kinnock rounded on the militants. He singled out and savaged Derek Hatton, a key figure behind the total shambles in which the Liverpool Labour Party had landed the City. It was an electric performance and I watched spellbound. The public watching on television liked what they saw. As Labour's poll rating immediately rose our lead vanished overnight. Now I saw we would be confronting an increasingly realistic Labour Party. We had to consolidate our position urgently, which involved my criss-crossing the country for meetings aimed at local television and newspapers, while being ready to return at short notice to the House of Commons. I still believed that it was in the House of Commons that the SDP would best prosper and Ian Wrigglesworth, Bob Maclennan and Charles Kennedy worked very hard in keeping up the SDP profile on every occasion.

On 15 November Margaret Thatcher and Garret Fitzgerald, the Irish Taoiseach, signed the Anglo-Irish Agreement. I wanted to believe it would work but had profound doubts. It seemed to be one of those rare occasions when Margaret Thatcher had given too much ground while negotiating. It was very understandable: Garret was not only one of the nicest persons in international politics but an indefatigable negotiator, as I had learnt to Britain's cost at many European Community Foreign Ministers' meetings. It must have been agony for Margaret Thatcher to sign the Agreement, for she is a believer in the Union and this was giving a *droit de regard* to the South which was without precedent. It also provoked the resignation of Ian Gow, perhaps her closest confidant. My anxiety was that the Agreement would offend mainstream opinion in the North without such compensating gains as the restoration of a devolved Assembly. It was generally felt by moderate Unionists to be unbalanced and that Garret Fitzgerald had scored too many points on behalf of John Hulme and the Catholic SDLP. But the Alliance Commission members were all in favour, including the sensible chairman, Lord Donovan, so I felt bound to support the Agreement in my speech in the House, but was more tentative and cautious than some would have wished, and Bob Maclennan shared my doubts. To me everything now depended on whether cross-border security improved. It was indefensible that the Irish and British armies were never in direct communication and the only contact was between the Garda and the RUC. I had been convinced for years that, until the border was no longer an open door, the IRA would never feel the pressure of living with their back against a wall. Also for a fellow member of the Community to have a claim to another's territory was hard to live with. Nevertheless a dialogue between Dublin and London was vital and this was the Agreement's great achievement. But the moderates had yet to be convinced. It would only, I thought, prosper when they in Belfast felt the advantages of having a formalized dialogue with Dublin.

On 19 November Mikhail Gorbachev and Ronald Reagan met in

Geneva. In all they spent six hours talking by the fire, with only interpreters present, and concluded with a joint press conference. For generations brought up on Soviet-American hostility the change of style was dramatic. It was obvious, though not yet to the most committed unilateralists, that the US policy of hanging tough had paid off. There would not just be a freeze on nuclear arsenals but real cuts. Nor had Reagan's emphasis on the Star Wars programme ruled out negotiations. It was possible even to hope that Reagan's gamble of going for the total removal of SS-20s in exchange for giving up the modernization of existing Pershing missiles and the deployment of cruise missiles, the so-called zero-zero option, might succeed. We were at the start of a positive phase in US-Soviet relations and I was delighted. I long regarded Reagan as a more interesting figure than it was then fashionable to suppose, ever since I had met him for the first time in November 1978. I had liked the way he handled himself – the unpretentious, friendly nature of the man, his refusal to appear as a smart ass and the readiness to admit ignorance. These were signs of strength. I had wanted to see if he was an isolationist in relation to NATO; he had wanted to talk about Africa. His last comment to me typified his style, 'Well, Dr Owen, I can't say you have convinced me on everything but you have convinced me on one thing – I won't be making any more speeches on Africa.' Sometimes it is a good thing to have an assured self-confident President, even if a rather simplistic one, in the White House and 1985 was just such a time. The uncertainties in Europe and the flux in the Soviet Union meant that we were fortunate to have a US President who could bargain without a political imperative for a deal with the Russians. Reagan was in his second term, having won an overwhelming victory in November 1984, his constituency was hard-line anti-Soviet and any deal he made would almost certainly carry Congress. There would be no repetition of President Carter's inability to obtain ratification in Congress. I felt genuinely optimistic.

On the evening of 3 December, more than fifteen million people stopped what they were doing and watched our Party Political Broadcast. Apart from a James Bond movie and *EastEnders* it was the biggest TV audience that week. Over 5,000 people telephoned after the broadcast and over 2,000 wrote in to express their support. It started with John Cleese mid-yawn saying 'I am sorry but this is a Party Political Broadcast and you know how boring they are. This one, I am afraid, promises to be outstandingly tedious.' He suggested switching over to snooker on the other side! His subject was Proportional Representation. He showed the grotesque unfairness of the British electoral system and lampooned the traditional argument that coalition governments are weak and indecisive. There were rollicking jokes about countries like poor, weak, old Germany and other countries with proportional representation whose standard of living far surpassed ours. For some time we had been breaking new ground in Party Political Broadcasts thanks to party members freely giving their skills, but this was easily the best we had done and we achieved a good deal of favourable press coverage.

The year ended with the Intergovernmental Conference, under article 236 of the Treaty of Rome, reaching agreement in Luxembourg. Here was Margaret Thatcher agreeing to majority voting on an extensive scale to introduce a single market by 1993. The powers of the European Parliament were increased to allow them to amend single market decisions, there was an extension of Community competence and political co-operation over foreign affairs was now formalized under the Treaty. Margaret Thatcher then proceeded to carry this far-reaching legislation through the House of Commons with hardly any protest. This was an example of Margaret Thatcher the pragmatist. She wanted a single market and to achieve it she was ready to compromise on a specific issue with well defined boundaries to it. Because of this readiness to grapple with Europe on a practical level there was no real political controversy over Europe prior to the 1987 election. And for some of the conservative Europeans the knowledge that she reacted responsibly over the single market meant they were less excitable and anti-Thatcher when the Westland case blew up a few weeks later.

32

SDP LEADER – 1986

At the beginning of 1986 Michael Heseltine walked out of a Cabinet meeting and resigned. The Westland affair had lit a fire that smouldered for half a decade. In retrospect it was his resignation which paved the way for Margaret Thatcher's overthrow in November 1990, bringing together the two critical ingredients – attitudes to the European Community and the authoritarian style with which Margaret Thatcher governed.

As so often in politics it was the personality clash between Heseltine and Thatcher that lit the fuse. Michael Heseltine was elected to Parliament for the constituency neighbouring on mine, Tavistock, at the same time as me in 1966. I had watched him carefully over the years that we were political neighbours and after. The most important aspect of his politics is that he is an unabashed Tory in the old-fashioned sense of the word. He believes in privilege and he has no egalitarian instinct. It is wholly in keeping with his character that he should have striven from the start to become very rich and that he lives in a grand country house in which the ironwork gates incorporate his own initials. Yet, despite the flamboyance of his wealth, his concern, first evidenced when Secretary of State for the Environment in the early 1980s to reverse the squalor of inner-city decay, notably in Liverpool, was genuine. He retained this interest after he resigned as a backbencher, and on his return to Government in 1990 showed every sign of continuing to devote time and effort to the regeneration of urban areas. The Tavistock constituency Conservative Association was very Right-wing in the late 1960s and early 1970s, but Michael never equivocated on racial questions, either over the admission of Kenyan and then Ugandan Asians. Nor did he shift his ground over the abolition of hanging. He was a Heath with passion, never a wet of the Pym or Prior variety. He later left Tavistock for Henley to obtain a more convenient seat nearer London. Apart from his interest in preserving Dartmoor National Park, I never felt that he identified with the West Country nor did he or his wife appear to enjoy the constituency.

Michael's European commitment is very strong and after his resignation we served together on the Monnet Action Committee for Europe. Although he denies being a federalist, he appeared to me to be constrained more by the recognition that federalism would offend some MPs whose votes he would need in a leadership election than any intrinsic dislike of the concept of a United States of Europe. His support for a European solution to the problem of rationalizing the helicopter industry was perfectly in character and the preferred option of many within the Ministry of Defence. His decision to resign was gestating for some many months. He knew that Margaret Thatcher distrusted him and had never really forgiven him for lifting the Mace up in the House of Commons when Labour MPs had been singing the Red Flag, an incident better known as 'Tarzan swings the Mace'. She also appeared to be jealous of his capacity to stir the Conservative Party Conference, tossing his long golden hair like a lion. She appointed him to cut defence spending, probably guessing that this would alienate a number of Conservative MPs. Eventually she would have sacked him in the same way as she had unceremoniously removed so many of her Cabinet Ministers. But Michael Heseltine showed every sign of wanting to get his resignation in first. Westland was the issue on which he decided to break. At any time, in the month before and even during the fateful Cabinet meeting when he decided to walk out, he could have quietly backed off without any loss of face. The fact that he chose not to demonstrates that, consciously or subconsciously, he was intent on challenging her authority. He knew that he would advance no higher in the Cabinet and that she would do her best to block his route to being Prime Minister. By resigning apparently on impulse, he left himself open to the charge of impetuosity, but by immediately widening the issue from Westland to the way Margaret Thatcher had destroyed Cabinet Government he laid the foundation for his challenge in 1990.

That it might have toppled her at the time was because the Attorney-General and the Solicitor-General became incensed and just might have resigned, calling in question the conduct of the Prime Minister. I was in Pakistan and India with the Palme Commission at the time of Michael Heseltine's resignation, but on my return the new twist to the saga was that it had become obvious that Margaret Thatcher and Leon Brittan had wanted to embarrass Heseltine by using the advice of the Solicitor-General against him. Who leaked it is less important than that Leon Brittan thought she was ready to have it leaked. It was inconceivable to me that people of the undoubted calibre of her Press Secretary, Bernard Ingham, or her Private Secretary from the Foreign Office, Charles Powell, who was handling Westland, would authorize any action without knowing her mind or without telling her afterwards what had been done. It was obvious too that her answers in the House of Commons had been carefully crafted. In a speech in Bath, I quoted these words of Kipling to her: 'The truthful well-weighed answer that tells the blacker lie,' and warned that in the House of Commons debate we would need answers to questions that had been covered up. On Monday 27 January 1986, just before the key debate, she told her closest friends 'I may not be Prime Minister by 6 o'clock tonight.' We are now asked to believe that this was a joke. I wonder, it seemed very far from a joke at the time.

In that House of Commons debate I spoke immediately after the Prime Minister and I focused on the question she had not answered – what conversations she had had over what would happen if the material inaccuracies – provisionally thought by the Solicitor-General to have occurred in Michael Heseltine's letter – were to be confirmed in the Solicitor-General's follow-up letter expected shortly. Normally the advice of the Law Officers is revealed only in the most exceptional circumstances. What is at issue, I argued, 'goes to the core of the Government and their integrity in relation to the position of the Law Officers'. If the civil servants in her private office had acted without reference to her they should be subjected to the normal disciplinary procedures. If they were not disciplined we had to conclude they had been authorized. I went on:

> 'It is not often realized that the Prime Minister's Principal Private Secretary has his desk as close to the Prime Minister sitting in the No. 10 Cabinet Room as you are to Mr Speaker. It is extraordinary that throughout this period, from the moment when the Prime Minister admits that she talked to her officials on 7 January, she did not ask them point blank what the view of the Rt. Hon. and learned Member for Richmond (Leon Brittan) was.'

The debate required Conservative MPs to break ranks to catch fire but they did not do so. Instead they bided their time. Michael Heseltine would have been well advised to say nothing for he made a hypocritical speech and Michael Foot reminded him of what Winston Churchill had said, 'Its all right to rat but you cannot re-rat,' to which Sir Peter Tapsell intervened to say 'The point about Sir Winston Churchill is he did re-rat.' While Margaret Thatcher remained Prime Minister, she lost the votes of many Conservative MPs that day; the very ones that would have ensured an outright victory on the first ballot in 1990 against Heseltine.

In February I had a long-standing engagement to have lunch with the editor of the *Sun*, Kelvin Mackenzie. But then a strike was called at the Wapping plant of News International which I passed every day on my way to work. I was informed that lunch would be at Wapping, not, as I would normally have expected, in an hotel. I could see this was a try-on to see if I would cross the picket line. Since I believed the printing unions were wrong, I agreed to go into the plant for lunch. No sooner had I accepted than the television news people got in touch, having been tipped off to fix a time to film me crossing the picket. I rang Kelvin up in a fury to protest and started to tear a strip off him only to find him

unexpectedly contrite and apologetic, admitting that he had informed the
television people. I was so amazed at his confession that I agreed to keep
our lunch date, but I went in too early for the cameras to be in position
and looked around the plant first, ending up with lunch in the canteen
with Kelvin and Rupert Murdoch. I rather expected a brick through my
window in Limehouse, but nothing came and eventually the strike ended
after a lot of misery. Nevertheless it revolutionized newspaper publishing
costs. Without Wapping I doubt it would have been possible for *The
Independent* to have been successfully launched and many small
newspapers became viable. Symbolically breaking the stranglehold of the
print unions was important. With them and the miners beaten within a
year, the toughest elements in the TUC had been forced to accept that
militancy and vested interest were now going to be challenged everywhere.

That month for the first time I overhauled David Steel in the leaders'
rating lists, and this was thought to be due to my intervention in the
debate on Westland. We had been level-pegging for some months on the
question of which party leader would make the best Prime Minister, but
in the early months of my leadership David Steel had consistently been
ahead. The ratings had no significance other than being cited by Liberals,
when in David's favour, as a reason why he should be Leader of the
Alliance.

Sadly at the end of the month Olof Palme was assassinated and I went
to Stockholm for his funeral. I had lost a good friend and social
democracy one of its idealistic champions. We decided to continue the
Commission as a mark of respect but the spark went out of our work. On
the way back in the plane, I spoke to Robert Mugabe for the first time
since independence in Zimbabwe. He was travelling first class and I
economy – such are the fortunes of politics.

In March I gave the prizes at Granada's *What the Papers Say* lunch.
In my televised speech I advocated selling commercial television
franchises to the highest bidder. This outraged a large number of the
existing franchise holders in the audience. They were only too happy
with the comfortable arrangement of having licences handed out as part
of a system of allocation, which I always refer to as 'Lady Plowden's
bounty'. I also wanted independent producers to be guaranteed 25 per
cent of BBC output and something more done about the restrictive
practices of the television unions. These were very controversial proposals
at the time, but a few years later they were all adopted as Government
policy. Despite many complaints, they show every sign of creating a
much fairer and more competitive franchising system. The quality
threshold must be kept high, but once across that threshold there is every
reason, unless there are exceptional circumstances, for the tax payer to
benefit rather than the lobbyists or those who can exert influence behind
the scenes.

As the Westland affair began to die down the death of Conservative

MP Martin Stephens meant yet another by-election, this time in Fulham. Our candidate was Roger Liddle, Bill Rodgers's former political adviser. Since the Alliance was ahead in the national polls, some people in the SDP felt that this was a winnable seat and that we should talk up our prospects. I was determined not to have another Darlington and deliberately understated our prospects, saying truthfully that there were 560 other seats more winnable for the Alliance. It was lucky that we did not build our hopes too high because Labour chose a local candidate and made their theme, 'Nick Raynsford lives here'. They poured in money, huge numbers of people to canvass and for the first time we saw lavish, coloured literature. Labour under Neil Kinnock had thrown off the old Foot style and was now capable of effective campaigning.

All too soon the by-election resolved itself into a fight for second place between us and the Tories. In the process we were having to defend the Liberal Party's rather poor record in local government. Our campaign never captured people's imagination and we came third, a disappointing result. We had improved our share of the poll by 11–12 per cent in the four previous by-elections, but this time we only managed a 1 per cent improvement. It showed that in these sort of inner-city seats it is best to have a local candidate, preferably with a lot of charisma, if one is going to shift people's voting patterns. Following Fulham, Labour moved ahead of us in the opinion polls, though the Tories remained third. Yet Fulham was not a setback like Darlington for no one really expected us to win.

On the morning of 15 April 1986 I woke up to find that during the night the Americans had bombed terrorist targets in Libya using F-111 aircraft from bases in Britain. The Prime Minister was under immediate attack for authorizing their use and I quickly had to determine my attitude. Normally I would have supported action against terrorism, but this was illegal by any standard: the sort of retaliatory action which we had always condemned the Israelis for undertaking. For some weeks I had feared that this was going to happen, for the rhetoric and actions of the Reagan Administration had shown they were increasingly cavalier about remaining within the limits of international law when dealing with terrorists. Washington was disillusioned with the pitiful response of the European Community to any suggestion of applying tough sanctions against Libya for harbouring terrorists and determined to act.

In a speech to US correspondents in London five days earlier I had gone out of my way to warn that, desirable though it was to take action to stop Colonel Gaddafi from harbouring and training terrorists it was questionable whether any US action could be justified as being a proportionate use of force if it took the form of air strikes against Libya. Instead the US should ask the United Nations Security Council to impose a quarantine on Libya, stopping all movement of aircraft until Gaddafi ceased all terrorist and subversive activity.

Someone whose judgement I greatly valued took me to task on my *Times* article headed 'Bombing is not the answer'. He said bluntly that, from what he knew of me, if I had been Prime Minister I would have agreed to the American request to use British bases because to have refused would have very seriously undermined Anglo-American relations. His criticism struck a sensitive nerve for deep down I wondered whether he was right. Had I been Prime Minister I would have tried to steer the Americans much earlier towards an air and maybe even a maritime blockade of Libya. Yet though I believed passionately in respecting international law, I also knew that in government decisions have to be made where the choice is between two evils. The lesser evil in this case was to support President Reagan's request and try to pretend, as Margaret Thatcher had, that it was covered under Article 51 of the UN Charter as an act of self-defence.

Having been given crucial military support by President Reagan during the Falklands War, Margaret Thatcher knew that she owed him similar support. Given her personality, she would have found it impossible to refuse, and it is to her credit, in such trying circumstances, that she gave permission. She knew that Ronald Reagan had had doubts about the wisdom of her action in sending a task force to the South Atlantic, and that the Americans, under successive administrations, had never accepted our claim to the Falklands. Not only the President, but most of his advisers, believed the US's fragile relationship with Latin America would be gravely damaged by supporting us. Nevertheless Reagan agreed with his Defence Secretary, Caspar Weinberger, that the US could not refuse our request for help. Nor had the US ever made it a condition, as I was urging on the Prime Minister in the case of Libya, that their agreement should be subject to being involved in the operational decisions. They simply ensured that every request we made was delivered to our forces in the Southern Atlantic as soon as possible, sometimes accepting an operational penalty for their own forces. Weinberger richly deserved our thanks, as did the Pentagon for working round the clock, but none of this could have been done without Reagan's personal, private decision to help his friend Margaret and his favourite country, Britain, in their hour of need. Margaret Thatcher recognized all this and, in fulfilling her debt of honour, she offended some of her closest Cabinet colleagues like Norman Tebbit. She also went against the best Foreign Office legal advice. President Mitterrand refused President Reagan the right to overfly France and it can be argued that this did him no harm. But the Americans, and especially that President, were bound to expect different attitudes from Britain.

When history assesses whether Margaret Thatcher was a great Prime Minister, this decision deserves to be weighed in the balance. Her refusal would have done immense damage to our relations with the Reagan Administration. She showed courage and loyalty, but she also demonstrated one of the distinguishing features of great leadership – the ability to turn a blind eye to instructions or to legal niceties and just to follow one's instincts. In the event the bombing did deter the Libyans and Colonel Gaddafi, even though it was, by any legal standard, retaliation not self-defence and therefore outside the terms of the UN Charter.

I was soon to face a defence crisis of my own. In February I was alerted by David Dunn, one of our members on the Joint Alliance Defence Commission, that the Commission was looking for a compromise on Polaris. On 25 February I wrote back to him:

> On the key question I do not think we should find a form of words on the Polaris replacement. The words will come unstuck if there is any equivocation. Politically we will not be able to carry cancelling Trident unless we can say clearly that we will replace Polaris; unless there is a miracle and *all* nuclear weapons are negotiated away. How we replace Polaris is better left open. I cannot understand why Paddy Ashdown is so upset about submarine-launched cruise, whether the US Tomahawk, or built by British Aerospace, or preferably the Europeans. But my main worry is this idea of trying to find a formula of words. We may have to do this for an election manifesto, but if the Liberals are not yet ready to say Britain should remain a nuclear weapon state, then I think it is better for the SDP at this stage to hold firm in a gentle non-aggressive way and wait for the arms control negotiations.

By the middle of April I had become uneasy about the Joint Commission, suspecting it was up to no good. When I enquired about progress on the all important nuclear question which they had wisely left to the end, I was met by evasion. I twice raised the issue of what was going to be said about the nuclear deterrent with Bill Rodgers, once on the telephone from Buttermere and once when he came into my office. On both occasions I suspected that Bill was dissembling. I also raised the issue directly with David Steel on a number of occasions and was told each time that he had no idea what was going to be in the report, but would look into it.

Then on 30 April 1986 the world learnt of the nuclear disaster at Chernobyl. Civil nuclear power became the dominant issue. The *Guardian* carried a by-election report on 2 May under the title, 'Liberal team nukes voters', in which Des Wilson, the President-elect of the Liberal Party, was noted as saying, 'We would not further develop the nuclear power industry in any way whatever.' Interestingly Bill Rodgers had actually rung my office to express his anxiety about Des Wilson's comments which were in direct conflict with agreed policy. I agreed but I also realized we were dealing with a very emotional issue for the Liberal Party and also for David Steel personally. They were instinctively against all civil nuclear power stations and they were reacting to the widespread concern about the fall out of radiation from Chernobyl all over Europe. The agreed compromise between our two parties on nuclear power was coming apart at the seams. The Conservative candidate in the West Derbyshire by-election was a former miner and, with a tradition of coal-mining in one part of the constituency, the mood there was all in favour of coal-fired power stations. We were also finding considerable concern about nuclear power in the Ryedale by-election, where Elizabeth Shields, a local teacher, was fighting an effective campaign as a Liberal candidate on behalf of the Alliance.

During the West Derbyshire by-election David Steel and I were in Matlock to address a joint public meeting on 5 May and for a press conference the following day. I raised the nuclear deterrent question yet again with David, and did so with the utmost clarity so that there could be no possible misunderstanding between us. As we travelled together in the car, I proposed that the SDP should give ground on civil nuclear power to Liberal sentiment in exchange for Liberals giving ground to the SDP on nuclear deterrence. The SDP could not abandon support for a civil nuclear power programme but it was just about credible to agree to postpone the building of any new nuclear power stations provided we kept the existing ones going and increased investment in nuclear waste disposal. I explained that I could persuade the SDP to live with a manifesto commitment to build no more nuclear power stations in the five-year lifetime of an SDP/Liberal Alliance government provided, and only provided, he could persuade the Liberal Party to live with a commitment to retain a nuclear deterrent and replace Polaris. I had now seen the draft of the Commission report and I told him that they were coming up with a proposition to evade a commitment to replace Polaris. I emphasized that I could not accept any such idea. David again said he had not seen the draft report but agreed to raise my concern about the wording with his friend Richard Holme, who was a member of the Commission. I then proceeded to demonstrate my willingness to move on civil nuclear power.

In the joint press conference we held on Tuesday 6 May in Matlock no one was able to drive a wedge between us on our reaction to Chernobyl, as I had softened the SDP line. That night we both spoke at joint meetings in Ryedale and held another press conference there on the Wednesday. Once again on civil nuclear power, which was the issue concerning the press, the Alliance was speaking almost with one voice. I was not, however, as aggressively hostile as Des Wilson, for I was not prepared to be stampeded by Chernobyl into a total reversal of policy, but I was taking a much softer line than the SDP had hitherto done. As I drove back to London through West Derbyshire I sensed, on the eve of the poll, that we were within sight of winning there, while we were all confident of winning Ryedale. In the end we only got very close in West Derbyshire, but Elizabeth Shields had a brilliant victory in Ryedale.

On Tuesday 13 May I saw Bob Maclennan; his constituency interest in the nuclear power industry meant I had to clear my line with him before I spoke on it at a Council for Social Democracy meeting due to start in Southport on the Saturday. He was very upset about the way the Liberals were abandoning all the carefully agreed compromises on nuclear energy, but he was a realist and we discussed a form of words for my speech which envisaged softening our stance as part of the deal I had talked about with David Steel. I wanted to agree this with the Liberals and David Steel but I wanted first to agree words that would not embarrass Bob in his Highlands constituency where the fast breeder reactor at Dounreay was an important employer in the Thurso area. I had always protected Bob in the past from the more extreme Liberal policies on civil nuclear power and in the 1983 manifesto had gone to great lengths to safeguard his constituency position in the negotiations. He had been so desperate about the then draft he actually threatened to stand as an independent rather than endorse wording which could damage his constituency.

On Wednesday 14 May I sent a handwritten letter to David Steel, voicing my anxiety about what he had said about nuclear power on *Newsnight* the night before, and about Malcolm Bruce's speech in the House of Commons dealing with radioactive waste. I warned,

> This is not the response of a serious group of people intending to govern. I have watched in despair as ever since Chernobyl a variety of Liberal spokesmen have dumped the Alliance policy at the last election. I am a realist, of course we have to rethink in the light of that disaster, but what a spectacle we present if we do not at least stand back a little and look at the facts. We are also being repeatedly told that the new Sellafield plant should not go ahead, but no one says what else should take its place. Continue with the old, leaky, dangerous plant?

I went on, 'This is *not* serious. We may escape scrutiny because of Labour's divisions but even today with the Lobby we need a line. Can we meet at 4.15 to discuss?' We met and managed to agree a line before we talked to the lobby correspondents, as we regularly did every Wednesday afternoon. On nuclear policy I also explained what I intended to say at Southport. There was no hint from David Steel that he had or was about to give what was to prove a fateful interview on the nuclear deterrent to the *Scotsman*, indeed the subject was not even raised.

Next day David Steel and I sent out a joint letter to candidates. In many ways it marked the high water-mark of co-operation within the Alliance. We said we were looking forward to meeting the candidates in July for the launch of the initial draft of a policy document, entitled 'Priorities for the 1990s', which would be discussed at both our party conferences. After consultation it was to be the centrepiece of a rally we planned for the end of January 1987 as the launch pad for the election. The letter set out our basic strategy for dealing with the other parties after the next election when, as we thought likely, no party would have an overall majority. We asked candidates to make it plain that Liberals and Social Democrats would be indivisible in all stages of the negotiations after the election. The new SDP and Liberal MPs would meet separately and then together on the Saturday morning after polling day so that our opponents would know that we would be completely united and formidable in negotiation. We two Leaders were determined to act together in negotiation, reporting to our MPs for a final decision, and we said we would be ready for a second election if a minority government attempted to put through a programme without negotiation. 'The Alliance parties are willing to work with others to create consent for change. This applies whether we come first, second or third in seats in a balanced Parliament.' Fine words, but even as they were going out a time bomb was ticking away threatening our co-operation and personal relationships.

Early that Friday morning I drove to Southport, collecting Sue Robertson, our press officer, Alex de Mont, my economic adviser and Sandra Jantuah, a delightful person whose parents came from Ghana and who dealt with all policy questions in my office. My draft speech dealt mainly with civil nuclear power post-Chernobyl. As we drove up we were informed over the car telephone that the main front page article which had appeared in the *Scotsman* that morning had carried the headline: 'Owen's nuclear hopes dashed. Alliance report rejects UK deterrent', and it had gone on to say: 'Dr David Owen's attempts to commit the Alliance to a policy of replacing Polaris with a new independent nuclear deterrent have been dashed by a joint SDP/Liberal policy commission'. It continued:

> The Alliance Commission on Defence has unanimously rejected his suggestion that Britain should purchase a new nuclear deterrent at the end of the Polaris lifespan in the 1990s. The unanimity of the finding by the Commission, which is drawn equally from the SDP and the Liberals, means that the SDP Leader's favourite policy has been rejected by the specialist nominees of his own party. The finding will strengthen the hand of Mr David Steel, the Liberal Leader, in the difficult negotiations of ironing out the two parties' differences on nuclear defence policy.

The report was signed by Martin Dowle, the chief political correspondent, who, Sue Robertson knew, had recently talked to David Steel. We also knew that, the day before, a Liberal official, himself a unilateralist, was briefing the press about the Joint Commission report along very similar lines. The *Guardian*, we thought, also had the story but surprisingly had not run anything that Friday. Sue Robertson, who was well respected among lobby correspondents and had carefully followed what was happening, was convinced that we were facing a systematic briefing by the Liberal Party about the Commission's report. During the day we also heard that briefing had continued on the Friday for the Sunday newspapers.

David Steel admits in his own autobiography that he had lunch with

TIME TO DECLARE

Martin Dowle and that he had told him, foolishly but accurately, that the Commission's report made no commitment to a replacement of Polaris. He makes no mention in his book, though, of the letter which was published in the *Scotsman* on 19 May in which he professed to be most surprised by their chief political correspondent's lead story. He wrote, 'I must make it clear, as I did to him, that I have yet to see any text or draft.' This denial of his involvement was too much for the *Scotsman* to stomach and underneath the letter was the following explanation: '(the story was based on unambiguous information given to our reporters – Ed.)'. Much later I heard exactly what had gone on. There is no doubt that David leaked the report and then tried through the *Scotsman*'s letter column to pretend he had not done so.

The actual words of the final draft of the Commission report showed that Bill Rodgers had taken no account of my anxieties, for the critical wording which I had objected to had not been changed. Nor, I knew, had he communicated my anxieties either to John Cartwright or Jim Wellbeloved, who both sat on the Commission. On Trident, Bill had reverted to much the same position he had held in his paper in 1980 to members of the Labour Shadow Cabinet. When we had all witnessed how dominant an electoral issue nuclear weapons had been in the 1983 Election, to advance a formulation to delay a final decision on whether Britain should replace Polaris until after an election was amazing, particularly so coming from Bill. In the past he had been the strongest of the Gang of Four on nuclear questions, even at times criticizing me as at the Newcastle CSD for compromising too much with the Liberals.

Why did Bill Rodgers behave in this way? I shall never be sure. Part of the reason, I fear, lay in the deterioration in our personal relations. They had been declining over the last few years and I have little doubt that it was largely my fault. Having lost his seat, Bill had inevitably lost status in the Party. Shirley, as President, even though out of the House, had been able on the whole to maintain her position of influence. Immediately after the election Ian Wrigglesworth and Bob Maclennan, as MPs, were adamant that the Gang of Four had outlived its usefulness and should not continue. They were undoubtedly right; the Party now had its democratic structures and these needed to be respected. I had tried to offset Bill's isolation by asking him to take on responsible tasks like serving on this Commission, but regrettably I had not done enough to consult with him and to keep him fully in touch. He had resented my ousting of Roy as Leader, my determination that the Salford CSD should reject the principle of joint selection and my advocacy of the social market. He had resisted unsuccessfully the shift in economic policy at both the Buxton and Torquay CSDs and as a consequence had lost out all too publicly. This was bound to cause resentment in a proud man and I ought to have bent over backwards to counteract this. One of my great weaknesses is not taking enough trouble to soothe people's feelings, indeed too often unconsciously ruffling them when they are still sensitive. All this had combined to push Bill even further towards Roy Jenkins's view that the SDP should merge than I think was inevitable. But Roy's influence with him was pervasive and persistent.

Only a few weeks before the defence crisis on 25 April, Bill had written to me about the need for a Head of Communications in our HQ, which I supported. He mentioned his experience on the doorstep in Milton Keynes. There was, he told me, a key group of twenty-five- to thirty-five-year-olds wavering between us and Labour who were interested in policy, especially social policy, and alert to presentation. His letter warned me that we could not afford to lose these voters and he felt that they were starting to slip away. This was a fair point, for though we were advocating a very radical redistributive integrated tax and social security policy in the SDP, we had not been able to obtain enough headline publicity and few voters associated us with our innovative social agenda. But there was no mention of nuclear policy in that handwritten letter, even though he knew I was anxious; no hint that he was going to advocate a change from the SDP defence policy that we had agreed at Torquay in the Commission report.

One does not have to believe in conspiracy theories for I know that Bill's formulation was known to Shirley and perhaps to Roy. It was known as well by David Steel. I suppose in retrospect it had been a misjudgement to ask Bill to be a member of the Defence Commission in the first place and thereby, because of him having been a Minister of State in the Ministry of Defence, to be the *de facto* leader of the SDP members on the Commission rather than John Cartwright. I had also been unwise to make my representations only to him and not speak directly to John Cartwright. When I had discussed my worries with John Roper, our former Chief Whip, who was Secretary to the Commission, he had suggested that I should talk to Bill who was taking the lead on this issue.

The chairman of the Defence Commission was John Edmonds, formerly a diplomat in the Foreign Office, experienced in disarmament questions and someone I had suggested to David Steel. It was no criticism of the chairman that the Commission had put forward this wording on nuclear weapons. He was there to try and broker an agreement and if the SDP members were not upholding SDP policy it was not his job to do it for them. In our discussions both before and after he became chairman he had always known that Polaris replacement was going to be the most delicate question for the Commission. He had hoped, as I had, that David Steel and I would be able to sort it out through our intermediaries on the Commission. But Bill had deliberately decided to go his own way. The vast bulk of the Commission's report was excellent, as one would expect given the quality of its members, but this nuclear question was so highly political that it was understandable that many of the specialist members were bound to leave it predominantly to the more senior political members.

It was vital for me to act urgently if the Commission report was not to become Alliance policy. Once published, the Liberals would be bound to hold firmly to this quite unacceptable wording. I decided to spell out not just my views but the SDP position on both civil nuclear power and nuclear deterrence in my speech next day, and to do so in unequivocal terms. I judged it wiser not to refer directly to the Commission's report. It was still a draft and I hoped that John Cartwright and Jim Wellbeloved, seeing the interpretation that the Liberals were putting on the form of words there, would realize it was not acceptable and insist on clarifying this question further before the report was finalized. There was no doubt in my mind that I was embarking on a very risky course. If I lost I would have to consider giving up the leadership of the SDP.

That speech in Southport was a marker for the future, not just to a CSD. It started with a somewhat hyperbolic and emotional attack on Margaret Thatcher's style, perhaps in order to compensate for what was to follow, one of the strongest attacks I ever launched on her. An opinion poll had showed that a mere 6 per cent believed that she listened to reason. John Biffen, the Leader of the House, had just been rubbished in a briefing to the Lobby by her Press Secretary, Bernard Ingham, one further demonstration of the abuse of his position as a civil servant.

> Conservative MPs, wet by name and by nature, have not got the guts to challenge her. She buttresses her position or boosts the finances of the Conservative Party by showering patronage around with an ever-increasing number of peerages and knighthoods. The House of Commons has been systematically misled by this Prime Minister, on a number of occasions, most recently over Westland.

I said that contrary to the opinion of some Social Democrats, Margaret Thatcher was

> still a far more formidable opponent than many care to admit. The reason she is still formidable is not just that part of her message is right and ought to be maintained by any Prime Minister, but above all, she believes in what she says and carries conviction, even when she is wrong. Conviction is an asset for any leader. It could prove to be the winning asset at the next election if all of us in the three Opposition parties, SDP/Liberal Alliance and Labour, oppose her with leadership that does not carry the same conviction. If we oppose her with policies where the cracks are papered over, then she may still be able to squeeze home at the election, albeit with a massively reduced number of seats, because enough voters will have said to themselves, I do not like her, but at least we all know where she stands.

I warned she would 'fight like an alley cat to the last hour from her

Downing Street bunker'. This reflected my concern that, even in a
balanced Parliament, she might prefer to let Labour in than do a deal
over proportional representation, and try to pretend to her colleagues that
we were making absurd coalition demands. I had already taken steps
through Alan Clark to convince some Conservatives that she had to be
persuaded to talk seriously if there was a balanced Parliament. Alan, I
know, sent a memorandum about my concern to Willie Whitelaw,
Conservative Leader in the Lords, saying the SDP could be relied on to
negotiate sensibly in a balanced Parliament.

Only after I had warmed up the CSD did I turn to the two key
questions: Ought we to build any more nuclear power stations? Ought we
to remain a nuclear weapons state?

> There are voices that tell me that our policy on these two issues, as on
> others, should be determined on the basis not of the facts, not on the
> merits, but on whether we can find a form of words which will keep
> various strands of the Party happy, and even more importantly, keep
> our Liberal partners with us as well. I must tell you bluntly, that if
> that becomes the guiding principle, then we too will become vulnerable
> to the Thatcher challenge.

I then promised that the Party's working group under the chairmanship
of Sir Leslie Murphy would undertake an authoritative rethink, in the
light of Chernobyl, and if we were not satisfied about the risk of any
remotely comparable disaster occurring in this country, then we should
be prepared to take the fundamental decision to pull out of civil nuclear
power. At the very least, I said, the electorate were entitled to know
whether we would be prepared to order a new civil power station during
our five-year period of government. This was the form of words to pave
the way for our eventual manifesto commitment to build no new power
stations.

On the second critical question, whether we should or should not
remain a nuclear weapons state, I said that that too was a question on
which we would need to make up our minds before the next election:

> No leader of any political party can stand before the British electorate
> and refuse to answer the question. Mrs Thatcher believes in Trident.
> Mr Kinnock would cancel Trident, decommission Polaris and disown
> NATO's nuclear deterrent. I must tell you bluntly that I believe we
> should remain a nuclear weapons state.

I stated categorically that if we were to carry conviction in our decison to
cancel Trident after an election, we ought to be prepared to say that we
would find a replacement for Polaris, unless there had been such a
massive reduction in nuclear warheads by the Soviet Union and the
United States that we would feel it right to give up our nuclear weapons.

Certainly you should know quite clearly that I definitely do not believe that I would carry any conviction whatever in the next election were I to answer – on your behalf – on the question of the replacement of Polaris, that that would have to depend on the circumstances of the time. That would get and would deserve a belly laugh from the British electorate. That sort of fudging and mudging was what I left behind in the Labour Party.

Not many people in the hall realized what I was doing, but both Bill and Shirley knew full well that I had decided to confront their challenge head on. They would now have to defeat me using the democratic procedures of the Party if the Commission's wording on nuclear weapons were to form the basis of any general election manifesto. They started the attempt that day, trying to persuade people in the Party that the SDP's defence policy, as spelt out at Torquay, was not incompatible with the Commission's report. Meanwhile I spoke to John Cartwright who had just flown in from America and he agreed with Jim Wellbeloved to reopen the Commission's report. If the others would not amend it, he would make it clear that he stood by the SDP policy agreed at Torquay and could not accept the report.

My speech did not cause a public furore, indeed the newspaper reporting was modest, concentrating largely on my attack on Margaret Thatcher, which was what I had hoped would happen. In the meantime, a report in the *Sunday Telegraph* which covered my speech had 'one leading Liberal MP' saying: 'Liberals are walking around with their faces wreathed in smiles as we have ruled out a Polaris replacement.' The *Guardian* on Tuesday stressed that Liberal CND were trying to organize opposition to the Commission report on the basis that it would contain no concrete proposals for 'ending the Polaris threat or for removing cruise missiles from Greenham Common'. This was all part of a tactic to make it look as if the Commission, with its delaying form of words, was steering a sensible path between Liberal CND's wish to cancel Polaris and alleged hardliners in the SDP like myself who wanted a commitment to replace Polaris.

The fact that the speech had not made big news meant that there was a slight lull before the storm which would break with the official publication of the Commission's report on 10 June. The majority of the Commission decided to stick with their wording, but because of John Cartwright and Jim Wellbeloved's dissent the report was not now unanimous. The *Sunday Times* on 25 May warned about a Conservative attack under the headline, 'Tories draw battlelines for defence onslaught'. We had been warned. They were not going to confine their attacks to Labour. They hoped, we were told, to capitalize on our rift and they saw the document due to be published next month as favouring the Liberals' unilateral line and being evasive over a replacement for Polaris. Bill Rodgers then wrote to me with a form of words which he hoped I would use to give a qualified welcome to the Commission's report. I had no intention of doing any such thing. On 1 June I had already written an article in the *Observer* under the title 'Polaris must be replaced', in which I criticized Denis Healey for comporting himself in Moscow as if NATO did not exist. Denis was trying to pretend that we could now trade off our Polaris against an equivalent drop in Soviet strategic armaments. But, as I pointed out, there was no sort of equivalence in Britain's completely dropping all its sixty-four strategic missile launchers while leaving the Soviet Union with over 3,300 missile launchers.

I decided to follow up the *Observer* article with a detailed speech on defence in Bonn when I visited Germany on 5 June. My object was quite simply to ensure that when the Commission's report was published it would already have been exposed as an unacceptable fudge.

That same day, in the *Guardian*, Hugo Young suggested that I was 'entering one of the disturbing phases he has experienced before, in which style and image become his obsessive preoccupations. In particular a style and image most closely emulating that of Mrs Thatcher.' He argued that a true coalitionist would find a way of moderating his convictions. He was confused, as one would not expect from a columnist of his calibre, about the meaning and the compatibility of words like conviction, consensus, compromise and coalition in politics. Compromise is the art of politics, but in order for democratic politics to retain any foundation in principle, its practitioners must not feel obliged to compromise their core convictions. A coalition is not a vehicle for consensus but a mechanism for compromise and for creating a climate in which it is easier to reach a consensus. Within a coalition there can and indeed must be respect for conviction and, when compromise is not possible, an open acknowledgement of differences. This is the difference between multi-party coalitions and internal party coalitions, where collective responsibility is normally the rule. A coalition government in European Community countries is not bound like a British Cabinet by the doctrine of collective responsibility. When differences between political parties cannot be resolved there is an open acknowledgment of policy differences. The coalition partners fight the election on different platforms, even if they intend to resume the coalition after the election. This was the relationship I always sought between the SDP and the Liberals within the Alliance.

While it was better for us to agree policy in the Alliance, it could not be at any price, certainly not at the price of our country's security. Hugo Young and some like-minded people within the SDP seemed to believe that even differences over a defence policy issues of fundamental importance for the country should be papered over. For them, coalition seemingly meant compromising on everything, never allowing conviction to threaten the consensus of a coalition. That was exactly the sort of thinking that had contributed to the mess the Labour Party was in. They had developed the broad church tradition so far that members and MPs were expected to accept Conference decisions regardless of their convictions. The fact that a belief in nuclear deterrence was one of the reasons many of us had left the Labour Party was also being conveniently forgotten. It was inconceivable that on this of all issues I and many others in the SDP were going to abandon our convictions purely because the Liberals insisted on keeping their non-nuclear convictions. We would have to respect their convictions, but we would have to agree to differ.

David Watt now entered the field and his criticism or support really mattered to me. He was a personal friend of both myself and Bill Rodgers and I knew he would have pondered very hard on the issue, having heard both our arguments. He wrote on Friday 6 June in *The Times*, under the title 'When it's best to disagree', saying

> an agreement at all costs suits the Liberal mergerites and those who want to cut Dr Owen down to size; an agreement to disagree is a visible endorsement of Owen's view that important principles still separate the two partners. But in the end these are side issues. The problem actually resides in the policy itself. Where nuclear weapons policy is concerned, a chasm exists in the Liberal/SDP Alliance as it does in the country as a whole.

David described those members of the Commission who thought that Britain's nuclear status should be decided in the light of circumstances after the next election as being either terrified of the effect of disunity on the Alliance's electoral appeal or actually soft on the nuclear issue, or a combination of the two.

Journalists and politicians influence each other far more than either admit. I valued David Watt's judgement and when he came down on my side he stiffened my resolve. I took Hugo Young's criticism seriously, but I also saw it as part of his overall attitude to politics. Though a fine libertarian, informed and intelligent, he had shown in the *Guardian*, since leaving the *Sunday Times*, that, on defence, he lacked the cutting edge of David Watt's incisive mind. Having been the director of the Royal Institute for International Affairs at Chatham House, David had developed a greater breadth of judgement on international affairs. He was also temperamentally more interested in the decisions of a government than in the protestations of those who refused to accept the discipline of government. It is not that David and I always agreed. He wrote critically about me from time to time as did Peter Jenkins, another columnist whose judgement and friendship I valued. It is hard for journalists and politicians to remain close friends, and to do so each must respect the other's independence and not get too prickly when they differ.

We were now back where we started in Llandudno in 1981 when, within twenty-four hours, the Liberals both endorsed the Alliance and voted to campaign against the deployment of cruise missiles. Roy Jenkins had spent those intervening years trying to pretend that there were no differences between us. Having sniffed the two parties as if they were bottles of claret, his nose, he kept telling us, was unable to detect a Liberal from a Social Democrat. This Olympian assessment owed too much to dining with Mark Bonham-Carter and the type of old Asquithian Liberal who had little in common with the new community politicians and pavement politics. It not only meant conveniently ignoring repeated democratic votes in each of our parties, but also the realities among Liberal MPs and candidates. A very high percentage of Liberal parliamentary candidates were professed supporters of CND while in the SDP support for CND was a barrier even to being placed on the panel of candidates.

In Bonn I had a private chat with Chancellor Kohl (xliii) and found him earthy and sensible. He had shown courage in going ahead with cruise deployment. I asked him, as I had asked Helmut Schmidt some years before, did he want Britain to remain a nuclear weapon state. The answer was an unequivocal yes. Later, speaking to the Anglo-German Society, I argued that 'what is vital to Europe is that France should not be left as the only European nuclear weapon state.' I hoped the Liberals could be won around to a continuing deterrent by stressing the European dimension. It was not necessary for it to be of 'the super sophistication of Trident, but at a level of deterrence that can be seen, in combination with France, to provide a serious European contribution to NATO's twin-track strategy of conventional and nuclear deterrence'. By now the newspapers were inevitably giving the controversy considerable coverage. But since we were going to have to have a row, in my view it was better to have it now. The Commission formula which stated 'No decision on whether, and if so how, British nuclear weapons should be maintained beyond Polaris can properly be made except in the light of . . . ' was fraught with political danger. Yet the Commission had listed four sensible criteria which should be the basis for such a decision and I could accept these criteria. My aim was to force the Liberal Party to answer those criteria now and make the decision on 'whether' to have the argument out during the summer well before the election. Otherwise, the debate would take place during the campaign itself when it is not easy to duck an issue of this size and there would be huge penalties for attempting to avoid the question of whether we should replace Polaris.

Shirley Williams was arguing publicly that SDP policy was not to replace Polaris and that I was 'expressing a personal view'. Bill Rodgers said he was 'quite puzzled' by my statement. Yet John Cartwright was splendidly forthright – 'I cannot understand what Shirley is on about. What the hell did we all leave the Labour Party for? We are not prepared to play games with Britain's defences.' Privately my critics in the SDP were talking about 'machismo' and 'conviction à la Thatcher'. Yet a Gallup poll of Alliance candidates claimed that nine out of ten of the SDP candidates were opposed to Britain giving up nuclear weapons, whereas half of the Liberal candidates wanted to do so. Then we had 'STEEL READY TO REBUKE OWEN' as *The Times* headline; 'STEEL: I COULD MURDER OWEN' in the *Daily Mirror*, 'I COULD KILL HIM' in the *Sun*. This was because David had commented that his relationship with me was like Dame Sybil Thorndike's marriage with Lewis Casson; she had never contemplated divorce but frequently murder.

Then Peter Walker made a speech exposing our differences far more delicately:

> There is one prime reason why Dr Owen defends the need for Britain to retain an effective nuclear deterrent while the rest of the Alliance argue for unilateral disarmament. The reason is that he is the only personality in the entire Alliance who has ever had to exercise the responsibility of high office in international affairs.

The others had held office on the domestic scene, he said, and he warned me that I must face the fact that I might be rejected by the Alliance. I had indeed faced that fact and I knew the answer too. I would be rejected by the Alliance; my hope lay with the SDP. What had happened was exactly what many of us had begun to fear from within a few months of the SDP's foundation: a combination of Liberals and some SDP members, all activists, overturning democratically agreed SDP policy. In this case, David Steel with Roy, Shirley and Bill were apparently confident of victory. I was told I was isolated and alone. I feared it was going to be, in the words of the Duke of Wellington, 'A damned near thing – the nearest run thing you ever saw in your life.' The question was whether we had yet become a Liberal Party Mark II.

The first confrontation came at a meeting of the Parliamentary Advisory Committee, consisting of MPs and other senior Party figures outside Parliament. They were selected by the MPs so it was not strictly representative, but they were nevertheless a powerful group. They excoriated Shirley's fiction that the policy agreed at Torquay was unclear about replacing Polaris. People like Anthony Lester who were close to Roy said that was nonsense. Roy had been away and returned to the House of Commons fuming. I suggested a chat that afternoon, and so we went and had an unpleasant row in the Smoking Room. It was unlike the Great Yarmouth encounter for this time I was the Leader and I told him a few home truths which he did not care for at all. I asked him why he had written to me after our Conference in Torquay and the Liberals' in Dundee to say he agreed with me on policy and yet was now disowning the very defence policy which had been agreed at Torquay. He huffed and puffed about needing to take account of the Liberals, and was evidently uncomfortable when I asked acidly, 'What about the country?' As always, by then the Alliance meant everything and the SDP was secondary. I wondered if he had any policy sticking point.

The issue went to the National Committee on 19 June where to my surprise a very clear majority upheld the policy of the Party as decided at Torquay. Shirley told the Committee that she had no knowledge of the Commission report before Southport, but John Cartwright intervened to say crisply that he had given her a draft of the report weeks before. The Committee now knew exactly what they were dealing with and that there had been a conspiracy. Roy, Shirley and Bill had little option but to agree on the interpretation of SDP policy and it was minuted that there should be no further attempt to contest this. The policy of the Party was as agreed at Torquay:

> Social Democrats would not abandon Britain's existing nuclear capability and are willing to replace Polaris. A decision over any replacement will be taken in the light of disarmament negotiations and the views of our allies. We are prepared to include the British nuclear force as part of an overall East/West disarmament agreement.

On 30 June I spoke in the two-day House of Commons debate on the defence estimates and tried to answer George Younger, the Defence Secretary, who had, not unfairly, dubbed Alliance policy 'a shambles'. The *Daily Telegraph* parliamentary report summed up my speech in headline form, 'ALLIANCE TO LOOK FOR MINIMUM NUCLEAR DETERRENT - OWEN SEEKS CUT-PRICE EUROPEAN MISSILE SYSTEM'. At our Alliance joint policy committee meeting on 8 July we got broad agreement to this new European emphasis. Later that same day I flew to Moscow for a small working session of the Palme Commission. There I had an interesting conversation with Dobrynin, Gorbachev's principal foreign adviser, whom I had met when he was their Ambassador in Washington. I questioned him very carefully about underlying Soviet attitudes to Britain replacing Polaris. On my return I had a meeting with Mr Shevardnadze, the Soviet Foreign Minister, who was very impressive. From everything they said it was clear that the Soviet Union was ready to accept modernization of the UK nuclear deterrent and the replacement of Polaris as long as there was no increase in the overall levels of nuclear arsenals.

On 16 July David Steel and I released the defence section of our joint consultative document, *Partnership for Progress*. We agreed that we would consult not only with our own Party but would go round Europe consulting our main Community partners, both in government and in Opposition, exploring what contribution Britain's nuclear capability should make to European deterrence. This was to be done within the criteria suggested by the Alliance Joint Defence Commission. In effect I had forced the Alliance to accept that it was going to have to make up its mind about whether to remain a nuclear weapons state well before the election.

Though we could assemble some attractive European packaging there was no way that we could avoid the fact that the ultimate control of any nuclear weapon would be vested in the French President and the British Prime Minister. There was no other democratic mechanism short of a federalist solution, a United States of Europe, which I and the SDP had never favoured – another fundamental difference between us and the Liberals. A European deterrent would have two fingers on two buttons. This would be all the more credible in terms of forcing a US President to consult his principal European allies. In the very unlikely nightmare of an isolationist United States, two European decision points would make nuclear weapons states, such as the Soviet Union, at least hesitate before attempting to blackmail the democratic countries of Western Europe.

The series of rather unpleasant, but still vital, SDP meetings on defence came to its climax at the policy committee at the end of July. I had to use my casting vote to ensure that Bill Rodgers was not chosen to reply to the crucial defence debate due to take place at our September Conference in Harrogate. The resolution which the policy committee was putting to the Party formally welcomed the Joint Commission document, but we also deliberately reaffirmed SDP policy, so it would have been absurd for Bill, given what he had been saying, to speak on our behalf.

My public attitude to criticism that the Alliance was divided over defence was to admit it and not flannel around pretending otherwise. Sometimes in the past I had fallen into the trap of going too far in minimizing the differences. But I was comfortable defending the Alliance as a new concept in British politics and was ready to ride out the fact that our differences were real and not just being played up in the press. As long as David and I could be interviewed on television in the midst of even such a robust debate and demonstrate a constructive partnership, the electorate would realize that there was a basic strength to the Alliance.

All this time David and I were campaigning together for the by-election at Newcastle-under-Lyme on 17 July. At the start Michael Heseltine challenged me to disown the Liberal candidate because he was a supporter of CND. My reply was that I respected the pacifist Quaker tradition in Liberal politics, that the Liberal candidate had been chosen by Liberal members not Social Democrats and that voters sympathetic to the SDP could be confident in voting for someone committed to the concept of an Alliance partnership. Labour narrowly won the by-election, with the Liberal/SDP Alliance candidate only 794 votes behind. If the Labour candidate had not been Llin Golding, the wife of John Golding the former Labour MP, a militant moderate who had become General Secretary of the National Communications Union, the Alliance would have won this seat. Perhaps we might have won too if the Liberal candidate had not been a unilateralist. But it did show that even in the midst of public controversy between the Alliance partners, we could still poll very well, having improved our performance during the campaign. Only a fortnight earlier a poll had shown Labour way ahead with 49 per

SDP LEADER - 1986

cent, the Alliance on 25 per cent and the Conservatives with 21 per cent. The final result was impressive proof that an identical outlook between the two parties was not the only route to electoral success.

More evidence came in a MORI poll at the end of July which showed the Alliance on 25 per cent, up on our rating of 23 per cent in June and only 1 per cent below our 26 per cent rating in May. The party that had gained were the Tories, now on 36 per cent, running close to Labour who were still ahead but had dropped to 37 per cent. Interestingly I had become more popular among Alliance sympathizers and David Steel less so. There was, therefore, no polling evidence that this particular row over defence had been as damaging as we might have feared. What did upset the polls was Margaret Thatcher's apparent rift with the Queen over the future of the Commonwealth, which dented her own popularity quite considerably. This was reflected in a Marplan poll published in early August, which had the Alliance on 27.5 per cent, the Tories on 29.5 per cent and Labour well ahead on 41 per cent. The Alliance vote had only gone down 1.5 per cent from the previous month, which was not statistically significant.

Understandably, now I had asserted my authority on defence, David felt he had to assert his own policies. The *Spitting Image* picture of him in my pocket was always a caricature. Fortunately we had different strengths and weaknesses. David took the opportunity of the tenth anniversary of his leadership of the Liberal Party to make it clear that he believed a formal union between the Liberal and the Social Democratic Party was almost inevitable. Stressing that he believed in union rather than merger he emphasized that a decision would depend on the parties' defining the constitutional shape of their common future after the general election, but that it would be wrong to press on against any substantial minority in either of the parties. I dearly wish that he had stuck by these words, as do a substantial minority. I could take no exception to this speech, apart from wishing that we could get headlines on policy rather than on internal merger arguments. I conceded that merger was a legitimate subject for debate after the next election, though I was still personally opposed to it. I could already sense that there were many Social Democrats who would want to merge after the election. This was when I started to hope that if David really was prepared to accept that a minority could not be forced into a merger we might reach an agreement where some Social Democrats merged with the Liberals and others did not.

One symbol of the subterranean debate in the SDP came in a column by Hugo Young who, clearly briefed by some of my Party colleagues, returned to the attack on my personality in a piece published in the *Guardian* on 24 July: 'With brief lapses into collegiate mode he has become ever more dominant, ever more impatient and ever more convinced that hardly anyone else in the party is worth a row of beans.'

According to him my motive was to ensure that if there were a hung Parliament I would be unencumbered by the Liberals.

He has always found many of their attitudes uncongenial, and has the old Labour man's contempt for their nagging individualism. But far more important than that, in a certain configuration of seats, he would want to keep open the Tory option: to do a deal with a new Conservative leadership as the last hope of precluding what would be, for Owen personally, the ruin of his political life – the installation of Neil Kinnock in Downing Street.

By stressing personality Hugo's columns have, over the years, tended to disparage the possibility that there might ever be principle behind any politician's stand. Inasmuch as I would have expected SDP MPs in a hung Parliament to refuse to help install a government committed to unilateral nuclear disarmament, his surmise was quite correct. I was fearful that some Liberal MPs would be ready to install Neil Kinnock in Downing Street without safeguarding our national security. We had not created the SDP as a vehicle to let a Labour Government in by the back door, committed to all the dangerous damaging nonsense that was then still part of their party policy. Neil Kinnock's defence policy was in fact worse than Michael Foot's because it called for the removal of US nuclear bases from Britain as well as ending the British nuclear deterrent. The importance of what Hugo Young was writing was that it was what some in the SDP National Committee also believed. It was, however, so full of inaccuracies that both Ian Wrigglesworth and Mike Thomas wrote letters to the *Guardian* putting the record straight.

Our family spent August in America and when we came back towards the end of the month I travelled up to Scotland for a visit to the Edinburgh Festival with David and Judy Steel. It was an enjoyable occasion and I spent the night with them at Ettrick Bridge. We had election photographs taken together fishing, an event which was also covered by television, and we were able to prepare for our European visit in early September. We were not, as I had said to the press, 'bosom friends', but we had as good a partnership as any two politicians in a similar situation could expect to have had.

On Wednesday 3 September we visited NATO headquarters together with MP colleagues John Cartwright and Alan Beith. We met the American Supreme Allied Commander who was extraordinarily frank about Anglo-French nuclear co-operation. Since Mitterrand had taken office as President there had been clearly far more French nuclear co-operation with NATO than was generally known. We then went by train to Paris. This was the period of 'cohabitation' so it was natural to see key figures both on the Right and on the Left. We met the articulate young former socialist Prime Minister, Laurent Fabius. We also saw Michel Rocard who, though he had resigned from Mitterrand's Socialist Government before they left office, was still a force to be reckoned with and was later to become Prime Minister. The Minister for Foreign Affairs was cautious as befitted a professional diplomat appointed to serve the President without offending the Prime Minister. We had lunch with the Minister of Defence, who was a Chirac appointment and very keen on Anglo-French nuclear co-operation. The meeting with President Mitterrand was extremely positive. Finally, we met Prime Minister Jacques Chirac who was friendly about Margaret Thatcher, but did not disguise his disappointment that she would only look to the United States over nuclear co-operation.

François Mitterrand was dominating continental Europe by then in a way which we in Britain had insufficiently realized. Everyone agreed that he was the great survivor of French politics. But there was less agreement on why he had survived so long. No one does so without having rare political skills, some of them born out of adversity, and we were to see these flower even more after 1986.

I had first met Mitterrand in *Gauche Europeane* meetings in Paris in the mid-1960s and had been deeply unimpressed. His appearance was very unappealing and he spoke unattractively. Yet even so, I had felt grudging respect, for he had recently pushed General de Gaulle into a second ballot in the Presidential elections of December 1965 and demonstrated a formidable capacity to unify the vote of the Left across what many thought was an unbridgeable chasm between the Socialist Party and the Communists. In May 1968, in the month of the barricades, Mitterrand, as the leader of the Federation of the Left, challenged de Gaulle with virulent criticism. When de Gaulle resigned after the April 1969 referendum, Mitterrand declined to stand against Pompidou.

The French politician that I had known best over all those years was Michel Rocard, whom I had first met when he was in the *Inspection des Finances*. I had tended, therefore, to see Mitterrand from the perspective of Rocard and their antipathy was well known. Gradually, through the 1970s, I watched as Mitterrand's appearance and manner were changed. He began to cultivate an image of a man above the battle; a sage and seasoned politician. I met him when he came to the Labour Party Conference in the late 1970s and I had heard him speak at meetings but I had not chatted to him in any depth for some years.

In the first round of the 1981 Presidential elections in April, Mitterrand came a close second to Giscard d'Estaing, having squeezed the Communist vote down to 15 per cent, and voters felt safe in switching in the second ballot to Mitterrand. He became the first socialist President in the twenty years of the Fifth Republic.

For the first two years, he governed as a socialist; cut working hours, increased holidays, enlarged social security, nationalized industries and abolished the guillotine. In the process he also smothered French Communism. In an increasingly interdependent world economy, the French attempt at socialism in one country was a disaster. It ended in 1983 with a massive trade deficit, wage inflation and a gravely weakened franc. It was as bad as Wilson's period from 1964–67 which started with hope and ended in devaluation. Yet whereas Wilson had to accept the IMF, Mitterrand was luckier, he could realign within the discipline of the EMS. He held to that discipline thereafter with tenacity and the French economy progressively grew stronger all through the 1980s; but before the benefits could work through the National Assembly elections were coming up.

Seeing election defeat staring him in the face, Mitterrand switched to a proportional voting system for the National Assembly. It was a move of the utmost cynicism which provoked Rocard to resign as Minister of Agriculture. However, when the Socialists lost in the Assembly elections earlier in 1986, Mitterrand could claim that they had not been wiped out as they would have been under the old voting system. Also the extreme Right-wing Party Leader, Le Pen, had reduced Chirac's majority. President Mitterrand had insisted on staying in office and when David Steel and I saw him he was intent on showing that cohabitation was feasible, whereby a President and Prime Minister from different parties could work together. It was always going to be the biggest test for de Gaulle's constitution and ironic that Mitterrand, the foremost critic of the Fifth Republic's constitution made it work. That it survived cohabitation is a tribute not just to Mitterrand but also to Chirac. Cohabitation could, however, never have worked had it not been for the nature of Mitterrand's foreign policy. From the start it had been hard to criticize from the Right. President Mitterrand had gone to the German Bundestag and used his socialist credentials to urge German social democrats, then in Opposition, to support the deployment of cruise missiles and the modernization of Pershing I missiles to counter the Soviet SS-20 missile deployment. In doing so he forged a close working relationship with the Christian Democrat, Chancellor Kohl, and the Republican, President Reagan. Mitterrand had absolutely no sympathy with the prevalent mood of hostility to nuclear weapons among the socialists and social democrats of Northern Europe. When we arrived in Paris, we did not expect to hear different notes on nuclear policy from Mitterrand and Chirac and nor did we. Mitterrand make it quite clear to us that France would remain a nuclear weapon state and that he wanted Britain to do the same.

So we had Mitterrand and Chirac going to great lengths to demonstrate to the accompanying British press and television cameras that they wanted to co-operate on nuclear defence with Britain and were irritated by the reluctance of Margaret Thatcher to envisage a nuclear relationship with anyone other than the Americans. The warmth of our reception surprised even the most cynical people in Britain. While we had gone as a way of helping the Alliance parties to get safely through a tricky defence debate at the Liberal Party Conference, our trip had demonstrated, to some people's surprise, that Anglo-French nuclear co-operation was a real not imaginary prospect. By putting the red carpet down for us the French were signalling an important message to the British Government which I hope we will act on before the end of this century.

Before our visit I watched with amazement as Mitterrand readily acquiesced in Chirac reversing the proportional representation he had introduced, then turned the tables by beating Chirac convincingly for a second Presidential term in 1988. He did a tacit deal with Rocard that if Rocard supported him in the fight for Presidency he would appoint him Prime Minister. They then lived three years in an uneasy but successful partnership which ended only in 1991 when Mitterrand chose Madame Cresson to be France's first woman Prime Minister. The parting was all very civilized, with Michel Rocard relieved to go and with Mitterrand implying that he might be his successor as President. Whether indeed Rocard, with a few years to prepare to run for the Presidency, will be the choice of the Socialist Party will no doubt depend on whether Madame Cresson is a success. Rocard is more of a Euro-federalist.

Mitterrand has long been ready to work with the Americans on defence provided they paid public lip-service to his aspirations for French nuclear independence. Those who have visited French ballistic missile nuclear submarines say that the amount of unnamed American equipment is staggering. Certainly within NATO, successive SACEURs have found no difficulty in matching NATO's nuclear targeting strategy with that of the French. Ever the pragmatist Mitterrand has achieved a quiet revolution in the realities of French defence policy, if not yet its rhetoric. He wants and with luck will soon obtain Anglo-French nuclear co-operation from the British. During the build up to the liberation of Kuwait, Mitterrand waited while his Defence Minister, Chevenement, went out on a limb rejecting any French role in attacking Iraq and kept France outside any US command structure. When public opinion shifted towards French involvement, he sacked Chevenement, ensuring that France, albeit with a modest role, got maximum credit from contributing to the allied effort, dropped their previous insistence on not attacking Iraq and de facto accepted US command and control.

The unanswered question is in what direction does Mitterrand want the European Community to head. In early 1990 he appeared to be going along with Jacques Delors's wish for a United States of Europe. By the middle of 1991 Mitterrand proved to be too close to the heartbeat of France to surrender the substance of French nationhood to government from Brussels and the British and French Foreign Ministers were refusing to accept majority voting for foreign policy, but for how long?

Before the Party Conferences started, we celebrated Tristan's sixteenth birthday. It was the first time for thirteen years that we could feel safe in the knowledge that his leukaemia was cured. In an interview in *Woman's Own* Debbie and I had spoken a little more frankly than we would normally have done and this triggered a number of press stories, but they were all tactfully written and paid tribute to his bravery. Coping with a father in the public eye was not always easy for my children. When I was Foreign Secretary and loathed by the Right-wing press, the boys were sometimes teased at school. They were very conscious too that people's approach to them could be unduly influenced by who their father was rather than for what they were themselves. Strangely, older people, particularly teachers, were often worse in this respect than the boys' contemporaries. Whereas I had grown a thick skin to some of the personal criticism, they were on one occasion very upset by a *Panorama* programme at the time of the 1985 Torquay Conference. They were so angry that they never again agreed to be filmed. They had trusted a fawning TV producer and a presenter who won their trust. They then went off and broke it with cynical disregard. At last the BBC are doing something about that minority culture within it that appears based on a few people with massive chips on their shoulders. They may be the minority but they do enormous harm to the BBC and do not seem to have an equivalent in ITV. Above all, my children longed to go to the cinema or even fishing at sea without their father being recognized. As the years went on they grew ever more resistant to being photographed and some, but not many, photographers refused to take no for an answer. With the odd exception, though, I have found the media to be considerate of our need for some measure of privacy and I am deeply opposed to legislating to protect privacy.

By the time we drove into Harrogate for our Conference on Saturday 13 September, I was pleased with the progress we had made on the defence issue. Even defence experts were taking the emerging Alliance defence policy seriously. But the merger question would not go away and *The Times*, in an editorial entitled 'Merger mania', said,

Those in favour of merger tend to favour a deal with Labour, those against are in general more ready to deal with either Labour or the Conservatives. Much pro-merger fervour, of course, conceals simple envy and resentment of Dr Owen; many of his colleagues spend much of their time casting about for new engines to reinforce the long siege of their leader's independence ... At its foundation, many of Dr Owen's present opponents regarded the Party as a temporary vehicle to be led by Roy Jenkins into rapid merger with the Liberals. Mr Jenkins's dauphin, Mr David Steel, would then take over the combined entity and set out to replace the Labour Party as the principal opposition to Conservatism ... Dr Owen has not yet proved that the Alliance is a plausible candidate for government. But as he faces today's defence debate, he can reflect that he has brought off two commendable successes. He has maintained a position on the British deterrent which is defensible in principle and he has, at least, helped minimize the danger of the early summer split growing wider.

When we came to the defence debate the policy committee's tough stance on defence was supported by a margin of 4:1. John Cartwright put the issue very clearly to the Party and, though Charles Kennedy, in winding up, made a speech with too many cheap jibes at the Americans, he was nevertheless firm on the main issue. I was able to tell the press at the end, 'I've got what I wanted – the freedom to go for the Labour Party's jugular on the crucial question of defence at the next election.' My anxiety was whether we could get the same freedom from the Liberal Conference at Eastbourne.

In many ways the most important SDP debate at Harrogate was on the policy document, *Merging tax and benefits*. We had published the proposals a fortnight before and they were given a rough ride. Removing the married man's tax allowance was correct, but it was difficult to do without making many middle-income couples worse off and we had not solved the phasing-out problems. It is interesting that in 1991, Norman Lamont decided to freeze this allowance as a first step towards phasing it out. Another editorial in *The Times*, 'Tax and displease', agreed that the logic of integrating the tax and benefits system was undeniable. It also commended us for not pretending, like the Labour Party, that it could all be paid for by taxing the rich. But they were correct in pointing out that the burden of our integration plans would fall on the middle class and we knew this would not go down well in every house in suburbia. *The Times* concluded that 'Dr Owen may find that proving he is not Mrs Thatcher is not wholly to his advantage. David Steel expressed his anxiety that the proposals were a gift to Tory propagandists and we both agreed, having discussed it at Ettrick Bridge, that our presentation would have to be considerably improved. On the other hand, I was concerned that, whereas the toughness in SDP policy was always reported, the tenderness which was less newsworthy was too often ignored. A readiness to redistribute was essential to our claim to be Social Democrats and the Conference, far from rejecting the package, gave Dick Taverne, its chief architect, a well deserved standing ovation and strongly supported the policy. Dick and I did not agree on the merger question but this did not prevent us working closely on tax reform where his experience was invaluable. Because of the defence row the wider public had been fed only the tough image of the SDP in recent months so I set out to offset this by emphasizing the tender side in my final speech. I virtually ignored defence and tried to sell our tax reforms, not just for their redistributive social justice but for the simplification and modernization of the system. The *Guardian*, often critical of the SDP, concluded editorially that the net effect 'is of an SDP that, as well as challenging for votes from socially concerned Conservatives, is also now in a position to compete credibly and legitimately for votes on the Left.'

The mood of the Harrogate Conference was not ebullient like Torquay. It was more workmanlike, even mundane. Quite a sizeable element in the

Conference were alarmed about confronting the Liberals on defence and anxious about the forthcoming election. The divisions in the Gang of Four were obvious in little jabs and coded phrases, but by the end we had achieved perhaps a better balance of SDP policy than in any other Conference.

People often used to speculate on what the SDP membership was really like. I suppose inevitably I saw the grass roots membership from my constituency vantage point. In our Plymouth SDP there were many former Labour members and council tenants. We were not wealthy nor even a predominantly middle-class group but a genuine mix. There was hardly a claret drinker among them. Try as I might, however, I never succeeded in ridding the national Party of that claret image.

As we packed up to go home we knew an election was likely before we met again. I felt too that we were not yet over the defence hurdle. As a believer in the Liberal Party's capacity to mess anything up, I looked to the Liberal Conference in Eastbourne with some trepidation, for it was too quiet for comfort.

A warning about the Liberal Party Conference came on 20 September with the publication of a pamphlet written by three Liberal MPs, Simon Hughes, Archy Kirkwood and Michael Meadowcroft. They insisted that the European initiative being pursued by the leadership must be the means to a non-nuclear Europe and not a means towards a European pillar of NATO with a minimum deterrent. Next day the *News of the World* ran an article by David Steel entitled, 'Why I believe that the Liberals and the SDP will merge', but he wrote that it must evolve naturally. I cursed his obsession with merger as heartily as he no doubt cursed my separatism. At a Liberal Conference Sunday teach-in Bill Rodgers was disappointingly reported on the Monday as having reiterated the Commission's form of words which had been rejected by the SDP. Shirley Williams was also reported as saying, 'We would be mad if we attempted to throw out the idea of a compromise on defence.' So, despite Harrogate and all that had gone before it, I could not look to either of them for support, nor to Roy Jenkins.

When I rose to speak on the Monday I had been warned by Des Wilson that there was a likelihood of a walk-out by Liberal CND. Instead of a political speech, I therefore deliberately gave an academic lecture on disarmament, described by my wife as quite the most boring speech she had ever heard me make. It was so low key as to be lacklustre but it caused minimum offence and there were no walk outs. In the *Daily Telegraph* Edward Pearce wrote that

to see Dr Owen and Mr Des Wilson, the Liberal President, in contra-distinction on the same afternoon is like feeding junket through a grinder ... Dr Owen, having come here as a devil figure, with a Polaris substitute in his hip pocket was oppressively exact, flipping statistics of comparative warheads off the back of his wrist, concentrating minutely on the six-point type of disarmament negotiations.

He claimed perceptively that I had

> set out to elucidate the opposition into glazed-over cataleptic acquiescence. Force-fed, with expertise, the hungry sheep of the Liberal CND looked up in hope of heartless outrage, and were offered rich handfuls of statistical budgie-seed ... Some people are born boring. Others have boringness thrust upon them. Yesterday Dr Owen, with malicious forethought, *achieved* boringness.

Over tea afterwards David Steel and other Liberal leaders were very happy with my speech and extraordinarily confident that all would go well next day, talking of a huge majority. The press were interpreting my speech as being conciliatory because of the stress that I laid on disarmament. Even so I left Eastbourne that night with a nagging fear that all the delicate diplomacy of the last few months could be shattered in one Eastbourne afternoon.

Next day I actually watched the whole two-hour debate on television from my office in the House of Commons, so I must have been worried. In a highly emotional speech Simon Hughes spoke in favour of an amendment that any British contribution to collective European defence should be non-nuclear. As the tide of the debate turned against the platform, I willed David Steel to speak and put his leadership on the line. But he stayed firmly put, no doubt fearing another rejection like that of 1984. After a tense, passionate and at times hopelessly naïve debate, the Assembly backed the amendment by 652 votes to 625. This was a disaster for the Alliance and I was appalled as David went on television immediately afterwards trying to downplay its significance, describing the vote as 'only an irritant and not a serious setback'. In despair we closed down our office, refused to answer any phone calls and went to ground. For four hours, the future of the Alliance hung in the balance. If the Liberals had persisted with that defence policy, I would have had no other option than to bust the Alliance wide open. Probably aware of how the press were going to play it, David by the time of the *Nine o'Clock News* was singing a completely different tune, warning his MPs that the decision would have to be reversed.

Until that vote there had been an excellent prospect that the electorate would be given a three-way choice on defence between Conservatives supporting Trident, Labour committed to unilateralism and the Alliance advocating a minimum nuclear deterrent. Suddenly the newspapers had a field day. 'ALLIANCE SHATTERED', 'STEEL HUMILIATED', 'DEFEAT ON DEFENCE', 'DOCTOR IN DISTRESS', are just a sample. Once it became clear that David Steel was prepared to fight back and reverse the decision I knew that it was my duty to help him.

I was in no mood to crow or make life more difficult than it already was. Since the general election, I have sometimes wondered whether that was the moment when I should have broken up the Alliance. Such was the anger in the SDP with the Liberals that I have no doubt I could have done so. But it would have been a cynical act and would soon have been recognized as such. It would also have shattered the whole concept of co-operation between parties and the concept of coalition politics. However, it could be argued that since it was going to be shattered a year later anyway, we should have anticipated events. My answer to that is that, given David's readiness to try to reverse the vote, I had no honourable alternative to trying to put the pieces together with him. I thought David Steel deserved my support for his constructive response since his leaking of the Defence Commission Report. A joint television interview on Thursday for *This Week* had been arranged for some weeks. David flew up by helicopter from Eastbourne. It provided us with an opportunity to put a brave face on the Eastbourne decision. But the fault line in any Alliance defence policy was now very clearly exposed. I had little doubt that we would pay a heavy price in the polls and I was right. A MORI poll late that month had us below 20 per cent for the first time for years with a mere $17\frac{1}{2}$ per cent, a drop of 9 per cent since September, and the satisfaction ratings of both David Steel and me had dropped.

There was, however, a silver lining to Eastbourne's dark cloud. Having been buffeted in the press, the Liberal leadership and all Liberal MPs, irrespective of their views on defence, at long last began to exert a collective influence. The Party's Policy Committee on 22 October approved a statement acknowledging that a British minimum nuclear deterrent would be maintained – with necessary modernization – until it could be negotiated away as part of worldwide arms negotiation and that Britain's nuclear capacity would be frozen at a level no greater than that of the Polaris system. I had little difficulty in supporting that statement for it was broadly what I had insisted on. We had in effect knocked out the 'whether' from the Commission Report and answered the question using their criteria. The Alliance was now committed to replace Polaris, the decision which the Defence Commission had ducked. But the SDP had achieved this at the savage price of exposing the Liberal Party's equivocation over defence. The question now was whether or not this new statement should be put to a recalled special Liberal Assembly. Bob Maclennan was keen that it should be reconvened but David Steel was against it. If I had been more ruthless, I would have pressed David hard to do so. Perhaps it was a mistake not to, but I felt that I had pushed the Liberal Party as far as it could go. At least on 24 October the Liberal Party Council agreed the statement, so it now became official Party policy. But Bob Maclennan, and to a lesser extent Ian Wrigglesworth, were correct in sensing that only a reconvened conference and another vote would have buried public memories of Eastbourne. It was a high risk strategy and, as I had been balancing on the high wire ever since Southport, I relented, even though I too worried about the Conservative Party trying to pin the unilateralist label on the Alliance. I had every reason to fear Tory Chairman Norman Tebbit and his instinct for the political jugular.

As I looked back over those last few difficult months I asked myself whether I had been wise to reject the Defence Commission's recommendation over Polaris so completely at Southport. It seemed to me that that question could only be answered at the next election, now very likely some time in 1987. If defence and nuclear weapons, contrary to my predictions, proved to be a non-issue, then being bound by the Defence Commission's wording would not prove disastrous. If defence was by contrast a big issue, as I thought it was bound to be, then all the trauma would have been necessary.

What the Reykjavik Summit had shown in the middle of October was how dependent the domestic defence debate was on the shifting sands of international affairs. In his autobiography President Reagan describes how at Reykjavik 'my hopes for a nuclear-free world soared briefly, then fell during one of the longest, most disappointing – and ultimately angriest – days of my Presidency'. Right at the end when Reagan thought they had negotiated the most massive weapons reductions in history, Gorbachev added, with a smile on his face, 'This all depends, of course, on you giving up SDI.' Rightly or wrongly Reagan had always attached immense importance to his Strategic Defence Initiative, better known as Star Wars. It was only because he had faith in this concept of an impenetrable shield that he, unlike most Western leaders, could envisage a non-nuclear world. To Reagan SDI was his insurance policy; it gave him confidence to argue with the American military that all ballistic missiles could go. Without it he would never have dreamt of taking on the fears of his top military advisers. It was inevitable and logical that he should refuse. In his terms the Soviet leader was playing poker. But if Gorbachev had not made SDI his sticking point and Reykjavik had fulfilled all Reagan's hopes, whatever qualms we in Britain might have had about the abolition of all ballistic missiles, there would have been a dramatic change in the domestic climate over defence which would have had profound implications for the 1987 Election. Even if the INF Treaty had been agreed at the start of 1987 instead of at the end, it would have had an effect domestically.

But in the middle of October 1986 the mood in Britain and in the Western democracies was that the Reykjavik Summit marked the end of serious arms control negotiations. I was virtually alone in arguing in *The Times* of 16 October that Reykjavik was but the beginning, and my note of optimism was in marked contrast to the prevailing mood of pessimism. I claimed that in Iceland Reagan and Gorbachev had taken the sort of risks that distinguish the bureaucrat from the political leader. Hoping to bounce Reagan over the SDI hurdle Gorbachev had gambled by making dramatic changes in the Soviet arms control position right up to the end of the meeting. Reagan had gambled by giving the Russians their head in discussing a global settlement which was not on the official agenda for Iceland and hoped Gorbachev would not make SDI a sticking point. But neither leader gambled recklessly. Both had a clear view of their limits, but in negotiating to those limits both men had significantly loosened the bureaucratic log-jam that had bedevilled the negotiations on inter-mediate-range (INF) and strategic weapons (START). The armchair critics, particularly former presidential advisers in both Democratic and Republican administrations, were arguing that summit meetings should be held only for heads of government to sign previously negotiated text. That was the Foreign Office view throughout my time as Foreign Secretary, and it is why diplomatic negotiations drag on for years with barely any movement because each side is afraid to move first. When considering the role of diplomats and politicians it is worth recalling Vice President Lyndon Johnson's early enthusiasm for all the Kennedy intellectuals, like Bundy, Rusk and McNamara. Sam Rayburn, the wily old Speaker of the House of Representatives, said, 'Well, Lyndon, you may be right and they may be every bit as intelligent as you say, but I'd feel a whole lot better about them if just one of them had run for sheriff once.' Reykjavik was a classic example of why you need politicians in international affairs. Politicians win votes by having a go. They gamble and the best ones have the courage to call off the gamble if it does not look like succeeding. As I argued in *The Times*,

> politicians' virtues should be a readiness on occasion to take responsibil-ity and make decisions on their own initiative, cutting through the bureaucratic inertia. Those who now cry 'I told you so' are the small men. Reagan and Gorbachev were right to gamble and, given that neither gamble quite came off, both men were right to stand firm. Each will now think the better of the other for knowing that he has sticking points.

Turning back to domestic politics, by November 1986 I could at least start putting the knife into Labour's defence policy again. For the last six months I had operated under a self-imposed moratorium because it would have been ludicrous to rough Labour up while I had not won the battle within the SDP, let alone the Liberal Party. The fact that I was now able to do so was recognized in the *Mail on Sunday* of 14 December in an editorial entitled 'Dr Owen's vital decision to cut the Labour cord'. They concentrated on my recent statement that, as long as the Labour Party maintained its current defence policy, the Alliance would find it impossible, in the event of a hung Parliament, to throw their weight behind a Neil Kinnock attempt to form a government. 'Dr Owen, by finally cutting the umbilical cord with the Labour Party, is now firmly established as the leader of the real radical alternative to the Conservative Party.' Sadly, as events were to prove over the next six months, the umbilical cord linking David Steel's Liberal Party to the Labour Party had not been cut. Though we had a rational, firm defence policy, the Liberals were neither prepared to stand firmly behind it nor to abandon their traditional position of sitting even-handedly between the Labour and Conservative Parties even when, as was the case on defence, Labour was still not fit to govern.

Just before Christmas the Liberal Party, and we in the SDP too, were dealt a dreadful blow. David Penhaligon was killed in a motor accident in Cornwall at the age of forty-two. Debbie and I had grown to know him and Annette quite well, helped by having stayed at their house, which had quickly eroded some mutual suspicions. Few things gave Debbie and me greater pleasure than when Annette asked Debbie to be the literary agent for her book on David, entitled simply *Penhaligon*. Its sales confirmed that he had many admirers in the country. Refreshingly down-to-earth as a politician and a man, with a distinctive Cornish accent, he revelled in representing all that was best in the Cornish tradition of Liberal policy. He had genuine wit and was many people's favourite performer on *Question Time*. His personal example had done a great deal to overcome Liberal nonconformist self-consciousness over what had happened to Jeremy Thorpe and the Cornish Liberal MP Peter Bessell. I had always believed that if he had intervened in the Eastbourne debate he would have swung the few votes that were so crucially needed, for his attitude to defence was at times quite robust. He was always in favour of a merger, but for David it would have had to be a merger on Liberal terms. In all my many dealings with him at national and even more often at regional level, he was zealous in protecting the interests of the Liberal Party, particularly those west of the River Tamar. I suspect, and it may be wishful thinking, that had he lived he would have seen the merit of an agreement to merge voluntarily and to live and let live with people like me. He always acknowledged that only an SDP candidate could keep Devonport from going Labour and he was too much of a countryman not to recognize that you needed horses for courses.

33

SDP LEADER – 1987

The new year had me flat on my back with a slipped lumbar disc and, though I had it manipulated just before Christmas, for once it had not gone back. I am a very bad patient and, like most doctors, I always imagine the worst. By now I was suffering from the direst of all possible diagnoses – a pathological fracture of the spine caused by secondary deposits in the bone from cancer. The family were becoming very fed up with me and only Peter Mayer, who lived in a rented house in the Waters' farmyard across the road from us in Buttermere, came to my rescue. His theory, which he claimed had worked for him, was to apply boiling hot flannels to the back. What is more important he came and administered the treatment himself, wringing out the towels and nearly burning my skin. Much to my surprise it worked, and within a few days I was up and about, completely cured. Peter is the chief executive of the Penguin Group and is a publisher with considerable flair. He and Mary had grown to love Buttermere as had Lisa his daughter. It was nevertheless an unfashionable place to live, particularly since the farmyard in winter had mud up to the top of everyone's wellington boots. One rainy day Ed Victor, one of the brightest and flashiest of Debbie's fellow literary agents, arrived to visit the Mayers in a Rolls-Royce with white walled tyres. He drove into the farm only to find himself bogged down in the mire and promptly christened Buttermere the 'capital of shit'. So it becomes each winter and we tease our neighbours, Roger and Susan Waters, who just smile and say it is nature's safety device for slowing down speeding cars.

Later in January, Debbie and I travelled down by train to David Penhaligon's memorial service with many of his Liberal and SDP friends. The tragedy of David Penhaligon's death brought crowds twenty deep outside Truro Cathedral. Inside there was a packed congregation of 1,300 people with many hundreds more linked by video in the City Hall or in the nearby Methodist Church. It was as if the whole of the West Country were mourning a man who had been affectionately called the Voice of Cornwall.

On the return train journey, David Steel and I finalized a list of joint Alliance spokesmen which we had agreed we would announce just in advance of our Barbican rally. Prince Edward had just resigned from the Royal Marines and we cheered ourselves up with the thought of making him Education spokesman and returning Paddy Ashdown to the Marines! I had been persuaded that Alliance spokesmen were needed for the election campaign and once I was sure we had Alliance policy successfully negotiated I was happy to have them in place. We also discussed the forthcoming by-elections. On Christmas Eve Guy Barnett, the Labour MP for Greenwich, had died. This was an SDP seat and so we now faced two by-elections. It was feared that the Labour Party would choose to fight in Greenwich first and not agree to have them at the same time. David Steel was nervous that the SDP might be badly defeated just before Truro. I welcomed fighting in Greenwich, for it meant that we could do what I had long wanted the SDP to do, take the Labour Party apart in one of their safe seats. Greenwich had been held by Labour since 1945 and I relished the fact that on this occasion they had adopted a hard-line Left-wing candidate.

A Marplan poll in the middle of January had shown the Conservatives ahead with 38 per cent, Labour second on 36 per cent and the Alliance 23 per cent. The Labour Party was doing too well and we should have been cutting more deeply into their vote.

In a perceptive article in the *Sunday Times*, Brian Walden attacked me for pursuing the wrong strategy.

> What Dr Owen needs is for the Labour Party to lose the election, preferably by many millions of votes. Dr Owen knows this, yet somehow his brain has severed communication with his tongue. Most of what he says indirectly helps Labour. He is lighting his own funeral pyre.

What he wanted me to do, and what I wanted to do myself, was to say that Labour was unfit to govern, that under no circumstances could we form a pact with them, and that the Conservatives would win the coming election. What was important, was to build up the numbers of SDP and Liberal MPs so that we could become a more effective Opposition. It was the old bridgehead versus the breakthrough argument.

I agreed with Brian Walden that being anti-Labour was sellable to the electorate. It was not, however, sellable to the other members of the Gang of Four, a considerable part of the SDP, let alone to David Steel and the Liberal Party. I had after all tried and lost on this same argument within the SDP before the 1983 Election when the case for this strategy was even stronger. Then, after all, we were facing Michael Foot and Margaret Thatcher after the Falklands. Now with an election likely in the summer or autumn we not only faced a more voter-friendly Labour leader in Neil Kinnock but a Margaret Thatcher unleashing a consumer boom. It was still the right strategy to rule out a coalition with Labour, but I knew it was impossible to make it the official Alliance line.

The best I could hope for was that the polls would be sufficiently good for me to argue convincingly that we would hold the balance of power. Then, while nominally agreeing that we were prepared to form a coalition with either Labour or the Conservatives, I could point up the obstacles to doing so with the Labour Party in such a way that the electorate would know that we would not easily form a coalition with Labour. For the last three and-a-half years I had been nudging, cajoling and positioning the Alliance to adopt something close to this strategy. It was endlessly discussed in the Joint Leaders Advisory Committee and I suspect most people present knew it was the logical course. But logic and politics do not always coincide. The strategy we finally adopted of pretending that the Labour and Conservative parties were equally acceptable coalition partners was not merely silly but, as Brian Walden, with pardonable exaggeration said, quoting Mr Gladstone, touched the 'confines of lunacy'. Yet my experience of working within the Alliance meant that I was not convinced that I could hold even to my own compromise strategy of leaning towards the Conservatives as the favoured coalition partner. For now I had begun to doubt whether David Steel was personally capable of sustaining the impression that there were circumstances in which he might envisage working in a coalition under Margaret Thatcher. To say David hated her was hardly an exaggeration. At one stage he floated a suggestion of working in a coalition under Sir Geoffrey Howe, but that was predictably not only a trial balloon but a lead one. It is immensely difficult for the smaller grouping in a coalition to demand the head of the political leader of the largest party as their price. When that leader had twice been elected as Prime Minister and was in as dominant a position within the Party as Margaret Thatcher, to pretend that we could shunt her out was just incredible.

I found it profoundly depressing that what seemed to me a common sense electoral strategy was dismissed as crypto-Conservatism, in the same way as the social market had been. It ignored the electoral arithmetic and popular attitudes underpinning Margaret Thatcher's victory in 1979 and in 1983. To appeal to the people who had given her those majorities was not to be a Conservative. These people wanted what I wanted for Britain – a fairer society – but they would not vote Labour which appeared dangerous and damaging to them. If the SDP had played our cards right in 1983 and 1987, worked as a new and separate Party rather than as one merged electoral entity, and made some difficult choices, these people could have formed a permanent core vote for the SDP.

I understood David Steel's problem. In Scotland Margaret Thatcher was deeply unpopular, and almost all the Liberal activists throughout the UK loathed her. Within the SDP I had no such problem. The majority of the Party did not like Margaret Thatcher but they had come into

politics to co-operate, and possessed or developed an instinctive understanding of coalition politics. They also had enough sense to see that she
had some merits and that the Labour Party leadership was then far
worse. We had, however, a minority which included Roy Jenkins and
Shirley Williams, who perhaps because of past slights and present
aggravations over the European Community, would not allow themselves
to be seen to be even contemplating a coalition with Margaret Thatcher.
Had we been dealing then with John Major, the strategy that Brian
Walden was advocating and which I had constantly pressed for could
perhaps have been adopted by the Alliance in both the 1983 and 1987
Elections. We would have been rewarded with many more seats. Our
mistake was in pursuing the breakthrough once the opportunity had gone
in early 1982 and certainly after the Falklands War, thereby failing to
secure even a sizeable bridgehead for the SDP in either 1983 or 1987.

The dilemma the Alliance faced in developing its strategy was well
illustrated in the two by-elections which we were about to fight. In Truro
David Penhaligon's success had been virtually to dismantle the Labour
Party vote. I well understood in the West Country, how much he had
done, for in the 1966 election Reg Scott, a Plymouth journalist and
Labour Councillor, whom I knew well and liked, had fought in Truro
and had polled 17,093 votes, coming second to the Conservatives. To win
the by-election in Truro the Liberals needed many Labour votes as well
as those of the disillusioned Tories; they dared not offend Labour's
natural constituency. They planned, therefore, to lay off Labour in
public, putting the knife in only on the doorsteps where no one else could
hear. In Greenwich the SDP, by contrast, did not have to worry about
the sensibilities of Labour voters, many of whom were outraged both by
Labour's policies and by the candidate and were only too ready to vote
SDP. Our problem was to convince Conservative voters to trust us and
to believe that we had a chance to beat Labour.

Yet what I always tried to convince the Joint Leaders Advisory
Committee was that if we wanted to play big league politics, we had to
have a strategy which did not fundamentally differ whether we were
fighting in Truro or Greenwich. The Alliance throughout its six-year life
struggled to modify the old Liberal tactic of letting different constituencies have completely different strategies. Every party shifts the emphasis
but serious parties do not switch the policies. The SDP as a partner with
the Liberals did contribute more coherence in policy but the price was
having to tone down policies that either SDP or Liberal activists wanted
in full measure. Slowly, as we worked together and as those policies
gelled, the parties might have come together. I was a sufficient realist by
1987 to know that the Alliance concept could not be unscrambled
without paying a considerable price and that all we could hope was that
what emerged had as much of the SDP in it as the voters wanted.

On Monday 26 January we launched the joint policy document *The*

Time Has Come both in a shortened version and in a paperback format. We also unveiled our new Alliance colour: gold because no one was prepared to call it yellow. Our theme music was Purcell's Trumpet Tune in D. Perhaps symbolically it is often played at weddings. On Saturday, after a week of media activity, we held the Rally at the Barbican in the City of London. We had put together a very good media package with the help of experts from within our parties, in particular David Abbott of the Abbott, Mead, Vickers advertising agency who had been hired with money provided by David Sainsbury specifically for that purpose. Our new Alliance spokesmen addressed the Rally. Roy dealt with the economy in an authoritative way, albeit disowning the social market with every word and emphasis. Alan Beith for the Liberals spoke on foreign affairs. Shirley spoke for the Alliance on home affairs, John Cartwright on defence and Bill Rodgers on energy. Baroness Seear, a splendidly rumbustious character, who led the Liberals in the House of Lords, spoke on social security issues. We tried to get contributions from as many Alliance spokesmen as we could gather. The emphasis in both David Steel's speech and mine was on coalition. David, in a well delivered speech, much better than mine, said that what mattered was not which party we coalesced with, but that there should be an agreed programme, including 'progress towards proportional representation'. I stressed our appeal to thinking voters and underlined my concern with the national decline by drawing a parallel with France in 1958, before the return of General de Gaulle; saying that the lesson for us was not that Britain should have a powerful President but that constitutional change had preceded French economic recovery and indeed was the prerequisite for it.

Unfortunately David Steel and I, interviewed next day by David Frost on TV-am, virtually contradicted each other. David had declared that it was 'almost impossible' to work with Margaret Thatcher and I, perhaps unwisely, feeling that I had to intervene, said 'I think David has gone too far. I don't think she is the right person to lead the country and I don't think it would be easy for us to carry on a coalition government with her as head but, once we get into the business of telling other parties who is to be leader that goes down a dangerous course'. We had been warned – a potential split in our Alliance had emerged. We were to pay the price during the election campaign.

Two by-election polls were conducted by BBC 2 *Newsnight* at the start of February. In Greenwich it gave Labour 48 per cent (up 10 per cent since 1983), the Conservatives 26 per cent (down 9 per cent) and the SDP 24 per cent (down 1 per cent). In Truro it gave the Liberals 55 per cent (down 2 per cent since 1983), Conservatives 32 per cent (down 6 per cent) and Labour 12 per cent (up 8 per cent). Everybody expected the sympathy vote in Truro would ensure that the Liberal candidate, Matthew Taylor, would hold it for the Alliance. If there was to be a surprise it could only be in Greenwich.

We moved immediately into the attack on the politics of the Greenwich Labour candidate Deirdre Wood. I said she was unfit to be a Member of Parliament and typical of the type of extreme Left-winger who had invited members of Sinn Fein, the political wing of the IRA, to London. In Rosie Barnes we had chosen a charismatic, local and very determined campaigner. Building on John Cartwright's reputation in the neighbouring constituency, Woolwich, we had at last absolutely the right image for the SDP. John had represented Woolwich since 1974, when it was pronounced by Labour to be one of the safest seats in the country, winning by 12,425 votes. Self-taught after grammar school, he became Leader of Greenwich Council and was agent to Christopher Mayhew, their former Labour MP, from whom he took over when Chris resigned to join the Liberal Party. John is an extremely tough political in-fighter, a fact belied by his rather slight, bespectacled appearance. He had been on Labour's National Executive Committee for many years, standing for the Co-operative Party, and had been the scourge for years of Trotskyists and Labour infiltrators. He also had, for such a mild man, a surprisingly vivid turn of phrase, once saying, 'Asking Pat Wall to have nothing to do with the Militant Tendency is like asking Joan Collins to have nothing to do with sex,' which he later toned down to 'like asking Terry Wogan not to appear on television.'

Rosie Barnes had never been a member of any other political party, though if anything she had been more sympathetic to Labour. She lived in the constituency and her children went to school there. She is so warm and friendly that it was not long before everyone was simply calling her 'Rosie'. As a candidate her distinctive virtue was that at no time did she ever doubt that she was going to win, the advantage perhaps of being a political virgin but also the product of a self-assured, determined personality. We soon found that Deirdre Wood's unpopularity was a key factor and 'I'm not voting for that woman' was constantly heard on the doorstep. By and large Rosie eschewed personal attacks, leaving these to the popular national newspapers. Fortunately a poll after two weeks showed that, while Labour was still ahead with 43 per cent, we had moved up to second place with 31 per cent and the Conservatives had slipped to third place with 25 per cent. Also, in a *Today* survey, 43 per cent of voters said they would vote for Rosie if they thought she could win. We exploited these findings to the full to try and persuade Conservative voters to switch to Rosie.

Debbie and I were due to go to India with Helen and Paul Hamlyn to celebrate his birthday. Debbie had known Paul from her New York publishing days and the four of us became warm, or as Paul puts it 'cuddly', friends. I was longing to show Debbie India, but I dared not be abroad even for a week of such a crucial by-election, so with much heartrending we had to cancel. The talk in Greenwich was starting to concentrate on whether we could repeat our 'Bermondsey' triumph. The popular newspapers had by now adopted Rosie and pushed her candidacy hard, with the *Sunday Mirror* headline 'ALL COMING UP ROSIE'S' and the *Sun*'s, 'NECK AND NECK – DEIRDRE SLUMPS IN POLL SETBACK'. Rosie's spectacular win was richly deserved. Not only did she have a majority of 6,500 but an exit poll had shown that she had a good chance of winning the seat in any subsequent general election. The SDP now had eight MPs.

My joy at our victory was slightly marred on the following Sunday by John Horam announcing that he had joined the Conservatives. On top of this, Neville Sandelson was telling people to vote Conservative. With two former SDP MPs doing this, Liberal activists' suspicions of our attitude to the Conservatives grew. After all, I was the man the hated Margaret Thatcher had predicted would be the next non-Tory Prime Minister. The other members of the Gang of Three did not help by constantly hinting that I was a closet Tory. This was despite my saying and repeating that I would never join the Conservative Party. In fact Roy Jenkins, both in his attitudes and in his friends, was always far closer to the leading Conservatives than I, though admittedly he preferred the party of Carrington and Gilmour – rich, Tory and paternalist.

I soon toughened my stance towards Labour in an interview for the *People*, entitled 'Kinnock for PM?. No chance with us says David Owen.' I stated that 'on defence my disagreement with Kinnock is total' and that we would not vote for a Labour Government's Queen's Speech which had not been negotiated with us.

By March, the Tories were moving ahead in the polls. Marplan still had the Alliance third but up at 27 per cent, with Labour slipping to 32 per cent and the Tory lead enhanced with them on 38 per cent. On the following day, 12 March, the Liberals held Truro with an increased majority. Even their campaign managers had expected a slight dent in David Penhaligon's majority. With two victories the Alliance was feeling very confident.

The Budget on 17 March I described as cunning and seductive. All the good things would come in the pre-election period: the fall in interest rates, mortgage rates, lower income tax, relatively cheaper whisky, beer, cigarettes and petrol. 'But like all things based on deceit, the day of reckoning will come and perhaps sooner than any of us realize.' For Nigel Lawson it came two years later.

The Tory national lead remained stubbornly high and it was getting hard to sound convincing when talking about a balanced Parliament. The Conservative political fire was also being concentrated on the Alliance. Their line of attack that the SDP/Liberal Alliance stood for socialism by another name was clear and crude, with Margaret Thatcher giving the lead. The good news was that on 26 March *Today* carried a story under the headline 'OUCH, OUCH', saying we were poised to smash Labour into third place on the basis of a Marplan poll putting the Conservatives on 36 per cent, and with Labour and the Alliance on 31 per cent.

So we proceeded in the build-up towards the general election now only a matter of weeks away. Then, late on 27 March after a public meeting in Cardiff, I had a message to ring Debbie urgently, and discovered that David Watt was dead. He was my closest political friend, the person with whom I spent most time chewing over political decisions. I was shattered. It was the day after the great storm and strong winds had brought down an electric cable on the drive outside David's house in the country. He had lifted it up thinking the cable was dead and had been electrocuted. Debbie was consoling his wife, Susan, and their four boys at their London home. I could do nothing. I went to bed that night with a sense of deep loss. There was no one who could replace him in my life. Though never a practising politician, his journalism had always been focused on political questions, initially as labour correspondent, then covering the House of Commons before becoming a columnist and finally specializing in foreign affairs. When we walked in the countryside together we could switch from discussing our children, to arms control, to theology, to the economy, all the time having a common base of knowledge, even though our interpretation or judgement of events might differ, on rare occasions profoundly. Debbie had to fly to New York that Sunday but returned for the funeral on the following Friday. I was badly jolted and Maggie Smart recalls me breaking down and weeping in my office.

My attention had been focusing on Party Political Broadcasts for some time. We saw them as an important way of countering the BBC bias in reporting politics as if it were a mirror of the balance in the House of Commons. I had written one of my rare letters of actual complaint to Alistair Milne when in January the BBC had given no coverage at all to our announcement of what was in effect an Alliance Shadow Cabinet. The post-Barbican Alliance broadcast had, I felt, been bland and boring, a real let down since it was the first one done by our advertising agency. It was not even good technically with very poor lighting. They had developed the theme of a seesaw to depict the Labour-Conservative alternation and the privatization-nationalization switchback; the classic plague-on-both-your-houses message. The SDP planned a controversial knocking piece against Labour. Unfortunately Labour got wind of what we were intending to say about Islington and we were taken to court in an attempt to stop our broadcast. On 1 April Mr Justice Drake decided that the SDP could go ahead with its Party Political Broadcast. John Cleese's gag had pilloried Islington Council for accusing 'a five-year-old of reciting a racially offensive poem. You've got it – Baa, baa black sheep.' The Council claimed in the High Court that it was not their policy to ban the rhyme, the teacher had only written that it had been identified as 'racially derogative' and was 'discouraged' by the Council. The Judge refused to grant an injunction banning the joke. He said there was evidence the SDP could justify its allegation. Nevertheless because the child's mother specifically asked me not to broadcast that bit because she was unhappy about the effect of publicity on her child, I decided to cut it out, which angered the *Sun*. But the publicity certainly gave our Party Political Broadcast a boost and served to remind people of how way out many Labour controlled councils had become.

Meanwhile, Margaret Thatcher was making a triumphant trip to the Soviet Union from 28 March to 1 April. The television coverage of her meetings in the Kremlin and walkabouts in the street was massive. It was virtually a daily party political broadcast beaming back from Moscow, fantastic for the Conservatives. Here was the woman the Soviets had christened the Iron Lady being wooed by Mikhail Gorbachev. At a stroke the Labour Party's war-mongering propaganda against her blew up in their face. A BBC correspondent asked her if her trip had anything to do with electioneering and she snapped back 'enlarge your view'. In fairness to the BBC and ITN there was little they could do: though patently stage managed, it was news, not least that the Soviets were ready to co-operate in the stage management. It was obvious that Gorbachev was investing in Thatcher. So too was Reagan, as he showed when Neil Kinnock visited the United States. The fact that her Moscow visit was in such marked contrast to his trip to Washington did not escape the electorate. Neil Kinnock and Denis Healey were treated with utter disdain by the President. He started by mistaking Denis Healey for our Ambassador, very bad for Denis's *amour propre*; he is the biggest name-dropper on the international circuit, always referring to what Helmut or François said to him. But perhaps by then, not being known by an American President, particularly Reagan, was a battle honour for the old pugilist. There was also a humiliating argument about how long they had spent in the White House, and it turned out that I had spent longer with Reagan the year before. But the damage was done in the press briefing which made it abundantly clear that Neil Kinnock was regarded as a bad ally. It got very close to being an interference in British domestic politics and as such would have backfired, but Labour's mistake was in going to Washington in the first place.

These two visits completely altered the shape of British politics and influenced the election. The Conservative Party lead was consolidated in the polls. In early April MORI had the Conservatives on 41 per cent, Labour 29 per cent and the Alliance 29 per cent. A Marplan poll a few days later showed the Conservatives on 38 per cent, Labour on 32 per cent and the Alliance on 27 per cent. What was significant was that that poll exactly mirrored the same poll a month before and the Conservatives had had a steady lead at 38 per cent ever since January when we had been at 23 per cent.

We had what we thought was an authentic tip off from within the Conservative Central Office that there was a possibility of a general election being called to coincide with the 7 May council elections. So, after talking to our National Secretary, it was agreed that in order to put our troops on election alert I would publicly predict a 7 May election. Margaret Thatcher, however, resisted whatever pressure there was to go early. It prompted Roy Hattersley to make a rather good joke at my expense in the House of Commons: 'I understand that he has no prediction to make about the second coming since he believes that has already happened.' The problem with the joke was that it backfired since he had preceded it by noting, 'I am sorry to see that the Right Honourable Gentleman, the Leader of the Social Democratic Party, is not in his place.' In fact I had come in just seconds before his joke was launched. This caused much merriment and the 'collapse of stout party'.

During the Easter Recess I had been invited to give a lecture in Costa Rica on social democracy, as had Tony Crosland in 1975. We decided to make a family holiday of it knowing that an election was coming and feeling sun and sea would make a good break for us all. We flew on a package holiday to Miami and then my Costa Rican hosts arranged for us to fly down to San José. The President, Oscar Arias, went out of his way to be the host for our stay. He was a close friend of my old political adviser in the Foreign Office, David Stephen, having been at the University of Essex with him and David made the arrangements and helped me with that part of my lecture which dealt with the Latin American political scene. Costa Rica is a remarkable country, the oldest democracy in Latin America and with no armed forces. We all flew with Oscar Arias and one of his children across to the Pacific Coast for a holiday by the sea in the small light planes which constitute their air force. Unfortunately his wife had to stay behind with the other child who was unwell. It was a breathtakingly beautiful place, hot and dry, and made memorable by my catching a big game fish, two feet taller than myself. It was an incredibly hard struggle to bring it in. Once is enough and I have returned to catching mackerel in the sea outside the River Yealm with no sense of anticlimax. San José is a beautiful capital set in the hills and on our return we drove down to the contrasting Atlantic coast through a wild, tropical forest and, in humid heat, visited a banana plantation. Not surprisingly all five Owens long to return to Costa Rica.

Few doubted that a general election would be called after the May local elections. The Alliance was finalizing the draft of our manifesto, a rather depressing experience because of the difficulty of getting any new thoughts into it. Polly Toynbee, who was helping on the Alliance Planning Group for the election, was very conscious that we needed some new political ideas to liven up the rather bland and lengthy manifesto. It was based on the paperback *The Time Has Come*. We did not lack for policies, what we lacked was bite. I was myself now well and truly anaesthetized by the Alliance. I felt I was in a straitjacket. Of course I could not have the same freedom to campaign as in 1983. Then I had been a guerrilla leader. Now I was a joint allied commander and began to understand all the frustration of being a NATO commander.

Towards the end of April the Alliance switched its attack from Labour to the Conservatives. It was part of a deliberate strategy to bring back the possibility of a balanced Parliament, for if Labour continued to do so badly, we would suffer too by virtue of being thought irrelevant. We had to try and decrease the Tory lead for people to believe we could have an influence. So I said 'The time has come to shift the attack from Labour who clearly cannot win the next election to the Tories who clearly can but equally do not deserve to.' I listed the considerable price of eight years of Conservative rule. That there were disillusioned Conservatives was not in doubt but they had to be prised out and then held to vote for us, being vulnerable to switching back if they thought a vote for us might let Labour in. Fear of Labour was, as in 1983, still a big factor. We had carefully costed our Alliance manifesto and I was able to claim that we were offering a 'menu with prices'. We were becoming the civil servants' choice which worried me; a sign of being too cautious.

The council election results on Friday 8 May brought comfort to the Conservatives, bleak news for Labour, and a welcome advance for the Alliance. When Margaret Thatcher met her key political advisers at Chequers the following Sunday we knew an election would be announced either then or on the following day. On Monday morning a short announcement from No. 10 fixed 11 June as Polling Day.

Immediately after I had heard the news I went to St James's, Piccadilly for David Watt's memorial service. I had been very reluctant to speak, in part because I dislike memorial addresses, but also because I was not sure I could either do his memory justice or keep control of my emotions. Debbie persuaded me and I knew Susan wanted me to do it. Preparing the speech was at least a complete change from election preparations. I decided to let his words speak and chose passages from some of his writings which had an especial appeal. The service was attended by many people from different political parties and journalists with opposing political views. It was rather strange to be all together on the eve of battle, united at least in our admiration and affection for his life and courage. I tried to capture the image of this 'clergy boned' figure who had coped with teenage polio, which had left him with a damaged arm and difficulty in breathing; inconveniences which he resolutely refused to allow to interfere with his lifestyle.

As I returned to face the hustings I felt the Alliance would be lucky to do as well as at the last election and I knew that, in the disappointment of defeat, the merger debate would break with a vengeance for it offered faint hearts the scapegoat which they always need.

34

ELECTION 1987

A general election is like a military campaign except that there is a fixed moment after four weeks when the final exchanges cease. It has a daily rhythm to it, actions are taken, reactions given, temporary advantages exploited and weaknesses buttressed. The leaders of the parties have to take the battle to the constituencies. This means criss-crossing the country to bolster the morale of the troops. Under the Representation of the Peoples Act there is a statutory obligation on television and radio to be fair, and even the press feels obliged to project messages to the voters which their proprietors do not agree with. No party can buy TV advertising though there is no limit on press advertising. Candidates can only spend up to a modest statutory limit in their constituencies. Throughout the campaign almost every word a leader says is recorded and then examined; intonations, malapropisms, slips and mistakes are exploited and exaggerated. For a month a party leader lives like a goldfish in a bowl, with every movement watched, every statement weighed. Then suddenly, once the result is declared, the normal pattern of government and official Opposition in the framework of the House of Commons returns, and the smaller parties are left sidelined and yet again staggered by the distortion built into our first-past-the-post electoral system.

The Alliance was operating under severe constraints. All political parties fight elections under considerable constraints, but they contributed to making us unelectable. The first constraint in 1987 was that the election had been called by the Conservatives at a point in their cynical pre-election economic boom when they were certain of victory. Inflation was down to 4 per cent. Interest rates were at 9 per cent and unemployment was falling. Nigel Lawson had matched the economic cycle to the electoral cycle with consummate skill. The voters do not take kindly to Cassandra-like warnings. We found no resonance at all for arguments that the economic boom was not soundly based and that inflation would return. While the voters felt prosperous and wanted more prosperity, the Conservatives were bound to win. Yet the Alliance never felt able to admit that the Conservatives were going to win and that we were fighting at best for influence in a balanced Parliament. We had to instead pretend that we were going to win.

The second constraint was that we were giving the illusion that our two parties were closer in policies and in attitudes than in fact they were; we never felt free to admit to policy differences and to present our Alliance only as a potential coalition. Instead we pretended we were already in effect a government with shared spokesmen and a single programme which just happened to have two leaders.

The third constraint was that we were not free to say which party, Conservative or Labour, was our preferred coalition partner. We tried to hide the fact that the SDP would have preferred a coalition with the Conservatives, while the Liberals favoured Labour.

The fourth constraint reflected all the other constraints. Our manifesto contrived to cover up all these differences and in order to do so was bland. We could not openly endorse the social market for Liberals felt that positioned us too close to the Conservatives; we could not whole-heartedly support the British nuclear deterrent for the Liberals were still deeply divided on this issue. Nor could we present Labour as totally unfit to govern because that meant closing the option of being able to form a coalition with them. We could not choose because the Liberals did not want to choose. All political parties fight elections under self-induced handicaps. Ours were just about manageable, but they contributed to making us unelectable. They were constraints that could be traced back to the Liberal Assembly at Llandudno in 1981 and the flawed model for the Alliance that had been foisted on the SDP by an unelected and unrepresentative élite that really wanted a single large third party from the outset.

We had carefully planned the Alliance election campaign and managed to keep broadly to its outline throughout. As soon as the election was called David Steel and I issued a letter to the President of the National Council of Women of Great Britain challenging the other party leaders to an election debate. In the United States, ever since 1961 when Vice-President Richard Nixon and Senator John Kennedy debated, there had been two or three debates among the Presidential candidates arranged by their National Organization of Women. In the Federal Republic of Germany the leaders of the CDU, CSU, SPD and the FDP are always questioned together on television during the election period. We suggested that, though the BBC and the IBA would make all the technical arrangements and carry the cost, it would add considerably to the tone and quality of the election campaign if our National Council of Women would sponsor national debates in Britain between the party leaders. We sent copies of our letter to Neil Kinnock and Margaret Thatcher.

It was already obvious that Margaret Thatcher was going to refuse, but what was depressing was how cravenly the British newspapers accepted her refusal; a reflection, I fear, of the strong Conservative bias within our newspaper ownership. It is a disgrace that the voters are not given the chance to see a debate between the Prime Ministerial candidates. Sadly, incumbent Prime Ministers will not agree to a debate on television unless they are either so far behind that they have nothing to lose or they fear a penalty in terms of public displeasure if they are seen to refuse. The media, who have a strong interest in reporting such a debate, ought to be creating a climate in which future Prime Ministers would hesitate before refusing. Margaret Thatcher was too far ahead in the polls for there to be any hope of generating much controversy on this issue. But it was a useful gambit and we were in the business of making waves, though I fear this was just a ripple.

On Tuesday, as we had also planned, Roy Jenkins, Ian Wrigglesworth and Malcolm Bruce revealed the costings of the Alliance's Programme for Government to the press in advance of launching our manifesto. It was an attempt, before the campaign had officially started, to meet the charge that the Alliance was financially irresponsible and the country could not afford our prescription. The press gave it fairly good coverage and at least we had the appearance of having our act together.

The Campaign team was led by the 'two Johns' – John Pardoe, of whom I had great hopes, was chairman, with John Harris as his deputy. They were the two most experienced political figures in both parties who were not themselves involved in fighting a seat. John Pardoe, once Liberal Economics Spokesman, did not want to be an MP again. John Harris, initially a Labour peer and now an SDP one, had been Labour Party Press Officer under Hugh Gaitskell and Harold Wilson. He had years of experience and had worked very closely with Roy Jenkins. I hoped my readiness to involve him would be treated as an olive branch by Roy and would keep him committed to the campaign. Roy was too valuable to have sniping from the sidelines. We had asked him to be Alliance Economic Spokesman, even though I knew that this meant paying a slight penalty in terms of our social market identity. Roy would, I know, tend to play down market economics. He was, however, still a political heavyweight and added considerably to any claims that we would be credible in government. I felt John Harris's presence would ensure that Roy felt his interests would be protected during the campaign.

The Alliance Planning Group (APG) had been formed to plan the leaders' campaigns, the Party Election Broadcasts and the daily press conferences. We had started working together in the autumn of 1986 in the hope that we would get to know each other's minds well before the election. The problem was to keep it small and get decisions delegated. Everyone always wanted to be on every committee. Political parties love committees and insist on democratic decisions on all occasions.

It was always agreed that when David and I were campaigning, John

Pardoe would take the key decisions without reference to us, but if John
Harris disagreed, he would have the right of appeal to us. Paul Tyler,
David Steel's main assistant for the campaign, and Roland Freeman, who
advised me, had both been involved in public relations. Des Wilson had
forced his way onto the APG against David Steel's wishes. He
volunteered to produce an overnight press cutting service and analysis of
the TV coverage and forthcoming issues each morning and did this well.
He was always bubbling with ideas, some 'off the wall', others on the
button. Polly Toynbee was given the task of supervising our daily press
conferences and she did extremely well in difficult circumstances, trying
to get the Liberals to accept new policy initiatives. The two party
secretaries who were mainly responsible for each party's constituency
campaigns had been included in the run up to the actual campaign – but
we consciously wanted them to take responsibility for the party machines
and not focus on the London-based media campaign and the two leaders'
tours. In the SDP we had targeted our resources over a period of two
years, concentrating on a list of the twenty seats we considered most
winnable. We had also been running a direct mail programme in these
constituencies. In our politics the margin is everything. Had we not
concentrated our resources in these seats I do not believe that we would
have done so well and there was some polling evidence to confirm this. It
was a talented team and I doubt whether we could have assembled
anything better from our two parties. John Pardoe kept everyone's
morale up and worked long hours. John Harris had other commitments
and was less engaged, acting like a man who realized from the start that
the pattern for the election had been set. This was the key difficulty with
the entire campaign. Despite various false alarms, the polls never shifted
and the Alliance was firmly in third place with Labour in second from
the beginning to the end of the campaign. I organized private telephone
polls which, though not good for predicting results, are very sensitive to
any shift of opinion. At no time did they even show a blip to vary the
pattern. There was no justification whatever for the panic which seized
Margaret Thatcher on 'wobbly Thursday'; victory was never remotely
slipping away. Elections are won by what happens in the nine months
before – if the campaign has any real impact, it is for losing ground
rather than winning.

We had five Party Election Broadcasts, which was parity with the other
parties – in 1983 it had been 5–5–4. Our first PEB was widely judged to
be bad, but I have not to this day seen it. Instead of continuing the
seesaw theme developed for the post-Barbican rally broadcasts, John
Pardoe and John Harris decided to devote the whole programme to film
of Rosie Barnes. The film had originally been taken to provide only a few
shots to incorporate with others, but both 'Johns' felt Rosie had come
across so appealingly and with such freshness with her daughter and the
family rabbit that it should be devoted to her and her alone. It was one of

the few times in the campaign when John Harris actually enthused. We all teased them, saying they were middle-aged men who had lost their hearts to Rosie. It was unfortunate that their gamble did not come off. Instead of a boost from our first PEB, we had the activists complaining. This meant there was far too much recrimination, particularly when this was followed by another disappointing PEB by David Abbott and Justin Cartwright. David and I then insisted on being allocated one each and keeping them under our personal control, leaving the two Johns and David Abbott to concentrate on the last PEB appeal. At least in this way we could put ourselves across in a way we each felt comfortable with. David did his direct to camera which he is good at and I did it in the format of an interview but cutting out the questions.

On Wednesday 13 May David and I launched *The Great Reform Charter*, a revamped version of a document which spelt out the constitutional reforms we had always planned to highlight. Over the next two days, in a series of lightning visits, we travelled to all parts of the United Kingdom in an HS-125 jet loaned to David by Anthony Jacobs.

In retrospect what we lacked was a packed public meeting to show that we had mass support. On television that Friday night both Margaret Thatcher in Perth and Neil Kinnock in Northampton were seen holding large rallies while we were filmed talking either to the press or to a few people in the streets. The visual impression was that the Alliance was not part of the big league and it served to emphasize our position as third in the opinion polls. We also found that by Saturday's newspapers, the constitutional theme with which we had launched the campaign no longer played as well. It was, in effect, its third outing and we had to find other sub-themes for the next few days just to keep press interest. I had given constitutional reform a very high priority in Party Political Broadcasts, books, articles and speeches throughout my period as leader, but I found repeatedly that neither the press nor television were very interested. You could see and feel them stifling a yawn as soon as proportional representation was mentioned. Since then the cry from the activists has been that we should have emphasized these constitutional policies more. But that is hard to do unless it is judged to be a key issue of the campaign. The Alliance did not have the political clout to force issues on to the agenda so we had to be reactive. Probably only if the parties are so close that a balanced or hung Parliament looks likely will the media decide to give constitutional policies a central role in the way they report an election campaign. Electoral reform is a very difficult issue on which to whistle a catchy tune. It nevertheless continues to have the support of around 50 per cent of the voting public.

We continued to campaign together on Saturday, flying to Bristol for a press conference in the morning and then to Exeter. On the plane, David Steel was distressed by nasty newspaper accusations about his private life and was unsure whether to sue. He flew to Edinburgh to go to his constituency and I drove to Plymouth that evening for a press conference and joint adoption meeting with David Astor. David Astor was fighting the neighbouring Drake constituency and, unlike 1983, the SDP were this time fighting both Devonport and Drake to win, so there was no question of diverting resources from Drake to help me in Devonport. I spent Sunday morning finalizing texts of constituency leaflets with Jon Aarons, my young full-time agent who had been operating in Plymouth for over a year and had built up an effective organization which we had already tried out in the May Council elections. Although we had won eight council seats in May, as in 1983, the Labour Party had scored significantly more votes in Devonport than the SDP and they were claiming victory. Since they had got a bloody nose in 1983 when they claimed they were poised to win Devonport, not many believed them. This time there were no local polls to back their pre-election boasts.

On Sunday afternoon I flew back to London with my daughter Lucy in a small plane loaned by John Boyle, much to her excitement. We left Debbie to mastermind the Devonport campaign from then on, which she did with verve and skill. When I returned, the first meeting I had was with Oscar Arias, the Costa Rican President, who was on an official visit. Oscar consoled me with the fact that he had come from being behind in the polls all through his Presidential campaign to win. However, already the polling pattern for the campaign seemed set in concrete. The Conservative lead looked unassailable and Labour were clearly second. At the Alliance Campaign Committee we once again tried to establish whether, in the light of the polls, we were going to go on saying we were hell-bent on victory or whether we should, as I wanted, talk about holding the balance. We settled, with me dissenting, for victory talk. As to who was the main enemy, John Pardoe thought it should be Labour. David wanted it, as usual, to be the Conservatives and Labour equally, with the Conservatives the greater enemy. I knew the most I could hope for was to lean hard against Labour while criticizing the Conservatives. The whole problem of the Liberal Party stems from their resolute refusal to choose, in part because they are so accustomed to being the third party and therefore always feel they have to split the difference.

It was a difficult meeting. David Steel was preoccupied with the smear story which had first appeared in the *Sun* and the *Daily Star* on Saturday and was based on a rumour which, it was now alleged, had been started at the Tory Party Conference in Perth. Because it involved two of his close friends, David and Judy felt they should issue writs for defamation and it was this story which filled Monday's newspapers. It put a great deal of strain on David and was a thoroughly unpleasant way of starting the campaign. It is always a very difficult decision whether or not to sue. My own firm view is that a politician should never sue, almost regardless of the circumstances. I had felt this ever since seeing Peter Cook doing a wicked television skit after Harold Wilson's decision to sue. Peter Cook looked straight into camera and said deadpan, 'I suppose you could say that the biggest sue-er was Harold Wilson.' David's litigation did stop the story dead in its tracks, but damage had been done – how much we will never know. Certainly we did not get the lift in the polls that we had hoped for, and indeed felt we deserved, after hitting the deck running during that first week. In terms of activity and imagination we had far outpaced both the other parties. Yet the Sunday polling was not encouraging. The Harris poll conducted between 13–15 May had the Conservatives on 42 per cent, Labour 33 per cent and the Alliance 23 per cent; predicting a House of Commons with 359 Conservative MPs, 251 Labour MPs and 19 SDP/Liberal Alliance MPs. The only worry for the Tories was some evidence that their lead had been cut by Labour in their marginals, but this was balanced by the finding that we were failing to make up ground in those seats where we had been second last time.

On the Monday morning at our press conference in the basement of the National Liberal Club we launched our manifesto under the slogan 'Britain United'. It was well produced and aimed, as I explained in Cardiff that night, to 'reform, revive and rebuild a Britain efficient, caring, successful and united.' Good worthy stuff, but it was not dynamic or hard hitting enough, the product of a committee. We had a photocall with our matching yellow campaign buses before leaving on the campaign trail. It all looked good, but that did not stop some of the press commenting that we were heading off in two different directions!

The press reporting for our manifesto was extensive. 'THE OTHER VOICE OF RADICALISM' was the *Guardian* headline with 'RIGHT DOWN THE MIDDLE' in the *Financial Times* and 'LEAVING SOCIALISM?' in *The Times*. But some of our own confusions had been spotted. The *Guardian* concluded that

> the logic of the Alliance proposals is that they could more easily work with Labour than with the Conservatives. In German elections the Free Democrats always make a clear choice of this kind before the campaign rather than afterwards. The Alliance, too, should come off the fence.

The *Daily Telegraph* said 'The Alliance and its programme will win votes from those who crave a return to the politics of lowest common denominator of national consent'. The *Financial Times* thought that the bad proposal was 'the call for statutory reserve powers to impose a counter-inflation tax on companies which are judged [by whom?] to be paying too high wages'; seeing this, quite rightly, as a reversion to the past, an incomes policy by another name. They also criticized us for proposing Royal Commissions and changing the names and functions of Government Departments; 'taken together, the proposals sound positively Wilsonian.' But overall they gave praise, 'it is serious, comprehensive and it is costed. On this basis the Alliance would almost certainly be the second choice of the majority of both Labour and Conservative voters.' In the *Daily Mail* it was headlined 'OH WOULDN'T IT BE LUVVERLY!' and went on, 'In their sales catalogue there is something for everybody. The appeal is that of the plastic key to a bounteous togetherness where the waiting is taken out of wanting ... too soft an option to be entrusted with the burden of government.'

The quality of our campaign was already far slicker and more professional than anything we had attempted in 1983. It needed to be, because the Labour campaign was transformed from Michael Foot's leadership days into one of the most polished campaigns ever waged by any party in Britain. Labour's problem was that their product could not be sold whatever the packaging. It was obvious that Labour were going to try and paint the Alliance, and me in particular, as Tories because we were ready to do a deal with Margaret Thatcher. For example, their attack on our manifesto focused on our readiness to privatize British Steel, a policy which immediately caused some Liberal candidates in Scotland to disavow our manifesto commitments. At the same time Norman Tebbit, in order to frighten off any weakly attached Conservatives from voting Alliance, bluntly ruled out negotiations after an election with any party and specifically with us. The Tory tactic was to present the Alliance as being as bad as Labour and, since they did not think this label would stick on me, to avoid criticizing me unless I opened myself up for attack.

The SDP hired an HS-748 thirty-four-seater prop-plane for my campaign and Maggie Smart, who was masterminding it, sold most of the seats to journalists for £4,000 for the duration of the campaign. This meant that we offset a large part of our costs and could traverse the country in relative comfort. We visited Birmingham first and went to Handsworth where the riots in 1985 had left two dead and damage amounting to £16 million. I saw some of the same people I had seen two years before and we hoped this would stimulate TV news and the press to show flashback films or photographs reminding people of the divisiveness and urban unrest. We then flew to Cardiff and arrived back in London late. Our strategy was to cover at least two regional television areas a day and this could not be done by bus alone. We also wanted to keep a press corps constantly with me and not run the risk of being separated by travelling in different vehicles. Despite what looked a formidable timetable, we had allowed enough time for reflection and for liaison with headquarters. We tried to get back to London before midnight each night giving the journalists time to file reflective rather than simply reactive stories and then get a decent night's sleep.

It was something of a disadvantage that the Alliance had to start its press conferences at 8.30 a.m. before the other parties. This meant that quite a number of senior journalists did not come to us on a regular basis. However, following the other two parties would have been even worse.

Before the morning press conference, I conferred at my hotel with Roger Carroll, who travelled on the plane, Tom McNally, Alex de Mont, Danny Finkelstein and Maggie Smart. The press conference theme had usually been chosen the night before. Then the two leaders would go to a campaign meeting which had already focused on the key issues.

In general it was an effective campaign but, on occasions I did have some bad television pictures. Visiting a mosque, I had put a handkerchief over my head as a mark of respect. That was fine in the context of the mosque but on TV it just looked ludicrous. Also, touring a dairy in Dyfed and having to wear a hat as part of the health regulations looked odd. John F. Kennedy always refused to wear any form of headgear, and he was right.

After the press conference it was into the bus and off round the country on the day after our manifesto was released. I toured Kent constituencies, with Peter Luff always ready by my side to fend off the press, keep me to the schedule, remind me to smile and generally look after me. I then flew to Norwich where I succeeded in terrifying myself with the acceleration of a Lotus car on their test track, the compensation being that it gave attractive TV footage. Then on to the first joint leaders 'Ask the Alliance' rally with Shirley Williams in the Corn Exchange at Cambridge. That pattern followed day after day. The format of these rallies allowed only short speeches and then a lengthy Question and Answer session. They were interesting and enjoyable for those attending and, unlike the other parties, anyone could come for they were not 'ticket only'. But they did not make for dramatic television. The atmosphere was not that of the hustings. It was rare to have any heckling and, looking back, they were a mistake. I found I was far more telegenic speaking off-the-cuff to a more conventional political meeting and provoking heckling. That made my adrenalin surge and added a sparkle and excitement which, if captured on camera, sometimes made an electric television bite. Most of my TV bites in the campaign were too earnest and as a consequence we were not able to push ourselves up the order in the news bulletins. For the Alliance to be high in the order we had to be seen saying something original, amusing or hard-hitting.

In Cambridge Shirley Williams was facing a difficult fight. Her Conservative opponent, Robert Rhodes-James, was a liberal Tory MP and well respected. I know from conversations with him that he feared an SDP candidate, particularly Shirley. He was amazed when he found Shirley becoming more and more identified with the Liberals and less and less identified with the SDP, for he felt this posed far less of a problem for him. However, she was fighting a former Liberal seat and had been chosen by joint selection and was by then more comfortable conducting a totally Alliance campaign. It was pretty obvious that she had chosen to distance herself from me and to go for a softer image, and though I offered to come back later in the campaign if she wanted me to, she was never very keen. Once as main speaker at one of the press conferences, she was demonstrating the weapons that were freely available in the shops, and, finding herself unable to release the blade of a flick knife, passed it to me saying, 'David, you take it – you'll know how to do it.' The journalists roared with laughter, picking up on her anxiety that I was the bovver-booted Norman Tebbit of the Alliance. In fact poll after poll showed that my image was surprisingly soft. Sadly Shirley was never able in Cambridge to recapture the enthusiasm she engendered in Crosby, where, in the 1983 Election, she had managed to keep some special electoral fizz and élan, even though ill-served by the boundary changes. Cambridge is not like Oxford – it is suspicious of the trendy and, perhaps because of its scientific background, likes its politics tautly argued and hard-headed.

On that Tuesday both the Conservative and Labour manifestos were published. The issue which seemed to me to offer the juiciest target was the Conservatives lumping the Alliance in with Labour, saying we favoured one-sided disarmament. They actually had the nerve to refer to us as taking the country 'down the same disastrous road as the Labour Party towards a frightened and fellow-travelling Britain.' 'Fellow-traveller' was a term that had gone rather out of fashion since Hugh Gaitskell had used it against people in the Labour Party who were far too close to the Communists, but its meaning was still clear enough. I denounced the Conservative manifesto for containing a 'foul smear' and wrote to Margaret Thatcher demanding a retraction, saying it brought dishonour on her office to campaign on such a deeply offensive charge. Raising defence at this point was not without calculation. It would be better for us to get our defence policy out of the way early for it was never going to be our best issue. From our own private information and contacts we knew the Tories intended to concentrate on Labour's defence policy towards the end. If we could establish an independent Alliance position early and dissuade the Conservatives from linking us with Labour, they might hesitate before pursuing this line later in the election. I hoped any fair minded journalist would also see the Tory line as a smear, especially as the Tories proceeded to play the patriotic card again that night with a flag-waving PEB which virtually claimed that the country was only safe under Margaret Thatcher.

At our pre-press conference meeting on Wednesday none of the Liberals raised any objection to going for the Tories on defence and we agreed to devote Thursday's press conference to our own defence policy, asking John Cartwright and Alan Beith, as the respective defence and foreign affairs spokesmen, to put together a joint statement. At the press conference I said, 'It sticks in my gullet that there is this extraordinary belief that the union jack belongs to the Tory Party.' In London later that night I read our defence statement for the next day's press conference and it was excellent. The main talking point when we arrived at the

Royal Horse Guards Hotel, where I was sleeping the night, was not about defence at all. It was about the Labour Party PEB called simply 'Kinnock'. It was ten minutes of utter though very effective schmaltz made by the film director, Hugh Hudson, who had been involved with David Puttnam on *Chariots of Fire*. It sent a warning note to us and shivers up the spine of Conservatives. We were now dealing with Labour Party packaging which owed a lot to Andrex.

But then, at the Thursday morning meeting before the conference, there was a Liberal outcry over the defence statement, with both Des Wilson and the Liberal National Secretary in full cry. This was despite the fact that it had been agreed with Alan Beith. What they objected to was its detailed discussion of the possible options for replacing Polaris. As the argument went on and time was running out, I asked David Steel one simple question – could he live with it or not? He confessed worry, so we had no alternative. We could not issue it. Strangely those Liberals who were most anxious seemed quite happy for John Cartwright to speak the same words that were in the written statement. It was a sign of how divided we still really were on defence that they wanted nothing incriminating on paper, but nevertheless realized what was needed to satisfy the press. The press did not spot anything amiss and our attack on Margaret Thatcher was winning some plaudits. *The Independent* in an editorial, 'Nailing Mrs Thatcher's lie', said 'for the Conservatives to attack an Alliance dominated by Dr David Owen as unilateralist is both inept and dishonest,' and went on to make the telling point that the Conservative Party ought not 'to declare itself in favour of One Nation and then try to suggest that nobody but Conservatives can belong to that nation.' The press conference went well, John Cartwright being quite specific about possible nuclear replacements instead of Trident. I felt that now with a little luck we would not need to return to defence apart from swiping at the Labour Party. But the issue did not go away. That evening I did an interview for *This Week* in Liverpool and the Press Association report claimed that I had said that we would take advice from senior military figures about keeping a ballistic system, such as Trident. This was inaccurate. I had never used the words, 'such as Trident', but that did not stop the BBC *Nine o'Clock News* repeating the words and suggesting that my readiness to keep Trident would divide our two parties. David flew back in my plane to London and when we were driving back into town in separate cars we were told by the Campaign Committee on our car radios that one of us should go on *Newsnight* to clear the matter up. We wound down our car windows at the next lights and agreed that it would be better for David Steel to do it. It was a mischievous story which came back at our press conference on Friday. Fortunately I was able to show that I had not used the words on Trident and that we had actually referred to listening to advice on systems from the Chiefs of Staff in our defence statement published in November and again in January.

In the papers on the Friday morning there was an article by Matthew Symonds in *The Independent* following up their criticism of our manifesto as 'moderate *dirigisme*', under the headline 'Disappointing packaging buries the Alliance's ideals'. He said he could not find a single reference to the social market in the entire document and that 'until the Alliance realizes that you do not emphasize the "social" in the social market by diluting the role of the market, it will continue to lack the cutting edge which it requires.' Much has since been made of the fact that I did not fight to have the words 'social market' used in the document. It would have been pointless to try. We had decided to bring Roy Jenkins back as economics spokesman and to him the social market was a sub-Thatcherite term. Also, the Liberals saw the social market as Owenism. It was far wiser for Ian Wrigglesworth on the drafting committee to concentrate on establishing market principles and competition rather than forcing the term 'social market', which had become an anathema to Liberals, aided and abetted by snide comment from the other members of the Gang of Four whose economic thinking meant they were reluctant to accept any new market language. But *The Independent* was important to us in shaping the attitudes of what I called 'the thinking voter', and by being too bland we lost the chance to appeal to those who wanted a counter-revolution.

The Sunday press contained little comfort for us. Three polls showed the Conservatives in the early forties, Labour in the early thirties and us in the early twenties. In the first week of the campaign we had lost 2.5 per cent, the Tories 1.5 per cent while Labour had gained 3.5 per cent. Our telephone polls too were showing a remarkably static situation. Brian Walden in the *Sunday Times* called our campaign strategy 'staggeringly inept' because we were not attacking the Labour Party. It was this issue we discussed that evening, but all too briefly. Unfortunately we had television cameras outside the door and John Pardoe was given the thankless task of summing up a strategy which, as usual, was deadlocked on the issue of whether to attack Labour. He said our strategy was to present our own policies and attack no one, but in earlier interviews, unbeknown to him, I had implied we should attack Labour, and David that we should attack the Tories. Undoubtedly we looked a mess on the ITN bulletin on Sunday night.

Fortunately Neil Kinnock came to the rescue. In a rambling reply to David Frost on TV-am that morning, he had dropped two clangers: 'The alternatives are between the gesture, the threat or the use of nuclear weapons – and surrender,' explaining that his choice would be to 'make any occupation totally untenable'. John Cartwright ridiculed Labour's defence policy as 'the Mujahideen in Penge High Street seem to be expected to deter Soviet nuclear blackmail.' The issue stalled Labour just when they might have hoped to break the Tory lead. With the polls stuck, we had to erode the Labour vote. Picking up a crack which Des Wilson had given me at our press conference, 'Now we are told by Mr

Kinnock we must be ready to fight a Soviet occupation of Britain. Thanks a lot! ... He wants Dad's Army back and Captain Mainwaring returned to the colours.' Then referring to Neil Kinnock's belief in guerrilla warfare, I asked, 'Does his confidence stem from his own extensive experience of fifth columnists in the Labour Party?' It was rough stuff, but when I returned to London that night I was told that the newspapers were leading on the Dad's Army quote next day. David Frost is a deceptive interviewer who lulls one into indiscretions. We have become close friends with him and his wife, Carina, the more my political star has faded. Usually it is the other way around and it has amused us to watch those who only wanted to know us when my star was bright.

At Tuesday morning's press conference, a question on fifth columnists allowed me to open up the whole question of Militant within the Labour Party. But it was Nancy Seear's joke about Kinnock which had everyone laughing, saying that being a nice guy was not enough to be Prime Minister, 'it's not even enough to be a cook.' I then flew to Exeter and took the campaign bus through Exeter with Mike Thomas, our candidate, continuing to Plymouth where I put in my nomination papers. It is hard at times for a leader to remember that there is also a constituency battle going on with local press releases to write. Without a portable phone I would have been in great difficulty. The Plymouth campaign was easier than in 1983 and the coverage I was getting on national TV also helped far more. My main concern was not to give the impression I was taking their votes for granted.

Then at 8 o'clock came an important event. David Steel and I had a live interview with Sir Robin Day on *Panorama* with an estimated audience of 4.7 million. At first it went well, then near the end an exchange took place about which much has since been written. Robin Day questioned us both clearly about a hung Parliament and moved on to a different question:

DAY: Do you think that a Tory government would be a greater evil than a majority Labour government. A majority Tory government or a majority Labour government. Which is the greater evil in your view?

OWEN: In the last analysis, the one issue on which I will always judge anyone – and that is somebody who would put at jeopardy the defences and security of this country – unless the Labour Party changes its defence and security policy, in my judgement they are not fit to govern this country.

DAY: You are saying that a majority Labour government would, therefore, be a greater evil than a majority Tory government?

OWEN: In the final analysis, I don't want either. And I'm not prepared to support either. And I don't believe it's in many ways a fair question. But the one fundamental must remain the security of our country and the security of Western Europe. And on that big test, the Labour Party massively fails.

DAY: I'd put the same question to you, Mr Steel with apologies if you think it's unfair. But by submission, I think it's extremely fair.

STEEL: It's a question that you have put to me many times over the years and I can recall giving you exactly the same answer.

DAY: No, not this question. Not a majority government.

STEEL: Well, yes but you invited me as a Liberal over the years to make a preferential choice between the Conservative and Labour Party. Quite frankly, if I had such a preferential choice I might as well have joined them all those years ago. I don't believe either is capable of providing a government which can unite this country again. And that's a slightly different issue. I believe that the kind of programme which the Liberal Party and the SDP are putting forward together in this campaign has got a sporting chance of pulling together the diverse threads of this country in a way in which neither of the class-based parties can hope to do. And I am not going to be driven to making a choice between the two of them.

DAY: I'm not asking you to make a choice.

STEEL: You are.

DAY: I'm really saying which do you think would be the greater evil?

STEEL: Well, I don't believe either of them is going to be a successful government. I don't see why I've got to start getting out the measuring rod and saying 'Well, one would be slightly better on this one, slightly better on that one.'

There, in that exchange, was the whole dilemma of the way in which the Alliance had been structured since 1981. My answer expressed the reason why we were two parties and why we had two leaders. It even answered why the SDP had to be created if the old Liberal appeal in the Centre was to be widened out. No one listening could have failed to notice that we had a very different attitude to the Labour Party's defence policy: for me it was the disqualifying factor for being the government, for David it was one very good issue to measure Labour by, no more and no less. After the programme I took Polly Toynbee, Maggie Smart and Sue Robertson to Manzi's fish restaurant off Leicester Square, one of my favourite places to relax. Polly, her journalist's antennae ever alert, thought what I had said would be damaging and picked up in the press as a split. I was not so sure about the damage. I was more concerned about the millions watching than any press comment. I sensed that Robin Day was not going to let me escape with a David Steel-like refusal to make a preferential choice and he has since confirmed to me that he intended to go on until he got a real answer. I knew I would eventually give him such an answer. The viewer knew and was meant to know that defence was my sticking point. It was neither a gaffe nor an indiscretion. My fear was that we would not gain the votes of disillusioned Conservatives if they felt that we in the Alliance did not have a sticking point on defence. And it was not just Conservatives either. The Liberals never understood how many working-class voters were antagonized by Labour's defence policy. They were hardly likely to turn to us if they did not perceive us as totally unequivocal. Watching *Panorama* were millions more people than would ever read what the press said next day. What was important was that they realized that voting Alliance was not letting Labour and unilateralism in by the back door.

In many ways the rest of the campaign hinged on this question of attitudes to the Conservatives and Labour. Since David Steel could not convincingly give the impression that he could work with a Thatcher-led government, he did not want to talk about a coalition. The journalists following us around, travelling in my bus and comparing notes on their portable phones with colleagues in David's bus were bound to exploit this. The truth is that David was fairly reflecting the views of his party and I of mine. Those who wanted us to say the same thing were not recognizing that this was why we were two parties. It is like wanting the best of someone's personality while losing the worst parts. People are all of a piece and have to be taken with their strengths and their weaknesses. So are parties. When the Alliance tried to pretend we were one party it was a fraud. When we were relaxed about being two parties we were honestly divided on some issues, which is exactly what a coalition government reflects. Selling the Alliance for what it was would have been a far better strategy.

The next few days of campaigning followed much the same pattern as before. Roy Jenkins, John Harvey-Jones and David Sainsbury gave a press conference on economic and industrial policy, but it failed to excite. The anxiety at our pre-press conference meetings was our slippage in the polls, with Gallup showing us falling five points to 18 per cent. This proved to be a slightly rogue poll for Marplan then showed us steady at 21 per cent. Then we had a quite disastrous press conference in which Simon Hughes, talking about long hospital waiting lists, was meant to point to a computer print-out eight feet tall to illustrate the point. Unfortunately he claimed that these lists represented real people and, before he could be stopped, the journalists had pounced. He was forced to admit that they were not real names and there were cries of 'phoney' and 'bogus'. It took attention away from one of our best policies, whereby we would give patients the right to have an operation or treatment outside their area if they were faced by a long waiting list.

David Steel then did an effective PEB and we went into the weekend with the Alliance a little more focused. I had defined six issues on which to concentrate – reducing unemployment, spending more on education, reducing hospital waiting lists, sustaining trade union reform, maintaining a nuclear deterrent and strengthening the police.

Relations between everyone involved in the campaign were pretty good and at least no one was contemplating another Ettrick Bridge summit. Denis Healey was saying, 'Dr Owen continues to treat Mr Steel as Mrs Thatcher treats Sir Geoffrey Howe – as a portable punchbag. Instead of shooting himself in the foot he shoots poor Mr Steel.' This was far from the truth, indeed Simon Jenkins in the *Sunday Times* urged me to strike out on my own arguing that our campaign lacked leadership, passion, personality and guts. 'It suffers from Wordsworth's complaint: no single volume paramount, no code, no master spirit, no determined road.' I had already had to be quite sharp with one of my staff who had suggested to the newspapers that a speech I had given on the social market was a sign of my frustration with the campaign. I knew that the last thing we needed was internal backbiting.

Defence was now becoming the major issue. The Saatchi poster, 'Labour's policy on arms' showing a British soldier with arms raised in surrender, was by far the most effective knocking copy of the whole election. It went right to the heart of Labour's traditional working class vote, its C1 and C2 supporters. As I had predicted, defence had, as in 1983, become a major issue again. Yet the Alliance could not or would not exploit the issue. All the benefit was going to the Conservatives. Though correspondents were praising the Labour Party campaign with its red roses and soft packaging as extremely effective, this was not reflected in the polls. The MORI poll in the marginals showed no change in the Conservatives vote since 1983, and no change in our vote in Conservative-Labour marginals, but worryingly down some 8 per cent in Conservative-Alliance marginals.

We did have some more helpful polls at this stage in the campaign. *Today* agreed to publish polls on key SDP marginal seats. This showed us 4 per cent ahead of Chris Patten in Bath; in Birmingham, Hall Green we were running second, having leap-frogged ahead of Labour; in Cambridge Shirley was second behind Robert Rhodes-James and up on the 1983 result. And Ian Wrigglesworth in Stockton South had a 2 per cent lead over the Tories. This was all better news. I was visiting Ian's constituency that day and I hoped to be able to ram home that poll finding since Ian had only won by 103 votes last time.

We were still hoping for a last-minute surge as in 1983 but it was hard to find any evidence for it. In order to help the process along I tabled a draft press release at our Monday morning pre-press conference meeting which was effectively an all-out call for a coalition. It would give us credibility and would answer what was once more a central question – how do you stop a Tory landslide without getting a unilateralist, anti-EEC government? Yet, once again, most of those present were against this. They were expressing prejudices not producing rational arguments. Calling for coalition meant that the next question was with whom to coalesce, a question David Steel feared because he was not prepared to answer 'Margaret Thatcher'. No one was able to argue against the simple fact that our poll rating now meant that we did not have a chance of winning outright. I conceded gracefully, withdrawing my draft press release, but it was a marker and everyone knew that I would come back to it in a few days' time.

Peter Shore had meanwhile made public his doubts about his own party's defence policies. Naturally the press made much of it. Speaking as an elected member of the Shadow Cabinet, someone who under Labour's new rules would be an automatic member of a future Cabinet, Peter had said, 'No answer', when asked if he would serve in a Labour Cabinet, admitting 'it would raise all sorts of questions and difficulties.'

On the Tuesday morning *The Times* in an editorial, 'Bored or just calm?' analysed the mood of the electorate and detected a certain detachment. This followed a report that viewers were hiring video films to escape the saturation television coverage of the election. My own strong sense was that the electorate had made up their mind and were going to give Margaret Thatcher another turn. They were not bored, but as *The Times* argued,

> settled in its own mind, for more or less, the social market system which Mrs Thatcher's first two terms have launched, worried though they are about some of the social by-products in the period of transition. That is something, of course, which Dr Owen recognizes even if Mr Steel does not. The detachment of the electorate may well arise from a disinclination to waste too much more time on arguments it already understands.

Perhaps it was this growing conviction which led me – while in Kings Lynn helping Christopher Brocklebank-Fowler – to say that voting for us was a unique 'perhaps never to occur again opportunity', a statement translated by the Press Association into 'Alliance may not get another chance – Owen'. Perhaps it was a Freudian slip. I knew the Alliance would not hold after the election since it was already apparent that a merger coup was being planned. Towards the end of the campaign, our own campaign committee actually discussed a merger, much to the annoyance of Polly Toynbee. We had also been picking up more and more stories that the two parties' National Secretaries were ringing people up in the regions to advocate merger. Eric Woolfson, the composer of the Alan Parsons Project music with many golden discs to his name, had helped the party financially and in every other way from the outset. He was close to Shirley Williams, but was getting more and more incensed by the clandestine activity which he felt was a diversion from the campaign. He and his wife, Hazel, and two girls have since become family friends. The final confirmation of the seriousness of their intentions came when our National Secretary, Dick Newby, telephoned David Sainsbury in the final days of the campaign to find out if he would support a merged party and was sent away with a flea in his ear. So I knew that this was probably our last chance as an SDP/Liberal Alliance. It shows the penalties of speaking off-the-cuff for it does tend to reveal one's inner thoughts, and journalists have a sense for hidden meanings.

But the flipside of speaking in this way was that the same evening, using the same technique, I had probably the best meeting of the whole campaign, held in Finsbury Town Hall, and shown on TV. I had run into plenty of heckling as I let fly at the Left by saying that the Tories were only too happy to have Labour's Left around, 'They like them to be mad-hat, lethal or lunatic.'

As I was talking, David Steel was having dinner with Des Wilson in a Dolphin Square restaurant and confiding that he was now only concerned about winning in their hopeful target seats, which meant capturing tactical votes from Labour. Des Wilson claims that David Steel had said 'What it needs is for David Owen to say there is an anti-Thatcher majority out there, and that he is part of it.' If David Steel was right that Labour tactical votes were what was needed then this was indeed a reasonable strategy. But what he did not understand is that the real votes up for grabs, in the target seats as anywhere else, were the voters who would not vote Labour over defence, but would not vote Tory for fear of a landslide.

The idea of an 'anti-Thatcher' majority was an absurd one. People might not have liked her much but they *were* prepared to vote for her. We needed to stop people who were not prepared to vote Labour going over to her, for that is what was happening. We should not have been trying to twiddle around with a few tactical votes because there is absolutely no evidence that at constituency level people vote tactically in any numbers at general elections. The only tactical voting that really counted would be national and if people identified us with Labour we would squeeze ourselves, not them. So his strategy really would help only a few Liberal MPs and only a very little. We needed national tactical voting, with disillusioned Conservatives tactically voting for us against a landslide, confident that we in the Alliance were not going to climb into bed with Labour. That was why *Today*'s posters of me and David in bed with Margaret Thatcher were not damaging, even though they may have embarrassed David and some of our activists.

Next morning on BBC *Election Call* David Steel started to make his tactical campaign public. He was asked whether he would support Mrs Thatcher in a hung Parliament and said,

> I find it unimaginable that there would be any circumstance in which a minority government led by Mrs Thatcher could be sustained in office by us. Her whole style and the nature of her policies is one which would not lead to the kind of compromise, the kind of search for consensus, the wider agreements, the healing of wounds that is required in this country. She would be disqualified for a whole range of reasons from leading such a government.

Although David had made some very fair criticisms, the headline writers were set for a field day at our expense. Fortunately David agreed to issue a clarifying statement later that day saying,

> We are ready to negotiate with either the Labour or the Conservative
> Party and we will talk first to whichever has the largest number of MPs.
> We are not in the business of propping up Mr Kinnock or Mrs
> Thatcher and if they are not ready to listen to reason, if they are not
> ready to take account of the judgement of the voters, then let their
> parties find other leaders who are ready.

But no sooner was this statement issued to the press than David Steel
was saying that for Mrs Thatcher to stay on in such circumstances was
'wonderland', and was quoted in another newspaper as saying he would
refuse to serve under her. Not much was made about the differences in
the Thursday newspapers, above all perhaps because most people were
firmly convinced that Mrs Thatcher was going to remain Prime Minister
after the election. The biggest press we had were photographs of me
visiting Lucy at her primary school. She even had a drawing of the
family on display, but only *The Independent* diarist was unkind enough to
mention that there was a 'literacy crisis' with some of her spelling.

My Party Election Broadcast took the line that no one would win if
either the Conservatives or the Labour Party achieved an outright win. If
the Conservatives won:

> This country would remain divided between north and south, between
> those who are in a job and those who are out of a job. The Health
> Service would be neglected, some of our best scientists would leave the
> country and we would end up worse off, poorer and more divided than
> we've ever been before.

As to the Labour Party were they to win it would make us the laughing
stock of the world:

> We will be felt to have acted totally out of character. It is out of
> character for this country to be unilateralist; to abandon its responsibili-
> ties.

I warned about MPs on the hard Left who loathed the police, were no
respectors of civil liberties and were ready to trample on people.

> If you really care about this country, the National Health Service and
> education, you should not have to vote Labour and then have to accept
> unilateralism, anti-police attitudes, and reversing legislation over the
> trade unions.

At long last I had broken loose and put a hung Parliament at the core of
our appeal directly to millions of voters.

It was a tragedy that I had had to wait this long. The evidence was
very clear in private and in publicized polls that if people believed that we
would hold the balance they would vote for us in almost as many
numbers as if they thought we could win. It was if they only thought
we would win a few seats that our vote plummeted. Since 1983 the

number of people believing we could hold the balance increased and always more were prepared to believe we could hold the balance than said they would vote for us.

GALLUP POLL	SEPT. 86 per cent	SEPT. 85 per cent	SEPT. 84 per cent
Would you be likely to vote for the Alliance between the Liberals and the Social Democrats if you thought they:			
Would get a majority?			
Yes	49	59	47
No	45	38	43
Don't know	7	3	10
Were likely to hold the balance?			
Yes	45	50	44
No	47	42	46
Don't know	8	8	9
Would win only a few seats?			
Yes	24	31	23
No	67	59	66
Don't know	9	10	10

I had gambled by devoting my broadcast to a hung Parliament. Even so, when the first edit of the broadcast was shown to Maggie Smart, she was appalled to find the hard message had been left on the cutting-room floor. She rang me and I authorized her to go back and firm up the message and in effect to take over the editing, which she did. The filming had been done over the weekend in advance of the BBC *Newsnight* poll. Quite fortuitously the poll revealed on the Tuesday evening that in sixty marginal seats it was a much closer contest and showed a hung Parliament as a distinct possibility. I feared that we were pushing the idea of a balanced Parliament too late and I also knew that our own telephone polls showed no shift in the Conservative lead. So personally I thought we were not even remotely near to achieving a balance. Nevertheless the *Newsnight* poll gave me the credibility to push the idea that we would be part of the action after the election. All our polling evidence over three years showed that, unless people believed this was a possibility, loosely attached voters would not vote for us. Since few could possibly believe we would win outright they had to be convinced we could hold the balance.

Even as my recorded broadcast was going out David Steel was making the ludicrous equation of Margaret Thatcher with Arthur Scargill, saying they had a lot in common. As he said it I sat writhing in my chair in the Ask the Alliance rally in Nottingham. It was as if he and his Party had learned absolutely nothing from the miners' strike. To many voters the miners' strike was when Margaret Thatcher's qualities were better displayed than in either the Falklands or in dealing with the Soviet Union. I knew that I could not possibly persuade wavering Conservatives to vote for the Alliance if they thought that one of its leaders disliked Margaret Thatcher so much that he saw her as being as great a menace as Arthur Scargill. While I was trying to attract tactical voters from the Conservative Party by being tough on Labour, David Steel was trying to attract tactical voters from Labour by being tough on the Conservatives. Perhaps the different messages worked in holding our vote, but there was no doubt that the coherence of our campaign disintegrated in those last few days. We were following the old Liberal style of discordant messages. It showed something else too, that the Liberal Party, at least under David Steel, was essentially more of an anti-Conservative Party force than an anti-Labour Party force, whatever policies Labour followed. The labels of Left-wing or Right-wing were crucial to Steel's Liberals. It was the actual policies which were crucial to the SDP.

Yet for all our internal differences about positioning, the biggest problem by far in running the concept of a balanced Parliament was that Labour was not doing well enough. Another rogue poll on Thursday morning had the *Daily Telegraph*'s Gallup showing Labour within 4 per cent of the Conservatives and this riled the Tory high command. Saatchi and Saatchi were strongly criticized and, though at the time we only got a hint of what was going on, it has since been revealed that 'Wobbly Thursday' was also a personal crisis between Margaret Thatcher and Norman Tebbit. For the Alliance the danger was of a squeeze and the election starting to look like a two-horse race. That morning at the Conservative press conference, Margaret Thatcher showed her unease over the polls by making one of her few campaign mistakes. Asked about her own use of private health care she said 'I exercise my right as a free citizen to spend my own money in my own way, so that I can go on the day, the time, to the doctor I choose and get out fast.' It was hailed by the press as a gaffe. I likened her insensitive remarks to Marie Antoinette's famous 'Let them eat cake' comment to the starving poor in Paris.

By Friday, however, everything was back to normal. The Tories breathed again, with a Marplan poll showing no change since the previous week, with the Conservatives on 44 per cent, Labour 34 per cent and the Alliance 20 per cent. At the Alliance Planning Group John Pardoe perfectly reasonably remonstrated with David and me over all the conflicting stories about whether or not one could work with Margaret Thatcher in a balanced Parliament. He had reached the point where he did not care what we said as long as we said the same thing. But this too was a cop-out and not an acceptable position. The Alliance Planning Group, given a conflict between the leaders, should have tried to make a decision. The reason they could not do so is that they too were divided. John Pardoe and John Harris would not come down on one side or the other. This conflict between us two was later used to justify the impossibility of campaigning with two leaders and the necessity of having a single leader. In fact it came mostly from the same people who wanted to merge into a single party.

The press also began to show their frustration and write that the Alliance campaign was a disaster. John Pardoe later expressed this view in florid terms in a seminar following the election. I believe it is a mistake to exaggerate the adverse effect on the electorate of these differences. We were not one party and where we pretended that we were we tended to come unstuck. When David talked about our joint TV appearances early in the campaign as Tweedledum and Tweedledee, he gave the press their headline. There were differences, not just between the two leaders but between the two parties about policy. That mirrored conflicting views on our target audience within the electorate. Some potential Alliance voters saw some merit in the Conservatives, others could see none. Some feared a Labour Government, others could have tolerated it. All I knew throughout the campaign was that there were more people likely to vote Conservative than were ever going to vote Labour. Labour's vote was also down to a much harder core, having been compressed over its extremist years. For the Alliance to set itself against a coalition with the Conservative Party which was, by any polling standard, going to end up as the largest single party, was quite simply bad mathematics as well as bad politics.

The effect of the Conservative lead and of all these repeated differences led to the worst day of my whole campaign, not helped by the only foul-up in my entire campaign programme. We found ourselves in full view of TV and reporters being refused entry to a shipyard in Aberdeen which, considering the candidate was closely involved with the management, was extremely irritating. Flying down to Plymouth from Edinburgh that night, my own press corps detected a mood of dejection. But the next day the sea air and Plymouth, as it usually does, revived me and I was back in a buoyant mood. In the early evening I flew up to help Mike Hancock and we had a very successful meeting in Portsmouth.

The final days of the campaign were a matter of whistling in the dark and keeping everyone's spirits up. Every cameraman was waiting to catch a downcast or despondent look and I went around with an inane grin on my face. By then I knew the most we could hope for was ten SDP MPs and it might be far fewer.

Nevertheless at our riverside rally in Richmond on the final Sunday the spirit was amazingly good. In a spontaneous speech I made light of the differences between David and myself, saying that we were divided over 'whether or not our dear Prime Minister can listen to anyone else. David thinks she can listen to no one, and I don't think she can listen to anyone. On that remarkable difference the BBC and ITN managed to hang a great many newscasting programmes.'

*

We also had a splendid encounter with an eager policeman. Seeing David Steel's battlebus, waiting to take people to Richmond, double parked outside the National Liberal Club he climbed in and told the driver to proceed to the police pound in the Old Kent Road. Someone then decided to telephone our bus, with its appropriate slogan 'The time has come', and find out what was happening. Constable Rankin answered the telephone and when asked how soon the Alliance bus could be got back on the road said 'As soon as they come round here with £57. I suppose a cheque will do.'

To further liven life up Enoch Powell said you had to be barmy to believe that nuclear weapons had kept the peace in Europe for forty years, and fell just short of endorsing Labour. A more frivolous note was struck by *Woman's Own* who, in a survey, found that Maggie Thatcher was the person you would be most likely to trust with your money, David Owen was the choice for a romantic encounter, David Steel would be best to decorate the house and Neil Kinnock would make a great babysitter.

On Monday Margaret Thatcher was due to be in Venice for sixteen hours at the Economic Summit. Tom McNally suggested I should label it a 'one cornetto' publicity stunt and this made a good headline. I also said 'it has been easier to persuade Mrs Thatcher to catch a plane to an international summit than to catch a plane to one of Britain's deprived or depressed regions.' We tried once again to make constitutional reform an issue at our press conference and I pointed out how coalition governments were almost the inevitable consequence of proportional representation. But again there was not much interest. If it had ever looked as if we might hold the balance then the constitutional reform package would have been of the greatest interest.

On Tuesday I was watching TV-am over breakfast and saw Anne Diamond confront Denis Healey. It was electric stuff and Denis for once met his match. Denis started off by talking about Mrs Thatcher's face on *Panorama* 'being contorted with hate'. When Anne Diamond said the same thing could be said about his own face, he replied 'Oh no, look at me – genial, friendly old chap, quite different from Mrs Thatcher', but then Anne produced a copy of the *Sun* with its story alleging that Edna Healey had had a private hip operation. 'It is a TV-am dirty trick, isn't it,' said Denis. 'You brought me in here to talk about the Summit and you decided to talk about my wife.' He then asked Anne where she planned to have her baby, to which she replied she was not a politician and he, quite fairly, pointed out that his wife was not either. It ended with Denis storming out of the interview, poking TV-am's political editor Adam Bolton in the stomach and saying to Anne Diamond, off camera, 'You're a shit!' I decided to bring this vignette to the press conference since many of the journalists would not have seen it. I prefaced what I said by saying Edna Healey's private life was not a political issue but Denis's behaviour was.

I cannot tell you the unmitigated pleasure Anne Diamond's interview gave me. I was rolling on the floor with laughter. It was one of the best virtuoso performances. I doubt if Sir Robin Day, David Dimbleby and Co. would have hung in there so tenaciously. The old entertainer, Denis Healey, was rolled over, trampled on. It was lovely theatre.

I only realized much later how much offence my remarks had caused to Edna Healey. I have deeply regretted them ever since I knew. She is an enchanting person and over the years has been immensely kind to me. I should have realized the probable effect and ignored the whole incident. Yet it was all so unnecessary. If only Denis had kept his cool and said what is perfectly fair for any politician to say, when confronted with a conflict of loyalties between the best interests of their family and their own political views, 'So what, I have put the interests of my wife first.'

I have faced this dilemma over our youngest child, Lucy. Having put both our boys through the state education system and seeing their education suffer as a result of the teachers' strikes in London and the financial problems of the ILEA, Debbie and I decided that Lucy should go to a private co-educational school. I take no pride in the decision but I think it was the right one in our circumstances and I defend it as putting Lucy's interests first. But I have always believed in the right of anyone to spend their after-tax income in the way they choose and think it is quite wrong to try to prevent people by law from having access to private health or private education.

The way the press handled this Denis Healey story was truly amazing. Wednesday's *Daily Mail* led with 'HEALEY'S GIFT TO THE TORIES', 'Labour's attack on private medicine boomerangs in four-letter row over wife's cash operation.' The *Daily Express* headline was 'HEALEY THE HYPOCRITE'. The only person to come out of the whole row with any grace was Edna Healey herself who said of Anne Diamond, 'She should have asked me. I paid for the operation. I am an independent person. The operation transformed my life. What angers me is that 95 per cent of people do not have that choice.' It was a classic example of why politicians living in glass houses should not throw stones.

We held our last rally in Central Hall, Westminster on Tuesday evening. I stuck to my theme that people voted for the Conservatives out of fear not out of enthusiasm. They were afraid about what Labour would do.

Use your heads and your hearts; you can have the sound market economy, conventional and nuclear deterrence, the responsible trade unionism that your head tells you that Britain needs. You can have people back in work, with every pensioner enjoying a decent retirement, all our children fulfilling their potential, and with no one waiting years in pain for a routine operation – that your heart tells you Britain needs. You don't have to make the impossible choice. You don't have to cut yourself in two – half head, half heart.

Next morning we had our last press conference and I left for Plymouth. There had been a number of press articles writing my and the SDP's epitaph. Perhaps the most thoughtful was written by Matthew Symonds in *The Independent* under the title 'The political tragedy that may lie in wait for David Owen'.

> ... the prospects for Dr Owen are really rather bleak. There will be renewed and possibly irresistible pressure on him to acquiesce in the merger of the SDP with the Liberals – an outcome which he has with good reason bitterly resisted hitherto. But infinitely more serious for Dr Owen is the likelihood that history and the course of events will no longer be seen to be on his side. If the Labour Party loses this election respectably (that means taking about a third of the popular vote and more than 250 seats) it is in business. During the next five years the purge of the hard Left will continue, the policies – including defence – both fudged and brought up to date and the grip of the yuppie apparatchiks around the leader strengthened.

He went on to argue that old-style Liberal opportunism which might result in the occasional by-election spectacular was hardly mould-shattering and no strategy:

> A hand-to-mouth existence of this kind may not appal, may even appeal to, many Liberals, but to the SDP, and to Dr Owen in particular, it would be a kind of living death. The gamble, which began in 1981, would have failed. Under such circumstances Dr Owen may well not wish to stay in politics. The effort of leading a small, under-resourced party in our political system is almost unimaginable.

I too was beginning to ponder what would happen after the election. I knew the merger battle would break out and that I would not wish to be part of a merged party. Nothing that had happened since 1981 nor in the month of this election campaign could convince me that I should try or could successfully live within a party made up predominantly of Liberals. Quite definitely, if elected as a Social Democrat for Devonport, I would stay one for the lifetime of the next Parliament. That was a judgement made not in anger or in frustration but from my heart. I was not and never have been a British Liberal. I had no serious complaints about David Steel or the Liberal Party's conduct in the campaign. They were what they were. Yes, there were differences but they were honourable, political differences and we had accommodated each other and each other's parties with a considerable amount of give and take. I had then and have no wish now to make anyone a scapegoat for our election defeat.

To have started the campaign with polls showing us at 23 per cent and to have ended with 23 per cent in the ballot box was in some ways an achievement given that we lay third throughout and could well have expected to have our votes squeezed and eroded. It is invidious to single anyone out, but in the Alliance the contribution of John Pardoe and Polly

Toynbee was outstanding. In my own team Maggie Smart and Sue Robertson had performed some minor miracles and in Plymouth Debbie and Jon Aarons had ensured that I not only won my seat but increased my majority. But behind them there were many more volunteers putting in an immense effort. Of course there had been difficulties, but politics in the SDP was fun – far more so than it had ever been in the Labour Party – and I came to the end of my campaign feeling it had been enjoyable and worthwhile. I had pushed the Liberal Party to adopt a more sensible election strategy as far as human flesh and blood could go. If we had gone for Labour and been more forthcoming about the Conservatives, I believe we would have won twenty or so more seats. But I would think that! My problem was they did not agree.

On the eve of the poll I had three meetings in schools in Devonport and, for the first time in any election that I had fought, I went to bed that night certain that at least I was going to win my seat. I also feared that five of our eight MPs would lose their seats. It was obvious that Margaret Thatcher was heading for her third term as Prime Minister and that Labour still had a long way to go before it deserved to be the government of the country.

The Conservatives won 372 seats, Labour 229; the SDP had dropped from eight to five MPs. John Cartwright and Rosie Barnes had, to my immense relief, held their adjoining seats in Woolwich and Greenwich, Bob Maclennan and Charles Kennedy had, as I expected, held their adjoining seats in Caithness and Sutherland, and Ross, Cromarty and Skye. Roy Jenkins had, as I feared, lost Glasgow Hillhead by 3,251 votes. Mike Hancock narrowly lost in Portsmouth South by 205 votes, Ian Wrigglesworth lost in Stockton South by 774 votes. Shirley Williams had predictably failed to win Cambridge and had lost by 5,060 votes. Also Bill Rodgers had failed to win Milton Keynes by 13,701 votes. Yet George Cunningham had only failed to win back Islington South and Finsbury by 805 votes, Rosemary Brownlow had come very close in Blyth Valley – Labour holding on by 853 votes – and Chris Patten only managed to hold on in Bath by 1,412 votes. The Liberals had dropped from nineteen to seventeen MPs, losing Michael Meadowcroft and Clement Freud, both in their different ways great assets and people with whom I had enjoyed working despite our different views.

Like a General who has lost a battle, a political leader who has lost a general election either retires, is ousted or fights back. My firm belief was that, since Labour was still not fit to govern, the SDP still had a role to play. Only if Labour could become the government of the country without my losing sleep would I hang up my boots. Until that happened I would stay a Social Democrat, join no other party and fight for social democracy.

35

THE DEMISE OF THE SDP

Up most of the night coping with the fall-out of electoral defeat, I would have preferred to have had a few days' peace and quiet before considering what should be done about the Alliance. But there was no escaping the press – there they all were in the foyer of my Plymouth hotel on the morning of Friday 12 June waiting to pounce. We had travelled many miles together on the campaign and press relations had been excellent. I think they, like my team, had enjoyed the last month but they had a job to do and sympathy is not the journalist's stock in trade. I had promised to do a press conference after I had taken a walk on the Hoe to get some fresh air. Debbie and I strolled out of the hotel, past the statue of Sir Francis Drake and the famous bowling green, towards Seaton lighthouse (xli). We were accompanied initially by photographers but soon they left us in peace. As we walked and talked we both knew that when I returned to the hotel the merger issue would now be unavoidable. The press conference would present a dilemma. If I gave the impression that a merger might be acceptable the flood-gates would open but if, as the leader of a losing party, I appeared to be adamantly opposed, it would look like a refusal to listen. I decided to rely on the stock phrases which had been used throughout the campaign but I knew they would be subject to more publicity and scrutiny than hitherto.

So at the informal press conference the inevitable questions about merger began. Whether to merge, I said, was a 'legitimate question', but within the SDP

the endless examining of our own navels on whether or not we should exist is probably one of our greatest weaknesses. I have never doubted that we should exist. I knew we needed a fourth party, and I think everything that has happened since then has justified the decision. I am sticking to what I have always said. The partnership is of two parties and two strands of British politics – social democracy and liberalism. I will stay as SDP Leader as long as the SDP exists and they want me to stay as their leader.

I said the issue of merger, if people wished, would 'go to the membership, because we have within our constitution, provision for a one member-one vote democracy.'

It seemed to me that many in the SDP would wish to merge and I wanted them to do so with good will on all sides. I had no desire to prevent them, believing they had the right to unite with the Liberals if that was what they wanted. But, that morning on Plymouth Hoe, I never envisaged that any Social Democrat would try to stop me staying on as the SDP MP for Devonport. I was soon to realize that was exactly what they were planning – it was not enough for them to join up with the Liberals themselves; they also wanted to liquidate the SDP and make any of us who wished to remain in it illegitimate and without a party. The enormity of the proposition that those of us who had been elected should be deprived of the right to continue as social democrats in the party we loved, was never sufficiently appreciated.

Before I could fly back to London I had first to thank my own Devonport constituents for electing me. We said goodbye to the detectives who had been with us throughout the campaign and all five Owens jumped into the back of the campaign Land-Rover and set off, waving and smiling, as we were driven through the familiar streets of the constituency. Through the loud speaker I thanked all those who came out of their houses. My relationship with Plymouth and my constituents is not a remote business arrangement with visits treated as an inconvenience. Some people in the constituency had worked for years for me to be their representative. Some had supported me voluntarily for over twenty-one years, whether I was Labour or SDP, putting in long hours, sometimes in the cold and rain, canvassing to hold and win the crucial margin of votes. My dominant emotion that morning was gratitude and I suppressed all thought of the manoeuvring to precipitate a merger that I knew was going on.

In the early hours of the morning, I had talked to David Steel on the telephone; it seemed that it was unlikely he would come to London, but I told him I would stick to the plan that we would both thank the staff. So the press corps and my campaign team flew back to London, having a snack on the plane. I then went to our Alliance Headquarters in Cowley Street to thank everyone who had worked so hard. They were naturally disappointed and already merger talk was beginning to divide them. I avoided the subject and concentrated on giving their morale a boost. The family all returned that night to the peace of Buttermere with its never-failing capacity to re-charge our batteries.

The Saturday papers were predictably full of a possible merger. The Liberals were already talking about both Alliance parties drawing up merger proposals to go before special party conferences in the New Year. David Steel was also reported as having talked to me on the telephone about a formal uniting of our parties, which was news to me. The idea that we had a discussion about merger as dawn was breaking after electoral defeat is pure fantasy.

Later in the day the radio reported Roy Jenkins as having come out strongly in favour of an early merger. It was no surprise. It was perfectly reasonable for him to argue this now that the election was over. He had shown restraint before the election and was now totally free to speak his mind and force the issue. All the signs were that that was exactly what he intended to do.

That afternoon Robert Maclennan also rang and asked if he could come to see me. We agreed he would come down for lunch at Buttermere next day. On that Sunday we could both see the pressure building. The *Observer* carried a story about merger and the possibility was raised that Paddy Ashdown would put his hat in the ring for the leadership of the Liberal Party. It was good to talk with Bob. He and I had been friends ever since we had come into the House together in 1966. We went for a long walk before lunch. I expected his mood to be cautious and reflective. He had always been more enthusiastic for the Alliance than I and had seen the merits of merging. At times I felt he had been tempted by the logic but put off both emotionally and by the practical problems. Before the election, with the strongly pro-merger William Goodhart, he had produced a factual memo on the constitutional implications of merging which Shirley had sent to me. Like Charles Kennedy, he could easily win his seat, whether as a Liberal or Social Democrat, for the Liberals had always been fairly strong in his seat and he had taken much of the Labour vote into the SDP. It was a constituency where a conscientious member like Bob could build up a large personal following. Over the years, however, he had been extremely upset by the attitude of the Liberals to civil nuclear power. This affected his constituency and he had been one of their most hardline critics over the non-nuclear defence vote at Eastbourne. So I was uncertain which side of the argument he would take.

In the event he was far more robustly opposed to merging than I had expected. When I told him I had no intention of merging myself, he made no attempt to dissuade me. He even felt strongly that we needed to bring a swift end to having joint Alliance policy spokesmen so that we could revert to speaking with distinctive SDP and Liberal voices in the House of Commons.

While we were out walking David Steel telephoned from Ettrick Bridge and Debbie took the call. David said he was writing a memorandum on merger for his own party and that he wanted me to read it. They both then discussed when I would be coming back to London. When Debbie said I was coming back that night and could pick it up at his flat in Dolphin Square he said there was no problem and he would arrange for it to reach my office on Monday morning. The next telephone call Debbie took while Bob and I were still out was from Chris

Moncrieff of the Press Association. As always he was bright, friendly and on the ball. He not only knew all about the existence of David Steel's memorandum but seemed to have a lot of detail. Bob, Debbie and I had a good laugh about all this over lunch. It was so flagrant. David was mounting a clear takeover bid for the SDP, while trying hard to protect his own back from Paddy Ashdown and showing his party that he was not about to resign or take a sabbatical as he had done after the last election. It was later rumoured that David Steel had encouraged the *Observer* to run the story about Paddy Ashdown. Neither Bob nor I was surprised by David's demand to merge or by his tactic of trying to bounce us. We had grown used to his using that technique with his own party and we had no reason to expect that he would not try it with us. Our problem was going to be the other members of the Gang of Four. Their continued dominance was something Bob had long resented. We could see off David Steel or Roy, Shirley and Bill individually, but the combination of all four would be formidable. Bob went off after lunch, happy that we would oppose a merger, promising to talk to others, especially Charles Kennedy, in greater depth than he had been able to do up until then. I soon established that all the SDP MPs had said in private consultations that they were not prepared to merge with the Liberals.

The evening television news had film of David Steel in his home actually writing the memorandum – the same memorandum he had told Debbie he wanted me to read. It was all far too melodramatic. I refused to make any comment to the press all that Sunday, even though some tried to tempt me to comment by regaling me with what Shirley Williams had apparently said in favour of a merged party. This slightly surprised me since we had talked on the telephone the previous day and she had not mentioned that she was planning anything of the sort. We had instead agreed that at the National Committee meeting arranged for the Monday we would jointly suggest having a debate on merger at our Portsmouth conference, which was due to start over the August Bank Holiday weekend, and that the members would almost certainly want a ballot which would come after the conference. The SDP conference had been deliberately timed to start early, so we could hold it even if the election was in the early autumn.

By Monday morning the papers had more details of David Steel's memorandum and Bill Rodgers had joined the fray, declaring in favour of a merger. I rang Shirley that morning to say I could no longer agree to recommend a merger debate at Portsmouth. I wanted to think carefully about what would now be the best way of handling this new development. I told her that I feared a six-month public debate during which we might destroy ourselves and did not want to make any decisions that afternoon and intended to say very little at the meeting, preferring to listen to the arguments. I had been tipped off about a preemptive ballot motion.

I had also by now read David Steel's memorandum. His tone was not hostile, saying generously that he thought that we had both done as much as any two human beings could to work closely in the interests of Alliance unity. He claimed that if either one of us had been running the campaign as a single leader, it would have had a sharper image and strategy. He would have preferred a clear anti-Thatcher, non-socialist alternative while I wished for a more assertive balance of power coalition focus and it was 'futile' to blame our setback on the dual leadership. We were, however, now, whether we liked it or not, into 'presidential' elections and he felt we needed a single leader and one party. I was pleased that at least he had put down three options – separate politics, growing together, or democratic fusion – but he made it clear that it was the latter he wanted. He even named the new party the Liberal Democratic Alliance. It was what I would have expected – a shrewd, well-crafted document with a pre-emptive bid over the name for the merged party. I could have predicted that he would want to keep the word 'Liberal'. But it was predicated on a massive false assumption, one which proved extremely difficult to shake during the ensuing debate. The argument that the Alliance was an ineffective organization made a good deal of sense if one accepted we were identical parties which, clumsily, and accidentally had two leaders. But we never had been created to be two identical parties and, in so far as we had tried to become identical, I believed, and had consistently argued, that we had damaged both our appeal and purpose.

The memorandum also did not address the key fact that, even with the Centrist label pinned on us, the two-party Alliance had achieved persistently high levels of public support, particularly in 1981 and in 1985, when the distinctive SDP image was clearest; it was unmatched by anything the Liberals had achieved since the early part of the century. In both 1983 with 25 per cent and 1987 with 23 per cent we had broken through the 20 per cent barrier for the first time since 1929 and had done significantly better than Jeremy Thorpe's best performance of 19 per cent in 1974. Did David Steel think the Liberal Party on its own would have done better than the Alliance through the 1980s in either the opinion polls or in the two elections? And did he believe that a Liberal/ SDP merger that did not carry an overwhelming majority of members with it could hope to retain and build on Alliance levels of support? Those questions were ignored.

The National Committee of the SDP met that afternoon. Shirley put a paper to the Committee under her own name suggesting not just the open debate we had talked of, but that the National Committee should recommend to the Portsmouth Conference a ballot of all SDP members. It should determine whether to form a single new party with the Liberal Party. It even proposed the ballot wording, giving SDP members the bald choice of voting *for* union with the Liberal Party or *against* union with the Liberal Party. If a majority voted for union, then a working party should report back to the National Committee and the Council for Social Democracy on a constitution for a single merged party.

It was obvious that a concerted campaign to merge had been launched and that those who wanted this had co-ordinated their language and their tactics. There was no point in complaining. After the 1983 Election we had removed Roy to prevent a merger; after the 1987 Election they were now moving ahead to ensure a merger. The danger of Shirley's formulation, for those of us who did not want to merge, was obvious. She had chosen 'union', a phrase Bill had also used, as the description best calculated to appeal. She was asking for the positive vote to be for union which she favoured and the negative vote to be against union. Sensible tactics from her point of view. I was sure Shirley had calculated, as I had done, that there was a clear majority to merge in the Conference body, the CSD. So holding the ballot after Portsmouth virtually guaranteed that there would be a positive recommendation for a merger from the CSD. Moreover the campaign for merger would have months to organize and propagate their view, while I, as Leader, would be in an extremely difficult position to campaign against.

I knew there was a majority against merger on the National Committee and that many Party members were angry with David Steel and the Liberals for such an obvious bounce. I was not sure whether there was a majority against a merger in our membership but rather doubted it. I suspected that by early 1987 there was a majority in favour of a merger. Since 1982 we had progressively lost many of the members most opposed to working closely with the Liberals. Yet whether there was a majority or not really did not matter very much. What did matter was that there was a significant minority of people in the SDP who would simply not join a merged party. Also a large group who had no enthusiasm for merging – some would go along with it and others would not, depending on individual circumstances. All members had rights. To compel people by majority vote to renounce their right to belong to the party of their choice was quite wrong. I was facing a ballot in which individuals would be told that, if they lost the vote, they would no longer be members of the SDP. Our Party would be closed because others in the Party had found something else they wanted to try.

My task as Leader was to devise a mechanism, if possible, for everyone to respect the other's viewpoint. I was not going to use tricks to suppress the open debate. I believed this would be pointless. In the early years I felt it was right to resist merger and had succeeded in doing so. After two general elections and much experience of merged parties locally I felt that those who wanted to 'unite' with the Liberals should be allowed to do so; equally that others should be free to continue with a Social Democratic Party. It was not 'losing' or 'winning' a merger ballot that bothered me – it was the rights of all the individuals concerned. I did not want to keep anyone in the SDP who wanted to go. Shirley's paper was not accepted at the National Committee meeting, the view being vigorously expressed that four days after an election was hardly the ideal time to be making such vitally important decisions. This was the firm view of our two trustees. I said very little, confining myself to an election report. It was agreed that we should meet again on 29 June to discuss the matter further and decide then whether we wished to put forward a motion to the Portsmouth conference and if so in what form. A few days later, after her rebuff in the National Committee, Shirley wanted to send out a letter to all Area Parties which I thought was highly prejudicial. Luckily she agreed not to include the contentious wording, but relations were becoming very strained.

On Tuesday 16 June, only two days after writing his memorandum with three options, David Steel was telling the press it was merger or bust and there were in fact only two options, the option of a closer two-party Alliance having been peremptorily closed. The pro-merger force, Liberal and SDP, were now using identical language and the same tactics. I dreaded the results of fighting them. The Alliance's public image would be badly damaged by an open wrangle over merger. We had been concealing our differences, as all political parties do week after week in the House of Commons, and both parties had compromised with each other frequently; most of the time trying conscientiously to minimize differences. If we triggered a public debate these differences were going to be aired, inevitably exaggerated and exploited by both sides. I became convinced that the only way to maintain public support and to behave honourably among people who had worked together for many years was a friendly separation. Those who wanted to form a new party with the Liberals doing so, and allow others to remain members of a distinctive Social Democratic Party. The two groups would continue to co-operate. This seemed the only alternative to a divisive ballot and an unpleasant and electorally disastrous final split.

On Wednesday 17 June, after the House had met to elect a Speaker, the SDP Parliamentary Committee met for the first time since the election. All five MPs were present, as were Jack Diamond, Leader of the SDP Peers, Alastair Kilmarnock, Chief Whip in the Lords, and Sue Robertson, Secretary to the Parliamentary Committee. They unanimously re-elected me as Leader. I then put to them a draft resolution for the National Committee which I had considered very carefully over the six days since the election. I had tried to look at the situation from every angle, consulted widely and had concluded reluctantly and sadly that there was no possible way of keeping the SDP together. I recommended to my parliamentary colleagues that we embark openly on an amicable divorce.

I had often observed that the most certain recipe for maximum ill will and minimum mutual respect when a marriage broke down was to bring in the lawyers. I felt we could use our one member-one vote ballot system to enable individual members to choose their own course and also allow for a collective negotiation with the Liberals on behalf of those who were certain that they wanted a merger. I suggested a way in which this could be done while keeping open every party member's option to make their own final choices when they saw the result of the negotiations with the Liberal Party. The assets of the party could then be split to reflect the balance of the members' choice. The key passages in my resolution were:

> ... profoundly aware of the dangers of a deeply divisive debate being undertaken in which members of the party explain why they do or do not believe that a merger of the party is desirable against a background of 'winner takes all'.
> ... an immediate consultative ballot of all members of the SDP so as to allow for an amicable settlement between those SDP members who wish to open negotiations with the Liberal Party and those members who do not wish to do so and want to remain members of the SDP.
> Do you want your membership registration to remain with the SDP as a separate party?   YES / NO
> Do you want your membership registration to be transferred to an SDP group who will go into negotiation with the Liberal Party with the aim of forming a merged party?   YES / NO
> If you do not register your vote on this ballot paper, your membership will remain registered with the SDP as a separate party.
> The resources of the SDP, its financial and physical assets, will be split fairly on a proportional basis between those who decide to transfer their membership and those who remain members of the SDP. The National Committee will appoint an independent arbitrator to preside over such an allocation. The Electoral Reform Society will supervize the ballot. An independent returning officer will be appointed by the National Committee.
> ... it is vital that there is no personal acrimony between Social Democrats and our Liberal partners and that we retain the spirit of partnership that has been a feature of the Alliance in the past and will be important for the future.

Unfortunately, at that meeting, I completely failed to convince any of my colleagues that a split in the SDP was inevitable. None of them showed any interest or put forward any arguments for merging, but what they could not accept was the inevitability of a split. I, who knew the Party very well by virtue of being its Leader and travelling more than anyone else, was convinced that the grass roots were deeply and irretrievably divided. I knew that Shirley's ballot would stifle a legitimate desire to form a new party or dragoon people into a party they did not want. Either way what was left would be unworkable. Now that the campaign for merger had started there was no way of forcing the genie back into the bottle. Things could not stay as they were, a parting of ways was inevitable. But the parliamentarians just could not face that horror. No one, not even Charles Kennedy, expressed the slightest qualification about their opposition to merger and determination to remain members of the SDP. Jack Diamond, the oldest and most experienced person in the room, an old Treasury colleague of Roy Jenkins who had played a key role in the 1983 campaign, was resolutely opposed to a merger, but even he could not reconcile himself to a split. Bob Maclennan had not changed his mind in any way since Sunday but he thought I was overreacting and believed that a large majority of the party would want to stay separate but in a deeper Alliance. If anything, he was now even more determined and adamant that we should end the system of Alliance spokesmen. John Cartwright was not ready to accept a split either and all his old reflexes as a party agent were for a compromise solution to maintain the unity of the SDP. Rosie Barnes was for staying together within the SDP but felt we should concede a single leader for the Alliance before the next election.

They all felt I was being far too fatalistic about a split and they wanted to find a compromise along the lines of David Steel's growing-together option, in effect a halfway house. Even when I pointed out that David was already showing every sign of going back on this option of growing together, they believed we could still persuade people that this was the wisest course. I tried to explain the passions and the jealousies that had been bottled up for years over this issue but they had not had the same experience of those tensions. They had not felt as I had the personal trauma surrounding the disintegration of the Gang of Four. Even these people, close to the top of the Party as they were, did not understand the vehemence with which Roy Jenkins wanted to merge and how completely Bill and Shirley had now swung to his side.

I drew their attention to an article in the *Guardian* that morning by Richard Holme, whose views tended to be identical with David Steel's. It said that the options for the SDP and the Liberal Party were stark – to fight or unite, and although the Labour Party had not yet shown any sign of changing its general election policies, he was already talking about exploring common ground with Labour. I failed to convince my parliamentary colleagues of the need for an amicable separation and agreed instead that Bob Maclennan should be charged with trying to produce a resolution for the National Committee which would build on the option of growing together. My fellow parliamentarians had not convinced me that this was a viable option but since I had not convinced them either I felt I had no alternative but to go along with their views. The numbered copies of my original resolution were collected up and no one else has ever been allowed to have a copy. I have not published its wording until now.

I readily agreed to Rosie's suggestion, pressed by everyone, that by the next election there would have to be a single Leader for the two Alliance parties. My only *caveat*, and it was an important one, was that this leader should not be chosen until there was agreement on common policies in order to fight the election. In this way I at least hoped to preserve a two to three year period for a continuing dialogue on policy. The SDP, by retaining some measure of freedom to espouse more radical and realistic policies might eventually persuade the Liberal Party to adopt them as well. I had after all just emerged from a four-week election campaign where the pressure for unity could hardly have been stronger and even so we had had to paper over substantive policy differences.

John Cartwright wrote an article next day in the same series in the *Guardian* entitled 'Picking up the Pieces', in which he criticized the launching of a high pressure campaign for a total merger within hours of the polls closing, saying that there was a very real risk of a shotgun marriage alienating activists on both sides and though, from the lofty vantage point of Westminster, that might seem both perverse and illogical, 'it isn't pure logic which gets activists out on the doorsteps on rainy nights – that comes from a gut loyalty to ideas in which they believe and an organization which they have helped to build.' David Steel followed with an article in the *Guardian* on the Saturday saying that the relationship between the two parties could not remain static, it must either move forward to union or backward to separation. The battle lines were being drawn up.

All this time I refused to make any public comment. Writing in the *Social Democrat* that weekend John Cartwright showed his exasperation that 'those responsible for the pro-merger blitzkrieg in the Alliance seem to have combined the sensitivity of Genghis Khan with the strategic genius of Ethelred the Unready.' Yet Bill Rodgers, no doubt depressed by having no constituency to look after, was writing in the same edition that we had to enter into a union with the Liberals or accept that our mission had failed.

Meanwhile I was not short of advice. It showered in upon me from every quarter; sincere, kind and well-meant advice. Some of the letters were heartbreaking, from people who could not believe that having fought as a partnership of two parties only days before we were now at each other's throats. Simon Jenkins in the *Sunday Times* wrote suggesting I should pack in the Alliance and stop 'a-wastin' Christian kisses on an 'eathen idol's foot' and become a truly independent parliamentarian acting as the proportional representative of a generous swathe of the electorate. Douglas Hurd, in a speech designed to sunder the SDP from the Liberals, urged the SDP MPs to join the Conservatives, saying it might be less painful than falling prey to those Liberals who show more zeal for a takeover of the SDP than the 'most brazen of asset strippers'. The *Guardian* had an editorial saying that 'the Doctor isn't Tory', but they and the *Observer*, almost alone among the newspapers, wanted a merger.

In private I was talking continually to those people in the SDP on whom I had really been able to count whenever the going had got tough over the last six-and-a-half years: the people who had held out against joint selection and a merger by stealth in 1982 and 1983; who had supported the social market economy in 1984 and 1985 and who had insisted that we should stand firm on a commitment to replace Polaris in

1986 and 1987. They were not always the same people but they were the sort of people with whom one could go tiger hunting without worrying about one's back. Their views were depressing. There was a realism to their comments, benefiting as they did from a slight detachment from the hothouse atmosphere of either the House of Commons or our Cowley Street HQ. Almost to a man and woman they believed we were facing a takeover by the Liberal Party which we were too weak to resist. They agreed that an amicable separation was the only viable option, one which most of them doubted would be accepted by the pro-merger group. The vindictiveness associated with the takeover bid did not seem to allow for friendship: it looked as if the new party would try to crush anyone wanting to stay in a separate independent SDP, seeing our continued existence as a threat. The most depressing finding was that, whatever I did, they had no interest whatever in being active in a merged party. Many of them expected me to accept the inevitable and become the Leader of the merged party. While wishing me well they were at pains to make it clear that they had other priorities like their jobs or their home life. Even a really close friend like Mike Thomas refused to give me any advice, feeling that this was a decision the MPs could only make for themselves. Whatever course they took they would have to live with it in their constituencies and explain it day by day in the House of Commons.

Among the activists in my own constituency there was no enthusiasm at all for becoming, effectively, Liberals and fury that our own victory should have been blighted within hours by a controversy which they saw as a supreme irrelevance. In the other two Plymouth constituencies, Drake and Sutton, there was slightly more enthusiasm for a merger. But David Astor wanted nothing to do with the Liberals. We had had less than a handful of Liberal councillors in Plymouth since the war. The Liberals had been a negligible force in the City, despite being reasonably strong in the West Country. Our SDP councillors did not believe they could win their seats if we were merged with the Liberals and many questioned whether I could hold my own seat if we lost our independence. As in other parts of the country, some started to drift away.

Time and time again, from those activists up and down the country who were closest to me came the comment 'If I had wanted to join the Liberals I would have done it in –' and then they would add the particular year when their frustration with the Labour or Conservative Party had come to a head, the moment when they had wanted an alternative but had not seen it in the Liberals. Some people's memories went back to 1959 and the Clause 4 argument inside the Labour Party. Some went back to 1981 and their anger at massive and growing unemployment because of Conservative incompetence and insensitivity. For many of these people the SDP had fulfilled their hopes, even their dreams. Their commitment was not transferable. They would refuse to follow me into the Liberal Party.

The pitfall I had to avoid was being stuck in a predestined groove, feeling that because I had been against merger from 1981 to 1987 I must inevitably continue to oppose it. I really tried to think afresh and consider whether it was not a moment to cut my losses and accept merger as inevitable. I examined carefully whether it was possible for me to do a reverse takeover, to join a Liberal dominated party and turn it into an SDP Mark II. But my power base was far weaker than in 1983. Then I had been the new leader coming in to replace the *ancien regime*, now I was associated with a disappointing election result. In addition, of course, I would be fighting all these battles without the help of those who had sustained me in the past and surrounded almost solely by those who had resisted every policy move I had made. No one can lead any organization for long if he or she is too distant from its centre of gravity, and a merged party's centre of gravity would be far away from where my instincts lay. No doubt I could have initially held the line on policy, including the nuclear deterrent, but it would have been a constant battle, and again and again I asked myself whom would I be able to rely on?

I do not believe that time has invalidated this analysis. It is true that under Paddy Ashdown the Liberal Democrats accepted Trident, but after Neil Kinnock had changed Labour's policy, they shifted theirs as well. Then again Labour have in 1991 moved first to accept that while the Soviet Union has any nuclear weapons it is in the European interest for France and Britain to maintain a minimum nuclear deterrent. Take another crucial issue – Europe. Those who argue that I should have fought to become leader of a merged party must consider what would have happened when one of the first important issues since the last election hit the headlines – European federalism. I am totally opposed to it; the vast majority of Liberal Democrats are historically committed to it. It would have been impossible for me to lead the Liberals away from federalism. I doubt it would be right to even try for it is a good thing that there is one party that is federalist. There are also still problems over the Liberal Democrats' readiness to champion the market economy. This is not a pedantic matter of their refusal to use the term social market. It is simply that the plans they have advanced over the last few years cast doubt on the degree to which they are enthusiasts for the market idea. Now they have become more positive, but again the change in the Liberal Democrats reflected the movement towards market socialism by the Labour Party. They set the pace on the environment and the constitution.

I have never had any difficulty in believing that Liberal politicians are more than capable of moving with the tide of opinion. My problem is with their inability to hold a line against it. My analysis on which the SDP was created has never changed since 1981; it is that the soft Centre is insufficient to break through on its own, it needs to be broadened and strengthened by the development of the hard Centre. This is easier to do and better maintained if one can form a Centre coalition between two parties. The argument that there is not room for more than three parties is defeatist nonsense. The SDP was destined to be the hard Centre. It stiffened the policies of the Liberal Party and widened its appeal from 1981 to 1987. A continuation of the SDP as a national party from 1987 to 1990 stiffened the emerging policies of the Liberal Democrats and helped force the pace of the Labour Party reforms. The question which will not be answered for some years yet is whether, without the existence of an SDP pioneering policy, with independence as its ultimate weapon, the Liberal Democrats will slip back into being the predominantly soft Centre party the Liberals had been for so long.

Like any politician, I would not embark on an election in order to lose. If I had put myself up to be leader of the merged party I would do what so many SDP candidates had done in joint selection meetings, gravitate to where the votes were. To be elected leader I would have to tone down the policy differences with the Liberals on defence even further and spout the mudge and fudge which I had so often derided inside the Labour Party. We, in the SDP, had trimmed on policy time and again since 1981 in order to preserve the Alliance. I firmly believe that this obsessive policy closeness and consequent trimming damaged us, but at least it was done with an SDP voice and had to be negotiated with us. Without independent negotiation there would be more trimming still, and there was precious little room for that.

Of course it was encouraging that, if I stood, it was quite likely that I could be elected as the new leader of the merged party. Some Liberal MPs were very keen for me to be its leader and came to persuade me. I could rely on the votes of many SDP members and, surprisingly, on a substantial number of Liberal activists. Very probably they would have been sufficient to make me leader, even against David Steel. But I also knew that too many of those people, particularly some who wrote in to urge me to head up the merger, would not stand firm in the policy disputes that take place in any party and were inevitable in the merged party. Rightly or wrongly, I was by then a red rag to active Liberals, particularly the London based intelligentsia. Some of those urging me publicly to join and even saying they would vote for me as leader would, I knew, exact a price for their support. They wanted me Leader for electoral reasons because they thought I would attract votes, but they would try to make me a prisoner on policy. I could see a miserable marriage ahead, flawed from the start and bound to end in tears. I had not left the Labour Party to end up in the Liberal Party. Nor had I lost hope that the Labour Party could be reformed. Ever since Neil Kinnock started to deal with Militant I believed he would eventually move on policy. Meanwhile the SDP could try and survive. If the Labour Party remained unfit to govern there was a case for keeping the SDP, as long as we were realistic about our own chances of surviving if Labour moved on to our ground; if that happened we would die.

I took my time and listened in case my attitude to these questions had been distorted by the election aftermath. Though I was neither tired nor dejected, it is possible to make bad decisions after a time of sustained tension and activity, either overestimating the problems or underestimating the potential. Yet as the days passed, more and more of those people whose judgement I valued and who were prepared to hazard an opinion came down against my going along with the merger.

I drove over to David Sainsbury's house in the country on the Sunday ten days after polling day. He had just flown in from America having negotiated a major acquisition. We talked through all the options. I showed him my resolution for an amicable settlement but explained that the MPs could not accept that the Party had to split. He still wanted to get the Gang of Four together and I left him with the difficult task of ringing around to see if there was any compromise.

When one's family and close friends are unanimous, as they were in this case, then the decision is not hard. Wife, mother, sister, uncles, aunts, cousins and, though only seventeen, fifteen, and nine, all three children were against my merging with the Liberal Party. They knew the tensions and strains of keeping the Alliance on the road. They had seen and experienced them, some of them hour by hour, day by day. They had watched me hide my distress as my friendship with the other three members of the Gang of Four had deteriorated. Better, they felt, to stick with the SDP at least for the lifetime of the Parliament. They knew exactly what weight could be attributed to the protestations of David Steel and other Liberals about their commitment to the Alliance over those years. For Alliance read Liberal Party. They also knew how much weight to give to the pleading letters that I received. Some of those people's motives were transparently dishonest. An embarrassingly laudatory letter from one prominent SDP woman had arrived on polling day only to be followed within days by denunciation. The warning signs were all there.

But, in the end, the decision could only be mine. My head told me that the SDP was over, that it was only a matter of time before our membership shrank and our electoral appeal faded. My heart wanted to believe we could survive. I bent over backwards to be persuaded by the parliamentarians that the SDP could unite around the 'federal solution' – a single leader, joint policy formation and some joint selection of candidates – but I never believed its ambiguities would attract the majority. Even if that option were to win the ballot, which I doubted, there would be such a haemorrhage of members to the Liberals and such ill will because of the acrimonious debate already underway, that we would not be able to maintain the position of influence we had held since the 1983 election. Perhaps only I knew how fragile that position was; how much, since 1983, it had been illusion and how much reality. At least then we had had six MPs; now it was only five, and that was simply not enough. We were soon not even to have five. Unbeknown to us, Charles Kennedy was preparing to jump ship and join those who wanted a merger. In doing so he broke the crucial unanimity of the Parliamentary Party. Had I known he was going to do this, I would have insisted on putting the proposition that I had put to the MPs for an amicable settlement to the National Committee. When he did make his dramatic shift perhaps I should have revealed to the Committee my true wish for an amicable settlement. If I had done so, at least I would not have been open to the charge, later made, that I only advocated an amicable settlement after the ballot was lost.

The irony of this period was that the main drafter of the resolution for the federal option was Bob Maclennan. It was he who had insisted on the specific wording for the ballot paper, so viciously attacked by Shirley and others as highly prejudicial. Yet to read the press comment you would think I had personally drafted every word. It was virtually impossible to convince people that the other four MPs made up their own minds. Even when the four of them held a press conference putting forward their resolution on Wednesday 24 June, it was still reported as if it was my initiative. Bob Maclennan's draft of the question was as follows:

1. Do you want the National Committee to negotiate a closer constitutional framework for the Alliance, which preserves the identity of the SDP [as a separate party]?
OR
2. Do you want the National Committee to seek a total merger of the SDP with the Liberal Party [which involves the abolition of the SDP]?

Eventually to quieten the protest about 'abolition' of the SDP, from Shirley and others in the National Committee, Bob Maclennan asked that the words in square brackets should be removed, but, ironically, having had 'abolition' deleted at their request, it was abolition which they aggressively pursued once they had won the ballot.

On the Thursday I left for a meeting of the Palme Commission in Oslo. This meant long telephone calls to keep in touch and I was faxed Saturday's *Times*. Its main story came with the headline, 'STEEL'S ATTACK SEEMS SET TO ISOLATE OWEN'. David Steel was now adopting a completely different tone from that in his memorandum. He was reported as saying that 'any half-baked compromise which said little more than 'let's have two parties but one leader' would be doomed from the start.' Roy Jenkins was just about to go to the House of Lords, much to his chagrin, as a result of my nomination, because Margaret Thatcher had refused his attempt to get appointed in his own right. So it was that the soon-to-be-ennobled Lord Jenkins of Hillhead announced that 'the five SDP MPs have done more to damage the Alliance than anything Mrs Thatcher or Neil Kinnock could have concocted against it.' To add colour he was privately telling people that the other four MPs were terrified rabbits, mesmerized by me. Yet two of them, Charles and Bob, were soon to be his colleagues in the Liberal Democrats.

In view of all these attacks, which would obviously come out in the Sunday newspapers, my closest friends felt that I should make public the contents of a letter explaining why I had no intention of being persuaded to become a member of a merged party. The pro-mergerites had continually implied that I was so ambitious that I would eventually join and lead the new party. I agreed to do this from Oslo that Saturday. My silence had been interpreted by some as keeping my options open. It was felt if the federal option were to have any chance I had to make my position clear, indeed, since I was sure I was not going to join, it would be unfair to allow people to vote under a misapprehension. This was no sacrifice. I was not to be persuaded, I might gain a few votes by stating this clearly, as long as it did not appear to be an ultimatum or a threat. The only regret I had in going public was that it meant breaking my fortnight's silence before the National Committee on the Monday.

The crucial paragraphs in the letter were:

> I believe that the fight to maintain the SDP as a separate party is essential for the medium term at least. I do not want to spend hours on television and radio explaining why, but the truth is that, without the SDP, the Alliance would never have been able to maintain the policy stance that we did over the Falklands, over the miners' dispute, over the Right to Buy council-house legislation, over the market economy, over the Prevention of Terrorism Act, over deployment of cruise missiles that has led to the imminent INF agreements, over the integration of tax and social security, and over maintaining a minimum nuclear deterrent. There are a host of other policy areas where the SDP voice has been crucial and has only been influential in the last analysis with the Liberal Party because we had the power to take our own stance as a separate party.
>
> Obviously as a democrat, I will accept the judgement of the members of the Party. There are some on the National Committee who sincerely wish to merge our two parties, indeed some of them have wanted to do so from the beginning. If they win the ballot it will, I imagine, be for them to negotiate with the Liberals.
>
> I for my part will remain a member of the SDP as long as it exists but I have no intention of being persuaded to become a member of a merged party. Though I am naturally flattered by expressions of support for me to lead such a party, it is not for me. I will remain a social democrat ready to work at some future date with Liberals and others to realign British politics.

I flew back on Sunday night from Oslo and was met by the press and television cameras at London Airport. I had no bitterness, I was just resigned to the inevitable. I said to the press, 'I have watched with despair what has happened during the last fortnight, and listened with despair. I think we have let down the more than seven million people who voted for the Alliance in the election.' I used the word 'we' deliberately to include myself.

David Sainsbury rang me at home that evening. All that Roy Jenkins would agree to do was to postpone the ballot until after the Portsmouth CSD. That was no concession but exactly the same position as Shirley had advocated at the National Committee. It was designed to maximize their advantage since we believed they had a majority for merger in the CSD. I told him about my letter being released and said I could see no acceptable compromise other than an amicable settlement, which no one other than me in the Party leadership wanted.

Bill Rodgers accused me of putting a pistol to the heads of the members. *The Independent* in an editorial 'In defence of the Doctor' said:

> it is fashionable to accuse the ambitious Dr Owen of attempting to rig the projected referendum, of trying to blackmail his colleagues, of demanding a veto over the policies of a democratic party and of acting as a little Napoleon on St Helena, divorced from all reality. He, it is said, has brought his party and the Alliance to an appalling pass. (These are only a few of the more printable remarks passed in public by those who fought the general election as Dr Owen's allies and apparent friends.) Such accusations are wrong.
>
> The immediate crisis in the Alliance was precipitated, quite deliberately, by David Steel in the immediate aftermath of the election. With the support of Roy Jenkins, he attempted to bounce the SDP when the younger party looked at its most vulnerable. They reckoned without the determination of Dr Owen and the unity of the other four SDP Members of Parliament. These will, if pushed hard, declare UDI rather than be swallowed up by the Liberal Party.

Sadly this 'unity of the other four SDP Members of Parliament' was to be shattered in the National Committee that day. Although the National Committee voted by eighteen votes to thirteen for Bob Maclennan's resolution, Charles Kennedy voted against the resolution which he had helped to draft. Bob, who was closest to Charles, was apoplectic with rage and felt he had been betrayed, even saying 'Judas' to describe his conduct. Oddly, as things turned out, John, Rosie and I were rather more understanding. Charles was young and had been showing signs of strain and, we later learned, was under great pressure from, among others, Roy Jenkins with whom he had shared an office in the House of Commons for the last four years. The Ross, Cromarty and Skye constituency was essentially a Liberal one and many of the Liberals there felt it had been loaned to the SDP in 1983. He had already faced criticism from his Liberal activists, unhappy at the prospect of his staying in the SDP, and someone close to him told me it was a decision forced on him, not one he would have chosen. Though I was deeply disappointed and surprised, I did not feel bitter then, or since, about his change of mind. These were harsh choices for everyone. I did, however, realize that Charles's decision would do great damage to our chances of winning the membership ballot for a federal solution, for now the Parliamentary Party was divided. I was tempted, even at that late moment in the meeting, to break my silence and table my amicable settlement resolution, which I had brought to the meeting as a precaution. I still believed it was the only mechanism by which we could draw back from the warfare ahead. The blame for not tabling it is mine, and mine alone.

No account of the SDP can ever truly record the debt which the Party owed to David Sainsbury. It was not just his financial contributions, large and generous though they were. He contributed intellectually to the development of our thinking on industrial and economic questions and, as a trustee, was a wise counsellor and totally committed supporter. I had never met him before the Limehouse Declaration. He voted for Roy Jenkins in the 1982 leadership election and we only gradually became friends. He has a fine analytical mind and deep concerns which combine with his wife Susie's different intelligence and outlook to make them the most interesting and powerful philanthropic couple in Britain. Yet everything they do is done quietly, unassumingly and in a profoundly serious and sensitive way. Debbie and I count ourselves lucky to be their friends. In 1987 neither David Sainsbury nor I had faith in Labour, the Conservatives or the Liberals and it just seemed sensible to hold on to what we had in the SDP. In effect to wait and see and try to influence events from a greatly weakened SDP.

On 9 July David Sainsbury and Leslie Murphy, the two trustees of the Party, wrote an article for *The Times*, explaining why they would not join a merged party, under the title 'This murder of ideals by merger':

> Political parties are not companies. They depend totally on the enthusiasm of their members, and their destinies cannot be settled, therefore, by simple majority votes. The merger should, therefore, take place only if there is an overwhelming vote in favour. It is nonsense for anyone to propose to have a ballot on a merger when the leader of the Party, and majorities of the National Committee and the MPs, have declared themselves against it. Unless, that is, they want to destroy the Party.

The two most influential and independent members of the Party, who had been towers of strength, then went on to say what should probably have been said to Party members many years before. They exposed what Roy Jenkins had been up to:

> From the beginning the SDP was seen by some members of the Gang of Four as simply a device to get people out of the Labour Party. They thought, therefore, that as soon as possible it should be merged with the Liberal Party. This view, which was no doubt a careful political decision at the beginning, has become an article of faith, if not an obsession . . .

That obsession was now set to destroy not just the SDP and the Alliance but do considerable damage to the Liberal Party itself. Everything I feared and anticipated in my original amicable separation resolution occurred. Civil war broke out. It was reminiscent of those internal battles of the Labour Party, which had occupied so many years of my life, and it was heart-rending to endure them in the SDP. Whether politics has some unique quality which fosters such behaviour I do not know; perhaps it is just that the clashes are more obvious because politicians are so exposed to scrutiny. The most unpleasant incident was when Shirley spoke at an SDP local government councillors' meeting in Nottingham and released the text of her speech to the press. The *Guardian* headline was, 'OWEN A "VIVISECTOR" ALLEGES WILLIAMS'. She never actually spoke those words, no doubt because she found that many of the councillors present were already so angry with her for her readiness to give up the SDP. Next day I arrived to talk to the group of councillors who felt incensed that Shirley had betrayed the purpose of their meeting and it was then that I came under pressure from Rosemary Brownlow, who had nearly won Blyth Valley, to keep the SDP going even if there was a merger. I said it was not for me to decide but for the grass roots to respond. This triggered a spontaneous fight back with the formation of a 'Grass-roots Uprising' by Marina Carr, an SDP member in the south-east.

The toughest public comment I made was that 'the merger is basically defeatist. It is a lack of nerve, and it is classic, the lack of nerve comes from the liberal-minded people in this country because they are the people whose nerve always fails.' This was a charge to which Shirley Williams apparently took 'great exception' but I believed it when I said it and still do. David Steel accused me of 'petty apartheid' and used a Liberal Party Political Broadcast to campaign for a merger among SDP members. It actually went out while our ballot was going on, saying 'Six years is long enough for an engagement, it is time for wedding bells.'

There were two campaigns – 'Vote for the SDP' for Option 1, the federal closer Alliance solution; and 'Yes to Unity' for Option 2, for opening negotiations to merge. A statement from each side was issued to all members with the ballot paper and under the rules of the Party it was decided by the National Committee that there should be no canvassing, a rule which we more or less held to in the leadership election. At least there had been no direct mailings but telephoning had been fairly widespread. Sadly there was no longer any restraining discipline. The pro-mergerites campaigned on the basis that this was a fight to the finish, no doubt feeling that within a few months the SDP would be merged or they would have left politics. In a subsequent enquiry the 'pro-merger' campaign admitted to the Electoral Reform Society, who were asked by the National Committee to investigate the conduct of the ballot, that they had done a mass mailing to 30,000 members. This must have influenced the outcome of the ballot, by how much we will never know, though I doubt if it was sufficient to change the result. Nevertheless it was a flagrant abuse and it soured the atmosphere. If divorce had not been inevitable before the ballot, whatever the result, it was certainly inevitable once we had begun. The Electoral Reform Society concluded that in certain instances Area Party Secretaries had been approached for membership lists in direct contravention of the rules and that substantial parts of the membership information used by the pro-merger group must have originated from Area Parties. The pro-merger campaign in return complained about the advertisements which the 'Vote for the SDP' campaign placed in national newspapers when it became clear that a mass mailing was already underway by the other side. The Electoral Reform Society, however, found the anti-merger majority on the National Committee had not formulated in advance a set of rules so as to exclude mass mailings but allow newspaper advertising.

On Sunday 26 July Rosie, John and Bob came to dinner at Narrow Street and the four of us discussed how we would handle the aftermath of the ballot. I had known before the dinner that Bob Maclennan was having extensive discussions with Dick Newby, the SDP National Secretary who, since 1983, had believed in merger and who for the last year or more I had virtually regarded as a Liberal. My informant strongly suspected that Bob was shifting his ground. But there was no evidence of this at the dinner, for Bob actually declared to John Cartwright, somewhat insensitively, that he 'would leave politics rather than join a merged party, for unlike you, I have another career to which I can return.' Perhaps wrongly I did not raise the matter directly but I did say that, following Charles's change of mind without any prior warning, I thought it vital that we agreed that no one would change their position without at least discussing it among the four of us. It was noticeable that Bob was very unhappy about my belief that I would have to resign if we lost the ballot. He was due to leave for a holiday in America before the ballot result was announced. This would make consultation over resigning extremely difficult and was why I raised the issue. In retrospect we did not discuss the consequences of my resigning sufficiently, but none of them was left in any doubt that I felt it would be impossible to carry on if the ballot, as I expected, went in favour of opening merger negotiations.

On 6 August the ballot showed that 25,897 votes (57.4 per cent) were in favour of opening negotiations to merge and those who voted not to merge and for the federal option numbered 19,229 (42.6 per cent). This meant that merger negotiations would be opened and that the results would be put first to next year's CSD in Sheffield and then to another members' ballot. Once through these hoops, merger would be complete. In honour I had no option other than to resign. I had no intention of participating in the negotiations and had decided, whatever happened, to continue as the Social Democratic Member of Parliament for Devonport. I suspected that the pro-merger minority in the National Committee would have demanded my resignation and, what is more, they would have had the right to do so. The members' choice had to be respected and, if I hung on to office, there would always be the suspicion that I was doing so to sabotage the negotiations. Moreover by then I was fed up with the whole saga and deeply regretted not having advocated to the National Committee my resolution for an amicable settlement. Charles had gone and Bob was going. I had clearly attached too much to keeping the unity of the Parliamentary Committee. One advantage of doing so was that Rosie, John and I felt deeply committed to each other, and two more decent and determined colleagues cannot be imagined.

When the ballot result was announced I took the result through to my office where other National Committee members were waiting. After I had given them the news, I handed each a copy of my resignation statement. Rosie Barnes immediately wrung from me a pledge to speak at a fringe meeting at the forthcoming Portsmouth Conference, where we had agreed we would launch the Campaign for Social Democracy. Since she was being so understanding about my resignation, I had little alternative but to agree. Until that moment I had made not the slightest commitment to a continuing SDP and I did not believe it was viable. But by agreeing to address this meeting, I left the door ajar and gave the grass roots movement their opportunity, which they took, to push the door open.

One thing I made quite clear was that I would not be party to the Campaign if it sought to use the constitution, as it was still possible to do, to block those members of the Party who wished to merge with the Liberals. As far as I was concerned I was not going to participate in anything more to do with a merger, neither the negotiations nor the ballot after the negotiations. Belatedly too I now felt free to argue for an amicable settlement. However, even if that were rejected, I would not lend my name or indulge myself in any negative campaigning. I wanted the merger to take place as soon as possible and, until then, I would take a back seat and enjoy myself, go to the theatre, read novels and poetry and see more of Debbie and the children. For fourteen years I had been working flat out, since starting on the Private Member's Children's Bill in November 1973, through Government and Opposition, and now I felt like a break. If the grass roots movement mobilized enough members for a continuing SDP I would consider that possibility and, if persuaded, campaign positively for it. I hoped we could restore a working relationship with the merged party, but blocking a merger was not for me. I held to that conviction with a tenacity that infuriated some of my closest friends. When the debacle over the Steel/Maclennan policy document took place in 1988, they begged me to mobilize against the merger and organize, as was certainly possible, for a third of the conference members at the Sheffield Council for Social Democracy to vote against the merger. This would have been enough to block it. But what would that have left us with? I felt 1987 was the time to allow individuals to go their own way. I thereafter refused point blank to shift from what I considered was a principled position of non participation.

'A defeat for the radical Centre' was how *The Independent*, in an editorial summed up the SDP ballot.

> the soft Centre of British politics yesterday won a victory ... Dr Owen's central insight is that policy matters. He is not good at building up a party organization, it does not much interest him. Nor does he have the emollient manner which helps to smooth over differences of opinion among members of a party or coalition. He is not a diplomat, and his tactical judgement is questionable. But he has the ear of the House of Commons which David Steel does not. Dr Owen's straightforward manner, his wide knowledge of government and his wry sense of humour also make him a formidable performer on television. Above all, he is deeply interested in what a political party says, not just how it looks.

The *Guardian* had a perceptive article by John Carvel, 'A journey into darkness', which posed the question of whether I would become the Enoch Powell of the 1990s.

> It is a common criticism of politicians that they are too ready to abandon principle to achieve compromise and maximize their power. Dr Owen shows what happens when people get the alternative sort of politician they ask for but may not actually want.

The critics of my decision not to join the merged party have always had difficulty in squaring my alleged consuming ambition with my turning down the opportunity to lead the merged party. They find it very hard to understand that politics is not and never has been my whole life. I do not regard politics as a profession but as a transitory occupation. One can be voted in or out with no presumption that a political career is permanent. Perhaps this attitude was inculcated early because my seat was so marginal at first, or because my victory in 1966 so surprised me. Maybe medicine remained my first love. Whatever the reason, I view the prospect of no longer being in politics with equanimity.

Before I left with the family for a holiday in France I wrote an article for the *Sunday Times* in which I drew attention to the Campaign for Social Democracy which was being established under Rosie Barnes in Greenwich. Significantly I claimed only that it could have the power of influence and of generating ideas. I urged people, as they contemplated the folly and tragedy of the merger debate, to lift their sights and to remind themselves of Shelley's words in *Prometheus Unbound*, 'to hope till Hope creates from its own wreck the thing it contemplates.'

On the Monday, while staying with French friends in Normandy, I was rung up by Bob Maclennan. He was deeply upset by the press stories that Charles Kennedy was preparing to stand for the SDP leadership. I said Charles could only stand, under our rules, if he could get another MP to second him and, provided the four of us remained united, the leadership could, if we wanted, be left vacant. However, in subsequent telephone calls it became clear that Bob wanted to lead the negotiations for a merger. It came, therefore, as no surprise when it was eventually announced that he was going to stand as Leader of the Party on the nomination of Charles Kennedy. Rather him than me was my reaction. John Cartwright was abroad on holiday, but I eventually tracked him down. We agreed that we would consider whether he should stand for the leadership when we all returned from holiday. I told John he would have my total support if he wished to stand but he was reluctant, referring to it as Mickey Mouse politics.

Our holidays over, the five SDP MPs met in the House of Commons. John Cartwright announced that he would not contest the leadership. He, Rosie and I had agreed beforehand that we would let Bob and Charles negotiate for the majority without any hindrance from us. When the negotiations were completed we would continue with the Social Democratic Parliamentary Party. The House of Commons recognizes as a party any group of three or more MPs who accept the discipline of the whip. Whatever happened in the country, Parliament would be our base. We had made no decision at this stage about whether to continue with a party in the country. Our view was that it was not worth considering unless the Campaign for Social Democracy could rely on having at least 15,000, preferably 20,000, members by the time of any re-launch. We accepted Bob Maclennan as the SDP leader in the interim and both John and Rosie were content with the strategy of not attempting to block a merger. The Liberal and SDP negotiators would have no difficulty in agreeing a constitution, considerable difficulty in agreeing a name and, provided they kept any statement very general, no serious problems agreeing a policy statement.

The Portsmouth Conference followed soon afterwards. It was a sad affair. By agreement I spoke in the debate on the general election. The scene was described by Mark Lawson in *The Independent*:

> No doctor could close the gashes of the SDP but Dr Owen yesterday achieved something closer to faith healing than you could reasonably have expected.
>
> At 3.15 p.m., he sat slumped on the second row of the conference rostrum – the man now uniformly called tragic by ex-colleagues, a victim of political self-destruction. At 5.15 p.m., he was ducking under cheers, shutters clicking like crickets, even hands dabbing at eyes.
>
> What is to be made of these scenes? There was no hope of uniting the Party but a different speech might have ignited the rankle and back-stabbing.
>
> The best you could say by last night was that half the Party was at peace with itself and so was the other half. Dr Owen had managed a significant amendment to the emotions of the conference.

Its success was its unexpectedness. The media hordes had come to Portsmouth to watch the sensible party going barmy. In a tetchy conference, even conference chairperson Shirley Williams, was moved to snap that 'even a confused mind could grasp that point'. It looked petty and messy, the dregs of social democracy. Delegates bickered that general election defeats end in the generals blaming their unelected troops.

What could Dr Owen do? It was some minutes before he could speak 'This is one general who will not blame the poor bloody infantry,' he began.

He told them that, whatever happened now, the past six years had mattered; that social democracy was a child too young to die. Telling them what a swell party it had been touched something in both sects – whether sadness at their loss or a belief in his career to come.

A party alarmed by the prospect of a conference with no leader now had two on the platform. The real one had stood up and they returned the compliment. If he is headed for the wilderness he will hold there a searing memory of what could have been.

There were only two significant issues – whether to create a new party *incorporating* the SDP and the Liberal Party or to amicably give each member the choice to join the merged party or *continue as a member of the SDP*. The Council for Social Democracy voted by a majority to incorporate. But again there was a significant minority that wanted an amicable settlement. Incorporation in plain English meant that John, Rosie and I, despite having been elected as SDP MPs would be declared illegitimate in a few months' time. It was then claimed that we were no longer entitled even to be called Social Democrats, because the 'legitimate' Social Democrats had merged with the Liberal Party. The same would apply to elected councillors and to ordinary members of the Party. This was all justified on the basis of one member–one vote and of transforming the SDP constitution, by amendment, into the constitution of the merged party. As I had feared, we were like married couples who, having rejected voluntary conciliation and arbitration procedures, end up hating each other in the divorce courts and trying to squeeze every penny from the other. Charles Kennedy showed how far he had somersaulted by dismissing an amicable settlement as 'illogical nonsense', adding 'under our present political arithmetic, and system, the accommodation within British politics is already fully booked and there is no room at the inn for further parties.' It was not unreasonable to ask, why therefore had he joined the SDP in the first place?

The first Campaign for Social Democracy meeting, which as agreed was held as a conference fringe, was a runaway success, far exceeding our wildest expectations. The attendance figures were higher than for the conference itself. For the sceptics it was a triumphant demonstration that a very significant element in the SDP was not going to merge and dashed any hope that the initial 54 per cent would steadily increase to over 80 per cent in favour of a merger.

Once it was clear more than 20 per cent of the members did not want to merge, mutual respect should have dictated a negotiated settlement of the differences in the SDP. Once it was clear that it was more than 40 per cent, their survival instinct should have reversed engines and gone for an amicable settlement. Every single policy that the SDP had advocated in the industrial, social and legal field pointed to using conciliation, not constitutional, procedures. We were ending up practising first-past-the-post politics while still preaching the politics of proportional representation. Why? One significant reason is that too many of the SDP pro-merger leaders were never going to live with the consequences of their vindictiveness and would be leaving politics, going abroad or going to the House of Lords.

After my speech to the conference was over, in the privacy of my room my emotions got the better of me and for the first time I wept. The trigger was a chance remark recalling how Mary Lake with tears in her eyes, during our so-called victory celebration at Devonport, had said, 'How could they do this to us, David? How could Shirley, above everyone, do this?' Mary had been in the Labour Party with me, and had left with me. She had championed the SDP in the teeth of intense hostility from other members of the Labour Party in the early years on her council estate in St Budeaux. She had always adored Shirley Williams, in part because they were both Catholics, but in the main because she believed in her and thought Shirley shared her views about what the SDP was created to do. All she could repeat was 'Why are they taking our Party away from us?' Cynics may scoff, but these feelings are what drive a political party. Declaring oneself as a member of the SDP in a solid Labour ward in Devonport in the early years was not an easy thing to do. John Cartwright had experienced very much the same reaction among his party activists in Woolwich. They had put up with vilification and abuse for six years to find their own party about to be torn from them. It was significant that it was the three SDP MPs whose constituencies would normally be strong Labour constituencies who were the ones who wanted to stay with the SDP. We were not political innocents. We knew exactly what we were doing, what risks we were taking and why we were undertaking them. If the Labour Party were to become a social democratic party then my mission would be complete, but until it did I felt happier remaining in the House of Commons as a Social Democrat, for the next four years at least. I also felt it would give me as good, if not a better, chance of being re-elected a Member of Parliament for Devonport if I remained a Social Democrat. One change of party had been enough for me, I did not want to join a new party. As John Cartwright expressed it to the conference, 'No ballot gives anybody the right to tell me which political party I should be a member of. Those who take my view are not just numbers on a computer. We are flesh and blood human beings and our position will not be altered by threats to run candidates against us.'

There was one headline I could have done without. 'From one-man band to megalomaniac' was the title over Peter Jenkins's column in *The Independent*. Peter was a longstanding friend and we had managed that difficult relationship between journalist and politician remarkably well. His problem and mine was that his wife, Polly Toynbee, had become increasingly committed to the SDP. While Polly was writing, mainly but not exclusively, on women's issues in the *Guardian*, she was not encroaching on Peter's political turf. But more recently her involvement had become a complicating factor, for Polly, with her outstanding ability, had become an influential voice on the SDP National Committee. The problem came to a head with my invitation to her to serve on the Alliance Planning Group before and during the election. Now, her identification with the 'Vote for the SDP' campaign had meant that Peter was in danger of being sucked into and identified with a cause to which he was profoundly opposed.

> Dr Owen has no title to the SDP. The result of the ballot cannot reasonably be construed as a vote for 'amicable separation'. SDP members were asked whether they favoured the idea of merger or not and a majority said they did. They were not asked if they would support Dr Owen splitting the Party to set up one of his own.
>
> He hasn't a leg to stand on in his bunker. But there he is, surrounded by a last ditch entourage, inventing new schemes for the confounding of his enemies and moving imaginary armies on the map. The bitterness of defeat seems to have got the better of his judgement. The virtuoso one-man band performance which in the last Parliament made him the most impressive politician in the country after Margaret Thatcher has degenerated into a display of megalomania.
>
> It happens that I agree with Dr Owen about nuclear weapons and on other matters. I share his low opinion of the Liberal Party. But the politics of sectarian fantasy are even less attractive. There are – or rather, were – 23 per cent of the people who wish to vote for a third party. They should be allowed the best possible opportunity to do so.

Peter Jenkins had a powerful case and friendship should not have stopped him putting it. Yet in important respects he was wrong. Above all, it was not a 'third' party but an alliance of two parties for which that 23 per cent had voted. That is not a quibble or a pedantic point but a key fact. If David Steel had been leading the Liberal Party on its own in that election with no SDP I doubt if they would have polled as high as the 19 per cent they had achieved in February 1974. Polly knew better than most how little bitterness I felt at many going off to merge – resigned regret would be closer to my mood – and far from wanting to continue the SDP as a national party, I was one of its most reluctant recruits and even at this stage had not accepted it could be viable. As to Peter's motives, I knew he was finding that his journalistic access to leading figures in the pro- merger part of the SDP and in the Liberal Party was suffering. He was being seen,

quite wrongly, as a partisan figure. Although he wished me well personally, his practical judgement was that the course I had chosen could not
succeed. His own new paper, *The Independent*, was editorially against the
merger and sympathetic to my plight. I could well understand how Peter
began to feel fenced in and why he decided to establish his independence
both from Polly and me in such a dramatic way. It led to some stimulating encounters. On breakfast television Polly was asked how she could
associate with the man her husband thought was a megalomaniac. She
carried it off with a smile. I shrugged my shoulders and refused to be
drawn when asked by Peter's fellow journalists what I thought. Inwardly
I was of course hurt, but there has never been a friendship without pain. In
generous letters we both moved towards each other's position. Fortunately,
Polly was soon offered an excellent job as the social affairs editor for all
BBC News programmes. This meant she had to give up party politics
and made it much easier for both families to resume normal relations.

Although my decision not to join the new party was immutable, there
still remained the question as to what I should do. There were many who
argued that I should be an independent MP, a lone voice divorced from
party, an Enoch warning in the wilderness. But for everyone who argued
this course there were others warning against the danger of being without a
party, however small; that the House of Commons eats up individuals but
could not totally dismiss a party. I read everything I could about the life of
David Lloyd George following his electoral defeat in 1922. I learnt about
Winston Churchill's 'black dog' days when depression and despair blighted
his life, how Baldwin had been able to dismiss him even in 1937 as a
'beached whale stranded on the shore'. John Grigg, Lloyd George's
biographer, urged me to join and lead the merged party, and offered no
comfort from Lloyd George's history. At the same time Julian Amery
advised me of the vital need to secure funds and how Lloyd George's Fund
had been the *sine qua non* of his influence in the 1920s and 1930s and how
Joseph Chamberlain had needed the small party that he had.

Meanwhile all I could do was wait – wait until the negotiations were
over, wait and see whether we could build up the Campaign for Social
Democracy. We left Portsmouth bloodied but unbowed but the damaging
Owenite label had been firmly fixed around our neck by the BBC and
purportedly objective commentators, as well as by those who wished us
ill. It was only a matter of weeks before Bill Rodgers quit party politics
for a full-time job. Shirley Williams married an American professor, and
left Britain to live in the United States. She, however, generously invited
all sides of the merger dispute to her wedding and it was an enjoyable
occasion. But even Shirley's nearest and dearest were divided: her
mother's old secretary, an active SDP supporter, decided to stick with us
and refused to merge. It was like civil war – the merger divided families,
damaged friendships, all in support of the politics of winner takes all,
which we were supposed to despise.

The negotiations with the Liberals were thereafter masterminded by Bob Maclennan while I, together with the majority of the National Committee, deliberately stood aside. Although there were tensions between the five SDP MPs we managed to remain civil to each other and act as a Parliamentary Party. I took little interest in what was happening in the negotiations between the two parties and never believed they would be allowed to break down. Then we saw one sign that things were not going well: on 9 December John Grant, a former SDP MP, resigned from the negotiating team saying that it was proving to be a Liberal takeover. John had written a *Times* article in the form of an open letter to me before the Portsmouth Conference, urging me not to slam the door on a merger with the Liberals before the negotiations had even opened. Bob Maclennan had then persuaded John to serve on his negotiating team, wanting him to be a hardliner on some of the important policy questions. John, who had been a junior Minister in the Department of Employment under Callaghan, had gone back to the EETPU as Communications Officer after fighting for the SDP and losing his Islington seat in 1983. He was, like many trade unionists, never happier than when negotiating and extremely good at it. He had been to see me twice since Portsmouth and had actually paid a tribute to the toughness of Bob's negotiating stance on civil nuclear power and the nuclear deterrent. But gradually he had become more and more exasperated with the Liberals on the negotiating team. He has written that, from the start, Bob Maclennan's contempt for and distrust of David Steel were marked. Then over dinner John had told Bob Maclennan he had come to the conclusion that the merger should be rejected, and Bob admitted he too had come perilously close to walking out on the talks with the Liberals. He pledged to John he would not recommend a merger without a satisfactory declaration on the policies of the new party. But John decided he had had enough. It was clear to him that there was a basic incompatibility on policy.

In the New Year I wrote in the *Mail on Sunday* that 15,000 people had now signed up with the Campaign and were going to stick with the SDP and that I had no intention of heading for the political wilderness. The Campaign for Social Democracy had by then established a small office in Buckingham Gate and we were publishing policy pamphlets and holding policy conferences. John Cartwright, Rosie Barnes and I were beginning to think that perhaps it might be a strong enough base to support a national party. I still only thought of it acting as a guerrilla force, fighting by-elections only when it suited us and never routinely. The SDP was still registering in the few polls which tried to discover what levels of support we had, but the electorate was unsurprisingly confused so their preferences could not be relied upon.

On Tuesday 12 January the Liberal and Social Democratic negotiators met in Cowley Street to try and finalize their merger negotiations. In the early evening David Steel left the negotiators' meeting so that he could present the policy prospectus that he had agreed with Bob Maclennan to the Liberal Policy Committee. He found that not only were the passages on defence, nuclear power, VAT and tenants' rights unacceptable, but the whole flavour of the document was, as far as these Liberals were concerned, wrong. David Steel returned to Cowley Street to tell Bob Maclennan that the prospectus had to be changed, only to find the negotiators deadlocked over what to call the new party. The SDP wanted it to be called the Social and Liberal Democrats. The Liberals wanted 'Liberal and Social Democrats', and were not at all disconcerted when they were warned it would be known as LSD. Then, according to a senior Liberal, Bob Maclennan seemed to go completely off the rails, proclaiming, 'Right. You've got five minutes to change your mind on this or the merger is off.' The Liberals agreed to call themselves Social and Liberal Democrats but rejected the short title of Democrats. Three of their team then walked out. The constitutional questions were resolved, and the policy prospectus was amended throughout the night.

Next morning at 11 o'clock a press conference to launch the policy prospectus was due to start in the Jubilee Room. About eighty media representatives were present and the television cameras were all set to whirl. The prospectus had been distributed to the waiting journalists and the two leaders were expected any minute. As the delay lengthened people became more and more restless. Soon after 12 o'clock there was an announcement that David Steel first wanted to consider the prospectus with his parliamentary colleagues. It transpired that the Liberal MPs had revolted, demanding that the press launch be postponed. At 1 o'clock the Liberal MPs met with Bob Maclennan and Charles Kennedy. What happened then was described in a variety of different newspapers. Bob Maclennan was reported to have burst into tears during the angry and emotional meeting. Someone said the prospectus must have been drafted on another planet. By this time I had read a copy and was shocked by the recommendation to end universal child benefit. The extension of the base of VAT was by any standard a brave, if reckless, proposal which I doubt would have passed the SDP Policy Committee. It was no surprise that the Liberals were jibbing. What was incredible is that David Steel could have agreed to it in the first place. On nuclear defence I could recognize almost every word, for they had clearly based the statement on my own speeches, occasionally even employing my exact words. Whether David Steel had ever read the document was a matter of serious conjecture. Having once, during a by-election, watched spellbound as David Steel allowed a press release to be put out which he had never read, I could believe it. Nor had I forgotten how shocked Roger Carroll, the former SDP Communications Officer, had been during the 1987 Election when it emerged, halfway through, that David had not read all the Alliance manifesto. It was perfectly possible that he had done little more than give this policy prospectus a cursory glance. At one moment during the day some Liberals thought David Steel was about to resign. It was widely reported that he had rung his wife to say that he might well not be the leader by the end of the evening. A debacle was clearly unfolding with every hour. A reconvened press conference withdrew the policy prospectus and a new team were called in to recast the statement and to bring it back to the joint policy on which the two parties had fought the election.

We of the Campaign for Social Democracy could not resist the temptation to stir the pot a little, and, besides lampooning the proposals for their adverse effect on family poverty, we took the favourable political opportunity formally to establish the Social Democratic Parliamentary Party and remove the SDP whip from Bob Maclennan and Charles Kennedy, though it was deliberately done without any publicity. The embarrassment of Bob's leadership was mercifully over. It had been a trying time for everyone, most of all for him. It was very hard not to gloat and I was reminded of Willie Whitelaw when the 1979 Winter of Discontent was at its height saying 'I am told we should not gloat. Well, I tell you this, I am going to gloat. I am going to *gloat*. I am going to gloat like hell.' I had been told for months that I had been seen off by David Steel, that I had missed a historic opportunity to lead this grand new party and there they were, revealed to everyone as the 'shower'. I knew them to be incapable of fighting their way out of a paper bag. It was perfectly apparent that David Steel's leadership would not recover from this and he would have to step down before a new leader was chosen. One of his fellow MPs, Alex Carlile, was actually quoted as saying, 'People are looking for candidates now.' Des Wilson, who was on the new drafting committee, ever ready with a quote, buried the two leaders' policy prospectus by using John Cleese's dead parrot phrase in the Monty Python skit.

As the country laughed and some Liberals and Social Democrats wept, the new negotiating team cobbled up a policy statement for release late on Monday 18 January. The press were to have a field day comparing the two texts, for the policies were watered down on every point in the new version. Meanwhile John Grant telephoned my office that morning, asking to speak to me, and was told I was in Paris and not expected back until 6 o'clock in the evening. It later transpired that Bob Maclennan had rung John at 10 o'clock that morning to say that he thought that John had been right and that there should now be a 'No' vote against the merger. He said he was ready to recommend a 'No' vote if he got the right signals and some flexibility from me. Would I, Bob asked John, be prepared to call for a 'No' vote? John Grant told him that only a week before I had said that, in view of what had happened I thought a split in the SDP was now for the best. He discouraged Bob Maclennan from thinking that I would urge a 'No' vote because I simply wanted the merger to go ahead and had no intention of participating in a further ballot. Bob apparently wanted me to say that I sought a 'united party', which was by this stage totally impossible to conceive, and that I did not want to 'get rid' of anyone in the SDP. As far as the leadership was concerned, Bob said his role was only temporary and if there was a 'No' vote at the Council for Social Democracy meeting in Sheffield he would then step down. He clearly wanted a bargain and said that if I was not prepared to help then he would not call for a 'No' vote. John Grant described the conversation later as 'A curious combination of humility, contrition and bravado', with Bob even threatening that if I would not budge he would talk so tough on policy that the Liberal Assembly would reject the entire deal.

When I got back from Paris, I rang John Grant and he described the situation to me in almost the same words as he later used in an article in the *Sunday Times*, telling me what he thought might be negotiable with Bob. He deliberately did not say that he was passing on Bob's words, but only his interpretation of Bob's thoughts. John was a skilled negotiator and I got the message loud and clear. I readily gave the assurance that Bob Maclennan would himself be welcome as part of the SDP in Parliament because I genuinely liked him and certainly anyone who wanted to stay with a continuing SDP would be welcome too. But I could not turn round and say that amending the constitution with a 'Yes' or 'No' ballot was the proper way to proceed. The members should simply be invited to choose. I could not say that the process itself was legitimate and urge a 'No' vote in order to stop people who desperately wanted to merge from merging. However, we could, I suggested, work out a strategy together, and if Bob wanted to talk it all over I was very ready to do so. John said he would relay all this to Bob Maclennan who was due to meet the Liberals at 8.30 p.m. that evening. At 8.10 p.m. he rang John Grant who was able to tell him that not only I but also John Cartwright would welcome renewed co-operation and wanted no recrimination. He told him that we could not try to reunite the existing SDP by going back to the old backbiting National Committee with Shirley Williams in the chair. She was at that very moment in the process with Bill and Roy of actually endorsing the redrafted policy document. This was despite having publicly backed Bob Maclennan on the need for tough policy guarantees before agreeing to merge. It was clear she had no sticking point. By contrast Roy had never shown any interest in Bob Maclennan's negotiating stance. John Grant found Bob not interested in hearing about the nuances of the conversation, but keen only to find out whether I would see him, enquiring if I would be at home for the rest of the evening. John thought that Bob was tense and curiously abrupt. Then, three-quarters of an hour later, he saw the television news with a smiling Bob Maclennan emerging from Cowley Street describing the merger deal as 'magnificent' and announcing that he was off to see David

Owen to persuade him to join the new party and accept the merger. Not surprisingly, John Grant was stunned. The most charitable explanation of Bob Maclennan's conduct over those few days is that he was close to having a nervous breakdown following the rejection of his policy document, a document of which he had such high hopes and on which he had no doubt planned a genuine meeting with me. Indeed, with the earlier document, I would have been put seriously on the spot. There was no such difficulty with the new document which, unlike the old one, made no firm commitment on retaining the Trident missile system and was equivocal on the future of civil nuclear power. The net effect was of a watered down statement coming on top of a political debacle almost without parallel.

Meanwhile the Owen household was celebrating Lucy's ninth birthday. Soon after he had rung John Bob Maclennan had telephoned me and in a quick conversation asked if I would see him, urgently and soon. In view of my conversation with John I assumed he was coming to talk on the lines that had been explored already and as I had invited him to do through John. So, despite the birthday celebrations, I agreed to see him. Luckily I just happened to switch on the *Nine o'Clock News* and was staggered to see what John Grant had witnessed. This made me hopping mad. My first reaction was not to see him, to turn off our lights and let Bob, and the television cameras who would no doubt be accompanying him, knock on the door of an apparently empty house. But Debbie felt that it would be better to see him, however briefly. Soon there was a knock on the door, and there was Bob with Charles Kennedy. In icy tones I invited them both in and told them in no uncertain manner that their behaviour was disgraceful, that they had both known what my answer would be before they had come, and this was a set-up. I had thought we were going to have a serious conversation about how we could work together again and instead I was being used. The boys were listening at the air vents to try and hear what was happening down below and Lucy was listening halfway down the stairs, so her birthday was given extra spice. After five minutes I terminated the conversation and showed them the door before any television cameras arrived. I wanted no pictures with them outside or inside my house. Bob and Charles were left to talk to the press on our doorstep and I stayed inside. Given the lateness of the hour and the danger that the press might well misread what had happened, I had to spend the rest of the evening on the telephone to journalists explaining the exact nature of Bob's visit and why it reeked of insincerity. It was fortunate I did for some were tempted to write it up as a serious attempt to reach agreement, not the cheap publicity stunt that it was. Only when John Grant wrote his article in the *Sunday Times* later did people who had been critical of my brush-off know the truth. It was an unsavoury episode.

At the Liberals' Special Assembly in Blackpool on 23 January the fiasco of the merger negotiations was forgotten and, with 2,099 votes in favour and only 385 against, the merger was agreed. David Steel told them, 'The choice is a simple one – Yes for the chance to put Liberalism into practice or, No, for decades of division . . . I will be a Liberal to the day I die. I feel myself clothed in the aura of the word Liberal and all the associations which that has.' There was even some speculation that David Steel might be sufficiently rehabilitated to be able to stand as leader of the new party and he encouraged this by emphasizing that while there should be a contest he did not want a 'coronation'. Personally, I found it hard to believe that he could be regarded as a credible leader any longer and most people's money started moving towards Paddy Ashdown.

I repeatedly promised on television and to the press that I would not exploit the 'dead parrot' episode or use the disenchantment it had provoked to attempt to block the merger at our Sheffield Council for Social Democracy meeting due the following weekend. But my stance was extremely unpopular with some influential people in whom I trusted in the Campaign for Social Democracy. People like Edward Lyons had always felt we should stop the merger at all costs. Debbie and my mother also wanted to block the merger and when the ballot came, they still voted against as did some others close to me, like Maggie Smart. Some who had believed all along we should use the constitution to mobilize one-third of the CSD and block the merger started to organize a revolt. It was because I knew that some would vote 'no' that it was decided that I should not speak or even attend the debate at Sheffield. This would underline our recommendation to members not even to participate in a procedure which we saw as illegitimate.

Were we right? Undoubtedly we could have blocked the merger for we had the support of over a third, even if we did not have more than 50 per cent. But political parties are not legal bodies, they are unincorporated associations with no legal existence apart from the members who compose them. They are governed by rules or constitutions which are subject to the principles of natural justice. Political parties must therefore be guided first and foremost by common sense. When the SDP's constitution was ratified in 1982 and then later revised in 1985 it was never envisaged that it provided within it a mechanism for winding up the party. To use the procedure laid down for amending the SDP constitution was, in my judgement, wholly inappropriate as the means for creating a constitution for a new party. Throughout this period, those of us who were against merging still had a majority on the National Committee and it was our view that the procedures put forward by Shirley Williams as President to the Council for Social Democracy at Sheffield conformed neither to natural justice nor common sense. Hitherto the President's motion to the Council for Social Democracy had always been interpreted as the expression of the view of the majority on the National Committee, but suddenly

Shirley announced that the President's motion, a purely procedural device, had become the sole responsibility of the President. Her motion, according to the Standing Orders of the Council, ought to have been presented to the previous Council for prior debate and only then presented to the Council after six weeks' notice. Neither of these safeguards had been fulfilled. Some of my supporters argued that we should block the suspension of Standing Orders, but this would only have delayed the debate and exposed the SDP to even further public ridicule.

What was not sufficiently recognized was that those of us who were definitely continuing as the SDP had no interest in denigrating its good name. Even if we had blocked the amendment to the constitution we would then have been back with a fractious, deeply divided National Committee. The SDP would have looked absurd, however much we could have argued we were within our constitutional rights. Throughout the last few months I had been attacked by the pro-merger forces for ignoring the democratic institutions of the Party. Indeed, soon this attack became their primary battle cry. The truth is that we could, if we had wished, have used the democratic institutions of the Party to block their merger. Instead we gave them separation, but by then I fear there was very little amity around.

Our whole case against the way the merger was being conducted rested on the intrinsic right of an individual to choose which party he or she wished to be a member of. We would have been acting against our own principles if we had blocked the procedure, albeit we thought it illegitimate. In one important respect the pro-mergerites were forced to recognize that reality. Their legal advice was that no one's membership of the SDP could be automatically transferred to any new party even if it was called the Social and Liberal Democratic Party. So after the members' ballot to ratify the amended constitution, each member still had to be asked if they wished their membership to be transferred.

The Sheffield Conference began on a note of high farce. As in Portsmouth, the Campaign for Social Democracy had booked the conference hall for a rally. The booking had been made quite openly with SDP Headquarters in Cowley Street and confirmed in writing. Then on the Thursday evening the National Secretary wrote to the Campaign to cancel the booking. John Cartwright complained to Shirley Williams who, after some equivocation, defended the decision to cancel saying that the booking had been wrongly accepted by a Party official. Since we no longer always bothered to maintain a full presence on the National Committee and I was in New York addressing the Council on Foreign Relations, only due back in London early on Saturday morning, we deliberately had only a few representatives present when the National Committee met on the Friday. So, despite the fact that the matter was in the hands of lawyers, the Committee proceeded to endorse the ban. A High Court injunction had been sought by the Campaign for Social

Democracy, but when our QC arrived at the London home of Mr Justice Henry there was no sign of their QC. Shirley Williams had decided to give way and let the meeting go ahead. The Judge awarded us costs. The whole legal row erupted publicly when the BBC News showed Shirley Williams being corrected by Mike Thomas about the legal situation. How far we had come from 1981. Now Shirley, Bill and Roy were trying to stop John, Mike and me addressing a fringe meeting at a conference of the party we had all formed together.

Next day Shirley's opening speech, delivered while I was still travelling up from London Airport, was somewhat marred by her claim that Bob Maclennan's visit to my home had been 'spontaneous' and an attempt to 'reconcile' the SDP. She was apparently alternately booed and cheered when she went on to say 'David rejected it out of hand. Not for the first time in this Party's affairs I believe that Bob Maclennan acted with integrity and David Owen with impetuosity at a moment of crisis.' John Grant had warned Bob Maclennan and Shirley that if anyone continued to present Bob's visit to my home as a genuine olive branch, when they knew it was nothing of the sort, he would feel bound to reveal the truth. In the light of Shirley's speech he spelt it all out the following week in a long article for the *Sunday Times* entitled 'False Pretences', and concluded that it was now clear to him why Bob Maclennan's last telephone call to him that Monday evening had been so short and sharp. 'He knew that if he had told me I would have scuppered his visit to Limehouse and prevented the surrounding publicity which is what he really sought.'

At the campaign meeting of 1,000 people on the Saturday, claimed by John Cartwright as the meeting they could not stop, the mood was too euphoric for comfort and I warned 'We are embarked once again as in 1981 on a great adventure. It will require courage, nerve and commitment.' We still wanted to forge a workable coalition with the new merged party but we were not about to pack it in after only seven years. It was not a case of good riddance to the mergerites but

> we do say, in the certain knowledge that we have to know what we love and fight for, that it is far better now that the faint hearts leave and the strong hearts stay. There is only one majority we are deeply interested in, whether we can achieve a majority of the members of the SDP who of their own free will decide to remain members of the SDP.

Next day, despite the fact that we had urged all our supporters not to participate, some were so angry that they voted against merger. Fortunately this revolt was so small that it did not threaten the two-thirds majority necessary to carry the amended constitution. Few independent commentators doubted that we could have blocked it if we had wished to. It was now just a matter of time before the formal split took place. Paddy Ashdown was busy campaigning for the leadership throughout the two-day conference and, though the Social and Liberal Democrats formally came into existence in March under the interim dual leadership of David Steel and Bob Maclennan, a leadership election was fixed for the summer.

The SDP ballot result was announced on 2 March 1988. Only 18,722 members voted 'Yes', less than one-third of the SDP membership, which in July 1987 had been 58,357. The merger or bust campaign had alienated over two-thirds of the members. Despite our repeated urging of people not to vote 'No' in the ballot, some had done so. It was hard to be sure what was the exact split in the 1987 membership. It had certainly gone three ways with the largest number, slightly more than one-third, being so disenchanted with the whole post-election fracas that they no longer wished to be involved. A little less than one third had voted for the merger and are assumed to have joined the Social and Liberal Democrats. We were claiming at the time that the Campaign for Social Democracy had around 30,000 supporters and, allowing for 15 per cent slippage, that we could be sure of having 25,500 committed members. Some of those had joined without previously having been members of the SDP. Our claim was based on a computer printout which we invited the press to examine at our Headquarters. Adam Raphael of BBC *Newsnight*, perhaps the most sceptical, had taken up our invitation and checked out some of the names, apparently discovering nothing wrong.

We were to learn in May of next year that our figures had been wrong. We never had more than 18,000 supporters, let alone members. At my insistence we made a clean breast of this error as soon as it was discovered and admitted that our true membership by then was 11,000. Why this error was made we will never be totally sure. It was probably the result of an over-zealous member of our staff exaggerating the figures so as to persuade John Cartwright and me to abandon the Campaign for Social Democracy and re-establish the SDP. Everyone involved knew that we had made it crystal clear that without a certain minimum membership of the Campaign we could not relaunch the SDP. At the end of January, in an interview with the *Sunday Telegraph*, I was feeling confident that we would in a few months' time relaunch the party and I said 'I always thought 10,000 was a good campaign, 15,000 was halfway between a campaign and a party and 20,000 was a national party, although you have got to increase that.'

We now know that the continuing SDP never had a viable membership. Those who called us 'an Owenite rump' will feel their jibe was justified. Even so, they underestimated the extent to which the continuing SDP was composed of people of independent mind, determined to keep the SDP going and for whom my involvement was a bonus but not a prerequisite. One of the strengths of the SDP was its membership of political virgins, and it was these who were often the most adamant that the SDP should continue. Probably they were less aware of the difficulties of establishing a national party on a small membership. Their commitment to the SDP was uninhibited by the custom and practice of the old politics. Many of them, including my wife Debbie, thought John and, I were far too cautious in insisting that we would not relaunch without the certainty of 20,000 members and the prospect of more to come. Yet for all their enthusiasm, had we then known the true figures we would not have relaunched the SDP.

So, the merger went ahead and the SDP was re-established on 8 March 1988 as Britain's fourth national political party. Three of the five SDP MPs elected in 1987 continued to take the Party whip in the House of Commons, twenty-three out of forty SDP Peers continued to take the whip in the House of Lords with Baroness Stedman as their leader. John Cartwright was elected, unopposed, as the Party's President and the National Committee co-opted people like Marina Carr who had organized the grass roots campaign. It also appointed Fiona Wilson as the Party's National Secretary, who had previously been the Campaign organizer and before that a fundraiser for the SDP. We presented ourselves as a continuation of the SDP, retained the original constitution, filled the vacancies on the National Committee from the runners-up in previous elections and sought, in effect, to conduct ourselves as if there had been the amicable split we wanted. We fixed our annual conference for the middle of September in Torquay and set out to build up our membership. The previous trustees, Sir Leslie Murphy and David Sainsbury, stayed on and were joined by George Apter and Eric Woolfson. I warned the Party that

> there will be no quick fix to provide an instant solution to the years of hard grind that lie ahead. We have to painstakingly rebuild our credibility with the electorate and there is nothing flash about what lies in front of us. While the Tory lead remains very strong and until the aggro is knocked out of the merged party we are on a very bloody path.

On 15 March Nigel Lawson introduced his budget which cut higher rates from 60 to 40 per cent and took income tax down from 27p in the pound to 25. I called it the Blue Budget, 'rejoicing the heart of the Conservative voter, bringing the blues to many others'. I argued that if the £1.65 billion that the Chancellor had taken off from higher rate taxpayers had been clawed back by making National Insurance contributions progressive right up the scale, he would have been a truly radical Chancellor and taken this possibly one and only opportunity in this decade to integrate the tax and benefit system. But no one wanted to listen, least of all Nigel Lawson. He was on a high feeding inflation and Margaret Thatcher had caught his euphoria. Little did they realize that they were imperilling their whole anti-inflationary record.

On 8 May Brian Walden, acting on this occasion as a newspaper journalist rather than a TV commentator, interviewed Margaret Thatcher for the *Sunday Times*. Under the headline 'THATCHER WOOS OWEN BUT SNUBS TORY OLD GUARD' she revived the speculation that I would join the Conservatives. Historically the important part of the interview was that for the first time she gave a clear indication that she expected to be succeeded not by Geoffrey Howe, Nigel Lawson or Michael Heseltine but by the younger generation of Cabinet Ministers and there was a hint that John Major, then aged forty-five and Chief Secretary in the Treasury, was her favoured candidate. Of me, she said

> he has a very big decision to take, there are basically only two ways in which to run a country – one is the socialist way and one is the Conservative way – and I think he perhaps realizes that at the back of his mind. He has very little in common with socialism. The questions he asks are what I call 'splinter thoughts from the great stem of the oak tree' and he has to decide whether he is going to join the basic stem of the oak tree or not.

This public invitation to join the Conservatives forced me to reply that I would never become a Conservative:

> I would prefer to go out of politics than become a Tory ... I am in favour of coalition governments, I am willing to work with Labour or the Conservatives. I have never considered Margaret Thatcher to be a Tory, in some senses she's a populist, she is an instinctive politician, she is not afraid of change, she is not afraid to challenge vested interests and doesn't mind if they are Tory interests – this is where she has an appeal. You cannot deny her political acumen and skills. I am as different as chalk from cheese in other respects, but you don't have to rubbish everything she thinks or does.

John Biffen said of her courtship that it could

> only downgrade the already threatened status of Sir Geoffrey Howe. Owen has a big personal following. He would expect to be a member of the Cabinet. This would be strongly contested and resented by many Conservatives. He would be a cuckoo in the nest. He's more adept at busting things up than in creating them. A large number of Tories feel all the enthusiasm for him that their forebears thought about Lloyd George.

It was obvious that the Social and Liberal Democrats would have to choose a new leader when a poll of 800 SLD Councillors showed that 57 per cent supported Paddy Ashdown with only 15 per cent behind David Steel. Paddy Ashdown's chief rival was Alan Beith. When the election result was announced at the end of July, Ashdown had won easily. But before this a by-election was pending in Kensington following the death of Sir Brandon Rhys-Williams in early May. A MORI poll in early June showed the Conservatives on 44 per cent, Labour 40 per cent, the Social and Liberal Democrats on 7 per cent and what the press insisted on calling Dr David Owen's SDP on 6 per cent. Kensington was exactly the sort of seat Labour had to win if they were to have a hope of power at the next election. It was also a contest which many people in the SDP felt that we could not duck. I was very keen to put forward Roy Evans if we fought. He was an outstanding member of the National Committee, a former Conservative and active in the National Union of Students, he was black and aged thirty-three. He would have been an excellent candidate for that by-election. Unfortunately the extremely small local party voted for John Martin, one of their own local members. Though the National Committee had the power to choose a candidate for a by-election, we had never used it and, given the circumstances of our re-establishment, it would have been unwise to override the local choice.

I had barely known John Martin before but he turned out to be a most tiresome person. He was obsessed about many things, not least that the SDP should practise what he described as 'niche politics'. Unfortunately the niche he chose for himself, and by association the SDP, was the Notting Hill Carnival. There had been some unpleasant incidents sur-rounding the Carnival and there was a case for taking measures to prevent such incidents recurring, but this was hardly the basis for a by-election campaign. At one stage a group of SDP students protested to me that the tone of our campaign was damaging all the Party had achieved in establishing a high reputation for promoting good race relations. We were in danger of playing on the edge of a volcano and I made it clear that I wanted less on the Carnival and more on housing.

I was determined the SDP should avoid the example of Mosley who had left the Labour Party on the issue of unemployment to lead a new party and had then moved into the populist undergrowth of politics, inciting his black shirts in the East End against Jewish immigrants and ending up as a fascist. I had not fought against racism all my political life and spent two-and-a-half years having myself and my family subjected to racist filth when Foreign Secretary to allow any taint of racism attach to the SDP. A few years earlier Hugo Young had written an article in the *Sunday Times* which had deeply upset me by the mere fact that he had linked my name with Mosley. A mutual friend, unprompted by me, had told him that it still rankled and he kindly wrote to say that he was sorry and dismayed to find that it had been wounding to me. He had not meant there to be any remote comparison between us on any of the matters Mosley was most obviously remembered for. It was yet another example of how politicians and journalists interact. But it also showed the danger of labelling, for the *New Socialist* had adduced Hugo Young's article and actually had a cover entitled 'The New Mosley?' I was not, in our first by-election, going to risk that offensive label sticking.

We managed to put in a reasonable effort in Kensington but we suffered from a shortage of canvassers and it was a struggle to match the effort put in by the Social and Liberal Democrats. Their candidate, William Goodhart QC, had previously fought the seat for the SDP in 1987 and had been a fellow member, with John Martin, of the SDP area party. The Conservatives just scraped home with a much reduced majority of only 815 votes. We managed to save our deposit with 1,190 votes and the Social and Liberal Democrats came a poor third with 2,546 votes. Even the combined SLD-SDP vote at 16 per cent failed to match the 17 per cent William Goodhart had obtained for the Alliance in the 1987 election and few doubted that if the Alliance had still been in operation we would have polled substantially more than that although probably still coming third. All the signs were that we were now locked in an internecine war with the Social and Liberal Democrats. They for their part were about to embark on a dispute about their name with a strong groundswell for 'Liberal Democrats'. It was only a matter of time before they were Liberals once more. They were nevertheless doing quite well in local government and many former SDP councillors had joined them.

In July, Pan published my book, *Our NHS*, simultaneously in hardback and paperback. I had started it as a form of therapy after the Portsmouth conference. It had meant revisiting many parts of the National Health Service and I had been staggered at the changes over the twelve years since I had been Minister of Health. *Our NHS* gave me the opportunity not only to promote the ethical basis of the National Health Service but also to spell out a model for an internal market which the SDP had been advocating, in the teeth of opposition from the Conservative Government, since 1985. Trevor Clay, the widely respected General Secretary of the Royal College of Nursing, in a review in *Nursing Times* said:

> Many of the internal market measures which are described in his book I would support wholeheartedly. But I would support them because they are administrative reforms which should have happened ten years ago and could be done without any great threat to the principles of the Health Service but with a great increase in the happiness of people currently stuck on waiting lists.

The book was written in an attempt to influence Margaret Thatcher's review of the NHS and it spelt out in detail how one could introduce a hypothecated health tax and abolish the national insurance contribution. The tragedy for those of us who believe that establishing cost yardsticks and market disciplines internally within the NHS will bring substantial benefits over time, is that the Government proposals announced in January 1989 commercialized the whole NHS. They damagingly divided the hospital from the community services, reversing the integration of health care that had been progressively introduced by successive Health Ministers since Iain Macleod. In Prime Minister's Questions on the day the Government's reforms were announced, I challenged Margaret

Thatcher. In an almost Freudian revelation, she professed great surprise that I should be opposed to those who could afford private care doing so, thereby relieving NHS waiting lists. It was a dramatic demonstration of her wish to move towards a two-tier health service. The very concept of a health service designed for everyone's use was an intellectual anathema to her. She had not been able to win agreement for tax exemption from private health insurance for everyone because it had been opposed by every single Minister involved in the Review and particularly strongly by the Treasury. But she had cracked the principle by forcing a concession through for old age pensioners. Few people doubted that, given the opportunity, Margaret Thatcher would have extended the tax concession to everyone. Fortunately, John Major is more likely to be guided by the example of Iain Macleod on the NHS. The old demand of those in the Conservative Party opposed to the very principles of the NHS that private health should be encouraged by tax concessions, had been rejected by every Conservative Prime Minister until Margaret Thatcher. The best way for John Major to demonstrate that he has no intention of undermining the NHS by building up private health insurance is to say that this tax concession will not be widened. An internal market in the NHS could have carried broad-based support. Instead it has been blighted from the start, for the suspicion that it is a mechanism for destroying the NHS will last for years. In the hands of politicians who believe in the NHS, whether Conservative or Labour, an internal market can still become the best mechanism for reviving the NHS, but the way this internal market is designed and has been implemented has put off some of us who support and indeed first championed the concept.

In early September 1988 I went to Moscow to attend a conference on Human Rights organized in association with the United Nations. It was a good opportunity to reassess Gorbachev's regime and I spoke to many people. I had never been convinced that he was ready to challenge the Leninist tradition of authoritarianism. He wanted a managed democracy and a managed economy. There were, however, signs that perestroika and glasnost in his hands were leading to an ever greater opening up of the USSR. But that individual republics like Lithuania, Latvia and Estonia were going to have to struggle for their independence and talk of self-determination was for the UN not for the USSR. In a restaurant, the man at the next table was the nuclear physicist and Nobel Peace Prize winner Andrei Sakharov. We were introduced, and he thanked me for making representations on his behalf to Gromyko. It was a reminder of the changes, but in a short conversation he was scathingly critical of Gorbachev at the very time he was being lauded by the West.

The SDP Conference in Torquay was a nerve-racking business. None of us really knew how many people would turn up. A little empty on Saturday, it filled up by Sunday and we were able to breathe more easily.

The most important debate was that on the social market economy. It was based on a Green Paper whose principal author was Professor Robert Skidelsky, the definitive biographer of Keynes, and a driving force in making the SDP rethink its economic policy from that adopted in the 1983 General Election. We were at long last ready to abandon the ill-fated inflation tax which had hung round our necks like an albatross since 1982. Our social market policy was based on five elements: support for the market as the main system for supplying goods and services; insuring the market's social accountability; recognizing the limits of the market; compensating for market failure, and securing acceptable social conditions for buying and selling in the markets. The conference was a success. We had a good cricket match and morale was high, but we were a much smaller party and I could not be sure we could survive.

The Independent, in an editorial headlined 'The end of a beginning', said:

> The activists who persuaded David Owen that a continuing SDP was viable can therefore regard the present meeting in Torquay as a triumph. Despite all the doubts, their party still exists, still able to hold debates. Indeed its members can speak their minds with greater freedom now that they do not have to worry about exposing to the world their differences of opinion with the Liberals. It is not clear, however, what sort of victory the Torquay conference will represent in a longer perspective: whether a brave rearguard action on a road leading nowhere or the small beginnings of great things.
>
> The remaining activists have shown that they are extraordinarily determined. They have demonstrated, too, that they are far from being blind followers of Dr Owen: they are quite capable of rejecting proposals of which he approves. But though they declare that they themselves would be 'disenfranchised' if their party did not exist, they have yet to bring many voters to share that view.

The conference could not have been expected to have matched the 1985 SDP Torquay Conference but there was the same spirit there which surprised and delighted me. The *Sunday Telegraph* headline summed it up, 'Plenty of yeast, but where is the SDP loaf?', saying that members arrived in Torquay rather 'in the spirit of the man who has survived being blown up in an explosion, but who is not sure whether he still has a full complement of limbs.' Peter Jenkins in *The Independent*, still not reconciled to the SDP's survival, nevertheless said I had made the speech of my political lifetime.

> The berries and locusts of the wilderness seem to have put fire into his belly. With nothing any more to lose, he did what a politician rarely does – he spoke all of his mind ... Dr Owen envisaged the possibility of Labour returning to the social democratic fold. Who shall know whether he seriously believes this is likely or says it simply in order, as one Labour leader said, to 'shaft Ashdown'?

Yet after analysing what I had said he concluded 'the wilderness is the natural habitat of the prophet'.

For the first time I had begun to sense that Labour was pulling back from its extremist years. Paddy Ashdown's belief that he could replace Labour as the main party in opposition was coming too late. In an interview with John Carvel of the *Guardian*, having first disposed of the fantasy that I was about to become a member of the Tory Party, I said

> there is no question that I am wistful about Labour. If one of the penalties of the last year is that we can't make it, but that we make Labour a decent Government again, that is not the end of the world. You needn't go to your grave regretting that. Whether or not I personally join the Labour Party is immaterial.

But when asked, 'But not inconceivable?' I replied,

> No, it is not inconceivable, it is the only other party I'd join . . . I have said I would never join the Tory Party, never. It is quite deliberate that I have not used the word never about the Labour Party. Whether I would or not is a different question. But I could envisage circumstances when there were again two social democratic parties, the SDP and the Labour Party . . . At that juncture the SDP would have to consider what it wanted to do.

The reason I sensed a shift in the Labour Party's policy stance was that Jacques Delors, the former French Socialist Minister of Finance and now President of the Commission, had given a fraternal address to the TUC Conference where his reception had been so warm and his exposition about the Social Charter so well received that it was apparent that Labour was in the process of abandoning its hostility to membership of the European Community. That process continued at the Labour Party Conference with a series of policy papers, all moving closer to an acceptance of market economics. The old problem of the nuclear deterrent had not yet been resolved and Neil Kinnock's attempt to support unilateralism, bilateralism and multilateralism convinced no one, but it was nevertheless an indication that he personally was on the move, even though Ron Todd managed with the Transport and General Workers Union block vote to secure the passage of a hardline unilateralist resolution.

In November the Glasgow Govan by-election was held. After much debate, we decided not to field a candidate, though many of the Scottish SDP activists were upset by this decision. They felt we left ourselves open to the charge that we were not a national Party, but I saw no joy for the SDP in using precious resources to fight a campaign where, especially because of the SNP, we were certain to be seen as also-rans. It would not do our chances of survival any good if we lost our deposit. I was very attracted to the argument that the SDP should act as a guerrilla force, choosing to fight those by-elections which were demographically more favourable to us. This made a lot of sense even if it exposed us to the charge that as a guerrilla force we were merely a destructive element. But I did not really carry the new SDP National Committee on this; the zealots wanted to fight everywhere and it was this which eventually proved our undoing.

In December, there was another by-election, this time in Epping Forest. Michael Pettman, a solicitor, had fought the seat for the SDP in the general election and was a local councillor. He had also been against the merger. If we felt we should fight, he was ready to put his name forward. Another by-election was also pending in Richmond, Yorkshire, for Leon Brittan, having been forced to resign over Westland, had accepted being a Vice-President and Commissioner in Brussels. I imagine that it was this post that I had been sounded out over much earlier. On being asked if I would be interested, I had given a clear no. Neither of us wished to live in Brussels and I could see no enjoyment in being a Commissioner. I disliked the Euro-federalist stance of Jacques Delors and I could not have stood up to him as was needed without the necessary base in either the Conservative or Labour Party. I sympathized with much of Margaret Thatcher's dislike of the push towards a United States of Europe but I did not wish to be dependent only on her patronage. The Richmond seat had been fought previously for the SDP by Mike Potter, a local farmer and county councillor. He too had refused to join the merger and was an engaging and charismatic figure. We wanted to reach an agreement with the Social and Liberal Democrats that they would fight Epping and we would fight Richmond, but they rejected any and all co-operation at national level, referring every issue down to their local associations. So we raised it locally with the SLD in Epping and in Richmond. Michael Pettman had good personal relations with the probable candidate but unfortunately no deal emerged from the discussions. We could not forgo two consecutive by-elections so we decided that Michael Pettman should stand for the SDP. Conservative, it was the fifteenth safest in the country and had a great history. There was a time when the words of the Member of Parliament for Epping resonated around the world. Winston Churchill first won the seat in 1924 standing as a Constitutionalist on his way back to the Conservative Party. He had a somewhat uneasy relationship with the constituency party, particularly over India and Munich, and in a speech on 14 March 1938 Churchill defended his right to speak unfettered by Party restrictions. I recalled his words in the by-election in order to remind people of the virtues of independence in Parliament.

> What is the use of sending members to Parliament to say popular things of the moment, and saying things merely to give satisfaction to the Government whips and by cheering loudly every Ministerial

platitude? What is the value of our parliamentary institutions, and how can our parliamentary doctrines survive if constituencies tried to return only tame, docile, and subservient members and tried to stamp out every form of independent judgement?

I warned, as I had done often before, how Margaret Thatcher's power had increased as the power of the Party whip grew, how patronage which had expanded grotesquely was used to put ever more subtle pressures on Members of Parliament. I warned too how the status of Members and of the House of Commons itself had been diminished because there was no credible official Opposition and because the opposition within the party was wet both in name and nature.

We had a small team but an excellent candidate and Chris Hopson, previously the agent in Bath at the 1987 Election, masterminded our campaign. The result was declared on Friday 16 December and had the Conservatives ahead on 13,183 but with their majority slashed from 17,009 to 4,504. The SLD candidate came a creditable second with 8,879, Labour third with 6,261 and Michael Pettman fourth with 4,077. Nobody had any doubt that if we or the Social and Liberal Democrats had stood down then the Conservatives would have been defeated. The SLD accused us of spoiling tactics but it was they who turned down the opportunity to win the seat. The *Daily Telegraph* in an editorial 'Epping message' said that the Conservatives had blundered in not moving the writ for the Richmond by-election at the same time as Epping and warned that Ministers were already saying privately that a defeat in Richmond would not surprise them. But defeat in Richmond was only possible if the SLD came to a prior agreement and admitted that the SDP had by far the better candidate in Richmond; popular locally and politically experienced. Sadly they believed that their highest priority was to snuff us out in a war of attrition. I had little doubt that in the end their superior numbers, particularly in local government, would prevail. The question I thought they would answer was at what price? How much damage could they do not just to the SDP's appeal but to the basic appeal of the Liberal Party?

A MORI poll in early January 1989 gave the Conservatives a 10 per cent lead over Labour. The poll showed for the first time that the SDP, on 7 per cent, was ahead of the 'Democrats', as they were then insisting on being called in polling questions, who were on 6 per cent. This was good for our morale but I believed that if the word Liberal had been used in the polling questions they would have been ahead of us by three or four percentage points. Whatever the case, our battle was looking increasingly like a battle of the mice. Interestingly Margaret Thatcher had a 40 per cent satisfaction rating, seven points more than the Government at that stage. My personal rating had not been extinguished and, though she was more popular than me by nineteen points, she was twenty-one points more popular than Neil Kinnock and 22 points more popular than Paddy Ashdown.

The Independent was saying that this was the year in which Neil Kinnock must finally take his party by the scruff of the neck to retrieve its fortunes as well as his own. I felt that 1989 was going to be the critical year – if Labour really reformed itself then we in the continuing SDP would be far harder hit than the SLD. All the signs were that the SLD would change their name again and restore the word Liberal. They had not called themselves Liberal Democrats from the start, because of Shirley Williams. She had done them a disservice by winning that argument. Although she and Paddy Ashdown wanted the Party to be seen as a new one, it was obvious by then that it was the Liberal Party in all but name with an SDP input and a new Liberal Leader. The by-elections were showing that the old Liberal vote was still there. The SDP was also finding that it could not muster anywhere near the same number of troops on the ground as the SLD. In the last few days of the Epping campaign the SLD were able, through sheer numbers, to shift voters towards them. According to our membership we ought to have been able to rely on more supporters attending. But of course we were to discover a few months later why we were not attracting as much help as we had hoped. Our membership figures had been greatly exaggerated.

At the end of January Paddy Ashdown, under pressure from David Alton and David Steel, made a rather confused speech about electoral pacts and said that if Labour's interest in proportional representation meant that the realignment of British politics was on its way then he had been mistaken in slamming the door so firmly. He also said that he had never meant what he had said in earlier speeches about destroying Labour in one go. Yet, despite this, and all other efforts, the SLD still refused to stand down in Richmond in the name of realignment, so battle commenced both there and in Pontypridd, where we had again failed to reach an agreement.

Our Richmond candidate, Mike Potter, fought a splendid campaign. Popular in the SDP, he attracted people from all over the country to help. For the first time since Rosie Barnes' victory in Greenwich, we were mounting a really effective by-election campaign with Chris Hopson's team having moved straight up from Epping with only a short break for Christmas. Though our resources were stretched, morale was high. Unfortunately there were no constituency polls until the last week of the campaign. On Tuesday 21 February a poll for Tyne Tees Television showed the Tory vote slashed, down to 40 per cent, with the SLD on 19.5 per cent and the SDP 19 per cent. Since in the last election the Liberal standing for the Alliance had polled 27 per cent it was already clear that our combined total was far greater, but it was not clear the way the voters would go. On Wednesday 22 February, the day before the vote, a poll for Yorkshire Television showed Mike Potter four points ahead of Barbara Pearce, the SLD candidate. We did our best to publicize this in a last-minute leaflet and it was carried by Yorkshire

Television and the BBC. Unfortunately Tyne Tees ignored it despite the fact that they knew the findings. Next day when the ballot boxes were opened we did not appear to have done as well in the Tyne Tees area as in the Yorkshire TV area. We were agonizingly close but just unable to get our last minute bandwagon rolling quickly enough. As it was, William Hague polled 19,543, Mike Potter came second with 16,909 votes and Barbara Pearce third with 11,589. Labour, who lost their deposit, were fourth with 2,591 votes. The 24 per cent drop in the Conservative vote was their worst performance since Margaret Thatcher became Prime Minister. They had not been helped by the furore over eggs and their being in some people's view a health hazard.

No one doubted that if the old Alliance had been fighting we would have had an easy victory to match the Liberals in Orpington or the SDP in Crosby. It was widely reported as a triumph for the SDP but also an example of the folly of our fighting each other. The *Evening Standard* headline was 'THE REAL WINNER – OWEN IS SO CLOSE TO BY-ELECTION SENSATION', the *Daily Express* 'DAVID OWEN RIDES AGAIN – ASHDOWN WOOS FLYING DOCTOR AS HE SHOCKS TORIES'. Some in the SDP believe that if we had won our survival would have been assured. I am not convinced. As at Warrington, the media awarded us a moral victory but there was no surge in applications for membership. And the underlying message lay in the Pontypridd result that same day: in many places both parties were now of marginal significance, the SLD candidate having polled 3.9 per cent and the SDP candidate 3.1 per cent of the votes. The seat was won by Labour despite the surge in support for Plaid Cymru.

The Richmond result added greatly to the deep feeling of betrayal among many voters who had voted Alliance in 1987. I believe it was the last opportunity for those of us who had once worked in alliance to hold these votes and to rebuild the 30 per cent and more levels of public support we had kept from 1981–87. I hoped that we would be able quietly to reach some form of understanding with the SLD. David Alton, the SLD MP who had developed into the most far-sighted and conciliatory of all the SLD MPs, and John Cartwright, the SDP's President, publicly renewed their call for an electoral pact, saying 'a pointless competition for second and third places is about as rational and cost effective as subscribing to Conservative Party funds'. But Paddy Ashdown simply issued an immediate appeal for me to meet to discuss how the union of a single party could be achieved. Certainly I was ready to meet but obviously not on that basis. A *Times* editorial, 'A shock for the Centre', said

Dr Owen's original refusal to merge with the Liberals in the shot-gun marriage engineered by Mr Steel was justified. Mr Steel's way of trying to balance the sixties' social democratic reflexes with the anarchic impulses of the old Liberal Left would have undermined Dr Owen's realistic post-Thatcherite attitudes.

But much has since changed. Mr Steel has gone, the influx of Social Democrats into the SLD has altered its balance and the old Liberal Left has gone quiet. To the extent that Mr Ashdown has anything clear to say about policies, it has an Owenite tinge.

Indeed, part of his resistance to any kind of talking with Dr Owen may arise from a fear that the SDP Leader would outshine him in any new association. That, however, is no longer an affordable luxury.

With the Sunday press all urging some accommodation between the two parties, Paddy Ashdown then turned turtle and announced, without any consultation, a scheme for by-elections with a joint open selection of a candidate if the parties agreed locally. It was very difficult to understand what he was up to. In September 1988 he said 'no one is going to play footsie with David Owen'; in his New Year message to his Party, he had said 'our success will come by our own efforts, not by seeking accommodation with others'; in late January 1989 he said 'I believe pacts won't work. I underline that seventeen times.' Now he was making what most independent commentators thought was a clumsy attempt to put me in an awkward position so that I could be blamed for any lack of co-operation.

In retrospect I think I should have refused to be drawn publicly on the detail and just announced that we were arranging to meet. But I doubt whether we would have made progress. We were feeling fairly bullish after Richmond with a false sense of optimism, while the Liberal Democrats were bruised and suspicious and facing a Federal Conference on 4 March in Bournemouth. Nevertheless David Sainsbury did arrange for a private dinner at his house with Paddy Ashdown and myself on 16 March. I hoped that we might be able to reach some understanding over the forthcoming Welsh by-election and the Euro-elections, but although it was a pleasant occasion there was no sign that Paddy Ashdown was personally ready to advocate any understanding over the Euro-elections. He took refuge in saying he would support any local arrangements but I was left with the impression that he would not encourage them. A serious attempt was, however, under way to reach an agreement over who should fight the Vale of Glamorgan by-election. Following the bad result in Pontypridd, the SLD member for Brecon and Radnor, Richard Livesey, appeared genuinely to want to reach some form of understanding with Geoff Drake, the key SDP figure in Wales. Unfortunately it came to nothing and, rightly or wrongly, we felt a local agreement was being undermined by the Liberal Democrats nationally. Although it was becoming painfully apparent that the SDP could not go on sustaining fights in every by-election, if we did not stand we left the field open to the SLD and gave the impression that we were incapable of fighting as a national Party. It gave more credence to the 'Owenite rump' label that was so disparagingly fixed on us by some of the commentators. When we eventually fought the by-election the level of activity in the Vale of Glamorgan was very poor in comparison to the SLD and it was left to a few of our people to work their hearts out. In the Council elections due on 4 May, the same day as the Glamorgan by-election, the Green Party was fielding nearly double the number of candidates that we were and the SLD were fielding many more. This again emphasized how weak we were becoming on the ground.

In early April I flew to Karachi for a seminar to honour the memory of the former Prime Minister of Pakistan, Zulfiqar Ali Bhutto. It had been planned for a long time and none of us could have anticipated that his daughter Benazir would be the elected Prime Minister when it was held. There was I, a former British Foreign Secretary, who had tried to prevent Bhutto's death and Sardar Swaran Singh, a former Indian Foreign Minister, who had often negotiated on India-Pakistan problems with Mr Bhutto, speaking in the presence of his daughter as Prime Minister. Benazir's contribution to building a democracy in Pakistan over the next few years was formidable.

When I became Foreign Secretary Bhutto was the democratically elected leader of Pakistan. A general election was held on 7 March 1977, the first election to be called by a popularly elected government. But although Bhutto won there were strong allegations of ballot rigging and considerable division within the country. It culminated in a military coup on 5 July 1977 and Bhutto's imprisonment.

A human rights task that I had undertaken as Foreign Secretary was to try and persuade General Zia to release Bhutto and allow free elections. I received a letter from a Dr Niazi, Bhutto's personal dentist, describing the appallingly squalid conditions in which Bhutto was being held. The Foreign Office had wisely ensured that I was shown the letter because it was so movingly written. It stimulated me to do everything in my power to get Bhutto out. Dr Niazi was himself put in prison for his outspokenness and it was Niazi's daughter who brought messages to and from the prison between Mr Bhutto and Benazir. In desperation towards the end Jim Callaghan wrote to General Zia reminding him of the old soldier's saying, 'The grass grows swiftly over a battlefield but never over a scaffold.' Zia did not heed it and Bhutto was hanged.

So a scaffold hung hauntingly over our seminar; as stark, as sombre as when it was first erected. We hoped the seminar would be part of the process of healing, a kind of catharsis. Whatever the arguments about Bhutto's political legacy, and he was undoubtedly a controversial partisan leader, his overall record was one which deserved respect, and respect is the first step in reconciliation.

After the seminar we flew out to the Bhutto family home in the rural part of Sind Province and, driving from the airport along narrow dusty roads, I saw people coming from all parts of Pakistan to mark the tenth anniversary of Bhutto's death and to visit the family mausoleum. Local buses were overflowing, peasants in their thousands could be seen walking across the fields, some of them having made a four or five day journey just to be there. It was a massive crowd. Benazir arrived by helicopter to address the large rally. Her car was mobbed and I feared for her life as the security completely broke down. One hears the expression 'being carried off one's feet', and this is literally what happened as I was squeezed tight by the vast crowd. Everyone seemed delighted to see a European face and I was eventually set down near the dais where I sat on the floor listening to Benazir deliver an impassioned speech. Eventually we went back to the family house for lunch, after which I flew back with Benazir in her plane to Karachi.

Throughout the 1980s I had met Benazir at regular intervals and she had always come with a quietly spoken older man. I never realized he was the same Dr Niazi who had written to me, until he reminded me of his letter and my reply when he and his attractive daughter welcomed me on my arrival in Karachi. It was a moving visit to a country which had fascinated me in 1959 as a student. Its hold on democracy at the start of the 1990s remains tenuous and any government will need support and understanding if the military are to be held off from another coup.

Back in London I attended the speech delivered in the Guildhall by Mikhail Gorbachev before flying to Stockholm for the final meeting of the Palme Commission. Once again I was struck by how dramatic the changes had been since we started our work in 1980; now Eastern Europe was on the threshold of freedom. It was both a sad and happy occasion. For nine years the members of this Commission had worked together with remarkable harmony on disarmament and security issues. Many lasting friendships were made and in particular I was pleased to have the opportunity to work once more alongside Cyrus Vance. Olusegun Obasanjo from Nigeria was also a member of the Commission together with Gro Harlem Brundtland, the Prime Minister of Norway, Giorgi Arbatov of the Soviet Union and Sonny Ramphal, then the Commonwealth Secretary-General. Sonny chaired the final meeting in Stockholm and we issued our final report, *A World at Peace*.

When I look back at our despairing mood, and the fear that there would be no dialogue between President Reagan and President Brezhnev in the early 1980s, and contrast it with the relationship just starting between President Bush and President Gorbachev it is as if we were in a different age. The INF Treaty was not only signed and ratified but we were now actually witnessing the removal and destruction of Soviet SS-20 missiles and American cruise missiles. At long last it looked as if the United Nations might develop some of the 'sinews of power' that Winston Churchill had called for in his 1947 Fulton speech, best known for its description of the Iron Curtain that had fallen between East and West. Our final report focused on reform of the United Nations and widened our original concept to achieve common security through economic development, social justice and protection of the planet. Our detailed proposals for the UN Secretariat had the enhanced authority of the involvement of Brian Urquhart, the most distinguished of all UN peacekeepers, who had become a member of our Commission. The environmental aspects of our Report were also helped by the contribution of Gro Harlem Brundtland who, while being a member of the Palme Commission, was also Chairman of the Independent Commission on Environmental Issues.

I found it fascinating to watch the Soviet representative, Giorgi Arbatov, through the nine years. He was the Director of the Academy of Sciences of the USSR, essentially a policy analyst specializing in the United States. He skilfully retained the ear of successive Soviet Presidents, including Brezhnev and Andropov, though he looked as if he was going out of favour under Andropov's leadership. He was back under Chernenko and for a time surprisingly influential with Gorbachev, though now he appears as a critic and it would not surprise me to find him advising Yeltsin. Despite Gromyko's promise that he would be free to comment as an individual, his contributions to the Commission were at first pretty negative. But with the change of atmosphere in Moscow he became far more positive and by the end was making a very constructive contribution on how to make the UN more effective.

While the battle of the mice was going on between us and the Liberal Democrats, the Labour Party was making massive strides towards the Centre. A wholesale revisionist review had produced a set of papers which were described by *The Independent* – in my judgement accurately – as potentially as important as the decision taken by the German Social Democratic Party at Bad Godesberg some thirty years earlier to abandon its Marxist heritage. The review not only recommended abandoning unilateral nuclear disarmament, but came out in favour of retaining three Trident submarines. The papers also advocated continued membership of the European Community. There was market socialism too and a recommendation for entry into the Exchange Rate Mechanism of the EMS. Within the year John Smith, their Shadow Chancellor, had won acceptance for ERM as a discipline against inflation.

My mood, like that of John Cartwright at this moment, was near to despair with the Liberal Democrats and genuine pleasure that at long last the Labour Party for which we both, in our different ways, still had an underlying affection, was adopting the very policies which we had left the Labour Party in order to uphold. On the day of the local council elections and the Vale of Glamorgan by-election, John Cartwright was told by one of our employees that our membership figures had been deliberately exaggerated and that we had no more than 11,000 members. As the council election results came in it was apparent to everyone that the SDP was virtually non-existent at local council level. This mattered to John Cartwright, for it was where he had started in politics. In the Vale of Glamorgan by-election Labour overturned a Tory majority with the SLD candidate coming third but with only 4.2 per cent of the vote; the SDP came fourth after Plaid Cymru with 2.3 per cent. Speaking in the early hours of Friday morning on the BBC *Election Special* television programme John said, 'If Labour becomes truly a social democratic party, there would be no point in us continuing as a separate party.' It was an understandable verbal gaffe from a normally very sure-footed politician. I watched as he said it and winced.

It was fortunately too late for Friday newspapers to pick up on what John Cartwright had said and anyhow they had more important results to focus on. But it was picked up in Saturday's *Sun* and then seized on by the Radio 4 *Today* programme on the Saturday morning. I was at Ditchley Park chairing a conference on the Middle East. I was told the BBC wanted me to ring. Rather than go down to the basement and ring back on a pay telephone I preferred the warmth of a four poster bed with Debbie. On such human frailties do bigger events hang. I might have been able to defuse the story then and there, but by unwisely refusing to comment I allowed it to gather momentum. It was fuelled in the Sunday papers by some foolish comments I had made, saying that I would have no difficulty serving in a coalition government under Neil Kinnock and saw a role for the SDP in preventing a Labour-dominated coalition government from going back on the new realism set out in Labour's policy review. In many ways neither John nor I were saying anything different from what we had always said about the SDP being ready to work in coalition with other parties. What was new was John raising the question mark about the SDP's existence and the warmth of my welcome to Labour's policy changes. The press had got so used to hearing me attacking Labour that it was news to have me praising them.

The whole story was thus built up out of all proportion. This in turn provoked criticism from SDP members and fuelled the story further. On Monday *The Independent* ran a piece 'Supporters attack Owen for overtures to Labour'. It was being said that our remarks had had a destabilizing effect on the Party. While this was true, what our critics did not know was that the Party was already facing a membership crisis.

Over the next few weeks I had extensive discussions with the Trustees of the Party about whether the SDP could survive. David Sainsbury and I had always feared this point might come and had promised ourselves that we would not shirk from giving up our membership of the Party rather than let its existence drag on when it was no longer viable. David had made that clear publicly at our Portsmouth Conference in 1987. But a democratic party cannot just be folded from the top. We had already lived through the experience of others attempting to close us down and we could not do the same ourselves. I did believe that we were no longer viable and I was determined that David Sainsbury should be released from feeling any financial commitment to the Party and in particular from any commitment to help finance the elections for the European Parliament that were due in June. We had managed to persuade seventy-eight candidates to stand but many of them had no funds and precious few workers and were virtually paper candidates. We had promised therefore to finance an election address for all of them. This meant an outlay of nearly £150,000, money which in our now straitened circumstances could be far better spent. I had also been tipped off about polling evidence showing a surge in support for the Greens at the expense of the SLD and the SDP. I therefore proposed to David Sainsbury that we would withdraw our offer of financial support for Euro-candidates, and come clean publicly with our membership figures. I felt strongly that if we did not do this we would be guilty of a serious deception. The SDP had from 1981 been open about its membership and I did not intend to start now evading what I believe to be an obligation of a political party to divulge its true membership figures. In good faith we had claimed membership figures which we now knew to be false. We owed it to everyone to correct the record, however embarrassing. The Trustees accepted my proposals, with David Sainsbury the most reluctant. Far from wanting to withdraw financial support, he had to be persuaded by us all that it would be unwise to continue subsidizing the European elections, which were not likely to show a reasonable return. Once again the Party had cause to be grateful that its major financial supporter saw himself as just a normal member of the Party and resolutely refused to use his financial position to influence decisions.

We all believed that the SDP had to be allowed to die or live from now on within its own resources. While there would not be any more financial support from the Trustees neither they nor we on the National Committee were entitled to deprive the members of the opportunity of financing the Party themselves. All this was put to an emergency meeting of the National Committee on Saturday 13 May. In the midst of the meeting in St Ermin's Hotel we discovered a journalist from the *Mail on Sunday* with his ear against the door. Not knowing exactly what he had heard we decided that we had to go public ourselves on these decisions that afternoon.

We had decided to pre-empt any charge that we were only spoiling elections for the SLD and from now on we would fight only on a selective campaigning basis. In view of that we decided not to fight any Euro-constituency which had an SLD MP within it. This meant our standing down in my own Euro-constituency of Devon and Cornwall because Matthew Taylor had his seat there. I said that I personally would back the SLD candidate, Paul Tyler, whom I know and respect. In effect this meant we were going to fight around fifteen of the Euro-seats in all the television areas so as to keep some profile going. We gave the SLD the opportunity to step down for us, at least in John and

Rosie's Euro-constituencies. But they had neither the grace nor the good sense to make even that limited gesture. The *Mail on Sunday* and the *Sunday Times* led with the SDP story. The press generally wrote our obituary but in a fairly friendly fashion, using the words of one of our own members that our decision had been a 'rendezvous with reality'. The *Daily Mail* on Monday said it was a grisly end to a dream which had entranced millions of decent citizens. Criticizing David Steel for calling me a gadfly they wrote, 'hemmed in by his yapping adversaries and confronting the extinction of his hopes we see him as altogether more noble and potentially more tragic political beast: the stag at bay'.

Two by-elections were pending in Vauxhall and Glasgow Central on the same day as the Euro-elections. Having stood down in Govan and been castigated by the SLD, the Scottish SDP were very keen to fight and had an excellent enthusiastic candidate in Peter Kerr. In the event both the SDP and SLD lost their deposits and the merger in Scotland, where the Liberal Party had been strong, appeared to be in trouble. In Vauxhall the SLD were very keen to fight and we tried to negotiate. Ideally we would have liked them to let us fight the Euro-election constituency while they fought Vauxhall. But this proved impossible. What we did in the end negotiate was a package deal: we would recommend to our members that we would not fight the by-election or the next general election in Vauxhall or in Bermondsey, while the SLD would recommend to their members that they should not fight John or Rosie in Woolwich and Greenwich at the next election. A poll of the two parties' membership in all four constituencies eventually ratified this sensible arrangement. It was a tragedy that a similar arrangement to allow Mike Potter a free run at the next election and Elizabeth Shields, a former MP, to fight Ryedale again was voted down in Richmond by the SLD members.

The SDP's decision to fight only a few Euro-seats proved more enlightened than we could have hoped. The Green Party beat the SLD convincingly, making it a disaster for them. This time they had no excuse and no SDP to blame. The emergence of the Green Party was a severe jolt to those Liberals who had in the 1970s and 1980s set out very effectively to capture the green vote. Why had it happened? At the end of May Paddy Ashdown, following Labour's lead, had decided that they too would accept the continuation of Trident. Whether this was the final straw for the unilateralist Liberal sympathizers who were almost all by definition Green; whether it was Bob Maclennan's civil nuclear power commitment with David Steel in the Party prospectus or whether it was just that the Green Party's moment for protest had come, it was hard to be sure. Probably it was a combination of events. In the Euro-elections it was the Green Party who came third with 1,869,549 votes – 15.2 per cent of the electorate, a sensational result. The SLD had only 812,547 votes – 6.6 per cent. I was very glad that I had in effect taken the SDP out of the contest, for, though we might have got around 6 per cent, it was we who would have been blamed for the rise of the Greens. No one could be sure what would now happen to the Centre of British politics. Having been told by Roy Jenkins and David Steel that there was only room for three parties in British politics, after the 1987 Election it looked as if the SLD might have achieved the demise of the SDP, but at the price of a Green Party which, though destined to wane as well as wax, may not again disappear into the insignificance that was its fate before 1989.

The only way the SLD could recover was to change their name to Liberal Democrats. They did this at their Party Conference. For some former SDP members who opposed it this further name change was the final nail in the coffin of a supposedly new party. We were now back into predominantly two-party politics with the old Liberal Party set to attempt to recover the Green vote which they had temporarily lost. Paddy Ashdown was well equipped to do this for he was genuinely concerned about environmental questions, and personally opposed to civil nuclear power. Gradually the Green Party slipped back as people examined their detailed policies. But even though its polling strength may be only 2–3 per cent it is very unlikely that it will ever be totally marginalized. What the Green Party needed was for Jonathan Porritt to be their spokesman but their reluctance to have any identifiable leadership diffused their message and they never managed to hold on to that quite remarkable breakthrough.

At long last in the summer of 1989 Paddy Ashdown, pressurized by his MPs, began to talk to the SDP. John Cartwright, at David Alton's request, had talked to Bob Maclennan, with whom I had also been talking privately, to see if we could improve working relations. It sadly soon became obvious that through inadvertence or design Bob and John were at cross purposes and that Paddy Ashdown envisaged no change in his role and still wanted joint spokesmen, a single whip and in effect a merger. Admittedly the SDP was in no great shape to negotiate but nor was the SLD. There was no readiness on their part to take even a few small steps towards us. They wanted a takeover or nothing. If that was their position, it was better to stick with the SDP – at least we knew what we stood for.

The only surprise of the 1989 conference season was that the SDP managed to pull off a successful conference in Scarborough. It may prove to be the last SDP Conference. Morale was amazingly high and the press were glad to be back in Scarborough. Surprised to be witnessing a political resurrection, they gave us more coverage than we probably deserved. In policy terms we accepted independent grant aided schools, developed the right of patients to be treated under an internal NHS market and if confronted by long waiting lists to go to another hospital. We built up the social market philosophy to stress competition and the breaking up of monopoly power. We were also the first political party to advocate independence for the Bank of England and simultaneously question the desirability of a single currency with fixed exchange rates for the European Community. We specifically decided that the SDP was not in favour of a United States of Europe, a rejection hitherto implicit but never explicit.

The Conference ended with a bomb scare and we had to evacuate the conference hall just before I was due to make the Leader's set speech to end the Conference. When it became clear that we would not be able to go back in the hall for four or five hours and members had trains and buses to catch, I decided to speak from a makeshift loudspeaker outside. It became known as the Speech on the Beach and we got far more publicity than we would have ever had inside. Speaking off-the-cuff, I let slip one Freudian passage which journalists seized on:

> Sometimes people think that we will not continue to exist. Sometimes people say that we have to continue to exist. Do not worship at the altar of party. I think it has always been a great mistake of the old parties to think that parties have to live forever. What has to live forever are values and ideas.

As I drove away from Scarborough I knew that it was just a question of time before the majority of our dwindling membership accepted that their dream was dying. As always the death throes are the most painful. People want to hear that all is well and listen only to siren voices telling them what they want to hear rather than what they should hear. Having to live within the financial constraints imposed by a small membership meant that the members of the SDP slowly came to grips with reality. But even so the unreal voices were listened to more than they deserved. Good people were growing impatient, gradually doing less and less and drifting away.

In October the dramatic resignation of Nigel Lawson over Margaret Thatcher's adamant refusal to join the Exchange Rate Mechanism once again revealed how deep the divisions were within the Conservative Party over Europe. Her summer reshuffle when she had ignominiously dropped Geoffrey Howe as Foreign Secretary and replaced him with John Major was now revealed to have been her response to Howe and Lawson forcing her at the Madrid European Summit in the summer to state conditions under which Britain would join the ERM. We now know that they had both threatened resignation if she would not commit herself in specific terms and that in order to ensure that there should be no repeat of such ganging-up she had been determined to remove at least one of them.

Nigel Lawson, having seen the Foreign Office closed to him and realizing that he was being set up to carry the responsibility for the renewed inflation and consequential high interest rates was rather like Michael Heseltine ensuring that he went of his own volition rather than being pushed. He was using the inflammatory remarks made by Sir Alan

Walters, Mrs Thatcher's economic guru, for his own purposes. Nigel Lawson was thick-skinned enough to have shrugged these off if he had wanted to stay. The truth was he was seeking an opportunity to go which did not look like cutting and running. Alan Walters' remarks gave him a semi-valid opportunity. He used to great effect the traditional personal statement by a resigning Minister to the House of Commons. It allows for no interruption and is heard in silence after question time and is therefore bound to receive maximum media attention. It should have sounded a warning note to Margaret Thatcher about the dangers of a resigning senior Cabinet Minister using the House of Commons as a dramatic forum to launch damaging personal criticism. But as I listened to Nigel Lawson I never thought that a far more devastating resignation speech was yet to come, a year later, and that it would be delivered by that most unlikely figure, the Deputy Prime Minister, Sir Geoffrey Howe, huddled on the front bench and appearing to have been sidelined into oblivion.

The SDP decided to fight a by-election in Mid Staffordshire in March 1990. The result was a substantial swing to Labour who gained the seat from the Conservatives. The Liberal Democrats came third with 11.2 per cent of the vote and the SDP trailed a poor fourth with 2.5 per cent just ahead of the Green Party on 2.2 per cent. Two months later we fought a by-election in Northern Ireland where we had an excellent candidate who had long campaigned for the SDP not only to accept members but also to fight elections in Northern Ireland. Our candidate put in a good campaign talking much sense but we made little impact, and lost our deposit. The Conservatives had also fought for the first time and had done badly but at least the mainland parties had served notice that Northern Ireland might not continue to be given a free run and if sectarian politics proved impervious to reason, it might well be necessary to take mainland politics directly to the people of the Province. It was merely a marker for the future and it may serve to encourage the Northern Ireland parties to build more concrete links with the mainland politics. In as much as the SDP presence made it easier for the Conservatives to run we were fulfilling our catalytic role in UK politics.

Membership renewals in the first few months of 1990 slipped even further and I grew worried about the democratic base for the Party. It was then argued that we should put a candidate up to fight the Bootle by-election. Our few local supporters were not keen. John Cartwright was opposed but I reluctantly went along with the decision, as if sensing that a final humiliation was necessary before the SDP could force itself to face reality. So it proved to be. Despite a brave personal fight by our candidate we not only lost our deposit but were beaten by Lord Sutch of the Monster Raving Loony Party. This was the end of the road for most people in the Party and I knew we would now have to make the hard decision we had postponed last May. Twice during the campaign I visited Bootle and each time I was struck by seeing as many Labour posters on the council estates as there had been SDP posters for Shirley Williams in her by-election in 1981. The Labour Party had come back a long way in the last two years and the voters knew it. It was absurd for me to pretend otherwise and I was determined not to. Breakaway parties are too often unable to recognize any changes for the better in the party they left.

The press were clamouring for comment but with my family all staying at my parents' house in Plymouth that Friday, preparing to attend two family funerals that was neither the time nor the place. I refused to say anything because of the funeral of my sister's father-in-law and, next day, of my niece's baby. My generation had been spared the spectacle of the frequent funerals for infants in the pre-penicillin era. Indeed this was the first funeral I had ever been to when the coffin was so small that it could easily be carried by two members of the family. We were all devastated by this cot death and most wept as we watched the little coffin being lowered into the ground. It was a welcome opportunity for reflection.

We drove back to Buttermere that Saturday and over the Bank Holiday weekend I thought long and hard on what should be done about the SDP. I had known for some months that we were no longer viable as a democratic national party. After Bootle I believed that even the most committed of our activists would be ready to face the realities. In meetings over the next few days we three MPs and the Trustees all concluded that we should try to persuade the National Committee to put on ice that part of the Constitution that related to the Council for Social Democracy and area parties which were no longer operating on a proper democratic basis. In effect we would keep the shell of the Party in the country with the Parliamentary Party remaining intact. At a meeting on Sunday 3 June the overwhelming majority of the National Committee reluctantly accepted our recommendation and agreed that we should close our Headquarters and arrange generous redundancy terms for the small staff. Active local parties remained in different parts of the country but there was no pretence – we could no longer sustain a national Party.

People around that table had dedicated the last nine years of their life to the SDP. For all of us it was a very painful decision but done with dignity. For our beloved SDP it had been a lingering death and not everyone even then was ready to accept that this was the end. Like other members in the country they were hoping against hope that a miracle would happen and the SDP would revive. For some the decision was a relief; others the start of a grieving period that would last many months. Even when nearly two hundred of us met together again for dinner in the House of Commons on the tenth anniversary of the SDP the following March there were a few who had not yet fully adjusted. People are still fighting council elections and sometimes winning seats as SDP candidates. John Cartwright and Rosie Barnes are determined to defend their seats and there are some who are likely to stand as parliamentary candidates. They do so to serve their constituents and uphold the principles and philosophy of social democracy.

Next morning the obituaries started. Most were kind and showed a genuine regret. No one sought to deny that the political scene was vastly different in 1990 to that in 1981 and that the SDP had had an influence in changing the scene. There were different interpretations as to the extent of the influence. Where I believe our influence was most profound was in taking Labour votes under the noses of their activists in such large numbers that they could no longer deny that Labour's policies were disastrous and had to be changed. If the Liberals or the Conservatives had been taking their votes there would have been the usual Left-wing excuses. But for the SDP to do it was a humiliation they could not ignore. Even so it took three successive defeats for the Labour Party to transform itself. Between 1988–91 the Labour Party reversed almost every policy that was losing them votes and they moved from a party wholly unfit to govern to a party that in a few years might well be trusted again to govern the country.

My main sadness and I take my share of responsibility was that the Gang of Four never gave the SDP a chance to prove itself. Only for a few weeks were we the genuinely independent social democratic party that we had launched. By September 1982 I had written in my notebook that I feared that this was the moment when the historians would say we had lost our independence and I was unfortunately proven correct.

After the 1983 Election the obituary note was first struck when the Parliamentary Party dropped from twenty-nine to a mere six MPs. After the 1987 Election with only five MPs the obituary notices were ready but lost in the immediate debacle of the merger. The struggle we had had to re-establish our independence since 1987 was lost but if that fight had taken place in 1981 then the SDP would have won through. We would in the 1990s be an established political party with anything between twenty-five to fifty SDP MPs and in a powerful position to force proportional representation on to the statute book.

Yet few if any of us regretted the last ten years. Nor all the knocks and humiliation of the last four years, when we had made an honest try to rescue our Party from what had gone before. We had failed. But, as I had written in 1980, to win all you have to be prepared to risk all. There had been moments of great hope, happiness and human endeavour. We had contributed positively to British politics at a critically important time. Only historians will be able to judge the value of putting policies before party, the impact of the SDP's ideas, the extent of our influence and the worth of the policies we pioneered.

36

THE ROAD NOT TAKEN

Two roads diverged in a yellow wood,
And sorry I could not travel both
And be one traveller, long I stood
And looked down as far as I could
To where it bent in the undergrowth;

Robert Frost

The SDP was brought into existence by many of the same forces that projected Margaret Thatcher to victory in 1979. Ours was a desire for radical change; the wish for a strong, creative, individualist, irreverent society, a society whose government and institutions supported the diversity and variety of individuals and communities rather than stifling them in a centralized bureaucracy. After decades of creeping corporatism, the desire for a market-led change did not disappear in the first year or indeed in the eleven years of Margaret Thatcher's reign. Her single greatest achievement was in trade union reform, but privatization is probably the policy for which she will be best remembered. By cutting direct taxation while raising indirect taxation she convinced many that their taxes had fallen, though the take was greater than ever before. Her attempt at a counter-revolution – for that is what it amounted to – had a mixed reception. But in the end many returned with a sigh of relief to consensus. The SDP champions a broader based counter-revolution which promotes social justice. It was the determination to continue market-led change, but in the shape of a social market economy, which was our distinctive contribution through the 1980s. We devised a radical way of merging the tax and benefit system to alleviate poverty and a 'Careers Charter'. We advocated 'green growth', where the polluter paid. Interestingly, Margaret Thatcher eventually embraced the environment on the basis of a repairing lease held in trust for future generations. But she was slower to see the case for cherishing and promoting the arts. The voice of the consumer, which she had done much to release by market changes through the 1980s, found surprisingly little echo within her Government. In the NHS she refused to give patients the right to overcome long local waiting lists by being referred elsewhere, a consumer reform which should have been the hallmark for the internal market in health. There was no recognition that many had no other choice than to travel on old and deteriorating railway rolling stock and commuters detected Government animus against public investment. As the quality of public transport declined, so road users found the M25 round London snarled up, and even those who worked in the private sector felt there had to be more coherent transport planning. Industrialists looked with admiration at the way the French Government seemed better able to exploit the potential of the Channel tunnel.

Thus the unfettered market allocation of resources began to pall. The counter-revolution would not, I felt, be sustainable after the 1983 Election unless there was more of what I called tenderness and compassion to offset the market's casualties, and a greater acknowledgement of actions taken for the common good. It was also a paradox how centralization, not the decentralization which fitted better into a market culture, dominated the Government's legislation. After 1989, when it became ever more obvious that promises of an economic miracle had not been fulfilled, the counter-revolution was too much identified with the epithet of Thatcherism. If the good parts of Margaret Thatcher's legacy were to be sustained, I hoped that a new approach would develop around the social market economy and that the counter-revolution would not end with either the demise of the SDP or the decline and fall of Margaret Thatcher.

Three days after we had announced that the SDP was no longer operating nationwide I had lunch with David Ginsburg, who had lost his Dewsbury constituency fighting for the SDP in 1983. He was still fascinated by politics and he recalled how in 1950 Winston Churchill had insisted the Conservative candidate should stand down for Lady Violet Bonham-Carter in Colne Valley. She had lost and Labour had retained the seat but it had left a legacy of bitterness with the Conservatives. He had used this to demonstrate the difficulty of making any seat deals stick, even though he could see how important they could be in changing British politics. He gave me examples of people who, in his experience, had thought their political career was over and yet had come back against all predictions. His generally upbeat note surprised me, as did the emphasis he gave to keeping open the option of working with the Conservatives. He strongly believed that before this Parliament was over they would need and seek support from me; though he did not believe I should join the Conservative Party. There might be a valuable opportunity to keep alive the concept of co-operation across party political lines. He judged that the Labour Party would not be ready to co-operate with the Liberal Democrats or what might remain of the SDP until after another election defeat. Little did I know that within months I would be talking to the Conservatives.

On 14 July 1990 the *Spectator* had carried an interview with Nicholas Ridley where he had given vent to highly prejudiced anti-German sentiment. Although he was forced to resign from his post as Secretary of State for Trade and Industry, it was all too clear that Margaret Thatcher shared his basic hostility to Germany. That she totally miscalculated the speed and imperative driving German reunification was one of the first signs that her political judgement was suffering from her prejudices. In November 1989, when the Berlin Wall had come down, she had foolishly refused to believe that reunification was even on the immediate agenda. When it became obvious that it was, she began to talk far too emotionally in private about a Fourth Reich. She was haunted by the belief that the Germans were going to dominate Europe, and when she met with Mitterrand the two would play their fears off against each other. For my part, I am far more confident about post-war democratic Germany, and I think this is common among my generation.

The Germany I had grown to admire was exemplified by Helmut Schmidt and I believed his brand of social democracy had much to contribute, but it had gone awry after he ceased to be Chancellor – not as badly as the Labour Party but sufficient to shake the electors' confidence. In 1988 I had been asked to predict the future of social democracy in a book of essays written to mark his seventieth birthday, and I wrote then that

> if social democrats appear to the voters to be unsound on defence and naïve in their interpretation of the Soviet Union's ideological tendencies they will not be given enough opportunities in government to influence the evolution of Soviet Communism through economic and social reforms. That would be a tragedy, for one of the purposes for which social democracy is historically well designed is to assist the transformation of communism so that its ideology is revised to the point that it no longer challenges the pluralist democracy that social democrats stand for.

Most of the essays were written by German friends of Helmut Schmidt, but some people living outside Germany, like Yehudi Menuhin, Karl Popper, King Juan Carlos, Giscard d'Estaing and Jacques Delors, had written in German. The contributions in English were from Leonard Bernstein, Jim Callaghan, who wrote 'Far Cry from the Spirit of Rambouillet', Gerald Ford, Takeo Fukuda, Lee Kuan Yew, Robert McNamara, Mohammed Mubarak and George Schultz. These names were a reminder of how wide and deep were not just Helmut Schmidt's links, but those of post-war democratic Germany. It was the country which, after 1989, would inevitably play the key role in transforming communism, and this was well understood by President Bush. It was bad for Britain that Thatcher and Kohl, both from the political Right, had such poor personal relations. Chancellor Kohl had showed considerable political courage in campaigning in East Germany when the Christian

Democrats had very little support, and their victory right across a united Germany was his vindication. John Major's decision to build good personal relations was wise, but it will not alter Kohl's own commitment to a United States of Europe, something actually envisaged in the German constitution.

Most of my writing and speaking on international affairs at this time was focused on the Soviet Union and how we should respond to an empire in decline. For some years I had been speaking out against the naïve interpretation of what Mikhail Gorbachev was trying to achieve. I was not against Gorbachev personally, for he was by any standard a remarkable man and a deft political operator. What I was worried about was the wave of 'Gorbymania' that was then sweeping the West. We were underestimating his drive to retain power for himself and the elite around him. He had consciously abandoned the Soviet satellite nations in order to hold power and consolidate around the existing borders of the USSR. When the British Empire was declining and we gave independence to more and more nations previously under our rule, we did not admit that we were doing so out of economic weakness. We talked about democracy, freedom and independence to cloak our inability to retain our influence. Mikhail Gorbachev was paying us the compliment of using the same language, even talking at one stage of a Soviet Commonwealth. He was intent on covering a humiliating retreat, stimulated by profound economic weakness. Yet we were interpreting his motives along the propaganda lines set by the KGB.

Gorbachev came from the same KGB-dominated elite that, over a decade ago, had begun to question the extended empire of satellite nations. They were masterminding retrenchment to the borders of the USSR. The process had been precipitate in 1989, and neither they nor us had anticipated the speed with which the satellite countries would crumble to the new forces of democracy, or how dependent they had been on the threat of Soviet invasion to keep them in line. It was essential, I felt, to recognize that the basic decision to retrench came in Andropov's time, and that it was not done for democratic libertarian reasons; it was done for the preservation of the USSR. The power elite had no intention of allowing that process to trigger the fragmentation of the USSR. They were always prepared to use force, as was Gorbachev in Georgia, Lithuania and Latvia. What happens in Yugoslavia will be a considerable influence on whether Russia accepts a limited break up of the USSR in 1992 and beyond.

I had fiercely cricitized Gorbachev for clamping down on the Lithuanians in their capital, Vilnius. So I was especially pleased to visit for the first time Estonia, Latvia and Lithuania in a three-man, all-party, human rights delegation at the end of August 1990. I had become convinced that the vacillation of the Western democracies over the Baltic States had to end, and that it was essential to force Gorbachev to honour their right to self-determination and independence. If we could prise out of the USSR these three republics, which had been illegally occupied as a result of the infamous Hitler-Stalin pact of 1940, we would not only redress a historic wrong but start an irreversible process by which Soviet Communism would be transformed into a market economy and a genuine democracy. Once we had succeeded with Poland, Hungary, Czechoslovakia and the Baltic States, we could then edge in towards the big republics – the Russian Federation, Ukraine and Byelorussia.

Nearly everyone we saw in the Baltic capitals, Tallinn, Riga and Vilnius, was determined to win back their independence, but they were equally sure that Gorbachev would only concede their freedom under pressure from the Western democracies. It was fascinating to talk to people who were simultaneously negotiating with Mikhail Gorbachev and his Ministers, dedicated to the maintenance of the USSR, and to Boris Yeltsin and his team from the Russian Federation. Whereas Yeltsin was surrounded by genuine market economists, and even budding democrats, they felt that Gorbachev's advisers were opposed to risking their hold on power to the ballot box. I believed that Gorbachev himself only believed in a managed democracy and a managed economy, but his views were evolving. No one was sure what either Yeltsin or Gorbachev would concede under the differing pressures ahead of them. But they felt there was everything to play for with Yeltsin, and that his thinking was more in flux. In as much as the two were interacting with each other, some hoped this process could provide the momentum for substantive and radical change inside the Soviet Union. The unanimous view was that Gorbachev should be pressurized and that we in the West should listen more to what the Soviet people felt about him and his policies. My fear that we were falling for KGB propaganda was strengthened by all I heard. The West's approach was so nuanced it was almost deferential. It needed to be more robust, and that particularly applied to Margaret Thatcher, not someone I normally associated with soft pedalling.

In early August, before I left for the Baltic States, Saddam Hussein invaded Kuwait. It was one of those fortuitous acts of timing that within hours of the invasion Margaret Thatcher was due to meet President George Bush at Aspen in Colorado. How much influence she had on George Bush we will probably never know. Before he arrived in Aspen he had given no indication that he saw this invasion as the trigger for putting American forces into Saudi Arabia. Nevertheless, to have been told by a fellow leader for whom he had respect that this was an act of aggression that must be resisted, and that she would give him full support, must have concentrated the President's mind and steeled his resolve.

I shared Mrs Thatcher's view that this invasion had to be reversed, and wrote an article for the *Daily Express* on 3 August entitled 'This dictator must be halted or the world will regret it'. I had already crossed swords with Saddam's ugly Baathist regime in 1978 when, as Foreign Secretary, I decided to expel a group of Iraqi diplomats. My action was then provoked by the regime's campaign of violence against Iraqi residents in London. I found no difficulty in fully supporting George Bush's consummate handling of the West's response once the invasion of Kuwait had taken place, right up until the Iraqi troops had withdrawn. My differences came when Bush, for some unaccountable reason, refused to promote legal action to extradite Saddam Hussein for war crimes and did little to help those wanting to overthrow him. Yet it was Bush who saw how vital it was to send troops early to Saudi Arabia and persuaded King Fahd that this was of crucial importance if sanctions were ever to bite. This was the all-important decision for eventual success. Without it Saddam Hussein would have threatened Saudi Arabia every time we turned the sanction screw and Arab solidarity would have collapsed. It was a considerable risk to deploy US troops without heavy armament or adequate air cover in the early period. If Saddam Hussein had pushed right down into Saudi Arabia these token American forces would have been severely defeated and George Bush humiliated. It might have been hard to hold US public opinion as the US forces regrouped and built up their strength to attack the Iraqis. The Saudis would by then have very likely settled on Saddam Hussein's terms.

The House of Commons was recalled on 6 September. I warned that it could be very difficult to make sanctions work and that Saddam Hussein would prefer to give up Kuwait as a result of a military battle, and I predicted that a battle would eventually be necessary. I went on to say that, if we maintained the consensus that had developed among the multi-national force, 'there might be military action that would not last very long and would not involve a great deal of loss of life.

The invasion of Kuwait injected a wholly new political factor into domestic politics. Though there were few parallels with the Falklands – since in this case Britain was not in the lead role – Margaret Thatcher must have seen the potential to stage a political comeback and she might well have done so had she not been forced out before the fighting commenced.

The autumn of 1990 meant that for the first time in thirty years I had no party conference to attend. I wrote an article in the *Mail on Sunday* on the eve of the Labour Party conference, warmer than for many years to Labour, entitled 'What the Labour Party must do to win power', in which I urged them to make a commitment to proportional representation to attract votes from the moderate Centre. Labour, in policy terms, had transformed itself. It was now committed to the European Community and wanting to go into the ERM as an anti-inflationary discipline. It was ready to build three Trident submarines. It was rejecting state ownership of industry and talking at least some of the language of the private commercial marketplace. It was becoming hard to find areas in which they had not adopted SDP policy. And yet I had grave doubts that Neil Kinnock in particular could free himself in government from the influence of the public sector unions which were still a powerful vested interest with real power at every level within the Labour Party. The electoral college with the trade union block vote remained in place capable of being used to make or break a Prime Minister. Even so, deservedly, Labour was in a confident mood with its opinion poll lead building up. Yet, far from going out to widen its electoral appeal, it gratuitously slammed the door shut on any possible co-operation with us in the SDP On 2 October – the very day, incidentally, that the two Germanies reunified in a spirit of reconciliation – it passed the following resolution:

> This Conference resolves to oppose any rule changes on membership of the Labour Party, which can be construed as inducements for former members of the Social Democratic Party to re-join the Labour Party. Specifically this motion notes the twelve-month membership qualification for party office and resolves to oppose any attempt by the national leadership to alter the aforementioned rule with a view to offering an accommodation to the three surviving SDP Members of Parliament.

Up until this moment I had hoped that Labour would recognize that they would need every extra help that they could get to beat the Conservatives in an election due before July 1992. For after the election, unless Labour won, and once in government changed the voting system to proportional representation, as Mitterrand cynically did in France, the effect of the boundary changes which come into effect in 1993 would be adverse to them. I was, however, too optimistic; Labour was not prepared to heal the breach between social democrats and democratic socialists in order to maximize their appeal.

Why, knowing there was little concrete evidence that Labour would contemplate co-operation, had I felt it was my duty to try? I think because I needed for my own peace of mind to demonstrate publicly that Labour had had the opportunity but turned it down. Since Labour was ahead in the opinion polls in October 1990, they could have co-operated from a position of strength. I had long realized that I personally was too much of an anathema to the Labour activists to expect them to stand down for me in Devonport. Anyhow, I felt confident I could hold my seat against a Labour challenge if I decided to contest it. So I had made it clear to people close to Neil Kinnock that I would be ready to stand aside at the next election if a negotiated agreement were reached between the Labour Party and the SDP which would allow John and Rosie to stand in their constituencies unopposed by Labour. But I knew that meant them having a very necessary fight with the Left in the Borough of Greenwich. If this local difficulty had been overcome with a little give and take on both sides and more movement by Labour on constitutional reform and proportional representation, I would have had to overcome my doubts and help Labour. The mere act of them co-operating with the SDP was for me the test. Without co-operation my anxieties about whether Labour's change of heart was for real and not just undertaken for votes would remain. It had been in the wind since 1988 that Labour might be ready to adopt proportional representation for Scottish and European parliamentary elections, and that might even apply to electing peers to a reformed second chamber. I could sense Labour was moving towards a Bill of Rights, though hesitant over embracing proportional representation for the Westminster Parliament. Yet movement in these areas would still help convince Social Democratic voters to support Labour, though fewer activists than I expected were ready to join.

There was persistent polling evidence that we could marginally influence former SDP voters. More than seven million people had voted for SDP Liberal Alliance candidates in 1987; it only needed a few hundred voters in highly marginal seats, the crucial 1 or 2 per cent, to determine who won. They would be most influenced in the last fortnight of an election campaign, so we had time on our side. I knew too that co-operating with other political parties is the essential political change that has to come to achieve proportional representation. If Labour could have worked out a very small electoral arrangement with the SDP it would have underlined to many non-political people that it had really changed. A genuinely social democratic government might then have emerged. Sadly, as we have seen, it was not to be. In 1983 and in 1987, I had wanted the SDP to publicly rule out co-operating with Labour as their policies were far too extreme and miles apart from ours or those of the SDP/Liberal Alliance. Yet in 1990 Labour's policies had moved so far towards us that it was not unprincipled to see if we could co-operate. The fact that they were not interested reinforced my key doubt; for too many activists the policy conversion was not yet genuine.

One piece of good news did come out of the conference season. In October, during the weekend before the Conservative Party Conference, John Major at long last took Britain into the Exchange Rate Mechanism of the EMS. It was a feat of political adroitness that had eluded his predecessors, Geoffrey Howe and Nigel Lawson. I had talked to John Major that summer while we were both watching cricket at Lord's. It was striking how determined he was to get interest rates down before his party conference. He felt this was a political imperative as much as an economic one. Tying the cut in interest rates to ERM entry may have just tipped the balance in persuading Margaret Thatcher to enter the ERM, even though the linkage annoyed the Governor of the Bank of England. I suspect that Margaret Thatcher agreed to enter the ERM, despite feeling it would restrict her freedom to cut interest rates in the run-up to a general election, because she knew she could not fight on two fronts. She decided, correctly, that the more important battle was to resist the Euro-federalist package which Jacques Delors was trying to push through so as to tie the hands of those on the inter-governmental conferences on political and economic union. By joining the ERM she hoped that some of the Conservative MPs who were strongly European would be able to live with her vetoing any irreversible move towards a United States of Europe. Nevertheless, for the first time in over a decade of watching Margaret Thatcher very closely, I felt that ERM entry represented a personal defeat for her. She had used every tactic to avoid it, she had delayed and delayed taking action, and yet now she had no alternative. I do not believe that she ever accepted the virtue of managed exchange rates within the ERM. She merely resigned herself to it as part of the price that she was having to pay within her party for having helped Nigel Lawson to fuel inflation.

It could have been very different. If Britain had been inside the ERM in the autumn of 1989 it could have had near to zero inflation; instead we had inflation peaking at 10.9 per cent. On the eve of the 1989 Conservative Party Conference, Nigel Lawson had been forced to raise bank rates to 15 per cent and they had stayed at that level for a full year until John Major reduced them to 14 per cent. Instead of the Conservatives campaigning on the basis that they had transformed the economy, they were being attacked for bringing back the stop-go cycle of the past. Margaret Thatcher could no longer talk of an economic miracle and this had all happened as a result of miscalculating the force and persistence of the pre-election consumer boom. If the ERM discipline had been in opera- tion in 1986–89 it would undoubtedly have prevented Nigel Lawson from making those economic mistakes. Yet it was Margaret Thatcher who had point-blank refused entry despite being in a minority of one in the key Cabinet sub-committee. The only concession she agreed to make was to accept the formula 'Not if, but when'. She cannot evade, therefore, her share of the responsibility.

When he became Chancellor in 1983, Nigel Lawson was the figure in the Thatcher Cabinet who most interested me. I had first become aware of him when he was the editor of the *Spectator*, advocating devaluation in the late 1960s. For those Labour MPs who were devaluationists, he was one of the very few journalists with enough courage to stick his neck out, risking jibes that his advocacy was costing the country significant sums of money by eroding confidence and making intervention in support of the currency more likely. When the Grand Hotel in Brighton was bombed in 1985 and I thought the unthinkable – what would have happened if the Prime Minister had been killed – the only other significant figure was Nigel Lawson. He had been the architect of the Government's 1980 medium-term financial strategy and was starting to emerge as a strong Chancellor. His intellect was powerful enough to ensure that he did not have a closed mind. When he reveals in his memoirs how he gradually became disillusioned with monetary targets and became converted to the ERM it should be a fascinating story.

If Nigel Lawson had taken Britain into the ERM when he wanted to in 1985, then Margaret Thatcher's period of office would have been marked by a true economic miracle. In 1986, when world oil prices slipped from $30 a barrel to $10 a barrel, sterling weakened and Nigel Lawson seemed to be happy to help it drift down. Over eighteen months sterling lost over 30 per cent against the Deutschmark. This led to a further expansion of the economy. It was at that time Nigel Lawson decided to have a clandestine policy of shadowing the Deutschmark, which he conducted from the Treasury. It is claimed neither Margaret Thatcher nor the Governor of the Bank of England were aware for quite a long period what he was doing, but I find it impossible to credit that the Governor did not know. It was to say the least odd behaviour from a Chancellor who has since told us he advocated an independent role for the Governor of the Bank of England. The SDP supported independence for the Bank of England as part of a constitutional reform package. If even Margaret Thatcher could fuel inflation, then more banking checks and balances on politicians, as occurs in Germany and in the US, is as necessary as an independent judiciary. Which is one reason why I do not share Margaret Thatcher's view that an independent European Central Bank is necessarily destructive of Britain's nationhood, although it does represent a very substantial transfer of power away from the Prime Minister and Chancellor of the Exchequer.

All would have been well for the economy if Nigel Lawson had corrected the pre-election boom after victory. He wanted a global system of managed currencies, but then on 19 October 1987 came Black Monday when the world stock markets suffered. In the midst of the BP share sale, £50 billion was wiped off London share prices in one day, and £40 billion the following day. Under pressure from James Baker, then the US Treasury Secretary, there was a co-ordinated cut in world interest rates when really the domestic British economy needed a rise in interest rates. Yet even so inflation would have been less had Nigel Lawson not cut the standard rate of income tax from 27p to 25p in his budget of 1988. With the higher rate cut from 60 per cent to 40 per cent and changes in mortgage relief this further stimulated consumer spending. Tax relief of £4 billion was totally irresponsible, as I said at the time, and instead I urged lifting the national insurance threshold, which in effect would have meant only cutting the higher rate to 49 per cent. Far from restraining her Chancellor, Margaret Thatcher had encouraged him to cut both rates of tax and not just reduce the higher rate. So it was that the two politicians most associated with a determination to reduce inflation managed by the end of 1988 to induce a dangerous and wholly unnecessary rise in inflation. Inevitably interest rates had to rise too and it was then a mistake to raise them little by little. The whole period of 1986 to 1989 was one of such serious economic mismanagement that it has besmirched Margaret Thatcher's record as Prime Minister. It also weakened her politically to such an extent that she became vulnerable to Michael Heseltine's challenge.

In the middle of October I went to Venice for a meeting of the Trilateral Commission. It became very clear to me while talking to senior political figures that a head of steam was building up behind Jacques Delors' proposals and that the Rome European Heads of Government meeting would propose a treaty framework for political, economic and monetary union which would be overtly federalist, and if accepted would inexorably lead to a United States of Europe. Debbie had come with me to Venice along with Delia Smith and her husband, Michael Wynn-Jones, to celebrate twenty years working with Delia. It was one of those rare Indian summers with few people around and it appeared at times that we had Venice to ourselves.

I had been coming to Venice like a homing pigeon ever since 1960.

> I loved her from my boyhood; she to me
> Was as a fairy city of the heart,
> Rising like water columns from the sea,
> Of joy the sojourn, and of wealth the mart;

> Byron

What better place, I thought, to ponder how I, though an enthusiast for the European Community, could in the interests of Europe both help halt the seemingly inexorable slide towards a European state and also retain the advantages of a Europe of nation states. I kept questioning whether my deep-seated opposition to a United States of Europe was a generational question. I was still contemplating this when we returned to London for an invitation to dance among the dinosaurs at David Sainsbury's fiftieth birthday party in the National History Museum. It was the first occasion on which all five of the Owen family had been to an adult dance, with our sons Tristan and Gareth in evening dress and Lucy in a frock (xlvi). Would their generation be ready to live in a European state where an elected President and Cabinet had real executive power over those policies best conducted at a European level? Would they become impatient with a collective nation-state decision-making structure always dependent on broad consensus among the member states? Maybe I was the dinosaur. While all my training as a natural scientist told me that the answer lay in evolution, I feared that pragmatic piecemeal changes eschewing any national vision would mean the European Community gradually eroding the nation state. Yet neither of my sons wanted this. Both were taking independent decisions on many aspects of their lives, but on this issue, slightly to my surprise, they did not aspire to a European state. I think it is too glibly assumed that the young, who now travel freely all over Europe, feel less attached to the substance as distinct from the trappings of British nationhood.

On 22 October I attended the memorial service for Ian Gow who had been murdered by the IRA in a dastardly car bomb attack. He was a brave and principled parliamentarian. Our offices were close together in the Norman Shaw North building in Parliament. We had often talked about politics, and sometimes the ever-present risk of being blown up. Over time I discovered, as one so often does in cross-party relationships when the need for public political posturing is not there, how thoughtful and sincere other politicians can be. It was a moving service and St Margaret's, Westminster was packed. I could not stop thinking how on the eve of the 1979 Election I had attended a similar service for Airey Neave following a car bomb attack within the House of Commons precincts. It was as if the terrorists were saying, if we cannot get Margaret Thatcher we will get the politician closest to her. Both were psychologically deep blows to Margaret Thatcher. What fascinated me was that Geoffrey Howe gave the address, for I had never before realized how close he was to Ian Gow. In retrospect, I cannot help but wonder whether, if Ian Gow had been alive, events would have unfolded in quite the same way as they did over the next few weeks. I do not believe he could have stopped Howe's resignation, but he might well have stopped Margaret Thatcher putting down Sir Geoffrey afterwards and the consequential bitterness of his personal statement. I wondered too whether the intrusive security measures necessary for her protection were a contributory factor to her growing isolation. A democratic politician needs to 'touch the flesh', to feel people through the rough and tumble of the hustings. Margaret Thatcher was being forced to live a day-to-day life more remote from the people she led than any other Prime Minister in our history. She also missed Willie Whitelaw's common sense.

The Rome Summit took place the following weekend and it was clear that Andreotti, the Italian Prime Minister, had foolishly gone out of his way to isolate Margaret Thatcher. But what was alarming was that Whitehall had not picked up the mood which I had sensed in Venice about the coming ambush. Even people involved in the Community negotiations who were normally hostile to the Prime Minister were admitting that the Italian Presidency had behaved pretty disgracefully. On Tuesday 30 October Margaret Thatcher came to the House of Commons to make a statement, and I helped wind her up by my question supporting the use of the veto. It was already clear from her Rome press conference, when she came out with her series of 'No, no, no' statements, that she was on an emotional high and the adrenalin was pumping round her system as she handbagged every federalist proposal. She was taking her stand on the single currency, and even beginning to backtrack from the agreed Government position over the hard ecu. I watched Geoffrey Howe's face as she answered these questions; he looked miserable and unhappy, truly, I thought, a dead sheep. How wrong I proved to be.

On 1 November, the day Parliament prorogued, without any warning, Geoffrey Howe resigned as Deputy Prime Minister and Leader of the House. Margaret Thatcher's response to the Rome Summit had been the final straw for him. The resignation letter, ready to use for the last few years, was taken out, dusted and this time delivered. He had suffered a humiliating cycle of events following his removal from the Foreign Office. Even before that his consistent support for ERM entry back in 1985 and again before the Madrid European Summit in the summer of 1987 had so antagonized Margaret Thatcher that she could barely be in the same room as him. When he became Leader of the House and foolishly insisted on being called Deputy Prime Minister, the tension between them was there for all to see. A mild and decent man, he had been made to look ridiculous for too long. He was never a Tory wet and had made a quiet but distinguished contribution to the counter-revolution, though a less revolutionary figure would be hard to imagine.

At this crucial moment in domestic politics the former Norwegian Foreign Minister, who was the UN High Commissioner for Refugees, resigned in order to return to Oslo to join Gro Harlem Brundtland's new government. I was approached by some young activists within UNHCR in Geneva to ask if I would put my name forward. I rang Martin Morland, an old friend, who is the UK Ambassador to the UN in Geneva, and found out some details about the job. I became sufficiently interested to let Douglas Hurd know and he agreed that private soundings should be taken in UN circles in New York and among a few governments. While it was apparent that Perez de Cuellar had in mind someone within his own Secretariat it was also obvious that this did not command wide support. From the soundings that were made, it appeared that my candidature would have powerful support. I had to make up my mind quickly. At various times I had considered going back to medicine and not fighting a coming election, but I had never before contemplated resigning my seat.

Then to add to the complications, out of the blue on Thursday 8 November, I was telephoned by Maurice Saatchi to say he had a proposition to put to me and ask if I was free for lunch. We met that day at the Connaught hotel. He came straight to the point, arguing that the Conservative Party under Margaret Thatcher had to change its image if it was to win the election and that there was an overwhelming mutual interest in me joining the Conservatives and taking a high-profile job in a Conservative Cabinet. Maurice's company had the Conservative Party account, handling their advertising, party political broadcasts, polling and public relations. So I was talking to a person who knew the Conservative Party inside out. With total frankness I went through with him all the obstacles to this course of action. I explained why I had said publicly over five years ago that I would never become a Conservative and had repeated it endlessly ever since. I had not said this lightly, and though of course I could in theory change my mind and put up with the jibes for doing so, in practice I did not want to do so. I was not and never would be a natural member of the Conservative Party. I reminded him of my opposition to Margaret Thatcher's basic attitude to the National Health Service, and that while I agreed with her on a number of very important foreign policy issues, not least the danger of sliding imperceptibly into a United States of Europe, I simply could not see myself becoming a Conservative. There were circumstances in which I would serve as a Social Democrat in either a Conservative or Labour government. But I would need to feel I could carry some influence, even if only on the margin, on the policies of any such government and have at least the power to argue for some of the constitutional changes I thought necessary. Maurice was adamant that his strategy would only work if I were a prominent Cabinet Minister, for only that would give the necessary public profile to change people's perceptions.

It had been a fascinating lunch and Maurice Saatchi had handled his proposition with considerable skill. I gathered this was his own personal initiative and he never once gave any indication he had discussed it with any senior Conservative. Given that his company would know all the private polling information, I asked whether he had the numbers to show I would have such a beneficial effect and he confirmed that he had. Given his own links with Conservative Ministers, it would not have surprised me if he had consulted them, but as far as I was concerned it had been a private lunch and I told no one other than Debbie about it. Indeed I would not have disclosed it even now had it not been for the fact that the *Sunday Telegraph* on 10 February 1991 carried a detailed account of Maurice Saatchi's involvement with me under the headline 'THE TORIES GO OUT TO WOO DR OWEN'.

It was Margaret Thatcher in No. 10 Downing Street on 7 July 1988 who had last proposed quite directly to me that I should join the Conservatives. She had given a dinner for Lord Carrington to mark his retirement from the post of NATO Secretary-General and had quite deliberately taken both Debbie and me aside as we were leaving. In her blunt way she said to Debbie, 'Your husband has a big choice to make and it can no longer be avoided. There are only two serious parties in British politics and we women understand these things; it is time he made up his mind.' Debbie bridled and I politely refused to join the Conservative Party then, as I had refused Alan Clark and others who had raised the issue with me ever since the summer of 1983. It was a deliberate strategy of Margaret Thatcher's, which she had followed for a few years even before the SDP was formed, to attract the social democrats in the Labour Party to the Conservatives. Previously in interviews she had virtually invited me to join; this time it had been done in person. Her quoted remarks that I 'would be the next non-Conservative Prime Minister' had also been often misreported, with the word 'non' removed, much to my embarrassment. I had also found out since then, interestingly in view of what was to transpire, that John Major shared her strategy. He had asked me, half-jokingly, while watching cricket that summer with David Frost, whether I would ever consider joining the Conservatives when Margaret Thatcher retired. I had explained that in some ways the opposite was the case; I was more attracted to her because she was not in my eyes a typical Conservative. The Conservative Party for me, I said, still stood for privilege. Yet by no stretch of the imagination despite her ruthless use of patronage could one identify Margaret Thatcher with privilege, and an instinctive wish to challenge vested interest wherever she encountered it was one of her most refreshing characteristics. He grinned and appeared to take the point, and we left the matter there.

As the hours ticked by I knew I had to make a decision about whether to go for the UNHCR job. That Saturday I attended Lucy's new school, Alleyn's, for her first open day. Watching her excited and enthused, I shuddered at the idea of uprooting her, quite apart from asking Debbie to move to Switzerland. Her job continued to give her great personal satisfaction. Debbie felt that going to Geneva would mean she could not operate her literary agency, so I would be asking her to abandon the independence she had had since she had first gone out to work at the age of nineteen. At seventeen Debbie had spent nine months in Geneva. I like Switzerland and Geneva more than she does. She would joke that you could not flush a lavatory in an apartment after 10.30 at night, so ordered and controlled were the Genevois. So on Sunday, with some regrets but no reluctance, I let Douglas Hurd's office know that I did not want my name to go forward for consideration. For many years the whole family had sacrificed an immense amount for my career. It was not too much to ask me to do a little of the same for their happiness.

Meanwhile I flew off to Istanbul for a conference to tell the Turks that we could see no possibility of the boundaries of the European Community being extended to include them. This was not a very palatable message, especially since Turkey was behaving so robustly over the Iraqi invasion, applying sanctions and losing considerable revenue from the oil pipeline being shut down from the lack of trade across their borders. I was taking time off in Europe to write this book and was feeling very emotional as I re-lived my early life and I wondered whether I should have opened up a new chapter in my life working for refugees.

As I travelled through Europe, a drama was unfolding in the House of Commons in the debate on the Queen's Speech. On Tuesday 13 November, Geoffrey Howe, annoyed by attempts to protray his resignation as an argument about style and not substance, used his right to make a personal statement in the House to considerable effect. I wish I had been there. It was a full frontal attack, the speech of an assassin, with every word sharpened to penetrate ever deeper: 'The time has come for others to consider their response to the tragic conflict of loyalty with which I have perhaps wrestled for far too long.' I returned to London to find Michael Heseltine's mind had been made up for him by that speech and he announced he would challenge Margaret Thatcher for the leadership of the Conservative Party.

I did not want Michael Heseltine to become Prime Minister. First and foremost he is, as I have described earlier, an unabashed Tory in a way that I sense are neither Margaret Thatcher nor John Major. But there were deeper reasons than this. I had not been impressed by his judgement, whether over the mace-waving incident in the House of Commons, wearing a flak jacket when he dealt with CND or flouncing out of the Cabinet while in full session. It was all too theatrical and revealed a pattern of impetuousness. I was also appalled to read that Michael Heseltine did not believe that the European Community should expand to include Poland, Hungary or Czechoslovakia as a high priority. Taken with my anxiety about his readiness to concede too much ground towards a United States of Europe, it was all a sufficient disincentive, despite his many good qualities, to make me ready to put up with Margaret Thatcher for a little longer.

Sentiment and respect also meant I did not want Margaret Thatcher forced out of her great office in humiliating circumstances. My overriding anxiety was that this was an appalling time to change any Prime Minister. Her judgement and experience would have been a national asset in the forthcoming war against Iraq. War I felt was inevitable, and would start in January or February. Margaret Thatcher had proved her worth during the Falklands and, though Britain had only a secondary role in the Gulf, she would have an important influence on President Bush in the conduct of the war. Also, she believed that a readiness to veto Jacques Delors' proposals for political and monetary union was an essential British interest. I too thought this, though I believed she could achieve more if she were readier to build coalitions of interest with other member states on different issues and negotiate positively. For these international reasons I did not want a change of Prime Minister at that crucial stage.

Yet I wondered what would be the view of a Conservative MP. My case that it was in the broader national interest for her to stay on at least until the early summer would no doubt for some conflict with their knowledge that if she was not pushed now she would hang on beyond then. It was easy for me as a Social Democrat to ruminate that she might step down if she were still unpopular next year. But with no objective signs of her being ready to do so, a Conservative MP had to worry about winning his seat and losing the election, matters which were not my concern. Even those MPs still sympathetic must have feared that, if she stayed, by the summer she would have built up her public approval ratings on the back of a successful Gulf War sufficient to remain in power while still remaining an electoral liability. In this respect a vote for Michael Heseltine had its attractions, for he with no pretensions to the

Thatcher legacy would have abolished the poll tax immediately and gone to the country straight after the Gulf War. At the inevitable jibes of a khaki election he would have comforted himself with the fact that his hero David Lloyd George had won the most famous khaki election.

On Monday 19 November, while Margaret Thatcher was in Paris attending the CSCE conference, the result of the first ballot was announced. She had failed by four votes to have the requisite majority. It was a sensational rebuff. Even though Michael Heseltine was fifty-two votes behind her, under the complex rules the contest automatically went to a second ballot unless she had a majority of fifty-six votes. In the House of Commons the following Tuesday, she had to report on the Paris meeting. There was a strange generosity about the House that day, as if most of us sensed her days were numbered. Unless you are a member of the party involved, you feel removed from these inner party elections, and yet they were choosing our Prime Minister, not just their Party Leader. It was hard not to see a certain poetic justice in that the worms had turned and the wets, after having been reviled over all those years, had had their revenge in the secrecy of the ballot box.

On Thursday 22 November at 10 o'clock Margaret Thatcher resigned as Leader of the Conservative Party. She had been brought down over the European Community, not the poll tax. I quoted Mark Antony's words at the death of Caesar:

> O judgement thou art fled to brutish beasts
> And men have lost their reason, Bear with me
> My heart is in the coffin there with Caesar
> And I must pause till it come back to me.

As you walk through the door into the Members' Lobby in the House of Commons, you face two statues of Winston Churchill and Lloyd George, guarding the entrance to the Chamber of the House of Commons. On the right of the door is a statue of Clement Attlee and on the left a place left empty for another statue. There is no doubt that eventually Margaret Thatcher, the first woman Prime Minister, will occupy that position and deservedly so.

I did feel sentimental. She had beaten me in the 1987 Election and there is from the vanquished to the victor a certain gallantry due, and in my case genuinely felt. I sensed at times we were partners in the counter-revolution and I shared some of her convictions. Nevertheless, I did not share her attitude to a whole range of social and civil liberty issues. Above all, I was passionately opposed to her basic attitude to the NHS. I had been alarmed ever since she had announced her intentions of reviewing the NHS on *Panorama* in 1988, and when the results of her review were made available in January 1989 I felt it portended ill for the future. I knew that if she were to win an election she would extend tax concessions for private health insurance from the elderly to everyone, fuelling a two-tier health service. It was not the internal health market that I feared, for I still advocated it, albeit a better version; it was her encouragement for private health insurance that I abhorred. Hitherto she had wisely steered clear of the NHS, almost as if she knew her populist instincts were bound to clash with her ideological prejudices. Yet by then, in many areas, caution had been thrown to the winds and now she was reaping what she had sown.

So, with the country on the brink of war, I had to watch while Conservative MPs chose our Prime Minister. Geoffrey Howe and Nigel Lawson were out of the running. Douglas Hurd was well up to the job but would be beaten by Michael Heseltine. Under John Major, he would definitely stay as Foreign Secretary and be influential. It seemed to me that John Major was a far better choice than Michael Heseltine. I believed he would be less flashy over the Gulf and show the necessary quiet determination in the European inter-governmental conferences, winning concessions that Michael Heseltine might not even demand. I sensed too that John Major would be far better in creating a climate of social cohesion. Among some of my friends who thought John Major was a conventional Thatcherite, that judgement was vigorously questioned. Yet I felt confident that he was the nearest of the Conservative candidates to being a social democrat.

Margaret Thatcher's downfall was due to hubris. Her excessive self-confidence was by then being flaunted day by day in the face of friend or foe alike. The tragedy that the Greeks identified followed Nemesis. It came because she had pitted herself against her own source of power, the Conservative MPs. She had reached a stage where she was not only not listening to her parliamentary colleagues but was contemptuous of their views. The Cabinet had been reduced in stature and in quality. Majority opinion was frequently flouted or manipulated. People of substance, who well knew that Cabinet government was a great constitutional safeguard, had allowed this to develop over the years to the detriment of us all. It was not just because she was a woman that the Cabinet had been so supine but it was a material factor. With the Cabinet too weak to act, the Conservative MPs had shown their power.

I always knew when she or others had tried to persuade me to become a Conservative that my relationship with her could not have survived my becoming a creature of her patronage. Watching her style of government from the outside, I sensed in 1982 from the Franks Report that there was something seriously wrong. When a Foreign Secretary as formidable as Peter Carrington could be overriden on important issues by a mere Prime Ministerial memo, the system was not working. That he would not think it even worth putting his views to colleagues on the Defence and Overseas Policy Committee of the Cabinet was a sign of how dominating she had become. When she removed Geoffrey Howe from being Foreign Secretary, she was publicly warned not to sack him by Conservative MPs who waved their order papers and gave him a rousing welcome on his first attendance at the Commons as Leader of the House. It was a very meaningful signal to her but one which she totally ignored. She did not attempt to stop his resignation, thinking it would be an insignificant matter. As Chancellor and Foreign Secretary, Geoffrey Howe had accumulated many political debts, and to believe his resignation would not do serious damage was a clear sign that she had lost respect for the deeper-seated loyalties of the Conservative Parliamentary Party. Even her friends knew that since 1987 her political antennae were no longer receiving, only broadcasting.

The taunting of Michael Heseltine through the press, virtually inviting him to stand against her, was also a reflection of a Leader who was grossly underestimating her opponents – always a dangerous fault and one she had not hitherto committed. One of the most touching of the many stories that surround her is that she packed her bags in No. 10 before both the 1983 and 1987 Elections, in case she were defeated and to convince herself she was not to take victory for granted. Michael Heseltine's popularity in the country, the way he had concentrated on doing the circuit of constituency functions, meant that he too had earned the gratitude of a significant number of MPs in marginal seats. That she was oblivious to all this showed how the bunker mentality can develop in No. 10. She was by then focusing too much attention on foreign policy. The build up of the Gulf War, the Rome Community Summit and the Paris CSCE Summit had taken an inordinate amount of her time. She fell, however, on her own sword.

Even so Neil Kinnock, by foolishly going ahead with the censure debate, allowed her to make a sparkling speech the very day she had resigned, and she went out in great style. Dennis Skinner gave her the feed line to play with the House of Commons, telling us 'I am enjoying this!', while leaving us all with the prospect, to dread or relish according to taste, of her becoming the first Governor of an independent European Central Bank. Yet the harshness of the rejection was to eat away at her over the next few months.

Would John Major continue with the counter-revolution? I believed he would do so and in terms which most SDP supporters would approve. Nothing that has happened so far has made me change that initial judgement. He had only come into the House of Commons in 1979. I had not even registered his presence until he was a junior Minister in the Department of Health and Social Security in the middle 1980s. Because of my involvemment with the Disablement Income Group and my own time at the DHSS when Jack Ashley and Alf Morris had made a real attempt to improve facilities for the disabled, this was an area that I watched closely even as Party Leader. I had been very impressed by the concerned, careful, considerate way in which John Major as a junior Minister had handled these problems. What was also clear was that many of my friends outside Parliament in the disablement field who dealt with him had also been impressed. I did not meet him socially until after the 1987 Election, when Tristan Garel-Jones had invited John Cartwright and me to dinner at his home to talk to a number of Conservative MPs. Both Douglas Hurd and John Major had come and it had been a very friendly occasion. They had made no attempt to persuade us to become Conservatives – it was more of an occasion for gentle gossip and for them to question us about how we hoped to survive. They all appeared to have considerable sympathy with us for our refusal to merge with the Liberals. Of course they may have been feeling us out as to whether we would come over to the Conservatives, but nothing so indelicate was mooted. The Government was then riding high in the opinion polls and they had no need of our support.

On the Whitehall/Westminster grapevine I had also picked up intriguing comments about John Major from perceptive people I respected. As Chief Secretary to the Treasury he had shown a readiness to switch public expenditure priorities with a sensitivity to social problems most unusual for anyone holding that office, though he had held everyone toughly to previously agreed ceilings. In the Foreign Office, where he had only been for a short time, the wiser heads had found him thoughtful and ready to take an independent line. It was the trendy diplomats and effete politicians who had rubbished his short stay. Debbie too, slightly to my surprise, had found him an interesting figure. As Chancellor he had shown in debate and in odd conversations a sensible wish to enter the ERM but a wariness about the far-reaching consequences of economic and monetary union. He had also made it clear that he was very much in favour of enlarging the Community to include Hungary, Poland and Czechoslovakia. For all of these rather second-hand and somewhat incomplete reasons I believed he would make a good Prime Minister.

In numerous interviews on the day she announced she was going I stressed both the achievements and the disappointments of Margaret Thatcher's period in office, while supporting John Major as the man best suited to make the good parts of her legacy stick and to achieve for these a deserved and necessary permanence. In the evening I went on a special BBC *Question Time* with Jim Callaghan, Enoch Powell and Simon Jenkins, the editor of *The Times*. We were all asked about who should be the next Conservative Prime Minister and while they hedged I plumped for John Major. My justification for putting in my halfpenny worth was that the Conservative MPs were choosing our Prime Minister at a peculiarly vulnerable period of our history. What the country needed was a cool head in the war; someone who was not a believer in a Euro-state to deal with the Community; and a concerned person for the NHS and social security questions. What John Major needed at that stage was public recognition, for he was vulnerable to opinion polls showing Michael Heseltine to be the popular choice. Within a few days of the campaign starting, John Major's public opinion poll rating climbed spectacularly. It was as if through television people picked up his pleasant personality which had already made him one of the more popular members of the House of Commons. I was worried that I might be harming his chances with some of his MPs by pushing his candidature, so I spoke to him early that Friday evening on the telephone, just to check that what I was saying was not causing any problems. He was grateful, relaxed and quite happy for me to continue. We talked a bit about his campaign strategy, but far more important, to my surprise and pleasure, he was sounding certain about being the victor.

On 27 November John Major was elected the Conservative Leader and next day, having been appointed by the Queen as Prime Minister, on the steps of No. 10 said that he wanted 'to see us build a country that is at ease with itself', a sentiment which matched many people's mood.

As Margaret Thatcher drove away from No. 10 Downing Street, the iron will cracked and tears came to her eyes. I wrote to her and had a warm letter back, for both of us recognized similar instincts for what the British people wanted. All looked set for a far more dignified exit than ever seemed possible in the immediate aftermath of the first ballot. But she was bruised in the bone and those bruises last. At a private dinner some weeks afterwards, it was painfully apparent that her removal still rankled. Gradually she fell into the temptation to diminish John Major's efforts. Months afterwards she even started to talk of having had the option of staying on because she had never lost a vote in Parliament or in the country. That was sheer illusion. The fact that she had even been able to entertain it shows how far removed she had become from the real world.

We can all rerun history. Perhaps if she had not gone to Paris on that Monday she might have persuaded another two MPs to switch to her. She now claims she would have insisted Saddam Hussein was captured in Baghdad. I consider it is easier to say now than to have achieved then. President Bush was the victorious and dominant figure. Not only was he determined to end the 'Turkey shoot' on the road to Basra, but also adamant that he would not be sucked into street fighting in Baghdad. He was also obsessed with 'bringing the boys home', and haunted by Vietnam. I very much doubt whether Margaret Thatcher would have been able to do more for the Kurds than John Major did, and indeed she might not have been as ready to offend the Americans. The basic errors were in the military assessment that Saddam's Revolutionary Guard had been destroyed and also in the ceasefire arrangements negotiated between the generals which allowed the Iraqi forces to continue to use helicopters, supposedly for humanitarian reasons. When the Iraqis turned them into gunships the Allies' delay in responding was a disgrace. John Major's safe haven idea was then pushed through against American opposition in an exemplary manner, and with French support. Yet as long as Saddam

Hussein remains in power a pall will hang over the liberation of Kuwait. He should be brought to trial under international law as a war criminal and Kuwait should apply for an extradition order. The Western allies should not lift sanctions while Iraq refuses to comply with such an order, which cannot be evaded in law by claiming political refugee status.

The big difference if Margaret Thatcher had been Prime Minister through the Gulf War is that she would have shown little wish to maintain the all-party consensus. When Labour did have its big policy wobble on 7 January and urged continuing sanctions on the eve of war, she would have tried to open their divisions up. I am sure she would not have acted as John Major did, to close them down. It was not as if Labour did not provide the political ammunition. It is hard to be charitable about Denis Healey's contribution to the Gulf War. For a former Secretary of State for Defence, knowing that British forces could be involved in battle within weeks, to say on BBC radio that fear of appearing a 'wimp' was driving President Bush to act as 'a sort of ersatz Rambo, pushing an unwilling world into disaster', was so far below the level of events that one wondered why he did it. It looked as if he was now trying to do the same for Neil Kinnock as he did for Michael Foot over the Falklands War, when Michael's initial response was to endorse the use of force and Denis Healey influenced him in favour of relying on sanctions. But Neil Kinnock, having put down Labour's marker in case anything went wrong, wisely supported our armed forces fully thereafter. To his eternal credit, John Major tried to minimize differences throughout the war and never exploited Labour's divisions. Some will say there are penalties for being too nice a Prime Minister; I would like to believe it has its reward. His conduct of the Gulf War deserves to be remembered, for it was a formidably testing time for an unproven leader.

It may not come in my lifetime, but I look forward to the day when politicians of different parties work together in and outside government. We do this on Select Committees to considerable effect and the sooner politicians widen their cross-party contacts and stop the pretence of being poles apart on everything the better. I can envisage a time when no one considers it odd for an MP of one party to serve in a Cabinet formed by another, and not necessarily because of the need for votes in the House of Commons. This change of climate will come when we have proportional representation; but there is no good reason why it should only be dependent on this. The reason US Presidents have people from the other party in their Cabinets is that it widens the base of government, improves the quality of decision making and helps to widen their appeal. It is hard to see this philosophy developing in our political system, but it is worth persevering.

On Monday 10 December, at a party given by Simon Jenkins and Gayle Hunnicut in the newly opened and beautifully restored Spencer House at St James's Place, I was again approached by Maurice Saatchi.

He wanted to know whether I was prepared to have lunch with Kenneth
Baker, now Home Secretary. I said I would be delighted. Our respective
secretaries fixed a date for Tuesday 29 January and I was intrigued to see
if it would lead anywhere.

Early in the New Year I was telephoned by a close friend of mine to
pass on a conversation he had had with a person in regular contact with
John Major. He had commented that the Prime Minister hoped for my
endorsement at the next election, and did not even rule out standing
down in the three SDP MPs' seats, although it would be very difficult to
obtain agreement within the Conservative Party. I had no idea if this was
a deliberately placed piece of information, but it was important intelligence from a valuable source and it meant that I began to approach the
lunch with Maurice Saatchi and Kenneth Baker in a far more thoughtful
mood.

According to Frank Johnson, writing with wit but also with all the
main facts in the *Sunday Telegraph* on 10 February, the lunch with
Kenneth Baker, which he called a dinner, had come about as a result of a
letter written to the Prime Minister by Maurice Saatchi.

> Mr Major consulted his soothsayers. It was agreed that at this stage
> there should be nothing so portentous as a meal involving the Prime
> Minister, Mr Saatchi and Dr Owen. So Mr Saatchi's information was
> discussed over a meal attended by Mr Chris Patten, the Conservative
> Party Chairman, Mr Saatchi and Mr Michael Dobbs. It was still not
> thought time for serious eating between the Prime Minister and Dr
> Owen – serious being understood in politics as three courses plus
> closing Bendick's mints. So Mr Kenneth Baker, in his capacity as a
> former Party Chairman, was sent to raise the napkin on the Prime
> Ministerial behalf.

This only confirmed what I had suspected, that Kenneth Baker was not
acting on his own but had been used as a conduit to discover my intentions.

The main difference between the previous lunch with Maurice Saatchi
and the one with Kenneth Baker was that there was no longer any
attempt to persuade me to join the Conservative Party. It was a sophisticated conversation in which the reality that I would not join was
accepted and instead we explored all the possible permutations whereby I
could co-operate as a Social Democrat. With good will we discussed the
various options. For the Conservative Party it was clearly difficult, but
not judged impossible, to persuade their people to stand down in our
three SDP seats. It was understood that I was not prepared to do
anything which would damage John and Rosie's chances of being re-
elected. No one denied my assertion that the Conservatives could not
possibly win any of our three seats and that only Labour was the
challenger. My contention was not challenged either – that if I endorsed
the Conservative Party their local Conservative candidate and the Labour

candidate would exploit the news against John and Rosie. We three had stuck together since 1987 and I was not prepared to countenance any action which would harm them. Our independence was our best electoral asset, and not something to give up without a bankable return. Furthermore, we had an agreement with the Liberal Democrats covering those two seats and we expected that they would use any electoral arrangement as an excuse to break the agreement. If they were serious politicians, however, they should welcome it as a precursor of things to come.

I told them I did not wish to remain in politics if there were not a constructive role for me in a new Parliament. I had promised John and Rosie in 1987 that I would stay for the lifetime of this Parliament, but had specifically ruled out the promise to fight another election. It had been immensely difficult trying to influence events from my position below the gangway in the House of Commons over the last ten years. By early 1991 I knew I was becoming less effective, and also, it has to be admitted, bored. If I were to stay and fight the next election, and carry any influence with voters, I needed to be able to feel confident that I would have some influence on the decisions of any government I supported. That meant joining the Cabinet. Obviously that would present difficulties for the Government, and Kenneth Baker made it clear that was for the Prime Minister to determine. I said that alternatively I was content to step aside and not fight the next election, and, provided John and Rosie were not opposed, I was willing to consider endorsing John Major. Yet as we talked Maurice Saatchi made it clear he wanted the endorsement of an active parliamentary politician. It was a fascinating lunch and we had frankly exposed all the advantages and disadvantages. I took a lift with Kenneth Baker back in his car to the House of Commons. To Maurice as a businessman these problems were all solvable, but as politicians we both saw the obstacles as being too great to overcome.

Once again the party political battle in Britain was too sharply drawn for there to be any inter-party co-operation, at least in advance of an election. Although our lunch conversation was to say the least unusual in British politics, it would be considered quite normal in other European countries. However, in 1951 Winston Churchill had offered Clement Davies, then the Leader of the Liberal Party, a seat in his Cabinet, which he turned down. Edward Heath offered Jeremy Thorpe a seat in the Cabinet in February 1974. If in 1977 or 1978 Jim Callaghan had offered David Steel a seat in his Cabinet, I am sure David would have accepted.

Before the Frank Johnson article appeared in the *Sunday Telegraph*, an approach was made to a friend of mine by a person near to Neil Kinnock, and they met shortly after the article had come out. This meeting was not leaked to the press and so I feel it must remain private. The underlying message was that Neil Kinnock was anxious to reduce the offputting effect of the Conference Resolution, although that was not specifically mentioned. There was no question of Labour withdrawing from the fight in our seats and they promised nothing, but I appreciated the attempt to bury the hatchet, albeit privately. They had correctly judged that I still felt a debt to the Labour Party. Without Labour I would never have even been an MP, let alone Foreign Secretary. As they shed their dangerous and damaging policy commitments, so I felt more inhibited in attacking Labour. My problem was that I liked John Major far more than the Conservative Party. I did not know Neil Kinnock, but while I thought he was courageous to abandon so many of his past political views I was worried about him becoming Prime Minister having held those views.

To my immense surprise, a week or so later I was rung up by Kenneth Baker to ask if I would have dinner at his house with John Major and Chris Patten. I took this invitation to mean something serious was underway. For the first time I talked specifics rather than generalities with my two parliamentary colleagues. Then Kenneth Baker rang up to change the date of the dinner and I thought they might be backing off in the light of the *Sunday Telegraph* article. But in fact they were still keen, and the Prime Minister still intended coming despite the war having started. I did not tell even my parliamentary colleagues who I was having dinner with, though I did say that it was being considered at a high level. My colleagues' attitude was that they enjoyed being independent and did not want to give that up. Nevertheless, it was important to them to use whatever influence we had to promote the ideas and philosophy of social democracy. We had always favoured cross-party agreements, and they were ready for me to negotiate.

At the dinner on Sunday 24 February 1991, before anything other than pleasantries had been exchanged, Chris Patten made it clear he did not think his people would stand down in the three SDP seats. Once that had been stated there was no point in discussing any of the various options and co-operative arrangements that I had previously talked through with Kenneth Baker. I replied that there had always been formidable difficulties and it was not surprising that it was impossible to deliver. The last time the Conservatives had done a seat deal was with the Liberal Party in the four constituencies in Huddersfield and Bolton in the 1951 and 1955 General Elections, each party being given a clear run in two seats. Whether it was constituency resistance that was crucial I do not know. It is fair to assume that they would not have arranged the dinner unless they thought there was a chance of standing down their local candidates. But they had obviously tested the water since then. The reaction of their MPs was also important, for it would not have been worth my while to have entered a Conservative Cabinet if I were only to be given sullen or half-hearted co-operation. Since we were still in the midst of the Gulf War, we moved on to discuss that next. The poll tax was their chief concern and I urged them to slash the costs by taking police, fire and education out of local government's control to make them the agents of central government and in education the co-ordinator of self-governing schools. In retrospect, my only surprise was that they waited until the Budget to cut the poll tax and so it was not defused enough by the time of the council elections or the Ribble Valley by-election and it had to be abolished. The dinner ended with good will all round, but I left puzzled by what had happened, yet firmly believing that it would remain private and that I would hear no more about it.

The following Wednesday I had a longstanding lunch engagement with Sir Nicholas Lloyd, editor of the *Daily Express*. I did not reveal that I had met John Major or what we had discussed only three days before. Our discussion nevertheless focused on me joining the Conservative Cabinet under John Major while remaining a Social Democrat. Nick and I had discussed the issue before and he knew I had never ruled out co-operating with either Labour or the Conservative Party. He argued, not unreasonably, that my previous objections to the Conservatives no longer applied, since John Major would clearly not encourage a two-tier National Health Service. The *Daily Express* under his editorship was and remains a firm supporter of Margaret Thatcher. Over a good many years of talking as a friend, Nick knew exactly where I supported her and where I disagreed; there were few shades of grey in my attitude towards Margaret Thatcher. Yet it was a frustrating conversation because I could not tell Nick why I believed the whole issue was off the agenda without revealing Sunday night's dinner and who had been there. So I confined myself to saying there were substantial difficulties and that it would require a change of heart among Conservatives.

On the Friday the *Daily Express* had a major feature article on why it made sense for me to join a Tory Cabinet as a Social Democrat. There were some angry comments about that prospect from the Conservative Chairman in the Devonport constituency. Old enmities die slowly. At the same time Labour leaders were using the traditional argument against pre-election pacts to tweak the Conservatives, saying any talks with us would be a sign the Tories believed they could lose the election. In fact at that stage in the Gulf War the Conservatives and John Major were doing well in the polls and an early general election looked very much on the cards. There was some follow-up press comment, but then the whole matter seemed to fade away.

On the face of it an honest attempt had been made to break the convention that politicians of different parties cannot co-operate. I was disappointed that it had failed, but not because I was yearning to go back into government. I knew it would ignite all the old passions; I would be called a traitor by Labour and trigger envy from some Conservatives. It was because the counter-revolution with which Margaret Thatcher was so strongly identified had some very important elements within it which I wanted further developed. These needed to be sustained across the political divide. If the concept of inter-party co-operation could take hold, if the social market philosophy could become embedded, there would be real gains.

I would not be confirming any of this had it not been for the fact that on Monday 22 April, following a briefing by a Conservative, the *Daily Express* revealed the February dinner with John Major. Also this story had followed on from two front-page headline stories in the *Sunday Times* and the *Mail on Sunday* on 21 April, again briefed by Conservatives. To this day I do not know why they did this. On that Saturday evening I was about to go to bed in a hotel overlooking Lake Kariba in Zimbabwe, having just been out in a Land-Rover watching lions by spotlight. Kieran Prendergast, my old Assistant Private Secretary in the Foreign Office and now High Commissioner in Zimbabwe, told me that I was wanted on the telephone by his press officer in Harare. Over a radio telephone link I was warned that tomorrow's *Sunday Times* was going to carry a front-page story about my discussions with the Conservatives and the possibility of my endorsing them at the next election. I refused to comment. I had been rung up on the Friday before I left for Africa by the *Sunday Times* political editor, Michael Jones, so I knew something was brewing. But I had no idea that it would be such a big story or that the briefing had been so extensive. Nor had he any idea that a very similar story had been leaked to the *Mail on Sunday*.

The *Sunday Times* banner headline was 'MAJOR CONSIDERS CABINET POST FOR DAVID OWEN'. 'John Major and David Owen have discussed the possibility of the former Social Democrat Leader joining the Cabinet', it went on. Downing Street was reported as denying that I had ever discussed any position in the Cabinet with John Major, which was true. But I had discussed this question with Kenneth Baker, and it would have been relayed back because he had always made it clear that he could not speak for the Prime Minister on that subject. The *Mail on Sunday* headline, again on the front page, was 'OWEN IN SECRET TALKS WITH PM'. It went on to say:

> David Owen has held secret talks on his political future with Prime Minister John Major. The move, revealed by sources close to the Premier will intensify speculation that the former SDP Leader will back the Tories at the next general election. Officials confirmed last night that the channels of communication are open. Dr Owen has been given no promise that – even if he does join the Conservatives – he will return to the Cabinet.

I had never given the slightest hint that I would become a Conservative, so that part of the story was gratuitously damaging. The stories were given added credibility, however, because I had a few days before written an article in the *Daily Mail* strongly supporting John Major's achievement in twisting the arm of the US to support a safe haven for the Kurds. But this had come after my heavy criticism that nothing had been done earlier. Indeed I had been so critical that I had written to John Major, comparing the situation to the Russians encamped outside Warsaw watching and holding back as the Nazis crushed the Polish freedom fighters in the Jewish ghetto.

All four of these stories, *Sunday Telegraph*, *Sunday Times*, *Mail on Sunday*, and *Daily Express*, had been placed by the Conservatives. I had to ask myself why? I have good reason to believe that none had been authorized from No. 10. Perhaps the motivation was to obtain some good will for the Conservatives before the council elections. But I do not believe it was done to embarrass me and sour relations, for journalists were not briefed in such a way as to contradict the story. It did some damage to SDP councillors in my constituency in the midst of defending their seats. But it was foolish politics, for trust is crucial. Now that they have revealed it, I see no reason to be defensive about either our meeting or our attempt to reach an understanding of mutual benefit.

I credit John Major with even considering a co-operative arrangement. I am pleased that an honest attempt was made and I bear no ill will that it failed. I suspect that it gives more than a hint of how he wants to broaden out from our present deeply entrenched adversarial political system. He opposes proportional representation for the Westminster Parliament, but there are other ways of evolving and building bridges across our polarized politics. Chris Patten is wisely talking about fixed-term Parliaments. The alternative voting system practised in France, with a vote a week later which allows for thought is worth contemplating. A parliamentary candidate who failed to get 50 per cent would then have a run-off against their nearest rival. This is a far fairer system than the one we have, though not as fair as proportional representation. Neverthe-less, it might have some attractions to the Conservative Party. In Northern Ireland, if we could bring back an Assembly in Belfast, the Conservatives would be wise to rediscover Sir Alec Douglas-Home's blueprint for a Scottish Assembly and make a virtue of a move to federalism within the UK. Coupled with a reformed House of Lords, part elected and having Euro-MPs as participants, the evolution of our constitution could recom-mence after a period of total stagnation. Interestingly, the Christian Democrats in Europe are very keen that there is proportional representa-tion for elections to the European Parliament. If the Conservative Party are to join their group in the Parliament, a change would be greatly appreciated; for it is one thing to distort representation in our national Parliament, quite another to distort the European Parliament.

In our political culture of hostility to any form of inter-party co-operation it is never the right time to co-operate. If you are ahead in the polls, those who are anti say why do a deal? If you are behind, they say a deal will indicate you fear losing. The only way this sort of co-operation will come about is if politicians think voters will reward inter-party co-operation because they positively feel it provides for better government.

The opposition parties praised John Major for not exploiting the Gulf War. But no sooner was the war over than the politicians and the journalists heaved a sigh of relief and clambered back into the trenches to start firing political abuse. I do not believe the voters relished the resumption of political hostilities, and I am convinced they want a more civilized system. It is the vested interest of politicians that ensures that while they reform every other aspect of our lives they have not reformed the political system for more than a century.

From time to time press articles played up the possibility of there being some deal between the SDP and the Conservatives, but as far as I could see it was off the agenda. A particularly large banner headline on 16 June 1991 in the *Sunday Express*, 'OWEN DECLARES', carried factually what was by then a familiar story. They reported I was prepared to serve under John Major in his Cabinet, but only as a Social Democrat and provided the other two SDP MPs were not opposed by the Conservative Party. This was mildly unfortunate in that it provoked the usual rebuff stories from No. 10 which reiterated the truth that no Cabinet post had been offered by the Prime Minister and that he planned no immediate reshuffle. It seemed as clear to me in June as at the dinner at the end of February that, though there was innate good will, no co-operative arrangement was going to emerge. The *Sunday Express* story had followed my support in the House of Commons for John Major's stance over a single currency within the European economic and monetary union Treaty. His speech in Swansea on Friday 14 June had said that 'any Treaty would have to provide for the British Government and the British Parliament to only move to a single currency if they took a further, separate and explicit decision to do so. Not just when to do so. but whether to do so at all.' That was exactly what I had argued should happen in a speech to the Bruges Group the previous December, so I was bound to support it. It was absurd to say now we would join on a specific date. Only the zealots were attempting to do this. I felt I was back in 1978 trying to juggle the negotiations to allow us to join the EMS but leave open when to join the ERM. It did us little harm not being in the ERM from 1979–85, but immeasurable harm to stay out from 1985. Perhaps it would harm us to remain aloof from a single currency from the day it started, for we do have in the City of London vital interests to protect. But that judgement can only be sensibly undertaken by the House of Commons at the time of entry when all the relevant facts are known.

John Major has in my view already totally justified Margaret Thatcher's decision to support him as her successor. At no stage have I heard anything as remotely clear or concise about what the British monetary position should be from Neil Kinnock or anyone else in the Labour Party. On the most substantive issue of British politics, the European Community, John Major's Government was taking the same policy line as the SDP had agreed at its Scarborough Conference in

1989. The Liberal Democrats under Paddy Ashdown, advocates of a United States of Europe, had no wish to negotiate. They wanted just to sign up for a single currency and for fixed exchange rates to be imposed by the Treaty. They were now the Jo Grimond Liberal Party re-visited. The parallels in style and content with the 1963–64 pre-election period were becoming uncanny. But I saw John Major as a more formidable political operator than Sir Alec Douglas-Home, though an equally decent man.

On Monday 17 June, at a meeting of Foreign Ministers in Luxembourg, a paper was presented in which, for the first time in the history of the European Community, an explicit reference was made to the 'federal goal' of European Union, and proposing a further round of inter-governmental negotiations later in 1996 on a new federal constitution. Douglas Hurd immediately rejected these words on behalf of the British Government. At long last the federalists had broken cover and sought to build in an explicit goal for what had hitherto been for them implicit in 'an ever closer union'. It was of course only an aspiration and the background against which it was being put forward was one where already some of the Jacques Delors federalist proposals of the Rome summit had in part been turned back. Even so, journalists, diplomats and politicians tried unconvincingly to pretend that the word 'federalism' in this context only meant decentralization. Since this was then shortly followed by the break-up of the Yugoslavian Federation, it was apparent to everyone that national feelings were not easily harnessed within a single state. The controversy and argument over the word federalism would henceforth make it a little harder to argue that the Treaty of Rome had within it an inherent commitment to a federal United States of Europe.

In Britain, Edward Heath's attack on Margaret Thatcher exposed the polar extremes of European sentiment. Animosity apart, no longer constrained by Cabinet colleagues and by the need to carry the majority of Conservative MPs with them, both have reverted to their basic instincts. Edward Heath is quite happy to have majority voting for defence and foreign affairs. He soft-pedalled his belief in a European state in order to get acceptance from the British Parliament for entry in 1971–2. Margaret Thatcher was in Heath's Cabinet that took us in and was Prime Minister during the passage of the Single European Act in 1986 which brought more majority voting than any other legislation. She is really a believer in a free trade area, not the European Community. At long last Britain, as so often in our history only near the cliff edge, is waking up to the real threat to our nationhood. There are serious people committed to the European Community like Giscard d'Estaing who make no secret of their wish, within twenty years, to have a European President directly elected, a European Cabinet appointed by the President but approved by the European Parliament and answerable to that Parliament.

There are many more to whom this is a private aspiration to which they bend every effort. To go on pretending that the issue of a federal state is not on the political agenda for the European Community is to continue to deliberately evade a serious question and a legitimate debate.

37

THE SINEWS OF NATIONHOOD

Britain faces years of painstaking detailed negotiation over the evolution of the European Community. Contrary to the conventional wisdom since 1973 we have had considerable influence in shaping the Community. We were in favour of enlargement in the 1970s and the architects of allowing members to decide when and if they should join the ERM. The single market in the 1980s owed much to British enthusiasm. Negotiations will not end with a new Treaty in 1992, they are a continuous feature of life within the Community. The tide of federalism will go on beating for a United States of Europe, trying to erode the castles of nationhood. The idea of a European state was repulsed by de Gaulle in the 1960s. It has surged back now in the 1990s. It will probably never go away.

It is Britain's European destiny to resist tides of Euro-federalism, hopefully in combination with other nations. But, if necessary, we must do it alone, confidently insisting on retaining the essentials of nationhood within the Community. We should be positive in arguing that a single European state is not in the best interests of the European Community. We should not do so because we are afraid of any further losses of sovereignty, regardless of the rational case. Where it makes sense and the Community is following strictly the principle of subsidiarity, there are instances where further loss of sovereignty could be beneficial. The environment is an area where authority is needed across the member states. But transferring authority from the nation state must not be done just to suck in decisions to Brussels purely from habit or for reasons of prestige, only because the European level is the correct place for such decisions. Nor is the Community the only vehicle for European decisions. NATO succeeded brilliantly without ever having a vote among the member states and without even any provision for majority voting.

What are the essential sinews of nationhood which I wish to preserve inside a more united European Community? I want a British Prime Minister to be able to commit to action when faced by an invasion outside the NATO area with the same determination and authority as

Margaret Thatcher was able to do when discussing Kuwait with George
Bush. Nor am I ready to give up to the European Community the British
position as a permanent member of the UN Security Council. Every few
years an incident occurs which demonstrates that the Anglo-American
relationship is still very important. I leave to academics to argue whether
or not it is special. Its strength lies in actions often taken quickly,
informally and in an atmosphere of trust. Those of us who have operated
the relationship will have their own memories of why it matters. For me,
the ambivalence from the colonial past, the loyalties from adversity and
allied action, are summed up in one intimate incident. Kingman Brewster,
the US Ambassador in London, came to see me formally in the Foreign
Office to say that a specialized rifle which we had requested from the US
Army could not be sold to us. Normally our meetings were full of fun,
but on hearing this I became icily cold. He knew, and I knew, though it
was never said, that the decision had been made because of Congressional
pressure, aware that we would use the rifles in Northern Ireland. I flatly
refused to accept his message. He was ashamed and I was angry. I told
him that before I informed the Prime Minister, Cy Vance should repeat
these words to my face. I never heard anything about the subject again
and the rifles were bought by the British Army. The Anglo-American
relationship depends on personal relations at every level, but particularly
between US Presidents and Secretaries of State and their British
counterparts. Down-play or denigrate this relationship and it will be
Europe, not just Britain, that will suffer. The invasion of Kuwait, the
seizure of the Falklands, the bombing of Libya, are but three recent
examples in a long list of post-war incidents where it was tested and not
found wanting.

Europe has also gained immeasurably by the involvement of the US
and Canada. We still need NATO to harness their commitment, albeit
now in a sensibly reduced form. Europe should, however, build up the
Western European Union which is a specifically European defence
organization that has lain dormant while NATO predominated. It has
many advantages, not least its own mechanisms for involving parliamentarians from the member states. It allows for a European pillar excluding a
defence role for the Commission or the need to amend the Rome Treaty.
The terms of the treaty that governs WEU is robust on the commitment
of the member states to come to the defence of each other. If anything
this is stronger than that in the North Atlantic Treaty. Defence merits a
distinct European pillar like NATO accountable to the national parliaments, and not the European Parliament. If that could be agreed, we
would be going a long way towards defining the acceptable limits of
encroachment on the nation state. Particularly if it were linked with the
rejection of majority voting in foreign affairs within the agreed Community framework for foreign policy decision making. If Britain were
to concede to any selected areas proposed for common action by the

European Council on foreign policy to have majority voting, a United States of Europe would become unstoppable. This is an absolute threshold.

A European Community designed to be sui generis would continue with a Community of nation states and deliberately allow for a varied pattern of development. The Treaty of Rome would govern the social market. NATO and the WEU treaties would govern defence. This would ensure that we would not even be attempting to look like a United States of Europe. Community membership offers a disciplined framework to develop a social market economy and an opportunity for Britain to consolidate the market led counter-revolution, which dominated our politics throughout the 1980s and will hopefully run through the 1990s. It must be based on the Single Market and the need to promote and develop economic convergence among the member states. To satisfy our partners, it will be necessary for Britain to be more forthcoming than hitherto and accept more majority voting in the fields of social and environmental policy. That will be easier now it has been agreed that minimum wage legislation and industrial relations are national responsibilities.

Millions of people in their different ways knew in 1979 that Britain could not go on as we had through previous decades. It was our relative economic decline which triggered the 1979 counter-revolution. It had spluttered to life after a number of false starts. Harold Wilson had made an attempt in 1963 with his 'white heat of the technological revolution'. Edward Heath had tried to do it through the European Community in 1971. Jim Callaghan in 1976, through the discipline of the IMF. They had all failed. The importance of the counter-revolution that Margaret Thatcher started was that in essence it sought to reassert the centrality of the market place. The SDP rejected a *laissez faire* market approach in the middle 1980s with its advocacy of the social market. For a market economy to prosper it must be built on a foundation of social justice. It also needs this base if it is to survive the strains and stresses of alternating governments and to retain popular respect. For the market economy to be permanent and successful there has to be co-operation between the industrial partners, the parties within the United Kingdom and between the countries within the European Community. A social dimension within a market economy is not intrinsically wrong or hostile to market forces, but it has to complement the market, not distort or disrupt it.

When the historians seek parallels for the counter-revolution which took place in Britain under Margaret Thatcher, I think they will compare what happened here with what happened to France under General de Gaulle from 1956–68. Both leaders challenged their countries to do better, to think bigger and to reverse their relative decline. Both leaders drew heavily on a strident nationalism to galvanize their nations. Through their own hubris, both were ignominiously brought down by the people

on whom they had relied in order to exert immense and unprecedented
power – he by a referendum of the people, she by the votes of her
Conservative MPs. Both leaders sought regeneration from within, building up national pride and eschewing dilution through a United States of
Europe. Naturally there were also differences. Charles de Gaulle's anti-
Americanism was buttressed by Franco-German reconciliation. Margaret
Thatcher's Europhobia was off-set by an unprecedented reassertion of
the Anglo-American special relationship. De Gaulle left behind a new
constitution which has given a framework to his counter-revolution,
reinforcing the changes in attitude which were fostered in his time.
Margaret Thatcher was uninterested in constitutional change, and did
not see the importance of such reforms in reinforcing her inheritance.
But, taken as a whole, the similarities are striking. De Gaulle was
fortunate to be followed by Pompidou. Can John Major play the same
role? The problem for John Major is that she will not go to the
equivalent of Colombey-les-Deux-Eglises to say not a word on domestic
politics. She would be wiser if she concentrated almost exclusively on
international politics. But John Major has one consolation, that as yet she
is not behaving like Edward Heath. She has so far only taken a mild
stand on the poll tax and concentrated on the substantive issue of
Europe. She is close to the instincts of many British people on this. If
John Major can persuade her by example not to fall into the trap of
sounding anti the whole European Community, then she will be an
important influence; for this is John Major's key political card. His stance
in favour of playing a role in the heart of the European Community is
actually closer to the instincts of the British people than Margaret
Thatcher's hostile rhetoric. Soon, Neil Kinnock and the Labour Party
will have to define their position on Europe. Having flirted with all the
enthusiasm of the convert with a position closer to Euro-federalism than
Labour has ever before adopted, I hope they too will resist any treaty
that has within it a clear momentum towards a United States of Europe.

In 1983, as Leader of the SDP, I set out to identify with those parts of
Margaret Thatcher's counter-revolution with which I agreed. I wanted to
use the good will that this open-mindedness engendered to create a more
receptive climate for the constitutional reforms and social policy which I
believe are an essential complement to sustaining the market economy.
The one thing I dreaded most about those policy fights within the SDP
in 1984–5 was that I would be dragged away from supporting the
counter-revolution because Party members would be too afraid of
controversy. I was worried that we would merely cling to the status quo,
as most Centre parties do, fearful of annoying anyone.

The middle class, which some split into lower and upper, has been the
largest grouping in Britain since the late 1960s. In a real sense this was
their counter-revolution. It has by no means yet achieved all its objectives,
and its gains are not yet permanent. But it has begun to make much

needed changes in Britain. Its driving force and its chief architect has been Margaret Thatcher, but it is not solely her revolution, nor that of the Conservative Party. It has involved many people in the country who would not even consider themselves party political. Essentially it has been part of a movement against statism worldwide; a resolve to reassert the role of the individual and to roll back the frontiers of an intrusive state, whether it was manifested in the form of corporatism or communism. The stress on classlessness binds together the SDP and the Conservative counter-revolutionaries. It was Margaret Thatcher at the Conservative Conference in October 1990 who said:

> . . . the more we break down barriers – barriers between workers and bosses, skilled and unskilled, tenants and owners; barriers between private and public. That's the kind of open classless Britain I want to see. And it's the kind of Opportunity Britain the Conservative Party stands for.

It was John Major who picked that theme up only six weeks later, and it is very important for social democrats that he makes classlessness the leitmotif of his Prime Ministership.

In Britain the role of the state was repeatedly extended through two World Wars and consolidated in peacetime by Clement Attlee's Labour Government. The counter-revolution of the 1980s was not just a wish to reverse these state powers, it went deeper than this – it sought to reassert a national self-confidence, to rediscover the commercial market-orientated prosperity of the Victorian era which had not just been the product of Empire but owed much to British invention, design, entrepreneurship, and industrial skill. But it did not draw sufficiently on those other middle-class aspirations to serve the common good, to contribute to society as a whole, and indeed at times the Thatcher counter-revolution quite unnecessarily upset those who held these values.

In a class-ridden Britain, for decades past, the middle class had witnessed our country's decline with a mixture of stoicism and self-mockery. In amateur dramatic societies up and down the land they had sung lustily Gilbert and Sullivan's chorus in *Iolanthe* as the Peers processed by 'Bow, bow, ye lower middle-classes'. But what started as satire became too close to reality. Resentment began to build up as the middle class watched with a mixture of anxiety and anger as trade union leaders lorded it over not only their members but, all too often, the economic life of the country. For centuries they had been patronized by those with hereditary wealth and yet hitherto they had found they could escape from their backgrounds and by their own efforts create wealth. The crippling levels of personal taxation in the 1960s and 1970s, however, began to make it virtually impossible for the law-abiding, tax-paying, middle-class citizen to accumulate wealth. The Brain Drain and the fall-off in standards of public provision served as a reminder of our decline.

The artificially high price of land affected the yeoman farmer and his family. The crippling cost of a home began to put home ownership beyond the means of many young lower-middle-class couples. All the time the leaden hand of bureaucracy was stifling effort and enterprise.

Suddenly by 1979 the middle class had discovered that they had a champion in Margaret Thatcher, a person ready to fight, not just for the best interests of her country, but also unashamedly for the interests of her class. Fortunately in the main these two interests coincided. But it was both a strength and a weakness that her counter-revolution had so marked a class base. The SDP called for a classless society in the Limehouse Declaration and I watch with fascination as John Major develops this classless theme as Prime Minister. The political skill of Margaret Thatcher was her readiness, in a totally unabashed way, to mobilize the middle class. But it was a paradox of Margaret Thatcher's stress on the individual that she was ready to assume greater powers for centralized government, in order, as she saw it, to protect the individual. The antics of the Labour Left in local government legitimized rate-capping. Then the poll tax had a corrosive effect on the standing and authority of local government. A refusal to contemplate devolving power to a Scottish Parliament and her dismissive attitude to constitutional change meant that, while she was constantly condemning and exaggerating the centralizing tendencies of the European Commission in Brussels she was herself presiding over the most centralized country in the European Community.

The attractive feature of the social market is that it sees decentralization as a natural development within a market economy. We have sought to develop this by establishing the Social Market Foundation, a charity devoted to promoting the concept of the social market economy. I could not as an active politician, with the Charity Commissioner zealously guarding the political neutrality of charities, be too heavily involved, though I am a Trustee. Its executive director is Lord Kilmarnock and its chairman is Robert Skidelsky, who was made a Life Peer by John Major. Robert, who is Professor of Political Economy at Warwick University, became a close friend through the SDP. Little did we realize when we started the Foundation and decided to champion the social market that within the year a new Chancellor of the Exchequer, Norman Lamont, would be extolling the merits of the social market along with Chris Patten, the Conservative Party Chairman. It is a sign of the change, not just in tone but of philosophy, that has come in with John Major.

In 1989 a political hurricane hit Europe. It is difficult to describe in any other way the sudden tumbling of communism and the reassertion of nationhood in Eastern Europe. It was 1848 once more. When Poland, Hungary and Czechoslovakia overturned communism and restored democracy, we saw why nationhood cannot be stifled. It was their sense of national pride which was vital in defeating communism. Half a century of military occupation and imposed Marxist ideology still could not suppress hundreds of years of nationhood. The role of nationhood in defending liberty should not be forgotten by those libertarians who fear nationalism. The positive contribution of national feeling has, historically, been more significant than nationalism's excesses. Internationalism is by definition about the support and co-operation between nations. The UN, the GATT, IMF, World Bank, NATO, are all the result of a recognition that world order will not come through grandiose and illusory schemes for world government but through respecting the legitimacy of nationhood within a framework of collective co-operation and the rule of law. A greater degree of integration and pooling of sovereignty between nations can be achieved at regional rather than global level. The challenge for the twenty-first century is how to develop international groupings of nations, which will contribute to the cohesion of world order. For the European Community, as yet the most advanced and sophisticated of all such groupings, this is a formidable challenge; it has to harness nationhood so as not to lose its power. Becoming the mirror image of the United States of America is not compatible with European history. The best twenty-first century model for Europe is a decentralized, democratic, market-orientated, competitive and co-operative Community.

For very good reasons, the European Community has been driven most recently by the desire to complete a single market, something that has taken thirty-seven years. But while the European Community has had an economic strategy, it has barely begun to develop a geopolitical strategy. It is typical of the rather old-fashioned centralized model of the European Community that from 1989 we have been responding to the drama of Eastern Europe economically and not geopolitically. It is a tragic error that the Community is so reluctant to enlarge to help the new Eastern European countries and that it wants to become a single unified state at a time when artificial unions of states are breaking up.

Very few Western Europeans have started by asking themselves what the implications are of a failure by Poland, Hungary or Czechoslovakia to make the transition from communism to democracy? What are the consequences for a united Germany of the Polish economy failing to make the transition to a market economy? They are predominantly political. That inherently controversial border between Poland and Germany is now bolstered by a new treaty, but as the eastern part of Germany becomes more prosperous the sensitivity of that border will grow ever more acute. It is not too soon to warn that it could become the flashpoint for another European war. This time it would be a war between the 'haves', comfortably off in the European Community, and the 'have nots' outside the Community reverting to an aggressive authoritarianism. This could happen not just in Poland but in the Soviet Republics as well It would not necessarily be a reassertion of Soviet Communism but of authoritarianism. A Russian speaking demagogue

might be able to unite a fragmented USSR with some of its neighbours
and proceed to try and take what they cannot make.

There are major questions as to whether it is in the best interests of
the European Community to transfer resources in order to put economic
and monetary union for the twelve before Community membership for
Poland, Hungary, and Czechoslovakia. If Britain has to be the only
country posing that question so be it. There are historical reasons why we
have every right to insist that these questions are both asked and
answered. Britain went to war in 1939 to defend Poland and felt guilt
ridden about what happened to Czechoslovakia in 1938. Now a united
Germany has a debt of honour to Hungary whose brave decision to open
their border to Austria in 1989 started the process that brought down the
Berlin Wall. There are already deep fears in the European Community of
a mass migration of people from the USSR, and from Eastern Europe,
looking for work. The geopolitical arguments for holding back that
migration on Poland, Hungary and Czechoslovakia's border with the
USSR, rather than on their borders with the European Community, are
very powerful. It will be far more acceptable for an ex-communist
country to say no than to start policing the old NATO Warsaw Pact
frontier again. It is argued that these three countries cannot transform
their economies and need first associate membership and then a long
transition period for full Community membership. Quite apart from the
fact that much the same arguments were made against admitting Spain to
full membership in the late 1970s and they showed those doubts to be
unjustified, it is a hard argument to sustain when these three Eastern
European countries see what is being done for those who previously lived
in East Germany. The unification of Germany has been made a little
easier by the former trading links between the two Germanys that were
allowed for within the European Community from 1956 onwards. But
extending Community membership with a firm and detailed timetable for
restructuring is the best way of the Community fulfilling its democratic
and geopolitical purpose.

The western democracies, Europe, Japan and Northern America,
cannot afford to spread limited investment capital, skills and know-how
thinly across the whole of Eastern Europe and the Soviet Republics. In
that way, none will make a successful transition. We have to invest some
of our defence savings in a geopolitical stabilization programme. It means
focusing our contribution in a way that guarantees a successful transition
for, at the very least, Poland, Hungary and Czechoslovakia. Only with
success assured there can we reasonably hope to extend the process.

Yet such geopolitical considerations are not dominant within the
European Commission; most of the Commissioners want to move towards
a United States of Europe, indeed it has almost become a prerequisite to
being accountable to the European Parliament. The pure Euro-federalist
would prefer not to enlarge the Community at all until the process of

building the inner core of twelve is completed. Then if forced to enlarge, they would look first to the old EFTA countries, Norway and Sweden. The Community can of course easily absorb already well established democratic countries like Austria, Sweden, Norway and Finland, and possibly, those less likely in the first tranche, Switzerland and Iceland. Such an enlargement pattern is easily explicable in terms of a predominantly economic European Community. But a geopolitical strategy would be different. It would say to the Scandinavian countries: of course we will enlarge to include you, but for the moment our first priority must be to include Hungary, Poland and Czechoslovakia. It would add that it makes sense to take Austria in as part of the first tranche because Austria can make a special contribution to the transition process, particularly in Hungary. Everyone knows the Community cannot absorb too many countries at any one time. A Community of nation states has nothing to fear and much to gain from taking these former communist countries in soon, even before they are economically ready, because it is in Europe's interests that we buttress both their democracy and their market economy. We know that Community membership makes it easier for any country to tolerate the painful adjustments necessary to develop a real market economy. The Scandinavian countries would understand such priorities even if they did not welcome waiting longer for full membership.

Where are the leaders in Europe or in North America who are ready to advocate such a geopolitical vision? They should be urging Sweden, Norway and Finland to help Estonia, Latvia and Lithuania in the transition from communism and insisting that Mikhail Gorbachev let these Baltic Republics choose independence or receive no financial help. Such a geopolitical approach would not ignore the Soviet Republics. It would make support available to them on a hardheaded assessment of what will pay off in terms of laying the foundation for a market economy. Such an assessment means making it clear to Gorbachev that the new Union of Soviet Sovereign Republics will be a contradiction in terms if the sovereignty is merely titular and genuine self-determination is denied to the individual republics. The transition from communism will be much easier if those republics that feel themselves to be nations use the spirit of nationhood to make the sacrifices that will inevitably coincide with any successful transition to a market economy. The same goes for Yugoslavia. The US in particular was far too keen initially to hold these nations artificially together. Slovenia will find it easier to make the transition when it is an independent nation, as will Croatia.

The Russian Federation is a massive republic embracing both Europe and Asia. Russia has never had in all its long and fascinating history a proper market economy nor even a true democracy. The transition of the Russian Federation will present formidable difficulties. It will only succeed if our European investment concentrates help on the old Leningrad, now

St Petersburg, area in the west, with Japan, once the issue of the disputed Kurile islands is resolved, helping in the east.

It is against such a background that the European Community's own internal development should be judged. As Germany grapples with reunification, having made a gross underestimate of its cost and of the difficulty of sustaining a common currency when the two parts of the country have such widely divergent economies, a prudent European Community would hesitate before plunging towards a single currency and fixed exchange rates for all twelve countries. After all, even Bretton Woods after the end of the Second World War did not impose fixed exchange rates by statute. To draw up a timetable for economic and monetary union without being able to guarantee economic convergence is unreal. It is essential to ensure economic convergence first. That means substantial financial transfers to Greece and an insistence on a firm regime of implementation. A single currency and fixed exchange rates represents a quantum leap in the pooling of sovereignty. I would find it easier to accept if it were certain that the European Community were going to remain a grouping of nations and not a single European state. Of itself, a single currency does not for me mark an absolute threshold after which the emergence of a United States of Europe is certain. As I have said, an absolute threshold is majority voting on foreign affairs.

Until Iraq invaded Kuwait the prevailing wisdom in Washington was that the sooner the United Kingdom signed up for a United States of Europe the better. It was believed this would provide a stronger European voice and presence worldwide – a matching superpower. It was, and remains, a seductive argument for some Europeans. It was a flawed argument, but few adherents wish to hear its flaws exposed. A glazed look would come over American diplomats and commentators if one as much as hinted that part of Britain's reluctance to sacrifice our independent foreign policy had its roots in history; that Britain's refusal to countenance majority voting was a necessary safeguard for our security and theirs. After the Gulf War many more Americans now understand Britain's position. NATO has shown us that operating by consensus we can be both decisive and flexible, able to accommodate minority views, even on such sensitive issues as the siting of nuclear weapons.

The Europe of the 1940s was very different to the Europe of the 1990s. Britain can, however, never forget that when we were alone even the most powerful US President in America's history, Franklin D. Roosevelt, after winning his third term, was not able to take the US people and Congress into the Second World War until they were attacked by the Japanese at Pearl Harbor in 1941. We dare not lose the will or ability to defend ourselves.

I do not trust a single European state to stand firm against blackmail from an authoritarian coalition of countries in Eastern Europe that have failed to make the transition to a market economy. I have not adopted this position lightly, nor by dwelling on the 1940s, but on how European politics and public opinion has responded in the last decade.

It was no accident that of all the European countries, only Britain was immediately ready to see the invasion of Kuwait in August 1990 as an act of aggression that had to be reversed, if need be with force. It was part of our history that Margaret Thatcher was able to make that response on behalf of Britain. Nor was she the first Prime Minister prepared to come to the defence of Kuwait; we committed troops to their defence in 1961. It was John Major who in 1991 went against the indifference of President Bush about the plight of the Kurds and demanded and eventually obtained military help to provide safe havens for their return. So an independent capacity in foreign and defence policy is an essential safeguard not just for Britain but for the European Community and the United States. Margaret Thatcher was perceptive when she told George Bush at Aspen that at the end of the day he could rely on President Mitterrand to bring France along into an allied military response, but it is a fact that the French were still refusing to attack targets in Iraq when the allied forces first flew their air missions into Iraq. For months the then French Defence Minister, Chevenement, had argued that we should free Kuwait without attacking Iraq. Nor should it be forgotten that Belgium, wanting economic sanctions to work, refused to supply Britain with ammunition for fear it was going to be used in the Gulf War. Nor can it be ignored that Germany was unable to deploy troops in support of the allied cause, despite Chancellor Kohl's wish to do so. This failure has been laid at the door of the German constitution, but the SPD is still vigorously opposing the relevant amendments to the constitution, even after the successful outcome of the Gulf War. One of the reasons Kohl wants a Community foreign policy with majority voting is that this would be an easy way of changing their constitution. Fear of Germany is why Mitterrand is tempted by majority voting. He favours building Germany into a common foreign policy and inhibiting her freedom to operate bilaterally with the Soviets.

To believe that political union with majority voting on foreign and security policy within the Community would result in a stronger and more coherent European response defies the lessons of past and recent history. By far the most likely outcome of such a binding decision-making process would be to split differences and inhibit the United Kingdom, and on occasions France, from fulfilling global responsibilities in association with, or sometimes separate from, the United States. It is in this area that Britain must be ready to exercise the right to protect our vital interests. If necessary, John Major must be ready to use our veto, as General de Gaulle did in order to uphold French vital interests.

Lest anyone believe the Gulf War is but an isolated example, let them recall the pusillanimous way in which the European Community responded to the invasion of Afghanistan in 1979. The mealy-mouthed response of Community member states to Libya, Syria, Iran or the Lebanon's record on terrorism. This indicates that any collective decision procedure would lead to a neutered, not a strong, Europe. The strongest peace movement during the 1980s was in Western Europe. But for France and Britain, NATO would have had immense difficulty in carrying public opinion when going ahead with the deployment of cruise and Pershing in order to negotiate for the removal of all Soviet SS-20 missiles. Europe has much to be thankful for in that our defence posture in Europe ever since 1948 has been so strongly influenced by the American presence and position in NATO. The INF Treaty would never have been achieved if left to Western Europe to negotiate directly with the then Union of Soviet Socialist Republics. One only has to remember with some shame the way too many European leaders were ready to fawn over Brezhnev and his predecessors.

In too many European capitals there is too much wishful thinking about Gorbachev's true intentions. Lithuania's bid for freedom was seen as a tiresome upsetting of the status quo. Slovenia's was regarded in much the same way. Peacekeeping operations, whether multi-national or UN, have not been undertaken with a great deal of enthusiasm by most Community countries. It has been the Scandinavians who have been far readier to commit their forces to the UN and to sustain them in difficult circumstances.

Britain must argue again and again that without the sinews of nation-hood reinforcing the European Community there is a real danger of a mercantile, self-satisfied, insipid and introspective Europe. The United States of America would not be balanced by a United States of Europe. Such a Europe would neither seek nor sustain superpower status and if the United States of America were ever to retreat again into isolationism it would not provide a replacement. By contrast, a European Community that builds cohesion and unity while respecting the nationhood of member states can gain strength from their independent power of decision. The stimulus of being able to act independently may from time to time ensure the Community states respond collectively, and thus wield the influence of a great power. A Community readier to fulfil geopolitical objectives and expand its membership for political reasons would also be a more powerful force for democracy and stability.

This is no time for Britain to back off from continuing with radical reforms. We need to reinvigorate our counter-revolution through the 1990s and reinforce the counter-revolution against Soviet Communism throughout Europe. I believe that constitutional changes – fairer voting, fixed-term Parliaments and a Bill of Rights - will help, not hinder, the counter-revolution in Britain. In Europe a readiness to offer membership of the Community, at some cost to ourselves, to selected Eastern European countries is urgently required.

Given these strongly held views, some will say how can I possibly at fifty-three give up being a Member of Parliament. In fact my political age is nearer sixty-three. While there is truth in the old adage that politicians are never dead when they have a voice and a vote in the House of Commons, one can exaggerate the influence of an independent.

After the debacle of the takeover of part of the SDP by the Liberals I promised to stay as a Social Democrat Member of Parliament only for the lifetime of this Parliament. In November 1991 I will have overtaken Nancy Astor's record as being the longest-serving MP in Plymouth's history. When the SDP was formed it was with a sense of release that I abandoned the old animosities and was able to support or praise the policies of another party if I agreed with them. Yet in leaving Labour in 1981 I risked going outside the conventional bounds of party politics, and there was a price to pay for doing so. I gained immense freedom but had to build an alternative power-base in politics. Whatever the merits of the SDP/Liberal Alliance or the strains and stresses within it, for six-and-a-half years it provided me with an effective power-base. We were not on the fringe of British politics, but a contender for real power. At various times both the Labour and the Conservative parties feared us. Our levels of public support never fell below 20 per cent and were frequently over 30 per cent. We never looked remotely like the post-war Liberal Party, merely a vehicle for protest not power.

In 1987 the five SDP MPs faced a blunt choice to merge and become Liberals or to fight and stay Social Democrats. Three of us refused to merge but tried to go on co-operating with the Liberal Democrats. Our readiness to co-operate was repeatedly rebuffed and with every refusal a nail was driven into the coffin of the very concept of political parties co-operating together to build a power-base. Disillusioned, our supporters drifted away from the SDP/Liberal Alliance, helped by first Neil Kinnock's move to the Centre ground and then John Major taking over from Margaret Thatcher. It is always possible that the electoral arithmetic will give the Liberal Democrats a little leverage in the 1990s as it gave it to Jeremy Thorpe in 1974 and David Steel in 1977. But that is not a power-base. Whether, if this were to happen, Paddy Ashdown, who is a good Liberal Leader, could achieve proportional representation, is an open question. I suspect it is more likely in such circumstances to come from Labour making the change unilaterally. There is of course a continuing role for the Liberal Democrats, as there has been for the Liberal Party. There are, for example, benefits in having at least one political party advocating Euro-federalism and wanting a United States of Europe. Politics should reflect the spectrum and diversity of views.

Yet it is very apparent from all my years in politics that while deeply committed to the European Community it has always been within the context of Britain retaining the essentials of nationhood. This is no minor political issue, as we are discovering again in the 1990s. It was one of the numerous reasons why in West-Country politics in the 1960s I was never attracted to the Liberal Party. It was again a reason why I never felt it was possible for me to join, let alone attempt to lead, the Liberal Democrats.

I am genuinely pleased by the changes that Neil Kinnock has made in Labour Party policy since 1988 and it cannot have been easy for him to reverse his own position. But I ask myself, as I suspect do many voters, does he truly believe the policies he now espouses? Labour will, I am sure, come back into government sometime before the end of the 1990s. It is unhealthy for the Conservative Party to dominate government for such a long period. The NHS remains the issue above all on which the country quite rightly trusts Labour. Early in 1990 I had an anonymous letter and with it was my 1964 Torrington Election leaflet, pristine and with only two folds. Also an application to join the Labour Party with the focus on safeguarding the NHS. All my old sentimental attachments came welling back, for under Margaret Thatcher I did not trust her government with our NHS.

Had Margaret Thatcher still been Prime Minister with the poll tax still in place, it is hard to believe that the old political cry of 'time for a change' would not have won through. But the image of the Conservative Party has been transformed. Because of the dominance of Margaret Thatcher's personality, her going appears almost as a change of government. It may well be that the voters, seeing a consistent record in John Major's classless political views, will wait for a Labour leader with a more consistent record of supporting the new policies. Many still feel that Labour has been driven to accept its new policies on the back of electoral defeat, rather than having adopted them from conviction. Much may depend on how strongly John Major identifies with the common good and a classless society and makes greater social justice as the benchmark for the social market economy the Conservative Party now espouses. John Major shows signs of doing this, and if he also protects the NHS, he may well be given the chance to develop his own style of counter-revolution, and such an approach promises to be closer to the aspirations of the average citizen.

For my part, I have decided that since it is clear there is now no likelihood of arranging co-operation across party political battlelines, it is time to declare my party political innings over. It has been said that it is cussedness, megalomania, pride, arrogance, or any and all of these which has made me stubbornly choose to stay a Social Democrat. It may be inconvenient, but I am a Social Democrat. Like many others who have supported the SDP, I will remain a social democrat as a private citizen. I feel no Messianic need to tell others how to vote, particularly when I may have to make up my mind on the lesser of two evils. I have watched fading political idols haunt the corridors of power and I have no wish to follow them. Knowing when to cease battling is as important as knowing when to fight. Most of the policies I felt impelled to oppose in the 1980s have now been rejected. My concern is that the counter-revolution should continue; if it does not do so our relative decline is inevitable.

Looking back on all the big political decisions that I have had to take over the last twenty-five years, I have usually chosen on the basis that I could do no other. That is not to say that all the decisions were judged correctly, but at least they were taken, with very few exceptions, on the basis of what I genuinely believed was in the best interests of the country. I have not worshipped as much as conventional politicians do at the altar of party and I have willingly paid a price for this disdain. I gave my all to the SDP for ten years and, though I believe it has had a profound influence, I am sad that I have not been able to ensure that it will remain a permanent feature of British politics. But the combination of policies and the philosophy which guided the SDP will, I believe, stay beyond our association with them. Over the years many have helped me, strengthened me and loved me. They, I hope, know I am forever in their debt.

What then of ambition, that driving force which has been with me through boyhood, youth, doubt, manhood? What colour is ambition, does it ripen with time or does it canker? What is one ambitious for, is it only oneself, or can one also be ambitious for our country? Who can separate the two, who can weigh them in the balance? All I know is that with my eyes open I have chosen the least trodden path.

> I shall be telling this with a sigh
> Somewhere ages and ages hence:
> Two roads diverged in a wood, and I –
> I took the one less travelled by,
> And that has made all the difference.
>
> Robert Frost

INDEX